2005 edition

No 141

Annual Abstract
of Statistics

Editor: David Penny

Office for National Statistics

palgrave
macmillan

© Crown copyright 2005

Published with the permission of the Controller of Her Majesty's Stationery Office (HMSO).

This publication, excluding logos, may be reproduced free of charge, in any format or medium for research or private study subject to it being reproduced accurately and not used in a misleading context. The material must be acknowledged as crown copyright and the title of the publication specified. This publication can also be accessed at the National Statistics website: **www.statistics.gov.uk**

For any other use of this material please apply for a free Click-Use Licence on the HMSO website:
www.hmso.gov.uk/click-use-home.htm
or write to HMSO at The Licensing Division, St Clements House, 2-16 Colegate, Norwich, NR3 1BQ
Fax: 01603 723000 or e-mail: hmsolicensing@cabinetoffice.x.gsi.gov.uk

First published 2005 by
PALGRAVE MACMILLAN
Houndmills, Basingstoke, Hampshire RG21 6XS and
175 Fifth Avenue, New York, NY 10010
Companies and representatives throughout the world.

PALGRAVE MACMILLAN is the global academic imprint of the Palgrave Macmillan division of St. Martin's Press, LLC and of Palgrave Macmillan Ltd. Macmillan® is a registered trademark in the United States, United Kingdom and other countries. Palgrave is a registered trademark in the European Union and other countries.

ISBN 1-4039-9073-5
ISSN 0072-5730

This book is printed on paper suitable for recycling and made from fully managed and sustained forest sources.

A catalogue record for this book is available from the British Library.

10   9   8   7   6   5   4   3   2   1
14   13   12   11   10   09   08   07   06   05

Printed and bound in Great Britain by
Ashford Colour Press Ltd, Gosport.

A National Statistics publication

National Statistics are produced to high professional standards as set out in the National Statistics Code of Practice. They are produced free from political influence.

About the Office for National Statistics

The Office for National Statistics (ONS) is the government agency responsible for compiling, analysing and disseminating economic, social and demographic statistics about the United Kingdom. It also administers the statutory registration of births, marriages and deaths in England and Wales.

The Director of ONS is also the National Statistician and the Registrar General for England and Wales.

For enquiries about this publication, contact The Editor.
Tel: 020 7533 5086
E-mail: david.penny@ons.gsi.gov.uk

For general enquiries, contact the National Statistics Customer Contact Centre.
Tel: **0845 601 3034** (minicom: 01633 812399)
E-mail: info@statistics.gsi.gov.uk
Fax: 01633 652747
Post: Room 1015, Government Buildings,
          Cardiff Road, Newport NP10 8XG

You can also find National Statistics on the internet at
www.statistics.gov.uk

Contents

Contents

Contents

Contents

Contents

National accounts

17 Prices

18 Government finance

Contents

Contents

22 Production

Contents

Acknowledgements

The Editor would like to thank the following people for their help in producing this book:

Production team:
- Sharon Adhikari
- Nicola Amaranayake
- Michael Crawley
- Sunita Dedi
- Trish Duffy
- Jonathan Elphick
- Usuf Islam
- Dharma Mahesan
- Mark Nevill
- Sathees Sivagnanam
- Carol Summerfield
- Chris Randall
- Steve Whyman
- Brian Yin

Contributors

The Editor also wishes to thank all his colleagues in ONS, the rest of the Government Statistical Service and all contributors in other organisations for their generous support and helpful comments, without whose help this publication would not be possible.

Typesetting by the Desktop Publishing Unit, ONS Titchfield.

Units of measurement

Length

1 millimetre (mm)		= 0.03937 inch
1 centimetre (cm)	= 10 millimetres	= 0.3937 inch
1 metre (m)	= 1,000 millimetres	= 1.094 yards
1 kilometre (km)	= 1,000 metres	= 0.6214 mile
1 inch (in.)		= 25.40 millimetres or 2.540 centimetres
1 foot (ft.)	= 12 inches	= 0.3048 metre
1 yard (yd.)	= 3 feet	= 0.9144 metre
1 mile	= 1,760 yards	= 1.609 kilometres

Area

1 square millimetre (mm²)		= 0.001550 square inch
1 square metre (m²)	= one million square millimetres	= 1.196 square yards
1 hectare (ha)	= 10,000 square metres	= 2.471 acres
1 square kilometre (km²)	= one million square metres	= 247.1 acres
1 square inch (sq. in.)		= 645.2 square millimetres or 6.452 square centimetres
1 square foot (sq. ft.)	= 144 square inches	= 0.09290 square metre or 929.0 square centimetres
1 square yard (sq. yd.)	= 9 square feet	= 0.8361 square metre
1 acre	= 4,840 square yards	= 4,046 square metres or 0.4047 hectare
1 square mile (sq. mile)	= 640 acres	= 2.590 square kilometres or 259.0 hectares

Volume

1 cubic centimetre (cm³)		= 0.06102 cubic inch
1 cubic decimetre (dm³)	= 1,000 cubic centimetres	= 0.03531 cubic foot
1 cubic metre (m³)	= one million cubic centimetres	= 1.308 cubic yards
1 cubic inch (cu.in.)		=16.39 cubic centimetres
1 cubic foot (cu. ft.)	= 1,728 cubic inches	= 0.02832 cubic metre or 28.32 cubic decimetres
1 cubic yard (cu. yd.)	= 27 cubic feet	= 0.7646 cubic metre

Capacity

1 litre (l)	= 1 cubic decimetre	= 0.2200 gallon
1 hectolitre (hl)	= 100 litres	= 22.00 gallons
1 pint		= 0.5682 litre
1 quart	= 2 pints	= 1.137 litres
1 gallon	= 8 pints	= 4.546 litres
1 bulk barrel	= 36 gallons (gal.)	= 1.637 hectolitres

Weight

1 gram (g)		= 0.03527 ounce avoirdupois
1 hectogram (hg)	= 100 grams	= 3.527 ounces or 0.2205 pound
1 kilogram (kg)	= 1,000 grams or 10 hectograms	= 2.205 pounds
1 tonne (t)	= 1,000 kilograms	= 1.102 short tons or 0.9842 long ton
1 ounce avoirdupois (oz.)	= 437.5 grains	= 28.35 grams
1 pound avoirdupois (lb.)	= 16 ounces	= 0.4536 kilogram
1 hundredweight (cwt.)	= 112 pounds	= 50.80 kilograms
1 short ton	= 2,000 pounds	= 907.2 kilograms or 0.9072 tonne
1 long ton (referred to as ton)	= 2,240 pounds	= 1,016 kilograms or 1.016 tonnes
1 ounce troy	= 480 grains	= 31.10 grams

Energy

British thermal unit (Btu)	= 0.2520 kilocalorie (kcal) = 1.055 kilojoule (kj)
Therm	= 10^5 British thermal units = 25,200 kcal = 105,506 kj
Megawatt hour (MWh)	= 10^6 watt hours (Wh)
Gigawatt hour (GWh)	= 10^6 kilowatt hours = 34,121 therms

Food and drink

Butter	23,310 litres milk	= 1 tonne butter (average)
Cheese	10,070 litres milk	= 1 tonne cheese
Condensed milk	2,550 litres milk	= 1 tonne full cream condensed milk
	2,953 litres skimmed milk	= 1 tonne skimmed condensed milk
Milk	1 million litres	= 1,030 tonnes
Milk powder	8,054 litres milk	= 1 tonne full cream milk powder
	10,740 litres skimmed milk	= 1 tonne skimmed milk powder
Eggs	17,126 eggs	= 1 tonne (approximate)
Sugar	100 tonnes sugar beet	= 92 tonnes refined sugar
	100 tonnes cane sugar	= 96 tonnes refined sugar

Shipping

Gross tonnage	= The total volume of all the enclosed spaces of a vessel, the unit of measurement being a 'ton' of 100 cubic feet.
Deadweight tonnage	= Deadweight tonnage is the total weight in tons of 2,240 lb. that a ship can legally carry, that is the total weight of cargo, bunkers, stores and crew.

Area

Chapter 1

Area

The United Kingdom comprises Great Britain and Northern Ireland. Great Britain comprises England, Wales and Scotland only.

Physical Features

The United Kingdom (UK) constitutes the greater part of the British Isles. The largest of the islands is Great Britain. The next largest comprises Northern Ireland and the Irish Republic. Western Scotland is fringed by the large island chain known as the Hebrides, and to the north east of the Scottish mainland are the Orkney and Shetland Islands. All these, along with the Isle of Wight, Anglesey and the Isles of Scilly, have administrative ties with the mainland, but the Isle of Man in the Irish Sea and the Channel Islands between Great Britain and France are largely self-governing, and are not part of the United Kingdom. The UK is one of the 25 member states of the European Union (EU).

With an area of about 243 000 sq km (94 000 sq miles), the United Kingdom is just under 1 000 km (about 600 miles) from the south coast to the extreme north of Scotland and just under 500 km (around 300 miles) across at the widest point.

- Highest mountain: Ben Nevis, in the highlands of Scotland, at 1 343 m (4 406 ft)

- Longest river: the Severn, 354 km (220 miles) long, which rises in central Wales and flows through Shrewsbury, Worcester and Gloucester in England to the Bristol Channel

- Largest lake: Lough Neagh, Northern Ireland, at 396 sq km (153 sq miles)

- Deepest lake: Loch Morar in the Highlands of Scotland, 310 m (1 017 ft) deep

- Highest waterfall: Eas a'Chual Aluinn, from Glas Bheinn, in the highlands of Scotland, with a drop of 200 m (660 ft)

- Deepest cave: Ogof Ffynnon Ddu, Wales, at 308 m (1 010 ft) deep

- Most northerly point on the British mainland: Dunnet Head, north-east Scotland

- Most southerly point on the British mainland: Lizard Point, Cornwall

- Closest point to mainland continental Europe: Dover, Kent. The Channel Tunnel, which links England and France, is a little over 50 km (31 miles) long, of which nearly 38 km (24 miles) are actually under the Channel.

1.1 Area of the United Kingdom, 2003

	sq km		sq km
United Kingdom	242 514	Shropshire	3 197
		Staffordshire	2 620
Great Britain	228 937	Warwickshire	1 975
		West Midlands (Met County)	902
England and Wales	151 013	Worcestershire	1 741
		East	19 110
England	130 281	Luton UA	43
		Peterborough UA	343
North East	8 573	Southend-on-Sea UA	42
		Thurrock UA	163
Darlington UA	197		
Hartlepool UA	94	Bedfordshire	1 192
Middlesbrough UA	54	Cambridgeshire	3 046
Redcar and Cleveland UA	245	Essex	3 465
Stockton-on-Tees UA	204	Hertfordshire	1 643
		Norfolk	5 371
Durham	2 226	Suffolk	3 801
Northumberland	5 013		
Tyne and Wear (Met County)	540	**London**	1572
North West	14 106	Inner London	319
		Outer London	1 253
Blackburn with Darwen UA	137		
Blackpool UA	35	**South East**	19 069
Halton UA	79		
Warrington UA	181	Bracknell Forest UA	109
		Brighton and Hove UA	83
Cheshire	2 083	Isle of Wight UA	380
Cumbria	6 768	Medway UA	192
Greater Manchester (Met County)	1 276	Milton Keynes UA	309
Lancashire	2 903	Portsmouth UA	40
Merseyside (Met County)	645	Reading UA	40
		Slough UA	33
Yorkshire and the Humber	15 408	Southampton UA	50
		West Berkshire UA	704
East Riding of Yorkshire UA	2 408	Windsor and Maidenhead UA	197
Kingston upon Hull, City of UA	71	Wokingham UA	179
North East Lincolnshire UA	192		
North Lincolnshire UA	846	Buckinghamshire	1 565
York UA	272	East Sussex	1 709
		Hampshire	3 679
North Yorkshire	8 038	Kent	3 544
South Yorkshire (Met County)	1 552	Oxfordshire	2 605
West Yorkshire (Met County)	2 029	Surrey	1 663
		West Sussex	1 991
East Midlands	15 607		
		South West	23 837
Derby UA	78		
Leicester UA	73	Bath and North East Somerset UA	346
Nottingham UA	75	Bournemouth UA	46
Rutland UA	382	Bristol, City of UA	110
		North Somerset UA	374
Derbyshire	2 547	Plymouth UA	80
Leicestershire	2 083	Poole UA	65
Lincolnshire	5 921	South Gloucestershire UA	497
Northamptonshire	2 364	Swindon UA	230
Nottinghamshire	2 085	Torbay UA	63
West Midlands	12 998	Cornwall and the Isles of Scilly	3 563
		Devon	6 564
Herefordshire, County of UA	2 180	Dorset	2 542
Stoke-on-Trent UA	93	Gloucestershire	2 653
Telford and Wrekin UA	290	Somerset	3 451
		Wiltshire	3 255

3

	sq km		sq km
Wales	20 732	Dumfries and Galloway	6 426
		Dundee City	60
Blaenau Gwent	109	East Ayrshire	1 262
Bridgend	251	East Dunbartonshire	175
Caerphilly	278	East Lothian	679
Cardiff[1]	139		
Carmarthenshire[1]	2 394	East Renfrewshire	174
		Edinburgh, City of	264
Ceredigion[1]	1 792	Eilean Siar (Western Isles)	3 071
Conwy	1 126	Falkirk	297
Denbighshire	837	Fife	1 325
Flintshire	438		
Gwynedd	2 535	Glasgow City	175
		Highland	25 659
Isle of Anglesey	711	Inverclyde	160
Merthyr Tydfil	111	Midlothian	354
Monmouthshire	849	Moray	2 238
Neath Port Talbot	441		
Newport[1]	190	North Ayrshire	885
Pembrokeshire[1]	1 589	North Lanarkshire	470
		Orkney Islands	990
Powys	5 181	Perth and Kinross	5 286
Rhondda, Cynon, Taff	424	Renfrewshire	261
Swansea	378	Scottish Borders	4 732
Torfaen	126		
The Vale of Glamorgan[1]	331	Shetland Islands	1 466
Wrexham	504	South Ayrshire	1 222
		South Lanarkshire	1 772
		Stirling	2 187
Scotland	77 925	West Dunbartonshire	159
		West Lothian	427
Aberdeen City	186		
Aberdeenshire	6 313	**Northern Ireland**	13 576
Angus	2 182		
Argyll and Bute	6 909		
Clackmannanshire	159		

1 On boundaries as at 2001.

Source: Office for National Statistics

Parliamentary elections

2.1 Parliamentary elections[1]
United Kingdom

Thousands and percentages

	26 May 1955	8 Oct 1959	15 Oct 1964	31 Mar 1966	18 June 1970[1]	28 Feb 1974	10 Oct 1974	3 May 1979	9 June 1983	11 June 1987	9 April 1992	1 May 1997	7 June 2001
United Kingdom													
Electorate	34 852	35 397	35 894	35 957	39 615	40 256	40 256	41 573	42 704	43 666	43 719	43 846	44 403
Average-electors per seat	55.3	56.2	57.0	57.1	62.9	63.4	63.4	65.5	66.7	67.2	67.2	66.5	67.4
Valid votes counted	26 760	27 863	27 657	27 265	28 345	31 340	29 189	31 221	30 671	32 530	33 614	31 286	26 367
As percentage of electorate	*76.8*	*78.7*	*77.1*	*75.8*	*71.5*	*77.9*	*72.5*	*75.1*	*71.8*	*74.5*	*76.7*	*71.4*	*59.4*
England and Wales													
Electorate	30 591	31 109	31 610	31 695	34 931	35 509	35 509	36 695	37 708	38 568	38 648	38 719	39 228
Average-electors per seat	55.9	56.9	57.8	57.9	63.9	64.3	64.3	66.5	67.2	68.8	68.8	68.0	68.9
Valid votes counted	23 570	24 619	24 384	24 116	24 877	27 735	25 729	27 609	27 082	28 832	29 897	27 679	23 243
As percentage of electorate	*77.0*	*79.1*	*77.1*	*76.1*	*71.2*	*78.1*	*72.5*	*75.2*	*71.8*	*74.8*	*77.5*	*71.5*	*59.3*
Scotland													
Electorate	3 388	3 414	3 393	3 360	3 659	3 705	3 705	3 837	3 934	3 995	3 929	3 949	3 984
Average-electors per seat	47.7	48.1	47.8	47.3	51.5	52.2	52.2	54.0	54.6	55.5	54.6	54.8	55.3
Valid votes counted	2 543	2 668	2 635	2 553	2 688	2 887	2 758	2 917	2 825	2 968	2 931	2 817	2 313
As percentage of electorate	*75.1*	*78.1*	*77.6*	*76.0*	*73.5*	*77.9*	*74.5*	*76.0*	*71.8*	*74.3*	*74.2*	*71.3*	*58.1*
Northern Ireland													
Electorate	873	875	891	902	1 025	1 027	1 037	1 028	1 050	1 090	1 141	1 178	1 191
Average-electors per seat	72.8	72.9	74.2	75.2	85.4	85.6	86.4	85.6	61.8	64.1	67.1	65.4	66.2
Valid votes counted	647	576	638	596	779	718	702	696	765	730	785	791	810
As percentage of electorate	*74.1*	*65.8*	*71.7*	*66.1*	*76.0*	*69.9*	*67.7*	*67.7*	*72.9*	*67.0*	*68.8*	*67.1*	*68.0*
Members of Parliament elected: (Numbers)	630	630	630	630	630	635	635	635	650	650	651	659	659
Conservative	344	364	303	253	330	296	276	339	396	375	336	165	166
Labour	277	258	317	363	287	301	319	268	209	229	271	418	412
Liberal Democrat	6	6	9	12	6	14	13	11	17	17	20	46	52
Social Democratic Party	-	-	-	-	-	-	-	-	6	5	-	-	-
Scottish National Party	-	-	-	-	1	7	11	2	2	3	3	6	5
Plaid Cymru	-	-	-	-	-	2	3	2	2	3	4	4	4
Other[2]	3	2	1	2	6	15	13	13	18	18	17	20	20

1 The Representation of the People Act 1969 lowered the minimum voting age from 21 to 18 years with effect from 16 February 1970.
2 Including the Speaker.

Source: University of Plymouth for the Electoral Commission: 01752 233205

2.2 Parliamentary by-elections
United Kingdom

	April 1992 - April 1997	General[1] Election April 1992	May 1997 - June 2001	General[1,2] Election May 1997	June 2001 - November 2004	General[1] Election June 2001
Numbers of by-elections	18		17		6	
Votes recorded						
By party (percentages)						
Conservative	*21.4*	*40.1*	*27.0*	*25.1*	*16.9*	*21.2*
Labour	*39.5*	*36.2*	*29.7*	*40.1*	*38.8*	*58.3*
Liberal Democrat	*24.6*	*16.4*	*22.1*	*14.4*	*29.7*	*13.7*
Scottish National Party	*5.2*	*3.1*	*6.0*	*4.1*	-	-
Plaid Cymru	*0.5*	*0.2*	*2.5*	*2.3*	*2.6*	*2.1*
Other	*8.8*	*4.1*	*12.7*	*14.1*	*12.1*	*4.7*
Total votes recorded (percentages)	*100.0*	*100.0*	*100.0*	*100.0*	*100.0*	*100.0*
(thousands)	625	808	435	723	148	205

1 Votes recorded in the same seats in the previous General Election.
2 Proportions of 'other' votes inflated by the fact that votes were cast for the retiring Speaker as 'The Speaker seeking re-election' and not as a party candidate.

Source: University of Plymouth for the Electoral Commission: 01752 233205

International development

Chapter 3

International development

Overseas development assistance

(Tables 3.1 and 3.2)

The UK development assistance programme is administered by the Department for International Development (DFID) to promote the economic development and welfare of recipient countries. It is managed within financial years, the money being voted annually by Parliament. Since 1992 the statistics relating to the programme are also published on a financial year basis and on a calendar year basis for both international aid comparisons and for national purposes such as the balance of payments.

Aid flows can be measured before (gross) or after (net) deduction of repayments of principal on past loans. These tables show only the gross figures.

Assistance is provided in two main ways: bilateral, that is directly to recipient countries or to institutions in the United Kingdom for work on behalf of such countries, or multilateral, that is to international institutions for their development assistance programmes. Table 3.1 shows the main groups of multilateral agencies, the International Development Association being the largest in the World Bank Group.

Bilateral assistance takes various forms:

Project or sector aid is finance for investment schemes primarily designed to increase the physical capital of the recipient country, including contributions for local and recurrent costs.

Sector-wide programmes (typically in education, health or agriculture) comprise a combination of assistance including direct budget support, financial assistance in the form of projects and technical co-operation.

Programme aid is financial assistance to fund imports, sector support programmes or budgetary expenditure, usually as part of or in conjunction with a World Bank/IMF co-ordinated structural adjustment programme.

Technical co-operation is the provision of know-how in the form of personnel, training, research and associated costs.

Grants and other aid in kind are used to provide equipment and supplies, and support to the development work of UK and international voluntary organisations.

Humanitarian assistance comprises food aid and other disaster relief.

Aid and Trade Provision is a special allocation to soften the terms of credit to developing countries by mixing aid funds with private export credits. The ATP scheme lacked poverty elimination as its central focus and was closed in November 1997.

CDC Capital Partners (formerly The Commonwealth Development Corporation) invests in productive public or private sector projects in developing countries.

Other Government Departments' expenditure covers debt relief, drug-related assistance and support to the British Council or voluntary organisations.

Most of the expenditure not allocable by region in Table 3.2 is for assistance provided through organisations in the United Kingdom.

Fuller statistics of the UK's development assistance effort are published annually in *Statistics on International Development* (obtainable from Statistics Department, Abercrombie House, East Kilbride, Glasgow G75 8EA). International comparisons are available in the OECD Development Assistance Committee's annual report. The latest is *2002 Report: Development Co-operation* (available from The Stationery Office).

3.1 Gross public expenditure on aid (GPEX)[1]
United Kingdom

£ Thousand

		1995 /96	1996 /97	1997 /98	1998 /99	1999 /00	2000 /01	2001 /02	2002 /03	2003 /04
Bilateral Assistance										
Department for International Development										
Project or Sector Aid	LUJS	121 456	106 361	96 448	127 634	174 159	185 881	243 054	286 562	295 639
Programme Aid	LUJW	83 494	96 299	84 784	133 574	141 165	255 329	264 711	217 933	387 183
Technical Co-operation Projects	LUOS	446 788	457 060	487 003	479 621	518 095	547 231	594 267	713 228	697 259
Grants and Other Aid in Kind	LUOT	184 315	191 152	172 665	189 311	170 124	178 766	200 149	270 824	274 272
Humanitarian Assistance	LUOU	141 410	121 886	94 680	113 159	227 157	210 363	189 749	292 272	285 110
Debt Relief	LUOV	27 337	23 529	23 161	25 659	23 140	21 188	18 322	23 571	19 517
Aid and Trade Provision	LUOW	71 988	61 978	60 711	56 898	37 790	27 645	23 094	17 733	13 399
CDC Investments	LUOX	279 986	189 082	249 062	166 716	268 518	201 427	159 352	237 324	350 356
Other Government Departments	LUOY	61 606	34 224	170 171	87 147	100 721	149 128	319 536	487 522	287 535
Total	LUOZ	1 418 381	1 281 571	1 438 684	1 379 719	1 660 868	1 776 959	2 012 234	2 546 969	2 610 270
Multilateral Assistance										
European Community[2]	LUPA	693 690	636 418	557 287	754 549	752 473	727 685	756 885	901 059	1 104 476
World Bank Group	LUPB	206 877	174 398	189 851	175 254	167 297	270 367	243 016	239 794	402 543
International Monetary Fund	LUPC	30 000	20 000	20 000	18 000	17 000	–	11 147	11 434	8 417
UN Agencies	LUPD	116 772	130 775	141 300	133 983	175 730	245 299	226 292	189 105	207 947
Regional Development Banks	LUPE	69 513	58 833	60 411	66 295	67 178	54 803	75 382	90 647	80 391
Other	LUPF	27 036	30 665	30 846	30 357	32 450	36 607	41 976	43 837	76 781
Total	LUPG	1 143 887	1 051 089	999 695	1 178 438	1 212 128	1 334 761	1 354 698	1 475 876	1 880 555
Administrative costs	LUPH	72 198	82 133	91 436	98 645	104 601	119 893	112 222	129 008	246 894
Total Gross Public Expenditure on Aid	LUPI	2 634 465	2 414 793	2 529 815	2 656 802	2 977 597	3 231 613	3 479 154	4 151 853	4 737 719

1 See chapter text.
2 The institution, not the member states of the European Union.

Source: Department for International Development: 01355 843612

3.2 Total bilateral gross public expenditure on aid (GPEX): by main recipient countries and regions[1]
United Kingdom

£ Thousand

		1995 /96	1996 /97	1997 /98	1998 /99	1999 /00	2000 /01	2001 /02	2002 /03	2003 /04
Main recipients										
India	LUPJ	154 730	111 789	114 022	110 374	107 283	128 800	204 528	188 837	245 365
Iraq	C222	6 954	6 282	3 351	5 749	6 585	9 545	7 760	18 853	209 313
Tanzania	LUPK	29 900	56 414	51 437	78 085	75 099	112 034	205 812	98 912	162 551
Bangladesh	LUPM	54 282	44 329	39 078	67 361	71 794	77 033	62 983	77 441	155 855
Congo, Democratic Republic	C223	1 356	1 213	8 000	1 546	2 132	6 752	10 262	15 586	151 657
South Africa	LUPT	17 666	23 214	28 372	35 110	47 838	36 755	44 178	57 186	93 332
Afghanistan	C224	4 986	9 644	6 873	3 873	5 452	7 465	50 039	76 023	84 595
Ghana	LUPL	26 305	28 474	30 428	62 912	52 032	75 215	54 619	91 473	78 194
Pakistan	LUPY	60 234	59 365	32 654	26 904	23 471	16 345	44 911	47 062	66 548
Uganda	LUPN	40 590	49 207	59 325	64 261	90 286	97 572	68 724	54 868	59 614
Malawi	LUPP	35 720	44 876	30 651	52 629	49 337	57 499	50 679	55 421	57 722
Ethiopia	C225	25 716	8 371	11 867	9 793	7 299	16 484	12 091	44 240	43 694
China	LUPS	32 803	30 956	38 616	39 190	26 260	56 766	50 418	44 625	42 535
Mozambique	LUPV	22 026	26 610	48 311	28 902	70 630	43 304	134 671	39 617	36 870
Algeria	C226	150	46	120	39	5	–	150	–	34 932
Sierra Leone	ZBXQ	8 963	10 841	3 293	9 153	30 044	35 148	37 177	32 761	34 439
Zimbabwe	LUPX	20 191	21 007	13 715	29 394	17 363	14 716	15 726	30 145	34 172
Zambia	LUPO	58 915	40 529	46 742	33 567	46 779	93 488	59 288	45 705	33 196
Nigeria	C227	8 210	7 866	9 346	11 216	14 597	16 356	21 625	30 733	32 715
Nepal	LUQC	16 485	15 271	16 953	16 041	14 847	17 695	23 414	27 887	32 036
Total	LUQD	626 182	596 304	593 154	686 099	759 133	918 972	1 159 055	1 077 375	1 689 335
Total other countries	LUQE	792 199	685 267	845 529	693 620	901 735	857 987	853 179	1 469 594	920 935
Regional totals										
Africa	LUQF	437 146	445 153	450 076	574 289	630 662	781 731	878 685	904 288	1 066 481
America	LUQG	192 769	107 291	271 336	170 125	239 831	183 294	172 707	229 826	108 843
Asia	LUQH	465 945	401 402	391 763	349 939	381 890	418 279	545 264	621 548	949 657
Europe	LUQI	129 941	137 934	114 537	83 171	191 899	114 155	98 214	384 745	71 162
Pacific	LUQJ	14 053	12 458	26 890	20 251	7 248	5 134	7 042	5 496	4 511
World unallocated[2]	LUQK	178 527	177 333	184 081	181 943	209 338	274 366	310 322	401 066	409 615
Total Bilateral GPEX	LUQL	1 418 381	1 281 571	1 438 683	1 379 719	1 660 868	1 776 959	2 012 234	2 546 969	2 610 270

1 See chapter text.
2 World unallocated comprises block grants to the British Council, VSO, CSOs, Research Institutions and Commonwealth Organisations based in the UK, and some ATP Technical Co-operation.

Source: Department for International Development: 01355 843612

Defence

Chapter 4

Defence

This section includes figures on Defence expenditure, on the size and role of the Armed Forces and on related support activities.

Much of the material in this section can be found in *UK Defence Statistics 2004* (The Stationery Office).

Defence expenditure

(Table 4.1)

UK Defence Expenditure – the move from cash to resource accounting

Up until financial Year 1998/99, Government expenditure was accounted for on a Cash basis. For the years 1999/00 and 2000/01 there was a transitional period from Cash to Resource Accounting & Budgeting (RAB), whereby Government Departments continued to be controlled on a cash basis, but were required to produce consolidated resource accounts. Since 2001/02 Government expenditure has been accounted for on a resource basis only. The main difference arising from the adoption of RAB is that costs are accounted for as they are incurred, rather than when payment is made (the principle of accruals). This gives rise to timing differences in accounting between the Cash and RAB systems and also to the recognition of depreciation. Additionally, under RAB, departments are required to account for a cost of capital charge, equivalent to an interest charge on the capital (in the form of net assets) held on the Balance Sheet.

The change from cash based accounting to resource (accruals) based accounting, and the two stage introduction of RAB (outlined below) has affected the time series comparability of the data.

Please refer to UK Defence Statistics 2002 Chapter 1 – Resource Accounting & Budgeting section for a summary of the key events leading to the introduction of RAB. Back copies of this publication are available at *www.dasa.mod.uk/national statistics.*

Managing Resources

Under Resource Accounting, Government Departments are accountable for their spending against Resource and Capital Departmental Expenditure Limits (DELs). Spending against the Resource DEL covers current items such as in year personnel costs, equipment/stock consumption, maintenance of land and buildings etc. The Capital budget, whilst part of the overall DEL, reflects investment spending that will appear on the Department's balance sheet and be consumed over a number of years. Departments are also responsible for Annually Managed Expenditure (AME). This spending is demand led (for example, payment of War Pensions) and therefore cannot be controlled by Departments in the same way.

Stage 1 of RAB covered the financial years 2001/02 and 2002/03. Unlike cash, costs were accrued as they were incurred, rather than when payment was made. For 2001/02 and 2002/03 the Resource DEL did not include the non-cash costs associated with Resource Accounting, such as depreciation and the cost of capital charge. During the Stage 1 period these non-cash costs fell within Annually Managed Expenditure (AME) and were not controlled to the same degree as DELs. This arrangement was applied in Stage 1 only and allowed departments an interim period to gain experience of managing the new non-cash costs, to reconsider their holdings of stocks and fixed assets, which impact the non-cash costs, prior to the charge impacting on the more tightly controlled DELs.

Stage 2 of RAB began at the start of the financial year 2003/04. This involved the movement of the primary non-cash costs (depreciation and the cost of capital charge) from AME into the Resource DEL.

The change in definition of the DELs combined with volatile non-cash costs over the Stage 1 period make time series comparisons over the period 2001/02 – 2003/04 complex. Additionally, the mix of cash and non-cash costs may be subject to change in future years.

Factors affecting Cash to RAB data consistency

i) There are timing differences as to when payments are seen to be made.

ii) The movement of Non-Cash items of expenditure from AME into the Resource DEL from 2003/04 onwards has the 'apparent' effect of inflating the Resource DEL.

iii) In financial year 2003/04 the Cost of Capital Charge is reduced from 6 per cent to 3.5 per cent. This non-cash cost may change in future years.

Under Resource Accounting the individual headings consist of the following:

Equipment support: Internal and contracted out costs for equipment repair and maintenance.

Stock consumption: Consumption of armament, medical, dental, veterinary, oil, strategic weapon systems, clothing, and general stores.

Property management: Estate and facilities management services and costs for building's maintenance.

Movements: Cost of transportation of freight and personnel.

Accommodation and utilities: Charges include rent, rates, gas, electricity, water and sewerage costs.

Professional fees: Includes legal and consultancy fees.

Fuel: Relates to fuel consumption by military vehicles, ships and aircraft.

Expenditure on fixed asset categories: Includes disposal receipts but include in particular:

Intangible assets: comprise the development costs of major equipment projects and Intellectual Property Rights.

Assets in the course of construction: largely consist of major weapons platforms under construction in the Defence Procurement Agency (there is a smaller element of buildings under construction). Once construction is complete, those platforms will transfer to the relevant top level budget holder as Fighting Equipment.

Capital spares: are items of repairable material used to replace parts of assets undergoing repair, refurbishment, and maintenance, servicing, modification, enhancement or conversion. Examples include aircraft engines and ships.

Departmental Annually Managed Expenditure (AME) is spending that is outside the Departmental Expenditure Limit (DEL), but included in departmental budgets. This includes the provision for Armed Forces Pensions and non-cash items such as depreciation, cost of capital charges, and provision. At present, these non-cash items are not subject to the same controls and are included in Annually Managed Expenditure but from 2003/04 they will be included as part of the DEL.

For 2001/02 through to 2003/04, the 'other' category contains the sum of movements, cash release and cost of capital credit on nuclear provisions and also QinetiQ loan repayments. In addition, for 2001/02 and 2002/03 this category includes depreciation and the cost of capital charge. The 2002/03 figure includes a supplementary estimate for additional funding to cover the asset write off in this year.

Service personnel

(Tables 4.2, 4.4, 4.5, 4.8 and 4.10)

The Regular Forces consist entirely of volunteer members serving on a whole-time basis, figures for which include both Trained and Untrained personnel and exclude Gurkhas, Full Time Reserve Service personnel, the Home Service battalions of the Royal Irish Regiment, mobilised reservists and Naval Activated Reservists.

Locally Entered Personnel are recruited outside the United Kingdom for whole-time service in special formations with special conditions of service and normally restricted locations. The Brigade of Gurkhas is an example.

The Regular Forces are supported by Reserves and Auxiliary Forces. There are both regular and volunteer Reserves. Regular Reserves consist of former Service personnel with a Reserve liability. Volunteer Reserves are open to both former Service personnel and civilians. The call out liabilities of the various reserve forces differ in accordance with their roles.

All three Services run cadet forces for young people and the Combined Cadet Force, which is found in certain schools where education is continued to the age of 17 or above, may operate sections for any or all of the Services.

Full-Time Reserve Service personnel represent reserves serving full-time in regular posts. This was made possible by the Reserve Forces Act 1996. None existed before 1998. FTRS figures include Full Commitment (FC), Home Commitment (HC) and Limited Commitment (LC) individuals.

Home Service battalions of the Royal Irish Regiment. Up until 1 July 1992, this was the Ulster Defence Regiment. The figures for the Territorial Army include Officer Training Corps and non-regular permanent staff.

The figures for cadet forces for each service include the Combined Cadet Force. Naval Service figures include officers and civilian instructors. The Army and Royal Air Force figures exclude officers and civilian instructors.

Intake of UK regular forces from civilian life: by service

(Table 4.2)

This table shows all intakes to UK Regular Forces including re-enlistments and rejoined reservists.

Formation of the armed forces

(Table 4.3)

This table shows the number of units which comprise the 'teeth' elements of the Armed Forces and excludes supporting units.

Defence

Outflow of UK regular forces: by service

(Table 4.4)

This table does not include promotions to officer from other ranks and miscellaneous outflow.

Civilian personnel

(Table 4.6)

In previous years, the Ministry of Defence (MoD) civilian workforce definition has reflected the historical requirement to understand the number of civil servants being directly funded. However with changes in employment legislation and the requirement to plan the future of the civilian workforce there was a need to change the definition to a more inclusive one better reflecting modern human resources methods and policies. In the longer term it will be used for skills planning, ensuring that the MoD has a well-equipped workforce able to provide the best support to the UK Armed Forces.

In summary, the change over previous years is the addition of two further categories of individuals:

> *Casual staff* – those employed on a short-term casual contract;

> *Those not directly funded* – those staff who are employed by the MoD, but whose salaries are paid for by another Department/Agency etc. This includes staff on loan to other government departments or working for NATO, as well as those on a career break or long term sickness absence.

These additions allow two levels of definition to be established:

> *Definition – Level 1* This *includes* permanent and casual personnel, Royal Fleet Auxiliaries, but_*excludes* Trading Funds. This is generally used for internal reporting and planning.

> *Definition – Level 0* This contains all those at Level 1 *plus* Trading Funds and Locally Engaged Civilians. This is used for external reporting, including National Statistics publications CPS1 and UKDS, and Parliamentary business.

For more information on the revised civilian workforce definition, visit: *www.dasa.mod.uk/natstats/consultation/consultation.html*

Prior to April 1995 all part-timers were counted as half of full time. From that date they are counted as the number of hours worked as a proportion of normal conditioned hours.

As from 1 April 2000 a new top level budget was formed in the Centre called Defence Logistics Organisation, replacing the top level budgets CinC Fleet Support, Quarter Master General and RAF Logistics Command.

The QinetiQ portion of the Defence Evaluation and Research Agency was established as a private company in July 2001. The War Pensions Agency transferred from the Department of Work & Pensions in 2001. The Clyde Dockyards were contractorised in 2002.

The 1993 to 1995 Royal Fleet Auxiliary (RFA) figures used in calculating the Level 1 measure are estimates. Data on manually paid staff before 1999 is not available, so estimates are used.

Totals and subtotals have been rounded separately and so may not appear to be the sums of their parts.

Family accommodation and defence land holdings

(Table 4.7)

In November 1996 most of the MoD's housing stock in England and Wales was sold to a private company, Annington Homes. The homes retained for use by Service families were leased back, with the condition that the MoD release a certain number of houses each year for disposal by Annington. The proceeds of the sale are being used to upgrade the housing stock.

The table also presents statistics of land and foreshore in the United Kingdom owned or leased by the MoD or over which it has limited rights under grants or licences. Land declared as surplus to Defence requirements is also included.

Deployment of service personnel

(Table 4.8)

The figures for Service personnel in England, Wales, Scotland and Northern Ireland are obtained from a different source from that used to compile the United Kingdom total. Consequently the sum of the national figures can differ from the United Kingdom total. The figures for Northern Ireland include all personnel who are serving on emergency tours of duty but exclude the former Ulster Defence Regiment, now the Home Services element of the Royal Irish Regiment. The figures for overseas countries include service personnel who are on loan to countries in the areas shown. Royal Navy and Royal Marines personnel on board ship are included in the United Kingdom figure if the ship was in home waters on the situation date or otherwise against the appropriate overseas area. All Defence Attaches and Advisers and their staffs are included under 'Other Locations' and not identified within specific areas. From 2001 the grouping of overseas locations has been changed to give a more relevant overview.

UK regular forces – deaths

(Table 4.9)

Rates have been standardised to 2003 Tri-Service age and sex structure.

Health

(Table 4.10)

The Services operate a number of hospitals in this country and in areas abroad where there is a significant British military presence. These hospitals take as patients, members of all three Services and their dependants; in addition, the hospitals in the United Kingdom take civilian patients under arrangements agreed with the National Health Service. Medical support is also supplied by Service medical staff at individual units, ships and stations.

Defence services and the civilian community

(Table 4.11)

This table covers incidents in which Rescue Coordinating Centres (RCCs) in the United Kingdom coordinated search and rescue (SAR) action in which elements of the Armed Forces were involved. The table also includes urgent medical incidents in which the Forces SAR facilities gave assistance (e.g. inter-hospital transfers). More than one element of the SAR services are called to the same incident. Consequently, the number of callouts is likely to be greater than the number of incidents.

Persons rescued refers to civilian or military personnel who were removed from a hazardous environment or were transported from the scene by SAR Units in order to receive urgent medical attention. People assisted by Mountain Rescue Teams, but subsequently transported from the scene by helicopter, are credited as having been rescued by the helicopter unit concerned. The total incidents figure also includes any HM Coastguard incidents under the control of ARCC Kinloss.

The Ministry of Defence helps the civil community in a variety of ways, for example by providing assistance in time of natural disasters or other emergencies and by undertaking community projects which are of training value to the Services. In some cases facilities established primarily for defence purposes also provide benefits to the general public.

Service assistance may be provided during an industrial dispute at the request of the civil ministries in order to maintain services essential to the life of the community (e.g. maintenance of emergency fire services). Figures for the

number of man weeks spent by service personnel are no longer collected, so this has been removed from the table.

The Royal Navy Fishery Protection squadron operates within the British fishery limits under contract to the Department for Environment, Food and Rural Affairs. Boardings carried out by vessels of the Executive Environment and Rural Affairs Department and the Department of Agriculture for Northern Ireland are not included.

4.1 UK Defence expenditure[1]

£ million

		2001 /02	2002 /03	2003[2] /04	2004[3] /05
Defence Spending	C228	..	..	30 916	29 868
Departmental Expenditure Limits (DEL)	SNKJ	24 439	26 144	37 229	37 917
Resource DEL					
Expenditure on personnel	SNKK	9 456	9 969	10 435	10 567
Armed forces	SNKL	7 014	7 385	7 980	7 865
Civilians	SNKM	2 442	2 584	2 455	2 702
Depreciation/impairments	SNKN	..	..	6 313	8 049
Cost of capital	SNKO	..	..	2 770	2 894
Equipment support	SNKP	2 419	3 135	3 804	3 596
Stock consumption	SNKQ	1 294	1 222	1 060	1 409
Property management	SNKR	1 222	1 453	1 393	1 445
Movements	SNKS	718	505	492	412
Accommodation and utilities	SNKT	572	544	643	673
Professional fees	SNKU	559	468	549	544
Fuel	SNKV	160	185	161	159
Other	SNKW	2 121	2 477	3 701	1 843
Capital DEL					
Expenditure on fixed asset categories					
Intangible assets	SNKX	1 031	1 756	1 662	1 641
Land and buildings	SNKY	−163	−185	−211	232
Fighting equipment[4]	SNKZ	34	320	−77	5
Plant, machinery and vehicles	SNLA	99	132	61	84
IT and communications equipment	SNLB	84	94	37	86
Assets in the course of construction	SNLC	4 479	3 601	3 854	3 757
Capital spares	SNLD	353	467	581	522
Annually Managed Expenditure (AME)	SNLF	14 962	19 293	3 237	978
War pensions	SNLG	1 238	1 166	1 116	1 151
Other	SNLH	13 724	18 127	2 121	−173

1 See chapter text.
2 Provisional outturn.
3 Planned.

4 In 2004/05 there is a forecasted drop in fighting equipment spend due to a large disposal receipt.

Source: Ministry of Defence/DASA (Procurement): 0117 913 4585

4.2 Intake of UK regular forces from civilian life: by service[1]

Numbers

		1993 /94	1994 /95	1995 /96	1996 /97	1997[2] /98	1998 /99	1999 /00	2000 /01	2001 /02	2002 /03	2003 /04
All services:												
Male	KCJB	10 620	11 150	15 500	19 230	19 740	22 560	22 390	20 410	20 950	23 040	20 760
Female	KCJC	1 330	1 850	2 180	2 940	3 220	3 440	3 160	2 610	2 700	3 240	2 710
Total	KCJA	11 950	13 010	17 670	22 160	22 960	26 000	25 550	23 020	23 650	26 280	23 470
Naval service:												
Male	KCJE	1 280	960	2 010	3 400	3 540	4 110	4 250	3 990	4 270	4 420	3 530
Female	KCJF	260	340	350	560	570	660	700	630	740	800	580
Total	KCJD	1 540	1 300	2 360	3 960	4 110	4 770	4 950	4 620	5 010	5 220	4 120
Army:												
Male	KCJJ	8 760	9 490	11 510	13 580	13 500	15 010	14 750	13 450	13 620	15 060	13 930
Female	KCJK	810	1 190	1 380	1 940	1 970	1 980	1 750	1 320	1 240	1 550	1 260
Total	KCJI	9 580	10 680	12 890	15 520	15 470	16 990	16 500	14 770	14 850	16 610	15 190
Royal Air Force:												
Male	KCJM	580	700	1 980	2 250	2 700	3 450	3 380	2 980	3 070	3 550	3 290
Female	KCJN	260	320	450	430	680	800	710	660	720	890	870
Total	KCJL	840	1 020	2 420	2 680	3 380	4 250	4 100	3 630	3 780	4 450	4 160

1 See chapter text.
2 The definitions of intake used have been standardised from 1997/98 to give a more consistent picture across the three services.

Source: Ministry of Defence/DASA (Tri-Service): 020 7218 0390

4.3 Formation of the UK armed forces[1]
As at 1 April

Numbers

		Front Line Units	1994	1995	1996	1997	1998	1999	2000	2001	2002	2003	2004
Royal Navy[2]													
Submarines	KCGA	Vessels	23	16	15	15	15	15	16	16	16	16	15
Carriers and assault ships	KCGB	"	5	5	5	5	5	6	6	6	4	4	5
Cruisers, destroyers and frigates	KCGC	"	37	35	36	35	35	35	32	32	32	31	31
Mine counter-measure	KCGE	"	18	18	18	18	19	20	21	23	22	22	19
Patrol ships and craft	KCGF	"	34	32	32	34	28	24	24	23	23	22	26
Fixed wing aircraft[3]	KCGG	Squadrons	3	3	3	3	3	3	1	1	1	1	1
Helicopters[4]	KCGH	"	17	15	15	15	12	12	9	9	8	8	5
Royal Marines	KCGI	Commandos	3	3	3	3	3	3	3	3	3	3	3
Regular Army													
Royal Armoured Corps[5,6]	KCGJ	Regiments	12	11	11	11	11	11	11	10	10	10	10
Royal Artillery[5]	KCGK	"	16	16	16	16	15	15	15	15	15	15	14
Royal Engineers[7]	KCGL	"	12	10	10	10	10	10	11	11	11	11	11
Infantry	KCGM	Battalions	45	41	41	40	40	40	40	40	40	40	40
Special Air Service	KCGN	Regiments	1	1	1	1	1	1	1	1	1	1	1
Army Air Corps[4]	KCGO	"	6	5	5	5	5	5	–	–	–	–	–
Royal Air Force													
Strike/attack	KCGP	Squadrons	6	6	6	6	6	5	5	5	5	5	5
Offensive support[3]	KCGQ	"	5	5	5	5	5	5	2	2	2	2	2
Air defence	KCGR	"	6	6	6	6	6	5	5	5	5	4	4
Maritime patrol	KCGS	"	3	3	3	3	3	3	3	3	3	3	3
Reconnaissance	KCGT	"	5	5	5	5	5	5	5	5	5	5	5
Airborne early warning[8]	KCGU	"	1	1	2	2	2	2	2	2	2	2	2
Air transport and tankers and helicopters[3]	KCGV	"	15	14	14	13	14	14	8	9	9	9	9
Search and rescue	KCGX	"	2	2	2	2	2	2	2	2	2	2	2
Ground based air defence	KCGY	"	5	5	6	6	6	4	4	4	4	4	4
Field	KCGZ	"	5	5	5	5	5	5	5	6	6	6	6
Joint Helicopter Command													
Royal Navy Helicopter	JUAT	"	..	..	..	..	..	..	4	4	4	4	4
Army Aviation	JUAU	"	..	..	..	..	..	..	5	5	5	5	5
Royal Air Force Helicopter	JUAV	"	..	..	..	..	..	..	6	6	6	6	6
Joint Force Harrier													
Royal Navy	JUAW	"	..	..	..	..	..	..	3	3	3	3	2
Royal Air Force	JUAX	"	..	..	..	..	..	..	3	3	3	3	3

1 See chapter text.
2 Only active vessels are shown from 1995 onwards. All vessels are included before then.
3 From 2000 excludes aircraft transferred to the Joint Force Harrier squadron.
4 From 2000 excludes helicopters transferred to the Joint Helicopter command.
5 Figure for 1994 includes one training regiment.

6 From 2000 includes one Armoured Regiment which is committed to the new Joint Nuclear Biological and Chemical Regiment.
7 Figure for 2000 includes an additional Close Support Regiment formed as a result of the Stategic Defence Review.
8 Figure for 2001 includes an embedded Operational Conversion Unit at the Sentry Operation Establishments.

Source: Ministry of Defence/DASA (Tri-Service): 020 7218 0390

4.4 Outflow of UK regular forces: by service[1]

Numbers

		1993 /94	1994 /95	1995 /96	1996 /97	1997[2] /98	1998 /99	1999 /00	2000 /01	2001 /02	2002 /03	2003 /04
All Services:												
Male	KDNA	29 700	31 050	25 750	29 320	21 860	24 500	23 870	22 520	22 360	21 770	21 200
Female	KDNB	2 430	2 990	3 120	3 680	2 490	2 970	2 750	2 430	2 350	2 340	2 200
Total	KDNC	32 130	34 040	28 860	33 000	24 350	27 470	26 620	24 950	24 710	24 100	23 400
Naval Service:												
Male	KDND	4 610	5 500	4 310	6 190	4 650	4 920	5 160	4 480	5 110	4 680	4 230
Female	KDNE	490	680	630	940	620	610	630	550	690	620	540
Total	KDNF	5 110	6 180	4 940	7 130	5 270	5 530	5 800	5 040	5 800	5 300	4 770
Army:												
Male	KDNI	19 630	20 230	13 940	13 760	13 190	15 320	14 620	13 900	13 290	13 420	13 500
Female	KDNJ	1 290	1 650	1 510	1 600	1 280	1 730	1 580	1 330	1 090	1 140	1 090
Total	KDNK	20 920	21 880	15 440	15 350	14 470	17 050	16 200	15 230	14 380	14 560	14 600
Royal Air Force:												
Male	KDNL	5 450	5 310	7 500	9 380	4 020	4 250	4 080	4 140	3 960	3 670	3 470
Female	KDNM	650	660	980	1 140	590	640	540	540	570	580	570
Total	KDNN	6 100	5 970	8 480	10 520	4 610	4 890	4 620	4 680	4 530	4 250	4 040

1 See chapter text. Comprises all those who left the Regular Forces and includes deaths.
2 The definitions of outflow used have been standardised from 1997/98 to give a more consistent picture across the three services.

Source: Ministry of Defence/DASA (Tri-Service): 020 7218 0390

4.5 UK Defence: service manpower strengths[1]
As at 1 April

Thousands

UK service personnel		1994	1995	1996	1997	1998	1999	2000	2001	2002	2003	2004
Full-time trained strength[2]	ZBTR	248.4	226.3	211.6	197.4	194.0	..	..	189.2	187.1	188.5	190.2
Trained Naval Service	ZBTS	52.4	48.2	45.6	41.7	40.5	39.3	38.9	38.5	37.5	37.6	37.5
UK regulars	ZBTT	52.4	48.2	45.6	41.7	40.4	39.1	38.5	38.0	36.8	36.6	36.4
Full-time reserve service	ZBTU	..	..	..	..	0.1	0.3	0.3	0.5	0.7	1.0	1.1
Trained Army[2]	ZBTV	121.8	108.7	103.6	101.5	100.9	..	..	100.6	100.4	102.0	103.6
UK regulars	ZBTW	116.1	104.5	99.5	97.8	97.5	96.3	96.5	96.3	96.0	97.6	99.4
Full-time reserve service[2]	ZBTX	..	..	..	..	..	..	..	0.8	0.9	1.0	0.7
Gurkhas	ZBTY	5.6	4.2	4.0	3.8	3.4	3.4	3.4	3.5	3.4	3.4	3.4
Trained Royal Air Force	ZBTZ	74.2	69.4	62.5	54.2	52.7	51.9	51.2	50.1	49.2	48.9	49.1
UK regulars	ZBUA	74.2	69.4	62.5	54.2	52.7	51.8	51.0	49.8	48.9	48.5	48.7
Full-time reserve service	ZBUB	..	..	..	..	..	0.1	0.2	0.3	0.3	0.4	0.4
Untrained UK regulars	ZBUC	11.8	11.2	14.3	17.2	19.7	21.5	21.6	21.5	23.0	24.2	22.5
Naval Service	ZBUD	3.4	2.7	2.8	3.5	4.1	4.6	4.3	4.4	4.9	5.0	4.5
Army	ZBUE	6.9	7.2	9.3	11.1	12.4	13.4	13.6	13.2	14.0	14.5	13.3
Royal Air Force	ZBUF	1.5	1.3	2.2	2.7	3.2	3.5	3.7	3.9	4.1	4.7	4.7
Locally Entered Personnel (excluding Gurkhas)	ZBUG	1.2	0.6	0.6	0.4	0.4	0.4	0.4	0.3	0.4	0.4	0.4
Royal Irish Regiment Home Service batallions	ZBUH	5.4	5.3	5.0	4.8	4.6	4.4	4.2	3.8	3.6	3.5	3.4
Reserve personnel	ZBUI	334.1	329.6	327.3	323.5	319.4	307.0	294.8	284.2	273.4	259.7	246.7
Regular Reserves	ZBUJ	262.2	264.1	264.6	259.4	254.9	247.6	241.6	234.9	224.9	212.6	201.4
Naval Services	ZBUK	23.3	23.3	23.9	24.1	24.8	24.7	24.2	23.5	23.5	23.2	22.8
Army	ZBUL	192.5	195.3	195.5	190.1	186.2	180.5	175.5	169.8	161.1	151.5	141.9
of which mobilised:	SNEO	..	..	..	..	0.2	0.1	0.3	0.2	0.3	0.4	0.1
Royal Air Force	ZBUM	46.4	45.5	45.2	45.3	43.9	42.4	41.9	41.6	40.3	37.9	36.6
of which mobilised:	SNEP	..	..	..	..	..	–	–	–	–	–	–
Volunteer Reserves	ZBUN	71.9	65.5	62.6	64.1	64.5	59.4	53.2	49.3	48.5	47.1	45.4
Royal Naval Reserve and Royal Marine Reserve[3]	ZBUO	4.6	3.7	3.5	4.3	4.4	4.5	4.8	4.8	5.0	4.9	4.5
of which mobilised:	SNEQ	..	..	..	..	..	..	..	..	..	0.4	0.1
Territorial Army	ZBUP	65.0	59.7	57.3	57.6	57.6	52.3	45.6	41.9	40.9	39.6	38.3
of which mobilised:	SNER	..	..	..	..	0.6	0.5	0.8	0.4	0.5	4.1	2.9
Royal Auxilliary Air Force	ZBUQ	2.3	2.1	1.9	2.2	2.5	2.6	2.7	2.6	2.6	2.6	2.6
of which mobilised:	SNES	..	..	..	..	..	–	–	–	0.1	0.8	–
Cadet Forces	ZBUR	135.7	143.5	152.1	151.0	150.2	151.0	154.5	151.0	152.3	155.6	155.6
Naval Service	ZBUS	26.7	26.5	26.9	26.3	25.9	24.5	24.1	23.8	23.8	23.2	22.6
Army	ZBUT	65.2	65.0	74.2	74.1	73.9	74.6	77.4	75.4	75.8	78.7	80.5
Royal Air Force	ZBUU	43.8	52.2	51.0	50.7	50.5	51.9	53.0	51.8	52.7	53.7	52.5

1 See chapter text.
2 The recorded Army Officer FTRS strength shows a significant downward revison. This is due to the identification of discrepancies within the underlying raw data supplied to DASA. The process is currently under review and FTRS figures from 2001 have been supplied by the Army Personnel Centre and should be considered as provisional. Figures for 1999 and 2000 were not available at the time of publication.
3 Figures before 1997 do not include University Royal Navy Units.

Source: Ministry of Defence/DASA (Tri-Service): 020 7218 1546

4.6 UK Defence: civilian manpower strengths[1]
As at 1 April

Thousands: Full-time Equivalent

		1994	1995	1996	1997	1998	1999	2000	2001	2002	2003	2004
Ministry of Defence civilians												
Centre												
Non-industrial	KDQE	20.4	18.6	21.8	22.9	22.2	21.5	19.7	19.1	20.0	21.2	22.7
Industrial	KDQF	0.9	0.7	0.9	1.2	1.1	1.0	0.9	0.9	0.8	0.7	0.6
Defence Logistics Organisation												
Non-industrial	ZBTJ	..	..	..	..	..	..	19.7	17.8	17.3	16.4	16.6
Industrial	ZBTK	..	..	..	..	..	..	11.5	8.4	6.3	4.4	4.3
Naval Service												
Non-industrial	KYCW	16.3	15.7	14.3	13.2	12.8	12.0	3.8	3.7	3.8	3.7	4.0
Industrial	KYCX	13.3	12.3	10.0	9.1	8.2	6.9	2.7	2.6	2.3	2.2	2.0
Army												
Non-industrial	KDQK	23.6	23.4	22.9	22.4	21.7	21.6	16.3	16.4	16.0	16.0	15.0
Industrial	KDQL	15.7	15.2	14.4	13.8	12.1	10.6	5.8	5.7	5.5	5.4	5.3
Royal Air Force												
Non-industrial	KDQM	11.9	11.7	11.5	11.5	11.7	12.2	7.1	7.0	7.1	7.0	8.0
Industrial	KDQN	8.6	8.3	8.0	7.8	7.3	7.1	4.5	4.4	4.3	4.4	3.7
Procurement Executive												
Non-industrial	KDQO	15.9	15.7	–	–	–	–	–	–	–	–	–
Industrial	KDQP	3.1	2.5	–	–	–	–	–	–	–	–	–
Level 1 Total	C7PE	129.9	124.0	103.8	101.9	97.1	94.1	91.9	86.0	83.6	81.5	82.2
Non-industrial	C7PF	88.2	85.0	70.4	70.1	68.4	67.4	66.5	64.1	64.2	64.3	66.3
Industrial	C7PG	41.7	39.0	33.4	31.9	28.7	26.7	25.3	21.9	19.3	17.2	15.9
Locally engaged overseas	KDQA	20.9	17.3	17.1	15.9	15.2	14.9	14.8	13.3	14.1	13.8	15.4
Non-industrial	KDQT	7.3	6.6	7.1	7.0	6.7	6.7	6.7	6.3	6.5	6.5	7.3
Industrial	KDQU	13.6	10.7	10.0	8.9	8.4	8.1	8.2	7.0	7.6	7.4	8.1
Trading funds	GQHI	..	..	14.5	15.5	14.0	14.0	14.5	18.8	12.4	12.2	11.4
Level 0 Total	C7PH	150.8	141.3	135.4	133.3	126.3	123.0	121.3	118.2	110.1	107.6	109.0

1 See chapter text. Individuals on temporary and geographic (T&G) promotion are classed as non-industrial. From 2004, staff who cannot be correctly allocated to Top Level Budgets (TLBs) are included with the Centre figures. (numbering approx 60 in 2004).

Source: Ministry of Defence/DASA (Civilian): 020 7218 6019

4.7 Family accommodation and defence land holdings[1]
As at 1 April

			1994	1995	1996	1997	1998	1999	2000	2001	2002	2003	2004
Family accommodation													
United Kingdom: total	KDPA	Thousands	71.1	69.7	72.1	68.6	67.3	65.5	64.8	59.2	55.8	53.8	52.8
Land holdings		Thousand hectares											
United Kingdom													
Land[2]	KDPF	"	223.5	221.0	222.6	221.0	220.0	220.2	219.9	224.3	222.4	221.4	221.3
Foreshore[2]	KDPH	"	18.5	18.4	18.5	18.6	18.6	18.6	18.6	18.6	18.6	18.6	18.6
Rights held	KDPJ	"	100.4	122.3	124.3	124.5	124.5	124.8	124.8	124.8	124.9	131.1	131.1
Defence land													
Used for agricultural purposes	KDPL	"	107.6	107.9	107.4	96.2	103.5	114.5	92.2	98.6	91.8	103.0	100.5
Used for grazing only	KDPM	"	61.3	61.8	60.7	51.9	59.6	65.5	50.3	66.6	60.0	70.2	68.3
Full agricultural use	KDPN	"	46.3	46.1	46.7	44.3	43.9	49.0	41.9	32.0	31.8	32.8	32.2

1 See chapter text.
2 Freehold and leasehold.

Sources: Ministry of Defence/Defence Housing Executive: 020 7305 3051;
Ministry of Defence/Defence Estates: 0121 311 3818

4.8 Deployment of UK service personnel[1]
As at 1 July

Thousands

		1994	1995	1996	1997	1998	1999	2000	2001	2002	2003	2004
UK Service personnel, Regular Forces:												
UK distribution[2]												
In United Kingdom[3,4]	KDOB	192.1	182.2	177.4	171.6	173.4	171.7	170.3	172.0	..	..	..
England	KDOC	156.5	149.4	146.6	142.6	144.6	144.3	143.0	144.1	..	..	..
Wales	KDOD	4.8	5.2	4.3	3.3	3.2	3.3	3.2	2.6	..	..	..
Scotland	KDOE	18.4	16.9	15.5	13.9	14.2	14.9	15.1	14.5	..	..	..
Northern Ireland	KDOF	12.3	9.9	10.5	11.5	11.0	9.0	8.4	9.4	..	..	..
Global deployment[2]												
United Kingdom[3]	MKCN	193.6	180.7	172.0	167.5	165.0	161.0	163.1	162.8	..	..	..
Overseas	KDOG	56.2	50.0	48.5	42.6	43.1	47.1	43.0	40.9	..	..	..
Mainland European States[5]	KDOI	..	..	11.7	6.2	6.9	15.2	8.2	8.6	..	..	..
Germany[6]	KDOH	37.2	33.4	20.8	21.2	20.3	18.0	19.5	17.3	..	..	..
Balkans	MKCO	..	..	..	..	..	..	..	..	..	..	..
Mediterranean[7]	KDOM	2.4	0.6	0.5	0.3	1.2	1.3	1.1	2.3	..	..	..
Gibraltar	KDOJ	1.5	0.6	0.6	0.5	0.5	0.6	0.6	0.5	..	..	..
Cyprus	KDOL	4.1	4.4	4.0	3.9	3.6	3.6	3.5	3.5	..	..	..
Far East/Asia[8]	MKCT	2.0	1.2	1.2	1.5	0.3	0.3	1.0	0.3	..	..	..
Africa	MKCP	..	..	..	..	..	..	..	−	..	..	..
North America	MKCQ	..	..	..	..	..	..	..	2.5	..	..	..
Central/South America	MKCR	..	..	..	..	..	..	..	−	..	..	..
Falkland Islands	MKCS	..	..	..	..	..	..	..	0.8	..	..	..
Other locations, including unallocated	KDOQ	8.9	9.4	9.8	9.0	10.4	8.2	9.1	5.1	..	..	..
Locally entered service personnel:[9]												
United Kingdom	KDOS	1.5	1.8	1.7	2.1	2.1	2.0	2.1	2.3	2.6	2.6	2.6
Gibraltar	KDOT	0.2	0.2	0.2	0.2	0.4	0.4	0.3	0.4	0.4	0.4	0.4
Hong Kong	KDOV	3.7	1.8	1.6	0.7	..	..	..	..	..	..	..
Brunei	KDOW	0.7	0.9	0.7	1.0	0.9	0.8	0.8	0.8	0.8	0.8	0.7
India/Nepal	KDOX	0.2	0.5	0.7	0.9	0.5	0.5	0.5	0.4	0.3	0.4	0.4
Total	KDOK	7.1	5.1	4.9	4.7	4.0	3.7	3.7	3.9	4.2	4.1	4.1

1 See chapter text.
2 Data not available from 2002, because of concerns over the quality of source data. A review of data sources is being undertaken.
3 Figures for global deployment of service personnel are compiled using different methodologies to those for UK distribution. Comparison is therefore not possible between the two sets of UK personnel figures.
4 Includes personnel within the UK whose location is unknown on the 1st July.

5 Includes the Balkans until 2001.
6 Prior to 1996, figures for the Federal Republic of Germany and Mainland European States were combined.
7 Includes Med Near East and Middle East
8 Prior to 1997 figures include personnel serving in Hong Kong.
9 Including Gurkhas.

Source: Ministry of Defence/DASA (Tri-Service): 020 7218 0390

4.9 UK regular forces: deaths[1]

		1994	1995	1996	1997	1998	1999	2000	2001	2002	2003
Deaths											
Total Number	SNIA	216	201	142	160	162	139	148	140	148	170
Male	SNIB	209	192	140	151	154	136	144	137	139	163
Female	SNIC	7	9	2	9	8	3	4	3	9	7
Rates per thousand											
Tri-service	SNIH	0.89	0.94	0.64	0.80	0.77	0.67	0.72	0.68	0.72	0.82
Navy	SNII	0.70	0.57	0.63	0.86	0.63	0.61	0.62	0.79	0.66	0.90
Army[2]	SNIJ	1.09	0.98	0.73	0.92	0.85	0.72	0.81	0.71	0.85	0.79
RAF	SNIK	0.61	0.83	0.44	0.49	0.64	0.49	0.62	0.48	0.52	0.75

1 See chapter text.
2 Excludes Gurkhas.

Source: Ministry of Defence/DASA (Health Statistics): 01225 468008

4.10 Strength of uniformed UK medical staff[1]
As at 1 April

Numbers

		1994	1995	1996	1997	1998	1999	2000	2001	2002	2003	2004
Qualified doctors:												
Naval Service	KDMA	270	260	240	210	210	210	210	220	220	230	240
Army	KDMB	490	470	430	430	440	450	460	470	490	550	600
Royal Air Force	KDMC	360	330	270	220	210	200	180	180	180	190	200
All Services	KDMD	1 120	1 070	940	870	850	860	860	870	890	970	1 040
Qualified dentists:												
Naval Service	KDME	80	70	60	60	60	60	60	60	60	60	60
Army	KDMF	170	150	140	140	140	140	140	150	140	150	150
Royal Air Force	KDMG	120	110	100	90	80	80	80	80	70	70	80
All Services	KDMH	360	340	310	290	280	290	280	290	280	270	290
Support staff:[2]												
Naval Service	KDMI	1 400	1 410	1 290	1 020	950	1 060	1 100	1 060	1 110	1 180	1 200
Nursing services	ZBTL	..	..	..	..	..	220	220	230	260	300	310
Support	ZBTM	..	..	..	..	..	840	880	830	850	880	890
Army	KDMJ	3 760	3 460	3 280	3 020	3 090	3 120	3 210	3 260	3 320	3 410	3 560
Nursing services	ZBTN	..	..	..	..	..	520	570	610	650	710	770
Support	ZBTO	..	..	..	..	..	2 600	2 640	2 650	2 670	2 700	2 800
Royal Air Force	KDMK	1 840	1 800	1 400	1 210	1 190	1 360	1 460	1 480	1 500	1 600	1 680
Nursing services	ZBTP	..	..	..	..	..	330	400	420	450	470	480
Support	ZBTQ	..	..	..	..	..	1 030	1 060	1 070	1 050	1 130	1 200
All Services	KDML	7 000	6 660	5 980	5 260	5 230	5 540	5 760	5 800	5 930	6 180	6 440

1 See chapter text. Includes staff employed at units (including ships) and in hospitals.
2 Includes all members of the Nursing Services/Nursing Corps. From 1999, figures for support staff have been split so that nurses are separate from other support staff.

Source: Ministry of Defence/DASA (Tri- Service): 020 7218 0390

4.11 UK Defence services and the civilian community[1]

Numbers

		1993	1994	1995	1996	1997	1998	1999	2000	2001	2002	2003
Search and rescue operations at home												
Call outs of:	GPYC	2 145	2 017	2 297	2 164	1 941	1 898	1 912	1 941	1 763	1 684	1 714
Royal Navy helicopters	GPXO	606	560	665	512	495	463	499	499	502	436	424
Royal Air Force helicopters	GPXP	1 260	1 215	1 392	1 392	1 258	1 257	1 235	1 278	1 115	1 122	1 173
Contractorised and other helicopters	GPXQ	47	26	24	27	16	20	–	–	–	–	–
Royal Air Force Nimrod aircraft	GPXR	73	74	78	69	79	71	65	71	54	46	37
Other fixed wing aircraft[2]	GPXS	2	3	6	1	2	2	–	1	1	1	–
HM ships and auxilliary vessels[2]	KCMG	8	6	7	1	3	3	–	–	–	–	–
Royal Air Force mountain rescue teams	KCMH	149	133	125	162	88	82	113	92	91	79	80
Persons rescued: total	KCMI	1 503	1 390	1 382	1 550	1 226	1 243	1 204	1 316	1 182	1 224	1 270
By rescue service												
Royal Navy helicopters	GPXT	406	369	412	356	328	283	355	360	386	314	314
Royal Air Force helicopters	GPXU	947	892	918	1 084	877	937	832	934	781	900	920
Royal Air Force mountain rescue teams	GPXV	97	49	39	100	15	12	17	22	15	10	36
Other	GPXW	53	80	13	10	6	11	–	–	–	–	–
By type of rescue												
Rescue	GPXX	479	464	275	307	219	317	307	276	281	343	271
Medrescue	GPXY	764	766	824	921	721	667	640	713	629	654	785
Medivac	GPXZ	194	123	220	275	224	209	216	241	228	201	174
Recovery	GPYA	32	25	43	34	54	43	32	29	36	21	25
Other	GPYB	34	12	20	13	8	7	9	57	8	5	15
Search and rescue incidents: Total	KCMM	1 890	1 791	2 036	1 919	1 750	1 697	1 714	1 781	1 608	1 544	1 599

		1993	1994/95	1995/96	1996/97	1997/98	1998/99	1999/00	2000/01	2001/02	2002/03	2003/04
Fishery protection												
Vessels boarded	KCMO	2 540	1 556	1 707	1 884	1 715	1 879	1 716	1 603	1 464	1 375	1 710

1 See chapter text.
2 Not permanently on stand-by.

Source: Ministry of Defence/DASA (Logistics): 01225 468769/467249

Population and vital statistics

Chapter 5

Population and vital statistics

This section begins with a summary of population figures for the United Kingdom and constituent countries for 1851 to 2026 and for Great Britain from 1801 (Table 5.1). Table 5.2 analyses the components of population change. Table 5.3 gives details of the national sex and age structures for years up to the present date, with projected figures up to the year 2026. Legal marital condition of the population is shown in Table 5.4. The distribution of population at regional and local levels is summarised in Table 5.5.

In the main, historical series relate to census information, while mid-year estimates, which make allowance for under-enumeration in the census, are given for the recent past and the present (from 1961 onwards).

Population

(Tables 5.1 to 5.3)

Figures shown in these tables relate to the population enumerated at successive censuses, (up to 1951), mid-year estimates (from 1961 to 2003) and population projections (up to 2026). Population estimates for 1992 to 2002 were revised in light of the local authority population studies. Further information can be found on the National Statistics website www.statistics.gov.uk/popest.

Population projections are interim 2003-based and were published by the Government Actuary's Department on 30 September 2004. Further information can be found at www.gad.gov.uk/Population/index.asp

Definition of resident population

The estimated population of an area includes all those usually resident in the area, whatever their nationality. HM Forces serving abroad are excluded from, but non-UK Armed Forces stationed here are included within the estimates of resident population. Students are taken to be resident at their term-time addresses.

The projections of the resident population of the United Kingdom and constituent countries are prepared by the Government Actuary, in consultation with the Registrars General, as a common framework for use in national planning in a number of different fields. New projections are made every second year on assumptions regarding future fertility, mortality

and migration which seem most appropriate on the basis of the statistical evidence available at the time. The population projections in Tables 5.1 to 5.3 are based on the estimates of the population of the United Kingdom at mid-2003 made by the Registrars General.

Marital condition (*de jure*): estimated population

(Table 5.4)

This table shows population estimates by marital status. The mid-1991 to mid-2002 marital status estimates for England and Wales were revised in light of the local authority population studies.

Geographical distribution of the population

(Table 5.5)

The population enumerated in the Censuses for 1911–1951, and the mid-year population estimates for later years, are provided for standard regions of the United Kingdom, for metropolitan areas, for broad groupings of local authority districts by type within England and Wales, and for some of the larger cities. Projections of future subnational population levels are prepared from time to time by the Registrar General, but are not shown in this publication.

Migration into and out of the United Kingdom

(Tables 5.7 to 5.9)

A migrant is defined as a person who changes his or her country of usual residence for a period of at least a year, so that the country of destination effectively becomes the country of usual residence.

The main source of international migration data is the International Passenger Survey (IPS). This is a continuous voluntary sample survey that provides information on passengers entering and leaving the UK by the principal air, sea and tunnel routes. Being a sample survey, the IPS is subject to some uncertainty; therefore it should be noted that international migration estimates, in particular the difference between inflow and outflow, may be subject to large sampling errors. The IPS excludes routes between the Channel Islands and Isle of Man and the rest of the world.

The IPS data are supplemented with three types of additional information in order to provide a full picture of total international migration:

1. The IPS is based on intentions to migrate and intentions are liable to change. Adjustments are made for visitor switchers (those who intend to stay in the UK or abroad for less than one year but subsequently stay for longer and become migrants) and for migrant switchers (those who intend to stay in the UK or abroad for one year or more but then return earlier so are no longer migrants). These adjustments are primarily based on IPS data but for years prior to 2001, Home Office data on short-term visitors who were subsequently granted an extension of stay for a year or longer for other reasons have been incorporated.

2. Home Office data on applications for asylum and dependants of asylum seekers entering the UK are used to estimate inflows of asylum seekers and dependants not already captured by the IPS. In addition, Home Office data on removals and refusals are used to estimate outflows of failed asylum seekers not identified by the IPS.

3. Migration flows between the UK and the Irish Republic are added to these data, as the IPS did not cover this route until recently and the quality of these data are still being assessed. Migration flows are obtained mainly from the Quarterly National Household Survey and are agreed between the Irish Central Statistics Office and ONS.

The international migration estimates in Table 5.7 are derived from all these sources and represent total international migration. The estimates in Tables 5.8 and 5.9 are based on the International Passenger Survey only (without the three adjustments outlined above).

Acceptances for settlement in the United Kingdom

(Table 5.10)

This table presents in geographic regions, the statistics of individual nationalities, arranged alphabetically within each region. The figures are on a different basis from those derived from IPS (Tables 5.8 and 5.9) and relate only to people subject to immigration control. Persons accepted for settlement are allowed to stay indefinitely in the United Kingdom. They exclude temporary migrants such as students and generally relate only to non-EEA nationals. Settlement can occur several years after entry to the country.

Applications received for asylum in the United Kingdom, excluding dependants

(Table 5.11)

This table shows statistics of applications for asylum in the United Kingdom. Figures are shown for the main applicant

nationalities by geographic region. The basis of assessing asylum applications, and hence of deciding whether to grant asylum in the United Kingdom, is the 1951 United Nations Convention on Refugees.

Marriages

(Table 5.12)

The figures in this table relate to marriages solemnised in the constituent countries of the UK. They take no account of the growing trend towards marrying abroad.

Divorces

(Tables 5.13 and 5.14)

A marriage may be either dissolved following a petition for divorce and the granting of a decree absolute, or annulled, following a petition for nullity and the awarding of a decree of nullity. The first group of decrees are known as dissolutions of marriage and the second as annulments of marriage. In Table 5.13 the term 'divorce' includes both types of decrees, although strictly speaking, it should refer only to dissolutions.

Births

(Tables 5.15 to 5.17)

For Scotland and Northern Ireland the number of births relate to those registered during the year. For England and Wales the figures up to and including 1930–32 are for those registered, while later figures relate to births occurring in each year.

All data for England and Wales and for Scotland include births occurring in those countries to mothers not usually resident in them. Data for Northern Ireland, and hence UK, prior to 1981 include births occurring in Northern Ireland to non-resident mothers; from 1981, such births are excluded.

Deaths

(Tables 5.19 and 5.21)

The figures relate to the number of deaths registered during each calendar year. However, from 1993 onwards, the figures for England and Wales represent occurrences. This change has little effect on annual totals.

Infant and maternal mortality

(Table 5.20)

On 1 October 1992 the legal definition of a stillbirth was altered from a baby born dead after 28 completed weeks gestation or more, to one born after 24 completed weeks of gestation or more. The 258 stillbirths of 24 to 27 weeks gestation that which occurred between 1 October and 31 December 1992 are excluded from this table.

Life tables

(Table 5.22)

The current set of interim life tables are constructed from the estimated populations in 2001–2003 and the births, infant deaths and deaths by individual age occurring in those years for England and Wales and registered in those years for Scotland and Northern Ireland.

The estimates used in these interim life tables are the estimates, or revised estimates, following the 2001 Census issued on the following dates:

Mid-year population estimates			
	2001	**2002**	**2003**
England	September 2004	September 2004	September 2004
Wales	September 2004	September 2004	September 2004
Scotland	September 2002	June 2003	April 2004
Northern Ireland	September 2002	August 2003	August 2004

Adoptions

(Tables 5.23)

The figures shown within these tables relate to the date the adoption was entered in the Adopted Children Register. Figures based on the date of court order are available for England and Wales in the volume *Marriage, divorce and adoption statistics 2001* (no. 29 in the FM2 series) available on the National Statistics website *www.statistics.gov.uk* or from the enquiry point in ONS shown at the foot of the tables.

5.1 Population summary: by country and sex

Thousands

	United Kingdom[1]			England and Wales[1]			Wales[1]	Scotland			Northern Ireland		
	Persons	Males	Females	Persons	Males	Females	Persons	Persons	Males	Females	Persons	Males	Females

Enumerated population: Census figures

1801	..	..	..	8 893	4 255	4 638	587	1 608	739	869	..	..	..
1851	22 259	10 855	11 404	17 928	8 781	9 146	1 163	2 889	1 376	1 513	1 442	698	745
1901	38 237	18 492	19 745	32 528	15 729	16 799	2 013	4 472	2 174	2 298	1 237	590	647
1911	42 082	20 357	21 725	36 070	17 446	18 625	2 421	4 761	2 309	2 452	1 251	603	648
1921[2]	44 027	21 033	22 994	37 887	18 075	19 811	2 656	4 882	2 348	2 535	1 258	610	648
1931[2]	46 038	22 060	23 978	39 952	19 133	20 819	2 593	4 843	2 326	2 517	1 243	601	642
1951	50 225	24 118	26 107	43 758	21 016	22 742	2 599	5 096	2 434	2 662	1 371	668	703
1961	52 709	25 481	27 228	46 105	22 304	23 801	2 644	5 179	2 483	2 697	1 425	694	731

Resident population: mid-year estimates

	DYAY	BBAB	BBAC	BBAD	BBAE	BBAF	KGJM	BBAG	BBAH	BBAI	BBAJ	BBAK	BBAL
1968	55 214	26 784	28 429	48 511	23 554	24 957	2 715	5 200	2 498	2 702	1 503	733	770
1969	55 461	26 908	28 553	48 738	23 666	25 072	2 722	5 209	2 503	2 706	1 514	739	776
1970	55 632	26 992	28 641	48 891	23 738	25 153	2 729	5 214	2 507	2 707	1 527	747	781
1971	55 928	27 167	28 761	49 152	23 897	25 255	2 740	5 236	2 516	2 720	1 540	755	786
1972	56 097	27 259	28 837	49 327	23 989	25 339	2 755	5 231	2 513	2 717	1 539	758	782
1973	56 223	27 332	28 891	49 459	24 061	25 399	2 773	5 234	2 515	2 719	1 530	756	774
1974	56 236	27 349	28 887	49 468	24 075	25 393	2 785	5 241	2 519	2 722	1 527	755	772
1975	56 226	27 361	28 865	49 470	24 091	25 378	2 795	5 232	2 516	2 716	1 524	753	770
1976	56 216	27 360	28 856	49 459	24 089	25 370	2 799	5 233	2 517	2 716	1 524	754	770
1977	56 190	27 345	28 845	49 440	24 076	25 364	2 801	5 226	2 515	2 711	1 523	754	769
1978	56 178	27 330	28 849	49 443	24 067	25 375	2 804	5 212	2 509	2 704	1 523	754	770
1979	56 240	27 373	28 867	49 508	24 113	25 395	2 810	5 204	2 505	2 699	1 528	755	773
1980	56 330	27 411	28 919	49 603	24 156	25 448	2 816	5 194	2 501	2 693	1 533	755	778
1981	56 357	27 412	28 946	49 634	24 160	25 474	2 813	5 180	2 495	2 685	1 543	757	786
1982	56 291	27 364	28 927	49 582	24 119	25 462	2 804	5 165	2 487	2 677	1 545	757	788
1983	56 316	27 371	28 944	49 617	24 133	25 484	2 803	5 148	2 479	2 669	1 551	759	792
1984	56 409	27 421	28 989	49 713	24 185	25 528	2 801	5 139	2 475	2 664	1 557	761	796
1985	56 554	27 489	29 065	49 861	24 254	25 606	2 803	5 128	2 470	2 658	1 565	765	800
1986	56 684	27 542	29 142	49 999	24 311	25 687	2 811	5 112	2 462	2 649	1 574	768	805
1987	56 804	27 599	29 205	50 123	24 371	25 752	2 823	5 099	2 455	2 644	1 582	773	809
1988	56 916	27 652	29 265	50 254	24 434	25 820	2 841	5 077	2 444	2 633	1 585	774	812
1989	57 076	27 729	29 348	50 408	24 510	25 898	2 855	5 078	2 443	2 635	1 590	776	814
1990	57 237	27 819	29 419	50 561	24 597	25 964	2 862	5 081	2 444	2 637	1 596	778	818
1991	57 439	27 909	29 530	50 748	24 681	26 067	2 873	5 083	2 445	2 639	1 607	783	824
1992	57 585	27 977	29 608	50 876	24 739	26 136	2 878	5 086	2 445	2 640	1 623	792	831
1993	57 714	28 039	29 675	50 986	24 793	26 193	2 884	5 092	2 448	2 644	1 636	798	837
1994	57 862	28 108	29 754	51 116	24 853	26 263	2 887	5 102	2 453	2 649	1 644	802	842
1995	58 025	28 204	29 821	51 272	24 946	26 326	2 889	5 104	2 453	2 650	1 649	804	845
1996	58 164	28 287	29 877	51 410	25 030	26 381	2 891	5 092	2 447	2 645	1 662	810	851
1997	58 314	28 371	29 943	51 560	25 113	26 446	2 895	5 083	2 442	2 641	1 671	816	856
1998	58 475	28 458	30 017	51 720	25 201	26 519	2 900	5 077	2 439	2 638	1 678	819	859
1999	58 684	28 578	30 106	51 933	25 323	26 610	2 901	5 072	2 437	2 635	1 679	818	861
2000	58 886	28 690	30 196	52 140	25 438	26 702	2 907	5 063	2 432	2 631	1 683	820	862
2001	59 113	28 832	30 281	52 360	25 574	26 786	2 910	5 064	2 434	2 630	1 689	824	865
2002	59 322	28 963	30 359	52 570	25 702	26 868	2 923	5 055	2 432	2 623	1 697	829	868
2003	59 554	29 108	30 446	52 794	25 841	26 953	2 938	5 057	2 435	2 623	1 703	833	870

Resident population: projections (mid-year)[3]

	C59J	C59K	C59L	C59M	C59N	C59O	C59P	C59Q	C59R	C59S	C59T	C59U	C59V
2006	60 254	29 514	30 740	53 463	26 231	27 232	2 980	5 068	2 441	2 628	1 723	843	880
2011	61 401	30 160	31 241	54 615	26 880	27 735	3 020	5 034	2 423	2 611	1 753	857	895
2021	63 835	31 432	32 403	57 060	28 168	28 892	3 106	4 963	2 380	2 583	1 811	884	928
2026	64 902	31 955	32 947	58 163	28 718	29 445	3 138	4 907	2 346	2 562	1 832	891	940

1 Mid-1992 to mid-2002 population estimates for the UK, England and Wales are revised estimates in light of the local authority population studies.
2 Figures for Northern Ireland are estimated. The population at the Census of 1926 was 1 257 thousand (608 thousand males and 649 thousand females).
3 These projections are 2003-based. See chapter text for more detail.

Sources: Office for National Statistics: 01329 813318;
General Register Office for Scotland;
Northern Ireland Statistics and Research Agency;
Government Actuary's Department: 020 7211 2622

5.2 Population changes: by country

Thousands

	Population[1] at start of period	Average annual change — Overall annual change	Average annual change — Births	Average annual change — Deaths[2]	Average annual change — Natural change	Net migration and other changes
United Kingdom						
1901 - 1911	38 237	385	1 091	624	467	-82
1911 - 1921	42 082	195	975	689	286	-92
1921 - 1931	44 027	201	824	555	268	-67
1931 - 1951	46 038	213	793	603	190	22
1951 - 1961	50 225	258	839	593	246	12
1961 - 1971	52 807	312	962	638	324	-12
1971 - 1981	55 928	42	736	666	69	-27
1981 - 1991	56 357	108	757	655	103	5
1991 - 2001[3]	57 439	167	731	631	100	68
2001[3] - 2003	59 113	220	672	603	69	151
2011 - 2021	61 401	243	698	585	113	130
England and Wales						
1901 - 1911	32 528	354	929	525	404	-50
1911 - 1921	36 070	182	828	584	244	-62
1921 - 1931	37 887	207	693	469	224	-17
1931 - 1951	39 952	193	673	518	155	38
1951 - 1961	43 758	244	714	516	197	47
1961 - 1971	46 196	296	832	560	272	23
1971 - 1981	49 152	48	638	585	53	-5
1981 - 1991	49 634	111	664	576	89	23
1991 - 2001[3]	50 748	161	647	556	92	69
2001[3] - 2003	52 360	217	599	531	69	148
2011 - 2021	54 615	245	628	515	113	132
Scotland						
1901 - 1911	4 472	29	131	76	54	-25
1911 - 1921	4 761	12	118	82	36	-24
1921 - 1931	4 882	-4	100	65	35	-39
1931 - 1951	4 843	13	92	67	25	-12
1951 - 1961	5 096	9	95	62	34	-25
1961 - 1971	5 184	5	97	63	34	-30
1971 - 1981	5 236	-6	70	64	6	-11
1981 - 1991	5 180	-7	66	63	3	-10
1991 - 2001	5 083	-2	60	60	-1	-1
2001 - 2003	5 064	-3	52	58	-6	3
2011 - 2021	5 034	-7	49	55	-6	-2
Northern Ireland						
1901 - 1911	1 237	1	31	23	8	-6
1911 - 1921	1 251	1	29	22	7	-6
1921 - 1931	1 258	-2	30	21	9	-11
1931 - 1951	1 243	6	28	18	10	-4
1951 - 1961	1 371	6	30	15	15	-9
1961 - 1971	1 427	11	33	16	17	-6
1971 - 1981	1 540	-	28	17	11	-11
1981 - 1991	1 543	6	27	16	12	-5
1991 - 2001	1 607	8	24	15	9	-
2001 - 2003	1 689	7	21	14	7	-
2011 - 2021	1 753	6	21	15	6	-1

1 Census enumerated population up to 1951; mid-year estimates of resident population from 1961 to 2003 and mid-2003-based projections of resident population thereafter.

2 Including deaths of non-civilians and merchant seamen who died outside the country. These numbered 577 000 in 1911-1921 and 240 000 in 1931-1951 for England and Wales; 74 000 in 1911-1921 and 34 000 in 1931-1951 for Scotland; and 10 000 in 1911-1926 for Northern Ireland.

3 Mid-2001 and mid-2002 population estimates for the UK and England & Wales are revised in light of the local authority population studies.

Sources: Government Actuary's Department: 020 7211 2622;
Office for National Statistics: 01329 813318;
General Register Office for Scotland;
Northern Ireland Statistics and Research Agency

5.3 Age distribution of the resident population: by sex and country

Thousands

		United Kingdom														
		Population enumerated in Census			Estimated mid-year resident population							Projected mid-year resident population[1]				
		1901	1931	1951	1961	1971	1981	1991[2]	2001[3]	2002[3]	2003	2006	2011	2016	2021	2026
Persons: All ages	KGUA	38 237	46 038	50 225	52 807	55 928	56 357	57 439	59 114	59 322	59 554	60 254	61 401	62 618	63 835	64 902
Under 1	KGUK	938	712	773	..	899	730	790	663	661	679	690	681	697	705	696
1 - 4[4]	KABA	3 443	2 818	3 553	4 274	3 654	2 726	3 077	2 819	2 753	2 703	2 751	2 724	2 761	2 817	2 815
5 - 9	KGUN	4 106	3 897	3 689	3 819	4 684	3 677	3 657	3 735	3 689	3 650	3 501	3 463	3 428	3 481	3 545
10 - 14	KGUO	3 934	3 746	3 310	4 267	4 232	4 470	3 485	3 890	3 912	3 891	3 755	3 517	3 479	3 443	3 497
15 - 19	KGUP	3 826	3 989	3 175	3 748	3 862	4 735	3 719	3 678	3 761	3 855	3 956	3 809	3 572	3 535	3 499
20 - 29	KABB	6 982	7 865	7 154	6 570	7 968	8 113	9 138	7 499	7 401	7 379	7 627	8 179	8 300	7 920	7 648
30 - 44	KABC	7 493	9 717	11 125	10 529	9 797	10 956	12 125	13 405	13 499	13 519	13 253	12 446	12 010	12 405	12 812
45 - 59	KABD	4 639	7 979	9 558	10 605	10 202	9 540	9 500	11 168	11 316	11 424	11 764	12 325	13 113	12 952	12 186
60 - 64	KGUY	1 067	1 897	2 422	2 788	3 222	2 935	2 888	2 884	2 890	2 943	3 254	3 774	3 485	3 874	4 335
65 - 74	KBCP	1 278	2 461	3 689	3 977	4 764	5 195	5 067	4 947	4 969	5 005	5 053	5 554	6 415	6 628	6 780
75 - 84	KBCU	470	844	1 555	1 885	2 159	2 677	3 119	3 296	3 345	3 401	3 417	3 518	3 770	4 273	5 009
85 and over	KGVD	61	113	224	346	485	603	873	1 130	1 127	1 104	1 234	1 412	1 587	1 802	2 079
School ages (5-15)	KBWU	..	..	7 649	..	9 704	9 086	7 818	8 381	8 369	8 330	8 055	7 713	7 580	7 627	7 736
Under 18	KGUD	–	..	13 248	..	15 798	14 472	13 120	13 357	13 310	13 253	13 062	12 614	12 445	12 585	12 636
Pensionable ages[5]	KFIA	2 387	4 421	6 828	7 747	9 123	10 035	10 557	10 845	10 916	11 014	11 366	12 182	12 417	12 703	13 868
Males: All ages	KGWA	18 492	22 060	24 118	25 528	27 167	27 412	27 909	28 832	28 963	29 108	29 514	30 160	30 811	31 432	31 955
Under 1	KGWK	471	361	397	..	461	374	403	338	339	349	353	349	357	361	357
1 - 4[4]	KBCV	1 719	1 423	1 818	2 194	1 874	1 400	1 572	1 445	1 409	1 384	1 409	1 394	1 413	1 442	1 441
5 - 9	KGWN	2 052	1 967	1 885	1 956	2 401	1 889	1 871	1 913	1 890	1 869	1 789	1 770	1 750	1 778	1 811
10 - 14	KGWO	1 972	1 892	1 681	2 185	2 175	2 295	1 784	1 993	2 005	1 995	1 922	1 794	1 774	1 755	1 783
15 - 19	KGWP	1 898	1 987	1 564	1 897	1 976	2 424	1 905	1 879	1 930	1 983	2 028	1 948	1 820	1 801	1 782
20 - 29	KBCW	3 293	3 818	3 509	3 288	4 024	4 103	4 578	3 744	3 700	3 697	3 841	4 147	4 204	3 999	3 853
30 - 44	KBCX	3 597	4 495	5 461	5 237	4 938	5 513	6 045	6 645	6 690	6 701	6 575	6 186	6 009	6 238	6 465
45 - 59	KBUU	2 215	3 753	4 493	5 137	4 970	4 711	4 732	5 534	5 604	5 653	5 814	6 081	6 466	6 392	6 027
60 - 64	KGWY	490	894	1 061	1 250	1 507	1 376	1 390	1 412	1 414	1 439	1 592	1 841	1 698	1 891	2 111
65 - 74	KBWL	565	1 099	1 560	1 605	1 999	2 264	2 272	2 308	2 327	2 354	2 400	2 657	3 072	3 170	3 252
75 - 84	KBWM	196	335	617	675	716	922	1 146	1 308	1 339	1 371	1 415	1 524	1 680	1 926	2 267
85 and over	KGXD	23	36	70	105	126	141	212	312	316	313	376	469	567	680	807
School ages (5-15)	KBWV	–	..	3 895	..	4 982	4 666	4 001	4 294	4 289	4 269	4 121	3 938	3 867	3 891	3 947
Under 18	KGWD	–	..	6 753	..	8 108	7 430	6 711	6 845	6 822	6 794	6 687	6 447	6 356	6 427	6 453
Pensionable ages[5]	KFIB	785	1 471	2 247	2 385	2 841	3 327	3 630	3 928	3 982	4 038	4 191	4 650	5 319	5 777	6 325
Females: All ages	KGYA	19 745	23 978	26 107	27 279	28 761	28 946	29 530	30 281	30 359	30 446	30 740	31 241	31 806	32 403	32 947
Under 1	KGYK	466	351	376	..	437	356	387	324	323	331	337	332	340	344	340
1 - 4[4]	KBWN	1 724	1 397	1 735	2 079	1 779	1 327	1 505	1 375	1 344	1 319	1 342	1 329	1 348	1 375	1 374
5 - 9	KGYN	2 054	1 930	1 804	1 863	2 283	1 788	1 786	1 822	1 800	1 781	1 712	1 694	1 677	1 703	1 734
10 - 14	KGYO	1 962	1 854	1 629	2 083	2 057	2 175	1 701	1 897	1 907	1 896	1 832	1 723	1 705	1 688	1 714
15 - 19	KGYP	1 928	2 002	1 611	1 851	1 887	2 311	1 815	1 799	1 830	1 873	1 928	1 861	1 753	1 734	1 718
20 - 29	KBWO	3 690	4 047	3 644	3 282	3 945	4 009	4 560	3 755	3 701	3 682	3 786	4 032	4 096	3 922	3 795
30 - 44	KBWP	3 895	5 222	5 663	5 292	4 859	5 442	6 080	6 760	6 808	6 817	6 678	6 259	6 001	6 167	6 347
45 - 59	KBWR	2 424	4 226	5 065	5 467	5 231	4 829	4 769	5 634	5 713	5 771	5 950	6 244	6 647	6 560	6 159
60 - 64	KGYY	577	1 003	1 361	1 539	1 715	1 559	1 498	1 473	1 476	1 504	1 662	1 932	1 787	1 983	2 224
65 - 74	KBWS	713	1 361	2 127	2 372	2 765	2 931	2 795	2 640	2 641	2 651	2 653	2 897	3 343	3 458	3 529
75 - 84	KBWT	274	509	937	1 210	1 443	1 756	1 972	1 987	2 006	2 030	2 002	1 994	2 090	2 347	2 742
85 and over	KGZD	38	77	154	241	359	462	661	817	811	791	858	943	1 020	1 122	1 272
School ages (5-15)	KBWW	–	..	3 753	..	4 722	4 421	3 817	4 087	4 081	4 060	3 934	3 775	3 713	3 736	3 789
Under 18	KGYD	–	..	6 495	..	7 690	7 042	6 409	6 512	6 489	6 459	6 375	6 167	6 089	6 159	6 183
Pensionable ages[5]	KFIC	1 601	2 950	4 580	5 362	6 282	6 708	6 927	6 917	6 934	6 976	7 175	7 532	7 098	6 926	7 543

5.3 Age distribution of the resident population: by sex and country

continued

Thousands

| | | England | | | | | | | | Wales | | | | | | |
| | | Estimated mid-year resident population | | | | | Projected population[1] | | | Estimated mid-year resident population | | | | | Projected population[1] | |
		1981	1991[2]	2001[3]	2002[3]	2003	2011	2026		1981	1991[2]	2001[3]	2002[3]	2003	2011	2026
Persons: All ages	KCCI	46 821	47 875	49 450	49 647	49 856	51 595	55 025	KERY	2 813	2 873	2 910	2 923	2 938	3 020	3 138
Under 1	KCCJ	598	660	558	558	575	580	598	KFAC	36	38	32	30	31	32	31
1 - 4	KCCK	2 235	2 560	2 366	2 312	2 273	2 313	2 411	KFBX	136	153	136	132	129	129	130
5 - 9	KCCL	3 011	3 019	3 121	3 085	3 054	2 929	3 021	KFCA	185	186	185	183	181	163	169
10 - 14	KCCM	3 666	2 865	3 238	3 260	3 245	2 947	2 973	KFCB	222	177	196	197	197	176	171
15 - 19	KCCN	3 897	3 067	3 045	3 118	3 202	3 183	2 974	KFCC	233	187	186	191	196	194	172
20 - 29	KCEG	6 734	7 651	6 307	6 226	6 208	6 887	6 538	KFCD	381	415	336	334	336	391	347
30 - 44	KCEH	9 175	10 147	11 257	11 351	11 379	10 564	10 953	KFCE	536	583	608	611	611	551	586
45 - 59	KCEQ	7 948	7 920	9 327	9 448	9 533	10 287	10 343	KFCF	485	486	572	579	583	607	569
60 - 64	KCEW	2 449	2 399	2 395	2 397	2 438	3 149	3 632	KFCG	158	154	154	156	161	205	217
65 - 74	KCGD	4 347	4 222	4 113	4 130	4 159	4 623	5 636	KFCH	272	284	264	265	268	306	359
75 - 84	KCJG	2 249	2 626	2 764	2 804	2 852	2 941	4 201	KFCI	139	164	183	185	187	188	275
85 and over	KCKJ	511	739	959	956	936	1 194	1 747	KFCK	29	45	59	59	58	77	111
School ages (5-15)	KCWX	7 451	6 439	6 985	6 982	6 955	6 489	6 584	KFCL	453	397	420	419	417	376	374
Under 18	KCWY	11 871	10 840	11 146	11 118	11 082	10 633	10 773	KFCM	721	662	662	659	655	612	603
Pensionable ages[5]	KEAA	8 403	8 827	9 055	9 111	9 190	10 174	11 583	KFEB	525	573	584	589	596	663	745
Males: All ages	KEAB	22 795	23 291	24 166	24 288	24 415	25 407	27 184	KFEI	1 365	1 391	1 409	1 414	1 426	1 473	1 534
Under 1	KEAC	306	336	285	286	295	297	306	KFEJ	18	20	16	16	16	16	16
1 - 4	KEAD	1 147	1 307	1 212	1 183	1 164	1 184	1 234	KFEK	70	78	69	68	66	66	66
5 - 9	KEAE	1 547	1 545	1 599	1 580	1 564	1 497	1 544	KFEL	95	95	95	94	93	83	86
10 - 14	KEAF	1 883	1 467	1 658	1 671	1 664	1 503	1 516	KFFA	113	91	101	101	101	90	87
15 - 19	KECA	1 996	1 572	1 558	1 603	1 648	1 629	1 515	KFFN	119	95	94	97	100	99	87
20 - 29	KECB	3 404	3 835	3 155	3 117	3 113	3 492	3 293	KFHA	193	207	166	164	167	200	178
30 - 44	KECC	4 623	5 064	5 600	5 648	5 663	5 277	5 546	KFHB	270	289	297	297	297	267	294
45 - 59	KECD	3 938	3 957	4 624	4 682	4 721	5 092	5 151	KFHW	240	242	283	286	287	296	273
60 - 64	KECE	1 154	1 159	1 176	1 176	1 195	1 538	1 779	KFQO	73	74	75	77	79	100	105
65 - 74	KECF	1 902	1 900	1 928	1 944	1 965	2 218	2 712	KFQV	118	128	124	125	127	148	171
75 - 84	KECG	777	970	1 103	1 128	1 156	1 281	1 906	KFUK	48	60	73	74	75	82	125
85 and over	KECH	119	181	267	270	267	399	681	KFUL	7	11	16	16	16	26	44
School ages (5-15)	KECI	3 827	3 295	3 578	3 578	3 565	3 313	3 361	KFUV	232	204	215	215	214	193	191
Under 18	KECJ	6 096	5 545	5 712	5 698	5 681	5 435	5 504	KFVE	370	339	340	338	336	313	308
Pensionable ages[5]	KECK	2 798	3 050	3 298	3 342	3 388	3 898	5 299	KFVF	173	198	212	215	219	255	340
Females: All ages	KEJV	24 026	24 584	25 284	25 358	25 441	26 188	27 841	KFVL	1 448	1 482	1 502	1 509	1 512	1 547	1 604
Under 1	KEJW	292	324	273	272	280	283	292	KFYW	18	19	15	15	15	16	15
1 - 4	KEJX	1 088	1 253	1 154	1 129	1 109	1 129	1 176	KFZJ	66	75	66	65	63	63	63
5 - 9	KEKP	1 464	1 474	1 522	1 505	1 491	1 432	1 478	KGCK	90	91	90	89	88	79	83
10 - 14	KEKQ	1 783	1 399	1 580	1 589	1 581	1 444	1 456	KGCM	109	86	95	96	96	86	84
15 - 19	KEKR	1 901	1 495	1 487	1 516	1 554	1 554	1 459	KGCN	114	91	92	94	95	95	85
20 - 29	KEKS	3 330	3 816	3 152	3 108	3 095	3 395	3 245	KGCO	189	208	170	170	169	191	169
30 - 44	KENR	4 553	5 083	5 657	5 703	5 716	5 287	5 407	KGCP	265	294	312	314	314	284	292
45 - 59	KEOQ	4 009	3 964	4 702	4 766	4 812	5 195	5 192	KGGZ	246	244	289	293	296	311	296
60 - 64	KEOZ	1 295	1 239	1 219	1 220	1 243	1 611	1 853	KGIY	85	80	78	80	82	105	113
65 - 74	KEQJ	2 445	2 323	2 185	2 186	2 194	2 405	2 923	KGKR	154	156	141	140	141	159	188
75 - 84	KEQK	1 472	1 656	1 661	1 676	1 696	1 659	2 295	KGTQ	91	104	110	111	112	106	150
85 and over	KEQL	392	558	692	687	669	795	1 066	KGTZ	22	34	43	43	42	52	67
School ages (5-15)	KEQM	3 625	3 143	3 406	3 405	3 391	3 176	3 223	KGVG	221	194	204	204	203	184	183
Under 18	KEQN	5 775	5 295	5 434	5 420	5 401	5 197	5 269	KGVH	351	323	323	321	319	299	295
Pensionable ages[5]	KEQO	5 605	5 777	5 757	5 769	5 802	6 276	6 284	KGVK	352	375	372	374	377	408	405

5.3 Age distribution of the resident population: by sex and country

continued

Thousands

| | | Scotland | | | | | | | | Northern Ireland | | | | | | |
| | | Estimated mid-year resident population | | | | | Projected population[1] | | | Estimated mid-year resident population | | | | | Projected population[1] | |
		1981	1991[2]	2001[6]	2002	2003	2011	2026		1981	1991	2001[6]	2002	2003	2011	2026
Persons: All ages	KGVP	5 180	5 083	5 064	5 055	5 057	5 034	4 907	KIOY	1 543	1 607	1 689	1 697	1 703	1 753	1 832
Under 1	KHAQ	69	66	52	51	52	49	46	KIOZ	27	26	22	22	21	21	20
1 - 4	KHCT	249	258	224	217	212	197	191	KIPA	106	106	93	91	89	85	84
5 - 9	KHDN	348	320	306	299	294	262	246	KIPN	133	131	123	122	121	109	109
10 - 14	KHDQ	433	313	323	323	320	278	244	KIPP	148	129	132	131	129	117	108
15 - 19	KHDT	459	337	318	319	324	309	248	KIPQ	146	128	130	132	133	123	106
20 - 29	KHDU	771	820	630	619	614	650	549	KIPR	227	253	225	222	221	251	214
30 - 44	KHDV	971	1 080	1 163	1 158	1 150	981	907	KIPS	273	315	376	378	378	349	367
45 - 59	KHFK	880	853	979	993	1 008	1 089	937	KIPT	227	241	290	296	301	342	338
60 - 64	KHOZ	260	265	262	262	265	327	366	KIPU	68	70	74	75	78	93	120
65 - 74	KHTU	460	441	447	449	452	479	596	KIPV	116	120	123	125	126	146	189
75 - 84	KHUO	232	259	272	276	281	303	408	KIPW	57	69	77	79	81	87	126
85 and over	KHUQ	49	70	89	88	86	109	171	KIPX	14	19	23	24	24	31	50
School ages (5-15)	KHVV	871	697	694	687	679	598	539	KIPY	311	285	282	281	278	250	239
Under 18	KIMT	1 377	1 150	1 098	1 086	1 074	964	873	KIQL	504	467	451	447	443	405	386
Pensionable ages[5]	KIMU	882	912	944	950	958	1 040	1 174	KIQM	224	246	262	266	271	306	366
Males: All ages	KIMV	2 495	2 445	2 434	2 432	2 435	2 423	2 346	KIQN	757	783	824	829	833	857	891
Under 1	KIMW	35	34	26	26	26	25	24	KIQO	14	13	11	11	11	11	10
1 - 4	KIMX	128	132	115	111	108	101	97	KIQP	54	54	48	47	46	43	43
5 - 9	KIMY	178	164	156	153	151	133	125	KIQQ	69	67	63	63	62	56	55
10 - 14	KIMZ	222	161	166	165	164	141	124	KIQR	76	66	68	67	66	60	55
15 - 19	KINA	234	171	161	163	166	157	125	KIQS	75	66	66	68	68	63	54
20 - 29	KINB	390	410	311	308	306	327	273	KIQT	117	127	113	111	111	128	109
30 - 44	KINC	483	535	563	560	556	473	443	KIQU	137	156	185	186	186	169	181
45 - 59	KIND	424	415	483	490	496	525	443	KIQV	109	118	144	147	149	167	161
60 - 64	KINE	118	124	125	125	126	158	171	KIQW	32	32	35	36	38	45	57
65 - 74	KINR	194	192	200	202	204	223	277	KIRJ	50	53	56	56	57	69	91
75 - 84	KINS	77	91	103	106	108	125	180	KIRK	21	26	30	31	31	36	56
85 and over	KINT	11	16	23	23	23	35	63	KIRL	4	5	6	6	7	10	19
School ages (5-15)	KINU	446	357	356	352	348	305	274	KIRM	160	146	145	144	142	128	121
Under 18	KINV	706	588	562	556	550	491	444	KIRN	259	239	231	229	227	207	196
Pensionable ages[5]	KINW	282	299	327	331	336	383	520	KIRO	75	83	92	94	95	115	166
Females: All ages	KINX	2 685	2 639	2 630	2 623	2 623	2 611	2 562	KIRP	786	824	865	868	870	895	940
Under 1	KINY	33	32	26	25	25	24	23	KIRQ	13	13	10	11	10	10	10
1 - 4	KINZ	121	126	109	106	104	96	93	KIRR	52	52	45	44	43	41	41
5 - 9	KIOA	170	157	149	146	143	129	121	KIRS	65	64	60	59	59	54	53
10 - 14	KIOB	211	153	157	157	156	136	120	KIRT	72	63	65	64	63	57	53
15 - 19	KIOC	225	166	156	156	158	152	123	KIRU	70	62	64	65	65	60	52
20 - 29	KIOO	381	411	319	311	307	323	275	KISH	110	126	113	111	110	123	105
30 - 44	KIOP	488	545	600	598	595	509	463	KISI	137	159	191	192	193	179	186
45 - 59	KIOQ	456	437	496	504	512	564	494	KISJ	118	123	146	149	152	174	177
60 - 64	KIOR	142	141	137	137	139	169	195	KISK	37	38	38	39	40	48	63
65 - 74	KIOS	265	249	246	247	248	256	318	KISL	66	67	68	68	68	77	99
75 - 84	KIOT	155	168	169	171	173	178	228	KISM	37	44	47	48	49	51	70
85 and over	KIOU	38	54	66	65	63	75	108	KISN	10	14	17	17	17	21	31
School ages (5-15)	KIOV	424	340	339	335	331	294	265	KISO	151	139	138	137	135	122	118
Under 18	KIOW	671	562	536	530	524	472	429	KISP	245	228	220	218	215	198	190
Pensionable ages[5]	KIOX	600	612	617	619	622	657	654	KISQ	150	163	170	173	175	191	200

1 2003-based projections are made as described in the chapter text.
2 Data for mid 1991 for UK, England and Wales and Scotland are revised in light of the 2001 Census.
3 Data for mid-2001 and mid-2002 for UK, England and Wales are revised in light of the local authority population studies (9 September 2004).
4 1961 estimates are for ages 0 - 4.
5 The pensionable age population is that over state retirement age. The 2011 figures take account of planned changes in retirement age from 65 for men and 60 for women at present to 65 for both sexes. This change will be phased in between April 2010 and March 2020.

Sources: Office for National Statistics: 01329 813318;
General Register Office for Scotland;
Northern Ireland Statistics and Research Agency;
Government Actuary's Department: 020 7211 2622

5.4 Marital condition (*de jure*): estimated population: by age and sex
England and Wales

		Males							Females					
		1971	1981	1991[1]	2001[2]	2002[2]	2003		1971	1981	1991[1]	2001[2]	2002[2]	2003
All ages:														
Single	KRPL	10 507	10 614	11 131	12 270	12 422	12 582	KUBS	9 584	9 424	9 824	10 917	11 051	11 188
Married	KRPM	12 522	12 238	11 636	11 090	11 015	10 940	KVCC	12 566	12 284	11 833	11 150	11 073	11 000
Widowed	KRPN	682	698	727	733	731	728	KVCD	2 810	2 939	2 951	2 745	2 709	2 668
Divorced	KRPO	187	611	1 187	1 482	1 535	1 590	KVCE	296	828	1 459	1 975	2 035	2 096
Age groups:														
0 - 14: Single	KRPP	5 984	5 181	4 939	5 036	4 999	4 963	KVCF	5 672	4 910	4 720	4 796	4 760	4 722
15 - 19: Single	KRPQ	1 677	2 095	1 659	1 645	1 694	1 743	KVCG	1 491	1 923	1 554	1 560	1 595	1 637
Married	KRPR	34	20	8	5	4	4	KVCH	142	93	32	16	13	12
Widowed	KRPS	–	–	–	1	1	1	KVCI	–	–	–	1	1	1
Divorced	KRPT	–	–	–	1	1	1	KVCJ	–	–	–	1	1	–
20 - 24: Single	KRPU	1 211	1 420	1 717	1 501	1 534	1 573	KVCK	745	1 007	1 421	1 390	1 428	1 466
Married	KRPV	689	466	242	74	69	69	KVCL	1 113	811	490	178	166	161
Widowed	KRPW	–	1	–	1	1	1	KVCM	2	2	1	1	1	1
Divorced	KRPX	3	10	12	3	3	3	KVCN	9	27	29	8	8	8
25 - 34: Single	KRPY	637	906	1 652	2 227	2 238	2 253	KVCO	326	496	1 135	1 770	1 795	1 820
Married	KRPZ	2 450	2 508	2 028	1 391	1 293	1 206	KVCP	2 635	2 791	2 488	1 768	1 662	1 566
Widowed	KRQA	4	4	2	3	3	3	KVCQ	12	13	8	10	9	8
Divorced	KRQB	38	151	237	136	131	126	KVCR	63	218	312	231	219	208
35 - 44: Single	KRQC	317	316	477	963	1 031	1 089	KVEH	201	170	280	692	751	805
Married	KRQD	2 513	2 519	2 632	2 494	2 489	2 471	KVEI	2 529	2 540	2 760	2 649	2 650	2 634
Widowed	KRQE	13	12	11	12	12	12	KVEJ	48	41	34	36	35	34
Divorced	KRQF	48	178	384	411	424	435	KVEK	66	222	444	558	571	583
45 - 54: Single	KRQG	279	254	251	419	433	451	KVEL	248	169	144	256	271	289
Married	KUAR	2 605	2 338	2 347	2 511	2 433	2 379	KVEM	2 570	2 292	2 322	2 548	2 475	2 427
Widowed	KUBA	47	38	31	37	35	34	KVEN	187	150	118	111	105	99
Divorced	KUBB	46	134	290	448	455	466	KVEO	69	158	332	557	566	578
55 - 59: Single	KUBC	118	128	101	128	141	151	KVEP	148	108	69	74	81	87
Married	KUBD	1 250	1 192	1 050	1 156	1 240	1 280	KVEQ	1 154	1 130	982	1 125	1 211	1 258
Widowed	KUBE	49	46	34	34	36	37	KVER	213	186	136	112	115	114
Divorced	KUBF	20	49	95	174	195	210	KVES	31	63	107	210	235	256
60 - 64: Single	KUBG	105	98	104	97	97	100	KVET	174	109	80	62	61	62
Married	KUBH	1 140	1 029	997	980	976	989	KVEU	985	936	908	906	909	928
Widowed	KUBI	77	64	63	50	49	48	KVEV	332	284	250	178	172	167
Divorced	KUBJ	16	35	70	125	131	138	KVEW	25	51	82	151	158	168
65 - 74: Single	KUBK	132	149	150	155	154	154	KMGN	332	263	176	130	126	123
Married	KUBL	1 407	1 594	1 574	1 569	1 582	1 600	KMGO	1 133	1 291	1 317	1 322	1 336	1 354
Widowed	KUBM	226	234	229	188	184	179	KMGP	959	978	879	697	675	654
Divorced	KUBN	14	43	74	139	149	159	KMGQ	26	68	107	177	190	204
75 and over: Single	KUBO	47	67	81	99	101	104	KMGR	249	270	246	188	182	178
Married	KUBP	434	573	759	909	928	945	KMGS	304	401	536	639	651	661
Widowed	KUBQ	266	300	357	407	411	415	KMGT	1 056	1 285	1 526	1 598	1 597	1 590
Divorced	KUBR	3	11	25	44	48	52	KMGU	6	23	46	81	86	91

1 Mid-1991 marital status estimates are revised in light of the 2001 Census.
2 Mid-2001 and mid-2002 marital status estimates are revised in light of the local authority population studies.

Source: Office for National Statistics: 01329 813318

5.5 Geographical distribution of the population

Thousands

		Population enumerated in Census			Mid-year population estimates						
		1911	1931	1951	1961	1971	1981	1991	2001[1]	2002[1]	2003
United Kingdom	KIUR	42 082	46 074	50 225	52 807	55 928	56 357	57 439	59 113	59 322	59 554
Great Britain	KISR	40 831	44 795	48 854	51 380	54 388	54 815	55 831	57 424	57 625	57 851
England	KKOJ	33 650	37 359	41 159	43 561	46 412	46 821	47 875	49 450	49 647	49 856
Standard Regions											
North	KKNA	2 729	2 938	3 009	3 246	3 152	3 117	3 073	3 028	3 026	3 029
Yorkshire and Humberside	KKNB	3 896	4 319	4 567	4 630	4 902	4 918	4 936	4 977	4 993	5 009
East Midlands	KKNC	2 467	2 732	3 118	3 108	3 652	3 853	4 011	4 190	4 223	4 252
East Anglia	KKND	1 191	1 231	1 381	1 489	1 688	1 894	2 068	2 181	2 192	2 219
South East	KKNE	11 613	13 349	14 877	16 346	17 125	17 011	17 511	18 566	18 645	18 712
South West	KKNF	2 818	2 984	3 479	3 436	4 112	4 381	4 688	4 943	4 968	4 999
West Midlands	KKNG	3 277	3 743	4 423	4 762	5 146	5 187	5 230	5 281	5 304	5 320
North West	KKNH	5 659	6 062	6 305	6 545	6 634	6 459	6 357	6 285	6 296	6 315
Government Office Regions											
North East	JZBU	..	..	..	..	2 679	2 636	2 587	2 540	2 538	2 539
North West (including Merseyside)	JZBV	..	..	..	..	7 108	6 940	6 843	6 773	6 783	6 805
Yorkshire and The Humber	JZBX	..	..	..	..	4 902	4 918	4 936	4 977	4 993	5 009
East Midlands	JZBY	..	..	..	..	3 652	3 853	4 011	4 190	4 223	4 252
West Midlands	JZBZ	..	..	..	..	5 146	5 187	5 230	5 281	5 304	5 320
South West	JZCA	..	..	..	..	4 112	4 381	4 688	4 943	4 968	4 999
East	JZCB	..	..	..	..	4 454	4 854	5 121	5 400	5 422	5 463
London	JZCC	..	..	..	..	7 529	6 806	6 829	7 322	7 371	7 388
South East	JZCD	..	..	..	..	6 830	7 245	7 629	8 023	8 044	8 080
Wales	KKNI	2 421	2 593	2 599	2 635	2 740	2 813	2 873	2 910	2 923	2 938
Scotland	KGJB	4 761	4 843	5 096	5 184	5 236	5 180	5 083	5 064	5 055	5 057
Northern Ireland	KGJC	1 251	1 280[4]	1 371	1 427	1 540	1 543	1 607	1 689	1 697	1 703
Greater London	KKNJ	7 161	8 110	8 197	7 977	7 529	6 806	6 829	7 322	7 371	7 388
Inner London[2]	KISS	4 998	4 893	3 679	3 481	3 060	2 550	2 599	2 859	2 892	2 905
Outer London[2]	KITF	2 162	3 217	4 518	4 496	4 470	4 255	4 230	4 463	4 479	4 483
Metropolitan areas of England and Wales	KITG	9 716	10 770	11 365	11 686	11 862	11 353	11 085	10 888	10 908	10 925
Tyne and Wear	KGJN	1 105	1 201	1 201	1 241	1 218	1 155	1 124	1 087	1 084	1 083
West Yorkshire	KGJP	1 852	1 939	1 985	2 002	2 090	2 067	2 062	2 083	2 091	2 096
South Yorkshire	KGJO	963	1 173	1 253	1 298	1 331	1 317	1 289	1 266	1 269	1 273
West Midlands	KGJQ	1 780	2 143	2 547	2 724	2 811	2 673	2 619	2 568	2 576	2 578
Greater Manchester	KGJR	2 638	2 727	2 716	2 710	2 750	2 619	2 554	2 516	2 522	2 531
Merseyside	KGJS	1 378	1 587	1 663	1 711	1 662	1 522	1 438	1 368	1 365	1 364
Principal Metropolitan Cities[2]	KITH	3 154	3 906	3 915	4 204	3 910	3 550	3 415	3 344	3 355	3 361
Newcastle	KGJT	267	286	292	336	312	284	275	266	266	267
Leeds	KGJX	446	483	505	710	749	718	707	716	716	715
Sheffield	KGJV	455	512	513	581	579	548	520	513	513	513
Birmingham	KGKF	526	1 003	1 113	1 179	1 107	1 021	1 005	985	990	992
Manchester	KGKJ	714	766	703	657	554	463	433	423	429	432
Liverpool	KGKM	746	856	789	741	610	517	476	442	442	442
Other metropolitan districts[2]	KITI	6 562	6 864	7 450	7 482	7 952	7 803	7 670	7 544	7 552	7 565
Non-metropolitan districts of England and Wales	KITJ	19 194	21 072	24 196	26 533	29 761	31 475	32 834	31 239	31 368	31 543
Non-metropolitan cities[2,3]	KITK	..	..	..	4 670	4 715	4 617	..	..	..	..
Incl. Kingston-upon-Hull	KKNZ	278	314	299	302	288	274	263	250	248	248
Leicester	KKOA	227	239	285	286	285	283	281	283	284	284
Nottingham	KKNX	260	269	308	311	302	278	279	269	271	274
Bristol	KKNV	357	397	443	436	433	401	392	390	390	392
Plymouth	KITL	207	215	225	240	249	253	251	241	241	241
Stoke-on-Trent	KKOD	235	277	275	276	265	252	249	240	239	238
Cardiff	KKOB	182	224	244	289	291	281	297	310	313	315
Industrial districts[2,3]	KITM	..	..	..	6 004	6 486	6 713	..	..	..	..
New Towns[2,3]	KITN	..	..	..	1 552	1 895	2 194	..	..	..	..
Resort, port and retirement districts[2,3]	KITO	..	..	..	2 828	3 184	3 368	..	..	..	..
Urban and mixed urban/rural districts[2,3]	KITP	..	..	..	7 240	8 821	9 446	..	..	..	..
Remoter, mainly rural districts[2,3]	KITQ	..	..	..	4 239	4 661	5 137	..	..	..	..
City of Edinburgh local government district	KGKU	320	439	467	..	478	446	436	449	448	448
City of Glasgow local government district	KGKT	784	1 088	1 090	..	983	774	629	579	577	577
Belfast[4]	KGKV	387	438[4]	444	..	..	315	293	277	274	272

1 Mid-2001 and mid-2002 population estimates for the UK, Great Britain, England and Wales are revised in light of the local authority population studies.
2 Details of the classification by broad area type are given in recent issues of the ONS annual reference volume Key Population and Vital Statistics; local and health authority areas (Series VS). The ten broad area types include all local authorities in England and Wales.
3 The breakdown of non-metropolitan districts by area type has not been provided from mid-2001 onwards. This is because the effect of boundary changes due to the major local government reorganisation on 1 April 1995 and 1 April 1996 (particularly in Wales) make the comparison of 2001 data with data for earlier years invalid.

4 1931 figures shown for Northern Ireland and the City of Belfast relate to the 1937 Census.

Sources: Office for National Statistics: 01329 813318;
General Register Office for Scotland;
Northern Ireland Statistics and Research Agency

33

5.6 Population: by ethnic group and age, Spring 2002 - Winter 2002/03
United Kingdom
Average over the period

Percentages and thousands

	0 to 4	5 to 9	10 to 14	15 to 19	20 to 24	25 to 29	30 to 34	35 to 44	45 to 59	60 to 74	75 and over	All ages (=100%) (thousands)
White												
British[2]	5	6	7	6	6	6	7	16	20	14	7	51 010
Other[2]	4	4	4	4	8	12	11	18	18	11	6	1 946
Mixed												
White and Black Caribbean	19	21	16	12	8	5	4	9	-	-	-	234
White and Black African	19	19	12	10	-	11	-	11	-	-	-	72
White and Asian	19	15	14	11	7	7	8	10	4	-	-	129
Other Mixed	14	19	14	9	-	7	-	13	-	-	-	74
Asian												
Indian	7	7	7	8	9	9	10	17	18	8	1	1 016
Pakistani	11	11	11	10	11	9	8	12	11	5	1	718
Bangladeshi	14	12	10	10	10	12	9	11	6	5	-	273
Other Asian	8	7	7	6	8	13	12	17	14	6	-	302
Black												
Black Caribbean	8	7	7	8	6	5	8	25	12	11	3	584
Black African	12	11	8	8	8	8	11	20	10	3	-	541
Black Other	14	-	10	10	11	-	-	16	10	-	-	59
Chinese	4	5	5	9	15	12	9	19	15	6	-	199
Other	8	8	6	6	8	11	10	21	14	5	2	458
All[1]	6	6	7	6	6	6	8	16	19	13	7	59 330

1 Includes ethnic group not stated.
2 Great Britain only. Detailed level ethnicity questions are not asked of the White group in Northern Ireland.

Source: Office for National Statistics, Labour Force Survey

5.7 Total international migration estimates:[1] citizenship
United Kingdom

Thousands

	All citizenships	British	Non-British	European Union[2]	Commonwealth Old[3]	Commonwealth New	Other foreign[4]
Inflow							
	C58E	C58H	C58K	C58N	C58Q	C58T	C58W
1995	311.9	83.9	228.0	61.2	26.7	58.3	81.7
1996	317.8	93.6	224.2	72.5	29.0	49.2	73.5
1997	326.1	88.9	237.2	71.5	31.2	58.7	75.7
1998	390.3	103.1	287.3	81.8	53.9	51.0	100.5
1999	453.8	116.4	337.4	66.6	54.4	66.5	149.9
2000	483.4	104.1	379.3	63.1	57.2	90.9	168.1
2001	479.6	106.3	373.3	60.4	67.4	83.9	161.6
2002	512.8	94.6	418.2	62.8	65.6	92.9	196.8
2003	512.6	105.8	406.8	64.0	62.7	103.1	177.0
Outflow							
	C58F	C58I	C58L	C58O	C58R	C58U	C58X
1995	236.5	135.5	101.0	38.0	17.6	11.9	33.5
1996	263.7	155.7	108.0	44.0	17.3	14.3	32.4
1997	279.2	148.7	130.6	53.2	20.1	19.8	37.5
1998	251.5	125.8	125.7	48.9	19.7	13.2	44.0
1999	290.8	139.2	151.6	58.6	28.8	12.3	51.9
2000	320.7	161.1	159.6	57.0	32.2	14.9	55.5
2001	307.7	159.2	148.5	49.1	32.1	18.6	48.6
2002	359.4	185.7	173.7	51.7	42.3	15.8	63.9
2003	361.5	190.9	170.6	49.9	41.9	16.6	62.2
Balance							
	C58G	C58J	C58M	C58P	C58S	C58V	C58Y
1995	75.4	−51.6	127.0	23.3	9.2	46.5	48.2
1996	54.1	−62.1	116.2	28.5	11.7	34.9	41.1
1997	46.8	−59.8	106.6	18.3	11.2	38.9	38.2
1998	138.8	−22.7	161.6	33.0	34.2	37.9	56.6
1999	163.0	−22.8	185.8	8.0	25.6	54.2	98.0
2000	162.8	−57.0	219.7	6.1	25.0	76.0	112.6
2001	171.8	−53.0	224.8	11.2	35.2	65.4	113.0
2002	153.4	−91.1	244.5	11.1	23.4	77.1	132.9
2003	151.0	−85.2	236.2	14.2	20.8	86.5	114.8

1 Based mainly on data from the International Passenger Survey. Includes adjustments for (1) those whose intended length of stay changes so that their migrant status changes; (2) asylum seekers and their dependants not identified by the IPS; and (3) flows between the UK and the Republic of Ireland.
2 Figures for all years show EU as it was constituted on 1 January 1995.

These do not include the 10 new member states admitted to the EU in May 2004. However, these member states will be included in the 2004 international migration estimates for the EU.
3 Includes estimates for South African citizenship for all years.
4 Figures for all years include Hong Kong.

Source: Office for National Statistics: 01329 813255

5.8 Estimates of migration into and out of the United Kingdom[1] by usual occupation[2] and sex

Thousands

	Total			Professional and managerial			Manual and clerical			Not gainfully employed[3]		
	Persons	Males	Females	Persons	Males	Females	Persons	Males	Females	Persons	Males	Females
Inflow												
	KGOA	KGOB	KGOC	KGOD	KGOE	KGOF	KGOG	KGOH	KGOI	KGOJ	KGOK	KGOL
1995	235	125	111	83	55	28	44	19	25	108	51	57
1996	261	124	137	86	51	35	55	24	31	120	50	71
1997	273	137	136	89	57	33	42	23	19	141	57	84
1998	318	160	158	112	65	47	71	35	35	136	60	76
1999	354	181	173	131	77	54	77	41	36	146	63	83
2000	364	191	173	163	98	65	64	34	30	137	60	77
2001	372	187	185	142	78	63	77	38	39	154	71	82
2002	386	200	186	142	78	64	83	44	39	161	77	83
2003	431	212	220	144	77	67	98	46	52	189	89	100
Outflow												
	KGPA	KGPB	KGPC	KGPD	KGPE	KGPF	KGPG	KGPH	KGPI	KGPJ	KGPK	KGPL
1995	198	105	93	64	43	21	43	23	20	91	39	52
1996	223	109	114	87	54	32	48	23	24	89	31	58
1997	232	125	107	88	59	29	50	23	26	94	43	51
1998	206	103	103	82	48	34	42	22	21	82	33	48
1999	245	132	114	97	60	38	69	32	37	79	41	39
2000	278	154	124	128	80	48	59	36	23	90	37	53
2001	251	136	115	104	67	37	60	30	30	88	39	49
2002	306	162	144	124	79	45	80	41	40	102	42	59
2003	314	165	149	108	60	49	103	59	44	103	46	57
Balance												
	KGRA	KGRB	KGRC	KGRD	KGRE	KGRF	KGRG	KGRH	KGRI	KGRJ	KGRK	KGRL
1995	37	19	18	18	11	7	1	−4	6	17	12	5
1996	37	15	22	−1	−3	2	7	–	7	31	18	13
1997	40	12	29	1	−2	3	−7	−1	−7	47	14	33
1998	113	57	55	30	17	13	28	13	15	54	27	27
1999	109	49	60	33	17	16	8	9	−2	67	22	45
2000	87	38	49	35	18	17	5	−2	8	47	22	24
2001	121	51	69	38	11	26	17	8	10	66	33	34
2002	80	38	42	18	−1	19	3	4	−1	59	35	24
2003	118	47	71	36	17	18	−5	−14	9	87	43	44

1 See chapter text.
2 Refers to regular occupation before migration.
3 Includes housewives, students, children and retired persons.

Source: Office for National Statistics: 01329 813255

5.9 Estimates of migration into and out of the United Kingdom[1] by citizenship and country of last or next residence

Thousands

| | All migrants | British citizens | | | | | | European Union citizens[2] (excluding British) | | | |
| | | | Country of last/next residence | | | | | | Country of last/next residence | | |
	Total	Total	European[2] Union	Old[3] Common-wealth	New Common-wealth	United States of America	Other countries	Total	European[2] Union	Other Europe	Other countries
Inflow											
	KEZR	KGLA	KGLB	KGLC	KGLD	KGLE	KGLF	KGLG	KGLH	KGLI	KGLJ
1995	235	86	32	14	12	12	16	42	36	–	6
1996	261	97	33	18	16	13	17	55	49	1	5
1997	273	90	36	20	10	7	17	62	56	–	6
1998	318	104	29	29	14	16	16	70	62	–	7
1999	354	117	32	38	16	11	20	60	55	–	5
2000	364	104	34	29	14	8	19	59	53	–	6
2001	372	106	26	31	17	10	22	57	54	–	3
2002	386	94	29	22	10	9	24	59	53	3	3
2003	431	106	40	29	12	10	15	61	54	1	6
Outflow											
	KEZS	KGMA	KGMB	KGMC	KGMD	KGME	KGMF	KGMG	KGMH	KGMI	KGMJ
1995	198	122	38	35	10	18	21	20	16	–	4
1996	223	143	53	38	16	16	21	24	19	–	5
1997	232	135	41	38	13	16	27	32	27	1	4
1998	206	114	37	36	8	15	19	26	21	1	4
1999	245	115	37	41	8	14	14	47	41	–	6
2000	278	141	41	48	9	19	24	46	39	1	6
2001	251	134	43	47	7	15	22	40	34	1	5
2002	306	165	69	44	10	18	24	42	38	–	4
2003	314	170	71	55	9	13	22	42	33	3	5
Balance											
	KEZT	KGNA	KGNB	KGNC	KGND	KGNE	KGNF	KGNG	KGNH	KGNI	KGNJ
1995	37	−36	−6	−21	2	−6	−5	22	21	–	2
1996	37	−46	−20	−20	–	−3	−3	31	31	1	–
1997	40	−45	−5	−18	−2	−9	−10	30	29	−1	2
1998	113	−10	−8	−7	7	1	−3	44	41	−1	4
1999	109	2	−6	−3	7	−3	6	13	14	–	−2
2000	87	−37	−8	−19	6	−12	−4	13	14	−1	–
2001	121	−28	−17	−15	10	−6	–	17	20	−1	−1
2002	80	−70	−40	−21	–	−9	−1	17	15	3	−1
2003	118	−64	−31	−26	3	−3	−7	19	21	−3	1

Estimates of migration into and out of the United Kingdom[1] by citizenship and country of last or next residence

Thousands

| | Commonwealth citizens | | | | | | | | | | Other foreign citizens | | | | |
| | Country of last/next residence | | | | | | | | | | Country of last/next residence | | | | |
	Total	Aust-ralia	Canada	New Zealand	South Africa	Bangl-adesh, India, Sri Lanka	Pakistan	Other African Common-wealth	Carib-bean Common-wealth	Other count-ries	Total	Euro-pean[2] Union	Other Europe	United States of America	Other coun-tries
Inflow															
	KGLK	KGLL	KGLM	KGLN	KTDK	KGLO	KGLP	KGLQ	KGLR	KGLT	KGLU	KGLV	KGLW	KGLX	KGLY
1995	56	12	5	6	2	8	3	4	–	16	52	2	10	11	29
1996	59	14	3	7	4	8	7	6	1	10	49	–	7	15	27
1997	75	14	5	7	5	15	5	6	1	18	45	–	7	11	27
1998	88	24	5	13	11	10	4	10	1	11	56	4	7	18	27
1999	98	26	2	12	12	14	6	14	3	9	79	3	19	15	42
2000	114	23	6	11	14	21	9	13	1	16	87	2	11	13	61
2001	123	32	4	10	12	21	9	18	2	14	87	1	12	12	61
2002	124	22	5	9	20	27	6	23	2	9	109	2	11	16	81
2003	141	20	6	8	20	37	8	23	3	16	124	2	23	16	82
Outflow															
	KGMK	KGML	KGMM	KGMN	KTDL	KGMO	KGMP	KGMQ	KGMR	KGMT	KGMU	KGMV	KGMW	KGMX	KGMY
1995	27	6	1	4	2	1	1	2	1	9	30	–	5	9	16
1996	29	8	2	3	2	2	–	2	–	9	27	1	7	5	14
1997	36	7	1	5	5	2	2	2	1	12	29	2	5	9	13
1998	30	9	1	3	4	2	1	2	–	6	35	2	7	9	18
1999	38	11	2	6	4	1	–	1	–	11	45	–	9	14	21
2000	43	12	3	8	5	2	2	2	1	8	48	3	11	9	24
2001	44	15	3	6	5	3	1	2	1	7	33	1	9	7	16
2002	52	18	6	9	5	3	2	2	–	7	47	2	12	16	18
2003	53	19	2	8	9	4	1	2	–	8	48	2	12	8	26
Balance															
	KGNK	KGNL	KGNM	KGNN	KTDM	KGNO	KGNP	KGNQ	KGNR	KGNT	KGNU	KGNV	KGNW	KGNX	KGNY
1995	29	5	4	2	–	6	3	2	–1	7	22	2	5	2	13
1996	30	7	1	4	2	5	7	4	1	–	22	–1	–	10	13
1997	39	7	4	2	1	13	3	4	–	7	16	–2	2	3	14
1998	59	15	3	10	7	7	3	8	1	5	21	2	–	9	9
1999	60	15	–	6	8	13	6	12	3	–2	34	3	10	2	20
2000	71	11	3	3	9	19	8	10	–	7	40	–1	–	4	36
2001	79	17	–	4	7	18	9	16	1	7	53	–	3	5	45
2002	72	4	–1	–	15	24	4	21	2	2	61	–	–2	–	63
2003	87	1	3	–	11	33	7	21	3	8	75	–	11	8	56

1 A small weighting adjustment has been applied to IPS data for 1991 to 1998. This reflects the estimated effect of applying the weighting improvements made to IPS data from 1999 onwards.

2 Figures for all years show EU as it was constituted on 1 January 1995. These do not include the 10 new member states admitted to the EU in May 2004. However, these member states will be included in the 2004 international migration estimates for the EU.

3 Figures for all years include South Africa in the Old Commonwealth.

Source: Office for National Statistics: 01329 813255

5.10 Acceptances for settlement by nationality[1]
United Kingdom

Number of persons

Geographical region and nationality		2001	2002	2003	Geographical region and nationality		2001	2002	2003
All nationalities	KGFA	108 410	115 965	141 490	Africa (continued)				
					Somalia	KGHG	8 405	10 000	6 820
Europe[1]					South Africa	KGHH	4 755	6 135	8 930
					Sudan	KGHI	655	560	660
Bulgaria	KGFW	310	365	760	Tanzania	KGHJ	310	290	505
Cyprus	KGFN	260	270	565	Tunisia	KGHK	190	160	215
Former Czechoslovakia	KGFX	920	875	945	Uganda	KGHL	755	745	840
Of which,					Zambia	KGHM	345	330	575
Czech Republic[2]	LQLS	490	495	515	Zimbabwe	KGHN	1 040	3 530	3 510
Slovakia	LQLT	430	380	430	Other Africa	KOSU	2 015	2 550	3 125
Hungary	KGFZ	215	270	330					
Malta	KGFP	95	80	100	Total	KGHO	31 925	39 165	45 835
Poland	KGGA	945	875	1 310					
Romania	KGGB	360	390	575	Asia				
Switzerland[3]	KGFS	220	145	..					
Turkey	KGFT	3 310	2 920	4 340	Indian sub-continent				
Former USSR	KGGC	2 025	2 535	4 165	Bangladesh	KGHP	4 050	4 725	5 610
Of which,					India	KGHQ	7 320	8 005	11 460
Estonia	LQLU	40	50	75	Pakistan	KGHR	11 645	11 935	13 120
Latvia	LQLV	70	75	130					
Lithuania	LQLW	135	170	330	Total	KGHS	23 020	24 665	30 190
Russia[4]	LQLX	1 025	1 365	2 180					
Ukraine	LQLY	405	460	820	Middle East				
Other former USSR	LQLZ	340	415	630	Iran	KGHT	1 560	1 715	1 545
Former Yugoslavia	KGFU	5 080	2 830	1 990	Iraq	KGHU	1 715	1 955	1 415
Of which,					Israel	KGHV	320	375	525
Croatia	LQMA	710	310	290	Jordan	KGHW	175	170	180
Slovenia	LQMB	10	25	20	Kuwait	KGHX	30	65	65
Serbia & Montenegro[5]	LQMC	2 785	1 540	1 140	Lebanon	KGHY	265	365	310
Other former Yugoslavia	LQMD	1 575	955	540	Saudi Arabia	KGHZ	45	40	75
Other Europe	KOSO	255	190	315	Syria	KGIA	195	170	280
					Yemen	KOSV	380	300	420
Total[1]	KOSP	13 990	11 740	15 390	Other Middle East	KOSW	140	190	165
Americas					Total	KGIB	4 830	5 345	4 985
Argentina	KGGF	120	120	160					
Barbados	KGGG	115	100	160	Remainder of Asia				
Brazil	KGGH	575	510	755	China	KGIC	1 515	1 705	2 575
Canada	KGGI	1 320	1 300	1 730	Hong Kong[7]	KOSX	605	460	175
Chile	KGGJ	75	100	125	Indonesia	KGID	205	225	315
Colombia	KGGK	785	805	1 045	Japan	KGIE	1 695	1 785	1 875
Guyana	KGGM	210	190	280	Malaysia	KGIF	710	745	1 180
Jamaica	KGGN	2 855	2 675	4 500	Philippines	KGIG	1 355	1 505	3 845
Mexico	KGGO	130	160	250	Singapore	KGIH	225	220	275
Peru	KGGP	150	155	190	South Korea	KOTE	480	485	740
Trinidad and Tobago	KGGQ	365	410	670	Sri Lanka	KGII	4 240	2 935	2 560
USA	KGGR	4 385	4 355	5 695	Taiwan	KOSY	165	200	255
Venezuela	KGGT	85	80	135	Thailand	KGIJ	1 260	1 335	2 030
Other Americas	KOSR	810	720	1 040	Other Asia	KOSZ	3 840	4 980	4 200
Total	KGGU	11 975	11 680	16 735	Total	KGIL	16 305	16 575	20 015
Africa					Total	KGIM	44 155	46 585	55 190
Algeria	KGGV	775	855	1 115					
Angola	KOSS	280	660	640	Oceania				
Congo (Dem. Rep.)[6]	KOST	800	1 260	1 475	Australia	KGIN	3 205	3 500	4 160
Egypt	KGGW	420	500	630	New Zealand	KGIO	2 185	2 645	2 940
Ethiopia	KGGX	475	345	290	Other Oceania	KOTA	60	100	90
Ghana	KGGY	2 440	2 585	4 065					
Kenya	KGHA	1 025	1 055	1 600	Total	KGIP	5 455	6 250	7 185
Libya	KGHB	370	445	360					
Mauritius	KGHC	375	455	710	British Overseas citizens	KGIQ	520	330	830
Morocco	KGHD	575	520	685	Stateless[8]	KGIS	390	215	320
Nigeria	KGHE	5 045	5 325	7 695					
Sierra Leone	KGHF	875	855	1 380	All nationalities	KGFA	108 410	115 965	141 490

1 Excluding European Economic Area nationals
2 Includes Czechoslovakian passport holders.
3 Switzerland joined the EEA on 1 June 2002.
4 Includes Soviet Union passport holders.

5 Includes holders of passports of the former Yugoslavia.
6 Formerly known as Zaire.
7 Includes Hong Kong stateless persons.
8 Includes refugees from South East Asia.

Source: Home Office: 020 8760 8289

5.11 Applications[1] received for asylum in the United Kingdom, excluding dependants, by nationality

Number of principal applicants

		1994	1995	1996	1997	1998	1999[2]	2000[2]	2001	2002	2003[3]
Europe											
Albania	LQME	75	110	105	445	560	1 310	1 490	1 065	1 150	595
Czech Republic	LQMF	5	15	55	240	515	1 790	1 200	825	1 365	70
Macedonia	PTDW	..	..	15	20	50	90	65	755	310	60
Moldova	VQHP	5	10	..[4]	20	25	180	235	425	820	380
Poland	DMLX	360	1 210	900	565	1 585	1 860	1 015	615	990	95
Romania	KEAV	355	770	455	605	1 015	1 985	2 160	1 400	1 210	550
Russia	ZAEQ	..	..	205	180	185	685	1 000	450	295	280
SAM[5]	ZAFA	..	..	400	1 865	7 395	11 465	6 070	3 230	2 265	815
Turkey	KEAW	2 045	1 820	1 495	1 445	2 015	2 850	3 990	3 695	2 835	2 390
Ukraine	ZAER	..	..	235	490	370	775	770	445	365	300
Other Former USSR	ZAES	590	785	960	1 325	2 235	2 460	2 275	895	1 245	625
Other Former Yugoslavia	ZAET	1 385	1 565	620	375	535	2 625	2 200	85	90	50
Europe Other	ZAEU	535	770	1 035	1 575	1 260	200	415	335	300	80
Total	KEAZ	5 360	7 050	6 475	9 145	17 745	28 280	22 880	14 215	13 235	6 295
Americas											
Colombia	KEBZ	405	525	1 005	1 330	425	1 000	505	365	420	220
Ecuador	KYDB	105	250	435	1 205	280	610	445	255	315	150
Jamaica	PTDX	110	150	125	130	105	180	310	525	1 310	965
Americas Other	PTDY	265	415	205	165	165	240	155	170	240	230
Total	KECT	890	1 340	1 765	2 825	975	2 025	1 420	1 315	2 290	1 560
Africa											
Algeria	KOTB	995	1 865	715	715	1 260	1 385	1 635	1 140	1 060	550
Angola	KECU	605	555	385	195	150	545	800	1 015	1 420	850
Burundi	PTDZ	50	95	60	85	215	780	620	610	700	650
Cameroon	VQHU	75	85	105	175	95	245	355	380	615	505
Congo	PTEA	40	80	75	90	150	450	485	540	600	320
Congo (Dem. Rep.)	KEEH	775	935	680	690	660	1 240	1 030	1 370	2 215	1 540
Eritrea	PTEC	110	245	135	125	345	565	505	620	1 180	950
Ethiopia	KECW	730	585	205	145	345	455	415	610	700	640
Gambia	DMMA	140	1 170	245	125	45	30	50	65	130	95
Ghana	KECX	2 035	1 915	780	350	225	195	285	190	275	325
Ivory Coast	DMLZ	705	245	125	70	95	190	445	275	315	390
Kenya	KOTC	1 130	1 395	1 170	605	885	485	455	305	350	220
Liberia	C53K	140	390	330	205	70	65	55	115	450	740
Nigeria	KECY	4 340	5 825	2 900	1 480	1 380	945	835	810	1 125	1 010
Rwanda	ZAEV	100	135	80	90	280	280	820	760	530	655	260
Sierra Leone	KOTD	1 810	855	395	815	565	1 125	1 330	1 940	1 155	380
Somalia	KECZ	1 840	3 465	1 780	2 730	4 685	7 495	5 020	6 420	6 540	5 090
Sudan	KEEE	330	345	280	230	250	280	415	390	655	930
Tanzania	DMMC	205	1 535	225	90	80	80	60	80	40	30
Uganda	KEEG	360	365	215	220	210	420	740	480	715	705
Zimbabwe	GRFS	55	105	130	60	80	230	1 010	2 140	7 655	3 295
Africa Other	PTEB	390	360	275	220	305	400	615	555	845	895
Total	KEEJ	16 960	22 545	11 290	9 515	12 380	18 435	17 920	20 590	29 390	20 370
Middle East											
Iran	KEEK	520	615	585	585	745	1 320	5 610	3 420	2 630	2 875
Iraq	KEEL	550	930	965	1 075	1 295	1 800	7 475	6 680	14 570	4 015
Middle East Other	ZAEX	910	755	600	675	745	1 045	1 330	1 165	1 115	1 080
Total	KEGY	1 985	2 295	2 150	2 335	2 785	4 165	14 415	11 265	18 315	7 970
Asia											
Afghanistan	DMLY	325	580	675	1 085	2 395	3 975	5 555	8 920	7 205	2 280
Bangladesh	ZAEY	310	685	645	545	460	530	795	510	720	735
China	KEGZ	425	790	820	1 945	1 925	2 625	4 000	2 390	3 675	3 450
India	KEIL	2 030	3 255	2 220	1 285	1 030	1 365	2 120	1 850	1 865	2 290
Pakistan	KEIM	1 810	2 915	1 915	1 615	1 975	2 615	3 165	2 860	2 405	1 915
Sri Lanka	KEIN	2 350	2 070	1 340	1 830	3 505	5 130	6 395	5 510	3 130	705
Vietnam	VQIB	5	5	10	10	35	105	180	400	840	1 125
Asia Other	PTEE	260	385	270	255	615	1 120	1 025	1 040	915	655
Total	KEJO	7 515	10 685	7 885	8 570	11 940	17 465	23 230	23 480	20 755	13 155
Nationality not known[6]	KEJP	125	50	80	105	190	785	450	160	145	55
Grand Total	KEJQ	32 830	43 965	29 640	32 500	46 015	71 160	80 315	71 025	84 130	49 405

1 Figures rounded to the nearest 5.
2 May exclude some cases lodged at Local Enforcement Offices between January 1999 and March 2000.
3 Provisional figures.
4 Figure = 1 or 2.

5 Serbia and Montenegro (SAM) replaced Federal Republic of Yugoslavia (FRY) from 5 February 2003. SAM comprises the Republic of Serbia, the Republic of Montenegro, and the Province of Kosovo (administered by the UN on an interim basis since 1999).
6 Where the nationality was not known in 1994 the most likely nationality was recorded.

Source: Home Office: 020 8760 8274

5.12 Marriages: by previous marital status, sex, age and country

		1993	1994	1995	1996	1997	1998	1999	2000	2001	2002	2003
United Kingdom[1,2]												
Marriages	KKAA	341 608	331 232	322 251	317 514	310 218	304 797	301 083	305 912	286 129	293 021	306 214
Persons marrying per 1,000 resident population	KKAB	11.8	11.4	11.1	10.9	10.6	10.4	10.3	10.4	9.7	9.9	10.3
Previous marital status												
Bachelors	KKAC	245 996	236 619	227 717	221 826	216 237	214 005	211 820	213 777	202 690	206 196	215 574
Divorced men	KKAD	85 824	85 261	85 743	87 113	85 625	82 977	81 750	84 771	76 852	80 040	83 554
Widowers	KKAE	9 788	9 352	8 791	8 575	8 356	7 815	7 513	7 364	6 587	6 785	7 036
Spinsters	KKAF	248 063	237 241	228 462	221 697	216 776	215 399	213 246	215 865	205 048	208 385	217 828
Divorced women	KKAG	84 268	85 220	85 396	87 618	85 648	82 016	80 816	83 166	74 807	78 182	81 770
Widows	KKAH	9 277	8 771	8 393	8 199	7 794	7 382	7 021	6 881	6 274	6 454	6 576
First marriage for both partners	KMGH	210 567	200 910	192 078	185 293	181 135	180 404	178 759	180 020	171 912	174 374	182 938
First marriage for one partner	KMGI	72 925	72 040	72 023	72 937	70 743	68 596	67 548	69 602	63 914	65 833	67 526
Remarriage for both partners	KMGJ	58 116	58 282	58 150	59 284	58 340	55 797	54 776	56 290	50 303	52 814	55 700
Males												
Under 21 years	KKAI	8 767	7 091	6 302	5 497	5 126	5 173	5 234	5 019	4 625	4 396	4 275
21-24	KKAJ	65 129	56 877	49 432	42 488	36 875	32 723	29 390	28 467	25 840	26 293	26 853
25-29	KKAK	114 101	111 108	105 218	101 647	97 345	94 696	90 412	85 870	78 687	74 858	74 942
30-34	KKAL	63 848	65 490	68 245	69 867	70 904	71 096	72 129	73 809	70 657	72 592	75 292
35-44	KKAM	50 553	51 310	53 350	56 513	58 292	59 838	62 114	68 019	65 242	69 747	75 131
45-54	KKAN	23 841	24 136	24 786	26 252	26 472	26 118	26 581	28 791	26 122	27 801	30 212
55 and over	KKAO	15 369	15 220	14 918	15 250	15 204	15 153	15 223	15 937	14 956	17 334	19 469
Females												
Under 21 years	KKAP	26 839	22 903	20 643	18 485	17 254	16 793	16 082	15 938	13 874	13 194	13 400
21-24	KKAQ	93 125	84 171	75 071	66 191	59 549	54 645	50 350	48 578	45 687	45 789	46 903
25-29	KKAR	104 517	102 803	100 644	99 651	97 932	97 181	94 703	92 753	85 647	82 892	83 366
30-34	KKAS	49 546	52 359	54 819	57 752	58 589	59 349	60 446	62 478	59 859	62 279	65 471
35-44	KKAT	40 090	41 213	43 115	45 969	47 267	47 721	50 136	54 697	52 209	56 997	61 229
45-54	KKAU	18 800	19 280	19 720	21 025	21 038	20 708	20 822	22 621	20 459	22 187	24 593
55 and over	KKAV	8 691	8 503	8 239	8 441	8 589	8 400	8 544	8 847	8 394	9 683	11 212
England and Wales[1,2]												
Marriages	KKBA	299 197	291 069	283 012	278 975	272 536	267 303	263 515	267 961	249 227	255 596	267 700
Persons marrying per 1,000 resident population	KKBB	11.7	11.4	11.0	10.9	10.6	10.3	10.2	10.3	9.5	9.7	10.1
Previous marital status												
Bachelors	KKBC	213 476	206 077	198 208	193 306	188 268	186 329	184 266	186 113	175 721	179 121	187 510
Divorced men	KKBD	76 986	76 633	76 967	78 003	76 839	74 029	72 617	75 378	67 678	70 506	73 940
Widowers	KKBE	8 735	8 359	7 837	7 666	7 429	6 945	6 632	6 470	5 828	5 969	6 200
Spinsters	KKBF	214 987	206 332	198 603	192 707	188 457	187 391	185 328	187 717	177 506	180 675	189 170
Divorced women	KKBG	75 904	76 857	76 869	78 939	77 098	73 330	71 971	74 092	66 120	69 234	72 660
Widows	KKBH	8 306	7 880	7 540	7 329	6 981	6 582	6 216	6 152	5 601	5 687	5 830
First marriage for both partners	KMGK	181 956	174 200	166 418	160 680	156 907	156 539	155 027	156 140	148 642	151 014	158 560
First marriage for one partner	KMGL	64 551	64 009	63 975	64 653	62 911	60 642	59 540	61 550	55 943	57 768	59 560
Remarriage for both partners	KMGM	52 690	52 860	52 619	53 642	52 718	50 122	48 948	50 271	44 642	46 814	49 530
Males												
Under 21 years	KKBI	7 540	6 175	5 520	4 877	4 574	4 608	4 629	4 536	4 160	3 952	3 820
21-24	KKBJ	55 963	49 073	42 711	36 713	31 907	28 389	25 424	24 764	22 436	22 961	23 500
25-29	KKBK	99 314	96 862	91 607	88 338	84 644	82 135	78 364	74 367	67 934	64 619	64 930
30-34	KKBL	56 129	57 848	60 014	61 582	62 265	62 323	63 212	64 611	61 409	62 998	65 460
35-44	KKBM	44 863	45 514	47 330	50 038	51 654	52 812	54 528	59 834	56 872	61 196	65 800
45-54	KKBN	21 440	21 794	22 349	23 661	23 688	23 385	23 676	25 470	22 949	24 336	26 610
55 and over	KKBO	13 948	13 803	13 481	13 766	13 804	13 651	13 682	14 379	13 467	15 534	17 540
Females												
Under 21 years	KKBP	23 469	20 250	18 343	16 510	15 439	15 065	14 379	14 421	12 467	11 916	12 160
21-24	KKBQ	80 470	72 937	65 126	57 296	51 766	47 446	43 691	42 265	39 746	39 968	41 070
25-29	KKBR	91 134	89 941	87 680	86 838	85 352	84 399	82 250	80 312	73 799	71 540	72 090
30-34	KKBS	43 559	46 119	48 216	50 799	51 405	51 982	52 721	54 649	51 865	53 970	56 840
35-44	KKBT	35 662	36 651	38 367	40 889	41 838	42 245	44 199	48 245	45 672	49 984	53 650
45-54	KKBU	16 969	17 409	17 791	18 992	18 938	18 575	18 572	20 083	18 071	19 535	21 730
55 and over	KKBV	7 934	7 762	7 489	7 651	7 798	7 591	7 703	7 986	7 607	8 683	10 120

5.12

Marriages: by previous marital status, sex, age and country

continued

Numbers

		1993	1994	1995	1996	1997	1998	1999	2000	2001	2002	2003
Scotland[2]												
Marriages	KKCA	33 366	31 480	30 663	30 242	29 611	29 668	29 940	30 367	29 621	29 826	30 757
Persons marrying per 1,000 resident population	KKCB	13.1	12.3	12.0	11.9	11.7	11.7	11.8	12.0	11.7	11.8	12.2
Previous marital status												
Bachelors	KKCC	24 609	23 004	22 126	21 454	20 994	20 987	21 052	21 201	20 737	20 671	21 477
Divorced men	KKCD	7 879	7 654	7 741	8 048	7 845	7 934	8 142	8 427	8 238	8 475	8 574
Widowers	KKCE	878	822	796	740	772	747	746	739	646	680	706
Spinsters	KKCF	25 103	23 248	22 410	21 799	21 303	21 241	21 308	21 608	21 223	21 180	21 974
Divorced women	KKCG	7 469	7 487	7 542	7 718	7 621	7 754	7 949	8 141	7 825	8 008	8 157
Widows	KKCH	794	745	711	725	687	673	683	618	573	638	626
First marriage for both partners	KEZV	21 214	19 644	18 822	18 071	17 751	17 677	17 680	17 864	17 468	17 426	18 232
First marriage for one partner	KEZW	7 284	6 964	6 892	7 111	6 795	6 874	7 000	7 081	7 024	6 999	6 987
Remarriage for both partners	KEZX	4 868	4 872	4 949	5 060	5 065	5 117	5 260	5 422	5 129	5 401	5 538
Males												
Under 21 years	KKCI	902	680	577	452	406	421	490	364	371	367	361
21-24	KKCJ	6 870	5 693	4 915	4 191	3 494	3 147	2 853	2 720	2 489	2 395	2 507
25-29	KKCK	11 266	10 812	10 209	10 056	9 495	9 439	9 031	8 536	7 949	7 468	7 219
30-34	KKCL	6 214	6 176	6 574	6 574	6 911	6 988	7 179	7 419	7 464	7 692	7 752
35-44	KKCM	4 803	4 864	5 021	5 412	5 649	5 945	6 470	7 018	7 215	7 328	8 007
45-54	KKCN	2 093	2 050	2 124	2 288	2 459	2 412	2 575	2 960	2 816	3 033	3 213
55 and over	KKCO	1 218	1 205	1 243	1 269	1 197	1 316	1 342	1 350	1 317	1 543	1 698
Females												
Under 21 years	KKCP	2 461	1 959	1 728	1 423	1 302	1 289	1 322	1 171	1 111	996	1 007
21-24	KKCQ	9 506	8 291	7 264	6 474	5 568	5 248	4 778	4 581	4 343	4 171	4 199
25-29	KKCR	10 368	9 895	9 904	9 818	9 574	9 764	9 539	9 495	8 994	8 520	8 321
30-34	KKCS	5 002	5 145	5 401	5 675	5 927	6 036	6 433	6 463	6 618	6 832	7 110
35-44	KKCT	3 774	3 917	4 025	4 378	4 722	4 726	5 150	5 633	5 712	6 115	6 583
45-54	KKCU	1 606	1 648	1 689	1 794	1 844	1 900	1 994	2 279	2 147	2 322	2 589
55 and over	KKCV	649	625	652	680	674	705	724	745	696	870	948
Northern Ireland[2]												
Marriages	KKDA	9 045	8 683	8 576	8 297	8 071	7 826	7 628	7 584	7 281	7 599	7 757
Persons marrying per 1,000 resident population	KKDB	11.1	10.6	10.4	10.0	9.7	9.3	9.1	9.0	8.6	9.0	9.1
Previous marital status												
Bachelors	KKDC	7 911	7 538	7 383	7 066	6 975	6 689	6 502	6 463	6 232	6 404	6 587
Divorced men	KKDD	959	974	1 035	1 062	941	1 014	991	966	936	1 059	1 040
Widowers	KKDE	175	171	158	169	155	123	135	155	113	136	130
Spinsters	KKDF	7 973	7 661	7 449	7 191	7 016	6 767	6 610	6 540	6 319	6 530	6 684
Divorced women	KKDG	895	876	985	961	929	932	896	933	862	940	953
Widows	KKDH	177	146	142	145	126	127	122	111	100	129	120
First marriage for both partners	KEZY	7 397	7 066	6 838	6 542	6 477	6 188	6 052	6 016	5 802	5 934	6 146
First marriage for one partner	KEZZ	1 090	1 067	1 156	1 173	1 037	1 080	1 008	971	947	1 066	979
Remarriage for both partners	KFBI	558	550	582	582	557	558	568	597	532	599	632
Males												
Under 21 years	KKDI	325	236	205	168	146	144	115	119	94	77	94
21-24	KKDJ	2 296	2 111	1 806	1 584	1 474	1 187	1 113	983	915	937	846
25-29	KKDK	3 521	3 434	3 402	3 253	3 206	3 122	3 017	2 967	2 804	2 771	2 793
30-34	KKDL	1 505	1 466	1 657	1 711	1 728	1 785	1 738	1 779	1 784	1 902	2 080
35-44	KKDM	887	932	999	1 063	989	1 081	1 116	1 167	1 155	1 223	1 324
45-54	KKDN	308	292	313	303	325	321	330	361	357	432	389
55 and over	KKDO	203	212	194	215	203	186	199	208	172	257	231
Females												
Under 21 years	KKDP	909	694	572	552	513	439	381	346	296	282	233
21-24	KKDQ	3 149	2 943	2 681	2 421	2 215	1 951	1 881	1 732	1 598	1 650	1 634
25-29	KKDR	3 015	2 967	3 060	2 995	3 006	3 018	2 914	2 946	2 854	2 832	2 955
30-34	KKDS	985	1 095	1 202	1 278	1 257	1 331	1 292	1 366	1 376	1 477	1 521
35-44	KKDT	654	645	723	702	707	750	787	819	825	898	996
45-54	KKDU	225	223	240	239	256	233	256	259	241	330	274
55 and over	KKDV	108	116	98	110	117	104	117	116	91	130	144

1 2002 for England and Wales and the United Kingdom are provisional, all data for 2003 are provisional.

Sources: Office for National Statistics: 01329 813339;
General Register Office for Scotland;
Northern Ireland Statistics and Research Agency

5.13 Divorce: by duration of marriage, age of wife and country

Numbers

		1993	1994	1995	1996	1997	1998	1999	2000	2001	2002	2003
United Kingdom												
Decrees absolute granted[1]:												
Number	ZBRL	180 018	173 611	170 050	171 729	161 087	160 057	158 746	154 628	156 814	160 726	166 737
Duration of marriage:												
0-4 years	ZBRM	39 530	37 978	36 594	37 016	33 719	33 087	31 047	28 933	28 306	28 591	28 781
5-9 years	ZBRN	50 883	49 215	48 309	48 670	45 040	44 243	43 357	41 621	42 360	42 924	43 558
10-14 years	ZBRO	33 221	31 177	30 257	30 159	29 085	29 706	30 270	30 166	30 849	31 257	32 564
15-19 years	ZBRP	22 324	21 336	21 040	21 379	20 211	20 078	20 147	19 902	20 568	21 881	23 119
20 years and over	ZBRQ	34 055	33 898	33 840	34 487	33 020	32 935	33 916	34 000	34 729	36 073	38 713
Not stated	ZBRR	5	7	10	18	12	8	9	6	2	–	2
Age of wife at marriage:												
16-19 years	ZBRS	43 368	38 464	35 145	33 590	28 987	27 627	25 440	23 505	22 558	22 107	22 367
20-24 years	ZBRT	83 806	80 594	78 341	78 075	72 971	71 416	69 509	66 215	66 282	66 264	67 070
25-29 years	ZBRU	29 213	30 576	31 611	33 634	33 452	34 195	35 585	36 009	37 418	39 116	41 464
30-34 years	ZBRV	11 272	11 716	12 322	13 122	12 968	13 719	14 420	14 892	15 842	17 374	18 658
35-39 years	ZBRW	6 018	5 979	6 172	6 470	6 155	6 571	6 848	6 993	7 417	8 070	8 742
40-44 years	ZBRX	3 260	3 247	3 335	3 507	3 375	3 360	3 557	3 568	3 778	4 104	4 404
45 years and over	ZBRY	3 004	2 952	3 052	3 239	3 094	3 086	3 291	3 352	3 429	3 572	3 917
Not stated	ZBRZ	77	83	72	92	85	83	96	94	90	119	115
Age of wife at divorce:												
16-24 years	ZBSA	13 895	11 845	10 517	9 298	7 371	6 758	5 671	5 115	4 874	4 998	5 092
25-29 years	ZBSB	38 632	35 824	33 354	32 808	28 814	26 968	24 120	21 280	19 635	18 340	17 633
30-34 years	ZBSC	39 879	39 456	38 839	39 497	37 257	36 795	36 052	34 356	34 194	33 555	32 774
35-39 years	ZBSD	30 746	30 000	30 280	31 497	30 641	31 688	32 605	32 588	33 997	35 050	36 465
40-44 years	ZBSE	23 943	22 847	22 791	22 843	22 246	22 810	23 614	23 879	25 579	27 564	30 154
45 years and over	ZBSF	32 841	33 549	34 187	35 684	34 662	34 947	36 578	37 311	38 442	41 102	44 498
Not stated	ZBSG	82	90	82	102	96	91	106	99	93	117	121
Divorces in which there were:												
No children aged under 16[2]	ZBSH	78 803	78 913	78 844	..	..	..	..	..	..	..	..
One or more children aged under 16[2]	ZBSI	101 215	94 698	91 206	..	..	..	..	..	..	..	..
England and Wales												
Decrees absolute granted[1]:												
Number	KKEA	165 018	158 175	155 499	157 107	146 689	145 214	144 556	141 135	143 818	147 735	153 490
Rate per 1,000 married couples	KKEB	14.2	13.7	13.6	13.8	13.0	12.9	12.9	12.7	12.9	13.4	14.0
Duration of marriage:												
0-4 years	KKEC	37 252	35 695	34 507	34 924	31 767	31 136	29 307	27 474	26 987	27 344	27 511
5-9 years	KKED	46 536	44 769	44 304	44 609	41 260	40 239	39 676	38 206	39 079	39 730	40 599
10-14 years	KKEE	30 156	28 073	27 365	27 332	26 215	26 698	27 384	27 459	28 176	28 592	29 831
15-19 years	KKEF	20 233	19 200	18 943	19 321	18 027	17 934	18 072	17 870	18 603	19 784	20 923
20 years and over	KKEG	30 836	30 431	30 370	30 912	29 408	29 199	30 108	30 120	30 971	32 285	34 624
Not stated	KKEH	5	7	10	9	12	8	9	6	2	–	2
Age of wife at marriage:												
16-19 years	KKEI	38 811	34 069	31 322	29 927	25 579	24 276	22 486	20 930	20 218	19 828	20 063
20-24 years	KKEJ	76 853	73 291	71 360	71 123	66 167	64 453	62 853	59 874	60 211	60 353	61 057
25-29 years	KKEK	27 178	28 360	29 441	31 396	31 022	31 533	32 867	33 282	34 759	36 387	38 722
30-34 years	KKEL	10 593	11 007	11 585	12 335	12 094	12 788	13 507	13 972	14 890	16 339	17 567
35-39 years	KKEM	5 673	5 615	5 800	6 051	5 767	6 153	6 432	6 562	6 956	7 623	8 249
40-44 years	KKEN	3 091	3 064	3 121	3 254	3 156	3 135	3 331	3 378	3 559	3 841	4 154
45 years and over	KKEO	2 819	2 769	2 870	3 021	2 904	2 876	3 080	3 137	3 225	3 364	3 678
Age of wife at divorce:												
16-24 years	KKEP	12 924	10 956	9 783	8 615	6 871	6 298	5 318	4 839	4 643	4 808	4 867
25-29 years	KKEQ	35 362	32 608	30 563	30 075	26 435	24 586	22 173	19 650	18 231	17 227	16 539
30-34 years	KKER	36 300	35 848	35 538	36 274	33 967	33 446	32 837	31 420	31 489	30 982	30 345
35-39 years	KKES	28 162	27 195	27 550	28 727	27 715	28 605	29 663	29 820	31 164	32 282	33 519
40-44 years	KKET	21 891	20 765	20 739	20 774	20 125	20 521	21 325	21 469	23 190	25 017	27 610
45 years and over	KKEU	30 374	30 796	31 316	32 633	31 564	31 750	33 231	33 931	35 099	37 419	40 608
Not stated	KKEV	5	7	10	9	12	8	9	6	2	–	2
Divorces in which there were:												
No children aged under 16[2]	ZBSJ	70 103	69 684	69 632	70 174	66 019	64 738	65 258	64 359	64 541	66 738	69 681
One or more children aged under 16[2]	ZBSK	94 915	88 491	85 867	86 933	80 670	80 476	79 298	76 776	79 277	80 997	83 809

5.13 Divorce: by duration of marriage, age of wife and country

continued

		1993	1994	1995	1996	1997	1998	1999	2000	2001	2002	2003
Scotland												
Decrees absolute granted[1]												
Number	KKFA	12 787	13 133	12 249	12 308	12 222	12 384	11 864	11 143	10 631	10 826	10 928
Rate per 1,000 married couples	KKFB	11.1	11.5	10.8	10.9	11.0	11.3	10.9	10.3	9.7	10.0	10.2
Duration of marriage:												
0-4 years	KKFC	2 092	2 095	1 908	1 914	1 793	1 766	1 588	1 304	1 159	1 128	1 141
5-9 years	KKFD	3 722	3 790	3 399	3 432	3 224	3 360	3 095	2 890	2 721	2 689	2 450
10-14 years	KKFE	2 539	2 592	2 407	2 310	2 385	2 456	2 368	2 168	2 163	2 183	2 222
15-19 years	KKFF	1 745	1 786	1 698	1 709	1 804	1 729	1 686	1 622	1 562	1 705	1 773
20 years and over	KKFG	2 689	2 870	2 837	2 934	3 016	3 073	3 127	3 159	3 026	3 121	3 342
Not stated	ZBSL	–	–	–	9	–	–	–	–	–	–	–
Age of wife at marriage:												
16-19 years	ZBSM	3 768	3 641	3 091	2 939	2 749	2 654	2 374	2 043	1 839	1 845	1 816
20-24 years	ZBSN	5 890	6 197	5 845	5 822	5 714	5 744	5 453	5 142	4 873	4 823	4 869
25-29 years	KKFJ	1 812	1 926	1 887	1 933	2 151	2 314	2 333	2 318	2 233	2 316	2 307
30-34 years	KKFK	612	628	654	697	791	824	829	805	827	895	958
35-39 years	KKFL	312	329	338	393	360	382	379	378	401	407	432
40-44 years	KKFM	152	163	196	234	199	198	208	170	193	235	219
45 years and over	KKFN	164	166	166	198	173	185	192	193	175	186	212
Not stated	KKFO	77	83	72	92	85	83	96	94	90	119	115
Age of wife at divorce:												
16-24 years	KKFP	844	767	622	583	426	377	301	232	182	180	191
25-29 years	KKFQ	2 775	2 750	2 353	2 269	2 021	1 957	1 597	1 330	1 109	974	884
30-34 years	KKFR	3 037	3 045	2 747	2 708	2 736	2 767	2 642	2 381	2 215	2 174	1 943
35-39 years	KKFS	2 212	2 390	2 290	2 307	2 469	2 562	2 450	2 298	2 311	2 281	2 388
40-44 years	KKFT	1 771	1 788	1 734	1 761	1 819	1 951	1 929	1 999	1 963	2 110	2 106
45 years and over	KKFU	2 071	2 310	2 431	2 587	2 667	2 687	2 848	2 810	2 760	2 990	3 297
Not stated	KKFV	77	83	72	93	84	83	97	93	91	117	119
Divorces in which there were:												
No children aged under 16[2]	KKFW	6 951	7 390	7 515	..	..	..	..	..	..	..	..
One or more children under 16[2]	KKFX	5 836	5 743	4 734	..	..	..	..	..	..	..	..
Northern Ireland												
Decrees absolute granted:[1,3]												
Number	ZBSO	2 213	2 303	2 302	2 314	2 176	2 459	2 326	2 350	2 365	2 165	2 319
Duration of marriage:												
0-4 years	ZBSP	186	188	179	178	159	185	152	155	160	119	129
5-9 years	ZBSQ	625	656	606	629	556	644	586	525	560	505	509
10-14 years	ZBSR	526	512	485	517	485	552	518	539	510	482	511
15-19 years	ZBSS	346	350	399	349	380	415	389	410	403	392	423
20 years and over	ZBST	530	597	633	641	596	663	681	721	732	667	747
Age of wife at marriage:												
16-19 years	ZBSU	789	754	732	724	659	697	580	532	501	434	488
20-24 years	ZBSV	1 063	1 106	1 136	1 130	1 090	1 219	1 203	1 199	1 198	1 088	1 144
25-29 years	ZBSW	223	290	283	305	279	348	385	409	426	413	435
30-34 years	ZBSX	67	81	83	90	83	107	84	115	125	140	133
35-39 years	ZBSY	33	35	34	26	28	36	37	53	60	40	61
40-44 years	ZBSZ	17	20	18	19	20	27	18	20	26	28	31
45 years and over	ZBTA	21	17	16	20	17	25	19	22	29	22	27
Age of wife at divorce:												
16-24 years	ZBTB	127	122	112	100	74	83	52	44	49	10	34
25-29 years	ZBTC	495	466	438	464	358	425	350	300	295	139	210
30-34 years	ZBTD	542	563	554	515	554	582	573	555	490	399	486
35-39 years	ZBTE	372	415	440	463	457	521	492	470	522	487	558
40-44 years	ZBTF	281	294	318	308	302	338	360	411	426	437	438
45 years and over	ZBTG	396	443	440	464	431	510	499	570	583	693	593
Divorces in which there were:												
No children aged under 16[2]	ZBTH	1 749	1 839	1 697	1 676	1 573	1 807	1 649	1 051	1 054	972	1 050
One or more children aged under 16[2]	ZBTI	464	464	605	638	603	652	677	1 299	1 311	1 193	1 269

1 Includes decrees of nullities.
2 Children of the family as defined by the Matrimonial Causes Act 1973.
3 Marital estimates are not available for Northern Ireland - no divorce rate for Northern Ireland and the United Kingdom.

Sources: Office for National Statistics: 01329 813339;
General Register Office for Scotland;
Northern Ireland Statistics and Research Agency

5.14 Divorce proceedings: by country

		1993	1994	1995	1996	1997	1998	1999	2000	2001	2002	2003
United Kingdom												
Dissolution of marriage[1]												
Decree absolute/decree granted	ZBXR	179 539	173 178	169 621	171 309	160 733	159 688	158 418	154 273	156 562	160 529	166 536
On grounds of:												
Adultery	ZBXS	45 759	42 743	41 313	41 127	38 652	37 302	35 545	34 082	33 452	33 389	33 844
Behaviour	ZBXT	78 686	75 029	71 733	72 581	68 546	68 685	67 851	65 687	66 818	68 499	70 866
Desertion	ZBXU	1 193	1 185	1 196	1 101	956	828	748	722	718	727	697
Separation (2 years and consent)	ZBXV	41 002	41 144	41 969	42 265	39 398	39 627	40 368	39 763	40 699	42 579	44 012
Separation(5 years)	ZBXW	12 183	12 317	12 699	13 547	12 552	12 697	13 389	13 653	14 575	15 076	16 831
Combination of more than one ground and other	ZBXX	716	760	711	688	629	549	517	366	300	259	286
Decree absolute/decree granted to[2]:												
the wife	ZBXY	128 797	123 256	118 869	119 570	111 912	111 556	109 828	106 958	107 345	108 106	114 665
the husband	ZBXZ	50 407	49 507	50 268	51 247	48 393	47 764	48 236	47 069	49 015	52 251	51 691
both	ZBYA	345	423	490	493	430	369	358	247	202	173	181
Nullity of marriage												
Decree absolute/decree granted	ZBYB	479	433	429	420	354	369	328	355	252	198	201
England and Wales												
Dissolution of marriage												
Petitions filed	KKGA	184 471	175 510	173 966	177 970	163 769	165 870	162 137	157 809	161 580	171 054	167 591
Decree nisi granted	KKGM	160 625	154 241	155 739	157 588	148 310	144 231	143 106	143 729	146 932	160 943	162 503
Decree absolute granted	KKGN	164 556	157 756	155 076	156 692	146 339	144 851	144 233	140 783	143 568	147 538	153 294
On grounds of:												
Adultery	KKGB	44 466	41 449	40 178	40 012	37 592	36 319	34 584	33 310	32 839	32 829	33 331
Behaviour	KKGC	74 583	70 932	68 168	68 986	65 047	65 257	64 816	63 182	64 768	66 480	68 944
Desertion	KKGD	1 118	1 062	1 108	1 030	912	790	713	680	689	681	665
Separation (2 years and consent)	KKGE	34 144	33 996	35 030	35 422	32 638	32 394	33 482	32 820	33 703	35 476	36 931
Separation(5 years)	KKGF	9 556	9 589	9 930	10 626	9 592	9 616	10 193	10 498	11 355	11 896	13 239
Combination of more than one ground and other	ZBYC	689	728	662	616	558	475	445	293	214	176	184
Decree absolute granted to:												
the wife	ZBYD	118 127	112 415	108 764	109 489	102 173	101 583	100 469	98 227	98 992	102 676	106 208
the husband	ZBYE	46 084	44 918	45 823	46 712	43 739	42 902	43 413	42 311	44 378	44 694	46 915
both	ZBYF	345	423	489	491	427	366	351	245	198	168	171
Nullity of marriage												
Petitions filed	KKGO	634	822	881	702	485	505	549	452	657	758	368
Decree nisi granted	KKGR	365	705	425	332	248	281	495	274	297	158	137
Decree absolute granted	KKGS	462	419	423	415	350	363	323	352	250	197	196
Judicial separation												
Petitions filed	KKGT	2 251	4 358	3 349	2 795	1 078	916	882	650	535	499	359
Decrees granted	KKGW	1 413	1 350	1 543	1 199	589	519	696	540	925	331	145

5.14 Divorce proceedings: by country
continued

		1993	1994	1995	1996	1997	1998	1999	2000	2001	2002	2003
Scotland												
Dissolution of marriage[1]												
Decree granted	ZBYG	12 777	13 125	12 243	12 307	12 220	12 383	11 860	11 142	10 631	10 826	10 927
On grounds of:												
Adultery	ZBYH	1 092	1 099	956	943	909	832	770	610	473	428	401
Behaviour	ZBYI	3 757	3 711	3 203	3 184	3 081	3 005	2 611	2 099	1 639	1 656	1 537
Desertion	ZBYJ	56	103	72	61	33	28	18	34	24	43	23
Separation (2 years and consent)	ZBYK	5 800	6 078	5 846	5 835	5 773	6 121	5 908	5 878	5 943	6 101	6 016
Separation(5 years)	ZBYL	2 072	2 134	2 166	2 284	2 424	2 397	2 553	2 521	2 552	2 598	2 950
Decree granted to[2]												
the wife	ZBYM	9 190	9 278	8 545	8 559	8 266	8 329	7 774	7 191	6 775	4 025	6 927
the husband	ZBYN	3 597	3 855	3 704	3 749	3 956	4 055	4 090	3 952	3 856	6 802	4 001
Nullity of marriage												
Decree granted	ZBYO	10	8	6	1	2	1	4	1	–	1	1
Northern Ireland												
Dissolution of marriage												
Petitions filed	ZBYP	2 610	2 875	2 875	2 695	2 808	2 760	2 414	3 005	2 869	2 929	2 319
Decree nisi granted	ZBYQ	2 384	2 535	2 535	2 419	2 532	2 904	2 393	2 456	2 615	2 454	2 616
Decree absolute granted	ZBYR	2 206	2 296	2 302	2 310	2 174	2 454	2 325	2 348	2 363	2 165	2 315
On grounds of:												
Adultery	ZBYS	201	195	179	172	151	151	191	162	140	132	112
Behaviour	ZBYT	346	386	362	411	418	423	424	406	411	363	385
Desertion	ZBYU	19	20	16	10	11	10	17	8	5	3	9
Separation (2 years and consent)	ZBYV	1 059	1 072	1 093	1 010	991	1 112	978	1 065	1 053	1 002	1 065
Separation(5 years)	ZBYW	555	594	603	637	536	684	643	634	668	582	642
Combination of more than one ground and other	ZBYX	26	29	49	70	67	74	72	73	86	83	102
Decree absolute granted to:												
the wife	ZBYY	1 480	1 562	1 560	1 522	1 473	1 644	1 585	1 540	1 578	1 405	1 530
the husband	ZBYZ	726	734	741	786	698	807	733	806	781	755	775
both	ZBZA	–	–	1	2	3	3	7	2	4	5	10
Nullity of marriage												
Petitions filed	ZBZB	2	5	5	5	7	5	1	2	1	5	4
Decree nisi granted	ZBZC	2	3	5	5	2	6	2	5	2	2	5
Decree absolute granted	ZBZD	7	7	–	4	2	5	1	2	2	–	4
Judicial separation												
Petitions filed	ZBZE	44	57	84	63	70	64	50	54	40	27	35
Decrees granted	ZBZF	6	15	30	22	34	40	31	23	25	15	22

1 The terms petition filed, decree nisi granted, decree absolute and judicial separation are not used in Scotland. Decree absolute granted to 'both' and 'Combination of more than one ground and other' are not procedures used in Scotland.

2 Information on Decree granted for the wife or husband for Scotland includes nullities (these are identified separately under 'Nullity of marriage'); figures excluding nullities are not available.

Sources: Office for National Statistics: 01329 813339;
General Register Office for Scotland;
Northern Ireland Statistics and Research Agency;
The Court Service (E&W and NI);
Scottish Courts Administration

5.15 Births:[1] by country and sex

	Live births				Rates				
	Total	Male	Female	Sex ratio[2]	Crude birth rate[3]	General fertility rate[4]	TFR[5]	Still-births[6]	Still-birth rate[6]
United Kingdom[7]									
1900 - 02	1 095	558	537	1 037	28.6	115.1	..	..	..
1910 - 12	1 037	528	508	1 039	24.6	99.4	..	..	..
1920 - 22	1 018	522	496	1 052	23.1	93.0	..	..	..
1930 - 32	750	383	367	1 046	16.3	66.5	..	..	..
1940 - 42	723	372	351	1 062	15.0	..	1.89	..	..
1950 - 52	803	413	390	1 061	16.0	73.7	2.21	..	..
1960 - 62	946	487	459	1 063	17.9	90.3	2.80	18.6	19.2
1970 - 72	880	453	427	1 064	15.8	82.5	2.36	11.3	12.7
1980 - 82	735	377	358	1 053	13.0	62.5	1.83	5.0	6.8
1990 - 92	790	405	385	1 051	13.8	63.7	1.81	3.6	4.6
2000 - 02	672	345	328	1 052	11.4	54.7	1.64	3.6	5.4
	BBCA	KBCZ	KBCY	KMFW	KBCT	KBCS	KBCR	KBCQ	KMFX
1993	762	391	371	1 054	13.2	62.4	1.76	4.4	5.7
1994	750	385	365	1 054	13.0	61.6	1.74	4.3	5.8
1995	732	375	357	1 052	12.6	60.1	1.71	4.1	5.6
1996	733	376	357	1 055	12.6	60.2	1.73	4.1	5.5
1997	727	372	354	1 051	12.5	59.6	1.72	3.9	5.3
1998	717	367	350	1 052	12.3	58.8	1.71	3.9	5.4
1999	700	359	341	1 056	11.9	57.3	1.69	3.7	5.3
2000	679	348	331	1 051	11.5	55.4	1.64	3.6	5.3
2001	669	343	326	1 050	11.3	54.3	1.63	3.6	5.3
2002	669	343	327	1 054	11.3	54.2	1.64	3.8	5.6
2003	696	357	339	1 052	11.7	56.2	1.72	4.0	5.7
England and Wales									
1900 - 02	932	475	458	1 037	28.6	114.7	..	..	..
1910 - 12	884	450	433	1 040	24.5	98.6	..	..	..
1920 - 22	862	442	420	1 051	22.8	91.1	..	..	..
1930 - 32	632	323	309	1 047	15.8	64.4	..	27.0	..
1940 - 42	607	312	295	1 057	15.6	61.3	1.81	22.0	..
1950 - 52	683	351	332	1 058	15.6	72.1	2.16	16.0	..
1960 - 62	812	418	394	1 061	17.6	88.9	2.77	15.6	18.9
1970 - 72	764	394	371	1 061	15.6	81.4	2.31	9.7	12.5
1980 - 82	639	328	311	1 053	12.9	61.8	1.81	4.3	6.7
1990 - 92	698	358	340	1 051	13.8	63.8	1.82	3.2	4.5
2000 - 02	598	307	292	1 052	11.4	55.2	1.65	3.2	5.4
	BBCB	KMFY	KMFZ	KMGA	KMGB	KMGC	KMGD	KMGE	KMGF
1993	673	346	328	1 056	13.2	62.7	1.76	3.9	5.7
1994	665	341	323	1 055	13.0	62.0	1.75	3.8	5.7
1995	648	332	316	1 051	12.6	60.5	1.72	3.6	5.5
1996	649	333	316	1 055	12.6	60.6	1.74	3.5	5.4
1997	643	330	314	1 051	12.5	60.0	1.73	3.4	5.3
1998	636	326	310	1 051	12.3	59.2	1.72	3.4	5.3
1999	622	319	303	1 055	12.0	57.8	1.70	3.3	5.3
2000	604	310	295	1 050	11.6	55.9	1.65	3.2	5.3
2001	595	305	290	1 050	11.4	54.7	1.63	3.2	5.3
2002	596	306	290	1 055	11.3	54.7	1.65	3.4	5.6
2003	621	318	303	1 051	11.8	56.8	1.73	3.6	5.7

Births:[1] by country and sex

Thousands

	Live births				Rates				
	Total	Male	Female	Sex ratio[2]	Crude birth rate[3]	General fertility rate[4]	TFR[5]	Still-births[6]	Still-birth rate[6]
Scotland									
1900 - 02	132	67	65	1 046	29.5	120.6	..	..	..
1910 - 12	123	63	60	1 044	25.9	107.4	..	..	..
1920 - 22	125	64	61	1 046	25.6	105.9	..	..	..
1930 - 32	93	47	45	1 040	19.1	78.8	..	..	..
1940 - 42	89	46	43	1 051	18.5	73.7	..	4.0	..
1950 - 52	91	47	44	1 060	17.9	81.4	2.41	2.0	..
1960 - 62	102	53	50	1 060	19.7	97.8	2.98	2.2	20.8
1970 - 72	84	43	41	1 057	16.1	83.3	2.46	1.1	13.5
1980 - 82	68	35	33	1 051	13.1	62.2	1.80	0.4	6.3
1990 - 92	66	34	32	1 052	13.0	59.2	1.68	0.4	5.7
2000 - 02	52	27	26	1 046	10.3	48.6	1.48	0.3	5.6
	BBCD	KMEU	KMEV	KMEW	KMEX	KMEY	KMEZ	KMFM	KMFN
1993	63	32	31	1 046	12.4	57.4	1.61	0.4	6.4
1994	62	31	30	1 038	12.0	56.0	1.58	0.4	6.1
1995	60	31	29	1 043	11.7	54.6	1.55	0.4	6.6
1996	59	31	29	1 061	11.6	54.1	1.56	0.4	6.4
1997	59	31	29	1 055	11.6	54.4	1.58	0.3	5.3
1998	57	29	28	1 060	11.3	52.7	1.55	0.4	6.1
1999	55	28	27	1 050	10.9	50.9	1.51	0.3	5.2
2000	53	27	26	1 051	10.5	49.2	1.48	0.3	5.6
2001	53	27	26	1 041	10.4	48.8	1.49	0.3	5.7
2002	51	26	25	1 047	10.1	48.1	1.48	0.3	5.4
2003	52	27	26	1 054	10.4	49.4	1.54	0.3	5.6
Northern Ireland[7]									
1900 - 02	..	..	..	..	..	..	..	..	..
1910 - 12	..	..	..	..	..	..	..	..	..
1920 - 22	31	16	15	1 048	24.2	105.9	..	..	..
1930 - 32	26	13	12	1 047	20.5	78.8	..	..	..
1940 - 42	27	14	13	1 078	20.8	73.7	..	..	..
1950 - 52	29	15	14	1 066	20.9	81.4	..	..	..
1960 - 62	31	16	15	1 068	22.5	111.5	3.47	0.7	22.0
1970 - 72	31	16	15	1 074	20.4	105.7	3.13	0.5	14.3
1980 - 82	28	14	13	1 048	18.0	87.5	2.59	0.2	8.4
1990 - 92	26	13	13	1 051	16.1	74.8	2.15	0.1	4.6
2000 - 02	22	11	11	1 054	12.8	58.8	1.78	0.1	5.0
	BBCE	KMFO	KMFP	KMFQ	KMFR	KMFS	KMFT	KMFU	KMFV
1993	25	13	12	1 025	15.1	70.3	2.01	0.1	5.2
1994	24	12	12	1 053	14.7	68.0	1.95	0.2	6.3
1995	24	12	11	1 078	14.4	66.6	1.91	0.1	6.1
1996	24	12	12	1 032	14.7	67.8	1.96	0.2	6.2
1997	24	12	12	1 048	14.4	66.4	1.93	0.1	5.4
1998	24	12	12	1 039	14.1	65.0	1.90	0.1	5.1
1999	23	12	11	1 084	13.7	62.9	1.86	0.1	5.7
2000	22	11	10	1 070	12.8	58.7	1.75	0.1	4.3
2001	22	11	11	1 058	13.0	59.7	1.80	0.1	5.1
2002	21	11	11	1 035	12.6	58.1	1.77	0.1	5.7
2003	22	11	10	1 080	12.7	59.0	1.81	0.1	5.0

1 See chapter text.
2 Males per 1,000 females (calculated using whole numbers).
3 Rate per 1,000 population and produced using whole numbers.
4 Rate per 1,000 women aged 15 - 44.
5 Total period fertility rate is the average number of children which would be born to a woman if she experienced the age-specific fertility rates of the period in question throughout her child-bearing life span. UK figures for the years 1970-72 and earlier are estimates.

6 On 1 October 1992 the legal definition of a stillbirth was changed from a baby born dead after 28 completed weeks gestation or more to one born dead after 24 completed weeks gestation or more. Between 1 October and 31 December 1992 in the UK there were 258 babies born dead between 24 and 27 completed weeks gestation (216 in England and Wales, 35 in Scotland and 7 in Northern Ireland). If these babies were included in the stillbirth figures given, the stillbirth rate would be 4.7 for the UK and England and Wales, while Scotland and Northern Ireland stillbirth rate would remain as stated.
7 From 1981, data for the United Kingdom and Northern Ireland have been revised to exclude births in Northern Ireland to non-residents of Northern Ireland.

Sources: Office for National Statistics: 01329 813339;
General Register Office for Scotland;
Northern Ireland Statistics and Research Agency

5.16 Birth occurrence inside and outside marriage by age of mother[1]

Thousands

	Inside marriage						Outside marriage					
	All ages	Under 20	20 - 24	25 - 29	Over 30	Mean[2] age (Years)	All ages	Under 20	20 - 24	25 - 29	Over 30	Mean[2] age (Years)
United Kingdom[3]												
	KKEY	KKEZ	KKFY	KKFZ	KKGX	KKGY	KKGZ	KKIC	KKID	KKIE	KKIF	KKIG
1961	890	55	273	280	282	27.7	54	13	17	10	13	25.5
1971	828	70	301	271	185	26.4	74	24	25	13	12	23.8
1981	640	36	193	231	180	27.3	91	30	33	16	13	23.4
1986	596	21	159	231	185	27.9	158	45	60	31	22	23.7
1987	598	18	153	235	192	28.1	178	48	68	37	26	23.9
1988	589	16	144	234	195	28.2	198	51	76	42	29	24.1
1989	570	14	130	228	198	28.4	207	49	79	46	32	24.3
1990	576	13	121	233	209	28.6	223	51	83	53	37	24.5
1991	556	10	109	224	213	28.9	236	50	87	58	41	24.8
1992	540	9	98	216	218	29.1	241	46	86	62	46	25.1
1993	520	8	87	204	221	29.3	242	44	84	64	50	25.4
1994	510	7	78	194	231	29.6	240	41	80	65	55	25.7
1995	486	6	69	180	232	29.8	246	42	79	66	60	25.9
1996	473	6	61	170	237	30.1	260	45	80	69	66	26.0
1997	460	6	55	159	240	30.3	267	47	79	71	71	26.1
1998	447	6	51	149	243	30.5	270	49	77	70	74	26.2
1999	428	6	47	136	239	30.7	272	49	77	68	77	26.3
2000	411	5	44	126	237	30.9	268	47	77	66	78	26.4
2001	401	5	44	116	236	30.9	268	45	77	64	82	26.7
2002	397	5	44	109	239	31.1	272	44	80	62	85	26.7
2003[4]	407	5	44	110	249	31.2	288	45	86	65	92	26.8
Great Britain												
	KKIH	KKII	KKIJ	KKIK	KKIL	KKIM	KKIN	KKIO	KKIP	KKIQ	KKIR	KKIS
1961	859	53	264	270	272	27.7	53	13	17	10	13	25.5
1971	797	68	293	261	176	26.4	73	24	25	13	12	23.8
1981	614	34	186	223	171	27.2	89	29	32	16	13	23.3
1986	572	20	153	222	177	27.9	155	44	59	30	22	22.9
1987	574	17	147	227	184	28.0	174	46	66	36	25	23.4
1988	566	16	138	226	186	28.2	194	49	74	42	29	23.6
1989	549	13	125	220	190	28.4	202	48	77	45	32	24.2
1990	554	12	116	225	201	28.6	218	49	81	52	36	24.6
1991	535	10	105	216	205	28.9	231	48	85	57	41	24.8
1992	520	9	94	208	210	29.1	235	45	84	61	46	25.1
1993	500	7	84	196	213	29.3	236	42	82	62	49	25.4
1994	492	7	75	188	222	29.6	235	41	78	63	53	25.7
1995	468	6	66	173	223	29.8	240	40	77	65	59	25.9
1996	455	6	59	163	227	30.1	254	44	78	68	65	26.0
1997	442	6	53	152	231	30.3	261	46	76	69	69	26.2
1998	430	6	49	143	233	30.5	263	48	74	68	73	26.3
1999	412	6	46	131	230	30.7	265	48	74	67	76	26.4
2000	396	5	43	121	228	30.9	261	46	74	65	77	26.5
2001	386	5	43	112	227	30.9	261	44	75	62	80	26.6
2002	383	5	43	105	230	31.1	265	43	77	61	84	26.7
2003[4]	393	4	43	106	239	31.2	281	44	83	64	90	26.9

1 Figures may not add up due to rounding.
2 The mean ages presented in this table do not take into account the changing population distribution of women.
3 From 1981, data for the United Kingdom exclude births in Northern Ireland to non-residents of Northern Ireland.
4 Provisional

Sources: Office for National Statistics: 01329 813339;
General Register Office for Scotland;
Northern Ireland Statistics and Research Agency

5.17 Live births: by age of mother and country

	Under 20	20 - 24	25 - 29	30 - 34	35 - 39	40 - 44	45 and over	All ages
United Kingdom								
All live births[1]								
	KMDV	KMDW	KMDX	KMDY	KMDZ	KMES	KMET	KMBZ
1993	51 463	171 096	267 413	193 565	66 235	11 123	582	761 526
1994	47 874	157 468	259 367	202 880	70 871	11 432	536	750 480
1995	47 646	147 056	246 017	204 601	73 945	12 008	585	731 882
1996	50 793	141 090	238 857	210 490	78 335	12 832	638	733 163
1997	52 851	133 257	229 429	212 162	84 508	13 731	618	726 622
1998	54 822	127 230	218 072	212 876	88 729	14 453	640	716 888
1999	54 921	124 036	204 808	208 986	91 272	15 210	695	699 976
2000	52 060	120 304	191 583	202 893	95 400	16 032	708	679 029
2001	50 157	121 664	179 776	202 017	97 379	17 271	831	669 123
2002	49 164	123 845	171 852	203 260	101 379	18 274	968	668 777
2003[2]	49 875	129 866	175 473	210 071	109 038	20 233	933	695 549
Age-specific fertility rates								
	KMBR	KMBS	KMBT	KMBU	KMBV	KMBW	KMBX	KMBY
1993	30.8	81.6	114.6	87.2	33.8	5.8	0.3	62.4
1994	28.7	77.9	112.3	89.1	35.4	6.0	0.3	61.6
1995	28.2	75.4	108.4	88.1	36.1	6.4	0.3	60.1
1996	29.6	75.7	106.6	89.6	37.2	6.8	0.3	60.2
1997	30.2	74.9	104.2	89.8	39.1	7.1	0.3	59.6
1998	31.1	73.6	101.4	90.5	40.4	7.4	0.3	58.9
1999	30.7	71.8	98.0	89.4	40.2	7.6	0.4	57.3
2000	29.2	68.7	93.9	87.7	41.0	7.8	0.4	55.4
2001	27.9	68.0	91.5	88.0	41.3	8.2	0.4	54.5
2002	26.9	68.1	91.3	89.7	42.6	8.4	0.5	54.2
2003[2]	26.6	70.1	95.9	94.5	45.9	9.1	0.5	56.2
England and Wales								
All live births								
	KGSA	KGSB	KGSC	KGSD	KGSE	KGSF	KGSG	KGSH
1993	45 121	151 975	235 961	171 061	58 824	9 986	539	673 467
1994	42 026	140 240	229 102	179 568	63 061	10 241	488	664 726
1995	41 938	130 744	217 418	181 202	65 517	10 779	540	648 138
1996	44 667	125 732	211 103	186 377	69 503	11 516	587	649 485
1997	46 372	118 589	202 792	187 528	74 900	12 332	582	643 095
1998	48 285	113 537	193 144	188 499	78 881	12 980	575	635 901
1999	48 375	110 722	181 931	185 311	81 281	13 617	635	621 872
2000	45 846	107 741	170 701	180 113	84 974	14 403	663	604 441
2001	44 189	108 844	159 926	178 920	86 495	15 499	761	594 634
2002	43 467	110 959	153 379	180 532	90 449	16 441	895	596 122
2003[2]	44 236	116 622	156 931	187 214	97 386	18 205	875	621 469
Age-specific fertility rates								
	KGSI	KGSJ	KGSK	KGSL	KGSM	KGSN	KGSO	KGSP
1993	30.9	82.5	114.4	87.4	34.1	5.9	0.3	62.7
1994	28.9	79.0	112.2	89.4	35.8	6.1	0.3	62.0
1995	28.5	76.4	108.4	88.3	36.3	6.5	0.3	60.5
1996	29.7	77.0	106.6	89.8	37.5	6.9	0.3	60.6
1997	30.2	76.0	104.3	89.8	39.4	7.3	0.3	60.0
1998	30.9	74.9	101.5	90.6	40.4	7.5	0.3	59.2
1999	30.9	73.0	98.3	89.6	40.6	7.7	0.4	57.8
2000	29.3	70.0	94.3	87.9	41.4	8.0	0.4	55.9
2001	28.0	69.0	91.7	88.0	41.5	8.4	0.5	54.7
2002	27.0	69.2	91.6	89.8	43.0	8.6	0.5	54.7
2003[2]	26.8	71.2	96.4	96.4	46.4	9.3	0.5	56.8

5.17 Live births: by age of mother and country

continued

	Under 20	20 - 24	25 - 29	30 - 34	35 - 39	40 - 44	45 and over	All ages
Scotland								
All live births[1]								
	KGTA	KGTB	KGTC	KGTD	KGTE	KGTF	KGTG	KGTH
1993	4 750	13 923	22 758	16 088	5 049	697	23	63 337
1994	4 303	12 637	21 851	16 705	5 346	736	26	61 656
1995	4 280	11 913	20 395	16 803	5 799	811	26	60 051
1996	4 544	11 026	19 511	17 038	6 126	891	32	59 296
1997	4 835	10 607	18 782	17 455	6 740	936	19	59 440
1998	4 802	9 804	17 477	17 207	6 893	1 027	43	57 319
1999	4 755	9 440	16 011	16 722	7 034	1 096	41	55 147
2000	4 599	8 962	14 676	16 233	7 395	1 133	29	53 076
2001	4 444	9 121	13 763	16 206	7 701	1 224	40	52 527
2002	4 195	9 267	12 694	16 038	7 727	1 267	47	51 270
2003[2]	4 155	9 626	12 725	16 085	8 310	1 432	39	52 432
Age-specific fertility rates								
	KGTI	KGTJ	KGTK	KGTL	KGTM	KGTN	KGTO	KGTP
1993	31.2	72.5	110.0	79.8	28.0	4.1	0.1	57.4
1994	28.5	68.2	106.5	81.3	28.8	4.4	0.2	56.0
1995	28.2	66.6	101.3	80.6	30.4	4.8	0.1	54.6
1996	29.7	64.5	98.5	81.9	31.4	5.2	0.2	54.1
1997	31.0	65.5	97.4	83.9	34.0	5.3	0.1	54.4
1998	30.6	62.8	94.3	83.2	34.1	5.7	0.3	52.7
1999	30.3	61.0	90.4	82.0	34.3	5.9	0.2	50.9
2000	29.3	57.6	86.5	81.3	35.6	6.0	0.2	49.2
2001	28.4	57.8	85.1	82.2	36.9	6.3	0.2	48.8
2002	26.8	58.3	83.3	83.6	37.1	6.4	0.3	48.1
2003[2]	26.3	60.1	86.5	86.8	40.0	7.1	0.2	49.4
Northern Ireland								
All live births								
	KMDF	KMDG	KMDH	KMDI	KMDJ	KMDK	KMDL	KMDM
1993	1 592	5 198	8 694	6 416	2 362	440	20	24 722
1994	1 545	4 591	8 414	6 607	2 464	455	22	24 098
1995	1 428	4 399	8 204	6 596	2 629	418	19	23 693
1996	1 582	4 332	8 243	7 075	2 706	425	19	24 382
1997	1 644	4 061	7 855	7 179	2 868	463	17	24 087
1998	1 735	3 889	7 451	7 170	2 955	446	22	23 668
1999	1 791	3 874	6 866	6 953	2 957	497	19	22 957
2000	1 615	3 601	6 206	6 547	3 031	496	16	21 512
2001	1 524	3 699	6 087	6 891	3 183	548	30	21 962
2002	1 502	3 619	5 779	6 690	3 203	566	26	21 385
2003[2]	1 484	3 618	5 817	6 772	3 342	596	19	21 648
Age-specific fertility rates								
	KMDN	KMDO	KMDP	KMDQ	KMDR	KMDS	KMDT	KMDU
1993	26.1	83.3	136.1	104.3	43.9	8.9	0.4	70.3
1994	25.4	75.0	131.2	104.9	44.3	9.2	0.4	68.0
1995	23.4	73.5	129.1	102.7	45.5	8.4	0.4	66.6
1996	25.7	73.8	129.4	108.3	45.4	8.4	0.4	67.8
1997	26.4	71.1	124.2	109.2	46.6	8.8	0.3	66.4
1998	27.8	69.6	119.0	108.4	47.2	8.2	0.4	65.0
1999	28.6	70.6	112.3	105.6	46.1	8.9	0.4	62.9
2000	25.6	66.0	103.9	100.4	46.2	8.5	0.3	58.7
2001	23.9	67.5	105.1	106.0	48.0	9.1	0.6	59.7
2002	23.3	66.0	102.9	104.2	48.2	9.2	0.5	58.1
2003[2]	22.9	65.5	106.8	107.0	50.2	9.8	0.3	59.0

1 The 'All ages' figure for Scotland includes births to mothers whose age was
  not known. There were 49 in 1993, 52 in 1994, 24 in 1995, 128 in 1996, 66
  in 1997, 66 in 1998, 48 in 1999, 49 in 2000, 28 in 2001 and 35 in 2002 and
  60 in 2003.
2 Provisional

Sources: Office for National Statistics: 01329 813339;
General Register Office for Scotland;
Northern Ireland Statistics and Research Agency

5.18 Legal abortions: by age for residents

	All ages	Under 15	15	16 - 19	20 - 24	25 - 29	30 - 34	35 - 39	40 - 44	45 and over	Not stated
England and Wales											
	C53Z	C542	C543	C544	C545	C546	C547	C548	C549	C54A	C54B
1986	147 619	924	2 970	33 819	45 316	28 656	18 005	12 977	4 521	409	22
1987	156 191	907	2 858	35 167	49 256	31 243	18 960	12 639	4 757	390	14
1988	168 298	859	2 709	37 928	54 067	34 584	20 000	12 681	5 047	412	11
1989	170 463	803	2 580	36 182	54 880	36 604	21 284	12 713	5 020	388	9
1990	173 900	873	2 549	35 520	55 281	38 770	22 431	12 956	5 104	404	12
1991	167 376	886	2 272	31 130	52 678	38 611	23 445	13 035	4 901	408	10
1992	160 501	905	2 095	27 589	49 052	38 430	23 870	13 252	4 844	452	12
1993	157 846	964	2 119	25 806	46 846	38 139	24 690	13 885	4 889	494	14
1994	156 539	1 080	2 166	25 223	44 871	38 081	25 507	14 156	5 008	440	7
1995	154 315	946	2 324	24 945	43 394	37 254	25 759	14 352	4 868	457	16
1996	167 916	1 098	2 547	28 790	46 356	39 311	28 228	16 118	5 027	428	13
1997	170 145	1 020	2 414	29 947	44 960	40 159	28 892	16 858	5 413	482	–
1998	177 871	1 103	2 656	33 236	45 766	40 366	30 449	18 174	5 576	511	34
1999	173 701	1 066	2 537	32 807	45 004	38 492	29 139	18 341	5 755	502	58
2000	175 542	1 048	2 700	33 218	47 099	37 852	28 735	18 589	5 794	459	48
2001	176 364	1 066	2 592	33 431	48 267	36 506	28 782	19 146	6 094	456	24
2002	175 932	1 075	2 658	32 985	48 359	35 795	28 503	19 450	6 531	457	119
2003	181 582	1 171	2 796	34 247	51 124	36 018	28 749	19 868	7 032	500	77
Scotland[1]											
	C54C	C54D	C54E	C54F	C54G	C54H	C54I	C54J	C54K	C54L	
1986	9 628	74	236	2 529	2 985	1 744	1 081	708	249	22	
1987	9 460	70	210	2 417	2 996	1 729	1 082	697	242	17	
1988	10 128	65	218	2 529	3 304	1 970	1 107	663	257	15	
1989	10 209	53	209	2 561	3 202	1 968	1 229	706	266	15	
1990	10 219	54	186	2 539	3 242	2 063	1 161	700	253	21	
1991	11 068	77	203	2 571	3 486	2 253	1 445	743	262	28	
1992	10 818	73	174	2 377	3 389	2 291	1 444	799	254	17	
1993	11 076	92	193	2 300	3 368	2 447	1 492	891	264	29	
1994	11 392	78	215	2 312	3 486	2 431	1 648	877	315	30	
1995	11 143	79	233	2 169	3 399	2 438	1 609	887	296	33	
1996	11 978	87	236	2 362	3 571	2 603	1 801	960	331	27	
1997	12 109	85	204	2 431	3 444	2 651	1 854	1 093	322	25	
1998	12 485	73	213	2 707	3 426	2 749	1 807	1 149	339	22	
1999	12 168	69	182	2 635	3 354	2 554	1 810	1 180	361	23	
2000	11 997	93	181	2 610	3 355	2 403	1 769	1 177	381	28	
2001	12 128	66	210	2 722	3 462	2 322	1 818	1 127	378	23	
2002	11 772	80	192	2 633	3 419	2 157	1 728	1 156	378	29	
2003[2]	12 217	71	242	2 772	3 654	2 223	1 712	1 107	409	27	

1 Refers to therapeutic abortions notified in accordance with the Abortion Act 1967.
2 Provisional

Sources: Department of Health;
Scottish Executive

5.19 Deaths: by sex and age[1]

	All ages[2]	Under 1 year	1-4	5-9	10-14	15-19	20-24	25-34	35-44	45-54	55-64	65-74	75-84	85 and over
United Kingdom														
Males														
1900 - 02	340 664	87 242	37 834	8 429	4 696	7 047	8 766	19 154	24 739	30 488	37 610	39 765	28 320	6 563
1910 - 12	303 703	63 885	29 452	7 091	4 095	5 873	6 817	16 141	21 813	28 981	37 721	45 140	29 397	7 283
1920 - 22	284 876	48 044	19 008	6 052	3 953	5 906	6 572	13 663	19 702	29 256	40 583	49 398	34 937	7 801
1930 - 32	284 249	28 840	11 276	4 580	2 890	5 076	6 495	12 327	16 326	29 376	47 989	63 804	45 247	10 022
1940 - 42	314 643	24 624	6 949	3 400	2 474	4 653	4 246	11 506	17 296	30 082	57 076	79 652	59 733	12 900
1950 - 52	307 312	14 105	2 585	1 317	919	1 498	2 289	5 862	11 074	27 637	53 691	86 435	79 768	20 131
1960 - 62	318 850	12 234	1 733	971	871	1 718	1 857	3 842	8 753	26 422	63 009	87 542	83 291	26 605
1970 - 72	335 166	9 158	1 485	1 019	802	1 778	2 104	3 590	7 733	24 608	64 898	105 058	82 905	30 027
1980 - 82	330 495	4 829	774	527	652	1 999	1 943	3 736	6 568	19 728	54 159	105 155	98 488	31 936
1990 - 92	312 521	3 315	623	372	396	1 349	2 059	4 334	6 979	15 412	40 424	87 849	106 376	43 032
2000 - 02	288 261	2 065	365	233	326	1 032	1 502	4 270	7 181	15 370	32 328	66 808	98 363	58 419
	KHUA	KHUB	KHUC	KHUD	KHUE	KHUF	KHUG	KHUH	KHUI	KHUJ	KHUK	KHUL	KHUM	KHUN
1992	308 535	2 954	559	346	377	1 144	1 932	4 379	6 845	15 236	39 033	87 075	104 261	44 394
1993[1]	317 796	2 746	582	325	401	1 072	1 907	4 442	6 672	15 631	38 734	90 160	105 693	49 431
1994	303 333	2 660	497	319	400	1 041	1 829	4 741	6 661	14 983	36 469	86 896	98 982	47 855
1995	310 722	2 595	447	314	388	1 115	1 810	4 748	6 754	15 644	36 068	85 459	103 324	52 056
1996	305 323	2 562	489	267	352	1 104	1 693	4 746	6 789	15 796	35 033	81 333	102 090	53 069
1997	300 414	2 391	456	300	364	1 111	1 712	4 583	6 667	15 689	33 707	77 870	101 365	54 199
1998	300 160	2 327	463	283	343	1 058	1 539	4 684	6 902	15 825	33 778	75 718	101 468	55 772
1999	300 368	2 318	456	257	319	1 085	1 553	4 516	6 946	15 849	33 338	73 736	101 795	58 200
2000	290 186	2 120	380	253	326	1 042	1 491	4 397	7 081	15 470	32 556	69 499	98 075	57 496
2001	286 760	2 042	347	223	330	1 061	1 508	4 262	7 156	15 515	32 005	66 111	97 816	58 384
2002	287 837	2 032	368	223	321	992	1 508	4 150	7 305	15 126	32 423	64 814	99 198	59 377
2003	288 604	2 029	351	214	289	969	1 467	3 823	7 408	14 689	32 825	63 574	100 933	60 033
Females														
1900 - 02	322 058	68 770	36 164	8 757	5 034	6 818	8 264	18 702	21 887	25 679	34 521	42 456	34 907	10 099
1910 - 12	289 608	49 865	27 817	7 113	4 355	5 683	6 531	15 676	19 647	24 481	32 813	46 453	37 353	11 828
1920 - 22	274 772	35 356	17 323	5 808	4 133	5 729	6 753	14 878	18 121	24 347	34 026	48 573	45 521	14 203
1930 - 32	275 336	21 072	9 995	3 990	2 734	4 721	5 931	12 699	15 373	24 695	39 471	59 520	56 250	18 886
1940 - 42	296 646	17 936	5 952	2 743	2 068	4 180	5 028	11 261	14 255	23 629	42 651	70 907	71 377	24 658
1950 - 52	291 597	10 293	2 098	880	625	1 115	1 717	5 018	8 989	18 875	37 075	75 220	92 848	36 844
1960 - 62	304 871	8 887	1 334	627	522	684	811	2 504	6 513	16 720	36 078	73 118	105 956	51 117
1970 - 72	322 968	6 666	1 183	654	459	718	900	2 110	5 345	15 594	36 177	75 599	109 539	68 024
1980 - 82	330 269	3 561	585	355	425	733	772	2 099	4 360	12 206	32 052	72 618	117 760	82 743
1990 - 92	328 218	2 431	485	259	255	520	714	1 989	4 340	9 707	25 105	61 951	115 467	104 994
2000 - 02	317 356	1 586	283	188	208	446	536	1 877	4 426	10 270	20 549	47 324	101 650	128 012
	KIUA	KIUB	KIUC	KIUD	KIUE	KIUF	KIUG	KIUH	KIUI	KIUJ	KIUK	KIUL	KIUM	KIUN
1992	325 703	2 187	455	249	228	489	704	1 994	4 262	9 705	24 013	61 635	113 119	106 663
1993[1]	340 685	2 084	436	239	283	465	659	2 121	4 204	9 973	23 900	63 767	114 905	117 649
1994	324 303	1 989	410	205	232	406	626	2 053	4 285	10 081	22 401	62 069	106 816	112 730
1995	334 771	1 931	370	224	250	449	592	2 140	4 203	10 389	22 093	60 988	110 247	120 895
1996	330 701	1 904	355	214	224	493	589	2 140	4 215	10 301	21 406	57 889	109 578	121 393
1997	329 332	1 862	333	215	239	487	574	1 960	4 323	10 412	20 999	55 687	108 276	123 965
1998	329 012	1 752	347	213	215	486	568	1 971	4 289	10 430	20 874	54 200	107 135	126 532
1999	331 694	1 727	338	195	240	473	553	1 924	4 372	10 430	21 045	52 240	106 841	131 316
2000	318 180	1 671	277	177	203	449	535	1 961	4 509	10 459	20 533	48 994	101 711	126 701
2001	315 508	1 622	297	208	207	439	552	1 821	4 385	10 287	20 481	46 964	100 907	127 338
2002	318 379	1 465	276	180	214	449	521	1 849	4 385	10 063	20 633	46 013	102 333	129 998
2003	322 584	1 657	312	176	221	424	539	1 802	4 482	9 830	20 962	45 364	105 158	131 657

5.19 Deaths: by sex and age[1]

continued

	All ages[2]	Under 1 year	1-4	5-9	10-14	15-19	20-24	25-34	35-44	45-54	55-64	65-74	75-84	85 and over
England and Wales														
Males														
1900 - 02	288 886	76 095	32 051	7 066	3 818	5 611	7 028	15 869	21 135	26 065	31 600	33 568	23 835	5 144
1910 - 12	257 253	54 678	24 676	5 907	3 348	4 765	5 596	13 603	18 665	24 820	32 217	38 016	24 928	6 036
1920 - 22	240 605	39 796	15 565	5 151	3 314	4 901	5 447	11 551	17 004	25 073	34 639	42 025	29 685	6 455
1930 - 32	243 147	23 331	9 099	3 844	2 435	4 354	5 580	10 600	14 041	25 657	41 581	54 910	39 091	8 624
1940 - 42	268 876	19 393	5 616	2 834	2 051	3 832	3 156	9 484	14 744	25 983	50 058	68 791	51 779	11 158
1950 - 52	266 879	11 498	2 131	1 087	778	1 248	1 947	4 990	9 489	23 815	46 948	75 774	69 496	17 677
1960 - 62	278 369	10 157	1 444	812	742	1 523	1 624	3 278	7 524	22 813	54 908	77 000	73 180	23 364
1970 - 72	293 934	7 818	1 259	860	677	1 524	1 788	3 079	6 637	21 348	56 667	92 389	73 365	26 522
1980 - 82	290 352	4 168	657	452	555	1 716	1 619	3 169	5 590	16 909	47 144	92 485	87 338	28 551
1990 - 92	275 550	2 926	545	325	338	1 157	1 757	3 717	6 057	13 258	34 977	77 063	94 672	38 757
2000 - 02	253 706	1 836	323	200	282	862	1 244	3 619	6 104	13 184	27 696	58 114	87 481	52 761
	KHVA	KHVB	KHVC	KHVD	KHVE	KHVF	KHVG	KHVH	KHVI	KHVJ	KHVK	KHVL	KHVM	KHVN
1992	271 732	2 606	487	302	322	969	1 621	3 751	5 952	13 117	33 674	76 357	92 662	39 912
1993[1]	279 561	2 407	510	276	340	912	1 596	3 813	5 784	13 416	33 347	78 881	93 754	44 525
1994	267 555	2 367	432	278	331	843	1 550	4 065	5 769	12 923	31 320	76 270	88 230	43 177
1995	274 449	2 305	391	269	340	910	1 533	4 043	5 880	13 487	30 973	74 970	92 291	47 057
1996	268 682	2 272	441	236	291	925	1 409	4 064	5 843	13 565	30 066	71 046	90 708	47 816
1997	264 865	2 137	412	267	325	947	1 442	3 940	5 707	13 484	28 907	68 024	90 207	49 066
1998	264 707	2 070	413	240	291	875	1 292	4 013	5 895	13 595	29 052	66 099	90 450	50 422
1999	264 299	2 075	405	218	275	902	1 270	3 847	5 934	13 620	28 689	64 296	90 431	52 337
2000	255 547	1 886	335	217	284	872	1 224	3 755	6 048	13 367	27 898	60 593	87 126	51 942
2001	252 426	1 808	318	185	281	882	1 266	3 633	6 065	13 271	27 469	57 492	87 013	52 743
2002	253 144	1 813	315	197	280	833	1 243	3 470	6 198	12 915	27 721	56 258	88 304	53 597
2003	253 852	1 809	305	189	244	808	1 229	3 260	6 318	12 694	28 221	55 118	89 629	54 028
Females														
1900 - 02	269 432	60 090	30 674	7 278	4 010	5 265	6 497	15 065	18 253	21 474	28 424	35 307	29 118	7 977
1910 - 12	242 079	42 642	23 335	5 883	3 519	4 522	5 256	12 742	16 363	20 611	27 571	38 489	31 363	9 782
1920 - 22	229 908	29 178	14 174	4 928	3 456	4 719	5 533	12 244	15 142	20 580	28 633	41 010	38 439	11 871
1930 - 32	233 915	16 929	8 013	3 338	2 293	3 969	5 039	10 716	13 022	21 190	33 798	50 844	48 531	16 234
1940 - 42	253 702	14 174	4 726	2 265	1 695	3 426	4 198	9 470	12 093	20 413	36 814	60 987	61 891	21 550
1950 - 52	252 176	8 367	1 727	732	520	893	1 365	4 131	7 586	16 161	31 875	65 087	81 154	32 579
1960 - 62	266 849	7 409	1 103	527	444	591	700	2 147	5 576	14 389	31 083	63 543	93 548	45 789
1970 - 72	284 181	5 677	1 020	562	396	620	806	1 814	4 585	13 417	31 222	65 817	96 952	61 293
1980 - 82	290 026	3 064	511	301	365	635	670	1 821	3 740	10 420	27 606	63 023	103 676	74 194
1990 - 92	288 851	2 161	420	227	217	455	625	1 718	3 765	8 347	21 466	53 783	101 752	93 914
2000 - 02	279 482	1 412	251	168	182	382	455	1 629	3 805	8 893	17 659	40 734	89 387	114 525
	KIVA	KIVB	KIVC	KIVD	KIVE	KIVF	KIVG	KIVH	KIVI	KIVJ	KIVK	KIVL	KIVM	KIVN
1992	286 581	1 933	387	214	199	432	615	1 722	3 717	8 336	20 585	53 423	99 548	95 470
1993[1]	299 238	1 835	374	194	246	394	575	1 802	3 625	8 614	20 423	55 245	100 947	104 964
1994	285 639	1 753	364	187	204	357	535	1 771	3 669	8 688	19 039	53 921	94 197	100 954
1995	295 234	1 677	333	196	210	382	502	1 859	3 644	9 001	18 891	52 987	97 162	108 390
1996	291 453	1 687	320	175	196	430	507	1 852	3 658	8 852	18 244	50 195	96 679	108 658
1997	290 416	1 663	297	177	209	426	490	1 718	3 737	9 016	17 949	48 293	95 508	110 933
1998	290 308	1 555	309	177	189	407	480	1 724	3 678	9 066	17 927	46 894	94 713	113 189
1999	291 819	1 546	300	168	215	385	470	1 668	3 786	9 029	18 031	45 100	93 878	117 243
2000	280 117	1 491	246	156	179	384	466	1 688	3 874	9 090	17 635	42 174	89 310	113 424
2001	277 947	1 432	270	188	178	378	467	1 591	3 768	8 917	17 610	40 465	88 808	113 875
2002	280 383	1 314	236	159	189	384	432	1 608	3 772	8 672	17 733	39 564	90 043	116 277
2003	284 402	1 497	281	153	193	353	461	1 569	3 860	8 514	17 989	38 991	92 670	117 871

5.19 Deaths: by sex and age[1]

continued

	All ages[2]	Under 1 year	1-4	5-9	10-14	15-19	20-24	25-34	35-44	45-54	55-64	65-74	75-84	85 and over
Scotland														
Males														
1900 - 02	40 224	9 189	4 798	1 083	672	1 069	1 292	2 506	2 935	3 591	4 597	4 531	3 117	834
1910 - 12	35 981	7 510	3 935	962	595	826	910	1 969	2 469	3 325	4 356	5 113	3 182	813
1920 - 22	34 649	6 757	2 847	710	489	747	791	1 616	2 128	3 314	4 785	5 624	3 928	911
1930 - 32	32 476	4 426	1 771	610	365	568	706	1 352	1 848	2 979	5 095	6 906	4 839	1 010
1940 - 42	36 384	3 973	1 011	449	321	668	888	1 643	2 090	3 348	5 728	8 556	6 317	1 337
1950 - 52	32 236	1 949	349	175	105	200	265	693	1 267	3 151	5 574	8 544	8 094	1 871
1960 - 62	32 401	1 578	222	121	102	146	185	456	1 013	2 986	6 682	8 505	7 980	2 425
1970 - 72	32 446	944	168	119	93	178	233	396	875	2 617	6 641	10 176	7 383	2 624
1980 - 82	31 723	451	80	56	71	206	233	423	776	2 280	5 601	10 152	8 804	2 591
1990 - 92	29 421	287	57	34	40	137	230	485	744	1 730	4 402	8 611	9 311	3 353
2000 - 02	27 526	165	30	23	30	119	196	523	882	1 775	3 781	7 038	8 535	4 430
	KHWA	KHWB	KHWC	KHWD	KHWE	KHWF	KHWG	KHWH	KHWI	KHWJ	KHWK	KHWL	KHWM	KHWN
1992	29 334	265	51	28	36	123	238	511	731	1 716	4 313	8 541	9 225	3 556
1993[1]	30 504	240	50	39	37	107	225	490	725	1 817	4 375	9 031	9 470	3 898
1994	28 416	212	42	27	48	133	212	538	715	1 684	4 114	8 575	8 446	3 670
1995	28 791	197	37	30	30	152	195	563	698	1 746	4 144	8 449	8 604	3 946
1996	29 223	206	41	23	46	139	212	556	755	1 845	4 087	8 259	8 926	4 128
1997	28 305	186	32	22	27	114	208	521	788	1 794	3 876	7 909	8 791	4 037
1998	28 132	183	37	34	39	134	200	524	843	1 796	3 828	7 746	8 585	4 183
1999	28 605	161	31	23	33	138	215	545	818	1 820	3 773	7 569	8 908	4 571
2000	27 511	173	33	24	28	115	198	512	842	1 716	3 789	7 224	8 523	4 334
2001	27 324	155	22	27	35	131	179	510	902	1 820	3 751	6 950	8 433	4 409
2002	27 743	167	34	17	27	111	211	546	901	1 789	3 804	6 940	8 648	4 548
2003	27 832	146	35	15	31	122	186	469	893	1 634	3 787	6 797	8 994	4 723
Females														
1900 - 02	39 891	7 143	4 477	1 162	747	1 058	1 246	2 625	2 732	3 130	4 485	5 273	4 305	1 508
1910 - 12	36 132	5 854	3 674	981	618	836	910	2 149	2 473	2 909	3 960	5 636	4 588	1 552
1920 - 22	34 449	5 029	2 602	687	489	711	889	1 947	2 266	2 828	4 157	5 587	5 443	1 814
1930 - 32	32 377	3 319	1 602	527	339	568	666	1 508	1 812	2 731	4 380	6 630	6 178	2 117
1940 - 42	33 715	2 852	921	373	283	595	656	1 382	1 672	2 528	4 630	7 674	7 613	2 536
1950 - 52	31 525	1 432	284	115	84	185	293	714	1 127	2 188	4 204	8 157	9 310	3 431
1960 - 62	30 559	1 107	170	80	63	72	87	287	762	1 897	4 115	7 752	9 991	4 177
1970 - 72	30 978	694	118	69	46	73	74	231	608	1 769	4 036	7 823	10 112	5 324
1980 - 82	32 326	337	49	37	44	74	73	213	493	1 456	3 565	7 781	11 333	6 871
1990 - 92	31 747	190	45	20	29	49	72	218	458	1 093	2 966	6 630	11 079	8 898
2000 - 02	30 235	123	24	14	21	50	64	199	493	1 110	2 341	5 326	9 785	10 685
	KIWA	KIWB	KIWC	KIWD	KIWE	KIWF	KIWG	KIWH	KIWI	KIWJ	KIWK	KIWL	KIWM	KIWN
1992	31 603	184	50	23	21	45	73	225	442	1 109	2 816	6 663	10 944	9 008
1993[1]	33 545	172	45	34	27	55	60	258	460	1 089	2 793	6 918	11 330	10 304
1994	30 912	170	29	11	19	33	74	229	495	1 102	2 723	6 617	10 008	9 402
1995	31 709	178	26	16	26	50	70	231	435	1 100	2 601	6 449	10 452	10 075
1996	31 448	159	24	31	21	49	67	218	453	1 172	2 573	6 206	10 256	10 219
1997	31 189	130	23	28	21	43	71	199	496	1 128	2 480	5 985	10 164	10 421
1998	31 032	137	26	28	19	55	68	198	485	1 106	2 416	5 955	9 913	10 626
1999	31 676	115	26	20	17	65	58	201	467	1 128	2 431	5 837	10 198	11 113
2000	30 288	132	20	10	21	46	56	222	510	1 086	2 324	5 512	9 875	10 474
2001	30 058	135	20	16	21	47	71	189	480	1 111	2 361	5 235	9 695	10 677
2002	30 360	103	32	15	20	58	65	185	489	1 134	2 339	5 232	9 784	10 904
2003	30 640	119	24	18	20	57	64	181	489	1 062	2 446	5 194	9 977	10 989

5.19 Deaths: by sex and age[1]

continued

	All ages[2]	Under 1 year	1-4	5-9	10-14	15-19	20-24	25-34	35-44	45-54	55-64	65-74	75-84	85 and over
Northern Ireland														
Males														
1900 - 02	11 554	1 958	985	280	206	367	446	779	669	832	1 413	1 666	1 368	585
1910 - 12	10 469	1 697	841	222	152	282	311	569	679	836	1 148	2 011	1 287	434
1920 - 22	9 622	1 491	596	191	150	258	334	496	570	869	1 159	1 749	1 324	435
1930 - 32	8 626	1 083	406	126	90	154	209	375	437	740	1 313	1 988	1 317	388
1940 - 42	9 383	1 258	322	117	102	153	202	379	462	751	1 290	2 305	1 637	405
1950 - 52	8 197	658	105	55	36	50	77	179	318	671	1 169	2 117	2 178	583
1960 - 62	8 080	499	67	38	27	49	48	108	216	623	1 419	2 037	2 131	816
1970 - 72	8 786	396	58	40	32	76	83	115	221	643	1 590	2 493	2 157	881
1980 - 82	8 420	211	37	20	26	77	92	144	202	539	1 414	2 518	2 346	795
1990 - 92	7 550	102	21	13	18	55	73	132	178	423	1 044	2 175	2 393	922
2000 - 02	7 029	64	13	11	14	50	62	128	195	411	851	1 656	2 347	1228
	KHXA	KHXB	KHXC	KHXD	KHXE	KHXF	KHXG	KHXH	KHXI	KHXJ	KHXK	KHXL	KHXM	KHXN
1992	7 469	83	21	16	19	52	73	117	162	403	1 046	2 177	2 374	926
1993[1]	7 731	99	22	10	24	53	86	139	163	398	1 012	2 248	2 469	1 008
1994	7 362	81	23	14	21	65	67	138	177	376	1 035	2 051	2 306	1 008
1995	7 482	93	19	15	18	53	82	142	176	411	951	2 040	2 429	1 053
1996	7 418	84	7	8	15	40	72	126	191	386	880	2 028	2 456	1 125
1997	7 244	68	12	11	12	50	62	122	172	411	924	1 937	2 367	1 096
1998	7 321	74	13	9	13	49	47	147	164	434	898	1 873	2 433	1 167
1999	7 464	82	20	16	11	45	68	124	194	409	876	1 871	2 456	1 292
2000	7 128	61	12	12	14	55	69	130	191	387	869	1 682	2 426	1 220
2001	7 010	79	7	11	14	48	63	119	189	424	785	1 669	2 370	1 232
2002	6 950	52	19	9	14	48	54	134	206	422	898	1 616	2 246	1 232
2003	6 920	74	11	10	14	39	52	94	197	361	817	1 659	2 310	1 282
Females														
1900 - 02	12 735	1 537	1 013	317	277	495	521	1 012	902	1 075	1 612	1 876	1 484	614
1910 - 12	11 397	1 369	808	249	218	325	365	785	811	961	1 282	2 328	1 402	494
1920 - 22	10 415	1 149	547	193	188	299	331	687	713	939	1 236	1 976	1 639	518
1930 - 32	9 044	824	380	125	102	184	226	475	539	774	1 293	2 046	1 541	535
1940 - 42	9 229	910	305	105	90	159	174	409	490	688	1 207	2 246	1 873	572
1950 - 52	7 896	494	87	33	21	37	59	173	276	526	996	1 976	2 384	834
1960 - 62	7 463	371	61	20	15	21	24	70	175	434	880	1 823	2 417	1 151
1970 - 72	7 809	295	45	23	17	25	20	65	152	408	919	1 959	2 475	1 407
1980 - 82	7 917	160	26	17	17	23	29	65	127	329	881	1 813	2 752	1 678
1990 - 92	7 620	80	20	12	9	16	17	53	117	267	672	1 538	2 636	2 182
2000 - 02	7 638	50	9	7	5	13	17	49	129	266	548	1 263	2 479	2 802
	KIXA	KIXB	KIXC	KIXD	KIXE	KIXF	KIXG	KIXH	KIXI	KIXJ	KIXK	KIXL	KIXM	KIXN
1992	7 519	70	18	12	8	12	16	47	103	260	612	1 549	2 627	2 185
1993[1]	7 902	77	17	11	10	16	24	61	119	270	684	1 604	2 628	2 381
1994	7 752	66	17	7	9	16	17	53	121	291	639	1 531	2 611	2 374
1995	7 828	76	11	12	14	17	20	50	124	288	601	1 552	2 633	2 430
1996	7 800	58	11	8	7	14	15	70	104	277	589	1 488	2 643	2 516
1997	7 727	69	13	10	9	18	13	43	90	268	570	1 409	2 604	2 611
1998	7 672	60	12	8	7	24	20	49	126	258	531	1 351	2 509	2 717
1999	8 199	66	12	7	8	23	25	55	119	273	583	1 303	2 765	2 960
2000	7 775	48	11	11	3	19	13	51	125	283	574	1 308	2 526	2 803
2001	7 503	55	7	4	8	14	14	41	137	259	510	1 264	2 404	2 786
2002	7 636	48	8	6	5	7	24	56	124	257	561	1 217	2 506	2 817
2003	7 542	41	7	5	8	14	14	52	133	254	527	1 179	2 511	2 797

1 See chapter text.
2 In some years the totals include a small number of persons whose age was not stated.

Sources: Office for National Statistics: 01329 813318;
General Register Office for Scotland;
Northern Ireland Statistics and Research Agency

5.20 Infant and maternal mortality[1]
(i) - By country. (ii) - Infant mortality by country, type of death and sex

| | Deaths of Infants under 1 year of age per thousand live births | | | | | | | | | | | | Maternal deaths per thousand live births[3] | | | |
| | United Kingdom | | | England and Wales[2] | | | Scotland | | | Northern Ireland | | | United Kingdom | England and Wales | Scotland | Northern Ireland |
	Total	Males	Females	Total	Males	Females	Total	Males	Females	Total	Males	Females				
1900 - 02	142	156	128	146	160	131	124	136	111	113	123	103	4.71	4.67	4.74	6.03
1910 - 12	110	121	98	110	121	98	109	120	97	101	110	92	3.95	3.67	5.65	5.28
1920 - 22	82	92	71	80	90	69	94	106	82	86	95	77	4.37	4.03	6.36	5.62
1930 - 32	67	75	58	64	72	55	84	94	73	75	83	66	4.54	4.24	6.40	5.24
1940 - 42	59	66	51	55	62	48	77	87	66	80	89	70	3.29	2.74	4.50	3.79
1950 - 52	30	34	26	29	33	25	37	42	32	40	45	36	0.88	0.79	1.09	1.09
1960 - 62	22	25	19	22	24	19	26	30	22	27	30	24	0.36	0.36	0.37	0.43
1970 - 72	18	20	16	18	20	15	19	22	17	22	24	20	0.17	0.17	0.17	0.12
1980 - 82	12	13	10	11	13	10	12	13	10	13	15	12	0.09	0.09	0.14	0.06
1990 - 92	7	8	6	7	8	6	7	8	6	7	8	6	0.07	0.07	0.10	-
2000 - 02	5	6	5	5	6	5	5	6	5	5	6	5	0.07	0.06	0.12	0.05
	KKAW	KKAX	KKAY	KKAZ	KKBW	KKBX	KKBY	KKBZ	KKCW	KKCX	KKCY	KKCZ	KKDW	KKDX	KKDY	KKDZ
1992	6.6	7.4	5.7	6.6	7.4	5.8	6.8	7.9	5.7	6.0	6.4	5.6	0.07	0.07	0.11	—
1993	6.3	7.0	5.6	6.3	7.0	5.6	6.5	7.4	5.6	7.1	7.8	6.3	0.06	0.05	0.11	—
1994	6.2	6.9	5.4	6.2	6.9	5.4	6.2	6.8	5.6	6.1	6.5	5.6	0.08	0.08	0.15	—
1995	6.2	6.9	5.4	6.1	6.9	5.3	6.2	6.4	6.1	7.1	7.5	6.6	0.07	0.07	0.10	—
1996	6.1	6.8	5.4	6.1	6.9	5.4	6.2	6.7	5.5	5.8	6.7	4.8	0.07	0.07	0.10	0.04
1997	5.8	6.4	5.3	5.9	6.5	5.3	5.3	6.1	4.5	5.6	5.5	5.8	0.06	0.06	0.07	—
1998	5.7	6.3	5.0	5.7	6.4	5.0	5.6	6.2	4.9	5.6	6.1	5.1	0.07	0.07	0.09	0.04
1999	5.8	6.4	5.1	5.8	6.5	5.1	5.0	5.7	4.3	6.4	6.8	5.9	0.05	0.05	0.13	—
2000	5.6	6.1	5.0	5.6	6.1	5.1	5.7	6.4	5.1	5.1	5.5	4.6	0.07	0.06	0.15	—
2001	5.5	6.0	5.0	5.4	5.9	4.9	5.5	5.8	5.2	6.1	7.0	5.2	0.07	0.07	0.11	0.09
2002	5.2	5.9	4.5	5.2	5.9	4.5	5.3	6.4	4.1	4.7	4.8	4.6	0.06	0.06	0.10	0.05
2003	5.3	5.7	4.9	5.3	5.7	4.9	5.1	5.4	4.7	5.2	6.5	3.9	0.10	0.07	0.10	0.14

Deaths per thousand live births

		1993	1994	1995	1996	1997	1998	1999	2000	2001	2002	2003
Total												
United Kingdom:												
Stillbirths[4]	KHNQ	5.7	5.8	5.6	5.5	5.3	5.4	5.3	5.3	5.3	5.6	5.7
Perinatal[4]	KHNR	9.0	8.9	8.9	8.7	8.3	8.3	8.2	8.1	8.0	8.3	8.5
Neonatal	KHNS	4.2	4.1	4.2	4.1	3.9	3.8	3.9	3.9	3.6	3.5	3.6
Post neonatal	KHNT	2.2	2.1	2.0	2.0	2.0	1.9	1.9	1.7	1.8	1.7	1.7
England and Wales:												
Stillbirths[4]	KHNU	5.7	5.7	5.5	5.4	5.3	5.3	5.3	5.3	5.3	5.6	5.7
Perinatal[4]	KHNV	8.9	8.9	8.7	8.6	8.3	8.2	8.2	8.2	8.0	8.3	8.5
Neonatal	KHNW	4.2	4.1	4.1	4.1	3.9	3.8	3.9	3.9	3.6	3.6	3.6
Post neonatal	KHNX	2.1	2.1	2.0	2.0	2.0	1.9	1.9	1.7	1.9	1.7	1.7
Scotland:												
Stillbirths[4]	KHNY	6.4	6.1	6.6	6.4	5.3	6.1	5.2	5.6	5.7	5.4	5.6
Perinatal[4]	KHNZ	9.6	9.0	9.6	9.2	7.8	8.7	7.6	8.4	8.5	7.6	8.0
Neonatal	KHOA	4.0	4.0	4.0	3.9	3.2	3.6	3.3	4.0	3.8	3.2	3.4
Post neonatal	KHOB	2.5	2.2	2.2	2.2	2.1	2.0	1.7	1.8	1.7	2.1	1.7
Northern Ireland:												
Stillbirths[4]	KHOC	5.2	6.3	6.1	6.3	5.4	5.1	5.7	4.3	5.1	5.7	4.9
Perinatal[4]	KHOD	8.8	9.7	10.4	9.4	8.2	8.1	10.0	7.3	8.5	8.9	8.0
Neonatal	KHOE	4.9	4.2	5.5	3.7	4.2	3.9	4.8	3.8	4.5	3.5	3.9
Post neonatal	KHOF	2.1	1.9	1.6	2.0	1.4	1.7	1.6	1.3	1.6	1.2	1.3
Males												
United Kingdom:												
Perinatal[4]	KHOG	9.7	9.6	9.4	9.1	8.7	8.8	8.7	8.7	8.6	8.9	8.8
Neonatal	KHOH	4.7	4.6	4.6	4.6	4.2	4.2	4.3	4.2	4.0	4.0	3.9
Infant mortality	KHOI	7.0	6.9	6.9	6.8	6.4	6.3	6.4	6.1	6.0	5.9	5.7
England and Wales:												
Perinatal[4]	KHOK	9.5	9.6	9.3	9.0	8.7	8.8	8.6	8.7	8.5	8.9	8.9
Neonatal	KHOL	4.6	4.6	4.6	4.6	4.2	4.3	4.3	4.2	3.9	4.0	3.8
Infant mortality	KHOM	7.0	6.9	6.9	6.9	6.5	6.4	6.5	6.1	5.9	5.9	5.7
Scotland:												
Perinatal[4]	KHOO	10.8	9.6	10.1	10.0	8.1	9.6	8.4	9.5	9.2	7.9	8.4
Neonatal	KHOP	4.5	4.4	4.1	4.3	3.4	4.0	3.8	4.5	4.0	3.7	3.6
Infant mortality	KHOQ	7.4	6.8	6.4	6.7	6.1	6.2	5.7	6.4	5.8	6.4	5.4
Northern Ireland:												
Perinatal[4]	KHOS	10.3	10.4	10.4	10.1	8.5	8.9	10.5	8.0	9.8	10.0	8.2
Neonatal	KHOT	5.9	4.3	5.7	4.3	4.3	4.4	5.5	4.2	5.3	3.8	4.6
Infant mortality	KHOU	7.8	6.5	7.5	6.7	5.5	6.1	6.8	5.5	7.0	4.8	6.5
Females												
United Kingdom:												
Perinatal[4]	KHOW	8.2	8.2	8.3	8.2	7.9	7.7	7.8	7.5	7.4	7.7	8.2
Neonatal	KHOX	3.6	3.6	3.7	3.6	3.5	3.3	3.4	3.5	3.3	3.1	3.4
Infant mortality	KHOY	5.6	5.4	5.4	5.4	5.3	5.0	5.1	5.0	5.0	4.5	4.9
England and Wales:												
Perinatal[4]	KHPA	8.3	8.1	8.1	8.2	7.9	7.7	7.8	7.6	7.3	7.7	8.2
Neonatal	KHPB	3.6	3.6	3.6	3.6	3.6	3.3	3.5	3.5	3.2	3.1	3.4
Infant mortality	KHPC	5.6	5.4	5.3	5.4	5.3	5.0	5.1	5.1	4.9	4.5	4.9
Scotland:												
Perinatal[4]	KHPE	8.3	8.4	9.2	8.4	7.5	7.9	6.7	7.2	7.8	7.2	7.7
Neonatal	KHPF	3.5	3.6	3.9	3.5	2.9	3.2	2.8	3.5	3.5	2.6	3.1
Infant mortality	KHPG	5.6	5.6	6.1	5.5	4.5	4.9	4.3	5.1	5.2	4.1	4.7
Northern Ireland:												
Perinatal[4]	KHPI	7.2	8.9	10.5	8.6	8.0	7.3	9.5	6.5	7.0	7.8	7.8
Neonatal	KHPJ	3.9	4.1	5.2	3.1	4.0	3.4	4.1	3.4	3.6	3.1	3.2
Infant mortality	KHPK	6.3	5.6	6.6	4.8	5.8	5.1	5.9	4.6	5.2	4.6	3.9

1 See chapter text.
2 From 1937 to 1956 death rates are based on the births to which they relate
  in the current and preceding years.
3 Deaths in pregnancy and childbirth.
4 Deaths per 1,000 live and stillbirths.

Sources: Office for National Statistics: 01329 813758;
General Register Office for Scotland;
Northern Ireland Statistics and Research Agency

5.21 Death rates by sex and age[1]
United Kingdom

	All ages	0-4	5-9	10-14	15-19	20-24	25-34	35-44	45-54	55-64	65-74	75-84	85 and over
Males													
1900 - 02	18.4	57.0	4.1	2.4	3.7	5.0	6.6	11.0	18.6	35.0	69.9	143.6	289.6
1910 - 12	14.9	40.5	3.3	2.0	3.0	3.9	5.0	8.0	14.9	29.8	62.1	133.8	261.5
1920 - 22	13.5	33.4	2.9	1.8	2.9	3.9	4.5	6.9	11.9	25.3	57.8	131.8	259.1
1930 - 32	12.9	22.3	2.3	1.5	2.6	3.3	3.5	5.7	11.3	23.7	57.9	134.2	277.0
1940 - 42	..	..	..	..	..	..	..	..	..	..	..	..	..
1950 - 52	12.6	7.7	0.7	0.5	0.9	1.4	1.6	3.0	8.5	23.2	55.2	127.6	272.0
1960 - 62	12.5	6.4	0.5	0.4	0.9	1.1	1.1	2.5	7.4	22.2	54.4	123.4	251.0
1970 - 72	12.4	4.6	0.4	0.4	0.9	1.0	1.0	2.4	7.3	20.9	52.9	116.3	246.1
1980 - 82	12.1	3.2	0.3	0.3	0.8	0.9	0.9	1.9	6.3	18.2	46.7	107.1	224.9
1990 - 92	11.2	2.0	0.2	0.2	0.7	0.9	1.0	1.8	4.6	14.2	38.6	93.0	201.4
2000 - 02	10.0	1.4	0.1	0.2	0.5	0.8	1.0	1.6	4.0	10.4	28.9	75.2	187.7
	KHZA	KHZB	KHZC	KHZD	KHZE	KHZF	KHZG	KHZH	KHZJ	KHZK	KHZL	KHZM	KHZN
1992	11.0	1.8	0.2	0.2	0.6	0.9	1.0	1.8	4.4	13.8	37.9	91.5	198.7
1993	11.3	1.7	0.2	0.2	0.6	0.9	1.0	1.7	4.4	13.6	38.6	94.8	208.6
1994	10.8	1.6	0.2	0.2	0.6	0.9	1.0	1.7	4.1	12.8	36.8	90.3	194.8
1995	11.0	1.6	0.2	0.2	0.6	0.9	1.0	1.7	4.2	12.6	36.7	90.0	202.1
1996	10.8	1.6	0.1	0.2	0.6	0.9	1.0	1.7	4.2	12.3	35.2	86.0	199.6
1997	10.6	1.5	0.2	0.2	0.6	1.0	1.0	1.7	4.1	11.8	33.9	83.2	196.7
1998	10.5	1.5	0.1	0.2	0.6	0.9	1.1	1.7	4.1	11.6	33.0	81.8	193.6
1999	10.5	1.5	0.1	0.2	0.6	0.9	1.0	1.7	4.1	11.2	32.2	80.9	195.7
2000	10.1	1.4	0.1	0.2	0.6	0.8	1.0	1.6	4.0	10.7	30.3	76.8	187.9
2001	9.9	1.3	0.1	0.2	0.6	0.8	1.0	1.6	4.0	10.4	28.6	74.8	186.9
2002	9.9	1.4	0.1	0.2	0.5	0.8	1.0	1.6	4.0	10.1	27.8	74.1	188.2
2003	9.9	1.4	0.1	0.1	0.5	0.8	1.0	1.6	3.9	9.9	27.0	73.6	191.7
Females													
1900 - 02	16.3	47.9	4.3	2.6	3.5	4.3	5.8	9.0	14.4	27.9	59.3	127.0	262.6
1910 - 12	13.3	34.0	3.3	2.1	2.9	3.4	4.4	6.7	11.5	23.1	50.7	113.7	234.0
1920 - 22	11.9	26.9	2.8	1.9	2.8	3.4	4.1	5.6	9.3	19.2	45.6	111.5	232.4
1930 - 32	11.5	17.7	2.1	1.5	2.4	2.9	3.3	4.6	8.3	17.6	43.7	110.1	246.3
1940 - 42	..	..	..	..	..	..	..	..	..	..	..	..	..
1950 - 52	11.2	6.0	0.5	0.4	0.7	1.0	1.4	2.3	5.3	12.9	35.5	98.4	228.8
1960 - 62	11.2	4.9	0.3	0.3	0.4	0.5	0.8	1.8	4.5	11.0	30.8	87.3	218.5
1970 - 72	11.3	3.6	0.3	0.2	0.4	0.4	0.6	1.6	4.5	10.5	27.5	76.7	196.1
1980 - 82	11.4	2.3	0.2	0.2	0.3	0.4	0.5	1.3	3.9	9.9	24.8	67.2	179.5
1990 - 92	11.1	1.5	0.1	0.2	0.3	0.3	0.4	1.1	2.9	8.4	22.1	58.7	157.2
2000 - 02	10.5	1.1	0.1	0.1	0.2	0.3	0.4	1.0	2.6	6.4	17.9	51.1	157.3
	KHZO	KHZP	KHZQ	KHZR	KHZS	KHZT	KHZU	KHZV	KHZW	KHZX	KHZY	KHZZ	KHZI
1992	11.0	1.4	0.1	0.1	0.3	0.3	0.4	1.1	2.8	8.1	21.9	58.1	155.7
1993	11.5	1.3	0.1	0.2	0.3	0.3	0.5	1.1	2.8	8.1	22.4	60.6	165.2
1994	10.9	1.3	0.1	0.1	0.2	0.3	0.4	1.1	2.8	7.6	21.7	57.5	154.8
1995	11.2	1.2	0.1	0.1	0.3	0.3	0.5	1.1	2.8	7.5	21.7	57.8	161.4
1996	11.1	1.2	0.1	0.1	0.3	0.3	0.5	1.1	2.7	7.3	21.0	56.4	159.4
1997	11.0	1.2	0.1	0.1	0.3	0.3	0.4	1.1	2.7	7.1	20.5	55.2	160.3
1998	11.0	1.2	0.1	0.1	0.3	0.3	0.4	1.0	2.7	7.0	20.2	54.4	159.8
1999	11.0	1.2	0.1	0.1	0.3	0.3	0.4	1.0	2.7	6.9	19.6	54.2	163.7
2000	10.5	1.1	0.1	0.1	0.3	0.3	0.5	1.0	2.7	6.6	18.5	51.6	155.8
2001	10.4	1.1	0.1	0.1	0.2	0.3	0.4	1.0	2.6	6.4	17.8	50.8	155.8
2002	10.5	1.0	0.1	0.1	0.2	0.3	0.4	1.0	2.6	6.2	17.4	51.0	160.3
2003	10.6	1.2	0.1	0.1	0.2	0.3	0.4	1.0	2.6	6.1	17.1	51.8	166.4

1 The figures for 1992 to 2000 have been revised using the latest population estimates.

Sources: Office for National Statistics: 01329 813318;
General Register Office for Scotland;
Northern Ireland Statistics and Research Agency

5.22 Interim life tables,[1] 2001-03

| | United Kingdom | | | | England and Wales | | | |
| | Males | | Females | | Males | | Females | |
Age(x)	l_x	$e^0{}_x$	l_x	$e^0{}_x$	l_x	$e^0{}_x$	l_x	$e^0{}_x$
0 years	100 000	75.9	100 000	80.5	100 000	76.2	100 000	80.7
5 years	99 313	71.5	99 432	76.0	99 315	71.7	99 431	76.1
10 years	99 255	66.5	99 380	71.0	99 258	66.8	99 379	71.2
15 years	99 177	61.6	99 324	66.0	99 183	61.8	99 323	66.2
20 years	98 917	56.7	99 206	61.1	98 936	57.0	99 208	61.3
25 years	98 513	51.9	99 059	56.2	98 554	52.2	99 069	56.4
30 years	98 077	47.2	98 885	51.3	98 143	47.4	98 898	51.5
35 years	97 551	42.4	98 634	46.4	97 640	42.6	98 651	46.6
40 years	96 894	37.7	98 263	41.6	97 012	37.9	98 288	41.8
45 years	95 950	33.0	97 663	36.8	96 103	33.2	97 704	37.0
50 years	94 470	28.5	96 677	32.2	94 665	28.7	96 742	32.3
55 years	92 229	24.1	95 170	27.6	92 490	24.3	95 266	27.8
60 years	88 703	20.0	92 866	23.3	89 063	20.1	93 022	23.4
65 years	83 063	16.1	89 236	19.1	83 597	16.3	89 489	19.2
70 years	74 683	12.6	83 656	15.2	75 377	12.7	84 046	15.3
75 years	62 342	9.6	74 767	11.7	63 170	9.7	75 295	11.7
80 years	45 866	7.2	61 363	8.7	46 653	7.2	61 968	8.7
85 years	27 999	5.1	43 554	6.1	28 614	5.2	44 165	6.2
90 years	12 176	3.7	23 483	4.3	12 498	3.7	23 902	4.3

| | Scotland | | | | Northern Ireland | | | |
| | Males | | Females | | Males | | Females | |
Age(x)	l_x	$e^0{}_x$	l_x	$e^0{}_x$	l_x	$e^0{}_x$	l_x	$e^0{}_x$
0 years	100 000	73.5	100 000	78.9	100 000	75.6	100 000	80.4
5 years	99 305	69.0	99 435	74.3	99 279	71.1	99 476	75.9
10 years	99 241	64.1	99 380	69.4	99 199	66.2	99 434	70.9
15 years	99 148	59.1	99 315	64.4	99 097	61.2	99 380	65.9
20 years	98 777	54.3	99 145	59.5	98 763	56.4	99 291	61.0
25 years	98 188	49.6	98 937	54.6	98 271	51.7	99 135	56.1
30 years	97 485	45.0	98 718	49.7	97 787	46.9	98 966	51.2
35 years	96 681	40.3	98 418	44.9	97 307	42.2	98 732	46.3
40 years	95 716	35.7	97 965	40.1	96 656	37.4	98 400	41.4
45 years	94 422	31.2	97 239	35.4	95 747	32.8	97 707	36.7
50 years	92 529	26.7	96 021	30.8	94 291	28.2	96 715	32.0
55 years	89 664	22.5	94 189	26.3	91 983	23.9	95 257	27.5
60 years	85 129	18.6	91 288	22.1	88 464	19.7	92 888	23.1
65 years	77 871	15.1	86 725	18.1	82 772	15.9	89 409	18.9
70 years	68 130	11.8	79 993	14.4	74 056	12.4	83 595	15.1
75 years	54 727	9.1	69 922	11.1	61 162	9.5	74 539	11.6
80 years	38 655	6.8	55 719	8.2	44 777	7.0	61 412	8.5
85 years	22 371	4.9	37 923	5.9	27 004	5.0	43 109	6.0
90 years	9 274	3.6	19 729	4.1	11 458	3.5	22 769	4.1

Note Column l_x shows the number who would survive to exact **age**(x), out of 100,000 born, who were subject throughout their lives to the death rates experienced in the three-year period indicated. Column $e^0{}_x$ is 'the expectation of life', that is, the average future lifetime which would be lived by a person aged exactly x if likewise subject to the death rates experienced in the three-year period indicated.

1 See chapter text.

Source: Government Actuary's Department: 020 7211 2622

	All ages		Under 1		1-4		5-9		10-14		15-17	
	Numbers	Percentages	Numbers	Percentages	Numbers	Percentages	Numbers	Percentages	Numbers	Percentages	Numbers	Percentages
United Kingdom **Persons**												
	VOXI	VOXJ	VOXK	VOXL	VOXM	VOXN	VOXO	VOXP	VOXQ	VOXR	VOXS	VOXT
1998	4 996	100	213	4	1 647	33	1 793	36	1 098	22	245	5
1999	4 951	100	234	5	1 795	36	1 714	35	957	19	251	5
2000	5 503	100	283	5	2 203	40	1 745	32	1 025	19	247	4
2001[1,2]	6 588	100	272	4	2 874	44	2 047	31	1 103	17	292	4
2002	6 240	100	314	5	2 737	44	1 937	31	999	16	253	4
2003[3]	5 429	100	211	4	2 484	46	1 717	32	790	15	227	4
Males												
	VOXU	VOXV	VOXW	VOXX	VOXY	VOXZ	VOYA	VOYB	VOYC	VOYD	VOYE	VOYF
1998	2 514	100	110	4	854	34	880	35	562	22	108	4
1999	2 428	100	115	5	903	37	833	34	459	19	118	5
2000	2 740	100	144	5	1 115	41	867	32	491	18	123	4
2001[4,5]	3 314	100	138	4	1 483	45	1 006	30	547	17	140	4
2002	3 140	100	176	6	1 425	45	935	30	488	16	116	4
2003[6]	2 635	100	103	4	1 225	46	845	32	351	13	111	4
Females												
	VOYG	VOYH	VOYI	VOYJ	VOYK	VOYL	VOYM	VOYN	VOYO	VOYP	VOYQ	VOYR
1998	2 482	100	103	4	793	32	913	37	536	22	137	6
1999	2 523	100	119	5	892	35	881	35	498	20	133	5
2000	2 763	100	139	5	1 088	39	878	32	534	19	124	4
2001[4,7]	3 274	100	134	4	1 391	42	1 041	32	556	17	152	5
2002	3 100	100	138	4	1 312	42	1 002	32	511	16	137	4
2003[8]	2 794	100	108	4	1 259	45	872	31	439	16	116	4
England and Wales **Persons**												
	GQTP	GQTQ	GQTR	GQTS	GQTT	GQTU	GQTV	GQTW	GQTX	GQTY	GQTZ	GQUA
1998	4 386	100	195	4	1 489	34	1 545	35	937	21	220	5
1999	4 317	100	196	5	1 627	38	1 477	34	803	19	214	5
2000	4 940	100	251	5	2 019	41	1 549	31	906	18	215	4
2001[1]	5 981	100	246	4	2 648	44	1 845	31	983	16	257	4
2002	5 681	100	288	5	2 532	45	1 748	31	900	16	213	4
2003	4 821	100	182	4	2 263	47	1 504	31	684	14	188	4
Males												
	GQUB	GQUC	GQUD	GQUE	GQUF	GQUG	GQUH	GQUI	GQUJ	GQUK	GQUL	GQUM
1998	2 214	100	100	5	775	35	755	34	489	22	95	4
1999	2 115	100	96	5	816	39	712	34	390	18	101	5
2000	2 452	100	127	5	1 022	42	759	31	434	18	110	4
2001[4]	3 011	100	124	4	1 370	45	904	30	494	16	118	4
2002	2 871	100	160	6	1 324	46	846	29	443	15	98	3
2003	2 340	100	90	4	1 116	48	738	32	301	13	95	4
Females												
	GQUN	GQUO	GQUP	GQUQ	GQUR	GQUS	GQUT	GQUU	GQUV	GQUW	GQUX	GQUY
1998	2 172	100	95	4	714	33	790	36	448	21	125	6
1999	2 202	100	100	5	811	37	765	35	413	19	113	5
2000	2 488	100	124	5	997	40	790	32	472	19	105	4
2001[4]	2 970	100	122	4	1 278	43	941	32	489	16	140	5
2002	2 810	100	128	5	1 208	43	902	32	457	16	115	4
2003	2 481	100	92	4	1 147	46	766	31	383	15	93	4

5.23 Adoptions by date of entry in Adopted Children Register: by sex, age and country

	All ages		Under 1		1-4		5-9		10-14		15-17	
	Numbers	*Percentages*	Numbers	*Percentages*	Numbers	*Percentages*	Numbers	*Percentages*	Numbers	*Percentages*	Numbers	*Percentages*
Scotland **Persons**												
	GQUZ	GQVA	GQVB	GQVC	GQVD	GQVE	GQVF	GQVG	GQVH	GQVI	GQVJ	GQVK
1998	490	*100*	16	*3*	126	*26*	198	*40*	128	*26*	22	*4*
1999	489	*100*	34	*7*	135	*28*	176	*36*	117	*24*	27	*6*
2000	391	*100*	24	*6*	140	*36*	123	*31*	85	*22*	19	*5*
2001[2]	468	*100*	18	*4*	176	*38*	161	*34*	92	*20*	21	*4*
2002	385	*100*	13	*3*	143	*37*	130	*34*	73	*19*	26	*7*
2003[3]	468	*100*	25	*5*	153	*33*	170	*36*	88	*19*	32	*7*
Males												
	GQVL	GQVM	GQVN	GQVO	GQVP	GQVQ	GQVR	GQVS	GQVT	GQVU	GQVV	GQVW
1998	235	*100*	8	*3*	63	*27*	94	*40*	60	*26*	10	*4*
1999	247	*100*	17	*7*	71	*29*	91	*37*	54	*22*	14	*6*
2000	210	*100*	13	*6*	75	*36*	71	*34*	43	*20*	8	*4*
2001[6]	241	*100*	11	*5*	93	*39*	83	*34*	40	*17*	14	*6*
2002	193	*100*	8	*4*	75	*39*	60	*31*	37	*19*	13	*7*
2003[7]	228	*100*	11	*5*	78	*34*	85	*37*	43	*19*	11	*5*
Females												
	GQVX	GQVY	GQVZ	GQWA	GRFK	GRFL	GRFM	GRFN	GRFO	GRFP	GRFQ	GRFR
1998	255	*100*	8	*3*	63	*25*	104	*41*	68	*27*	12	*5*
1999	242	*100*	17	*7*	64	*26*	85	*35*	63	*26*	13	*5*
2000	181	*100*	11	*6*	65	*36*	52	*29*	42	*23*	11	*6*
2001[7]	227	*100*	7	*3*	83	*37*	78	*34*	52	*23*	7	*3*
2002	192	*100*	5	*3*	68	*35*	70	*36*	36	*19*	13	*7*
2003[8]	240	*100*	14	*6*	75	*31*	85	*35*	45	*19*	21	*9*
Northern Ireland **Persons**												
	VOYS	VOYT	VOYU	VOYV	VOYW	VOYX	VOYY	VOYZ	VOZA	VOZB	VOZC	VOZD
1998	120	*100*	2	*2*	32	*27*	50	*42*	33	*28*	3	*3*
1999	145	*100*	4	*3*	33	*23*	61	*42*	37	*26*	10	*7*
2000	172	*100*	8	*5*	44	*26*	73	*42*	34	*20*	13	*8*
2001	139	*100*	8	*6*	50	*36*	41	*29*	28	*20*	12	*9*
2002	174	*100*	13	*7*	62	*36*	59	*34*	26	*15*	14	*8*
2003	140	*100*	4	*3*	68	*49*	43	*31*	18	*13*	7	*5*
Males												
	VOZE	VOZF	VOZG	VOZH	VOZI	VOZJ	VOZK	VOZL	VOZM	VOZN	VOZO	VOZP
1998	65	*100*	2	*3*	16	*25*	31	*48*	13	*20*	3	*5*
1999	66	*100*	2	*3*	16	*24*	30	*45*	15	*23*	3	*5*
2000	78	*100*	4	*5*	18	*23*	37	*47*	14	*18*	5	*6*
2001	62	*100*	3	*5*	20	*32*	19	*31*	13	*21*	7	*11*
2002	76	*100*	8	*11*	26	*34*	29	*38*	8	*11*	5	*7*
2003	67	*100*	2	*3*	31	*46*	22	*33*	7	*10*	5	*7*
Females												
	VOZQ	VOZR	VOZS	VOZT	VOZU	VOZV	VOZW	VOZX	VOZY	VOZZ	VPAA	VPVD
1998	55	*100*	–	*–*	16	*29*	19	*35*	20	*36*	–	*–*
1999	79	*100*	2	*3*	17	*22*	31	*39*	22	*28*	7	*9*
2000	94	*100*	4	*4*	26	*28*	36	*38*	20	*21*	8	*9*
2001	77	*100*	5	*6*	30	*39*	22	*29*	15	*19*	5	*6*
2002	98	*100*	5	*5*	36	*37*	30	*31*	18	*18*	9	*9*
2003	73	*100*	2	*3*	37	*51*	21	*29*	11	*15*	2	*3*

1 Includes two cases where age was greater than 17 - these have been included in the '15-17' age group.
2 Includes four adoptions where age was greater than 17 - these have been included in the '15-17' age group.
3 Includes three adoptions where age was greater than 17 - these have been included in the '15-17' age group.
4 Includes one case where age was greater than 17 - this has been included in the '15-17' age group.
5 Includes one adoptions where age was greater than 17 - these have been included in the '15-17' age group.
6 Includes two adoptions where age was greater than 17 - this has been included in the '15-17' age group.
7 Includes three adoptions where age was greater than 17 - these have been included in the '15-17' age group.
8 Includes one adoption where age was greater than 17 - this has been included in the '15-17' age group.

Sources: Office for National Statistics: 01329 813339;
General Register Office for Scotland;
Northern Ireland Statistics and Research Agency

Education

Chapter 6

Education

Educational establishments in the United Kingdom are administered and financed in several ways. Most schools are controlled by local education authorities (LEAs), which are part of the structure of local government, but some are 'assisted', receiving grants direct from central government sources and being controlled by governing bodies which have a substantial degree of autonomy. Completely outside the public sector are non-maintained schools run by individuals, companies or charitable institutions.

For the purposes of UK education statistics, schools fall under the following broad categories:

Mainstream state schools (Grant-aided mainstream schools in Northern Ireland)

These schools work in partnership with other schools and local education authorities and they receive funding from LEAs. Since 1 September 1999, the categories (typically in England) are:

Community – schools formerly known as 'county' plus some former Grant-maintained (GM) schools;

Foundation – most former GM schools;

Voluntary Aided – schools formerly known as 'aided' and some former GM schools;

Voluntary Controlled – schools formerly known as 'controlled'.

Non-maintained mainstream schools

Consisting of:

(a) Independent schools

Schools which charge fees and may also be financed by individuals, companies or charitable institutions. These include Direct Grant schools, where the governing bodies are assisted by Departmental grants and a proportion of the pupils attending them do so free or under an arrangement by which local education authorities meet tuition fees. City technology colleges and Academies (applicable in England only) are also included as independent schools.

(b) Non-maintained schools

Run by voluntary bodies who may receive some grant from central government for capital work and for equipment, but their current expenditure is met primarily from the fees charged to the LEAs for pupils placed in schools.

Special schools

Provide education for children with special educational needs (SEN) (Record of Needs, in Scotland) who cannot be educated satisfactorily in an ordinary school. Maintained special schools are run by LEAs, while non-maintained special schools are financed as shown at (b) above.

Pupil Referral Units

Pupil Referral Units (PRUs) operate in England and Wales and provide education outside of a mainstream or special school setting, to meet the needs of difficult or disruptive children.

Schools in Scotland are categorised as Education Authority, Grant-Aided, Opted-out/Self-governing (these three being grouped together as 'Publicly funded' schools), Independent schools and Partnership schools.

The home Government Departments dealing with education statistics are:

Department for Education and Skills (DfES);

National Assembly for Wales (NAfW);

Scottish Executive (SE);

Northern Ireland Department of Education (DENI);

Northern Ireland Department for Employment and Learning (DELNI).

Each of the home Education Departments in Great Britain, along with the Northern Ireland Department of Education, have overall responsibility for funding the schools sectors in their own country.

Up to March 2001, further education (FE) courses in FE sector colleges in England and in Wales were largely funded through grants from the respective Further Education Funding Councils. In April 2001, however, the Learning and Skills Council (LSC) took over the responsibility for funding the FE sector in England, and the National Council for Education and Training for Wales (part of Education and Learning Wales – ELWa) did so for Wales. The LSC in England is also responsible for funding provision for FE and some non-prescribed higher education in FE sector colleges; it also funds some FE provided by LEA maintained and other institutions referred to as 'external institutions'. In Wales, the National Council – ELWa, funds FE provision made by FE institutions via a third party or sponsored arrangements. The Scottish Further Education Funding Council (SFEFC) funds FE colleges in Scotland, while the Department for Employment and Learning funds FE colleges in Northern Ireland.

Higher education courses in higher education establishments are largely publicly funded through block grants from the HE funding councils in England and Scotland, the Higher Education Council – ELWa in Wales, and the Department of Employment and Learning in Northern Ireland. In addition, some designated HE (mainly HND/HNC Diplomas and Certificates of HE) is also funded by these sources. The FE sources mentioned above fund the remainder.

Statistics for the separate systems obtained in England, Wales, Scotland and Northern Ireland are collected and processed separately in accordance with the particular needs of the responsible Departments. Since 1994/95 the Higher Education Statistics Agency (HESA) has undertaken the data collection for all higher education institutions (HEIs) in the UK. This includes the former Universities Funding Council (UFC) funded UK universities previously collected by the Universities Statistical Record. There are some structural differences in the information collected for schools, further and higher education in each of the four home countries and in some tables the GB/UK data presented are amalgamations from sources that are not entirely comparable.

Stages of education

There are five stages of education: foundation, primary, secondary, further and higher education, and education is compulsory for all children between the ages of five (four in Northern Ireland) and sixteen. The non-compulsory fourth stage, further education, covers non-advanced education, which can be taken at both further (including tertiary) education colleges, higher education institutions and increasingly in secondary schools. The fifth stage, higher education, is study beyond A levels and their equivalent which, for most full-time students, takes place in universities and other higher education institutions.

Foundation education

In recent years there has been a major expansion of pre-school education, and in England, the National Curriculum has been extended to include the Foundation stage and covers children's education from the age of three to the end of reception year, when most are just five and some almost six years old. Children under five attend a variety of settings including state nursery schools, nursery classes within primary schools and, in England and Wales, reception classes within primary schools, as well as settings outside the state sector such as voluntary pre-schools or privately run nurseries.

Primary education

The primary stage covers three age ranges: nursery (under five), infant (five to seven or eight) and junior (up to 11 or 12) but in Scotland and Northern Ireland there is generally no distinction between infant and junior schools. Most public sector primary schools take both boys and girls in mixed classes. It is usual to transfer straight to secondary school at age 11 (in England, Wales and Northern Ireland) or 12 (in Scotland), but in England some children make the transition via middle schools catering for various age ranges between eight and 14. Depending on their individual age ranges middle schools are classified as either primary or secondary.

Secondary education

Public provision of secondary education in an area may consist of a combination of different types of school, the pattern reflecting historical circumstance and the policy adopted by the local education authority. Comprehensive schools largely admit pupils without reference to ability or aptitude and cater for all the children in a neighbourhood, but in some areas they co-exist with grammar, secondary modern or technical schools. In 2003/04, 88 per cent of secondary pupils in England attended comprehensive schools while all secondary schools in Wales are comprehensive schools. The majority of education authority secondary schools in Scotland are comprehensive in character and offer six years of secondary education; however in remote areas there are several two-year and four-year secondary schools. In Northern Ireland, post primary education is provided by secondary intermediate and grammar schools. In England, the Specialist Schools Programme helps schools, in partnership with private sector sponsors and supported by additional Government funding, to establish distinctive identities through their chosen specialisms and achieve their targets to raise standards. Specialist schools have a special focus on their chosen subject area but must meet the National Curriculum requirements and deliver a broad and balanced education to all pupils. Any maintained secondary school in England can apply to be designated as a specialist school in one of ten specialist areas: arts, business & enterprise, engineering, humanities, language, mathematics & computing, music, science, sports and technology. Schools can also combine any two specialisms.

Education

Special schools

Special schools (day or boarding) provide education for children who require specialist support to complete their education, for example because they have physical or other difficulties. Many pupils with special educational needs are educated in main-stream schools. All children attending special schools are offered a curriculum designed to overcome their learning difficulties and to enable them to become self-reliant.

Further education

The term further education may be used in a general sense to cover all non-advanced courses taken after the period of compulsory education, but more commonly it excludes those staying on at secondary school and those in higher education, i.e. courses in universities and colleges leading to qualifications above GCE A Level, SCE H Grade, GNVQ/NVQ level 3, and their equivalents. Since 1 April 1993 sixth form colleges in England and Wales have been included in the further education sector.

Higher education

Higher education is defined as courses that are of a standard that is higher than GCE A level, the Higher Grade of the Scottish Certificate of Education, GNVQ/NVQ level 3 or the Edexcel (formerly BTEC) or SQA National Certificate/ Diploma. There are three main levels of HE course: (i) postgraduate courses leading to higher degrees, diplomas and certificates (including postgraduate certificates of education and professional qualifications) which usually require a first degree as entry qualification; (ii) first degrees which includes first degrees, first degrees with qualified teacher status, enhanced first degrees, first degrees obtained concurrently with a diploma, and intercalated first degrees; (iii) other undergraduate courses which includes all other higher education courses, for example HNDs and Diplomas in HE. As a result of the 1992 Further and Higher Education Act, former polytechnics and some other higher education institutions were designated as universities in 1992/93. Students normally attend HE courses at higher education institutions, but some attend at further education colleges. Some also attend institutions which do not receive public grant (such as the University of Buckingham) and these numbers are excluded from the tables.

6.1 Schools[1] and establishments of further and higher education: by type and country
Academic years

Numbers

		1990/91	1997/98	1998/99	1999/00	2000[2]/01	2001[2]/02	2002[2]/03	2003/04
United Kingdom:									
Public sector mainstream									
Nursery[3,4]	KBFK	1 364	1 681	2 369	2 864	3 228	3 227	3 394	3 438
Primary[5]	KBFA	24 135	23 230	23 125	23 036	22 902	22 800	22 638	22 509
Secondary[6]	KBFF	4 790	4 434	4 418	4 405	4 337	4 306	4 284	4 255
of which 6th form colleges	KPGM	116	..	..	..	..	..	..	..
Non-maintained mainstream[1]	KBFU	2 508	2 499	2 482	2 457	2 414	2 409	2 380	2 524
Special - all	KBFP	1 830	1 517	1 522	1 523	1 498	1 483	1 471	1 463
maintained	KPVX	..	1 419	1 428	1 426	1 401	1 387	1 367	1 360
non maintained	KPGO	..	98	94	97	97	96	104	103
Pupil referral units	KXEP	..	332	325	325	338	340	390	457
Universities (including Open University)[7]	KAHG	48	88	88	88	89	90	89	89
All other further and higher education institutions	KJPQ	588	596	581	574	546	541	526	525
Higher education institutions	KPVY	..	63	58	58	55	58	60	60
Further education institutions	KSNY	..	533	523	516	491	483	466	465
of which 6th form colleges	KPGP	..	108	107	105	103	101	103	102
England:									
Public sector mainstream									
Nursery	KBAK	566	533	520	514	506	494	475	468
Primary	KBAA	19 047	18 312	18 234	18 158	18 069	17 985	17 861	17 762
Secondary[6]	KBAF	3 897	3 567	3 560	3 550	3 481	3 457	3 436	3 409
of which 6th form colleges	KPGS	114	..	..	..	..	..	..	..
Non-maintained	KBAU	2 289	2 244	2 231	2 204	2 205	2 206	2 180	2 330
Special - all	KBAP	1 380	1 229	1 209	1 197	1 175	1 161	1 160	1 148
maintained	KPGT	..	1 164	1 148	1 134	1 113	1 098	1 088	1 078
non maintained	KPGU	..	65	61	63	62	63	72	70
Pupil referral units	KXEQ	..	309	298	295	308	312	360	426
Universities (including Open University)[7]	KAHM	37	71	70	70	72	73	72	72
All other further and higher education institutions	KJPR	460	491	482	458	446	441	428	427
Higher education institutions	KPXA	..	48	47	47	43	45	47	47
Further education institutions	KPWC	..	443	435	411	403	396	381	380
of which 6th form colleges	KPGV	..	108	107	105	103	101	103	102
Wales:									
Public sector mainstream									
Nursery	KBBK	54	47	46	42	41	40	37	34
Primary	KBBA	1 717	1 673	1 660	1 644	1 631	1 624	1 602	1 588
Secondary[6]	KBBF	230	228	229	228	229	227	227	227
of which 6th form colleges	KPGY	2	..	..	..	..	..	..	..
Non-maintained	KBBU	71	57	54	55	54	56	59	60
Special (Maintained)	KBBP	61	50	48	47	45	44	43	43
Pupil referral units	KZBF	..	23	27	30	30	28	30	31
Universities[7]	KAHS	1	2	2	2	2	2	2	2
All other further and higher education institutions	KJQP	38	30	28	28	28	28	27	27
Higher education institutions	KSNZ	..	4	4	4	4	4	4	4
Further education institutions	KPGZ	..	26	24	24	24	24	23	23
Scotland:									
Public sector mainstream									
Nursery[4]	KBDK	659	1 010	1 712	2 213	2 586	2 597	2 782	2 836
Primary	KBDA	2 372	2 300	2 291	2 293	2 278	2 271	2 258	2 248
Secondary	KBDF	424	401	392	389	389	387	386	386
Non-maintained[1]	KBDU	131	176	175	176	129	122	119	117
Special - all	KBDP	343	191	218	229	230	230	221	225
maintained	KYCZ	343	158	185	195	195	197	189	192
non-maintained	KYDA	..	33	33	34	35	33	32	33
Universities[7]	KAHX	8	13	14	14	13	13	13	13
All other further and higher education institutions	KJRA	64	56	52	52	53	53	53	53
Higher education institutions	KPWE	..	9	5	5	6	7	7	7
Further education institutions	KPHB	..	47	47	47	47	46	46	46
Northern Ireland:									
Grant aided mainstream									
Nursery[3]	KBEK	85	91	91	95	95	96	100	100
Primary[5]	KBEA	999	945	940	941	924	920	917	911
Secondary	KBEF	239	238	237	238	238	235	235	233
Non-maintained	KBEU	17	22	22	22	26	25	22	17
Special (Maintained)	KBEP	46	47	47	50	48	48	47	47
Universities	KIAD	2	2	2	2	2	2	2	2
Colleges of education	KIAE	2	2	2	2	2	2	2	2
Further education colleges	KIAG	24	17	17	17	17	17	16	16

1 See chapter text. From 1997/98 to 1999/00, non-maintained schools in Scotland with more than one department have been counted once for each department e.g. a school with nursery, primary and secondary departments has been counted 3 times. Subsequent figures for Scotland show primary and secondary only.

2 Includes revised data.

3 Excludes voluntary and private pre-school education centres in Northern Ireland (383 in total in 2003/04).

4 Nursery schools figures for Scotland prior to 1998/99 only include data for Local Authority pre-schools. Data thereafter include partnership pre-schools.

5 From 1995/96, includes Preparatory Departments in Northern Ireland Grammar Schools (19 in total in 2003/04).

6 From 1993/94 excludes sixth form colleges in England and Wales which were reclassified as further education colleges on 1 April 1993.

7 From 1993/94 includes former polytechnics and colleges which became universities as a result of the Further and Higher Education Act 1992.

Source: Education Departments: 01325 392754

67

6.2 Full-time and part-time pupils in school by age[1,2] and sex
United Kingdom
All schools at January[3]

		1994	1995	1996	1997	1998	1999	2000	2001	2002	2003	2004[4]
Age at previous 31 August[5]												
Boys and girls												
2 - 4[6]	KBIF	1 103	1 135	1 146	1 148	1 149	1 154	1 184	1 187	1 180	1 189	1 147
5 - 10	KBIG	4 462	4 517	4 583	4 628	4 668	4 661	4 629	4 597	4 537	4 489	4 407
11	KBIH	713	718	717	744	746	762	783	771	783	791	785
12 - 14	KBII	2 179	2 179	2 157	2 151	2 182	2 211	2 256	2 297	2 320	2 343	2 355
15	KBIK	651	700	722	716	701	706	705	732	737	751	774
16	KBIL	259	259	279	289	288	283	285	287	298	290	314
17	KBIM	180	181	191	206	217	218	213	219	223	217	238
18 and over	KBIN	23	24	22	22	24	25	27	27	23	24	32
Boys												
14	KBIO	367	376	370	365	368	367	381	384	391	401	394
15	KBIP	333	358	368	365	358	361	359	374	377	384	393
16	KBIQ	128	127	137	141	140	137	138	139	145	140	150
17	KBIR	88	88	92	100	104	104	101	105	107	104	112
18 and over	KBIS	12	13	12	12	13	13	14	15	13	13	17
Girls												
14	KBIT	347	358	355	349	350	352	364	365	373	384	378
15	KBIU	318	342	354	351	343	345	346	358	360	368	379
16	KBIV	131	132	143	148	149	146	147	148	153	150	161
17	KBIW	92	93	99	107	113	114	111	114	116	113	124
18 and over	KBIX	11	11	10	10	11	11	13	12	11	11	15
United Kingdom	KBIE	9 571	9 714	9 816	9 907	9 975	10 020	10 081	10 116	10 102	10 095	10 051
England	KBIA	7 883	8 013	8 110	8 195	8 261	8 310	8 346	8 374	8 369	8 367	8 335
Wales	KBIB	498	504	508	510	513	513	512	512	511	509	509
Scotland[1]	KBIC	841	845	846	848	850	844	874	882	876	874	866
Northern Ireland[2]	KBID	349	351	353	354	352	352	349	348	346	345	341

1 Figures for Scotland, up to 2002/03, are estimates using the stage rolls.
2 In Northern Ireland, a split is not collected by age but is available by year group and so this is used as a proxy.
3 In Scotland, as at the previous September.

4 Provisional.
5 1 July for Northern Ireland and 31 December for Scotland.
6 Includes the so-called "rising 5s" (i.e. those pupils who become 5 during the autumn term).

Source: Education Departments: 01325 392754

6.3 Pupils and teachers, and pupil:teacher ratios:[1] by school type
United Kingdom
At January[2]

Numbers

		1999	2000[3]	2001[3]	2002[3]	2003[3,4]	2004[3,5]
All schools or departments							
Total							
Pupils (thousands)							
Full-time and full-time equivalent of part-time	KBCA	9 782.6	9 828.3	9 856.3	9 858.1	9 852.3	9 812.6
Teachers[6] (thousands)	KBCB	540.4	545.6	553.1	558.3	561.6	563.6
Pupils per teacher[6]:							
United Kingdom	KBCC	18.2	18.1	17.9	17.7	17.6	17.5
England	KBCD	18.4	18.3	18.1	18.0	17.9	17.8
Wales	KBCE	18.8	18.7	18.4	18.1	18.1	18.2
Scotland	KBCF	15.4	15.4	15.4	15.4	14.9	15.0
Northern Ireland	KBCG	17.1	16.9	16.6	16.4	16.3	16.5
Public sector mainstream schools or departments							
Nursery							
Pupils (thousands)							
Full-time and full-time equivalent of part-time	KBFM	61.1	75.3	77.5	85.6	84.8	83.9
Teachers[6] (thousands)	KBFN	3.0	3.1	3.4	3.6	3.6	3.6
Pupils per teacher[6]	KBFO	20.6	24.2	23.1	23.6	23.6	23.6
Primary[7]							
Pupils (thousands)							
Full-time and full-time equivalent of part-time	KBFB	5 202.5	5 167.9	5 130.5	5 083.4	5 021.9	4 953.9
Teachers[6] (thousands)	KBFD	226.7	228.0	229.6	231.5	228.8	226.2
Pupils per teacher[6]	KBFE	22.9	22.7	22.3	22.0	21.9	21.9
Secondary[8]							
Pupils (thousands)							
Full-time and full-time equivalent of part-time	KBFG	3 793.3	3 859.0	3 915.5	3 948.0	3 994.0	4 014.1
Teachers[6] (thousands)	KBFH	230.4	232.9	237.0	241.2	243.3	244.6
Pupils per teacher[6]	KBFI	16.5	16.6	16.5	16.4	16.4	16.4
Special schools - maintained							
Pupils (thousands)							
Full-time and full-time equivalent of part-time	KPGE	108.5	107.4	106.5	105.4	104.5	102.2
Teachers[6] (thousands)	KPGG	16.9	17.0	17.0	17.0	17.0	16.9
Pupils per teacher[9]	KPGI	6.4	6.3	6.3	6.2	6.1	6.0

1 'All schools' pupil:teacher ratios exclude Pupil Referral Units and non-maintained special schools.
2 In Scotland, as at the previous September.
3 Nursery schools for Scotland refer to pre-school education centres and are not therefore directly comparable with earlier years.
4 Includes revised data.
5 Provisional.

6 Figures of teachers and of pupil:teacher ratios take account of the full-time equivalent of part-time teachers.
7 Includes preparatory departments attached to grammar schools in Northern Ireland.
8 Includes voluntary grammar schools in Northern Ireland.
9 England and Scotland only.

Source: Education Departments: 01325 392754

Full-time and part-time pupils with special educational needs (SEN),[1] 2003/04[2,3]
United Kingdom
By type of school

Thousands and percentages

	United Kingdom	England	Wales[3]	Scotland	Northern Ireland
All schools					
Total pupils	10 057.0	8 334.9	509.2	865.6	347.4
SEN pupils with statements	290.7	247.6	16.0	16.1	11.0
Incidence *(Percentages)[4]*	*2.9*	*3.0*	*3.1*	*1.9*	*3.2*
Maintained schools[5]					
Nursery[6]					
Total pupils	156.4	39.0	2.1	103.1	12.2
SEN pupils with statements	1.8	0.5	-	1.3	0.1
Incidence *(Percentages)[4]*	*1.1*	*1.2*	*0.6*	*1.2*	*0.5*
Placement *(Percentages)[7]*	*0.6*	*0.2*	*0.1*	*7.8*	*0.6*
Primary[8]					
Total pupils	5 111.4	4 252.5	278.7	406.0	174.2
SEN pupils without statements	712.6	685.7	..	..	26.9
SEN pupils with statements	83.0	69.6	5.8	4.0	3.6
Incidence *(Percentages)[4]*	*1.6*	*1.6*	*2.1*	*1.0*	*2.1*
Placement *(Percentages)[7]*	*28.5*	*28.1*	*36.1*	*24.8*	*32.6*
Secondary					
Total pupils	4 013.1	3 325.0	214.3	318.4	155.4
SEN pupils without statements	461.3	450.1	..	..	11.2
SEN pupils with statements	92.3	78.5	6.1	4.8	3.0
Incidence *(Percentages)[4]*	*2.3*	*2.4*	*2.8*	*1.5*	*1.9*
Placement *(Percentages)[7]*	*31.8*	*31.7*	*38.0*	*29.7*	*26.9*
Special[9,10]					
Total pupils	103.2	86.9	3.8	7.7	4.8
SEN pupils with statements	98.1	84.3	3.7	5.7	4.4
Incidence *(Percentages)[4]*	*95.0*	*96.9*	*98.5*	*73.9*	*90.8*
Placement *(Percentages)[7]*	*33.7*	*34.0*	*23.3*	*35.3*	*39.9*
Pupil referral units[9,11]					
Total pupils	13.4	13.0	0.4	..	..
SEN pupils with statements	2.4	2.3	0.1	..	..
Incidence *(Percentages)[4]*	*17.9*	*17.6*	*25.5*	*..*	*..*
Placement *(Percentages)[7]*	*0.8*	*0.9*	*0.7*	*..*	*..*
Other schools					
Independent					
Total pupils	653.6	613.6	9.8	29.3	0.8
SEN pupils with statements	8.1	7.8	0.3	-	..
Incidence *(Percentages)[4]*	*1.2*	*1.3*	*3.0*	*0.1*	*..*
Placement *(Percentages)[7]*	*2.8*	*3.1*	*1.9*	*0.2*	*..*
Non-maintained special[9]					
Total pupils	5.9	4.8	..	1.1	..
SEN pupils with statements	5.1	4.7	..	0.4	..
Incidence *(Percentages)[4]*	*86.0*	*97.2*	*..*	*34.7*	*..*
Placement *(Percentages)[7]*	*1.7*	*1.9*	*..*	*2.3*	*..*

1 See chapter text. For Scotland, pupils with a Record of Needs including some who had an Individualised Educational Programme.

2 Provisional.

3 Data for Wales refer to 2002/03.

4 Incidence of pupils - the number of pupils with statements within each school type expressed as a proportion of the total number of pupils on roll in each school type.

5 Grant-Aided schools in Northern Ireland.

6 Includes pupils in Voluntary and Private Pre-School Centres in Northern Ireland funded under the Pre-School Expansion Programme which began in 1998/99.

7 Placement of pupils - the number of pupils with statements within each school type expressed as a proportion of the number of pupils with statements in all schools.

8 Includes nursery classes (except for Scotland, where they are included with Nursery Schools) and reception classes in primary schools.

9 England and Wales figures exclude dually registered pupils.

10 Including general and hospital special schools.

11 England and Wales only.

Source: Education Departments: 01325 392754

6.5 GCE, GCSE and SCE[1] and vocational qualifications obtained at a typical age,[2,3] and by students of any age

United Kingdom

Percentages and thousands

	Pupils in their last year of compulsory education[2]					Pupils/students in education[3]			
						% achieving GCE A Levels and equivalent			Population
	5 or more grades A*-C[4]	1-4 grades A*-C[4]	Grades D-G[5] only	No graded results	Total (=100%) (Thousands)	2 or more passes[6,7]	1 pass[8]	1 or more passes	aged 17 (thousands)
Students at a typical age (percentages and thousands)									
1998/99									
All	49.1	24.8	20.3	5.9	703.6	33.7	6.7	40.3	744.2
Males	43.8	25.2	24.1	6.9	359.6	30.1	6.1	36.2	381.4
Females	54.6	24.3	16.3	4.8	344.0	37.4	7.3	44.7	362.8
1999/00[1]									
All	50.4	24.5	19.7	5.5	703.7	34.5	6.5	41.0	732.2
Males	45.0	25.0	23.6	6.4	357.7	30.5	6.0	36.6	376.0
Females	55.9	23.9	15.7	4.5	346.0	38.6	7.1	45.6	356.3
2000/01[1,9]									
All	51.0	24.1	19.4	5.5	729.7	36.5	4.8	41.3	735.4
Males	45.7	24.6	23.1	6.5	372.1	32.3	4.5	36.9	378.5
Females	56.5	23.6	15.5	4.4	357.6	41.0	5.0	46.0	356.9
2001/02[1,9]									
All	52.5	23.7	18.4	5.4	732.5	37.6	4.7	42.3	735.2
Males	47.2	24.4	22.0	6.4	374.0	33.2	4.5	37.8	377.0
Females	58.0	23.1	14.6	4.3	358.5	42.1	5.0	47.1	358.2
2002/03[1]									
All	53.5	23.1	18.2	5.2	750.2	38.5	3.8	42.3	769.0
Males	48.3	23.6	21.8	6.3	382.7	34.1	3.8	37.9	395.1
Females	58.8	22.7	14.4	4.1	367.6	43.2	3.8	47.0	373.9

	GCSE and SCE S Grade/Standard Grade (SG)				GCE A Level and SCE/NQ Higher Grade		
	5 or more grades A*-C[4,10]	1-4 grades A*-C[4,10]	Grades D-G[5,11] only	No graded results[12]	2 or more passes[6,7]	1 pass[8]	Total 1 or more passes
Students of all ages (thousands)							
1998/99							
All	341.0	323.7	229.8	31.2	257.9	69.9	327.8
Males	162.3	150.6	128.1	15.6	118.4	30.6	149.0
Females	178.7	173.2	101.7	15.6	139.5	39.3	178.8
1999/00[1]							
All	357.7	311.6	224.4	30.3	258.8	65.6	324.4
Males	162.8	150.9	125.3	15.2	118.0	28.7	146.6
Females	194.9	160.7	99.1	15.1	140.9	36.9	177.7
2000/01[1]							
All	375.1	335.0	227.3	31.8	280.8	64.2	345.1
Males	171.8	164.1	127.3	16.0	128.4	29.1	157.5
Females	203.3	170.9	100.1	15.8	152.4	35.2	187.6
2001/02[1]							
All	394.9	381.1	234.2	50.6	286.7	67.8	354.5
Males	182.4	188.7	131.1	27.9	130.0	31.6	161.6
Females	212.4	192.3	103.1	22.7	156.7	36.2	192.9
2002/03[1]							
All	409.4	340.9	234.2	51.7	309.1	60.8	369.9
Males	189.6	168.1	131.2	28.3	140.5	28.7	169.3
Females	219.9	172.9	103.0	23.4	168.6	32.0	200.6

1 From 1999/00 National Qualifications (NQ) were introduced in Scotland but not all are shown until 2000/01. NQs include Standard Grades, Intermediate 1 & 2 and Higher Grades. The figures for Higher Grades combine the new NQ Higher and the old SCE Higher and include Advanced Highers.
2 Pupils aged 15 at the start of the academic year, pupils in year S4 in Scotland.
3 Pupils in schools and students in further education institutions generally aged 16-18 at the start of the academic year in England, Wales and Northern Ireland as a percentage of the 17 year old population. Data for 2002/03 for Wales and Northern Ireland however, relate to schools only. Pupils in Scotland generally sit Highers one year earlier and the figures relate to results of pupils in Year S5/S6.
4 Standard Grades 1-3/Intermediate 2 A-C/Intermediate 1 A-B in Scotland.
5 Grades D-G at GCSE and Scottish Standard Grades 4-6/Intermediate 1 (C)/Access 3 (pass).

6 3 or more SCE/NQ Higher Grades/ 2 or more Advanced Highers/ 1 Advanced Higher with more than 2 Higher passes in Scotland.
7 Includes Vocational Certificates of Education (VCE) and, previously, Advanced level GNVQ/GSVQ which is equivalent to 2 GCE A levels or AS equivalents/3 SCE/NQ Higher grades.
8 2 AS levels or 2 Highers/ 1 Advanced Higher or 1 each in Scotland, count as 1 A Level pass. Includes those with 1.5 A level passes.
9 Includes revised data.
10 Includes GNVQ/GSVQ Intermediate Part 1, Full and Language unit which are equivalent to 2, 4 and 0.5 GCSE grades A*-C/SCE Standard grades 1-3 respectively. Figures include those with 4.5 GCSEs.
11 Includes GNVQ/GSVQ Foundation Part 1, Full and Language unit which are equivalent to 2, 4 and 0.5 GCSE grades D-G/SCE Standard grades 4-6 respectively.
12 Figures for Scotland include students in Year S4 only.

Source: Education Departments: 01325 392754

71

6.6 Students in further education:[1] by country, mode of study,[2] sex and age,[3] 2002/03
Home and overseas students

Thousands

	United Kingdom		England[4]		Wales		Scotland[5]		Northern Ireland	
	Full-time	Part-time	Full-time	Part-time	Full-time	Part-time	Full-time	Part-time	Full-time	Part-time
All persons										
Age under 16	5.8	45.5	2.6	5.7	0.9	5.6	2.1	30.9	0.1	3.3
16	268.9	75.5	238.0	52.0	14.1	4.1	9.5	14.7	7.3	4.6
17	227.6	83.2	200.1	59.2	11.7	4.8	9.0	15.5	6.9	3.6
18	102.5	80.3	87.0	62.6	5.5	4.7	6.1	10.5	3.9	2.4
19	42.8	74.8	36.2	59.9	2.2	4.6	3.1	8.5	1.3	1.9
20	25.5	70.1	21.8	57.3	1.2	4.4	1.9	6.9	0.5	1.5
21	21.0	73.4	18.4	61.5	0.9	4.4	1.4	6.2	0.3	1.4
22	18.7	79.1	16.7	67.0	0.6	4.6	1.1	6.1	0.2	1.4
23	16.3	77.0	14.7	65.5	0.5	4.3	0.9	5.9	0.1	1.2
24	14.4	73.2	13.1	62.6	0.4	3.8	0.8	5.6	0.1	1.2
25	13.2	71.9	12.1	62.0	0.4	3.7	0.7	5.1	0.1	1.1
26	13.0	74.0	12.0	63.7	0.4	3.8	0.6	5.4	-	1.1
27	12.6	75.3	11.7	64.9	0.3	3.9	0.5	5.5	-	1.0
28	12.4	76.9	11.4	66.5	0.4	4.0	0.5	5.4	-	1.0
29	12.1	79.4	11.2	68.6	0.3	4.1	0.5	5.7	-	1.0
30+	218.5	2 565.1	205.8	2 202.0	4.9	146.0	7.3	191.5	0.5	25.7
Unknown	1.5	27.0	1.4	23.6	0.1	2.9	-	-	-	0.5
All ages	1 026.7	3 701.6	914.5	3 104.7	44.8	213.7	46.0	329.3	21.5	54.0
Males										
Age under 16	3.2	23.5	1.3	2.5	0.6	3.2	1.2	15.6	0.1	2.1
16	132.5	36.7	115.5	26.0	7.3	2.1	5.3	6.5	4.3	2.1
17	109.9	41.0	95.8	29.0	5.7	2.7	4.6	7.7	3.8	1.6
18	52.4	39.0	44.3	28.9	2.7	2.7	3.1	6.2	2.3	1.2
19	23.2	34.7	19.5	26.3	1.2	2.5	1.7	5.0	0.8	0.9
20	13.6	30.5	11.6	24.1	0.7	2.2	1.0	3.6	0.3	0.6
21	10.5	29.9	9.2	24.3	0.4	2.0	0.7	3.0	0.1	0.5
22	9.2	31.3	8.3	26.1	0.3	2.0	0.5	2.7	0.1	0.5
23	8.0	29.9	7.3	25.2	0.2	1.8	0.4	2.5	0.1	0.4
24	7.0	28.7	6.4	24.4	0.2	1.6	0.4	2.4	0.1	0.4
25	6.5	28.4	6.0	24.4	0.2	1.6	0.3	2.1	-	0.4
26	6.4	29.0	6.0	24.9	0.2	1.6	0.3	2.1	-	0.3
27	6.2	30.0	5.8	26.0	0.1	1.5	0.2	2.1	-	0.3
28	6.0	30.1	5.7	26.0	0.1	1.7	0.2	2.1	-	0.3
29	5.8	30.9	5.5	26.7	0.1	1.6	0.2	2.3	-	0.3
30+	107.9	940.0	103.4	805.8	1.8	55.3	2.6	71.2	0.1	7.7
Unknown	0.9	10.1	0.9	8.7	-	1.2	-	-	-	0.2
All ages	509.3	1 423.9	452.6	1 179.4	21.8	87.4	22.6	137.3	12.3	19.8
Females										
Age under 16	2.6	22.0	1.3	3.1	0.3	2.4	0.9	15.3	0.1	1.2
16	136.5	38.8	122.5	26.0	6.8	2.0	4.2	8.2	3.0	2.5
17	117.7	42.1	104.4	30.2	6.0	2.1	4.3	7.9	3.1	2.0
18	50.1	41.2	42.7	33.7	2.7	2.0	3.1	4.3	1.6	1.2
19	19.6	40.1	16.7	33.6	1.0	2.1	1.4	3.5	0.5	0.9
20	11.9	39.5	10.3	33.2	0.6	2.2	0.9	3.3	0.2	0.9
21	10.5	43.5	9.2	37.1	0.5	2.4	0.7	3.2	0.1	0.9
22	9.4	47.8	8.4	40.9	0.3	2.6	0.6	3.4	0.1	0.9
23	8.3	47.0	7.4	40.4	0.3	2.5	0.5	3.4	0.1	0.9
24	7.4	44.5	6.7	38.3	0.2	2.2	0.5	3.2	0.1	0.8
25	6.7	43.5	6.1	37.6	0.2	2.1	0.4	3.0	-	0.8
26	6.5	45.0	6.0	38.7	0.2	2.3	0.3	3.2	-	0.8
27	6.4	45.4	5.9	38.9	0.2	2.4	0.3	3.4	-	0.7
28	6.3	46.8	5.7	40.5	0.2	2.4	0.3	3.2	-	0.7
29	6.2	48.6	5.7	41.9	0.2	2.5	0.3	3.4	-	0.7
30+	110.6	1 625.1	102.4	1 396.2	3.1	90.7	4.7	120.3	0.3	18.0
Unknown	0.6	16.9	0.6	14.9	-	1.7	-	-	-	0.3
All ages	517.5	2 277.7	462.0	1 925.2	23.0	126.3	23.3	192.0	9.2	34.2

1 Further education (FE) institution figures are whole year counts except for Northern Ireland, which are on a snapshot basis. Higher education (HE) institution figures are based on the HESA July 'standard registration' count.
2 Full-time includes sandwich. Part-time comprises both day and evening, including block release and open/distance learning.
3 Ages as at 31 August 2002 (1 July in Northern Ireland and 31 December in Scotland).

4 Further education institution figures for England include LSC funded students only and are not therefore directly comparable with previous years.
5 Figures for Scotland further education colleges are enrolments rather than headcounts.

Source: Education Departments: 01325 392754

6.7 Students in further education:[1] by country, mode of study,[2] sex and area of learning,[3] 2002/03

Home and overseas students

Thousands

	United Kingdom		England[4]		Wales		Scotland[5]		Northern Ireland	
	Full-time	Part-time	Full-time	Part-time	Full-time	Part-time	Full-time	Part-time	Full-time	Part-time
All persons										
Business Administration, Management & Professional	64.0	339.8	56.3	295.6	-	-	4.6	33.2	3.1	10.9
Construction	41.0	102.6	32.6	85.0	-	-	4.5	15.2	3.9	2.4
Engineering, Technology and Manufacturing	40.7	106.0	33.3	83.7	-	0.1	5.1	18.9	2.3	3.3
English, Languages and Communications	42.5	178.9	40.5	143.7	-	0.1	2.0	35.0	-	-
Foundation programmes	77.0	281.9	76.6	278.1	..	..	0.4	3.8	-	-
Hairdressing and Beauty Therapy	44.2	87.8	38.9	78.7	..	..	3.7	6.6	1.5	2.5
Health, Social Care and Public Services	154.8	487.4	144.2	428.5	..	..	8.2	54.9	2.4	4.0
Hospitality, Sports, Leisure and Travel	59.1	237.2	52.1	203.8	..	..	4.6	31.2	2.3	2.2
Humanities	66.3	83.6	64.1	73.5	-	-	2.2	10.1	-	-
Information & Communication Technology	81.6	733.2	76.4	644.0	..	..	3.6	76.2	1.6	13.0
Land-based provision	15.8	49.2	14.4	42.1	..	..	1.3	6.8	0.1	0.2
Retailing, Customer Service and Transportation	7.1	66.2	6.8	60.0	..	..	0.3	5.4	-	0.8
Science and Mathematics	50.6	96.8	47.1	79.8	..	..	1.1	6.8	2.4	10.2
Visual and Performing Arts & Media	80.5	155.5	74.4	126.2	..	..	4.3	25.0	1.8	4.3
Other Subjects[6]	16.1	82.0	15.8	74.9	0.3	6.9	-	0.2	-	-
Unknown	185.4	613.6	141.0	407.0	44.4	206.6	-	-	-	-
All areas of learning	1 026.7	3 701.6	914.5	3 104.7	44.8	213.7	46.0	329.3	21.5	54.0
Males										
Business Administration, Management & Professional	28.5	102.5	25.7	88.1	-	-	1.3	11.0	1.5	3.3
Construction	39.2	94.7	31.2	79.6	-	-	4.2	12.7	3.8	2.3
Engineering, Technology and Manufacturing	36.0	90.7	28.8	72.1	-	0.1	4.9	15.5	2.3	3.1
English, Languages and Communications	16.5	69.4	15.5	55.1	-	-	1.0	14.2	-	-
Foundation programmes	39.2	118.7	39.0	117.0	..	..	0.2	1.8	-	-
Hairdressing and Beauty Therapy	2.8	15.1	2.7	14.7	..	..	0.1	0.3	-	0.1
Health, Social Care and Public Services	63.7	154.6	62.2	134.9	..	..	1.4	19.4	0.1	0.4
Hospitality, Sports, Leisure and Travel	30.1	81.9	26.2	68.3	..	..	2.6	12.8	1.2	0.8
Humanities	24.7	24.2	23.8	21.0	-	-	0.8	3.2	-	-
Information & Communication Technology	52.8	268.2	48.9	236.5	..	..	2.6	27.5	1.3	4.2
Land-based provision	8.1	21.4	7.3	17.5	..	..	0.8	3.8	-	0.1
Retailing, Customer Service and Transportation	4.7	26.2	4.5	21.9	..	..	0.2	4.0	-	0.3
Science and Mathematics	26.5	35.8	24.9	29.4	..	..	0.5	2.6	1.1	3.7
Visual and Performaing Arts & Media	35.0	45.4	32.0	35.6	..	..	2.0	8.3	0.9	1.5
Other Subjects[6]	5.8	32.3	5.7	29.8	0.1	2.4	-	-	-	-
Unknown	95.9	242.9	74.2	158.0	21.7	84.9	-	-	-	-
All areas of learning	509.3	1 423.9	452.6	1 179.4	21.8	87.4	22.6	137.3	12.3	19.8
Females										
Business Administration, Management & Professional	35.5	237.3	30.6	207.5	-	-	3.3	22.2	1.6	7.6
Construction	1.8	7.9	1.5	5.4	-	-	0.3	2.5	0.1	0.1
Engineering, Technology and Manufacturing	4.8	15.3	4.5	11.6	-	-	0.3	3.4	-	0.3
English, Languages and Communications	26.0	109.5	25.0	88.6	-	0.1	1.0	20.8	-	-
Foundation programmes	37.7	163.2	37.6	161.2	..	..	0.2	2.0	-	-
Hairdressing and Beauty Therapy	41.3	72.7	36.2	64.0	..	..	3.7	6.3	1.5	2.4
Health, Social Care and Public Services	91.1	332.7	81.9	293.6	..	..	6.9	35.5	2.3	3.6
Hospitality, Sports, Leisure and Travel	29.0	155.2	25.9	135.5	..	..	2.0	18.3	1.1	1.4
Humanities	41.6	59.4	40.3	52.5	..	..	1.3	6.9	-	-
Information & Communication Technology	28.7	465.0	27.5	407.5	..	..	1.0	48.7	0.3	8.8
Land-based provision	7.8	27.8	7.2	24.6	..	..	0.5	3.0	0.1	0.1
Retailing, Customer Service and Transportation	2.4	40.0	2.3	38.1	..	..	-	1.4	-	0.5
Science and Mathematics	24.2	61.1	22.2	50.4	..	..	0.6	4.1	1.3	6.5
Visual and Performing Arts & Media	45.6	110.1	42.4	90.6	..	..	2.3	16.7	0.9	2.8
Other Subjects[6]	10.3	49.7	10.1	45.1	0.2	4.5	-	0.2	-	-
Unknown	89.5	370.7	66.8	249.0	22.7	121.7	-	-	-	-
All areas of learning	517.5	2 277.7	462.0	1 925.2	23.0	126.3	23.3	192.0	9.2	34.2

1 Further education (FE) institution figures are whole year counts except for Northern Ireland, which are collected on a snapshot basis. Higher education (HE) institution figures are based on the HESA July 'standard registration' count.

2 Full-time includes sandwich. Part-time comprises both day and evening including block release.

3 Data are shown by area of learning and are not directly comparable with subject groups previously shown. The UK individual area of learning totals exclude students for Wales, where the individual area of learning was not known, which are included in the 'Unknown' rows.

4 Further education institution figures for England include LSC funded students only and are not therefore directly comparable with previous years.

5 Figure on colleagues are enrolments rather than headcounts.

6 For UK higher education institutions, includes the previous subject groups not allocated to specific areas of learning, i.e, medicine & biological, veterinary, physical, mathematical, computing and social (inc law) sciences, creative arts & design and education.

Source: Education Departments: 01325 392754

6.8 Students in higher education:[1] by level, mode of study,[2] sex and age,[3] 2002/03[4,5]
United Kingdom
Home and overseas students

Thousands

	Postgraduate level						First degree		Other undergraduate		Total higher education[6]	
	PhD and equivalent		Masters and others		Total Postgraduate							
	Full-time	Part-time	Full-time	Part-time	Full-time	Part-time	Full-time	Part-time	Full-time	Part-time	Full-time	Part-time
All persons												
Age under 16	-	-	-	-	-	-	-	-	-	0.3	-	0.3
16	-	-	-	-	-	-	0.3	-	0.8	1.9	1.2	1.9
17	-	-	-	-	-	-	10.5	0.1	4.7	1.8	15.2	1.9
18	-	-	0.1	-	0.1	-	160.2	0.6	20.5	6.2	180.9	6.8
19	-	-	0.1	-	0.1	-	214.4	2.4	29.0	11.0	243.7	13.5
20	-	-	1.4	0.2	1.4	0.2	217.9	4.3	22.8	13.0	242.2	17.6
21	0.8	-	15.3	1.4	16.1	1.5	149.3	6.2	15.7	14.0	181.3	21.8
22	3.1	0.2	24.7	5.2	27.8	5.4	71.6	6.9	11.0	15.6	110.4	27.9
23	5.0	0.3	23.0	8.4	28.0	8.7	35.9	5.8	8.5	15.8	72.4	30.4
24	5.4	1.2	17.1	9.3	22.5	10.5	20.5	4.6	6.5	15.3	49.4	30.5
25	4.3	2.5	12.8	9.4	17.1	11.9	13.9	4.1	5.2	15.0	36.2	31.1
26	3.4	2.5	10.0	9.8	13.4	12.3	10.4	3.8	4.8	15.1	28.5	31.3
27	3.0	2.3	8.2	9.8	11.2	12.0	8.4	3.7	4.3	15.0	23.9	30.8
28	2.5	2.0	6.8	9.9	9.3	12.0	7.0	3.6	4.0	15.4	20.3	31.1
29	2.1	2.0	5.7	10.1	7.8	12.1	6.3	3.7	3.6	15.8	17.7	31.7
30+	13.8	29.7	38.6	176.1	52.4	205.8	63.6	67.8	46.5	386.4	162.7	662.0
Unknown	0.1	0.1	0.2	2.5	0.3	2.6	0.3	0.3	0.2	14.5	0.7	17.4
All ages	43.5	42.8	164.0	252.2	207.5	295.0	990.3	117.9	188.1	572.2	1 386.7	988.2
Males												
Age under 16	-	-	-	-	-	-	-	-	-	0.2	-	0.2
16	-	-	-	-	-	-	0.1	-	0.2	0.8	0.4	0.8
17	-	-	-	-	-	-	4.6	0.1	1.9	0.8	6.6	0.9
18	-	-	-	-	-	-	71.9	0.3	9.1	3.4	81.0	3.7
19	-	-	0.1	-	0.1	-	98.2	1.4	13.7	6.0	112.1	7.4
20	-	-	0.7	0.1	0.7	0.1	100.5	2.5	10.3	6.5	111.5	9.2
21	0.4	-	6.4	0.5	6.8	0.5	73.1	3.4	7.0	6.6	86.9	10.6
22	1.8	0.1	11.2	2.0	13.0	2.1	37.6	3.6	4.8	6.4	55.4	12.2
23	3.0	0.2	10.8	3.3	13.8	3.4	19.2	2.9	3.4	6.0	36.4	12.3
24	3.1	0.6	8.2	3.6	11.3	4.2	10.9	2.2	2.5	5.7	24.6	12.2
25	2.4	1.5	6.3	3.7	8.7	5.2	7.1	1.8	1.9	5.4	17.8	12.4
26	1.9	1.4	4.9	4.0	6.8	5.4	5.2	1.5	1.7	5.5	13.7	12.5
27	1.6	1.2	4.2	4.0	5.8	5.2	4.0	1.4	1.4	5.6	11.2	12.3
28	1.3	1.1	3.5	4.3	4.8	5.4	3.2	1.4	1.3	5.7	9.4	12.5
29	1.2	1.1	3.0	4.5	4.1	5.6	2.8	1.5	1.2	6.1	8.2	13.3
30+	8.2	16.9	20.6	80.2	28.8	97.1	22.3	22.2	12.3	138.2	63.5	258.3
Unknown	-	0.1	0.1	1.0	0.2	1.1	0.2	0.1	0.1	5.2	0.4	6.3
All ages	25.0	24.2	79.8	111.1	104.8	135.3	461.1	46.4	72.8	214.1	639.1	397.1
Females												
Age under 16	-	-	-	-	-	-	-	-	-	0.2	-	0.2
16	-	-	-	-	-	-	0.2	-	0.6	1.1	0.8	1.1
17	-	-	-	-	-	-	5.9	-	2.8	1.0	8.7	1.0
18	-	-	0.1	-	0.1	-	88.3	0.3	11.5	2.8	99.9	3.1
19	-	-	0.1	-	0.1	-	116.1	1.1	15.3	5.0	131.6	6.1
20	-	-	0.7	0.1	0.7	0.1	117.4	1.8	12.5	6.4	130.7	8.4
21	0.3	-	9.0	0.9	9.3	0.9	76.3	2.8	8.7	7.4	94.3	11.2
22	1.3	0.1	13.5	3.2	14.8	3.3	34.0	3.3	6.2	9.1	55.0	15.8
23	2.1	0.1	12.2	5.1	14.2	5.3	16.7	2.9	5.1	9.8	36.0	18.0
24	2.3	0.6	8.9	5.7	11.2	6.3	9.6	2.4	4.0	9.6	24.8	18.3
25	1.9	1.0	6.5	5.7	8.4	6.7	6.8	2.3	3.3	9.6	18.5	18.7
26	1.6	1.1	5.0	5.8	6.6	6.9	5.1	2.3	3.1	9.6	14.8	18.9
27	1.4	1.1	4.1	5.8	5.4	6.8	4.3	2.2	2.9	9.4	12.6	18.5
28	1.1	0.9	3.3	5.7	4.5	6.6	3.8	2.2	2.6	9.7	10.9	18.6
29	0.9	0.9	2.8	5.6	3.6	6.5	3.4	2.1	2.4	9.7	9.5	18.4
30+	5.6	12.8	18.0	95.9	23.6	108.7	41.3	45.6	34.2	248.1	99.2	403.8
Unknown	-	-	0.1	1.5	0.1	1.5	0.1	0.2	0.1	9.4	0.3	11.1
All ages	18.5	18.6	84.2	141.1	102.6	159.7	529.3	71.5	115.4	358.0	747.6	591.1

1 Includes Open University students. Part-time figures include dormant modes, those writing up at home and on sabbaticals.
2 Full-time includes sandwich. Part-time comprises both day and evening, including block release and open/distance learning.
3 Ages as at 31 August 2002 (1 July in Northern Ireland and 31 December in Scotland).
4 Figures for higher education (HE) institutions are based on the HESA July 'standard registration' count. Figures for further education (FE) institutions (other than in Scotland FE colleges) are snapshots counted at a particular point in the year [November for FE institutions in England and Northern Ireland, and December for FE institutions in Wales].
5 FE institution figures for England include Learning and Skills Council (LSC) funded students only.
6 Includes data for higher education students in further education institutions in Wales which cannot be split by level.

Source: Education Departments: 01325 392754

6.9 Students in higher education:[1] by level, mode of study,[2] sex and subject group,[3] 2002/03[4,5]

United Kingdom: Home and overseas students

Thousands

	Postgraduate level						First degree		Other undergraduate		Total higher education[6]	
	PhD and equivalent		Masters and others		Total Postgraduate							
	Full-time	Part-time	Full-time	Part-time	Full-time	Part-time	Full-time	Part-time	Full-time	Part-time	Full-time	Part-time
All persons												
Medicine & Dentistry	2.8	3.8	2.7	6.2	5.5	10.0	33.1	0.1	0.3	0.1	38.8	10.1
Allied Medicine	2.2	2.8	5.1	24.4	7.3	27.2	62.7	30.0	69.2	72.4	139.2	129.6
Biological Sciences	6.6	4.6	6.1	7.9	12.7	12.6	90.1	4.7	2.4	3.6	105.3	20.8
Vet. Science, Agriculture & related	0.9	0.7	1.4	1.3	2.3	2.0	10.0	0.6	3.8	3.0	16.2	5.6
Physical Sciences	6.9	3.2	5.2	3.1	12.0	6.3	46.7	1.8	0.9	3.4	59.6	11.6
Mathematical and Computing Sciences	3.3	2.0	14.0	10.7	17.2	12.7	94.7	7.3	13.7	23.1	125.7	43.1
Engineering & Technology	6.8	4.4	13.3	12.1	20.1	16.5	71.8	8.5	11.2	24.1	103.0	49.1
Architecture	0.6	0.7	4.5	7.0	5.1	7.7	19.8	6.7	3.0	11.7	27.9	26.1
Social Sciences	4.4	5.1	27.4	24.6	31.8	29.7	133.0	16.1	9.4	35.8	174.2	81.6
Business & Administrative Studies	1.7	2.9	33.0	58.4	34.7	61.4	135.1	15.6	28.2	74.1	198.1	151.0
Mass Communication & Documentation	0.3	0.3	4.3	4.0	4.6	4.3	28.8	1.2	2.4	2.4	35.8	7.9
Languages	2.5	2.9	6.1	4.9	8.6	7.8	73.2	4.4	4.6	32.2	86.4	44.4
Historical and Philosophical Studies	2.5	3.4	4.8	8.9	7.3	12.3	47.9	5.6	1.6	30.2	56.8	48.1
Creative Arts & Design	1.2	1.4	6.9	4.5	8.1	5.9	96.9	4.2	13.6	11.5	118.6	21.7
Education[7]	0.8	4.4	29.1	57.0	29.9	61.4	32.6	6.8	2.9	38.9	65.4	107.1
Other subjects[8]	-	0.1	0.1	16.7	0.1	16.7	7.4	2.6	4.1	184.5	11.6	203.8
Unknown[6]	-	-	0.1	0.4	0.1	0.4	6.4	1.6	16.8	21.2	24.1	26.4
All subjects	43.5	42.8	164.0	252.2	207.5	295.0	990.3	117.9	188.1	572.1	1 386.7	988.2
Males												
Medicine and Dentistry	1.1	2.1	1.1	2.8	2.3	4.9	14.2	-	0.1	-	16.5	5.0
Allied Medicine	0.9	1.1	1.5	6.1	2.4	7.3	14.1	3.9	9.3	7.8	25.8	18.9
Biological Sciences	2.8	2.0	2.3	2.6	5.1	4.6	32.6	1.6	1.4	1.3	39.0	7.6
Vet. Science, Agriculture & related	0.5	0.4	0.7	0.6	1.2	1.0	3.4	0.2	1.6	1.3	6.2	2.5
Physical Sciences	4.6	2.2	2.9	1.7	7.5	3.9	27.8	1.1	0.5	2.0	35.8	7.0
Mathematical and Computing Sciences	2.5	1.5	10.4	7.3	12.8	8.8	71.7	5.4	11.2	11.7	95.8	25.9
Engineering & Technology	5.4	3.7	10.8	10.3	16.1	13.9	60.5	7.8	9.8	22.3	86.5	44.0
Architecture	0.4	0.5	2.7	4.5	3.1	5.0	14.2	5.3	2.4	9.2	19.7	19.4
Social Sciences	2.3	2.7	12.2	10.0	14.5	12.7	54.0	6.1	2.0	9.1	70.6	27.8
Business & Administrative Studies	1.0	1.9	17.9	30.7	18.9	32.5	65.7	6.7	12.7	27.5	97.3	66.7
Mass Communication & Documentation	0.1	0.2	1.5	1.3	1.6	1.5	11.4	0.4	1.3	0.9	14.3	2.8
Languages	1.0	1.2	2.0	1.6	3.0	2.8	20.3	1.3	2.0	12.4	25.4	16.5
Historical and Philosophical Studies	1.4	2.0	2.2	4.0	3.7	6.0	21.4	2.1	0.5	10.1	25.6	18.3
Creative Arts & Design	0.6	0.8	2.9	1.8	3.5	2.6	38.2	1.4	5.9	3.7	47.6	7.7
Education[7]	0.3	1.9	8.8	16.4	9.1	18.4	6.1	1.5	1.1	11.1	16.3	31.0
Other subjects[8]	-	-	-	9.2	-	9.2	2.9	0.9	2.1	75.7	5.0	85.8
Unknown[6]	-	-	-	0.1	-	0.1	2.5	0.6	8.7	8.0	11.7	10.1
All subjects	25.0	24.2	79.8	111.1	104.8	135.3	461.1	46.4	72.8	214.1	639.1	397.1
Females												
Medicine & Dentistry	1.6	1.7	1.6	3.3	3.2	5.0	18.9	-	0.2	0.1	22.3	5.1
Allied Medicine	1.2	1.7	3.6	18.3	4.9	20.2	48.6	26.2	59.9	64.6	113.4	110.7
Biological Sciences	3.9	2.6	3.8	5.3	7.7	8.0	57.5	3.1	1.1	2.2	66.3	13.3
Vet. Science, Agriculture & related	0.4	0.4	0.7	0.7	1.1	1.1	6.6	0.3	2.2	1.6	10.0	3.0
Physical Sciences	2.3	1.1	2.3	1.4	4.6	2.4	18.9	0.8	0.3	1.4	23.8	4.6
Mathematical and Computing Sciences	0.8	0.5	3.6	3.5	4.4	3.9	23.0	1.9	2.5	11.4	29.9	17.2
Engineering & Technology	1.4	0.8	2.5	1.8	3.9	2.6	11.3	0.7	1.3	1.8	16.6	5.1
Architecture	0.2	0.2	1.8	2.5	2.0	2.7	5.7	1.4	0.6	2.5	8.2	6.6
Social Sciences	2.1	2.4	15.2	14.6	17.2	17.0	79.1	10.0	7.4	26.7	103.7	53.7
Business & Administrative Studies	0.7	1.1	15.1	27.8	15.8	28.8	69.4	8.9	15.5	46.6	100.8	84.4
Mass Communication & Documentation	0.2	0.2	2.9	2.6	3.0	2.8	17.3	0.8	1.1	1.6	21.5	5.2
Languages	1.5	1.6	4.1	3.4	5.6	5.0	52.9	3.1	2.5	19.9	61.0	28.0
Historical and Philosophical Studies	1.1	1.4	2.6	4.9	3.6	6.3	26.5	3.5	1.1	20.1	31.2	29.9
Creative Arts & Design	0.6	0.6	4.1	2.7	4.6	3.4	58.7	2.8	7.7	7.8	71.0	14.0
Education[7]	0.5	2.5	20.3	40.6	20.8	43.0	26.5	5.3	1.8	27.8	49.0	76.1
Other subjects[8]	-	-	-	7.5	-	7.5	4.5	1.8	2.0	108.7	6.6	118.0
Unknown[6]	-	-	0.1	0.3	0.1	0.3	3.9	1.0	8.1	13.2	12.4	16.3
All subjects	18.5	18.6	84.2	141.1	102.6	159.7	529.3	71.5	115.4	358.0	747.6	591.1

1 Higher Education Statistics Agency (HESA) higher education institutions include Open University students. Part-time figures include dormant modes, those writing up at home and on sabbaticals.
2 Full-time includes sandwich. Part-time comprises both day and evening, including block release and open/distance learning.
3 For HE students in further education institutions in England, includes those areas of learning which cannot be allocated to specific subject groups shown.
4 FE institution figures for England include Learning and Skills Council (LSC) funded students only.

5 Figures for higher education (HE) institutions are based on the HESA July 'standard registration' count. Figures for further education (FE) institutions (other than in Scotland FE colleges) are snapshots counted at a particular point in the year [November for FE institutions in England and Northern Ireland, and December for FE institutions in Wales]. Students starting courses after these dates will not therefore be counted. Figures for Scotland, however, are whole year (not snapshot) enrolments (rather than headcounts).
6 Includes data for higher education students in further education institutions in Wales which cannot be split by level.
7 Including ITT and INSET.
8 Includes Combined and general categories.

Source: Education Departments: 01325 392754

Students[1] obtaining higher education qualifications:[2] by level, sex and subject group, 2002/03

United Kingdom

Thousands

	Sub-degree[3]	First degree	Postgraduate			Total higher education
			PhD and equivalent	Other	Total	
All persons						
Medicine & Dentistry	0.1	6.1	0.9	1.7	2.7	8.9
Subjects Allied to Medicine	27.8	22.3	0.8	5.8	6.5	56.6
Biological Sciences	1.5	23.2	1.9	3.8	5.7	30.5
Vet. Science, Agriculture & related	1.2	2.7	0.3	0.9	1.1	5.0
Physical Sciences	1.0	12.1	1.8	2.7	4.5	17.6
Mathematical & Computer Sciences	6.2	22.5	0.6	7.8	8.5	37.2
Engineering & Technology	4.0	18.8	1.7	6.7	8.3	31.1
Architecture, Building & Planning	1.8	6.3	0.1	3.2	3.3	11.4
Social Sciences[4]	9.2	35.9	1.2	20.1	21.3	66.5
Business & Financial Studies	11.0	38.7	0.5	27.1	27.6	77.3
Librarianship & Info Science	0.8	7.2	-	3.0	3.0	11.0
Languages	2.5	19.7	0.7	3.8	4.6	26.8
Humanities	1.0	13.1	0.7	3.4	4.1	18.2
Creative Arts & Design	3.9	26.1	0.3	4.8	5.0	35.0
Education[5]	7.6	9.3	0.5	32.1	32.6	49.6
Combined, gen.	14.8	9.3	-	4.8	4.8	28.9
All subjects	94.4	273.4	11.8	131.9	143.7	511.5
Males						
Medicine and Dentistry	-	2.8	0.4	0.7	1.2	4.0
Subjects Allied to Medicine	3.3	4.2	0.3	1.4	1.8	9.3
Biological Sciences	0.7	8.0	0.8	1.3	2.1	10.8
Vet. Science, Agriculture & related	0.5	1.0	0.1	0.4	0.6	2.1
Physical Sciences	0.7	6.9	1.2	1.4	2.6	10.2
Mathematical & Computer Sciences	4.6	16.3	0.5	5.4	5.9	26.7
Engineering & Technology	3.6	15.7	1.4	5.4	6.7	26.0
Architecture, Building & Planning	1.3	4.5	0.1	1.9	2.0	7.8
Social Sciences[4]	2.5	14.0	0.7	8.6	9.2	25.7
Business & Financial Studies	4.5	17.5	0.3	14.3	14.6	36.6
Librarianship & Info Science	0.4	2.6	-	1.0	1.0	4.0
Languages	1.0	5.2	0.3	1.1	1.5	7.6
Humanities	0.4	5.7	0.4	1.5	2.0	8.1
Creative Arts & Design	1.8	10.1	0.2	1.9	2.1	14.0
Education[5]	2.1	1.8	0.2	9.0	9.3	13.2
Combined, gen.	5.0	3.9	-	2.8	2.8	11.7
All subjects	32.4	120.3	6.9	58.2	65.1	217.9
Females						
Medicine & Dentistry	0.1	3.3	0.5	1.0	1.5	4.9
Subjects Allied to Medicine	24.5	18.1	0.4	4.4	4.8	47.3
Biological Sciences	0.8	15.2	1.1	2.6	3.7	19.7
Vet. Science, Agriculture & related	0.6	1.7	0.1	0.4	0.6	2.9
Physical Sciences	0.3	5.2	0.6	1.3	1.9	7.4
Mathematical & Computer Sciences	1.6	6.3	0.1	2.4	2.6	10.5
Engineering & Technology	0.4	3.1	0.3	1.3	1.6	5.1
Architecture, Building & Planning	0.5	1.8	-	1.3	1.3	3.6
Social Sciences[4]	6.7	21.9	0.5	11.6	12.1	40.7
Business & Financial Studies	6.4	21.2	0.2	12.9	13.0	40.6
Librarianship & Info Science	0.4	4.6	-	2.0	2.0	7.0
Languages	1.5	14.6	0.4	2.7	3.1	19.2
Humanities	0.6	7.4	0.3	1.9	2.1	10.1
Creative Arts & Design	2.1	16.0	0.1	2.8	2.9	21.0
Education[5]	5.5	7.5	0.3	23.1	23.4	36.4
Combined, gen.	9.7	5.4	-	2.0	2.0	17.2
All subjects	61.9	153.1	4.9	73.7	78.6	293.6

1 Includes students on Open University courses.
2 Includes higher education in higher education institutions in the UK only. Excludes qualifications from the private sector and higher education qualifications in further education institutions (approximately 6% of the total number of students).

3 Excludes students who successfully completed courses for which formal qualifications are not awarded.
4 Includes Law.
5 Includes ITT and INSET.

Source: Education Departments: 01325 392754

6.11 Qualified teachers: by type of school and sex

	Public sector mainstream schools		Non-maintained mainstream schools	All special schools	Total
	Nursery and primary	Secondary[1]			
All full-time teachers					
Great Britain					
1990/91	200.3	223.2	44.9	18.2	486.6
1996/97	202.8	211.4	48.2	16.3	478.7
United Kingdom					
1998/99	210.8	221.7	50.5	16.7	499.7
1999/00[2]	211.1	223.0	51.2	16.6	502.0
2000/01[3,4,5]	211.2	225.7	52.3	16.5	505.7
2001/02[3]	211.2	227.1	52.8	16.3	507.3
2002/03[7]	209.0	230.5	53.6	17.1	510.2
of which:					
England and Wales[6]	179.5	197.3	51.0	14.3	442.1
Scotland	21.5	23.1	2.5	2.1	49.1
Northern Ireland	8.1	10.1	0.1	0.7	19.0
Full-time male teachers					
Great Britain					
1990/91	35.8	116.0	20.6	5.8	178.2
1996/97	33.0	101.7	20.6	5.1	160.4
United Kingdom					
1998/99	33.0	103.4	20.8	5.1	162.4
1999/00[2]	32.6	102.9	21.1	5.0	161.6
2000/01[3,4,5]	32.1	102.9	21.3	5.0	161.3
2001/02[3]	31.8	102.6	21.5	4.9	160.8
2002/03[7]	31.4	102.6	21.6	5.1	160.7
of which:					
England and Wales[6]	28.4	88.1	20.6	4.5	141.6
Scotland	1.6	10.4	1.0	0.5	13.5
Northern Ireland	1.4	4.0	-	0.1	5.6
Full-time female teachers					
Great Britain					
1990/91	164.5	107.1	24.3	12.4	308.4
1996/97	169.8	109.7	27.6	11.2	318.3
United Kingdom					
1998/99[3]	177.8	118.3	29.6	11.6	337.3
1999/00[2]	178.5	120.1	30.2	11.6	340.4
2000/01[3,4,5]	179.1	122.8	30.9	11.6	344.4
2001/02[3]	179.4	124.5	31.2	11.4	346.5
2002/03[7]	177.7	127.9	32.0	12.0	349.6
of which:					
England and Wales[6]	151.1	109.2	30.4	9.8	300.5
Scotland	19.9	12.6	1.5	1.6	35.7
Northern Ireland	6.7	6.0	0.1	0.6	13.4
All full time equivalents (FTE) of part-time teachers					
Great Britain					
1990/91	..	..	..	..	30.0
1996/97	17.8	15.7	9.4	1.4	44.3
United Kingdom					
1998/99	19.7	16.8	9.8	1.5	47.8
1999/00[2]	20.0	17.3	10.3	1.6	49.2
2000/01[3,4,5]	21.9	16.7	10.2	1.6	50.4
2001/02[3]	23.4	17.4	10.4	1.8	53.0
2002/03[7]	24.0	17.8	11.1	1.7	54.6

1 From 1993/94 excludes sixth form colleges in England and Wales which were reclassified as further education colleges on 1 April 1993.
2 Includes 1998/99 data for Northern Ireland.
3 Includes revised data.
4 Includes 1999/00 pre-school data for Scotland.
5 Includes 2001/02 data for Northern Ireland.

6 A gender breakdown of public sector teachers in England and Wales is only available from the Database of Teachers Records (DTR) where some in service teachers may be shown as not in service because their service details are not recorded. A complete coverage of teachers in England and Wales is available from the Form 618G survey, and published in *Statistics of Education: School workforce in England (including teachers pay for England and Wales).*
7 Provisional. Includes 2001/02 pre-school and 2003/04 school data for Scotland

Source: Education Departments: 01325 392754

Labour market

Chapter 7

Labour market

Labour Force Survey

(Tables 7.1 to 7.3, 7.6, 7.8 to 7.10, 7.12 and 7.15 to 7.17)

Background

The LFS is the largest regular household survey in the United Kingdom. LFS interviews are conducted continuously throughout the year. In any three-month period, a nationally representative sample of approximately 102,000 people aged 16 or over in around 57,000 households are interviewed. Each household is interviewed five times, at three-monthly intervals. The initial interview is done face-to-face by an interviewer visiting the address. The other interviews are done by telephone wherever possible. The survey asks a series of questions about respondents' personal circumstances and their labour market activity. Most questions refer to activity in the week before the interview.

The concepts and definitions used in the LFS are agreed by the International Labour Organisation (ILO) – an agency of the United Nations. The definitions are used by European Union member countries and members of the Organisation for Economic Co-operation and Development (OECD).

The Labour Force Survey was carried out every two years from 1973 to 1983. The ILO definition was first used in 1984. This was also the first year in which the survey was conducted on an annual basis with results available for every spring quarter (representing an average of the period from March to May). The survey moved to a continuous basis in spring 1992 in Great Britain and in winter 1994/95 in Northern Ireland, with average quarterly results published four times a year for seasonal quarters: spring (March to May), summer (June to August), autumn (September to November) and winter (December to February). From April 1998, results are published 12 times a year for the average of three consecutive months.

The LFS collects information on a sample of the population. To convert this information to give estimates for the population the data must be grossed. This is achieved by calculating weighting factors (often referred to simply as weights) which can be applied to each sampled individual in such a way that the weighted-up results match estimates or projections of the total population in terms of age distribution, sex, and region of residence.

Strengths and limitations of the LFS

The LFS produces coherent labour market information on the basis of internationally standard concepts and definitions. It is a rich source of data on a wide variety of labour market and personal characteristics. It is the most suitable source for making comparisons between countries. The LFS is designed so that households interviewed in each three-month period constitute a representative sample of UK households. The survey covers those living in private households and nurses in National Health Service accommodation. Students living in halls of residence have been included since 1992 as information about them is collected at their parents' address.

However the LFS has its limitations. It is a sample survey and is therefore subject to sampling variability. The survey does not include people living in institutions such as hostels or residential homes. 'Proxy' reporting (when members of the household are not present at the interview, another member of the household answers the questions on their behalf) can affect the quality of information on topics such as earnings, hours worked, benefit receipt and qualifications. Around one third of interviews are conducted 'by proxy', usually by a spouse or partner but sometimes by a parent or other near relation.

Sampling Variability

Survey estimates are prone to *sampling variability*. The easiest way to explain this concept is by example. In the September to November 1997 period, ILO unemployment in Great Britain (seasonally adjusted) stood at 1,847,000. If we drew another sample for the same period we could get a different result, perhaps 1,900,000 or 1,820,000.

In theory, we could draw many samples, and each would give a different result. This is because each sample would be made up of different people who would give different answers to the questions. The spread of these results is the sampling variability. Sampling variability is determined by a number of factors including the sample size, the variability of the population from which the sample is drawn and the sample design. Once we know the sampling variability we can calculate a range of values about the sample estimate that represents the expected variation with a given level of assurance. This is called a confidence interval. For a 95 per cent confidence interval we expect that in 95 per cent of the samples (19 times out of 20) the confidence interval will contain the true value that would be obtained by surveying the entire population. For the example given above, we can be 95 per cent confident that the true value was in the range 1,791,000 to 1,903,000.

Small estimates

Some Labour Force Survey estimates are based on small sample sizes and are therefore subject to a higher degree of sampling variability. They should therefore be treated with caution

Non-Response

Non-response can introduce bias to a survey, particularly if the people not responding have characteristics that are different from those who do respond. The LFS has a response rate of around 75 per cent to the first interview and at each subsequent intrview, a response rate of approximately 90 per cent is achieved. Any bias from non-response is minimised by *weighting* the results.

Weighting (or grossing) converts sample data to represent the full population. In the LFS, the data are weighted separately by age, sex and area of residence to population estimates based on the Census. Weighting also adjusts for people not in the survey and thus minimises non-response bias.

Labour Force Survey Concepts and Definitions

Discouraged workers – a sub-group of the economically inactive population, defined as those neither in employment nor unemployed (on the ILO measure) who said they would like a job and whose main reason for not seeking work was because they believed there were no jobs available.

Economically active – people aged 16 and over who are either in employment or ILO unemployed.

Economic activity rate – the percentage of people aged 16 and over who are economically active.

Economically inactive – people who are neither in employment nor unemployed. This group includes, for example, all those who were looking after a home or retired.

Employment – people aged 16 or over who did at least one hour of paid work in the reference week (whether as an employee or self-employed); those who had a job that they were temporarily away from (on holiday, for example); those on Government-supported training and employment programmes (from spring 1983); and those doing unpaid family work (from spring 1992).

Employees – the division between employees and self-employed is based on survey respondents' own assessment of their employment status.

Full Time – the classification of employees, self-employed and unpaid family workers in their main job as full-time or part-time is on the basis of self-assessment. Up until autumn 1995, people who were on government work-related training programmes are classified as full-time or part-time according to whether their usual hours of work per week were over 30 or 30 and under; from winter 1995/96 onwards, the full-time/part-time classification for this group has been changed to self-assessment, in line with the other groups outlined above. People on Government-supported training and employment programmes who are at college in the survey reference week are classified, by convention, as part-time.

Government-supported training and employment programmes – comprise all people aged 16 and over participating in one of the Government's employment and training programmes (Youth Training, Training for Work and Community Action), together with those on similar programmes administered by Training and Enterprise Councils in England and Wales, or Local Enterprise Companies in Scotland.

Hours worked – respondents to the LFS are asked a series of questions enabling the identification of both their usual hours and their actual hours. Total hours include overtime (paid and unpaid) and exclude lunchbreaks.

Unemployment – Unemployment figures from the Labour Force Survey (LFS), which are based upon the International Labour Organisation (ILO) definition, were re-labelled 'unemployment' rather than 'ILO unemployment' in January 2003. This emphasises that the LFS figures provide the official and only internationally comparable measure of unemployment in the UK. For more details see the National Statistics website at *www.statistics.gov.uk/ cci/ nugget.asp?id=251*

The International Labour Office (ILO) measure of unemployment used throughout this supplement refers to people without a job who were available to start work in the two weeks following their LFS interview and who had either looked for work in the four weeks prior to interview or were waiting to start a job they had already obtained. This definition of unemployment is in accordance with that adopted by the 13th International Conference of Labour Statisticians, further clarified at the 14th ICLS, and promulgated by the ILO in its publications.

Unemployment (rate) – the percentage of economically active people who are unemployed on the ILO measure.

Unemployment (duration) – defined as the shorter of the following two periods: (a) duration of active search for work; and (b) length of time since employment.

Labour market

Part-Time – see full-time

Second jobs – jobs which LFS respondents hold in addition to a main full-time or part-time job.

Self-employment – See Employees

Temporary employees – in the LFS these are defined as those employees who say that their main job is non permanent in one of the following ways: fixed period contract; agency temping; casual work; seasonal work; other temporary work.

Unpaid Family Workers – the separate identification from spring 1992 of this group in the LFS is in accordance with international recommendations. The group comprises persons doing unpaid work for a business they own or for a business that a relative owns.

Distribution of workforce

(Table 7.4)

Claimant unemployed – those people who were claiming unemployment-related benefits (contributions or income related Jobseeker's Allowance and/or National Insurance credits) at Jobcentre Plus local offices on the day of the monthly count. The seasonally-adjusted claimant unemployment series allows for all relevant changes which, unless adjusted for, would distort comparisons over time.

Workforce jobs (formerly workforce in employment) – comprises employee jobs, self-employment jobs (from the Labour Force Survey), HM Forces and government supported trainees.

HM Forces (provided by Ministry of Defence) – represent the total number of UK service personnel, male and female, in HM Regular Forces, wherever serving and including those on leave.

Self-employed jobs – estimates are based on the results of the Labour Force Survey. The Northern Ireland estimates are not seasonally adjusted.

Government-supported trainees – include all participants on government training and employment programmes who are receiving some work experience on their placement but who do not have a contract of employment (those with a contract are included in the employee jobs series). The numbers are not subject to seasonal adjustment.

Persons employed in local authorities

The old table 7.8 (Annual Abstract 2004) on Persons employed by local authorities has been dropped from this edition. The methodology underlying this has been reviewed as part of the review of public sector employment, and has been found to be below the standard required for publication.

Jobseekers allowance claimant count

(Tables 7.13 and 7.14)

This is a count of all those people who are claiming Jobseeker's Allowance (JSA) at Jobcentre Plus local offices. People claiming JSA must declare that they are out of work capable of, available for and actively seeking work during the week in which the claim is made. All people claiming Jobseeker's Allowance (JSA) on the day of the monthly count are included in the claimant count, irrespective of whether they are actually receiving benefits.

Economically inactive

(Table 7.17)

An improved Table 7.17 is introduced into the *Annual Abstract*. The new format provides a clearer, more easily readable table of reasons for inactivity by showing an aggregated total for both those who do not want a job and those who do, by reason.

Labour disputes

(Table 7.18)

These figures exclude details of stoppages involving fewer than ten workers or lasting less than one day except any in which the aggregate number of working days lost is 100 or more. There may be some under-recording of small or short stoppages; this would have much more effect on the total of stoppages than of working days lost. Some stoppages which affected more than one industry group have been counted under each of the industries but only once in the totals. Stoppages have been classified using Standard Industrial Classification (SIC) 1992.

The figures for working days lost and workers involved have been rounded and consequently the sum of the constituent items may not agree with the totals. Classifications by size are based on the full duration of stoppages where these continue into the following year. Working days lost per thousand employees are based on the latest available mid-year (June) estimates of employee jobs.

Earnings

(Tables 7.19 to 7.24)

The total gross remuneration employees receive before any statutory deductions (tax, national insurance). Income in kind and pension funds are excluded.

Annual Survey of Hours and Earnings

(Tables 7.19, 7.20, 7.23 and 7.24)

The Annual Survey of Hours and Earnings (ASHE) is a new survey that has been developed to replace the New Earnings Survey (NES). The ASHE includes improvements to the coverage of employees and to the weighting of earnings estimates. The data variables collected remain broadly the same, although an improved questionnaire will be introduced for the 2005 survey. The change in methodology means that statistics on pay and hours published from the ASHE, including the calculation of ONS's low pay statistics, are discontinuous with previous NES surveys.

To improve coverage and make the survey more representative, supplementary information was collected for the 2004 ASHE survey on businesses not registered for VAT and for people who changed or started new jobs between sample selection and the survey reference period. The 2004 ASHE results are therefore discontinuous with the results for 2003, for which no supplementary information was collected. However, for 2004 two sets of results are available; the headline results that include supplementary information and results that exclude this information. These second set of results are given solely for comparison to earlier results.

The ASHE methodology includes imputation and weighting, the main impact of these changes when applied to existing NES data for 1998 to 2003 are:

To increase the estimates of the level of average weekly pay over estimates published from the NES.

For males the increase in estimates of earnings is more than the increase for females. In particular this affects hourly pay excluding overtime, which is used in the calculation of the ONS's preferred measure of the gender pay gap. The estimate of hourly pay for males is increased more then the estimate for females, which widens the estimate of the gap between male and female hourly pay.

Estimates of the level of earnings for people working in London are increased more than estimates for other regions. This widens the estimate of the difference in pay between London and other regions of the UK.

Average earnings index

(Tables 7.21 and 7.22)

The Average Earnings Index (AEI) is designed to measure changes in the level of earnings, i.e. wage inflation in Great Britain. Average earnings are calculated as the total wages and salaries paid by firms, divided by the number of employees paid. Like all indices, changes are measured against a base year, whose index value is set to 100. The current base year is 2000 for Tables 7.21 and 7.22.

Users should note that the data contained in Table 7.22 of the *Annual Abstract* since 2003 are not comparable with that published up until 2002. Table 7.22 now shows the set of 20 industry sectors. That better reflect the current state of the economy, and supersedes the previous set of 26 industry sectors. The new series are available in the format of excluding bonus index, including bonus index, and an annual percentage change for including and excluding bonuses. An article covering the reasons for the change can be found on our *website www.statistics.gov.uk/labour.*

The *AEI* is published monthly in the *Labour Market Statistics First Release.* The main indicator of growth, the headline rate, is based on the annual change in the seasonally adjusted index values for the latest three months compared with the same period a year ago. The use of a three-month average reduces the level of volatility seen in the data on a month-on-month basis.

Strengths of the AEI

The AEI, based on monthly survey data, is a timely indicator of changes in the level of earnings.

Limitations of the AEI

The index is not adjusted for any changes in the composition of the workforce such as changes in the share of full-time and part-time workers, or in the share of skilled and unskilled workers. Similarly, the index does not account for changes in the number of hours worked, or any temporary factors that affect earnings.

The sample of the Monthly Wages and Salaries Survey on which the AEI is based is not designed to provide information on the level of earnings. The sample is not completely representative of the economy as firms with fewer than 20 employees are excluded, as are the earnings of self employed persons.

The AEI only covers earnings in Great Britain as earnings information is not collected for Northern Ireland and regional data are not available.

Labour market

Vacancies at jobcentres

(Table 7.25)

Publication of the jobcentre vacancy statistics has been deferred. This publication contains vacancy data only up to April 2001 because the figures from May 2001 are affected by the introduction of Employer Direct. Employer Direct is a major change, which involved the transfer the vacancy taking process from local Jobcentres to regional Customer Service Centres. In addition, the numbers of notified vacancies appear to be substantially affected by a drive (from April 2003) by Jobcentre Plus to market their services and increase notifications from many employers in chosen sectors. Recent changes in these figures would therefore not necessarily signify developments in the labour market. ONS and Department for Work and Pensions are continuing to monitor and review the data with a view to publishing more statistics when it is appropriate to do so. Vacancies notified to and placings made by jobcentres do not represent the total number of vacancies/engagements in the economy. Inflow, outflow and placings figures are collected for four or five-week periods between count dates; the figures in this table are converted to a standard $4\frac{1}{3}$ week month. Table excludes vacancies on Enterprise Ulster and Action for Community Employment (ACE) which are included in the seasonally adjusted figures for Northern Ireland.

> *Vacancy* – This is a job opportunity notified by an employer to a Jobcentre.

> *Unfilled vacancy* – (also known as 'Stock of vacancies') This is the number of vacancies which have not been filled or cancelled on the count date.

> *Inflow of vacancy* – (also known as 'Notified vacancies') This is the number of job opportunities notified by employers to Jobcentres in the period between two successive count dates.

> *Outflow of vacancy* – This is a derived statistic which represents the total of vacancies filled plus cancelled between count dates. This concept can also be expressed as 'vacancy stock' at the beginning of the period plus notified vacancies (inflows) minus 'vacancy stock' at the end of the period.

> *Placings* – This is the number of Jobseekers placed into employment by individual Jobcentres.

Trade unions

(Table 7.26)

The statistics relate to all organisations of employees known to Certification Officer with head offices in the United Kingdom that fall within the appropriate definition of a trade union in the 1992 Trade Union and Labour Relations Act. Included in the data are home and overseas membership figures of contributory and non-contributory members. Employment status of members is not provided and the figures may therefore include some people who are self-employed, unemployed or retired.

The membership part of this table was revised in 2001, so that statistics presented here are on a consistent basis with the GB table produced by the Certification Officer in his Annual Report and with tables produced in the annual *Labour Market Trends* Trade Union article. There is a break in the time series for the figures in this table between the years 1988 (contained within previous publications) and 1989. GB data for 1989–95 are DTI analyses of annual returns, with 1996–1999 as published in the Certification Officer's Annual Report. Data for Northern Ireland for 1989–1991 are DTI analyses of annual returns, with 1992–1999 from the Certification Officer's Annual Report.

7.1 Labour force summary:[1] by sex
United Kingdom
Spring each year. Seasonally adjusted

Thousands and percentages

	Total[2]	Total economically active	Total in employment	Total unemployed	Economically inactive	Economic activity rate 16-59/64[3]	Employment rate all aged 16 and over[4]	Employment rate 16-59/64[5]	Unemployment rate[6]
			All aged 16 and over			Percentages			
All									
	MGSL	MGSF	MGRZ	MGSC	MGSI	MGSO	MGSR	MGSU	MGSX
1994	45 072	28 201	25 451	2 750	16 871	78.4	56.5	70.6	9.8
1995	45 189	28 202	25 731	2 470	16 988	78.2	56.9	71.2	8.8
1996	45 342	28 345	26 000	2 344	16 997	78.4	57.3	71.8	8.3
1997	45 497	28 492	26 448	2 045	17 004	78.4	58.1	72.7	7.2
1998	45 661	28 497	26 713	1 783	17 164	78.3	58.5	73.3	6.3
1999	45 862	28 811	27 052	1 759	17 051	78.7	59.0	73.8	6.1
2000	46 107	29 071	27 434	1 638	17 035	78.9	59.5	74.4	5.6
2001	46 413	29 122	27 691	1 431	17 292	78.5	59.7	74.6	4.9
2002	46 704	29 404	27 861	1 542	17 300	78.6	59.7	74.4	5.2
2003	46 995	29 648	28 159	1 489	17 347	78.7	59.9	74.7	5.0
2004	47 293	29 821	28 382	1 438	17 473	78.6	60.0	74.7	4.8
Men									
	MGSM	MGSG	MGSA	MGSD	MGSJ	MGSP	MGSS	MGSV	MGSY
1994	21 646	15 709	13 903	1 806	5 938	85.5	64.2	75.5	11.5
1995	21 710	15 682	14 091	1 591	6 028	85.0	64.9	76.3	10.1
1996	21 794	15 686	14 163	1 524	6 108	84.9	65.0	76.6	9.7
1997	21 876	15 687	14 405	1 283	6 189	84.7	65.8	77.7	8.2
1998	21 961	15 647	14 571	1 076	6 314	84.2	66.3	78.3	6.9
1999	22 071	15 774	14 704	1 070	6 297	84.4	66.6	78.6	6.8
2000	22 202	15 882	14 908	974	6 320	84.6	67.1	79.3	6.1
2001	22 377	15 867	15 020	847	6 510	84.0	67.1	79.5	5.3
2002	22 550	15 969	15 051	918	6 581	83.9	66.7	79.0	5.7
2003	22 723	16 159	15 257	901	6 564	84.1	67.1	79.3	5.6
2004	22 898	16 179	15 351	829	6 719	83.6	67.0	79.3	5.1
Women									
	MGSN	MGSH	MGSB	MGSE	MGSK	MGSQ	MGST	MGSW	MGSZ
1994	23 425	12 492	11 548	944	10 933	70.9	49.3	65.4	7.6
1995	23 479	12 520	11 640	879	10 959	70.9	49.6	65.8	7.0
1996	23 547	12 658	11 838	820	10 889	71.4	50.3	66.7	6.5
1997	23 621	12 805	12 043	762	10 815	71.8	51.0	67.4	6.0
1998	23 700	12 850	12 143	707	10 850	72.0	51.2	67.9	5.5
1999	23 791	13 037	12 348	689	10 754	72.5	51.9	68.6	5.3
2000	23 905	13 189	12 526	663	10 716	72.9	52.4	69.1	5.0
2001	24 036	13 255	12 672	583	10 781	72.7	52.7	69.4	4.4
2002	24 154	13 435	12 810	624	10 719	73.0	53.0	69.6	4.6
2003	24 272	13 489	12 901	588	10 783	73.0	53.2	69.7	4.4
2004	24 395	13 642	13 032	610	10 754	73.2	53.4	69.8	4.5

1 See chapter text. The data in this table have been adjusted to reflect the latest 2001 Census population data.
2 Population in private households and student halls of residence.
3 Economically active of working age as a percentage of all persons of working age.
4 Total employed as a percentage of all persons 16 and over.
5 Total employed of working age as a percentage of all persons of working age (men 16-64, women 16-59).
6 Total unemployed as a percentage of all economically active.

Source: Labour Force Survey, Office for National Statistics

7.2 Employment status: full-time/part-time, second jobs and temporary employees[1]
United Kingdom
Spring each year. Seasonally adjusted

Thousands

	All in employment[2]					Total employment[2]		Employees[2]		Self-employed[2]			
	Total	Employees	Self employed	Unpaid family workers	Government supported training and employment programmes[3]	Full-time	Part-time	Full-time	Part-time	Full-time	Part-time	Workers with second jobs[4]	Temporary employees
All													
	MGRZ	MGRN	MGRQ	MGRT	MGRW	YCBE	YCBH	YCBK	YCBN	YCBQ	YCBT	YCBW	YCBZ
1994	25 451	21 483	3 494	145	329	19 219	6 233	16 206	5 277	2 829	666	1 135	1 473
1995	25 731	21 752	3 562	139	279	19 449	6 282	16 405	5 347	2 869	692	1 279	1 607
1996	26 000	22 155	3 475	127	244	19 485	6 516	16 548	5 607	2 772	703	1 282	1 646
1997	26 448	22 635	3 479	118	216	19 788	6 660	16 888	5 746	2 744	735	1 242	1 760
1998	26 713	23 052	3 386	103	172	20 001	6 712	17 243	5 809	2 632	754	1 169	1 714
1999	27 052	23 485	3 311	101	156	20 249	6 803	17 561	5 923	2 581	730	1 262	1 681
2000	27 434	23 922	3 260	111	141	20 515	6 918	17 884	6 038	2 526	734	1 172	1 696
2001	27 691	24 161	3 281	99	150	20 708	6 983	18 026	6 135	2 578	703	1 166	1 704
2002	27 861	24 319	3 339	98	106	20 796	7 066	18 138	6 181	2 583	756	1 130	1 572
2003	28 159	24 448	3 530	88	93	20 867	7 292	18 127	6 321	2 678	852	1 130	1 505
2004	28 382	24 526	3 628	104	124	20 997	7 385	18 137	6 389	2 781	848	1 075	1 492
Men													
	MGSA	MGRO	MGRR	MGRU	MGRX	YCBF	YCBI	YCBL	YCBO	YCBR	YCBU	YCBX	YCCA
1994	13 903	11 065	2 576	49	213	12 823	1 080	10 358	706	2 351	225	499	645
1995	14 091	11 223	2 647	43	177	12 959	1 132	10 454	770	2 403	245	534	738
1996	14 163	11 409	2 560	43	151	12 956	1 207	10 551	858	2 314	246	539	727
1997	14 405	11 684	2 551	38	132	13 120	1 285	10 740	944	2 285	266	543	798
1998	14 571	11 967	2 464	29	111	13 274	1 296	11 014	953	2 184	279	509	757
1999	14 704	12 128	2 438	36	103	13 361	1 343	11 125	1 003	2 169	269	529	790
2000	14 908	12 432	2 354	37	85	13 537	1 371	11 402	1 029	2 073	281	489	770
2001	15 020	12 478	2 406	37	99	13 636	1 384	11 422	1 056	2 143	263	476	776
2002	15 051	12 504	2 454	31	62	13 602	1 449	11 407	1 098	2 150	304	465	723
2003	15 257	12 594	2 577	31	55	13 659	1 598	11 400	1 194	2 219	358	461	685
2004	15 351	12 569	2 665	43	74	13 718	1 632	11 355	1 213	2 312	354	458	696
Women													
	MGSB	MGRP	MGRS	MGRV	MGRY	YCBG	YCBJ	YCBM	YCBP	YCBS	YCBV	YCBY	YCCB
1994	11 548	10 418	918	96	116	6 395	5 153	5 848	4 570	477	441	636	828
1995	11 640	10 529	914	96	101	6 490	5 150	5 952	4 577	467	448	745	870
1996	11 838	10 746	915	84	93	6 529	5 309	5 997	4 750	458	457	743	920
1997	12 043	10 951	928	80	84	6 668	5 375	6 148	4 803	459	469	699	962
1998	12 143	11 085	922	74	62	6 727	5 416	6 230	4 856	448	474	660	957
1999	12 348	11 357	873	66	53	6 888	5 461	6 437	4 920	412	461	733	891
2000	12 526	11 491	906	73	56	6 979	5 547	6 482	5 009	453	453	683	926
2001	12 672	11 683	875	62	51	7 073	5 599	6 604	5 079	435	440	690	928
2002	12 810	11 814	885	67	44	7 193	5 617	6 732	5 083	432	452	665	848
2003	12 901	11 855	953	57	37	7 207	5 694	6 728	5 127	460	493	670	820
2004	13 032	11 957	963	62	50	7 279	5 753	6 782	5 176	469	494	617	796

1 See chapter text. The data in this table have been adjusted to reflect the latest 2001 Census population data.
2 People whose main job is full or part-time.
3 Those on employment and training programmes are classified as in employment. Some of those on programmes may consider themselves to be employees or self employed so appear in other categories.
4 Second jobs reported in LFS in addition to person's main full or part-time job.

Source: Labour Force Survey, Office for National Statistics

7.3 Employment: by sex and age[1]
United Kingdom
At Spring each year. Seasonally adjusted

Thousands and percentages

	All aged 16 and over	16-59/64	16-17	18-24	16-24	25-34	35-49	50-64 (m) 50-59 (f)	65+ (m) 60+ (f)
Thousands									
All									
	MGRZ	YBSE	YBTO	YBTR	PXLA	YBTU	YBTX	MGUW	MGUZ
1996	26 000	25 230	659	3 286	3 945	6 853	9 514	4 918	770
1997	26 448	25 645	696	3 232	3 928	6 998	9 561	5 158	803
1998	26 713	25 938	694	3 199	3 893	6 972	9 675	5 398	776
1999	27 052	26 235	675	3 205	3 880	6 942	9 827	5 585	818
2000	27 434	26 602	670	3 265	3 935	6 887	10 044	5 737	832
2001	27 691	26 872	670	3 292	3 962	6 752	10 222	5 935	820
2002	27 861	26 974	652	3 383	4 035	6 553	10 383	6 003	888
2003	28 159	27 225	658	3 384	4 042	6 389	10 565	6 229	934
2004	28 382	27 388	643	3 510	4 153	6 289	10 669	6 276	995
Men									
	MGSA	YBSF	YBTP	YBTS	PXLB	YBTV	YBTY	MGUX	MGVA
1996	14 163	13 897	333	1 705	2 038	3 793	5 090	2 977	266
1997	14 405	14 137	339	1 696	2 035	3 852	5 123	3 127	268
1998	14 571	14 298	344	1 677	2 021	3 848	5 187	3 243	273
1999	14 704	14 418	332	1 679	2 011	3 799	5 257	3 350	286
2000	14 908	14 623	333	1 715	2 048	3 774	5 387	3 415	285
2001	15 020	14 755	335	1 727	2 062	3 702	5 457	3 534	264
2002	15 051	14 762	321	1 767	2 088	3 586	5 536	3 551	289
2003	15 257	14 921	322	1 779	2 101	3 495	5 641	3 684	336
2004	15 351	15 015	310	1 854	2 164	3 422	5 715	3 714	335
Women									
	MGSB	YBSG	YBTQ	YBTT	PXLC	YBTW	YBTZ	MGUY	MGVB
1996	11 838	11 333	327	1 580	1 907	3 061	4 424	1 941	505
1997	12 043	11 508	357	1 536	1 893	3 146	4 438	2 031	535
1998	12 143	11 640	351	1 522	1 873	3 124	4 488	2 155	503
1999	12 348	11 817	343	1 527	1 870	3 143	4 570	2 234	532
2000	12 526	11 979	337	1 550	1 887	3 113	4 657	2 322	547
2001	12 672	12 116	336	1 565	1 901	3 049	4 765	2 401	556
2002	12 810	12 211	331	1 615	1 946	2 967	4 847	2 451	599
2003	12 901	12 304	336	1 606	1 942	2 894	4 924	2 545	597
2004	13 032	12 372	333	1 655	1 988	2 867	4 955	2 562	660
Rates[2]									
All									
	MGSR	MGSU	YBUA	YBUD	PXLD	YBUG	YBUJ	YBUM	YBUP
1996	57.3	71.8	46.6	65.8	61.5	75.7	79.7	63.5	7.6
1997	58.1	72.7	47.9	66.5	62.2	77.7	79.9	64.5	7.9
1998	58.5	73.3	47.9	66.6	62.1	78.4	80.6	65.4	7.6
1999	59.0	73.8	47.0	66.6	62.1	79.3	81.1	66.1	7.9
2000	59.5	74.4	46.7	67.6	62.8	80.1	81.7	66.7	8.0
2001	59.7	74.6	45.6	67.4	62.3	80.0	81.9	67.9	7.9
2002	59.7	74.4	43.3	68.0	62.2	79.6	81.9	67.8	8.5
2003	59.9	74.7	43.2	66.4	61.0	79.5	82.1	69.8	8.9
2004	60.0	74.7	41.4	67.4	..	79.7	81.9	69.9	9.3
Men									
	MGSS	MGSV	YBUB	YBUE	PXLE	YBUH	YBUK	YBUN	YBUQ
1996	65.0	76.6	46.2	68.3	63.3	84.6	85.9	65.8	7.3
1997	65.8	77.7	45.9	69.8	64.3	86.4	86.4	67.3	7.3
1998	66.3	78.3	46.7	69.9	64.3	87.5	87.3	67.9	7.4
1999	66.6	78.6	45.5	70.0	64.3	87.8	87.6	68.6	7.7
2000	67.1	79.3	45.5	71.3	65.2	88.8	88.6	68.7	7.6
2001	67.1	79.5	44.5	71.0	64.6	88.7	88.4	70.2	6.9
2002	66.7	79.0	41.6	71.1	64.1	88.0	88.3	69.8	7.5
2003	67.1	79.3	41.2	69.6	62.9	87.8	88.7	71.8	8.6
2004	67.0	79.3	39.0	70.8	..	87.5	88.8	71.8	8.5
Women									
	MGST	MGSW	YBUC	YBUF	PXLF	YBUI	YBUL	YBUO	YBUR
1996	50.3	66.7	46.9	63.3	59.7	67.0	73.5	60.2	7.7
1997	51.0	67.4	49.9	63.2	60.2	69.2	73.6	60.6	8.2
1998	51.2	67.9	49.1	63.2	60.0	69.5	74.1	62.1	7.7
1999	51.9	68.6	48.6	63.3	59.9	71.0	74.6	62.8	8.1
2000	52.4	69.1	47.9	64.0	60.4	71.6	74.9	63.8	8.3
2001	52.7	69.4	46.8	63.9	60.0	71.6	75.5	64.7	8.4
2002	53.0	69.6	45.0	64.9	60.3	71.4	75.6	65.1	9.1
2003	53.2	69.7	45.2	63.2	59.2	71.4	75.7	67.0	9.0
2004	53.4	69.8	44.0	64.0	..	72.1	75.2	67.2	9.9

1 See chapter text. The data in this table have been adjusted to reflect the latest 2001 Census population data.
2 Total in employment as a percentage of all persons in the relevant group.

Source: Labour Force Survey, Office for National Statistics

7.4 Distribution of the workforce:[1] by sex
At mid-June each year. Seasonally adjusted

Thousands

		1994	1995	1996	1997	1998	1999	2000	2001	2002	2003	2004
United Kingdom												
Claimant count	BCJD	2 625	2 294	2 135	1 572	1 344	1 263	1 094	962	949	948	849
Males	DPAE	2 016	1 756	1 625	1 208	1 028	969	836	733	719	713	634
Females	DPAF	609	538	509	364	317	294	258	229	230	236	215
Workforce jobs	DYDC	27 307	27 660	28 025	28 426	28 632	29 038	29 431	29 737	29 875	30 213	30 440
Males	KAMS	14 486	14 669	14 729	15 038	15 211	15 553	15 721	15 921	15 945	16 224	16 400
Females	KAMT	12 821	12 991	13 296	13 387	13 421	13 484	13 710	13 816	13 930	13 989	14 040
HM Forces	KAMU	250	230	222	210	210	209	207	204	204	207	206
Males	KAMV	232	214	206	195	194	192	190	188	187	189	188
Females	KAMW	18	16	16	15	16	16	17	17	17	18	18
Self-employment jobs	DYZN	3 736	3 820	3 777	3 724	3 588	3 614	3 518	3 526	3 585	3 801	3 860
Males	KAMZ	2 719	2 776	2 753	2 661	2 571	2 597	2 517	2 547	2 577	2 738	2 794
Females	KANA	1 016	1 044	1 024	1 063	1 017	1 016	1 001	980	1 008	1 063	1 066
Employees jobs	BCAJ	23 005	23 370	23 834	24 320	24 703	25 085	25 588	25 905	25 990	26 105	26 264
Males	KANC	11 335	11 523	11 651	12 077	12 370	12 683	12 941	13 124	13 123	13 237	13 352
Females	KAND	11 670	11 847	12 182	12 243	12 333	12 402	12 646	12 781	12 867	12 868	12 912
of whom												
Total, production and construction industries	KANF	5 195	5 244	5 292	5 358	5 496	5 365	5 341	5 192	4 969	4 817	4 733
Total, all manufacturing industries	KANG	3 971	4 073	4 138	4 151	4 179	4 042	3 951	3 803	3 599	3 415	3 282
Government-supported trainees	KANH	317	240	194	171	131	131	119	101	96	100	109
Males	KANI	199	156	119	105	76	81	73	63	58	60	66
Females	KANJ	118	84	75	66	55	50	46	39	38	40	43
Great Britain												
Claimant count	DPAG	2 527	2 207	2 048	1 510	1 287	1 212	1 052	922	912	913	818
Males	ZSDP	1 940	1 687	1 559	1 159	983	929	804	702	691	686	610
Females	ZSDQ	1 940	1 687	1 559	1 159	983	929	804	702	691	686	610
Workforce jobs	KANQ	26 647	26 965	27 331	27 711	27 909	28 304	28 680	28 973	29 103	29 424	29 642
Males	KANR	14 122	14 289	14 351	14 651	14 819	15 157	15 315	15 508	15 533	15 802	15 974
Females	KANS	12 525	12 677	12 980	13 060	13 090	13 147	13 365	13 465	13 570	13 622	13 667
HM Forces	BCAH	250	230	222	210	210	209	207	204	204	207	206
Males	KANU	232	214	206	195	194	192	190	188	187	189	188
Females	KANV	18	16	16	15	16	16	17	17	17	18	18
Self-employment jobs	KANW	3 650	3 715	3 678	3 622	3 493	3 518	3 418	3 420	3 484	3 691	3 750
Males	KANX	2 645	2 692	2 671	2 579	2 493	2 520	2 435	2 459	2 495	2 648	2 704
Females	KANY	1 005	1 024	1 007	1 043	1 000	998	983	961	989	1 043	1 046
Employee jobs	KANZ	22 447	22 795	23 254	23 722	24 090	24 458	24 946	25 254	25 325	25 434	25 583
Males	KAOA	11 056	11 238	11 365	11 780	12 065	12 372	12 623	12 803	12 798	12 911	13 022
Females	KAOB	11 390	11 558	11 889	11 942	12 024	12 087	12 322	12 450	12 527	12 523	12 562
of whom												
Total, production and construction industries	KAOC	5 070	5 115	5 159	5 217	5 354	5 222	5 197	5 050	4 830	4 684	4 602
Total, all manufacturing industries	KAOD	3 868	3 968	4 034	4 043	4 072	3 936	3 848	3 701	3 502	3 322	3 193
Government-supported trainees	KAOE	301	224	178	157	117	120	110	94	89	93	103
Males	KAOF	189	145	109	96	67	73	67	58	53	55	61
Females	KAOG	112	79	69	61	50	47	43	36	36	38	41

1 See chapter text. The data in this table have not been adjusted to reflect the 2001 Census population data. Totals may include some employees whose industrial classification could not be ascertained.

Source: Earnings and Employment Division, Office for National Statistics: 01633 812318

7.5 Employee jobs: by industry[1]
Standard Industrial Classification 1992
At June each year. Not seasonally adjusted

Thousands

			United Kingdom							Great Britain					
		SIC 1992	1999	2000	2001	2002	2003	2004		1999	2000	2001	2002	2003	2004
All sections	KAOH	A - O	25 058	25 557	25 873	25 965	26 070	26 226	LMAB	24 434	24 917	25 223	25 302	25 401	25 548
Index of production and construction industries	KAOI	C - F	5 366	5 336	5 185	4 961	4 810	4 725	LMAH	5 224	5 193	5 042	4 823	4 677	4 595
Index of production industries	KAOJ	C - E	4 256	4 153	4 009	3 797	3 599	3 457	LMAF	4 145	4 044	3 902	3 694	3 501	3 363
of which, manufacturing industries	KAOK	D	4 051	3 954	3 802	3 597	3 413	3 281	KAPQ	3 946	3 850	3 700	3 499	3 321	3 192
Service industries	KAOL	G - O	19 375	19 900	20 410	20 748	21 032	21 276	LMAJ	18 908	19 418	19 917	20 238	20 511	20 741
Agriculture, hunting and forestry and fishing	KAOM	A/B	318	321	279	256	228	226	KAPS	302	305	264	242	213	211
Agriculture hunting and forestry	KPHI	A	305	310	270	246	221	219	KOVW	290	295	255	231	207	204
Agriculture hunting & related activities	KPHJ	01	297	304	259	235	210	209	KOVX	282	288	245	221	196	195
Fishing	KPHK	B	13	11	9	10	7	7	KOVY	12	11	9	10	7	7
Mining and quarrying	KPHL	C	74	73	72	68	62	58	KOVZ	72	71	70	66	60	56
Mining and quarrying of energy producing materials	KPHM	CA	46	44	43	41	38	34	KOWA	45	43	43	41	37	34
Mining	KAPG	10/12	..	..	..	..	..	..	KOWB	14	13	13	12	10	9
Extraction of crude petroleum	KPHN	11	..	..	..	..	..	..	KOWC	31	31	30	29	27	25
Mining and quarrying except of energy producing materials	KPHO	CB(13/14)	28	29	29	27	24	24	KOWD	27	28	28	25	23	22
Energy and water supply industries	KAOO	C/E	205	200	207	200	186	176	LMAM	199	194	202	195	181	171
Manufacturing	KPHP	D	4 051	3 954	3 802	3 597	3 413	3 281	LMAD	3 946	3 850	3 700	3 499	3 321	3 192
Manufacture of food products Beverages and tobacco	KPHQ	DA	499	493	478	464	455	444	LMAN	480	474	459	445	437	425
Of food	KPHR	151 to 158	..	..	..	..	..	..	KOWH	425	421	406	393	387	377
Of beverages and tobacco	KPHS	159/16	..	..	..	..	..	..	KOWI	54	53	53	52	50	48
Manufacture of textiles and textile products	KPHT	DB	294	258	224	193	164	143	KOWJ	275	242	210	181	155	137
Of textiles	KPHU	17	162	149	135	119	107	96	KOWK	152	141	127	113	101	91
Of made-up textile articles except apparel	KPHV	174	..	..	..	..	..	..	KOWL	34	34	34	33	31	29
Of textiles excluding made-up textile	KPHW	Rest of 17	..	..	..	..	..	..	KOWM	118	106	93	80	70	62
Of wearing apparel, dressing and dyeing of fur	KPHX	18	133	109	89	74	58	48	KOWN	123	101	83	69	54	46
Manufacture of leather and leather products including footwear	KPHY	DC	30	26	21	18	14	12	KOWO	30	25	20	18	14	12
Of leather and leather goods	KPHZ	191/192	..	..	..	..	..	..	KOWP	11	10	9	8	6	6
Of footwear	KPIA	193	..	..	..	..	..	..	KOWQ	19	15	11	10	8	6
Manufacture of wood and wood products	KPIB	DD(20)	84	83	82	84	82	85	LMAP	81	80	78	80	79	81
Manufacture of pulp paper and paper products, publishing and printing	KPIC	DE	469	464	451	440	426	414	LMAQ	463	458	445	434	420	408
Of pulp paper and paper products	KPID	21	104	100	95	89	87	82	KOWT	102	98	93	87	85	80
Publishing printing and reproduction of recorded media	KPIE	22	365	364	356	351	340	332	KOWU	361	360	352	346	335	328
Manufacture of coke refined petroleum products and nuclear fuel	KPIF	DF(23)	26	26	28	26	25	23	KOWV	26	26	27	26	25	23
Manufacture of chemicals, chemical products and man-made fibres	KPIG	DG(24)	249	238	234	233	226	212	LMAR	246	235	230	229	222	208
Manufacture of rubber and plastics	KPIH	DH(25)	244	237	228	221	214	215	LMAS	237	230	221	214	206	208
Manufacture of other non-metallic mineral products	KPII	DI(26)	140	140	134	127	121	117	KOWZ	135	135	129	121	115	111
Manufacture of basic metals and fabricated metal products	KPIJ	DJ	534	521	491	462	442	427	KOXA	528	515	484	455	435	420
Of basic metals	KPIK	27	124	117	108	98	92	87	KOXB	124	116	108	97	91	86
except machinery	KPIL	28	410	404	383	364	350	340	KOXC	405	398	377	358	344	334

89

Employee jobs: by industry[1]
Standard Industrial Classification 1992
At June each year. Not seasonally adjusted

Thousands

		SIC 1992	United Kingdom							Great Britain					
			1999	2000	2001	2002	2003	2004		1999	2000	2001	2002	2003	2004
Manufacture of Machinery and Equipment not elsewhere classified	KPIM	DK(29)	372	358	348	326	301	284	**LMAU**	365	351	341	320	294	277
Manufacture of electrical and optical equipment	KPIN	DL	497	494	481	426	381	357	**LMAV**	486	481	468	415	371	347
Of office machinery and computers	KPIO	30	51	53	50	42	37	34	**KOXF**	49	51	48	40	34	31
Of electrical machinery and apparatus	KPIP	31	181	178	169	153	139	127	**KOXG**	179	175	166	150	135	124
Of electric motors etc control apparatus and insulated cable	KPIQ	311 to 313	..	..	..	..	..	..	**KOXH**	103	101	96	86	74	67
Of accumulators, primary cells, batteries, lamps and electrical equipment	KPIR	314 to 316	..	..	..	..	..	..	**KOXI**	76	74	70	64	61	57
Radio television and communication equipment	KPIS	32	125	129	126	99	82	76	**KOXJ**	120	123	120	95	79	73
Of electronic components	KPIT	321	..	..	..	..	..	..	**KOXK**	50	45	40	33	30	29
Of radio TV and telephone apparatus, sound and video recorders	KPIU	322/323	..	..	..	..	..	..	**KOXL**	70	78	80	62	49	45
Of medical precision and optical equipment, watches	KPIV	33	140	134	135	131	124	120	**KOXM**	138	132	134	130	123	118
Manufacture of transport equipment	KPIW	DM	399	400	388	371	358	346	**LMAW**	386	387	375	358	347	336
Of motor vehicles and trailers	KPIX	34	228	224	212	210	206	200	**KOXO**	224	220	207	206	202	196
Of other transport equipment	KPIY	35	171	176	176	160	152	146	**KOXP**	163	168	168	153	145	139
Manufacturing not elsewhere classified	KPIZ	DN(36/37)	211	216	215	207	204	203	**KOXQ**	207	212	211	203	200	199
Electricity gas and water supply	KPJA	E	131	127	135	132	124	118	**KOXR**	127	123	132	129	121	115
Electricity gas steam and hot water supply	KPJB	40	..	..	..	..	..	..	**KOXT**	97	92	97	95	91	90
Collection purification and distribution of water	KPJC	41	..	..	..	..	..	..	**KOXU**	30	31	35	33	30	25
Construction	KPJD	F(45)	1 110	1 183	1 176	1 164	1 211	1 268	**LMAY**	1 079	1 148	1 140	1 128	1 176	1 232
Services	KPJE	G - O	19 375	19 900	20 410	20 748	21 032	21 276	**KOXX**	18 908	19 418	19 917	20 238	20 511	20 741
Wholesale and retail trade; Repair of motor vehicles, motorcycles and personal household goods	KPJF	G (50 - 52)	4 325	4 378	4 485	4 537	4 537	4 562	**LMAZ**	4 223	4 272	4 379	4 424	4 422	4 445
Sale maintenance and repair of motor vehicles, retail of automotive fuel	KPJG	50	576	567	565	573	564	560	**KOXZ**	562	553	550	557	548	545
Sale of motor vehicles, motorcycles and parts, motorcycle repair and sale of automotive fuel	KPJH	501/503 - 505	..	..	..	..	..	..	**KOYA**	405	387	385	390	381	375
Maintenance and repair of motor vehicles	KPJI	502	..	..	..	..	..	..	**KOYB**	158	166	165	166	167	169
Wholesale trade and commission trade except motor vehicles	KPJJ	51	1 167	1 175	1 159	1 134	1 124	1 119	**KOYC**	1 144	1 153	1 136	1 111	1 101	1 097
Wholesale on a fee of contract basis	KPJK	511	..	..	..	..	..	..	**KOYD**	58	62	60	56	59	59
Wholesale agricultural raw materials and live animals	KPJL	512	..	..	..	..	..	..	**KPLD**	24	23	24	23	23	23
Wholesale food beverages & tobacco	KPJM	513	..	..	..	..	..	..	**KPLE**	206	199	192	189	188	187
Wholesale household goods	KPJN	514	..	..	..	..	..	..	**KPLF**	254	266	270	266	264	264
Wholesale of non-agricultural intermediate products waste & scrap	KPJO	515	..	..	..	..	..	..	**KPLG**	239	243	233	235	232	236
Wholesale machinery eqpt. & supplies	KPJP	516	..	..	..	..	..	..	**KPLH**	256	252	251	243	238	229
Other wholesale	KPJQ	517	..	..	..	..	..	..	**KPLI**	107	107	106	100	98	99
Retail trade except of motor vehicles and motorcycles; repair of personal and household goods	KPJR	52	2 582	2 636	2 762	2 830	2 849	2 883	**KPLJ**	2 517	2 567	2 692	2 756	2 773	2 803
Non-specialised stores selling mainly food beverages & tobacco	KPJS	5211/5221-4,5227	..	..	..	..	..	..	**KPLK**	968	999	1 083	1 144	1 145	1 120
Other non-specialised stores second hand shops & sales not in stores	KPJT	5212/525-526	..	..	..	..	..	..	**KPLL**	381	381	379	367	364	359

Employee jobs: by industry[1]
Standard Industrial Classification 1992
At June each year. Not seasonally adjusted

Thousands

		SIC 1992	United Kingdom							Great Britain					
			1999	2000	2001	2002	2003	2004		1999	2000	2001	2002	2003	2004
Alcoholic & other beverages, tobacco	KPJU	5225 to 5226	..	..	..	..	..	..	KPLM	70	68	68	64	56	59
Pharmaceutical & medical goods cosmetics & toilet articles	KPJV	523	..	..	..	..	..	..	KPLN	88	89	92	96	93	99
Clothing footwear & leather goods	KPJW	5242/5243	..	..	..	..	..	..	KPLO	339	352	355	340	369	405
Textile furniture lighting equipment electrical household appliances radio and TV paints glass hardware and household goods not elsewhere classified	KPJX	5241/5244-46	..	..	..	..	..	..	KPLP	266	278	291	303	297	300
Books newspapers and stationery, other retail in specialised stores	KPJY	5247/5248	..	..	..	..	..	..	KPLQ	384	378	400	416	421	436
Repair of personal and household goods	KPJZ	527	..	..	..	..	..	..	KPLR	20	23	24	26	27	26
Hotels and restaurants	KPKA	H	1 649	1 685	1 698	1 748	1 798	1 828	LMBA	1 613	1 647	1 660	1 708	1 759	1 788
Hotels camp sites short-stay accom.	KPKB	551/552	..	..	..	..	..	..	KPLT	371	376	371	365	370	373
Restaurants	KPKC	553	..	..	..	..	..	..	KPLU	478	493	509	547	576	586
Bars	KPKD	554	..	..	..	..	..	..	KPLV	534	543	525	531	541	556
Canteens and catering	KPKE	555	..	..	..	..	..	..	KPLW	229	237	256	265	272	273
Transport, storage and communication	KPKF	I	1 459	1 523	1 589	1 581	1 586	1 561	KPLX	1 434	1 497	1 562	1 553	1 558	1 534
Land transport, transport via pipelines	KPKG	60	519	514	522	518	516	518	KPLY	508	503	510	506	504	506
Transport via railways	KPKH	601	..	..	..	..	..	..	KPLZ	49	49	50	49	48	47
Other land transport and via pipelines	KPKI	602/603	..	..	..	..	..	..	KPMA	460	453	461	457	456	459
Water transport	KPKJ	61	20	19	17	18	17	16	KPMB	20	18	17	17	16	16
Air transport	KPKK	62	89	94	93	88	90	85	KPMC	88	93	92	87	90	85
Supporting and auxiliary transport activities, activities of travel agents	KPKL	63	354	381	403	403	412	426	KPMD	349	376	398	398	407	421
Travel agencies and tour operators	KPKM	633	..	..	..	..	..	..	KPME	115	125	132	128	128	138
Post and telecommunications	KPKN	64	477	515	555	554	551	515	LMBC	469	506	545	545	542	507
National post and courier activities	KPKO	641	..	..	..	..	..	..	KPMG	276	282	299	295	297	272
National post activities	KPKP	6411	..	..	..	..	..	..	KPMH	216	216	229	220	216	200
Courier activities	KPKQ	6412	..	..	..	..	..	..	KPMI	60	66	70	75	81	72
Telecommunications	KPKR	6420	..	..	..	..	..	..	KPMJ	193	223	246	249	245	235
Financial intermediation	KPKS	J	1 072	1 068	1 088	1 112	1 108	1 095	LMBD	1 058	1 053	1 072	1 095	1 091	1 078
Financial intermediation except insurance and pension funding	KPKT	65	618	605	616	638	644	646	KPML	609	595	605	627	633	635
Insurance and pension funding except compulsory social security	KPKU	66	232	227	228	223	214	201	KPMM	230	225	226	221	212	199
Activities auxiliary to financial intermediation	KPKV	67	221	236	244	251	249	248	KPMN	219	233	241	248	246	244
Except insurance and pension funding	KPKW	671	..	..	..	..	..	..	KPMO	79	95	107	111	114	113
Auxiliary to insurance and pension funding	KPKX	672	..	..	..	..	..	..	KPMP	140	138	134	137	133	132
Real estate renting & business activities	KPKY	K	3 572	3 746	3 933	3 956	4 007	4 072	KPMQ	3 526	3 697	3 881	3 901	3 950	4 010
Real estate activities	KPKZ	70	313	350	364	369	382	394	LMBE	310	347	360	365	378	390
Activities with own property, letting of own property	KPLA	701/702	..	..	..	..	..	..	KPMS	187	213	219	218	224	231
Activities on a fee or contract basis	KPLB	703	..	..	..	..	..	..	KPMT	122	133	141	147	154	159

7.5 Employee jobs: by industry[1]
Standard Industrial Classification 1992
At June each year. Not seasonally adjusted

Thousand

		SIC 1992	United Kingdom							Great Britain					
			1999	2000	2001	2002	2003	2004		1999	2000	2001	2002	2003	2004
Renting of machinery and equipment without operator & of personal & household goods	KPLC	71	148	154	156	157	151	150	KPMU	146	152	154	155	149	148
Construction and civil engineering machinery	KOUU	7132	..	..	..	..	..	..	KPMV	39	42	45	45	42	39
All other goods and equipment	KOUV	Rest of 71	..	..	..	..	..	..	KPMW	108	109	109	110	108	109
Computer and related equipment	KOUW	72	418	460	503	494	503	492	KPMX	415	455	497	489	498	487
Research and development	KOUX	73	97	100	104	108	106	100	KPMY	96	98	102	106	105	98
Other business activities	KOUY	74	2 595	2 683	2 806	2 829	2 865	2 936	KPMZ	2 560	2 646	2 767	2 786	2 820	2 887
Legal, accounting,book-keeping & auditing activities	KOUZ	741	..	..	..	..	..	..	KPNA	663	698	724	741	778	831
Legal activities	KOVA	7411	..	..	..	..	..	..	KPNB	233	240	240	248	250	253
Accounting, book-keeping auditing, tax consultancy	KOVB	7412	..	..	..	..	..	..	KPNC	190	206	207	195	192	194
Market research business and consultancy activities	KOVC	7413/7414	..	..	..	..	..	..	KPND	202	219	246	270	275	288
Management activities of holding companies[2]	KOVD	7415	..	..	..	..	..	..	KPNE	..	..	..	..	..	96
Architectural engineering activities and related technical consultancy, technical testing	KOVE	742/743	..	..	..	..	..	..	KPNF	324	324	331	332	332	336
Advertising	KOVF	744	..	..	..	..	..	..	KPNG	83	86	93	87	83	78
Industrial cleaning	KOVG	747	..	..	..	..	..	..	KPNH	445	427	425	418	416	415
Public administration and defence, compulsory social security	KOVH	L(75)	1 360	1 377	1 385	1 432	1 491	1 518	LMBG	1 302	1 318	1 325	1 372	1 428	1 454
Education	KOVI	M(80)	2 098	2 137	2 153	2 192	2 258	2 313	LMBH	2 033	2 071	2 087	2 125	2 189	2 245
Health and social work	KOVJ	N	2 600	2 694	2 752	2 810	2 879	2 951	LOJV	2 506	2 599	2 654	2 711	2 777	2 843
Human health, veterinary activities	KOVK	851/852	..	..	..	..	..	..	KPNL	1 600	1 693	1 745	1 799	1 856	1 908
Social work activities	KOVL	853	..	..	..	..	..	..	KPNM	906	906	909	912	920	936
Other community social and personal service activities,private households with employed persons, extra-territorial organisations and bodies	KOVM	O	1 240	1 290	1 328	1 379	1 368	1 376	LMBK	1 213	1 262	1 299	1 349	1 337	1 345
Sewage and refuse disposal; sanitation	KOVN	90	110	99	109	106	95	100	KPNO	107	97	106	103	92	97
Activities of membership organisations	KOVO	91	212	219	215	226	220	215	KPNP	205	212	207	218	212	206
Recreational cultural and sporting activities	KOVP	92	625	660	684	717	732	742	KPNQ	612	646	670	702	716	726
Motion picture video radio TV news agencies and entertainment activities	KOVQ	921 to 924	..	..	..	..	..	..	KPNR	203	211	215	227	220	227
Library archives museums and other cultural activities	KOVR	925	..	..	..	..	..	..	KPNS	74	80	79	84	92	89
Sporting activities and other recreational activities	KOVS	926/927	..	..	..	..	..	..	KPNT	335	355	377	392	405	411
Other service activities,private households with employed persons, extra territorial organisations	KOVT	93/95/99	293	312	319	330	321	320	KPNU	289	308	315	325	317	315
Washing, dry cleaning of textile and fur products	KOVU	9301	..	..	..	..	..	..	KPNV	46	45	48	46	46	42
Hairdressing, other beauty treatment, physical and well-being activities	KOVV	9302/9304	..	..	..	..	..	..	KPNW	97	100	100	102	103	101

1 See chapter text. The data in this table have not been adjusted to reflect the 2001 Census population data.
2 Head office and holding company local units were reclassified to Class 74.15 (within Section K) from December 2003 as a result of the SIC 2003 update.

Sources: Department of Manpower Services (Northern Ireland); Earnings and Employment Division, ONS: 01633 812318

7.6 Weekly hours worked: by sex[1,2]
United Kingdom
At Spring each year. Seasonally adjusted

Hours

| | All workers' weekly hours[3] | | Average actual weekly hours of work | | |
	Total (millions)	Average	Full-time employment[3,4]	Part-time employment[4]	Second jobs[5]
All					
	YBUS	YBUV	YBUY	YBVB	YBVE
1994	840.8	33.2	38.4	15.0	9.1
1995	856.4	33.4	38.7	15.1	9.1
1996	860.9	33.2	38.7	15.1	8.9
1997	878.0	33.3	38.7	15.2	9.4
1998	885.4	33.2	38.7	15.2	9.1
1999	887.3	32.9	38.2	15.3	9.0
2000	893.3	32.6	37.9	15.4	8.9
2001	906.1	32.8	38.0	15.7	9.4
2002	907.3	32.6	37.9	15.6	9.4
2003	903.4	32.1	37.4	15.6	9.3
2004	906.8	32.0	37.3	15.6	9.1
Men					
	YBUT	YBUW	YBUZ	YBVC	YBVF
1994	538.2	38.9	40.4	14.9	9.8
1995	549.5	39.2	40.8	14.7	10.0
1996	549.9	39.0	40.7	14.8	9.7
1997	558.7	38.9	40.7	14.9	10.7
1998	564.0	38.8	40.7	15.0	9.8
1999	560.4	38.2	40.1	15.0	9.7
2000	564.2	37.9	39.8	15.1	9.4
2001	569.6	38.0	39.9	15.6	10.2
2002	566.0	37.7	39.7	15.0	10.2
2003	563.0	36.9	39.1	15.4	10.2
2004	566.8	37.0	39.2	15.7	10.2
Women					
	YBUU	YBUX	YBVA	YBVD	YBVG
1994	302.5	26.3	34.5	15.0	8.5
1995	306.9	26.4	34.4	15.2	8.5
1996	311.1	26.3	34.5	15.1	8.2
1997	319.2	26.6	34.7	15.3	8.4
1998	321.3	26.5	34.6	15.3	8.6
1999	326.9	26.5	34.5	15.3	8.5
2000	329.2	26.3	34.1	15.4	8.6
2001	336.5	26.6	34.4	15.7	8.8
2002	341.3	26.7	34.4	15.7	8.8
2003	340.4	26.4	34.1	15.7	8.7
2004	340.0	26.1	33.7	15.6	8.3

1 See chapter text. The data in this table have been adjusted to reflect the latest 2001 Census population data.
2 Average hours actually worked in the reference week which includes hours worked in second jobs.
3 Main and second job.

4 People whose main job is full-time or part-time.
5 Second jobs reported in the LFS in addition to persons' main full time job.

Source: Labour Force Survey, Office for National Statistics

7.7 Civil Service staff: by ministerial responsibility[1,2]

At 1 April each year

Full-time equivalents (thousands)[3]

		1994	1995	1996	1997	1998	1999	2000	2001	2002	2003	2004
Agriculture, Fisheries and Food	BCDA	11.0	10.6	10.8	10.1	10.8	11.7	10.8	11.4	..	..	..
Cabinet Office	BBGD	12.0	11.7	12.3	7.8	7.7	7.6	6.9	6.9	6.9	7.1	7.0
Chancellor of the Exchequer's Departments:												
Customs and Excise	BCDC	25.0	24.1	23.2	23.1	23.4	22.5	21.9	21.7	21.8	22.2	22.6
Inland Revenue	BCDD	64.0	59.1	56.5	54.4	53.4	61.3	66.3	66.9	68.2	75.6	80.1
Department for National Savings	BCDE	6.0	5.4	4.7	4.3	4.1	0.1	0.1	0.1	0.1	0.1	0.1
Treasury and others	BCDF	5.0	4.3	6.0	5.1	5.1	5.0	5.5	5.5	5.6	5.8	6.1
Total	BCDB	99.0	92.9	90.3	86.8	86.0	89.0	93.8	94.2	95.7	103.7	108.9
Culture, Media and Sport	DMTC	..	..	..	..	0.6	0.6	0.6	0.6	0.7	0.7	0.7
Education	BCDG	2.0	2.5	..	..	..	..	..	..	..	..	..
Education and Employment	BBFT	..	..	40.8	34.1	33.6	34.6	36.5	38.3	..	..	..
Education and Skills	LNFW	..	..	..	..	..	..	..	..	7.2	7.5	7.7
Environment	BCDJ	10.0	9.4	10.9	9.6	..	..	..	..	..	..	..
Environment, Food and Rural Affairs	LNFX	..	..	..	..	..	..	..	..	14.6	14.5	15.4
Environment, Transport and the Regions	CKUZ	..	..	..	..	21.2	21.8	23.2	25.4	..	..	..
Foreign and Commonwealth	BCDK	8.0	7.5	7.1	6.6	5.4	5.5	5.5	5.5	5.7	6.0	6.0
Health	BAKR	7.0	6.2	4.8	4.7	4.6	4.8	7.0	7.2	5.1	4.5	4.2
Home	BCDL	51.0	51.4	50.8	50.4	50.7	50.0	53.6	60.1	61.0	65.6	69.9
International Development	DMUA	..	..	..	..	1.1	1.2	1.2	1.3	1.5	1.6	1.8
Legal Departments	BBGE	29.0	28.7	27.8	26.3	25.4	25.5	24.9	25.0	26.9	28.2	28.8
National Heritage	BBGF	1.0	1.0	1.0	1.0	..	..	..	..	..	..	..
Northern Ireland	BBGG	..	0.2	0.2	0.2	0.2	0.2	0.2	0.2	0.2	0.2	0.2
Office of the Deputy Prime Minister	YEGA	..	..	..	..	..	..	..	..	..	4.6	5.2
Scotland	BCDN	13.0	12.1	11.7	11.8	12.0	12.5	13.6	13.7	14.3	14.8	15.3
Social Security	BAKS	90.0	89.2	91.5	93.1	87.2	81.6	83.5	81.9	..	..	..
Trade and Industry	BCDQ	11.3	11.1	11.2	10.3	10.4	10.5	11.0	11.4	12.0	12.2	11.9
Transport	BCDR	14.0	12.9	11.3	11.4	..	..	..	..	..	20.8	15.9
Transport, Local Government and the Regions	LNFZ	..	..	..	..	..	..	..	..	23.9	..	..
Welsh Office	BCDS	2.0	2.2	2.1	2.2	2.1	2.3	2.7	3.2	3.5	3.7	4.4
Work and Pensions	LNGA	..	..	..	..	..	..	..	..	122.0	124.4	129.0
Total civil departments	BCDU	418.0	400.8	384.6	366.3	359.1	359.1	375.1	384.4	401.2	420.0	432.2
Defence	BCDW	122.0	116.1	109.9	109.2	104.2	100.9	100.3	98.3	89.0	91.3	91.4
Total all departments	BCDX	540.0	516.9	494.5	475.6	463.3	460.0	475.4	482.7	490.2	511.3	523.6
of which												
Non-industrial staff	BCDY	494.0	474.1	458.7	439.6	430.5	429.2	446.0	453.8	462.9	490.2	503.6
Industrial staff	BCDZ	46.0	42.0	35.9	36.0	32.8	30.8	29.4	28.9	27.3	21.1	20.0

1 The figures include non-industrial and industrial staff but exclude casual or seasonal staff and employees of the Northern Ireland Civil Service.

2 A comprehensive list of Machinery of Government changes is listed on the Cabinet Office's web site at: *www.civil-service.gov.uk/statistics*

3 Figures included are measured as 'full-time equivalent' staff. Part-time staff are recorded as a proportion of full-time employees according to the proportion of a full week that they work.

Source: Cabinet Office: 020 7276 1532

7.8 Unemployment: number by sex and age group[1]
United Kingdom

At Spring each year. Seasonally adjusted

Thousands

	All aged 16 and over	16-59/64	16-17	18-24	16-24	25-34	35-49	50-64 (m) 50-59 (w)	65+ (m) 60+ (w)
All									
	MGSC	YBSH	YBVH	YBVN	PXLG	PXLJ	PXLM	PXLP	PXLS
1996	2 344	2 324	165	557	722	641	610	357	21
1997	2 045	2 021	168	489	657	518	533	318	24
1998	1 783	1 763	159	437	596	468	435	268	21
1999	1 759	1 740	169	424	593	425	459	269	20
2000	1 638	1 621	177	403	580	372	414	261	17
2001	1 431	1 416	146	375	521	328	382	191	15
2002	1 542	1 521	163	395	558	349	388	218	22
2003	1 489	1 472	176	407	583	312	363	211	18
2004	1 438	1 420	173	392	565	..	..	..	..
Men									
	MGSD	YBSI	YBVI	YBVO	PXLH	PXLK	PXLN	PXLQ	PXLT
1996	1 524	1 512	97	359	456	400	393	270	12
1997	1 283	1 271	90	304	394	325	331	227	12
1998	1 076	1 067	85	262	347	278	253	194	..
1999	1 070	1 062	101	250	351	246	278	195	..
2000	974	968	96	239	335	216	238	186	..
2001	847	840	85	221	306	190	212	139	..
2002	918	908	91	245	336	202	227	144	10
2003	901	894	100	246	346	188	211	149	..
2004	829	819	101	216	317	..	..	..	..
Women									
	MGSE	YBSJ	YBVJ	YBVP	PXLI	PXLL	PXLO	PXLR	PXLU
1996	820	812	68	198	266	241	216	87	..
1997	762	750	78	184	262	194	202	90	12
1998	707	696	74	175	249	191	183	74	11
1999	689	678	68	173	241	179	181	75	11
2000	663	654	81	164	245	157	176	75	10
2001	583	576	61	154	215	138	171	51	..
2002	624	613	72	150	222	148	161	73	12
2003	588	578	76	161	237	123	152	62	10
2004	610	601	72	177	249	..	..	..	..

1 See chapter text. The data in this table have been adjusted to reflect the latest 2001 Census population data.

Source: Labour Force Survey, Office for National Statistics

7.9 Unemployment: percentage by sex and age group[1,2]
United Kingdom

At Spring each year. Seasonally adjusted

Percentages

	All aged 16 and over	16-59/64	16-17	18-24	16-24	25-34	35-49	50-64 (m) 50-59 (w)	65+ (m) 60+ (w)
All									
	MGSX	YBTI	YBVK	YBVQ	PXLV	PXLY	PXMB	PXME	PXMH
1996	8.3	8.4	20.0	14.5	15.5	8.5	6.0	6.8	2.6
1997	7.2	7.3	19.4	13.1	14.3	6.9	5.3	5.8	2.9
1998	6.3	6.4	18.7	12.0	13.2	6.3	4.3	4.7	2.6
1999	6.1	6.2	20.0	11.7	13.3	5.7	4.5	4.6	2.4
2000	5.6	5.7	20.9	11.0	12.9	5.1	4.0	4.4	2.0
2001	4.9	5.0	17.9	10.2	11.6	4.6	3.6	3.1	1.8
2002	5.2	5.3	20.0	10.5	12.2	5.0	3.6	3.5	2.4
2003	5.0	5.1	21.1	10.7	12.6	4.7	3.3	3.3	1.9
2004	4.8	4.9	21.2	10.1	..	..	..	..	..
Men									
	MGSY	YBTJ	YBVL	YBVR	PXLW	PXLZ	PXMC	PXMF	PXMI
1996	9.7	9.8	22.6	17.4	18.3	9.5	7.2	8.3	4.3
1997	8.2	8.2	20.9	15.2	16.2	7.7	6.1	6.8	4.3
1998	6.9	6.9	19.8	13.5	14.6	6.7	4.6	5.6	..
1999	6.8	6.9	23.3	13.0	14.9	6.0	5.0	5.5	..
2000	6.1	6.2	22.3	12.2	14.1	5.4	4.2	5.2	..
2001	5.3	5.4	20.3	11.4	13.0	4.8	3.7	3.8	..
2002	5.7	5.8	22.0	12.2	13.9	5.3	4.0	3.9	3.3
2003	5.6	5.7	23.7	12.1	14.2	5.1	3.6	3.9	..
2004	5.1	5.2	24.6	10.4	..	..	..	..	..
Women									
	MGSZ	YBTK	YBVM	YBVS	PXLX	PXMA	PXMD	PXMG	PXMJ
1996	6.5	6.7	17.2	11.1	12.2	7.3	4.7	4.3	..
1997	6.0	6.1	18.0	10.7	12.1	5.8	4.4	4.3	2.2
1998	5.5	5.6	17.5	10.3	11.7	5.8	3.9	3.3	2.2
1999	5.3	5.4	16.6	10.2	11.5	5.4	3.8	3.2	2.0
2000	5.0	5.2	19.4	9.5	11.4	4.8	3.7	3.1	1.8
2001	4.4	4.5	15.4	8.9	10.1	4.3	3.5	2.1	..
2002	4.6	4.8	17.9	8.5	10.3	4.7	3.2	2.9	1.9
2003	4.4	4.5	18.5	9.1	10.8	4.1	3.0	2.4	1.7
2004	4.5	4.6	17.8	9.6	..	..	..	..	..

1 See chapter text. The data in this table have been adjusted to reflect the latest 2001 Census population data.

2 Total unemployment as a percentage of all economically active persons in the relevant age group.

Source: Labour Force Survey, Office for National Statistics

7.10 Duration of unemployment: by sex[1,2]
United Kingdom
At Spring each year. Seasonally adjusted

Thousands

		1994	1995	1996	1997	1998	1999	2000	2001	2002	2003	2004
All												
All unemployed	MGSC	2 750	2 470	2 344	2 045	1 783	1 759	1 638	1 431	1 542	1 489	1 438
Duration of unemployment												
Less than 6 months	YBWF	1 065	1 021	1 041	973	969	997	961	847	979	965	915
6 months & less than 1 year	YBWG	457	394	393	305	248	263	239	216	232	205	232
1 year or more	YBWH	1 228	1 055	910	767	566	499	437	368	332	319	291
1 year or more as % of total	YBWI	*44.7*	*42.7*	*38.8*	*37.5*	*31.7*	*28.4*	*26.7*	*25.7*	*21.5*	*21.4*	*20.2*
Men												
All unemployed	MGSD	1 806	1 591	1 524	1 283	1 076	1 070	974	847	918	901	829
Duration of unemployment												
Less than 6 months	MGYK	599	563	587	533	514	550	518	454	531	546	489
6 months & less than 1 year	MGYM	292	248	249	186	162	162	139	130	155	129	143
1 year or more	MGYO	915	780	688	564	401	358	317	263	232	226	197
1 year or more as % of total	YBWJ	*50.6*	*49.0*	*45.1*	*44.0*	*37.2*	*33.4*	*32.6*	*31.1*	*25.3*	*25.1*	*23.8*
Women												
All unemployed	MGSE	944	879	820	762	707	689	663	583	624	588	610
Duration of unemployment												
Less than 6 months	MGYL	465	458	455	439	455	446	443	393	448	419	427
6 months & less than 1 year	MGYN	165	146	144	120	87	101	101	86	77	76	90
1 year or more	MGYP	314	276	222	203	165	142	120	105	99	93	93
1 year or more as % of total	YBWK	*33.2*	*31.3*	*27.1*	*26.6*	*23.3*	*20.6*	*18.0*	*18.0*	*15.9*	*15.8*	*15.3*

1 All aged 16 and over. See chapter text.
2 The data in this table have been adjusted to reflect the latest 2001 Census population data.

Source: Labour Force Survey, Office for National Statistics

7.11 Claimant count:[1] by age and duration
Computerised claims only
United Kingdom. Seasonally adjusted

Thousands

		1998	1999	2000	2001	2002	2003	2004
Annual averages								
Males								
All ages								
All durations	AGNG	1 022.7	946.1	826.1	733.6	708.3	693.1	631.0
Up to 6 months	AGXK	533.3	522.8	481.4	449.4	457.4	451.3	409.0
Over 6 and up to 12 months	ELNP	188.1	166.3	142.7	125.4	124.2	127.1	113.8
All over 12 months	ELON	301.4	257.1	202.0	158.8	126.7	114.6	108.2
All over 24 months	IKBS	169.8	128.9	102.4	77.5	50.7	37.6	34.5
Aged 18 to 24								
All durations	JLGC	237.5	205.2	182.3	167.9	168.1	171.9	162.0
Up to 6 months	JLGD	159.8	160.9	149.6	141.4	141.0	143.7	134.5
Over 6 and up to 12 months	JLGE	44.2	34.3	28.3	23.4	23.8	24.5	23.3
All over 12 months	JLGF	33.6	10.0	4.4	3.1	3.3	3.6	4.2
All over 24 months	JLGH	10.7	2.3	0.5	0.3	0.3	0.4	0.5
Aged 25 to 49								
All durations	AGMA	619.4	582.9	506.1	445.9	421.8	404.9	362.4
Up to 6 months	JLHG	303.2	291.3	266.8	248.2	254.9	248.2	221.3
Over 6 and up to 12 months	JLHH	117.3	107.4	92.8	83.1	80.9	83.0	73.0
All over 12 months	JLHI	198.9	184.3	146.5	114.7	86.1	73.8	68.1
All over 24 months	JLHK	112.4	88.0	70.5	52.4	29.2	17.0	14.1
Aged 50 and over								
All durations	JLHL	165.8	158.0	137.7	119.8	118.4	116.3	106.7
Up to 6 months	JLHM	70.3	70.6	65.0	59.9	61.6	59.4	53.3
Over 6 and up to 12 months	JLHN	26.6	24.6	21.6	18.9	19.6	19.7	17.5
All over 12 months	JLHO	69.0	62.8	51.1	41.0	37.3	37.2	35.9
All over 24 months	JLHQ	46.7	38.6	31.5	24.8	21.1	20.2	19.9
Females								
All ages								
All durations	JLGI	315.6	289.9	254.8	227.9	226.8	230.2	214.9
Up to 6 months	JLGK	197.2	189.6	172.5	160.4	163.6	166.4	153.2
Over 6 and up to 12 months	JLGJ	54.2	47.7	40.9	35.1	35.5	37.3	35.0
All over 12 months	JLGL	64.3	52.6	41.4	32.5	27.6	26.6	26.7
All over 24 months	JLGN	30.9	22.9	18.2	13.9	9.7	8.1	8.0
Aged 18 to 24								
All durations	JLGO	101.6	88.9	79.3	73.4	75.0	77.3	74.1
Up to 6 months	JLGP	72.5	71.2	65.7	62.1	62.9	64.9	61.5
Over 6 and up to 12 months	JLGQ	17.3	13.9	11.7	9.8	10.4	10.5	10.5
All over 12 months	JLGR	11.8	3.8	1.9	1.4	1.8	1.8	2.0
All over 24 months	JLGT	3.3	0.8	0.2	0.2	0.2	0.2	0.3
Aged 25 to 49								
All durations	JLHR	157.4	147.0	128.0	113.3	111.4	112.2	102.1
Up to 6 months	JLHS	96.1	90.3	80.8	74.4	76.7	77.4	69.0
Over 6 and up to 12 months	JLHT	27.0	24.6	21.3	18.6	18.5	19.9	18.2
All over 12 months	JLHU	34.3	32.1	25.9	20.4	16.2	14.9	14.9
All over 24 months	JLHW	16.9	13.4	10.9	8.2	4.7	3.1	2.9
Aged 50 and over								
All durations	JLHX	56.7	54.0	47.5	41.3	40.4	40.8	38.8
Up to 6 months	JLHY	28.6	28.1	26.0	23.9	24.1	24.1	22.7
Over 6 and up to 12 months	JLHZ	9.9	9.1	7.9	6.7	6.6	6.8	6.3
All over 12 months	JLIA	18.1	16.7	13.6	10.7	9.7	9.8	9.8
All over 24 months	JLIC	10.7	8.7	7.1	5.5	4.8	4.7	4.8

1 Count of claimants of unemployment-related benefits.

Source: Office for National Statistics: 020 7533 6094

7.12 Unemployment rates: by region[1,2]

At Spring each year. Not seasonally adjusted

Percentages

		1994	1995	1996	1997	1998	1999	2000	2001	2002	2003	2004
North East	BENU	12.7	11.5	10.9	9.9	8.1	10.2	9.1	7.4	6.8	6.6	5.4
North West	BENV	10.4	9.1	8.4	6.8	6.6	6.2	5.3	5.1	5.4	4.8	4.4
Yorkshire and Humber	BENY	10.0	8.8	8.1	8.1	7.0	6.5	6.0	5.0	5.4	5.4	4.4
East Midlands	BENZ	8.4	7.6	7.5	6.4	4.9	5.2	5.2	5.0	4.2	4.1	4.1
West Midlands	BEOA	10.2	9.1	9.4	6.9	6.3	6.9	6.2	5.1	5.5	5.6	5.5
East	BEOB	10.2	9.1	9.4	6.9	6.3	6.9	6.2	5.1	5.5	5.6	5.5
London	BEOC	13.4	11.8	11.5	9.3	8.2	7.5	7.1	5.9	6.7	6.8	6.5
South East	BEOD	7.3	6.5	6.2	5.3	4.4	3.7	3.4	3.0	4.0	3.8	3.8
South West	BEOE	7.6	8.0	6.5	5.3	4.6	4.8	4.2	3.5	3.6	3.7	3.3
Wales	BEOG	9.6	8.9	8.4	8.4	6.8	7.1	6.1	5.8	6.0	4.5	4.7
Scotland	BEOH	10.2	8.5	8.8	8.6	7.4	7.5	7.6	5.8	6.8	5.5	6.1
Northern Ireland	BEOI	11.8	11.3	9.7	7.6	7.3	7.3	7.1	6.3	5.5	5.4	4.8

1 All aged 16 and over. See chapter text.
2 The data in this table have been adjusted to reflect the latest 2001 Census population data.

Source: Labour Force Survey, Office for National Statistics

7.13 Claimant count rates: by region[1]

Seasonally adjusted annual averages

Percentages

		1993	1994	1995	1996	1997	1998	1999	2000	2001	2002	2003
United Kingdom	BCJE	9.7	8.8	7.6	7.0	5.3	4.5	4.1	3.6	3.2	3.1	3.0
North East	DPDM	12.1	11.7	10.8	9.6	7.7	7.0	7.0	6.3	5.6	5.1	4.5
North West	IBWC	10.0	9.3	8.1	7.4	5.8	5.1	4.6	4.1	3.7	3.5	3.2
Yorkshire and the Humber	DPBI	9.7	9.1	8.1	7.4	6.0	5.4	5.0	4.3	3.9	3.6	3.4
East Midlands	DPBJ	9.0	8.3	7.1	6.4	4.7	3.9	3.6	3.4	3.1	2.8	2.8
West Midlands	DPBN	10.3	9.4	7.7	6.8	5.2	4.5	4.4	4.0	3.7	3.5	3.5
East	DPDP	8.8	7.6	6.2	5.7	4.0	3.2	2.9	2.4	2.0	2.1	2.1
London	DPDQ	10.9	10.1	8.9	8.3	6.3	5.1	4.5	3.7	3.3	3.6	3.6
South East	DPDR	8.1	6.9	5.6	4.9	3.3	2.6	2.3	1.9	1.6	1.6	1.7
South West	DPBM	9.0	7.7	6.5	5.8	4.1	3.4	3.0	2.5	2.1	1.9	1.9
England	VASQ	9.7	8.7	7.5	6.8	5.1	4.3	3.9	3.4	3.0	2.9	2.9
Wales	DPBP	9.8	8.9	8.1	7.6	6.1	5.4	5.0	4.4	4.0	3.6	3.4
Scotland	DPBQ	9.2	8.7	7.5	7.2	6.0	5.4	5.0	4.5	4.0	3.9	3.8
Northern Ireland	DPBR	13.6	12.6	11.2	10.8	8.1	7.3	6.4	5.3	4.9	4.5	4.2
Great Britain	DPAJ	9.6	8.7	7.5	6.9	5.2	4.4	4.1	3.5	3.1	3.0	3.0

1 The number of unemployment-related benefit claimants as a percentage of the estimated total workforce (the sum of claimants, employee jobs, self-employed, participants on work-related government training programmes and HM Forces) at mid-year. Excluded are claimants under 18, consistent with current coverage. See chapter text.

Source: Office for National Statistics: 020 7533 6094

7.14 Claimant count:[1] by region
Seasonally adjusted

Thousands

		North East	North West	Yorkshire and the Humber	East Midlands	West Midlands	East	London	South East	South West	England	Wales	Scotland	Great Britain	Northern Ireland	United Kingdom
		DPDG	IBWA	DPAX	DPAY	DPBC	DPDJ	DPDK	DPDL	DPBB	IBWK	DPBE	DPBF	DPAG	DPBG	BCJD
1990	Jan	112.5	243.7	159.5	93.8	151.1	74.3	199.4	95.5	86.5	1 215.7	84.4	207.9	1 508.6	97.3	1 605.9
	Apr	109.3	238.0	154.0	92.7	145.0	75.3	194.7	95.1	86.5	1 189.9	82.8	200.8	1 474.2	96.0	1 570.2
	Jul	109.1	237.7	156.1	96.1	147.1	83.8	203.9	107.2	94.1	1 234.7	83.2	194.3	1 512.6	94.4	1 607.0
	Oct	112.3	248.0	165.0	104.8	157.3	98.2	226.6	127.5	106.4	1 345.5	88.7	197.3	1 632.1	93.8	1 725.9
1991	Jan	116.7	261.8	176.4	113.1	171.0	112.5	255.8	149.7	122.2	1 478.8	95.0	200.9	1 775.1	96.0	1 871.1
	Apr	126.2	285.9	197.5	132.0	203.5	138.5	303.2	190.5	146.9	1 723.9	108.8	212.7	2 045.7	97.9	2 143.6
	Jul	130.5	305.4	211.9	145.5	225.4	158.9	342.3	221.3	165.7	1 906.8	115.5	220.1	2 242.5	98.8	2 341.3
	Oct	133.2	318.2	219.6	154.5	240.0	172.4	368.9	240.9	178.6	2 025.9	119.3	224.0	2 369.6	100.5	2 470.1
1992	Jan	133.9	325.4	222.7	160.4	250.6	183.3	389.8	258.4	188.4	2 112.6	121.3	228.0	2 462.2	102.2	2 564.4
	Apr	135.7	332.8	227.6	168.0	260.0	196.0	409.6	277.7	199.0	2 205.5	123.4	231.8	2 561.6	103.4	2 665.0
	Jul	136.7	335.2	232.4	172.1	266.1	205.1	426.2	288.9	206.6	2 268.9	124.1	235.2	2 628.6	104.6	2 733.2
	Oct	141.4	343.6	240.2	178.8	277.4	218.6	448.0	308.4	215.3	2 371.1	129.2	242.4	2 743.3	105.1	2 848.4
1993	Jan	146.2	348.3	247.5	185.2	286.2	229.5	464.6	325.2	222.6	2 454.4	131.4	245.3	2 832.0	105.5	2 937.5
	Apr	148.0	345.2	246.5	183.6	285.1	228.2	469.5	321.4	220.0	2 446.6	130.3	243.2	2 821.0	104.5	2 925.5
	Jul	148.5	338.0	240.9	180.8	278.7	223.5	466.3	314.0	214.4	2 404.4	129.3	241.2	2 775.6	102.5	2 878.1
	Oct	147.5	331.1	237.8	177.8	271.5	216.6	460.4	306.6	208.4	2 356.8	127.8	236.6	2 722.1	101.8	2 823.9
1994	Jan	145.6	325.1	233.7	174.7	262.3	210.0	451.4	296.7	203.6	2 302.3	126.7	236.0	2 665.8	100.2	2 766.0
	Apr	141.6	314.5	227.4	170.7	252.0	200.4	440.4	280.9	194.5	2 221.7	123.3	231.7	2 577.4	98.9	2 676.3
	Jul	139.1	304.2	222.7	166.3	242.3	191.0	428.1	268.1	188.1	2 148.8	119.0	227.4	2 496.3	97.2	2 593.5
	Oct	136.0	291.7	215.9	160.1	230.5	180.5	415.4	251.1	178.9	2 059.0	112.9	218.1	2 391.1	93.8	2 484.9
1995	Jan	133.0	280.1	210.6	153.2	218.5	172.3	401.4	237.9	171.4	1 977.5	108.3	209.3	2 296.0	91.3	2 387.3
	Apr	130.0	270.8	206.8	148.1	211.0	167.1	395.0	229.7	166.0	1 923.8	106.2	200.3	2 231.0	88.6	2 319.6
	Jul	128.2	266.1	204.6	145.3	206.9	165.0	390.2	225.1	162.5	1 892.8	106.7	195.3	2 195.9	87.6	2 283.5
	Oct	126.4	260.9	200.7	142.3	201.3	160.7	383.2	219.1	159.4	1 852.7	105.4	193.5	2 152.9	85.8	2 238.7
1996	Jan	123.1	255.8	197.0	140.0	196.5	157.2	376.8	213.3	155.6	1 814.6	104.0	193.2	2 112.5	85.9	2 198.4
	Apr	121.7	254.9	195.7	137.7	194.2	153.5	367.9	207.6	152.3	1 785.1	104.6	194.9	2 085.0	86.1	2 171.1
	Jul	116.9	248.2	188.8	131.8	187.6	146.8	357.5	198.9	146.8	1 722.5	101.8	191.9	2 017.0	86.4	2 103.4
	Oct	110.5	238.4	181.1	124.9	177.8	138.5	341.6	185.5	137.9	1 635.0	98.2	186.3	1 920.7	81.7	2 002.4
1997	Jan	101.0	218.5	166.4	111.8	160.1	123.5	312.6	163.3	126.0	1 483.2	90.3	173.8	1 747.3	71.1	1 818.4
	Apr	95.2	201.3	154.7	102.4	147.3	110.6	284.9	144.4	112.1	1 352.9	82.5	162.2	1 597.6	65.0	1 662.6
	Jul	92.4	188.9	148.2	95.0	138.0	102.5	264.3	131.0	100.7	1 261.0	78.1	153.6	1 492.7	61.4	1 554.1
	Oct	90.4	177.6	142.0	87.6	131.7	94.3	246.4	120.4	93.0	1 183.4	73.6	146.5	1 403.5	60.6	1 464.1
1998	Jan	87.6	170.6	137.2	82.8	126.1	88.5	234.3	112.3	88.7	1 128.1	70.9	141.6	1 340.6	59.9	1 400.5
	Apr	84.1	165.4	134.1	79.9	122.3	85.2	229.4	108.0	85.1	1 093.5	69.3	138.7	1 301.5	57.9	1 359.4
	Jul	81.8	163.7	133.3	80.0	121.4	83.7	225.2	105.5	84.1	1 078.7	68.6	139.4	1 286.7	57.3	1 344.0
	Oct	82.1	160.9	130.9	79.9	121.4	82.0	219.3	102.5	81.8	1 060.8	68.1	136.9	1 265.8	56.1	1 321.9
1999	Jan	82.6	159.5	129.5	79.0	122.6	80.3	214.5	101.2	81.2	1 050.4	67.8	135.6	1 253.8	55.9	1 309.7
	Apr	82.5	157.2	127.0	78.2	123.1	79.1	207.8	98.8	78.4	1 032.1	67.1	133.9	1 233.1	55.0	1 288.1
	Jul	80.3	153.8	122.4	75.9	120.2	76.6	202.2	94.4	74.9	1 000.7	63.8	130.2	1 194.7	50.0	1 244.7
	Oct	76.7	150.0	118.3	73.6	115.9	73.6	196.5	91.1	71.4	967.1	61.0	126.1	1 154.2	46.5	1 200.7
2000	Jan	75.7	145.7	114.6	73.2	112.1	70.3	189.4	87.2	68.0	936.2	59.3	123.2	1 118.7	44.2	1 162.9
	Apr	73.6	139.9	108.9	70.0	108.1	66.9	181.6	81.3	63.8	894.1	57.8	119.0	1 070.9	42.4	1 113.3
	Jul	72.0	135.4	104.9	68.7	107.2	62.5	172.0	77.5	61.1	861.3	57.1	115.1	1 033.5	41.2	1 074.7
	Oct	69.5	131.0	102.5	67.7	106.5	60.7	165.0	74.3	58.1	835.3	56.4	111.7	1 003.4	41.3	1 044.7
2001	Jan	66.2	127.4	99.9	66.6	104.0	57.2	158.2	69.7	54.9	804.1	54.9	108.8	967.8	40.8	1 008.6
	Apr	63.2	124.9	97.6	65.1	100.8	54.8	151.8	66.1	53.6	777.9	52.4	105.3	935.6	39.9	975.5
	Jul	61.4	121.5	95.1	63.0	97.4	53.7	151.0	65.1	52.1	760.3	49.8	102.4	912.5	39.3	951.8
	Oct	61.5	121.4	93.2	61.6	95.7	54.3	156.3	65.9	51.1	761.0	49.2	104.2	914.4	38.6	953.0
2002	Jan	60.9	121.3	91.4	60.5	95.4	55.3	162.9	68.7	51.0	767.4	48.1	104.3	919.8	38.1	957.9
	Apr	59.4	119.5	89.7	59.6	93.9	56.5	166.5	70.8	51.1	767.0	47.7	104.7	919.4	37.7	957.1
	Jul	58.4	117.9	88.9	58.3	93.2	57.3	167.3	72.0	50.0	763.3	46.8	101.5	911.6	36.2	947.8
	Oct	55.9	116.3	87.7	58.0	93.7	57.3	167.6	72.3	49.4	758.2	46.8	100.3	905.3	35.1	940.4
2003	Jan	54.6	115.2	86.5	57.6	94.1	57.2	168.3	72.7	48.6	754.8	46.1	100.0	900.9	35.0	935.9
	Apr	53.6	112.9	84.6	59.0	95.3	58.5	172.0	75.7	48.8	760.4	45.5	99.7	905.6	34.3	939.9
	Jul	52.5	112.1	84.0	59.7	94.9	58.6	171.6	76.2	49.1	758.7	45.0	99.8	903.5	34.1	937.6
	Oct	51.3	109.5	81.9	59.1	94.2	57.5	170.2	76.0	47.6	747.3	43.2	99.4	889.9	34.7	924.6
2004	Jan	49.1	103.2	77.4	55.6	92.6	56.3	167.2	74.5	44.6	720.5	41.5	96.2	858.2	33.5	891.7
	Apr	47.4	101.3	75.9	53.7	90.4	56.1	165.8	72.3	42.9	705.8	41.7	94.5	842.0	32.0	874.0
	Jul	45.3	96.9	71.8	50.9	86.9	54.4	161.9	69.0	40.6	677.7	39.6	89.8	807.1	29.2	836.3
	Oct	45.6	97.5	71.5	51.3	86.0	55.4	159.4	69.5	40.8	677.0	39.5	90.4	806.9	29.8	836.7

1 The figures are based on the number of claimants receiving unemployment related benefits and are adjusted for seasonality and discontinuities to be consistent with current coverage. See chapter text. The latest national and regional seasonally adjusted claimant count figures are provisional and subject to revision in the following month.

Source: Office for National Statistics: 020 7533 6094

7.15 Economic activity: by sex and age[1]
United Kingdom
At Spring each year. Seasonally adjusted

Thousands and percentages

	All aged 16 and over	16-59/64	16-17	18-24	16-24	25-34	35-49	50-64 (m) 50-59 (w)	65+ (m) 60+ (w)
Thousands									
All									
	MGSF	YBSK	YBZL	YBZO	PXMK	YBZR	YBZU	YBZX	YCAD
1996	28 345	27 554	824	3 843	4 667	7 490	10 122	5 276	791
1997	28 492	27 666	864	3 721	4 585	7 513	10 093	5 475	826
1998	28 497	27 700	854	3 636	4 490	7 437	10 107	5 666	796
1999	28 811	27 974	844	3 629	4 473	7 366	10 283	5 852	837
2000	29 071	28 223	846	3 668	4 514	7 259	10 455	5 995	848
2001	29 122	28 288	817	3 667	4 484	7 078	10 602	6 124	834
2002	29 404	28 495	814	3 778	4 592	6 905	10 775	6 223	909
2003	29 648	28 697	834	3 791	4 625	6 703	10 928	6 441	951
2004	29 821	28 808	817	3 902	4 719	6 582	11 034	6 473	1 013
Men									
	MGSG	YBSL	YBZM	YBZP	PXML	YBZS	YBZV	YBZY	YCAE
1996	15 686	15 409	430	2 064	2 494	4 187	5 481	3 247	277
1997	15 687	15 408	429	2 000	2 429	4 172	5 453	3 354	279
1998	15 647	15 365	429	1 939	2 368	4 122	5 438	3 436	282
1999	15 774	15 480	433	1 929	2 362	4 042	5 533	3 544	295
2000	15 882	15 590	428	1 954	2 382	3 988	5 621	3 599	292
2001	15 867	15 596	420	1 949	2 369	3 890	5 665	3 673	271
2002	15 969	15 670	412	2 013	2 425	3 786	5 763	3 697	299
2003	16 159	15 815	422	2 024	2 446	3 684	5 853	3 832	344
2004	16 179	15 834	411	2 070	2 481	3 598	5 905	3 849	345
Women									
	MGSH	YBSM	YBZN	YBZQ	PXMM	YBZT	YBZW	YBZZ	YCAF
1996	12 658	12 145	395	1 778	2 173	3 303	4 640	2 029	514
1997	12 805	12 258	436	1 721	2 157	3 341	4 640	2 121	547
1998	12 850	12 336	425	1 697	2 122	3 315	4 670	2 230	514
1999	13 037	12 494	411	1 700	2 111	3 324	4 751	2 309	543
2000	13 189	12 633	418	1 714	2 132	3 271	4 834	2 396	557
2001	13 255	12 692	397	1 718	2 115	3 189	4 936	2 452	563
2002	13 435	12 824	403	1 765	2 168	3 119	5 012	2 525	610
2003	13 489	12 883	412	1 767	2 179	3 019	5 076	2 609	607
2004	13 642	12 974	405	1 832	2 237	2 983	5 129	2 624	668
Rates[2]									
All									
	MGWG	MGSO	YCAG	YCAJ	PXMN	YCAM	YCAP	MGWP	MGWS
1996	62.5	78.4	58.2	76.9	72.8	82.8	84.8	68.1	7.8
1997	62.6	78.4	59.4	76.5	72.6	83.5	84.4	68.5	8.1
1998	62.4	78.3	58.9	75.6	71.6	83.6	84.2	68.7	7.8
1999	62.8	78.7	58.8	75.4	71.6	84.2	84.8	69.3	8.1
2000	63.1	78.9	59.0	76.0	72.0	84.4	85.0	69.7	8.2
2001	62.7	78.5	55.6	75.1	70.5	83.9	84.9	70.0	8.0
2002	63.0	78.6	54.1	76.0	70.8	83.9	85.0	70.3	8.7
2003	63.1	78.7	54.7	74.4	69.8	83.4	85.0	72.2	9.0
2004	63.1	78.6	52.6	75.0	..	83.5	84.7	72.1	9.5
Men									
	MGWH	MGSP	YCAH	YCAK	PXMO	YCAN	YCAQ	MGWQ	MGWT
1996	72.0	84.9	59.7	82.6	77.5	93.4	92.5	71.8	7.6
1997	71.7	84.7	58.0	82.4	76.7	93.6	92.0	72.2	7.6
1998	71.2	84.2	58.3	80.9	75.4	93.7	91.5	71.9	7.6
1999	71.5	84.4	59.3	80.5	75.6	93.4	92.2	72.5	7.9
2000	71.5	84.6	58.6	81.2	76.0	93.8	92.4	72.4	7.7
2001	70.9	84.0	55.9	80.1	74.3	93.2	91.8	72.9	7.1
2002	70.8	83.9	53.4	81.0	74.5	92.9	91.9	72.7	7.7
2003	71.1	84.1	54.1	79.2	73.3	92.5	92.0	74.7	8.8
2004	70.7	83.6	51.7	79.1	..	92.0	91.8	74.4	8.7
Women									
	MGWI	MGSQ	YCAI	YCAL	PXMP	YCAO	YCAR	MGWR	MGWU
1996	53.8	71.4	56.7	71.3	68.0	72.3	77.1	62.9	7.8
1997	54.2	71.8	60.8	70.7	68.5	73.5	76.9	63.3	8.4
1998	54.2	72.0	59.6	70.4	67.9	73.7	77.1	64.3	7.8
1999	54.8	72.5	58.3	70.4	67.7	75.1	77.6	64.9	8.3
2000	55.2	72.9	59.5	70.8	68.2	75.2	77.8	65.9	8.5
2001	55.1	72.7	55.3	70.1	66.8	74.8	78.2	66.1	8.5
2002	55.6	73.0	54.8	71.0	67.2	75.1	78.2	67.1	9.3
2003	55.6	73.0	55.4	69.5	66.4	74.4	78.0	68.7	9.1
2004	55.9	73.2	53.5	70.8	..	75.0	77.9	68.9	10.0

1 See chapter text. The data in this table have been adjusted to reflect the latest 2001 Census population data.
2 Total economically active as a percentage of all persons in the relevant age group.

Source: Labour Force Survey, Office for National Statistics

7.16 Economically inactive: by sex and age[1]
United Kingdom
At Spring each year. Seasonally adjusted

Thousands and percentages

	All aged 16 and over	16-59/64	16-17	18-24	16-24	25-34	35-49	50-64 (m) 50-59 (w)	65+ (m) 60+ (w)
Thousands									
All									
	MGSI	YBSN	YCAS	YCAV	PXMQ	YCAY	YCBB	MGWA	MGWD
1996	16 997	7 592	591	1 151	1 742	1 560	1 820	2 470	9 405
1997	17 004	7 608	591	1 140	1 731	1 488	1 866	2 523	9 396
1998	17 164	7 697	595	1 171	1 766	1 457	1 891	2 583	9 468
1999	17 051	7 589	591	1 181	1 772	1 384	1 840	2 593	9 462
2000	17 035	7 542	587	1 159	1 746	1 340	1 843	2 612	9 493
2001	17 292	7 729	653	1 217	1 870	1 356	1 883	2 619	9 563
2002	17 300	7 749	692	1 195	1 887	1 324	1 908	2 630	9 551
2003	17 347	7 752	690	1 306	1 996	1 334	1 935	2 486	9 595
2004	17 473	7 842	736	1 304	2 040	1 305	1 988	2 510	9 631
Men									
	MGSJ	YBSO	YCAT	YCAW	PXMR	YCAZ	YCBC	MGWB	MGWE
1996	6 108	2 736	290	434	724	295	443	1 274	3 372
1997	6 189	2 790	310	428	738	283	475	1 294	3 399
1998	6 314	2 889	307	458	765	277	504	1 342	3 426
1999	6 297	2 858	297	468	765	283	467	1 342	3 439
2000	6 320	2 847	302	451	753	262	460	1 371	3 473
2001	6 510	2 970	332	486	818	284	507	1 362	3 540
2002	6 581	3 018	360	473	833	288	507	1 389	3 563
2003	6 564	2 994	359	533	892	297	507	1 298	3 571
2004	6 719	3 098	384	547	931	313	531	1 323	3 621
Women									
	MGSK	YBSP	YCAU	YCAX	PXMS	YCBA	YCBD	MGWC	MGWF
1996	10 889	4 856	301	717	1 018	1 264	1 377	1 196	6 033
1997	10 815	4 818	281	712	993	1 205	1 391	1 229	5 998
1998	10 850	4 808	288	712	1 000	1 180	1 387	1 240	6 042
1999	10 754	4 731	294	713	1 007	1 100	1 373	1 251	6 023
2000	10 716	4 695	285	708	993	1 078	1 383	1 241	6 020
2001	10 781	4 758	321	731	1 052	1 073	1 376	1 257	6 023
2002	10 719	4 731	332	722	1 054	1 037	1 401	1 241	5 988
2003	10 783	4 758	332	774	1 106	1 037	1 429	1 187	6 025
2004	10 754	4 744	352	756	1 108	992	1 457	1 187	6 010
Rates[2]									
All									
	YBTC	YBTL	LWEX	LWFA	PXNF	LWFD	LWFG	LWFJ	LWFM
1996	37.5	21.6	41.8	23.1	27.2	17.2	15.2	31.9	92.2
1997	37.4	21.6	40.6	23.5	27.4	16.5	15.6	31.5	91.9
1998	37.6	21.7	41.1	24.4	28.4	16.4	15.8	31.3	92.2
1999	37.2	21.3	41.2	24.6	28.4	15.8	15.2	30.7	91.9
2000	36.9	21.1	41.0	24.0	28.0	15.6	15.0	30.3	91.8
2001	37.3	21.5	44.4	24.9	29.5	16.1	15.1	30.0	92.0
2002	37.0	21.4	45.9	24.0	29.2	16.1	15.0	29.7	91.3
2003	36.9	21.3	45.3	25.6	30.2	16.6	15.0	27.8	91.0
2004	36.9	21.4	47.4	25.0	..	16.5	15.3	27.9	90.5
Men									
	YBTD	YBTM	LWEY	LWFB	PXNG	LWFE	LWFH	LWFK	LWFN
1996	28.0	15.1	40.3	17.4	22.5	6.6	7.5	28.2	92.4
1997	28.3	15.3	42.0	17.6	23.3	6.4	8.0	27.8	92.4
1998	28.8	15.8	41.7	19.1	24.6	6.3	8.5	28.1	92.4
1999	28.5	15.6	40.7	19.5	24.4	6.6	7.8	27.5	92.1
2000	28.5	15.4	41.4	18.8	24.0	6.2	7.6	27.6	92.3
2001	29.1	16.0	44.1	19.9	25.7	6.8	8.2	27.1	92.9
2002	29.2	16.1	46.6	19.0	25.5	7.1	8.1	27.3	92.3
2003	28.9	15.9	45.9	20.8	26.7	7.5	8.0	25.3	91.2
2004	29.3	16.4	48.3	20.9	..	8.0	8.2	25.6	91.3
Women									
	YBTE	YBTN	LWEZ	LWFC	PXNH	LWFF	LWFI	LWFL	LWFO
1996	46.2	28.6	43.3	28.7	32.0	27.7	22.9	37.1	92.2
1997	45.8	28.2	39.2	29.3	31.5	26.5	23.1	36.7	91.6
1998	45.8	28.0	40.4	29.6	32.1	26.3	22.9	35.7	92.2
1999	45.2	27.5	41.7	29.6	32.3	24.9	22.4	35.1	91.7
2000	44.8	27.1	40.5	29.2	31.8	24.8	22.2	34.1	91.5
2001	44.9	27.3	44.7	29.9	33.2	25.2	21.8	33.9	91.5
2002	44.4	27.0	45.2	29.0	32.8	24.9	21.8	32.9	90.7
2003	44.4	27.0	44.6	30.5	33.6	25.6	22.0	31.3	90.9
2004	44.1	26.8	46.5	29.2	..	25.0	22.1	31.1	90.0

1 See chapter text. The data in this table have been adjusted to reflect the latest 2001 Census population data.

2 Total economically inactive as a percentage of all persons in the relevant age group.

Source: Labour Force Survey, Office for National Statistics

7.17 Economically inactive:[1] by reason and sex
United Kingdom
At Spring each year. Seasonally adjusted

	Student	Looking after family/home	Temporary sick	Long-term sick	Discouraged workers[2]	Retired	Other	Does not want a job	Wants a job	All economically inactive
			Economic inactivity by reason:					by:		

Thousands

All

	BEDZ	BEEC	BEBK	BEBN	YCFO	BEEI	BEEL	YBVZ	YBWC	YBSN
1997	1 406	2 551	216	2 145	88	479	722	5 242	2 365	7 608
1998	1 417	2 568	205	2 201	72	506	728	5 323	2 374	7 697
1999	1 452	2 444	178	2 179	68	524	745	5 285	2 305	7 589
2000	1 406	2 376	184	2 157	63	545	812	5 233	2 309	7 542
2001	1 518	2 391	189	2 207	35	589	800	5 529	2 200	7 729
2002	1 522	2 381	179	2 236	34	592	806	5 492	2 257	7 749
2003	1 623	2 400	195	2 124	36	570	804	5 621	2 131	7 752
2004	1 662	2 342	198	2 165	33	598	844	5 818	2 024	7 842

Men

	BEEX	BEAQ	BEDI	BEDL	YCFP	BEDR	BEDU	YBWA	YBWD	YBSO
1997	698	156	106	1 201	50	327	252	1 874	916	2 790
1998	702	177	94	1 259	44	344	269	1 928	961	2 889
1999	706	171	76	1 235	40	353	277	1 936	922	2 858
2000	681	163	87	1 205	34	377	300	1 923	924	2 847
2001	733	176	90	1 237	23	396	315	2 061	909	2 970
2002	744	182	89	1 248	21	397	337	2 072	946	3 018
2003	813	178	88	1 172	21	392	329	2 101	892	2 994
2004	847	192	95	1 182	22	413	348	2 241	856	3 098

Women

	BEBL	BEBO	BEEG	BEEJ	YCFQ	BEEP	BEES	YBWB	YBWE	YBSP
1997	708	2 396	110	944	38	152	470	3 368	1 450	4 818
1998	715	2 391	111	943	28	162	458	3 395	1 413	4 808
1999	746	2 273	102	944	28	171	468	3 348	1 383	4 731
2000	725	2 213	97	952	29	168	512	3 310	1 385	4 695
2001	786	2 215	99	970	11	193	484	3 468	1 290	4 758
2002	778	2 199	90	988	13	194	468	3 420	1 311	4 731
2003	809	2 222	106	952	15	179	475	3 520	1 238	4 758
2004	815	2 150	104	983	11	185	496	3 576	1 168	4 744

Percentages

All

	BEDJ	BEDM	BEDP	BEDS	BEDV	BEDY	BEEB	BEEE	BEBM	BEAR
1997	18.5	33.5	2.8	28.2	1.2	6.3	9.5	68.9	31.1	100.0
1998	18.4	33.4	2.7	28.6	0.9	6.6	9.5	69.2	30.8	100.0
1999	19.1	32.2	2.3	28.7	0.9	6.9	9.8	69.6	30.4	100.0
2000	18.6	31.5	2.4	28.6	0.8	7.2	10.8	69.4	30.6	100.0
2001	19.6	30.9	2.5	28.6	0.4	7.6	10.3	71.5	28.5	100.0
2002	19.6	30.7	2.3	28.9	0.4	7.6	10.4	70.9	29.1	100.0
2003	20.9	31.0	2.5	27.4	0.5	7.4	10.4	72.5	27.5	100.0
2004	21.2	29.9	2.5	27.6	0.4	7.6	10.8	74.2	25.8	100.0

Men

	BEEH	BEEK	BEEN	BEEQ	BEET	BEEW	BEEZ	BEAS	BEGT	BEBP
1997	25.0	5.6	3.8	43.1	1.8	11.7	9.0	67.2	32.8	100.0
1998	24.3	6.1	3.3	43.6	1.5	11.9	9.3	66.7	33.3	100.0
1999	24.7	6.0	2.6	43.2	1.4	12.3	9.7	67.7	32.3	100.0
2000	23.9	5.7	3.0	42.3	1.2	13.3	10.5	67.6	32.4	100.0
2001	24.7	5.9	3.0	41.6	0.8	13.3	10.6	69.4	30.6	100.0
2002	24.7	6.0	2.9	41.4	0.7	13.2	11.2	68.7	31.3	100.0
2003	27.2	6.0	3.0	39.2	0.7	13.1	11.0	70.2	29.8	100.0
2004	27.3	6.2	3.1	38.2	0.7	13.3	11.2	72.4	27.6	100.0

Women

	BEGZ	BEHC	BEHF	BEHI	BEHL	BEHO	BEBQ	BEHR	BEHU	BEGW
1997	14.7	49.7	2.3	19.6	0.8	3.2	9.7	69.9	30.1	100.0
1998	14.9	49.7	2.3	19.6	0.6	3.4	9.5	70.6	29.4	100.0
1999	15.8	48.0	2.2	19.9	0.6	3.6	9.9	70.8	29.2	100.0
2000	15.4	47.1	2.1	20.3	0.6	3.6	10.9	70.5	29.5	100.0
2001	16.5	46.5	2.1	20.4	0.2	4.1	10.2	72.9	27.1	100.0
2002	16.4	46.5	1.9	20.9	0.3	4.1	9.9	72.3	27.7	100.0
2003	17.0	46.7	2.2	20.0	0.3	3.8	10.0	74.0	26.0	100.0
2004	17.2	45.3	2.2	20.7	0.2	3.9	10.5	75.4	24.6	100.0

1 All persons aged 16 - 59/64. See chapter text.
2 People whose reason for not seeking work was that they believed no jobs were available.

Source: Labour Force Survey, Office for National Statistics

		1997	1998	1999	2000	2001	2002	2003
Working days lost through all stoppages in progress (thousands)	KBBZ	235	282	242	499	525	1 323	499
Analysis by industry								
Mining, quarrying, electricity, gas and water	DMME	2	–	–	3	25	–	–
Manufacturing	BBFX	86	34	57	52	43	21	63
Construction	DMMG	17	13	49	49	10	17	14
Transport, storage and communication	BBFY	36	139	50	97	107	96	126
Public administration and defence	BBFZ	29	28	35	50	216	488	138
Education	BBGA	28	6	25	50	43	376	131
Health and social work	BBGB	7	16	5	122	73	148	15
Other community, social and personal services	DMML	5	30	7	36	4	107	10
All other industries and services	DMMM	25	15	12	40	4	70	2
Analysis by number of working days lost in each stoppage								
Under 250 days	KBFC	12	8	11	12	9	7	6
250 and under 500 days	KBFJ	6	11	13	9	11	8	6
500 and under 1,000 days	KBFL	17	11	16	21	15	15	13
1,000 and under 5,000 days	KBFY	72	48	69	71	59	47	69
5,000 and under 25,000 days	KBFZ	101	118	133	85	140	104	46
25,000 and under 50,000 days	KBGS	26	–	–	–	72	122	112
50,000 days and over	KBGT	–	86	–	301	220	1 021	248
Working days lost per 1 000 employees all industries and services	KBHA	10	11	10	20	20	51	19
Workers directly and indirectly involved (thousands)	KBHB	130	93	141	183	180	943	151
Analysis by industry								
Mining, quarrying, electricity, gas and water	DMMN	–	1	–	1	3	–	–
Manufacturing	DMMO	28	14	31	28	17	10	18
Construction	DMMP	13	2	18	16	3	17	2
Transport, storage and communications	DMMQ	24	39	42	39	69	33	52
Public administration and defence	DMMR	20	4	17	29	46	171	56
Education	DMMS	15	4	28	17	34	388	15
Health and social work	DMMT	5	2	–	28	6	144	3
Other community, social and personal services	DMMU	1	22	2	13	1	103	3
All other industries and services	DMMV	23	4	2	12	1	76	1
Analysis by duration of stoppage								
Not more than 5 days	KBHM	108	57	129	82	98	828	78
Over 5 but not more than 10 days	KBHN	7	32	8	9	43	57	23
Over 10 but not more than 20 days	KBJQ	14	1	3	8	4	3	31
Over 20 but not more than 30 days	KBJR	–	–	–	–	–	1	–
Over 30 but not more than 50 days	KBJS	1	1	–	83	6	1	–
Over 50 days	KBJT	–	1	–	1	30	55	20
Numbers of stoppages in progress: total	KBLG	216	166	205	212	194	146	133
Analysis by industry								
Mining, quarrying, electricity, gas and water	DMMW	1	1	–	3	3	2	1
Manufacturing	DMMX	53	36	37	38	32	33	43
Construction	DMMY	11	13	20	16	9	3	4
Transport, storage and communications	DMMZ	68	57	91	116	94	51	45
Public administration and defence	DMNA	23	10	17	7	22	20	12
Education	DMNB	35	19	21	18	16	16	15
Health and social work	DMNC	7	6	4	10	12	14	7
Other community, social and personal services	DMND	8	17	8	13	10	11	9
All other industries and services	DMNE	12	7	8	5	9	12	4
Analysis of number of stoppages by duration								
Not more than 5 days	KBNH	184	130	179	187	162	118	113
Over 5 but not more than 10 days	KBNI	15	21	8	14	15	16	10
Over 10 but not more than 20 days	KBNJ	8	3	9	5	7	3	5
Over 20 but not more than 30 days	KBNK	2	4	4	1	1	3	1
Over 30 but not more than 50 days	KBNL	6	3	3	3	4	1	1
Over 50 days	KBNM	1	5	2	2	5	5	3

1 See chapter text.

Source: Labour Market Statistics, Office for National Statistics: 01633 819205

7.19

Average earnings and hours of full-time employees by industry division:[1] by sex
United Kingdom
At April. Standard Industrial Classification 1992

	Agriculture, Hunting and Forestry	Fishing	Mining and Quarrying	Manufacturing	Electricity, Gas and Water Supply	Construction	Wholesale and Retail Trade; repair of motor vehicles, cycles, personal and household goods
All employees							
Weekly earnings							
	C5V5	C5V8	C5VB	C5VE	C5VU	C5W8	C5WB
2000	289.2	374.2	538.2	417.2	520.8	420.8	368.1
2001	302.6	397.7	581.1	439.9	532.1	445.6	386.8
2002	336.1	350.7	591.7	455.6	543.0	466.4	403.6
2003	340.5	392.7	657.0	476.5	561.5	489.8	414.6
2004[2]	354.2	419.4	625.1	495.6	603.5	508.2	436.5
	349.9	414.4	620.4	493.5	600.7	507.3	435.6
Hours worked							
	C5V6	C5V9	C5VC	C5VF	C5VV	C5W9	C5WC
2000	43.9	44.4	44.1	41.3	39.4	44.2	40.4
2001	43.7	45.4	44.0	41.3	39.9	44.1	40.5
2002	44.7	43.4	43.2	41.0	39.9	43.4	40.5
2003	44.9	42.9	45.3	40.9	39.6	43.4	40.4
2004[2]	44.5	43.5	43.6	41.0	40.1	43.1	40.6
		43.8	43.4		40.0	43.2	
Hourly earnings							
	C5V7	C5VA	C5VD	C5VG	C5VW	C5WA	C5WD
2000	6.59	8.42	12.21	10.10	13.23	9.52	9.10
2001	6.92	8.76	13.21	10.66	13.33	10.10	9.55
2002	7.52	8.08	13.68	11.12	13.61	10.75	9.95
2003	7.59	9.15	14.51	11.65	14.17	11.28	10.27
2004[2]	7.97	9.63	14.35	12.09	15.06	11.78	10.75
	7.86	9.46	14.29	12.04	15.01	11.73	10.73
Males employees							
Weekly earnings							
	C6C3	C6C4	C6C5	C6C6	C6C7	C6C8	C6C9
2000	299.7	375.7	559.1	445.6	552.8	429.8	413.5
2001	312.4	..	601.4	469.5	568.9	456.4	431.7
2002	350.5	353.4	608.8	482.9	584.7	478.5	453.7
2003	356.2	391.4	671.2	503.2	595.7	503.8	464.4
2004[2]	365.1	433.1	643.5	521.3	630.4	520.7	485.8
	360.0	424.5	638.6	519.5	629.3	519.5	485.4
Hours worked							
	C6D6	C6D7	C6D8	C6D9	C6DA	C6DB	C6DC
2000	44.7	44.6	44.8	42.0	39.9	44.8	41.4
2001	44.6	..	44.8	41.9	40.4	44.7	41.5
2002	45.8	44.1	44.1	41.6	40.6	44.0	41.5
2003	46.1	43.4	46.5	41.5	40.1	44.0	41.5
2004[2]	45.5	45.4	44.5	41.6	40.5	43.7	41.6
	45.6	45.6	44.4			43.8	
Hourly earnings							
	C6E2	C6E3	C6E4	C6E5	C6E6	C6E7	C6E8
2000	6.70	8.42	12.48	10.62	13.87	9.59	9.98
2001	7.01	..	13.43	11.21	14.06	10.21	10.41
2002	7.65	8.02	13.81	11.62	14.42	10.88	10.92
2003	7.73	9.02	14.43	12.13	14.87	11.44	11.19
2004[2]	8.02	9.53	14.45	12.54	15.57	11.91	11.69
	7.90	9.32	14.40	12.49	15.55	11.86	11.67
Female employees							
Weekly earnings							
	C6CP	C6CQ	C6CR	C6CS	C6CT	C6CU	C6CV
2000	242.0	..	376.4	312.1	395.4	324.5	280.2
2001	253.5	..	437.6	332.2	410.9	343.9	297.2
2002	272.3	..	478.6	350.8	405.1	356.9	310.1
2003	270.8	..	566.5	372.8	426.0	370.8	321.6
2004[2]	302.0	..	513.1	392.8	477.8	399.9	342.2
	301.2		510.0	390.6	472.2	398.5	341.7
Hours worked							
	C6DL	C6DM	C6DN	C6DO	C6DP	C6DQ	C6DR
2000	40.1	43.2	38.3	38.9	37.4	37.7	38.5
2001	39.5	..	38.6	39.0	38.1	38.4	38.6
2002	39.8	40.0	37.8	38.8	37.7	38.2	38.7
2003	39.6	39.8	37.6	38.7	37.9	38.3	38.3
2004[2]	39.3	36.5	37.7	38.7	38.1	38.1	38.7
					38.0		
Hourly earnings							
	C6EH	C6EI	C6EJ	C6EK	C6EL	C6EM	C6EN
2000	6.03	..	9.82	8.02	10.57	8.61	7.28
2001	6.42	..	11.35	8.52	10.78	8.95	7.71
2002	6.84	..	12.67	9.04	10.75	9.34	8.02
2003	6.83	..	15.08	9.64	11.23	9.69	8.39
2004[2]	7.68	..	13.62	10.14	12.54	10.51	8.84
	7.67		13.52	10.08	12.41	10.46	8.82

Average earnings and hours of full-time employees by industry division:[1] by sex
United Kingdom
At April. Standard Industrial Classification 1992

	Hotels and restaurants	Transport, Storage and Communication	Financial Inter-mediation	Real Estate, Renting and Business	Public Administration and Defence; compulsory social security	Educa-tion	Health and Social work	Other community, social and personal service activities
All employees								
Weekly earnings								
	C5WE	C5WH	C5WK	C5WN	C5WQ	C5WT	C5WW	C5WZ
2000	273.2	429.8	587.5	489.6	419.0	419.7	381.0	407.5
2001	283.1	443.0	628.8	533.1	437.9	438.8	407.7	424.0
2002	295.9	462.3	671.0	564.4	456.7	459.6	427.7	468.4
2003	311.3	476.3	660.6	568.5	469.9	481.6	446.8	486.8
2004[2]	319.5	505.0	699.0	580.5	496.4	497.3	472.7	514.5
	317.9	503.4	702.4	573.4	495.4	496.8	472.2	509.7
Hours worked								
	C5WF	C5WI	C5WL	C5WO	C5WR	C5WU	C5WX	C5X2
2000	40.4	43.5	36.3	39.4	38.0	35.0	38.4	39.7
2001	40.6	43.0	36.4	39.4	38.3	35.3	38.6	40.0
2002	40.7	42.7	36.3	39.3	38.5	35.5	38.5	39.6
2003	40.7	43.0	36.1	39.3	39.1	35.6	38.5	39.4
2004[2]	41.2	42.7	36.3	39.3	39.2	35.5	38.6	39.8
	41.3	42.8						
Hourly earnings								
	C5WG	C5WJ	C5WM	C5WP	C5WS	C5WV	C5WY	C5X3
2000	6.76	9.87	16.19	12.43	11.01	12.00	9.93	10.26
2001	6.97	10.30	17.27	13.53	11.42	12.43	10.56	10.61
2002	7.27	10.83	18.49	14.36	11.87	12.94	11.10	11.82
2003	7.64	11.07	18.29	14.47	12.01	13.52	11.60	12.34
2004[2]	7.76	11.82	19.24	14.78	12.65	13.99	12.26	12.93
	7.70	11.77	19.33	14.60	12.63	13.98	12.23	12.80
Males employees								
Weekly earnings								
	C6CA	C6CB	C6CC	C6CD	C6CE	C6CF	C6CG	C6CH
2000	307.5	451.1	745.5	549.4	463.7	460.4	495.6	463.9
2001	320.8	463.9	794.1	601.0	488.4	480.8	532.8	482.4
2002	332.9	480.4	855.9	635.3	506.0	504.3	549.9	536.3
2003	351.9	493.5	832.1	636.7	522.5	528.8	581.1	562.2
2004[2]	346.3	521.6	874.9	645.5	547.8	545.4	612.7	592.5
	342.7	520.9	878.1	638.5	546.4	544.5	612.1	587.9
Hours worked								
	C6DD	C6DE	C6DF	C6DG	C6DH	C6DI	C6DJ	C6DK
2000	41.3	44.6	36.3	40.3	38.7	36.1	39.6	41.0
2001	41.6	44.1	36.5	40.3	38.9	36.4	39.9	41.1
2002	41.7	43.7	36.4	40.2	39.1	36.6	39.8	40.7
2003	41.8	44.0	36.3	40.1	40.0	36.7	39.4	40.4
2004[2]	42.2	43.6	36.4	40.1	40.1	36.5	39.5	40.9
			36.5				39.6	
Hourly earnings								
	C6E9	C6EA	C6EB	C6EC	C6ED	C6EE	C6EF	C6EG
2000	7.44	10.11	20.51	13.64	11.98	12.76	12.51	11.32
2001	7.71	10.51	21.78	14.91	12.55	13.19	13.34	11.73
2002	7.98	10.98	23.53	15.81	12.96	13.79	13.82	13.17
2003	8.41	11.20	22.95	15.86	13.06	14.40	14.73	13.90
2004[2]	8.21	11.97	24.01	16.08	13.65	14.93	15.50	14.49
	8.12	11.93	24.08	15.91	13.63	14.91	15.47	14.37
Female employees								
Weekly earnings								
	C6CW	C6CX	C6CY	C6CZ	C6D2	C6D3	C6D4	C6D5
2000	231.7	355.3	406.6	381.6	349.0	389.6	337.2	328.4
2001	238.5	372.9	440.5	414.6	357.7	407.1	359.9	343.1
2002	249.8	402.9	463.7	436.3	377.6	425.7	380.1	375.7
2003	262.2	410.0	463.7	446.4	390.9	445.9	394.0	379.1
2004[2]	285.4	443.1	493.0	461.1	418.6	462.8	416.5	406.6
	284.9	438.6	492.2	455.0	418.2	462.4	415.4	402.3
Hours worked								
	C6DS	C6DT	C6DU	C6DV	C6DW	C6DX	C6DY	C6DZ
2000	39.4	39.7	36.2	37.8	37.0	34.2	37.9	38.0
2001	39.4	39.2	36.3	37.8	37.4	34.4	38.1	38.3
2002	39.5	39.2	36.2	37.8	37.6	34.7	38.1	38.2
2003	39.4	39.1	35.9	37.7	37.8	34.8	38.1	38.0
2004[2]	39.9	39.5	36.2	37.7	37.9	34.8	38.2	38.2
	40.0							38.3
Hourly earnings								
	C6EO	C6EP	C6EQ	C6ER	C6ES	C6ET	C6EU	C6EV
2000	5.89	8.96	11.23	10.10	9.43	11.40	8.90	8.65
2001	6.05	9.51	12.12	10.96	9.55	11.83	9.44	8.95
2002	6.32	10.27	12.81	11.55	10.05	12.27	9.99	9.84
2003	6.65	10.49	12.90	11.82	10.35	12.81	10.33	9.97
2004[2]	7.15	11.22	13.62	12.23	11.05	13.29	10.91	10.63
	7.12	11.11	13.60	12.06	11.04	13.28	10.87	10.50

1 See chapter text. Employees on adult rates whose pay for the survey pay-period was not affected by absence.

2 For 2004, two sets of figures are shown. The first does not included supplementary information and therefore is comparable with earlier years. The second includes supplementary information and so is discontinuous with previous years (where the two figures are equal, only one appears).

Sources: Annual Survey of Hours and Earnings;
Office for National Statistics: 01633 819024

7.20 Average earnings and hours of full-time employees:[1] by sex
United Kingdom
At April

	All Industries				Manufacturing industries			
	Average weekly earnings	Average hours (numbers)	Average hourly earnings		Average weekly earnings	Average hours (numbers)	Average hourly earnings	
			including overtime	excluding overtime			including overtime	excluding overtime
All employees								
	C5TJ	C5TM	C5TP	C5TS	C5TV	C5TY	C5U3	C5U6
1999	407.8	37.8	10.26	10.28	402.7	41.2	9.76	9.72
2000	425.1	37.9	10.71	10.70	417.2	41.3	10.10	10.00
2001	449.7	37.9	11.33	11.35	439.9	41.3	10.66	10.62
2002	472.1	39.6	11.93	11.97	455.6	41.0	11.12	11.09
2003	487.1	38.0	12.32	12.34	476.5	40.9	11.65	11.62
2004[2]	506.9	39.6	12.81	12.86	495.6	41.0	12.09	12.07
	504.9		12.75	12.80	493.5		12.04	12.02
Male employees								
	C5TK	C5TN	C5TQ	C5TT	C5TW	C5TZ	C5U4	C5U7
1999	453.4	38.5	11.03	11.10	431.7	41.9	10.31	10.28
2000	471.7	38.6	11.50	11.53	445.6	42.0	10.62	10.54
2001	498.6	38.6	12.16	12.24	469.5	41.9	11.21	11.19
2002	523.3	40.8	12.82	12.92	482.9	41.6	11.62	11.62
2003	539.3	40.8	13.21	13.28	503.2	41.5	12.13	12.12
2004[2]	558.6	40.8	13.68	13.78	521.3	41.6	12.54	12.54
	556.8		13.63	13.73	519.5		12.49	12.49
Female employees								
	C5TL	C5TO	C5TR	C5TU	C5TX	C5U2	C5U5	C5U8
1999	331.0	36.7	8.83	8.83	299.3	39.0	7.68	7.65
2000	344.7	36.7	9.22	9.20	312.1	38.9	8.02	7.97
2001	366.9	36.7	9.79	9.79	332.2	39.0	8.52	8.50
2002	386.8	37.5	10.32	10.32	350.8	38.8	9.04	9.03
2003	400.7	37.4	10.71	10.70	372.8	38.7	9.64	9.62
2004[2]	422.3	37.5	11.26	11.27	392.8	38.7	10.14	10.15
	420.2		11.19	11.21	390.6		10.08	10.09

1 See chapter text. Employees on adult rates whose pay for the survey period was not affected by absence.

2 For 2004, two sets of figures are shown. The first does not included supplementary information and therefore is comparable with earlier years. The second includes supplementary information and so is discontinuous with previous years (where the two figures are equal only one appears).

Sources: Annual Survey of Hours and Earnings; Office for National Statistics: 01633 819024

Average earnings index:[1] **all employees by main industrial sectors**
Great Britain
Analyses by industry based on Standard Industrial Classification 1992

Indices (2000=100)

	Not seasonally adjusted												
	Annual averages	Jan-uary	Feb-ruary	March	April	May	June	July	August	Sept-ember	Oct-ober	Nov-ember	Dec-ember
Whole economy (Divisions 01 - 93)													
	LNMM												
2002	108.1	106.4	110.8	111.6	107.2	106.5	107.8	107.6	106.3	106.3	107.3	108.1	111.3
2003	111.7	109.9	113.8	116.8	110.0	110.0	111.2	111.8	110.2	110.4	110.9	111.2	114.7
2004	116.8	118.2	118.1	122.2	115.0	114.8	116.1	115.4	114.8	114.9	115.7	116.2	119.6
Manufacturing industries (Divisions 15 - 37)													
	LNMN												
2002	107.9	105.1	106.3	110.5	107.8	107.2	107.3	108.4	106.8	106.8	108.1	108.8	112.0
2003	111.7	109.1	111.0	117.9	110.5	110.5	110.4	111.8	109.8	110.6	111.5	112.3	115.4
2004	115.9	112.8	114.9	122.1	115.6	115.5	114.9	116.1	113.6	114.2	115.4	115.7	120.0
Production industries (Divisions 10 - 41)													
	LNMO												
2002	107.8	105.0	106.2	110.9	107.7	107.1	107.6	108.2	106.7	106.8	107.8	108.6	111.7
2003	111.6	108.9	110.7	118.2	110.7	110.4	110.9	111.6	109.7	110.4	111.2	112.0	114.9
2004	115.8	112.6	115.1	122.1	115.9	115.2	115.3	115.7	113.4	113.9	115.4	115.6	119.6
Service industries (Divisions 50 - 93)													
	LNMP												
2002	108.1	106.9	112.3	111.5	107.0	106.3	107.7	107.3	106.0	105.9	107.0	107.8	111.0
2003	111.7	110.1	114.9	116.3	109.9	110.0	111.3	111.9	110.4	110.1	110.6	110.7	114.3
2004	116.8	119.8	119.0	122.0	114.7	114.4	116.1	115.1	115.0	114.8	115.6	115.7	119.1
Private sector services (Divisions 50-99)													
	JJGF												
2002	107.6	107.2	114.5	113.3	106.3	105.4	107.0	106.3	104.8	104.5	105.3	106.0	110.2
2003	110.6	109.6	115.9	117.5	108.2	108.5	109.8	110.3	108.1	108.1	108.8	108.7	113.0
2004	115.5	121.0	119.7	123.7	113.1	112.6	114.0	113.1	112.3	112.2	113.5	113.6	117.7

	Seasonally adjusted												
	Annual averages	Jan-uary	Feb-ruary	March	April	May	June	July	August	Sept-ember	Oct-ober	Nov-ember	Dec-ember
Whole economy (Divisions 01 - 93)													
	LNMQ												
2002	108.2	106.3	107.0	106.2	107.9	107.9	108.1	108.5	108.5	108.8	109.2	109.8	109.7
2003	111.8	109.9	110.2	110.6	110.7	111.3	111.5	112.6	112.3	112.9	113.1	113.2	113.5
2004	116.7	118.3	114.5	115.3	115.6	115.8	116.1	116.3	116.9	117.3	117.8	118.2	118.5
Manufacturing industries (Divisions 15 - 37)													
	LNMR												
2002	108.0	106.0	105.8	106.8	107.3	107.6	108.1	108.3	108.8	108.8	109.3	109.4	109.9
2003	111.9	110.0	110.4	113.9	110.1	110.9	111.2	111.7	112.1	112.6	112.8	113.4	113.5
2004	116.0	113.9	114.3	118.1	115.2	115.6	115.7	115.9	115.8	116.1	116.6	116.6	117.8
Production industries (Divisions 10 - 41)													
	LNMS												
2002	107.9	105.9	105.6	106.9	107.1	107.5	107.9	108.2	108.7	108.7	109.2	109.3	109.8
2003	111.7	109.9	110.1	113.8	110.1	110.8	111.2	111.6	111.9	112.4	112.7	113.2	113.2
2004	115.8	113.7	114.4	117.7	115.2	115.4	115.5	115.6	115.6	115.9	116.4	116.5	117.5
Service industries (Divisions 50 - 93)													
	LNMT												
2002	108.1	106.3	107.1	106.2	107.8	107.9	108.1	108.5	108.3	108.7	109.0	110.0	109.5
2003	111.8	109.7	109.9	110.3	110.6	111.4	111.6	112.9	112.4	112.8	113.0	113.2	113.3
2004	116.7	119.4	113.9	115.4	115.4	115.6	116.0	116.2	116.9	117.3	117.9	118.3	118.4
Private sector services (Divisions 50-93)													
	JJGH												
2002	107.7	106.0	106.9	105.6	107.7	107.6	107.9	108.1	108.0	108.2	108.4	109.4	108.6
2003	110.7	108.7	108.8	109.2	109.5	110.6	110.6	111.9	111.2	111.7	111.9	112.1	112.0
2004	115.6	120.2	112.6	114.4	114.3	114.4	114.7	114.9	115.5	116.0	116.6	117.0	117.1

1 See chapter text.

Source: Office for National Statistics: 01633 819024

7.22 Average earnings index:[1] all employee jobs: by industry
Great Britain
Not seasonally adjusted

Indices (2000=100)

Excluding bonuses

SIC 1992	Agriculture, forestry and fishing (A,B)	Mining and quarrying (C)	Food products, beverages and tobacco (DA)	Textiles, leather and clothing (DB,DC)	Chemicals and man-made fibres (DG)	Basic metals and metal products (DJ)	Engineering and allied industries (DK, DL,DM)	Other manufacturing (DD,DE,DF, DH,DI,DN)	Electricity, gas and water supply (E)	Construction (F)
	JVUZ	JVVA	JVVB	JVVC	JVVD	JVVE	JVVF	JVVG	JVVH	JVVI
2002	112.7	106.8	108.5	108.2	108.3	106.6	109.1	109.4	103.3	110.5
2003	118.2	112.6	112.4	112.8	112.1	110.5	112.8	112.2	106.4	113.6
2002 Feb	108.0	104.3	105.3	105.2	105.5	104.7	107.1	107.1	103.4	109.7
Mar	113.3	103.6	107.2	106.1	106.0	104.8	107.8	107.3	102.1	109.8
Apr	110.5	106.3	107.7	108.0	108.3	107.6	108.5	109.1	103.0	110.3
May	109.4	106.4	108.3	106.8	108.6	106.5	109.0	110.2	101.5	110.5
Jun	110.6	107.8	109.3	108.0	108.7	106.7	109.9	109.6	103.3	111.4
Jul	110.2	106.9	107.8	111.0	109.6	107.7	110.3	109.8	104.0	111.8
Aug	114.8	107.7	109.1	107.8	108.3	105.8	109.4	109.3	103.7	109.4
Sep	119.5	108.2	109.0	109.3	109.6	107.1	109.1	110.3	104.9	110.9
Oct	113.9	106.8	109.6	110.7	109.2	108.0	110.1	111.1	104.3	111.2
Nov	115.9	107.2	110.4	109.6	108.5	108.0	110.5	111.5	104.5	111.9
Dec	118.8	111.9	112.2	110.6	111.0	108.0	111.2	111.2	103.6	111.7
2003 Jan	114.9	111.0	110.2	110.2	108.9	108.1	110.6	110.3	103.3	111.3
Feb	118.2	108.6	110.3	109.3	109.4	109.8	111.0	111.1	103.7	112.3
Mar	119.9	112.1	110.6	111.2	110.7	109.0	112.2	111.0	106.2	113.4
Apr	116.3	110.5	113.8	111.4	111.3	109.3	112.7	110.9	104.9	112.3
May	115.7	112.3	113.5	111.2	111.3	111.2	113.1	111.6	107.0	111.9
Jun	116.7	111.5	112.1	112.7	112.8	110.8	113.2	112.3	105.4	114.0
Jul	117.1	114.3	112.0	116.0	112.5	111.4	113.3	112.5	107.3	113.6
Aug	118.1	114.8	112.5	113.6	113.1	109.7	112.3	112.3	108.5	111.0
Sep	120.4	114.4	112.6	114.8	113.5	111.4	112.8	113.1	106.9	114.9
Oct	118.6	112.9	112.8	114.0	113.1	112.3	113.7	113.4	107.4	115.2
Nov	119.2	113.3	113.2	113.6	114.1	112.1	114.6	113.8	108.2	116.2
Dec	122.7	115.1	115.8	115.8	115.0	110.9	114.5	114.3	108.0	117.1
2004 Jan	119.8	114.1	115.1	115.1	113.5	113.4	114.1	114.1	109.4	116.3
Feb	120.7	116.2	114.5	114.3	116.1	113.1	114.2	114.5	108.9	117.5
Mar	119.6	114.5	115.8	116.4	117.1	115.2	115.7	115.5	109.7	119.8
Apr	123.7	115.1	117.2	114.4	117.7	113.2	116.7	115.2	112.1	119.2
May	120.1	116.0	118.7	116.1	118.1	115.3	117.2	116.4	111.0	118.7
Jun	123.9	116.2	117.6	117.6	119.5	115.5	117.1	116.0	113.3	119.5
Jul	122.5	116.1	117.8	119.6	119.0	117.3	118.3	116.3	111.4	120.4
Aug	120.5	114.6	118.0	117.2	118.9	116.7	117.5	115.2	110.9	119.7
Sep	123.2	115.9	116.8	118.4	118.6	116.6	117.3	115.9	109.4	120.9

Percentage change on the year

	JVVT	JVVU	JVVV	JVVW	JVVX	JVVY	JVVZ	JVWA	JVWB	JVWC
2003 Feb	9.4	4.1	4.8	3.9	3.7	4.9	3.6	3.8	0.3	2.4
Mar	5.8	8.2	3.2	4.7	4.4	4.0	4.1	3.4	4.0	3.3
Apr	5.2	3.9	5.7	3.2	2.7	1.6	3.9	1.6	1.8	1.8
May	5.8	5.5	4.8	4.2	2.4	4.4	3.8	1.2	5.4	1.3
Jun	5.5	3.4	2.5	4.3	3.8	3.8	3.0	2.5	2.1	2.3
Jul	6.3	6.9	3.8	4.5	2.6	3.5	2.7	2.5	3.2	1.6
Aug	2.9	6.5	3.1	5.3	4.3	3.7	2.6	2.7	4.5	1.5
Sep	0.8	5.7	3.3	5.0	3.6	4.0	3.4	2.6	1.9	3.5
Oct	4.2	5.7	2.9	3.0	3.6	4.0	3.3	2.1	3.0	3.6
Nov	2.9	5.7	2.5	3.6	5.2	3.8	3.7	2.1	3.5	3.8
Dec	3.3	2.8	3.1	4.6	3.7	2.7	3.0	2.8	4.2	4.9
2004 Jan	4.3	2.8	4.4	4.5	4.2	4.9	3.1	3.4	5.9	4.5
Feb	2.1	7.0	3.7	4.6	6.1	3.0	2.9	3.0	5.0	4.7
Mar	−0.2	2.2	4.7	4.7	5.8	5.7	3.1	4.0	3.3	5.6
Apr	6.4	4.1	2.9	2.6	5.8	3.6	3.5	3.8	6.9	6.1
May	3.8	3.3	4.6	4.4	6.1	3.7	3.6	4.3	3.7	6.1
Jun	6.2	4.2	4.9	4.4	5.9	4.3	3.5	3.3	7.5	4.8
Jul	4.6	1.6	5.2	3.1	5.8	5.2	4.4	3.4	3.7	6.0
Aug	2.0	−0.1	4.9	3.2	5.1	6.3	4.6	2.5	2.3	7.8
Sep	2.3	1.3	3.7	3.1	4.5	4.7	4.0	2.5	2.3	5.2

7.22 Average earnings index:[1] all employee jobs: by industry
Great Britain
continued Not seasonally adjusted

Indices (2000=100)

	Wholesale trade	Retail trade and repairs	Hotels and restaurants	Transport, storage and communication	Financial interm-ediation	Real estate renting and business activities	Public admini-stration	Education	Health and social work	Other services
Excluding bonuses										
SIC 1992	(G:51)	(G:50,52)	(H)	(I)	(J)	(K)	(L)	(M)	(N)	(O)
	JVVJ	JVVK	JVVL	JVVM	JVVN	JVVO	JVVP	JVVQ	JVVR	JVVS
2002	105.4	106.7	111.2	108.2	108.4	110.7	109.0	109.5	112.9	105.4
2003	109.0	111.1	116.2	112.6	111.7	113.3	113.6	115.4	119.3	106.1
2002 Feb	104.8	103.4	107.2	105.9	108.1	109.5	107.1	105.8	108.6	104.5
Mar	105.7	105.3	110.4	107.6	106.9	109.9	107.1	106.0	109.2	105.0
Apr	105.8	106.6	109.7	107.1	108.2	110.6	108.4	108.1	112.7	104.3
May	105.9	106.7	111.1	107.5	108.2	111.1	107.8	108.3	112.9	105.0
Jun	105.5	109.3	112.2	108.6	108.1	111.2	108.2	109.0	114.0	106.0
Jul	105.5	107.7	112.8	108.4	108.3	111.1	108.3	109.5	115.1	106.3
Aug	105.5	108.4	113.6	107.4	108.1	110.1	107.7	111.2	113.5	106.3
Sep	105.3	108.1	111.3	109.5	108.3	110.5	108.2	111.4	113.8	103.7
Oct	105.2	107.1	112.1	109.5	109.1	111.7	112.0	113.5	114.8	104.8
Nov	105.7	106.9	111.7	109.8	110.0	112.0	115.3	113.3	114.8	106.3
Dec	106.3	106.5	116.4	110.3	110.2	111.5	110.6	112.7	116.2	107.0
2003 Jan	107.5	109.2	113.2	110.5	110.3	112.3	110.2	111.6	116.6	106.5
Feb	107.8	108.1	112.9	108.5	111.5	112.6	111.4	112.0	115.0	104.9
Mar	108.5	108.8	113.2	110.9	111.4	112.9	112.1	112.1	115.9	104.2
Apr	108.5	110.3	116.3	111.6	111.6	112.1	113.0	115.5	117.7	106.2
May	108.8	113.0	116.2	112.0	112.8	113.0	113.1	114.7	118.0	106.2
Jun	109.4	111.7	116.0	112.9	112.5	113.1	112.9	115.7	119.1	106.2
Jul	109.2	112.2	116.8	113.0	112.2	113.4	114.0	116.9	121.8	106.6
Aug	109.3	112.9	117.7	113.2	111.0	113.3	114.0	117.7	122.3	107.2
Sep	109.1	113.0	116.5	114.0	111.1	113.4	114.4	118.2	120.6	105.9
Oct	109.6	111.1	116.5	114.4	111.5	114.2	114.3	116.8	120.9	106.6
Nov	109.2	110.5	116.9	114.7	112.4	114.5	117.8	116.2	121.1	106.3
Dec	110.7	111.9	121.5	115.5	112.2	114.7	116.1	117.0	121.9	106.8
2004 Jan	110.7	112.9	118.6	116.4	113.9	115.7	115.5	115.4	122.4	111.6
Feb	110.8	111.4	118.1	114.9	113.2	116.5	116.4	116.1	121.5	110.7
Mar	112.2	112.7	119.7	115.9	114.8	117.1	116.4	116.1	122.1	110.0
Apr	112.7	114.6	120.6	117.4	114.9	117.4	117.6	118.8	125.6	110.3
May	113.3	114.5	121.1	117.9	115.1	118.7	118.0	119.2	126.1	110.7
Jun	112.9	114.7	121.9	119.7	115.1	117.5	118.1	119.0	130.2	111.9
Jul	112.8	114.8	123.5	119.1	114.9	118.4	118.2	119.5	128.3	114.1
Aug	113.0	115.4	124.2	119.8	115.2	118.2	119.7	123.2	128.1	114.3
Sep	113.6	115.3	122.8	120.4	114.9	118.2	121.7	123.2	128.4	112.4
Percentage change on the year										
	JVWD	JVWE	JVWF	JVYJ	JVYK	JVYL	JVYM	JVYN	JVYO	JVYP
2003 Feb	2.9	4.5	5.4	2.5	3.1	2.9	4.0	5.9	5.9	0.4
Mar	2.7	3.3	2.5	3.0	4.2	2.7	4.7	5.8	6.1	−0.7
Apr	2.6	3.5	6.0	4.2	3.1	1.3	4.3	6.8	4.5	1.7
May	2.7	5.9	4.6	4.2	4.3	1.7	4.9	5.9	4.6	1.1
Jun	3.7	2.2	3.4	4.0	4.1	1.7	4.3	6.2	4.5	0.2
Jul	3.5	4.2	3.6	4.2	3.7	2.1	5.3	6.8	5.8	0.3
Aug	3.6	4.1	3.6	5.4	2.7	2.9	5.9	5.9	7.7	0.9
Sep	3.6	4.5	4.7	4.1	2.5	2.6	5.8	6.0	6.0	2.1
Oct	4.1	3.7	4.0	4.5	2.3	2.3	2.1	3.0	5.3	1.8
Nov	3.3	3.4	4.7	4.5	2.1	2.3	2.2	2.6	5.5	–
Dec	4.1	5.1	4.4	4.6	1.8	2.9	5.0	3.9	4.9	−0.2
2004 Jan	3.0	3.4	4.8	5.3	3.3	3.0	4.8	3.4	4.9	4.9
Feb	2.7	3.0	4.6	5.9	1.5	3.4	4.5	3.7	5.6	5.6
Mar	3.4	3.5	5.8	4.6	3.0	3.7	3.8	3.6	5.3	5.6
Apr	3.8	3.9	3.7	5.2	3.0	4.8	4.1	2.9	6.7	3.9
May	4.0	1.3	4.2	5.2	2.0	5.0	4.4	3.9	6.8	4.2
Jun	3.3	2.7	5.1	6.1	2.3	3.8	4.7	2.8	9.3	5.4
Jul	3.3	2.3	5.7	5.4	2.4	4.4	3.6	2.2	5.4	7.0
Aug	3.4	2.2	5.6	5.8	3.8	4.3	4.9	4.6	4.8	6.6
Sep	4.2	2.0	5.4	5.6	3.4	4.3	6.4	4.3	6.4	6.2

7.22 continued Average earnings index:[1] all employee jobs: by industry
Great Britain
Not seasonally adjusted

Indices (2000=100)

	Agriculture, forestry and fishing	Mining and quarrying	Food products, beverages and tobacco	Textiles, leather and clothing	Chemicals and man-made fibres	Basic metals and metal products	Engineering and allied industries	Other manufacturing	Electricity, gas and water supply	Construction
Including bonuses										
SIC 1992	(A,B)	(C)	(DA)	(DB,DC)	(DG)	(DJ)	(DK, DL,DM)	(DD,DE,DF, DH,DI,DN)	(E)	(F)
	JVUF	JVUG	JVUH	JVUI	JVUJ	JVUK	JVUL	JVUM	JVUN	JVUO
2002	112.0	112.6	106.2	106.1	108.7	106.7	108.7	108.2	103.1	109.4
2003	117.0	118.6	110.4	109.2	114.5	110.4	113.5	110.2	105.4	112.4
2002 Feb	107.1	106.6	104.9	104.4	111.0	104.4	106.7	106.0	102.2	107.4
Mar	113.4	127.1	112.6	108.5	120.7	105.8	109.4	109.9	111.1	114.3
Apr	110.2	112.6	103.9	105.3	110.6	108.5	108.4	107.7	102.0	109.5
May	109.1	112.0	105.1	104.2	106.1	104.9	108.4	108.5	100.5	108.2
Jun	109.1	112.2	105.7	105.9	105.0	105.7	108.7	108.0	110.9	109.7
Jul	108.2	109.3	105.0	107.2	107.8	108.9	109.5	108.5	102.4	110.2
Aug	112.9	110.3	105.4	104.6	109.0	104.0	108.0	106.6	101.8	107.4
Sep	118.1	114.4	105.2	105.5	105.3	105.6	107.5	107.9	101.5	109.3
Oct	112.4	110.1	105.7	106.9	104.9	109.3	108.9	108.6	101.0	108.7
Nov	114.4	111.1	107.1	106.6	104.9	108.2	110.2	109.6	101.0	109.8
Dec	121.6	119.0	110.4	111.1	114.8	109.2	113.1	111.8	100.4	113.1
2003 Jan	114.0	113.3	108.1	107.6	107.5	109.2	110.4	108.5	102.4	109.5
Feb	116.9	113.7	109.8	106.4	115.9	109.5	112.2	109.7	101.6	109.8
Mar	121.4	138.7	119.9	110.7	138.2	111.5	118.6	113.6	113.1	119.3
Apr	114.8	132.0	110.0	106.6	115.0	110.0	112.4	107.8	101.8	109.8
May	113.8	114.8	108.2	107.1	109.8	109.8	113.5	108.9	104.1	108.5
Jun	115.0	113.9	107.7	107.2	110.6	109.4	112.8	109.5	118.7	111.3
Jul	115.8	115.4	109.8	111.1	110.9	114.1	113.4	110.1	104.8	111.7
Aug	115.5	116.4	108.9	108.7	112.4	108.2	111.2	108.6	103.9	108.0
Sep	118.0	117.1	110.8	109.6	111.3	108.7	111.8	109.7	102.8	112.9
Oct	117.0	114.6	108.1	109.3	110.6	113.7	113.0	110.6	103.9	113.4
Nov	117.5	115.0	109.5	109.2	112.0	110.8	115.2	111.2	104.0	114.8
Dec	124.0	118.3	114.3	117.3	120.2	110.4	117.0	114.1	104.2	119.2
2004 Jan	118.0	117.3	111.1	111.7	113.5	114.7	114.2	110.9	105.5	114.6
Feb	118.9	129.6	112.0	110.8	120.8	114.1	118.1	111.4	109.3	116.5
Mar	119.6	127.3	120.7	114.2	148.9	114.9	124.4	115.7	119.9	124.6
Apr	122.7	132.6	115.0	110.7	125.6	116.0	117.6	110.9	110.6	117.1
May	119.0	115.8	115.2	113.8	116.9	114.2	117.6	113.3	109.3	118.5
Jun	123.9	116.1	112.4	114.4	117.3	115.1	117.5	112.1	123.1	117.7
Jul	122.2	114.8	112.9	116.9	117.6	120.5	118.1	112.4	109.1	119.5
Aug	118.8	114.2	111.2	113.6	115.0	115.4	116.8	109.7	108.8	116.4
Sep	122.6	118.2	112.8	114.3	113.6	115.3	116.8	111.6	106.4	118.4
Percentage change on the year										
	JVYQ	JVYR	JVYS	JVYT	JVYU	JVYV	JVYW	JVYX	JVYY	JVYZ
2003 Feb	9.2	6.6	4.7	2.0	4.4	4.9	5.1	3.4	−0.5	2.2
Mar	7.1	9.1	6.5	2.1	14.5	5.4	8.4	3.4	1.7	4.4
Apr	4.2	17.2	5.9	1.3	4.0	1.3	3.7	0.1	−0.2	0.2
May	4.3	2.5	3.0	2.8	3.5	4.7	4.7	0.3	3.6	0.3
Jun	5.4	1.4	1.9	1.2	5.4	3.5	3.8	1.4	7.1	1.5
Jul	7.0	5.6	4.6	3.6	2.8	4.7	3.6	1.5	2.3	1.4
Aug	2.3	5.5	3.3	3.9	3.2	4.0	3.0	1.8	2.1	0.6
Sep	−0.1	2.4	5.3	3.8	5.7	2.9	4.0	1.7	1.3	3.3
Oct	4.1	4.1	2.3	2.3	5.5	4.0	3.8	1.8	2.9	4.4
Nov	2.7	3.5	2.2	2.5	6.7	2.4	4.6	1.4	3.0	4.6
Dec	2.0	−0.6	3.5	5.5	4.7	1.1	3.5	2.1	3.7	5.4
2004 Jan	3.6	3.5	2.8	3.8	5.6	5.1	3.4	2.3	3.0	4.7
Feb	1.7	14.0	2.0	4.1	4.2	4.2	5.3	1.5	7.6	6.1
Mar	−1.5	−8.2	0.6	3.2	7.7	3.0	4.9	1.8	6.0	4.4
Apr	6.9	0.5	4.5	3.8	9.2	5.5	4.6	2.9	8.7	6.6
May	4.5	0.8	6.4	6.2	6.4	4.0	3.6	4.0	5.0	9.2
Jun	7.7	1.9	4.4	6.7	6.0	5.2	4.1	2.3	3.7	5.7
Jul	5.5	−0.5	2.8	5.2	6.1	5.7	4.2	2.1	4.1	6.9
Aug	2.8	−2.0	2.2	4.5	2.3	6.7	5.0	1.0	4.7	7.7
Sep	3.9	0.9	1.9	4.4	2.1	6.1	4.5	1.7	3.5	4.9

Average earnings index:[1] all employee jobs: by industry
Great Britain

Not seasonally adjusted

Indices (2000=100)

	Wholesale trade	Retail trade and repairs	Hotels and restaurants	Transport, storage and communication	Financial interm- ediation	Real estate renting and business activities	Public admini- stration	Education	Health and social work	Other services
Including bonuses										
SIC 1992	(G:51)	(G:50,52)	(H)	(I)	(J)	(K)	(L)	(M)	(N)	(O)
	JVUP	JVUQ	JVUR	JVUS	JVUT	JVUU	JVUV	JVUW	JVUX	JVUY
2002	105.8	107.0	114.1	107.6	104.7	107.8	108.4	109.4	113.0	105.9
2003	111.3	110.9	119.2	111.3	105.2	109.7	113.1	115.2	119.3	108.4
2002 Feb	105.6	105.3	110.3	106.9	158.0	108.4	106.6	105.9	108.5	107.1
Mar	117.3	107.4	112.7	107.7	132.8	110.3	106.8	105.8	109.3	107.1
Apr	103.9	108.0	112.1	106.6	101.2	107.1	107.8	108.0	112.9	103.3
May	105.6	107.1	114.7	108.0	90.8	107.7	107.1	108.2	112.8	103.6
Jun	104.0	111.6	114.3	112.5	90.7	109.3	107.9	108.9	114.0	104.9
Jul	104.1	107.3	115.6	106.7	94.8	108.5	107.7	109.4	115.1	106.4
Aug	103.1	107.8	116.2	105.6	89.6	106.0	107.1	111.0	113.5	105.2
Sep	101.6	108.1	113.1	106.9	88.7	106.3	107.5	111.3	113.8	102.5
Oct	105.0	106.4	114.6	107.1	89.3	106.9	111.3	113.3	114.7	105.6
Nov	105.2	105.6	117.5	107.9	91.3	107.4	114.6	113.2	115.0	107.9
Dec	110.0	105.1	120.1	111.1	112.3	109.3	109.9	112.7	116.3	111.1
2003 Jan	107.6	106.8	116.1	107.6	112.6	108.3	109.5	111.7	116.7	110.2
Feb	108.3	109.0	117.4	106.5	155.2	111.3	110.8	111.8	115.2	107.0
Mar	122.2	111.7	117.2	112.2	143.3	112.9	111.6	112.0	116.2	108.7
Apr	108.7	109.8	118.3	108.5	101.5	106.9	112.3	115.3	117.9	107.5
May	109.1	111.6	120.0	110.6	93.7	109.1	112.5	114.4	118.1	107.8
Jun	111.6	112.1	118.1	117.8	92.0	110.5	112.2	115.6	119.1	108.2
Jul	110.1	112.1	119.4	111.8	97.6	110.7	113.3	116.8	121.9	109.8
Aug	107.8	111.7	119.3	110.4	90.4	108.5	114.4	117.4	122.3	108.2
Sep	108.3	112.6	118.5	110.8	90.3	108.1	113.7	117.9	120.6	106.2
Oct	110.4	110.3	118.7	111.3	91.7	109.4	113.8	116.5	120.9	108.9
Nov	112.7	109.2	120.1	112.1	92.3	108.6	117.1	116.1	121.2	107.6
Dec	118.3	113.8	127.8	115.6	101.7	112.3	115.5	116.9	122.0	110.5
2004 Jan	114.1	111.3	120.7	113.5	164.8	112.1	114.7	115.0	122.3	113.8
Feb	113.7	112.8	123.1	115.1	149.5	113.6	115.6	115.8	121.5	113.2
Mar	122.4	115.4	122.8	116.4	151.6	121.1	115.7	115.9	122.1	113.4
Apr	113.6	114.9	122.6	115.8	99.4	113.7	116.8	118.5	125.7	111.1
May	111.1	113.2	125.1	116.5	93.9	115.1	117.4	118.9	126.0	112.4
Jun	114.7	115.1	124.0	126.1	93.3	113.4	117.3	118.7	130.1	120.9
Jul	114.1	114.0	126.2	117.0	92.1	114.8	117.5	119.3	128.3	116.4
Aug	113.2	114.1	126.6	116.8	90.9	112.7	121.2	123.0	128.0	115.3
Sep	113.8	114.7	125.7	117.4	90.2	111.4	121.1	122.9	128.3	115.1
Percentage change on the year										
	JVZA	JVZB	JVZC	JVZD	JVZE	JVZF	JVZG	JVZH	JVZI	JVZJ
2003 Feb	2.6	3.5	6.4	−0.4	−1.7	2.7	3.9	5.6	6.2	−0.1
Mar	4.2	4.0	4.0	4.2	7.8	2.3	4.5	5.9	6.3	1.4
Apr	4.6	1.7	5.5	1.8	0.3	−0.2	4.2	6.8	4.5	4.2
May	3.3	4.2	4.6	2.5	3.2	1.3	5.0	5.8	4.7	4.1
Jun	7.2	0.4	3.4	4.7	1.5	1.1	4.0	6.1	4.5	3.1
Jul	5.8	4.5	3.2	4.7	3.0	2.1	5.2	6.7	5.8	3.3
Aug	4.5	3.6	2.7	4.5	0.9	2.4	6.8	5.8	7.8	2.9
Sep	6.5	4.2	4.8	3.6	1.8	1.7	5.7	6.0	5.9	3.7
Oct	5.1	3.7	3.6	3.9	2.7	2.4	2.2	2.9	5.4	3.1
Nov	7.1	3.4	2.2	3.9	1.1	1.1	2.2	2.5	5.4	−0.2
Dec	7.6	8.4	6.4	4.1	−9.4	2.7	5.2	3.7	4.9	−0.5
2004 Jan	6.0	4.2	4.0	5.4	46.4	3.5	4.8	3.0	4.9	3.2
Feb	5.0	3.4	4.8	8.1	−3.7	2.1	4.4	3.6	5.5	5.8
Mar	0.2	3.3	4.8	3.8	5.8	7.3	3.7	3.5	5.0	4.3
Apr	4.5	4.7	3.6	6.7	−2.0	6.3	4.0	2.8	6.6	3.3
May	1.8	1.4	4.3	5.3	0.2	5.5	4.4	3.9	6.7	4.3
Jun	2.8	2.7	5.0	7.1	1.4	2.6	4.6	2.7	9.3	11.8
Jul	3.6	1.7	5.7	4.7	−5.6	3.7	3.7	2.2	5.3	6.0
Aug	5.1	2.1	6.1	5.8	0.6	3.8	5.9	4.7	4.6	6.6
Sep	5.1	1.8	6.0	5.9	−0.1	3.1	6.5	4.2	6.4	8.3

1 See chapter text.

Source: Office for National Statistics: 01633 819024

7.23 Gross weekly and hourly earnings of full-time employees:[1] by sex
United Kingdom
At April

£

	Gross weekly earnings					Gross hourly earnings				
	Lowest decile	Lower quartile	Median	Upper quartile	Highest decile	Lowest decile	Lower quartile	Median	Upper quartile	Highest decile
All employees										
	C5U9	C5UC	C5UF	C5UI	C5UL	C5UO	C5UR	C5UU	C5V2	C5UX
1999	189.3	248.0	345.5	484.5	660.5	4.79	6.17	8.60	12.55	17.75
2000	195.8	256.6	359.0	501.8	685.4	4.99	6.40	8.91	13.04	18.37
2001	205.0	268.2	375.9	527.8	731.1	5.20	6.67	9.32	13.73	19.60
2002	214.4	279.1	390.9	551.8	767.8	5.44	6.97	9.74	14.36	20.60
2003	222.7	288.0	404.0	572.6	794.2	5.68	7.23	10.07	14.82	21.27
2004[2]	_231.9_	_301.3_	_423.0_	_595.5_	_828.6_	_5.91_	_7.53_	_10.56_	_15.42_	_22.19_
	230.3	299.6	422.1	593.9	825.3	5.87	7.49	10.51	15.36	22.09
Male employees										
	C5UA	C5UD	C5UG	C5UJ	C5UM	C5UP	C5US	C5UV	C5V3	C5UY
1999	211.5	278.4	383.9	531.5	731.7	5.10	6.61	9.21	13.45	19.19
2000	220.0	287.9	397.7	549.8	760.1	5.30	6.82	9.56	13.94	19.96
2001	229.5	299.6	415.7	575.8	813.3	5.52	7.13	9.99	14.62	21.43
2002	239.0	310.2	430.1	599.9	857.5	5.78	7.41	10.40	15.32	22.56
2003	246.6	320.3	444.6	622.8	881.9	6.00	7.68	10.75	15.83	23.17
2004[2]	_254.8_	_333.8_	_463.7_	_648.5_	_917.9_	_6.21_	_7.99_	_11.24_	_16.43_	_24.11_
	251.8	331.5	462.0	646.4	915.0	6.15	7.93	11.18	16.38	24.04
Female employees										
	C5UB	C5UE	C5UH	C5UK	C5UN	C5UQ	C5UT	C5UW	C5V4	C5UZ
1999	168.2	213.6	288.5	408.5	529.6	4.41	5.58	7.63	11.07	15.32
2000	174.3	221.7	298.1	422.6	549.4	4.58	5.80	7.89	11.51	15.87
2001	183.1	231.3	314.3	449.4	585.5	4.82	6.07	8.28	12.15	16.77
2002	192.1	241.8	330.7	474.0	623.7	5.04	6.35	8.70	12.80	17.66
2003	201.3	251.6	343.0	490.2	645.7	5.30	6.63	9.07	13.28	18.33
2004[2]	_210.6_	_265.1_	_360.5_	_515.8_	_679.3_	_5.53_	_6.95_	_9.55_	_13.96_	_19.18_
	210.0	263.4	358.0	512.5	677.6	5.50	6.92	9.49	13.87	19.07

1 See chapter text. Employees on adult rates whose pay for the survey period was not affected by absence.
2 For 2004, two sets of figures are shown. The first does not included supplementary information and therefore is comparable with earlier years. The second includes supplementary information and so is discontinuous with previous years.

Sources: Annual Survey of Hours and Earnings; Office for National Statistics: 01633 819024

7.24 Average earnings by age group of full-time employees:[1,2] by sex, 2004
United Kingdom
At April

£ and numbers

	Average gross weekly pay excluding overtime	Average gross weekly overtime pay	Average weekly hours (numbers)		Average gross hourly earnings excluding overtime pay
			Total	Overtime	
All employees					
18 to 21	246.6	12.1	39.8	1.5	6.4
22 to 29	393.3	14.6	39.3	1.4	10.4
30 to 39	521.4	19.1	39.6	1.6	13.7
40 to 49	545.6	21.9	39.7	1.8	14.4
50+	490.4	19.4	39.6	1.7	12.9
All ages	486.1	18.8	39.6	1.6	12.8
Male employees					
18 to 21	257.8	16.4	41.0	2.0	6.6
22 to 29	412.9	21.0	40.6	1.9	10.7
30 to 39	555.5	25.5	40.7	2.1	14.4
40 to 49	604.3	29.2	40.9	2.3	15.6
50+	537.3	26.0	41.0	2.3	13.9
All ages	531.3	25.6	40.8	2.1	13.7
Female employees					
18 to 21	233.2	6.9	38.4	0.9	6.2
22 to 29	370.4	7.1	37.8	0.7	10.0
30 to 39	459.8	7.6	37.5	0.7	12.5
40 to 49	442.0	9.0	37.5	0.8	12.1
50+	405.6	7.7	37.2	0.7	11.1
All ages	412.4	7.8	37.5	0.8	11.2

1 See chapter text. Employees on adult rates whose pay for the survey period was not affected by absence.
2 Data collected including supplementary surveys to improve coverage therefore these data are not directly comparable with those from previous years.

Sources: Annual Survey of Hours and Earnings, Office for National Statistics; 01633 819024

7.25 Vacancies at Jobcentres[1]
United Kingdom
Seasonally adjusted

Thousands

	January	February	March	April	May	June	July	August	September	October	November	December
Numbers of vacancies remaining unfilled DPCB												
1991	140.0	138.9	133.9	119.8	110.2	105.6	106.0	109.2	112.5	109.6	111.8	117.4
1992	117.0	118.2	118.2	117.1	118.8	119.8	120.2	118.6	113.1	112.9	114.4	117.0
1993	119.0	120.3	124.3	123.6	125.9	124.8	129.2	129.8	129.5	133.2	136.3	138.2
1994	140.4	142.7	143.4	146.2	149.1	154.9	158.8	165.0	165.4	175.3	176.9	177.6
1995	175.2	174.3	177.5	186.0	185.4	182.9	181.8	181.7	184.5	181.7	185.2	186.7
1996	190.4	189.3	196.9	201.2	209.2	220.7	233.0	238.8	247.4	248.7	257.5	265.5
1997	272.6	279.2	279.6	279.4	277.3	283.9	288.0	295.2	297.2	293.7	275.2	278.2
1998	275.0	285.0	286.3	288.2	298.1	300.1	302.8	302.7	301.5	302.9	304.4	303.2
1999	305.3	300.8	298.5	295.7	304.6	305.6	307.8	315.8	314.7	336.5	338.5	347.4
2000	340.3	341.7	344.6	355.7	354.3	357.2	362.9	361.6	365.6	364.5	374.3	376.5
2001	395.7	391.6	394.9	387.8	..	..	..	..	..	..	..	..
Inflow of vacancies DRYW												
1991	185.4	167.8	168.0	182.8	182.2	163.9	165.6	168.7	170.7	168.3	164.9	167.1
1992	166.4	166.9	171.7	166.0	166.2	176.4	173.3	164.0	167.1	171.3	164.7	173.8
1993	180.2	175.9	181.5	179.3	180.2	183.5	190.5	183.4	191.5	189.6	193.9	197.2
1994	199.2	199.5	199.1	203.7	205.2	212.2	208.3	223.6	216.6	219.1	223.1	226.8
1995	218.2	219.5	215.2	205.4	227.7	223.1	225.6	230.9	226.5	231.9	232.9	222.1
1996	228.9	222.2	219.8	231.7	221.4	219.5	224.4	223.1	221.7	203.4	230.2	232.8
1997	202.9	239.3	242.9	239.1	236.2	226.2	226.4	220.8	227.6	222.6	217.9	216.2
1998	184.2	218.5	219.2	216.3	218.2	225.0	222.0	221.4	221.8	229.9	223.1	219.4
1999	237.7	222.8	221.8	229.6	224.4	226.2	231.2	234.0	230.2	235.0	235.3	236.7
2000	227.9	226.1	228.8	225.3	213.2	222.3	220.6	219.0	225.6	221.3	220.2	222.8
2001	224.9	233.2	232.8	237.6	..	..	..	..	..	..	..	..
Outflow of vacancies DRZL												
1991	176.4	168.7	172.4	197.5	197.1	168.3	165.0	164.9	168.7	170.2	159.9	160.8
1992	169.7	165.6	170.5	168.4	168.6	174.1	172.5	164.1	170.5	169.8	160.8	170.6
1993	178.8	173.6	176.6	180.1	181.0	184.0	185.6	182.0	189.8	186.4	191.0	195.3
1994	196.8	196.7	198.3	202.3	203.4	205.8	202.8	217.1	214.8	210.8	221.6	227.0
1995	219.0	220.6	214.1	195.1	229.0	225.0	224.6	230.4	225.5	237.1	229.7	219.2
1996	225.6	222.1	213.8	222.7	212.9	211.1	214.3	218.4	213.9	200.9	220.9	229.8
1997	208.5	232.1	238.0	236.8	234.1	220.9	225.0	215.0	216.8	224.2	232.5	219.9
1998	207.2	208.7	213.1	214.0	209.0	222.3	219.3	221.2	218.5	228.7	220.4	223.5
1999	236.9	224.4	220.9	232.3	219.4	225.2	227.6	226.5	229.0	219.6	233.6	231.1
2000	240.6	223.6	224.1	218.9	213.9	218.6	214.6	219.2	221.8	217.1	211.8	220.4
2001	212.1	237.6	226.1	241.1	..	..	..	..	..	..	..	..
Number of placings DTQR												
1991	129.4	122.5	127.6	148.4	148.4	123.9	123.2	120.9	122.1	122.7	114.8	115.9
1992	124.6	119.7	123.6	122.6	123.0	126.5	126.5	119.6	125.9	127.6	120.6	130.2
1993	134.3	132.1	131.7	134.0	134.9	136.3	139.0	136.1	144.1	140.6	146.4	148.2
1994	149.5	150.6	151.5	156.6	157.7	161.9	157.7	169.6	166.4	162.3	170.3	173.2
1995	166.2	169.1	164.6	145.8	179.8	173.6	174.4	178.5	172.5	183.5	179.7	167.4
1996	176.1	164.6	151.5	152.8	151.6	148.2	149.7	153.6	148.9	135.4	150.4	159.3
1997	147.9	157.7	163.6	164.0	151.8	143.1	138.6	127.1	126.4	123.1	120.2	116.9
1998	109.0	113.9	115.5	114.1	110.5	115.9	115.8	116.4	117.8	121.4	118.0	117.2
1999	119.8	120.3	116.7	126.5	118.1	121.0	123.0	121.8	122.7	120.3	123.1	122.6
2000	121.1	116.4	115.7	111.4	108.1	109.5	107.3	109.9	111.3	109.9	107.1	108.4
2001	110.2	108.6	109.1	117.5	..	..	..	..	..	..	..	..

1 See chapter text.

Source: Office for National Statistics: 020 7533 6094

7.26 Trade unions[1]
United Kingdom
At end of year

Percentages

		1992	1993	1994	1995	1996	1997	1998	1999	2000	2001	2002
Number of trade unions	KCLB	315	302	281	271	261	257	243	241	230	220	218
Analysis by number of members:												
Under 100 members	KCLC	14.3	15.9	16.4	15.5	13.0	16.0	16.9	18.7	22.2	19.1	20.6
100 and under 500	KCLD	22.9	24.8	23.1	23.2	27.2	22.2	21.4	20.3	17.8	18.6	19.3
500 and under 1,000	KCLE	9.8	7.6	8.9	10.0	8.0	12.1	10.7	9.5	9.6	11.4	10.1
1,000 and under 2,500	KCLF	17.1	15.2	15.3	15.1	17.2	14.8	13.2	14.1	12.2	10.0	10.6
2,500 and under 5,000	KCLG	8.9	8.9	9.3	8.9	7.7	7.8	9.5	9.5	9.1	11.4	10.6
5,000 and under 10,000	KCLH	6.0	6.3	6.4	5.9	5.7	5.8	6.2	5.4	5.7	4.5	5.0
10,000 and under 15,000	KCLI	1.6	2.0	2.1	3.0	2.7	2.7	2.1	1.7	1.7	2.7	3.2
15,000 and under 25,000	KCLJ	3.8	3.0	2.8	2.6	2.3	2.3	2.9	4.1	5.2	5.9	4.1
25,000 and under 50,000	KCLK	6.3	7.0	7.1	7.4	7.7	7.4	8.2	7.9	7.0	6.8	7.3
50,000 and under 100,000	KCLL	2.9	3.0	2.5	2.6	1.9	2.3	2.5	2.1	2.6	2.3	1.8
100,000 and under 250,000	KCLM	3.5	3.3	3.6	3.0	3.1	3.1	2.5	2.1	2.2	2.3	2.8
250,000 and over	KCLN	2.9	3.0	2.5	3.0	3.4	3.5	4.1	4.6	4.8	5.0	4.6
All sizes	KCLP	100	100	100	100	100	100	100	100	100	100	100
Membership												
Analysis by size of union:												
Under 100 members	KCLQ	–	–	–	–	–	–	–	–	–	–	–
100 and under 500	KCLR	0.2	0.2	0.2	0.2	0.3	0.2	0.2	0.2	0.2	0.2	0.2
500 and under 1,000	KCLS	0.2	0.2	0.2	0.2	0.2	0.3	0.2	0.2	0.2	0.2	0.2
1,000 and under 2,500	KCLT	1.0	0.9	0.9	0.9	0.9	0.8	0.7	0.7	0.6	0.5	0.5
2,500 and under 5,000	KCLU	1.1	1.1	1.1	1.1	0.9	0.9	1.1	1.1	0.9	1.2	1.1
5,000 and under 10,000	KCLV	1.5	1.5	1.6	1.4	1.3	1.3	1.4	1.2	1.2	0.9	1.0
10,000 and under 15,000	KCLW	0.6	0.8	0.9	1.3	1.2	1.1	0.9	0.7	0.6	0.9	1.1
15,000 and under 25,000	KCLX	2.3	1.8	1.7	1.5	1.3	1.3	1.6	2.3	2.8	3.3	2.2
25,000 and under 50,000	KCLY	8.0	8.6	8.9	9.1	8.8	8.1	8.4	8.2	7.1	6.8	7.2
50,000 and under 100,000	KCLZ	7.0	7.3	5.9	5.9	3.9	4.5	4.5	3.8	4.6	4.0	3.1
100,000 and under 250,000	KCMA	18.6	18.2	19.3	16.3	15.2	15.3	11.9	9.9	9.8	9.5	10.1
250,000 and over	KCMB	59.4	59.2	59.3	62.0	66.0	66.1	69.1	71.7	72.0	72.5	73.5
All sizes	KCMC	100	100	100	100	100	100	100	100	100	100	100
Total membership (thousands)	KCMD	9 171	8 848	8 297	8 111	7 982	7 841	7 894	7 940	7 823	7 796	7 783

1 See chapter text.

Source: Department of Trade and Industry: 020 7215 5780

Personal income, expenditure and wealth

Chapter 8

Personal income, expenditure and wealth

Distribution of total incomes

(Table 8.1)

The information shown in Table 8.1 comes from the Survey of Personal Incomes for the financial years 1999/00, 2000/01, 2001/02 and 2002/03. This is an annual survey that covers approximately 300,000 individuals across the whole of the UK. It is based on administrative data held by Inland Revenue offices on individuals who could be liable to tax.

The table relates only to those individuals who are taxpayers. The distributions cover only incomes as computed for tax purposes and above a level which for each year corresponds approximately to the single person's allowance. Incomes below these levels are not shown because the information about them is incomplete.

Investment income from which tax has been deducted at source is not always known to local tax offices. Estimates of missing bank and building society interest and dividends from United Kingdom companies are included in these tables. The missing investment income is distributed, in a manner consistent with information from the Expenditure and Food Survey (EFS) and the National Accounts, to individuals for whom there is no investment income already reported by the tax office.

Superannuation contributions are estimated and included in total income. They have been distributed among earners in the Survey of Personal Incomes sample by a method consistent with information about the number of employees who are contracted in or out of the State Earnings Related Pension Scheme and the proportion of their earnings contributed.

When comparing results of these surveys across years, it should be noted that the Survey of Personal Incomes is not a longitudinal survey. However, sample sizes have increased in recent years to increase precision.

Estimates of self-employment income in the annual survey for 1998/99 are incomplete due to the absence of data from a limited number of sole trader sources. The deficiency is estimated to be worth about ½ per cent of total income.

Average incomes of households

(Table 8.2)

Original income is the total income in cash of all the members of the household before the deduction of taxes or the addition of state benefits. It includes income from employment, self-employment, investment income, etc. The addition of cash benefits (retirement pensions, child benefit, etc) and the deduction of income tax, council tax, water charges, domestic rates and employees' National Insurance contributions give disposable income. By further allowing for taxes paid on goods and services purchased, such as VAT, an estimate of 'post-tax' income is derived. These income figures are derived from estimates made by the Office for National Statistics, based largely on information from the Expenditure and Food Survey, and published each year in *Economic Trends*, and available on the National Statistics website.

A retired household is defined as one where the combined income of retired members amounts to at least half the total gross income of the household, where a retired person is defined as anyone who describes themselves as 'retired' or anyone over the minimum NI pension age describing themselves as 'unoccupied' or 'sick or injured but not intending to seek work.'

Children are defined as persons aged under 16 or aged between 16 and 18, unmarried and receiving full-time non-advanced further education.

Expenditure and Food Survey

(Tables 8.3 to 8.5)

The Expenditure and Food Survey (formerly the Family Expenditure Survey), introduced in 1957, covers all types of private households in the United Kingdom. It is a continuous survey with fieldwork carried out in every month of the year. In 2002–03 around 6,900 households in the UK provided information. The main purpose of the survey is to provide a source for the weighting pattern for the Index of Retail Prices, so it is primarily concerned with household expenditure on goods and services. However, it does have several other important uses.

Although the survey is primarily concerned with the expenditure of private households, much additional information is collected about income and the characteristics of co-operating households. Consequently, the survey provides a unique fund of important economic and social data.

Like all surveys based on a sample of the population, its results are subject to sampling error, and to some bias due to non-response.

The results of the survey are published in an annual report, the latest being *Family Spending 2002–2003*. The report includes a list of definitions used in the survey, items on which information is collected and a brief account of the fieldwork procedure.

8.1 Distribution of total income before and after tax
United Kingdom
Years ending 5 April

	1999/2000 Annual Survey					2000/01 Annual Survey			
	Number of individuals (Thousands)	£ million				Number of individuals (Thousands)	£ million		
		Total income before tax	Total tax	Total income after tax			Total income before tax	Total tax	Total income after tax
Lower limit of range of income					**Lower limit of range of income**				
All incomes[1]	27 200	533 000	93 200	439 800	All incomes[1]	29 300	594 700	105 600	489 100
Income before tax (£)					Income before tax (£)				
4 335	730	3 420	23	3 390	4 385	786	3 690	23	3 660
5 000	1 100	6 070	118	5 950	5 000	1 360	7 470	139	7 330
6 000	3 110	21 700	932	20 800	6 000	3 270	22 800	986	21 800
8 000	2 970	26 800	2 090	24 700	8 000	2 960	26 700	2 070	24 600
10 000	2 750	30 300	3 070	27 200	10 000	2 740	30 200	3 030	27 100
12 000	2 490	32 300	3 830	28 500	12 000	2 590	33 600	3 950	29 700
14 000	2 200	32 900	4 300	28 600	14 000	2 340	35 100	4 540	30 500
16 000	1 900	32 200	4 500	27 700	16 000	2 040	34 600	4 730	29 900
18 000	1 610	30 600	4 560	26 000	18 000	1 750	33 300	4 850	28 400
20 000	4 850	117 800	19 000	98 800	20 000	5 400	131 000	20 800	110 200
30 000	2 390	88 400	17 000	71 300	30 000	2 780	103 500	19 700	83 800
50 000	817	54 000	14 500	39 500	50 000	961	65 500	16 900	46 600
100 000	182	24 200	7 730	16 500	100 000	216	28 800	9 150	19 600
200 000 and over	70	32 400	11 600	20 800	200 000 and over	88	40 600	14 700	25 900
Income after tax (£)					Income after tax (£)				
4 335	800	3 770	28	3 740	4 385	891	4 220	30	4 190
5 000	1 280	7 260	162	7 100	5 000	1 490	8 390	175	8 210
6 000	3 790	27 900	1 470	26 500	6 000	3 980	29 300	1 540	27 800
8 000	3 660	36 200	3 300	32 900	8 000	3 560	35 200	3 160	32 000
10 000	3 280	40 700	4 630	36 100	10 000	3 370	41 700	4 730	37 000
12 000	2 750	41 100	5 380	35 700	12 000	2 940	43 800	5 650	38 100
14 000	2 340	40 700	5 780	35 000	14 000	2 490	43 300	6 020	37 300
16 000	1 870	37 300	5 630	31 600	16 000	2 060	41 100	6 080	35 000
18 000	1 450	32 700	5 150	27 600	18 000	1 630	36 500	5 640	30 800
20 000	3 880	112 000	19 000	93 000	20 000	4 410	127 500	21 300	106 200
30 000	1 540	73 100	16 700	56 400	30 000	1 820	86 400	19 500	66 900
50 000	424	39 400	11 700	27 800	50 000	502	46 500	13 800	32 800
100 000	87	17 500	5 860	11 600	100 000	105	21 200	7 100	14 100
200 000 and over	33	23 300	8 420	14 900	200 000 and over	43	29 700	10 900	18 900

Distribution of total income before and after tax
United Kingdom
Years ending 5 April

| | 2001/02 Annual Survey | | | | | 2002/03 Annual Survey | | | |
| | Number of individuals (Thousands) | £ million | | | | Number of individuals (Thousands) | £ million | | |
		Total income before tax	Total tax	Total income after tax			Total income before tax	Total tax	Total income after tax
Lower limit of range of income					**Lower limit of range of income**				
All incomes[1]	28 600	611 600	107 000	504 700	All incomes[1]	28 900	624 000	108 800	515 200
Income before tax (£)					Income before tax (£)				
4 535	525	2 500	12	2 490	4 615	439	2 110	8	2 100
5 000	1 070	5 890	98	5 790	5 000	1 050	5 760	88	5 670
6 000	2 890	20 200	696	19 500	6 000	2 860	20 100	652	19 400
8 000	2 800	25 200	1 670	23 500	8 000	2 840	25 600	1 630	23 900
10 000	2 650	29 100	2 600	26 500	10 000	2 660	29 200	2 550	26 600
12 000	2 580	33 400	3 600	29 800	12 000	2 520	32 600	3 470	29 200
14 000	2 340	35 100	4 220	30 900	14 000	2 310	34 600	4 130	30 500
16 000	2 040	34 600	4 490	30 100	16 000	2 060	34 900	4 510	30 400
18 000	1 700	32 200	4 440	27 700	18 000	1 740	33 100	4 540	28 600
20 000	5 510	134 300	20 500	113 800	20 000	5 700	138 900	21 200	117 700
30 000	3 160	116 900	21 500	95 400	30 000	3 300	122 400	22 500	100 000
50 000	1 050	69 800	18 500	51 300	50 000	1 090	72 100	19 100	53 000
100 000	237	31 500	10 000	21 500	100 000	249	33 100	10 600	22 500
200 000 and over	91	41 000	14 600	26 500	200 000 and over	91	39 500	13 900	25 700
Income after tax (£)					Income after tax (£)				
4 535	577	2 770	14	2 750	4 615	488	2 350	10	2 340
5 000	1 190	6 680	121	6 560	5 000	1 160	6 510	109	6 400
6 000	3 440	25 100	1 060	24 100	6 000	3 390	24 800	983	23 800
8 000	3 400	33 100	2 570	30 600	8 000	3 440	33 400	2 490	30 900
10 000	3 310	40 500	4 130	36 300	10 000	3 280	40 000	4 000	36 000
12 000	2 940	43 400	5 180	38 200	12 000	2 930	43 100	5 090	38 000
14 000	2 500	43 000	5 640	37 400	14 000	2 500	43 000	5 600	37 400
16 000	2 020	39 800	5 570	34 200	16 000	2 110	41 600	5 800	35 800
18 000	1 670	37 100	5 490	31 600	18 000	1 720	38 200	5 620	32 500
20 000	4 730	136 000	21 830	114 200	20 000	4 900	140 900	22 600	118 300
30 000	2 140	100 000	21 880	78 100	30 000	2 270	105 700	23 000	82 600
50 000	560	52 200	15 390	36 800	50 000	578	53 800	16 000	37 900
100 000	111	22 500	7 560	14 900	100 000	113	22 800	7 690	15 100
200 000 and over	44	29 400	10 520	18 900	200 000 and over	43	27 900	9 840	18 100

1 See chapter text. All figures have been independently rounded.

Source: Board of Inland Revenue: 020 7417 2917

8.2 Average income of households before and after taxes and benefits,[1] 2002/03
United Kingdom

	Retired households		Non-retired households									
	1 adult	2 or more adults	1 adult	2 adults	3 or more adults	1 adult with children	2 adults with 1 child	2 adults with 2 children	2 adults with 3 or more children	3 or more adults with children	All house-holds
Number of households in the population (thousands)	3 226	3 113	3 375	5 284	2 149	1 487	1 790	2 191	852	880	24 346
Average per household (£ per year)											
Original income	4 211	10 900	18 259	34 549	44 258	8 924	38 090	38 868	33 769	37 618	25 271
Disposable income	9 432	16 932	15 859	28 310	37 327	14 435	31 172	32 356	31 478	34 438	23 483
Post-tax income	7 893	13 476	12 919	23 007	29 931	11 402	25 261	26 374	25 350	27 477	19 002

1 See chapter text. Redistribution of Income, included in the Effects of taxes and benefits on household income, 2002/03, analysis published on the National Statistics website www.statistics.gov.uk/taxesbenefits and in the June 2004 edition of Economic Trends.

Source: Office for National Statistics: 020 7533 5772

8.3 Sources of gross household income[1]
United Kingdom

		1992	1993	1994 /95	1995 /96	1996 /97	1997 /98	1998[2] /99	1999[2] /00	2000[2] /01	2001[2] /02	2002[2] /03
Number of households supplying data	KPDA	7 418	6 979	6 853	6 797	6 415	6 409	6 630	7 097	6 637	7 473	6 927
Average weekly household income by source (£)												
Wages and salaries	KPCB	222.70	228.30	237.90	245.00	256.30	280.20	309.20	315.40	336.70	376.80	373.90
Self-employment	KPCC	29.60	29.20	35.30	32.90	37.50	32.90	37.20	46.00	44.50	43.80	44.50
Investments	KPCD	20.80	18.00	16.20	18.10	17.80	18.70	18.80	21.80	20.00	19.60	18.80
Annuities and pensions (other than social security benefits)	KPCE	19.60	21.90	23.50	26.00	26.00	28.90	30.30	32.80	35.00	36.10	39.90
Social security benefits	KPCF	45.00	48.90	49.90	52.40	54.10	55.00	55.80	58.00	60.10	63.50	68.50
Other sources	KPCH	5.20	6.70	6.50	6.60	5.30	5.20	5.70	5.90	6.20	6.70	6.70
Total	KPCI	342.90	353.00	369.30	380.90	396.90	420.80	457.00	479.90	502.50	546.50	552.30
Sources of household income as a percentage of total household income												
Wages and salaries	KPCJ	65	65	64	64	65	67	68	66	67	69	68
Self-employment	KPCK	9	8	10	9	9	8	8	10	9	8	8
Investments	KPCL	6	5	4	5	5	4	4	5	4	4	3
Annuities and pensions (other than social security benefits)	KPCM	6	6	6	7	7	7	7	7	7	7	7
Social security benefits	KPCN	13	14	14	14	14	13	12	12	12	12	12
Other sources	KPCP	2	2	2	2	1	1	1	1	1	1	1
Total	KPCQ	100	100	100	100	100	100	100	100	100	100	100

1 See chapter text.
2 Income based on weighted data.

Source: Expenditure and Food Survey, Office for National Statistics: 020 7533 5755

8.4 Households and their expenditure at current prices[1]
United Kingdom

		1992	1993	1994/95	1995/96	1996/97	1997/98	1998[2]/99	1999[2]/00	2000[2]/01	2001[2]/02	2002[2]/03
Number of households supplying data	KPDA	7 418	6 979	6 853	6 797	6 415	6 409	6 630	7 097	6 637	7 473	6 927

Average weekly household expenditure on commodities and services (£)

		1992	1993	1994/95	1995/96	1996/97	1997/98	1998[2]/99	1999[2]/00	2000[2]/01	2001[2]/02	2002[2]/03
Housing	KPEV	47.40	44.90	46.40	48.30	49.10	51.50	57.20	57.00	63.90	66.60	66.70
Fuel and power	KPEW	13.00	13.20	13.00	12.90	13.40	12.70	11.70	11.30	11.90	11.70	11.70
Food	KPEX	47.70	50.00	50.40	52.90	55.20	55.90	58.90	59.60	61.90	62.30	64.30
Alcoholic drink	KPEY	11.10	12.00	12.30	11.40	12.40	13.30	14.00	15.30	15.00	14.60	14.80
Tobacco	KPEZ	5.40	5.60	5.60	5.80	6.10	6.10	5.80	6.00	6.10	5.60	5.40
Clothing and footwear	KCWC	16.40	17.40	17.10	17.20	18.30	20.00	21.70	21.00	22.00	22.50	22.00
Household goods	KCWH	21.90	23.10	22.70	23.50	26.70	26.90	29.60	30.70	32.60	33.10	33.80
Household services	KCWI	13.40	15.40	15.10	15.10	16.40	17.90	18.90	18.90	22.00	23.80	23.30
Personal goods and services	KCWJ	10.20	11.00	10.80	11.60	11.60	12.50	13.30	13.90	14.70	14.90	15.20
Motoring expenditure	KCWK	35.70	36.30	36.20	37.00	41.20	46.60	51.70	52.60	55.10	58.50	61.70
Fares and other travel costs	KCWL	7.20	7.00	6.60	6.20	7.50	8.10	8.30	9.20	9.50	9.50	9.70
Leisure goods	KCWM	13.30	13.30	13.90	13.20	15.20	16.40	17.80	18.50	19.70	19.90	20.50
Leisure services	KCWN	27.60	25.60	31.20	32.10	34.00	38.80	41.90	43.90	50.60	52.30	53.60
Miscellaneous	KCWO	1.80	2.10	2.30	2.40	2.20	2.00	1.20	1.40	0.70	1.90	2.00
Total	KCWP	271.80	276.70	283.60	289.90	309.10	328.80	352.20	359.40	385.70	397.20	404.70

Expenditure on commodity or service as a percentage of total expenditure

		1992	1993	1994/95	1995/96	1996/97	1997/98	1998[2]/99	1999[2]/00	2000[2]/01	2001[2]/02	2002[2]/03
Housing	KPFH	17	16	16	17	16	16	16	16	17	17	16
Fuel and power	KPFI	5	5	5	5	4	4	3	3	3	3	3
Food	KPFJ	18	18	18	18	18	17	17	17	16	16	16
Alcoholic drink	KPFK	4	4	4	4	4	4	4	4	4	4	4
Tobacco	KPFL	2	2	2	2	2	2	2	2	2	1	1
Clothing and footwear	KPFM	6	6	6	6	6	6	6	6	6	6	5
Household goods	KCWQ	8	8	8	8	9	8	8	9	8	8	8
Household services	KCWR	5	6	5	5	5	5	5	5	6	6	6
Personal goods and services	KCWS	4	4	4	4	4	4	4	4	4	4	4
Motoring expenditure	KCWT	13	13	13	13	13	14	15	15	14	15	15
Fares and other travel costs	KCWU	3	3	2	2	2	3	2	3	2	2	2
Leisure goods	KCWV	5	5	5	5	5	5	5	5	5	5	5
Leisure services	KCWW	10	9	11	11	11	12	12	12	13	13	13
Miscellaneous	KPFR	1	1	1	1	1	1	–	–	–	–	–
Total	KPFS	100	100	100	100	100	100	100	100	100	100	100

1 See chapter text.
2 Averages based on grossed number of households. Expenditure based on weighted data and including children's expenditure.

Source: Expenditure and Food Survey, Office for National Statistics: 020 7533 5756

8.5 Households with selected durable goods[1]
United Kingdom

Percentages

		1992	1993	1994/95	1995/96	1996/97	1997/98	1998[2]/99	1999[2]/00	2000[2]/01	2001[2]/02	2002[2]/03
Number of households supplying data	KPDA	7 418	6 979	6 853	6 797	6 415	6 409	6 630	7 097	6 637	7 473	6 927
Car	KPDB	68	69	69	70	69	70	72	71	72	74	74
One	KPDC	45	46	45	47	43	44	44	43	44	44	44
Two	KPDD	19	19	20	19	22	21	23	21	22	24	25
Three or more	KPDE	4	4	4	4	5	5	5	6	6	6	6
Central heating, full or partial	KPDF	82	83	84	85	87	89	89	90	91	92	93
Washing machine	KPDG	88	89	89	91	91	91	92	91	92	93	94
Refrigerator or fridge/freezer	KPDH	99	99	99	99	..	..	..	..	..	..	..
Fridge/freezer or deep freezer	KPDI	84	87	86	87	91	90	92	91	94	95	96
Refrigerator	KPDJ	..	..	..	..	49	51	52	53	..	..	..
Dishwasher	GPTL	..	..	18	20	20	22	23	23	25	27	29
Television	KPDK	98	..	..	..	..	..	..	..	..	..	..
Telephone	KPDL	88	90	91	92	93	94	95	95	93	94	94
Home computer	KPDM	19	..	..	..	27	29	33	38	44	50	55
Video recorder	KPDN	69	73	76	79	82	84	85	86	87	90	90
Internet access	ZBUZ	..	..	..	..	..	..	10	19	32	40	45

1 See chapter text.
2 Percentages based on grossed number of households.

Source: Expenditure and Food Survey, Office for National Statistics: 020 7533 5756

Health

Chapter 9

Health

Hospital and family health services

(Table 9.1)

The courses of treatment are for the General Dental Services (GDS). A course of treatment is complete when the treatment that is required – or such of it that the patient is willing to undergo – has been carried out. A dentist in accepting a patient for continuing care (adults) or capitation (children), undertakes to provide the care and treatment necessary to secure and maintain oral health.

Deaths: analysed by cause

(Table 9.6)

All figures in this table for England and Wales represent the number of deaths *occurring* in each calendar year. All data for Scotland and Northern Ireland relate to the number of deaths *registered* during each calendar year. From 2001, all three constituent countries of the United Kingdom are coding their causes of death using the latest, tenth, revision of the International Statistical Classification of Diseases and Related Health Problems (ICD-10). All cause of death information from 2001 (also for 2000 for Scotland) presented in this table is based on the revised classification.

To assist users in assessing any discontinuities arising from the introduction of the revised classification, bridge-coding exercises were carried out on all deaths registered in 1999 in England and Wales and also in Scotland. For further information about ICD-10 and the bridge-coding carried out by the Office for National Statistics, see the ONS Report: Results of the ICD-10 bridge-coding study, England and Wales, 1999. *Health Statistics Quarterly* 14 (2002), pages 75–83 or on the National Statistics website at: *www.statistics.gov.uk*. For information on the Scottish bridge-coding exercise, consult the *Annual Report of the General Register Office for Scotland* or log on to their website at: *www.gro-scotland.gov.uk*. No bridge-coding exercise was conducted for Northern Ireland.

Neonatal deaths and homicide and assault

For England and Wales, neonatal deaths (those at age under 28 days) are included in the number of total deaths but excluded from the cause figures. This has particular impact on the totals shown for the chapters covered by the ranges P and Q, 'Conditions originating in the perinatal period' and

'Congenital malformations, deformations and chromosomal abnormalities'. These are considerably lower than the actual number of deaths because it is not possible to assign an underlying cause of death from the neonatal death certificate used in England and Wales.

Also, for England and Wales only, the total number shown for Homicide and assault, X85–Y09, will not be a true representation because the registration of these deaths is often delayed by adjourned inquests.

Occupational ill health

(Tables 9.8 and 9.9)

There are a number of sources of data on the extent of occupational or work-related ill health in Great Britain. For some potentially severe lung diseases caused by exposures which are highly unlikely to be found in a non-occupational setting, it is useful to count the number of death certificates issued each year. This is also true for mesothelioma, a cancer affecting the lining of the lungs and stomach, for which the number of cases with non-occupational causes is likely to be larger (although still a minority). Table 9.9 shows the number of deaths for mesothelioma and asbestosis (linked to exposure to asbestos), pneumoconiosis (linked to coal dust or silica), byssinosis (linked to cotton dust) and some forms of allergic alveolitis (including farmer's lung). For asbestos-related diseases the figures are derived from a special register maintained by HSE. Most conditions which can be caused or made worse by work can also arise from other factors. The remaining sources of data on work-related ill health rely on attribution of individual cases of illness to work causes. In The Health and Occupation Reporting Network (THOR), this is done by specialist doctors – either occupational physicians or those working in particular disease specialisms (covering musculoskeletal, psychological, respiratory, skin, audiological and infectious disease). Table 9.7 presents data from THOR for the last three years. It should be noted that not all cases of occupational disease will be seen by participating specialists; for example, the number of deaths due to mesothelioma (shown in Table 9.9) is known to be greater than the number of cases reported to THOR.

Injuries at work

(Table 9.10)

The appropriate 'responsible person' is required to report injuries arising from workplace activities to HSE or the local authority under the Reporting of Injuries, Diseases and Dangerous Occurrences Regulations 1995 (RIDDOR 95). This includes fatal injuries, nonfatal major injuries, as defined by the

Regulations, and other injuries causing incapacity for work for more than 3 days. As of 1 April 2001, reports are to be made to an Incident Centre (ICC), based at Caerphilly.

HSE gets to know about virtually all workplace fatalities. However, it is known that employers and others do not report all non-fatal reportable injuries. To estimate the level of under-reporting by employers, HSE place questions each year with the Labour Force Survey (LFS), asking respondents if they have suffered a workplace injury in the past year.

The results from the latest LFS show that in Great Britain employers report around 43 per cent of reportable injuries (2002/03). When compared to the previous year, these results also indicate a drop of in the non-fatal injury rate of 4.6 per cent. The self-employed report around five per cent of reportable non-fatal injuries.

9.1 Hospital and family health services
England and Wales

			England						Wales				
			1998	1999	2000	2001	2002		1999	2000	2001	2002	2003
Hospital services[1]													
Average daily number of available beds	KNMY	Thousands	190	186	186	185	184	KNHY	14.7	14.6	14.4	14.3	14.2
Average daily occupation of beds:													
All departments	KNMX	"	157	154	156	157	157	KNHX	11.8	11.7	11.7	11.8	11.8
Psychiatric departments	KNMW	"	37	34	34	..	..	KNGZ	2.6	2.5	2.5	2.4	2.3
Persons waiting for admission at 31 March[2]	KNMV	"	1 298	1 037	1 007	1 035	992	KNGY	65.3	79.9	65.6	70.6	74.6
Finished consultant episodes													
Day case admissions	KNLY	"	3 421	3 593	3 629	3 588	3 703	KNBZ	123.7	135.3	136.2	111.6	..
Ordinary admissions	KIBS	"	8 563	8 604	8 636	8 750	9 012	KNEO	515.1	513.8	509.4	493.0	503.5
Out-patients													
New cases	KNLX	"	11 778	12 136	12 466	12 714	13 032	KNBY	694.1	698.9	697.1	737.3	739.5
Total attendances	KNLW	"	42 154	43 041	43 569	44 008	44 598	KNBX	2 706.2	2 736.8	2 761.9	2 842.5	2 868.3
Accident and Emergency:													
New cases	KOTH	"	12 811	13 167	12 953	12 853	12 945	KTCO	868.0	853.7	877.7	888.7	915.7
Total attendances	KOTI	"	14 280	14 629	14 293	14 044	14 046	KTCP	1 026.4	986.2	1 009.8	1 004.7	1 035.6
Ward attendances	KOTJ	"	1 068	1 073	1 078	1 089	1 179	KTCQ	..	..	..	..	..
Family health services[3]													
Medical services:													
Doctors on the list[4]	KNKX	Numbers	..	..	..	..	..	KNBR	1 761	1 775	1 785	1 782	1 783
Number of UPEs[5]	LQZZ	"	27 392	27 591	27 704	27 843	28 031	ZCMA	1 767	1 880	1 796	1 793	1 804
Number of patients per doctor	KNKW	"	1 866	1 845	1 853	1 841	1 838	KNBQ	1 694	1 695	1 685	1 704	1 695
Paid to doctors[6]	KNKV	£ million	3 242	3 348	..	..	..	KNBP	201	213	222	241	269
Pharmaceutical services:[7,8]													
Number of prescription forms	KWUK	Millions	291	294	300	315	326	VQEU	..	..	..	23	..
Number of prescription items	KWUL	"	513	530	552	587	617	KNBO	42	44	46	49	51
Total cost	KWUM	£ million	5 231	5 620	5 967	6 488	7 162	KNBN	404	434	472	..	..
Average total cost per prescription	KWUN	£	10.2	10.6	10.8	11.1	11.6	KNBK	9.6	9.9	10.0	..	..
Income from patients	KWUO	£ million	341	367	387	408	423	KNBM	22	23	23	23	23
Dental services:													
Principals on an FHSA/HA list at 30 September[9]	KIAZ	Numbers	15 820	16 089	16 276	16 451	16 445	KIBG	913	928	931	927	919
Number of adult courses of treatments[10]	KIBA	Thousands	26 171	25 915	26 353	26 318	26 284	KIBH	1 525	1 557	1 564	1 886	1 629
Number of adult patients accepted into continuing care provision at 30 September[11]	KIBB	"	16 721	16 649	16 813	16 793	16 739	KIBI	1 055	1 074	1 063	1 065	1 078
Number of children accepted into capitation at 30 September[11]	KIBC	"	6 775	6 821	6 845	6 784	6 733	KIBJ	408.0	411.5	403.3	399.9	396.6
Gross expenditure[12]	KIBD	£ million	1 438	1 477	1 555	–	–	KIBK	86 093	91 498	95 222	99 480	103 577
Paid by patients[12]	KIBE	"	420	431	453	–	–	KIBL	23 456	24 634	24 374	25 455	27 489
Paid out of public funds[12]	KIBF	"	1 018	1 046	1 102	–	–	KIBM	62 637	66 864	70 848	74 025	76 088
General ophthalmic services:													
Sight tests[13]	KNJL	Thousands	6 992	9 399	9 567	9 807	9 662	KNBD	631	659	668	647	646
Pairs of spectacles for which NHS vouchers redeemed	KNJK	"	3 777	3 662	3 575	3 607	3 472	KNBC	275	273	273	252	252
Cost of services (gross)[12]	KNJJ	£ million	265	307	306	311	304	KNBA	20	21	22	22	22
Paid out of public funds:[12]													
For sight testing	KNJH	"	114	160	163	167	166	KMZZ	10	10	11	11	11
For cost of vouchers[11]	WMPC	"	150	147	142	143	137	KMZX	9	10	10	9	9

1 Data shown reflect data for the financial year commencing the year in the heading (for example, the figures under 1999 reflects 1999/2000 data). Out-patient figures do not include accident and emergency figures or ward attenders which are given separately. Information on general practitioner maternity clinics is not collected separately in England but is included for Wales.

2 People awaiting elective admission at NHS Trusts in England and Wales, as an inpatient or a day case.

3 Welsh FHS expenditure and income is based upon cash payments and receipts in each financial year, as accrued gross expenditure is not available in a common format for all years shown in this series. Welsh Dental Services data excludes refunds of dental charges.

4 For Wales, Principals providing unrestricted services as at 1 October.

5 UPE's include Unrestricted Principals, PMS Contracted GP's and PMS salaried GP's.UPE data are at 1 October.

6 For Wales, includes PFMA but excludes GPFH drugs and payments to providers.

7 Welsh data are based on pricing bureau totals of prescriptions dispensed in a calendar year and paid during the financial year. Data shown reflects data for the year commencing the year in the heading (for example, the figures under 1999 reflects 1999/2000 data). Financial year is from 1 April to 31 March.

8 The data cover all prescription items dispensed by community pharmacists and appliance contractors, dispensing doctors and prescriptions submitted by prescribing doctors for items personally administered. Total cost refers to the cost of the drug less discounts and includes on cost allowance, dispensing fees, container allowance, oxygen payments and VAT. Income from patients relates to financial years and from 2001/2002 is taken from HA annual accounts. Previous years taken from the Appropriation Account. Income includes charges retained by pharmacists & dispensing doctors, sales of pre-payment certificates and recoveries from patients.

9 Principals only. Assistants and vocational trainees are not included. Some dentists may have a contract with more than one Family Health Service /Health Authority. These dentists have been counted once only.

10 Data shown reflect data for the financial year commencing the year in the heading (for example, the figures under 2001 represent 2001/2002 data).

11 Figures for 1998 onwards are affected by the shortening of the registration period to 15 months.

12 Figures for England are based on provisional outturn figures, with gross gross expenditure and patient figures having been adjusted from previous publications to include refunds of dental charges. For Wales, figures are for the financial year and based on the Appropriation account.

13 Number of NHS sight tests paid for by FHSAs/HAs in the period.

Sources: Department of Health;
National Assembly for Wales: 029 2082 5080

9.2 Hospital and primary care services
Scotland

			1993	1994	1995	1996	1997	1998	1999	2000	2001	2002	2003
Hospital and community services													
In-patients:[1,2]													
Average available staffed beds	KDEA	Thousands	46.7	44.2	42.4	40.6	38.4	36.8	35.2	33.5	32.1	30.9	..
Average occupied beds:													
All departments	KDEB	"	38.1	35.9	34.3	32.8	30.9	29.5	28.2	26.9	25.8	25.1	..
Psychiatric and learning disability	KDEC	"	14.6	13.2	12.6	11.7	10.8	10.0	9.1	8.3	7.6	7.0	..
Discharges or deaths[3]	KDED	"	942	952	960	973	965	978	977	965	957	952	..
Outpatients:[2,4]													
New cases	KDEE	"	2 457	2 503	2 577	2 666	2 675	2 715	2 734	2 766	2 744	2 743	..
Total attendances	KDEF	"	6 086	6 145	6 241	6 338	6 272	6 331	6 424	6 451	6 382	6 291	..
Medical and dental staff:[5]	JYXO	Numbers	8 078	8 317	8 524	8 774	9 098	9 157	9 367	9 325	9 646	10 256	10 381
Whole-time	KDEG	"	5 767	5 937	6 102	6 433	6 707	7 052	7 202	6 896	7 218	7 759	8 325
Part-time	KDEH	"	1 730	1 827	1 854	1 819	1 886	1 613	1 685	1 966	1 989	2 063	1 633
Honorary	JYXN	"	582	563	579	534	522	506	495	495	468	468	438
Professional and technical staff:[6]													
Whole-time	KDEI	"	9 953	10 062	10 452	10 584	10 740	10 884	11 261	11 261	11 705	12 265	12 942
Part-time	KDEJ	"	3 434	3 753	4 075	4 370	4 738	4 928	5 218	5 483	5 852	6 273	6 708
Nursing and midwifery staff:[7]													
Whole-time	KDEK	"	33 284	32 956	32 693	32 560	32 218	32 156	32 356	32 401	33 334	34 294	34 961
Part-time	KDEL	"	30 459	30 532	30 580	29 917	29 736	29 178	29 242	29 131	29 004	29 015	29 356
Administrative and clerical staff:[8]													
Whole-time	KDEM	"	15 125	15 723	15 815	15 155	14 707	14 564	14 541	14 710	15 361	16 200	17 238
Part-time	KDEN	"	6 113	6 624	7 005	6 986	7 174	7 265	7 456	7 677	8 075	8 630	9 305
Domestic, transport, etc, staff:[9]													
Whole-time	KDEO	"	10 205	9 574	9 037	8 596	8 187	8 090	7 972	7 848	7 625	7 768	8 234
Part-time	KDEP	"	15 403	14 464	14 105	13 554	13 082	12 716	12 424	12 272	11 522	11 915	12 588
Cost of services (gross)[10]	KDEQ	£ million	2 940.5	3 050.5	3 269.5	3 430.6	3 610.3	3 856.0	4 309.7	4 862.6	5 378.6	5 919.5	..
Payments by patients[10]	KDER	"	2.30	0.40	0.02	0.01	0.01	0.01	0.01	0.01	–	..	..
Payments out of public funds[10]	KDES	"	2 938.2	3 050.1	3 269.5	3 430.6	3 610.3	3 855.9	4 309.7	4 862.6	5 378.6	5 919.5	..
Primary care services													
Medical services													
Doctors on the list:[11]													
Principals[12]	KDET	Numbers	3 456	3 490	3 524	3 573	3 625	3 660	3 698	3 707	3 756	3 765	..
Assistants	KDEU	"	22	25	28	22	22	27	19	25	39	37	..
Average number of patients per principal doctor[13]	KDEV	"	1 542	1 524	1 506	1 488	1 468	1 450	1 441	1 425	1 409	1 392	..
Payments to doctor[14]	KDEW	£ million	275.3	291.7	311.9	333.2	356.4	365.9	377.5	404.7	429.6	467.5	..
Pharmaceutical services[15]													
Prescriptions dispensed	KDEX	Millions	48.18	49.27	51.08	54.62	56.64	58.52	60.36	62.34	65.56	68.81	..
Payments to pharmacists (gross)	KDEY	£ million	406.1	434.9	474.2	543.4	588.4	627.2	693.7	731.0	788.6	868.9	..
Average gross cost per prescription	KDEZ	£	8.4	8.8	9.3	10.0	10.4	10.7	11.5	11.7	12.0	12.6	..
Dental services													
Dentists on list[16]	KDFA	Numbers	1 772	1 763	1 764	1 772	1 798	1 854	1 833	1 831	1 866	1 891	..
Number of courses of treatment completed	KDFB	Thousands	2 647	2 723	2 711	2 825	3 406	3 349	3 406	3 395	3 390	3 148	..
Payments to dentists (gross)	KDFC	£ million	128.4	136.1	137.3	139.2	154.9	157.5	160.6	162.9	165.1	172.3	..
Payments by patients	KDFD	"	40.0	42.2	41.7	41.4	45.9	47.4	48.8	50.6	52.3	54.7	..
Payments out of public funds	KDFE	"	88.4	93.9	95.6	97.8	109.0	110.1	111.8	112.3	112.9	117.6	..
Average gross cost per course	KDFF	£	37.0	38.0	38.0	40.1	36.5	38.0	38.0	37.0	38.0	42.0	..
General ophthalmic services													
Number of sight tests given[17]	KDFG	Thousands	568	..	614	618	635	656	657	850	861	877	..
Number of pairs of glasses supplied[18]	KDFH	"	463	..	473	461	474	488	485	494	439	463	..
Payments out of public funds for sight testing and dispensing	KDFK	£ million	22.2	24.4	25.8	27.7	29.1	29.8	32.0	33.1	..	42.9	..

1 Excludes joint user and contractual hospitals.
2 In year to 31 March.
3 Includes transfers out and emergency inpatients treated in day bed units.
4 Including attendances at accident and emergency consultant clinics.
5 As at 30 September. Figures exclude officers holding honorary locum appointments. Part-time includes maximum part-time appointments. There is an element of double counting of "heads" in this table as doctors can hold more than one contract. For example, they may hold contracts of different type, eg part time and honorary. Doctors holding two or more contracts of the same type, eg part time, are not double counted. Doctors, whose sum of contracts amounts to whole time, are classed as such.
6 As at 30 September. Comprises Scientific and Professional, Allied Health Professionals and Technical staff.
7 As at 30 September. Includes Health Care Assistants.
8 As at 30 September. Comprises Senior Management and Administrative and Clerical staff.
9 As at 30 September. Comprises Ambulance, Works, Ancillary and Trades.

10 These figures are for Health Boards only and do not include the 2 NHS Trusts in 1995 and 47 in 1995/96. Estimated from financial years.
11 At 1 October.
12 Unrestricted principals in post.
13 Unrestricted principals: establishment.
14 Data relate to financial year, eg 1997 data are for year ending 31 March 1998. As 1994/95 data are unavailable for Dumfries & Galloway Health Board, 1993/94 data have been substituted for that board only.
15 For prescriptions dispensed in calendar year by all community pharmacists (including stock orders), dispensing doctors and appliance suppliers.
16 Comprises principals only.
17 This figure represents sight tests paid for by health boards, hospital eye service referrals and GOS(s) ST (v) claimants. From 1995, data refers to financial year (eg 1995 data is for year ending 31 March 1995). 1994 calander year data is missing.
18 Does not include hospital eye service.

Source: NHS National Services Scotland and The Scottish Executive: 0131 551 8899

			1994	1995	1996	1997	1998	1999	2000	2001	2002	2003
Hospital services[1]												
In-patients:												
Beds available[2]	KDGA	Numbers	10 356	10 054	9 464	9 006	8 818	8 639	8 571	8 419	8 301	8 358
Average daily occupation of beds	KDGB	Percentages	_78.1_	_77.7_	_78.9_	_80.8_	_81.9_	_81.5_	_82.0_	_83.3_	_84.3_	_84.2_
Discharges or deaths[3]	KDGC	Thousands	298	304	300	305	335	332	333	328	327	332
Out-patients:[4]												
New cases	KDGD	"	873	940	933	952	962	984	994	997	992	1 014
Total attendances	KDGE	"	2 051	2 087	2 070	2 084	2 091	2 111	2 114	2 131	2 122	2 161
General health services												
Medical services[1]												
Doctors (principals) on the list[5,6]	KDGF	Numbers	991	1 005	1 028	1 039	1 042	1 054	1 066	1 073	1 091	1 096
Number of patients per doctor	KDGG	"	1 738	1 725	1 698	1 690	1 693	1 678	1 661	1 651	1 632	1 783
GrossPayments to doctors[7]	KDGH	£ thousand	62 849	65 130	67 872	69 889	71 385	78 604	82 471	84 664	88 194	96 894
Pharmaceutical services[8]												
Prescription forms dispensed	KDGI	Thousands	11 152	12 017	12 802	13 246	13 489	13 454	13 666	14 277	14 622	15 158
Number of prescriptions	KDGJ	"	18 560	19 893	21 203	22 047	22 754	23 249	23 985	24 705	25 495	26 656
Gross cost	KDGK	£ thousand	173 064	197 579	219 978	236 746	248 845	266 535	278 405	303 489	327 045	362 389
Charges	KDGL	"	6 507	6 455	6 224	6 784	7 007	8 183	8 499	9 074	9 597	9 786
Net Cost	KDGM	"	166 764	191 324	213 950	229 962	241 837	258 353	269 906	294 415	317 448	352 603
Average gross cost per prescription	KDGN	£	9.32	9.93	10.38	10.74	10.94	11.46	11.61	12.28	12.83	13.59
Dental services[8,9]												
Dentists on the list[5]	KDGO	Numbers	568	581	596	609	634	660	674	673	689	696
Number of courses of paid treatment	KDGP	Thousands	825	832	928	1 053	1 088	1 097	1 120	1 129	1 126	1 107
Gross cost	KDGQ	£ thousand	46 318	48 780	51 512	53 733	56 835	58 712	61 561	64 454	66 201	66 371
Patients	KDGR	"	11 231	11 530	11 870	12 433	13 686	14 358	15 302	16 041	16 824	16 868
Contributions (Net cost)	KDGS	"	35 086	37 250	39 642	41 300	43 149	44 354	46 260	48 413	49 376	49 503
Average gross cost per paid treatment	KDGT	£	56	59	56	51	52	54	55	57	59	60
Ophthalmic services[8]												
Number of sight tests given[10]	KDGU	Thousands	182	196	212	227	237	298	305	314	322	334
Number of optical appliances supplied[11]	KDGV	"	139	146	153	159	161	157	160	166	168	170
Cost of service (gross)[12]	KDGW	£ thousand	7 127	8 568	9 555	10 271	10 452	11 365	11 975	12 490	13 473	13 980
Health and social services[13]												
Medical and dental staff:												
Whole-time	KDGZ	Numbers	2 358	2 053	2 107	2 156	2 196	2 231	2 224	2 281	2 411	2 607
Part-time	KDHA	"	694	1 154	1 094	1 041	1 009	1 014	580	597	626	620
Nursing and midwifery staff:												
Whole-time	KDHB	"	11 047	10 896	10 578	10 114	10 117	10 135	9 926	9 828	10 248	10 729
Part-time	KDHC	"	8 662	9 169	8 943	9 015	8 287	8 813	7 591	7 814	8 395	8 706
Administrative and clerical staff:												
Whole-time	KDHD	"	7 006	7 078	7 055	6 915	7 019	7 230	7 373	7 536	7 966	8 370
Part-time	KDHE	"	2 186	2 306	2 518	2 708	2 776	2 910	2 972	3 136	3 372	3 609
Professional and technical staff:												
Whole-time	KDHF	"	2 786	2 862	2 939	2 933	3 014	3 177	3 642	3 762	3 975	4 163
Part-time	KDHG	"	804	921	985	1 060	1 146	1 226	1 283	1 369	1 499	1 616
Social services staff(excluding casual home helps):												
Whole-time	KDHH	"	3 480	3 470	3 441	3 349	3 262	3 319	3 017	3 127	3 284	3 461
Part-time	KDHI	"	1 933	2 110	2 250	2 394	2 241	2 358	868	911	986	1 105
Ancillary and other staff:												
Whole-time	KDHJ	"	4 364	3 982	3 812	3 569	3 423	3 426	3 506	3 472	3 426	3 418
Part-time	KDHK	"	4 609	3 685	3 558	3 482	3 558	3 913	4 508	4 925	5 125	5 420
Cost of services (gross)[14]	KDHL	£ thousand	1 043 745	1 111 507	1 120 563	1 153 741	1 292 348	1 422 920	1 576 657	1 639 283	1 868 538	2 113 453
Payments by recipients	KDHM	"	20 629	32 685	40 725	49 498	59 484	65 533	71 411	78 478	88 860	87 999
Payments out of public funds	KDHN	"		1 023 116	1 078 822	1 079 838	1 104 243	1 232 864	1 357 387	1 505 246	1 560 805	1 779 678	2 025 454

1 Financial Year.
2 Average available beds in wards open overnight during the year.
3 Includes transfers to other hospitals.
4 Includes consultant outpatient clinics and Accident and Emergency departments.
5 At beginning of period.
6 Doctors include assistants.
7 These costs refer to the majority of non-cash limited services: further expenditure under GMS is allocated through HSS Boards on a cash limited basis. Change between 2002 and 2003 is due to advance payments being made in relation to the new GMS contract introduced in April 2004.
8 From 1995 onwards figures are taken from financial year.
9 Due to changes in the Dental Contract which came into force in October 1990 dentists are paid under a combination of headings relating to Capitation and Continuing Care patients. Prior to this, payment was simply on an item of service basis, which made statistics such as 'Number of courses of treatment completed' and Average gross cost per course' relevant and meaningful. This is no longer the case.

10 Excluding sight tests given in hospitals and under the school health service and in the home.
11 Relates to the number of vouchers supplied and excludes repair/replace spectacles.
12 Gross cost is defined as net ingredient costs plus on-cost, fees and other payments.
13 Workforce figures until 1999 refer to 31st December and are taken from the Trust and Board payroll system. Figures from 2000 onwards are at 30th September and are taken from the Trust and Board Human Resource Management Systems. Figures for 2000 onwards exclude all home helps and all agency/bank staff but include Ambulance and Works staff in the Ancillary & Other Staff category. As a result, backward comparison of the workforce is not advisable as definitions differ. Some figures for 2000 have been revised.
14 Figures relate to the costs of the hospital, community health and personal social services, and have been estimated from financial year data.

Sources: Central Services Agency Northern Ireland: 028 9032 4431;
Dept of Health, Social Services & Public Safety Northern Ireland: 028 9052 2509;

(Figures on Hospital Services: 028 9052 2800)

9.4 Health services: workforce summary[1]
Great Britain
As at 30 September.

Whole-time equivalent

		1994	1995[2]	1996	1997	1998	1999	2000	2001	2002	2003
Health service staff and practitioners											
Medical staff: total	KDBC	56 736	60 172	62 176	64 316	67 408	69 089	70 939	73 206	78 024	82 294
Hospital medical staff: total	KDBD	53 787	57 299	59 592	61 937	65 088	66 812	68 767	71 107	76 122	80 537
Consultant	KDBE	18 808	20 246	21 066	21 699	23 139	24 250	25 067	26 106	27 951	29 566
Staff grade	KADJ	1 536	2 037	2 440	2 785	3 458	3 868	4 423	4 720	5 409	5 462
Associate specialist	KDBF	1 013	1 128	1 223	1 340	1 439	1 527	1 572	1 609	1 780	1 993
Registrar group[3]	KWUG	..	..	11 898	12 435	12 863	13 299	13 372	13 826	14 530	15 580
Senior registrar	KDBG	4 281	4 540	..	..	..	..	..	..	..	..
Registrar	KDBH	7 273	7 294	..	..	..	..	..	..	..	..
Senior house officer	KDBI	14 942	15 661	16 616	17 353	17 760	17 518	17 945	18 377	19 850	21 525
House officer	KADK	3 781	4 003	4 025	4 163	4 287	4 364	4 518	4 560	4 944	4 985
Hospital practitioner	KDBL	178	197	212	198	220	230	231	223	248	247
Clinical assistant	KDBM	1 964	2 182	2 094	1 924	1 907	1 744	1 638	1 684	1 407	1 179
Other staff	KDBK	11	11	18	38	16	11	1	1	3	–
Community health medical staff	KDBN	2 948	2 873	2 584	2 379	2 320	2 278	2 172	2 100	1 902	1 756
Dental staff: total	KDBO	2 947	3 070	3 127	3 078	3 193	3 147	3 107	3 152	3 357	3 429
Hospital dental staff: total	KDBP	1 597	1 687	1 737	1 696	1 807	1 816	1 781	1 816	1 944	1 981
Consultant	KDBQ	537	549	556	524	570	581	580	578	610	664
Staff grade	KADL	39	54	67	86	99	113	118	135	154	158
Associate specialist	KDBR	62	69	65	62	68	70	73	74	75	79
Registrar group[3]	LQMZ	..	..	..	..	309	314	295	311	339	329
Senior registrar	KDBS	124	123	138	169	..	..	..	..	..	..
Registrar	KDBT	178	186	183	125	..	..	..	..	..	..
Senior house officer	KDBU	394	446	490	491	531	496	497	513	572	584
Dental house officer	KDBV	101	86	68	58	59	68	60	61	60	38
Hospital practitioner	KDBX	20	17	23	22	21	23	21	18	20	20
Clinical assistant	KDBY	141	158	145	152	144	146	136	126	112	108
Other staff	KDBW	2	–	3	6	5	6	–	–	1	–
Community health dental staff	KDBZ	1 350	1 383	1 390	1 382	1 386	1 331	1 326	1 336	1 413	1 448
Non-medical staff: total	KWUH	..	804 148	856 732	849 426	855 305	870 921	890 282	927 831	974 390	1 022 837
Nursing and midwifery staff:[4,5] (excluding agency): total	KDCA	..	387 436	410 693	407 760	409 045	415 786	423 737	437 417	455 361	474 263
of which:											
qualified	KSBR	..	282 200	300 371	298 483	299 654	303 644	309 682	320 685	335 313	349 701
unqualified	KSBS	..	99 946	106 181	106 313	106 773	109 687	111 931	114 532	117 582	121 896
learners	KSBT	..	4 580	2 804	2 356	2 178	1 961	2 054	2 201	2 387	2 591
All Professional and Technical staff (excluding works)[6]	KSBM	..	106 544	118 403	120 439	123 902	128 116	131 943	138 348	146 804	155 507
Health care assistants	KWUI	..	13 090	18 025	19 268	22 026	22 746	24 919	30 047	33 301	36 027
Support staff	KWUJ	..	74 540	75 836	72 608	71 043	69 883	68 449	69 245	69 628	69 553
Ancillary, Works & Maintainance	KSBN	..	29 466	27 603	26 037	25 131	24 468	23 962	23 013	23 430	23 820
Administrative and Clerical staff	KSBO	..	172 948	183 049	183 112	184 711	190 421	197 327	209 004	224 490	241 634
Ambulance staff	KSBP	..	16 744	18 655	18 751	18 382	18 552	19 209	19 888	20 864	21 449
Others	KSBQ	..	3 180	4 159	1 079	906	780	746	711	512	584

1 Figures exclude locums and occasional seasonal staff
2 1995 data do not include Wales. A new system for classifying NHS non-medical staff was used for the first time in Sptember 1995 non-medical workforce census classifying staff according to what they do (known as new occupation codes). Data for years prior to 1995 for all classes of non- medical staff are incomparable.
3 Includes Specialist Registrar (SpR), Senior Registrar and Registrar. The SpR grade was introduced formally on 1 April 1996.

4 Excludes bank nurses for Wales.
5 Nursing total includes qualified, unqualified and others only.
6 GP Registrars were formerly referred to as Trainees.

Sources: Department of Health; National Assembly for Wales.; Scottish Health Service Common Services Agency

9.5 Health and personal social services: workforce summary
Great Britain

		1994	1995	1996	1997	1998	1999[3]	2000	2001	2002	2003
Family Health services:											
General medical practitioners[1]											
All practitioners: total[2,3]	GPYL	..	..	..	..	..	36 949	37 572	38 162	38 649	40 013
All practitioners (excluding GP Retainers)	LQZN	34 421	34 594	34 825	35 205	35 611	35 951	36 225	36 754	37 278	38 764
Unrestricted Principals & equivalents (UPE's)	LQZO	31 767	31 945	32 164	32 477	32 801	33 049	33 186	33 384	33 578	34 152
of which GMS UP's	LQZP	31 767	31 945	32 164	32 477	32 414	32 140	31 869	29 475	26 785	23 669
PMS contracted/salaried	PTKJ	..	..	..	..	..	387	908	1 317	3 909	6 793	10 483
Restricted principals	LQZS	156	137	126	111	108	99	94	102	92	86
Assistants	LQZT	626	684	890	891	751	691	675	533	505	518
GP Registrars[4]	LQZU	1 841	1 790	1 605	1 678	1 830	1 903	2 028	2 278	2 386	2 626
of which GMS[5]	LQZV	1 841	1 790	1 605	1 678	1 796	1 825	1 920	1 956	1 738	1 800
Salaried Doctors	LQZW	–	–	–	–	60	117	159	160	127	149
PMS Other	LQZX	–	–	–	–	12	43	33	246	547	956
Associates	LQZY	31	38	40	48	52	50	51	49	44	43
GP Retainers	GPYM	–	–	–	–	–	997	1 347	1 408	1 371	1 250
General dental practitioners: total[6]	KDCQ	18 600	18 736	19 139	19 598	20 216	20 840	21 316	21 929	22 194	22 891
General Dental Service	GPYN	18 600	18 736	19 139	19 598	20 216	20 750	21 124	21 462	21 538	21 701
Personal Dental Service	GPYO	..	..	..	..	..	90	192	467	656	1 190
Ophthalmic medical practitioners[7]	KDCT	775	789	799	833	863	827	819	754	686	674
Ophthalmic opticians[7]	KDCU	7 185	7 333	7 582	7 790	8 024	8 423	8 742	8 650	8 761	9 123
Personal Social Services staff: total	KDDE	237 752	233 861	233 655	229 439	223 500	221 700	217 200	212 000	208 300	212 000
of which:											
Home help service	KSBU	59 391	56 961	55 430	53 573	50 417	47 227	42 583	40 200	37 300	35 000
Field Social Workers	KSBX	29 820	31 926	32 140	32 990	33 400	33 900	34 700	35 200	35 800	37 200
Day care establishments staff	KADV	31 270	31 109	31 605	30 839	30 300	30 800	30 800	29 500	29 300	28 900
Residential care staff	KADW	72 155	68 651	67 975	65 422	62 100	59 200	56 600	53 800	51 400	51 400

1 All GP data as at 1 October except England and Wales as at 30 September from 2000.

2 The 'All practioners' totals for some years do not add up to the sum of their parts, having been adjusted in respect of some Scotish GPs who have posts in two separate categories.

3 All Practioners data for 1999 does not include Scotland retainers as these were first collected in April 2000.

4 GP Registrars were formerly referred to as Trainees.

5 GP Registrars in GMS Partnerships.

6 Includes principals, assistants and Vocational Dental Practioners and PDS dentists not working in the GDS. Some dentists may have a contract with more than one Health Authority. These dentists have been counted only once. PDS pilots are only in operation in England until 2002 and in only England and Wales 2003.

7 Figures for Scotland are as at 31 March, and figures for England and Wales are as at December 31, of that year. Count of OMPs and OOs holding contracts with FHSAs/HA's/LHBs and/ or Scotish Health Boards to carry out NHS Sight Tests. Practitioners with contracts in both England and Scotland are counted twice for these statistics. The OMP figure for 2003 (644) includes an estimate of 22 OMP's for Scotland, the OMP figure for Scotland being unavailable for 2003.

Sources: Department of Health;
National Assembly for Wales;
Scottish Health Service Common Services Agency

9.6 Deaths: by cause
International Statistical Classification of Diseases, Injuries and Causes of Death
Ninth Revision 1979 and Tenth Revision 1999.

Numbers

	ICD-9 code	England and Wales			
		1997	1998	1999	2000
Total deaths		555 281	555 015	556 118	535 664
Deaths from natural causes	001-799	536 453	536 396	537 166	516 803
Certain infectious and parasitic diseases	001-139	3 496	3 410	3 613	3 767
Intestinal infectious diseases	001-009	384	418	476	547
Respiratory and other tuberculosis including late effects	010-018,137	437	453	437	427
Meningococcal infection	036	242	210	217	199
Viral hepatitis	070	165	173	179	200
AIDS (HIV - disease)	042-044	259	163	155	182
Neoplasms	140-239	137 618	138 306	136 181	134 793
Malignant neoplasms	140-208	135 647	136 329	134 135	132 686
Malignant neoplasm of oesophagus	150	5 855	5 952	6 040	6 061
Malignant neoplasm of stomach	151	6 613	6 442	6 139	5 779
Malignant neoplasm of colon	153	10 448	10 170	9 911	9 554
Malignant neoplasm of rectum and anus	154.1-154.8	4 177	4 182	4 059	4 024
Malignant neoplasm of pancreas	157	5 782	5 801	5 956	6 105
Malignant neoplasm of trachea, bronchus and lung	162	29 976	30 199	29 493	29 029
Malignant neoplasm of skin	172	1 378	1 468	1 476	1 536
Malignant neoplasm of breast	174-175	12 047	11 835	11 670	11 433
Malignant neoplasm of cervix uteri	180	1 225	1 158	1 107	1 106
Malignant neoplasm of prostate	185	8 523	8 573	8 533	8 293
Leukaemia	204-208	3 587	3 551	3 680	3 570
Diseases of the blood and blood-forming organs and certain disorders involving the immune mechanism	279-289	2 056	1 978	1 907	1 829
Endocrine, nutritional and metabolic diseases	240-278	7 335	7 501	7 508	7 209
Diabetes mellitus	250	5 890	5 938	5 963	5 773
Mental and behavioural disorders	290-319	9 725	10 430	11 173	10 865
Vascular and unspecified dementia	290	6 731	7 124	7 654	7 173
Alcohol abuse (inc. alcoholic psychosis)	291,303	344	350	347	331
Drug dependence and non-dependent abuse of drugs	292,304-305	736	895	935	1 049
Diseases of the nervous system and sense organs	320-389	9 772	10 035	10 192	9 632
Meningitis (including meningococcal)	320-322	224	216	182	206
Alzheimer's disease	331.0	2 185	2 374	2 406	2 182
Diseases of the circulatory system	390-459	228 446	226 677	219 087	207 228
Ischaemic heart diseases	410-414	122 432	121 037	115 119	108 418
Cerebrovascular diseases	430-438	57 747	57 516	56 051	52 516
Diseases of the respiratory system	460-519	92 517	90 192	97 755	92 461
Influenza	487	347	129	585	509
Pneumonia	480-486	56 719	54 631	59 273	56 329
Bronchitis, emphysema and other chronic obstructive pulmonary diseases	490-492,496	25 097	24 878	26 114	23 538
Asthma	493	1 439	1 366	1 364	1 272
Diseases of the digestive system	520-579	20 406	21 025	21 698	22 134
Gastric and duodenal ulcer	531-533	3 959	3 935	4 011	4 007
Chronic liver disease	571	4 107	4 494	4 718	4 770
Diseases of the skin and subcutaneous tissue	680-709	1 025	1 070	1 152	1 266
Diseases of the musculo-skeletal system and connective tissue	710-739	3 559	3 566	3 554	3 407
Rheumatoid arthritis and juvenile arthritis	714	797	778	697	675
Osteoporosis	733.0-733.1	1 282	1 273	1 335	1 268
Diseases of the genito-urinary system	580-629	6 757	6 946	7 299	7 270
Diseases of the kidney and ureter	580-594	3 767	3 803	3 844	3 799
Complications of pregnancy, childbirth and the puerperium	630-676	35	43	30	38
Certain conditions originating in the perinatal period (excluding neonatals)[1]	760-779	131	124	116	83
Congenital malformations, deformations and chromasomal abnormalities (excluding neonatals)[1]	740-759	1 283	1 247	1 194	1 165
Congenital malformations of the nervous system	740-742	121	124	104	116
Congenital malformations of the circulatory system	745-747	689	643	621	617
Symptoms, signs and abnormal clinical and laboratory findings not elsewhere classified	780-799	12 292	13 846	14 707	13 656
Senility without mention of psychosis (old age)	797	11 028	12 615	13 473	12 458
Sudden infant death syndrome	798.0	327	236	222	180
Deaths from external causes	E800-E999	16 311	16 201	16 517	16 526
All accidents	E800-E929	10 661	10 351	10 625	10 771
Land transport accidents	E800-E829	3 291	3 023	3 098	2 985
Accidental falls	E880-E888	3 885	3 865	3 993	4 281
Accidental poisonings	E850-E869	1 058	1 045	1 030	1 064
Suicide and intentional self-harm	E950-E959	3 424	3 614	3 690	3 480
Homicide and assault[1]	E960-E969	290	285	293	380
Event of undetermined intent	E980-E989	1 914	1 931	1 886	1 872

133

9.6
continued

Deaths: by cause
International Statistical Classification of Diseases, Injuries and Causes of Death
Ninth Revision 1979 and Tenth Revision 1999.

	ICD-9 code	ICD-10 code	England and Wales		
			2001	2002	2003
			ICD-10		
Total deaths			530 373	533 527	538 254
Deaths from natural causes	001-799	A00-R99	511 667	515 262	519 297
Certain infectious and parasitic diseases	001-139	A00-B99	4 253	4 330	4 763
Intestinal infectious diseases	001-009	A00-A09	777	847	1 063
Respiratory and other tuberculosis including late effects	010-018,137	A15-A19,B90	446	443	451
Meningococcal infection	036	A39	201	115	118
Viral hepatitis	070	B15-B19	196	170	209
AIDS (HIV - disease)	042-044	B20-B24	180	198	224
Neoplasms	140-239	C00-D48	139 135	140 174	139 360
Malignant neoplasms	140-208	C00-97	135 839	136 777	135 955
Malignant neoplasm of oesophagus	150	C15	6 107	6 330	6 427
Malignant neoplasm of stomach	151	C16	5 606	5 588	5 285
Malignant neoplasm of colon	153	C18	9 436	9 504	9 152
Malignant neoplasm of rectum and anus	154.1-154.8	C20-C21	3 927	3 907	3 982
Malignant neoplasm of pancreas	157	C25	6 011	6 142	6 242
Malignant neoplasm of trachea, bronchus and lung	162	C33-C34	28 728	28 806	28 765
Malignant neoplasm of skin	172	C43	1 470	1 480	1 585
Malignant neoplasm of breast	174-175	C50	11 638	11 557	11 276
Malignant neoplasm of cervix uteri	180	C53	1 039	1 001	951
Malignant neoplasm of prostate	185	C61	8 912	8 973	9 166
Leukaemia	204-208	C91-C95	3 781	3 911	3 916
Diseases of the blood and blood-forming organs and certain disorders involving the immune mechanism	279-289	D50-D89	1 000	1 086	1 065
Endocrine, nutritional and metabolic diseases	240-278	E00-E90	7 711	7 897	8 016
Diabetes mellitus	250	E10-E14	6 119	6 192	6 316
Mental and behavioural disorders	290-319	F00-F99	14 143	14 444	14 846
Vascular and unspecified dementia	290	F01,F03	12 572	12 753	13 401
Alcohol abuse (inc. alcoholic psychosis)	291,303	F10	477	435	469
Drug dependence and non-dependent abuse of drugs	292,304-305	F11-F16,F18-F19	798	882	655
Diseases of the nervous system and sense organs	320-389	G00-H95	14 372	14 796	15 793
Meningitis (including meningococcal)	320-322	G00-G03	189	173	229
Alzheimer's disease	331.0	G30	4 579	4 771	5 055
Diseases of the circulatory system	390-459	I00-I99	211 842	209 433	205 508
Ischaemic heart diseases	410-414	I20-I25	105 895	102 833	99 790
Cerebrovascular diseases	430-438	I60-I69	58 517	59 068	57 808
Diseases of the respiratory system	460-519	J00-J99	67 391	69 900	75 138
Influenza	487	J10-J11	38	38	77
Pneumonia	480-486	J12-J18	31 636	32 631	34 400
Bronchitis, emphysema and other chronic obstructive pulmonary diseases	490-492,496	J40-J44	23 700	24 159	25 765
Asthma	493	J45-J46	1 268	1 264	1284
Diseases of the digestive system	520-579	K00-K93	23 386	24 124	24 948
Gastric and duodenal ulcer	531-533	K25-K27	3 802	3 746	3 678
Chronic liver disease	571	K70,K73-K74	5 234	5 376	5 844
Diseases of the skin and subcutaneous tissue	680-709	L00-L99	1 291	1 470	1 661
Diseases of the musculo-skeletal system and connective tissue	710-739	M00-M99	4 588	4 647	4 634
Rheumatoid arthritis and juvenile arthritis	714	M05-M06,M08	970	966	907
Osteoporosis	733.0-733.1	M80-M81	1 542	1 605	1 583
Diseases of the genito-urinary system	580-629	N00-N99	7 682	8 452	9 120
Diseases of the kidney and ureter	580-594	N00-N29	3 848	4 072	4 135
Complications of pregnancy, childbirth and the puerperium	630-676	O00-O99	42	34	45
Certain conditions originating in the perinatal period (excluding neonatals)[1]	760-779	P00-P96	200	208	207
Congenital malformations, deformations and chromasomal abnormalities (excluding neonatals)[1]	740-759	Q00-Q99	1 280	1 233	1299
Congenital malformations of the nervous system	740-742	Q00-Q07	119	127	142
Congenital malformations of the circulatory system	745-747	Q20-Q28	592	541	540
Symptoms, signs and abnormal clinical and laboratory findings not elsewhere classified	780-799	R00-R99	13 351	13 034	12 894
Senility without mention of psychosis (old age)	797	R54	11 900	11 645	11 394
Sudden infant death syndrome	798.0	R95	195	137	136
Deaths from external causes	E800-E999	V01-Y89	16 569	16 139	16 693
All accidents	E800-E929	V01-X59,Y85,Y86	10 733	10 382	10 979
Land transport accidents	E800-E829	V01-V89	2 949	2 929	2 943
Accidental falls	E880-E888	W00-W19	2 617	2 509	2 732
Accidental poisonings	E850-E869	X40-X49	1 037	814	835
Suicide and intentional self-harm	E950-E959	X60-X84,Y87.0	3 264	3 269	3 270
Homicide and assault[1]	E960-E969	X85-Y09,Y87.1	386	373	318
Event of undetermined intent	E980-E989	Y10-Y34, Y87.2	1 803	1 754	1 776

Deaths: by cause
International Statistical Classification of Diseases, Injuries and Causes of Death
Ninth Revision 1979 and Tenth Revision 1999.

Numbers

	ICD-9 code	ICD-10 code	Scotland 1998	1999	2000	2001	2002	2003
				ICD-9	ICD-10			
Total deaths			59 164	60 281	57 799	57 382	58 103	58 472
Deaths from natural causes	001-799	A00-R99	56 785	57 831	55 415	54 961	55 689	56 161
Certain infectious and parasitic diseases	001-139	A00-B99	498	601	476	558	651	660
Intestinal infectious diseases	001-009	A00-A09	34	31	51	65	96	85
Respiratory and other tuberculosis including late effects	010-018,137	A15-A19,B90	58	65	66	54	52	59
Meningococcal infection	036	A39	20	14	18	12	13	5
Viral hepatitis	070	B15-B19	22	17	14	6	13	23
AIDS (HIV - disease)	042-044	B20-B24	32	23	23	33	33	33
Neoplasms	140-239	C00-D48	14 907	14 966	15 255	15 475	15 391	15 412
Malignant neoplasms	140-208	C00-C97	14 752	14 789	14 958	15 196	15 051	15 116
Malignant neoplasm of oesophagus	150	C15	730	776	708	752	763	776
Malignant neoplasm of stomach	151	C16	680	650	649	678	621	579
Malignant neoplasm of colon	153	C18	996	1 018	1 052	1 062	975	966
Malignant neoplasm of rectum and anus	154.1-154.8	C20-21	448	474	400	405	384	368
Malignant neoplasm of pancreas	157	C25	607	574	633	595	562	641
Malignant neoplasm of trachea, bronchus and lung	162	C33-34	3 984	3 961	3 948	3 915	4 039	3 893
Malignant neoplasm of skin	172	C43	144	131	115	145	132	146
Malignant neoplasm of breast	174-175	C50	1 147	1 136	1 122	1 150	1 110	1 149
Malignant neoplasm of cervix uteri	180	C53	145	122	117	113	100	120
Malignant neoplasm of prostate	185	C61	677	769	773	777	775	786
Leukaemia	204-208	C91-C95	329	313	325	350	330	367
Diseases of the blood and blood-forming organs and certain disorders involving the immune mechanism	279-289	D50-D89	222	204	114	124	122	148
Endocrine, nutritional and metabolic diseases	240-278	E00-E90	797	870	828	891	902	958
Diabetes mellitus	250	E10-E14	574	670	616	695	676	709
Mental and behavioural disorders	290-319	F00-F99	1 725	1 901	2 309	2 425	2 446	2 637
Vascular and unspecified dementia	290	F01,F03	690	783	1 684	1 809	1 763	1 997
Alcohol abuse (inc. alcoholic psychosis)	291,303	F10	329	358	330	341	339	356
Drug dependence and non-dependent abuse of drugs	292,304-305	F11-F16,F18-F19	182	230	245	238	294	228
Diseases of the nervous system and sense organs	320-389	G00-H95	894	971	1 315	1 243	1 317	1 303
Meningitis (including meningococcal)	320-322	G00-G03	6	19	15	16	6	19
Alzheimer's disease	331.0	G30	142	140	329	324	388	354
Diseases of the circulatory system	390-459	I00-I99	25 153	24 787	23 657	22 666	22 688	22 102
Ischaemic heart diseases	410-414	I20-I25	13 419	13 337	12 412	11 914	11 692	11 441
Cerebrovascular diseases	430-438	I60-I69	6 900	6 785	6 803	6 621	6 722	6 497
Diseases of the respiratory system	460-519	J00-J99	8 011	8 870	6 547	6 435	6 806	7 454
Influenza	487	J10-J11	12	62	131	5	6	15
Pneumonia	480-486	J12-J18	4 064	4 526	2 312	2 370	2 466	2 859
Bronchitis, emphysema and other chronic obstructive pulmonary diseases	490-492,496	J40-J44	2 662	2 941	2 825	2 836	2 840	3 014
Asthma	493	J45-J46	120	119	131	101	131	98
Diseases of the digestive system	520-579	K00-K93	2 578	2 787	2 922	3 063	3 153	3 215
Gastric and duodenal ulcer	531-533	K25-K27	337	321	348	308	350	316
Chronic liver disease	571	K70,K73-K74	806	896	956	1 061	1 128	1 170
Diseases of the skin and subcutaneous tissue	680-709	L00-L99	94	90	89	90	118	131
Diseases of the musculo-skeletal system and connective tissue	710-739	M00-M99	284	295	405	357	384	369
Rheumatoid arthritis and juvenile arthritis	714	M05-M06,M08	86	87	126	125	133	103
Osteoporosis	733.0-733.1	M80-M81	46	53	58	56	59	70
Diseases of the genito-urinary system	580-629	N00-N99	890	936	844	969	1 013	1 056
Diseases of the kidney and ureter	580-594	N00-N29	644	619	563	638	627	670
Complications of pregnancy, childbirth and the puerperium	630-676	O00-O99	5	7	8	6	5	7
Certain conditions originating in the perinatal period	760-779	P00-P96	165	137	170	167	155	149
Congenital malformations, deformations and chromosomal abnormalities	740-759	Q00-Q99	176	157	154	172	168	172
Congenital malformations of the nervous system	740-742	Q00-Q07	23	13	25	16	31	23
Congenital malformations of the circulatory system	745-747	Q20-Q28	81	59	56	65	60	63
Symptoms, signs and abnormal clinical and laboratory findings not elsewhere classified	780-799	R00-R99	398	355	322	320	370	388
Senility without mention of psychosis (old age)	797	R54	111	185	161	172	191	236
Sudden infant death syndrome	798.0	R95	37	41	33	32	32	43
Deaths from external causes	E800-E999	V01-Y89	2 379	2 450	2 384	2 421	2 414	2 311
All accidents	E800-E929	V01-X59,Y85,Y86	1 303	1 359	1 341	1 350	1 315	1 326
Land transport accidents	E800-E829	V01-V89	394	326	338	367	321	357
Accidental falls	E880-E888	W00-W19	613	713	675	626	668	668
Accidental poisonings	E850-E869	X40-X49	38	30	34	50	37	30
Suicide and intentional self-harm	E950-E959	X60-X84,Y87.0	649	637	648	609	636	560
Homicide and assault	E960-E969	X85-Y09,Y87.1	94	121	93	92	118	101
Event of undetermined intent	E980-E989	Y10-Y34, Y87.2	229	237	230	278	263	234

135

9.6
continued

Deaths: by cause
International Statistical Classification of Diseases, Injuries and Causes of Death
Ninth Revision 1979 and Tenth Revision 1999.

Numbers

	ICD-9 code	ICD-10 code	Northern Ireland 1998	1999	2000 ICD-9	2001 ICD-10	2002	2003
Total deaths			14 993	15 663	14 903	14 513	14 586	14 462
Deaths from natural causes	001-799	A00-R99	14 424	15 054	14 296	13 968	13 949	13 912
Certain infectious and parasitic diseases	001-139	A00-B99	53	47	73	117	134	157
Intestinal infectious diseases	001-009	A00-A09	-	1	4	7	11	13
Respiratory and other tuberculosis including late effects	010-018,137	A15-A19,B90	6	7	7	6	10	11
Meningococcal infection	036	A39	6	4	9	4	7	4
Viral hepatitis	070	B15-B19	1	2	6	-	-	-
AIDS (HIV - disease)	042-044	B20-B24	1	2	1	-	3	2
Neoplasms	140-239	C00-D48	3 769	3 654	3 647	3 802	3 766	3 882
Malignant neoplasms	140-208	C00-C97	3 648	3 552	3 541	3 696	3 652	3 757
Malignant neoplasm of oesophagus	150	C15	154	161	150	155	163	154
Malignant neoplasm of stomach	151	C16	215	187	180	174	164	165
Malignant neoplasm of colon	153	C18	329	303	301	271	270	313
Malignant neoplasm of rectum and anus	154.1-154.8	C20-C21	98	95	84	100	90	103
Malignant neoplasm of pancreas	157	C25	154	142	159	176	194	173
Malignant neoplasm of trachea, bronchus and lung	162	C33-C34	775	781	792	782	802	810
Malignant neoplasm of skin	172	C43	28	33	31	37	38	40
Malignant neoplasm of breast	174-175	C50	299	286	289	316	278	291
Malignant neoplasm of cervix uteri	180	C53	33	36	30	24	25	31
Malignant neoplasm of prostate	185	C61	220	195	213	214	193	217
Leukaemia	204-208	C91-C95	93	104	91	87	93	85
Diseases of the blood and blood-forming organs and certain disorders involving the immune mechanism	279-289	D50-D89	24	24	24	32	24	37
Endocrine, nutritional and metabolic diseases	240-278	E00-E90	85	118	122	200	238	246
Diabetes mellitus	250	E10-E14	55	93	89	145	187	190
Mental and behavioural disorders	290-319	F00-F99	145	190	207	381	411	341
Vascular and unspecified dementia	290	F01,F03	58	75	66	298	329	284
Alcohol abuse (inc. alcoholic psychosis)	291,303	F10	35	46	46	75	74	52
Drug dependence and non-dependent abuse of drugs	292,304-305	F11-F16,F18-F19	11	25	38	2	6	3
Diseases of the nervous system and sense organs	320-389	G00-H95	240	285	245	467	531	481
Meningitis (including meningococcal)	320-322	G00-G03	4	3	6	9	5	3
Alzheimer's disease	331.0	G30	80	98	81	211	246	224
Diseases of the circulatory system	390-459	I00-I99	6 367	6 422	5 776	5 829	5 729	5 448
Ischaemic heart diseases	410-414	I20-I25	3 654	3 568	3 234	3 148	2 948	2 843
Cerebrovascular diseases	430-438	I60-I69	1 602	1 679	1 469	1 531	1 573	1 531
Diseases of the respiratory system	460-519	J00-J99	2 627	3 161	3 019	1 975	1 883	2 082
Influenza	487	J10-J11	2	5	39	-	1	4
Pneumonia	480-486	J12-J18	1 727	2 130	2 027	1 028	951	1 025
Bronchitis, emphysema and other chronic obstructive pulmonary diseases	490-492,496	J40-J44	627	704	610	584	553	660
Asthma	493	J45-J46	44	38	33	38	36	32
Diseases of the digestive system	520-579	K00-K93	499	507	531	556	581	587
Gastric and duodenal ulcer	531-533	K25-K27	80	80	89	76	62	77
Chronic liver disease	571	K70,K73-K74	104	92	101	133	166	156
Diseases of the skin and subcutaneous tissue	680-709	L00-L99	36	27	21	24	21	15
Diseases of the musculo-skeletal system and connective tissue	710-739	M00-M99	30	54	40	94	90	93
Rheumatoid arthritis and juvenile arthritis	714	M05-M06,M08	6	13	26	31	21	26
Osteoporosis	733.0-733.1	M80-M81	4	11	5	12	19	16
Diseases of the genito-urinary system	580-629	N00-N99	265	242	292	278	333	327
Diseases of the kidney and ureter	580-594	N00-N29	184	173	201	192	246	225
Complications of pregnancy, childbirth and the puerperium	630-676	O00-O99	1	-	-	2	1	3
Certain conditions originating in the perinatal period	760-779	P00-P96	64	69	62	63	62	62
Congenital malformations, deformations and chromasomal abnormalities	740-759	Q00-Q99	70	93	57	83	53	69
Congenital malformations of the nervous system	740-742	Q00-Q07	9	9	14	16	7	12
Congenital malformations of the circulatory system	745-747	Q20-Q28	17	32	19	24	17	16
Symptoms, signs and abnormal clinical and laboratory findings not elsewhere classified	780-799	R00-R99	149	161	180	65	92	82
Senility without mention of psychosis (old age)	797	R54	105	122	146	37	63	63
Sudden infant death syndrome	798.0	R95	4	3	-	2	0	-
Deaths from external causes	E800-E999	V01-Y89	569	609	607	545	637	550
All accidents	E800-E929	V01-X59,Y85,Y86	381	430	364	361	424	364
Land transport accidents	E800-E829	V01-V89	131	134	142	148	144	120
Accidental falls	E880-E888	W00-W19	127	161	131	52	60	44
Accidental poisonings	E850-E869	X40-X49	36	38	25	13	30	30
Suicide and intentional self-harm	E950-E959	X60-X84,Y87.0	126	121	163	141	162	132
Homicide and assault	E960-E969	X85-Y09,Y87.1	36	24	56	20	27	30
Event of undetermined intent	E980-E989	Y10-Y34,Y87.2	24	33	22	17	21	12

1 See chapter text

Sources: Office for National Statistics;
General Register Office, Scotland;
Northern Ireland Statistics and Research Agency

9.7 Notifications of infectious diseases: by country

		1993	1994	1995	1996	1997	1998	1999	2000	2001	2002	2003
United Kingdom												
Measles	KHQD	12 018	23 517	9 017	6 866	4 844	4 540	2 951	2 865	2 661	3 675	2 726
Mumps	KWNN	2 726	3 143	2 400	2 182	2 264	1 917	2 000	3 367	3 433	2 333	4 565
Rubella	KWNO	12 300	9 650	7 674	11 720	4 205	4 064	2 575	2 064	1 782	2 002	1 525
Whooping cough	KHQE	4 718	4 837	2 399	2 721	3 669	1 902	1 461	866	1 059	1 051	509
Scarlet fever	KHQC	7 341	8 031	6 863	6 101	4 639	4 708	2 956	2 544	2 320	2 749	3 252
Dysentery	KHQG	7 577	7 538	5 498	2 643	2 427	1 934	1 630	1 613	1 495	1 167	1 144
Food poisoning	KHQH	76 711	91 128	92 604	94 923	105 579	105 060	96 866	98 076	95 752	81 562	79 073
Typhoid and Paratyphoid fevers	KHQB	277	390	386	291	249	252	278	205	254	183	277
Hepatitis	KWNP	6 142	4 285	3 823	2 876	3 601	3 781	4 365	4 530	4 419	5 035	5 203
Tuberculosis	KHQI	6 565	6 230	6 176	6 238	6 367	6 605	6 701	7 100	7 204	7 239	6 863
Malaria	KWNQ	1 281	1 219	1 363	1 743	1 549	1 163	1 038	1 166	1 118	866	820
England and Wales[1]												
Measles	KHRD	9 612	16 375	7 447	5 614	3 962	3 728	2 438	2 378	2 250	3 187	2 488
Mumps	KWNR	2 153	2 494	1 936	1 747	1 914	1 587	1 691	2 162	2 741	1 997	4 204
Rubella	KWNS	9 724	6 326	6 196	9 081	3 260	3 208	1 954	1 653	1 483	1 660	1 361
Whooping cough	KHRE	4 091	3 964	1 869	2 387	2 989	1 577	1 139	712	888	883	409
Scarlet fever	KHRC	5 855	6 193	5 296	4 873	3 569	3 339	2 086	1 933	1 756	2 159	2 553
Dysentery	KHRG	6 841	6 956	4 651	2 312	2 274	1 813	1 538	1 494	1 388	1 087	1 047
Food poisoning	KHRH	68 587	81 833	82 041	83 233	93 901	93 932	86 316	86 528	85 468	72 649	70 895
Typhoid and Paratyphoid fevers	KHRB	268	370	370	276	241	243	276	204	250	175	275
Viral hepatitis	KWNT	5 557	3 722	3 296	2 437	3 186	3 183	3 424	3 541	3 388	3 859	4 004
Tuberculosis[2]	KHRJ	5 921	5 591	5 608	5 654	5 859	6 087	6 144	6 572	6 714	6 753	6 518
Malaria	KWNU	1 198	1 139	1 300	1 659	1 476	1 110	1 005	1 128	1 081	847	791
Total meningitis	KHRO	2 082	1 800	2 285	2 686	2 345	2 072	2 094	2 432	2 623	1 545	1 472
Meningococcal meningitis	KHRP	1 053	938	1 146	1 164	1 220	1 152	1 145	1 164	1 020	706	646
Meningococcal septicaemia	KWNV	398	430	707	1 129	1 440	1 509	1 822	1 614	1 238	842	732
Ophthalmia neonatorum	KHRI	340	268	245	246	224	198	163	176	115	91	102
Scotland												
Measles	KHSE	1 911	6 192	1 307	1 055	762	700	434	395	315	399	181
Mumps	KWNW	458	546	371	368	282	251	216	199	155	259	181
Rubella	KWNX	2 048	2 916	1 258	2 449	818	745	548	349	234	292	130
Whooping cough	KHSF	493	639	399	186	545	225	214	93	106	99	60
Scarlet fever	KHSD	911	1 319	1 065	750	645	883	438	301	281	376	395
Dysentery	KHSH	607	446	575	176	124	103	82	95	85	73	83
Food poisoning[3]	KHSI	7 170	8 291	9 297	10 234	10 144	9 186	8 517	9 263	8 640	7 693	6 910
Typhoid and Paratyphoid fevers	KHSB	7	18	16	14	6	6	2	1	3	4	2
Viral hepatitis	KWNY	290	296	405	360	359	490	863	943	1 008	1 165	1 159
Tuberculosis[4]	KHSL	554	546	478	509	433	457	496	469	442	418	307
Malaria	KWUC	75	74	58	70	57	30	20	27	24	17	28
Meningococcal infection	KWUD	207	201	190	201	271	313	329	301	256	175	117
Erysipelas	KHSC	130	118	125	84	95	66	64	41	39	41	28
Northern Ireland												
Measles	KHTD	495	950	263	197	120	112	79	92	96	89	57
Mumps	KHTR	115	103	93	67	68	79	93	1 006	537	77	180
Rubella	KHTQ	528	408	220	190	127	111	73	62	65	50	34
Whooping cough	KHTE	134	234	131	148	135	100	108	61	65	69	40
Scarlet fever	KHTC	575	519	502	478	425	486	432	310	283	214	304
Dysentery	KHTG	129	136	272	155	29	18	10	24	22	7	14
Food poisoning	KHTH	954	1 004	1 266	1 456	1 534	1 942	2 033	2 285	1 644	1 220	1 268
Typhoid and Paratyphoid fevers	KHTB	2	2	–	1	2	3	–	–	1	4	–
Infective hepatitis	KHTO	295	267	122	79	56	108	78	46	23	11	40
Tuberculosis	KHTI	90	93	90	75	75	61	61	59	48	68	38
Malaria	KWUE	8	6	5	14	16	23	13	11	13	2	1
Acute encephalitis/meningitis	KHTM	122	144	116	105	91	64	99	130	97	98	88
Meningococcal septicaemia	KWUF	34	39	42	67	56	87	145	123	90	98	76
Gastro-enteritis (children under 2 years)	KHTP	1 379	888	1 072	745	896	1 371	1 121	1 205	1 106	882	867

1 The figures show the corrected number of notifications, incorporating revisions of diagnosis, either by the notifying medical practitioner or by the medical superintendent of the infectious diseases hospital. Cases notified in Port Health Authorities are included.

2 Formal notifications of new cases only. The figures exclude chemoprophylaxis.

3 Scotland's food poisoning includes 'otherwise ascertained' for the first time in 1995.

4 Figures include cases of tuberculosis not notified before death.

Sources: Information and Statistics Division, NHS in Scotland; Communicable Disease Surveillance Centre (Northern Ireland); HPA Centre for Infections CDSC: 020 8200 6868

9.8 Estimated number of cases of work-related disease reported by specialist physicians to THOR[1]

Great Britain

Numbers

	All physicians			Disease specialist			Occupational physicians		
	2001	2002	2003	2001	2002	2003	2001	2002	2003
Musculoskeletal disorders					MOSS			OPRA	
Upper limb	4 930	5 254	3 243	1 824	1 708	1 473	3 106	3 546	1770
Spine/ back	2 294	2 084	1 973	432	436	501	1 862	1 648	1 472
Lower limb	528	489	352	84	81	40	444	408	312
Other	360	303	199	84	51	67	276	252	132
Total number of diagnoses	8 292	8 206	5 863	2 484	2 328	2 117	5 808	5 878	3 746
Total number of individuals[2]	7 871	7 970	5 687	2 328	2 260	2 061	5 543	5 710	3 626
Mental ill health					SOSMI			OPRA	
Stress/ anxiety/ depression	6 903	6 591	6 373	2 316	1 851	1 705	4 587	4 740	4 668
Other	1 212	954	868	888	666	604	324	288	264
Total number of diagnoses	8 115	7 653	7 241	3 204	2 565	2 309	4 911	5 088	4 932
Total number of individuals[2]	7 575	6 946	6 579	3 096	2 410	2 175	4 479	4 536	4 404
Respiratory disease					SWORD			OPRA	
Asthma	649	670	647	414	398	347	235	272	300
Malignant mesothelioma	973	882	875	966	870	869	7	12	6
Benign pleural disease	865	935	1 087	853	899	1 075	12	36	12
Other	938	706	807	708	458	548	230	248	259
Total number of diagnoses	3 425	3 193	3 416	2 941	2 625	2 839	484	568	577
Total number of individuals[2]	3 353	3 118	3 317	2 869	2 562	2 752	484	556	565
Skin disease					EPIDERM			OPRA	
Contact dermatitis	2 724	2 878	2 574	1 702	1 922	1 663	1 022	956	911
Skin neoplasia	545	392	361	545	380	361	-	12	-
Other	403	389	437	245	163	214	158	226	223
Total number of diagnoses	3 684	3 807	3 372	2 492	2 613	2 238	1 192	1 194	1 134
Total number of individuals[2]	3 647	3 600	3 308	2 467	2 431	2 174	1 180	1 169	1 134
Audiological disease					OSSA			OPRA	
Sensorineural hearing loss	341	219	322	149	27	58	192	192	264
Other	126	16	71	78	16	47	48	-	24
Total number of diagnoses	467	235	393	227	43	105	240	192	288
Total number of individuals[2]	395	222	352	155	30	64	240	192	288
Infections					SIDAW				
Diarrhoeal diseases	..	..	..	539	2051	934	..	..	..
Other	..	..	..	155	182	94	..	..	..
Total number of diagnoses	..	..	..	694	2 233	1 028	..	..	..
Total number of individuals[2]	..	..	..	694	2 233	1 028	..	..	..

1 See chapter text. THOR the Health and Occupation Reporting Network (formerly know as ODIN) comprises of the following schemes: OPRA: Occupational Physicians Reporting Activity; MOSS: Musculoskeletal Occupational Surveillance Scheme; SOSMI: Surveillance of Occupational Stress and Mental Illness; SWORD: Surveillance of Work-related and Occupational Respiratory Disease; EPIDERM: Occupational Skin Disease Surveillance by Dermatologists; OSSA: Occupational Surveillance Scheme for Audiologists; SIDAW: Surveillance of Infectious Disease at Work.
2 Individuals may have more than one diagnosis.

Source: Health and Safety Executive: 0151 951 3479/4355

9.9 Deaths due to occupationally related lung disease[1]
Great Britain

Numbers

		1992	1993	1994	1995	1996	1997	1998	1999	2000	2001	2002
Asbestosis (without mesothelioma)[2]	KADY	150	173	174	166	196	191	165	171	186	208	194
Mesothelioma [2]	KADZ	1 097	1 152	1 246	1 317	1 322	1 367	1 541	1 615	1 631	1 848	1 862
Pneumoconiosis (other than asbestosis)	KAEA	274	281	276	287	223	230	268	321	279	240	271
Byssinosis	KAEB	21	11	7	6	3	5	5	6	4	2	–
Farmer's lung and other occupational allergic alveolitis	KAEC	4	12	10	10	1	5	8	9	7	7	6
Total	KAED	1 546	1 629	1 713	1 786	1 745	1 798	1 987	2 122	2 107	2 305	2 333

1 See chapter text.
2 By definition every case of asbestosis is due to asbestos; the association with mesothelioma is also very strong, though there is thought to be a low natural background incidence.

Sources: Office for National Statistics; Health and Safety Executive: 0151 951 3479/4355

9.10 Injuries to workers:[1] by industry and severity of injury
Great Britain
As reported to all enforcing authorities

Numbers

				Fatal				Major				Over 3 Days[2]		
		Section	SIC (92)	2000 /01	2001 /02	2002 /03		2000 /01	2001 /02	2002 /03		2000 /01	2001 /02	2002 /03
Agriculture, hunting, forestry and fishing[3]	KSYS	A,B	01,02,05	46	39	36	KSZN	655	695	642	KTAZ	1 398	1 597	1 320
Energy and water supply industries	KSYT	C,E	10-14,40/41	8	14	3	KSZO	472	459	443	KTBH	2 375	2 261	1 890
Mining and quarrying	KSYU	C	10-14	8	9	1	KSZP	296	282	276	KTBI	1 481	1 417	1 086
Mining and quarrying of energy producing materials	KSON	CA	10-12	3	7	–	KSZQ	174	174	163	KTBJ	1 040	979	751
Mining and quarrying except energy producing materials	KSOO	CB	13/14	5	2	1	KSZR	122	108	113	KTBK	441	438	335
Electricity, gas and water supply	KSOP	E	40/41	–	5	2	KSZS	176	177	167	KTBL	894	844	804
Manufacturing	KSOQ	D	15-37	50	48	43	KSZT	7 459	7 180	6 789	KTBM	38 187	35 034	33 195
of food products; beverages and tobacco	KSOR	DA	15/16	4	7	3	KSZU	1 344	1 418	1 308	KTBN	9 417	8 779	8 685
of textile and textile products	KSOS	DB	17/18	4	–	1	KSZV	252	215	177	KTBO	1 131	973	903
of leather and leather products	KSOT	DC	19	–	1	–	KSZW	22	19	21	KTBP	161	120	112
of wood and wood products	KSOU	DD	20	4	2	2	KSZX	349	411	343	KTBQ	1 060	1 107	1 139
of pulp, paper and paper products; publishing and printing	KSOV	DE	21/22	–	3	–	KSZY	466	473	459	KTBR	2 544	2 365	2 105
of coke, refined petroleum products and nuclear fuel	KSOW	DF	23	–	2	1	KSZZ	42	19	18	KTBS	115	103	79
of chemicals, chemical products and man-made fibres	KSOX	DG	24	–	2	2	KTAE	395	406	407	KTBT	1 846	1 708	1 569
of rubber and plastic products	KSOY	DH	25	5	4	4	KTAF	619	608	557	KTBU	3 306	3 100	3 021
of other non-metallic mineral products	KSOZ	DI	26	5	2	4	KTAG	417	404	383	KTBV	2 052	1 929	1 827
of basic metals and fabricated metal products	KSYV	DJ	27/28	19	12	13	KTAH	1 534	1 333	1 285	KTBW	6 070	5 133	4 731
of machinery and equipment not elsewhere classified	KSYW	DK	29	4	3	4	KTAI	629	541	544	KTBX	2 876	2 731	2 468
of electrical and optical equipment	KSYX	DL	30-33	2	–	3	KTAJ	428	371	356	KTBY	2 321	2 053	1 774
of transport equipment	KSYY	DM	34/35	1	2	3	KTAK	654	586	538	KTBZ	3 799	3 351	3 171
Manufacturing not elsewhere classified	KSYZ	DN	36/37	2	8	3	KTAL	308	376	393	KTCA	1 489	1 582	1 611
Construction	KSZA	F	45	105	80	70	KTAM	4 708	4 595	4 721	KTCB	9 796	9 695	9 578
Total service industries	KSZB	G-Q	50-99	83	70	75	KTAN	14 860	16 011	16 597	KTCC	83 064	81 985	83 152
Wholesale and retail trade, and repairs	KSZC	G	50-52	15	13	19	KTAO	3 045	3 445	3 618	KTCD	15 154	14 376	15 379
Hotel and restaurants	KSZD	H	55	4	1	1	KTAP	754	936	997	KTCE	3 358	3 215	3 367
Transport, storage and communication[4]	KSZE	I	60-64	40	23	28	KTAQ	3 061	3 068	3 237	KTCF	22 596	22 531	23 340
Financial intermediation	KSZF	J	65-67	1	1	2	KTAR	152	228	252	KTCG	586	857	919
Real estate, renting and business activities	KSZG	K	70-74	7	13	9	KTAS	1 031	1 623	1 645	KTCH	3 474	4 882	5 206
Public administration and defence	KSZH	L	75	2	4	5	KTAT	2 165	2 183	2 362	KTCI	15 067	14 296	13 941
Education	KSZI	M	80	2	2	–	KTAU	1 462	1 447	1 338	KTCJ	4 682	4 373	4 290
Health and social work	KSZJ	N	85	2	2	–	KTAV	1 857	1 800	1 877	KTCK	13 400	13 061	12 576
Other community, social and personal services activities	KSZK	O-Q	90-99	10	11	11	KTAW	1 333	1 281	1 271	KTCL	4 747	4 394	4 134
All industries	KSZM			292	251	227	KTAY	28 154	28 940	29 192	KTCN	134 820	130 572	129 135

1 See chapter text.
2 Injuries causing incapacity for normal work for more than 3 days.
3 Excludes sea fishing.

4 Injuries arising from shore based services only. Excludes incidents reported under merchant shipping legislation.

Source: Health and Safety Executive (HSE): 0151 951 4842

Social
protection

Chapter 10

Social protection

Social security

(Tables 10.2 to 10.11, 10.13 and 10.15 to 10.18)

Tables 10.2 to 10.6, 10.9 – 10.11 and 10.13 to 10.18 give details of contributors and beneficiaries under the National Insurance and Industrial Injury Acts, supplementary benefits and war pensions.

There are three types of contributor:

Class 1   Employed people, that is, people working for employers. Their contributions are paid partly by themselves and partly by their employers. They are covered for all benefits.

Class 2   Self-employed people, that is, people working on their own account. They are covered for all benefits other than unemployment and industrial injuries.

Class 3   Non-employed people, that is, people who do not work for gain. These people pay contributions on a voluntary basis. They are covered for benefits other than unemployment, sickness, industrial injuries and maternity allowances.

Class 4   Payable, in addition to Class 2 by self-employed people, and the amount payable is proportionate to profits or gains between a lower and upper limit in any one year.

An employer must pay a contribution for every employee whose earnings exceed a base level. Most employed people pay the full employee's contribution, but retirement pensioners working for an employer do not, and some married women and some widows who are working need not, unless they so wish, contribute except for industrial injuries benefit. Thus the total numbers in the analysis by benefit for which the contributions were payable are less than the total numbers in the analysis by class of contributor.

Jobseeker's Allowance

(Table 10.6)

Jobseeker's Allowance (JSA) replaced Unemployment Benefit and Income Support for unemployed claimants on 7 October 1996. It is a unified benefit with two routes of entry:

contribution-based which depends mainly upon national insurance contributions and income-based which depends mainly upon a means test. Some claimants can qualify by either route. In practice they receive income-based JSA but have an underlying entitlement to the contribution-based element.

Sickness Benefit, Invalidity Benefit and Incapacity Benefit

(Tables 10.7 and 10.8)

Incapacity Benefit replaced Sickness Benefit and Invalidity Benefit from 13 April 1995. The first condition for entitlement to these contributory benefits is that the claimants are incapable of work because of illness or disablement. Secondly, that they satisfy the contribution conditions which depend on contributions paid as an employed (Class 1) or self-employed person (Class 2). Under Sickness and Invalidity Benefits the contribution conditions were automatically treated as satisfied if a person was incapable of work because of an industrial accident or prescribed disease. Under Incapacity Benefit those who do not satisfy the contribution conditions in this case do not have them treated as satisfied. Class 1A contributions paid by employers are in respect of the benefit of cars provided for the private use of employees, and the free fuel provided for private use. These contributions do not provide any type of benefit cover.

Since 6 April 1983, most people working for an employer and paying National Insurance contributions as employed persons, receive Statutory Sick Pay (SSP) from their employer when they are off work sick. SSP was payable for a maximum of eight weeks until 5 April 1986, and 28 weeks thereafter. People who do not work for an employer, and employees who are excluded from the SSP scheme, or those who have run out of SSP before reaching the maximum of 28 weeks and are still sick can claim benefit. Any period of SSP is excluded from the tables.

Spells of incapacity of three days or less do not count as periods of interruption of employment, and are excluded from the tables. Exceptions are where people are receiving regular weekly treatment by dialysis, or treatment by radiotherapy, chemotherapy or plasmapheresis where two days in any six consecutive days make up a period of interruption of employment, and those whose incapacity for work ends within three days of the end of SSP entitlement.

At the beginning of a period of incapacity, benefit is subject to three waiting days, except where there was an earlier spell of incapacity of more than three days in the previous eight weeks. Employees entitled to SSP for less than 28 weeks and who are still sick can get Sickness Benefit or Incapacity Benefit Short Term (Low) until they reach a total of 28 weeks provided they satisfy the conditions. After 28 weeks SSP and/or Sickness Benefit (SB), Invalidity Benefit (IVB) was payable up to pension age for as long as the incapacity lasts. From pension age Invalidity Benefit was paid at the person's State Pension rate, until entitlement ceases when SP is paid or at deemed pension age (70 for a man, 65 for a woman). For people on Incapacity Benefit under State pension age there are two short-term rates: the lower rate is paid for the first 28 weeks of sickness and the higher rate for weeks 29 to 52. From week 53 the Long Term rate Incapacity Benefit is payable. The Short Term rate Incapacity Benefit is based on State Pension entitlement for people over State Pension age and is paid for up to a year if incapacity began before pension age.

The Long Term rate of Incapacity Benefit applies to people under State Pension age who have been sick for more than a year. People with a terminal illness or who are receiving the higher rate care component of Disability Living Allowance will get the Long Term rate. The Long Term rate is not paid for people over pension age.

Under Incapacity Benefit, for the first 28 weeks of incapacity, people previously in work will be assessed on the 'own occupation' test – the claimant's ability to do their own job. Otherwise, incapacity will be based on a personal capability assessment, which will assess ability to carry out a range of work-related activities. The test will apply after 28 weeks of incapacity or from the start of the claim for people who did not previously have a job. Certain people will be exempted from this test.

The tables exclude all men aged over 65 and women aged over 60 who are in receipt of State Pension, and all people over deemed pension age (70 for a man and 65 for a woman), members of the Armed Forces, mariners while at sea, and married women and certain widows who have chosen not to be insured for sickness benefit. The tables include a number of individuals who were unemployed prior to incapacity.

The Short Term (Higher) and Long Term rates of Incapacity Benefit are treated as taxable income.

There were transitional provisions for people who were on Sickness or Invalidity Benefit on 12 April 1995. They were automatically transferred to Incapacity Benefit, payable on the same basis as before. Former IVB recipients continue to get Additional Pension entitlement, but frozen at 1994 levels. Also their IVB is not subject to tax. If they were over State Pension age on 12 April 1995 they may get Incapacity Benefit for up to five years beyond pension age.

Child Benefits

(Table 10.9)

Child Benefit is paid to those responsible for children. Here 'children' includes all those aged under 16. It also includes young people aged under 19 who are in full-time non-advanced education, or are entered for future external examinations, or are in the period between leaving (or exams finishing) and the week containing the first Monday in September (or similar dates after Easter and in early January, if earlier). It also includes young people aged under 18 who have moved directly from full-time education to being registered for work or training with the Careers service or with Connexions. Awards are also subject to residence criteria being satisfied.

Guardian's Allowance is an additional allowance for people bringing up a child because one or both of their parents has died. They must be getting Child Benefit for the child.

The table show the number of families in the United Kingdom in receipt of Child Benefit. The numbers shown in the table are estimates based on a random five per cent sample of awards current at 31 August and are therefore subject to sampling error. The figures take no account of new claims, or revisions to claims that were received or processed after 31 August even if they are backdated to start before 31 August.

Family Credit/ Working Families' Tax Credit

(Table 10.10)

Working Families' Tax Credit (WFTC) replaced Family Credit from 5 October 1999.

Family Credit was, and Working Families' Tax Credit is, available to families with at least one adult in remunerative work for at least 16 hours per week and who is responsible for at least one child under 16 (under 19 if in full time education up to A-level or equivalent standard). The rate of payment of WFTC depends on the number of such children and expenditure incurred on eligible childcare. It is also higher if the worker works for at least 30 hours per week, or if there are disabled children or severely disabled adults in the family. It is tapered away above an income threshold. Further details can be obtained from the Inland Revenue.

Child and Working Tax Credits (New Tax Credits)

(Table 10.11)

Child and Working Tax Credits (NTC's) replaced Working Families' Tax Credit (WFTC) from 6 April 2003.

Social protection

CTC and WTC are claimed by individuals, or jointly by couples, whether or not they have children.

Child Tax Credit (CTC) provides support to families for the children (up to the 31 August after their 16th birthdays) and the 'qualifying' young people (in full-time non-advanced education until their 19th birthdays) for which they are responsible. It is paid in addition to Child Benefit.

Working Tax Credit (WTC) tops up the earnings of families on low or moderate incomes. People working for at least 16 hours a week can claim it if they (a) are responsible for at least one child or qualifying young person, (b) have a disability which puts them at a disadvantage in getting a job, or (c) in the first year of work, having returned to work aged at least 50 after a period of at least six months receiving out-of-work benefits. Other adults also qualify if they are aged at least 25 and work for at least 30 hours a week.

Widow's Benefit and Bereavement Benefit

(Table 10.12 and 10.13)

Widow's Benefit is payable to women widowed on or after 11 April 1988 and up to and including 8 April 2001. There are three types of widow's benefits: Widow's Payment, Widowed Mother's Allowance and Widow's Pension. Women widowed before 11 April 1988 continue to receive Widow's Benefit based on the rules that existed before that date. Bereavement Benefit was introduced on 9 April 2001 as a replacement of Widows Benefit, payable to both men and women widowed on or after 9 April 2001. There are three types of Bereavement Benefits available: Bereavement Payment, Widowed Parent's Allowance and Bereavement Allowance.

Government expenditure on social services and housing

(Table 10.19 to 10.24)

The tables of general government expenditure on social services and housing in the United Kingdom comprise a summary table followed by separate tables for each of the social services and housing. The definition of government expenditure used in these tables follows that in Table 9.4 of the Blue Book 2002 Edition, and covers both current and capital expenditure of the central government (including the National Insurance Fund) and local authorities. The housing table also includes the capital expenditure of public corporations concerned with housing. As in the Blue Book, government expenditure is measured after deducting fees and charges for services. Expenditure on administration includes the cost of

common services (accommodation, stationery and printing, superannuation, etc) some of which is not directly borne by the departments administering each service. Transfers from one part of government to another have been eliminated to avoid double counting. The figures relate to years ended 31 March.

It should be noted that the figures no longer include imputed rents for the use of fixed assets owned and used by general government. In the Blue Book, imputed rents have been replaced by capital consumption. Capital consumption, however, cannot be allocated to individual services and is therefore not included in these tables.

The following notes give brief descriptions of each of the main services shown in the tables.

Education

(Table 10.20)

This covers expenditure by the Education Departments, local education authorities and the University Grants Committee on education in schools, training colleges, technical institutions and universities. It includes expenditure on school meals.

National Health Service

(Table 10.21)

This covers expenditure by central government on hospital and community health, family practitioner and other health services. The expenditure by local authorities on the provision of health centres, health visiting, home nursing, ambulance services, vaccination and immunisation, etc, was transferred to central government on 1 April 1974. Only the net costs of providing these services are included in total government expenditure, receipts from patients being shown separately.

Welfare services

(Table 10.22)

Personal social services: This covers local authority expenditure on the aged, handicapped and homeless, child care, care of mothers and young children, mental health, domestic help, etc. Also included are central government grants to voluntary approved schools.

Welfare foods: This covers the cost of providing welfare foods at reduced prices to children and expectant mothers. Only the net costs of providing these services are included in the total government expenditure, payments by the recipients of the services being shown separately.

Social security

(Table 10.23)

This comprises both benefits under the Social Security schemes and non-contributory benefits and allowances, administered by the Department for Work and Pensions. The analysis by type of Income Support is not exact; the estimates are derived from average numbers in receipt of benefit and average amounts paid. Unified housing benefit (rent rebates and allowances) is also included as social security expenditure and not as housing expenditure. This is now mainly administered by local authorities who receive grants from central government.

Housing

(Table 10.24)

The table shows, in addition to government expenditure on housing, the capital expenditure of public corporations and the total expenditure of the public sector on housing. The government expenditure figures cover subsidies paid by the housing departments towards the provision of housing by local authorities, new town development corporations and housing associations; subsidies by local authorities to their housing revenue accounts; rent rebates for tenants of housing owned by local authorities and new towns; rent allowances for tenants of privately-owned housing; grants to persons for the reduction of mortgage interest payments; capital expenditure on the provision of houses for letting; capital grants to housing associations; grants by local authorities towards the cost of conversion and improvement of privately-owned houses; net lending by the central government and local authorities for private house purchase; and improvement and loans for first time purchasers. The public corporations' figures cover capital expenditure on the provision of houses for letting and lending by the Housing Corporation to housing associations.

10.1 National Insurance Fund
United Kingdom
Years ended 31 March

£ million

		1994/95	1995/96	1996/97	1997/98	1998/99	1999/00	2000/01	2001/02	2002/03
Receipts										
Opening balance	KJFB	4 672	7 042	8 045	7 869	9 763	12 625	14 909	19 868	24 177
Contributions	JXVM	38 712	40 875	42 806	46 755	50 023	51 852	55 627	58 050	59 658
State Scheme Premiums[1]	C59W	..	..	..	..	..	..	..	..	194
Grant from Consolidated Fund	KOTF	6 445	3 680	1 952	966	3	2	..	..	..
Compensation for SSP/SMP	KJQM	563	475	542	601	576	625	688	710	775
Transfers from Great Britian	KOTG	145	125	75	150	315	230	200	110	350
Income from investments	KJFE	365	459	489	474	667	724	884	1 146	1 457
Other receipts	KJFF	61	76	85	97	92	127	112	67	80
Redundancy receipts	KIBQ	25	24	26	25	21	21	23	22	24
Total	JYJO	50 989	52 756	54 020	56 937	61 462	66 206	72 442	79 972	86 716
Expenditure										
Total benefits	JYJP	42 271	43 198	44 518	45 321	46 822	50 026	50 960	54 550	54 201
Unemployment[2]	KJFH	1 331	1 131	605	..	..	..	..	..	..
Jobseeker's Allowance (Contributory)[2]	LUQW	..	..	341	489	489	475	449	478	519
Sickness[3]	KJFI	351	15	..	..	..	..	..	..	..
Invalidity[3]	KJFJ	8 009	600	..	..	..	..	..	..	..
Incapacity[3]	JYXL	..	7 623	7 993	7 739	7 574	7 206	6 982	7 074	7 104
Maternity	KETY	28	30	34	37	39	40	46	57	70
Widows' pensions	KEWU	1 057	1 051	1 017	1 021	1 008	1 020	1 008	1 132	1 142
Guardian's allowances and Child's special allowance[4]	KJFK	1	2	2	2	2	2	2	2	2
Retirement pensions[5]	JYJV	31 367	32 620	34 736	36 396	38 072	41 157	42 350	45 677	45 240
Pensioners' lump sum payments	KAAW	126	127	132	126	128	126	123	131	124
Other payments	KAAZ	9	14	17	19	18	19	21	29	27
Administration	KABE	1 324	1 219	1 065	1 073	1 053	847	1 197	873	1 280
Transfers to Northern Ireland	KABF	145	125	75	150	315	230	200	110	350
Redundancy payments	KIBR	199	155	134	120	140	174	195	232	255
Personal Pensions	C59X	..	..	..	..	..	..	..	..	3 336
Total	JYJU	43 947	44 711	46 151	47 173	48 837	51 297	52 574	55 795	59 449
Accumulated funds	KABH	7 042	8 045	7 869	9 763	12 625	14 909	19 868	24 177	27 267

1 State Scheme Premiums are payable in respect of employed persons who cease to be covered, in certain circumstances, by a contracted out pension scheme.
2 Jobseeker's Allowance (Contributory) was introduced in October 1996 and replaced Unemployment Benefit.
3 Incapacity Benefit replaced Sickness Benefit and Invalidity Benefit from April 1995.
4 Includes Child's special allowance for Northern Ireland
5 Includes personal pensions up to 2001/02.

Sources: Board of Inland Revenue: 020 7438 7370;
Department for Work and Pensions: 01253 856123 Ext 62436;
Department of Health, Social Services and Public Safety (Northern Ireland);
028 9052 2062

10.2 Persons who paid National Insurance contributions in a tax year:[1] by sex
United Kingdom

Millions

		Total				Men				Women		
		2000/01	2001/02	2002/03		2000/01	2001/02	2002/03		2000/01	2001/02	2002/03
Total[2]	KABI	28.22	28.51	28.66	KEYF	15.76	15.86	15.86	KEYP	12.46	12.65	12.80
Class 1	KABJ	25.49	25.68	25.81	KEYG	13.71	13.75	13.75	KEYQ	11.79	11.93	12.06
Not contracted out[3]	KABK	16.09	16.32	16.62	KEYH	8.92	9.08	9.26	KEYR	7.17	7.24	7.36
Contracted out	KABL	7.60	7.57	7.57	KEYI	4.01	3.90	3.80	KEYS	3.59	3.68	3.77
Mixed contracted in/out[4]	KABM	1.66	1.67	1.52	KEYJ	0.78	0.77	0.69	KEYT	0.88	0.90	0.83
Class 1 Reduced rate (including standard rate)	KABO	0.14	0.12	0.09	KEYL	..	..	..	KEYV	0.14	0.12	0.09
Class 2 exclusively	KABP	2.07	2.14	2.17	KEYM	1.62	1.66	1.66	KEYW	0.45	0.48	0.51
Mixed Class 1 and Class 2	KABQ	0.48	0.54	0.57	KEYN	0.34	0.38	0.39	KEYX	0.14	0.17	0.18
Class 3 exclusively[5]	KABR	0.16	0.15	0.11	KEYO	0.09	0.08	0.06	KEYY	0.08	0.07	0.05

1 See chapter text. The tax year commences on 6 April and ends on 5 April of the following year.
2 Components may not sum to totals as a result of rounding.
3 Includes those persons with an Appropriate Personal Pension (such persons pay contributions at the not contracted out rate but then receive a rebate).
4 Not included in the above rows.
5 Persons who paid a mixture of Class 3 contributions and others are not included in this category.

Source: Board of Inland Revenue: 020 7147 3082

£

		1994	1995	1996	1997	1998	1999	2000	2001	2002	2003	2004
Unemployment Benefit:[2,3]												
Men and women	KJNA	45.45	46.45	48.25	..	..	..	..	..	..	..	..
Jobseeker's Allowance:[3]												
Personal allowances												
Single												
Aged under 18 (depending	KXDH	..	..	..	29.60	30.30	30.95	31.45	31.95	32.50	32.90	33.50
on their circumstances)	KXDI	..	..	..	38.90	39.85	40.70	41.35	42.00	42.70	43.25	44.05
Aged 18 - 24	KXDJ	..	..	..	38.90	39.85	40.70	41.35	42.00	42.70	43.25	44.05
Aged 25 or over	KXDK	..	..	..	49.15	50.35	51.40	52.20	53.05	53.95	54.65	55.65
Couple												
Both aged under 18[4]	KXDL	..	..	..	58.70	30.30	30.95	31.45	31.95	32.50	32.90	33.50
One or both aged												
18 or over	KXDM	..	..	..	77.15	79.00	80.65	81.95	83.25	84.65	85.75	87.30
Dependant children and												
young people												
Aged under 11	KXDN	..	..	..	16.90	17.30	20.20	26.60	31.45	33.50	38.50	42.27
Aged 11 - 16	KXDO	..	..	..	24.75	25.35	25.90	26.60	31.45	33.50	38.50	42.27
Aged 16 - 18	KXDP	..	..	..	29.60	30.30	30.95	31.75	32.25	34.30	38.50	42.27
Sickness Benefit:[2,5]	KJNB	43.45	..	..	..	..	..	..	..	..	..	..
Invalidity Benefit:[5]												
Invalidity pension	KJNC	57.60	..	..	..	..	..	..	..	..	..	..
Invalidity Allowance:[5]												
High rate	KJND	12.15	12.40	12.90	13.15	13.60	14.05	14.20	14.65	14.90	15.15	15.55
Middle rate	KJNE	7.60	7.80	8.10	8.30	8.60	8.90	9.00	9.30	9.50	9.70	10.00
Low rate	KJNF	3.80	3.90	4.05	4.15	4.30	4.45	4.50	4.65	4.75	4.85	5.00
Increase for dependants:[5]												
Adult	KJNG	34.50	35.25	36.60	37.35	38.70	39.95	40.40	41.75	42.45	43.15	44.35
Each child[6]	KJNH	11.00	11.05	11.15	11.20	11.30	11.35	11.35	11.35	11.35	11.35	11.35
Incapacity Benefit:												
Short term (Lower) Under pension age	KOSB	..	44.40	46.15	47.10	48.80	50.35	50.90	52.60	53.50	54.40	55.90
Increase for adult dependant	KOSC	..	27.50	28.55	29.15	30.20	31.15	31.50	32.55	33.10	33.65	34.60
Short term (Lower) Over pension age	KOSD	..	56.45	58.65	59.90	62.05	64.05	64.75	66.90	68.05	69.20	71.15
Increase for adult dependant	KOSE	..	33.85	35.15	35.90	37.20	38.40	38.80	40.10	42.45	41.50	42.65
Short term (Higher)	KOSF	..	52.50	54.55	55.70	57.70	59.55	60.20	62.20	63.25	64.35	66.15
Increase for dependants:												
Adult	KOSG	..	27.50	28.55	29.15	30.20	31.15	31.50	32.55	33.10	33.65	34.60
Child[6]	KOSH	..	11.05	11.15	11.20	11.30	11.35	11.35	11.35	11.35	11.35	11.35
Long term	KOSI	..	58.85	61.15	62.45	64.70	66.75	67.50	69.75	70.95	72.15	74.15
Increase for dependants:												
Adult	KOSJ	..	35.25	36.60	37.35	38.70	39.95	40.40	41.75	42.45	43.15	44.35
Child[6]	KOSK	..	11.05	11.15	11.20	11.30	11.35	11.35	11.35	11.35	11.35	11.35
Incapacity age addition:[7]												
Higher rate	KOSL	..	12.40	12.90	13.15	13.60	14.05	14.20	14.65	14.90	15.15	15.55
Lower rate	KOSM	..	6.20	6.45	6.60	6.80	7.05	7.10	7.35	7.45	7.60	7.80
Attendance Allowance:												
Higher rate	KJNI	45.70	46.70	48.50	49.50	51.30	52.95	53.55	55.30	56.25	57.20	58.80
Lower rate	KJNJ	30.55	31.20	32.40	33.10	34.30	35.40	35.80	37.00	37.65	38.30	39.35
Disability Living Allowance:												
Care component												
Higher rate	KXDC	45.70	46.70	48.50	49.50	51.30	52.95	53.55	55.30	56.25	57.20	58.80
Middle rate	KXDD	30.55	31.20	32.40	33.10	34.30	35.40	35.80	37.00	37.65	38.30	39.35
Lower rate	KXDE	12.15	12.40	12.90	13.15	13.60	14.05	14.20	14.65	14.90	15.15	15.55
Mobility component												
Higher rate	KXDF	31.95	32.65	33.90	34.60	35.85	37.00	37.40	38.65	39.30	39.95	41.05
Lower rate	KXDG	12.15	12.40	12.90	13.15	13.60	14.05	14.20	14.65	14.90	15.15	15.55

Weekly rates of principal social security benefits[1]
Great Britain
At April

£

		1994	1995	1996	1997	1998	1999	2000	2001	2002	2003	2004
Maternity Benefit:												
Maternity allowances for insured women[8]												
Higher rate	KOSN	..	52.50	54.55	55.70	57.70	59.55	60.20	..	..	..	..
Lower rate[9]	KJNL	44.55	45.55	47.35	48.35	50.10	51.70	52.25				
Standard rate[10]	GPTJ	..	..	..	..	..	..	..	62.20	75.00	100.00	102.80
Threshold[11]	GPTK	..	..	..	..	..	..	..	30.00	30.00	30.00	30.00
Guardian's Allowance	KJNN	11.00	11.05	11.15	11.20	11.30	11.35	11.35	11.35	11.35	11.55	11.85
Widow's Benefit:												
Widow's pension	KJNO	57.60	58.85	61.15	62.45	64.70	66.75	67.50	72.50	75.50	77.45	79.60
Widowed mother's allowance	KJNP	57.60	58.85	61.15	62.45	64.70	66.75	67.50	72.50	75.50	77.45	79.60
Addition for each child	KJNQ	11.00	11.05	11.15	11.20	11.30	11.35	11.35	11.35	11.35	11.35	11.35
Bereavement Benefit:												
Bereavement allowance	WMPF	..	..	..	..	..	..	..	72.50	75.50	77.45	79.60
Widowed parent's allowance	WMOZ	..	..	..	..	..	..	..	72.50	72.50	77.45	79.60
Addition for each child	WMPA	..	..	..	..	..	..	..	11.35	11.35	11.35	11.35
State Pension contributory:[12]												
Single person	KJNR	57.60	58.85	61.15	62.45	64.70	66.75	67.50	72.50	75.50	77.45	79.60
Married couple	KJNS	92.10	94.10	97.75	99.80	103.40	106.70	107.90	115.90	120.70	122.80	127.25
State Pension non contributory:												
Single person	KJNT	34.50	35.25	36.60	37.35	38.70	39.95	40.40	43.40	45.20	45.45	47.65
Married woman	KJNU	20.65	21.10	21.90	22.35	23.15	23.90	24.15	24.95	27.00	27.70	28.50
Industrial Injuries Benefit:												
Disablement pension at 100 per cent rate	KJNW	93.20	95.30	99.00	101.10	104.70	108.10	109.30	112.90	114.80	116.80	120.10
Widow's or widower's pension	KJNX	57.60	58.85	61.15	62.45	..	..	..	..	..	..	..
Increase for dependants:[13]												
Adult	KJNY	28.05	28.65	29.75	..	..	..	..	..	..	..	..
Child Benefit:												
First child	KJOA	10.20	10.40	10.80	11.05	11.45	14.40	15.00	15.50	15.75	16.05	16.50
Subsequent children	KETZ	8.25	8.45	8.80	9.00	9.30	9.60	10.00	10.35	10.55	10.75	11.05
Family Credit[14]												
(maximum awards payable):[15]												
Families with 1 child												
Birth to September following 11th birthday	KJOB	55.15	56.50	58.20	59.70	61.15	64.95	..	..	..	..	..
From September following 11th birthday to September following 16th birthday	KJOC	62.45	64.00	65.90	67.60	69.25	70.70	..	..	..	..	..
From September following 16th birthday to day before 19th birthday	KJOD	67.00	68.55	70.60	72.45	74.20	75.95	..	..	..	..	..
Increase for each additional child												
Birth to September following 11th birthday	KJOF	11.15	11.40	11.75	12.05	12.35	15.15	..	..	..	..	..
From September following 11th birthday to September following 16th birthday	KJOG	18.45	18.90	19.45	19.95	20.45	20.90	..	..	..	..	..
From September following 16th birthday to day before 19th birthday	KJOH	23.00	23.45	24.15	24.80	25.40	25.95	..	..	..	..	..
War pension:												
Ex-private (100 per cent assessment)	KJOJ	98.90	101.10	105.00	107.20	111.10	114.70	116.00	119.80	121.80	..	..
War widow	KJOK	74.70	76.35	79.35	81.00	83.90	86.60	87.55	90.45	92.00	..	..

Weekly rates of principal social security benefits[1]
Great Britain
At April

£

		1994	1995	1996	1997	1998	1999	2000	2001	2002	2003	2004
Income Support:												
Personal allowances[16]												
Single												
aged 16-17 either	KJOW	27.50	28.00	28.85	29.60	30.30	30.95	31.45	31.95	32.50	32.90	33.50
or depending on their circumstances	KABS	36.15	36.80	37.90	38.90	39.85	40.70	41.35	42.00	42.70	43.25	44.05
aged 18-24	KJOX	36.15	36.80	37.90	38.90	39.85	40.70	41.35	42.00	42.70	43.25	44.05
aged 25 or over	KJOY	45.70	46.50	47.90	49.15	50.35	51.40	52.20	53.05	53.95	54.65	55.65
Couple												
both aged under 18[4]	KJOZ	54.55	55.55	57.20	58.70	60.10	61.35	..	..	..	..	..
one or both 18 or over	KJPA	71.70	73.00	75.20	77.15	79.00	80.65	81.95	83.25	84.65	85.75	87.30
Lone parent												
aged 16-17 either	KJPB	27.50	28.00	28.85	29.60	30.30	30.95	31.45	31.95	32.50	32.90	33.50
or depending on their circumstances	KABT	36.15	36.80	37.90	38.90	39.85	40.70	41.35	42.00	42.70	43.25	44.05
aged 18 or over	KJPC	45.70	46.50	47.90	49.15	50.35	51.40	52.20	53.05	53.95	54.65	55.65
Dependant children and young people[16]												
1994 to 1996												
aged under 11	KJPD	15.65	15.95	16.45	..	..	..	..	..	..	..	..
aged 11-15	KJPE	23.00	23.40	24.10	..	..	..	..	..	..	..	..
aged 16-17	KJPF	27.50	28.00	28.85	..	..	..	..	..	..	..	..
aged 18	KABU	36.15	36.80	37.90	..	..	..	..	..	..	..	..
From 1997 to 1999												
Birth to September following 11th birthday	KXDQ	..	..	..	16.90	17.30	20.20					
From September following 11th birthday to September following 16th birthday	KXDR	..	..	..	24.75	25.35	25.90	..	..		..	..
From September following 16th birthday to day before 19th birthday	KXDS	..	..	..	29.60	30.30	30.95	..	..		..	..
From 2000												
Birth to September following 16th birthday	WMOD	..	..	..	..	..	..	26.60	31.45	33.50	38.50	42.27
From September following 16th birthday to day before 19th birthday	WMOP	..	..	..	..	..	..	31.75	32.25	34.30	38.50	42.27
Pension Credit[17]												
Standard minimum guarantee:												
single	C59Y	..	..	..	..	..	..	..	..	..	102.10	105.45
couple	C59Z	..	..	..	..	..	..	..	..	..	155.80	160.95
Additional amount for severe disability												
single	C5A2	..	..	..	..	..	..	..	..	..	42.95	44.15
couple (one qualifies)	C5A3	..	..	..	..	..	..	..	..	..	42.95	44.15
couple (both qualifies)	C5A4	..	..	..	..	..	..	..	..	..	85.90	88.30
Additional amount for careers	C5A8	..	..	..	..	..	..	..	..	..	25.10	25.55
savings credit												
threshold single	C5A9	..	..	..	..	..	..	..	..	..	77.45	79.60
threshold couple	C5AA	..	..	..	..	..	..	..	..	..	123.80	127.25
maximum single	C5AB	..	..	..	..	..	..	..	..	..	14.79	15.51
maximum couple	C5AC	..	..	..	..	..	..	..	..	..	19.20	20.22

1 See chapter text
2 Persons under the age of 18 are entitled to the appropriate adult rate.
3 Jobseeker's Allowance, introduced 7 October 1996, replaced Unemployment Benefit and Income Support for the unemployed.
4 From 12 April 1999 the personal allowance for couples where both members are not yet 18 or one of the couples is aged 18 or over depends on the couple's circumstances. They may be entitled to a couple allowance or a single person's allowance dependant on certain criteria.
5 Incapacity benefit introduced from 13 April 1995, has replaced sickness benefit and invalidity benefit.
6 For the first child only the Child Dependency increase is reduced by £1.30 to £9.90 because of child benefit.
7 The rate of age addition depends on age at date of onset of incapacity: higher rate for under age 35 and lower rate for age 35-44.
8 Following a EU Directive, employee's maternity benefit is aligned with the state benefit they would receive if off work sick.
9 Women who were either not employed or self-employed received the lower rate.

10 New Standard rate introduced from April 2000.
11 MA Earnings Threshold introduced April 2000.
12 Retirement pensioners over 80 receive 25p addition.
13 An allowance for one adult dependent was payable, where appropriate, with unemployment benefit, sickness benefit, retirement pension, injury benefit and maternity allowance.
14 Age bandings for children's personal allowances were revised on 7 April 1997. Some children have protected rights. Further information is available from the Department for Work and Pensions.
15 Maximum award does not include the 30 hour credit.
16 In addition to personal allowances, a claimant may also be entitled to premiums. The types of premiums are family, lone parent, pensioner, higher pensioner, disability, severe disability and disabled child.
17 Pension Credit replaced Minimum Income Guarantee (MIG) for Income Support for those aged 60 and over on 6th Ocotober 2003.

Sources: Department for Work and Pensions;
Information and Analysis Directorate : 0191 225 7373;
Board of Inland Revenue: 020 7438 7370;
Ministry of Defence/DASA (Pay & Pensions): 020 7218 4271

	Employee's standard contibutions[1]		Employer's standard contributions[1]	
	not contracted- out rate	contracted-out rate[2]	not contracted- out rate	contracted-out rate[3]

Class 1

Weekly earnings

1998/99

Below 64.00 (LEL)	-	-	-	-
64.00-109.99	2% on first £64.00;	2% on first £64.00;	3.0%	-
110.00-154.99	10% on balance	8.4% on balance	5.0%	2.0%
155.00-209.99			7.0%	4.0%
210.00-485.00			10.0%	7.0%
Above 485.00 (UEL)	£43.38	£36.64	10.0%	10.0%

1999/00

Below 66.00 (LEL)	-	-	-	-
66.00-82.99	10.0%	8.4%	-	-
83.00-500.00	10.0%	8.4%	12.2%	9.2%
Above 500.00 (UEL)	£43.40	£36.46	12.2%	12.2%

2000/01

Below 67.00 (LEL)	-	-	-	-
67.00-75.99 (PT)	-	See note 4	-	See note 5
76.00-83.99 (ST)	10.0%	8.4%	-	
84.00-535.00 (UEL)	10.0%	8.4%	12.2%	9.2%
Above 535.00 (UEL)	£45.90	£38.41	12.2%	12.2%

2001/02

Below 72.00 (LEL)	-	-	-	-
72.00-86.99 (PT/ST)	-	See note 4	-	See note 5
87.00-575.00 (UEL)	10.0%	8.4%	11.9%	8.9%
Above 575.00 (UEL)	£48.80	£40.75	11.9%	11.9%

2002/03

Below 75.00 (LEL)	-	-	-	-
75.00-88.99 (PT/ST)	-	See note 4	-	See note 6
89.00-585.00 (UEL)	10.0%	8.4%	11.8%	8.3%
Above 585.00 (UEL)	£49.60	£41.44	11.8%	11.8%

2003/04

Below 77.00 (LEL)	-	-	-	-
77.00-88.99 (PT/ST)	-	See note 4	-	See note 6
89.00-595.00 (UEL)	11.0%	9.4%	12.8%	9.3%
Above 595.00 (UEL)	1.0%	1.0%	12.8%	12.8%

2004/05

Below 79.00 (LEL)	-	-	-	-
79.00-90.99 (PT/ST)	-	See note 4	-	See note 6
91.00-610.00 (UEL)	11.0%	9.4%	12.8%	9.3%
Above 610.00(UEL)	1.0%	1.0%	12.8%	12.8%

	1998/99	1999/00	2000/01	2001/02	2002/03	2003/04	2004/05
Class 2							
Flat rate weekly	£6.35	£6.55	£2.00	£2.00	£2.00	£2.00	£2.05
Small earnings exception[7] (per annum)	£3,590	£3,770	£3,825	£3,955	£4,025	£4,095	£4,215
Class 3							
Flat-rate voluntary weekly contributions	£6.25	£6.45	£6.55	£6.75	£6.85	£6.95	£7.15
Class 4 (Self-employed; profit-related)							
Rate on profits between LPL and UPL	6.0%	6.0%	7.0%	7.0%	7.0%	8.0%	8.0%
Rate on profits above UPL	..	..	..	..	..	1.0%	1.0%
Lower profits limit (LPL)	£7,310	£7,530	£4,385	£4,535	£4,615	£4,615	£4,745
Upper profits limit (UPL)	£25,220	£26,000	£27,820	£29,900	£30,420	£30,940	£31,720

Note: LEL: Lower Earnings Limit; UEL: Upper Earnings Limit. PT: Primary Threshold; ST: Secondary Threshold.

1 Married women opting to pay contributions at the reduced rate at 3.85% before 2003-04 and 4.95% from 2003-04 earn no entitlement to contributory National Insurance benefits as a result of these contributions. No women have been allowed to exercise this option since 1977, but around 100,000 women who have been continually married or widowed and in the labour market since that time have retained their right to pay the reduced rate.

2 The contracted-out rebate for employees' contributions is applied only between LEL and UEL. Earnings below LEL are charged at the appropriate not contracted-out rate (which depends on total earnings). Earnings above the UEL are not subject to employee NICs before 2003-04.

3 The rates shown only apply to Contracted-Out Salary Related schemes. (COSR). Earnings below the LEL and above the UEL are charged at the appropriate not-contracted out rate. The employers' contracted-out rate applies only between the LEL and the UEL.

4 The contracted-out rebate for primary contributions is 1.6 per cent of earnings between the LEL and the UEL for all forms of contracting-out.

5 The contracted-out rebate for secondary contributions is 3.0 per cent of earnings between the LEL and the UEL.

6 The contracted-out rebate for secondary contributions is 3.5 per cent of earnings between the LEL and the UEL.

7 If earnings from self-employment are below this annual limit and the contributor applies for and is granted a small earnings exception Class 2 contributions need not be paid. Class 2 or 3 contributions may be paid voluntarily.

Source: Board of Inland Revenue: 020 7147 3082

10.5 Social Security Acts: number of persons receiving benefit[1]
Great Britain
At any one time

Thousands

		1994	1995	1996	1997	1998	1999	2000	2001	2002	2003	2004
Persons receiving:												
Unemployment Benefit[2]	KJHA	540.8	414.6	397.8	..	..	..	..	..	..	..	..
Jobseeker's Allowance[2,3]	JYXM	..	..	..	1 406.3	1 181.2	1 105.8	972.7	848.3	827.5	832.3	755.2
Sickness and Invalidity Benefit[4,5]	KJHB	1 808.6	1 894.1	..	..	..	..	..	..	..	..	..
Incapacity benefit[6]	KXDT	..	..	1 812.8	1 749.2	1 671.2	1 557.1	1 504.3	1 515.2	1 496.9	1 506.5	1 486.6
Attendance Allowance[7]	KXDU	962.4	1 046.5	1 120.6	1 183.2	1 225.6	1 243.8	1 249.6	1 290.0	1 288.2	1 340.7	1 391.9
Disability Living Allowance[8]	KXDW	1 329.1	1 534.2	1 729.2	1 886.5	1 995.9	2 061.3	2 130.5	2 240.5	2 353.5	2 498.0	2 606.7
Widows' Benefits[9]	KJHF	329.8	323.2	308.9	296.4	278.7	267.6	261.0	255.5	226.4	196.1	167.5
Bereavement Benefits[9]	VQAA	..	..	..	..	..	..	..	..	36.8	44.4	46.4
National Insurance												
State pension contributory[5]:												
Males[9]	KJHH	3 555.9	3 590.1	3 688.2	3 786.5	3 880.4	3 956.3	4 039.4	4 083.9	4 141.5	4 205.5	4 261.0
Females[9]	KJHL	6 668.1	6 686.4	6 733.5	6 783.2	6 850.7	6 886.3	6 928.0	6 959.7	6 982.5	7 037.0	7 107.8
Total[9]	KJHG	10 224.0	10 276.5	10 421.7	10 569.7	10 731.1	10 842.6	10 967.4	11 043.6	11 124.0	11 242.5	11 368.8
State pension non contributory[5]:												
Males[9]	KJHI	5.5	5.4	5.7	5.6	5.5	5.1	5.2	5.1	5.0	5.4	5.5
Females[9]	KJHJ	22.2	21.8	22.3	20.9	19.8	18.8	18.0	18.2	18.2	18.1	17.8
Total[9]	KJHK	27.7	27.2	28.0	26.5	25.2	23.9	23.2	23.3	23.3	23.5	23.3
Industrial Injuries Disablement Pensions assessments[10,11]	KJHN	225.6	235.2	249.2	257.8	269.1	278.2	280.8	280.4	278.2	267.1	266.5
Reduced Earnings Allowance/ Retirement Allowance assessments[10,11]	KEYC	154.3	152.1	154.9	155.6	152.8	153.5	153.5	152.3	148.7	143.0	140.0
Family Credit[12]	ZCGF	550.9	607.6	693.0	748.0	767.5	791.2	–	..	..	..	..
Income Support[13,14]	KABV	5 691.9	5 667.7	5 545.8	3 958.0	3 853.1	3 814.4	3 810.5	3 927.9	3 929.8	3 982.2	2 171.5
Pension Credit[14]	C5AP	..	..	..	..	..	..	..	..	..	..	2 492.6
Housing Benefit and Council Tax Benefit												
Rent rebate	KABY	3 016.1	2 964.3	2 898.3	2 792.3	2 664.1	2 518.5	2 287.8	2 133.5	2 037.6	1 838.1	1 808.0
Rent allowance[15]	KABZ	1 633.9	1 770.1	1 877.6	1 847.1	1 810.6	1 794.6	1 745.5	1 740.9	1 775.0	1 958.3	2 071.4
Council tax benefit[16]	KJPO	5 496.5	5 623.9	5 611.2	5 498.3	5 325.7	5 166.1	4 830.1	4 673.4	4 601.7	4 627.8	4 800.2
War pensions[5]	KJHR	309.2	315.4	327.5	320.7	302.0	306.0	295.7	284.3	272.7	260.7	247.5

1 See chapter text. Caseload counts at a specific date in the year which varies from benefit to benefit.
2 At May each year.
3 Jobseeker's Allowance introduced 7 October 1996, replacing Unemployment Benefit and Income Support for the unemployed.
4 A relatively small number of claims do not result in the payment of benefit but are included here because they indicate notified incapacity for work.
5 Includes overseas cases. As at end of March.
6 Incapacity Benefit replaced Sickness Benefit and Invalidity Benefit from 13 April 1995. Figures are taken at the last day in February.
7 Attendance Allowance figures are based at 31 March until 1995 then at the end of May.
8 At May of each year.
9 Includes overseas cases up to 2002.
10 A person may be in receipt of either IIDB or REA or both. The figure for 2003 has been amended.
11 Industrial Injuries Disablement Pension, Reduced Earnings Allowance/ Retirement Allowance assessments starting first Monday in April. Includes an allowance for late returns. From 2003 data is person based as at March.

12 Family Credit was replaced by Working Families' Tax Credit from October 1999.
13 From 9 October 1996 Income Support for the unemployed was replaced by Income-based Jobseeker's Allowance. Figures in this table up to and including 1996 include unemployed Income Support claimants. Figures from 1997 exclude unemployed who will be counted in the Jobseeker's Allowance claims.
14 From November 2003 the Income Support figure is severely affected by the introduction of Pension Credit, which replaced Minimum Income Guarantee (MIG) on 6th October 2003 and extended Income Support entitlement to customers aged 60+. It is not possible to produce comparisons across 6th October 2003 on a consistent basis whether Pension Credit cases are included or not.
15 Rent Allowance figures include registered social landlord tenants.
16 Figure excludes Second Adult Rebate Claims.

Sources: Department for Work and Pensions;
Information and Analysis Directorate : 0191 225 7373;
Board of Inland Revenue: 020 7438 7370;
Ministry of Defence/DASA (Pay & Pensions): 020 7218 4271

10.6 Jobseeker's Allowance[1] claimants: by benefit entitlement
Great Britain
As at May

		1998	1999	2000	2001	2002	2003	2004
All Persons								
All with benefit - total	KXDX	1 181.2	1 105.8	972.7	848.3	827.5	832.3	755.2
Contribution-based JSA only	KXDY	154.2	158.2	148.2	147.0	162.6	167.3	141.4
Contribution based JSA & income-based JSA	KXDZ	23.5	27.1	19.0	18.3	19.4	18.9	14.5
Income-based JSA only payment	KXEA	1 003.6	920.4	805.5	683.1	645.5	646.1	599.3
No benefit in payment	KXEB	114.5	118.7	94.6	93.7	91.1	91.7	84.0
Total	KXEC	1 295.8	1 224.5	1 067.3	942.0	918.5	924.0	839.2
Males								
All with benefit - total	KXED	918.2	862.3	755.0	659.4	634.6	631.7	569.2
Contribution-based JSA only	KXEE	101.6	109.0	104.2	104.5	116.0	119.0	101.3
Contribution based JSA & income-based JSA	KXEF	20.7	24.4	17.2	16.7	17.5	16.6	13.2
Income-based JSA only payment	KXEG	795.9	728.9	633.6	538.2	501.1	496.1	454.6
No benefit in payment	KXEH	75.5	79.2	63.4	61.9	62.3	62.9	56.9
Total	KXEI	993.6	941.5	818.4	721.3	696.9	694.6	626.1
Females								
All with benefit - total	KXEJ	263.0	243.4	217.7	188.9	192.9	200.6	186.1
Contribution-based JSA only	KXEK	52.6	49.2	44.0	42.5	46.6	48.3	40.1
Contribution based JSA & income-based JSA	KXEL	2.8	2.7	1.8	1.5	1.9	2.3	1.3
Income-based JSA only payment	KXEM	207.7	191.5	171.9	144.9	144.4	150.0	144.7
No benefit in payment	KXEN	39.1	39.5	31.2	31.8	28.8	28.7	27.0
Total	KXEO	302.1	283.0	248.9	220.8	221.7	229.3	213.1

1 See chapter text. Jobseeker's Allowance (JSA) has two routes of entry: contribution-based which depends mainly upon national insurance contributions and income-based which depends mainly on a means test. Some claimants can qualify by either route. In practice they receive income-based JSA but have an underlying entitlement to the contribution-based element.

Sources: Department for Work and Pensions;
Information and Analysis Directorate: 0191 225 7373

10.7 Sickness Benefit, Invalidity Benefit and Incapacity Benefit[1] claimants: by sex, age and duration of spell

Great Britain. At end of statistical year

Thousands

		1994[2]	1995[3]	1996	1997	1998	1999	2000	2001	2002	2003	2004
Age at 1 March[4]												
Males												
All durations: All ages	KJJA	1 544.4	1 629.9	1 627.0	1 577.9	1 530.1	1 458.4	1 432.0	1 458.5	1 454.7	1 467.3	1 466.2
Under 20	KJJB	6.8	7.8	8.7	8.8	10.7	10.7	11.2	10.2	12.7	21.2	20.3
20-29	KJJC	97.2	106.0	119.3	118.8	119.1	115.0	114.2	119.1	123.1	130.7	135.2
30-39	KJJD	160.4	189.7	202.6	208.5	216.6	217.6	222.5	234.8	236.4	239.6	242.5
40-49	KJJE	245.2	260.4	274.3	272.4	271.4	271.0	277.0	285.2	291.7	297.0	304.8
50-59	KJJF	441.7	468.7	475.4	473.4	474.1	467.3	469.8	473.5	468.9	465.5	457.5
60-64	KJJG	356.6	362.5	352.1	349.7	344.2	336.0	334.2	334.3	321.9	313.3	305.8
65 and over	KJJH	236.5	234.8	194.6	146.2	94.0	40.7	3.1	1.4	–	–	–
Over six months: All ages	KJJI	1 361.5	1 442.1	1 440.9	1 385.7	1 349.2	1 287.0	1 344.8	1 293.4	1 299.6	1 311.6	1 317.7
Under 20	KJJJ	2.9	3.0	3.9	3.6	4.7	4.9	7.4	4.7	5.6	13.8	13.4
20-29	KJJK	65.7	74.3	86.4	83.1	84.5	81.4	97.8	87.8	91.9	99.8	105.2
30-39	KJJL	126.5	152.1	165.1	166.8	177.2	181.2	203.9	197.6	201.6	205.4	207.0
40-49	KJJM	208.6	219.7	235.9	232.3	234.0	237.6	260.0	253.6	261.8	267.1	275.9
50-59	KJJN	389.2	418.2	426.5	423.8	428.2	423.8	446.8	431.6	431.7	428.1	423.2
60-64	KJJO	332.6	340.2	329.7	330.4	326.8	317.6	325.8	316.7	307.0	297.5	293.0
65 and over	KJJP	236.0	234.6	193.3	145.6	93.7	40.6	3.1	1.4	–	–	–
Females												
All durations: All ages	KJJQ	704.7	776.5	779.1	795.1	810.8	815.5	827.5	865.9	883.0	920.6	940.0
Under 20	KJJR	11.0	12.0	12.5	12.3	13.0	14.1	13.7	13.7	13.7	20.5	19.8
20-29	KJJS	74.9	79.4	88.6	89.0	87.8	85.3	84.6	85.1	87.3	96.1	98.7
30-39	KJJT	108.5	122.4	134.6	137.6	144.7	149.4	153.5	159.1	163.3	166.2	166.5
40-49	KJJU	176.0	200.7	201.9	206.5	209.7	217.2	221.0	232.0	237.1	246.3	253.4
50-59	KJJV	266.6	290.7	285.1	303.3	323.1	333.2	349.9	371.5	381.3	391.2	401.3
60 and over	KJJW	67.7	71.3	56.3	46.4	32.5	16.3	4.8	4.6	0.3	0.3	0.4
Over six months: All ages	KJJX	611.4	673.1	672.9	686.6	701.7	707.9	776.2	768.2	790.0	820.4	844.8
Under 20	KJJY	4.7	4.2	6.2	4.8	5.7	6.1	9.9	6.8	6.0	11.3	11.8
20-29	KJJZ	55.9	60.3	66.3	66.1	65.8	64.2	73.9	66.7	68.9	76.6	81.0
30-39	KJKA	92.3	103.2	113.2	117.5	120.9	126.3	142.4	139.4	143.6	146.3	147.7
40-49	KJKB	151.8	170.8	176.4	179.6	183.3	190.1	208.8	207.2	215.1	222.0	229.6
50-59	KJKC	239.9	263.7	256.6	273.1	294.1	305.2	336.5	343.5	356.4	364.1	374.5
60 and over	KJKD	66.8	70.9	54.3	45.4	31.9	16.0	4.6	4.5	0.1	0.2	0.2

1 See chapter text. Figures are based on a 1 per cent sample up to 1995 and 5 per cent sample thereafter.
2 The end of the statistical year was Saturday 2nd April.
3 The statistical year for 1994/95 was extended to 12 April 1995, the day before the introduction of the new Incapacity Benefit which replaced Sickness and Invalidity Benefit.

4 At 31 March until 1995/96. From 1995/96 the duration is taken on the the last day of February.

Sources: Department for Work and Pensions; Information and Analysis Directorate: 0191 225 7373

10.8 Sickness, Invalidity and Incapacity Benefit: days of certified incapacity

Great Britain analysis by age at end of period[1]

Years starting on first Monday in April[2]

Millions

		1991 /92	1992 /93	1993 /94	1994[3] /95	1995 /96	1996 /97	1997 /98	1998 /99	1999 /00	2000 /01	2001 /02
Age at 31 March[4]												
Males: All ages	KJKH	402.7	445.5	468.8	507.9	596.2	576.3	563.5	538.6	526.7	531.7	536.1
Under 20	KJKI	1.7	1.5	1.6	1.8	3.4	3.1	3.5	3.7	3.3	2.6	3.5
20 - 29	KJKJ	21.6	24.5	27.0	30.4	43.7	42.4	43.2	41.7	38.3	38.9	40.4
30 - 39	KJKK	36.1	41.4	46.6	56.0	72.3	73.9	77.7	78.2	75.8	81.3	84.0
40 - 49	KJKL	57.1	64.6	72.7	78.9	98.5	98.5	97.7	97.6	98.0	103.9	106.0
50 - 59	KJKM	112.8	121.7	129.8	141.4	172.0	170.7	172.2	170.0	161.9	165.9	168.5
60 - 64	KJKN	96.1	102.4	107.3	112.6	127.9	127.8	126.7	124.3	126.0	125.8	120.2
65 and over	KJKO	77.4	80.4	83.9	86.8	78.4	59.9	41.7	23.0	23.4	13.3	13.4
Females: All ages	KJKP	170.8	190.7	211.4	237.5	279.5	285.8	292.8	294.8	315.0	325.1	338.7
Under 20	KJKQ	2.2	2.1	2.4	2.6	4.8	4.1	4.4	4.5	4.0	3.5	3.9
20 - 29	KJKR	19.7	22.1	22.1	23.9	31.9	32.0	32.1	31.3	30.7	30.3	32.3
30 - 39	KJKS	25.6	28.5	32.7	37.6	48.0	49.8	51.4	53.4	54.9	58.9	59.9
40 - 49	KJKT	41.2	46.6	51.5	58.9	72.1	74.0	75.8	77.1	79.1	82.8	88.9
50 - 59	KJKU	63.8	71.3	79.1	88.4	101.0	107.5	115.3	120.0	134.3	142.2	145.9
60 and over	KJKV	18.2	20.1	23.6	26.1	21.7	18.4	13.8	8.4	12.0	7.3	7.9

1 See chapter text. The end of the statistical year up to 1993/94 was the Saturday before the first Monday in April.
2 Up to and including 1994/95 years start first Monday in April. The 1995/96 year started 13 April and ended 31 March. From 1996/97 years start 1 April.

3 The statistical year for 1994/95 was extended to 12 April 1995, the day before the introduction of the new Incapacity Benefit which replaced Sickness and Invalidity Benefit.
4 Until 1995/96 then at 1 March.

Sources: Department for Work and Pensions; Information and Analysis Directorate: 0191 225 7373

10.9 Child benefits[1]

Thousands

		Great Britain As at 31 December						United Kingdom As at 31 August					
		1995	1996	1997[2]	1998[2]	1999[3]		1999	2000	2001	2002	2003	2004
Families receiving allowances:													
Total	KJMU	6 996	7 024	6 956	6 976	7 102	VOWX	7 335	7 340	7 335	7 336	7 342	7 353
With 1 child	KJMV	2 970	2 983	..	..	3 015	VOWY	3 105	3 128	3 143	3 162	3 189	3 219
2 children	KJMW	2 783	2 794	..	..	2 822	VOWZ	2 905	2 898	2 891	2 894	2 890	2 885
3 children	KJMX	928	929	..	..	943	VOXA	983	977	970	954	942	931
4 children	KJMY	231	236	..	..	241	VOXB	255	251	247	242	239	235
5 or more children	KJMZ	84	82	..	..	82	VOXC	88	86	84	83	82	82
Families receiving Guardian's Allowance	VOXG	2.1	2.2	2.3	2.3	2.3	VOXH	2.3	2.5	2.3	2.5	2.6	2.9

1 See chapter text.
2 Figures provided by Child Benefit Centre Management Information Statistics as a new scan was being developed.
3 As at 31 August.

Source: Board of Inland Revenue: 020 7438 7370

10.10 Family Credit/ Working Families' Tax Credit[1,2]

Thousands

		Great Britain As at 31 December						United Kingdom As at 30 November			
		1993	1994	1995	1996	1997	1998		1999	2000	2001	2002
Families in receipt:												
Total	KJTO	518.3	578.0	646.5	716.7	751.4	779.7	ZCMK	965.3	1 167.8	1 293.7	1 377.3
Two-parent families: total	KJTP	291.0	324.6	356.9	390.2	388.0	383.4	ZCML	467.6	565.9	617.2	639.8
With 1 child	KJTQ	73.3	80.1	89.7	98.6	96.6	95.4	ZCMM	116.8	144.8	151.6	159.0
2 children	KJTR	110.1	122.4	135.1	146.1	144.4	141.7	ZCMN	178.4	220.1	243.5	252.7
3 children	KJTS	66.9	76.4	83.4	91.1	91.4	89.1	ZCMO	107.8	129.2	142.9	147.3
4 children or more children	ZIYM	40.7	45.8	48.6	54.4	55.6	57.3	ZCMP	64.6	71.8	79.2	80.8
One-parent families: total	KJTW	227.3	253.4	289.6	326.5	363.4	396.3	ZIYI	497.8	601.8	676.5	737.6
With 1 child	KJTX	117.8	133.8	152.2	170.4	189.3	203.4	ZIYJ	259.6	313.7	349.5	381.2
2 children	KJTY	79.2	86.0	99.1	111.2	121.8	136.1	ZIYK	169.6	207.6	238.7	261.6
3 or more children	KJTZ	30.4	33.5	38.3	45.0	52.3	56.9	ZIYL	68.6	80.5	88.3	94.8

1 See chapter text. Family Credit was replaced by Working Families Tax Credit (WFTC) in October 1999. The WFTC figures for December 1999 include Family Credit awards made before October 1999 and still current (both FC and WFTC awards last for 26 weeks).
2 WFTC was replaced by Child Credit and Working Tax Credit on 6th April 2003. See table 10.11.

Sources: Board of Inland Revenue: 020 7438 7370;
Department for Work and Pensions;
Information and Analysis Directorate: 0191 225 7373

10.11 In-work families with Child Tax Credit or Working Tax Credit awards[1]
United Kingdom

Thousands

		2003[2]
In-work families with award:	C5PF	4 647
With children	C5PG	4 368.5
Receiving Working Tax Credit[3] and Child Tax Credit	C5PH	1 588.6
Receiving Child Tax Credit only	C5PI	2 726.8
Zero award[4]	C5PJ	53.1
Without children	C5PK	278.5
Receiving Working Tax Credit	C5PL	187.7
Zero award[4]	C5PM	90.7

1 Child and Working Tax Credits replaced Working Families' Tax Credit on 6th April 2003. See chapter text.
2 Figures for 2003 are based on awards current at 5th January 2004.
3 Includes 57.7 thousand families (31.8 thousand couples and 25.9 thousand singles) whose Working Tax Credit (WTC) is less than or equal to the childcare element and is therefore all paid together with Child Tax Credit (CTC).

4 Claimed, and eligible for, CTC or WTC at the reference date, but with zero awards based on their circumstances at that date and their annual income reported by that date. These families may have positive awards at other times in the year, based on their circumstances then, and may finally qualify for positive annual awards based on all their circumstances in the year and their current year incomes.

Source: Board of Inland Revenue: 020 7084 5501

10.12 Widows' Benefit (excluding widows' payment[1]): by type of benefit and age of widow

Great Britain. Number in payment at March

Thousands

		1997	1998	1999	2000	2001	2002	2003	2004
All Widows' Benefit (excluding widows' allowance)									
All ages	KJGA	296.4	278.8	267.6	261.0	255.5	226.4	196.1	167.5
Under 30	KJGB	1.3	1.2	1.1	1.0	0.9	0.7	0.4	0.3
30 - 39	KJGC	12.5	12.5	11.2	11.4	10.6	9.0	7.2	5.3
40 - 49	KJGD	46.7	41.7	39.5	38.1	37.2	31.0	24.7	20.2
50 - 59	KJGE	194.3	189.8	183.1	182.2	179.1	158.4	136.5	116.2
60 and over	KJGF	41.7	33.5	32.6	28.4	27.7	27.3	27.3	25.4
Widowed mothers' allowance - with dependant children									
All ages	KJGG	50.4	48.5	46.7	47.0	46.6	40.4	33.1	27.6
Under 30	KJGH	1.3	1.1	1.1	1.0	0.9	0.6	0.4	0.3
30 - 39	KJGI	11.8	12.1	10.8	11.0	10.2	8.6	6.9	5.1
40 - 49	KJGJ	26.2	23.9	23.5	23.3	23.7	20.1	16.2	13.8
50 - 59	KJGK	10.7	11.2	11.2	11.6	11.5	10.8	9.2	8.0
60 and over	KJGL	0.4	0.2	0.2	0.2	0.4	0.3	0.4	0.3
Widowed mothers' allowance - without dependant children									
All ages	KJGM	4.9	3.8	3.1	2.9	2.5	2.2	1.9	1.6
Under 30	KJGN	–	–	–	0.1	–	–	–	–
30 - 39	KJGO	0.6	0.4	0.4	0.4	0.4	0.4	0.4	0.2
40 - 49	KJGP	2.4	1.8	1.6	1.2	1.1	1.0	0.9	0.8
50 - 59	KJGQ	1.8	1.4	1.1	1.1	1.0	0.8	0.6	0.5
60 and over	KJGR	0.1	0.1	–	0.1	–	–	0.1	0.1
Widows' pension									
All ages	KJGS	76.5	65.3	59.3	54.5	53.0	42.2	32.5	24.0
40 - 49	KJGT	–	–	–	–	–	–	–	–
50 - 59	KJGU	43.5	39.7	36.0	35.6	34.8	25.5	17.2	10.5
60 and over	KJGV	33.0	25.6	23.3	18.9	18.2	16.7	15.3	13.5
Age-related widows' pension[2]									
All ages	KJGW	164.6	161.1	158.4	156.6	153.4	141.6	128.6	114.3
40 - 49	KJGX	18.2	16.1	14.4	13.5	12.4	9.9	7.5	5.6
50 - 59	KJGY	138.2	137.5	134.8	133.8	131.9	121.3	109.5	97.2
60 and over	KJGZ	8.2	7.5	9.1	9.3	9.2	10.3	11.5	11.5

1 This is an especially high rate of benefit which is payable for the first 26 weeks of widowhood, provided that the widow is under pensionable age (age 60) or, if she is over that age, provided that her husband was not entitled to retirement pension.

2 Figures for widows' basic pension are included in age-related widows' pension.

Sources: Department for Work and Pensions; Information and Analysis Directorate: 0191 225 7373

10.13 Bereavement Benefit[1] (excluding bereavement payment): by sex, type of benefit and age of widow/er

Great Britain. Number in payment at March

Thousands

		Males				Females		
		2002	2003	2004		2002	2003	2004
All Bereavement Benefit (excluding bereavement allowance)								
All ages	WLSX	14.2	15.6	14.8	WLTC	22.6	28.8	31.6
Under 30	WLTD	–	–	–	WLTE	0.1	0.3	0.5
30 - 39	WLTQ	1.4	1.5	1.3	WLTR	1.5	3.2	4.1
40 - 49	WLTV	4.2	4.9	5.1	WLTW	4.8	7.3	10.1
50 - 59	WLTY	5.7	6.6	5.8	WLTZ	16.1	17.9	16.8
60 and over	WLUB	2.9	2.6	2.6	WLUC	..	..	..
Widowed parents' allowance - with dependant children								
All ages	WLUD	7.7	8.9	9.0	WLUH	5.7	11.3	16.6
Under 30	WLUI	–	–	–	WLUJ	0.1	0.3	0.5
30 - 39	WLUV	1.4	1.5	1.3	WLUW	1.5	3.1	4.1
40 - 49	WLUY	3.6	4.4	4.7	WLUZ	2.8	5.4	8.4
50 - 59	WLVD	2.4	2.8	2.9	WLVE	1.3	2.5	3.6
60 and over	WLVI	0.3	0.3	0.2	WLVJ	–	–	–
Widowed parents' allowance - without dependant children								
All ages	WLVK	–	0.1	0.1	WMMR	0.1	0.2	0.3
Under 30	WMMU	–	–	–	WMNI	–	–	–
30 - 39	WMNZ	–	–	–	WMOA	–	0.1	0.1
40 - 49	WMNQ	–	0.1	0.1	WMNR	–	0.1	0.1
50 - 59	WMNT	–	–	–	WMNW	–	–	0.1
60 and over	WMNX	–	–	–	WMNY	–	–	–
Age-related bereavement allowance								
All ages	WMOB	2.0	2.2	1.5	WMOC	8.0	8.3	6.3
40 - 49	WMOQ	0.5	0.5	0.4	WMOR	1.9	1.8	1.6
50 - 59	WMOS	1.5	1.7	1.1	WMOU	6.1	6.4	4.7
60 and over	WMOV	–	–	–	WMOW	..	..	..
Bereavement allowance (not age related)								
All ages	WMOX	4.5	4.4	4.2	WMOY	8.8	9.1	8.4
40 - 49	WMPG	–	–	–	WMPH	–	–	–
50 - 59	WMPI	1.9	2.0	1.8	WMPJ	8.8	9.0	8.4
60 and over	WMPK	2.6	2.4	2.4	WMPM	..	..	..

1 Bereavement Benefit replaced Widow's Benefit and is payable to both men and women widowed on or after 9 April 2001. Figures include overseas cases.

Source: Department for Work and Pensions: 0191 225 7874

10.14 Contributory and non-contributory retirement pensions:[1] by sex and age of claimant

Great Britain. Numbers in payment at end of March

Thousands and percentages

		1997	1998	1999	2000	2001	2002	2003	2004
Men:									
Age-groups:									
65-69	KJSB	1 142.8	1 199.3	1 243.2	1 288.8	1 287.5	1 296.1	1 319.4	1 336.9
Percentage	KJSC	*30.1*	*30.9*	*31.4*	*31.9*	*31.5*	*31.3*	*31.3*	*31.3*
70-74	KJSD	1 113.9	1 107.0	1 109.3	1 117.5	1 125.9	1 133.9	1 142.4	1 147.1
Percentage	KJSE	*29.4*	*28.5*	*28.0*	*27.6*	*27.5*	*27.3*	*27.1*	*26.9*
75-79	KJSF	790.3	838.3	872.3	867.4	860.5	862.0	861.7	871.2
Percentage	KJSG	*20.8*	*21.6*	*22.0*	*21.4*	*21.0*	*20.8*	*20.5*	*20.4*
80-84	KJSH	467.9	449.1	433.6	457.7	493.6	524.3	560.2	584.7
Percentage	KJSI	*12.3*	*11.6*	*10.9*	*11.3*	*12.1*	*12.6*	*13.3*	*13.7*
85-89	KJSJ	206.7	216.0	224.6	231.1	237.0	239.9	232.0	226.0
Percentage	KJSK	*5.5*	*5.6*	*5.7*	*5.7*	*5.8*	*5.8*	*5.5*	*5.3*
90 and over	KJSL	70.4	76.1	78.3	82.1	84.6	90.4	95.1	100.6
Percentage	KJSM	*1.9*	*2.0*	*2.0*	*2.0*	*2.1*	*2.2*	*2.3*	*2.4*
Total all ages	KJSA	3 792.1	3 885.9	3 961.4	4 044.6	4 089.0	4 146.5	4 210.9	4 266.5
Women:									
Age-groups:									
60-64	KJSO	1 185.4	1 245.2	1 284.9	1 332.2	1 339.4	1 346.2	1 376.0	1 416.2
Percentage	KJSP	*17.4*	*18.1*	*18.6*	*19.2*	*19.2*	*19.2*	*19.5*	*19.9*
65-69	KJSQ	1 422.1	1 415.9	1 406.7	1 396.5	1 392.4	1 396.5	1 416.5	1 440.3
Percentage	KJSR	*20.9*	*20.6*	*20.4*	*20.1*	*20.0*	*19.9*	*20.1*	*20.2*
70-74	KJSS	1 379.0	1 358.6	1 344.7	1 339.8	1 341.9	1 333.1	1 328.0	1 317.6
Percentage	KJST	*20.3*	*19.8*	*19.5*	*19.3*	*19.2*	*19.0*	*18.8*	*18.5*
75-79	KJSU	1 144.5	1 201.8	1 246.9	1 227.9	1 196.0	1 179.1	1 164.7	1 156.0
Percentage	KJSV	*16.8*	*17.5*	*18.1*	*17.7*	*17.1*	*16.8*	*16.5*	*16.2*
80-84	KJSW	858.5	815.4	775.9	793.2	843.3	878.3	925.3	963.3
Percentage	KJSX	*12.6*	*11.9*	*11.2*	*11.4*	*12.1*	*12.5*	*13.1*	*13.5*
85-89	KJSY	530.0	536.2	540.8	546.0	543.5	537.8	510.2	487.8
Percentage	KJSZ	*7.8*	*7.8*	*7.8*	*7.9*	*7.8*	*7.7*	*7.2*	*6.8*
90 and over	KJTA	284.9	297.7	305.1	310.7	321.6	329.9	334.5	344.4
Percentage	KJTB	*4.2*	*4.3*	*4.4*	*4.5*	*4.6*	*4.7*	*4.7*	*4.8*
Total all ages	KJSN	6 804.5	6 870.8	6 905.1	6 946.3	6 978.0	7 000.8	7 055.2	7 125.6

1 See chapter text. Including pensions payable to persons residing overseas.

Sources: Department for Work and Pensions;
Information and Analysis Directorate: 0191 225 7373

10.15 War pensions: estimated number of pensioners[1]
Great Britain
At 31 March each year

Thousands

		1994	1995	1996	1997	1998	1999	2000	2001	2002	2003	2004
Disablement	KADH	245.44	260.30	265.37	264.59	259.16	248.93	240.76	231.62	222.25	212.59	201.97
Widows and dependants	KADI	50.86	49.54	58.37	60.05	58.49	55.85	54.92	52.71	50.48	48.13	45.56
Total	KADG	296.30	309.84	323.74	324.64	317.65	306.06	295.67	284.33	272.72	260.73	247.52

1 See chapter text. From 1914 war, 1939 war and later service.

Source: Ministry of Defence/DASA (Pay & Pensions): 020 7218 0031

10.16 Income support: number of claimants receiving weekly payment[1]
Great Britain
On a day in May

Thousands

		1998	1999	2000	2001	2002	2003	2004
All income support[2]	KACC	3 853	3 814	3 811	3 928	3 930	3 982	2 172
All aged 60 and over[2]	KACD	1 659	1 624	1 615	1 717	1 746	1 778	12
State pensioners	KACE	1 338	1 308	1 305	1 406	1 428	1 450	–
In receipt of other NI benefit[3]	KACF	74	67	64	69	75	78	4
Others	KACG	248	249	246	242	244	250	8
All under 60	KACH	2 194	2 190	2 196	2 211	2 184	2 204	2 160
Disabled with contributory benefit[3]	KACK	195	196	207	220	229	232	225
Disabled without contributory benefit[3]	KFBJ	685	718	755	797	838	868	891
Lone parent premium not in other groups[4]	KACL	961	936	910	889	856	847	810
Others	KACM	353	341	324	306	261	257	234
Pension Credits[2]	C5AD	..	..	..	..	..	..	2 493
State pensioners	C5AE	..	..	..	..	..	..	2 157
In receipt of other NI benefit[3]	C5AF	..	..	..	..	..	..	79
Others	C5AG	..	..	..	..	..	..	257

1 See chapter text. Data are extracted from the Quarterly Statistical Enquiries undertaken each May from 1998-2004.
2 From November 2003 IS figures are severely affected by the introduction of Pension Credit, which replaced Minimum Income Guarantee on 6th October 2003 and extended Income Support entitlement to customers aged 60+.

3 Contributory/NI benefits other than State Pension are:
(i) Incapacity Benefit and Widows Benefit from 1998 until 2000;
(ii) Incapacity Benefit, Widow's Benefit and Bereavement Benefit from 2001.
4 Figures relate to one-parent families headed by a man or a woman, where the claimant is not receiving a pensioner or disability premium.

Sources: Department for Work and Pensions; Information and Analysis Directorate: 0191 225 7373

10.17 Income support[1]: number of persons provided for
Great Britain
On a day in May

Thousands

		1998	1999	2000	2001	2002	2003	2004
Number of regular weekly payments	KACN	3 853	3 814	3 811	3 928	3 930	3 982	2 172
Total number of persons provided for	KACO	6 769	6 689	6 666	6 782	6 749	6 809	4 544
Number of dependants	KACP	2 379	2 344	2 317	2 289	2 242	2 230	2 083
Partners	KACQ	537	531	539	565	577	596	290
Total children under 16 years	KACR	2 224	2 188	2 158	2 123	2 074	2 054	1 922
Under 11	KACS	1 605	1 557	1 524	1 489	1 441	1 421	1 340
11 - 15 years	KACT	618	631	634	634	633	633	582
16 - 17 years	KACU	129	128	131	138	138	144	133
Other dependants 18 years and over	KACV	26	28	28	28	30	32	28

1 See chapter text. Data are extracted from the Quarterly Statistical Enquires.
2 From November 2003 IS figures are severely affected by the introduction of Pension Credit, which replaced MIG on 6th October 2003 and extended Income Support entitlement to customers aged 60+. Pension Credit cases are not included in the figures in the table. It is not possible to produce comparisons across 6th October 2003 on a consistent basis whether Pension Credit cases are included or not.

3 Figures in this table may be affected by the introduction of New Tax Credits in April 2003 when child dependency increases paid with non-income related benefits were abolished for new claims. A small number of IS/JSA(IB) recipients will no longer be eligible once Child Tax Credit is in payment as it will raise them above the IS/JSA(IB) threshold.

Sources: Department for Work and Pensions; Information and Analysis Directorate: 0191 225 7373

10.18 Income support: average weekly amounts of benefit[1,2]
Great Britain

May

£ per week

		1997	1998	1999	2000	2001	2002	2003	2004
All income support	KACW	58.03	58.72	61.42	65.72	70.21	69.64	73.40	91.82
All aged 60 and over	KJUB	42.24	42.29	45.30	48.18	50.73	49.69	50.76	..
State pensioners	KACX	34.90	34.50	36.99	39.50	41.20	40.35	40.66	..
In receipt of other NI benefit	KJUD	30.73	32.42	35.58	40.76	47.18	47.06	49.72	..
Others	KACY	85.56	87.29	91.70	96.20	107.13	105.22	109.71	..
All under 60	KACZ	70.17	71.14	73.36	78.61	85.34	85.60	91.65	91.78
Disabled with contributory benefit[3]	KADC	33.87	33.56	34.40	36.85	41.81	41.33	44.59	44.77
Disabled without contributory benefit[3]	KADD	70.38	72.86	75.88	79.25	84.81	86.63	90.74	91.15
Lone parent premium not in other groups[4]	KADE	79.21	79.67	82.01	91.21	101.44	105.39	115.72	114.61
Others	KADF	63.24	65.38	66.71	68.37	71.26	56.16	57.87	60.32

1 See chapter text. Data are extracted from the Quarterly Statistical Enquiries undertaken in each May from 1997-2004.
2 From November 2003 IS figures are severely affected by the introduction of Pension Credit, which replaced MIG on 6th October 2003 and extended Income Support entitlement to customers aged 60+. It is not possible to produce comparisons across 6th October 2003 on a consistent basis whether Pension Credit cases are included or not.

3 Contributory/NI benefits other than State pension are:
(i) Incapacity Benefit and Widow's Benefit from 1997 until 2000;
(ii) Incapacity Benefit, Widow's Benefit and Bereavement Benefit from 2001.
4 Figures relate to one-parent families headed by a man or a woman, where the claimant is not receiving a pensioner or disability premium.

Sources: Department for Work and Pensions;
Information and Analysis Directorate: 0191 225 7373

10.19 Summary of government expenditure on social services and housing[1]
Years ended 31 March

£ million

		1993 /94	1994 /95	1995 /96	1996 /97	1997 /98	1998 /99	1999 /00	2000 /01	2001 /02	2002 /03
Education[2]	KJAA	33 540	35 390	36 807	37 950	39 077	38 981	40 895	44 350	49 733	53 815
National Health Service	KJAB	37 259	39 879	40 691	42 383	43 878	47 194	48 362	53 039	59 852	66 271
Welfare services	CSWL	7 700	9 016	10 312	11 521	11 713	11 984	12 168	12 995	14 009	16 088
Social security benefits	KJAE	85 805	87 941	90 534	92 217	92 146	93 929	97 077	98 899	106 504	108 982
Housing	QYXD	8 716	8 306	8 405	6 996	6 721	6 135	4 660	5 017	6 504	7 653
Total government expenditure	KJAG	173 020	180 532	186 749	191 067	193 535	198 223	203 162	214 300	236 602	252 809
Current expenditure	KJAH	165 509	173 030	179 199	184 749	187 667	193 846	199 789	210 128	230 837	246 745
Capital expenditure	KJAI	7 511	7 502	7 550	6 318	5 868	4 377	3 373	4 172	5 765	6 064
Total government expenditure	KJAG	173 020	180 532	186 749	191 067	193 535	198 223	203 162	214 300	236 602	252 809
Central government	KJAK	126 371	130 819	134 954	137 487	142 670	158 494	163 098	171 010	189 019	201 328
Local authorities	KJAL	46 649	49 713	51 795	53 580	50 865	39 729	40 064	43 290	47 583	51 481
Total government expenditure	KJAG	173 020	180 532	186 749	191 067	193 535	198 223	203 162	214 300	236 602	252 809
Total government expenditure on social services and housing as a percentage of GDP[3]		26.55	26.17	25.62	24.67	23.57	22.79	22.15	22.32	23.54	23.90

1 See chapter text.
2 Includes school meals.
3 GDP adjusted to take account of change from rates to community charge.

Source: Office for National Statistics: 020 7533 5990

10.20 Government expenditure on education[1]
Years ended 31 March

£ million

		1992/93	1993/94	1994/95	1995/96	1996/97	1997/98	1998/99	1999/00	2000/01	2001/02	2002/03
Current expenditure												
Nursery and primary schools	KEZN	8 262	8 712	9 094	9 352	9 697	10 405	23 069	24 441	27 066	30 227	31 546
Secondary schools	KJBC	8 347	8 615	8 875	8 844	9 194	9 322	..	..	..	..	..
Special schools	KJBD	1 354	1 420	1 451	1 493	1 578	1 655	..	..	..	..	..
Universities[2]	KJBG	3 361	..	..	..	..	..	..	..	..	..	..
Other higher, further and adult education[3]	KJBE	4 136	..	..	..	..	..	..	..	..	..	..
Higher Education Funding Council[3,4]	CSWM	..	4 908	5 192	5 472	5 729	5 693	4 726	5 166	5 843	5 628	6 239
Further Education Funding Council[5]	CSWO	..	3 072	3 200	3 392	3 694	3 718	5 064	5 216	5 194	6 810	6 085
Continuing Education	CSWP	..	380	294	1 801	1 891	1 960	..	..	..	..	..
Other education expenditure	KJBH	1 009	905	963	948	1 277	1 355	4 611	4 278	3 881	3 989	6 508
Related current expenditure:												
School welfare[6]	KJBJ	270	346	359	328	336	372	..	..	..	..	..
School meals[7]	KJBK	161	149	147	148	147	138	..	..	..	..	..
Youth service and physical training	KJBL	393	392	401	396	389	389	..	..	..	..	..
Maintenance grants and allowances to pupils and students[8]	KJBM	1 705	1 972	2 204	1 660	1 440	1 289	..	..	..	..	..
Transport of pupils	KJBN	417	444	486	507	526	584	..	..	..	..	..
Miscellaneous expenditure	KJBO	8	10	31	31	49	45	..	..	..	..	..
Total current expenditure[9]	KJBQ	29 424	31 325	32 697	34 372	35 947	36 925	37 470	39 101	41 984	46 294	50 378
Capital expenditure												
Nursery and primary schools	KEZP	384	414	517	497	482	546	1 357	1 472	1 730	2 044	2 185
Secondary schools	KJBT	518	485	565	482	515	601	..	..	..	..	..
Special schools	KJBU	32	31	37	51	52	44	..	..	..	..	..
Universities[2]	KJBX	236	..	..	..	..	..	..	..	..	..	..
Other higher, further and adult education[3]	KJBV	285	..	..	..	..	..	..	..	..	..	..
Higher Education Funding Council[3,4]	CSWQ	..	406	412	424	74	61	31	113	208	342	392
Further Education Funding Council[5]	CSWR	..	194	201	187	33	29	44	97	253	459	475
Continuing Education	CSWS	..	6	8	8	5	–	–	–	–	–	–
Other education expenditure	KJBY	25	12	45	25	24	30	57	111	174	234	385
Related capital expenditure	KJBZ	17	23	25	17	20	24	22	..	..	..	..
Total capital expenditure[9]	KJCA	1 496	1 571	1 810	1 691	1 205	1 335	1 511	1 793	2 365	3 079	3 438
VAT refunds to local authorities	KJBP	656	648	860	747	801	818	816	906	..	..	..
Total expenditure												
Central government	KJCB	4 722	8 186	9 490	10 853	11 388	12 167	11 422	13 177	14 421	16 678	18 629
Local authorities	KJCC	26 853	25 354	25 900	25 954	26 562	26 910	27 559	27 718	29 929	32 330	35 186
Total government expenditure[10]	KJAA	31 575	33 540	35 390	36 807	37 950	39 077	38 981	40 895	44 350	49 733	53 815
Total government education expenditure as a percentage of GDP[11]		5.12	5.15	5.13	5.05	4.90	4.76	4.48	4.46	4.62	4.95	5.09

1 See chapter text. From 1998/99 figures have been taken from HM Treasury Public Expenditure Statistical Analyses. They are not comparable with earlier years which used different sources. Schools expenditure no longer separately identifiable
2 Includes expenditure on University departments of Education for England and Wales
3 Includes tuition fees.
4 Includes expenditure on higher education institutions in Northern Ireland.
5 Includes expenditure on further education institutions in Northern Ireland.
6 Expenditure on the school health service is included in the National Health Service.
7 Expenditure on school meals in England has been recharged across other expenditure headings.

8 Excludes the secondment of teachers on further training. Includes student loans expenditure.
9 Due to rounding constituent figures may not sum to totals.
10 Excludes additional adjustment to allow for Capital consumption made for National Accounts purposes. From 1995/96, figures include expenditure on training programmes in England (such as Work Based Training for Young People) reclassified as education. Therefore the figures are not comparable with earlier years.
11 GDP includes adjustments to remove the distortion caused by the abolition of domestic rates.

Sources: Department for Education and Skills; Office for National Statistics: 020 7533 5990

10.21 Government expenditure on the National Health Service[1]
Years ended 31 March

£ million

		1993/94	1994/95	1995/96	1996/97	1997/98	1998/99	1999/00	2000/01	2001/02	2002/03
Current expenditure[2]											
Hospitals and Community Health Services[3] and Family Health Services[4]	KJQA	35 567	37 698	38 514	39 425	40 993	43 600	48 275	52 599	59 050	65 331
less Payments by patients:											
Hospital services	KJQC	−368	−111	−42	−42	−48	−84	−138	−138	−155	−172
Pharmaceutical services	KJQD	−324	−342	−383	−376	−396	−391	−405	−425	−478	−528
Dental services	KJQE	−440	−464	−494	−447	−475	−470	−483	−506	−568	−628
Total	KJQG	−1 132	−917	−919	−865	−919	−945	−1 026	−1 068	−1 199	−1 326
Departmental administration	KJQH	270	256	242	265	245	227	231	324	364	402
Other central services	KJQI	1 651	2 304	2 538	3 124	3 242	4 980	1 601	1 931	2 885	2 858
Total current expenditure	KJQJ	36 356	39 341	40 375	41 949	43 561	46 910	48 055	52 707	59 477	65 938
Capital expenditure[2]	KJQK	903	538	316	434	317	284	307	332	375	333
Total government NHS Expenditure[2]	KJAB	37 259	39 879	40 691	42 383	43 878	47 194	48 362	53 039	59 852	66 271
Total NHS expenditure as a percentage of GDP[5]		*5.72*	*5.78*	*5.58*	*5.47*	*5.34*	*5.43*	*5.27*	*5.52*	*5.96*	*6.27*

1 See chapter text.
2 By central government.
3 Including the school health service.
4 General Medical Services have been included in the expenditure of the Health Authorities. Therefore, Hospitals and Community Health Services and Family Practitioner Services (now Family Health Services) are not identifiable separately.
5 GDP adjusted to take account of change from rates to community charge.

Source: Office for National Statistics: 020 7533 5990

10.22 Government expenditure on the welfare services[1]
Years ended 31 March

£ million

		1992/93	1993/94	1994/95	1995/96	1996/97	1997/98	1998/99	1999/00	2000/01	2001/02	2002/03
Personal social services												
Central government current expenditure	KJCG	202	216	197	140	101	73	53	50	49	56	64
Local authorities current expenditure:												
Running expenses	CTKQ	6 122	7 113	8 400	9 716	10 947	11 131	11 378	11 563	12 405	13 331	15 309
Capital expenditure	KJCI	189	190	235	229	210	204	199	145	132	147	169
Total	KJAC	6 513	7 519	8 832	10 085	11 258	11 408	11 630	11 758	12 586	13 534	15 542
Welfare foods service												
Central government current expenditure on welfare foods (including administration)	KJCK	171	182	185	228	264	306	355	411	411	477	547
less Receipts from the public	KJCL	−1	−1	−1	−1	−1	−1	−1	−1	−2	−2	−2
Total	KJAD	170	181	184	227	263	305	354	410	409	475	545
Total government expenditure	CSWL	6 683	7 700	9 016	10 312	11 521	11 713	11 984	12 168	12 995	14 009	16 088
Total government expenditure as a percentage of GDP[2]		*1.08*	*1.18*	*1.31*	*1.41*	*1.49*	*1.43*	*1.38*	*1.33*	*1.35*	*1.39*	*1.52*

1 See chapter text.
2 GDP adjusted to take account of change from rates to community charge.

Source: Office for National Statistics: 020 7533 5990

10.23 Government expenditure on social security benefits[1]
Years ended 31 March

£ million

		1992 /93	1993 /94	1994 /95	1995 /96	1996 /97	1997 /98	1998 /99	1999 /00	2000 /01	2001 /02	2002 /03
Government current expenditure												
National Insurance fund:												
Retirement pensions	EKXK	27 076	28 481	28 925	30 162	32 146	33 643	35 782	37 918	39 361	43 222	48 863
Lump sums to pensioners	KJDB	115	122	123	124	129	118	120	123	128	134	137
Widows and Guardians allowances	CSDH	1 014	1 041	1 034	1 018	974	992	973	990	982	1 113	1 092
Unemployment Benefit	CSDI	1 761	1 623	1 277	1 099	588	1	–	–1	–1	–	–
Jobseeker's Allowance[2]	CJTJ	–	–	–	–	379	590	474	462	435	441	520
Sickness Benefit[3]	CSDJ	365	294	426	12	–	–	–	–	–	–	–
Invalidity Benefit[3]	CSDK	6 198	7 146	8 042	271	–	–	–	–	–	–	–
Incapacity Benefit[3]	CUNL	–	–	–	7 615	7 668	7 471	7 295	6 897	6 677	6 836	6 837
Maternity Benefit	CSDL	42	32	17	28	32	36	39	40	52	56	69
Statutory sick pay	CSDQ	688	688	24	24	24	28	28	28	36	32	–
Statutory maternity pay	GTKZ	416	440	498	476	500	516	552	585	611	652	708
Total	ACHH	37 675	39 867	40 366	40 829	42 440	43 395	45 263	47 043	48 281	52 486	58 226
Redundancy Fund	GTKN	321	110	208	128	108	88	116	148	196	194	230
Social Fund	GTLQ	175	189	183	216	203	200	360	920	1 957	1 859	1 940
Non-contributory benefits:												
War pensions [4]	KJDP	976	913	1 083	1 247	1 352	1 284	1 262	1 254	1 201	1 182	..
Family benefits:												
Child Benefit	KJDQ	5 950	6 347	6 294	6 332	6 645	7 095	7 327	8 212	8 528	8 685	8 897
One parent benefit	KJDR	275	282	289	310	317	9	–	–	–	–	–
Family Credit	KAAA	929	1 208	1 441	1 739	2 084	2 338	2 430	1 927	–788	–	–
Income support/Supplementary benefits:												
Income Support	KAAB	15 578	16 997	16 387	16 650	14 438	11 998	11 793	12 227	13 076	14 222	10 003
Other non-contributory benefits:												
Old persons' pensions	KJDX	36	36	35	36	30	29	29	28	28	27	29
Lump sums to pensioners	KJDY	13	14	13	15	15	17	17	17	17	17	17
Attendance Allowance	KJDZ	1 553	1 795	1 963	2 194	2 393	2 640	2 682	2 834	2 957	3 121	3 259
Invalid Care Allowance	KJEA	345	442	526	617	736	745	783	814	849	924	999
Mobility Allowance	KJEB	68	–	–	–	–	–	–	–	–	–	–
Disability Living Allowance	EKXL	1 973	2 772	3 125	3 802	4 498	5 018	5 367	5 653	6 021	6 567	7 081
Disability Working Allowance	EKYE	3	7	11	19	34	44	49	40	–	–	–
Severe Disablement Allowance	KJEC	640	703	776	820	906	1 007	984	1 016	1 024	1 034	960
Industrial Injury benefits	EKXM	668	687	706	731	744	754	–	–	–	–	–
Housing Benefit	KJED	7 670	9 163	10 345	10 773	11 276	11 315	11 311	11 247	11 616	11 923	12 977
Administration	KJEE	3 998	4 273	4 190	4 076	3 998	4 170	4 349	3 737	3 936	4 253	4 364
Total government expenditure	KJAE	78 846	85 805	87 941	90 534	92 217	92 146	93 929	97 077	98 899	106 504	108 982
Total government benefit expenditure as a percentage of GDP[5]		12.79	13.17	12.75	12.42	11.91	11.22	10.80	10.58	10.30	10.60	10.30

1 See chapter text.
2 Jobseeker's allowance was introduced in October 1996 to replace Unemployment benefit and Income Support for the unemployed.
3 Sickness benefit and Invalidity benefit were replaced by a single incapacity benefit in 1995.
4 From 2002/03 War Pensions are administered by the Ministry of Defence.
5 GDP adjusted to take account of change from rates to community charge.

Source: Office for National Statistics: 020 7533 5990

10.24 Government and other public sector expenditure on housing and community amenities[1]

Years ended 31 March

£ million

		1993/94	1994/95	1995/96	1996/97	1997/98	1998/99	1999/00	2000/01	2001/02	2002/03	2003/04
Final consumption expenditure												
Compensation of employees	QYSV	837	952	852	704	745	870	898	945	970	1 481	1 354
Other current expenditure on goods and services	QYSW	695	735	782	484	1 047	999	904	1 100	1 460	1 762	2 392
Capital consumption	QYSY	383	394	547	962	1 039	1 103	1 210	1 278	1 371	1 488	1 556
Total	QYSZ	1 915	2 081	2 181	2 150	2 831	2 972	3 012	3 323	3 801	4 731	5 302
Subsidies												
Paid to public corporations	C5AN	241	243	256	237	248	223	214	168	143	161	233
Paid to local authorities	CTMN	874	814	687	717	711	737	466	438	976	873	904
Other subsidies	C5DR	180	207	215	216	214	−19	21	21	5	18	..
Other current transfers	QZNY	25	19	15	43	14	40	29	38	18	32	18
Gross Fixed Capital Formation	QYVH	1 364	1 822	2 173	909	466	−146	−1 109	−894	102	−664	..
Capital transfers												
LA improvement grants	ADCE	1 287	1 105	846	918	1 157	1 181	1 130	902	985	969	852
LA capital grants to public corporations	ADCF	2	1	1	2	29	13	17	36	16	16	101
Central Government grants to Housing Associations	GTDI	1 841	1 507	1 243	1 140	761	883	1 022	986	1 143	1 220	2 211
Others	C5AO	987	507	788	602	290	653	222	−19	−881	297	..
Total government expenditure	QYXD	8 716	8 306	8 405	6 996	6 721	6 135	4 660	5 017	6 504	7 653	..
Total public sector housing expenditure as a percentage of GDP[3]		*1.34*	*1.20*	*1.15*	*0.90*	*0.82*	*0.71*	*0.51*	*0.52*	*0.65*	*0.72*	*..*

1 See chapter text.

Source: Office for National Statistics: 020 7533 5990

Crime and justice

Chapter 11

Crime and justice

There are differences in the legal and judicial systems of England and Wales, Scotland and Northern Ireland which make it impossible to provide tables covering the United Kingdom as a whole in this section. These differences concern the classification of offences, the meaning of certain terms used in the statistics, the effects of the several Criminal Justice Acts, and recording practices.

Recorded crime statistics

(Table 11.2)

Crimes recorded by the police provide a measure of the amount of crime committed. The statistics are based on counting rules, revised with effect from 1 April 1998, which are standard for all the police forces in England, Wales and Northern Ireland and now include all indictable and triable-either-way offences together with a few summary offences which are closely linked to these offences. The new rules have changed the emphasis of measurement more towards one crime per victim, and have also increased the coverage of offences. These changes have particularly impacted on the offence groups of violence against the person, fraud and forgery, drugs offences and other offences.

For a variety of reasons many offences are either not reported to the police or not recorded by them. The changes in the number of offences recorded do not necessarily provide an accurate reflection of changes in the amount of crime committed.

In order to further improve the consistency of recorded crime statistics, and to take a more victim oriented approach to crime recording, the National Crime Recording Standard (NCRS) was introduced in England, Wales and Northern Ireland from 1 April 2002. Some police forces implemented the principles of NCRS in advance of its implementation across all forces in April 2002. The NCRS had the effect of increasing the number of offences recorded by the police.

Further information is available from the Home Office: *Crime in England and Wales 2002/2003,* ed: Jon Simmons and Tricia Dodd.

Court proceedings and police cautions

(Tables 11.3 to 11.7, 11.13 to 11.17, 11.20 to 11.22)

The statistical basis of the tables of court proceedings is broadly similar in England and Wales, Scotland and Northern Ireland; the tables show the number of persons found guilty, recording a person under the heading of the principal offence of which he is found guilty, excluding additional findings of guilt at the same proceedings. A person found guilty at a number of separate court proceedings is included more than once.

The statistics on offenders cautioned in England and Wales cover only those who, on admission of guilt, were given a formal caution by, or on the instructions of, a senior police officer as an alternative to prosecution. Written warnings by the police for motor offences and persons paying fixed penalties for certain motoring offences are excluded. Formal cautions are not issued in Scotland. There are no statistics on cautioning available for Northern Ireland.

The Crime and Disorder Act 1998 created provisions in relation to reprimands and final warnings, new offences and orders which have been implemented nationally since 1 June 2000. They replace the system of cautioning for offenders aged under 18. Reprimands can be given to first-time offenders for minor offences. Any further offending results in either a final warning or a charge.

For persons proceeded against in Scotland, the statistics relate to the High Court of Justiciary, the Sheriff Court and the District Court. The High Court deals with serious solemn (ie Jury) cases and has unlimited sentencing power. The Sheriff Court is limited to imprisonment of three years for solemn cases, or three months (six months when specified in legislation for second or subsequent offences and 12 months for certain statutory offences) for summary (i.e. non-Jury) cases. The District Court deals only with summary cases and is limited to 60 days imprisonment and level 4 fines. Stipendiary Magistrates sit in Glasgow District Court and have the summary sentencing powers of a Sheriff.

In England and Wales, indictable offences are offences which are:

(a) *Triable only on indictment.* These offences are the most serious breaches of the criminal law and must be tried at the Crown Court. 'Indictable-only' offences include murder, manslaughter, rape and robbery.

(b) *Triable either way.* These offences may be tried at the Crown Court or Magistrates' Court.

The Criminal Justice Act 1991 led to the following main changes in the sentences available to the courts in England and Wales:

(a) introduction of combination orders;

(b) introduction of the 'unit fine scheme' at Magistrates' courts;

(c) abolishing the sentence of detention in a young offender institution for 14 year old boys and changing the minimum and maximum sentence lengths for 15 to 17 year olds to 10 and 12 months respectively; and

(d) abolishing partly suspended sentences of imprisonment and restricting the use of a fully suspended sentence.

The Criminal Justice Act 1993 abolished the 'Unit Fine Scheme' in Magistrates' courts which had been introduced under the Criminal Justice Act 1991.

A *charging standard for assault* was introduced in England and Wales on 31 August 1994 with the aim to promote consistency between the police and prosecution on the appropriate level of charge to be brought.

The Criminal Justice and Public Order Act 1994 created several new offences in England and Wales, mainly in the area of Public Order, but also including male rape (there is no statutory offence of 'male rape' in Scotland, although such a crime may be charged as serious assault). The Act also:

(a) extended the provisions of section 53 of the Children and Young Persons Act 1993 for 10 to 13 year olds;

(b) increased the maximum sentence length for 15 to 17 year olds to two years;

(c) increased the upper limit from £2,000 to £5,000 for offences of criminal damage proceeded against as if triable only summarily;

(d) introduced provisions for the reduction of sentences for early guilty pleas; and

(e) increased the maximum sentence length for certain firearm offences.

Provisions within the Crime (Sentences) Act 1997 (as amended by the Powers of Criminal Courts Sentencing Act 2000), in England and Wales, and the Crime and Punishment (Scotland) Act 1997, in Scotland, included:

a) an automatic life sentence for a second serious violent or sexual offence unless there are exceptional circumstances (this provision has not been enacted in Scotland);

b) a minimum sentence of seven years for an offender convicted for a third time of a class A drug trafficking offence unless the court considers this to be unjust in all the circumstances, and, in England and Wales;

c) the new section 38A of the Magistrates' Courts' Act 1980 extending the circumstances in which a magistrates' court may commit a person convicted of an offence triable either way to the Crown Court for sentence – it was implemented in conjunction with section 49 of the Criminal Procedure and Investigations Act 1996, which involves the magistrates' courts in asking defendants to indicate plea before the mode of trial decision is taken and compels the court to sentence or commit for sentence any defendant who indicates a guilty plea.

Under the Criminal Justice and Court Service Act 2000 new terms were introduced for certain orders. Community rehabilitation order is the new name for a probation order. A community service order is now known as a community punishment order. Finally, the new term for a combination order is community punishment and rehabilitation order. In April 2000 the secure training order was replaced by the detention and training order. Section 53 of the Children and Young Persons Act 1993 was repealed on 25 August 2000 and its provisions were transferred to Sections 90–92 of the Powers of Criminal Courts (Sentencing) Act 2000. Reparation and Action plan order were implemented nationally from 1 June 2000. Drug treatment and testing order was implemented nationally from October 2000. And Referral order was implemented nationally from April 2000. These changes are now reflected in Table 11.7.

The system of Magistrates' courts and Crown Courts in Northern Ireland operates in a similar way to that in England and Wales. A particularly significant statutory development, however, has been the Criminal Justice (NI) Order 1996 which introduces a new sentencing regime into Northern Ireland, largely replicating that which was introduced into England and Wales by the Criminal Justice Acts of 1991 and 1993. The order makes many changes to both community and custodial sentences, while introducing new orders such as the combination order, the custody probation order and orders for release on licence of sexual offenders.

Crime and justice

Previous convictions of prisoners

(Tables 11.8 and 11.9)

Standard list offences consist of all the indictable offences plus some of the more serious summary offences. From 1 January 1996 a number of summary motoring offences became standard list offences. Excluding the new standard lists from the analysis presented in the table would slightly alter the percentages with previous convictions.

Information on previous convictions of prisoners published prior to 1995 was based upon Prison Service records. However, details of a prisoner's previous conviction were often not recorded (e.g. this information was missing for 44 per cent of the 1990 male receptions under sentence). To overcome this problem the Home Office Offenders Index (a computerised database containing details of convictions for standard list offences) is now being used to provide information on prisoners' previous convictions. Unfortunately, this means that the most up-to-date information on previous convictions is not directly comparable with that previously published. Standard list offences include indictable offences and some of the more serious summary offences so the coverage is not as complete. The published information also does not relate to 'prison receptions' but to those sentenced to immediate custody for standard list offences (which accounted for 98 per cent of those sentenced to custody in 2002).

The problems with non-availability of previous history information are much less acute using the Offenders Index data source. Previous convictions were found for 95 per cent of the 1993 prison population sample. Some of the cases where information is missing would be accounted for by prisoners who are not sentenced for a standard list offence and have no previous record for such offences.

Expenditure on penal establishments in Scotland

(Table 11.19)

The results shown in this table are reported on a cash basis for financial years 1991–92 to 2000–01 in line with funding arrangements. Financial year 2001–02 is reported on a resource accounting basis in line with the introduction of Resource Budgeting. Capital Charges were introduced with Resource Accounting and Budgeting.

11.1 Police force strength: by country and sex
End of year

Numbers

		1993	1994	1995[1]	1996[1]	1997[1]	1998[1]	1999[1]	2000[1]	2001[1]	2002[1]	2003[1]
England and Wales												
Regular police												
Strength:												
Men	KERB	108 967	108 030	107 022	106 549	105 691	104 606	103 083	101 683	103 156	104 483	106 996
Women	KERC	16 571	17 263	17 688	18 501	19 124	19 659	19 967	20 519	21 794	22 784	24 430
Seconded:[2]												
Men	KERD	1 938	1 881	1 896	1 864	1 814	2 007	2 158	2 077	1 967	2 031	1 689
Women	KERE	182	184	202	209	233	232	256	307	294	305	251
Additional officers:[3]												
Men	KERF	63	97	105	111	200	267	324	361	493	567	375
Women	KERG	12	17	22	57	158	514	582	519	509	564	709
Special constables												
Enrolled strength:												
Men	KERH	13 240	12 772	12 751	12 594	12 483	11 331	10 667	9 120	8 238	8 014	7 718
Women	KERI	7 326	7 060	6 904	6 857	6 680	5 965	5 060	4 367	3 816	3 584	3 319
Scotland												
Regular police												
Strength[4]:												
Men	KERK	12 580	12 634	12 630	12 627	12 752	12 753	12 545	12 374	12 547	12 513	12 590
Women	KERL	1 559	1 679	1 693	1 885	2 037	2 227	2 265	2 325	2 602	2 738	2 897
Central service:[4,5]												
Men	KERM	73	79	96	94	85	85	88	95	87	116	131
Women	KERN	5	4	7	8	4	6	9	13	10	12	17
Seconded:[4,6]												
Men	KERO	109	110	108	105	101	101	85	130	140	133	166
Women	KERP	16	16	16	16	13	10	12	18	14	18	24
Additional regular police:												
Men	HFVM	55	88	85	81	71	88	85	80	83	80	79
Women	HFVN	3	3	5	5	1	9	6	4	5	12	10
Special constables												
Strength:												
Men	KERS	1 466	1 518	..	1 411	1 336	1 286	1 229	981	924	812	711
Women	KERT	431	474	..	467	450	437	422	355	336	307	280
Northern Ireland												
Regular police[7]												
Strength:												
Men	KERU	7 646	7 640	7 528	7 531	7 562	7 527	7 406	6 916	6 058	5 908	6 027
Women	KERV	818	853	887	897	923	933	987	978	918	1 032	1 185
Reserve[8]												
Strength:												
Men	KERW	4 027	4 052	3 976	3 727	3 587	3 469	3 199	2 959	2 620	2 223	1 983
Women	KERX	545	638	709	675	719	705	641	606	554	510	553

1 The 2002 and 2003 figures for England and Wales are for 31 March, with the previous years' figures being for 30 September. Figures for Scotland are as at 31 December until 1994 and from 1995 onwards as at 31 March. From 1999, figures for Northern Ireland reflect the position at the end of the financial year, i.e. 1999 and 2000 figures are as at 31 March 2000 and 31 March 2001 respectively. Prior to this, the figures were as at 31 December.
2 NCS, NCIS, other inter-force units and officers in central service.
3 Includes Police Officers on loan to organisations outside the British Police Service such as the Royal Hong Kong police, those on career breaks, and those on maternity leave.

4 'Strength' includes central service and seconded police.
5 Instructors at Training Establishments, etc, formerly shown as secondments.
6 Scottish Crime Squad, officers on courses, etc.
7 Does not include officers on secondment or student officers.
8 Includes Part-Time Reserve, 864 at 31 March 2004 (546 males and 318 females).

Sources: Home Office: 020 7273 2583;
The Scottish Executive Justice Department: 0131 244 2148;
The Police Service of Northern Ireland: 028 9065 0222 ext 24135

11.2 Recorded crime statistics: by offence group[1]
England and Wales

Thousands

		1993	1994	1995	1996	1997	1998[2,3] /99		1998[3] /99	1999 /00	2000 /01	2001[4] /02	2002[4] /03	2003 /04
Violence against the person	BEAB	205.1	218.4	212.6	239.3	250.8	230.8	LQMP	502.8	581.0	600.9	650.3	834.9	955.8
Sexual offences	BEAC	31.3	32.0	30.3	31.4	33.2	34.9	LQMQ	36.2	37.8	37.3	41.4	48.6	52.1
Burglary	BEAD	1 369.6	1 256.7	1 239.5	1 164.6	1 015.1	951.9	LQMR	953.2	906.5	836.0	878.5	888.8	818.6
Robbery	BEAE	57.8	60.0	68.1	74.0	63.1	66.2	LQMS	66.8	84.3	95.2	121.4	108.0	101.2
Theft and handling stolen goods	BEAF	2 751.9	2 564.6	2 452.1	2 383.9	2 165.0	2 126.7	LQMT	2 191.4	2 223.6	2 145.4	2 267.1	2 365.2	2 268.1
Fraud and forgery	BEAG	162.8	145.3	133.0	136.2	134.4	173.7	LQMU	279.5	334.8	319.3	317.4	330.1	317.9
Criminal damage	BEAH	906.7	928.3	914.0	951.3	877.0	834.4	LQMV	879.6	945.7	960.1	1 064.5	1 109.3	1 205.6
Drug offences[5]	LQMO	..	..	..	..	..	21.3	LQYT	135.9	121.9	113.5	121.3	141.1	141.1
Other offences[5]	BEAI	41.0	47.7	29.4	33.6	36.6	42.0	LQYU	63.6	65.7	63.2	65.3	72.5	74.2
Total	BEAA	5 526.3	5 253.0	5 100.2	5 036.6	4 598.3	4 481.8	LQYV	5 109.1	5 301.2	5 170.8	5 527.1	5 898.6	5 934.6

1 See chapter text.
2 Estimates.
3 The counting rules were revised on 1 April 1998
4 The National Crime Recording Standard (NCRS) was introduced in England and Wales from 1 April 2002. For more details about the inflationary effects of the NCRS on the 2001/02 and 2002/03 figures see chapter text.

5 Prior to 1 April 1998 the offence of drug trafficking was included in the 'Other offences' group. From 1 April 1999, under the new counting rules, drug trafficking became part of a new 'Drug offences' group which, with the expanded coverage, now includes possession and other drug offences. For 1998/99, under the old counting rules, drug trafficking - the only drugs offence counted - has been listed under drugs offences.

Source: Home Office: 020 7273 2583

11.3 Offenders found guilty: by offence group[1]
England and Wales
Magistrates' courts and the Crown Court

Thousands

		1993	1994	1995	1996	1997	1998	1999	2000	2001	2002	2003
All ages[2]												
Indictable offences												
Violence against the person:	KJEJ	38.9	37.6	29.1	30.0	34.6	35.7	34.4	34.0	35.3	37.7	38.0
Murder	KESB	0.2	0.2	0.2	0.3	0.3	0.3	0.3	0.3	0.3	0.3	0.3
Manslaughter	KESC	0.2	0.2	0.2	0.3	0.3	0.3	0.3	0.3	0.3	0.3	0.2
Wounding	KESD	37.4	36.1	27.4	28.3	32.7	35.2	33.9	33.5	33.5	35.7	35.9
Other offences of violence against the person	KESE	1.0	1.0	1.2	1.2	1.3	1.3	1.3	1.3	1.2	1.4	1.5
Sexual offences	KESF	4.3	4.5	4.7	4.4	4.5	4.6	4.3	3.9	3.8	4.4	4.4
Burglary	KESG	40.3	38.0	35.3	32.2	31.7	30.8	29.3	26.2	24.8	26.7	25.7
Robbery	KESH	5.1	4.9	5.2	5.9	5.6	5.5	5.6	6.0	6.8	7.7	7.3
Theft and handling stolen goods	KESI	121.6	121.6	116.1	114.5	118.4	125.7	131.2	128.0	127.0	127.3	119.1
Fraud and forgery	KESJ	17.5	18.4	17.2	16.3	17.0	19.8	20.3	19.2	18.3	18.1	18.0
Criminal damage	KESK	9.4	10.0	9.6	9.8	10.5	10.9	10.9	10.2	10.7	11.0	11.2
Drugs	KBWX	21.9	27.8	31.6	34.1	40.7	48.8	48.7	44.6	45.6	49.0	51.2
Other offences (excluding motoring)	KESL	37.8	39.4	42.2	43.5	47.6	49.6	47.9	44.5	44.2	48.0	51.4
Motoring offences	KESM	10.8	12.0	11.2	9.9	9.5	9.0	8.1	7.6	7.7	8.2	8.7
Total	KESA	307.6	314.1	302.2	300.6	320.1	341.7	342.0	325.5	324.2	338.3	335.1
Summary offences[3]												
Assaults[4]	KESO	19.0	21.9	29.3	30.0	32.0	35.3	37.5	37.4	37.7	40.7	45.6
Betting and gaming	KESP	–	–	–	–	–	–	–	–	–	–	–
Offences with pedal cycles	KBWY	1.2	1.0	1.1	1.3	1.5	2.1	1.3	0.8	0.6	0.5	0.6
Other Highways Acts offences	KBWZ	3.6	3.4	2.6	2.8	3.2	3.1	2.9	2.7	2.4	2.2	1.9
Breach of local or other regulations	KESQ	10.5	9.4	6.7	5.9	6.4	5.8	6.5	5.0	4.3	3.9	3.4
Intoxicating Liquor Laws:												
Drunkenness	KESR	18.8	20.2	19.8	24.2	28.8	30.8	28.7	27.2	26.2	26.9	27.7
Other offences	KESS	0.8	0.7	0.7	0.5	0.6	0.6	0.5	0.4	0.3	0.4	0.7
Education Acts	KEST	2.3	2.8	3.1	3.5	3.7	5.0	5.1	5.1	5.6	5.8	5.8
Game Laws	KESU	0.6	0.6	0.4	0.4	0.3	0.4	0.3	0.2	0.2	0.3	0.2
Labour Laws	KESV	0.1	0.1	0.1	–	0.1	0.1	0.1	0.1	–	–	0.1
Summary offences of criminal damage and malicious damage	KESW	21.6	22.7	22.6	23.4	24.7	26.5	27.9	28.0	26.9	28.3	29.8
Offences by prostitutes	KESX	8.2	7.7	6.8	6.6	6.6	6.0	4.0	4.1	3.7	4.2	3.9
Railway offences	KESY	4.0	5.6	6.2	9.1	11.4	12.6	15.2	17.4	22.6	29.4	34.8
Revenue Laws[3]	KESZ	123.0	126.2	123.8	139.1	143.5	174.7	165.8	175.0	146.9	167.8	172.5
Vagrancy Acts	KETB	1.7	1.9	1.6	2.0	2.0	2.2	2.7	3.3	3.2	3.8	3.8
Wireless Telegraphy Acts[3]	KETC	168.7	162.9	113.8	164.9	77.0	76.6	55.8	105.7	83.8	96.6	79.9
Other summary offences	KETD	69.0	67.8	71.5	74.7	74.7	80.9	79.3	78.1	77.8	76.4	82.9
Motoring offences (summary)[3]	KETA	664.7	638.7	642.4	649.0	649.3	665.2	632.9	607.5	583.3	595.8	662.6
Total	KESN	1 117.7	1 093.5	1 052.4	1 137.4	1 065.8	1 128.0	1 066.5	1 098.2	1 025.5	1 083.0	1 156.1
Persons aged 10 to under 18[3,5]												
Indictable offences												
Violence against the person:	KETF	5.1	5.8	4.7	5.3	5.9	5.9	6.2	6.4	6.9	6.9	6.6
Murder	KBXA	–	–	–	–	–	–	–	–	–	–	–
Manslaughter	KBXB	–	–	–	–	–	–	0.2	–	–	–	–
Wounding	KBXC	5.1	5.7	4.7	5.3	5.8	5.9	5.9	6.3	6.8	6.8	6.5
Other offences of violence against the person	KCAA	–	–	–	–	0.1	0.1	–	0.1	0.1	0.1	0.1
Sexual offences	KETG	0.4	0.4	0.4	0.4	0.5	0.5	0.5	0.5	0.5	0.6	0.4
Burglary	KETH	8.7	8.9	9.1	8.6	8.6	8.5	7.8	6.8	6.3	6.4	5.8
Robbery	KETI	1.5	1.7	2.0	2.4	2.3	2.2	2.0	2.2	2.8	2.8	2.6
Theft and handling stolen goods	KETJ	14.1	14.4	18.2	19.0	19.6	21.9	22.7	21.0	20.6	18.4	16.5
Fraud and forgery	KETK	0.4	0.5	0.6	0.7	0.8	1.0	1.1	1.0	1.0	1.2	0.8
Criminal damage	KETL	1.7	2.0	2.1	2.2	2.3	2.3	2.7	2.6	2.9	2.9	2.9
Drugs	KCAB	0.8	1.1	1.3	1.6	1.8	2.7	3.1	3.7	4.3	5.0	5.1
Other offences (excluding motoring)	KETM	2.4	2.8	3.3	3.8	4.2	4.2	4.3	4.4	4.4	4.4	4.3
Motoring	KETN	0.3	0.3	0.4	0.4	0.4	0.4	0.4	0.6	0.7	0.8	0.8
Total	KETE	35.4	37.9	42.2	44.4	46.4	49.7	50.6	49.2	50.3	49.1	46.0
Summary offences[3]												
Offences with pedal cycles	KETP	0.1	0.1	0.2	0.2	0.2	0.3	0.3	0.2	0.2	0.2	0.2
Breach of local or other regulations	KETR	0.1	0.1	0.2	0.3	0.2	0.2	0.2	0.2	0.2	0.1	0.1
Summary offences of criminal damage and malicious damage	KETS	2.2	2.9	3.4	3.9	4.4	5.2	6.1	6.7	6.9	7.0	7.2
Railway offences	KETT	0.2	0.3	0.4	0.4	0.5	0.5	0.5	0.4	0.4	0.4	0.3
Other summary offences	KETU	8.3	9.7	7.2	8.8	10.1	12.1	11.7	11.3	11.6	11.7	10.3
Motoring offences (summary)[3]	KCAC	8.9	8.6	9.3	10.8	10.8	11.3	12.6	14.5	16.7	17.1	17.8
Total	KETO	19.9	21.7	25.6	30.3	22.0	36.8	39.6	42.2	45.2	45.4	46.6

1 See chapter text.
2 Includes 'Companies', etc.
3 It is estimated that in 1995 there was a shortfall of 75,100 offenders found guilty for certain summary offences.

4 A new charging standard was introduced for assault in 1994.
5 Figures for persons aged 10 to under 18 are included in the totals above.

Source: Home Office: 020 8760 1404

11.4 Offenders cautioned: by offence group[1]
England and Wales

Thousands

		1993	1994	1995	1996	1997	1998	1999	2000	2001	2002	2003
All ages[2]												
Indictable offences												
Violence against the person	KELB	20.4	21.8	20.4	21.8	23.6	23.5	21.2	19.9	19.5	23.6	28.8
Murder	KCAD	–	–	–	–	–	–	–	–	–	–	–
Manslaughter	KCAE	–	–	–	–	–	–	–	–	–	–	–
Wounding	KCAF	20.1	21.4	20.1	21.4	23.3	22.9	20.6	19.3	18.9	22.9	27.9
Other violence against the person	KCAG	0.3	0.4	0.3	0.4	0.4	0.6	0.6	0.6	0.6	0.7	0.9
Sexual offences	KELC	2.3	2.0	2.3	2.0	1.9	1.7	1.5	1.3	1.2	1.1	1.4
Burglary	KELD	10.5	10.2	10.5	10.2	9.4	8.4	7.7	6.6	6.4	5.8	5.6
Robbery	KELE	0.6	0.6	0.6	0.6	0.7	0.6	0.6	0.6	0.5	0.4	0.4
Theft and handling stolen goods	KELF	104.9	93.6	104.9	93.6	82.8	83.6	75.4	67.6	63.5	54.2	54.5
Fraud and forgery	KELG	7.9	7.5	7.9	7.5	7.2	7.4	7.2	6.2	5.8	5.3	5.5
Criminal damage	KELH	3.8	3.1	3.8	3.1	2.8	2.7	3.0	3.2	3.4	3.1	3.7
Drug offences	KCAI	48.2	47.5	48.2	47.5	56.0	58.7	49.4	41.1	39.4	44.9	45.7
Other offences	KELI	4.0	4.4	4.0	4.4	5.0	5.0	4.6	4.4	4.2	4.4	5.3
All offenders cautioned	KELA	202.6	190.8	202.6	190.8	189.4	191.7	170.6	150.9	143.9	142.9	150.7
Summary offences												
Assaults[3]	KELK	3.1	4.2	8.1	9.1	9.1	–	17.0	17.2	18.2	17.3	19.8
Betting and gaming	KELL	–	–	–	–	–	–	–	–	–	–	–
Offences with pedal cycles	KCAK	0.9	0.8	0.8	0.9	0.9	0.8	0.6	0.3	0.2	0.1	0.1
Other Highways Acts offences	KCAL	1.0	0.9	0.9	0.8	0.8	0.8	0.7	0.4	0.3	0.2	0.3
Breach of local or other regulations	KELM	1.1	1.1	0.9	0.8	0.9	0.9	0.7	0.5	0.3	0.3	0.2
Intoxicating Liquor Laws: Drunkenness	KELN	41.1	37.7	22.9	25.9	25.7	22.8	20.3	18.1	16.6	16.2	18.1
Other offences	KELO	1.2	1.0	1.0	0.9	0.9	0.7	0.4	0.2	0.3	0.3	0.3
Education Acts	KELP	–	–	–	–	–	–	–	–	–	–	0.1
Game Laws	KELQ	0.2	0.1	0.1	0.1	0.1	0.1	0.1	–	–	–	–
Labour Laws	KELR	–	–	–	–	–	–	–	–	–	–	–
Summary offences of criminal damage and malicious damage	KELS	22.1	23.1	25.1	27.7	27.6	28.3	28.7	26.8	26.7	24.7	27.6
Offences by prostitutes	KELT	4.0	3.6	3.3	3.5	3.5	3.5	2.1	1.3	1.0	1.8	1.3
Railway offences	KELU	0.2	0.2	0.3	0.2	0.1	–	–	–	–	–	–
Revenue Laws	KELV	0.5	0.2	0.2	0.1	0.1	0.1	0.1	–	–	–	–
Vagrancy Acts	KELX	1.5	1.0	1.0	0.6	0.6	1.2	0.8	0.4	0.3	0.3	0.3
Wireless Telegraphy Acts	KELY	–	–	–	–	–	–	–	–	–	–	–
Other summary offences	KELZ	24.9	24.6	24.2	24.7	22.3	37.0	24.1	22.5	21.9	21.0	22.9
All offenders cautioned	KELJ	101.8	98.7	88.7	95.4	92.7	96.2	95.6	88.1	85.9	82.4	91.1
Persons aged 10 to under 18[4]												
Indictable offences												
Violence against the person	KEMB	9.4	9.4	9.4	9.4	9.6	9.5	8.5	8.3	8.7	9.3	11.0
Murder	KCAN	–	–	–	–	–	–	–	–	–	–	–
Manslaughter	KCAO	–	–	–	–	–	–	–	–	–	–	–
Wounding	KCAP	9.4	9.4	9.4	9.4	9.6	9.4	8.4	8.2	8.6	9.2	10.9
Other violence against the person	KCCE	–	–	–	–	–	0.1	0.1	0.1	0.1	0.1	0.1
Sexual offences	KEMC	0.8	0.7	0.8	0.7	0.7	0.6	0.6	0.5	0.5	0.4	0.5
Burglary	KEMD	8.5	8.2	8.5	8.2	7.5	6.7	6.1	5.4	5.3	4.6	4.4
Robbery	KEME	0.5	0.6	0.5	0.6	0.6	0.5	0.5	0.5	0.5	0.4	0.4
Theft and handling stolen goods	KEMF	57.4	48.2	57.4	48.2	40.9	44.0	39.6	36.9	35.2	28.1	28.3
Fraud and forgery	KEMG	1.6	1.5	1.6	1.5	1.4	1.6	1.7	1.5	1.3	1.1	1.0
Criminal damage	KEMH	2.4	2.0	2.4	2.0	1.8	1.7	1.9	2.1	2.3	1.9	2.3
Drug offences	KCCF	8.7	7.9	8.7	7.9	9.7	11.0	9.6	7.9	8.5	9.5	9.6
Other offences	KEMI	1.3	1.3	1.3	1.3	1.5	1.5	1.4	1.3	1.3	1.3	1.4
All offenders cautioned	KEMA	90.6	79.9	90.6	79.9	73.7	77.2	69.8	64.3	63.5	56.6	58.7
Summary offences												
Offences with pedal cycles	KEMK	0.4	0.5	0.4	0.5	0.5	0.4	0.3	0.2	0.1	0.1	0.1
Breach of local or other regulations	KEMM	0.3	0.4	0.3	0.3	0.3	0.3	0.2	0.2	0.1	0.1	0.1
Summary offences of criminal damage and malicious damage	KEMN	11.4	12.5	12.8	13.8	13.5	14.2	14.7	14.4	15.2	12.6	14.3
Railway offences	KEMO	0.1	0.1	0.1	0.1	0.1	–	–	–	–	–	–
Other summary offences	KEMP	15.3	15.6	10.3	10.8	9.1	13.8	9.9	9.2	9.5	8.5	9.2
All offenders cautioned	KEMJ	27.5	29.2	30.0	33.2	30.8	32.5	34.2	33.2	34.5	29.9	33.3

1 See chapter text.
2 Includes 'Companies', etc.
3 A new charging standard was introduced for assault in 1994.
4 Figures for persons aged 10 to under 18 are included in the totals above.

Source: Home Office: 020 8760 8270

11.5 Offenders found guilty of offences: by age and sex[1]
England and Wales
Magistrates' courts and the Crown Court

Thousands

		1993	1994	1995	1996	1997	1998	1999	2000	2001	2002	2003
Males												
Indictable offences												
All ages	KEFA	268.2	273.2	263.2	261.1	276.5	292.9	291.7	276.5	275.5	287.1	283.4
10 and under 15 years	KEFB	5.5	6.9	7.1	6.6	7.1	8.1	8.9	8.7	9.0	8.8	8.0
15 and under 18 years	KEFC	26.2	28.7	30.2	32.5	33.6	35.2	35.1	33.8	34.4	33.7	31.4
18 and under 21 years	KEFD	53.0	50.3	47.4	46.3	48.4	51.8	52.6	49.9	48.2	46.6	43.8
21 years and over	KEFE	183.4	187.4	178.6	175.6	187.3	197.9	195.0	184.0	183.9	198.0	200.2
Summary offences[2]												
All ages	KEFF	892.0	871.0	862.0	903.6	880.9	929.0	886.6	881.0	826.6	866.4	937.1
10 and under 15 years	KEFG	1.8	2.3	2.9	2.8	3.0	3.9	5.1	5.8	6.2	6.1	6.1
15 and under 18 years	KEFH	16.8	17.7	20.5	24.6	25.9	28.5	30.3	32.2	34.5	34.6	35.3
18 and under 21 years	KEFI	85.7	82.9	84.0	88.4	91.0	96.3	94.8	93.0	92.2	94.7	99.9
21 years and over	KEFJ	787.7	768.2	754.6	787.9	761.0	800.3	756.5	750.0	693.6	731.0	795.8
Females												
Indictable offences												
All ages	KEFK	37.8	39.5	37.5	38.0	42.2	47.3	49.0	47.7	47.4	50.0	50.2
10 and under 15 years	KEFL	0.7	1.0	1.0	1.0	1.0	1.4	1.4	1.5	1.6	1.6	1.6
15 and under 18 years	KEFM	3.1	3.8	4.0	4.2	4.6	5.1	5.2	5.2	5.3	5.1	4.9
18 and under 21 years	KEFN	6.3	6.2	5.7	5.7	6.3	7.1	7.6	7.5	7.0	6.9	6.2
21 years and over	KEFO	27.7	28.6	26.8	27.2	30.4	33.7	34.7	33.5	33.5	36.5	37.5
Summary offences[2]												
All ages	KEFP	213.3	211.5	180.5	222.9	174.9	188.3	171.0	208.3	190.2	208.7	210.5
10 and under 15 years	KEFQ	0.2	0.2	0.4	0.4	0.5	0.6	0.8	0.9	0.9	1.1	1.2
15 and under 18 years	KEFR	1.2	1.5	1.8	2.6	3.4	3.8	3.4	3.3	3.6	3.6	4.0
18 and under 21 years	KEFS	10.0	9.6	10.4	12.1	11.1	12.1	10.8	11.8	11.1	11.6	12.6
21 years and over	KEFT	201.9	200.2	167.9	207.9	160.0	171.7	155.4	192.3	174.7	192.4	192.7
Companies, etc												
Indictable offences	KEFU	1.7	1.4	1.5	1.5	1.3	1.5	1.3	1.3	1.3	1.2	1.4
Summary offences[2]	KEFV	12.5	10.9	9.9	10.9	10.0	10.7	8.9	8.8	8.6	7.9	8.6

1 See chapter text.
2 It is estimated that in 1995 there was a shortfall of 75,100 offenders found guilty for certain summary offences.

Source: Home Office: 020 8760 8270

11.6 Persons cautioned by the police: by age and sex[1]
England and Wales

Thousands

		1993	1994	1995	1996	1997	1998	1999	2000	2001	2002	2003
Males												
Indictable offences												
All ages	KEGA	153.6	153.6	149.3	142.6	143.3	142.9	126.1	109.7	103.8	104.4	109.8
10 and under 15 years	KEGB	31.4	32.3	29.2	25.1	22.9	23.7	22.0	20.3	19.7	16.7	16.9
15 and under 18 years	KEGC	37.1	35.5	35.3	33.0	32.0	32.0	28.7	25.0	24.5	23.3	24.1
18 and under 21 years	KEGD	24.5	25.0	24.8	24.3	25.2	25.7	22.7	20.1	18.5	18.9	19.4
21 years and over	KEGE	60.6	60.7	60.0	60.2	63.2	61.5	52.7	44.3	41.2	45.6	49.4
Summary offences												
All ages	KEGF	86.3	83.6	73.8	79.2	75.7	76.9	76.1	69.6	68.0	63.8	70.9
10 and under 15 years	KEGG	9.4	10.5	10.1	10.3	9.9	10.6	11.7	12.0	12.7	10.3	10.9
15 and under 18 years	KEGH	14.4	14.7	15.4	18.0	16.1	16.1	16.1	14.9	15.2	13.3	15.1
18 and under 21 years	KEGI	11.4	11.3	11.1	13.0	12.9	13.2	13.0	11.9	11.0	11.0	12.4
21 years and over	KEGJ	51.0	47.0	37.1	37.9	36.9	37.0	35.3	30.9	29.0	29.2	32.5
Females												
Indictable offences												
All ages	KEGK	55.9	56.2	53.3	48.2	46.0	48.8	44.5	41.2	40.1	38.5	41.0
10 and under 15 years	KEGL	12.8	15.2	14.0	10.8	9.2	11.1	9.8	10.0	10.1	8.4	8.6
15 and under 18 years	KEGM	12.8	12.4	12.2	10.9	9.5	10.3	9.3	9.0	9.3	8.3	9.1
18 and under 21 years	KEGN	6.7	6.1	6.0	5.6	5.7	5.9	5.7	5.2	4.9	4.8	4.9
21 years and over	KEGO	23.6	22.4	21.1	20.9	21.5	21.4	19.6	17.0	15.9	17.0	18.4
Summary offences												
All ages	KEGP	18.5	15.1	14.8	16.2	17.0	19.2	9.4	18.5	18.0	18.6	20.2
10 and under 15 years	KEGQ	1.3	1.5	1.7	1.8	1.7	2.1	2.5	2.8	2.9	2.7	3.0
15 and under 18 years	KEGR	2.3	2.5	2.7	3.2	3.2	3.7	3.9	3.7	3.8	3.6	4.3
18 and under 21 years	KEGS	2.1	1.9	1.9	2.1	2.3	2.6	2.7	2.5	2.3	2.4	2.7
21 years and over	KEGT	9.8	9.2	8.6	9.1	9.9	10.8	10.3	9.6	9.0	9.8	10.2

1 See chapter text.

Source: Home Office: 020 8760 8270

11.7 Sentence or order passed on offenders sentenced for indictable offences: by sex[1]
England and Wales
Magistrates' courts and the Crown Court

Percentages and thousands

		1993	1994	1995	1996	1997	1998	1999	2000	2001	2002	2003
Males												
Sentence or order												
Absolute discharge	KEJB	0.9	0.8	0.8	0.8	0.7	0.7	0.6	0.6	0.6	0.8	0.9
Conditional discharge	KEJC	18.6	17.4	16.2	15.6	15.5	15.3	15.0	14.1	13.4	12.4	13.0
Fine	KEJF	33.8	31.8	30.0	28.6	28.2	28.4	27.7	25.7	24.5	23.9	24.0
Community rehabilitation order	KEJD	9.3	10.2	10.0	9.9	10.0	10.0	10.1	10.1	10.7	10.6	10.1
Supervision order	KEJE	2.0	2.4	2.7	2.9	2.7	2.7	2.7	2.4	2.3	2.1	1.8
Community punishment order	KEJG	11.4	11.1	10.6	9.9	9.5	9.3	9.3	9.5	9.0	8.6	8.3
Attendance centre order	KEJH	1.9	2.0	2.0	1.9	1.8	1.7	1.8	1.5	1.2	0.7	0.6
Community punishment and rehabilitation order	KIJW	2.1	2.7	3.0	3.5	3.7	3.8	3.7	3.6	2.6	2.6	2.6
Curfew order	LUJP	..	..	..	0.1	0.1	0.2	0.3	0.5	0.7	1.1	1.6
Reparation order	SNFI	..	..	..	..	..	..	..	0.7	1.3	0.8	0.4
Action plan order	SNFJ	..	..	..	..	..	..	..	0.9	1.7	1.1	0.7
Drug treatment and testing order	SNFK	..	..	..	..	..	..	..	0.1	1.2	1.4	1.9
Referral order	SNFL	..	..	..	..	..	..	..	..	..	3.0	4.0
Fully suspended	KEJL	0.9	0.7	0.7	0.8	0.8	0.7	0.6	0.7	0.6	0.5	0.5
Imprisonment												
Sec 90-92	LUJQ	0.1	0.1	0.1	0.2	0.3	0.2	0.2	0.2	0.2	0.2	0.2
Detention and training order	LUJR	..	..	..	..	..	..	..	1.4	1.9	1.8	1.5
Young offender institution	KEJK	0.8	4.9	5.6	6.1	6.1	6.0	6.2	5.2	4.5	4.2	3.6
Unsuspended	KEJM	12.0	13.6	16.0	17.2	17.9	18.2	18.7	19.9	20.0	20.9	20.6
Other sentence or order	KEJN	2.5	2.3	2.2	2.4	3.0	2.6	3.1	3.1	3.4	3.3	3.5
Total number of offenders (thousands) = 100 per cent	KEJA	267.5	272.6	262.9	260.8	275.4	292.4	291.3	277.1	274.6	285.6	282.3
Females												
Sentence or order												
Absolute discharge	KEKB	0.9	0.9	0.8	0.9	0.8	0.7	0.7	0.6	0.6	0.9	1.0
Conditional discharge	KEKC	35.4	34.4	32.4	30.6	29.4	28.7	26.9	24.9	23.9	22.0	22.5
Fine	KEKF	29.2	25.6	24.1	22.5	21.8	21.3	20.8	20.1	18.6	17.9	18.5
Community rehabilitation order	KEKD	15.4	17.5	18.0	19.0	19.1	19.1	19.4	19.6	19.1	19.2	17.0
Supervision order	KEKE	1.8	2.4	2.7	2.9	2.9	3.1	2.9	2.8	2.7	2.1	2.1
Community punishment order	KEKG	6.1	6.4	6.6	6.5	6.5	6.5	7.1	7.5	7.3	6.8	6.6
Attendance centre order	KEKH	0.5	0.8	1.0	1.0	1.0	0.9	0.9	0.8	0.6	0.4	0.3
Community punishment and rehabilitation order	KIJX	1.4	2.1	2.4	3.0	3.2	3.4	3.3	3.0	2.1	2.1	1.8
Curfew order	LUJT	..	..	..	–	0.1	0.1	0.3	0.4	0.6	0.8	1.4
Reparation order	SNFX	..	..	..	..	..	..	..	0.8	1.6	0.8	0.4
Action plan order	SNFZ	..	..	..	..	..	..	..	1.0	2.0	1.2	0.8
Drug treatment and testing order	SNGA	..	..	..	..	..	..	..	0.1	1.4	1.7	2.4
Referral order	SNGB	..	..	..	..	..	..	..	..	..	3.9	5.1
Fully suspended	KEKL	1.2	1.1	1.4	1.5	1.6	1.5	1.3	1.3	1.2	1.1	1.0
Imprisonment												
Sec 90-92	LUJU	–	–	0.1	0.1	0.1	..	0.1	0.1	0.1	0.1	0.1
Detention and training order	LUJV	..	..	..	..	..	..	..	0.6	0.8	0.8	0.7
Young offender institution	KEKK	1.1	1.1	1.5	1.8	1.9	2.2	2.4	2.2	2.0	1.9	1.7
Unsuspended	KEKM	5.0	5.9	7.4	8.4	9.4	10.0	11.0	11.5	12.1	12.7	12.8
Other sentence or order	KEKN	1.9	1.7	1.8	2.0	2.2	2.5	3.0	2.9	3.5	3.4	3.8
Total number of offenders (thousands) = 100 per cent	KEKA	37.7	39.5	37.5	38.0	42.1	47.2	49.0	47.8	47.3	49.9	50.2

1 See chapter text.

Source: Home Office: 020 8760 8270

11.8 Offenders sentenced to immediate custody for standard list offences: by sex and number of previous convictions[1]

England and Wales

Percentages[2] and numbers

Year and sex	Nil	1 - 2	3 - 6	7 - 10	11 and over	Total sentenced for standard list offences	Total sentenced to custody for all offences
1998							
Males	20	14	20	15	30	91 800	94 000
Females	37	16	18	10	18	6 400	6 600
Total	22	14	20	15	29	98 200	100 600
1999							
Males	32	22	19	10	17	95 500	97 800
Females	49	23	15	6	7	7 300	7 500
Total	34	22	19	9	16	102 800	105 300
2000							
Males	30	17	14	11	28	95 700	98 300
Females	40	17	15	10	17	7 700	7 900
Total	31	17	14	11	27	103 400	106 200
2001							
Males	22	15	17	13	33	95 905	98 200
Females	33	15	18	14	20	7 903	8 100
Total	23	15	17	13	32	103 808	106 300
2002							
Males	14	12	19	16	39	100 389	102 800
Females	22	12	23	17	26	8 675	8 800
Total	14	12	19	16	38	109 064	111 600

1 See chapter text. Counting one conviction per court appearance.

2 The percentages are based on samples of 7 562, 6 096, 17 771, 6 863 and 7231 males and 459, 426, 1 361, 603 and 618 females in the years 1998, 1999, 2000, 2001 and 2002 respectively. Percentages are rounded and therefore may not add to 100.

Source: Home Office: 020 7217 1941

11.9 Population in Prison Service establishments under sentence: by sex and number of previous convictions[1,2]

England and Wales, on 30 June each year:

Percentages[3] and numbers

Year and sex	Previous convictions not found[3]	Nil	1 - 2	3 - 6	7 - 10	11 and over	Number of prisoners[4]
1998							
Males	5	16	14	19	15	31	49 793
Females	11	35	17	17	8	13	2 366
Total	5	17	14	19	14	30	52 159
1999							
Males	8	12	15	21	15	28	47 989
Females	16	27	18	17	9	13	2 486
Total	9	13	15	21	15	27	50 475
2000							
Males	9	14	15	19	14	29	50 437
Females	10	32	15	17	10	14	2 633
Total	9	15	15	19	14	28	53 070
2001							
Males	9	15	13	19	14	29	51 623
Females	13	33	15	16	10	13	2 909
Total	9	16	14	19	13	28	54 532
2002							
Males	9	15	13	18	14	30	53 971
Females	12	36	13	16	9	13	3 302
Total	9	17	13	18	14	29	57 273

1 Excludes fine defaulters.

2 In some cases it was not possible to find details on previous convictions. This can happen when a prisoner is not sentenced for a standard list offence and has no previous record for such offences. See chapter text.

3 The percentages are based on samples of 12 303, 12 341, 12 833, 13225 and 13 814 males in 1998, 1999, 2000, 2001 and 2002 respectively. All females are sampled. Percentages are rounded and therefore may not add to 100.

4 These numbers are based on a weighted sample and may therefore differ slightly from the exact from the exact figures published elsewhere.

Source: Home Office: 020 7217 1941

11.10 Receptions and average population in custody
England and Wales

Numbers

		1993	1994	1995	1996	1997	1998	1999	2000	2001	2002	2003
Receptions												
Type of inmate:												
Untried	KEDA	53 565	57 079	55 287	58 888	62 066	64 697	64 572	54 892	53 467	58 708	58 696
Convicted, unsentenced	KEDB	30 098	34 563	32 039	34 987	36 424	43 387	45 893	43 889	46 851	53 301	53 246
Sentenced	KEDE	72 966	83 657	89 173	82 861	87 168	91 282	93 965	93 671	91 978	94 807	93 495
Immediate custodial sentence	KEDF	50 563	61 188	69 016	74 306	80 832	85 908	90 238	91 195	90 523	93 615	92 245
Young offenders	KEDG	13 205	14 956	16 244	17 593	18 743	19 599	21 020	21 333	20 969	20 236	18 179
Up to 12 months	KEDH	8 867	10 520	11 308	11 285	11 867	12 942	14 330	14 639	14 234	12 891	11 850
12 months up to 4 years	KEDJ	3 815	3 921	4 393	5 497	5 949	5 921	5 904	5 877	5 856	6 355	5 412
4 years up to and including life	KEDL	523	515	543	811	927	736	786	817	879	990	917
Adults	KFBO	37 358	46 232	52 772	56 713	62 089	66 309	69 218	69 862	69 554	73 379	74 066
Up to 12 months	KEDV	21 050	28 197	33 053	34 864	38 702	42 513	45 662	46 759	46 146	47 870	48 962
12 months up to 4 years	KEDW	12 540	14 146	15 328	16 560	17 546	18 100	17 751	17 290	17 116	18 313	17 968
4 years up to and including life	KEDX	3 768	3 889	4 391	5 289	5 841	5 696	5 805	5 813	6 292	7 196	7 136
Committed in default of payment												
of a fine	KEDY	22 403	22 469	20 157	8 555	6 336	5 374	3 727	2 476	1 455	1 192	1 250
Young offenders	KEEA	3 353	3 268	2 846	885	555	568	366	216	138	110	116
Adults	KAFQ	19 050	19 201	17 311	7 670	5 781	4 806	3 361	2 260	1 317	1 082	1 134
Non-criminal prisoners	KEDM	5 073	4 507	3 789	3 128	3 204	3 290	3 271	3 153	4 630	2 674	3 142
Immigration Act 1971	KEDN	1 837	1 641	1 825	1 857	2 122	2 348	2 443	2 455	4 035	2 093	2 457
Others	KEDO	3 236	2 866	1 964	1 271	1 082	942	828	698	595	581	685
Average population												
Total in custody	KEDP	44 565	48 794	51 047	55 281	61 114	65 298	64 771	64 602	66 301	70 861	73 038
Total in prison service												
establishments	KFBQ	44 551	48 621	50 962	55 281	61 114	65 298	64 771	64 602	66 301	70 778	73 038
Police cells[1]	KFBN	14	173	85	–	–	–	–	–	–	83	–
Untried	KEDQ	7 960	9 047	8 352	8 374	8 453	8 157	7 947	7 098	6 924	7 727	7 862
Convicted, unsentenced	KEDR	2 700	3 181	2 954	3 238	3 678	4 411	4 571	4 177	4 314	5 064	5 060
Remanded for medical												
examination	KEDS	12	15	9	6	8	9	8	..	40	..	..
Others	KEDT	2 688	3 166	2 945	3 232	3 670	4 402	4 563	..	4 274	..	..
Sentenced	KEDU	33 317	35 753	39 040	43 043	48 413	52 176	51 691	52 685	54 051	57 222	59 007
Immediate custodial sentence	KFBR	32 825	35 308	38 636	42 863	48 272	52 045	51 596	52 620	54 006	57 184	58 959
Young offenders	KFBS	5 054	5 258	5 752	6 700	7 821	8 490	8 335	8 435	8 559	8 777	8 422
Up to 12 months[2]	KFBU	2 671	2 736	1 721	1 788	1 820	1 964	1 997	2 414	2 330	2 051	1 899
12 months up to 4 years[3]	KFBV	1 800	1 902	2 987	3 748	4 466	4 795	4 674	4 517	4 562	4 867	4 525
4 years up to and including life	KFBW	583	620	1 042	1 164	1 534	1 730	1 665	1 504	1 667	1 860	1 997
Adults	KFCO	27 771	30 050	32 902	36 162	40 451	43 555	43 261	44 186	45 447	48 408	50 536
Up to 12 months[2]	KFCP	7 054	8 051	4 930	5 136	5 428	5 898	5 635	6 053	5 904	5 755	6 000
12 months up to 4 years[3]	KFCQ	8 445	9 164	11 976	13 383	15 073	16 079	15 048	15 161	15 525	16 845	16 664
4 years up to and including life	KFCR	12 272	12 835	15 998	17 644	19 950	21 580	22 578	22 971	24 021	25 808	27 871
Committed in default of payment												
of a fine	KFCS	492	446	403	180	141	131	95	64	45	37	48
Young offenders	KFEW	77	62	54	22	13	15	9	4	6	2	3
Adults	KFEX	415	384	349	158	128	116	86	60	39	35	45
Non-criminal prisoners	KEEB	574	640	615	626	571	554	558	641	1 012	847	1 107
Immigration Act 1971	KEEC	431	487	483	516	485	476	485	576	955	777	995
Others	KEED	143	153	132	111	87	78	73	63	57	70	112

1 Mostly untried prisoners.
2 Figures before 1995 relate to sentence length defined as 'up to 18 months'.
3 Figures before 1995 relate to sentence length defined as '18 months up to 4 years'.

Source: Home Office: 020 7217 5567

11.11 Prison population serving sentences: by age and offence[1]
England and Wales

	15 - 17	18 - 20	21 - 24	25 - 29	30 - 39	40 - 49	50 - 59	60 and over	Total
At 30 June 1998									
Offences									
Males									
Total	1 627	5 807	8 780	10 590	14 109	5 485	2 608	896	49 902
Violence against the person	235	1 028	1 670	2 215	3 239	1 345	594	204	10 530
Sexual offences	51	140	224	560	1 366	1 113	872	455	4 781
Burglary	432	1 502	2 256	2 179	1 799	298	65	10	8 541
Robbery	449	1 244	1 319	1 427	1 587	350	61	15	6 452
Theft, handling, fraud & forgery	190	556	906	1 071	1 535	587	300	48	5 193
Drugs offences	38	308	944	1 616	2 569	1 092	441	95	7 103
Other offences	137	690	1 087	1 132	1 461	509	215	46	5 277
Offence not known	95	339	374	390	553	191	60	23	2 025
Females									
Total	62	210	425	501	709	332	116	12	2 367
Violence against the person	11	44	68	80	116	68	27	6	420
Sexual offences	1	1	1	2	5	5	1	-	16
Burglary	6	17	27	32	28	6	2	-	118
Robbery	24	45	33	36	28	8	3	-	177
Theft, handling, fraud & forgery	6	36	97	107	169	72	26	1	514
Drugs offences	3	32	134	181	267	131	44	2	794
Other offences	8	22	42	41	65	30	8	2	218
Offences not known	3	13	23	22	31	12	5	1	110
At 30 June 1999									
Offences									
Males									
Total	1 643	5 633	8 245	10 080	14 072	5 552	2 678	1 053	48 956
Violence against the person	250	1 070	1 548	2 033	3 260	1 428	608	238	10 435
Sexual offences	48	99	236	485	1 448	1 133	935	546	4 930
Burglary	447	1 441	2 207	2 230	1 899	322	73	7	8 626
Robbery	410	1 126	1 384	1 272	1 556	353	58	16	6 175
Theft, handling, fraud and forgery	208	585	886	1 065	1 418	529	279	57	5 027
Drugs offences	36	338	866	1 614	2 720	1 132	476	121	7 303
Other offences	185	742	968	1 120	1 422	541	197	49	5 224
Offence not known	59	232	150	261	349	114	52	19	1 236
Females									
Total	67	224	427	491	798	301	108	20	2 436
Violence against the person	17	65	50	77	125	63	25	7	429
Sexual offences	-	2	1	-	5	7	1	1	17
Burglary	7	27	37	38	41	6	2	-	158
Robbery	15	24	36	33	41	6	3	-	158
Theft, handling, fraud and forgery	11	33	113	99	159	58	24	5	502
Drugs offences	2	50	131	184	340	129	35	4	875
Other offences	13	9	45	43	68	26	16	-	220
Offence not known	2	14	14	17	19	6	2	3	77
At 30 June 2000									
Offences									
Males									
Total	1 788	5 911	8 691	10 060	14 454	5 720	2 749	1 140	50 514
Violence against the person	256	1 092	1 658	1 964	3 440	1 480	690	226	10 807
Sexual offences	58	139	261	460	1 424	1 157	937	635	5 070
Burglary	453	1 426	2 165	2 291	2 040	359	77	13	8 824
Robbery	399	1 087	1 343	1 315	1 556	387	57	14	6 158
Theft, handling, fraud and forgery	312	798	1 006	1 118	1 419	483	233	53	5 422
Drugs offences	43	405	949	1 591	2 765	1 188	480	106	7 526
Other offences	225	818	1 180	1 161	1 616	598	236	76	5 909
Offence not known	43	148	131	160	194	67	38	16	797
Females									
Total	65	266	457	563	863	335	102	15	2 666
Violence against the person	22	46	56	71	122	62	26	6	410
Sexual offences	-	1	1	1	7	5	2	2	20
Burglary	10	24	33	45	40	5	1	-	158
Robbery	13	43	39	39	50	10	1	-	195
Theft, handling, fraud and forgery	7	61	117	154	196	74	24	4	638
Drugs offences	6	58	151	200	354	141	34	2	947
Other offences	5	26	47	40	70	31	9	1	229
Offence not known	2	7	13	12	23	7	5	-	69

	15 - 17	18 - 20	21 - 24	25 - 29	30 - 39	40 - 49	50 - 59	60 and over	Total
At 30 June 2001									
Offences									
Males									
Total	1 918	5 864	9 051	9 964	14 538	6 044	2 723	1 211	51 313
Violence against the person	343	1 180	1 810	1 997	3 432	1 631	702	252	11 347
Sexual offences	53	145	265	406	1 368	1 172	953	686	5 048
Burglary	383	1 176	2 039	2 190	2 158	389	61	15	8 410
Robbery	429	1 191	1 436	1 309	1 652	360	60	12	6 449
Theft, handling, fraud & forgery	318	742	1 086	1 080	1 362	510	217	55	5 370
Drugs offences	47	423	1 126	1 686	2 828	1 278	479	113	7 980
Other offences	285	840	1 146	1 163	1 541	616	213	66	5 868
Offence not known	61	165	143	133	196	90	40	13	841
Females									
Total	63	305	493	589	906	406	119	18	2 899
Violence against the person	18	63	55	72	123	81	24	6	441
Sexual offences	-	2	1	1	7	10	2	2	25
Burglary	9	29	44	29	36	5	2	-	153
Robbery	10	53	63	54	55	13	1	-	248
Theft, handling, fraud & forgery	12	53	100	155	178	64	29	4	594
Drugs offences	3	72	183	215	411	193	49	4	1 130
Other offences	8	27	40	50	82	32	9	2	249
Offence not known	3	7	8	14	14	9	4	-	59
At 30 June 2002									
Offences									
Males									
Total	1 986	5 821	9 722	10 196	15 415	6 630	2 832	1 365	53 967
Violence against the person	336	1 187	1 942	1 937	3 490	1 769	749	267	11 678
Sexual offences	58	167	262	406	1 347	1 241	996	794	5 270
Burglary	396	1 130	2 159	2 331	2 379	448	58	15	8 917
Robbery	503	1 285	1 647	1 390	1 865	443	66	10	7 208
Theft, handling, fraud and forgery	302	570	1 055	1 105	1 416	480	213	62	5 203
Drugs offences	43	431	1 255	1 763	3 142	1 496	495	129	8 754
Other offences	275	875	1 195	1 103	1 555	640	205	73	5 921
Offence not known	72	174	207	162	222	113	50	15	1 016
Females									
Total	103	356	596	662	1 030	439	134	19	3 339
Violence against the person	27	67	73	85	163	84	33	6	538
Sexual offences	-	1	-	1	11	6	3	1	23
Burglary	9	37	58	54	68	12	1	-	239
Robbery	19	63	89	65	60	14	3	1	314
Theft, handling, fraud and forgery	22	56	103	139	168	68	20	4	581
Drugs offences	8	94	206	256	474	216	60	6	1 319
Other offences	12	32	52	50	73	34	9	1	262
Offence not known	6	7	16	13	13	5	4	-	63
At 30 June 2003									
Offences									
Males									
Total	1 724	5 740	10 112	10 441	16 304	7 252	2 975	1 413	55 962
Violence against the person	310	1 257	2 112	2 068	3 733	1 932	780	290	12 482
Sexual offences	42	183	310	390	1 376	1 353	1 023	838	5 514
Burglary	289	919	2 003	2 204	2 555	527	71	11	8 579
Robbery	436	1 370	1 910	1 546	2 022	514	69	12	7 879
Theft, handling, fraud & forgery	291	543	1 020	1 060	1 437	472	201	45	5 069
Drugs offences	43	452	1 256	1 791	3 215	1 579	528	127	8 993
Other offences	271	884	1 329	1 218	1 760	787	263	69	6 581
Offence not known	42	133	172	164	205	89	40	21	865
Females									
Total	57	305	670	702	1 100	492	123	28	3 477
Violence against the person	10	61	91	66	155	82	32	7	506
Sexual offences	-	-	2	1	11	7	3	2	26
Burglary	1	24	64	60	77	12	2	-	240
Robbery	21	60	105	100	93	24	4	-	407
Theft, handling, fraud & forgery	10	56	117	128	199	70	18	11	609
Drugs offences	6	73	226	271	453	253	54	8	1 343
Other offences	7	27	58	66	108	39	6	-	311
Offence not known	2	3	8	10	5	4	4	-	36

1 Includes persons committed in default of payment of a fine.

Source: Home Office: 020 7217 5567

11.12 Expenditure on prisons
England and Wales

Operating cost and total capital employed, years ending 31 March

£ thousand

		1997 /98	1998 /99	1999 /00	2000 /01	2001 /02	2002 /03	2003 /04
Expenditure								
Staff costs	KWUV	939 700	995 200	1 044 700	1 094 500	1 138 400	1 259 500	1 364 200
Accommodation costs	KXCO	116 200	163 400	149 300	153 700	193 100	200 000	194 000
Other operating costs	KXCP	472 600	538 800	584 300	654 200	706 100	756 200	653 000
Depreciation	KXCQ	160 200	146 100	115 700	117 200	128 100	132 600	129 600
Cost of capital	KXCR	231 300	262 500	254 900	259 900	284 900	292 700	164 400
Total expenditure	KXCS	1 920 000	2 106 000	2 148 900	2 279 500	2 450 600	2 641 000	2 505 200
Income								
Contributions from industries	KXCT	−7 900	−8 300	−10 400	−10 600	−11 600	−10 100	−11 000
Other operating income	KXCU	−8 500	−8 500	−9 600	−10 300	−13 100	−15 500	−21 000
Income from other Government Departments[1]	GDPM	..	..	..	−123 900	−180 600	−210 200	−368 000
Total income	KXCV	−16 400	−16 800	−20 000	−144 800	−205 300	−235 800	−400 000
Net operating costs	KXCW	1 903 600	2 089 200	2 128 900	2 134 700	2 245 300	2 405 200	2 105 200
Total capital employed	KXCX	4 116 900	4 345 100	4 382 600	4 726 200	4 859 600	4 821 500	5 228 600

1 Income from the Youth Justice Board (a non-departmental public body of the Home Office) for the provision of juvenile custody within the Prison Service and Department for Education and Skills for the provision of education services.

Source: Home Office: 020 7217 5567

11.13 Crimes and offences recorded by the police: by crime group[1]
Scotland

Thousands

		1993	1994	1995	1996	1997	1998	1999	2000	2001	2002	2003
Non-sexual crimes of violence												
against the person	BEBC	14.3	14.5	14.7	14.7	13.2	14.3	15.5	15.2	15.1	16.5	15.2
Serious assault, etc	KAFS	6.5	6.7	6.9	7.0	6.1	6.6	7.2	7.0	7.3	7.6	7.5
Robbery	KAFU	5.6	5.3	5.3	5.3	4.5	5.0	5.1	4.4	4.2	4.9	4.2
Other	KAFV	2.1	2.5	2.4	2.5	2.6	2.8	3.3	3.8	3.6	3.9	3.5
Crimes involving indecency	BEBD	6.0	6.0	5.5	5.7	7.1	7.4	6.0	5.8	6.0	6.6	6.6
Rape and attempted rape[2]	OXBQ	0.5	0.6	0.6	0.6	0.7	0.8	0.8	0.7	0.8	0.9	1.0
Indecent assault[2]	OXBR	1.1	1.0	1.0	1.1	1.2	1.4	1.2	1.1	1.2	1.3	1.4
Lewd and indecent behaviour	KAFY	2.7	2.7	2.4	2.5	3.0	3.0	2.4	2.3	2.4	2.7	2.5
Other	KAFZ	1.7	1.7	1.5	1.5	2.2	2.3	1.7	1.6	1.7	1.6	1.6
Crimes involving dishonesty	BEBE	374.9	350.3	321.2	295.4	267.2	275.4	276.2	260.9	239.9	235.7	210.9
Housebreaking	KAGB	97.8	88.4	74.2	64.5	55.5	56.6	53.8	48.7	44.9	43.8	36.7
Theft by opening lockfast places	KAGC	84.8	74.9	66.5	60.5	51.1	51.8	50.2	45.0	39.7	40.0	34.7
Theft of a motor vehicle	KAGD	42.8	42.0	37.5	34.2	28.6	28.4	29.8	26.2	23.2	22.5	17.8
Shoplifting	KAGE	26.7	26.6	28.0	26.9	26.3	29.6	32.0	32.3	31.6	29.5	27.7
Other theft	KAGF	93.3	88.9	87.7	82.6	79.6	80.1	81.1	78.1	74.7	75.0	71.9
Fraud	KAGG	19.1	17.7	17.1	16.1	15.7	18.6	18.6	21.2	17.4	16.6	15.1
Other	KAGH	10.3	12.0	10.2	10.8	10.3	10.2	10.6	9.4	8.4	8.2	6.9
Fire-raising, vandalism, etc	BEBF	84.2	88.5	86.5	89.0	81.0	79.2	79.6	83.2	94.9	95.5	100.0
Fire-raising	KAGJ	4.1	3.6	3.3	3.3	2.8	2.5	2.3	2.4	2.8	3.6	4.0
Vandalism, etc	KAGK	80.1	85.0	83.2	85.7	78.2	76.6	77.2	80.8	92.2	91.8	96.0
Other crimes	BEBG	37.8	40.7	47.7	47.1	52.1	55.2	58.4	58.1	65.2	72.9	74.3
Crimes against public justice	KAGM	14.5	16.0	16.4	16.1	16.6	16.9	18.5	18.4	20.3	22.7	24.8
Handling offensive weapons[3]	KAFT	5.2	5.3	6.5	6.8	6.0	6.7	7.9	8.2	8.7	9.7	8.9
Drugs	KAGN	18.0	19.3	24.8	24.0	29.4	31.5	31.9	31.4	36.2	40.4	40.5
Other	KAGO	0.2	0.2	0.2	0.1	0.1	0.1	0.1	0.1	0.1	0.1	0.2
Total crimes	KAGQ	517.2	500.1	475.7	452.0	420.6	431.6	435.7	423.2	421.1	427.0	407.0
Miscellaneous offences	BEBH	126.6	133.2	134.4	146.1	155.9	153.7	151.0	153.8	162.5	167.5	176.7
Petty assault	KAGS	41.3	45.1	46.6	47.6	50.1	51.0	54.0	54.8	54.9	54.7	55.6
Breach of the peace	KAGT	61.4	65.5	66.1	70.8	73.1	71.7	71.0	70.0	72.6	74.2	76.7
Drunkenness	KAGU	10.1	10.3	9.7	9.6	9.7	8.5	7.8	7.8	7.9	7.1	7.5
Other	KAGV	13.7	12.3	11.9	18.0	23.1	22.6	18.2	21.3	27.1	31.6	36.8
Motor vehicle offences	BEBI	315.1	330.7	317.5	305.9	331.0	362.1	353.4	345.8	362.1	341.3	409.5
Dangerous and careless driving	KAGX	20.0	21.1	18.7	17.3	16.3	15.8	14.0	12.3	12.0	12.7	12.3
Drunk driving	KAGY	10.9	10.8	10.7	11.8	11.2	10.6	10.8	10.7	11.4	11.8	11.6
Speeding	KAGZ	85.4	85.8	85.1	82.4	91.9	115.5	125.3	116.8	123.2	111.8	180.9
Unlawful use of a motor vehicle	KAHA	85.8	88.7	83.4	79.1	79.1	75.5	77.8	85.2	88.1	91.1	93.3
Vehicle defect offences	KAHB	51.4	56.9	56.3	53.5	60.1	63.6	52.9	48.3	47.3	46.3	41.2
Other	KAHC	61.7	67.4	63.2	61.8	72.3	81.2	72.5	72.5	80.1	67.7	70.2
Total offences	KAHD	441.7	463.9	451.9	452.0	486.9	515.8	504.5	499.6	524.6	508.9	586.2
Total crimes and offences	BEBB	959.0	964.0	927.6	903.9	907.5	947.3	940.2	922.8	945.7	935.9	993.1

1 See chapter text.
2 The category of 'sexual assault' was split into 'rape and attempted rape' and 'indecent assault' with effect from 2001, allowing the Police Statutory Performance Indicator of serious violent crime to be readily calculated. The statutory Performance Indicator of serious violent crime includes all
3 'Handling offensive weapons' used to be included in the group 'non-sexual crimes of violence'.

Source: The Scottish Executive Justice Department: 0131 244 2225

11.14 Persons proceeded against: by crime group[1]
Scotland

		1992	1993	1994	1995	1996	1997	1998	1999	2000	2001	2002[2]
Non-sexual crimes of violence	KEHC	1 979	2 022	1 867	1 786	2 008	2 028	1 942	2 079	1 958	2 011	2 189
Homicide	KEHD	111	114	94	111	133	108	88	106	95	99	86
Serious assault, etc	KEHE	775	856	831	809	944	1 037	1 004	1 085	1 052	1 109	1 276
Robbery	KEHG	740	785	737	664	720	665	627	683	623	623	609
Other violence	KEHH	353	267	205	202	211	218	223	205	188	180	218
Crimes of indecency	KEHI	1 403	1 509	1 427	1 306	979	1 200	1 327	910	657	617	559
Rape and attempted rape	HFVU	64	72	54	56	55	52	62	51	42	66	37
Sexual assault	KEHJ	77	79	82	79	69	84	85	82	66	52	57
Lewd and libidinous practices	KEHK	303	309	333	291	300	334	324	316	252	288	290
Other indecency	KEHL	959	1 049	958	880	555	730	856	461	297	211	175
Crimes of dishonesty	KEHM	33 696	31 034	30 021	28 197	26 965	25 666	24 728	23 293	20 866	21 446	21 806
Housebreaking	KEHN	5 830	5 219	5 064	4 470	3 838	3 275	2 978	3 021	2 686	2 711	2 736
Theft by opening lockfast places	KEHO	2 889	2 817	2 844	2 458	2 327	2 092	1 802	1 658	1 497	1 501	1 472
Theft of motor vehicle	KEHP	2 633	2 399	2 492	2 411	2 357	2 146	1 853	1 642	1 444	1 339	1 338
Shoplifting	KEHQ	7 697	7 437	6 633	6 510	7 080	7 194	7 611	7 649	7 419	8 123	8 931
Other theft	KEHR	8 129	7 129	6 427	6 318	6 052	5 960	5 701	5 260	4 498	4 321	3 965
Fraud	KEHS	2 163	2 188	2 511	2 307	2 011	2 010	1 973	1 635	1 458	1 490	1 450
Other dishonesty	KEHT	4 355	3 845	4 050	3 723	3 300	2 989	2 810	2 428	1 864	1 961	1 914
Fire-raising, vandalism, etc	KEHU	5 568	4 896	4 781	4 878	5 176	4 951	4 645	4 115	3 949	4 017	4 129
Fire-raising	KEHV	164	146	172	142	144	119	122	108	103	120	135
Vandalism, etc	KEHW	5 404	4 750	4 609	4 736	5 032	4 832	4 523	4 007	3 846	3 897	3 994
Other crime	KEHX	11 576	12 841	13 817	14 730	15 389	14 609	13 762	13 165	12 520	13 762	13 363
Crime against public justice	KFBK	5 939	6 592	6 913	7 316	6 935	5 346	4 738	4 622	4 845	5 317	4 998
Handling offensive weapons[3]	KEHF	1 494	1 552	1 491	1 782	2 240	2 194	2 062	2 080	2 238	2 695	2 589
Drugs offences	KFBL	4 114	4 675	5 386	5 599	6 183	7 027	6 929	6 438	5 424	5 731	5 763
Other	KFBM	29	22	27	33	31	42	33	25	13	19	13
Total crimes	KEHB	54 222	52 302	51 913	50 897	50 517	48 454	46 404	43 562	39 950	41 853	42 046
Miscellaneous offences	KEHZ	54 553	48 762	44 011	45 810	46 816	45 502	41 582	34 502	33 440	34 404	35 996
Common assault	KEIA	12 036	11 765	11 404	11 956	12 330	12 455	11 952	10 886	10 241	10 845	11 294
Breach of the peace	KEIB	18 353	17 456	16 775	17 989	19 411	19 416	18 109	14 398	13 226	13 775	14 124
Drunkenness	KEIC	2 161	1 735	1 429	1 313	1 103	928	725	478	434	371	384
Breach of social work orders	HFVT	2 162	2 197	2 385	2 783	3 176	3 554	4 180	4 564	4 690	4 446	4 974
Other miscellaneous offences	KEID	19 841	15 609	12 018	11 769	10 796	9 149	6 616	4 176	4 849	4 967	5 220
Motor vehicle offences	KEIE	68 708	61 742	63 254	60 000	55 754	56 552	51 894	49 494	44 757	44 032	46 908
Dangerous and careless driving	KEIF	6 673	5 426	4 839	4 962	4 847	4 732	3 908	3 369	2 816	3 217	3 420
Drunk driving	KEIG	8 113	7 632	7 426	7 595	8 065	8 519	7 287	6 899	6 691	6 792	8 856
Speeding[2]	KEIH	19 526	15 558	16 693	15 125	12 672	12 213	12 536	14 262	11 315	9 977	9 636
Unlawful use of vehicle	KEII	20 716	20 804	21 680	20 288	19 726	20 339	18 772	16 638	16 922	17 804	18 905
Vehicle defect offences	KEIJ	3 763	3 007	3 262	3 340	3 209	3 323	2 659	2 004	1 576	1 252	1 398
Other motor vehicle offences	KEIK	9 917	9 315	9 354	8 690	7 235	7 426	6 732	6 322	5 437	4 990	4 693
Total offences	KEHY	123 261	110 504	107 265	105 810	102 570	102 054	93 476	83 996	78 197	78 436	82 904
Total crimes and offences	KEHA	177 483	162 806	159 178	156 707	153 087	150 508	139 880	127 558	118 147	120 289	124 950

1 See chapter text.
2 Figures for 2002 for some categories dealt with by the High Court - including homicide, rape and major drugs cases - underestimated slightly due to late recording of disposals on SCRO.

3 'Handling an offensive weapon' has been moved from 'Non-sexual crimes of violence' to 'other crime'.

Source: Scottish Executive Justice Department: 0131 244 2229

11.15 Persons with a charge proved: by court procedure[1]
Scotland

		1992	1993	1994	1995	1996	1997	1998	1999	2000	2001	2002
Court procedure												
High Court[2]	KEIQ	1 091	1 235	964	1 096	1 099	1 120	1 048	1 174	1 099	1 076	892
Sheriff Court	KEIU	86 798	82 936	84 278	84 602	85 438	83 332	78 607	74 530	70 939	75 979	82 313
District Court[3]	KEIV	78 735	68 966	63 784	61 336	57 672	57 260	53 217	45 890	41 844	38 382	41 745
Stipendiary Magistrate Court[3]	KEIW	10 814	9 667	10 146	9 670	8 878	8 794	7 008	5 963	4 265	4 846	..
Total called to court[4]	KEIZ	177 483	162 806	159 178	156 707	153 087	150 508	139 880	127 558	118 147	120 289	124 950

1 See chapter text.
2 Including cases remitted to the High Court from the Sheriff Court. Figure for 2002 may be an underestimate due to late recording of disposals on SCRO.

3 District Court figure for 2002 includes the Stipendiary Magistrate Court.
4 Includes court type not known.

Source: Scottish Executive Justice Department: 0131 244 2229

11.16 Persons with charge proved: by main penalty[1]
Scotland

Numbers

Main penalty		1992	1993	1994	1995	1996	1997	1998	1999	2000	2001	2002
Restriction of liberty order[2]	ZBRE	..	..	..	..	..	..	71	206	215	201	495
Supervised attendance order[3]	ZBRF	..	..	..	..	8	73	68	107	75	48	74
Drug treatment and testing order[4]	OEWA	..	..	..	..	..	..	..	..	80	277	448
Absolute discharge	KEXA	967	989	839	939	1 000	1 065	957	986	967	987	1 096
Admonition or caution	KEXB	17 441	16 976	16 243	15 857	15 859	15 041	13 893	12 916	11 804	11 973	12 587
Probation	KEXC	5 385	5 722	6 145	6 145	6 435	6 817	7 146	7 350	7 377	8 179	9 182
Remit to children's hearing	KEXD	72	83	124	172	193	219	177	136	106	159	210
Community service order	KEXE	5 473	5 079	5 320	5 339	5 711	5 709	5 246	4 889	4 690	4 879	5 009
Fine	KEXF	131 842	116 918	112 748	110 337	105 384	103 861	94 917	83 482	76 238	75 672	77 636
Compensation order	KEXG	1 575	1 578	1 535	1 527	1 415	1 304	1 298	1 154	1 111	1 138	1 282
Insanity, hospital, guardianship order	KYAN	133	138	133	136	159	164	131	137	109	113	114
Prison	KEXI	10 085	10 832	11 583	11 561	12 134	11 663	11 496	11 684	11 046	12 408	13 131
Young offenders' institution	KEXJ	4 488	4 461	4 472	4 646	4 744	4 563	4 460	4 494	4 318	4 239	3 663
Detention of child	KEXM	22	30	36	48	45	29	20	17	11	16	23
Total persons with charge proved	KEXO	177 483	162 806	159 178	156 707	153 087	150 508	139 880	127 558	118 147	120 289	124 950

1 See chapter text.
2 A community sentence introduced by Section 5 of the Crime and Punishment (Scotland) Act 1995 and available on a pilot basis to 3 Scottish sheriff courts since August 1998. This sentence was made available to High Court, Sheriff Courts and Stipendiary Magistrates court from 1 May 2002.
3 The pilot scheme under the Crime and Punishment (S) Act 1995, where fines for 16 & 17 year olds were replaced by supervised attendance orders, was discontinued in December 1999. The majority of supervised attendance orders recorded from the year 2000 onwards were disposals relating to the breach of an existing order.

4 Drug treatment and testing orders are new measures made available on a pilot basis to the High Court and to Sheriff Courts for residents in Glasgow (from October 1999), Fife (from July 2000) and Aberdeen/Aberdeenshire (From December 2001).

Source: Scottish Executive Justice Department: 0131 244 2229

11.17 Persons with charge proved[1]: by age and sex
Scotland

Numbers

		1992	1993	1994	1995	1996	1997	1998	1999	2000	2001	2002
Males	KEWA	147 693	136 127	136 533	133 330	130 961	129 519	120 533	110 440	101 338	103 790	106 096
Under 16	KEWB	138	138	171	180	149	138	135	75	55	76	125
16 to 20	KEWC	36 494	32 589	30 708	30 113	31 704	31 319	29 319	26 948	24 361	25 165	24 756
21 to 30	KEWD	59 561	56 052	56 519	54 184	52 218	50 714	46 149	41 715	38 583	39 803	40 873
Over 30	KEWE	49 094	45 701	47 788	47 648	45 799	46 299	44 062	40 831	37 594	38 322	40 299
Age not known	KEWF	2 406	1 647	1 347	1 205	1 091	1 049	868	871	745	424	43
Females	KEWG	28 051	25 405	21 650	22 412	21 308	20 246	18 670	16 548	16 374	16 146	18 499
Under 16	KEWH	9	6	8	17	12	11	5	6	9	5	3
16 to 20	KEWI	3 885	3 589	2 939	3 098	3 302	3 424	3 361	3 275	3 052	2 918	3 030
21 to 30	KEWJ	11 998	10 557	9 190	9 284	8 461	8 095	7 458	6 496	6 285	6 381	7 185
Over 30	KEWK	11 409	10 611	9 002	9 439	8 894	8 266	7 532	6 499	6 769	6 725	8 271
Age not known	KEWL	750	642	511	574	639	450	314	272	259	117	10
Males and Females	KEWM	175 744	161 532	158 183	155 742	152 269	149 765	139 203	126 988	117 712	119 936	124 595
Under 16	KEWN	147	144	179	197	161	149	140	81	64	81	128
16 to 20	KEWO	40 379	36 178	33 647	33 211	35 006	34 743	32 680	30 223	27 413	28 083	27 786
21 to 30	KEWP	71 559	66 609	65 709	63 468	60 679	58 809	53 607	48 211	44 868	46 184	48 058
Over 30	KEWQ	60 503	56 312	56 790	57 087	54 693	54 565	51 594	47 330	44 363	45 047	48 570
Age not known	KEWR	3 156	2 289	1 858	1 779	1 730	1 499	1 182	1 143	1 004	541	53
Companies	KEWS	1 717	1 263	991	961	812	737	675	551	399	308	341
Total persons with charge proved[2]	KEWT	177 483	162 806	159 178	156 707	153 087	150 508	139 880	127 558	118 147	120 289	124 950

1 See chapter text.
2 Includes sex unknown.

Source: Scottish Executive Justice Department: 0131 244 2229

11.18 Penal establishments: average daily population and receptions
Scotland

		1993	1994	1995	1996	1997	1998	1999	2000	2001	2002	2003
Average daily population												
Male	KEPB	5 466	5 408	5 451	5 673	5 900	5 825	5 817	5 666	5 889	6 126	6 227
Female	KEPC	171	177	175	189	184	193	212	203	249	277	297
Total	KEPA	5 637	5 585	5 626	5 862	6 084	6 018	6 029	5 869	6 137	6 404	6 524
Analysis by type of custody												
Remand	KEPD	948	1 015	998	1 000	947	938	1 012	894	960	1 222	1 220
Persons under sentence: total	KEPE	4 686	4 569	4 624	4 924	5 134	5 077	5 016	4 973	5 176	5 180	5 303
Adult prisoners	KEPF	3 866	3 849	3 906	4 128	4 345	4 362	4 318	4 319	4 526	4 583	4 726
Young offenders	KEPI	819	720	719	796	789	715	697	654	650	597	577
Persons recalled from supervision/licence[1]	KEPN	40	37	44	46	46	72	93	129	193	244	290
Others[1]	KEPO	32	28	38	18	20	17	28	31	47	6	7
Persons sentenced by court martial[1]	KEPP	2	1	3	..	1	2	1	1	–	–	–
Civil prisoners[1]	KEPQ	1	1	..	1	1	1	1	1	1	2	1
Receptions to penal establishments												
Remand	KEPR	13 412	14 922	14 253	14 977	14 826	15 098	15 291	13 945	15 433	18 726	18 870
Male	KEPS	12 478	13 985	13 377	13 976	13 850	13 979	14 090	12 916	14 166	17 092	17 064
Female	KEPT	934	937	876	1 001	976	1 119	1 201	1 029	1 267	1 634	1 806
Persons under sentence: total	KEPU	22 157	21 111	19 030	22 155	23 202	22 269	20 741	18 916	19 247	19 687	18 872
Male	KEPV	20 741	19 697	17 737	20 869	21 936	20 862	19 465	17 739	18 035	18 440	17 577
Female	KEPW	1 416	1 414	1 293	1 286	1 266	1 407	1 276	1 177	1 212	1 247	1 295
Imprisoned: Adults:												
directly	KEPX	9 444	9 349	8 730	10 040	9 698	9 959	9 484	8 713	9 617	10 408	10 135
in default of fine	KEPY	7 956	7 377	6 299	7 432	8 873	7 866	7 154	6 542	6 088	6 056	5 873
in default of compensation order[2]	KEPZ	41	26	13	..	..	..	..	..	..	..	..
Sentenced to young offenders' institution:												
directly	KEQA	3 052	2 855	2 772	3 111	2 784	2 844	2 687	2 500	2 414	2 205	1 979
in default of fine	KEQB	1 660	1 498	1 210	1 567	1 847	1 593	1 411	1 161	1 128	1 018	885
in default of compensation order[2]	KEQC	4	6	4	..	..	..	..	..	..	..	..
Persons recalled from supervised release orders	JYYD	..	..	2	5	11	7	5	–	–	–	–
Persons sentenced by court martial	KEQH	7	5	4	4	4	5	3	2	1	3	2
Civil prisoners[3]	KEQI	37	27	25	32	23	10	14	12	9	12	7

1 'Persons recalled from supervision/licence' and 'others' are included in total persons under sentence as well as adult and young offender figures. In years before 1997, the figures include a small number of prisoners under 21 who were recalled from supervision/licence or were 'other' prisoners (less than 1 in each category). 'Persons sentenced by court martial' and 'civil prisoners' are not included in persons under sentence.

2 From 1996 compensation orders are included in the figures for default of fine.
3 For 1995 and 1996 data are estimated.

Source: The Scottish Executive Justice Department: 0131 244 2225

11.19 Expenditure on penal establishments[1]
Scotland
Years ended 31 March

£ thousand

		1993 /94	1994 /95	1995 /96	1996 /97	1997 /98	1998 /99	1999 /00	2000 /01	2001 /02	2002 /03	2003 /04
Departmental Expenditure												
Manpower and Associated Services	KPHC	135 301	140 009	135 941	143 107	137 890	144 660	170 347	160 242	172 490	168 593	169 784
Prisoner and Associated Costs	KPHD	10 795	11 679	12 373	13 377	16 313	18 891	22 930	23 501	24 652	23 363	51 070
Capital Expenditure	KPHE	11 845	15 636	15 377	22 577	22 136	23 697	28 918	24 283	24 955	36 519	34 617
Gross Expenditure	KPHF	157 941	167 324	163 691	179 061	176 339	187 248	222 195	208 026	222 097	228 475	255 471
Less Receipts	KPHG	3 598	3 042	2 800	2 600	2 810	8 160	6 668	8 380	8 194	3 485	3 298
Net Departmental Expenditure	KPHH	154 343	164 282	160 891	176 461	173 529	179 088	215 527	199 646	213 903	224 990	252 173
Plus Annually Managed Expenditure Capital Charges	DSJI	..	..	..	..	..	..	..	..	31 341	40 432	41 728
Total Net Expenditure	DSNX	154 343	164 282	160 891	176 461	173 529	179 088	215 527	199 646	245 244	265 422	293 901

1 See chapter text.

Source: The Scottish Executive Justice Department: 0131 244 2225

11.20 Recorded crime statistics: by offence group[1]
Northern Ireland

Thousands

		Old counting rules							New counting rules					
		1993	1994	1995	1996	1997	1998 /99		1998 /99	1999 /00	2000 /01	2001 /02	2002 /03	2003 /04
Violence against the person	RVCP	4.6	4.8	5.2	5.6	5.2	6.6	RVCQ	18.5	21.4	21.4	26.1	28.5	29.0
Sexual offences	RVCR	1.2	1.3	1.7	1.7	1.4	1.5	RVCS	1.6	1.3	1.2	1.4	1.5	1.8
Burglary	RVCT	15.7	16.9	16.5	16.1	14.3	15.5	RVCU	15.5	16.1	15.8	17.1	18.7	16.4
Robbery	RVCV	1.7	1.6	1.5	1.7	1.7	1.4	RVCW	1.4	1.4	1.8	2.2	2.5	2.0
Theft	RVCX	33.2	33.2	33.5	32.8	29.5	34.6	RVCY	35.4	37.0	36.9	41.7	41.9	35.7
Fraud and forgery	RVCZ	5.6	5.1	4.9	4.1	3.8	5.3	RVDA	6.8	7.9	8.0	8.6	8.8	6.3
Criminal damage	RVDB	2.9	3.1	3.8	4.8	4.7	9.8	RVDC	27.7	31.2	32.3	40.0	36.6	32.4
Offences against the state	RVDD	0.4	0.4	0.3	0.4	0.5	0.5	RVDE	0.6	0.7	0.8	1.2	1.8	1.3
Other notifiable offences	RVDF	1.0	1.4	1.5	1.2	1.1	1.5	RVDG	1.7	2.1	1.7	1.4	2.4	3.2
of which drug offences	RVDH	0.8	1.3	1.4	1.1	1.0	1.4	RVDI	1.4	1.7	1.5	1.1	1.9	2.6
Total	RVDR	66.2	67.9	68.8	68.5	62.2	76.6	RVDS	109.1	119.1	119.9	139.8	142.5	128.0

1 See chapter text.

Source: The Police Service of Northern Ireland

11.21 Persons found guilty at all courts: by offence group[1]
Northern Ireland

Numbers

		1992	1993	1994	1995	1996	1997	1998	1999	2000	2001	2002
Violence against the person	KYCT	1 558	1 674	1 498	1 685	1 597	1 594	1 596	1 699	1 858	1 621	1 790
Sexual offences	KEVG	184	126	148	182	184	130	128	90	130	112	84
Burglary	KYBW	1 149	1 114	979	951	801	715	647	703	703	496	595
Robbery	KYBX	202	159	168	195	161	166	134	129	122	121	152
Theft	KYBY	3 158	3 254	3 044	3 128	2 765	2 596	2 342	1 995	2 111	1 831	1 695
Fraud and forgery	KYBZ	683	633	568	533	467	491	426	476	403	398	362
Criminal damage	KYCA	967	1 145	1 134	1 008	1 076	1 163	1 043	931	1 060	917	957
Offences against the state	KYCB	187	184	137	166	147	165	198	178	174	158	215
Other indictable[2]	KYCC	448	606	669	863	899	739	936	943	700	495	453
Total indictable[3]	KYCD	8 536	8 895	8 345	8 711	8 097	7 759	7 450	7 144	7 261	6 149	6 303
Summary[4]	KYCE	4 115	4 307	4 369	4 137	4 402	4 435	4 062	3 598	3 967	3 735	3 453
Motoring[5]	KYCF	20 808	21 882	21 502	20 124	18 177	18 770	15 369	15 782	15 390	14 466	14 344
All offences	KYCG	33 459	35 084	34 216	32 972	30 676	30 964	26 881	26 524	26 618	24 350	24 100

1 See chapter text.
2 1998 and 1999 figures include 'dangerous driving' (a triable-either-way offence).
3 From 2000, includes 'indictable-only' motoring offences.
4 Excludes motoring offences.
5 Prior to 2000, includes all motoring offences (except for note 2 above). From 2000, includes summary and triable-either-way motoring offences.

Source: Northern Ireland Office: 028 9052 7534

11.22 Juveniles found guilty at all courts:[1] by offence group
Northern Ireland

Numbers

		1992	1993	1994	1995	1996	1997	1998	1999	2000	2001	2002
Violence against the person	KYCH	46	43	49	51	75	49	97	73	77	66	82
Sexual offences	KAHF	11	7	8	7	4	8	12	12	4	1	6
Burglary	KYCI	165	155	180	170	137	124	108	117	125	73	77
Robbery	KYCJ	8	4	9	22	13	18	4	7	15	8	14
Theft	KYCK	247	280	283	345	338	334	304	227	254	244	212
Fraud and forgery	KYCL	16	14	14	21	14	11	4	10	2	9	3
Criminal damage	KYCM	82	94	117	116	121	136	139	102	143	152	132
Offences against the state	KYCN	6	1	8	9	6	10	11	12	8	10	20
Other indictable[2]	KYCO	8	2	6	14	24	10	20	17	10	12	7
Total indictable[3]	KYCP	589	600	674	755	732	700	699	577	638	575	553
Summary[4]	KYCQ	113	125	131	180	182	198	187	163	180	203	194
Motoring[5]	KYCR	40	44	74	74	58	57	98	97	82	102	89
All offences	KYCS	742	769	879	1 009	972	955	984	837	900	880	836

1 See chapter text. Juveniles are aged 10 - 16 years inclusive.
2 1998 and 1999 figures include 'dangerous driving'.
3 From 2000, includes 'indictable-only' motoring offences.
4 Excludes motoring offences.
5 Prior to 2000 includes all motoring offences (except for note 2 above). From 2000, includes summary motoring offences.

Source: Northern Ireland Office: 028 9052 7534

11.23 Disposals given to those convicted by court
Northern Ireland

Numbers

		1992	1993	1994	1995	1996	1997	1998	1999	2000	2001	2002
Magistrates court - all offences												
Prison[1]	KYAO	830	1 027	945	1 046	1 003	989	996	1 278	1 356	1 048	1 107
Young offenders centre	KYAP	588	575	499	483	443	430	326	243	191	209	288
Training school[2]	KYAQ	120	125	193	169	147	148	136	13	..	..	..
Juvenile Justice Centre order[2]	OEUX	..	..	..	..	..	..	..	22	78	72	58
Total immediate custody	KYAR	1 538	1 727	1 637	1 698	1 593	1 567	1 458	1 556	1 625	1 329	1 453
Prison suspended	KYAS	1 420	1 529	1 558	1 674	1 722	1 506	1 025	1 080	1 247	1 215	1 278
YOC suspended	KYAT	507	447	447	385	444	461	139	104	93	77	100
Attendance centre	KYAU	66	94	89	101	91	66	55	14	20	37	84
Probation/supervision	KYAV	849	881	1 017	1 137	1 134	1 155	1 473	1 246	1 096	1 070	1 005
Community supervision order	KYAW	464	536	551	547	591	561	622	678	726	587	643
Combination order	OEUZ	..	..	..	..	..	..	38	7	48	24	36
Fine[3]	KYAX	23 418	25 166	24 390	22 726	20 612	21 313	17 955	18 076	17 716	16 439	15 968
Recognizance	KYAY	713	858	961	1 001	1 203	1 267	1 134	1 089	1 357	810	912
Conditional discharge	KYAZ	1 965	2 021	1 830	1 928	1 679	1 597	1 538	1 439	1 286	1 559	1 497
Absolute discharge	KYBA	732	690	661	608	509	424	303	223	242	209	163
Penalty points[3]	OEVA	..	..	..	..	..	..	44	105	1	–	–
Fine plus Disqualification[4]	KYBB	640	6	6	2	5	2	57	97	9	27	69
Other	KYBC	12	7	11	8	10	6	23	19	47	34	35
Total	KYBD	32 324	33 962	33 158	31 815	29 593	29 925	25 864	25 733	25 513	23 417	23 243
Crown court - all offences												
Prison[1]	KYBE	447	555	471	533	469	475	520	386	521	407	410
Young offenders centre	KYBF	119	130	87	76	106	111	63	67	32	42	23
Training school[2]	KYBG	5	2	5	6	–	4	2	–	..	..	..
Juvenile Justice Centre order[2]	VQEV	..	..	..	..	..	..	..	–	–	–	2
Total immediate custody	KYBH	571	687	563	615	575	590	585	453	553	449	435
Prison suspended	KYBI	249	211	277	265	253	220	199	185	313	262	220
YOC suspended	KYBJ	63	37	43	63	71	60	49	41	48	37	35
Combination order	ZAEP	..	..	..	..	..	..	13	6	7	5	18
Attendance centre	KYBK	–	–	1	–	–	–	–	–	–	–	1
Probation/supervision	KYBL	95	73	58	60	49	47	70	43	68	48	49
Community supervision order	KYBM	79	48	59	60	54	37	33	24	29	45	25
Fine[3]	KYBN	17	33	23	27	39	40	25	20	40	38	32
Recognizance	KYBO	9	5	16	–	7	10	7	–	4	11	12
Conditional discharge	KYBR	36	19	15	64	30	31	23	17	38	36	20
Absolute discharge	KYBS	8	3	2	1	–	1	6	–	3	–	6
Fine plus Disqualification[4]	KYBT	2	–	–	–	–	–	1	–	1	–	1
Other	KYBU	6	6	1	2	3	3	6	2	1	2	3
Total	KYBV	1 135	1 122	1 058	1 157	1 081	1 039	1 017	791	1 105	933	857

1 Figures include custody probation orders.
2 The Juvenile Justice Centre order replaced the training school order from 31st January 1999.
3 From 2000, fine incorporates 'fine plus disqualification' and 'fine plus penalty points'.
4 From 2000, figures relate to disqualification only.

Source: Northern Ireland Office: 028 9052 7534

11.24 Prisons and Young Offenders Centres
Northern Ireland

Receptions and average population

		1993	1994	1995	1996	1997	1998	1999	2000	2001	2002	2003
Receptions:												
Reception of untried prisoners	KEOA	2 045	2 043	2 003	2 292	2 188	2 284	2 497	2 197	1 922	2 337	2 439
Reception of sentenced prisoners:												
Imprisonment under sentence of immediate custody[1]	KEOB	1 135	1 029	1 070	1 070	1 062	949	963	1 001	791	916	1 032
Imprisonment in default of payment of a fine	KEOC	1 221	1 190	1 248	1 374	1 513	1 530	1 423	1 261	1 090	990	1 140
Total	KEOD	2 356	2 219	2 318	2 444	2 575	2 479	2 386	2 262	1 881	1 906	2 172
Reception into Young Offender Centres:												
Detention under sentence of immediate custody	KEOE	416	346	371	362	331	347	346	282	252	315	268
Detention in default of payment of a fine	KEOF	353	276	351	373	366	385	417	389	303	250	313
Total	KEOG	769	622	722	735	697	732	763	671	555	565	581
Other receptions[2]	KEOL	21	13	45	27	42	70	38	56	58	57	117
Daily average population:												
Unconvicted[3]	KEON	427	440	322	337	376	383	377	317	272	347	393
Convicted[4]	KEOP	1 507	1 459	1 440	1 302	1 256	1 124	867	751	638	679	767
Total	KEOM	1 934	1 899	1 762	1 639	1 632	1 507	1 244	1 068	910	1 026	1 160

1 Includes those detained under Section 73 of the Children and Young Persons (NI) Act 1968.

2 Non-criminal prisioners including those imprisoned for non-payment of maintenance, non-payment of debt, contempt of court or are being held under the terms of an Immigration Act.

3 Prisoners on remand or awaiting trial and prisoners committed by civil process.

4 Includes those sentenced to immediate custody and fine defaulters.

Source: Northern Ireland Office: 028 9052 7534

Lifestyles

Chapter 12

Lifestyles

Expenditure by the Department for Culture, Media and Sport

(Table 12.1)

The figures in this table are taken from the Department's Annual Report and are outturn figures for each of the headings shown (later figures are the estimated outturn). The Department's planned expenditure for future years is also shown.

Cinema statistics

(Table 12.3)

This table now includes data from CAA/Gallup/Nielsen EDI which replaces the previous ONS Inquiry data which are no longer collected.

Tourist attractions

(Table 12.5)

The figures in this table are compiled using data from the Survey of Visits to Visitor Attractions. The tourist attractions included within the headings shown are as follows:

Country parks: Country parks and forest parks.

Farms: Farms, rare breeds, shire horse centres and farm animals.

Gardens: Gardens, arboretums and botanical gardens.

Historic properties: Historic houses, palaces, castles, forts, historic monuments, places of worship, archaeological sites, historic ships and other historic properties.

Leisure and theme parks: Leisure parks and theme parks.

Museums and art galleries: Museums and/or art galleries and science centres.

Steam and heritage railways: Steam railways and heritage railways.

Visitor and heritage centres: Visitor and heritage centres.

Wildlife attractions: Nature reserves, wetlands, wildlife trips, safari parks, zoos, aquariums and aviaries.

Workplaces: Distilleries, vineyards, breweries and industrial or craft premises.

Domestic tourism

(Table 12.6)

The figures in this table are compiled using data from the United Kingdom Tourism Survey (UKTS) and represent trips of one or more nights away from home. The UKTS changed survey methodology in 2000. Data from 1995 to 1999 were reworked to allow comparisons to be made with 2000 and later data.

International tourism and holidays abroad

(Tables 12.7 and 12.8)

The figures in these tables are compiled using data from the International Passenger Survey. A holiday abroad is a visit made for holiday purposes. Business trips and visits to friends and relatives are excluded.

Attendances at leisure and cultural activities

(Table 12.9)

The definitions used in this table differ from those normally used to define regular attendees by the Department for Culture, Media and Sport.

Gambling

(Table 12.10)

The National Lottery figures in this table are the latest figures at the time of going to press which have been released by the National Lottery Commission, and represent ticket sales (money staked) for each of the games which comprise the lottery. The figures have been adjusted to real terms using the Retail Prices Index.

The National Lottery commenced on 19 November 1994, with the first instant ticket being sold in March 1995. Various other games have been started since, the latest shown in the table being the Euromillions game. The sum of the individual games may not agree exactly with the figures for total sales. Total sales also includes the Easy Play games which commenced in 1998, but were dropped in 1999.

The other gambling figures in this table are obtained from the Gaming Board and H.M. Customs and Excise. The figures have been adjusted to real terms using the Retail Prices Index.

The money staked at bingo clubs refers to licensed clubs only. Prior to 1994–95 the figures for bingo clubs relate to the year ending August.

Expenditure by the Department for Culture, Media and Sport[1]

£ million

	Museums, galleries and libraries[2]	The arts (England)	Sports (UK)	Historic buildings, monuments, and sites (England)	The Royal Parks (UK)	Tourism (UK)	Broadcasting and media (UK)	Administration and research	Other gambling and gaming bodies	Commemorative services (Queen's Golden Jubilee)	European regional development fund	Culture online
	GQIF	KWFP	KWFQ	KWFR	LQYY	KWFS	KWFT	GQIG	SNKA	SNKB	JYXQ	GQII
1993/94	335	235	54	164	23	46	85	22	–	..	..	..
1994/95	372	195	53	164	24	44	93	21	–	..	..	..
1995/96	399	200	54	164	25	45	98	20	–	..	6	..
1996/97	336	195	52	162	23	46	97	21	–	..	16	..
1997/98	321	196	50	156	22	45	43	21	–	..	26	..
1998/99	363	192	46	138	23	44	99	23	–	..	33	..
1999/00	377	230	51	144	27	48	104	28	–	..	28	..
2000/01	411	239	52	144	24	48	104	29	–	..	35	1
2001/02	313	254	67	139	42	68	105	33	–1	–	27	1
2002/03	408	286	126	147	26	75	108	38	2	4	19	–
2003/04[3]	868	334	82	347	26	58	118	50	4	–	6	1
2004/05[4]	535	367	121	155	26	55	123	46	4	–	6	–
2005/06[4]	560	412	123	157	25	55	122	50	3	–	6	–

1 See chapter text.
2 Includes museums and galleries (England), libraries (UK) and museums library archives (UK).
3 Data are estimated outturn.
4 Data are plans.

Source: Department for Culture, Media and Sport: 020 7211 6121

Employment in tourism related industries[1]
Great Britain

Non seasonally adjusted. At June each year

Thousands

	Hotels and other tourist accommodation	Restaurants, cafes etc.	Bars, public houses and nightclubs	Travel agents, tour operators	Libraries, museums and other cultural activities	Sport and other recreation activities	All tourism related industries All	Of which: Employee jobs	Of which: Self-employment jobs
	KWFV	KWFW	KWFX	KWFY	KWFZ	KWGA	LQZA	KWGB	KWGC
1996	400.4	491.1	506.1	104.0	74.2	353.2	1 929.0	1 706.3	222.6
1997	372.5	506.9	553.5	115.7	75.8	359.3	1 983.7	1 762.1	221.6
1998	385.5	522.4	555.6	110.9	74.8	346.4	1 995.6	1 809.0	186.6
1999	410.4	535.0	554.9	123.0	77.6	367.9	2 068.7	1 906.7	162.1
2000	411.1	554.3	558.9	135.9	84.6	396.3	2 141.0	1 971.1	169.9
2001	401.2	569.3	543.8	145.7	80.4	412.0	2 152.4	1 995.1	157.3
2002	394.2	587.5	557.6	136.7	82.8	423.3	2 182.1	2 019.1	163.0
2003	392.7	590.4	568.2	117.2	86.7	412.9	2 168.1	2 012.3	155.8

1 DCMS will release revised tourism employment estimates in 2005 following the completion of the Tourism Satellite Account project.

Sources: Department for Culture, Media and Sport: 020 7211 6121; using data from Labour Force Survey, Office for National Statistics

12.3 Cinema statistics[1,2]
United Kingdom

	Sites (numbers)	Screens (numbers)	Total number of admissions[3] (millions)	Gross box office takings (£ million)	Revenue per admission[3] (£)	Revenue per screen (£ thousand)
	JMHX	JMHY	JMHZ	JMIA	JMIB	JMIC
1995	728	2 003	114.6	354.2	3.09	176.8
1996	742	2 166	123.5	407.2	3.30	188.0
1997	747	2 383	138.9	486.2	3.50	204.0
1998	761	2 638	135.2	504.9	3.73	191.4
1999	751	2 825	139.1	549.7	3.95	194.6
2000	754	3 017	142.5	572.8	4.02	189.9
2001	766	3 248	155.9	645.0	4.14	198.6
2002	775	3 402	175.9	755.3	4.29	222.0
2003	776	3 433	167.3	742.0	4.44	216.1

1 See chapter text.
2 Includes Isle of Man and the Channel Islands.
3 Admissions are based on all cinemas taking advertising.

Source: CAA/Gallup/Nielsen EDI

12.4 Films
United Kingdom

Numbers and £ million

	Production of UK films		Expenditure on feature films (Current prices)				
	Films produced in the UK (numbers)	Production costs (1998 prices)	UK box office	Video rental	Video retail	Subscriptions to movie channels	Box office, video, subscription channels
	KWGD	KWGE	KWHU	KWHV	KWHW	KWHX	KWHY
1992	47	208.6	291	389	506	283	1 469
1993	67	214.0	319	350	643	350	1 662
1994	84	436.0	364	339	698	540	1 941
1995	78	421.0	385	351	789	721	2 246
1996	128	726.0	426	382	803	1 319	2 930
1997	116	558.0	506	369	858	..	1 733
1998	88	487.0	515	437	940	..	1 892
1999	100	570.0	606	408	882	..	1 896
2000	98	792.5	628	444	1 104	..	2 176
2001	96	..	692	465	1 490	..	..
2002	90	..	668	..	..	..	..

Source: UK Film Council

12.5 Visits to tourist attractions[1]
United Kingdom

Indices (1989=100)

	Country Parks	Farms	Gardens	Historic properties	Leisure and theme parks	Museums and art galleries	Steam and heritage railways	Visitor and heritage centres	Wildlife attractions and zoos	Workplaces	All attractions
	MKDZ	MKEA	LQZC	LQZB	MKEB	LQZD	MKEC	MKED	LQZE	MKEE	LQZG
1989	100	100	100	100	100	100	100	100	100	100	100
1990	105	117	102	102	102	106	101	103	101	102	103
1991	108	123	106	98	100	107	99	100	95	101	102
1992	106	127	105	98	99	110	95	103	87	101	102
1993	107	141	111	100	103	109	98	106	89	106	104
1994	110	148	116	99	106	110	98	108	87	108	105
1995	118	153	122	103	106	108	100	112	86	106	107
1996	118	160	125	106	106	111	107	117	90	112	110
1997	122	165	127	108	106	111	108	117	92	115	112
1998	117	165	118	107	103	112	108	116	92	113	110
1999	120	176	122	106	106	111	112	115	94	113	111
2000	119	162	120	101	105	108	115	114	92	108	109
2001	112	122	124	94	110	110	112	109	88	105	107
2002	125	178	138	99	110	118	119	119	99	108	115

1 See chapter text.

Source: VisitBritain: 020 8563 3320

12.6 Domestic tourism[1]
United Kingdom

	Number of trips (millions)	Number of nights spent (millions)	Expenditure at current prices (£ million)	Average nights spent (numbers)	Average expenditure per trip (£)
	GQGY	GQGZ	GQHA	GQHB	GQHC
1995	147.8	526.0	20 072	3.6	135.8
1996	154.2	532.8	22 041	3.5	142.9
1997	162.2	555.3	24 137	3.4	148.8
1998	148.8	515.9	22 814	3.5	153.3
1999	173.1	568.6	25 635	3.3	148.1
2000	175.4	576.4	26 132	3.3	149.0
2001	163.1	529.6	26 094	3.2	160.0
2002	167.3	531.9	26 699	3.2	159.6
2003	151.0	490.5	26 482	3.2	175.4

1 See chapter text.

Source: United Kingdom Tourism Survey, VisitBritain: 020 8563 3320

12.7 International tourism[1]

Thousands and £ million

	Visits to the UK by overseas residents (thousands)	Spending in the UK by overseas residents		Visits overseas by UK residents (thousands)	Spending overseas by UK residents	
		Current prices	Constant 1995 prices		Current prices	Constant 1995 prices
	GMAA	GMAK	CQPR	GMAF	GMAM	CQPS
1993	19 863	9 487	10 188	36 720	12 972	13 184
1994	20 794	9 786	10 050	39 630	14 365	14 852
1995	23 537	11 763	11 763	41 345	15 386	15 386
1996	25 163	12 290	11 954	42 050	16 223	15 897
1997	25 515	12 244	11 542	45 957	16 931	18 652
1998	25 745	12 671	11 573	50 872	19 489	21 847
1999	25 394	12 498	11 133	53 881	22 020	24 676
2000	25 209	12 805	11 102	56 837	24 251	27 281
2001	22 835	11 306	9 528	58 281	25 332	27 710
2002	24 180	11 737	9 641	59 377	26 962	29 311
2003	24 715	11 855	9 451	61 424	28 550	28 677

1 See chapter text.

Sources: International Passenger Survey, Office for National Statistics;
020 7533 5765

12.8 Holidays abroad:[1] by destination

Percentages

		1971	1981	1991	1996	1997	1998	1999	2000	2001	2002	2003
Spain[2]	JTKC	34.3	21.7	21.3	25.5	26.3	27.5	27.2	27.8	27.9	28.5	29.8
France	JTKD	15.9	27.2	25.8	23.4	23.1	20.2	19.7	18.3	18.3	19.0	18.1
Greece	JTKF	4.5	6.7	7.6	4.9	4.7	5.3	6.5	6.8	7.8	7.0	6.6
United States	JTKE	1.0	5.5	6.8	7.4	6.7	7.0	7.5	7.3	6.3	5.4	5.5
Italy	JTKG	9.2	5.8	3.5	3.8	4.2	4.0	4.1	4.2	4.3	4.6	5.0
Portugal	JTKH	2.6	2.8	4.8	3.6	4.0	3.6	3.7	3.9	3.6	4.0	4.0
Ireland	JTKI	..	3.6	3.0	3.4	3.6	3.5	5.5	4.6	4.1	4.1	3.7
Cyprus	JTKL	1.0	0.7	2.4	2.3	2.2	2.6	2.4	3.3	3.5	3.0	2.7
Netherlands	JTKK	3.6	2.4	3.5	2.5	2.8	2.7	2.4	2.2	2.6	2.8	2.6
Turkey	JTKJ	..	0.1	0.7	3.5	3.1	3.0	2.1	1.8	2.0	2.2	2.3
Belgium	JTKM	..	2.1	2.1	2.3	2.2	2.3	1.9	1.8	2.1	2.0	2.2
Germany	JTKN	3.4	2.6	2.7	1.6	1.7	1.8	1.6	1.7	1.4	1.5	1.2
Austria	JTKP	5.5	2.5	2.4	1.1	1.1	1.3	1.0	1.0	1.1	1.4	1.1
Malta	JTKO	..	2.6	1.7	1.4	1.2	1.3	1.0	1.1	1.0	1.0	1.0
Other countries	JTKQ	19.0	13.7	11.8	13.3	13.2	13.9	13.3	14.1	13.8	13.6	14.2

1 See chapter text.
2 Excludes the Canary Islands prior to 1981.

Sources: International Passenger Survey, Office for National Statistics;
020 7533 5765

12.9 Attendance at leisure and cultural activities[1]
Great Britain

At Spring

Percentages

		1993/94	1994/95	1995/96	1996/97	1997/98	1998/99	1999/00	2000/01	2001/02	2002/03	2003/04
Attendance by men at:												
Cinema	JSPR	50	53	53	55	55	57	58	57	58	62	59
Plays	JSPS	22	22	21	21	20	20	21	20	21	22	23
Art galleries and exhibitions	JSPT	21	22	22	22	20	20	21	21	22	23	24
Classical music	JSPU	12	12	12	12	11	10	11	12	12	12	13
Ballet	JSPV	5	5	4	4	4	4	4	4	4	5	5
Opera	JSPW	6	6	6	6	6	5	6	6	6	6	6
Contemporary dance	JSPX	3	3	3	3	4	3	3	3	3	4	5
Sporting events	JSPY	89	89	88	87	87	86	85	85	78	76	73
Pop/rock concerts	C3Q8	..	..	..	..	..	..	..	..	..	25	26
Attendance by women at:												
Cinema	JSQA	49	51	50	52	54	57	54	54	57	60	62
Plays	JSQB	26	26	25	26	25	23	25	25	26	27	27
Art galleries and exhibitions	JSQC	22	21	22	23	22	22	22	22	23	25	24
Classical music	JSQD	13	12	13	12	13	12	12	12	13	13	14
Ballet	JSQE	9	9	9	9	8	8	9	8	8	9	10
Opera	JSQF	8	7	7	7	7	7	7	7	7	8	8
Contemporary dance	JSQG	4	4	5	5	5	5	5	5	6	6	7
Sporting events	JSQH	73	72	72	69	67	66	65	65	56	58	55
Pop/rock concerts	C3Q9	..	..	..	..	..	..	..	..	..	21	23
Attendance by all persons at:												
Cinema	JSQJ	50	52	51	54	55	57	56	55	57	61	61
Plays	JSQK	24	24	23	24	22	22	23	23	24	24	25
Art galleries and exhibitions	JSQL	22	21	22	22	21	21	22	21	22	24	24
Classical music	JSQM	12	12	12	12	12	11	12	12	12	13	13
Ballet	JSQN	7	7	7	7	6	6	6	6	6	7	8
Opera	JSQO	7	7	6	7	6	6	6	6	6	7	8
Contemporary dance	JSQP	3	4	4	4	5	4	4	4	5	5	6
Sporting events	JSQQ	80	80	80	78	78	76	75	75	67	68	63
Pop/rock concerts	C3QA	..	..	..	..	..	..	..	..	..	23	25

1 Percentage of resident population aged 15 and over attending 'these days'.
See chapter text.

Source: Target Group Index, BMRB International: 020 8433 4125

12.10 Gambling[1]
United Kingdom

£ million at 2002/03 prices[2]

		1993/94	1994/95	1995/96	1996/97	1997/98	1998/99	1999/00	2000/01	2001/02	2002/03	2003/04
Money staked on gambling												
National Lottery - Total[3]	C229	..	1 417	6 404	5 603	6 325	5 809	5 450	5 315	5 029	4 670	4 614
On-line	C3PU	..	1 404	4 526	4 564	5 408	5 064	4 641	4 416	4 038	3 479	3 225
Instants[4]	C3PV	..	13	1 878	1 039	917	744	612	590	606	592	641
Thunderball	C3PW	..	..	..	..	..	..	197	257	254	287	351
Lottery Extra	C3PX	..	..	..	..	..	..	..	51	131	90	78
HotPicks	C3PY	..	..	..	..	..	..	..	..	..	222	244
Christmas draw	C3PZ	..	..	..	..	..	..	..	..	..	..	15
Euromillions	C3Q2	..	..	..	..	..	..	..	..	..	..	15
Daily Play	C3Q3	..	..	..	..	..	..	..	..	..	..	45
Lotteries (excluding the National Lottery)[5]	C3Q4	55	49	96	136	144	179	114	114	114	134	127
Bingo clubs	C3Q5	1 014	1 017	1 101	1 148	1 170	1 159	1 179	1 190	1 221	1 256	1 381
Football pools	C3Q6	1 191	1 121	727	548	400	286	221	185	151	124	112
Off-course betting[6]	C3Q7	8 232	8 233	7 671	7 972	7 869	7 916	7 996	7 689	9 969	17 985	32 265

1 See chapter text.
2 Adjusted to real terms using the Retail Prices Index.
3 Includes Easy Play tickets which are not shown separately.
4 From 2003/04 includes Inter-active games.
5 From 2002/03 includes Hotspot lotteries.
6 From 2001/02 includes Fixed Odds Betting Terminals.

Sources: National Lottery Commission;
Gaming Board for Great Britain: 020 7306 6253;
Department for Culture, Media and Sport: 020 7211 6121

Environment

Chapter 13

Environment

Air emissions

(Tables 13.1 to 13.7)

Emissions of air pollutants arise from a wide variety of sources. The National Atmospheric Emissions Inventory (NAEI) is prepared annually for the Government and the devolved administrations by the National Environmental Technology Centre (NETCEN), with the work being co-ordinated by the Department for Environment, Food and Rural Affairs (Defra). Information is available for a range of point sources, including the most significant polluters. However, a different approach has to be taken for diffuse sources such as transport and domestic emissions where this type of information is not available and estimates for these are derived from statistical information and from research on emission factors for stationary and mobile sources. Although for any given year considerable uncertainties surround the emission estimates for each pollutant, trends over time are likely to be more reliable.

UK national emission estimates are updated annually and any developments in methodology are applied retrospectively to earlier years. Adjustments in the methodology are made to accommodate new technical information and to improve international comparability.

Three different classification systems are used in the tables presented here: a National Accounts basis (Table 13.1); the format required by the Inter-governmental Panel on Climate Change (IPCC) (Table 13.2); and the EMEP format used by the United Nations Economic Commission for Europe (UNECE) (Tables 13.3–13.7).

The EMEP source categories are detailed below, together with details of the main sources of these emissions.

Power stations: Public power plants, including power generation from waste incineration.

Refineries: Petroleum refineries combustion.

Combustion in fuel extraction and transformation: Combustion in smokeless fuel plant, collieries, oil and gas plant, offshore industry (not flaring).

Domestic combustion: Combustion in residential plant, including domestic boilers and fires.

Commercial, public and agricultural combustion: Commercial and institutional plants; plants in agriculture, forestry and aquaculture.

Power generation within industry: Boilers, gas turbines and other stationary engines for power generation within industry, including iron and steel industry.

Other iron and steel combustion: Iron and steel reheating furnaces, sinter plant, foundries.

Other industrial combustion: Industrial combustion plants, furnaces, industrial production.

Production processes: Processes in petroleum, iron and steel, non-ferrous metal, chemical, wood, food, drink and other industries.

Extraction and distribution of fossil fuels: Extraction of solid, liquid and gaseous fossil fuels, including off-shore activities (apart from gas flaring); liquid fuel, gasoline and gas distribution.

Solvent use: Paint application; degreasing; chemical products manufacturing or processing; other use of solvents.

Road transport: Passenger cars, light and heavy duty vehicles, mopeds, motorcycles; gasoline evaporation from vehicles, tyre and brake wear.

Military: Military aircraft and naval vessels, military machinery (military road vehicles are included in road transport).

Railways: Railway locomotives.

Shipping: Inland waterways boats; domestic navigation, fishing vessels.

Civil aircraft: Domestic and international ground movement and take off and landing cycles up to 1 km from the airport.

Other mobile sources: Agricultural machinery; gardening, construction and aircraft support equipment; mobile industrial equipment powered by diesel or petrol engines.

Waste treatment and disposal: Treatment of domestic, industrial and other waste, including landfill, but excluding incineration with energy recovery; off shore gas flaring.

Agriculture: Culture with and without fertilisers; stubble straw burning; enteric fermentation and manure management of animals; managed forests.

Forests: Volatile organic compounds emissions from managed and unmanaged forests only.

In Tables 13.3 and 13.5, the figures on emissions from individual large combustion plants (LCPs) for 1991 onwards are totals of those reported by the Environment Agency to Defra. For 1970–1990, estimates are made assuming all power station emissions from coal, fuel oil and orimulsion stations are included, plus 79 per cent of refineries' emissions, 12 per cent of iron and steel emissions and 38 per cent of other (Table 13.3), and 88 per cent of refineries' emissions, 11 per cent of iron and steel emissions and 40 per cent of other industrial combustions in fuel extraction and transformation (Table 13.5). It is not possible to calculate LCP figures from the categories presented in these tables as refineries and other industrial combustion are both included in more than one category.

Estimated atmospheric emissions on a National Accounts basis

(Table 13.1)

The National Accounts figures in Table 13.1 differ from those on an IPCC basis in that they include estimated emissions from fuels purchased by UK residents either at home or abroad, including emissions from UK international shipping and aircraft operators and exclude emissions in the UK resulting from the activities of non-residents.

Greenhouse gases include carbon dioxide, methane, nitrous oxide, hydro-fluorocarbons, perfluorocarbons and sulphur hexafluoride which are expressed in thousand tonnes of carbon dioxide equivalent.

Acid rain precursors include sulphur dioxide, nitrogen oxides and ammonia which are expressed as thousand tonnes of sulphur dioxide equivalent.

PM^{10} are carbon particles in the air arising from incomplete combustion.

Further details on the methodology used to allocate emissions using the National Accounts measure are available from the Environmental Accounts website.

Estimated total emissions of greenhouse gases on a IPCC basis

(Table 13.2)

The IPCC classification is used to report greenhouse gas emissions under the Framework Convention on Climate Change and includes land use change and all emissions from domestic aviation and shipping, but excludes international marine and aviation bunker fuels. Estimates of the relative contribution to global warming of the main greenhouse gases, or classes of gases, is presented weighted by their global warming potential.

Emissions of PM^{10}

(Table 13.4)

Emissions of PM^{10} includes particles which pass through a size selective inlet with a 50 per cent efficiency cut-off at 10μm aerodynamics diameter.

Emissions of nitrogen oxides

(Table 13.5)

Most of the figures in this table are based on a single NO_x emission factor for each fuel which is held constant over time. Emissions are expressed as nitrogen dioxide equivalent.

Emissions of carbon monoxide

(Table 13.6)

Most of the figures in this table are based on a single carbon monoxide emission factor for each fuel held constant over time.

Emissions of volatile organic compounds

(Table 13.7)

Most of the figures in this table are based on a single volatile organic compound emission factor for each source held constant over time.

Biological and chemical quality of rivers and canals

(Table 13.9)

The chemical quality of river and canal waters is monitored in a series of separate national surveys in England and Wales and Northern Ireland. The General Quality Assessment (GQA) Scheme used in the surveys provides a rigorous and objective method for assessing the basic chemical quality of rivers and canals based on three determinants – dissolved oxygen, biochemical oxygen demand (BOD), and ammoniacal nitrogen. The GQA grades river stretches into six categories (A-F) of chemical quality and these in turn have been grouped into four broader groups – good (classes A and B), fair (C and D), poor (E) and bad (F).

To provide a more comprehensive picture of the health of rivers and canals, biological testing has also been carried out. The biological grading is based on the monitoring of tiny animals (invertebrates) which live in or on the bed of the river. Research has shown that there is a relationship between species composition and water quality. Using a procedure known as the River Invertebrate Prediction and Classification System (RIVPACS), species groups recorded at a site were compared with those which would be expected to be present in the absence of pollution, allowing for the different environmental characteristics in different parts of the country. Two different summary statistics (known as ecological quality indices (EQI)) were calculated and then the biological quality was assigned to one of six bands based on a combination of these two statistics.

River length stretches were allocated to Government Office Regions using a 1995 digitised map. This provides consistently smaller total river lengths for local areas than the equivalent Environment Agency figures. This is because of differences between stretch lengths used by the Environment Agency and those calculated using the map, and because it was not possible to link all stretch codes to the map, so some stretches were excluded. It should be noted that the monitoring network only covers stretches the Environment Agency are required to monitor, that is rivers and streams with a flow greater than 1m³/second. On this basis 40,000 km of river network are monitored in England and Wales out of an estimated total river length of 150,000 km. No canals are classified in Northern Ireland. The figures in table 13.9 are rounded to the nearest 10km and may not sum to totals.

Water quality of rivers and canals

(Table 13.10)

In Scotland, river and canal water quality is based upon the Scottish River Classification Scheme of 20 June 1997 which combines chemical, biological, nutrient and aesthetic quality using the following classes: excellent (A1), good (A2), fair (B), poor (C) and seriously polluted (D). The figures in the table are also rounded to the nearest 10km and may not sum to totals.

During 2000 a new digitised river network (DRN) was developed, based on 1:50,000 ordnance survey data digitised by the Institute of Hydrology. The new network ensures consistency between all SEPA areas and includes the Scottish Islands which were not previously covered. Data based on this network are published for the first time in the 2004 edition of *Annual Abstract* and are not consistent with data which have previously been published. The DRN includes:

> all mainland and islands rivers with a catchment area of 10 km² or more. This is known as the 'baseline network'.

> mainland and islands stream stretches with a catchment of less than 10 km² which are classified as fair, poor or seriously polluted and have been monitored. These are added to the baseline network to give a 'classification network'.

It is intended that future emphasis will be placed on the baseline network, which is likely to be reportable for the purposes of the EC Water Framework Directive. Efforts to improve the quality of the downgraded smaller streams will continue, but once this has been sustainably achieved, their monitoring may be reduced. Many of these streams are the subject of current attention because of their influence on the quality of larger classification network rivers.

Using the DRN scheme, data for every routine sampling point are automatically applied to an identified river stretch of predetermined length. The loss in total river length in moving to the DRN (i.e. despite the first time inclusion of islands rivers) arises mainly from the exclusion from classification of thousands of small remote headwater streams which were never monitored, but assumed to be of excellent quality. The smaller reduction in length of downgraded waters arises mainly from using 1:50,000 maps for the DRN; in the former system lengths were hand measured from 1:10,000 maps, so more minor channel bends were included.

Water industry expenditure

(Table 13.12)

The table is informed by the annual and regulatory accounts of water and sewerage companies and water companies of England and Wales. Figures are given based on current cost rather than historical cost accounting principles. The elements which make up operating expenditure are as follows: manpower costs, other costs of employment, power, agencies, associated companies, Environment Agency charges, bulk supply imports, general and support, customer services, scientific services, other business activities, local authority rates, water charges, local authority sewerage agencies, materials and consumables, hired and contracted services, charge for bad and doubtful debts, depreciation, infrastructure renewals expenditure, infrastructure renewals accrual, exceptional items and other operating costs. Capital expenditure figures are the addition to tangible fixed assets including management and general expenditure but excluding infrastructure renewals expenditure. Adopted assets at nil cost are also included.

Water pollution incidents

(Table 13.13)

The Environment Agency responds to complaints and reported incidents of pollution in England and Wales. Each incident is then logged and categorised according to its severity. The category describes the impact of each incident on our water, land and air. The impact of an incident on each medium is considered and reported separately. If no impact has occurred for a particular medium, the incident is reported as a Category 4. Before 1999, the reporting system was used only for water pollution incidents, thus the total number of substantiated incidents was lower as it did not include incidents not relating to the water environment.

Bathing waters

(Table 13.14)

Under the EC Bathing Water Directive 76/160/EEC, eleven physical, chemical and microbiological parameters are measured including total and faecal coliforms which are generally considered to be the most important indicators of the extent to which water is contaminated by sewage. The mandatory value for total coliforms is 10,000 per 100 ml, and for faecal coliforms 2,000 per 100 ml. For a bathing water to comply with the coliform standards, the Directive requires that at least 95 per cent of samples taken for each of these parameters over the bathing season are less than or equal to the mandatory values. In the UK a minimum of 20 samples are normally taken at each site. In practice this means that where 20 samples are taken, a maximum of only one sample may exceed the mandatory value for the bathing water to comply, and where less than 20 samples are taken none may exceed the mandatory value for the bathing water to comply.

The bathing water season is from mid-May to end-September in England and Wales, but shorter in Scotland and Northern Ireland. Bathing waters which are closed for the season are excluded for that year.

The table shows Environment Agency (EA) regions for England and Wales. The boundaries of which are based on river catchment areas and not county borders. In particular, the figures shown for Wales are the EA Welsh Region, the boundary of which does not coincide with the boundary of Wales.

Surface and groundwater abstractions

(Table 13.15)

From 1991 data were collected on a different basis. Figures are therefore not strictly comparable with those in previous years. Some regions report licensed and actual abstracts for financial rather than calendar years. As figures represent an average for the whole year expressed as daily amounts, differences between amounts reported for financial and calendar years are small.

The following changes have occurred in the classification of individual sources:

Public water supply: The 1991 figures include some private water supply.

Spray irrigation: This category includes small amounts of non-agricultural spray irrigation.

Mineral washing: From 1999 was not reported as a separate category, licences for mineral washing are now contained in 'Other industry'.

Private water supply: was shown as separate category from 1992 and includes private abstractions for domestic use and individual households.

Fish farming, cress growing, amenity ponds: Includes amenity ponds, but excludes miscellaneous from 1991.

Other: The figure for 1991 included some private domestic water supply wells and boreholes, public water supply transfer licences and frost protection use.

Radioactive wastes

(Table 13.16)

Solid radioactive wastes are not discharged to the environment but stored and conditioned by processes such as supercompaction, cementation or turning into glass. Such wastes cover a wide range of materials and can be classified, according to the nature and quantity of radioactivity associated with them, as high level wastes (HLW), intermediate level wastes (ILW) or low level wastes (LLW). HLW result from the reprocessing of irradiated nuclear fuel and are intensely radioactive. They contain over 95 per cent of all the radioactivity in wastes from nuclear establishments. HLWs are of relatively small in volume, but have a high heat output as a result of the energy from radioactive decay. ILW include the irradiated metal cladding for nuclear reactor fuel, reactor components, and chemical process residues and filters. They have a lower radioactivity and heat output than HLW but their radioactivity content exceeds the upper limits for LLW. LLW includes concrete, rubble and soil from building demolition, discarded protective clothing and worn out or damaged plant and equipment. LLW do not normally require shielding against radiation emissions during handling and transport. LLW volumes are reported, in most cases, as the volumes before supercompaction and grouting before disposal.

The table shows recent trends in the volume of radioactive waste stocks for particular groups of nuclear sites. Data are presented in two physical states – as stored and conditioned. 'As stored' is the form in which the waste is currently stored. For the majority of LLW, storage is short term prior to disposal. 'Conditioned' is the form of waste suitable for long-term storage (i.e. vitrified) in the case of HLW or ultimate disposal to deep underground repositories in the case of ILW. There is no simple relationship between as-stored and conditioned volumes of waste, since the effects of conditioning can vary with different wastes. Conditioning of HLW has yet to start at Dounreay. Volume indicates predicted final conditioned volume. Estimates of conditioned wastes are indicative only and should be interpreted with care.

The table excludes waste from defence establishments prior to 1991. Such ILW and LLW will add no more than 20 per cent to the volumes of radioactive waste from civil sources before 1991.

Annual waste arisings

(Table 13.17)

Agriculture: The estimate is derived from a survey of agricultural waste commissioned by Defra and relates to Great Britain. It includes all waste streams, e.g. excreta from all livestock (both housed and grazing animals) and other wastes including straw, plastics and packaging, animal carcasses and slurries.

Mining and quarrying: The minerals waste estimate is based on ratios of waste to product.

Sewage sludge: The estimate of sewage sludge arisings has been made on the basis of dry weight (wet weight can be estimated on the basis of four per cent solid content on average – giving a total of 26,450,000 tonnes).

Dredged material: The data for dredged material are for all UK waters.

Municipal waste: The UK estimate for municipal waste is based on returns made by Waste Disposal Authorities in England and Wales to a Defra/National Assembly for Wales survey.

Commercial and industrial: UK totals estimated from figures for England and Wales, based on survey by EA.

Demolition and construction: UK total estimated from figures for England and Wales, based on survey by the Office of the Deputy Prime Minister (ODPM).

Noise complaints

(Table 13.19)

The table shows trends in the number of complaints received by local authority Environmental Health Officers (EHOs). The figures are from those authorities making returns and are calculated per million people based on the population of the authorities making returns.

Most complaints about traffic noise are usually addressed to highways authorities or Department for Transport (DfT) Regional Directors, and will not necessarily be included in the figures. Similarly, complaints about noise from civil aircraft are generally received by aircraft operators, the airport companies, the DfT or Civil Aviation Authority. Complaints about military flying are dealt with either by Station Commanding Officers or by Ministry of Defence headquarters. It is also true that railway noise will be reported elsewhere. Thus the figures in this table will not necessarily include these complaints and are likely to be considerably understated. Therefore the information reported to the EHOs is considered to give, at best, only a very approximate indication of the trend in noise complaints from these sources.

Over time some of the categories shown in this table have changed. These have included: Up until 1996/97 Section 62 of the Control of Pollution Act 1974 covered noise in the streets – it primarily included the chimes of ice-cream vendors and the use of loudspeakers other than for strictly defined purposes. From 1997/98 all complaints about noise in the street are included with 'vehicles machinery and equipment in streets'. From 1997/98 complaints about road works are included with 'vehicles machinery and equipment in streets'. The use of the category 'Other' was discontinued in England and Wales from 1997/98. It included some complaints not covered by the other specified sources, but also those where the source was not certain or was due to more than one source. From 1997/98 in England and Wales more vigorous procedures have allocated complaints to the most appropriate source.

Material flows

(Table 13.20)

Economy-wide material flow accounts record the total mass of natural resources and products that are used by the UK economy, either directly in the production and distribution of products and services, or indirectly through the movement of materials which are displaced in order for production to take place.

The direct movement of materials into the economy derives primarily from domestic extraction, that is from biomass (agricultural harvest, timber, fish and animal grazing), fossil fuel extraction (such as coal, crude oil and natural gas) and mineral extraction (metal ores, industrial minerals such as pottery clay, and construction material such as crushed rock, sand and gravel). This domestic extraction is supplemented by the imports of products, which may be of raw materials such as unprocessed agricultural products, but can also be semi-manufactured or finished products. In a similar way the UK produces exports of raw materials, semi-manufactured and finished goods which can be viewed as inputs to the production and consumption of overseas economies.

Indirect flows of natural resources consist of the unused material resulting from domestic extraction such as mining and quarrying overburden and the soil removed during construction and dredging activities. Estimates of indirect flows have been revised following the implementation of the recommendations made by the University of Manchester in a review of indirect flow methodology that took place in 2003. Details of this review are due to be published on the Environmental Accounts website shortly. They also include the movement of used and unused material overseas which is associated with the production and delivery of imports. Water – except for that included directly in products – is excluded from the accounts.

There are three main indicators used to measure inputs. The *Direct Material Input (DMI)* measures the input of used materials into the economy, that is all materials which are of economic value and are used in production and consumption activities (including the production of exports). *Domestic Material Consumption (DMC)* measures the total amount of material directly used in the economy, ie it includes imports but excludes exports. The *Total Material Requirement (TMR)* measures the total material basis of the economy, that is the total primary resource requirements of all the production and consumption activities. It includes not only the direct use of resources for producing exports, but also indirect flows from the production of imports and the indirect flows associated with domestic extraction. Although TMR is widely favoured as a resource use indicator, the estimates of indirect flows are less reliable than those for materials directly used by the economy, and the indicator therefore needs to be considered alongside other indicators.

Designated areas

(Table 13.21)

National Parks, Areas of Outstanding Natural Beauty (AONB's) in England, Wales and Northern Ireland and National Scenic Areas in Scotland are the major areas which have been designated to protect their landscape importance. National Scenic Areas in Scotland are the equivalent of AONB's in England, Wales and Northern Ireland.

Some areas may be in more than one category. All areas shown in the table are at March 2004, except for Green Belt land which relates to 1 January 1997.

The area for Green Belt land is based on a new methodology in which the extent of Green Belt land is captured in digital form.

This approach provides much more reliable figures than those previously published in earlier years.

Further details regarding Tables 13.1 and 13.20 can be found in *Environmental Accounts* on the National Statistics website at: *www.statistics.gov.uk/statsbase/Product.asp?vlnk=3698*.

Further details regarding Tables 13.2 to 13.7, 13.9, 13.13 to 13.18 and 13.21 can be found in Defra's e-Digest of *Environmental Statistics* (on the Defra website at: *www.defra.gov.uk/environment/statistics/index.htm*). If you would like to discuss the tables, Adrian Redfern can be contacted at Defra on 020 7082 8608.

13.1 Estimated atmospheric emissions on a National Accounts basis,[1] 2002
United Kingdom

Thousand tonnes

	Greenhouse gases[2]	Acid rain precursors[3]	Emissions affecting air quality						Lead (Tonnes)	Cadmium (Tonnes)	Mercury (Tonnes)
			PM_{10}	Carbon monoxide	Volatile organic compounds[4]	Benzene	Butadiene				
Agriculture	51 749	505	19.13	50.9	145.0	0.141	0.112	0.16	0.009	0.003
Mining and quarrying	31 848	67	22.82	50.9	199.9	0.318	0.031	0.25	0.012	0.010
Manufacturing	122 817	443	35.10	816.6	363.5	2.821	0.665	113.61	3.052	3.832
Electricity, gas and water supply	175 925	937	10.42	102.4	75.7	0.849	0.047	24.20	0.558	1.501
Construction	3 620	15	5.95	47.2	55.4	0.147	0.085	5.60	0.033	0.013
Wholesale and retail trade	18 314	52	6.67	92.7	77.5	0.308	0.211	0.21	0.016	0.005
Transport and communication	88 227	574	18.20	191.4	50.1	2.205	1.001	2.59	0.108	0.033
Financial intermediation	11 604	27	4.52	91.8	10.3	0.230	0.093	0.15	0.011	0.001
Public administration	10 705	54	1.51	22.6	3.4	0.276	0.033	0.44	0.007	0.038
Education, health and social work	10 901	16	1.74	12.7	2.6	0.065	0.012	0.53	0.009	0.048
Other services	16 049	44	1.69	24.3	13.7	0.936	0.049	3.28	0.357	2.086
Domestic	154 710	320	38.90	1 798.5	338.4	7.266	1.442	13.46	0.347	0.483
Total	696 470	3 053	166.7	3 302.1	1 335.6	15.6	3.8	164.5	4.5	8.1
Of which, emissions from road transport	125 259	538	39.9	1 940.7	214.7	4.5	2.8	1.5	0.17	0.001

1 See chapter text.
2 Thousand tonnes of carbon dioxide equivalent.
3 Thousand tonnes of sulphur dioxide equivalent.
4 Excluding methane, but including benzene and 1,3-butadiene.

Sources: National Environmental Technology Centre;
Office for National Statistics: 020 7533 5904

13.2 Estimated total emissions[1] of greenhouse gases on IPCC basis[2]
United Kingdom

Million tonnes (Carbon dioxide equivalent[3])

		1990	1991	1992	1993	1994	1995	1996	1997	1998	1999	2000	2001	2002
Carbon dioxide	JZCK	603.6	607.4	592.6	577.3	573.0	564.0	584.3	559.7	562.7	554.2	557.9	571.1	551.0
Methane	GXDO	76.9	75.9	74.3	71.3	64.9	64.3	62.8	59.6	56.4	52.6	48.8	46.0	44.1
Nitrous oxide	GXDP	67.9	65.9	59.1	55.4	59.7	57.0	59.1	60.8	58.1	45.0	44.8	42.5	41.0
Hydrofluorocarbons	JZCN	11.38	11.85	12.32	13.00	14.01	15.49	16.72	19.18	17.27	10.83	9.08	9.73	10.42
Perfluorocarbons	JZCO	1.39	1.16	0.57	0.49	0.48	0.46	0.50	0.45	0.44	0.45	0.54	0.44	0.38
Sulphur hexafluoride	JZCP	1.08	1.13	1.18	1.22	1.24	1.29	1.32	1.28	1.31	1.47	1.85	1.46	1.59
Total	GXDQ	762	763	740	719	713	703	725	701	696	665	663	671	648
1990 Baseline[4]	GXJK	766	..	..	..	..	..	..	..	..	..	..	..	..
Percentage change from 1990 baseline	GXDR	..	−0.3	−3.3	−6.1	−6.8	−8.2	−5.4	−8.4	−9.1	−13.2	−13.4	−12.3	−15.3

1 Weighted by global warming potential. Emissions inventories based on the methodology developed by the Intergovernmental Panel on Climate Change (IPCC) are used to report UK emissions to the Climate Change Convention.
2 See chapter text.
3 12 tonnes of carbon is equivalent to 44 tonnes of carbon dioxide.

4 The 1990 baseline, used for comparison with the Kyoto target, is the sum of 1990 totals for carbon dioxide, methane and nitrous oxide and 1995 totals for hydrofluorocarbons, perfluorocarbons and sulphur hexafluoride.

Sources: National Environmental Technology Centre;
for Department for Environment, Food and Rural Affairs 020 7082 8608

13.3 Estimated emissions of sulphur dioxide (SO$_2$): by source[1]
United Kingdom

Thousand tonnes

By source category (UNECE/EMEP)		Percentage of total in 2002	1970	1980	1990	1992	1993	1994	1995	1996	1997	1998	1999	2000	2001	2002
Power stations	JZCR	68	2 913	3 007	2 723	2 434	2 083	1 762	1 591	1 320	1 025	1 072	776	821	742	680
Refineries	GPKK	7	242	262	153	146	148	135	142	144	134	98	93	72	72	66
Combustion in fuel extraction and transformation	JZCT	-	231	25	8	6	5	4	3	3	6	7	9	10	8	5
Domestic	JZCU	4	522	226	108	103	113	92	67	71	63	53	52	45	46	39
Commercial, public and agricultural combustion	JZCV	1	451	218	93	90	95	81	60	57	47	34	27	17	17	12
Power generation within industry	ESYA	9	1 696	816	359	439	438	364	273	221	199	161	116	94	103	93
Other iron and steel combustion	ESYB	1	35	10	18	18	18	16	17	17	17	15	15	11	12	10
Other industrial combustion	ESYC	3	99	80	58	44	42	46	50	49	50	46	43	39	39	34
Production processes	GPLN	3	120	95	71	62	59	57	57	56	51	52	45	38	40	33
Extraction and distribution of fossil fuels	GPKD	-	5	5	16	7	5	6	6	7	6	6	1	1	1	1
Road transport	JZCZ	-	44	42	63	62	59	63	51	37	27	23	14	6	3	3
Military	GPKX	1	9	9	9	9	8	8	8	8	8	6	6	6	6	5
Railways	GPUX	-	14	7	3	3	2	2	2	2	1	1	1	1	1	1
Shipping	GPUY	1	35	25	27	29	30	29	29	30	27	25	22	20	16	14
Civil Aircraft	GPUZ	-	–	–	–	–	–	–	–	–	–	–	–	–	–	–
Other mobile sources	GPLD	-	35	19	8	8	8	7	5	5	5	5	5	4	4	5
Waste treatment and disposal	GPVA	-	5	6	5	5	4	3	3	2	2	2	5	3	5	1
Total	JZDC	100	6 455	4 852	3 721	3 463	3 117	2 676	2 363	2 028	1 670	1 607	1 229	1 189	1 115	1 002

Emissions from large combustion plants

			1970	1980	1990	1992	1993	1994	1995	1996	1997	1998	1999	2000	2001	2002
Large plants	ZBZK		3 626	3 430	2 929	2 674	2 329	1 969	1 756	1 468	1 107	1 207	894	899	822	745
Index (1980=100)	ZBZL		106	100	85	78	68	57	51	43	32	35	26	26	24	22

1 See chapter text.

Sources: National Environmental Technology Centre; Environment Agency; for Department for Environment, Food and Rural Affairs 020 7082 8608

13.4 Estimated emissions of PM$_{10}$: by source[1]
United Kingdom

Thousand tonnes

By source category (UNECE/EMEP)		Percentage of total in 2002	1970	1980	1990	1992	1993	1994	1995	1996	1997	1998	1999	2000	2001	2002
Power stations	JZDN	6	67	76	70	66	55	49	38	35	24	25	20	21	18	10
Refineries	GQOZ	1	5	5	3	4	4	4	4	4	4	4	3	3	2	2
Combustion in fuel extraction and transformation	GQPA	-	16	2	–	–	–	–	–	–	–	–	–	–	–	–
Domestic	GQPB	17	222	103	52	52	53	43	33	35	33	33	35	28	31	28
Commercial, public & agricultural combustion	JZDP	3	19	11	8	8	7	7	6	6	7	6	5	5	5	4
Power generation within industry	EUID	5	66	27	18	22	20	19	17	14	13	11	11	7	9	8
Other iron and steel combustion	EVNZ	2	18	8	9	8	8	7	7	6	6	5	4	4	3	3
Other industrial combustion	EVPN	4	13	11	11	9	9	10	9	11	10	10	9	7	7	6
Production processes in industry	GQPE	7	16	14	16	15	15	16	15	15	15	15	14	12	11	11
Construction, mining and quarrying	GQPF	16	31	25	35	29	30	32	30	28	28	28	26	26	26	26
Road transport	JZDS	24	42	51	60	58	57	56	54	53	49	47	45	40	39	39
Other transport and mobile sources	GQPG	5	15	13	13	12	12	12	11	12	11	11	10	10	9	8
Waste treatment and disposal	GQPH	1	2	4	3	3	3	3	2	2	2	2	2	2	5	1
Agriculture	GQPI	8	11	12	12	12	12	12	12	13	13	14	14	14	14	14
Total	JZGA	100	543	361	311	298	285	270	240	235	215	210	199	179	180	161

1 See chapter text.

Sources: National Environmental Technology Centre; for Department for Environment, Food and Rural Affairs 020 7082 8608

13.5 Estimated emissions of nitrogen oxides (NOₓ): by source[1]
United Kingdom

Thousand tonnes

By source category (UNECE/EMEP)		Percentage of total in 2002	1970	1980	1990	1992	1993	1994	1995	1996	1997	1998	1999	2000	2001	2002
Power stations	JZGB	24	812	861	781	671	567	527	495	449	372	365	338	365	379	379
Refineries	JZGC	2	43	42	40	40	37	36	35	35	33	38	31	28	28	31
Combustion in fuel extraction and transformation	JZGD	4	56	42	61	63	65	75	47	47	47	50	53	53	53	64
Domestic	JZGE	5	62	64	64	69	72	69	66	75	69	71	71	72	75	74
Commercial, public and agricultural combustion	JZGF	2	74	46	38	40	38	38	38	39	36	34	34	32	32	28
Power generation within industry	GWDV	6	292	183	133	137	136	135	126	123	124	118	115	107	108	102
Other iron and steel combustion	GWDW	1	20	6	10	10	10	13	13	13	14	13	14	13	13	9
Other industrial combustion	GWEL	2	108	96	99	77	79	84	80	113	94	79	59	44	38	37
Production processes	JZGI	-	13	14	11	8	8	7	4	4	4	4	4	4	3	2
Extraction and distribution of fossil fuels	GQRZ	-	–	–	1	1	–	1	1	1	1	1	1	1	1	1
Road transport	JZGJ	45	762	978	1 295	1 217	1 160	1 117	1 081	1 079	1 026	973	910	826	760	711
Military	GQSB	1	32	32	35	31	29	28	28	28	28	22	23	22	21	20
Railways	GQSC	1	24	16	21	19	18	14	15	14	12	12	11	11	10	9
Shipping	GQSD	2	62	66	72	72	71	66	64	69	66	62	56	55	44	37
Civil aircraft	GQSE	-	1	2	3	3	3	3	3	3	3	4	4	4	4	4
Other mobile sources	GQSA	4	120	104	89	92	90	88	85	89	87	88	81	78	73	69
Waste treatment and disposal	JZGL	-	6	12	9	9	7	8	8	7	5	5	4	4	4	4
Agriculture	JZGM	-	10	15	9	6	–	–	–	–	–	–	–	–	–	–
Other sources and sinks	C22P	-	–	–	–	–	–	–	–	–	–	–	–	–	–	–
Total[2]	JZGO	100	2 499	2 580	2 771	2 566	2 391	2 311	2 188	2 190	2 022	1 938	1 810	1 718	1 647	1 582

Emissions from large combustion plants

			1970	1980	1990	1992	1993	1994	1995	1996	1997	1998	1999	2000	2001	2002
Large plants	ZBZM		926	948	854	742	636	572	524	471	371	369	333	341	348	338
Index (1980=100)	ZBZN		98	100	90	78	67	60	55	50	39	39	35	36	37	36

1 See chapter text.
2 Excludes emissions from animal pyres in 2001 of 0.6 thousand tonnes, due to the Foot and Mouth epidemic.

Sources: National Environmental Technology Centre; Environment Agency; for Department for Environment, Food and Rural Affairs 020 7082 8608

13.6 Estimated emissions of carbon monoxide (CO): by source[1]
United Kingdom

Thousand tonnes

By source category (UNECE/EMEP)		Percentage of total in 2002	1970	1980	1990	1992	1993	1994	1995	1996	1997	1998	1999	2000	2001	2002
Power stations	JZGP	2	117	121	114	110	99	106	104	102	71	73	61	70	72	71
Refineries	GPVW	-	8	8	7	7	8	7	8	8	8	8	7	6	4	4
Combustion in fuel extraction and transformation	JZGQ	1	45	24	22	20	20	20	22	23	23	26	27	28	27	26
Domestic	JZGR	6	1 237	608	345	347	369	324	260	268	246	239	244	215	229	208
Commercial, public and agricultural combustion	JZGS	1	46	26	23	21	21	20	19	19	19	18	18	18	18	17
Power generation within industry	HFLY	1	103	40	33	39	34	35	33	29	28	25	24	19	22	19
Other iron and steel combustion	HFLZ	8	757	215	385	377	378	342	348	347	353	339	343	241	281	253
Other industrial combustion	HFMA	4	137	101	97	83	86	87	89	94	89	77	113	114	115	118
Production processes	GPVZ	5	217	182	238	218	218	227	231	235	240	217	200	214	211	154
Extraction and distribution of fossil fuels	GPWA	-	2	2	7	3	2	3	3	3	3	3	1	1	1	1
Road transport	GPWB	59	5 266	5 302	5 375	4 959	4 615	4 337	4 064	4 044	3 705	3 384	3 035	2 548	2 183	1 916
Military	GPWD	-	11	11	13	10	10	10	10	10	9	8	8	7	7	8
Railways	GPWE	-	9	6	6	6	5	4	4	4	3	3	3	3	3	3
Shipping	GPWF	-	8	9	9	9	9	9	8	9	9	8	7	7	6	5
Civil aircraft	GPWG	-	1	2	3	3	3	3	3	4	4	4	4	4	4	4
Other transport and mobile sources	GPWC	12	584	512	428	453	439	428	407	408	407	407	406	405	404	404
Waste treatment and disposal	GPWH	1	6	48	34	31	30	38	28	28	23	24	20	19	40	18
Agriculture	JZGY	-	288	449	266	165	4	–	–	–	–	–	–	–	–	–
Other sources and sinks	C22H	-	..	..	10	10	10	10	10	10	10	10	10	10	10	10
Total	JZHA	100	8 842	7 669	7 417	6 872	6 361	6 010	5 651	5 644	5 251	4 874	4 531	3 928	3 636	3 238

1 See chapter text.

Sources: National Environmental Technology Centre; Environment Agency; for Department for Environment, Food and Rural Affairs 020 7082 8608

13.7 Estimated emissions of volatile organic compounds:[1] by source[2]
United Kingdom

Thousand tonnes

By source category (UNECE/EMEP)		Percentage of total in 2002	1970	1980	1990	1992	1993	1994	1995	1996	1997	1998	1999	2000	2001	2002
Power stations	JZHB	1	7	8	7	7	7	8	8	9	8	6	8	8	8	9
Refineries	GQJF	-	1	1	1	1	1	1	1	1	1	1	1	1	1	1
Combustion in fuel extraction and transformation	GQJG	-	2	2	2	3	3	3	1	1	1	1	1	1	1	1
Domestic	JZHC	2	292	128	63	61	61	48	37	40	37	38	41	32	35	32
Commercial, public and agricultural combustion	GQJH	-	4	3	3	4	4	4	4	4	4	4	4	4	4	3
Power generation within industry	GWEO	-	6	5	4	4	4	5	5	5	5	5	5	5	5	4
Other iron and steel combustion	GWEP	-	1	–	–	–	–	1	1	1	1	1	1	–	–	–
Other industrial combustion	GWEQ	-	12	9	5	3	3	3	3	3	3	3	2	3	3	3
Production processes	GQJL	13	292	308	341	331	322	315	321	307	283	262	215	208	185	175
Extraction and distribution of fossil fuels	GQJM	20	64	208	300	294	292	317	307	315	348	315	283	289	288	277
Solvent use	GQJN	29	596	583	675	602	585	579	538	526	512	497	462	429	404	390
Road transport[3]	JZHG	15	527	657	869	811	742	695	631	556	500	431	370	300	249	211
Military	GQJP	-	2	2	2	2	2	2	2	2	2	1	1	1	1	1
Railways	GQJQ	-	4	3	3	3	3	2	2	2	2	2	2	2	1	1
Shipping	GQJR	-	2	2	3	3	3	2	2	3	2	2	2	2	2	1
Civil aircraft	GQJJ	-	–	–	1	1	1	1	1	1	1	1	1	1	1	1
Other transport and mobile sources	GQJO	4	70	64	58	59	58	58	56	57	56	57	56	55	55	54
Waste treatment and disposal	JZHI	1	12	58	45	41	40	48	39	38	33	31	26	22	22	20
Agriculture	JZHJ	-	37	58	35	22	–	–	–	–	–	–	–	–	–	–
Forests[4]	JZHK	13	178	178	178	178	178	178	178	178	178	178	178	178	178	178
Total	JZHM	100	2 107	2 278	2 597	2 430	2 309	2 268	2 136	2 047	1 978	1 836	1 657	1 542	1 443	1 364

1 Excluding methane.
2 See chapter text.
3 Includes evaporative emissions from the petrol tank and carburettor of petrol-engined vehicles.

4 An order of magnitude estimate of natural emissions from managed and unmanaged forests.

Sources: National Environmental Technology Centre; Environment Agency; for Department for Environment, Food and Rural Affairs 020 7082 8608

13.8 Annual rainfall:[1] by region
United Kingdom

Millimetres and percentages

			Annual rainfall as a percentage of the 1961-1990 average										
			1993	1994	1995	1996	1997	1998	1999	2000	2001	2002	2003
Region[2]		1961 - 1990 rainfall average (= 100%) millimetres											
United Kingdom	JSJB	1 080	104	110	95	85	95	117	115	124	97	119	83
North West	JSJC	1 201	93	109	81	78	90	115	109	129	92	118	84
Northumbria	JSJD	853	107	98	91	81	93	120	103	129	104	122	79
Severn Trent	JSJE	754	108	111	87	80	96	116	121	133	105	120	82
Yorkshire	JSJF	821	107	106	82	83	92	114	109	135	99	124	81
Anglian	JSJG	596	120	106	90	78	95	120	115	130	125	120	87
Thames	JSLK	688	111	108	99	78	89	119	112	140	118	130	82
Southern	JSLL	778	114	119	96	82	99	111	107	149	115	131	86
Wessex	JSLM	839	111	119	107	90	101	119	121	140	103	136	86
South West	JSLN	1 173	115	123	98	94	100	121	116	131	94	124	80
England	JSLO	823	108	109	90	81	94	116	112	133	105	122	82
Wales[3]	JSLP	1 355	102	117	89	86	94	122	117	135	100	120	84
Scotland	JSLQ	1 436	99	108	100	85	95	117	116	113	91	113	84
Northern Ireland	JSLR	1 059	110	111	102	103	98	119	117	115	85	133	88

1 Monthly rainfall data for all years have been revised since the last edition. The 1961-1990 average is unchanged.
2 The regions of England shown in this table correspond to the original nine English regions of the National Rivers Authority (NRA); the NRA became part of the Environment Agency upon its creation in April 1996.

3 The figures in this table relate to the country of Wales, not the Environment Agency Welsh Region.

Sources: The Met Office; Centre for Ecology and Hydrology, Wallingford: 01491 838800

13.9 Biological[1] and chemical[2] quality of rivers and canals[3]
England, Wales and Northern Ireland

Kilometres and percentages

| | | Length surveyed | | | | | | | Percentage of total | |
| | | Good | | Fair | | | | | | |
	Years	A	B	C	D	Poor E	Bad F	Total	Good or fair	Poor or bad
Biological quality										
North East	1990	590	770	300	160	140	30	1 990	91	9
	2003	900	760	200	130	40	10	2 030	98	2
North West	1990	450	1 210	630	340	710	460	3 790	69	31
	2003	1 000	1 490	970	650	500	70	4 690	88	12
Yorkshire and the Humber	1990	790	500	340	250	210	220	2 330	81	19
	2003	1 300	830	700	400	250	50	3 540	91	9
East Midlands	1990	340	800	1 160	320	160	40	2 830	93	7
	2003	840	1 130	960	270	80	30	3 310	97	3
West Midlands	1990	480	610	560	360	120	80	2 200	91	9
	2003	960	950	890	380	250	110	3 540	90	10
East	1990	620	1 140	930	240	100	20	3 050	96	4
	2003	1 500	1 240	490	140	40	-	3 410	99	1
London	1990	-	30	80	80	80	20	290	65	35
	2003	20	90	90	100	70	-	360	81	19
South East	1990	1 020	1 210	700	240	130	30	3 330	95	5
	2003	1 780	1 450	740	220	40	-	4 230	99	1
South West	1990	2 380	2 300	720	220	120	60	5 800	97	3
	2003	3 690	1 810	520	160	80	10	6 270	99	1
England[4]	1990	6 980	9 010	5 640	2 300	1 850	990	26 770	89	11
	2003	12 750	10 410	5 920	2 630	1 460	290	33 460	95	5
Wales	1990	1 240	1 380	480	180	50	10	3 330	98	2
	2003	1 390	2 230	790	110	30	10	4 570	99	1
Northern Ireland	1991	710	950	410	100	10	-	2 190	100	-
	2003	810	2 130	1 510	610	120	10	5 190	97	3
Chemical quality										
North East	1990	540	840	320	130	140	50	2 030	91	9
	2003	650	1 090	210	60	70	10	2 090	96	4
North West	1990	820	1 230	760	650	890	420	4 770	72	28
	2003	1 900	1 420	1 090	510	440	70	5 430	91	9
Yorkshire and the Humber	1990	670	1 130	480	410	660	170	3 530	76	24
	2003	1 050	1 320	870	380	380	50	4 050	89	11
East Midlands	1990	80	640	1 270	760	580	80	3 410	81	19
	2003	520	1 400	1 140	310	160	20	3 550	95	5
West Midlands	1990	210	1 170	920	650	550	90	3 590	82	18
	2003	720	1 480	970	440	300	20	3 920	92	8
East	1990	50	690	1 350	800	570	70	3 530	82	18
	2003	200	1 210	1 220	580	340	20	3 580	90	10
London	1990	-	50	120	110	110	10	390	71	29
	2003	-	140	60	100	120	-	420	71	29
South East	1990	340	1 400	1 350	590	630	60	4 370	84	16
	2003	830	1 790	1 110	450	260	10	4 440	94	6
South West	1990	1 620	2 350	1 310	730	380	60	6 460	93	7
	2003	2 720	2 500	910	220	190	10	6 530	97	3
England[4]	1990	4 200	9 160	7 670	4 640	4 300	770	30 740	84	16
	2003	9 580	12 510	7 630	3 640	2 290	210	35 860	93	7
Wales	1990	1 830	1 210	270	130	60	30	3 520	98	2
	2003	3 300	1 120	210	60	80	10	4 780	98	2
Northern Ireland	1991	100	640	680	170	60	20	1 680	95	5
	2003	410	2 080	1 050	470	300	10	4 320	93	7

1 Based on the River Invertebrate Prediction and Classification System (RIVPACS).
2 Based on the General Quality Assessment (GQA) chemical classification system.
3 See chapter text.

4 Figures for the English regions will not add to the national figure for England because a small amount of river lengths which are located along the border between England and Wales are counted in both the national figures for England and Wales.

Sources: Environment Agency;
Environment and Heritage Service

13.10 Water quality of rivers and canals[1]
Scotland

Kilometres and percentages

| | Year | Length surveyed | | | | | | | Percentage of total | |
		Excellent A1	Good A2	Unclassified assumed good	Fair B	Poor C	Seriously polluted D	Total	Good or fair[2]	Poor or seriously polluted
Scottish Environment Protection Agency Regions										
Highlands, Islands and Grampian	1999	..	..	..	480	150	30	11 400	..	2
	2000	960	1 650	8 260	390	140	10	11 400	99	1
	2001	1 420	1 560	7 950	380	90	20	11 420	99	1
	2002	2 020	3 480	5 140	660	90	10	11 400	99	1
	2003	2 610	4 310	3 950	430	90	10	11 390	99	1
South East Scotland	1999	1 120	1 890	2 700	900	450	20	7 090	93	7
	2000	1 430	2 270	2 120	920	390	20	7 160	94	6
	2001	1 520	2 450	1 670	1 000	520	20	7 170	93	7
	2002	2 260	2 800	610	980	510	10	7 160	93	7
	2003	2 570	2 810	430	990	360	10	7 160	95	5
South West Scotland	1999	580	2 260	2 340	1 200	470	40	6 890	93	7
	2000	780	2 170	2 440	1 150	320	30	6 900	95	5
	2001	930	2 320	2 340	960	320	40	6 920	95	5
	2002	1 000	2 370	2 230	930	310	40	6 880	95	5
	2003	1 630	2 430	1 530	960	300	40	6 880	95	5
Scotland	1999	..	..	..	2 580	1 080	90	25 380	..	5
	2000	3 170	6 090	12 820	2 450	850	70	25 450	96	4
	2001	3 870	6 320	11 960	2 340	930	80	25 510	96	4
	2002	5 280	8 660	7 990	2 560	900	60	25 440	96	4
	2003	6 820	9 540	5 900	2 370	750	50	25 440	97	3

1 See chapter text.
2 Classes A1, A2, B and unclassified.

Source: Scottish Environmental Protection Agency: 01786 457700

13.11 Water reservoir stocks:[1] by month
England and Wales

Percentages

		1994	1995	1996	1997	1998	1999	2000	2001	2002	2003	2004
January	JTAS	94.9	95.1	61.2	79.1	90.5	95.8	95.8	94.8	86.5	95.1	79.9
February	JTAT	96.6	97.9	71.3	75.6	93.1	97.0	95.9	94.4	93.7	95.0	93.8
March	JTAU	95.5	98.3	81.8	91.6	92.3	96.5	97.4	95.0	95.5	92.1	92.1
April	JTAV	97.3	97.3	84.9	92.3	96.9	96.9	95.2	95.5	94.5	92.3	94.4
May	JTAW	95.8	92.7	86.2	87.1	97.0	97.0	97.0	96.7	91.9	88.6	94.7
June	JTAX	91.5	87.6	88.1	87.7	93.9	95.4	95.7	91.9	97.0	93.1	90.5
July	JTAY	86.6	79.5	82.2	87.8	95.1	92.0	93.8	85.1	94.9	87.0	84.8
August	JTAZ	76.2	69.1	73.4	81.3	93.5	82.6	88.5	80.7	91.1	81.1	78.5
September	JTBA	68.8	52.8	63.0	73.8	88.3	76.9	83.2	77.9	85.9	69.9	82.4
October	JTBB	71.7	47.3	54.6	70.6	86.6	79.7	88.0	77.0	77.3	60.4	84.2
November	JTBC	74.7	51.6	63.3	69.1	93.3	81.7	95.2	85.5	82.9	53.0	87.5
December	JTBD	85.6	56.5	77.3	76.4	93.1	84.9	96.7	87.9	91.8	60.9	86.2

1 Reservoir stocks are the percentage of useable capacity based on a representative selection of reservoirs; the percentages relate to beginning of each month.

Sources: Water PLCs;
Environment Agency;
Centre for Ecology and Hydrology, Wallingford: 01491 838800

13.12 Water industry expenditure[1]
England and Wales

£ million

		1993 /94	1994 /95	1995 /96	1996 /97	1997 /98	1998 /99	1999 /00	2000 /01	2001 /02	2002 /03	2003 /04
Operating expenditure												
Water supply	KQQX	2 113.5	2 215.0	2 319.6	2 314.9	2 339.3	2 386.1	2 448.1	2 391.0	2 426.9	2 544.2	2 676.5
Sewerage services	KQQY	1 757.0	1 764.0	1 738.4	1 780.7	1 854.6	1 971.3	2 069.8	2 087.1	2 167.6	2 265.2	2 319.4
Capital expenditure												
Water supply	KQSX	1 386.7	1 081.0	1 074.5	1 314.3	1 467.2	1 294.1	1 290.0	935.0	1 132.5	1 347.1	1 346.4
Sewerage	KQSY	410.7	381.0	375.6	479.9	455.2	507.5	488.5	352.0	362.4	507.2	617.6
Sewage treatment and disposal	KQSZ	735.3	763.0	773.0	959.4	1 296.3	1 374.5	1 440.8	1 040.9	996.0	1 066.2	1 235.6

1 See chapter text.

Source: Office of Water Services: 0121 625 1312

205

13.13 Water pollution incidents[1]
United Kingdom

Numbers

		1992	1993	1994	1995	1996	1997	1998		1999[2]	2000[2]	2001[2]	2002[2]
Categories 1 to 3													
Environment Agency Regions													
North West	JZIA	3 270	3 656	3 532	3 717	2 818	2 160	2 201	MKDB	1 668	1 757	1 734	1 805
North East	JZIB	3 059	3 642	3 243	2 576	2 143	2 404	1 993	MKDC	1 828	1 822	1 952	1 789
Midlands	JZKR	4 420	4 876	4 895	4 259	4 305	4 411	4 061	MKDD	2 804	3 106	2 862	2 843
Anglian	JZKS	2 462	2 625	2 819	2 156	2 417	2 411	2 163	MKDE	1 726	1 369	1 606	1 716
Thames	JZKT	1 955	2 071	2 006	1 972	1 959	1 917	1 819	MKDF	1 208	1 379	1 510	1 630
Southern	JZKU	1 089	1 355	1 316	1 235	1 189	1 174	1 138	MKDG	1 317	1 540	1 585	1 511
South West	JZKV	4 278	4 129	4 340	4 558	3 042	2 847	2 603	MKDH	2 463	2 294	2 292	1 929
Welsh	JZKW	2 798	2 945	3 264	2 990	2 285	2 247	1 885	MKDI	1 360	1 395	1 475	1 287
England and Wales	JZKX	23 331	25 299	25 415	23 463	20 158	19 571	17 863	MKDJ	14 374	14 662	15 016	14 510
Scotland[3]	JZKY	3 020	3 081	3 170	2 752	2 878	3 356	2 329	MKDK	2 306	2 345	1 829	1 409
Northern Ireland	JZKZ	..	..	..	..	2 087	1 826	1 644	MKDL	1 507	1 705	1 546	1 510
By category in England and Wales													
Category 1	MKCW	388	331	229	199	156	194	128	MKDM	90	77	118	82
Category 2	MKCX	..	6 768	6 567	2 194	1 510	1 354	1 238	MKDN	863	758	860	784
Category 3	MKCY	..	18 200	18 619	21 070	18 492	18 023	16 497	MKDO	13 421	13 827	14 038	13 644
Category 4[2,4]	MKCZ	..	..	..	..	..	..	..	MKDP	16 548	21 744	18 706	15 370
Total substantiated incidents[4]	MKDA	23 331	25 299	25 415	23 463	20 158	19 571	17 863	MKDQ	30 922	36 406	33 722	29 880

1 See chapter text. Substantiated incidents to water, unless otherwise specified.
2 From 1999, categories 1-3 do not include all substantiated incidents to water. An additional category (Category 4) was introduced which includes all incidents which were substantiated, but which had no impact on the water environment. Therefore, data are not comparable to previous years

3 Data for all years refer to financial years.
4 Category 4 and Total substantiated incidents include incidents to other media (air, land), which did not involve the water environment.

Sources: Environment Agency;
Scottish Environment Protection Agency;
Environment and Heritage Service

13.14 Bathing water:[1] by region
United Kingdom

Numbers and percentages

		Compliance with EC Bathing Water Directive coliform standards during the bathing season												*Percentage complying*
		Identified bathing waters (numbers)						Numbers complying						
		2000	2001	2002	2003	2004		2000	2001	2002	2003	2004		2004
Coastal bathing waters														
Environment Agency Regions														
United Kingdom	GPKA	545	546	547	554	556	GPKN	514	520	535	545	543	GPLA	98
North East	GPKB	56	55	56	55	55	GPKO	51	55	55	53	53	GPLB	96
North West	GPKC	34	34	34	34	34	GPKP	28	30	33	33	33	GPLC	97
Anglian	GPKE	37	37	38	38	38	GPKR	37	36	38	38	38	GPLE	100
Thames	GPKF	3	5	5	8	8	GPKS	3	5	5	8	8	GPLF	100
Southern	GPKG	79	79	79	79	79	GPKT	77	78	78	79	78	GPLG	99
South West	GPKH	187	187	186	188	190	GPKU	179	184	183	186	187	GPLH	98
England	GPKI	396	397	398	402	404	GPKV	375	388	392	397	397	GPLI	98
Wales	GPKJ	75	75	75	78	78	GPKW	74	70	75	77	78	GPLJ	100
Scotland	GPKL	58	58	58	58	58	GPKY	49	49	53	55	54	GPLL	93
Northern Ireland	GPKM	16	16	16	16	16	GPKZ	16	13	15	16	14	GPLM	88
Inland bathing waters														
United Kingdom	JTIG	11	11	11	11	11	JTIH	9	11	11	11	11	JTII	100

1 See chapter text.

Sources: Environment Agency;
Scottish Environment Protection Agency;
Environment and Heritage Service, Northern Ireland

13.15 Estimated abstractions from all surface and groundwater sources: by purpose[1]
England and Wales

Megalitres per day

		1992	1993	1994	1995	1996	1997	1998	1999	2000	2001	2002
Public water supply	JZLA	17 953	16 651	16 735	17 346	17 453	16 820	16 765	16 255	16 990	16 231	16 937
Spray irrigation	JZLB	269	164	283	352	369	292	282	325	291	259	248
Agriculture (excl spray irrigation)	JZLC	129	139	115	103	136	108	111	142	152	108	120
Electricity supply industry[2,3]	JZLD	37 693	26 581	27 732	29 510	31 294	33 307	34 587	26 515	31 546	32 263	35 447
Other industry	JZLE	5 326	6 017	4 292	3 808	4 960	4 352	4 964	5 428	5 433	4 772	4 883
Mineral washing	JZLF	213	198	222	262	250	297	223	..	..	..	..
Fish farming, cress growing, amenity ponds	JYXG	4 479	3 818	3 985	4 268	4 338	4 211	5 495	4 867	4 709	4 657	3 215
Private water supply	JZLG	53	81	82	98	171	162	175	91	102	92	54
Other	JZLH	1 794	93	194	223	531	408	289	526	559	108	77
Total	JZLI	67 909	53 742	53 640	55 970	59 503	59 957	62 891	54 148	59 782	58 489	60 981

1 See chapter text.
2 In South West region in 1992, Hydroelectric licences were classified as "Other", in 1993 they were classified as "Other industry" and from 1994 they were classified correctly as "Electricity supply".

3 A new power station was commissioned in the Thames region in 1994 and began abstracting from tidal waters in 1995. In the Southern region a power station was demolished and rebuilt in 1998-1999.

Source: Environment Agency: 01225 487635

13.16 Radioactive waste stocks and arisings[1,2,3]
Great Britain

Stocks in cubic metres

		1986	1987	1988	1989	1991	1994	1998	2001
High level waste									
As stored	JTCG	1 351	1 430	1 463	1 575	1 686	1 639	1 804	1 961
Sellafield	JTBE	1 200	1 250	1 250	1 320	1 415	1 476	1 577	1 766
Dounreay[4]	JTBF	151	180	213	255	271	163	227	195
Conditioned	JTCH	436	517	594	674	681	653	717	765
Sellafield	JTBG	430	445	509	572	573	640	701	740
Dounreay[4]	JTBH	6	72	85	102	108	13	16	25
Intermediate level waste									
As stored	JTCI	41 887	43 602	47 783	45 313	51 558	61 494	70 948	75 415
Sellafield	JTBI	28 200	29 000	32 900	30 500	33 100	40 000	47 620	51 913
Dounreay	JTBJ	1 620	1 740	1 810	1 900	2 278	3 316	3 636	3 558
Other BNFL sites[5]	JTBK	78	78	73	74	92	61	55	61
Other UKAEA[6]	JTBL	2 340	2 620	2 680	2 630	3 000	3 117	3 370	2 808
Power stations[7]	JTBM	9 520	9 780	9 920	9 820	10 762	11 938	12 580	12 624
Amersham plc	JTBN	129	384	400	389	380	290	293	358
URENCO[8]	JTBO	–	–	–	–	–	27	1	1
Ministry of Defence	JTBP	..	..	..	..	1 946	2 745	3 393	4 092
Conditioned	JTCJ	56 211	59 479	66 020	81 762	78 512	66 102	74 131	74 466
Sellafield	JTBQ	43 600	44 500	51 600	64 100	57 084	37 360	43 942	47 874
Dounreay	JTBR	3 230	3 050	3 100	3 330	3 606	7 092	6 052	5 679
Other BNFL sites[5]	JTBS	99	85	84	81	92	100	121	130
Other UKAEA[6]	JTBT	2 680	2 800	2 800	5 460	5 655	5 808	6 058	3 020
Power stations[7]	JTBU	6 220	8 520	7 870	8 210	9 494	12 606	14 959	14 531
Amersham plc	JTBV	382	524	566	581	605	597	293	345
URENCO[8]	JTBW	–	–	–	–	–	54	1	1
Ministry of Defence	JTBX	..	..	..	..	1 976	2 485	2 705	2 886
Low level waste									
As stored	JTCK	2 429	2 343	1 002	13 752	6 252	7 882	7 983	14 584
Sellafield	JTBY	120	540	523	601	423	1 633	1 913	1 580
Dounreay	JTBZ	–	–	–	12 000	2 686	–	1 086	5 639
Other BNFL sites[5]	JTCA	827	669	151	259	1 042	2 833	2 046	3 474
Other UKAEA[6]	JTCB	810	831	91	229	393	555	226	489
Power stations[7]	JTCC	672	303	237	663	454	780	937	1 682
Amersham plc	JTCD	–	–	–	–	55	5	–	–
URENCO[8]	JTCE	–	–	–	–	–	–	79	70
Ministry of Defence	JTCF	..	..	..	..	1 199	2 076	1 696	1 650

1 See chapter text.
2 Up to 1991 as at 1st January and from 1994 as at 1st April.
3 Excludes waste from defence establishments before 1991.
4 The fall between 1991 and 1994 is due to increased evaporation of liquid waste and its planned vitrification.
5 Includes Calder Hall, Chapelcross, Capenhurst and Springfields.

6 UKAEA (United Kingdom Atomic Energy Authority) includes wastes from minor producers. Some of this is stored at Harwell, while low level waste suitable for disposal goes to Drigg.
7 Includes all BNFL Magnox stations (except Calder Hall and Chapelcross), British Energy power stations and Berkeley Centre.
8 In 1993, BNFL's enrichment business at Capenhurst was transferred to the newly formed Urenco (Capenhurst) Ltd.

Sources: Electrowatt Ekono (UK) Ltd for;
Department for Environment, Food and Rural Affairs 020 7082 8608

13.17 Estimated total annual waste arisings: by sector[1]
United Kingdom

Million tonnes

Sector		Annual arisings						Percentage of total arisings
		1997	1998	1999	2000	2001		2001[2]
Non controlled waste[3]								
Agriculture[4]	JSNA	..	..	87	..	..	JSNP	20
Minerals (Mining and quarrying)								
Colliery	JSNB	15	12	10	9	..	JSNU	2
Coal	JSNC	9	8	8	7	..	JSNV	2
China clay	JSND	26	22	21	22	..	JSNW	5
Clay	JSNE	14	14	14	14	..	JSNX	3
Slate	JSNF	7	9	7	7	..	JSNY	2
Quarrying	JSNG	47	36	47	34	..	JSNZ	8
Controlled waste[5]								
Sewage sludge	JSNH	1	1	..	..	..	JSOA	–
Dredged material	JSNI	22	17	33	..	..	JSOB	8
Municipal waste	JSNJ	31	32	33	34	35	JSOC	8
of which household	JSNK	28	28	30	30	31	JSOD	7
Commercial	JSNL	..	28	..	..	..	JSOE	6
Industrial	JSNM	..	55	..	..	..	JSOF	13
Demolition and construction	JSNN	..	..	80	..	102	JSOG	24
Total (latest available year)	JSNO	..	..	..	..	434	JSOH	100

1 See chapter text.
2 Or latest available year.
3 Not classed as a controlled waste under the terms of the Environmental Protection Act (Controlled Waste Regulations) 1992.
4 Great Britain only.
5 Classed as controlled wastes under the terms of the Environmental Protection Act (Controlled Waste Regulations) 1992.

Sources: Department for Environment, Food and Rural Affairs 020 7082 8608;
Environment Agency;
Water UK

13.18 Recycling[1] of selected materials
United Kingdom

Scrap reused as a percentage of consumption

		1993	1994	1995	1996	1997	1998	1999[2]	2000	2001	2002	2003
Aluminium packaging	C4VH	..	..	..	..	..	..	..	..	24	25	26
Copper	JYWS	35	32	34	36	37	38	47	45	46	..	..
Ferrous	JYWQ	42	42	40	44	45	35	35	34	31	29	33
Glass	JYWW	22	22	22	22	21	22	27	33	34	34	35
Lead	JYWT	67	74	71	73	69	66	64	67	64	60	60
Paper and board	JYWV	32	34	37	38	38	38	38	38	37	38	38
Plastics	C22N	2	3	3	3	3	3	5	6	6	8	10
Waste paper used in newsprint	C22O	31	33	35	44	47	52	55	60	64	65	68
Zinc	JYWU	21	20	20	19	19	18	18	17	16	14	..

1 The ratios shown reflect the amount of secondary material used (scrap collected less exported scrap plus imported scrap) in the UK in a year as a proportion of consumption in that year.
2 Ferrous recycling level for 1999 is estimated.

Sources: Department for Environment, Food and Rural Affairs 020 7082 8608;
Alupro;
World Bureau of Metal Statistics;
Customs and Excise;
Corus;
British Glass Manufacturers Confederation;
Environment Agency;
British Paper & Board Industry Federation;
British Plastics Federation;
The Paper Federation of Great Britain

13.19 Noise complaints received by Environmental Health Officers[1]

Number per million people

England and Wales

		1993/94	1994/95	1995/96	1996/97		1998/99	1999/00	2000/01	2001/02	2002/03	2003/04
Not controlled by the Environmental Protection Act 1990:												
Road traffic	JZLJ	59	60	66	62	JZLJ	39	38	44	37	36	32
Aircraft	JZLK	64	111	48	58	JZLK	109	121	26	101	104	120
Railway						JTHH	14	17	16	12	18	21
Other[2]	JZLL	84	91	90	74							
Total	JZLM	207	262	204	194	JUZR	162	176	86	150	158	173
Controlled by the Environmental Protection Act 1990:												
Industrial/commercial premises	JZLN	1 120	1 320	1 466	1 455	JZLN	1 280	1 368	1 381	1 273	1 315	1 480
Road works, construction and demolition	JZLO	168	300	229	242	SNLE	248	292	325	347	325	335
Domestic premises	JZLP	3 468	3 949	4 895	5 051	JZLP	4 330	5 149	5 001	5 540	5 573	5 973
Vehicles, machinery and equipment in streets[3]	JZLQ	..	249	225	206	JZLQ	252	269	365	372	377	346
Total	JZLR	4 756	5 818	6 815	6 954	JZLR	6 110	7 078	7 072	7 532	7 590	8 134
Controlled by Section 62 of the Control and Pollution Act 1974:												
Noise in streets	JZLS	92	89	109	..							
Total complaints received	JZLT	5 055	6 169	7 128	7 259	JUZS	6 272	7 254	7 158	7 682	7 748	8 307

		1993/94	1994/95	1995/96	1996/97	1997/98		1998/99	1999/00	2000/01	2001/02	2002/03	2003/04
Scotland[4]													
Not controlled by the Environmental Protection Act 1990:													
Road traffic	JZLU	..	..	..	24	21	SNMB	16	..	14	..	..	..
Aircraft	JZLV	..	..	..	14	7	SNMC	5	..	8	..	..	..
Other	JZLW	..	..	..	304	229	SNMD	4	..	6	..	..	..
Total	JZLX	..	..	..	342	257	SNME	25	..	28	..	..	..
Controlled by the Environmental Protection Act 1990:													
Industrial/commercial premises	JZLY	..	..	..	845	504	SNMF	424	..	451	..	..	..
Road works, construction and demolition	JZLZ	..	..	..	206	177	SNMG	114	..	154	..	..	..
Domestic premises	JYWN	..	..	..	754	787	SNMH	660	..	769	..	..	..
Vehicles, machinery and equipment in streets[3]	JYXH	..	..	..	12	41	SNMI	19	..	20	..	..	..
Total	JYWO	..	..	..	1 817	1 509	SNMJ	1 218	..	1 394	..	..	..
Controlled by Section 62 of the Control and Pollution Act 1974:													
Noise in streets	JYXI	..	..	..	27	22							
Total complaints received	JYWP	..	..	..	2 186	1 788	SNMK	1 244	..	1 422	..	..	..

1 See chapter text.
2 In addition, in 1997/98 there were 210 complaints in the "Other" category which have not been included in this table.
3 Noise & Statutory Nuisance Act 1993 applies.
4 The method of collection changed from 1998/99. Data have been slightly reallocated to correspond as closely as possible to the existing categories.

Sources: The Chartered Institute of Environmental Health;
The Royal Environmental Health Institute of Scotland

13.20 Material flows[1]
United Kingdom

		1970	1975	1980	1985	1990	1995	1999	2000	2001	2002	2003
Domestic extraction												
Biomass												
Agricultural harvest	JKUN	42	38	47	47	46	47	52	51	45	51	48
Timber	JKUO	3	3	4	5	6	8	7	7	8	7	7
Animal grazing	JKUP	49	49	49	48	46	45	43	43	43	43	43
Fish	JKUQ	1	1	1	1	1	1	1	1	1	1	1
Total	JKUR	96	92	101	100	100	101	104	102	97	102	100
Minerals												
Ores	JKUS	12	5	1	1	—	—	—	—	—	—	—
Clay	JKUT	38	33	25	23	21	18	15	15	14	14	14
Other industrial minerals	JKUU	5	4	4	4	4	3	3	3	3	3	3
Sand and gravel	JKUV	122	131	110	112	128	106	105	106	105	98	92
Crushed stone	JKUW	156	169	150	160	212	200	179	176	183	173	170
Total	JKUX	333	342	290	299	366	327	302	299	305	287	279
Fossil fuels												
Coal	JKUY	149	129	130	94	94	53	37	31	32	30	28
Natural gas	JKUZ	11	37	39	37	43	71	99	109	106	104	103
Crude oil	JKVA	—	2	80	128	92	130	138	126	118	117	106
Total	JKVB	161	168	249	259	229	254	274	266	256	250	237
Total domestic extraction	JKVC	589	601	641	658	695	682	680	668	658	640	616
Imports												
Biomass	JKVD	38	33	30	31	38	40	42	42	46	46	49
Minerals	JKVE	30	32	24	34	41	51	50	49	52	53	53
Fossil fuels	JKVF	123	111	74	76	89	73	70	83	99	95	102
Other products	JKVG	5	6	13	14	19	23	29	34	34	32	34
Total	JKVH	197	183	140	156	187	187	191	208	230	226	238
Exports												
Biomass	JKVI	3	5	8	11	13	15	16	17	13	15	19
Minerals	JKVJ	17	20	26	22	25	39	45	44	42	41	44
Fossil fuels	JKVK	23	19	60	102	67	103	108	115	118	119	103
Other products	JKVL	5	7	8	11	12	17	19	20	20	20	20
Total	JKVM	47	51	101	146	117	174	187	196	193	195	187
Indirect flows												
From domestic extraction[2], excluding soil erosion	JKVN	525	521	587	580	635	589	566	539	543	533	515
Of which:												
Unused biomass	JKVO	25	23	32	36	37	37	41	40	35	40	38
Fossil fuels	JKVP	169	202	287	274	309	276	259	230	241	225	208
Minerals and ores	JKVQ	139	105	78	77	93	77	67	68	67	67	66
Soil excavation and dredging	JKVR	193	191	191	195	197	199	200	201	202	201	203
From production of imports	JKVS	394	395	368	423	457	527	549	614	711	648	671
Summary aggregates												
Direct material input (Domestic extraction + imports)	JKVT	786	784	781	814	882	869	871	876	888	866	854
Domestic material consumption (Domestic extraction + imports - exports)	JKVU	739	733	680	669	765	695	684	680	695	671	667
Total material requirement (Direct material input + indirect flows)	JKVV	1 705	1 700	1 737	1 817	1 974	1 984	1 986	2 028	2 142	2 047	2 041

1 See chapter text.
2 Indirect flows from domestic extraction relate to unused material which is moved during extraction, such as overburden from mining and quarrying.

Sources: Wuppertal Institute;
Office for National Statistics: 020 7533 5904

13.21 Designated areas:[1] by region, 2004[2]

	National Parks		Areas of Outstanding Natural Beauty[3]		Green Belt Land		Defined Heritage Coasts length (km)
	Area (thousand hectares)	Percentage of total area in region	Area (thousand hectares)	Percentage of total area in region	Area (thousand hectares)	Percentage of total area in region	
United Kingdom	1 972	8	3 377	14	2 032	8	1 568
North East	111	13	143	17	53	6	138
North West	261	18	153	11	252	18	6
Yorkshire and the Humber	315	21	92	6	264	17	80
East Midlands	92	6	52	3	80	5	-
West Midlands	20	2	123	10	267	21	..
East	30	2	110	6	237	12	121
London	-	-	..	..	36	22	..
South East	-	-	637	31	356	19	74
South West	165	7	708	30	106	4	638
England	994	7	2 018	16	1 650	13	1 057
Wales	410	20	72	4	..	..	511
Scotland	568	6	1 002	13	155	2	..
Northern Ireland	-	-	285	20	227	16	..

1 See chapter text.
2 At March 2004, except for Green Belt land which relates to 1 January 1997.
3 National Scenic Area in Scotland. The South East includes London.

Source: Department for Environment, Food and Rural Affairs 020 7082 8608

Housing

Chapter 14

Housing

Permanent dwellings completed

(Table 14.1)

Local housing authorities include the Commission for the New Towns and New Towns Development Corporations, Communities Scotland and the Northern Ireland Housing Executive. The figures shown for housing associations include dwellings provided by housing associations other than the Communities Scotland and the Northern Ireland Housing Executive and provided or authorised by government departments for the families of police, prison staff, the Armed Forces and certain other services.

Homeless households living in temporary accommodation

(Table 14.9)

Comprises households in accommodation arranged by local authorities pending enquiries or after being accepted as homeless under the 1996 Act (includes residual cases awaiting re-housing under the 1985 Act). Excludes 'homeless at home' cases.

Private sector accommodation: Comprises dwellings operated by Registered Social Landlords or local authorities on lease or under licence from the private sector, or placed directly with a private sector landlord.

14.4 Stock of dwellings: Estimated annual gains and losses
England

Thousands of dwellings

		1992 /93	1993 /94	1994 /95	1995 /96	1996 /97	1997 /98	1998 /99	1999 /00	2000[2] /01	2001 /02	2002 /03
Dwelling stock at start of financial year	GRWM	19 836	19 987	20 139	20 305	20 468	20 622	20 778	20 927	21 075	21 207	21 330
Gains to dwelling stock:												
Housebuilding completions	GRWN	142.5	147.7	158.0	154.6	146.2	149.6	138.6	141.8	133.7	130.1	137.9
Conversions (net gain)[1]	GRWO	8.3	7.5	9.9	8.9	8.6	2.8	4.2	3.5	2.8	5.1	3.8
Change of use	GRWP	..	..	..	..	..	11.6	15.9	13.9	9.2	14.8	16.2
Non-permanent dwellings additions	GRWQ	..	..	..	..	..	0.2	0.2	0.3	0.3	0.3	0.7
Losses from dwelling stock:												
Slum clearance (non LA owned dwelling demolished)	GRWR	2.0	3.9	3.0	2.7	2.9	1.3	1.3	1.4	1.7	1.6	1.2
Other demolitions[1]	GRWS	4.3	5.2	5.8	4.8	4.1	12.8	13.2	15.8	18.3	24.7	22.0
Change of use	GRWT	..	..	..	..	..	0.7	1.4	0.8	0.7	0.8	1.2
Non-permanent dwelling losses	GRWU	..	..	..	..	..	0.1	0.2	0.1	0.3	0.3	0.2
New gain in year	GRWV	144.5	146.2	159.0	156.0	147.8	149.3	143.0	141.3	125.0	122.8	134.0
Adjustment[3]	VQDN	6.6	6.6	6.6	6.6	6.6	6.6	6.6	6.6	6.6	–	–
Dwelling stock at end of financial year	GRWW	19 987	20 139	20 305	20 468	20 622	20 778	20 927	21 075	21 207	21 330	21 464

1 Figures prior to 1997/98 include change of use, and zero for net non-permanent dwellings.

2 Figures for 2000/01 conversions, change of use and non permanent dwellings are based on reported figures and do not include estimates for missing returns.

3 Series has been adjusted so that the 2000/01 estimates matches the 2001 Census.

Source: Office of the Deputy Prime Minister: 0117 372 8055

14.5 Housebuilding completions: by number of bedrooms

Percentages

		1993 /94	1994 /95	1995 /96	1996 /97	1997 /98	1998 /99	1999 /00	2000 /01	2001 /02	2002 /03	2003 /04
England												
1 bedroom	JUWJ	14	12	11	8	7	7	7	7	7	6	8
2 bedrooms	JUWK	33	32	32	29	27	27	26	27	25	29	33
3 bedrooms	JUWL	33	34	35	36	38	36	35	34	31	30	29
4 or more bedrooms	JUWM	19	22	23	26	28	30	32	32	37	34	30
All houses and flats	JUWN	100	100	100	100	100	100	100	100	100	100	100
Wales												
1 bedroom	JUWO	10	7	8	5	4	3	5	5	4	6	6
2 bedrooms	JUWP	33	30	30	27	24	21	19	18	19	18	20
3 bedrooms	JUWQ	43	47	44	47	46	46	43	42	39	35	37
4 or more bedrooms	JUWR	15	15	18	21	26	30	34	34	38	41	37
All houses and flats	JUWS	100	100	100	100	100	100	100	100	100	100	100

Sources: Office of the Deputy Prime Minister;
National Assembly for Wales

14.6 Mortgages
United Kingdom

		1993	1994	1995	1996	1997	1998	1999	2000	2001	2002	2003
Mortgages[1] (Thousands)	JUTH	10 137	10 410	10 521	10 637	10 738	10 821	10 982	11 173	11 270	11 364	11 452
Arrears and repossessions[1] (Thousands)												
Loans in arrears at end-period												
By 6-12 months	JUTI	165	134	127	101	74	74	57	48	41	34	29
By over 12 months	JUTJ	152	117	85	67	45	35	30	21	18	16	13
Properties repossessed in period	JUTK	59	49	49	43	33	34	30	23	17	12	8
Type of mortgage for house purchase[2] (Percentages)												
Standard repayment	JUTL	20.9	25.7	33.7	38.3	39.6	42.7	46.1	59.9	71.9	81.4	78.4
Endowment	JUTM	64.3	61.0	50.6	37.5	35.3	33.1	26.6	17.1	10.4	4.8	3.2
Other[3]	JUTN	14.7	13.3	15.7	24.2	25.1	24.3	27.3	23.0	17.7	13.8	18.4

1 Estimates cover only members of the Council of Mortgage Lenders; these account for 98 per cent of all mortgages outstanding.
2 Includes new mortgages advanced by building societies and other major lenders. Includes sitting tenants.
3 Includes interest only, PEP/ISA and pension.

Sources: Council of Mortgage Lenders; Office of the Deputy Prime Minister

14.7 County Court mortgage possession orders:[1] by region

Thousands

		1991	1996	1997	1998	1999	2000	2001	2002	2003
Actions entered										
England and Wales	JURS	186.6	79.8	67.0	84.8	81.6	73.0	65.0	61.7	64.2
North East	JURT	6.0	3.5	3.0	4.3	4.2	4.0	3.4	3.1	3.0
North West	JURU	22.3	12.7	10.9	14.2	13.8	12.4	11.7	10.7	7.8
Yorkshire and the Humber	JURV	14.1	7.6	6.9	8.2	8.1	7.8	6.9	6.2	5.5
East Midlands	JURW	13.5	5.9	4.9	6.4	6.8	5.7	5.4	4.7	4.7
West Midlands	JURX	17.7	7.6	6.7	8.1	9.5	9.8	7.6	6.3	7.2
East	JURY	18.6	8.3	6.7	8.5	7.3	6.2	5.5	5.4	6.2
London	JURZ	35.3	11.4	9.2	11.4	10.0	8.1	7.4	8.7	10.1
South East	JUSA	32.2	11.6	9.1	11.2	9.4	8.6	8.2	8.0	8.9
South West	JUSB	16.7	6.3	5.7	7.3	7.0	5.2	4.4	4.1	4.4
England	JUSC	176.4	74.9	63.1	79.6	77.1	67.7	60.5	57.1	60.1
Wales	JUSD	10.2	4.9	3.9	5.4	5.5	5.3	4.5	4.7	4.1
Northern Ireland[2]	JUSE	3.1	1.2	1.2	1.6	1.9	1.7	1.6	1.6	..
Suspended orders										
England and Wales	JUSF	69.1	43.4	34.8	40.8	36.6	31.7	27.9	23.5	23.4
North East	JUSG	2.9	2.0	1.6	2.3	2.3	1.9	1.6	1.2	1.2
North West	JUSH	8.6	7.7	5.5	6.4	6.0	5.7	5.0	4.5	3.9
Yorkshire and the Humber	JUSI	5.1	3.9	3.5	4.3	4.1	3.7	3.2	2.5	2.1
East Midlands	JUSJ	4.5	3.0	2.6	3.1	2.8	2.4	2.4	1.8	1.6
West Midlands	JUSK	6.5	3.9	3.4	3.8	4.0	3.7	3.5	2.5	2.7
East	JUSL	6.0	4.0	3.0	3.9	3.5	2.5	2.2	2.0	2.2
London	JUSM	13.1	6.4	4.7	5.3	4.5	3.1	2.7	2.7	3.3
South East	JUSN	13.2	6.6	5.4	5.8	4.4	3.9	3.4	2.9	3.1
South West	JUSO	5.8	3.3	2.7	3.0	2.8	2.3	1.8	1.7	1.7
England	JUSP	65.6	40.7	32.4	37.9	34.9	29.1	25.8	21.7	21.7
Wales	JUSQ	3.5	2.7	2.4	2.8	2.2	2.6	2.1	1.9	1.7
Northern Ireland[2]	JUSR	..	..	..	0.2	0.3	0.2	0.2	0.2	..
Orders made										
England and Wales	JUSS	73.9	27.8	22.5	25.3	23.6	20.4	17.8	16.2	16.4
North East	JUST	1.9	1.1	1.0	1.2	1.1	1.1	1.1	0.8	0.8
North West	JUSU	7.5	4.0	3.3	3.7	3.7	3.7	3.4	3.0	2.6
Yorkshire and the Humber	JUSV	5.7	2.6	2.3	3.1	3.0	2.4	2.2	1.7	1.6
East Midlands	JUSW	5.2	2.0	1.7	1.7	1.8	1.6	1.4	1.4	1.1
West Midlands	JUSX	6.9	2.1	2.0	2.4	2.3	2.3	2.1	1.7	1.7
East	JUSY	8.4	3.4	2.5	2.6	2.2	1.6	1.4	1.3	1.6
London	JUSZ	14.4	4.8	3.4	3.5	3.4	2.1	1.8	2.3	2.8
South East	JUTA	13.2	4.0	3.1	3.4	2.7	2.6	1.9	1.8	2.1
South West	JUTB	6.5	2.4	1.9	2.1	2.0	1.3	1.1	1.0	1.0
England	JUTC	69.9	26.4	21.2	23.7	22.2	18.7	16.4	15.0	15.2
Wales	JUTD	4.0	1.4	1.3	1.7	1.4	1.6	1.4	1.2	1.2
Northern Ireland[2]	JUTE	..	..	..	0.5	0.7	0.6	0.7	0.5	..

1 Local authority and private.
2 Mortgage possession actions are heard in Chancery Division of Northern Ireland High Court.

Sources: The Court Service: 020 7210 1752; Northern Ireland Court Service: 028 9032 8594

14.8 Sales and transfers of local authority dwellings
Great Britain

Numbers

		1993	1994	1995	1996	1997	1998	1999	2000	2001	2002	2003
Right to buy sales	JUQV	60 448	65 241	49 599	44 980	58 056	55 965	66 773	71 290	66 563	78 523	95 625
Large scale voluntary transfers	JUQW	27 500	41 019	47 676	29 862	21 116	36 871	88 672	111 443	100 753	102 467	104 626
Other sales and transfers[1]	JUQX	6 021	4 560	3 161	2 962	3 414	2 660	3 349	2 405	1 593	1 407	613
Total sales and transfers	JUQY	93 969	110 820	100 436	77 804	82 586	95 496	158 794	185 138	168 909	182 397	200 864

1 Excludes transfers in Wales.

Sources: Office of the Deputy Prime Minister;
National Assembly for Wales;
Scottish Executive

14.9 Homeless households living in temporary accommodation[1]
England
As at 31 March of each year

Thousands

		1994	1995	1996	1997	1998	1999	2000	2001	2002	2003	2004
Bed and breakfast hotels[2]	JUWF	4 920	4 480	4 750	4 100	4 820	6 570	8 680	10 860	11 840	12 070	7 170
Hostels/women's refuges	JUWG	10 460	10 380	10 090	9 680	9 730	9 840	10 300	10 610	9 610	10 010	10 850
Private sector accommodation	JXVN	20 860	14 130	11 410	14 040	14 820	19 270	20 060	25 610	28 370	37 130	50 080
Other accommodation[3]	JXVO	16 100	17 360	16 990	13 430	18 150	20 900	26 130	28 120	30 620	30 210	29 190
All accommodation	JUWI	52 340	46 350	43 240	41 250	47 520	56 580	65 170	75 200	80 440	89 400	97 290

1 See chapter text.
2 Private sector properties leased by social sector landlords, and households placed directly with a private sector landlord. From 2002 some self-contained accommodation in Annexe-style units, previously recorded under Bed and breakfast hotels, is now more appropriately attributed to private sector accommodation.
3 Includes local authorities' and Registered Social Landlords' own stock.

Source: Office of the Deputy Prime Minister

Transport and communications

Chapter 15

Transport and communications

Road data

(Tables 15.4, 15.5, 15.6 and 15.7)

The Department for Transport (DfT) has undertaken significant development work over the last two years to improve its traffic estimates and measurement of traffic flow on particular stretches of the road network. This work has previously been outlined in a number of publications (*Road Traffic Statistics: 2001 SB(02)23, Traffic in Great Britain Q4 2002 Data SB(03)5* and *Traffic in Great Britain Q1 2003 SB(03)6*).

The main point to note is that figures for 1993 to 2003 have been calculated on a different basis from years prior to 1993. Therefore, figures prior to 1993 are not directly comparable with estimates for later years. Estimates on the new basis for 1993 and subsequent years were first published by the Department on 8 May 2003 in Traffic in Great Britain Q1 2003 SB(03)6.

A summary of the main methodological changes to take place over the last couple of years appears below:

Traffic estimates are now disaggregated for roads in urban and rural areas rather than between built-up and non built-up roads. Built-up roads were defined as those with a speed limit of 40mph or lower. This created difficulties in producing meaningful disaggregated traffic estimates because an increasing number of clearly rural roads were subject to a 40mph speed limit for safety reasons. The urban/rural split of roads is largely determined by whether roads lie within the boundaries of urban areas with a population of 10,000 or more with adjustments in some cases for major roads at the boundary. At the time of publication the urban areas based on the 2001 Census had not been finalised, the figures in this bulletin are therefore provisional.

Traffic estimates are based on the results of many 12-hour manual counts in every year which are grossed up to estimates of annual average daily flows using expansion factors based on data from automatic traffic counters on similar roads. These averages are needed so that traffic in off-peak times, at weekends and in the summer and winter months (when only special counts are undertaken) can be taken into account when assessing the traffic at each site. For this purpose roads are now sorted into 22 groupings (previously there were only seven) and this allows a better match of manual count sites with our automatic count sites. These groupings are based on a detailed analyses of the results from all the individual automatic count sites and take into account regional groupings, road category (i.e. both the urban/rural classification of the road and the road class) and traffic flow levels. The groupings range from lightly-trafficked, rural minor roads in holiday areas such as Cornwall and Devon, to major roads in Central London.

With the increasing interest in sub-regional statistics, we have undertaken a detailed study of traffic counts on minor roads carried out in the last ten years. This has been done in conjunction with a Geographic Information System to enable us to establish general patterns of minor road traffic in each local authority. As a result of this, we have been able to produce more reliable estimate of traffic levels in each authority in our base year of 1998. This in turn has enabled us to produce better estimates of traffic levels back to 1993, as well as more reliable estimates for 1999 onwards.

The Department created a database for major roads based on a Geographic Information System and Ordnance Survey data. This was checked by local authorities and discussed with Government Regional Offices and the Highways Agency to ensure that good local knowledge supplemented the available technical data.

Road class

(Tables 15.5 and 15.6)

Urban major and minor roads, from 1993 onwards are defined as being within an urban area with a population of more than 10,000 people, these are based on the 2001 urban settlements. The definition for 'urban settlement' is 'Urban and rural area definitions: a user guide which can be found on the Office of the Deputy Prime Minister website at *www.odpm.gov.uk/stellent/groups/odpm_planning/ documents/page/odpm_plan_609188.hcsp*.

Rural major and minor roads, from 1993 onwards, are defined as being outside an urban settlement.

New vehicle registrations

(Table 15.9)

Special concession group

Various revisions to the vehicle taxation system were introduced on 1 July 1995 and on 29 November 1995. Separate taxation classes for farmers' goods vehicles were abolished on 1 July 1995; after this date new vehicles of this type were registered as HGVs. The total includes 5,900 vehicles registered between 1 January and 30 June in the (now abolished) agricultural and special machines group in classes which were not eligible to register in the special concession group. The old agricultural and special machines taxation group was abolished at the end of June 1995. The group includes agricultural and mowing machines, snow ploughs and gritting vehicles. Electric vehicles are also included in this group and are no longer exempt from 'Vehicle Excise Duty' (VED). Steam propelled vehicles were added to this group from November 1995.

Other licensed vehicles

Includes three wheelers, pedestrian controlled vehicles, general haulage and showmen's tractors and recovery vehicles. Recovery vehicle tax class introduced in January 1988.

Special vehicles group

The special vehicles group was created on 1 July 1995 and consists of various vehicle types over 3.5 tonnes gross weight but not required to pay VED as heavy goods vehicles. The group includes mobile cranes, works trucks, digging machines, road rollers and vehicles previously taxed as showman's goods and haulage. Figure shown for 1995 covers period from 1 July to 31 December only.

Full car driving licence holders – National Travel Survey data

(Table 15.11)

The 2003 National Travel Survey (NTS) is the latest in a series of household surveys designed to provide a databank of personal travel information for Great Britain. The survey is part of a continuous survey that began in July 1988, following *ad hoc* surveys since the mid-1960s. The survey is designed to pick up long-term trends and is not suitable for monitoring short-term trends.

The drawn sample size for 2002 onwards was nearly trebled compared with previous years following recommendations in a National Statistics Review of the National Travel Survey. This enables key results to be presented on a single year basis for the first time since the survey became continuous.

Changes to the methodology in 2002 mean that there are some inconsistencies with data for earlier years. The 2003 results presented in the table should be regarded as provisional.

During 2003, individuals in over 8,200 households provided details of their personal travel by filling in travel diaries over a period of seven days, compared with nearly 3,500 households in 2001. Previously, data have been shown for a three year time period because of the smaller sample size.

Travel details provided by respondents include trip purpose, method of travel, time of day and trip length. The households also provided personal information, such as their age, sex,

working status, and driving licence holding, and details of the cars available for their use.

Because estimates made from a sample survey depend upon the particular sample chosen they generally differ from the true values of the population. This is not usually a problem when considering large samples (such as all car trips in Great Britain), but may give misleading information when considering data from small samples.

The most recent editions of all NTS publications are available on the DfT website at *www.transtat.dft.gov.uk*. Bulletins of key results are published annually. The most recent bulletin is *National Travel Survey: 2003 Update*. More detailed data for 2002/2003 combined will be published in *Focus on Personal Travel* early in 2005.

Activity at civil aerodromes

(Table 15.28)

Figures exclude Channel Island airports. 'Other' covers local pleasure flights, scheduled service, positioning flights and non-transport charter flights for reward (for example: aerial survey work, crop dusting and delivery of empty aircraft) and 'Non-commercial' covers test and training flights, private, aeroclub, military and official flights, and Business Aviation, etc.

International passenger movements by air and sea

(Table 15.31)

Figures shown in the table are for arrivals plus departures.

EC Europe includes Azores, Madeira, Canary and Cape Verde Islands, Austria, Finland and Sweden joined the EC in 1995, but are included in the EC section for all years to show a consistent time series. Other Western Europe includes Iceland and the Faroe Islands.

For Pleasure cruises, passengers are included at both departure and arrival if their journeys begin and end at the United Kingdom seaports.

Postal services and television licences

(Table 15.32)

Data for letters, postal orders and telegrams sent, is shown up to 31 March of each year and data for television licences is at 31 March each year.

Letters posted category includes printed papers, newspapers, postcards and sample packets, Airmail includes letters without special charge for air transport. Business reply and freepost is now known as Response Services.

15.1 Trips per person per year: by main mode[1] and purpose, 2002/03[2]
Great Britain

Numbers

	Walk	Bicycle	Car/van driver	Car/van passenger	Motor-cycle	Other private
Commuting	15	5	90	16	2	1
Business	3	-	25	2	-	-
Education	28	1	2	19	-	4
Escort education	19	-	21	6	-	-
Shopping	51	2	82	42	-	-
Other escort	11	-	52	29	-	-
Other personal business	29	1	44	23	-	1
Visiting friends at home	24	2	44	40	-	-
Visiting friends elsewhere	13	-	12	13	-	-
Social/entertainment	9	1	25	24	-	1
Holidays/day trips	2	2	13	14	-	1
Other, including just walk	40	-	-	-	-	-
All purposes	244	15	410	228	3	8

	Local bus	Non-local bus	London Under-ground	Surface rail	Taxi/minicab	Other public	All modes
Commuting	11	-	3	5	1	1	150
Business	1	-	1	1	-	-	33
Education	9	-	1	1	1	-	65
Escort education	1	-	-	-	-	-	47
Shopping	17	-	-	1	2	-	197
Other escort	2	-	-	-	-	-	95
Other personal business	6	-	-	1	1	-	106
Visiting friends at home	6	-	-	1	2	-	119
Visiting friends elsewhere	2	-	-	-	3	-	45
Social/entertainment	3	-	-	1	1	-	65
Holidays/day trips	1	1	-	1	-	-	35
Other, including just walk	-	-	-	-	-	-	40
All purposes	59	1	6	12	11	2	998

1 Main mode is that used for the longest part of the trip.
2 This is an average of the 2002 and 2003 calendar years and not a financial year.

Source: Department for Transport 020 7944 3097

15.2 Retail Prices Index: real changes in the cost of transport and disposable income
Great Britain

Constant prices

Indices (1974=100)

	Petrol/oil	All motoring	Rail	Bus and coach fares	Disposable income
	ZCFV	ZCFW	ZCFX	ZCFY	ZCFZ
1982	107.4	101.0	146.5	133.3	113.0
1983	109.8	103.2	148.5	134.7	115.4
1984	108.2	100.7	142.0	131.1	119.6
1985	108.5	99.4	142.4	128.9	123.8
1986	91.3	94.7	147.0	135.2	128.9
1987	88.4	96.3	148.4	137.4	133.5
1988	83.4	95.9	151.3	140.1	140.9
1989	82.9	93.9	153.2	140.2	147.5
1990	84.6	91.0	152.2	135.1	152.7
1991	85.9	92.3	158.8	145.5	155.7
1992	85.2	95.0	164.2	150.2	160.1
1993	90.5	97.6	173.0	154.3	164.5
1994	92.4	98.5	176.3	154.6	166.9
1995	93.9	97.0	178.1	155.0	170.7
1996	96.3	97.5	180.3	156.9	174.9
1997	102.7	99.6	178.9	157.6	182.2
1998	104.2	99.3	180.1	157.3	182.8
1999	111.3	100.2	183.8	160.6	188.6
2000	122.4	101.0	181.6	162.3	200.4
2001	114.0	98.7	185.3	166.1	209.6
2002	108.7	96.3	186.5	168.5	213.2
2003	109.4	94.8	184.3	170.6	218.2

Source: Office for National Statistics: 020 7533 5874

224

15.3 Domestic freight transport: by mode
Great Britain

		1993	1994	1995	1996	1997	1998	1999	2000	2001	2002	2003
Goods moved (billion tonnes kilometres)												
Petroleum products												
Road[1]	ZBZP	5.0	5.1	5.7	6.1	5.8	5.1	4.9	6.3	5.8	5.2	5.4
Rail	ZBZQ	1.9	1.8	1.8	..	..	1.6[3]	1.5	1.4	1.2	1.1	1.2
Water[2]	ZBZR	41.7	43.0	42.5	45.9	38.3	45.2	48.6	52.7	43.5	51.7	..
of which: coastwise	ZBZS	28.9	28.9	31.4	38.7	33.8	36.4	33.3	26.0	23.1	24.2	..
Pipeline	ZBZT	11.6	12.0	11.1	11.6	11.2	11.7	11.6	11.4	11.5	10.9	10.5
All modes	ZBZU	60.2	61.9	61.1	63.6[4]	55.3[4]	63.6	66.6	73.9	62.0	68.9	..
Coal and coke												
Road[1]	ZBZV	3.1	2.9	2.7	2.5	2.7	2.0	2.2	1.5	2.1	1.5	1.5
Rail	ZBZW	3.9	3.3	3.6	3.9	4.4	4.5[3]	4.8	4.8	6.2	5.7	5.8
Water[2]	ZBZX	1.5	1.4	2.3	0.6	0.6	0.5	0.5	0.2	0.5	0.3	..
All modes	ZBZY	8.5	7.6	8.6	6.9	7.7	7.0	7.5	6.5	8.8	7.5	7.3
Other traffic												
Road[1]	ZBZZ	126.4	135.7	141.2	145.3	148.6	152.4	149.6	150.2	149.0	150.6	152.4
Rail	ZCAA	7.9	7.9	7.9	11.2	12.5	11.2[3]	11.9	11.9	12.0	11.9	11.9
Water[2]	ZCAB	8.0	7.8	8.3	8.7	9.2	11.2	9.6	14.6	14.8	15.2	..
All modes	ZCAC	142.3	151.4	157.4	165.3	170.3	174.8	171.1	174.5	175.8	177.7	164.3
All traffic												
Road[1]	KCTA	134.5	143.7	149.6	153.9	157.1	159.5	156.7	158.0	156.9	157.3	159.3
Rail	KCTB	13.8	13.0	13.3	15.1	16.9	17.3[3]	18.2	18.1	19.4	18.7	18.9
Water[2]	ZCAD	51.2	52.2	53.1	55.3	48.1	56.9	58.7	67.4	58.8	67.2	..
Pipeline	KCTE	11.6	12.0	11.1	11.6	11.2	11.7	11.6	11.4	11.5	10.9	10.5
All modes	KCTF	211.1	220.9	227.1	235.9	233.3	245.4	245.2	254.9	246.6	254.7	..
Percentage of all traffic												
Road[1]	ZCAE	*64*	*65*	*66*	*65*	*67*	*65*	*64*	*62*	*64*	*62*	*..*
Rail	ZCAF	*7*	*6*	*6*	*6*	*7*	*7[3]*	*7*	*7*	*8*	*7*	*..*
Water[2]	ZCAG	*24*	*24*	*23*	*23*	*21*	*23*	*24*	*26*	*24*	*26*	*..*
Pipeline	ZCAH	*5*	*5*	*5*	*5*	*5*	*5*	*5*	*4*	*5*	*4*	*..*
All modes	ZCAI	*100*	*100*	*100*	*100*	*100*	*100*	*100*	*100*	*100*	*100*	*..*
Goods lifted (million tonnes)												
Petroleum products												
Road[1]	ZCAJ	67	68	71	75	73	61	61	74	74	59	64
Rail	ZCAK	9	8	6	..	..	..	..	..	..	..	..
Water[2]	ZCAL	64	70	72	71	69	76	72	72	60	67	..
of which: coastwise	ZCAM	42	43	47	54	52	55	52	40	34	36	..
Pipeline	ZCAN	125	161	168	157	148	153	155	151	151	146	141
All modes	ZCAO	265	307	317	303[4]	290[4]	290[4]	288[4]	297	285	272	..
Coal and coke												
Road[1]	ZCAP	48	42	34	32	37	22	28	22	21	17	22
Rail	ZCAQ	49	43	45	52	50	45	44[5]	46	46	41	42
Water[2]	ZCAR	5	4	4	3	4	3	3	3	3	2	..
All modes	ZCAS	102	89	83	87	91	70	75	71	70	60	..
Other traffic												
Road[1]	ZCAT	1 500	1 579	1 596	1 623	1 630	1 646	1 572	1 593	1 565	1 632	1 639
Rail	ZCAU	45	47	50	50	55	57	48[5]	50	48	46	47
Water[2]	ZCAV	65	66	67	67	69	70	70	62	68	70	..
All modes	ZCAW	1 610	1 692	1 713	1 740	1 754	1 773	1 690	1 709	1 681	1 748	..
All traffic												
Road[1]	KCTG	1 615	1 689	1 701	1 730	1 740	1 727	1 661	1 689	1 660	1 708	1 725
Rail	KCTH	103	97	101	102	105	102	92[5]	95	94	87	89
Water[2]	ZCAX	134	140	143	142	142	149	144	137	131	139	..
Pipeline	KCTK	125	161	168	157	148	153	155	151	151	146	141
All modes	KCTL	1 977	2 087	2 113	2 131	2 135	2 131	2 052	2 072	2 037	2 080	..
Percentage of all traffic												
Road[1]	ZCAY	*82*	*81*	*80*	*81*	*81*	*81*	*81*	*81*	*81*	*82*	*..*
Rail	ZCAZ	*5*	*5*	*5*	*5*	*5*	*5*	*4[5]*	*5*	*5*	*4*	*..*
Water[2]	ZCBA	*7*	*7*	*7*	*7*	*7*	*7*	*7*	*7*	*6*	*7*	*..*
Pipeline	ZCBB	*6*	*8*	*8*	*7*	*7*	*7*	*8*	*7*	*7*	*7*	*..*
All modes	ZCBC	*100*	*100*	*100*	*100*	*100*	*100*	*100*	*100*	*100*	*100*	*..*

1 All goods vehicles, including those under 3.5 tonnes gross vehicle weight. These estimates were revised following a survey in 1993.
2 Figures for water are for UK traffic.
3 Figures for goods moved by rail is a new series from 1998.
4 Excludes rail.
5 Figures for goods lifted by rail have been revised from 1999.

Source: Department for Transport

15.4 Passenger transport:[1] by mode
Great Britain

		1993	1994	1995	1996	1997	1998	1999	2000	2001	2002	2003
Billion passenger kilometres												
Road												
Buses and coaches[2]	GRXK	44	44	43	43	44	45	46	47	47	47	47
Cars, vans and taxis	GRXG	607	614	618	625	632	635	641	639	654	677	678
Motor cycles	GRXH	4	4	4	4	4	4	5	5	5	5	6
Pedal cycles	GRXI	4	4	4	4	4	4	4	4	4	4	5
All road	GRXJ	659	666	669	676	684	688	696	695	710	734	736
Rail[3]	KCTN	37	35	37	39	42	44	46	47	47	48	49
Air	KCTM	5.1	5.5	5.9	6.3	6.8	7.0	7.3	7.6	7.7	8.5	9.1
All modes[4]	GRXM	701	706	712	721	733	738	750	749	765	791	794
Percentages												
Road												
Buses and coaches[2]	GRXN	6	6	6	6	6	6	6	6	6	6	6
Cars, vans and taxis	GRXO	87	87	87	87	86	86	85	85	85	86	85
Motor cycles	GRXP	1	1	1	1	1	1	1	1	1	1	1
Pedal cycles	GRXQ	1	1	1	1	1	1	1	1	1	1	1
All road	GRXR	94	94	94	94	93	93	93	93	93	93	93
Rail[3]	ZCBJ	5	5	5	5	6	6	6	6	6	6	6
Air	ZCBK	0.7	0.8	0.8	0.9	0.9	1.0	1.0	1.0	1.0	1.1	1.2
All modes[4]	GRXU	100	100	100	100	100	100	100	100	100	100	100

1 See chapter text.
2 Data for 2003 are provisional.
3 Financial years. Former British Rail companies and Urban Rail systems.

4 Excluding travel by water within the United Kingdom (including the Channel Islands), estimated at 0.7 billion passenger kilometres in 2000.

Source: Department for Transport

15.5 Motor vehicle traffic: by road class[1]
Great Britain

Billion vehicle kilometres

		1993	1994	1995	1996	1997	1998	1999	2000	2001	2002	2003
Motorways	JSZV	68.2	70.7	73.9	78.3	82.1	85.7	87.8	88.4	90.8	92.6	92.9
Rural major roads												
Trunk	JSZW	55.0	56.5	57.9	60.4	62.5	63.3	64.7	64.2	65.9	64.2	59.9
Principal	JSZX	58.4	60.0	61.6	63.1	64.1	65.4	66.0	65.8	67.4	72.3	79.5
All	JSZY	113.3	116.5	119.5	123.5	126.6	128.7	130.7	130.0	133.3	136.5	139.4
Urban major roads												
Trunk	JSZZ	13.7	13.9	13.8	13.9	13.8	13.8	14.0	14.0	7.6	7.4	6.4
Principal	JTAA	63.6	64.7	66.2	67.0	67.1	67.5	67.9	67.7	74.2	74.7	75.3
All	JTAB	77.3	78.5	80.1	80.9	80.9	81.3	81.9	81.7	81.8	82.1	81.6
Minor roads												
Minor rural roads	JTAC	56.1	57.6	57.8	58.9	60.0	60.4	61.3	61.5	61.6	64.5	64.4
Minor urban roads	JTAD	97.4	98.1	98.5	99.6	100.7	102.4	105.3	105.5	106.9	110.8	111.9
All	JTAE	153.5	155.7	156.2	158.5	160.7	162.8	166.6	167.0	168.5	175.3	176.4
All roads	JTAF	412.3	421.5	429.7	441.1	450.3	458.5	467.0	467.1	474.4	486.6	490.3

1 See chapter text.

Source: Department for Transport: 020 7944 3095

15.6 Public road length:[1] by road type
Great Britain

		1993	1994	1995	1996	1997	1998	1999	2000	2001	2002	2003
Trunk motorway	JSZD	3 139	3 170	3 197	3 253	3 333	3 376	3 405	3 422	3 432	3 432	3 431
Principal motorway	JSZE	72	72	72	45	45	44	45	45	45	45	46
Rural major roads:												
Trunk[2]	JSZF	10 521	10 500	10 510	10 598	10 690	10 585	10 611	10 627	10 607	9 926	8 778
Principal[2]	JSZG	24 559	24 609	24 759	24 592	24 636	24 783	24 852	24 866	24 915	25 599	26 739
Total	JSZH	35 080	35 109	35 269	35 190	35 326	35 369	35 463	35 493	35 522	35 525	35 517
Urban major roads:												
Trunk[2]	JSZI	1 159	1 146	1 133	1 117	1 108	1 096	1 087	1 074	762	714	563
Principal[2]	JSZJ	9 882	9 893	9 902	9 885	9 923	9 931	10 019	10 040	10 370	10 423	10 553
Total	JSZK	11 041	11 039	11 035	11 002	11 031	11 027	11 106	11 114	11 132	11 136	11 116
Rural minor roads:												
B roads	JSZL	24 625	24 618	24 610	24 603	24 594	24 586	24 579	24 570	24 562	24 554	24 547
C roads	JSZM	72 938	73 031	73 124	73 218	73 312	73 405	73 500	73 593	73 688	73 783	73 878
Unclassified	JSZN	110 050	110 265	110 481	110 698	110 915	111 132	111 350	111 568	111 787	112 006	112 232
All	JSZO	207 613	207 914	208 215	208 518	208 820	209 123	209 429	209 731	210 037	210 343	210 657
Urban minor roads:												
B roads	JSZP	5 604	5 608	5 611	5 615	5 618	5 622	5 626	5 630	5 633	5 638	5 642
C roads	JSZQ	10 878	10 900	10 922	10 943	10 966	10 986	11 009	11 031	11 054	11 076	11 098
Unclassified	JSZR	111 412	111 747	112 081	112 417	112 754	113 093	113 432	113 772	114 114	114 456	114 816
All	JSZS	127 894	128 254	128 614	128 975	129 338	129 702	130 068	130 432	130 802	131 169	131 556
All minor roads	JSZT	335 506	336 168	336 828	337 494	338 158	338 825	339 496	340 163	340 838	341 512	342 212
All roads	JSZU	384 839	385 557	386 401	386 983	387 893	388 641	389 515	390 237	390 969	391 650	392 321

1 See chapter text. A number of minor revisions have been made to the lengths of major roads for all years.
2 Figures for trunk and principal roads in England, from 2001 onwards, are affected by the detrunking programme.

Source: Department for Transport 020 7944 3095

15.7 Road traffic:[1] by type of vehicle
Great Britain

Billion vehicle kilometres

		1993	1994	1995	1996	1997	1998	1999	2000	2001	2002	2003
Cars and taxis	JTAH	338.1	345.0	351.1	359.9	365.8	370.6	377.4	376.8	382.8	392.9	393.0
Motor cycles etc.	JTAI	3.8	3.8	3.8	3.8	4.0	4.1	4.5	4.6	4.8	5.1	5.6
Larger buses and coaches	JTAJ	4.6	4.6	4.9	5.0	5.2	5.2	5.3	5.2	5.2	5.2	5.4
Light vans[2]	JTAK	41.6	43.3	44.5	46.2	48.6	50.8	51.6	52.3	53.7	55.0	57.9
Goods vehicles:												
2 axles rigid	JTAL	10.7	10.8	10.7	10.9	11.0	11.1	11.6	11.7	11.5	11.6	11.7
3 axles rigid	JTAM	1.4	1.4	1.6	1.6	1.6	1.9	1.7	1.7	1.8	1.8	1.8
4 or more axles rigid	JTAN	1.5	1.5	1.5	1.5	1.5	1.6	1.5	1.5	1.5	1.5	1.6
3 and 4 axles artic.	JTAO	3.6	3.6	3.3	3.3	3.2	3.0	3.0	2.7	2.5	2.3	2.2
5 axles artic.	JTAP	5.7	5.8	6.4	6.6	7.1	7.3	7.2	6.7	6.4	6.4	6.2
6 or more axles artic.	JTAQ	1.5	1.8	2.0	2.3	2.5	2.9	3.3	4.1	4.5	4.8	5.0
All	JTAR	24.3	24.8	25.4	26.2	26.9	27.7	28.1	28.2	28.1	28.3	28.5
All motor vehicles	JURA	412.3	421.5	429.7	441.1	450.3	458.5	467.0	467.1	474.4	486.6	490.3
Pedal cycles	JURB	4.0	4.0	4.1	4.1	4.1	4.0	4.1	4.2	4.2	4.4	4.5

1 See chapter text.
2 Not exceeding 3,500 kgs gross vehicle weight.

Source: Department for Transport 020 7944 3095

15.8 Motor vehicles currently licensed
Great Britain
At end of year

Thousands

| | Private and light goods | | | | | | | | | Body type cars | | |
	Body type cars	Other vehicles	Motor cycles, scooters and mopeds	Public transport vehicles[1]	Goods vehicles	Special machines/ special conces-sionary[2]	Other vehicles	Crown and exempt vehicles[2]	Special vehicles group	All vehicles	All	Percent-age of company cars
	BMBJ	BMBK	BMBB	BMBE	BMBD	KSBY	BMBF	BMBL	KSBZ	BMBI	ZCGR	ZCGS
1993	20 102	2 187	650	107	428	318	55	979	..	24 826	20 755	10.7
1994	20 479	2 192	630	107	434	309	50	1 030	..	25 231	21 199	10.4
1995[3]	20 505	2 217	594	74	421	274	44	1 169	28	25 369[4]	21 394	10.4
1996	21 172	2 267	609	77	413	254	40	1 424	48	26 302	22 238	10.3
1997	21 681	2 317	626	79	414	249	38	1 522	48	26 974	22 832	10.5
1998	22 115	2 362	684	80	412	243	37	1 558	47	27 538	23 293	10.4
1999	22 785	2 427	760	84	415	241	36	1 573	47	28 368	23 975	10.0
2000	23 196	2 469	825	86	418	233	34	1 590	46	28 898	24 406	10.3
2001	23 899	2 544	882	89	422	233	33	1 602	45	29 747	25 126	9.7
2002	24 543	2 622	941	92	425	243	32	1 855	46	30 557	25 782	9.0
2003	24 985	2 730	1 005	96	426	258	32	1 887	47	31 207	26 240	8.4

1 Includes taxis for years up to 1994. Taxation group now restricted to only vehicles with 9 or more seats.

2 Vehicles in this taxation class are exempt from duty and form part of the crown and exempt class with effect from January 2002.

3 The vehicle taxation system was subject to substantial revision from 1 July 1995.

4 Contains 44,000 vehicles still taxed in classes abolished from 1 July 1995.

Source: Department for Transport 020 7944 3077

15.9 New vehicle registrations by taxation class
Great Britain

Thousands

		1993	1994	1995	1996	1997	1998	1999	2000	2001	2002	2003
Total	BBKD	2 073.9	2 249.0	2 306.5	2 410.1	2 597.7	2 740.3	2 765.8	2 870.9	3 137.7	3 229.4	3 231.9
Private and light goods												
Private cars	BMAA	1 694.6	1 809.1	1 828.3	1 888.4	2 015.9	2 123.5	2 100.4	2 174.9	2 431.8	2 528.8	2 497.1
Other vehicles	BMAE	158.8	182.6	195.7	205.0	228.4	244.5	241.6	254.9	277.9	286.8	323.5
Total	BMAK	1 853.4	1 991.7	2 024.0	2 093.4	2 244.3	2 368.0	2 342.0	2 429.8	2 709.7	2 815.6	2 820.7
Motor cycles, etc:												
Up to 50 c.c.	KCUH	6.5	6.9	6.3	8.9	14.2	22.6	36.2	49.4	45.6	35.6	34.9
Other	KCUI	51.9	57.7	62.6	80.7	107.1	120.7	132.2	133.5	131.5	126.6	122.4
Total	BMAL	58.4	64.6	68.9	89.6	121.3	143.3	168.4	182.9	177.1	162.2	157.3
Public road passenger vehicles												
Buses, coaches, taxis, etc												
Not over 8 seats[1]	KCUJ	1.8	2.5	1.3	..	..	..	..	..	..	..	..
Over 8 seats	KCUK	3.6	4.2	5.2	6.5	6.6	7.4	8.0	7.5	6.8	7.8	8.4
Total	BBJZ	5.4	6.7	6.5	6.5	6.6	7.4	8.0	7.5	6.8	7.8	8.4
Heavy general goods and farmers[2]												
Goods vehicles: by weight	BBJY	32.8	41.1	48.0	45.5	41.8	49.1	48.3	50.4	48.6	44.9	48.4
Special concession group	BBKA	..	..	33.3	25.7	21.7	15.2	17.3	16.9	19.8	23.1	24.1
Other licensed vehicles	KCUM	1.4	1.3	1.0	1.0	1.5	1.5	1.5	1.2	1.2	1.3	1.2
Special vehicles group	DMNR	..	..	3.3	8.1	8.6	7.6	7.6	6.5	7.0	7.2	8.1
Exempt from licence duty												
Crown vehicles	KCUN	3.1	4.1	3.3	1.2	0.7	1.1	1.1	1.0	1.0	1.4	1.4
All other exempt vehicles[3]	KCUO	89.4	104.3	118.1	139.1	150.7	146.6	170.4	173.9	166.5	166.1	162.1
Total	KCUP	92.4	108.4	121.4	140.3	151.4	147.7	171.6	174.9	167.5	167.5	163.5

1 From 1 July 1995 separate taxation of public transport vehicles with 8 or fewer seats was abolished. After this date new vehicles of this type were re-gistered as PLG.

2 Until June 1995 included Agricultural vans and Lorries and Showman's goods vehicles licensed to draw trailers. From 1st July 1995 separate taxa-tion group for Farmers and Showman were abolished.

3 Between 1980 and 30 June 1995 electric vehicles were exempt from duty. From 1 July 1995 electric vehicles pay VED as part of the special concession group.

Source: Department for Transport: 020 7944 3077

15.10 Driving test pass rates: by sex and type of vehicle licence
Great Britain

		1989 /90	1991 /92	1996 /97	1997 /98	1998 /99	1999 /00	2000 /01	2001 /02	2002 /03
Males										
Motorcycle	JTRB	72	69	69	70	69	67	68	67	66
Car	JTRC	58	57	50	52	51	48	48	47	47
Bus	JTTG	..	..	50	48	48	49	47	46	44
Lorry	JTTH	..	..	49	53	52	53	53	50	50
All males	JTTI	..	..	..	..	..	51	51	50	49
Females										
Motorcycle	JTTJ	68	63	58	65	63	55	56	55	54
Car	JTTK	47	46	40	43	42	40	40	40	40
Bus	JTTL	..	..	40	49	47	46	45	40	40
Lorry	JTTM	..	..	37	53	50	49	53	47	46
All females	JTTN	..	..	..	..	..	40	41	41	40
All										
Motorcycle	JTTO	..	..	68	69	68	66	66	66	65
Car	JTTP	..	..	45	47	46	44	44	43	43
Bus	JTTQ	..	..	49	45	48	49	47	45	44
Lorry	JTTR	..	..	47	53	52	53	52	50	49
All persons	JTTS	..	..	..	..	..	46	46	46	45

Source: Driving Standards Agency 0115 901 2873

15.11 Full car driving licence holders by sex and age[1]
Great Britain

	17-20	21-29	30-39	40-49	50-59	60-69	70 or over	Estimated number of licence holders (millions)
All adults								
1975/76	28	59	67	60	50	35	15	19.4
1985/86	33	63	74	71	60	47	27	24.3
1991/93	49	75	81	78	70	57	34	29.1
1992/94	48	75	82	79	72	57	33	29.0
1996/98	43	73	82	82	76	64	38	30.4
1999/01	36	73	83	84	78	71	44	31.7
	C98J	C98K	C98L	C98M	C98N	C98O	C98P	C98Q
2002	32	67	82	84	81	70	45	32.1
2003[2]	28	68	82	84	79	73	45	32.3
Males								
1975/76	36	78	85	83	75	58	32	13.4
1985/86	37	73	86	87	81	72	51	15.1
1991/93	58	84	90	88	87	80	59	17.1
1992/94	54	83	91	88	88	81	59	17.1
1996/98	48	79	89	90	88	82	64	17.2
1999/01	41	81	89	91	88	86	69	17.6
	C98R	C98S	C98T	C98U	C98V	C98W	C98X	C98Y
2002	34	74	88	91	89	85	68	17.7
2003[2]	31	74	88	91	90	87	69	17.9
Females								
1975/76	20	43	48	37	24	15	4	6.0
1985/86	29	54	62	56	41	24	11	9.2
1991/93	40	68	73	68	54	37	17	12.1
1992/94	42	68	73	70	57	37	16	12.1
1996/98	38	68	75	73	63	48	20	13.2
1999/01	31	66	77	77	69	57	25	14.0
	C98Z	C992	C993	C994	C995	C996	C997	C998
2002	31	60	77	79	74	56	28	14.4
2003[2]	24	62	77	78	69	59	27	14.4

1 See chapter text.
2 Data are provisional.

Source: Department for Transport: 020 7944 3097

15.12 Households with regular use of cars[1]
Great Britain

Percentages and millions

	No car	One car	Two cars	Three or more cars	Total (millions)
	ZCGA	ZCGB	ZCGC	ZCGD	ZCGE
1992	32	45	20	4	22.6
1993	31	45	20	4	22.8
1994	32	45	20	4	23.1
1995	30	45	21	4	23.3
1996	30	45	21	4	23.5
1997	30	45	21	5	23.7
1998	28	44	23	5	23.9
1999	28	44	22	5	24.1
2000	27	45	23	5	24.4
2001	26	45	23	5	24.1
2002	26	44	24	5	24.3

	No car	One car	Two or more cars	Total
Government Office Regions, 2002				
Great Britain	26	44	29	100
North East	37	43	20	100
North West	27	45	28	100
Yorkshire and the Humber	30	46	24	100
East Midlands	22	45	33	100
West Midlands	26	43	31	100
East	19	45	36	100
London	38	42	20	100
South East	18	44	38	100
South West	18	46	36	100
England	26	44	30	100
Wales	27	45	27	100
Scotland	34	45	21	100

	No car	One car	Two or more cars	Total
Area type, 2003				
Great Britain	27	44	30	100
London	39	41	20	100
Metropolitan areas	35	41	24	100
Other urban areas with population:				
Over 250,000	25	43	31	100
25,000 - 250,000	25	46	29	100
10,000 - 25,000	27	45	28	100
3,000 - 10,000	20	44	36	100
Rural areas	14	43	43	100

1 Includes cars and light vans normally available to the household.

Sources: Office for National Statistics; Department for Transport 020 7944 3097

15.13 Vehicles with current licences[1]
Northern Ireland

		1993	1994	1995	1996[2]	1997	1998	1999	2000	2001[3]	2002	2003
Private cars, etc	KNKA	515 185	514 760	521 610	540 083	575 923	584 706	608 316	615 180	644 968	666 731	711 913
Cycles and tricycles	KNKB	8 634	8 775	9 142	10 026	10 932	11 663	13 087	14 116	15 205	17 598	23 903
Public road passenger vehicles:												
Taxis up to 4 seats	KNKD	462	623	739	..	..	..	..	..	..	..	..
Buses, coaches, over 4 seats	KNKE	2 217	2 455	1 353	2 090	2 144	2 175	2 204	2 266	2 315	2 322	2 353
Total	KNKC	2 679	3 078	2 092	2 090	2 144	2 175	2 204	2 266	2 315	2 322	2 353
General (HGV) goods vehicles:	KNKF	14 576	14 810	16 338	17 401	18 172	18 312	17 075	17 864	19 415	20 244	22 100
Farmers' goods vehicles[4]	KNKJ	5 498	5 904	..	..	..	..	..	..	..	..	..
Agricultural tractors and engines, etc[4]	KNKM	7 201	7 317	9 074	5 911	6 378	5 906	5 505	5 048	4 901	5 731	7 503
Other	KNKN	329	354	1 257	1 019	1 188	1 193	1 446	1 287	1 366	1 347	1 588
Vehicles exempt from duty:												
Government owned	KNKP	4 828	4 818	3 872	3 753	3 705	3 785	4 032	3 822	6 427	6 383	6 172
Other:												
Ambulances	KNKQ	101	104	250	371	389	425	417	452	318	299	325
Fire engines	KNKR	205	194	301	292	291	285	286	290	181	174	170
Other exempt[5]	KNKS	27 089	35 837	47 626	58 340	64 447	66 981	68 277	70 405	72 209	73 648	76 715
Total	KNKO	32 223	40 953	52 049	62 756	68 832	71 476	73 012	74 969	79 135	80 504	83 382
Total	KNKT	586 325	595 951	611 562	639 286	683 569	695 431	720 645	730 730	767 305	794 477	852 742

1 Licences current at any time during the quarter ended December.
2 Due to a revision of taxation classes, 1996 data are not directly comparable with previous years.
3 Taxation classes have been revised from 2001.
4 Owned by a farmer and available for hauling produce and requisites for his farm. From 1 July 1995 farmers goods taxation classes have been abolished

5 Changes in the Mobility Allowance (DWP) have contributed to the increase in Other exempt.

Source: Driver and Vehicle Licensing, Northern Ireland: 028 7034 1461

15.14 New vehicle registrations
Northern Ireland

Numbers

		1993	1994	1995	1996	1997	1998	1999	2000	2001	2002	2003
Private cars, etc	KNLA	65 360	70 765	73 718	77 817	83 968	91 141	89 078	84 973	88 592	83 402	87 506
Cycles and tricycles	KNLB	1 885	1 943	2 362	2 803	3 376	4 307	5 310	6 010	5 591	5 596	6 804
Public road passenger vehicles	KNLC	466	1 143	622	724	714	486	568	565	451	439	609
Goods vehicles:												
General haulage vehicles:												
Under 3.5 tonnes	KNLH	6 468	6 908	7 357	7 232	8 468	10 107	11 054	12 617	13 274	12 007	10 716
3.5 tonnes and over	KNLJ	2 593	2 668	2 935	3 492	3 521	3 572	3 697	3 502	4 534	3 669	3 776
Agricultural tractors[1]	KNLM	1 658	1 558	1 619	1 292	1 364	971	987	1 313	301	1	9
Vehicles exempt from duty	KNLR	4 550	6 423	8 333	10 520	10 885	10 718	11 083	10 789	12 126	12 515	11 907
General haulage and special types	JTAG	..	..	..	..	..	..	..	..	..	15	12
Total	KNLS	82 980	91 408	96 946	103 880	112 296	121 302	121 777	119 769	124 869	117 644	121 339

1 Agricultural tractors driven on public roads. From April 2001 tractors are exempt.

Source: Driver and Vehicle Licensing, Northern Ireland: 028 7034 1461

15.15 Local bus services: passenger journeys: by area

Millions

		1992 /93	1993 /94	1994 /95	1995 /96	1996 /97	1997 /98	1998 /99	1999 /00	2000 /01	2001 /02	2002 /03
Great Britain	ZCET	4 475	4 381	4 414	4 378	4 345	4 326	4 244	4 276	4 304	4 342	4 452
London	KILS	1 129	1 117	1 167	1 205	1 242	1 294	1 279	1 307	1 359	1 434	1 542
English Metropolitan Counties	KILT	1 383	1 337	1 331	1 292	1 246	1 232	1 195	1 162	1 165	1 150	1 149
English Shire Counties	KILU	1 302	1 268	1 271	1 260	1 260	1 243	1 242	1 258	1 232	1 214	1 206
All outside London	ZCES	3 346	3 264	3 247	3 173	3 103	3 032	2 965	2 969	2 945	2 908	2 910
England	ZCER	3 814	3 722	3 769	3 757	3 748	3 768	3 715	3 728	3 756	3 798	3 897
Scotland	KILV	532	525	513	494	467	438	413	434	435	441	445
Wales	KILW	129	133	132	127	130	120	116	114	113	104	109

Source: Department for Transport 020 7944 3076

15.16 Local bus services: fare indices: by area
Current prices

Indices (1995=100)

		1993 /94	1994 /95	1995 /96	1996 /97	1997 /98	1998 /99	1999 /00	2000 /01	2001 /02	2002 /03	2003 /04
Great Britain	KNEU	92.4	96.7	101.2	106.3	112.0	117.1	122.0	126.4	130.6	134.5	139.1
London	KNEP	90.9	96.2	101.1	105.4	109.3	113.7	117.2	117.2	115.5	114.8	116.9
English Metropolitan Counties	KILD	92.9	96.4	101.5	106.9	113.3	118.7	124.6	129.9	137.4	142.7	148.0
English Shire Counties	KILE	93.1	97.0	101.1	106.0	111.5	116.7	122.0	128.6	135.2	141.7	148.5
All outside London	ZCEQ	92.8	96.8	101.2	106.6	112.8	118.2	123.4	129.2	135.3	140.8	146.3
England	ZCEP	92.5	96.7	101.2	106.1	111.4	116.5	121.5	125.9	130.3	134.2	139.1
Scotland	KILF	91.3	96.9	100.8	108.0	116.5	121.8	125.3	129.9	131.8	134.5	136.8
Wales	KILG	93.8	97.4	100.7	104.4	110.1	116.3	122.2	127.5	133.5	139.5	145.5
Retail Prices Index (1995=100)	KNEV	94.9	97.5	100.7	103.1	106.5	109.9	111.6	114.9	116.6	119.1	122.4

Source: Department for Transport 020 7944 3076

15.17 Road accident casualties: by road user type and severity
Great Britain

Numbers

		1993	1994	1995	1996	1997	1998	1999	2000	2001	2002	2003
Child pedestrians:												
Killed	ZCDH	165	160	132	131	138	103	107	107	107	79	74
Killed or seriously injured	KIJS	4 231	4 610	4 400	4 132	3 954	3 737	3 457	3 226	3 144	2 828	2 381
All severities	ZCDI	18 250	19 263	18 590	18 510	18 407	17 971	16 876	16 184	15 819	14 231	12 544
Adult pedestrians:												
Killed	ZCDJ	1 072	953	897	858	835	803	760	750	712	688	695
Killed or seriously injured	KIJT	8 260	8 114	7 716	7 300	6 925	6 592	6 221	6 112	5 745	5 644	5 422
All severities	ZCDK	28 750	28 129	27 178	26 827	26 223	25 827	24 806	24 481	23 463	23 258	22 531
Child pedal cyclists:												
Killed	ZCDL	37	42	48	54	33	32	36	27	25	22	18
Killed or seriously injured	KIJU	1 146	1 234	1 249	1 231	1 016	915	950	758	674	594	595
All severities	ZCDM	7 386	8 075	8 133	8 217	7 899	6 930	7 920	6 260	5 451	4 809	4 769
Adult pedal cyclists:												
Killed	ZCDN	148	129	164	148	150	126	135	98	111	107	95
Killed or seriously injured	KIJV	2 598	2 710	2 673	2 517	2 542	2 345	2 172	1 954	1 951	1 801	1 776
All severities	ZCDO	16 115	16 097	16 140	15 778	16 181	15 326	14 834	13 630	12 974	11 712	11 643
Motorcyclists[1] and passengers:												
Killed	ZCDP	427	444	445	440	509	498	547	605	583	609	693
Killed or seriously injured	ZCDQ	6 882	6 666	6 615	6 208	6 446	6 442	6 908	7 374	7 305	7 500	7 652
All severities	BMDH	25 094	24 354	23 524	23 133	24 492	24 610	26 192	28 212	28 810	28 353	28 411
Car drivers and passengers:												
Killed	ZCDS	1 760	1 764	1 749	1 806	1 795	1 696	1 687	1 665	1 749	1 747	1 769
Killed or seriously injured	ZCDT	22 833	23 892	23 461	24 048	23 191	21 676	20 368	19 719	19 424	18 728	17 291
All severities	ZCDU	187 479	195 154	194 027	205 336	211 448	210 474	205 735	206 799	202 802	197 425	188 342
Bus/coach drivers and passengers:												
Killed	ZCDV	35	21	35	11	14	18	11	15	14	19	11
Killed or seriously injured	KCUZ	725	815	836	695	601	631	611	578	562	551	500
All severities	ZCDW	9 307	10 090	9 278	9 345	9 439	9 839	10 252	10 088	9 884	9 005	9 068
LGV drivers and passengers:												
Killed	ZCDX	91	64	69	61	64	67	65	66	64	70	72
Killed or seriously injured	ZCDY	1 082	1 101	1 106	989	928	949	867	813	811	780	765
All severities	ZCDZ	7 420	7 558	7 200	7 215	7 476	7 672	7 124	7 007	7 304	7 007	6 897
HGV drivers and passengers:												
Killed	ZCEA	59	41	57	63	45	60	52	55	54	63	44
Killed or seriously injured	ZCEB	635	571	635	555	573	560	540	571	500	524	429
All severities	ZCEC	3 333	3 370	3 331	3 245	3 302	3 444	3 484	3 597	3 388	3 178	3 061
All road users:[2]												
Killed	BMDC	3 814	3 650	3 621	3 598	3 599	3 421	3 423	3 409	3 450	3 431	3 508
Killed or seriously injured	ZCEE	48 834	50 190	49 154	48 097	46 583	44 255	42 545	41 564	40 560	39 407	37 215
All severities	BMDA	306 135	315 359	310 687	320 578	327 803	325 212	320 310	320 283	313 309	302 605	290 607

1 Includes mopeds and scooters.
2 Includes other motor or non-motor vehicle users, and unknown road user
  type and casualty age.

Source: Department for Transport 020 7944 3078

15.18 Freight transport by road: goods moved by goods vehicles over 3.5 tonnes[1]
Great Britain

Billion tonne kilometres

		1993	1994	1995	1996	1997	1998	1999	2000	2001	2002	2003
By mode of working												
Mainly public haulage	KNND	93.2	100.8	106.5	109.1	112.2	114.3	110.9	113.0	114.7	110.6	114.3
Mainly own account	KNNC	35.4	37.0	37.2	37.7	37.4	37.6	38.3	37.5	34.7	39.2	37.4
All modes	KNNB	128.6	137.8	143.7	146.8	149.6	151.9	149.2	150.5	149.4	149.8	151.7
By gross weight of vehicle												
Rigid vehicles:												
3.5-17 tonnes	ZCIL	18.7	19.9	18.7	19.5	19.2	17.8	17.9	15.8	13.1	11.9	10.1
17-25 tonnes	ZCIM	6.6	6.1	5.6	5.3	4.7	4.2	4.3	4.8	5.7	6.3	6.8
25 tonnes and over	ZCIN	11.3	12.4	13.3	13.5	14.3	14.7	15.3	15.4	15.6	17.3	18.3
All rigids	ZCIO	36.5	38.4	37.5	38.3	38.1	36.6	37.5	36.0	34.5	35.6	35.2
Articulated vehicles:												
3.5-33 tonnes	ZCIP	16.5	16.9	15.9	15.9	14.3	14.4	14.0	14.0	12.8	9.9	8.8
33 tonnes and over	ZCIQ	75.6	82.5	90.2	92.6	97.1	100.9	97.7	100.4	102.1	104.4	107.7
All articulated vehicles	ZCIR	92.1	99.4	106.1	108.5	111.4	115.3	111.7	114.4	114.9	114.3	116.5
All vehicles												
3.5-25 tonnes	ZCIS	25.9	26.6	24.7	25.3	24.3	22.5	22.7	21.3	19.3	18.7	17.3
25 tonnes and over	KNNG	102.7	111.2	119.0	121.5	125.2	129.4	126.5	129.2	130.1	131.1	134.4
All weights	ZCIT	128.6	137.8	143.7	146.8	149.6	151.9	149.2	150.5	149.4	149.8	151.7
By commodity												
Food, drink and tobacco	ZCIU	35.9	36.5	37.5	39.3	40.8	42.5	41.5	44.3	41.4	43.1	42.2
Wood, timber and cork	ZCIV	3.1	3.3	3.2	3.8	3.5	3.6	3.8	3.7	3.9	3.8	4.1
Fertiliser	ZCIW	1.5	1.3	1.4	1.5	1.3	1.2	1.4	1.2	1.2	1.2	1.2
Crude minerals	ZCIX	12.6	14.1	13.5	13.5	13.6	13.3	12.7	12.4	13.0	13.9	13.8
Ores	ZCIY	1.6	1.4	1.5	1.3	1.7	1.1	1.3	1.2	1.2	1.1	1.2
Crude materials	ZCIZ	1.7	2.0	1.9	2.1	2.1	2.6	2.6	2.6	2.3	2.7	2.3
Coal and coke	ZCJA	3.1	2.9	2.7	2.5	2.7	2.0	2.2	1.5	2.1	1.5	1.5
Petrol and petroleum products	ZCJB	5.0	5.1	5.7	6.1	5.8	5.2	5.0	6.4	5.8	5.2	5.5
Chemicals	ZCJC	7.2	8.1	7.4	7.7	8.2	7.9	7.4	6.8	7.2	6.5	6.8
Building materials	ZCJD	9.3	10.0	10.7	9.6	11.1	10.7	10.6	10.6	11.7	10.9	12.0
Iron and steel products	ZCJE	6.4	6.7	7.8	7.2	7.9	7.7	6.8	6.8	5.7	5.3	5.4
Other metal products[2]	ZCJF	1.9	2.0	1.7	1.7	1.5	1.7	1.7	1.7	1.4	1.5	1.5
Machinery and transport equipment	ZCJG	5.7	6.8	7.4	7.7	8.4	9.1	8.7	9.1	8.9	8.5	8.7
Miscellaneous manufactures[2]	ZCJH	12.4	13.4	13.3	14.2	14.2	15.9	15.7	15.1	15.4	16.2	15.8
Miscellaneous transactions[3]												
All commodities	ZCJJ	128.6	137.8	143.7	146.8	149.6	151.9	149.2	150.5	149.4	149.8	151.7

1 Rigid vehicles or articulated vehicles (tractive unit and trailer) with gross vehicle weight over 3.5 tonnes.
2 Includes not elsewhere specified.
3 Includes not elsewhere specified and commodity not known.

Source: Department for Transport 020 7944 3093

15.19 Freight transport by road: goods lifted by goods vehicles over 3.5 tonnes[1]
Great Britain

Million tonnes

		1993	1994	1995	1996	1997	1998	1999	2000	2001	2002	2003
By mode of working												
Mainly public haulage	ZCJK	911	980	987	1 011	1 044	1 041	991	1 038	1 052	1 019	1 053
Mainly own account	ZCJL	612	618	622	618	599	589	576	556	529	608	590
All modes	ZCJM	1 523	1 597	1 609	1 628	1 643	1 630	1 567	1 593	1 581	1 627	1 643
By gross weight of vehicle												
Rigid vehicles:												
3.5-17 tonnes	ZCJN	322	317	298	306	294	268	254	229	203	188	159
17-25 tonnes	ZCJO	211	202	162	133	120	106	86	87	86	90	100
25 tonnes and over	ZCJP	307	332	373	371	380	401	408	424	443	491	506
All rigids	ZCJQ	840	852	833	811	793	776	748	741	733	768	765
Articulated vehicles:												
3.5-33 tonnes	ZCJR	144	142	139	138	124	125	113	107	97	81	69
33 tonnes and over	ZCJS	540	604	637	679	726	729	706	746	751	778	809
All articulated vehicles	ZCJT	683	746	776	817	850	854	819	852	848	859	878
All vehicles												
3.5-25 tonnes	ZCJU	541	527	467	447	419	382	346	325	294	283	265
25 tonnes and over	ZCJV	982	1 070	1 142	1 181	1 224	1 248	1 221	1 268	1 287	1 343	1 378
All weights	ZCJW	1 523	1 597	1 609	1 628	1 643	1 630	1 567	1 593	1 581	1 627	1 643
By commodity												
Food, drink and tobacco	ZCJX	300	302	308	326	342	346	333	346	321	339	333
Wood, timber and cork	ZCJY	25	24	24	27	26	27	28	26	28	28	32
Fertiliser	ZCJZ	12	10	11	13	10	9	11	10	9	11	12
Crude minerals	ZCKA	310	355	319	320	329	327	297	308	298	333	327
Ores	ZCKB	21	18	18	18	25	18	20	16	16	17	21
Crude materials	ZCKC	14	16	16	18	17	20	20	18	20	21	19
Coal and coke	ZCKD	48	42	34	32	37	26	28	22	21	17	22
Petrol and petroleum products	ZCKE	67	68	71	75	73	61	61	75	74	59	64
Chemicals	ZCKF	47	51	50	51	53	53	47	49	50	41	47
Building materials	ZCKG	153	156	161	142	156	161	159	165	165	167	165
Iron and steel products	ZCKH	45	47	54	52	55	54	48	49	44	39	41
Other metal products[2]	ZCKI	20	17	17	15	16	18	17	16	14	14	16
Machinery and transport equipment	ZCKJ	46	57	61	59	71	73	67	69	70	68	66
Miscellaneous manufactures[2]	ZCKK	81	84	85	88	90	96	91	97	97	105	98
Miscellaneous transactions[3]	ZCKL	332	351	379	393	343	342	340	328	353	367	379
All commodities	ZCKM	1 523	1 597	1 609	1 628	1 643	1 630	1 567	1 593	1 581	1 627	1 643

1 Rigid vehicles or articulated vehicles (tractive unit and trailer) with gross vehicle weight over 3.5 tonnes.
2 Includes not elsewhere specified.
3 Includes not elsewhere specified and commodity not known.

Source: Department for Transport 020 7944 3093

		1993/94	1994/95	1995/96	1996/97	1997/98	1998/99	1999/00[1]	2000/01[1]	2001/02[1]	2002/03	2003/04
Passenger journeys (millions)												
National Rail network[2]	ZCKN	740	735	761	801	846	892	931	957	960	976	1 014
London Underground	KNOE	735	764	784	772	832	866	927	970	953	942	948
Docklands Light Railway	ZCKO	8	12	14	17	21	28	31	38	41	46	49
Glasgow Underground	ZCKP	14	15	14	14	14	15	15	14	14	13	13
Tyne and Wear Metro	ZCKQ	39	37	36	35	35	34	33	33	33	37	38
West Midlands Metro[3]	ZCKR	..	..	..	..	..	..	5	5	5	5	5
Croydon Tramlink[4]	GEOE	..	..	..	..	..	..	..	15	18	19	20
Manchester Metrolink[5]	ZCKS	11	12	13	13	14	13	14	17	18	19	19
Stagecoach Supertram (Sheffield)	ZCKT	..	2	5	8	9	10	11	11	11	12	12
Nottingham NET[6]	C3MI	..	..	..	..	..	..	..	..	..	..	−
All rail	ZCKU	1 547	1 577	1 627	1 660	1 771	1 858	1 967	2 061	2 054	2 068	2 118
of which: light rail[7]	GENZ	58	63	68	73	79	85	94	120	127	136	143
Passenger receipts												
(£ million at current prices)												
National Rail network[2]	KNDL	2 193	2 171	2 379	2 573	2 821	3 089	3 368	3 413	3 548	3 663	3 893
London Underground	KNOA	637	718	765	797	899	977	1 058	1 129	1 151	1 138	1 161
Docklands Light Railway	ZCKV	5	6	9	12	14	20	22	29	32	36	37
Glasgow Underground	ZCKW	7	7	8	8	9	9	10	11	10	10	10
Tyne and Wear Metro	ZCKX	19	19	20	21	22	23	24	24	25	29	31
West Midlands Metro[3]	ZCKY	..	..	..	..	..	..	..	3	4	5	5
Croydon Tramlink[4]	GEOF	..	..	..	..	..	..	..	12	13	15	16
Manchester Metrolink[5]	ZCKZ	10	10	11	13	14	..	..	18	20	21	21
Stagecoach Supertram (Sheffield)	ZCLA	..	2	4	5	6	6	7	7	8	10	9
Nottingham NET[6]	C3MJ	..	..	..	..	..	..	..	..	..	..	−
All rail	ZCLB	2 871	2 933	3 196	3 429	3 785	..	..	4 646	4 810	4 926	5 185
of which: light rail[7]	GEOA	34	37	44	51	56	..	..	93	102	115	120
Passenger kilometres (millions)												
National Rail network[2]	KNDZ	30 400	28 700	30 000	32 100	34 700	36 300	38 454	38 218	39 104	39 700	40 900
London Underground	KNOI	5 814	6 051	6 337	6 153	6 479	6 716	7 171	7 470	7 451	7 367	7 340
Docklands Light Railway	ZCLC	39	55	70	86	103	144	172	200	207	232	236
Glasgow Underground	ZCLD	41	43	41	40	45	47	47	46	44	43	43
Tyne and Wear Metro	ZCLE	273	271	261	254	249	238	230	229	238	275	284
West Midlands Metro[3]	ZCLF	..	..	..	..	..	..	50	56	50	50	54
Croydon Tramlink[4]	GEOG	..	..	..	..	..	..	..	96	99	100	105
Manchester Metrolink[5]	ZCLG	73	79	81	86	88	117	126	152	161	167	169
Stagecoach Supertram (Sheffield)	ZCLH	..	8	20	29	34	35	37	38	39	40	42
Nottingham NET[6]	C3MK	..	..	..	..	..	..	..	..	..	..	2
All rail	ZCLI	36 640	35 206	36 810	38 748	41 698	43 597	46 287	46 505	47 394	47 974	49 174
of which: light rail[7]	GEOB	385	412	432	455	474	534	615	771	795	864	891
Route kilometres open for												
passenger traffic (numbers)												
National Rail network[2]	ZCLJ	14 357	14 359	15 002	15 034	15 024	15 038	15 038	15 042	15 042	15 042	15 042
London Underground	ZCLK	394	392	392	392	392	392	408	408	408	408	408
Docklands Light Railway	ZCLM	14	22	22	22	22	22	27	27	27	27	27
Glasgow Underground	ZCLN	11	11	11	11	11	11	11	11	11	11	11
Tyne and Wear Metro	ZCLO	59	59	59	59	59	59	59	59	77	78	78
West Midlands Metro[3]	ZCLP	..	..	..	..	..	..	21	20	20	20	20
Croydon Tramlink[4]	GEOH	..	..	..	..	..	..	..	28	28	28	28
Manchester Metrolink[5]	ZCLQ	31	31	31	31	31	31	39	39	39	39	39
Stagecoach Supertram (Sheffield)	ZCLR	7	22	29	29	29	29	29	29	29	29	29
Nottingham NET[6]	C3ML	..	..	..	..	..	..	..	..	..	..	14
All rail	ZCLS	14 873	14 896	15 546	15 578	15 568	15 582	15 632	15 663	15 682	15 682	15 696
of which: light rail[7]	GEOC	111	134	141	141	141	141	175	202	221	221	235
Stations served (numbers)												
National Rail network[2]	ZCLT	2 493	2 489	2 497	2 498	2 495	2 499	2 503	2 508	2 508	2 508	2 508
London Underground	KNOO	245	245	245	245	245	246	253	253	253	253	253
Docklands Light Railway	ZCLU	27	27	28	28	29	29	34	34	34	34	34
Glasgow Underground	ZCLV	15	15	15	15	15	15	15	15	15	15	15
Tyne and Wear Metro	ZCLW	46	46	46	46	46	46	46	46	58	58	58
West Midlands Metro[3]	ZCLX	..	..	..	..	..	..	23	23	23	23	23
Croydon Tramlink[4]	GEOI	..	..	..	..	..	..	..	38	38	38	38
Manchester Metrolink[5]	ZCLY	26	26	26	26	26	26	36	36	36	37	37
Stagecoach Supertram (Sheffield)	ZCLZ	9	37	45	45	46	47	47	47	48	48	48
Nottingham NET[6]	C3MM	..	..	..	..	..	..	..	..	..	..	23
All rail	ZCLL	2 861	2 885	2 902	2 903	2 902	2 908	2 957	3 000	3 013	3 014	3 037
of which: light rail[7]	GSOC	108	136	145	145	147	148	186	224	237	238	261

1 National Rail passenger journeys and passenger kilometres revised by the Strategic Rail Authority.
2 Franchised train operating companies from February 1996 following rail privatisation.
3 West Midlands Metro opened in 1999.
4 Croydon tramlink opened in 2000.
5 Transfer of 20 stations from the national rail network to Manchester Metrolink.
6 Nottingham Express Transit (NET) opened in March 2004.
7 Light rail excludes London Underground and Glasgow Underground.

Sources: Railtrack; Strategic Rail Authority; Transport for London; Passenger Transport Executives and operators

15.21 National railways freight[1]
Great Britain

Billion tonne kilometres

		1993 /94	1994 /95	1995 /96	1996 /97	1997 /98	1998 /99	1999 /00	2000 /01	2001 /02	2002 /03	2003 /04
Moved by commodity												
Coal	ZCGG	3.9	3.3	3.6	3.9	4.4	4.5	4.8	4.8	6.2	5.7	5.8
Metals	ZCGH	2.1	1.7	1.7	..	..	2.1	2.2	2.1	2.4	2.7	2.4
Construction	ZCGI	2.3	2.5	2.3	..	..	2.1	2.0	2.4	2.8	2.6	2.7
Oil and petroleum	ZCGJ	1.9	1.8	1.8	..	..	1.6	1.5	1.4	1.2	1.1	1.2
Other traffic	ZCGK	3.5	3.8	3.9	11.3	12.5	7.1	7.6	7.4	7.0	6.5	6.8
All traffic	VOXD	13.8	13.0	13.3	15.1	16.9	17.3	18.2	18.1	19.4	18.7	18.9
Lifted by commodity												
Coal	ZCGL	48.9	42.5	45.2	52.2	50.3	45.3	44.3	45.7	46.1	40.7	42.0
Metals	ZCGM	15.8	16.9	15.1	..	..	..	..	..	..	..	..
Construction	ZCGN	16.1	16.8	11.5	..	..	..	..	..	..	..	..
Oil and petroleum	ZCGO	9.0	8.1	6.3	..	..	..	..	..	..	..	..
Other traffic	ZCGP	13.4	13.0	22.6	49.6	55.1	56.8	47.6	49.7	48.3	46.4	46.9
All traffic	VOXE	103.2	97.3	100.7	101.8	105.4	102.1	91.9	95.4	94.4	87.0	88.9

1 Because of changes in the way freight traffic has been estimated following privatisation, figures since 1996/97 are not strictly comparable with those or previous years. The series calculation was revised again from 1998/99 and from 1999/00 due to revisions from freight operators.

Source: Department for Transport: 020 7944 4977

15.22 Railways: permanent way and rolling stock
Northern Ireland
At end of year

Numbers

		1993	1994	1995	1996	1997	1998	1999	2000	2001	2002	2003
Length of road open for traffic[1] (Km)	KNRA	330	331	333	335	335	335	335	356	334	334	334
Length of track open for traffic (Km)												
Total	KNRB	504	503	506	506	505	526	526	547	480	480	480
Running lines	KNRC	463	462	464	464	464	484	484	505	464	464	464
Sidings (as single track)	KNRD	41	41	42	42	42	42	42	42	16	16	16
Locomotives												
Diesel-electrics	KNRE	9	11	11	8	6	5	6	6	6	6	5
Passenger carrying vehicles												
Total	KNRF	112	112	112	112	112	120	108	108	106	106	100
Rail motor vehicles:												
Diesel-electric, etc	KNRG	30	30	30	30	30	28	30	30	29	28	28
Trailer carriages:												
Total locomotive hauled	KNRH	28	28	28	28	28	38	21	21	25	22	22
Ordinary coaches	KNRI	26	26	26	26	26	36	19	19	23	20	20
Restaurant cars	KNRJ	2	2	2	2	2	2	2	2	2	2	2
Rail car trailers	KNRK	54	54	54	54	54	54	54	54	52	50	50
Rolling stock for maintenance and repair	KNRT	42	41	41	41	41	26	18	18	18	18	39

1 The total length of railroad open for traffic irrespective of the number of tracks comprising the road.

Source: Department for Regional Development, Northern Ireland: 028 9054 0801

15.23 Operating statistics of railways
Northern Ireland

		Unit	1993	1994	1995	1996	1997	1998	1999	2000	2001	2002	2003
Maintenance of way and works													
Material used:													
Ballast	KNSA	Thousand m²	16.0	33.2	22.5	27.0	51.3	38.5	40.0	47.0	80.0	40.0	130.0
Rails	KNSB	Thousand tonnes	2.00	1.80	1.76	2.12	0.37	2.50	3.00	3.50	2.50	1.00	4.50
Sleepers	KNSC	Thousands	14.60	22.40	22.90	27.50	5.10	32.00	30.00	40.00	50.00	5.00	40.00
Track renewed	KNSD	Km	16.00	12.00	16.00	20.00	2.40	22.50	7.00	29.00	15.00	5.00	25.75
New Track laid	KPGD	Km	..	3.2	2.5	–	–	–	–	21.0	–	–	–
Engine kilometres													
Total[1]	KNSE	Thousand Km	3 640	3 640	4 000	4 100	4 100	4 100	4 100	4 100	4 056	4 056	4 170
Train kilometres:													
Total	KNSF	"	3 210	3 210	3 570	3 670	3 670	3 670	3 670	3 670	3 626	3 626	3 704
Coaching	KNSG	"	3 206	3 206	3 566	3 666	3 666	3 666	3 666	3 666	3 622	3 622	3 700
Freight	KNSH	"	4	4	4	4	4	4	4	4	4	4	4

1 Including shunting, assisting, light, departmental, maintenance and repair.

Source: Department for Regional Development, Northern Ireland: 028 9054 0801

15.24 Main output of United Kingdom airlines

Available tonne kilometres (millions)

		1993	1994	1995	1996	1997	1998	1999	2000	2001	2002	2003
All services	KNTA	25 144	27 714	29 904	32 210	35 538	40 021	42 002	43 379	42 370	40 550	42 784
Percentage growth on previous year	KNTB	*8.5*	*10.2*	*7.4*	*7.7*	*10.3*	*12.5*	*5.0*	*3.6*	*−2.4*	*−4.3*	*5.5*
Scheduled services	KNTC	18 605	20 360	22 016	23 793	26 504	29 756	31 815	32 938	31 866	30 433	31 492
Percentage growth on previous year	KNTD	*9.0*	*9.4*	*8.1*	*8.1*	*11.4*	*12.3*	*6.9*	*3.5*	*−3.3*	*−4.5*	*3.5*
Non-scheduled services	KNTE	6 510	7 265	7 695	8 044	9 034	10 265	10 186	10 440	10 505	10 117	11 293
Percentage growth on previous year	KNTF	*7.1*	*13.0*	*5.9*	*4.5*	*7.3*	*13.3*	*−0.7*	*4.1*	*0.6*	*−3.7*	*11.6*

Source: Civil Aviation Authority: 020 7453 6246

15.25 Air traffic between the United Kingdom and abroad[1]

Thousands

		1993	1994[2]	1995	1996	1997	1998	1999	2000	2001	2002	2003
Flights												
United Kingdom airlines												
Scheduled services	KNUA	290.8	325.8	342.1	373.0	410.3	443.7	480.9	520.3	536.7	531.3	517.7
Non-scheduled services	KNUB	215.2	195.0	204.8	198.0	208.2	218.7	212.6	216.2	208.5	218.6	211.0
Overseas airlines[3]												
Scheduled services	KNUC	336.2	351.3	363.3	390.0	399.6	426.4	467.6	467.6	496.8	487.5	487.0
Non-scheduled services	KNUD	38.0	35.1	31.5	31.3	32.5	34.8	31.7	31.7	26.0	36.7	27.1
Total	KNUE	880.2	907.2	941.7	992.3	1 050.6	1 123.6	1 192.8	1 235.8	1 268.0	1 274.1	1 242.8
Passengers carried												
United Kingdom airlines												
Scheduled services	KNUF	29 798.2	32 578.0	34 934.7	37 902.2	41 854.7	46 747.7	50 148.5	54 522.8	53 591.7	54 360.0	56 476.7
Non-scheduled services	KNUG	24 777.1	19 501.0	20 484.5	26 304.4	28 699.5	31 616.6	32 603.8	33 185.9	34 009.1	33 935.7	33 385.6
Overseas airlines[3]												
Scheduled services	KNUH	31 163.4	35 134.5	34 568.5	36 992.1	39 900.7	42 554.5	46 628.0	46 627.9	51 107.8	51 317.6	54 504.0
Non-scheduled services	KNUI	3 638.0	3 509.5	4 244.2	4 416.3	4 413.0	4 569.7	4 156.5	4 156.5	3 966.1	3 956.3	3 947.1
Total	KNUJ	89 376.7	90 723.0	94 231.9	105 615.0	114 867.9	125 488.5	133 536.8	138 493.1	142 674.7	143 569.6	148 313.4

1 Excludes travel to and from the Channel Islands.
2 Due to the introduction of European licencing, off shore helicopter movements are no longer included in this figure.
3 Includes airlines of overseas UK Territories.

Source: Civil Aviation Authority: 020 7453 6246

15.26 Operations and traffic on scheduled services: revenue traffic
United Kingdom airlines[1]

		Unit	1993	1994	1995	1996	1997	1998	1999	2000	2001	2002	2003
All services													
Aircraft stage flights:													
Number	KNFA	Numbers	601 620	621 272	658 958	702 492	749 806	797 682	835 031	878 582	921 556	911 518	895 095
Average length	KNFB	Kilometres	971	1 023	1 032	1 047	1 079	1 111	1 134	1 156	1 138	1 149	1 215
Aircraft-kilometres flown	KNFC	Millions	584.3	663.2	679.9	735.3	809.2	886.3	946.9	1 016.3	1 048.6	1 047.1	1 088.0
Passengers uplifted	KNFD	"	40.1	43.9	47.5	51.1	56.3	61.7	65.4	70.3	69.7	72.2	76.3
Seat-kilometres used	KNFE	"	94 670.1	104 294.5	115 347.1	124 846.5	136 388.2	151 969.1	160 336.4	170 469.0	158 650.7	156 493.9	164 806.3
Cargo uplifted:[2]	KNFF	Tonnes	541 986	618 067	643 181	690 806	782 855	831 436	860 291	897 184	742 705	768 736	800 645
Tonne-kilometres used:		Millions											
Passenger	KNFH	"	8 905.3	9 789.2	11 171.5	12 189.6	13 287.2	14 754.9	15 517.7	16 507.0	15 258.0	15 035.1	15 418.8
Freight	KNFI	"	2 919.6	3 378.1	3 567.3	3 831.9	4 454.0	4 663.3	4 924.9	5 159.9	4 548.3	4 940.5	5 187.0
Mail	KNFJ	"	141.5	147.3	151.1	176.0	172.2	177.7	153.0	179.2	101.9	56.6	54.5
Total	KNFG	"	11 966.4	13 314.6	14 889.9	16 197.5	17 913.4	19 595.9	20 595.6	21 846.1	19 908.2	20 032.2	20 660.3
Domestic services													
Aircraft stage flights:													
Number	KNFK	Numbers	300 416	301 652	318 884	331 109	336 218	352 936	354 864	353 525	365 881	359 400	345 954
Average length	KNFL	Kilometres	311.3	314.8	317.0	320.0	330.0	333.1	337.0	343.5	350.3	350.0	356.5
Aircraft-kilometres flown	KNFM	Millions	93.5	94.9	101.1	105.8	111.0	117.6	119.6	121.4	128.2	126.0	123.0
Passengers uplifted	KNFN	"	12.1	13.0	14.0	15.0	15.9	16.6	17.1	18.0	18.2	19.8	20.7
Seat-kilometres used	KNFO	"	4 933.8	5 334.0	5 753.6	6 204.3	6 645.7	6 947.5	7 183.9	7 541.8	7 644.5	8 321.9	8 903.6
Cargo uplifted:[2]	KNFP	Tonnes	30 660	32 670	33 659	35 432	30 679	31 879	25 964	24 644	19 498	16 755	17 248
Tonne-kilometres used:		Millions											
Passenger	KNFR	"	405.2	417.3	485.0	527.8	568.9	592.6	609.9	640.2	648.5	702.8	737.9
Freight	KNFS	"	5.6	6.3	6.9	7.4	6.1	6.0	6.0	5.8	4.1	3.6	3.4
Mail	KNFT	"	6.5	6.7	6.6	6.4	6.0	6.0	4.0	3.7	3.5	2.8	3.0
Total	KNFQ	"	417.3	430.3	498.5	541.6	581.0	604.7	619.9	649.7	656.1	709.2	744.3
International services													
Aircraft stage flights:													
Number	KNFU	Numbers	301 204	319 620	339 714	371 400	413 588	444 746	480 167	525 057	555 675	552 118	549 141
Average length	KNFV	Kilometres	1 629.0	1 693.0	1 703.0	1 695.0	1 688.0	1 729.0	1 723.0	1 704.0	1 656.0	1 670.0	1 757.7
Aircraft-kilometres flown	KNFW	Millions	490.8	541.4	578.8	629.5	698.2	768.8	827.3	894.9	920.5	921.1	965.0
Passengers uplifted	KNFX	"	28.0	30.9	33.5	36.1	40.4	45.1	48.2	52.2	51.5	52.4	55.5
Seat-kilometres used	KNFY	"	89 736.3	98 960.5	109 593.4	118 642.2	129 742.5	145 021.6	153 152.5	162 927.2	151 005.5	148 172.1	155 902.6
Cargo uplifted:[2]	KNFZ	Tonnes	511 326	585 397	609 522	655 374	752 176	799 557	834 327	872 540	723 206	751 975	783 397
Tonne-kilometres used:		Millions											
Passenger	KNJX	"	8 500.1	9 352.3	10 686.4	11 661.9	12 718.2	14 162.3	14 908.0	15 867.0	14 609.5	14 331.6	14 680.9
Freight	KNJY	"	2 914.0	3 371.8	3 560.4	3 824.5	4 448.0	4 657.2	4 919.0	5 154.1	4 544.3	4 936.9	5 183.6
Mail	KNJZ	"	135.0	140.5	144.4	169.5	166.3	171.7	149.0	175.5	98.3	53.8	51.4
Total	KNJW	"	11 549.1	12 864.6	14 391.2	15 655.9	17 332.5	18 991.2	19 976.0	21 196.6	19 252.1	19 322.3	19 915.9

1 Includes services of British Airways and other UK private companies.
2 Freight and mail.

Source: Civil Aviation Authority: 020 7453 6246

15.27 Accidents on scheduled fixed wing passenger-carrying services[1,2]
United Kingdom airlines

| | Passenger casualties | | Crew casualties | | Thousand aircraft stage flights per fatal accident | Million aircraft-kms. flown per fatal accident | Thousand passengers carried per passenger killed | Million passenger kms. flown per passenger killed | Fatal accidents | | Passengers killed per hundred million passenger-kms. |
	Number of fatal accidents	Killed	Seriously injured	Killed	Seriously injured					per 100 000 aircraft stage flights	per hundred million aircraft-kms.	
1950-54	7	194	9	28	4	107.4	61.8	46.1	50.1	0.93	1.62	2.00
1955-59	7	123	28	29	8	158.3	92.1	155.2	158.5	0.63	1.09	0.63
1960-64	5	104	35	21	6	303.7	182.2	373.4	390.6	0.33	0.55	0.26
1965-69	6	273	2	32	2	282.7	194.9	222.2	255.2	0.35	0.51	0.39
1970-74	2	167	5	14	2	889.5	737.1	464.3	657.7	0.11	0.14	0.15
1975-79	1	54	6	9	-	1 773.0	1 523.5	1 688.2	3 239.9	0.06	0.07	0.03
1980-84	-	-	4	-	1	-	-	-	-	-	-	-
1985-89	2	47	79	1	8	1 220.0	1 014.5	3031.0	6 262.9	0.08	0.10	0.02
1990-94	-	-	1	-	9	-	-	-	-	-	-	-
1995-99	1	9	1	3	3	3 699.9	4 026.0	31 265.6	76 539.4	0.03	0.02	0.001
	KCVN	KCVO	KCVP	KCVQ	KCVR							
2000	-	-	1	-	-	-	-	-	-	-	-	-
2001	-	-	-	-	-	-	-	-	-	-	-	-
2002	-	-	-	-	3	-	-	-	-	-	-	-
2003	-	-	1	-	1	-	-	-	-	-	-	-

1 Excluding accidents involving the deaths of third parties only.
2 Following a review of historical data for this table, some revisions have been made to earlier years.

Source: Civil Aviation Authority: 01293 573346

15.28 Activity at civil aerodromes
United Kingdom[1]

Thousands and tonnes

		1994	1995	1996	1997	1998	1999	2000	2001	2002	2003
Movement of civil aircraft (thousands)											
Commercial											
Transport	KNQC	1 552	1 615	1 686	1 764	1 871	1 959	2 045	2 095	2 094	2 160
Other	KNQD	112	124	128	143	162	159	159	150	120	117
Total	KNQB	1 664	1 739	1 814	1 907	2 033	2 118	2 204	2 245	2 214	2 277
Non-commercial	KNQE	1 684	1 809	1 281	1 330	1 343	1 263	1 186	1 207	1 100	1 186
Total	KNQA	3 348	3 548	3 095	3 237	3 376	3 381	3 390	3 452	3 314	3 463
Passengers handled											
Terminal	KNQG	122 159	129 369	135 810	146 657	158 856	168 363	179 885	181 231	188 761	199 950
Transit	KNQH	1 565	1 490	1 486	1 405	1 226	1 156	1 167	1 087	1 054	990
Total	KNQF	123 724	130 859	137 296	148 062	160 082	169 519	181 052	182 318	189 815	200 940
Commercial freight handled[2] (tonnes)											
Set down	KNQJ	788 995	849 226	886 507	981 861	1 072 127	1 135 065	1 174 635	1 093 142	1 124 026	1 172 552
Picked up	KNQK	799 793	854 267	885 080	960 859	1 008 358	1 053 902	1 139 292	1 052 379	1 071 407	1 035 680
Total	KNQI	1 588 788	1 703 493	1 771 587	1 942 720	2 080 485	2 188 967	2 313 927	2 145 521	2 195 433	2 208 232
Mail handled											
Set down	KNQM	70 776	72 376	80 937	88 366	88 766	92 974	101 743	98 690	90 738	86 415
Picked up	KNQN	89 780	93 700	105 964	115 066	113 993	114 752	123 352	117 389	99 747	93 096
Total	KNQL	160 556	166 076	186 901	203 432	202 759	207 726	225 095	216 079	190 485	179 511

1 See chapter text.
2 With effect from 2001, passengers, freight and mail handled; excludes traffic carried on air taxi operations.

Source: Civil Aviation Authority: 020 7453 6258

15.29 United Kingdom ports: foreign, coastwise and one-port traffic

Thousand tonnes

		1992	1993	1994	1995	1996	1997	1998	1999	2000	2001	2002
Inwards:												
Foreign												
Liquid bulk	JURC	64 640	68 824	63 512	58 512	59 309	61 060	61 346	56 528	70 534	74 495	62 811
Other traffic	JURD	117 946	120 633	126 575	131 789	133 393	144 634	147 933	147 053	150 147	163 869	158 113
All traffic	HHEL	182 586	189 457	190 087	190 302	192 702	205 694	209 279	203 581	220 681	238 364	220 924
Coastwise												
Liquid bulk	JURE	40 134	41 893	44 178	48 393	52 354	49 981	51 514	48 164	36 999	37 008	38 694
Other traffic	JURF	18 060	17 540	19 102	19 504	17 563	17 526	19 222	18 811	20 803	20 268	19 521
All traffic	HHEO	58 194	59 433	63 279	67 898	69 917	67 508	70 736	66 975	57 801	57 276	58 215
One-port												
Liquid bulk	JURG	14 107	10 063	13 725	10 848	10 861	6 871	10 587	20 220	24 965	18 245	25 886
Other traffic	JURH	14 871	13 739	14 851	15 878	14 244	14 974	15 498	16 187	12 896	15 005	15 802
All traffic	HHER	28 978	23 802	28 577	26 726	25 105	21 844	26 085	36 407	37 862	33 250	41 688
Total inwards												
Liquid bulk	JURI	118 881	120 780	121 415	117 754	122 524	117 912	123 446	124 913	132 498	129 748	127 391
Other traffic	JURJ	150 876	151 912	160 528	167 171	165 200	177 134	182 654	182 050	183 846	199 142	193 436
All traffic	HHEU	269 758	272 692	281 943	284 926	287 724	295 046	306 100	306 963	316 344	328 890	320 828
Outwards:												
Foreign												
Liquid bulk	JURK	90 947	96 616	113 936	111 651	106 169	104 654	106 041	110 591	118 074	110 321	107 516
Other traffic	JURL	59 249	60 874	65 052	67 150	69 620	74 644	75 620	73 776	74 599	70 062	70 657
All traffic	HHEX	150 196	157 490	178 988	178 801	175 790	179 298	181 661	184 367	192 673	180 383	178 173
Coastwise												
Liquid bulk	JURM	42 696	44 557	46 135	51 459	57 146	53 753	52 622	51 966	42 488	36 049	37 535
Other traffic	JURN	18 093	17 469	18 664	20 676	18 169	18 251	19 324	19 132	19 812	18 877	19 796
All traffic	HHFA	60 789	62 027	64 799	72 134	75 316	72 004	71 946	71 098	62 300	54 926	57 331
One-port												
Liquid bulk	JURO	9 472	9 137	8 850	8 882	8 847	8 560	4 365	126	488	647	693
Other traffic	JURP	5 437	4 878	3 550	3 487	3 566	3 621	4 430	3 059	1 244	1 520	1 301
All traffic	HHFD	14 908	14 015	12 400	12 369	12 413	12 181	8 794	3 186	1 732	2 167	1 994
Total outwards												
Liquid bulk	JURQ	143 114	150 311	168 921	171 992	172 163	166 967	163 028	162 684	161 050	147 017	145 744
Other traffic	JURR	82 779	83 222	87 266	91 312	91 356	96 516	99 374	95 967	95 656	90 460	91 753
All traffic	HHFH	225 893	233 532	256 187	263 304	263 519	263 484	262 402	258 651	256 706	237 477	237 497
Total goods handled	HHFI	495 651	506 224	538 130	548 230	551 243	558 530	568 502	565 614	573 050	566 366	558 325

Source: Department for Transport; 020 7944 3087

15.30 Roll-on/roll-off ferry and Channel Tunnel traffic; road goods vehicles outward to mainland Europe: by country of registration

Thousands

		1993	1994	1995	1996	1997	1998	1999	2000	2001	2002	2003
Powered vehicles:												
United Kingdom	ZCGT	398.0	453.1	486.0	531.1	543.2	544.3	562.7	544.8	517.6	493.3	471.3
Austria	ZCGU	..	..	9.7	8.6	5.4	10.2	14.9	17.0	42.0	45.8	42.9
Belgium/Luxembourg	ZCGV	29.4	37.1	45.7	41.0	53.6	74.5	96.7	114.1	119.3	121.4	104.3
Denmark	ZCGW	4.9	5.0	4.5	4.6	5.5	7.3	8.7	9.5	12.0	16.9	13.7
Finland	ZCGX	..	..	0.3	0.2	0.1	0.6	0.7	0.9	3.1	2.0	1.1
Germany	ZCGY	27.7	28.1	28.0	30.4	39.3	52.4	73.1	111.5	132.0	148.2	155.7
France	ZCGZ	144.0	163.2	154.9	181.7	234.2	272.4	319.1	338.8	352.4	363.1	363.2
Greece	ZCHA	1.5	1.3	1.8	2.1	2.6	1.9	2.6	2.9	2.6	2.8	3.6
Irish Republic	ZCHB	35.6	32.4	31.0	30.1	32.3	38.8	44.7	48.5	46.6	44.6	30.8
Italy	ZCHC	13.0	22.7	29.3	28.9	30.4	35.3	45.8	67.8	91.1	127.8	132.4
Netherlands	ZCHD	73.3	76.3	84.6	87.2	107.0	125.4	153.3	185.1	187.5	186.3	210.2
Spain	ZCHE	29.5	35.2	38.4	39.4	45.1	56.3	67.7	81.8	93.9	102.2	105.9
Sweden	ZCHF	..	..	0.7	0.9	8.9	10.3	1.0	1.4	1.8	1.8	1.4
Portugal	ZCHG	3.3	3.7	3.4	3.1	5.1	6.7	9.2	10.7	10.2	11.0	9.4
European Union (excluding UK)[1]	ZCHH	362.2	405.2	432.2	458.1	569.5	690.3	837.3	990.0	1 094.5	1 174.0	1 174.5
Non-European Union	ZCHI	30.2	34.2	29.0	26.3	20.9	33.6	47.4	52.9	79.4	116.2	147.1
Unknown	ZCHJ	5.8	4.0	3.0	2.2	5.7	4.5	6.3	17.7	20.5	18.1	19.1
All countries	ZCHK	796.2	896.5	950.2	1 017.7	1 146.4	1 274.5	1 453.7	1 605.4	1 711.9	1 801.5	1 812.0
Unaccompanied trailers	ZCHL	593.4	701.6	677.4	626.4	740.0	737.5	737.8	712.9	686.4	726.0	780.4
Powered vehicles and unaccompanied trailers	ZCHM	1 335.6	1 598.1	1 627.6	1 644.1	1 886.4	2 012.3	2 191.4	2 318.3	2 398.3	2 527.5	2 592.5

1 As constituted before 1 May 2004.

Source: Department for Transport; 0117 987 8484

15.31 United Kingdom international passenger movements by air and sea[1]

Thousands

		1993	1994	1995	1996	1997	1998	1999	2000	2001	2002	2003
By air												
European Union[2]	ZCDD	51 506	58 042	59 987	60 949	66 089	73 360	79 003	84 930	87 534	91 419	97 768
Other Western Europe	ZCDE	8 507	8 797	9 364	9 473	10 385	11 089	11 246	11 897	12 062	12 053	12 477
Rest of the world	ZCDF	27 335	28 915	31 542	34 499	37 594	40 263	42 619	45 293	42 591	42 611	43 400
All air passenger movements	KMUP	87 348	95 754	100 893	104 921	114 068	124 712	132 868	142 120	142 187	146 082	153 644
By sea												
Irish Republic, European continent and Mediterranean Sea area	ZCDG	34 685	36 733	34 321	34 543	36 258	33 226	31 381	28 516	27 754	28 726	26 523
Rest of the world[3]	BMMF	37	34	33	24	29	23	26	26	27	32	25
Pleasure cruises[3,4]	KMRQ	193	236	207	233	..	..	445	461	469	540	698
All sea passenger movements	KMUO	34 915	37 002	34 562	34 792	36 288	33 249	31 852	29 003	28 249	29 298	27 246

1 See chapter text.
2 As constituted before 1 May 2004.
3 Figures for 2003 are provisional.
4 Cruise passengers, like other passengers are included at both departure and arrival if their journeys begin and end at United Kingdom seaports.

Sources: Civil Aviation Authority: 020 7453 6246; Department for Transport: 020 7944 6246

15.32 Postal services and television licences[1]
United Kingdom

		1994	1995	1996	1997	1998	1999	2000	2001	2002	2003	2004
Letters, etc posted (millions)	**KMRA**	16 651	17 468	18 322	18 101	18 350	18 878	19 711	20 076	20 648	21 979	22 837
of which:												
Registered and insured	**KMRB**	21.8	21.5	23.5	25.6	28.7	31.6	30.2	32.3	36.1	38.5	41.4
Airmail (Commonwealth and foreign)	**KMRC**	545.0	567.1	655.1	684.5	658.4	693.2	672.3	659.2	600.7	541.6	512.0
Business reply and freepost items	**KMRD**	482.9	477.6	493.1	505.8	524.7	503.6	475.3	487.4	486.2	434.4	397.7
Postal orders												
Total issued (thousands)[2]	**KMRH**	39 089	37 901	35 542	33 404	31 907	30 289	30 153	30 931	29 150	28 666	28 888
Television licences (thousands)												
In force on 31 March	**KMQL**	20 413	20 732	21 105	21 305	21 723	22 240	22 625	22 839	23 157	23 486	23 899
of which:												
Colour	**KMQM**	19 524	19 957	20 505	20 849	21 344	21 944	22 413	22 684	23 040	23 392	23 824

1 See chapter text.
2 Excluding those issued on HM ships, in many British possessions and in other places abroad. Up to 1998 includes Postal Orders issued Overseas and by Ministry of Defence.

Sources: Royal Mail: 01246 547012;
Capita Business Services Limited: 0117 3021003;
Post Office Counters Limited: 020 7921 9384

National accounts

Chapter 16

National accounts

National accounts

(Tables 16.1 to 16.22)

The tables which follow are based on those in the Blue Book 2004 edition. Some of the figures are provisional and may be revised later; this applies particularly to the figures for 2002 and 2003.

The accounts are based on the European System of Accounts 1995 (ESA95). The Blue Book contains an introduction to the system of the UK accounts outlining some of the main concepts and principles of measurement used. It explains how key economic indicators are derived from the sequence of accounts and how the figures describing the whole economy are broken down by sector and by industry. A detailed description of the structure for the accounts is provided in a separate ONS publication *United Kingdom National Accounts: Concepts, Sources and Methods* (TSO, 1998). Further information on the financial accounts is given in the *Financial Statistics Explanatory Handbook*.

In the tables in this chapter on national income, analyses by industry are based, as far as possible, on the Standard Industrial Classification Revised 1992. The principal aggregate measured in these tables is the *Gross domestic product* (GDP). This is a concept of the value of the total economic activity taking place in UK territory. It can be viewed as incomes earned, as expenditures incurred, or as production. Adding all primary incomes received from the rest of the world and deducting all primary incomes payable to non-residents produces *Gross national income* (previously known as gross national product). This is a concept of the value of all incomes earned by UK residents.

ESA95, the internationally compatible accounting framework, provides a systematic and detailed description of the UK economy. It includes the sector accounts which provide, by institutional sector, a description of the different stages of the economic process from production through income generation, distribution and use of income to capital accumulation and financing; and the input-output framework, which describes the production process in more detail. It contains all the elements required to compile such aggregate measures as GDP, Gross national income (GNI) and saving.

Gross domestic product and national income

(Tables 16.1 to 16.3)

Table 16.1 shows the main national accounts aggregates, both at current prices and chained volume measures.

Table 16.2 shows the various money flows which generate the gross domestic product and gross national income. The output approach to GDP shows the total output of goods and services, the use of goods and services in the production process (intermediate consumption) and taxes and subsidies on products. The expenditure approach to GDP shows consumption expenditure by households and government, gross capital formation and expenditure on UK exports by overseas purchasers. The sum of these items overstates the amount of income generated in the United Kingdom by the value of imports of goods and services; this item is therefore subtracted to produce gross domestic product at market prices. The income approach to GDP shows gross operating surplus, mixed income and compensation of employees (previously known as income from employment). Taxes are added and subsidies are deducted to produce the total of the income-based components at market prices.

Table 16.2 also shows the primary incomes received from the rest of the world, which are added to GDP and primary incomes payable to non-residents, which are deducted from GDP, to arrive at *Gross national income*. Primary income comprises compensation of employees, taxes less subsidies on production and property and entrepreneurial income.

Table 16.3 shows the expenditure approach to the chained volume measure of GDP. When looking at the change in the economy over time the main concern is usually whether more goods and services are actually being produced now than at some time in the past. Over time changes in current price GDP show changes in the monetary value of the components of GDP and, as these changes in value can reflect changes in both price and volume, it is difficult to establish how much of an increase in the series is due either to increased activity in the economy or to an increase in the price level. As a result, when looking at the real growth in the economy over time it is useful to look at volume estimates of GDP. In chained volume series, volume measures for each year are produced in prices of the previous year. These volume measures are then 'chain-linked' together to produce a continuous time series.

Industrial analysis

(Tables 16.4 and 16.5)

The analysis of gross value added by industry at current prices shown in Table 16.4 reflects the estimates based on the Standard Industrial Classification, Revised 1992 (SIC92). The table is based on current price data reconciled through the input-output process for 1992 to 2002. The estimates are valued at basic prices, that is, the only taxes included in the price will be taxes paid as part of the production process, such as business rates, and not any taxes specifically levied on the production of a unit of output, for example VAT.

Table 16.5 shows chained volume measures of gross value added at basic prices by industry. Chained volume measures of gross value added (output approach) provides the lead indicator of economic change in the short-term. The output analysis of gross value added is estimated in terms of change and expressed in index number form. It is therefore inappropriate to show as a statistical adjustment any divergence of an output measure of GDP derived from it from other measures of GDP. Such an adjustment does, however, exist implicitly.

Sector analysis – Distribution of income accounts and capital account

(Tables 16.6 to 16.13)

The National Accounts accounting framework includes the sector accounts which provide, by institutional sector, a description of the different stages of the economic process from production through income generation, distribution and use of income to capital accumulation and financing.

Tables 16.6–16.12 show the allocation of primary income account and the secondary distribution of income account for the non-financial corporations, financial corporations, government and households sectors. Additionally, Table 16.12 shows the use of income account for the households sector and Table 16.13 provides a summary of the capital account. The full sequence of accounts is shown in the Blue Book.

The allocation of primary income account shows the resident units and institutional sectors as recipients rather than producers of primary income. It demonstrates the extent to which operating surpluses are distributed to the owners of the enterprises. The resources side of the allocation of primary income accounts includes the components of the income approach to measurement of GDP. The balance of this account is the gross balance of primary income (B.5g) for each sector, and if the gross balance is aggregated across all sectors of the economy the result is **Gross national income**.

The secondary distribution of income account describes how the balance of income for each sector is allocated by redistribution; through transfers such as taxes on income, social contributions and benefits and other current transfers. The balancing item of this account is gross disposable income (B.6g). For the households sector, the chained volume measure of gross disposable income is shown as real household disposable income.

Table 16.12 shows, for the households sector, the use of disposable income where the balancing item is saving (B.8g). For the non-financial corporations sector the balancing item of the secondary distribution of income account, gross disposable income (B.6g) is equal to saving (B.8g).

The summary capital account (Table 16.13) brings together the saving and investment of the several sectors of the economy. It shows saving, capital transfers, gross capital formation and net acquisition of non-financial assets for each of the four sectors.

Household and non-profit institutions serving households (NPISH) consumption expenditure at current market prices and chained volume measures

(Tables 16.14 to 16.17)

Household and NPISH consumption expenditure is a major component of the expenditure measure of gross domestic product both at current prices (Table 16.2) and chained volume measures (Table 16.3).

Household final consumption expenditure includes the value of income-in-kind and imputed rent of owner-occupied dwellings but excludes business expenditure allowed as deductions in computing income for tax purposes. It includes expenditure on durable goods, for instance motor cars, which from the point of view of the individual might more appropriately be treated as capital expenditure. The only exceptions are the purchase of land and dwellings and costs incurred in connection with the transfer of their ownership and expenditure on major improvements by occupiers, which are treated as personal capital expenditure.

The estimates of household consumption expenditure include purchases of second-hand as well as new goods, *less* the proceeds of sales of used goods.

The most detailed figures are published quarterly in *Consumer Trends* (available as a web-only publication on the National Statistics website *www.statistics.gov.uk*).

Change in inventories (previously known as value of physical increase in stocks and work in progress)

(Table 16.18)

This table gives a broad analysis by industry, and, for manufacturing industry, by asset, of the value of entries less withdrawals and losses of inventories (stocks).

Gross fixed capital formation

(Tables 16.19 to 16.22)

Gross fixed capital formation comprises expenditure on the replacement of, and additions to, fixed capital assets located in the United Kingdom, including all ships and aircraft of UK ownership.

16.1

United Kingdom national and domestic product[1]
Main aggregates
At current prices and chained volume measures, reference year 2001

Indices (2001=100) and £ million

		1995	1996	1997	1998	1999	2000	2001	2002	2003
INDICES (2001=100)										
VALUES AT CURRENT PRICES										
Gross domestic product at current market prices ("money GDP")	YBEU	72.2	76.7	81.5	86.4	90.8	95.6	100.0	105.0	110.6
Gross value added at current basic prices	YBEX	72.5	77.1	81.7	86.4	90.5	95.2	100.0	105.1	110.8
CHAINED VOLUME MEASURES										
Gross domestic product at market prices	YBEZ	83.6	85.9	88.8	91.5	94.1	97.8	100.0	101.8	104.1
Gross national disposable income at market prices	YBFP	81.3	83.9	88.0	91.9	93.2	96.9	100.0	103.2	105.6
Gross value added at basic prices	CGCE	83.6	86.0	88.8	91.9	94.3	98.0	100.0	101.5	103.4
PRICES										
Implied deflator of GDP at market prices	YBGB	86.4	89.2	91.8	94.4	96.5	97.8	100.0	103.2	106.3
VALUES AT CURRENT PRICES (£ million)										
Gross measures (before deduction of fixed										
capital consumption) at current market prices										
Gross Domestic Product ("money GDP")	YBHA	718 383	762 610	810 138	858 616	903 167	950 561	994 309	1 044 145	1 099 896
Employment, property and entrepreneurial income from the rest of the world (receipts *less* payments)	YBGG	2 101	1 204	3 905	12 906	−1 116	5 208	11 652	21 475	22 097
Subsidies (receipts) *less* taxes (payments) on products from/to the rest of the world	−QZOZ	−5 220	−3 116	−2 919	−3 651	−3 288	−3 838	−3 772	−2 355	−2 233
Other subsidies on production from/to the rest of the world	−IBJL	293	253	206	246	309	292	298	519	..
Gross National Income (GNI)	ABMX	715 557	760 959	811 332	868 112	899 101	952 266	1 002 771	1 063 784	1 120 353
Current transfers from the rest of the world (receipts *less* payments)	−YBGF	−2 649	−1 902	−3 209	−4 966	−4 435	−6 253	−3 426	−6 764	−8 217
Gross National Disposable Income	NQCO	712 908	759 057	808 123	863 146	894 666	946 013	999 345	1 057 020	1 112 136
Adjustment to current basic prices										
Gross Domestic Product (at current market prices)	YBHA	718 383	762 610	810 138	858 616	903 167	950 561	994 309	1 044 145	1 099 896
Adjustment to current basic prices (*less* taxes *plus* subsidies on products)	−NQBU	−79 268	−83 084	−90 573	−97 077	−106 051	−112 071	−113 146	−117 870	..
Gross Value Added (at current basic prices)	ABML	639 115	679 526	719 565	761 539	797 116	838 490	881 163	926 275	976 148
Net measures (after deduction of fixed										
capital consumption) at current market prices	−NQAE	−82 792	−86 570	−88 301	−91 243	−96 935	−101 774	−105 838	−111 870	−115 342
Net domestic product	NHRK	631 069	675 379	721 024	765 536	803 684	845 709	885 368	929 353	981 487
Net national income	NSRX	628 243	673 728	722 218	775 032	799 618	847 414	893 830	948 992	1 001 943
Net national disposable income	NQCP	625 594	671 826	719 009	770 066	795 183	841 161	890 404	942 228	993 726
CHAINED VOLUME MEASURES (Reference year 2001, £ million)										
Gross measures (before deduction of fixed										
capital consumption) at market prices										
Gross Domestic Product	ABMI	831 104	854 517	882 522	909 819	935 818	971 937	994 309	1 011 892	1 034 618
Terms of trade effect ("Trading gain or loss")	YBGJ	−13 976	−11 375	−2 953	2 314	3 863	1 575	−	7 494	9 689
Real gross domestic income	YBGL	817 128	843 142	879 569	912 133	939 681	973 512	994 309	1 019 386	1 044 307
Real employment, property and entrepreneurial income from the rest of the world (receipts *less* payments)	YBGI	2 385	1 329	4 232	13 697	−1 161	5 330	11 652	20 995	21 024
Subsidies (receipts) *less* taxes (payments) on production from/to the rest of the world	−QZPB	−7 145	−6 371	−2 075	−2 944	−2 900	−4 089	−3 772	−2 892	−2 884
Other subsidies on production from/to the rest of the world	−IBJN	264	230	180	212	295	301	582	631	617
Gross National Income (GNI)	YBGM	815 230	840 827	882 398	923 228	936 076	975 029	1 002 771	1 038 120	1 063 064
Real current transfers from the rest of the world (receipts *less* payments)	−YBGP	−3 008	−2 099	−3 478	−5 270	−4 612	−6 399	−3 426	−6 613	−7 818
Gross National Disposable Income	YBGO	812 224	838 733	878 924	917 956	931 464	968 628	999 345	1 031 507	1 055 246
Adjustment to basic prices										
Gross Domestic Product (at market prices)	ABMI	831 104	854 517	882 522	909 819	935 818	971 937	994 309	1 011 892	1 034 618
Adjustment to basic prices (*less* taxes *plus* subsidies on products)	−NTAQ	−94 663	−96 812	−100 464	−100 366	−105 309	−108 816	−113 146	−117 857	−123 309
Gross Value Added (at basic prices)	ABMM	736 618	757 869	782 248	809 585	830 586	863 228	881 163	894 035	911 309
Net measures (after deduction of fixed										
capital consumption) at market prices	−CIHA	−88 819	−91 016	−93 222	−96 234	−100 317	−103 151	−105 838	−109 683	−112 212
Net national income at market prices	YBET	723 096	746 314	785 758	823 659	832 435	868 845	893 830	925 224	946 781
Net national disposable income at market prices	YBEY	720 080	744 221	782 281	818 384	827 819	862 440	890 404	918 611	938 963

1 See chapter text.

Source: Office for National Statistics: 020 7533 6031

16.2 United Kingdom gross domestic product and national income[1]
Current prices

£ million

		1995	1996	1997	1998	1999	2000	2001	2002	2003
Gross domestic product: Output										
Gross value added, at basic prices										
Output of goods and services	NQAF	1 343 623	1 436 904	1 518 586	1 610 029	1 689 186	1 790 997	1 868 990	1 948 458	..
less intermediate consumption	-NQAJ	−704 508	−757 378	−799 021	−848 490	−892 070	−952 507	−987 827	−1 022 183	..
Total Gross Value Added	ABML	639 115	679 526	719 565	761 539	797 116	838 490	881 163	926 275	976 148
Value added taxes (VAT) on products	QYRC	48 113	51 050	55 109	56 702	61 719	64 464	67 549	71 586	77 864
Other taxes on products	NSUI	37 995	39 724	43 003	46 933	50 512	54 086	52 246	52 890	53 599
less subsidies on products	-NZHC	−6 840	−7 690	−7 539	−6 558	−6 180	−6 479	−6 649	−6 606	−7 715
Gross Domestic Product at market prices	YBHA	718 383	762 610	810 138	858 616	903 167	950 561	994 309	1 044 145	1 099 896
Gross domestic product: Expenditure										
Final consumption expenditure										
Actual individual consumption										
Household final consumption expenditure	ABPB	443 367	474 311	503 813	536 933	570 440	603 349	635 583	665 896	693 551
Final consumption expenditure of NPISH	ABNV	16 481	18 338	19 509	21 053	22 069	23 188	24 345	26 359	27 532
Individual government final consumption expenditure	NNAQ	80 624	84 666	86 933	91 347	99 103	106 432	114 159	127 031	140 870
Total actual individual consumption	NQEO	540 472	577 315	610 255	649 333	691 612	732 969	774 087	819 286	861 953
Collective government final consumption expenditure	NQEP	59 614	60 843	60 437	61 792	66 536	70 658	75 565	81 835	89 022
Total final consumption expenditure	ABKW	600 086	638 158	670 692	711 125	758 148	803 627	849 652	901 121	950 975
Households and NPISH	NSSG	459 848	492 649	523 322	557 986	592 509	626 537	659 928	692 255	721 083
Central government	NMBJ	85 998	89 255	90 623	93 739	99 522	105 916	113 802	126 471	139 876
Local government	NMMT	54 240	56 254	56 747	59 400	66 117	71 174	75 922	82 395	90 016
Gross capital formation										
Gross fixed capital formation	NPQX	117 448	126 291	133 776	150 540	154 647	161 210	165 504	171 695	178 916
Changes in inventories	ABMP	4 512	1 771	4 621	5 026	6 060	5 271	6 189	2 213	2 504
Acquisitions less disposals of valuables	NPJO	−121	−160	−27	429	229	3	396	214	−40
Total gross capital formation	NQFM	121 839	127 902	138 370	155 995	160 936	166 484	172 089	174 122	181 380
Exports of goods and services	KTMW	203 509	223 969	233 027	230 334	238 794	267 007	272 369	273 720	277 539
less imports of goods and services	-KTMX	−207 051	−227 419	−231 951	−238 838	−254 711	−286 557	−299 801	−304 818	−310 212
External balance of goods and services	KTMY	−3 542	−3 450	1 076	−8 504	−15 917	−19 550	−27 432	−31 098	−32 673
Statistical discrepancy between expenditure components and GDP	RVFD	–	–	–	–	–	–	–	–	214
Gross Domestic Product at market prices	YBHA	718 383	762 610	810 138	858 616	903 167	950 561	994 309	1 044 145	1 099 896
Gross domestic product: Income										
Operating surplus, gross										
Non-financial corporations										
Public non-financial corporations	NRJT	9 162	9 070	7 769	8 183	7 497	7 123	7 481	6 784	7 149
Private non-financial corporations	NRJK	142 165	157 745	168 871	174 261	177 452	184 005	183 869	186 669	201 522
Financial corporations	NQNV	17 838	17 135	14 806	18 436	12 432	11 269	10 971	27 838	33 802
Adjustment for financial services	-NSRV	−23 215	−22 580	−22 396	−27 998	−26 768	−33 659	−33 575	−40 728	−45 294
General government	NMXV	7 479	8 588	8 848	9 139	9 681	9 987	10 163	10 335	10 722
Households and non-profit institutions serving households	QWLS	38 165	40 113	43 054	47 959	51 580	54 390	59 615	63 498	67 757
Total operating surplus, gross	ABNF	191 594	210 071	220 952	229 980	231 874	233 115	238 524	254 396	275 658
Mixed income	QWLT	46 647	49 564	51 040	50 876	54 181	56 967	60 874	65 006	68 681
Compensation of employees	HAEA	386 718	405 835	433 306	465 854	495 596	532 318	565 313	590 154	614 917
Taxes on production and imports	NZGX	101 322	105 819	113 298	119 450	128 713	135 597	137 870	143 265	150 583
less subsidies	-AAXJ	−7 898	−8 679	−8 458	−7 544	−7 197	−7 436	−8 272	−8 676	−10 436
Statistical discrepancy between income components and GDP	RVFC	–	–	–	–	–	–	–	–	493
Gross Domestic Product at market prices	YBHA	718 383	762 610	810 138	858 616	903 167	950 561	994 309	1 044 145	1 099 896

16.2 United Kingdom gross domestic product and national income[1]
Current prices
continued

		1995	1996	1997	1998	1999	2000	2001	2002	2003
Gross Domestic Product at market prices	YBHA	718 383	762 610	810 138	858 616	903 167	950 561	994 309	1 044 145	1 099 896
Compensation of employees										
receipts from the rest of the world	KTMN	887	911	1 007	840	960	1 032	1 087	1 121	1 116
less payments to the rest of the world	−KTMO	−1 183	−818	−924	−850	−759	−882	−1 021	−1 054	−1 057
Total	KTMP	−296	93	83	−10	201	150	66	67	59
less Taxes on products paid to the rest of the world										
plus Subsidies received from the rest of the world	−QZOZ	−5 220	−3 116	−2 919	−3 651	−3 288	−3 838	−3 772	−2 355	−2 233
Other subsidies on production	−IBJL	293	253	206	246	309	292	298	519	..
Property and entrepreneurial income										
receipts from the rest of the world	HMBN	87 132	91 621	95 337	103 667	99 729	134 436	141 178	124 393	125 224
less payments to the rest of the world	−HMBO	−84 735	−90 510	−91 515	−90 751	−101 046	−129 378	−129 592	−102 985	−103 186
Total	HMBM	2 397	1 111	3 822	12 916	−1 317	5 058	11 586	21 408	22 038
Gross National Income at market prices	ABMX	715 557	760 959	811 332	868 112	899 101	952 266	1 002 771	1 063 784	1 120 353

1 See chapter text.

Source: Office for National Statistics: 020 7533 6031

16.3 United Kingdom gross domestic product[1]
Chained volume measures, reference year 2001

£ million

		1995	1996	1997	1998	1999	2000	2001	2002	2003
Gross domestic product: expenditure approach										
Final consumption expenditure										
Actual individual consumption										
Household final consumption expenditure	ABPF	505 114	524 115	543 493	564 239	590 275	616 515	635 583	655 865	671 013
Final consumption expenditure of non-profit institutions serving households	ABNU	21 230	21 296	21 779	23 300	23 095	24 875	24 345	25 818	26 593
Individual government final consumption expenditure	NSZK	102 107	104 403	105 948	107 339	109 554	111 763	114 159	117 238	120 288
Total actual individual consumption	YBIO	628 250	650 156	672 108	696 661	724 888	754 444	774 087	798 921	817 894
Collective government final consumption expenditure	NSZL	68 692	68 703	66 667	67 334	71 148	73 173	75 565	79 624	83 386
Total final consumption expenditure	ABKX	696 085	717 604	737 172	761 728	793 836	826 249	849 652	878 545	901 280
Gross capital formation										
Gross fixed capital formation	NPQR	120 432	127 283	135 924	153 202	155 631	161 267	165 504	169 928	173 623
Changes in inventories	ABMQ	4 533	1 848	4 009	4 905	6 416	5 262	6 189	2 513	2 467
Acquisitions less disposals of valuables	NPJP	−28	−43	−3	57	28	3	396	226	9
Total gross capital formation	NPQU	124 954	129 285	140 342	158 346	161 954	166 590	172 089	172 668	176 099
Gross domestic final expenditure	YBIK	819 666	845 524	876 804	920 253	955 837	992 822	1 021 741	1 051 212	1 077 379
Exports of goods and services	KTMZ	191 774	208 304	225 828	232 057	241 978	264 810	272 369	272 635	272 949
Gross final expenditure	ABME	1 008 680	1 052 622	1 102 788	1 152 018	1 197 551	1 257 636	1 294 110	1 323 847	1 350 328
less imports of goods and services	−KTNB	−184 573	−202 472	−222 227	−242 789	−261 942	−285 837	−299 801	−311 955	−315 911
Statistical discrepancy between expenditure components and GDP	GIXS	−	−	−	−	−	−	−	−	201
Gross Domestic Product at market prices	ABMI	831 104	854 517	882 522	909 819	935 818	971 937	994 309	1 011 892	1 034 618
of which External balance of goods and services	KTNC	7 201	5 832	3 601	−10 732	−19 964	−21 027	−27 432	−39 320	−42 962

1 See chapter text.

Source: Office for National Statistics: 020 7533 6031

16.4

Gross value added at current basic prices: by industry[1,2]
United Kingdom

£ million

		1995	1996	1997	1998	1999	2000	2001	2002	2003
Agriculture, hunting, forestry and fishing	EWSH	11 766	12 058	10 239	9 546	9 359	8 915	8 703	8 978	9 476
Production										
Mining and quarrying										
Mining and quarrying of energy producing materials										
Mining of coal	QTOQ	1 223	1 045	988	817	643	611	549	474	479
Extraction of mineral oil and natural gas	QTOR	13 703	17 125	15 435	13 204	15 044	22 833	22 141	20 891	24 862
Other mining and quarrying	QTOS	1 442	1 599	1 695	1 645	1 717	1 795	1 762	1 479	2 160
Total mining and quarrying	EWSL	16 369	19 768	18 118	15 666	17 403	25 239	24 452	22 844	27 500
Manufacturing										
Food; beverages and tobacco	QTOU	18 261	19 891	20 329	20 013	20 226	20 300	20 936	21 141	22 232
Textiles and textile products	QTOV	6 821	7 264	7 734	6 988	6 450	6 003	5 589	5 122	5 519
Leather and leather products	QTOW	946	892	845	823	808	750	649	626	593
Wood and wood products	QTOX	1 918	2 026	2 237	2 328	2 248	2 335	2 371	2 542	2 523
Pulp, paper and paper products; publishing and printing	QTOY	17 582	18 154	18 405	18 995	19 880	20 556	20 463	20 326	20 343
Coke, petroleum products and nuclear fuel	QTOZ	2 924	2 530	2 381	2 576	2 664	2 513	2 572	2 573	3 012
Chemicals, chemical products and man-made fibres	QTPA	15 311	15 724	15 338	15 083	15 337	15 183	16 199	16 652	15 409
Rubber and plastic products	QTPB	6 789	7 222	8 015	8 237	7 944	7 842	7 901	7 665	7 914
Other non-metal mineral products	QTPC	5 158	5 188	5 196	5 017	4 952	5 014	5 091	5 156	5 499
Basic metals and fabricated metal products	QTPD	16 124	16 410	17 120	17 632	16 674	16 024	15 713	15 125	15 210
Machinery and equipment not elsewhere classified	QTPE	12 273	12 467	13 402	13 592	12 731	12 341	12 274	11 612	12 022
Electrical and optical equipment	QTPF	17 758	18 592	20 020	20 176	20 792	20 839	18 793	16 898	16 874
Transport equipment	QTPG	13 066	14 318	15 611	16 089	15 944	15 886	15 986	15 496	18 133
Manufacturing not elsewhere classified	QTPH	4 857	5 394	6 028	6 297	6 422	6 556	6 710	6 524	7 520
Total manufacturing	EWSP	139 789	146 071	152 658	153 844	153 071	152 147	151 247	147 462	152 803
Electricity, gas and water supply	EWST	15 586	16 280	16 141	16 087	15 968	16 112	16 044	16 140	14 924
Total production	QTPK	171 744	182 119	186 917	185 597	186 444	193 499	191 743	186 446	195 227
Construction	EWSX	33 004	34 644	36 932	39 001	41 721	45 475	50 002	55 491	61 538
Service industries										
Wholesale and retail trade (including motor trade); repair of motor vehicles, personal and household goods	QTPM	74 612	79 319	86 002	92 901	99 170	103 592	110 559	115 619	123 630
Hotels and restaurants	QTPN	18 254	20 276	22 439	24 434	26 224	27 914	29 310	30 918	33 222
Transport, storage and communication										
Transport and storage	QTPO	33 044	34 973	37 309	39 773	40 850	42 860	43 841	44 947	43 593
Communication	QTPP	18 296	18 731	20 115	22 588	24 146	27 194	27 572	29 245	32 044
Total	EWTF	51 341	53 705	57 424	62 362	64 996	70 054	71 413	74 192	75 634
Financial intermediation	QTPR	40 089	40 852	40 512	45 211	40 050	41 663	42 705	61 656	52 041
Adjustment for financial services (FISIM)	-NSRV	−23 215	−22 580	−22 396	−27 998	−26 768	−33 659	−33 575	−40 728	−45 294
Real estate, renting and business activities										
Letting of dwellings including imputed rent of owner occupiers	QTPS	45 083	46 717	50 272	55 714	59 588	62 710	68 597	72 623	75 306
Other real estate, renting and business activities	QTPT	73 970	82 406	93 170	108 041	118 548	129 447	141 361	148 071	167 411
Total	QTPU	119 052	129 122	143 444	163 756	178 137	192 157	209 958	220 695	242 717
Public administration and defence (PAD)[3]	EWTN	38 378	40 334	40 388	40 360	41 824	43 733	46 116	48 472	50 489
Education[3]	QTPW	35 722	37 005	39 247	41 663	44 980	48 080	51 761	55 304	55 752
Health and social work	QTPX	41 134	42 664	44 663	47 403	50 772	54 550	57 552	61 314	71 294
Other social and personal services, private households with employees and extra-territorial organisations	EWTV	27 234	30 008	33 753	37 307	40 208	42 520	44 915	47 922	50 421
Total service industries	QTPZ	422 600	450 706	485 477	527 395	559 594	590 603	630 715	675 360	709 907
All industries	ABML	639 115	679 526	719 565	761 539	797 116	838 490	881 163	926 275	976 148

1 See chapter text. Components may not sum to totals as a result of rounding.
2 Because of differences in the annual and monthly production inquiries, estimates of current price output and value added by industry derived from the current price input-output supply-use balances are not consistent with the equivalent measures of constant price growth given in Table 16.5. These differences do not affect GDP totals. For further information see "Experimental Constant Price Input-Output Supply-Use Balances: An approach to improving the quality of the national accounts" Nadim Ahmad, *Economic Trends*, July 1999 (No. 548).

3 Central government expenditure on education is included in PAD in 1995. For 1996 onwards it is included in Education.

Source: Office for National Statistics: 020 7533 6031

16.5 Gross value added at basic prices: by industry[1,2,3,4]
Chained volume indices
United Kingdom

	Weight per 1000[1] 2001		1995	1996	1997	1998	1999	2000	2001	2002	2003
Agriculture, hunting, forestry and fishing	9.9	GDQA	104.2	101.9	104.2	107.1	110.7	110.0	100.0	111.9	109.0
Production											
Mining and quarrying											
Mining and quarrying of energy producing materials											
Mining of coal	0.6	CKZP	170.8	163.1	154.3	130.7	115.9	99.0	100.0	94.0	88.8
Extraction of mineral oil and natural gas	25.1	CKZO	97.7	103.1	102.4	105.0	110.0	106.2	100.0	98.8	93.2
Other mining and quarrying	2.0	CKZQ	103.1	90.3	89.2	95.4	102.7	106.6	100.0	114.6	111.8
Total mining and quarrying	27.7	CKYX	100.6	103.8	102.8	104.9	109.3	105.8	100.0	99.7	94.3
Manufacturing											
Food; beverages and tobacco	23.8	CKZA	97.7	99.3	101.2	100.0	99.9	99.2	100.0	101.0	100.8
Textiles and textile products	6.3	CKZB	141.2	138.7	135.6	126.1	117.0	114.3	100.0	93.2	92.9
Leather and leather products	0.7	CKZC	129.6	127.7	134.0	116.6	110.2	97.2	100.0	87.5	71.7
Wood and wood products	2.7	CKZD	107.5	105.8	102.8	101.4	97.1	99.7	100.0	101.6	102.1
Pulp, paper and paper products; publishing and printing	23.2	CKZE	99.5	97.4	98.2	99.0	99.2	99.6	100.0	100.1	98.6
Coke, petroleum products and nuclear fuel	2.9	CKZF	125.8	116.0	119.6	111.8	100.8	106.1	100.0	102.3	95.8
Chemicals, chemical products and man-made fibres	18.4	CKZG	82.5	83.0	85.5	86.3	89.4	94.2	100.0	100.0	101.1
Rubber and plastic products	9.0	CKZH	101.8	100.6	101.0	104.2	103.7	103.8	100.0	95.8	96.6
Other non-metallic mineral products	5.8	CKZI	100.0	96.1	99.1	96.6	96.3	99.3	100.0	97.2	102.8
Basic metals and fabricated metal products	17.8	CKZJ	100.5	101.0	103.3	102.5	100.1	102.2	100.0	96.0	93.6
Machinery and equipment not elsewhere classified	13.9	CKZK	107.6	105.4	104.6	104.3	98.1	98.1	100.0	94.4	95.5
Electrical and optical equipment	21.3	CKZL	74.8	78.6	80.8	85.0	94.1	108.1	100.0	86.8	86.7
Transport equipment	18.1	CKZM	88.1	94.2	98.4	103.1	105.7	102.4	100.0	96.7	102.5
Manufacturing not elsewhere classified	7.6	CKZN	95.0	96.6	98.4	99.9	102.5	101.0	100.0	100.6	101.0
Total manufacturing	171.6	CKYY	95.1	95.8	97.6	98.2	98.9	101.4	100.0	96.9	97.3
Electricity, gas and water supply	18.2	CKYZ	85.7	89.9	90.2	93.1	95.6	97.7	100.0	99.5	101.7
Total production	217.6	CKYW	94.9	96.2	97.5	98.5	99.7	101.6	100.0	97.5	97.4
Construction	56.7	GDQB	90.6	93.1	95.6	96.7	97.0	98.2	100.0	103.8	108.9
Service industries											
Wholesale and retail trade (including motor trade); repair of motor vehicles, personal and household goods	125.5	GDQC	81.7	85.6	88.1	91.5	94.0	97.0	100.0	105.0	107.3
Hotels and restaurants	33.3	GDQD	87.3	87.9	91.5	95.4	99.2	100.5	100.0	103.7	109.2
Transport, storage and communication											
Transport and storage	49.8	GDQF	80.2	80.8	85.3	91.6	92.3	98.3	100.0	101.3	100.8
Communication	31.3	GDQG	49.8	56.2	63.8	69.4	81.0	93.1	100.0	101.2	105.9
Total	81.0	GDQH	67.1	70.5	76.4	82.4	87.8	96.2	100.0	101.3	102.8
Financial intermediation	48.5	GDQI	77.4	79.8	83.1	87.2	90.2	94.9	100.0	98.8	100.6
Adjustment for financial services (FISIM)	−38.1	GDQJ	73.0	78.0	81.3	86.5	88.6	95.4	100.0	102.9	114.1
Real estate, renting and business activities											
Letting of dwellings, including imputed rent of owner occupiers	77.8	GDQL	90.0	90.7	92.5	95.5	98.3	97.7	100.0	101.7	103.3
Other real estate, renting and business activities	160.4	GDQK	67.4	71.3	77.6	84.7	88.0	94.8	100.0	103.3	110.2
Total	238.3	GDQM	74.4	77.4	82.3	88.1	91.2	95.7	100.0	102.8	107.9
Public administration and defence (PAD)[4]	55.6	GDQO	98.1	96.9	95.8	96.0	96.1	98.3	100.0	102.7	104.8
Education[4]	58.7	GDQP	91.9	92.8	93.4	94.6	97.9	99.5	100.0	101.2	101.6
Health and social work[4]	62.3	GDQQ	81.9	85.3	86.9	89.6	92.0	96.4	100.0	103.8	107.7
Other social and personal services, private households with employees and extra-territorial organisations	51.0	GDQR	79.1	82.8	84.8	90.8	93.2	96.7	100.0	102.8	101.9
Total service industries	715.8	GDQS	79.8	82.3	85.5	89.7	92.8	96.8	100.0	102.7	105.3
All industries	1 000.0	CGCE	83.6	86.0	88.8	91.9	94.3	98.0	100.0	101.5	103.4

1 See chapter text. The weights are in proportion to total gross value added (GVA) in 2001. and are used to combine the industry output indices to calculate the totals for 2002 and 2003. For 2001 and earlier, totals are calculated using the equivalent weight for the previous year (eg totals for 2001 use 2000 weights).

2 As GVA is expressed in index number form, it is inappropriate to show as a statistical adjustment any divergence from the other measures of GDP. Such an adjustment does, however, exist implicitly.

3 See footnote 2 to Table 16.4.

4 The GVA for PAD, education and Health and social work in this table follows the SIC(92) and differs from that used in Table 2.3, which is based on Input-Output groups. The administration costs of the NHS are included in PAD in this table but are included in Health and social work in Table 2.3. Central government expenditure on teachers is included in this table but, for 1995 only, are included in PAD in Table 16.4.

Source: Office for National Statistics: 020 7533 6031

16.6 Non-financial corporations[1]
Allocation of primary income account[2]
United Kingdom. ESA95 sector S.11

£ million

		1995	1996	1997	1998	1999	2000	2001	2002	2003
Resources										
Operating surplus, gross	NQBE	151 327	166 815	176 640	182 444	184 949	191 128	191 350	193 453	208 671
Property income, received										
Interest	EABC	9 328	9 642	9 868	13 913	10 814	14 349	13 453	8 952	9 151
Distributed income of corporations	EABD	22 367	22 919	26 548	25 086	21 501	26 631	36 868	32 210	..
Reinvested earnings on direct foreign investment	HDVR	11 376	13 417	11 747	10 979	16 214	20 118	22 950	27 098	10 394
Attributed property income of insurance policy-holders	FAOF	395	423	386	463	338	489	280	302	..
Rent	FAOG	110	114	118	118	117	117	117	118	..
Total	FAKY	43 576	46 517	48 684	50 558	48 955	61 392	74 388	67 647	73 432
Total resources	FBXJ	194 903	213 332	225 324	233 002	233 904	252 520	265 738	261 100	282 103
Uses										
Property income, paid										
Interest	EABG	25 390	24 923	26 457	31 609	31 514	37 671	40 326	36 839	38 003
Distributed income of corporations	NVCS	71 532	76 136	80 805	78 299	87 100	83 202	100 810	91 868	..
Reinvested earnings on direct foreign investment	HDVB	4 662	6 117	5 187	3 117	2 776	7 348	1 699	3 760	4 188
Rent	FBXO	719	815	756	584	564	1 319	1 896	1 853	..
Total	FBXK	102 303	107 957	113 251	113 568	121 799	131 419	149 815	134 833	143 822
Balance of primary incomes, gross	NQBG	92 600	105 375	112 073	119 434	112 105	121 101	115 923	126 267	138 281
Total uses	FBXJ	194 903	213 332	225 324	233 002	233 904	252 520	265 738	261 100	282 103
After deduction of fixed capital consumption	-DBGF	−56 850	−53 856	−53 770	−55 666	−58 328	−60 886	−62 630	−64 771	−66 950
Balance of primary incomes, net	FBXQ	35 750	51 519	58 303	63 768	53 777	60 215	53 293	61 496	71 331

1 See chapter text.
2 Before deduction of fixed capital formation.

Source: Office for National Statistics: 020 7533 6031

16.7 Non-financial corporations[1]
Secondary distribution of income account
United Kingdom. ESA95 sector S.11

£ million

		1995	1996	1997	1998	1999	2000	2001	2002	2003
Resources										
Balance of primary incomes, gross	NQBG	92 600	105 375	112 073	119 434	112 105	121 101	115 923	126 267	138 281
Social contributions										
Imputed social contributions	NSTJ	3 329	3 200	3 173	3 801	3 983	4 312	4 500	4 738	4 506
Current transfers other than taxes, social contributions and benefits										
Non-life insurance claims	FCBP	4 716	5 508	4 190	4 849	4 151	4 456	4 565	7 789	..
Miscellaneous transfers	NRJY	494	537	557	595	611	622	619	616	..
Total	NRJB	4 716	5 508	4 190	4 849	4 151	5 923	5 000	5 978	6 532
Total resources	FCBR	100 645	114 083	119 436	128 084	120 239	131 336	125 423	136 983	149 319
Uses										
Current taxes on income, wealth etc.										
Taxes on income	FCBS	19 252	23 348	28 932	27 256	22 948	26 406	26 151	24 548	24 183
Social benefits other than social transfers in kind	NSTJ	3 329	3 200	3 173	3 801	3 983	4 312	4 500	4 738	4 506
Current transfers other than taxes, social contributions and benefits										
Net non-life insurance premiums	FCBY	4 716	5 508	4 190	4 849	4 151	4 456	4 565	7 789	..
Miscellaneous current transfers	FDBI	400	1 518	479	444	569	413	411	422	430
Total, other current transfers	FCBX	5 116	7 026	4 669	5 293	4 720	6 336	5 411	6 400	6 962
Gross Disposable Income	NRJD	72 948	80 509	82 662	91 734	88 588	94 282	89 361	101 297	113 668
Total uses	FCBR	100 645	114 083	119 436	128 084	120 239	131 336	125 423	136 983	149 319
After deduction of fixed capital consumption	-DBGF	−56 850	−53 856	−53 770	−55 666	−58 328	−60 886	−62 630	−64 771	−66 950
Disposable income, net	FCCF	16 098	26 653	28 892	36 068	30 260	33 396	26 731	36 526	46 718

1 See chapter text.

Source: Office for National Statistics: 020 7533 6031

16.8 General government[1]
Allocation of primary income account
United Kingdom. ESA95 sector S.13 Unconsolidated

£ million

		1995	1996	1997	1998	1999	2000	2001	2002	2003
Resources										
Operating surplus, gross	NMXV	7 479	8 588	8 848	9 139	9 681	9 987	10 163	10 335	10 722
Taxes on production and imports, received										
Taxes on products										
Value added tax (VAT)	NZGF	43 268	46 579	51 712	52 474	57 908	60 260	63 974	68 778	75 124
Taxes and duties on imports excluding VAT										
Import duties	NMXZ	–	–	–	–	–	–	–	–	–
Taxes on imports excluding VAT and import duties	NMBT	–	–	–	–	–	–	–	–	–
Taxes on products excluding VAT and import duties	NMYB	35 482	37 380	40 621	44 815	48 442	51 956	50 146	50 946	51 639
Total taxes on products	NVCC	78 750	83 959	92 333	97 289	106 350	112 216	114 120	119 724	126 763
Other taxes on production	NMYD	15 214	15 045	15 186	15 815	16 482	17 047	18 075	18 789	19 120
Total taxes on production and imports, received	NMYE	93 964	99 004	107 519	113 104	122 832	129 263	132 195	138 513	145 877
less Subsidies, paid										
Subsidies on products	-NMYF	−4 702	−3 991	−4 679	−3 863	−3 587	−3 983	−4 746	−4 209	−5 248
Other subsidies on production	-LIUF	−765	−728	−711	−745	−679	−622	−1 041	−1 551	−2 129
Total	-NMRL	−5 467	−4 719	−5 390	−4 608	−4 266	−4 605	−5 787	−5 760	−7 121
Property income, received										
Total Interest	NMYL	7 430	7 883	7 334	7 912	7 334	7 344	7 336	6 663	7 045
Distributed income of corporations	NMYM	6 915	6 882	6 527	7 456	7 102	7 203	7 605	7 081	7 126
Property income attributed to insurance policy holders	NMYO	32	28	33	48	33	54	24	22	22
Rent										
from sectors other than general government	NMYR	684	780	721	547	528	1 283	1 862	1 879	1 525
Total	NMYU	15 061	15 573	14 615	15 963	14 997	15 884	16 827	15 645	15 718
Total resources	NMYV	111 037	118 446	125 592	133 598	143 244	150 529	153 398	158 733	164 946
Uses										
Property income, paid										
Total interest	NRKB	30 044	31 874	33 792	34 824	30 645	30 556	27 911	25 379	27 004
Total	NMYY	30 044	31 874	33 792	34 824	30 645	30 556	27 911	25 379	27 004
Balance of primary incomes, gross	NMZH	80 993	86 572	91 800	98 774	112 599	119 973	125 487	133 354	137 942
Total uses	NMYV	111 037	118 446	125 592	133 598	143 244	150 529	153 398	158 733	164 946
After deduction of fixed capital consumption	-NMXO	−7 479	−8 588	−8 848	−9 139	−9 681	−9 987	−10 163	−10 335	−10 722
Balance of primary incomes, net	NMZI	73 514	77 984	82 952	89 635	102 918	109 986	115 324	123 019	127 220

1 See chapter text.

Source: Office for National Statistics: 020 7533 6031

16.9 General government[1]
Secondary distribution of income account
United Kingdom. ESA95 sector S.13 Unconsolidated

£ million

		1995	1996	1997	1998	1999	2000	2001	2002	2003
Resources										
Balance of primary incomes, gross	NMZH	80 993	86 572	91 800	98 774	112 599	119 973	125 487	133 354	137 942
Current taxes on income, wealth etc.										
Taxes on income	NMZJ	95 014	99 267	107 717	124 104	129 485	140 306	147 665	142 463	145 725
Other current taxes	NVCM	11 937	13 510	14 778	15 953	17 191	18 223	19 626	21 236	23 428
Total	NMZL	106 951	112 777	122 495	140 057	146 676	158 529	167 291	163 699	169 153
Social contributions										
Actual social contributions										
Employers' actual social contributions	NMZM	25 917	27 344	29 038	30 593	32 805	36 292	38 233	38 798	43 622
Employees' social contributions	NMZN	21 091	21 700	24 121	25 234	26 645	27 506	28 785	29 310	33 654
Social contributions by self- and non-employed persons	NMZO	1 541	1 771	1 848	1 729	1 784	1 973	2 112	2 284	2 805
Total	NMZP	48 549	50 815	55 007	57 556	61 234	65 771	69 130	70 392	80 081
Imputed social contributions	NMZQ	5 279	5 299	5 356	5 880	5 823	6 157	6 501	6 812	5 608
Total	NMZR	53 828	56 114	60 363	63 436	67 057	71 928	75 631	77 204	85 689
Other current transfers										
Non-life insurance claims	NMZS	377	371	349	499	410	403	353	423	463
Current transfers within general government	NMZT	58 587	59 464	59 513	60 455	64 820	66 462	71 970	77 194	85 023
Current international cooperation	NMZU	1 233	2 424	1 739	1 384	3 176	2 084	4 568	3 112	3 570
Miscellaneous current transfers										
from sectors other than general government	NMZX	455	411	459	433	308	228	398	320	273
Other current transfers	NNAA	60 652	62 670	62 060	62 771	68 714	69 177	77 289	81 049	89 329
Total resources	NNAB	302 424	318 133	336 718	365 038	395 046	419 607	445 698	455 306	482 113
Uses										
Social benefits other than social transfers in kind	NNAD	110 381	113 081	117 004	117 593	121 161	126 630	136 609	141 079	150 280
Other current transfers										
Net non-life insurance premiums	NNAE	377	371	349	499	410	403	353	423	463
Current transfers within general government	NNAF	58 587	59 464	59 513	60 455	64 820	66 462	71 970	77 194	85 023
Current international cooperation	NNAG	2 224	1 814	1 700	1 705	1 667	2 418	2 434	2 573	2 715
Miscellaneous current transfers										
to sectors other than general government	NNAI	10 120	12 027	13 376	15 225	16 694	18 016	18 749	22 793	26 383
Of which: GNP based fourth own resource	NMFH	1 826	2 454	2 458	3 920	4 632	4 379	3 858	5 335	6 772
Other current transfers	NNAN	71 308	73 676	74 938	77 884	83 591	87 299	93 506	102 983	114 256
Gross Disposable Income	NNAO	120 735	130 773	143 975	168 731	189 433	204 818	214 681	210 368	216 735
Total uses	NNAB	302 424	318 133	336 718	365 038	395 046	419 607	445 698	455 306	482 113
After deduction of fixed capital consumption	-NMXO	-7 479	-8 588	-8 848	-9 139	-9 681	-9 987	-10 163	-10 335	-10 722
Disposable income, net	NNAP	113 256	122 185	135 127	159 592	179 752	194 831	204 518	200 033	206 013

1 See chapter text.

Source: Office for National Statistics: 020 7533 6031

16.10 Households and non-profit institutions serving households[1]
Allocation of primary income account
United Kingdom. ESA95 sectors S.14 and S.15

£ million

		1995	1996	1997	1998	1999	2000	2001	2002	2003
Resources										
Operating surplus, gross	QWLS	38 165	40 113	43 054	47 959	51 580	54 390	59 615	63 498	67 757
Mixed income, gross	QWLT	46 647	49 564	51 040	50 876	54 181	56 967	60 874	65 006	68 681
Compensation of employees										
Wages and salaries	QWLW	336 973	352 651	377 272	404 715	428 073	457 273	486 302	505 659	523 192
Employers' social contributions	QWLX	49 449	53 277	56 117	61 129	67 724	75 195	79 077	84 562	91 784
Total	QWLY	386 422	405 928	433 389	465 844	495 797	532 468	565 379	590 221	614 976
Property income										
Interest	QWLZ	26 468	23 790	26 614	30 064	24 168	28 200	26 732	20 482	20 619
Distributed income of corporations	QWMA	32 279	33 810	36 590	37 312	39 244	43 508	49 283	44 181	46 612
Attributed property income of insurance policy holders	QWMC	42 358	48 356	51 068	53 408	53 200	53 107	53 080	52 045	54 087
Rent	QWMD	99	103	105	105	105	105	105	106	107
Total	QWME	101 204	106 059	114 377	120 889	116 717	124 920	129 200	116 814	121 425
Total resources	QWMF	572 438	601 664	641 860	685 568	718 275	768 745	815 068	835 539	872 839
Uses										
Property income										
Interest	QWMG	40 288	38 442	42 042	51 446	47 682	53 205	52 649	51 996	54 122
Rent	QWMH	202	210	216	216	215	215	215	216	218
Total	QWMI	40 490	38 652	42 258	51 662	47 897	53 420	52 864	52 212	54 340
Balance of primary incomes, gross	QWMJ	531 948	563 012	599 602	633 906	670 378	715 325	762 204	783 327	818 499
Total uses	QWMF	572 438	601 664	641 860	685 568	718 275	768 745	815 068	835 539	872 839
After deduction of										
fixed capital consumption	-QWLL	−19 575	−21 088	−22 923	−24 374	−27 261	−29 739	−32 122	−35 255	−36 054
Balance of primary incomes, net	QWMK	513 026	541 363	577 711	611 524	645 262	688 692	733 524	752 029	785 685

1 See chapter text.

Source: Office for National Statistics: 020 7533 6031

16.11 Households and non-profit institutions serving households[1]
Secondary distribution of income account
United Kingdom. ESA95 sectors S.14 and S.15

£ million

		1995	1996	1997	1998	1999	2000	2001	2002	2003
Resources										
Balance of primary incomes, gross	QWMJ	531 948	563 012	599 602	633 906	670 378	715 325	762 204	783 327	818 499
Imputed social contributions	RVFH	455	429	410	478	450	476	502	530	505
Social benefits other than social transfers in kind	QWML	149 123	156 560	165 765	170 975	181 607	198 453	208 258	215 999	223 356
Other current transfers										
Non-life insurance claims	QWMM	14 123	19 360	14 004	15 224	13 762	16 150	15 607	18 701	20 430
Miscellaneous current transfers	QWMN	17 833	20 358	20 868	21 577	22 620	24 623	25 698	28 483	30 466
Total	QWMO	31 956	39 718	34 872	36 801	36 382	40 773	41 305	47 184	50 896
Total resources	QWMP	713 482	759 719	800 649	842 160	888 817	955 027	1 012 269	1 047 040	1 093 256
Uses										
Current taxes on income, wealth etc										
Taxes on income	QWMQ	74 315	74 163	75 242	89 697	96 460	105 604	112 283	111 862	114 669
Other current taxes	NVCO	11 937	12 907	13 977	15 123	16 330	17 363	18 724	20 360	22 586
Total	QWMS	86 252	87 070	89 219	104 820	112 790	122 967	131 007	132 222	137 255
Social contributions										
Actual social contributions										
Employers' actual social contributions	QWMT	39 934	43 925	46 773	50 499	57 020	63 760	67 092	71 978	80 663
Employees' social contributions	QWMU	53 747	59 228	64 248	67 336	71 400	72 527	70 883	74 507	76 463
Social contributions by self and non-employed	QWMV	1 541	1 771	1 848	1 729	1 784	1 973	2 112	2 284	2 805
Total	QWMW	95 222	105 587	115 511	124 239	128 989	138 279	140 844	146 432	..
Imputed social contributions	QWMX	9 515	9 352	9 344	10 630	10 704	11 435	11 987	12 604	11 121
Total	QWMY	104 737	114 948	124 855	133 584	144 272	153 093	155 584	159 755	..
Social benefits other than social transfers in kind	QWMZ	925	899	880	950	922	948	977	1 006	980
Other current transfers										
Net non-life insurance premiums	QWNA	14 123	19 360	14 004	15 224	13 762	16 150	15 607	18 701	20 430
Miscellaneous current transfers	QWNB	8 327	8 434	9 346	9 677	10 033	10 646	11 019	11 274	11 638
Total	QWNC	22 450	27 794	23 350	24 901	23 795	26 796	26 626	29 975	32 068
Gross Disposable Income[2]	QWND	499 118	529 680	564 987	581 295	610 402	654 621	701 585	722 464	751 901
Total uses	QWMP	713 482	759 719	800 649	842 160	888 817	955 027	1 012 269	1 047 040	1 093 256
After deduction of fixed capital consumption	-QWLL	−19 575	−21 088	−22 923	−24 374	−27 261	−29 739	−32 122	−35 255	−36 054
Disposable income, net	QWNE	480 196	507 359	540 454	555 523	581 922	624 590	670 301	688 656	716 144

1 See chapter text.
2 Gross household disposable income revalued by the implied households and NPISH's final consumption expenditure deflator. For more details see table 6.1.4 on page 217 in *United Kingdom National Accounts* (the *Blue book*).

Source: Office for National Statistics: 020 7533 6031

16.12 Households and non-profit institutions serving households[1]
Use of disposable income account
United Kingdom. ESA95 sectors S.14 and S.15

£ million and percentages

		1995	1996	1997	1998	1999	2000	2001	2002	2003
Resources										
Disposable income, gross	QWND	499 118	529 680	564 987	581 295	610 402	654 621	701 585	722 464	751 901
Adjustment for the change in net equity of households in pension funds	NSSE	11 690	14 152	12 489	12 715	12 723	5 222	4 002	8 361	11 333
Total resources	NSSF	510 808	543 832	577 476	594 010	623 125	659 843	705 587	730 825	763 234
Uses										
Final consumption expenditure										
Individual consumption expenditure	NSSG	459 848	492 649	523 322	557 986	592 509	626 537	659 928	692 255	721 083
Saving, gross	NSSH	50 960	51 183	54 154	36 024	30 616	33 306	45 659	38 570	42 151
Total uses	NSSF	510 808	543 832	577 476	594 010	623 125	659 843	705 587	730 825	763 234
Saving ratio (percentages)	RVGL	10.0	9.4	9.4	6.1	4.9	5.0	6.5	5.3	5.5

1 See chapter text.

Source: Office for National Statistics: 020 7533 6031

£ million and indices (2001=100)

		1995	1996	1997	1998	1999	2000	2001	2002	2003
Net lending/borrowing by:										
Non-financial corporations	EABO	4 615	5 924	−3 497	−4 637	−12 910	−9 698	−16 360	297	14 604
Financial corporations	NHCQ	2 979	−2 414	−1 423	−2 384	−14 514	−23 628	−17 536	7 730	11 996
General government	NNBK	−42 001	−32 071	−17 834	523	9 384	14 335	7 862	−17 268	−36 060
Households and NPISH's	NSSZ	25 925	22 820	22 799	3 042	−5 603	−3 576	4 849	−8 113	−8 366
Rest of the world	NHRB	8 482	5 741	−45	3 456	23 643	22 567	21 185	17 354	19 187
Private non-financial corporations										
Gross trading profits										
Continental shelf profits	CAGJ	12 124	15 702	13 978	11 696	13 864	21 458	20 397	18 742	..
Others	CAED	125 151	133 508	145 693	150 975	153 954	153 342	149 885	156 800	169 657
Rental of buildings	FCBW	9 379	9 493	9 561	10 837	11 435	12 271	13 263	13 904	14 539
less Holding gains of inventories	−DLQZ	−4 489	−958	−361	753	−1 801	−2 941	434	−3 295	−1 630
Gross operating surplus	NRJK	142 165	157 745	168 871	174 261	177 452	184 005	183 869	186 669	201 522
Households and NPISH										
Household gross disposable income	QWND	499 118	529 680	564 987	581 295	610 402	654 621	701 585	722 464	751 901
Implied deflator of household and NPISH individual consumption expenditure indicies (2001=100)	YBFS	87.4	90.3	92.6	95.0	96.6	97.7	100.0	101.6	103.4
Real household disposable income:										
Chained volume measures (Reference year 2001)	RVGK	571 105	586 303	610 183	611 966	631 836	670 075	701 585	711 431	727 421
Indices (2001=100)	OSXR	81.4	83.6	87.0	87.2	90.1	95.5	100.0	101.4	103.7
Gross saving	NSSH	50 960	51 183	54 154	36 024	30 616	33 306	45 659	38 570	42 151
Households total resources	NSSJ	591 432	628 498	664 409	685 357	722 228	766 275	819 746	857 856	904 104
Saving ratio (percentages)	RVGL	*10.0*	*9.4*	*9.4*	*6.1*	*4.9*	*5.0*	*6.5*	*5.3*	*5.5*

1 See chapter text.

Source: Office for National Statistics: 020 7533 6031

16.14

Household final consumption expenditure: by purpose[1]
Current market prices
United Kingdom

£ million

		1995	1996	1997	1998	1999	2000	2001	2002	2003
Durable goods										
Furnishings, household equipment and routine maintenance of the house	LLIJ	13 508	14 321	15 250	15 873	16 566	17 798	19 276	20 228	19 092
Health	LLIK	1 401	1 453	1 549	1 717	1 881	1 997	2 109	2 406	3 436
Transport	LLIL	23 588	26 469	29 444	30 851	31 854	33 171	35 704	35 730	37 142
Communication	LLIM	244	276	282	440	512	601	636	634	604
Recreation and culture	LLIN	9 388	10 592	11 920	12 853	14 262	14 778	15 970	16 166	16 481
Miscellaneous goods and services	LLIO	2 963	3 094	3 295	3 320	3 398	3 403	3 750	4 205	4 548
Total durable goods	UTIA	51 092	56 205	61 740	65 054	68 473	71 748	77 445	79 369	81 303
Semi-durable goods										
Clothing and footwear	LLJL	27 426	28 865	30 270	31 540	32 561	34 759	36 312	38 564	40 453
Furnishings, household equipment and routine maintenance of the house	LLJM	7 990	8 429	9 091	9 751	10 577	11 877	12 399	13 233	13 266
Transport	LLJN	2 165	2 293	2 529	2 925	3 018	2 772	2 783	3 108	3 535
Recreation and culture	LLJO	11 770	12 887	14 724	17 292	19 049	20 405	21 605	23 812	24 178
Miscellaneous goods and services	LLJP	1 497	1 581	1 700	1 816	1 926	2 018	2 427	2 729	3 062
Total semi-durable goods	UTIQ	50 848	54 055	58 314	63 324	67 131	71 831	75 526	81 446	84 494
Non-durable goods										
Food & drink	ABZV	49 790	53 025	53 832	55 192	57 025	58 563	59 974	61 170	63 082
Alcohol & tobacco	ADFL	18 776	20 439	21 553	22 459	24 458	24 617	25 158	25 960	27 342
Housing, water, electricity, gas and other fuels	LLIX	21 357	22 757	22 656	22 094	21 800	22 265	23 076	23 361	24 966
Furnishings, household equipment and routine maintenance of the house	LLIY	2 374	2 433	2 495	2 505	2 657	2 786	2 973	3 168	3 349
Health	LLIZ	2 518	2 746	2 828	2 975	3 111	3 268	3 613	3 897	4 034
Transport	LLJA	11 986	12 767	13 818	14 396	15 200	16 711	15 676	14 922	14 921
Recreation and culture	LLJB	10 408	11 192	11 788	12 136	12 665	12 959	13 109	13 581	13 649
Miscellaneous goods and services	LLJC	7 257	8 014	8 383	8 727	9 121	9 463	9 884	10 931	11 999
Total non-durable goods	UTII	124 466	133 373	137 353	140 484	146 037	150 632	153 463	156 990	163 342
Total goods	UTIE	226 406	243 633	257 407	268 862	281 641	294 211	306 434	317 805	329 139
Services										
Clothing and footwear	LLJD	604	620	631	698	714	720	730	742	739
Housing, water, electricity, gas and other fuels	LLJE	60 055	63 173	67 558	74 103	79 411	83 389	90 391	95 498	100 493
Furnishings, household equipment and routine maintenance of the house	LLJF	2 415	2 545	2 686	2 873	3 046	3 206	3 326	3 400	3 382
Health	LLJG	2 916	3 048	3 189	3 389	3 537	3 722	4 064	4 414	4 669
Transport	LLJH	24 994	26 929	29 667	32 115	34 121	37 002	38 397	41 161	42 390
Communication	LLJI	8 823	9 083	9 732	10 607	11 493	12 755	13 521	14 049	14 893
Recreation and culture	LLJJ	19 509	20 737	21 539	22 967	23 756	24 075	25 321	28 405	29 405
Education	ADIE	6 197	6 405	7 440	7 814	8 943	9 634	9 239	8 629	9 649
Restaurants and hotels	ADIF	50 383	54 848	57 266	61 759	64 413	68 424	71 493	76 734	81 188
Miscellaneous goods and services	LLJK	40 612	42 951	45 793	49 377	53 987	59 270	63 143	64 496	65 110
Total services	UTIM	216 508	230 339	245 501	265 702	283 421	302 197	319 625	337 528	351 918
Final consumption expenditure in the UK by resident and non-resident households (domestic concept)	ABQI	442 914	473 972	502 908	534 564	565 062	596 408	626 059	655 333	681 057
Final consumption expenditure outside the UK by UK resident households	ABTA	13 721	14 377	14 942	16 913	19 690	21 654	22 907	24 435	26 702
less Final consumption expenditure in the UK by households resident in the rest of the world	CDFD	–13 268	–14 038	–14 037	–14 544	–14 312	–14 713	–13 383	–13 872	–14 208
Final consumption expenditure by UK resident households in the UK and abroad (national concept)	ABPB	443 367	474 311	503 813	536 933	570 440	603 349	635 583	665 896	693 551

1 See chapter text. Additional detail is published in *Consumer Trends* and table A7 of *UK Economic Accounts*, available from the National Statistics website *www.statistics.gov.uk/statbase/Product.asp?vlnk=1904.*

Source: *Office for National Statistics: 020 7533 6031*

16.15 Household final consumption expenditure: by purpose[1]
Chained volume measures, reference year 2001
United Kingdom

£ million

		1995	1996	1997	1998	1999	2000	2001	2002	2003
Durable goods										
Furnishings, household equipment and routine maintenance of the house	LLME	14 327	14 650	15 400	15 898	16 541	17 980	19 276	20 070	18 868
Health	LLMF	2 901	2 721	2 601	2 481	2 333	2 216	2 109	2 181	2 886
Transport	LLMG	23 323	25 389	27 072	28 536	30 013	32 192	35 704	35 982	37 943
Communication	LLMH	159	183	208	349	465	584	636	689	659
Recreation and culture	LLMI	5 789	6 569	7 544	9 079	11 558	13 363	15 970	17 494	19 687
Miscellaneous goods and services	LLMJ	3 219	3 319	3 509	3 464	3 485	3 447	3 750	4 157	4 338
Total durable goods	UTIC	47 475	50 911	54 725	58 793	64 045	69 640	77 445	80 573	84 381
Semi-durable goods										
Clothing and footwear	LLNG	24 259	25 692	26 730	28 058	29 795	33 151	36 312	40 599	43 293
Furnishings, household equipment and routine maintenance of the house	LLNH	7 945	8 267	8 854	9 458	10 323	11 845	12 399	13 283	13 462
Transport	LLNI	2 436	2 468	2 636	2 985	3 031	2 759	2 783	3 062	3 417
Recreation and culture	LLNJ	11 304	12 156	13 765	16 087	18 302	20 338	21 605	24 364	25 665
Miscellaneous goods and services	LLNK	1 462	1 565	1 688	1 801	1 922	2 039	2 427	2 755	3 048
Total semi-durable goods	UTIS	47 448	50 217	53 699	58 355	63 325	70 110	75 526	84 063	88 885
Non-durable goods										
Food & drink	ADIP	53 413	55 142	56 133	56 896	58 660	60 620	59 974	60 724	61 777
Alcohol & tobacco	ADIS	24 358	25 422	25 747	25 475	26 218	25 352	25 158	25 517	25 978
Housing, water, electricity, gas and other fuels	LLMS	20 982	22 032	22 177	22 055	21 764	22 336	23 076	22 914	24 062
Furnishings, household equipment and routine maintenance of the house	LLMT	2 379	2 416	2 514	2 482	2 578	2 758	2 973	3 202	3 459
Health	LLMU	2 996	3 134	3 107	3 181	3 253	3 333	3 613	3 859	3 996
Transport	LLMV	16 787	17 076	16 924	16 774	16 317	15 860	15 676	15 337	14 794
Recreation and culture	LLMW	12 125	12 432	12 847	12 981	13 279	13 223	13 109	13 428	13 210
Miscellaneous goods and services	LLMX	8 265	8 759	8 823	8 720	8 940	9 522	9 884	11 126	12 374
Total non-durable goods	UTIK	140 965	146 124	148 049	148 392	150 870	152 984	153 463	156 107	159 650
Total goods	UTIG	233 004	244 552	254 304	264 148	277 462	292 456	306 434	320 743	332 916
Services										
Clothing and footwear	LLMY	750	747	734	771	759	746	730	717	686
Housing, water, electricity, gas and other fuels	LLMZ	83 995	84 974	86 208	88 015	89 093	89 682	90 391	91 796	92 595
Furnishings, household equipment and routine maintenance of the house	LLNA	3 302	3 333	3 370	3 433	3 471	3 419	3 326	3 213	3 023
Health	LLNB	4 125	4 064	4 045	4 036	3 964	3 999	4 064	4 192	4 253
Transport	LLNC	32 709	33 843	35 299	36 646	38 791	40 432	38 397	39 764	39 780
Communication	LLND	7 258	7 632	8 368	9 234	10 267	11 855	13 521	13 812	14 509
Recreation and culture	LLNE	22 139	22 732	22 965	23 779	24 045	24 170	25 321	25 897	25 904
Education	ADMJ	8 490	8 423	9 305	9 258	10 018	10 208	9 239	8 167	8 482
Restaurants and hotels	ADMK	63 335	66 457	66 879	69 105	69 524	71 328	71 493	73 656	76 116
Miscellaneous goods and services	LLNF	53 399	54 147	55 186	56 164	59 150	61 780	63 143	63 144	61 756
Total services	UTIO	277 950	285 044	291 244	299 636	308 469	317 266	319 625	324 358	327 104
Final consumption expenditure in the UK by resident and non-resident households (domestic concept)	ABQJ	508 674	527 906	544 307	562 749	585 260	609 396	626 059	645 101	660 020
Final consumption expenditure outside the UK by UK resident households	ABTC	12 672	12 894	15 027	17 286	20 147	22 254	22 907	24 267	24 416
less Final consumption expenditure in the UK by households resident in the rest of the world	CCHX	−15 860	−16 231	−15 732	−15 790	−15 146	−15 151	−13 383	−13 503	−13 423
Final consumption expenditure by UK resident households in the UK and abroad (national concept)	ABPF	505 114	524 115	543 493	564 239	590 275	616 515	635 583	655 865	671 013

1 See chapter text. Additional detail is published in *Consumer Trends* and table A7 of *UK Economic Accounts*, available from the National Statistics website *www.statistics.gov.uk/statbase/Product.asp?vlnk=1904*.

Source: Office for National Statistics: 020 7533 6031

16.16 Individual consumption expenditure: by households, NPISHs and general government[1] Current market prices

United Kingdom. Classified by function (COICOP/COPNI/COFOG)[2]

£ million

		1995	1996	1997	1998	1999	2000	2001	2002	2003
FINAL CONSUMPTION EXPENDITURE OF HOUSEHOLDS										
Food and non-alcoholic beverages	ABZV	49 790	53 025	53 832	55 192	57 025	58 563	59 974	61 170	63 082
Food	ABZW	44 324	47 323	47 996	49 134	50 670	51 840	52 882	53 792	55 261
Non-alcoholic beverages	ADFK	5 466	5 702	5 836	6 058	6 355	6 723	7 092	7 378	7 821
Alcoholic beverages and tobacco	ADFL	18 776	20 439	21 553	22 459	24 458	24 617	25 158	25 960	27 342
Alcoholic beverages	ADFM	7 257	8 174	8 905	9 096	10 166	10 395	10 700	11 338	12 051
Tobacco	ADFN	11 519	12 265	12 648	13 363	14 292	14 222	14 458	14 622	15 291
Clothing and footwear	ADFP	28 030	29 485	30 901	32 238	33 275	35 479	37 042	39 306	41 192
Clothing	ADFQ	23 711	25 158	26 500	27 799	28 932	31 048	32 323	33 995	35 526
Footwear	ADFR	4 319	4 327	4 401	4 439	4 343	4 431	4 719	5 311	5 666
Housing, water, electricity, gas and other fuels	ADFS	81 412	85 930	90 214	96 197	101 211	105 654	113 467	118 859	125 459
Actual rentals for housing	ADFT	17 906	18 784	19 821	21 155	22 584	23 595	25 223	25 560	26 327
Imputed rentals for housing	ADFU	37 479	39 548	42 426	47 336	51 003	53 732	58 913	62 910	66 923
Maintenance and repair of the dwelling	ADFV	6 526	6 943	7 920	8 396	8 650	8 762	9 649	10 640	11 726
Water supply and miscellaneous dwelling services	ADFW	4 290	4 558	4 772	4 961	5 201	5 033	5 059	5 239	5 469
Electricity, gas and other fuels	ADFX	15 211	16 097	15 275	14 349	13 773	14 532	14 623	14 510	15 014
Furnishings, household equipment and routine maintenance of the house	ADFY	26 287	27 728	29 522	31 002	32 846	35 667	37 974	40 029	39 089
Furniture, furnishings, carpets and other floor coverings	ADFZ	9 843	10 471	11 072	11 667	12 437	13 758	14 362	15 546	14 475
Household textiles	ADGG	3 020	3 227	3 404	3 676	3 972	4 465	4 636	4 953	4 712
Household appliances	ADGL	4 405	4 609	4 997	5 080	5 038	4 948	5 758	5 553	5 302
Glassware, tableware and household utensils	ADGM	2 767	2 887	3 159	3 410	3 722	4 431	4 609	4 647	4 676
Tools and equipment for house and garden	ADGN	1 911	1 998	2 179	2 332	2 586	2 722	2 977	3 383	3 828
Goods and services for routine household maintenance	ADGO	4 341	4 536	4 711	4 837	5 091	5 343	5 632	5 947	6 096
Health	ADGP	6 835	7 247	7 566	8 081	8 529	8 987	9 786	10 717	12 139
Medical products, appliances and equipment	ADGQ	3 919	4 199	4 377	4 692	4 992	5 265	5 722	6 303	7 470
Out-patient services	ADGR	1 781	1 825	1 893	2 005	2 092	2 178	2 359	2 569	2 587
Hospital services	ADGS	1 135	1 223	1 296	1 384	1 445	1 544	1 705	1 845	2 082
Transport	ADGT	62 733	68 458	75 458	80 287	84 193	89 656	92 560	94 921	97 988
Purchase of vehicles	ADGU	23 588	26 469	29 444	30 851	31 854	33 171	35 704	35 730	37 142
Operation of personal transport equipment	ADGV	23 861	25 556	28 044	29 826	31 440	33 783	33 313	34 541	35 336
Transport services	ADGW	15 284	16 433	17 970	19 610	20 899	22 702	23 543	24 650	25 510
Communication	ADGX	9 067	9 359	10 014	11 047	12 005	13 356	14 157	14 683	15 497
Postal services	CDEF	967	960	951	1 064	899	873	870	856	885
Telephone & telefax equipment	ADWO	244	276	282	440	512	601	636	634	604
Telephone & telefax services	ADWP	7 856	8 123	8 781	9 543	10 594	11 882	12 651	13 193	14 008
Recreation and culture	ADGY	51 075	55 408	59 971	65 248	69 732	72 217	76 005	81 964	83 713
Audio-visual, photographic and information processing equipment	ADGZ	10 862	11 974	13 501	15 032	16 312	16 934	17 580	17 983	17 453
Other major durables for recreation and culture	ADHL	2 133	2 548	2 854	3 089	3 582	3 944	4 325	4 568	5 281
Other recreational items and equipment; flowers, garden and pets	ADHZ	11 284	12 758	14 488	16 237	17 655	18 636	20 216	22 347	22 748
Recreational and cultural services	ADIA	18 241	19 246	20 005	21 357	22 127	22 435	23 586	26 510	27 493
Newspapers, books and stationery	ADIC	8 555	8 882	9 123	9 533	10 056	10 268	10 298	10 556	10 738
Package holidays[3]	ADID	–	–	–	–	–	–	–	–	–
Education										
Education services	ADIE	6 197	6 405	7 440	7 814	8 943	9 634	9 239	8 629	9 649
Restaurants and hotels	ADIF	50 383	54 848	57 266	61 759	64 413	68 424	71 493	76 734	81 188
Catering services	ADIG	42 182	46 219	48 332	52 623	55 190	58 886	62 322	67 016	71 074
Accommodation services	ADIH	8 201	8 629	8 934	9 136	9 223	9 538	9 171	9 718	10 114
Miscellaneous goods and services	ADII	52 329	55 640	59 171	63 240	68 432	74 154	79 204	82 361	84 719
Personal care	ADIJ	10 378	11 361	11 887	12 574	13 229	13 883	14 626	16 222	17 517
Personal effects not elsewhere classified	ADIK	3 898	4 083	4 351	4 490	4 673	4 748	5 455	5 990	6 440
Social protection	ADIL	8 187	8 220	8 241	8 332	8 446	8 643	8 963	9 169	10 028
Insurance	ADIM	16 306	16 520	17 841	19 513	21 789	23 807	26 962	26 869	25 327
Financial services not elsewhere classified	ADIN	5 853	6 966	7 935	8 582	9 856	11 819	11 539	11 783	12 218
Other services not elsewhere classified	ADIO	7 707	8 490	8 916	9 749	10 439	11 254	11 659	12 328	13 189
Final consumption expenditure in the UK by resident and non-resident households (domestic concept)	ABQI	442 914	473 972	502 908	534 564	565 062	596 408	626 059	655 333	681 057
Final consumption expenditure outside the UK by UK resident households	ABTA	13 721	14 377	14 942	16 913	19 690	21 654	22 907	24 435	26 702
less Final consumption expenditure in the UK by households resident in the rest of the world	CDFD	−13 268	−14 038	−14 037	−14 544	−14 312	−14 713	−13 383	−13 872	−14 208
Final consumption expenditure by UK resident households in the UK and abroad (national concept)	ABPB	443 367	474 311	503 813	536 933	570 440	603 349	635 583	665 896	693 551

Individual consumption expenditure: by households, NPISHs and general government[1] Current market prices
United Kingdom. Classified by function (COICOP/COPNI/COFOG)[2]

£ million

		1995	1996	1997	1998	1999	2000	2001	2002	2003
FINAL CONSUMPTION EXPENDITURE OF UK RESIDENT HOUSEHOLDS										
Final consumption expenditure of UK resident households in the UK and abroad	ABPB	443 367	474 311	503 813	536 933	570 440	603 349	635 583	665 896	693 551
FINAL INDIVIDUAL CONSUMPTION EXPENDITURE OF NPISH										
Final individual consumption expenditure of NPISH	ABNV	16 481	18 338	19 509	21 053	22 069	23 188	24 345	26 359	27 532
FINAL INDIVIDUAL CONSUMPTION EXPENDITURE OF OF GENERAL GOVERNMENT										
Health	QYOT	38 469	41 152	42 197	44 933	49 761	53 471	57 896	63 909	71 464
Recreation and culture	QYSU	3 518	3 462	3 476	3 488	3 735	3 967	3 968	4 600	5 010
Education	QYSE	25 510	25 931	26 573	27 708	29 021	30 920	33 480	36 691	39 606
Social protection	QYSP	13 127	14 121	14 687	15 218	16 586	18 074	18 815	21 831	24 790
Housing	QYXO	–	–	–	–	–	–	–	–	..
Final individual consumption expenditure of general government	NNAQ	80 624	84 666	86 933	91 347	99 103	106 432	114 159	127 031	140 870
Total, individual consumption expenditure/ actual individual consumption	NQEO	540 472	577 315	610 255	649 333	691 612	732 969	774 087	819 286	861 953

1 See chapter text.
2 "Purpose" or "function" classifications are designed to indicate the "soci-economic objectives" that institutional units aim to achieve through various kinds of outlays. COICOP is the Classification of Individual Consumption by Purpose and applies to households. COPNI is the Classification of the Purposes of Non-Profit Institutions Serving Households and COFOG the Classification of the Functions of Government. The introduction of ESA95 coincides with the redefinition of these classifications and data will be available on a consistent basis for all European Union member states.
3 Package holidays data are dispersed between components (transport etc).

Source: Office for National Statistics: 020 7533 6031

16.17 Individual consumption expenditure: by households, NPISH and general government[1] Chained volume measures, reference year 2001

United Kingdom. Classified by function (COICOP/COPNI/COFOG)[2]

£ million

		1995	1996	1997	1998	1999	2000	2001	2002	2003
FINAL CONSUMPTION EXPENDITURE OF HOUSEHOLDS										
Food and non-alcoholic beverages	ADIP	53 413	55 142	56 133	56 896	58 660	60 620	59 974	60 724	61 777
Food	ADIQ	47 484	49 240	50 253	50 993	52 434	53 914	52 882	53 360	53 969
Non-alcoholic beverages	ADIR	5 966	5 936	5 914	5 940	6 256	6 724	7 092	7 364	7 808
Alcoholic beverages and tobacco	ADIS	24 358	25 422	25 747	25 475	26 218	25 352	25 158	25 517	25 978
Alcoholic beverages	ADIT	7 614	8 473	9 130	9 179	10 179	10 347	10 700	11 369	11 910
Tobacco	ADIU	17 445	17 447	16 918	16 549	16 134	15 032	14 458	14 148	14 068
Clothing and footwear	ADIW	24 962	26 404	27 438	28 802	30 537	33 890	37 042	41 316	43 979
Clothing	ADIX	21 071	22 429	23 290	24 536	26 282	29 481	32 323	35 918	38 242
Footwear	ADIY	3 946	4 029	4 205	4 318	4 283	4 414	4 719	5 398	5 737
Housing, water, electricity, gas and other fuels	ADIZ	104 916	107 194	108 526	110 079	110 785	111 986	113 467	114 710	116 657
Actual rentals for housing	ADJA	24 595	24 807	24 985	25 070	25 100	25 085	25 223	24 813	24 843
Imputed rentals for housing	ADJB	53 137	54 015	54 906	56 698	57 882	58 282	58 913	60 305	61 205
Maintenance and repair of the dwelling	ADJC	8 095	8 249	8 939	9 121	9 217	9 058	9 649	10 317	11 096
Water supply and miscellaneous dwelling services	ADJD	4 936	4 981	4 986	4 911	4 920	5 067	5 059	5 116	5 144
Electricity, gas and other fuels	ADJE	13 994	14 758	14 477	14 241	13 750	14 501	14 623	14 159	14 369
Furnishings, household equipment and routine maintenance of the house	ADJF	27 798	28 524	30 023	31 174	32 847	35 988	37 974	39 768	38 812
Furniture, furnishings, carpets and other floor coverings	ADJG	11 187	11 309	11 639	12 037	12 682	14 028	14 362	15 315	13 988
Household textiles	ADJH	2 993	3 129	3 289	3 524	3 827	4 457	4 636	5 022	4 818
Household appliances	ADJI	4 031	4 234	4 654	4 783	4 819	4 904	5 758	5 612	5 495
Glassware, tableware and household utensils	ADJJ	2 820	2 878	3 119	3 351	3 665	4 423	4 609	4 607	4 629
Tools and equipment for house and garden	ADJK	1 864	1 941	2 096	2 261	2 538	2 703	2 977	3 401	3 994
Goods and services for routine household maintenance	ADJL	5 052	5 151	5 297	5 258	5 345	5 491	5 632	5 811	5 888
Health	ADJM	9 804	9 784	9 646	9 633	9 517	9 532	9 786	10 232	11 135
Medical products, appliances and equipment	ADJN	5 679	5 722	5 602	5 597	5 554	5 534	5 722	6 040	6 882
Out-patient services	ADJO	2 576	2 494	2 472	2 429	2 355	2 327	2 359	2 441	2 382
Hospital services	ADJP	1 556	1 575	1 577	1 609	1 609	1 671	1 705	1 751	1 871
Transport	ADJQ	74 167	77 939	81 304	84 468	87 761	90 950	92 560	94 145	95 934
Purchase of vehicles	ADJR	23 323	25 389	27 072	28 536	30 013	32 192	35 704	35 982	37 943
Operation of personal transport equipment	ADJS	32 309	33 091	33 903	34 422	34 215	33 865	33 313	34 000	33 153
Transport services	ADJT	19 590	20 262	20 970	22 037	23 962	25 187	23 543	24 163	24 838
Communication	ADJU	7 392	7 792	8 552	9 576	10 731	12 438	14 157	14 501	15 168
Postal services	CCGZ	1 045	1 012	985	1 093	926	883	870	853	854
Telephone & telefax equipment	ADQF	160	184	208	348	464	584	636	689	659
Telephone & telefax services	ADQG	6 313	6 703	7 446	8 211	9 373	10 982	12 651	12 959	13 655
Recreation and culture	ADJV	48 933	51 749	55 358	60 708	66 686	70 909	76 005	81 183	84 466
Audio-visual, photographic and information processing equipment	ADJW	6 855	7 626	8 778	10 720	13 378	15 476	17 580	19 395	20 979
Other major durables for recreation and culture	ADJX	2 405	2 732	2 968	3 161	3 601	3 967	4 325	4 462	5 005
Other recreational items and equipment; flowers, gardens and pets	ADJY	11 141	12 359	13 880	15 566	17 241	18 570	20 216	22 902	24 182
Recreational and cultural services	ADJZ	20 504	20 901	21 150	21 952	22 263	22 454	23 586	24 089	24 168
Newspapers, books and stationery	ADKM	10 413	10 221	10 261	10 379	10 617	10 555	10 298	10 335	10 132
Package holidays[3]	ADMI	–	–	–	–	–	–	–	–	–
Education										
Education services	ADMJ	8 490	8 423	9 305	9 258	10 018	10 208	9 239	8 167	8 482
Restaurants and Hotels	ADMK	63 335	66 457	66 879	69 105	69 524	71 328	71 493	73 656	76 116
Catering services	ADML	52 892	55 690	56 128	58 543	59 212	61 222	62 322	64 282	66 473
Accommodation services	ADMM	10 523	10 846	10 826	10 616	10 354	10 127	9 171	9 374	9 643
Miscellaneous goods and services	ADMN	66 275	67 795	69 236	70 156	73 471	76 771	79 204	81 182	81 516
Personal care	ADMO	12 333	12 985	13 061	13 108	13 413	14 147	14 626	16 195	17 429
Personal effects not elsewhere classified	ADMP	4 118	4 270	4 532	4 610	4 737	4 781	5 455	5 965	6 252
Social protection	ADMQ	11 239	10 788	10 294	9 955	9 598	9 225	8 963	8 730	8 937
Insurance	ADMR	21 593	21 325	21 993	22 666	24 259	25 170	26 962	26 138	23 869
Financial services not elsewhere classified	ADMS	7 013	7 729	8 464	8 424	9 687	11 243	11 539	12 648	13 505
Other services not elsewhere classified	ADMT	10 509	11 111	11 193	11 735	11 991	12 258	11 659	11 506	11 524
Final consumption expenditure in the UK by resident and non-resident households (domestic concept)	ABQJ	508 674	527 906	544 307	562 749	585 260	609 396	626 059	645 101	660 020
Final consumption expenditure outside the UK by UK resident households	ABTC	12 672	12 894	15 027	17 286	20 147	22 254	22 907	24 267	24 416
less Final consumption expenditure in the UK by households resident in the rest of the world	CCHX	−15 860	−16 231	−15 732	−15 790	−15 146	−15 151	−13 383	−13 503	−13 423
Final consumption expenditure by UK resident households in the UK and abroad (national concept)	ABPF	505 114	524 115	543 493	564 239	590 275	616 515	635 583	655 865	671 013

16.17
continued

Individual consumption expenditure: by households, NPISH and general government[1] Chained volume measures, reference year 2001

United Kingdom. Classified by function (COICOP/COPNI/COFOG)[2]

£ million

		1995	1996	1997	1998	1999	2000	2001	2002	2003
FINAL CONSUMPTION EXPENDITURE OF UK RESIDENT HOUSEHOLDS										
Final consumption expenditure of UK resident households in the UK and abroad	ABPF	505 114	524 115	543 493	564 239	590 275	616 515	635 583	655 865	671 013
FINAL INDIVIDUAL CONSUMPTION EXPENDITURE OF NPISH										
Final individual consumption expenditure of NPISH	ABNU	21 230	21 296	21 779	23 300	23 095	24 875	24 345	25 818	26 593
FINAL INDIVIDUAL CONSUMPTION EXPENDITURE OF GENERAL GOVERNMENT										
Health	EMOA	48 767	50 686	51 352	52 297	53 936	55 576	57 896	60 258	62 719
Recreation and culture	QYXK	3 923	3 760	3 779	3 716	3 930	4 051	3 968	4 470	4 717
Education	EMOB	31 433	31 776	32 393	32 795	33 096	33 343	33 480	33 587	33 718
Social protection	QYXM	18 020	18 248	18 495	18 611	18 638	18 810	18 815	18 923	19 134
Housing	QYXN	–	–	–	–	–	–	–	–	–
Final individual consumption expenditure of general government	NSZK	102 107	104 403	105 948	107 339	109 554	111 763	114 159	117 238	120 288
Total, individual consumption expenditure/ actual individual consumption	YBIO	628 250	650 156	672 108	696 661	724 888	754 444	774 087	798 921	817 894

1 See chapter text.
2 "Purpose" or "function" classifications are designed to indicate the "socio-economic objectives" that institutional units aim to achieve through various kinds of outlays. COICOP is the Classification of Individual Consumption by Purpose and applies to households. COPNI is the Classification of the Purposes of Non-Profit Institutions Serving Households (NPISH) and COFOG the Classification of the Functions of Government. The introduction of ESA95 coincides with the redefinition of these classifications and data will be available on a consistent basis for all European Union member states.
3 Package holidays data are dispersed between components (transport etc).

Source: Office for National Statistics: 020 7533 6031

16.18

Change in inventories[1,2] Chained volume measures, reference year 2001

United Kingdom

Reference year 2001, £ million

	Mining and quarrying	Manufacturing industries				Electricity, gas and water supply	Distributive trades		Other industries[4]	Change in inventories
		Materials and fuel	Work in progress	Finished goods	Total		Wholesale[3]	Retail[3]		
	FADO	FBID	FBIE	FBIF	DHBH	FADP	FAJM	FBYH	DLWV	ABMQ
1994	−581	118	220	309	643	−536	454	1 132	–	4 874
1995	−181	458	1 086	887	2 402	−173	529	892	944	4 533
1996	−68	−93	−206	5	−287	12	605	702	1 044	1 848
1997	81	359	−1 266	303	−533	87	1 525	880	2 304	4 009
1998	375	643	−558	324	466	−130	488	1 087	3 226	4 905
1999	−315	608	−114	−421	102	−134	1 565	1 623	4 053	6 416
2000	−254	648	503	425	1 576	235	1 760	1 380	310	5 262
2001	96	−406	513	168	275	49	709	1 014	4 046	6 189
2002	−30	−95	−322	−507	−924	−223	663	1 594	1 433	2 513
2003	−113	−307	−543	410	−440	−93	469	1 591	1 053	2 467

1 See chapter text. Estimates are given to the nearest £ million but cannot be regarded as accurate to this degree.
2 Components may not sum to totals due to rounding.

3 Wholesaling and retailing estimates exclude the motor trades.
4 Quarterly alignment adjustment included in this series.

Source: Office for National Statistics 020 7533 6031

16.19 Gross fixed capital formation at current purchasers' prices: by broad sector and type of asset[1,2]

United Kingdom. Total economy

£ million

		1995	1996	1997	1998	1999	2000	2001	2002	2003
Private sector										
New dwellings, excluding land	DFDF	18 860	20 205	22 017	23 317	23 921	25 604	27 085	31 455	36 424
Other buildings and structures	EQBU	18 023	20 763	25 228	28 403	31 017	32 041	32 727	33 690	35 775
Transport equipment	EQBV	10 224	11 325	12 107	15 279	14 303	12 726	14 435	15 712	14 724
Other machinery and equipment and cultivated assets	EQBW	42 157	47 586	49 376	57 469	57 335	60 504	57 309	52 513	49 339
Intangible fixed assets	EQBX	3 179	3 278	3 395	3 555	3 624	4 004	4 320	4 628	..
Costs associated with the transfer of ownership of non-produced assets	EQBY	5 173	6 726	7 647	7 453	9 859	11 206	12 696	15 416	16 151
Total	EQBZ	97 616	109 300	120 157	135 781	138 913	143 699	144 826	152 019	..
Public non-financial corporations										
New dwellings, excluding land	DEER	162	163	123	49	8	–	–	–	–
Other buildings and structures	DEES	2 399	2 171	1 647	1 334	1 681	1 761	1 850	2 302	2 021
Transport equipment	DEEP	354	225	190	171	154	168	160	104	67
Other machinery and equipment and cultivated assets	DEEQ	453	406	402	438	586	503	576	601	670
Intangible fixed assets	DLXJ	496	585	595	605	625	551	397	556	623
Costs associated with the transfer of ownership of non-produced assets	DLXQ	126	101	267	352	–8	6	59	–41	–197
Total	FCCJ	3 990	3 651	3 224	2 949	3 046	2 988	3 042	3 522	3 184
General government										
New dwellings, excluding land	DFHW	2 642	2 148	1 788	1 856	1 771	1 790	2 721	3 062	4 061
Other buildings and structures	EQCH	11 421	9 891	8 580	9 304	8 982	10 076	10 804	11 316	14 240
Transport equipment	EQCI	717	672	675	693	610	550	599	570	738
Other machinery and equipment and cultivated assets	EQCJ	2 402	2 205	1 755	1 605	1 845	1 691	2 090	2 419	2 986
Intangible fixed assets	EQCK	264	273	259	387	396	367	334	358	367
Costs associated with the transfer of ownership of non-produced assets	EQCL	–1 604	–2 432	–2 275	–1 730	–2 062	–2 382	–2 623	–2 966	–3 978
Total	NNBF	15 842	12 757	10 782	12 115	11 542	12 093	13 925	14 759	18 414
Total gross fixed capital formation	NPQX	117 448	126 291	133 776	150 540	154 647	161 210	165 504	171 695	178 916

1 See chapter text.
2 Components may not sum to totals due to rounding.

Source: Office for National Statistics: 020 7533 6031

16.20 Gross fixed capital formation at current purchasers' prices: by type of asset[1,2]

United Kingdom. Total economy

£ million

		1995	1996	1997	1998	1999	2000	2001	2002	2003
Tangible fixed assets										
New dwellings, excluding land	DFDK	21 664	22 516	23 928	25 222	25 700	27 394	29 806	34 517	40 485
Other buildings and structures	DLWS	31 843	32 825	35 455	39 041	41 680	43 878	45 381	47 308	52 036
Transport equipment	DLWZ	11 295	12 222	12 972	16 143	15 067	13 444	15 194	16 386	15 529
Other machinery and equipment and cultivated assets	DLXI	45 012	50 197	51 533	59 512	59 766	62 698	59 975	55 533	52 995
Total	EQCQ	109 814	117 760	123 888	139 918	142 213	147 414	150 356	153 744	161 045
Intangible fixed assets	DLXP	3 939	4 136	4 249	4 547	4 645	4 966	5 016	5 542	5 895
Costs associated with the transfer of ownership of non-produced assets	DFBH	3 695	4 395	5 639	6 075	7 789	8 830	10 132	12 409	11 976
Total gross fixed capital formation	NPQX	117 448	126 291	133 776	150 540	154 647	161 210	165 504	171 695	178 916

1 See chapter text.
2 Components may not sum to totals due to rounding.

Source: Office for National Statistics: 020 7533 6031

16.21 Gross fixed capital formation: by broad sector and type of asset[1,2,3]
Chained volume measures, reference year 2001
United Kingdom. Total economy

£ million

		1995	1996	1997	1998	1999	2000	2001	2002	2003
Private sector										
New dwellings, excluding land	DFDP	24 825	24 629	26 079	26 377	25 508	25 604	27 085	29 176	31 477
Other buildings and structures	EQCU	20 422	23 497	28 540	31 739	32 538	32 759	32 727	33 018	35 343
Transport equipment	EQCV	10 607	11 337	12 420	15 486	14 276	12 640	14 435	15 870	14 849
Other machinery and equipment and cultivated assets	EQCW	32 669	36 801	39 668	48 898	51 548	57 137	57 309	55 453	53 072
Intangible fixed assets	EQCX	3 758	3 721	3 870	3 809	3 781	4 123	4 285	4 595	4 782
Costs associated with the transfer of ownership of non-produced assets	EQCY	11 900	12 260	12 482	10 510	11 485	11 206	12 696	13 643	12 659
Total	EQCZ	100 421	111 248	122 069	138 674	141 268	146 277	148 537	151 754	152 182
Public non-financial corporations										
New dwellings, excluding land	DEEW	209	190	141	55	9	–	–	–	–
Other buildings and structures	DEEX	3 494	2 884	2 159	1 677	1 904	1 907	1 850	2 219	1 922
Transport equipment	DEEU	386	242	199	174	154	168	160	104	64
Other machinery and equipment and cultivated assets	DEEV	155	146	193	286	466	444	576	630	742
Intangible fixed assets	EQDE	576	663	654	642	654	560	397	547	602
Costs associated with the transfer of ownership of non-produced assets	EQDF	−78	−94	−239	−278	4	6	59	−37	−186
Total	EQDG	4 326	3 855	3 354	2 985	3 081	2 987	3 042	3 463	3 144
General government										
New dwellings, excluding land	DFID	3 261	2 592	2 121	2 125	1 917	1 851	2 721	2 963	3 847
Other buildings and structures	EQDI	13 275	11 103	9 719	9 956	9 448	10 361	10 804	10 918	13 249
Transport equipment	EQDJ	745	681	715	677	591	540	599	513	639
Other machinery and equipment and cultivated assets	EQDK	1 736	1 581	1 285	1 305	1 612	1 576	2 090	2 540	3 253
Intangible fixed assets	EQDL	314	303	311	419	413	375	334	361	384
Costs associated with the transfer of ownership of non-produced assets	EQDM	−4 253	−5 868	−4 960	−3 247	−2 924	−2 814	−2 623	−2 585	−3 075
Total	EQDN	15 175	10 493	9 172	10 086	9 935	10 412	13 925	14 711	18 297
Total gross fixed capital formation	NPQR	120 432	127 283	135 924	153 202	155 631	161 267	165 504	169 928	173 623

1 See chapter text.
2 For the years before 2000, the total differs from the sum of their components.
3 Components may not sum to totals due to rounding.

Source: Office for National Statistics: 020 7533 6031

16.22 Gross fixed capital formation: by type of asset[1,2,3]
Chained volume measures, reference year 2001
United Kingdom. Total economy

£ million

		1995	1996	1997	1998	1999	2000	2001	2002	2003
Tangible fixed assets										
New dwellings, excluding land	DFDV	28 367	27 358	28 278	28 490	27 372	27 394	29 806	32 139	35 324
Other buildings and structures	EQDP	36 927	37 415	40 420	43 396	43 906	45 035	45 381	46 155	50 514
Transport equipment	DLWJ	11 694	12 251	13 328	16 337	15 020	13 348	15 194	16 487	15 552
Other machinery and equipment and cultivated assets	DLWM	34 966	38 601	41 154	50 450	53 617	59 133	59 975	58 623	57 067
Total	EQDS	108 029	114 209	121 764	138 824	140 711	146 217	150 356	153 404	158 457
Intangible fixed assets	EQDT	4 441	4 692	4 840	4 871	4 846	5 058	5 016	5 503	5 768
Costs associated with the transfer of ownership of non-produced assets	DFDW	7 073	7 773	8 928	8 329	9 023	8 830	10 132	11 021	9 398
Total gross fixed capital formation	NPQR	120 432	127 283	135 924	153 202	155 631	161 267	165 504	169 928	173 623

1 See chapter text.
2 For the years before 2000, the total differs from the sum of their components.
3 Components may not sum to totals due to rounding.

Source: Office for National Statistics: 020 7533 6031

Prices

Chapter 17

Prices

Producer price index numbers

(Tables 17.1 and 17.2)

The producer price indices (PPIs) were published for the first time in August 1983, replacing the former wholesale price indices. Full details of the differences between the two indices were given in an article published in *British Business*, 15 April 1983. The producer price indices are calculated using the same general methodology as that used by the wholesale price indices.

The high level index numbers in Tables 17.1 and 17.2 are constructed on a net sector basis. That is to say, they are intended to measure only transactions between the sector concerned and other sectors. Within sector transactions are excluded. Index numbers for the whole of manufacturing are thus not weighted averages of sector index numbers.

The index numbers for selected industries in Tables 17.1 and 17.2 are constructed on a gross sector basis, i.e. all transactions are included in deriving the weighting patterns, including sales within the same industry.

All the index numbers are compiled exclusive of value-added tax. Excise duties on cigarettes, manufactured tobacco and alcoholic liquor are included, as is the duty on hydrocarbon oils.

The indices relate to the average prices for a year. The movement in these prices are weighted to reflect the relative importance of the composite products in a chosen year (known as the base year), currently 2000.

Since July 1995, PPIs have been published fully reclassified to the 1992 version of the Standard Industrial Classification (SIC).

Further details are available from the National Statistics website: *www.statistics.gov.uk/ppi*.

Purchasing power of the pound

(Table 17.3)

Changes in the internal purchasing power of a currency may be defined as the 'inverse' of changes in the levels of prices; when prices go up, the amount which can be purchased with a given sum of money goes down. Movements in the internal purchasing power of the pound are based on the consumers' expenditure deflator (CED) prior to 1962 and on the General index of retail prices (RPI) from January 1962 onwards. The

CED shows the movement in prices implied by the national accounts estimates of consumers' expenditure valued at current and at constant prices, whilst the RPI is constructed directly by weighting together monthly movements in prices according to a given pattern of household expenditure derived from the Expenditure and Food Survey. If the purchasing power of the pound is taken to be 100p in a particular month (quarter, year), the comparable purchasing power in a subsequent month (quarter, year) is:

$$100 \quad \times \quad \frac{\text{earlier period price index}}{\text{later period price index}}$$

where the price index used is the CED for years 1946–1961 and the RPI for periods after 1961.

Consumer prices index

(Table 17.4)

The consumer prices index (CPI) is the main United Kingdom domestic measure of inflation for macro-economic purposes. Like the RPI (see below) it measures the average change from month to month in the prices of consumer goods and services purchased in the UK, but there are differences in coverage and methodology. A detailed description of these differences is given in the paper entitled '*The New Inflation Target: the Statistical Perspective*'. This paper is available on the National Statistics website:*www.statistics.gov.uk/StatBase/Product.asp?vlnk=10913*.

Since 10 December 2003, the Government inflation target for the UK has been defined in terms of the CPI measure of inflation. Prior to that the CPI had been published in the UK as the harmonised index of consumer prices (HICP); the two shall remain one and the same index.

The HICPs are calculated in each Member State of the European Union (EU), according to rules specified in a series of European Regulations developed by the EU statistical office in conjunction with the EU Member States. The HICPs are used to compare inflation rate across the EU. Since January 1999 it has also been used by the European Central Bank (ECB) as the measure of price stability across the euro area. Additional information on HICPs is available from the National Statistics website: *www.statistics.gov.uk/hicp*

CPI inflation rates prior to 1997 and index levels prior to 1996 are estimated. See article on National Statistics website: *www.statistics.gov.uk/cci/article.asp?ID=31*. Also the coverage of CPI categories for health, education and miscellaneous goods and services have been extended between 2000 and 2002. Details are given in articles available on the website: *www.statistics.gov.uk/cci/searchres2.asp?ct=6&term=HICP*

Further details on the CPI are available from the National Statistics website: *www.statistics.gov.uk/cpi*

Retail prices index

(Table 17.5)

The retail prices index (RPI) is the most familiar general purpose measure of inflation in the UK, measuring the percentage changes month by month in the average level of prices of the goods and services purchased by the great majority of households in the United Kingdom. The uses of the RPI include indexation of pensions, state benefits and index-linked gilts. The expenditure pattern on which the index is based is revised each year using information from the Expenditure and Food Survey. The expenditure of certain higher income households and households of retired people dependent mainly on social security benefits is excluded.

The index covers a large and representative selection of more than 650 separate goods and services, for which price movements are regularly measured in around 150 locations throughout the country. Around 120,000 separate price quotations are used in compiling the index.

Further details are available from the National Statistics website: *www.statistics.gov.uk/rpi*

Tax and price index (TPI)

(Table 17.6)

The purpose and methodology of the TPI were described in an article in the August 1979 issue (No 310) of *Economic Trends* (The Stationery Office). The TPI measures the change in gross taxable income needed for taxpayers to maintain their purchasing power, allowing for changes in retail prices. The TPI thus takes account of the changes to direct taxes (and employees' National Insurance contributions) facing representative cross-section of taxpayers as well as changes in the retail prices index (RPI).

When direct taxation or employees' National Insurance contributions change, the TPI will rise by less than or more than the RPI according to the type of changes made. Between Budgets, the monthly increase in the TPI is normally slightly larger than that in the RPI, since all the extra income needed to offset any rise in retail prices is fully taxed.

Index numbers of agricultural prices

(Tables 17.7 and 17.8)

The Indices of producer prices of agricultural products are currently based on the calendar year 2000. They are designed to provide short-term and medium-term indications of movements in these prices. All annual series are base-weighted Laspeyres type, using value weights derived from the Economic Accounts for Agriculture prepared for the Statistical Office of the European Union. Prices are measured exclusive of VAT. For Table 17.7 it has generally been necessary to measure the prices of materials (inputs) ex-supplier. For Table 17.8, it has generally been necessary to measure the prices received by producers (outputs) at the first marketing stage. The construction of the indices enables them to be combined with similar indices for other member countries of the European Union to provide an overall indication of trends within the Union which appears in the Union's Eurostat series of publications.

Index numbers at a more detailed level and for earlier based series are available from the Department for Environment and Rural Affairs, Food Chain Analysis Division, SSP, Room 133a Foss House, Kingspool 1-2 Peasholme Green, York, YO1 7PX Tel 01904 455253

17.1

Producer price index of materials and fuels purchased: by all manufacturing and selected industries SIC(92)[1]

United Kingdom: Annual averages

			1996	1997	1998	1999	2000	2001	2002	2003
Net sector										
Materials and fuel purchased by manufacturing industry[2]	RNNK	6292000050	113.0	103.7	94.3	93.1	100.0	98.8	94.4	95.6
Materials	PLKX	6292000010	114.6	104.5	93.6	92.3	100.0	98.1	93.7	95.2
Fuels[2]	RNNL	6292000060	103.8	99.9	103.8	103.6	100.0	107.1	103.4	102.1
Materials and fuels purchased by manufacturing industry- seasonally adjusted[2]	RNPE	6292008950	113.0	103.6	94.3	93.1	100.0	98.8	94.3	95.6
Materials and fuels purchased by manufacturing industry other than food, beverages, petroleum and tobacco[2]	RNNQ	6292990050	112.0	104.9	100.0	96.4	100.0	98.7	94.0	93.7
Materials	RWCJ	6292990010	114.4	106.5	99.7	95.8	100.0	98.1	93.2	93.0
Fuel[2]	RNNS	6292990060	107.8	103.7	103.9	103.7	100.0	106.8	103.1	101.8
Materials and fuels purchased by manufacturing industries other than food, beverages, petroleum and tobacco- seasonally adjusted[2]	RNPF	6292998950	112.0	104.8	100.0	96.4	100.0	98.7	94.0	93.7
Gross sector[3]										
All manufacturing	RBBO	6192000000	106.5	102.9	98.3	96.3	100.0	99.3	97.1	98.4
Other mining and quarrying products[4]	RABE	6112140000	88.3	89.2	87.5	90.2	100.0	96.9	92.3	93.1
Manufacture of food products	RBBQ	6192151600	114.2	107.8	104.0	102.3	100.0	103.2	102.3	105.2
Food products and beverages	RABF	6112150000	111.3	106.5	104.0	102.3	100.0	103.3	102.3	105.1
Tobacco products	RABG	6112160000	112.9	107.1	102.3	100.8	100.0	100.0	101.2	106.8
Manufacture of textiles	RBBR	6192171800	109.6	106.3	102.8	98.7	100.0	100.5	98.4	99.2
Textiles	RABH	6112170000	110.3	106.7	102.7	98.7	100.0	100.5	98.6	99.8
Wearing apparel	RABI	6112180000	108.7	105.8	103.1	98.5	100.0	100.3	97.8	98.0
Manufacture of leather	RBBS	6192190000	107.1	104.2	99.8	97.9	100.0	101.9	100.0	101.1
Manufacture of wood and wood products	RBBT	6192200000	113.7	112.6	105.6	100.2	100.0	99.2	96.5	96.8
Manufacture of pulp, paper, publishing and printing	RBBU	6192212200	107.7	101.1	98.5	97.0	100.0	100.9	99.2	99.4
Pulp and paper products	RABL	6112210000	108.6	102.1	98.7	96.0	100.0	100.7	97.5	96.5
Printed matter and recording material	RABM	6112220000	107.4	100.7	98.4	97.4	100.0	101.0	100.0	100.8
Manufacture of coke	RBBV	6192230000	76.5	69.6	51.1	65.4	100.0	92.1	89.2	95.4
Manufacture of chemical products	RBBW	6192240000	106.0	103.1	99.6	96.1	100.0	101.1	99.4	103.0
Manufacture of rubber products	RBBX	6192250000	110.7	105.4	99.3	96.6	100.0	99.1	97.7	99.5
Manufacture of other non-metallic mineral products	RBBY	6192260000	98.3	98.0	97.6	97.4	100.0	100.5	99.6	100.7
Manufacture of basic metals	RBBZ	6192272800	105.8	103.6	100.2	94.8	100.0	98.5	96.6	99.8
Basic metals	RABV	6112270000	106.1	103.4	98.9	93.4	100.0	98.6	96.8	101.3
Fabricated metal products	RABW	6112280000	105.3	103.8	101.3	96.1	100.0	98.4	96.4	98.6
Manufacture of machinery and equipment not elsewhere classified	RBCA	6192290000	103.1	102.8	100.9	97.8	100.0	98.9	97.1	97.8
Manufacture of electrical and optical equipment	RBCB	6192303300	117.1	111.5	104.6	99.8	100.0	97.2	92.5	88.8
Office machinery and computers	RABY	6112300000	128.9	116.6	104.7	99.5	100.0	95.5	87.4	80.7
Electrical machinery and apparatus not elsewhere classified	RACB	6112310000	107.6	105.7	101.6	98.1	100.0	98.5	95.8	94.5
Radio, television and communication equipment	RACC	6112320000	113.3	109.5	103.8	99.0	100.0	98.1	94.5	92.1
Medical, precision, optical instruments and clocks	RACD	6112330000	111.8	108.5	103.2	99.0	100.0	98.2	95.2	92.3
Manufacture of transport equipment	RBCC	6192343500	103.1	103.3	102.1	99.6	100.0	99.1	97.3	98.1
Motor vehicles, trailers and semi-trailers	RACE	6112340000	104.4	104.4	103.1	100.3	100.0	99.3	98.1	99.3
Other transport equipment	RACF	6112350000	100.0	100.4	99.8	97.8	100.0	98.7	95.4	95.5
Manufacturing not elsewhere classified	RBCD	6192363700	105.8	104.6	101.4	97.8	100.0	99.1	97.8	99.9
Electricity including Climate Change Levy	RCVR	7167850000	114.7	107.7	107.5	107.5	100.0	96.2	92.5	89.3
Gas including Climate Change Levy	RCVW	7167860000	84.8	87.8	92.4	91.9	100.0	140.7	136.5	141.3
Collected and purified water	PQNB	7167870000	88.5	92.5	97.7	102.4	100.0	101.6	103.4	107.0

1 See chapter text.
2 These indices include the Climate Change Levy which was introduced in April 2001.
3 The Climate Change Levy is excluded from the detailed industry input index.
4 These indices include the Aggregates Levy which was introduced in April 2002.

Source: Office for National Statistics: 01633 812106

17.2

Producer price index of output: by all manufacturing and selected industries SIC(92)[1]

United Kingdom: Annual averages

Indices (2000=100)

			1996	1997	1998	1999	2000	2001	2002	2003
Net sector										
Output of manufactured products	PLLU	7209200000	97.2	98.1	98.1	98.5	100.0	99.7	99.8	101.3
All manufacturing excluding duty	PVNP	7209200010	100.3	100.4	99.4	99.0	100.0	99.7	99.7	101.2
All manufacturing excluding duty - seasonally adjusted	PVNQ	7209200890	100.3	100.4	99.4	99.0	100.0	99.7	99.8	101.3
Products of manufacturing industries other than the food, beverages, petroleum and tobacco manufacturing industries - not seasonally adjusted	PLLV	7209299000	102.1	102.3	101.3	100.2	100.0	99.4	99.3	100.6
All manufacturing excluding food, beverages, tobacco and petroleum - seasonally adjusted	PLLW	7209299890	102.1	102.3	101.3	100.2	100.0	99.4	99.3	100.6
Gross sector										
Manufactured products excluding duty	POKE	7109200000	101.3	100.6	98.3	97.8	100.0	99.4	99.1	100.8
Manufactured products excluding food, drink, tobacco and petroleum	POKF	7109299000	103.7	102.9	101.5	100.1	100.0	99.4	99.3	100.5
Other mining and quarrying products[2]	ROFV	7112148000	88.5	91.1	94.8	96.2	100.0	104.4	120.3	126.9
Food products, beverages and tobacco excluding duty	POKH	7111151600	100.5	100.5	100.3	100.5	100.0	101.9	103.3	104.6
Food products, beverages and tobacco including duty	RBGA	7111151680	96.3	96.9	97.8	99.1	100.0	102.0	103.3	104.7
Food products and beverages including duty	RPUN	7112150080	101.2	100.7	100.4	100.4	100.0	101.5	102.6	103.6
Food products excluding beverages	RBGD	7112159900	103.0	102.0	101.1	100.9	100.0	101.7	102.7	103.7
Alcoholic beverages including duty	RPUX	7113159080	92.7	94.2	97.3	98.7	100.0	101.6	103.1	103.7
Tobacco products including duty	RPUS	7112160080	70.0	75.3	81.8	91.6	100.0	105.0	107.8	111.2
Textiles and textile products	POKI	7111171800	97.3	99.2	100.3	99.9	100.0	99.2	98.8	98.7
Textiles	POKZ	7112170000	98.5	100.2	101.0	100.2	100.0	99.4	99.2	99.4
Wearing apparel: Furs	POLA	7112180000	94.6	97.3	98.8	99.2	100.0	99.0	97.9	97.2
Leather and leather products	POKJ	7111190000	100.3	101.0	100.4	99.2	100.0	102.5	102.7	102.9
Wood and wood products	POKK	7111200000	105.1	106.7	104.9	101.5	100.0	99.9	100.0	101.8
Pulp, paper and paper products, recorded media and printing services	POKL	7111212200	99.6	98.3	98.4	98.2	100.0	101.5	102.1	104.0
Pulp, paper and paper products	POLD	7112210000	104.3	99.5	98.2	96.8	100.0	101.0	100.3	100.1
Printed matter and recorded media	POLE	7112220000	97.4	97.8	98.5	98.8	100.0	101.7	102.7	105.5
Chemicals, chemical, products and manmade fibres	POKN	7111240000	104.1	102.5	98.5	97.2	100.0	100.2	100.5	103.9
Rubber and plastic products	POKO	7111250000	105.2	104.6	102.2	100.4	100.0	100.3	100.4	100.5
Other non-metallic mineral products	POKP	7111260000	92.7	94.9	97.6	99.3	100.0	101.9	105.0	107.8
Base metals and fabricated metal products	POKQ	7111272800	103.8	103.0	102.5	98.7	100.0	99.9	99.5	101.3
Base metals	POLJ	7112270000	110.1	106.9	103.1	94.7	100.0	98.4	96.0	99.2
Fabricated metal products, except machinery and equipment	POLK	7112280000	100.3	101.2	102.2	100.6	100.0	100.6	101.1	102.3
Machinery and equipment not elsewhere classified	POKR	7111290000	94.9	97.4	98.3	99.1	100.0	100.9	101.8	101.9
Electrical and optical equipment	POKS	7111343500	131.2	122.6	112.2	106.2	100.0	94.7	90.0	87.5
Office machinery and computers	POLM	7112300000	236.2	193.5	146.6	124.1	100.0	75.2	64.6	57.1
Electrical machinery and apparatus not elsewhere classified	POLN	7112310000	102.0	102.5	102.3	101.3	100.0	99.9	100.4	100.6
Radio, television and communication equipment and apparatus	POLO	7112320000	124.1	116.7	109.4	104.2	100.0	97.3	88.0	84.3
Medical precision and optical instruments, watches and clocks	POLP	7112330000	97.1	97.8	98.7	99.2	100.0	101.1	102.4	103.3
Transport equipment	POKT	7111343500	95.7	97.1	99.0	100.9	100.0	98.4	98.8	99.2
Motor vehicles, trailers and semi-trailers	POLQ	7112340000	98.9	100.2	101.9	102.3	100.0	96.6	96.3	96.1
Other transport	POLR	7112350000	88.1	89.8	92.9	98.0	100.0	102.3	103.8	105.8
Furniture: other manufactured goods not elsewhere classified	POLS	7112360000	99.2	100.6	101.7	100.9	100.0	100.3	100.9	103.8

1 See chapter text.
2 These indices include the Aggregates Levy which was introduced in April 2002. These indices do not feed into Net Sector output (PLLU).

Source: Office for National Statistics: 01633 812106

271

17.3 Internal purchasing power of the pound[1,2]
United Kingdom

Pence

	Year in which purchasing power was 100p																			
	1985	1986	1987	1988	1989	1990	1991	1992	1993	1994	1995	1996	1997	1998	1999	2000	2001	2002	2003	2004
	BAMR	BAMS	BAMT	BAMU	BAMV	BAMW	BASX	CZVM	CBXX	DOFX	DOHR	DOLM	DTUL	CDQG	JKZZ	ZMHO	IKHI	FAUI	SEZH	C687
1985	100	103	108	113	122	133	141	146	149	152	158	161	166	172	175	180	183	186	192	197
1986	97	100	104	109	118	129	136	142	144	147	152	156	161	167	169	174	177	180	185	191
1987	93	96	100	105	113	124	131	136	138	141	146	150	155	160	162	167	170	173	178	183
1988	88	92	95	100	108	118	125	130	132	135	139	143	147	152	155	159	162	165	170	175
1989	82	85	88	93	100	109	116	120	122	125	129	133	137	141	144	148	150	153	157	162
1990	75	78	81	85	91	100	106	110	112	114	118	121	125	129	131	135	137	140	144	148
1991	71	73	76	80	86	94	100	104	105	108	112	114	118	122	124	128	130	132	136	140
1992	68	71	74	77	83	91	96	100	102	104	108	110	114	118	119	123	125	127	131	135
1993	67	70	72	76	82	90	95	98	100	102	106	109	112	116	118	121	123	125	129	133
1994	66	68	71	74	80	88	93	96	98	100	103	106	109	113	115	118	120	122	126	130
1995	63	66	68	72	77	85	90	93	94	97	100	102	106	109	111	114	116	118	122	125
1996	62	64	67	70	75	83	87	91	92	94	98	100	103	107	108	112	113	115	119	122
1997	60	62	65	68	73	80	85	88	89	92	95	97	100	103	105	108	110	112	115	119
1998	58	60	63	66	71	77	82	85	86	88	92	94	97	100	102	105	106	108	111	115
1999	57	59	62	65	70	76	81	84	85	87	90	92	95	98	100	103	105	107	110	113
2000	56	57	60	63	68	74	78	81	83	85	88	90	92	96	97	100	102	103	106	110
2001	55	56	59	62	66	73	77	80	81	83	86	88	91	94	95	98	100	102	105	108
2002	54	56	58	61	65	72	76	79	80	82	85	87	89	92	94	97	98	100	103	106
2003	52	54	56	59	64	70	74	76	78	79	82	84	87	90	91	94	96	97	100	103
2004	51	52	55	57	62	68	72	74	75	77	80	82	84	87	89	91	93	94	97	100

1 See chapter text. These figures are calculated by taking the inverse ratio of
the respective annual averages of the Retail Prices Index (RPI).
2 To find the purchasing power of the pound in 1995, given that it was 100
pence in 1990, select the column headed 1990 and look at the 1995 row.
The result is 85 pence.

Source: Office for National Statistics: 020 7533 5874

17.4 Consumer Prices Index:[1] detailed figures by division
United Kingdom

Indices (1996=100)

	Food and non-alcoholic beverages	Alcoholic beverages and tobacco	Clothing and footwear	Housing, water, electricity, gas & other fuels	Furniture, household equipment & routine maintenance	Health	Transport	Communication	Recreation and culture	Education	Restaurants and hotels	Miscellaneous goods and services	CPI (overall index)
COICOP Division	01	02	03	04	05	06	07	08	09	10	11	12	
Weights 2004	106	46	62	103	75	22	151	26	150	16	137	106	1000
	CHVK	CHVL	CHVM	CHVN	CHVO	CHVP	CHVQ	CHVR	CHVS	CHVT	CHVU	CHVV	CHVJ
2002 Sep	104.8	129.6	71.1	112.3	98.8	121.1	113.7	84.1	106.2	139.2	124.6	117.8	108.7
Oct	105.0	129.4	70.7	112.5	97.9	121.4	113.5	84.4	106.4	147.6	124.9	119.2	108.9
Nov	104.9	129.0	71.7	112.5	98.7	121.5	112.2	84.5	106.5	147.6	125.1	119.1	108.9
Dec	104.9	128.4	70.3	112.7	100.1	121.4	115.1	84.4	106.3	147.6	125.4	119.6	109.3
2003 Jan	104.9	129.3	67.4	112.8	96.8	122.2	114.4	84.5	105.8	147.6	125.6	118.6	108.6
Feb	105.6	129.4	68.2	113.0	97.4	122.6	115.0	84.5	106.0	147.6	125.8	118.8	109.0
Mar	105.9	129.4	68.7	113.0	98.9	122.7	116.0	84.6	105.8	147.6	126.2	119.0	109.4
Apr	106.3	130.8	68.6	113.7	97.5	123.3	117.8	84.5	105.7	147.6	126.7	119.1	109.7
May	106.9	131.2	68.7	113.7	98.8	123.7	116.8	84.6	105.2	147.6	127.1	119.2	109.7
Jun	106.3	131.3	68.1	113.8	98.2	123.9	116.7	83.9	104.8	147.6	127.5	119.4	109.6
Jul	106.3	131.4	65.5	114.2	97.1	125.0	118.1	84.6	104.2	147.6	127.8	120.1	109.5
Aug	106.3	132.1	66.9	114.3	97.3	125.1	118.7	84.6	104.4	147.6	128.0	120.6	109.9
Sep	107.1	132.0	68.7	114.6	98.5	125.4	117.4	85.0	104.4	151.3	128.3	121.0	110.2
Oct	107.3	132.2	68.4	114.9	97.6	125.8	117.2	84.7	104.3	154.5	128.5	122.5	110.4
Nov	107.6	131.1	68.6	115.0	98.4	125.9	116.4	84.2	104.1	154.5	128.9	122.5	110.3
Dec	108.0	130.7	67.8	115.2	99.5	125.0	118.5	84.2	104.0	154.5	129.1	122.7	110.7
2004 Jan	107.6	131.5	65.7	115.4	96.6	125.4	117.9	84.2	103.2	154.5	129.3	123.6	110.1
Feb	107.9	131.5	65.5	115.5	97.7	125.1	118.5	84.7	103.0	154.5	129.4	123.9	110.4
Mar	107.9	131.8	65.6	116.0	98.2	125.4	118.5	84.8	103.1	154.5	130.1	123.9	110.6
Apr	107.6	133.5	65.4	117.6	97.9	126.0	119.4	85.1	103.4	154.5	130.5	123.7	111.0
May	108.0	133.8	65.6	117.9	98.7	126.2	121.1	85.0	103.1	154.5	130.9	123.8	111.4
Jun	107.1	133.8	64.9	118.1	98.5	126.4	121.2	84.7	103.6	154.5	131.2	123.7	111.3
Jul	106.4	134.2	62.3	118.3	96.4	126.6	122.7	83.7	103.4	154.5	131.4	124.1	111.0
Aug	106.1	134.7	63.1	118.6	97.0	126.5	123.2	83.6	103.4	154.5	131.7	124.4	111.3
Sep	106.4	134.9	64.7	118.9	98.0	127.1	121.3	82.8	103.4	158.2	131.8	124.7	111.4
Oct	106.7	134.8	64.8	119.9	97.2	127.6	121.2	82.9	103.3	162.2	132.2	126.3	111.7
Nov	107.1	134.1	65.0	120.7	98.0	127.7	121.2	82.6	103.2	162.2	132.6	126.4	111.9
Dec	107.8	133.4	64.2	121.4	100.2	127.5	123.3	82.3	103.4	162.2	132.9	126.7	112.5

Percentage change on a year earlier

	CJYS	CJYT	CJYU	CJYV	CJYW	CJYX	CJYY	CJYZ	CJZA	CJZB	CJZC	CJZD	CJYR
2002 Sep	0.2	2.0	−6.8	2.0	−0.3	3.9	0.4	−0.1	1.7	2.9	3.4	1.8	1.0
Oct	0.2	1.6	−6.7	2.5	−0.2	4.0	1.0	−0.4	1.9	8.5	3.3	3.0	1.4
Nov	0.4	1.7	−5.9	2.6	−0.7	3.5	2.0	0.1	2.0	8.5	3.3	2.9	1.6
Dec	−0.2	1.7	−7.4	2.6	−0.8	3.3	4.4	−	1.6	8.5	3.4	3.0	1.7
2003 Jan	−1.1	1.7	−5.6	2.1	−0.7	3.3	3.6	0.5	1.3	8.5	3.4	1.8	1.4
Feb	−0.4	1.6	−4.3	2.2	−1.0	3.8	4.0	0.2	1.3	8.5	3.4	2.0	1.6
Mar	−0.3	1.6	−4.6	2.2	−0.9	3.5	4.1	1.0	0.9	8.5	3.4	2.1	1.6
Apr	0.3	2.5	−4.3	1.6	−1.0	3.1	4.2	0.7	0.3	8.5	3.3	1.3	1.5
May	1.2	1.9	−4.6	1.4	−0.5	3.1	2.9	1.1	−	8.5	3.2	1.1	1.2
Jun	1.3	2.2	−4.5	1.4	−0.3	2.8	2.3	−	−0.7	8.5	3.2	1.5	1.1
Jul	1.4	1.5	−2.2	1.8	−0.1	3.9	2.2	1.0	−1.0	8.5	3.1	2.4	1.3
Aug	1.6	2.4	−1.2	1.8	−0.3	3.4	2.4	0.7	−1.5	8.5	3.0	2.6	1.4
Sep	2.2	1.9	−3.4	2.0	−0.3	3.6	3.3	1.1	−1.7	8.7	3.0	2.7	1.4
Oct	2.2	2.2	−3.3	2.1	−0.3	3.6	3.3	0.4	−2.0	4.7	2.9	2.8	1.4
Nov	2.6	1.6	−4.3	2.2	−0.3	3.6	3.7	−0.4	−2.3	4.7	3.0	2.9	1.3
Dec	3.0	1.8	−3.6	2.2	−0.6	3.0	3.0	−0.2	−2.2	4.7	3.0	2.6	1.3
2004 Jan	2.6	1.7	−2.5	2.3	−0.2	2.6	3.1	−0.4	−2.5	4.7	2.9	4.2	1.4
Feb	2.2	1.6	−4.0	2.2	0.3	2.0	3.0	0.2	−2.8	4.7	2.9	4.3	1.3
Mar	1.9	1.9	−4.5	2.7	−0.7	2.2	2.2	0.2	−2.6	4.7	3.1	4.1	1.1
Apr	1.2	2.1	−4.7	3.4	0.4	2.2	1.4	0.7	−2.2	4.7	3.0	3.9	1.2
May	1.0	2.0	−4.5	3.7	−0.1	2.0	3.7	0.5	−2.0	4.7	3.0	3.9	1.5
Jun	0.8	1.9	−4.7	3.8	0.3	2.0	3.9	1.0	−1.1	4.7	2.9	3.6	1.6
Jul	0.1	2.1	−4.9	3.6	−0.7	1.3	3.9	−1.1	−0.8	4.7	2.8	3.3	1.4
Aug	−0.2	2.0	−5.7	3.8	−0.3	1.1	3.8	−1.2	−1.0	4.7	2.9	3.2	1.3
Sep	−0.7	2.2	−5.8	3.8	−0.5	1.4	3.3	−2.6	−1.0	4.6	2.7	3.1	1.1
Oct	−0.6	2.0	−5.3	4.4	−0.4	1.4	3.4	−2.1	−1.0	5.0	2.9	3.1	1.2
Nov	−0.5	2.3	−5.2	5.0	−0.4	1.4	4.1	−1.9	−0.9	5.0	2.9	3.2	1.5
Dec	−0.2	2.1	−5.3	5.4	0.7	2.0	4.1	−2.3	−0.6	5.0	2.9	3.3	1.6

1 See chapter text. Prior to 10 December 2003, the consumer prices index (CPI) was published in the UK as the harmonised index of consumer prices (HICP).

Source: Office for National Statistics: 020 7533 5874

17.5 Retail Prices Index[1]
United Kingdom

Indices (13 January 1987=100)

	All items (RPI)	All items excluding mortgage interest payments (RPIX)	mortgage interest payments and depreciation	housing	food	seasonal food[2]	Food and catering	Alcohol and tobacco	Housing and household expenditure	Personal expenditure	Travel and leisure	Consumer durables	All items excluding mortgage interest payments & indirect taxes (RPIY)[3]
Weights													
	CZGU	CZGY	DOGZ	CZGX	CZGV	CZGW	CBVV	CBVW	CBVX	CBVY	CBVZ	CBWA	
1996	1 000	958	929	810	857	978	191	113	353	92	251	116	
1997	1 000	961	932	814	864	981	185	114	351	96	254	122	
1998	1 000	955	923	803	870	982	178	105	359	95	263	121	
1999	1 000	958	928	807	872	980	179	100	358	95	268	127	
2000	1 000	960	924	805	882	982	170	95	355	101	279	126	
2001	1 000	954	914	795	884	982	169	97	362	96	276	125	
2002	1 000	964	924	801	886	980	166	99	363	94	278	126	
2003	1 000	961	919	797	891	983	160	98	365	92	285	126	
2004	1 000	961	914	791	889	981	160	97	367	93	283	121	
Annual averages													
	CHAW	CHMK	CHON	CHAZ	CHAY	CHAX	CHBS	CHBT	CHBU	CHBV	CHBW	CHBY	CBZW
1996	152.7	152.3	152.3	149.3	154.9	153.4	148.9	175.9	153.0	135.1	152.8	117.1	148.2
1997	157.5	156.5	156.4	152.9	160.5	158.5	150.4	183.2	158.4	137.7	159.0	117.3	151.5
1998	162.9	160.6	160.3	156.2	166.5	163.8	153.4	192.3	166.2	139.9	162.8	115.9	154.5
1999	165.4	164.3	163.6	158.9	169.4	166.5	155.4	202.6	167.7	139.6	165.6	112.3	157.1
2000	170.3	167.7	166.4	161.3	175.1	171.4	156.7	210.3	176.2	137.2	170.3	108.0	159.9
2001	173.3	171.3	169.5	163.7	178.0	174.3	162.2	216.9	180.0	135.7	172.0	105.0	163.7
2002	176.2	175.1	172.5	166.0	181.1	177.2	164.8	222.3	184.6	133.2	174.2	101.9	167.5
2003	181.3	180.0	176.2	168.9	186.7	182.4	167.9	228.0	194.3	133.2	177.0	99.8	172.0
2004	186.7	184.0	179.1	170.9	192.8	187.9	170.0	233.6	207.4	131.5	178.1	97.7	175.5
Monthly figures													
2001 Dec	173.4	172.5	170.5	164.5	177.9	174.3	163.8	218.2	180.0	136.1	170.6	106.1	165.0
2002 Jan	173.3	172.4	170.3	164.2	177.6	174.0	164.9	219.2	179.5	132.3	171.7	101.1	165.0
Feb	173.8	172.8	170.7	164.7	178.1	174.6	164.9	219.6	179.9	133.0	172.2	102.0	165.4
Mar	174.5	173.5	171.4	165.5	178.9	175.2	165.3	220.2	180.8	134.1	172.7	103.7	166.1
Apr	175.7	174.7	172.7	166.1	180.4	176.6	165.1	220.9	182.7	134.2	174.8	102.7	166.9
May	176.2	175.2	173.0	166.4	181.0	177.2	165.0	222.3	183.6	134.4	174.8	103.1	167.3
Jun	176.2	175.1	172.7	166.1	181.2	177.3	164.4	222.6	184.2	133.6	174.7	102.2	167.2
Jul	175.9	174.8	172.1	165.4	180.9	177.0	164.3	223.6	184.8	129.5	174.6	99.5	167.0
Aug	176.4	175.3	172.4	165.7	181.5	177.6	164.4	223.5	185.6	130.7	174.8	100.1	167.6
Sep	177.6	176.4	173.4	166.8	182.8	178.7	164.7	224.0	187.2	134.1	175.1	102.3	168.7
Oct	177.9	176.6	173.5	166.9	183.1	179.0	165.0	224.2	188.0	133.8	175.1	101.5	169.1
Nov	178.2	177.0	173.7	167.1	183.5	179.3	165.1	224.0	188.7	134.7	175.1	102.2	169.6
Dec	178.5	177.2	173.8	167.2	183.9	179.6	165.1	223.7	190.2	133.6	174.8	102.6	169.8
2003 Jan	178.4	177.1	173.5	166.8	183.8	179.5	165.3	224.6	189.7	130.6	176.1	98.4	169.8
Feb	179.3	177.9	174.4	167.8	184.6	180.4	166.1	224.9	190.3	132.9	176.7	99.9	170.6
Mar	179.9	178.7	175.2	168.7	185.3	181.0	166.6	225.6	190.8	133.8	177.5	101.4	171.4
Apr	181.2	180.0	176.5	169.0	186.7	182.3	167.2	227.4	193.1	133.9	178.4	100.3	171.8
May	181.5	180.2	176.6	169.1	186.8	182.4	168.2	228.3	193.9	133.8	177.4	100.8	171.9
Jun	181.3	180.0	176.4	168.8	186.8	182.4	167.8	228.7	194.2	133.0	177.2	99.9	171.7
Jul	181.3	179.9	176.1	168.5	186.7	182.4	168.0	229.0	194.7	130.6	177.1	97.8	171.6
Aug	181.6	180.4	176.5	168.9	187.1	182.7	168.1	229.6	194.8	132.5	177.2	98.7	172.2
Sep	182.5	181.3	177.2	169.7	188.0	183.5	168.9	229.7	196.3	134.6	177.0	100.4	173.2
Oct	182.6	181.3	177.2	169.6	188.0	183.6	169.2	230.0	196.7	134.3	176.7	99.7	173.1
Nov	182.7	181.4	177.2	169.6	188.1	183.7	169.4	229.4	197.4	134.5	176.2	100.0	173.1
Dec	183.5	181.8	177.6	169.9	189.0	184.5	169.9	229.1	199.4	133.4	176.7	100.3	173.5
2004 Jan	183.1	181.4	177.1	169.3	188.6	184.2	169.7	229.8	198.9	130.9	177.1	97.0	173.2
Feb	183.8	182.0	177.7	170.0	189.3	184.9	170.1	230.0	200.0	131.6	177.6	98.0	173.9
Mar	184.6	182.5	178.1	170.4	190.2	185.7	170.2	231.2	201.9	132.1	177.4	98.5	174.3
Apr	185.7	183.6	179.1	170.8	191.6	186.9	170.2	233.4	204.5	132.2	177.8	98.2	174.9
May	186.5	184.3	179.7	171.4	192.4	187.6	170.6	233.8	205.8	132.3	178.5	98.6	175.6
Jun	186.8	184.2	179.5	171.2	193.0	188.1	169.8	234.2	207.4	131.7	178.5	98.5	175.6
Jul	186.8	183.8	178.9	170.5	193.1	188.2	169.2	234.7	208.3	129.0	178.8	95.6	175.1
Aug	187.4	184.3	179.3	170.9	193.8	188.8	169.1	235.2	209.3	130.1	179.1	96.4	175.7
Sep	188.1	184.7	179.4	171.1	194.6	189.5	169.3	235.3	211.3	132.0	178.1	97.7	176.1
Oct	188.6	185.1	179.8	171.3	195.1	189.9	169.9	235.5	212.5	132.2	177.9	97.2	176.6
Nov	189.0	185.4	180.1	171.6	195.5	190.3	170.4	235.0	213.4	132.6	177.9	97.6	176.9
Dec	189.9	186.4	180.9	172.5	196.4	191.2	171.2	234.7	215.6	131.8	178.6	99.1	177.9

1 See chapter text.
2 Seasonal food is defined as items of food the prices of which show significant seasonal variations. These are fresh fruit and vegetables, fresh fish, eggs and home-killed lamb.

3 There are no weights available for RPIY.

Source: Office for National Statistics: 020 7533 5874

Indices and percentages

Tax and Price Index: (January 1987=100)

DQAB

	1990	1991	1992	1993	1994	1995	1996	1997	1998	1999	2000	2001	2002	2003	2004
January	113.9	123.6	128.1	128.7	132.1	137.2	141.6	143.6	147.1	150.5	152.7	156.7	156.5	161.4	166.9
February	114.7	124.3	128.8	129.6	132.9	138.2	142.3	144.2	147.9	150.8	153.7	157.6	157.0	162.3	167.6
March	115.9	124.9	129.3	130.2	133.4	138.8	143.0	144.6	148.4	151.2	154.6	157.8	157.7	163.0	168.4
April	118.2	125.4	129.6	131.3	135.3	140.3	141.7	143.8	149.7	151.2	155.7	156.3	158.6	164.9	168.9
May	119.4	125.8	130.2	131.8	135.8	141.0	142.0	144.4	150.6	151.7	156.3	157.4	159.1	165.2	169.7
June	119.9	126.5	130.2	131.7	135.8	141.2	142.1	145.0	150.5	151.7	156.7	157.6	159.1	165.0	170.0
July	120.0	126.2	129.6	131.4	135.1	140.4	141.5	145.0	150.1	151.1	156.1	156.5	158.8	165.0	170.0
August	121.4	126.5	129.7	132.1	135.8	141.3	142.2	146.0	150.8	151.5	156.1	157.2	159.3	165.4	170.6
September	122.7	127.0	130.3	132.7	136.1	142.0	143.0	146.9	151.5	152.3	157.3	157.8	160.6	166.3	171.3
October	123.8	127.5	130.8	132.6	136.4	141.2	143.0	147.1	151.6	152.6	157.2	157.5	160.9	166.4	171.8
November	123.4	128.1	130.6	132.4	136.5	141.2	143.1	147.2	151.5	152.8	157.7	156.8	161.2	166.5	172.2
December	123.3	128.2	130.1	132.7	137.2	142.1	143.6	147.6	151.5	153.4	157.8	156.6	161.5	167.3	173.1

Retail Prices Index: (January 1987=100)

CHAW

	1990	1991	1992	1993	1994	1995	1996	1997	1998	1999	2000	2001	2002	2003	2004
January	119.5	130.2	135.6	137.9	141.3	146.0	150.2	154.4	159.5	163.4	166.6	171.1	173.3	178.4	183.1
February	120.2	130.9	136.3	138.8	142.1	146.9	150.9	155.0	160.3	163.7	167.5	172.0	173.8	179.3	183.8
March	121.4	131.4	136.7	139.3	142.5	147.5	151.5	155.4	160.8	164.1	168.4	172.2	174.5	179.9	184.6
April	125.1	133.1	138.8	140.6	144.2	149.0	152.6	156.3	162.6	165.2	170.1	173.1	175.7	181.2	185.7
May	126.2	133.5	139.3	141.1	144.7	149.6	152.9	156.9	163.5	165.6	170.7	174.2	176.2	181.5	186.5
June	126.7	134.1	139.3	141.0	144.7	149.8	153.0	157.5	163.4	165.6	171.1	174.4	176.2	181.3	186.8
July	126.8	133.8	138.8	140.7	144.0	149.1	152.4	157.5	163.0	165.1	170.5	173.3	175.9	181.3	186.8
August	128.1	134.1	138.9	141.3	144.7	149.9	153.1	158.5	163.7	165.5	170.5	174.0	176.4	181.6	187.4
September	129.3	134.6	139.4	141.9	145.0	150.6	153.8	159.3	164.4	166.2	171.7	174.6	177.6	182.5	188.1
October	130.3	135.1	139.9	141.8	145.2	149.8	153.8	159.5	164.5	166.5	171.6	174.3	177.9	182.6	188.6
November	130.0	135.6	139.7	141.6	145.3	149.8	153.9	159.6	164.4	166.7	172.1	173.6	178.2	182.7	189.0
December	129.9	135.7	139.2	141.9	146.0	150.7	154.4	160.0	164.4	167.3	172.2	173.4	178.5	183.5	189.9

Percentage changes on one year earlier[1]

	1991	1992	1993	1994	1995	1996	1997	1998	1999	2000	2001	2002	2003	2004

Tax and Price Index[1]

	1991	1992	1993	1994	1995	1996	1997	1998	1999	2000	2001	2002	2003	2004
January	8.5	3.6	0.5	2.6	3.9	3.2	1.4	2.4	2.3	1.5	2.6	−0.1	3.1	3.4
February	8.4	3.6	0.6	2.5	4.0	3.0	1.3	2.6	2.0	1.9	2.5	−0.4	3.4	3.3
March	7.8	3.5	0.7	2.5	4.0	3.0	1.1	2.6	1.9	2.2	2.1	−0.1	3.4	3.3
April	6.1	3.3	1.3	3.0	3.7	1.0	1.5	4.1	1.0	3.0	0.4	1.5	4.0	2.4
May	5.4	3.5	1.2	3.0	3.8	0.7	1.7	4.3	0.7	3.0	0.7	1.1	3.8	2.7
June	5.5	2.9	1.2	3.1	4.0	0.6	2.0	3.8	0.8	3.3	0.6	1.0	3.7	3.0
July	5.2	2.7	1.4	2.8	3.9	0.8	2.5	3.5	0.7	3.3	0.3	1.5	3.9	3.0
August	4.2	2.5	1.9	2.8	4.1	0.6	2.7	3.3	0.5	3.0	0.7	1.3	3.8	3.1
September	3.5	2.6	1.8	2.6	4.3	0.7	2.7	3.1	0.5	3.3	0.3	1.8	3.5	3.0
October	3.0	2.6	1.4	2.9	3.5	1.3	2.9	3.1	0.7	3.0	0.2	2.2	3.4	3.2
November	3.8	2.0	1.4	3.1	3.4	1.3	2.9	2.9	0.9	3.2	−0.6	2.8	3.3	3.4
December	4.0	1.5	2.0	3.4	3.6	1.1	2.8	2.6	1.3	2.9	−0.8	3.1	3.6	3.5

Retail Prices Index

	1991	1992	1993	1994	1995	1996	1997	1998	1999	2000	2001	2002	2003	2004
January	9.0	4.1	1.7	2.5	3.3	2.9	2.8	3.3	2.4	2.0	2.7	1.3	2.9	2.6
February	8.9	4.1	1.8	2.4	3.4	2.7	2.7	3.4	2.1	2.3	2.7	1.0	3.2	2.5
March	8.2	4.0	1.9	2.3	3.5	2.7	2.6	3.5	2.1	2.6	2.3	1.3	3.1	2.6
April	6.4	4.3	1.3	2.6	3.3	2.4	2.4	4.0	1.6	3.0	1.8	1.5	3.1	2.5
May	5.8	4.3	1.3	2.6	3.4	2.2	2.6	4.2	1.3	3.1	2.1	1.1	3.0	2.8
June	5.8	3.9	1.2	2.6	3.5	2.1	2.9	3.7	1.3	3.3	1.9	1.0	2.9	3.0
July	5.5	3.7	1.4	2.3	3.5	2.2	3.3	3.5	1.3	3.3	1.6	1.5	3.1	3.0
August	4.7	3.6	1.7	2.4	3.6	2.1	3.5	3.3	1.1	3.0	2.1	1.4	2.9	3.2
September	4.1	3.6	1.8	2.2	3.9	2.1	3.6	3.2	1.1	3.3	1.7	1.7	2.8	3.1
October	3.7	3.6	1.4	2.4	3.2	2.7	3.7	3.1	1.2	3.1	1.6	2.1	2.6	3.3
November	4.3	3.0	1.4	2.6	3.1	2.7	3.7	3.0	1.4	3.2	0.9	2.6	2.5	3.4
December	4.5	2.6	1.9	2.9	3.2	2.5	3.6	2.7	1.8	2.9	0.7	2.9	2.8	3.5

1 See chapter text.

Source: Office for National Statistics: 020 7533 5874

17.7 Index of purchase prices of the means of agricultural production[1]
United Kingdom
Annual averages

		Weights	1993	1994	1995	1996	1997	1998	1999	2000	2001	2002	2003
Goods and services currently consumed[2]	C3FU	100	102.4	102.4	105.7	110.7	105.5	99.5	98.1	100.0	104.4	103.7	106.2
Seeds	C3FV	3.3	113.3	116.1	136.7	136.3	119.2	119.2	109.0	100.0	109.2	105.5	113.1
Energy, lubricants	C3FW	8.1	80.0	81.1	79.7	82.2	82.1	75.1	82.4	100.0	96.7	92.4	100.5
Fuels for heating	C3FX	1.0	72.2	65.6	67.9	81.9	77.3	61.6	66.6	100.0	95.5	87.2	104.5
Motor fuel	C3FY	5.1	67.7	71.0	69.6	71.0	73.1	66.7	77.8	100.0	96.7	91.6	100.7
Electricity	C3FZ	1.8	118.9	117.7	114.1	113.4	109.6	104.8	102.9	100.0	97.0	96.2	96.7
Lubricants	C3G2	0.2	82.7	84.8	84.8	84.9	86.2	88.5	98.1	100.0	101.2	106.2	112.7
Fertilisers and soil improvers	C3G3	9.1	89.8	95.5	103.1	109.5	106.6	95.3	93.3	100.0	115.8	110.3	119.0
Straight nitrogen	C3G4	3.9	89.6	97.4	109.8	121.5	104.4	87.0	82.9	100.0	129.1	120.2	133.1
Compound fertilisers	C3G5	4.6	90.6	94.3	98.0	100.3	109.6	101.9	101.3	100.0	106.7	103.0	109.1
Other fertiliser (mainly lime and chalk)	C3G6	0.4	80.0	83.9	85.2	92.0	93.5	95.9	96.7	100.0	100.5	104.0	103.4
Plant protection products	C3G7	7.2	105.3	110.4	108.8	115.8	116.6	108.2	105.8	100.0	96.8	95.8	95.7
Animal feedstuffs	C3G8	26.4	136.0	127.4	130.6	140.6	125.4	106.5	99.1	100.0	107.4	103.5	105.2
Feed wheat	C3G9	2.2	176.9	154.6	166.2	168.5	133.4	113.6	102.2	100.0	110.8	97.2	107.4
Whole barley	C3GA	2.1	176.0	155.0	161.0	159.5	125.3	108.5	111.5	100.0	101.8	89.6	103.2
Whole oats	C3GB	0.2	192.6	153.7	140.8	153.7	123.3	98.0	104.7	100.0	97.8	90.7	85.1
Maize glutten feed	C3GC	0.4	140.2	139.3	144.3	160.7	117.8	95.3	100.2	100.0	110.0	102.9	122.9
Oilcake	C3GD	2.1	119.3	110.7	109.1	139.8	131.5	91.9	83.5	100.0	109.4	100.4	109.5
White fish meal	C3GE	0.4	92.2	90.4	104.0	133.0	125.3	137.9	93.2	100.0	115.1	134.7	129.1
Other straight feedstuffs	C3GF	3.3	134.3	123.3	133.3	142.6	121.7	98.2	91.8	100.0	114.1	109.3	112.3
All straight feedstuffs	C3GG	10.6	149.4	134.0	141.1	151.5	127.3	104.1	97.1	100.0	109.7	101.3	108.9
Feedstuffs non-concentrates	C3GH	0.1	149.4	134.0	141.1	151.5	127.3	104.1	97.1	100.0	109.7	101.3	108.9
Compound feedstuffs for:	C3GI	15.8	127.1	122.9	123.7	133.3	124.1	108.1	100.4	100.0	105.8	104.9	102.7
Cattle and calves	C3GJ	6.2	127.3	121.7	120.8	130.5	122.0	105.0	99.9	100.0	106.4	105.9	102.5
Pigs	C3GK	3.5	136.4	130.5	132.9	142.0	130.5	112.8	101.9	100.0	105.9	103.3	101.0
Poultry	C3GL	5.0	123.5	120.6	121.7	131.5	121.7	108.7	100.6	100.0	105.9	104.5	105.0
Sheep	C3GM	1.1	112.3	116.4	119.1	129.2	126.5	108.3	98.0	100.0	102.2	106.2	99.4
Maintenance and repair of plant	C3GN	7.9	79.8	81.4	83.4	87.6	91.0	93.4	96.6	100.0	104.3	109.4	116.0
Maintenance and repair of buildings	C3GO	3.6	85.9	90.0	95.2	96.1	97.7	98.9	98.0	100.0	102.1	104.9	108.4
Veterinary services	C3GP	3.2	97.7	97.7	98.1	98.9	100.1	101.1	101.2	100.0	98.6	97.8	101.5
Other goods and services	C3GQ	31.2	89.8	92.9	95.7	98.0	95.6	98.4	99.8	100.0	102.5	105.5	104.3
Goods and services contributing to investment in agriculture	C3GR	100	88.1	89.7	91.9	95.3	98.1	99.8	100.2	100.0	99.0	100.0	101.5
Materials	C3GS	71.5	90.9	92.1	93.5	97.9	100.5	101.6	101.7	100.0	97.3	97.0	97.5
Machinery and other equipment	C3GT	28.4	85.0	85.8	88.3	92.2	95.0	97.7	99.2	100.0	97.4	95.7	95.1
Machinery and plant for cultivation	C3GU	8.0	77.7	79.2	81.5	89.7	93.3	97.7	99.1	100.0	99.6	98.6	98.7
Machinery and plant for harvesting	C3GV	14.3	88.3	88.3	91.1	93.9	96.8	98.4	100.0	100.0	92.3	88.8	88.2
Farm machinery and installations	C3GW	6.0	86.7	88.7	90.4	91.6	93.2	96.1	97.5	100.0	106.3	108.2	106.8
Tractors	C3GX	28.6	92.3	93.3	93.2	98.5	101.0	101.6	102.4	100.0	96.8	98.4	101.4
Other vehicles	C3GY	14.5	99.5	101.8	104.2	107.6	110.0	109.1	105.1	100.0	98.3	96.7	94.4
Buildings	C3GZ	19.5	80.8	84.2	88.6	90.1	93.2	95.6	96.6	100.0	103.3	107.8	112.1
Engineering and soil improvement operations	C3H2	9.0	87.8	87.9	91.2	86.1	89.8	94.8	96.9	100.0	101.4	107.2	110.3

1 See chapter text.
2 The sum of the percentages of categories included does not add up to 100% due to the exclusion of some minor categories.

Source: Department for Environment, Food and Rural Affairs: 01904 455253

17.8 Index of producer prices of agricultural products[1]
United Kingdom
Annual averages

Indices (2000=100)

		Weights	1993	1994	1995	1996	1997	1998	1999	2000	2001	2002	2003
All products[2]	C3H6	100	126.2	127.7	139.2	135.1	117.1	106.9	103.5	100.0	108.3	103.3	110.0
All crop products	C3H7	40.2	124.4	128.7	147.4	130.5	108.9	111.6	108.9	100.0	112.0	104.0	110.7
Cereals (including cereal seeds)	C3H8	13.3	175.7	156.0	166.5	166.2	132.4	113.8	111.0	100.0	107.8	95.0	105.2
Wheat for:													
breadmaking	C3H9	1.1	181.2	153.6	159.8	164.5	139.5	122.8	112.9	100.0	109.6	101.4	110.6
other milling	C3HA	1.5	173.5	151.6	162.8	165.0	133.7	116.0	110.9	100.0	107.5	92.9	104.1
feeding	C3HB	6.4	178.0	155.2	167.0	167.3	135.4	114.0	110.5	100.0	110.5	96.7	105.6
Barley for:													
feeding	C3HC	2.5	174.8	155.1	161.1	157.7	123.9	109.2	112.9	100.0	102.6	89.1	103.7
malting	C3HD	1.4	160.3	167.8	187.3	180.9	128.2	115.1	108.9	100.0	104.7	96.5	107.1
Oats for:													
milling	C3HE	0.1	195.3	163.6	158.5	161.1	128.8	104.9	109.9	100.0	109.8	89.0	90.7
feeding	C3HF	0.2	192.2	153.9	145.0	156.0	119.0	97.0	106.1	100.0	98.5	91.2	86.6
Potatoes:	C3HG	4.5	73.8	153.3	264.6	118.0	63.5	138.8	143.5	100.0	131.0	90.0	105.6
early	C3HH	0.4	63.7	134.5	93.2	68.2	46.3	100.7	51.9	100.0	114.5	73.0	90.0
main crop	C3HI	4.1	73.5	154.8	280.6	121.2	63.4	141.1	151.5	100.0	132.5	90.6	106.0
Industrial crops	C3HJ	4.3	139.5	139.5	147.9	154.4	127.9	118.4	103.4	100.0	111.9	114.3	120.1
Oilseed rape (non set-aside)	C3HK	1.2	130.8	157.1	151.9	164.4	135.6	140.0	102.0	100.0	119.2	121.2	140.3
Sugar beet	C3HL	2.2	144.9	139.3	150.1	152.5	124.9	111.4	108.7	100.0	107.3	114.8	112.0
Fresh vegetables	C3HM	7.7	96.5	100.0	107.5	105.3	97.4	105.2	99.2	100.0	113.6	112.7	125.7
Cauliflowers	C3HN	0.4	89.8	95.2	92.3	89.3	79.1	87.9	82.4	100.0	103.9	117.7	119.9
Lettuce	C3HO	0.7	115.2	112.4	108.7	96.5	114.0	98.6	102.9	100.0	129.2	128.6	151.1
Tomatoes	C3HP	0.7	96.1	88.2	92.9	106.6	86.9	91.8	100.3	100.0	100.1	107.6	135.6
Carrots	C3HQ	0.7	91.1	109.7	142.4	130.9	88.1	125.4	119.3	100.0	166.5	150.4	154.7
Cabbage	C3HR	0.4	95.6	81.0	100.7	104.4	83.2	94.5	94.2	100.0	123.0	109.8	120.0
Beans	C3HS	0.2	93.6	103.6	87.4	88.9	87.3	107.8	102.8	100.0	124.3	118.0	119.1
Onions	C3HT	0.5	146.6	181.3	149.0	107.3	122.8	165.8	104.7	100.0	128.6	126.7	136.3
Mushrooms	C3HU	1.3	98.5	97.0	107.7	110.6	99.1	98.9	98.1	100.0	91.0	95.9	100.6
Fresh fruit	C3HV	1.9	96.2	97.2	101.9	105.5	109.1	101.5	98.2	100.0	99.0	113.9	124.2
Dessert apples	C3HW	0.3	96.4	104.2	120.6	132.7	124.7	110.5	104.3	100.0	109.8	111.3	124.6
Dessert pears	C3HX	0.1	107.1	109.9	121.5	122.7	118.2	110.4	108.7	100.0	128.7	124.8	115.3
Cooking apples	C3HY	0.2	88.1	101.8	105.2	122.9	135.6	150.9	100.7	100.0	105.6	109.4	152.1
Strawberries	C3HZ	0.7	114.8	113.1	100.3	102.6	106.9	93.7	102.4	100.0	94.5	121.7	124.3
Raspberries	C3I2	0.2	80.2	73.4	102.9	92.8	103.3	84.6	91.3	100.0	102.9	128.9	125.9
Seeds (excluding cereal seeds)	C3I3	0.5	125.5	129.1	148.2	155.0	130.9	98.6	97.7	100.0	104.0	95.7	107.4
Flowers and plants	C3I4	5.9	92.9	98.4	99.0	98.3	102.4	103.1	105.3	100.0	105.3	106.8	107.9
Other crop products	C3I5	0.7	111.0	116.8	135.9	139.8	122.2	98.7	97.0	100.0	106.0	98.9	104.4
Animals and animal products	C3I6	59.8	127.5	127.0	133.7	138.3	122.6	103.8	99.9	100.0	105.8	102.8	109.5
Animals for slaughter	C3I7	35.3	125.7	123.5	126.0	132.4	118.0	97.2	95.2	100.0	101.3	103.2	109.3
Calves	C3I8	0.1	285.7	277.4	240.6	218.6	179.3	149.2	115.1	100.0	94.2	120.2	143.9
Clean cattle	C3I9	9.7	142.7	136.7	137.5	117.3	107.1	95.0	101.7	100.0	100.8	103.8	106.7
Clean pigs	C3IA	7.0	109.8	105.9	126.5	146.0	117.5	85.7	83.4	100.0	103.6	98.7	109.0
Sows and boars	C3IB	0.2	140.2	145.3	184.2	201.0	157.1	81.0	81.0	100.0	107.4	93.8	101.9
Clean sheep and lambs	C3IC	5.2	108.3	117.5	120.5	142.7	131.0	96.9	90.3	100.0	101.3	118.5	132.5
Ewes and rams	C3ID	0.4	145.6	138.8	137.0	189.6	198.5	116.1	81.3	100.0	152.4	149.6	188.2
All poultry	C3IE	11.5	121.4	120.1	113.0	126.7	116.8	103.4	99.1	100.0	98.6	97.2	99.4
Chickens	C3IF	7.9	135.0	131.3	120.2	136.3	126.6	105.9	101.4	100.0	100.1	99.5	100.2
Turkeys	C3IG	2.9	88.3	92.6	94.1	102.6	89.4	91.4	90.0	100.0	94.4	89.5	97.8
Cows' milk	C3IH	20.1	129.5	131.1	147.2	147.7	130.6	114.4	108.3	100.0	113.7	101.0	106.4
Eggs	C3II	3.2	135.1	137.1	127.5	142.2	121.0	109.3	98.1	100.0	104.8	109.6	131.4
Other animal products:	C3IJ	1.1	124.0	136.6	146.8	144.9	129.4	108.0	103.0	100.0	107.7	100.0	107.4
Wool (clip)	C3IK	0.2	125.4	191.8	189.0	173.5	150.1	98.6	93.5	100.0	87.0	96.4	108.4

1 See chapter text.
2 The sum of the percentages of all the categories does not add up to 100%
  due to the exclusion of some minor categories.

Source: Department for Environment, Food and Rural Affairs: 01904 455253

17.9 Commodity price trends[1]
United Kingdom

			1993	1994	1995	1996	1997	1998	1999	2000	2001	2002	2003
Wheat £ per tonne	KVAA	Average ex-farm price[2,3]	124.2	106.4	115.6	112.5	91.8	77.8	75.4	68.1	76.9	65.6	77.2
Barley £ per tonne	KVAB	Average ex-farm price[2,3]	113.6	105.4	107.6	103.7	86.3	79.2	74.2	70.1	72.1	64.8	75.5
Oats £ per tonne	KVAC	Average ex-farm price[2,3]	128.8	108.4	101.4	107.4	82.3	66.4	71.1	65.0	67.7	56.6	61.9
Rye £ per tonne	KVAD	Average ex-farm price[2]	113.40	112.80	107.90	113.90	..	..	..	..	..	..	..
Hops £ per tonne	KVAE	Average farm-gate price	3 357	4 005	3 595	3 360	3 550	3 679	4 003	3 861	3 532	2 832	3 048
Potatoes £ per tonne	KVAF	Average farm-gate price[4]	64.10	125.80	187.70	100.50	66.10	121.50	119.10	83.30	111.30	81.00	102.00
Sugar beet £ per tonne	KVAG	Producer price[5]	36.50	34.70	38.30	37.70	32.90	31.90	26.42	27.77	30.76	29.64	35.00
Oilseed rape £ per tonne	KVAH	Average market price[6]	153.00	185.40	177.70	186.90	160.20	164.30	112.90	120.40	148.35	148.15	171.60
Apples £ per tonne	KPUE	Dessert average farm-gate price[7]	297.7	391.4	437.3	493.6	525.0	476.1	405.0	359.8	352.2	385.2	460.3
" "	KVAI	Dessert average market price	368.3	447.4	465.7	523.5	462.0	431.5	405.4	408.7	418.2	453.1	551.3
" "	KVAJ	Culinary average market price	327.0	446.4	405.9	462.8	517.7	575.5	384.1	378.1	422.4	419.4	652.6
" "	KPUJ	Culinary average farm-gate price	230.8	232.3	248.2	286.8	335.1	297.3	209.9	236.0	175.7	285.7	471.7
Pears £ per tonne	KPUG	Average farm-gate price	385.7	412.6	453.0	445.7	441.9	405.1	426.4	283.3	352.1	402.9	344.0
" "	KVAK	Average market price	380.0	436.8	462.9	461.9	429.5	431.5	405.4	408.7	418.2	453.1	551.3
Tomatoes £ per tonne	LQMH	Average farm-gate price[7]	226.2	234.4	247.8	270.9	236.8	216.3	211.3	274.1	285.3	331.0	332.5
" "	KVAL	Average market price[7]	552.8	674.5	624.4	756.7	549.3	578.2	583.6	569.9	651.3	736.3	824.8
Cauliflowers £ per tonne	KPUI	Average farm-gate price[7]	590.3	685.0	585.1	742.4	546.9	594.6	576.3	751.6	725.4	793.6	1 039.6
" "	KVAM	Average market price[7]	296.9	317.7	328.9	363.0	309.8	284.8	242.5	282.9	304.9	365.6	368.2
Cattle (rearing) £ per head	KVAN	1st quality Hereford/cross bull calves[8,9,10]	185.95	182.06	166.32	131.81	146.95	107.86	88.24	79.98	..	85.20	112.70
"	KVAO	1st quality beef/ cross yearling steers[9,10]	478.00	471.00	475.00	445.00	427.00	369.00	382.00	400.05	..	398.14	445.50
Cattle (fat) p per kg liveweight	KVAP	Clean cattle[11]	128.04	121.71	123.15	105.52	96.89	86.10	92.12	89.68	87.53	91.38	94.20

			1993	1994	1995	1996	1997	1998	1999	2000	2001	2002	2003
Sheep (store) £ per head	KVAQ	1st quality lambs, hoggets and tegs[8]	35.56	40.02	44.46	46.83	53.42	31.28	28.62	34.50	..	..	37.70
Sheep (fat) p per kg estimated dressed carcase weight	KVAR	Great Britain[12]	218.96	236.88	236.40	283.13	239.02	192.46	180.27	196.44	..	233.40	260.10
	KVAS	Northern Ireland[13]	199.50	221.95	214.41	260.46	228.23	179.06	165.71	182.67	..	228.80	233.10
Pigs £ per kg deadweight	KVAT	Average price clean pigs	103.02	99.57	118.84	137.73	110.83	80.65	78.55	94.35	97.77	93.32	102.50
Broilers p per kg carcass weight	KVAU	Average producer price	87.4	87.1	84.0	90.9	86.1	76.6	72.1	70.7	70.4	68.7	68.6
Milk p per litre	KVAV	Average net return to producers[14]	22.68	23.19	24.94	25.02	22.12	19.37	18.35	16.93	19.26	17.11	18.02
Eggs p per dozen	KVAW	Average producer price[15]	41.90	42.31	38.23	45.70	39.33	36.23	34.12	36.67	35.73	39.89	46.95
Wool p per kg	KHWQ	Average producer price for clip paid to producers by the British Wool Marketing Board	62.00	98.90	95.00	86.90	74.90	48.00	46.60	51.30	47.00	50.00	53.30

1 This table gives indications of the movement in commodity prices at the first point of sale. The series do not always show total receipts by farmers; for some commodities additional premiums or deficiency payments are made to achieve support price levels.
2 Weighted average ex-farm prices of United Kingdom cereals.
3 Data from 1997 onwards have been revised and are not directly comparable with earlier years.
4 Weighted average price paid to growers for early and main crop potatoes in the United Kingdom (includes all potatoes and a value for sacks).
5 Returns to growers figures since 1986 prices per 'adjusted' tonne at 16% sugar content.
6 Typical contract price adjusted to delivered basis and 40 per cent oil content.
7 Weighted average wholesale prices for England and Wales. Average farm-gate price for England and Wales, crop year (June-May).

8 Average prices at representative markets in England and Wales.
9 Consists of Hereford/cross, Charolais/cross, Limousin/cross, Simmental/cross, Belgian/cross, other continental cross, other beef/dairy cross, other beef/beef cross.
10 From 2002 no differentiation between class 1 and class 2 animals.
11 Based on Meat and Livestock Commission all clean cattle prices.
12 Average of Great Britain weekly market prices as used to determine the level of ewe premium.
13 Average of Northern Ireland weekly market prices used to determine the level of ewe premium.
14 Derived by dividing total value of output by the total quantity of output available for human consumption.
15 Average price of all Class A eggs weighted according to quantity in each grade.

Source: Department for Environment, Food and Rural Affairs: 01904 455332

Government finance

Chapter 18

Government finance

Public sector

(Tables 18.1 to 18.3 and 18.5)

In Table 18.1 the term public sector describes the consolidation of central government, local government and public corporations. General government is the consolidated total of central government and local government. The table shows details of the key public sector finances' indicators, consistent with the European System of Accounts 1995 (ESA95), by sub sector.

The concepts in Table 18.1 are consistent with the format for public finances in the Economic and Fiscal Strategy Report (EFSR), published by HM Treasury on 11 June 1998, and The Budget. The public sector current budget is equivalent to net saving in national accounts plus capital tax receipts. Net investment is gross capital formation, plus payments less receipts of investment grants, less depreciation. Net borrowing is net investment less current budget. Net borrowing differs from the net cash requirement (see below) in that it is measured on an accruals basis whereas the net cash requirement is mainly a cash measure which includes some financial transactions Table 18.2 shows the Public sector key fiscal balances. The table shows the component detail of the public sector key fiscal balance by economic category. The tables are consistent with The Budget.

Table 18.3 shows public sector net debt. Public sector net debt consists of the public sector's financial liabilities at face value minus its liquid assets – mainly foreign currency exchange reserves and bank deposits. General government gross debt (consolidated) in Table 18.3 is consistent with the definition of general government gross debt reported to the European Commission under the requirements of the Maastricht Treaty.

More information on the concepts in Table 18.1, 18.2 and 18.3 can be found in a guide to monthly public sector finance statistics, GSS Methodology Series No 12, the ONS First Release *Public Sector Finances* and *Financial Statistics Explanatory Handbook*.

Table 18.5 shows the taxes and national insurance contributions paid to central government, local government, and to the institutions of the European Union. The table is the same as Table 11.1 of the National Accounts Blue Book. More information on the data and concepts in the table can be found in Chapter 11 of the Blue Book.

Consolidated Fund and National Loans Fund

(Tables 18.4, 18.6 and 18.7)

The central government embraces all bodies for whose activities a Minister of the Crown, or other responsible person, is accountable to Parliament. It includes, in addition to the ordinary government departments, a number of bodies administering public policy but without the substantial degree of financial independence which characterises the public corporations; it also includes certain extra-budgetary funds and accounts controlled by departments.

The government's financial transactions are handled through a number of statutory funds, or accounts. The most important of these is the Consolidated Fund which is the government's main account with the Bank of England. Up to 31 March 1968 the Consolidated Fund was virtually synonymous with the term 'Exchequer' which was then the government's central cash account. From 1 April 1968 the National Loans Fund, with a separate account at the Bank of England, was set up by the National Loans Act, 1968. The general effect of this Act was to remove from the Consolidated Fund most of the government's domestic lending and the whole of the government's borrowing transactions and to provide for them to be brought to account in the National Loans Fund.

Revenue from taxation and miscellaneous receipts, including interest and dividends on loans made from Votes, continue to be paid into the Consolidated Fund.

After meeting the ordinary expenditure on Supply Services and the Consolidated Fund Standing Services, the surplus or deficit of the Consolidated Fund (Table 18.4), is payable into or met by the National Loans Fund. Table 18.4 also provides a summary of the transactions of the National Loans Fund. The service of the National Debt, previously borne by the Consolidated Fund, is now met from the National Loans Fund which receives (a) interest payable on loans to the nationalised industries, local authorities and other bodies, whether the loans were made before or after 1 April 1968 and (b) the profits of the Issue Department of the Bank of England, mainly derived from interest on government securities, which were formerly paid into the Exchange Equalisation Account. The net cost of servicing the National Debt after applying these interest receipts and similar items is a charge on the Consolidated Fund as part of the standing services. Details of National Loans Fund loans outstanding are shown in Table 18.7. Details of borrowing and repayments of debt, other than loans from the National Loans Fund, are shown in Table 18.6.

Income tax

(Table 18.9, 18.10)

Following the introduction of Independent Taxation from 1990–91 the married couple's allowance was introduced. It is payable in addition to the personal allowance and between 1990–91 and 1992-93 went to the husband unless the transfer condition was met. The condition was that the husband was unable to make full use of the allowance himself and in that case he could transfer only part or all of the married couple's allowance to his wife. In 1993–94 all or half of the allowance could be transferred to the wife if the couple had agreed beforehand. The wife has the right to claim half the allowance. The married couple's allowance, and allowances linked to it, were restricted to 20 per cent in 1994–95 and to 15 per cent from 1995–96. From 2000–01 only people born before 6th April 1935 are entitled to married couple's allowance.

The age allowance replaces the single allowance, provided the taxpayer's income is below the limits shown in the table. From 1989–90, for incomes in excess of the limits, the allowance is reduced by £1 for each additional £2 of income until the ordinary limit is reached (before it was £2 for each £3 of additional income). The relief is due where the taxpayer is aged 65 or over in the year of assessment.

The additional personal allowance could be claimed by a single parent (or by a married man if his wife was totally incapacitated) who maintained a resident child at his or her own expense. Widow's bereavement allowance was due to a widow in the year of her husband's death and in the following year provided the widow had not remarried before the beginning of that year. Both the additional personal allowance and the widow's bereavement allowance were abolished from April 2000.

The blind person's allowance may be claimed by blind persons (in England and Wales, registered as blind by a local authority) and surplus blind person's allowance may be transferred to a husband or wife. Relief on life assurance premiums is given by deduction from the premium payable. From 1984–85, it is confined to policies made before 14 March 1984.

From 1993–94 until 1998–99 a number of taxpayers with taxable income in excess of the lower rate limit only paid tax at the lower rate. This was because it was only their dividend income and (from 1996–97) their savings income which took their taxable income above the lower rate limit but below the basic rate limit, and such income was chargeable to tax at the lower rate and not the basic rate.

In 1999–2000 the 10 per cent starting rate replaced the lower rate and taxpayers with savings or dividend income at the basic rate of tax are taxed at 20 per cent and 10 per cent respectively. Before 1999–2000 these people would have been classified as lower rate taxpayers.

Rateable values

(Table 18.11)

Major changes to local government finance in England and Wales took effect from 1 April 1990. These included the abolition of domestic rating – replaced by the community charge (replaced in 1993 by the council tax), the revaluation of all non-domestic properties, and the introduction of the Uniform Business Rate. Also in 1990, a new classification scheme was introduced which has resulted in differences in coverage. Further differences are caused by legislative changes which have changed the treatment of certain types of property. There was little change in the total rateable value of non-domestic properties when all these properties were revalued in April 1995. Rateable values for offices fell and there was a rise for all other property types shown in the table.

With effect from 1 April 2000 all non-domestic properties were revalued. Overall there was an increase in rateable values of over 25 per cent compared to the end of the 1995 list. The largest proportionate increase was for offices and cinemas, with all property types given in the table showing rises.

Sector analysis of key fiscal balances[1]
United Kingdom
Not seasonally adjusted

£ million[2]

		1993 /94	1994 /95	1995 /96	1996 /97	1997 /98	1998 /99	1999 /00	2000 /01	2001 /02	2002 /03	2003 /04
Surplus on current budget[3]												
Central Government	ANLV	−38 937	−30 283	−23 052	−20 841	−32	11 307	23 306	24 096	12 596	−9 169	−19 327
Local government	NMMX	2 768	2 016	446	−112	−457	−221	−2 428	−2 100	−1 735	−1 933	380
General Government	ANLW	−36 169	−28 267	−22 606	−20 953	−489	11 086	20 878	21 996	10 861	−11 102	−18 947
Public corporations	FDDP	−4 625	−4 893	−2 209	−969	−896	−1 081	−1 287	−1 453	−1 431	−2 805	−1 731
Public sector	ANMU	−40 794	−33 160	−24 815	−21 922	−1 385	10 005	19 591	20 543	9 430	−13 907	−20 678
Net investment[4]												
Central government	−ANNS	13 685	14 951	14 469	9 603	8 007	7 976	7 946	8 968	11 754	15 990	18 013
Local government	−ANNT	1 208	2 157	−220	−961	−552	−128	−1 485	−2 394	−803	−3 503	−1 591
General Government	−ANNV	14 893	17 108	14 249	8 642	7 455	7 848	6 461	6 574	10 951	12 487	16 422
Public corporations	−ANNU	−4 691	−7 058	−4 323	−3 111	−2 259	−1 415	−2 041	−1 420	−1 060	−1 240	−1 727
Public sector	−ANNW	10 202	10 050	9 926	5 531	5 196	6 433	4 420	5 154	9 891	11 247	14 695
Net borrowing[5]												
Central government	−NMFJ	52 622	45 234	37 521	30 444	8 039	−3 331	−15 360	−15 128	−842	25 159	37 340
Local government	−NMOE	−1 560	141	−666	−849	−95	93	943	−294	932	−1 570	−1 971
General Government	−NNBK	51 062	45 375	36 855	29 595	7 944	−3 238	−14 417	−15 422	90	23 589	35 369
Public corporations	−CPCM	−66	−2 165	−2 114	−2 142	−1 363	−334	−754	33	371	1 565	4
Public sector	−ANNX	50 996	43 210	34 741	27 453	6 581	−3 572	−15 171	−15 389	461	25 154	35 373
Net cash requirement												
Central government[6]	RUUX	49 121	39 660	36 153	25 199	2 751	−6 344	−10 664	−37 251	3 366	24 214	42 718
Local government	ABEG	−2 780	−961	−1 139	−843	−820	−404	979	−611	−423	−2 715	−2 692
General Government	RUUS	46 341	38 699	35 014	24 356	1 931	−6 748	−9 685	−37 862	2 943	21 499	40 026
Public corporations	ABEM	−210	−2 011	−3 529	−1 637	−669	−114	1 175	648	409	2 883	−491
Public sector	RURQ	46 131	36 688	31 485	22 719	1 262	−6 862	−8 510	−37 214	3 352	24 382	39 535
Public sector debt												
Public sector net debt (£ billion)	RUTN	249.4	289.3	321.3	348.4	352.0	348.5	340.9	306.9	311.7	341.9	375.7
Public sector net debt as a percentage of GDP	RUTO	37.2	40.8	42.7	43.6	41.6	39.1	36.3	31.3	30.2	31.5	32.8

1 National accounts entities as defined under the European System of Accounts 1995 (ESA95) consistent with the latest national accounts. See chapter text.
2 Unless otherwise stated
3 Net saving *plus* capital taxes.
4 Gross capital formation *plus* payments *less* receipts of investment grants *less* depreciation.

5 Net investment *less* surplus on current budget. A version of General government net borrowing is reported to the European Commision under the requirements of the Maastricht Treaty.
6 Central government net cash requirement (own account).

Source: Office for National Statistics: 020 7533 5984

18.2 Public sector transactions and fiscal balances[1]
United Kingdom

£ million

		1993 /94	1994 /95	1995 /96	1996 /97	1997 /98	1998 /99	1999 /00	2000 /01	2001 /02	2002 /03	2003 /04
Current receipts												
Taxes on income and wealth	ANSO	78 592	87 804	96 422	102 261	114 933	123 886	133 710	144 156	145 147	143 142	145 642
Taxes on production	NMYE	82 955	90 173	95 981	99 484	109 385	115 349	125 296	129 545	133 407	139 885	148 720
Other current taxes[2]	MJBC	10 535	11 312	12 130	13 162	14 214	15 468	16 541	17 519	19 247	20 752	23 224
Taxes on capital	NMGI	1 335	1 409	1 518	1 558	1 684	1 805	2 054	2 236	2 383	2 370	2 521
Social contributions	ANBO	40 136	42 832	45 007	47 219	51 692	54 746	57 163	62 068	63 161	63 528	75 065
Gross operating surplus	ANBP	13 745	14 519	17 540	17 259	17 009	16 963	16 547	16 478	17 326	16 852	18 153
Interest and dividends from private sector and Rest of World	ANBQ	4 275	4 133	4 435	4 365	4 481	5 033	4 261	6 040	4 717	4 520	4 413
Rent and other current transfers[3]	ANBS	955	1 107	1 125	1 325	1 041	835	930	1 875	2 161	2 143	1 599
Total current receipts	ANBT	232 528	253 289	274 158	286 633	314 439	334 085	356 502	379 917	387 549	393 192	419 337
Current expenditure												
Current expenditure on goods and services[4]	GZSN	131 134	137 267	141 956	145 277	147 591	155 753	167 357	179 896	194 076	213 609	233 300
Subsidies	NMRL	4 576	5 321	5 421	5 598	5 400	4 259	4 228	4 730	5 659	6 301	7 244
Social benefits	ANLY	95 266	97 715	100 660	104 948	106 830	107 645	111 310	116 827	124 897	128 927	135 092
Net current grants abroad[5]	GZSI	−371	553	458	−751	102	−847	−253	−146	−1 861	−626	−917
Other current grants	NNAI	9 814	9 275	10 403	13 047	13 887	15 584	16 368	18 725	19 484	23 294	28 089
Interest and dividends paid to private sector and Rest of World	ANLO	20 764	23 489	26 765	28 128	29 732	29 367	25 297	26 385	22 500	21 337	22 806
Total current expenditure	ANLT	261 183	273 620	285 663	296 247	303 542	311 761	324 307	346 417	364 755	392 842	425 614
Saving, gross plus capital taxes	ANSP	−28 655	−20 331	−11 505	−9 614	10 897	22 324	32 195	33 500	22 794	350	−6 277
Depreciation	−ANNZ	−12 139	−12 829	−13 310	−12 308	−12 282	−12 319	−12 604	−12 957	−13 364	−14 257	−14 401
Surplus on current budget	ANMU	−40 794	−33 160	−24 815	−21 922	−1 385	10 005	19 591	20 543	9 430	−13 907	−20 678
Net investment												
Gross fixed capital formation[6]	ANSQ	17 905	19 114	19 136	14 255	13 467	13 968	13 155	14 716	16 943	19 059	21 042
Less depreciation	−ANNZ	−12 139	−12 829	−13 310	−12 308	−12 282	−12 319	−12 604	−12 957	−13 364	−14 257	−14 401
Increase in inventories and valuables	ANSR	−224	−662	21	34	139	231	−472	−126	−16	−80	67
Capital grants to private sector and Rest of World	ANSS	5 153	4 854	4 432	4 032	4 388	4 920	4 768	4 277	7 267	7 416	9 287
Capital grants from private sector and Rest of World	−ANST	−493	−427	−353	−482	−516	−367	−427	−756	−939	−891	−1 300
Total net investment	−ANNW	10 202	10 050	9 926	5 531	5 196	6 433	4 420	5 154	9 891	11 247	14 695
Net borrowing[7]	−ANNX	50 996	43 210	34 741	27 453	6 581	−3 572	−15 171	−15 389	461	25 154	35 373
Financial transactions determining net cash requirement												
Net lending to private sector and Rest of World	ANSU	133	−1 167	−1 749	−655	−224	269	2 036	2 715	2 195	2 308	1 294
Net acquisition of UK company securities	ANSV	−5 194	−6 374	−2 344	−3 992	−1 526	565	−498	859	−562	1 002	788
Accounts receivable/payable	ANSW	917	75	3 139	−285	−656	−105	5 319	−22 358	2 086	−1 721	1 006
Adjustment for interest on gilts	ANSX	−791	−1 036	−1 895	−382	−2 349	−2 446	−1 295	−2 630	−361	−1 447	−1 186
Other financial transcations[8]	ANSY	70	1 980	−407	580	−564	−1 573	1 099	−411	−467	−914	2 260
Public sector net cash requirement	RURQ	46 131	36 688	31 485	22 719	1 262	−6 862	−8 510	−37 214	3 352	24 382	39 535

1 See chapter text.
2 Includes domestic rates, council tax, community charge, motor vehicle duty paid by household and some licence fees.
3 ESA95 transactions D44, D45, D74, D75 and D72-D71: includes rent of land, oil royalties, other property income and fines.
4 Includes non-trading capital consumption.
5 Net of current grants received from abroad.
6 Including net acquisition of land.
7 Net investment *less* surplus on current budget.
8 Includes statistical discrepancy, finance leasing and similar borrowing, insurance technical reserves and some other minor adjustments.

Source: Office for National Statistics: 020 7533 5984

18.3 Public sector net debt[1]
United Kingdom

£ million

		1995 /96	1996 /97	1997 /98	1998 /99	1999 /00	2000 /01	2001 /02	2002 /03	2003 /04
Central government sterling gross debt:										
British government stock										
Conventional gilts	BKPK	208 943	231 869	232 292	223 105	218 687	204 285	200 833	206 119	232 877
Index linked gilts	BKPL	46 133	51 535	58 729	62 289	65 740	70 316	70 417	75 966	78 982
Total	BKPM	255 075	283 404	291 021	285 394	284 427	274 601	271 250	282 085	311 859
Sterling Treasury bills	BKPJ	10 781	4 996	2 106	4 721	4 453	3 521	9 700	15 000	19 300
National savings	ACUA	56 965	61 754	63 271	64 346	63 331	62 611	62 275	63 087	66 482
Tax instruments	ACRV	1 222	853	706	574	535	491	478	376	407
Other sterling debt[2]	BKSK	26 746	26 345	25 108	26 027	26 550	27 773	25 647	29 722	30 375
Central government sterling gross debt total	BKSL	350 789	377 352	382 212	381 062	379 296	368 997	369 350	390 270	428 423
Central government foreign currency gross debt:										
US$ bonds	BKPG	4 524	4 294	4 180	4 338	4 388	4 924	2 107	–	1 632
DM bonds[3]	EYST	2 219	1 828	–	–	–	–	–	–	–
ECU bonds	EYSJ	2 059	1 777	1 606	1 672	1 500	–	–	–	–
ECU/Euro Treasury notes	EYSV	4 118	3 199	2 891	3 010	2 701	2 486	1 225	–	–
ECU/Euro Treasury bills	EYSN	2 883	2 488	2 249	2 341	–	–	–	–	–
Other foreign currency debt	BKPH	982	752	537	456	364	291	243	172	105
Central government foreign currency gross debt total	BKPI	16 785	14 338	11 463	11 816	8 954	7 701	3 575	172	1 738
Central government gross debt total	BKPW	367 574	391 690	393 675	392 878	388 250	376 698	372 925	390 442	430 161
Local government gross debt total	EYKP	50 552	49 856	50 193	51 039	51 702	52 517	52 561	51 324	50 512
less										
Central government holdings of local government debt	-EYKZ	–41 266	–42 348	–43 172	–45 045	–46 563	–47 789	–47 530	–44 836	–41 540
Local government holdings of central government debt	-EYLA	–153	–155	–170	–273	–77	–31	–29	–184	–510
General government gross debt (consolidated)	BKPX	376 707	399 043	400 526	398 599	393 312	381 395	377 927	396 746	438 623
Public corporations gross debt	EYYD	26 595	16 069	15 262	11 434	5 103	5 682	5 062	13 276	6 804
less:										
Central government holdings of public corporations debt	-EYXY	–25 980	–15 314	–14 590	–10 732	–4 307	–4 714	–4 308	–4 171	–5 188
Local government holdings of public corporations debt	-EYXZ	–	–1	–	–4	–123	–124	–122	–121	–123
Public corporations holdings of central government debt	-BKPZ	–5 723	–7 103	–7 313	–6 436	–6 126	–5 927	–4 615	–4 279	–3 896
Public corporations holdings of local government debt	-EYXV	–890	–134	–139	–108	–141	–106	–60	–50	–84
Public sector gross debt (consolidated)	BKQA	370 709	392 560	393 746	392 753	387 718	376 206	373 884	401 401	436 136
Public sector liquid assets:										
Official reserves	AIPD	30 463	25 547	21 293	22 147	21 498	30 423	28 055	26 348	25 231
Central government deposits[4]	BKSM	1 807	2 083	2 293	1 762	1 879	2 797	2 802	2 900	3 879
Other central government	BKSN	–	–	–	–	4 756	15 670	10 743	8 141	7 077
Local government deposits[4]	BKSO	10 229	11 313	11 828	12 301	10 221	11 522	11 570	12 535	14 530
Other local government short term assets	BKQG	2 826	3 256	3 693	4 335	5 468	5 719	5 990	6 061	5 599
Public corporations deposits[4]	BKSP	3 088	2 145	1 849	2 058	1 463	1 642	1 808	1 432	2 039
Other public corporations short term assets	BKSQ	1 054	686	668	1 300	1 128	1 212	1 180	1 979	2 225
Public sector liquid assets total	BKQJ	49 468	45 030	41 624	43 903	46 413	68 985	62 148	59 396	60 580
Public sector net debt	BKQK	321 241	347 530	352 122	348 850	341 305	307 221	311 736	342 005	375 556
as percentage of GDP[5]	RUTO	*42.7*	*43.6*	*41.6*	*39.1*	*36.3*	*31.3*	*30.2*	*31.5*	*32.8*

1 See chapter text.
2 Including overdraft with Bank of England.
3 Matured on 28 October 1997.
4 Bank and building society deposits.
5 Gross domestic product at market prices from 12 months centred on the end of the month.

Source: Office for National Statistics: 020 7533 5984

18.4 Consolidated Fund and National Loans Fund:[1] revenue and expenditure; receipts and payments

United Kingdom, years ending 31 March

£ million

		1994/95	1995/96	1996/97	1997/98	1998/99	1999/00	2000/01	2001/02	2002/03	2003/04
Consolidated Fund											
Revenue											
Inland Revenue	KCWZ	87 230.4	97 100.9	103 892.4	117 632.8	128 249.8	139 384.0	149 084.8	149 112.4	145 898.0	145 555.5
Customs and Excise	KCXA	72 485.6	76 668.6	82 351.6	89 839.6	94 018.3	97 291.5	102 168.0	104 854.8	108 719.8	115 656.3
Motor vehicle duties	KCXB	3 805.9	4 043.6	4 217.5	4 543.0	4 666.3	4 893.0	4 642.1	4 402.3	4 399.4	4 712.3
National Non-Domestic Rates	KPOI	11 469.8	13 373.4	14 269.3	14 036.9	15 878.3	13 403.8	15 482.0	16 009.3	17 592.9	16 579.3
Miscellaneous receipts	KCXE	16 280.3	10 289.3	12 634.6	14 176.6	10 737.1	8 799.0	29 329.4	7 796.6	9 425.0	10 548.9
Total revenue	KCXF	191 272.0	201 475.8	217 365.4	240 228.9	253 549.8	263 771.3	300 706.3	282 175.4	286 035.1	293 052.3
Expenditure											
Supply services	KCXG	207 465.8	211 403.3	214 226.0	209 440.8	213 439.2	226 989.6	241 685.1	271 998.6	290 183.0	313 071.9
Debt interest[2]	KCXH	16 039.8	18 423.1	20 702.3	21 605.7	21 320.8	18 535.3	16 629.2	15 325.6	14 680.9	14 502.4
Payments to Northern Ireland	KCXI	4 052.6	3 903.5	3 685.2	4 581.5	4 709.3	3 104.4	..	..	..	..
Payments to the European Union, etc	KCXJ	5 258.2	7 650.7	6 875.3	7 039.9	8 060.7	7 001.8	8 417.1	4 785.8	6 504.0	7 496.3
Other expenditure[3]	KCXL	271.6	−14.0	876.2	−53.8	−62.1	223.7	170.1	257.9	−72.4	203.8
Total expenditure	KCXM	233 088.0	241 366.5	246 365.0	242 614.1	247 467.9	255 854.8	266 901.5	292 367.9	311 295.5	335 274.4
Deficit met from the National Loans Fund	KCXN	41 816.0	39 890.7	28 999.6	2 385.2	−6 081.9	−7 916.5	−33 804.8	10 192.5	25 260.4	42 222.1
National Loans Fund											
Receipts											
Profits of the Issue Department of the Bank of England - income[4]	KZAW	955.2	1 275.5	1 200.9	1 604.8	1 600.9	1 327.3	1 603.0	1 362.9	1 240.2	1 247.8
Other miscellaneous receipts	KZAX	4.8	4.4	3.6	5.0	5.0	4.4	6.0	7.3	10.6	8.2
Interest on loans	KCXO	4 564.5	4 598.7	4 393.5	5 103.6	4 409.7	4 533.3	6 215.4	5 901.2	5 791.5	5 558.7
Service of the National Debt - balance met from the Consolidated Fund	KCXP	16 039.8	18 423.2	20 702.3	21 605.7	21 320.8	18 535.3	16 629.2	15 325.6	14 680.9	14 502.4
Gilt Edged Official Operations Account net income	KJDO	..	..	..	..	..	127.5	..	..	..	..
Total	KCXQ	21 564.3	24 301.8	26 300.3	28 319.1	27 336.4	24 527.8	24 453.6	22 597.0	21 723.2	21 967.1
Exchange Equalisation Account- sterling capital	KCXR	1 250.0	2 750.0	2 150.0	3 650.0	1 880.0	975.0	−5 205.0	4 849.0	4 620.0	330.0
Net borrowing[5]	KCXS	39 848.1	37 688.8	27 547.9	..	..	4 997.3	..	4 884.8	11 004.4	45 590.1
International Monetary Fund- maintenance of sterling holdings	KCXT	..	..	82.1	707.0	181.2	..	..	..	98.2	25.9
Profits of the Issue Department of the Bank of England: capital appreciation	KZAY	..	..	18.8	21.2	19.3	1.7	2.5	6.4	9.0	9.0
Reduction of National Debt Commissioners' Liability in respect of the National Savings Bank Investment Account	KCXU	..	..	..	..	..	..	..	..	..	..
Change in balances and other items	KCXV	..	..	..	..	..	..	..	..	..	..
NILO Gilt-Edged operations A/C	KJDL	2 500.0	2 500.0	2 000.0	2 500.0	2 500.0	5 000.0	..	..	..	..
Debt Management Account	GPJW	..	..	..	..	..	..	20 000.0	..	7 000.0	..
Total	KCXW	65 162.4	67 240.6	58 099.1	35 197.3	31 916.9	35 501.8	39 251.1	32 337.2	44 454.8	67 922.1
Payments											
Service of the National Debt:											
Interest	KJDM	21 334.7	24 004.0	25 942.5	27 877.8	26 792.1	24 073.7	23 855.8	22 041.2	21 297.2	21 477.2
Management and expenses	KCXY	229.6	297.8	357.8	441.3	544.3	454.1	597.8	555.8	426.0	490.0
Total	KCXZ	21 564.3	24 301.8	26 300.3	28 319.1	27 336.4	24 527.8	24 453.6	22 597.0	21 723.2	21 967.2
Consolidated Fund deficit met from the National Loans Fund	KCYA	41 816.0	39 890.7	28 999.6	2 385.2	−6 081.9	−7 916.5	−33 804.8	10 192.6	25 260.4	42 222.1
Net repayment[5]	KCYB	..	..	..	2 482.1	3 558.2	..	7 083.4	..	..	..
Net lending[6]	KCYC	−974.8	334.1	280.6	−4.2	1 766.3	1 255.9	1 496.5	−786.2	−2 532.4	−3 287.4
International Monetary Fund- maintenance of value of sterling holding	KCYD	226.2	202.1	..	..	..	126.1	21.2	315.2	..	..
International Monetary Fund- additional subscription	KCYE	..	..	..	..	2 826.5	..	..	..	..	..
NILO Gilt-Edged Operations A/C	KJDN	2 500.0	2 500.0	2 500.0	2 000.0	2 500.0	2 500.0	..	..	..	..
Discharge of Treasury Liability to the Bank of England Issue Department	KPUK	30.7	11.9	18.6	15.1	11.4	8.5	1.2	18.6	3.6	20.2
Debt Management Account	ZAFB	..	..	..	..	..	15 000.0	40 000.0	..	..	7 000.0
Total	KCYF	65 162.4	67 240.6	58 099.1	35 197.3	31 916.9	35 501.8	39 251.1	32 337.2	44 454.8	67 922.1

1 See chapter text.
2 Payment to National Loans Fund representing its payments for the service of the National Debt *less* its receipts of interest on loans outstanding, etc.
3 Includes net issues to Contingencies Fund.
4 Prior to 1996-97, receipts from the Bank of England for appreciation of the assets of the Issue Department were included in the total amount for the profits of the Issue Department.
5 See Table 18.6.
6 Minus sign indicates a net issue repayment.

Source: HM Treasury: 020 7270 4761

18.5 Taxes paid by UK residents to general government and the European Union[1]
Total economy sector S.1

£ million

		1994/95	1995/96	1996/97	1997/98	1998/99	1999/00	2000/01	2001/02	2002/03	2003/04
Generation of income											
Uses											
Taxes on production and imports											
Taxes on products and imports											
Value added tax (VAT)											
Paid to central government	NZGF	43 470	44 275	46 649	52 113	53 911	58 899	61 054	65 200	69 610	77 208
Paid to the European Union	FJKM	3 220	4 942	4 661	3 531	4 105	3 451	4 172	3 592	2 518	2 574
Total	QYRC	46 690	49 217	51 310	55 644	58 016	62 350	65 226	68 792	72 128	79 782
Taxes and duties on imports excluding VAT											
Paid to CG: import duties[2]	NMBS	–	–	–	–	–	–	–	–	–	–
Paid to EU: import duties	FJWE	2 185	2 468	2 290	2 261	2 042	2 049	2 103	2 024	1 893	1 957
Total	QYRB	2 185	2 468	2 290	2 261	2 042	2 049	2 103	2 024	1 893	1 957
Taxes on products excluding VAT and import duties											
Paid to central government											
Customs and Excise revenue											
Beer	GTAM	2 527	2 637	2 631	2 699	2 733	2 848	2 798	2 907	2 952	3 084
Wines, cider, perry & spirits	GTAN	3 017	2 983	2 999	3 057	3 301	3 652	3 814	4 068	4 430	4 526
Tobacco	GTAO	6 952	7 405	7 701	7 622	7 551	7 796	7 638	7 639	8 046	8 096
Hydrocarbon oils	GTAP	14 251	15 679	17 171	19 451	21 553	22 510	22 630	21 916	22 147	22 780
Car tax	GTAT	–	–	–	–	–	–	–	–	–	–
Betting, gaming & lottery	CJQY	1 233	1 591	1 460	1 539	1 527	1 500	1 517	1 317	977	922
Air passenger duty	CWAA	89	354	359	522	845	882	956	802	804	798
Insurance premium tax	CWAD	259	648	685	1 179	1 248	1 511	1 751	1 921	2 189	2 296
Landfill tax	BKOF	–	–	113	364	322	456	475	501	545	639
Other	ACDN	–	–	–	–	–	–	–	–	–	–
Fossil fuel levy	CIQY	1 379	1 272	880	256	164	84	52	92	9	–
Gas levy	GTAZ	211	171	199	188	−44	–	–	–	–	–
Stamp duties	GTBC	1 799	2 018	2 414	3 456	4 623	6 898	8 165	6 983	7 549	7 606
Levies on exports (Third country trade)	CUDF	–	–	–	–	–	–	–	–	–	–
Camelot payments to National Lottery Distribution Fund	LIYH	319	1 527	1 263	1 572	1 665	1 593	1 542	1 520	1 382	1 311
Purchase Tax	EBDB	–	–	–	–	–	–	–	–	–	–
Hydro-benefit	LITN	24	28	31	32	32	38	44	44	44	43
Aggregates Levy	MDUQ	–	–	–	–	–	–	–	–	293	356
Other taxes and levies	GCSP	–	–	–	–	–	–	–	–	–	–
Total paid to central government	NMBV	32 060	36 313	37 906	41 937	45 520	49 768	51 382	49 710	51 367	52 457
Paid to the European Union											
Sugar levy	GTBA	116	36	37	72	44	46	43	27	25	23
European Coal & Steel Community levy	GTBB	–	–	–	–	–	–	–	–	–	–
Total paid to the European Union	FJWG	116	36	37	72	44	46	43	27	25	23
Total taxes on products excluding VAT & import duties	QYRA	32 176	36 349	37 943	42 009	45 564	49 814	51 425	49 737	51 392	52 480
Total taxes on products and imports	NZGW	81 051	88 034	91 543	99 914	105 622	114 213	118 754	120 553	125 413	134 219
Production taxes other than on products											
Paid to central government											
Consumer Credit Act fees	CUDB	153	166	113	168	158	140	150	143	160	146
National non-domestic rates	CUKY	12 785	13 481	13 010	13 283	13 764	14 353	15 168	16 252	16 728	16 942
Old style non-domestic rates	NSEZ	124	124	126	136	130	123	132	131	123	120
Levies paid to CG levy-funded bodies	LITK	130	134	147	162	171	241	207	175	144	150
Selective employment tax	CSAH	–	–	–	–	–	–	–	–	–	–
National insurance surcharge	GTAY	–	–	–	–	–	–	–	–	–	–
London Regional Transport levy	GTBE	–	–	–	–	–	–	–	–	–	–
IBA levy	GTAL	–	–	–	–	–	–	–	–	–	–
Motor vehicle duties paid by businesses	EKED	1 290	1 331	1 365	1 405	1 503	1 559	1 230	751	736	815
Regulator fees	GCSQ	69	57	54	57	61	69	72	62	60	60
Climate change levy	LSNT	–	–	–	–	–	–	–	822	813	822
Total	NMBX	14 551	15 293	14 815	15 211	15 787	16 485	16 959	18 336	18 764	19 055
Paid to local government											
Old style non-domestic rates	NMYH	92	100	114	124	131	144	150	161	144	144
Total production taxes other than on products	NMYD	14 643	15 393	14 929	15 335	15 918	16 629	17 109	18 497	18 908	19 199
Total taxes on production and imports, paid											
Paid to central government	NMBY	90 081	95 881	99 370	109 261	115 218	125 152	129 395	133 246	139 741	148 720
Paid to local government	NMYH	92	100	114	124	131	144	150	161	144	144
Paid to the European Union	FJWB	5 521	7 446	6 988	5 864	6 191	5 546	6 318	5 643	4 436	4 554
Total	NZGX	95 694	103 427	106 472	115 249	121 540	130 842	135 863	139 050	144 321	153 418

18.5
Taxes paid by UK residents to general government and the European Union[1]
Total economy sector S.1

continued

£ million

		1994 /95	1995 /96	1996 /97	1997 /98	1998 /99	1999 /00	2000 /01	2001 /02	2002 /03	2003 /04
Secondary distribution of income											
Uses											
Current taxes on income, wealth etc											
Taxes on income											
Paid to central government											
Household income taxes	DRWH	70 361	74 974	75 191	81 895	89 739	96 967	106 866	108 556	110 435	114 585
Petroleum revenue tax	DBHA	711	968	1 729	963	502	853	1 518	1 310	958	1 179
Windfall tax	EYNK	–	–	–	2 610	2 614	–	–	–	–	–
Other corporate taxes	BMNX	17 031	20 748	25 715	29 844	31 263	36 164	35 878	35 338	31 830	30 965
Total	NMCU	88 103	96 690	102 635	115 312	124 118	133 984	144 262	145 204	143 223	146 729
Other current taxes											
Paid to central government											
Motor vehicle duty paid by households	CDDZ	2 556	2 686	2 802	3 045	3 116	3 296	3 039	3 540	3 600	3 944
Old style domestic rates	NSFA	80	79	104	115	114	117	108	109	117	120
Licences	NSNP	9	11	10	11	8	8	2	–	–	–
National non-domestic rates paid by non-market sectors	BMNY	–	–	930	929	971	1 002	997	1 065	1 011	993
Total	NMCV	2 645	2 776	3 846	4 100	4 209	4 423	4 146	4 714	4 728	5 057
Paid to local government											
Old style domestic rates	NMHK	56	60	61	64	62	68	76	80	72	72
Community charge	NMHL	–	–	–	–	–	–	–	–	–	–
Council tax	NMHM	8 611	9 294	10 059	10 850	12 037	12 918	14 155	15 371	16 809	18 958
Total	NMIS	8 667	9 354	10 120	10 914	12 099	12 986	14 231	15 451	16 881	19 030
Total	NVCM	11 312	12 130	13 966	15 014	16 308	17 409	18 377	20 165	21 609	24 087
Total current taxes on income, wealth etc											
Paid to central government	NMCP	90 748	99 466	106 481	119 412	128 327	138 407	148 408	149 918	147 951	151 786
Paid to local government	NMIS	8 667	9 354	10 120	10 914	12 099	12 986	14 231	15 451	16 881	19 030
Total	NMZL	99 415	108 820	116 601	130 326	140 426	151 393	162 639	165 369	164 832	170 816
Social contributions											
Actual social contributions											
Paid to central government											
(National Insurance Contributions)											
Employers' compulsory contributions	CEAN	23 334	24 533	25 950	27 761	29 779	31 717	35 087	35 702	35 397	41 061
Employees' compulsory contributions	GCSE	17 974	18 889	19 611	22 073	23 255	23 623	24 973	25 308	25 800	30 762
Self- and non-employed persons' compulsory contributions	NMDE	1 524	1 585	1 658	1 858	1 712	1 823	2 008	2 151	2 331	2 956
Total	AIIH	42 832	45 007	47 219	51 692	54 746	57 163	62 068	63 161	63 528	74 779
Capital account											
Changes in liabilities and net worth											
Other capital taxes											
Paid to central government											
Inheritance tax	GILF	1 383	1 484	1 517	1 649	1 764	2 016	2 181	2 346	2 323	2 488
Tax on other capital transfers	GILG	26	34	41	35	41	38	55	37	47	30
Development land tax and other	GCSV	–	–	–	–	–	–	–	–	–	–
Total	NMGI	1 409	1 518	1 558	1 684	1 805	2 054	2 236	2 383	2 370	2 521
Total taxes and compulsory social contributions											
Paid to central government	GCSS	225 070	241 872	254 628	282 049	300 096	322 776	342 107	348 708	353 590	377 803
Paid to local government	GCST	8 759	9 454	10 234	11 038	12 230	13 130	14 381	15 612	17 025	19 174
Paid to the European Union	FJWB	5 521	7 446	6 988	5 864	6 191	5 546	6 318	5 643	4 436	4 554
Total	GCSU	239 350	258 772	271 850	298 951	318 517	341 452	362 806	369 963	375 051	401 531
Total taxes and social contributions as percentage of GDP	GDWM	*34.7*	*35.5*	*35.0*	*36.3*	*36.5*	*37.2*	*37.8*	*36.8*	*35.4*	*35.9*

1 See chapter text.
2 These taxes existed before the UK's entry into the EEC in 1973

Sources: HM Treasury;
Office for National Statistics: 020 7533 5991

18.6 Borrowing and repayment of debt[1]
United Kingdom
Years ending 31 March

£ million

		1994/95	1995/96	1996/97	1997/98	1998/99	1999/00	2000/01	2001/02	2002/03	2003/04
Borrowing											
Government securities: new issues	KQGA	32 137.5	34 150.3	40 800.8	28 484.4	12 048.0	26 426.5	25 789.8	43 433.4	54 068.9	53 220.9
National savings securities:											
National savings certificates	KQGB	2 187.9	3 425.9	3 695.5	4 435.2	3 028.7	1 962.7	3 086.2	2 580.7	2 434.3	1 940.4
Capital bonds	KQGC	521.5	504.8	450.8	619.0	469.6	35.4	29.0	40.9	107.3	65.0
Income bonds	KQGD	1 255.7	780.7	1 272.7	1 043.4	1 371.7	653.4	760.5	625.6	484.8	415.3
Deposit bonds	KQGE	..	..	..	..	..	..	..	..	..	..
British savings bonds	KQGF	..	..	..	..	..	..	..	..	..	..
Premium savings bonds	KQGG	1 837.2	2 040.6	2 552.5	3 158.8	3 652.8	3 449.4	3 296.0	3 859.6	4 604.5	7 530.1
Save As You Earn	KQGH	66.5	50.8	34.1	20.7	11.4	5.0	0.3	..	..	..
Yearly plan	KQGI	116.5	94.1	..	..	5.2	..	..	..	..	..
National savings stamps and gift tokens	KQGJ	..	..	..	..	..	..	..	..	..	..
National Savings Bank Investments	KQGK	1 368.1	1 312.1	1 478.7	1 282.3	1 085.0	901.6	955.3	864.9	1 012.4	809.9
Children's Bonus Bonds	KGVO	118.9	144.9	352.4	255.3	205.0	58.5	53.4	45.0	54.0	51.7
First Option Bonds	KIAR	812.0	826.4	1 139.8	1 152.9	1 001.8	34.3	..	..	..	..
Pensioners Guaranteed Income Bond	KJDW	1 190.3	2 104.2	2 863.8	1 126.9	201.0	590.7	687.2	603.5	662.9	274.2
Treasurer's account	KWNF	..	..	21.1	39.9	17.1	13.6	12.5	15.2	19.4	13.9
Individual Savings Account	ZAFC	..	..	..	..	..	257.8	265.9	397.8	405.6	335.4
Fixed Rate Savings Bonds	ZAFD	..	..	..	..	..	175.9	284.7	192.7	193.0	82.0
Guaranteed Equity Bonds	ECPU	..	..	..	..	..	..	..	27.2	274.8	227.9
Easy Access Savings Account	C3OM	..	..	..	..	..	..	..	..	..	126.9
Certificate of tax deposit	KQGL	91.2	76.2	109.4	84.1	66.4	121.4	76.5	77.6	59.6	145.2
Nationalised industries', etc temporary deposits	KQGM	29 294.0	36 870.6	53 198.2	46 375.9	39 962.4	40 343.3	56 106.6	62 150.0	55 395.1	47 958.6
Sterling Treasury bills (net receipt)	KQGO	5 196.1	2 606.1	..	..	3 546.2	..	..	..	..	..
ECU Treasury bills (net receipt)	KQGP	..	..	..	..	..	..	..	..	..	..
ECU Treasury notes (net receipt)	KDZZ	429.8	..	..	..	..	721.1	..	..	..	..
Ways and means (net receipt)	KQGQ	8 891.7	1 162.3	511.1	..	183.6	5 599.0	12 126.0	12 095.3	3 899.9	22 700.2
Other debt : payable in sterling :											
Interest free notes	KQGR	382.6	247.4	99.2	32.4	2 130.9	373.5	972.7	1 427.2	754.0	1 213.2
Other debt : payable in external currencies	KHCY	..	..	2 565.2	..	..	..	..	..	..	1 792.5
Total receipts	KHCZ	85 897.5	86 397.4	111 145.3	88 111.2	68 986.8	81 723.1	104 502.6	128 436.6	124 430.5	138 903.3
Repayment of debt											
Government securities: redemptions	KQGS	9 333.3	4 652.7	14 488.4	20 678.9	18 575.5	19 815.8	33 722.2	43 642.3	42 109.9	35 087.4
Statutory sinking funds	KQGT	2.3	2.2	2.2	2.1	2.0	2.0	2.0	1.9	1.9	1.8
Terminable annuities:											
National Debt Commissioners	KQGU	..	..	..	..	..	..	..	..	..	..
National savings securities:											
National savings certificates	KQGV	1 612.6	2 258.4	3 263.7	4 058.5	3 449.0	2 405.2	4 546.8	4 177.7	4 146.7	2 769.1
Capital bonds	KQGW	647.7	509.0	698.3	1 160.5	888.3	324.2	375.0	175.9	155.9	116.9
Income bonds	KQGX	1 181.8	1 256.9	1 394.0	1 148.9	880.8	1 686.3	857.0	933.8	1 144.2	977.1
Deposit bonds	KQGY	72.3	72.5	64.8	72.6	84.2	70.2	71.1	45.4	369.9	4.4
Yearly Plan	KQGZ	77.0	101.9	96.3	113.2	120.0	141.8	18.4	4.5	3.0	2.0
British savings bonds	KQHA	..	..	..	..	..	..	..	..	..	..
Premium savings bonds	KQHB	333.0	590.1	869.3	1 203.1	1 398.4	1 923.8	1 872.6	1 942.9	2 343.3	2 967.4
Save As You Earn	KQHC	92.3	98.7	70.1	68.2	37.1	34.5	22.9	8.0	3.2	0.5
National savings stamps and gift tokens	KQHD	..	..	..	..	..	..	..	..	..	..
National Savings Bank Investments (repayments)	KQHE	1 745.3	1 755.8	1 837.0	2 175.7	2 027.0	1 886.3	1 654.1	1 415.8	1 350.1	1 342.7
Children's Bonus Bonds	KGVQ	4.3	0.1	257.8	187.9	183.2	69.3	95.0	114.5	92.6	79.8
First Option Bonds	KIAS	969.9	732.7	833.9	1 283.0	1 055.5	298.1	225.2	111.6	77.4	62.2
Pensioners Guaranteed Income Bond	KPOB	57.0	104.5	185.0	318.8	897.8	935.3	2 003.8	1 640.4	703.9	538.5
Treasurer's account	KWNG	..	..	1.2	11.8	13.7	16.4	13.9	16.5	16.9	14.2
Individual Savings Account	ZAFE	..	..	..	..	..	12.3	39.9	70.3	105.9	157.6
Fixed Rate Savings Bonds	ZAFF	..	..	..	..	..	2.8	62.1	110.1	133.6	153.1
Guaranteed Equity Bonds	JUWE	..	..	..	..	..	..	..	..	3.9	3.3
Easy Access Savings Account	C3ON	..	..	..	..	..	..	..	..	..	126.9
Certificates of tax deposit	KQHF	612.1	466.0	478.9	229.0	199.9	159.9	120.1	91.4	161.5	113.1
Tax reserve certificates	KQHG	..	..	..	..	..	..	..	..	..	..
Nationalised industries', etc temporary deposits	KQHH	28 557.8	35 263.1	51 979.3	46 835.7	41 776.9	41 089.4	56 004.0	63 127.9	55 695.6	47 757.7
Debt to the Bank of England	KPOC	11.0	..	..	..	..	..	..	..	..	..
Sterling Treasury bills (net repayment)	KQHJ	..	..	4 009.6	1 928.5	..	3 014.8	6 194.2	..	..	..
ECU Treasury bills (net repayment)	KJEG	..	..	..	..	..	2 492.9	..	..	..	..
ECU Treasury notes (net repayment)	KSPA	..	439.1	318.3	3.3	13.2	..	1 391.9	1 359.6	1 453.1	..
Ways and means (net repayment)	KQHK	..	..	..	5 815.4	..	..	..	..	..	..
Other debt: payable in sterling :											
Interest free notes	KQHL	225.2	301.3	87.6	1 215.5	850.5	246.4	458.2	1 723.3	1 393.3	990.5
Other	KQHM	..	..	..	..	..	..	..	..	..	..
Other debt : payable in external currencies	KQHN	514.5	103.6	2 661.7	2 082.7	92.0	98.1	1 835.6	2 838.1	1 960.3	47.0
Total payments	KQHO	46 049.4	48 708.6	83 597.4	90 593.3	72 545.0	76 725.8	111 586.0	123 551.9	113 426.1	93 313.2
Net borrowing	KQHP	39 848.1	37 688.8	27 547.9	..	..	4 997.3	..	4 884.7	11 004.4	45 590.1
Net repayment	KHDD	..	..	..	2 482.1	3 558.2	..	7 083.4	..	..	..

1 See chapter text.

Source: HM Treasury: 020 7270 4761

Consolidated Fund and National Loans Fund: assets and liabilities[1]
United Kingdom
At 31 March each year

£ million

		1995	1996	1997	1998	1999	2000	2001	2002	2003
CONSOLIDATED FUND										
Total estimated assets	KQIA	33 992.4	33 809.0	36 177.4	36 061.0	36 148.0	33 932.1	35 967.9	37 458.5	39 694.1
Subscriptions and contributions to international financial organisations	KQIB	5 898.1	6 470.8	6 528.9	6 660.8	7 059.7	6 903.6	7 298.4	7 564.4	8 540.3
International Bank for Reconstruction and Development	KQIC	265.2	271.6	265.0	262.5	266.0	267.1	279.2	279.0	268.2
International Finance Corporation	KQID	62.0	73.1	74.9	72.9	75.6	76.5	85.8	85.7	77.2
International Development Association	KQIE	3 005.5	3 205.8	3 372.7	3 562.2	3 733.3	3 900.0	4 134.0	4 347.8	4 567.5
African Development Bank	KQIF	141.2	148.3	162.9	180.0	199.1	215.7	229.8	259.8	293.9
Asian Development Bank	KQIG	201.5	214.6	240.4	272.5	304.6	339.3	365.5	393.3	420.4
Caribbean Development Bank	KQIH	32.6	34.2	34.1	34.6	36.8	40.7	41.9	44.0	49.1
European Investment Bank	KQII	1 876.4	2 166.6	2 036.5	1 840.7	2 083.1	1 706.6	1 767.3	1 742.1	2 419.2
European Bank for Reconstruction and Development	KPOD	146.3	189.4	175.6	164.2	179.2	170.0	187.4	197.6	239.3
Inter-American Development Bank	KQIJ	107.2	119.6	117.5	219.3	127.8	130.6	145.7	147.3	135.6
International Fund for Agricultural Development	KQIK	42.7	44.2	46.1	48.8	51.0	53.7	56.4	59.1	62.1
Multilateral Investment Guarantee Agency	KQIL	3.2	3.4	3.2	3.1	3.2	3.3	5.4	8.7	7.8
Loans from Votes	KQIP	13 599.7	12 967.0	13 684.7	14 050.0	11 546.3	3 970.3	7 015.3	9 006.1	11 097.1
Issues of public dividend capital:	KQIQ	11 467.0	12 161.1	12 424.8	13 157.1	16 238.5	21 338.3	20 083.6	19 546.2	18 982.3
Army Base Repair Organisation (ABRO)	C3QV	..	..	..	..	..	..	..	..	19.4
Royal Mint	KQIV	7.0	7.0	7.0	7.0	7.0	7.0	7.0	5.5	5.5
Welsh Development Agency	KQIY	10.9	9.8	8.9	8.8	8.6	9.1	9.1	11.0	12.7
British Shipbuilders	KQJA	1 598.3	1 598.3	1 598.5	1 598.3	50.0	21.0	21.0	21.0	21.0
Patent Office	KIAT	6.3	6.3	6.3	6.3	6.3	6.3	6.3	6.3	6.3
NHS Trusts	KIAU	9 603.1	10 173.8	10 349.7	11 078.0	14 158.7	19 216.6	19 539.2	19 184.1	18 600.7
Companies House	KIAV	15.9	15.9	15.9	15.9	15.9	15.9	15.9	15.9	15.9
Central Office of Information	KIAW	0.3	0.3	0.3	0.3	0.3	0.3	0.3	0.3	0.3
Chessington Computer Centre	KPOE	3.5	3.5	..	..	..	..	..	..	..
OGC Buying Solutions[2]	KWNH	0.1	0.4	0.4	0.4	0.4	0.4	0.4	0.4	0.4
Defence Aviation Repair Agency	JRVU	..	..	..	..	..	..	..	42.3	42.3
Defence Evaluation and Research Agency	KWNI	128.8	253.0	274.5	274.5	275.4	275.4	275.4	..	..
Defence Scientific Technology Laboratory	JRVV	..	..	..	..	..	..	..	50.4	50.4
Fire Service College	KWNJ	16.7	16.7	16.7	16.7	16.7	16.7	16.7	16.7	16.7
Forensic Science Service	GPVB	..	..	..	..	–	18.0	18.0	18.0	18.0
Hydrographic Office	GPVC	..	..	..	..	..	13.3	13.3	13.3	13.3
Land Registry	KWNK	55.4	55.4	61.5	61.5	61.5	61.5	61.5	61.5	61.5
Medicines Control Agency	KWNL	1.6	1.6	1.6	1.6	1.6	1.6	1.6	1.6	..
Meteorological Office	KZAZ	..	..	58.9	58.9	58.9	58.9	58.9	58.9	58.9
NHS Estates	GPVD	..	..	..	..	..	0.4	0.4	0.4	0.4
Registers of Scotland	KZBA	..	..	4.3	4.3	4.3	..	..	..	..
Vehicle Inspectorate	KWNM	19.1	19.1	20.3	20.3	20.3	20.3	20.3	20.3	20.3
Driving Standards Agency	LQMI	..	..	..	3.5	3.5	3.5	3.5	3.5	3.5
Ordnance Survey	GPVE	..	..	..	..	..	14.0	14.0	14.0	14.0
Queen Elizabeth II Conference Centre	LQMJ	..	..	..	0.8	0.8	0.8	0.8	0.8	0.8
Contingencies Fund - capital	KQJB	447.0	297.0	977.0	577.0	277.0	277.0	277.0	277.0	..
Balance on revenue accounts	KQJC	1 433.6	1 096.1	954.9	1 546.0	1 026.5	1 442.9	1 293.6	1 064.8	1 074.4
Privatisation receipts	KIAX	1 147.0	817.0	1 607.1	70.1	..	..	..	..	..
Total liabilities	KQJD	..	333 927.9	364 803.0	364 950.8	363 625.5	354 807.7	327 180.6	341 162.2	366 453.7
Liability to balance National Loans Fund	KQJE	286 055.9	331 164.9	362 506.5	362 582.5	361 065.3	351 626.3	324 336.7	338 550.1	362 496.5
Payment from Votes:	KQJF	64.3	63.4	62.4	61.3	60.2	59.0	57.7	56.4	54.9
Married quarters for Armed Forces	KQJG	64.3	63.4	62.4	61.3	60.2	59.0	57.7	56.4	54.9
Liability to Post Office										
Post-war credits outstanding and interest due - estimated	KQJI	46.0	45.9	45.9	45.9	45.9	45.8	45.8	45.8	45.8
Revenue paid over in advance of collection	KQJJ	37.0	..	28.2	13.8	177.9	259.7	301.7	635.6	1 293.7
Inland Revenue	KQJK	–	–	–	–	177.9	259.7	301.7	635.6	1 293.7
Customs and Excise	KQJL	..	..	28.2	..	..	..	..	..	..
Vehicle Excise Duty	KQJN	37.0	..	..	13.8	..	..	..	..	..
Promissory notes issued by Minister of Overseas Development	KQJQ	996.7	1 005.8	1 021.9	822.1	963.1	783.1	939.9	891.9	954.7
International Development Association	KQJR	656.5	663.2	673.6	484.0	612.3	445.6	553.1	509.7	589.4
African Development Fund	KQJS	93.2	86.2	95.3	95.2	105.6	89.1	141.6	145.5	152.3
Asian Development Bank	KQJT	–	–	–	–	–	1.9	2.5	2.4	2.3
Asian Development Fund	KQJU	140.5	127.6	136.0	120.5	105.4	87.8	78.6	73.2	68.3
Caribbean Development Bank	KQJV	1.3	1.4	1.3	1.3	1.3	1.3	1.5	1.5	1.4
Special Development Fund	KQKC	9.5	10.6	13.2	15.8	16.4	16.9	15.9	13.8	17.3
Inter-American Development Bank	KQJY	1.3	2.0	1.8	1.9	1.0	2.0	1.4	0.7	0.2

18.7
continued

Consolidated Fund and National Loans Fund: assets and liabilities[1]
United Kingdom
At 31 March each year

£ million

		1995	1996	1997	1998	1999	2000	2001	2002	2003
Promissory notes issued by										
Minister of Overseas Development (continued)										
Fund for special operations	KQJZ	13.1	11.3	8.8	6.3	2.6	2.1	1.1	..	..
International Fund for Agricultural Development	KQKA	15.8	14.2	12.3	14.2	16.5	18.4	15.6	12.9	9.9
International Bank for Reconstruction and Development	KQKB	39.2	60.7	71.7	81.9	94.3	105.9	112.5	114.6	88.5
European Bank for Reconstruction and Development	KIAY	20.9	21.0	6.1	..	7.7	12.1	16.1	17.6	19.8
United Nations Environment Programme	KJEH	5.4	7.6	1.8	1.0	..	..	..	..	5.3
Other contributions and instalments due in respect of international subscriptions, etc	KQYX	1 499.6	1 647.9	1 138.1	1 425.2	1 313.1	1 669.2	1 174.0	955.1	1 608.1
NATIONAL LOANS FUND										
Total assets	KQKD	349 159.5	390 681.8	419 548.9	418 444.7	421 635.7	426 239.2	425 955.6	434 544.6	448 006.3
Total National Loans Fund loans outstanding	KQKE	47 496.1	46 600.9	46 746.8	46 742.6	48 513.6	49 788.8	51 037.6	50 251.4	47 719.0
Loans to Public Corporations:										
Royal Mail Group plc	KQKF	..	..	..	..	..	..	500.0	500.0	550.0
Scottish Nuclear Ltd	KQKM	194.1	96.1	..	..	..	..	..	..	..
Railtrack	KTCR	1 287.7	..	..	..	..	..	..	..	..
European Passenger Services	KTCS	99.0	761.0	..	..	..	..	..	..	..
Civil Aviation Authority	KQKQ	453.3	476.1	447.5	420.9	365.7	342.5	92.5	9.8	8.8
British Railways Board	KQKS	749.2	718.3	601.2	573.7	546.2	518.7	481.3	..	..
British Waterways Board	KQKU	18.3	18.2	18.2	18.2	18.2	18.2	16.7	16.3	14.7
New Towns - Development Corporations and Commission	KQLD	1 008.8	314.3	122.2	36.2	8.0	8.0	8.0	8.0	7.9
Scottish Homes	KQLF	397.3	395.0	392.5	259.8	190.9	179.0	161.6	149.7	138.1
Housing Corporation (England)	KQLH	869.9	926.3	848.7	4.0	4.0	3.0	3.0	2.0	2.0
Housing for Wales	KQLI	69.2	59.0	..	..	..	..	..	..	..
Land Authority for Wales	KQLL	3.2	3.2	1.3	1.3	..	..	..	..	..
Scottish Enterprise	KQLM	1.3	0.6	0.5	0.1	..	..	..	..	..
Welsh Development Agency	KQLN	0.9	1.1	1.2	1.2	0.9	0.6	0.3	0.2	0.1
Land Registry Trading Fund	KPOF	..	..	..	..	..	..	..	..	..
Development Board for Rural Wales	KQLO	8.8	7.9	4.1	4.0	4.0	4.0	4.0	4.0	4.0
Royal Mint	KQLP	–	–	–	–	–	2.0	5.0	14.8	11.3
Crown Agents	KQLS	2.0	1.9	..	..	..	..	..	..	..
Her Majesty's Stationery Office	KQLT	..	7.0	..	..	..	..	..	..	..
Urban Development Corporations	KQLU	..	..	..	..	..	..	..	..	..
Harbour Authorities	KQLV	0.8	0.7	0.6	0.5	0.4	0.2	0.1	0.1	0.1
UK Atomic Energy Authority	KQLX	147.3	141.0	..	..	..	..	..	..	..
Ordnance Survey	GPVF	..	..	..	..	..	15.5	13.9	12.3	11.0
Central Office of Information	KJEI	0.5	0.3	..	..	..	..	..	..	..
Registers of Scotland	KZBB	..	..	6.4	5.6	5.1	4.5	4.0	3.7	3.6
East of Scotland Water Authority	KZBC	..	..	163.0	229.0	288.0	283.0	268.0	258.0	248.0
North of Scotland Water Authority	KZBD	..	..	155.0	189.2	242.0	236.5	236.5	236.5	231.5
West of Scotland Water Authority	KZBE	..	..	185.0	304.9	425.6	412.4	412.4	412.4	412.4
Loans to local authorities	KQLY	40 440.7	40 969.2	42 134.0	42 951.1	44 742.7	46 099.2	47 239.1	47 093.4	44 640.3
Loans to private sector:										
Housing associations	KGVS	13.2	12.7	0.5	0.5	0.5	0.5	0.5	..	..
Loans within central government:										
Northern Ireland Exchequer	KGVW	1 666.3	1 627.4	1 602.5	1 681.1	1 611.2	1 602.0	1 533.1	1 473.9	1 380.4
Married quarters for Armed Forces	KGVX	64.3	63.4	62.4	61.3	60.2	59.0	57.7	56.4	54.9
Other assets:										
Exchange Equalisation Account - capital	KGVZ	5 550.0	2 800.0	650.0	..	..	475.0	5 680.0	831.0	30.0
Subscriptions and contributions to international financial organisations:										
International Monetary Fund	KGXE	7 172.2	7 102.6	6 241.2	5 895.6	9 048.1	9 067.4	9 496.6	9 494.5	9 293.8
Gilt-Edged Official Operations Account -advances outstanding	KPUF	2 500.0	2 500.0	3 000.0	2 500.0	2 500.0	..	..	..	..
-surplus not paid to the National Loans Fund	KPUH	..	..	..	141.6	190.8	..	..	..	..
Borrowing included in national debt but not brought to account by 31 March	KGXF	385.2	513.4	404.7	568.6	317.9	281.6	405.9	417.5	467.1
Debt Management Account -advances outstanding	GPVG	..	..	..	..	..	15 000.0	35 000.0	35 000.0	28 000.0
Consolidated Fund liability	KCYI	286 055.9	331 164.9	362 506.2	362 596.4	361 065.3	351 626.3	324 335.5	338 550.2	362 496.5
Total liabilities										
National Loans Fund - national debt outstanding	KCYJ	349 159.5	390 681.8	419 548.9	418 444.7	421 635.7	426 239.2	425 955.6	434 544.6	448 006.3

1 See Chapter text.
2 Formerly The Buying Agency.

Source: HM Treasury: 020 7270 4761

18.8 British government and government guaranteed marketable securities[1]
Nominal values of official and market holdings by maturity[2,3]

At 31 March each year

£ million

		1994	1995	1996	1997	1998	1999	2000	2001	2002	2003	2004
Total holdings	**KQMO**	209 507	232 486	262 262	290 259	297 366	291 788	290 629	285 915	278 808	292 777	321 051
Up to 5 years	**KQMP**	58 437	69 011	81 122	90 357	86 094	95 112	95 131	92 090	92 780	106 074	88 678
Over 5 and up to 15 years	**KQMQ**	94 308	101 960	111 510	125 401	131 758	124 603	116 910	120 101	106 044	101 465	131 665
Over 15 years (including undated)	**KQMR**	56 762	61 515	69 630	74 501	79 515	72 074	78 587	73 724	79 984	85 238	97 500
Official holdings:[3]												
Total	**HHAW**	6 239	6 614	7 186	6 858	6 345	6 394	6 204	8 210	7 558	10 650	9 118
Up to 5 years	**HHAY**	1 685	2 007	2 345	2 850	2 499	2 600	2 849	4 652	3 928	4 797	3 321
Over 5 and up to 15 years	**HHAZ**	3 194	3 700	3 774	3 041	2 726	2 989	2 567	3 009	2 844	4 115	4 015
Over 15 years (including undated)	**HHBA**	1 359	907	1 068	967	1 120	805	788	549	786	1 738	1 540
Market holdings:												
Total	**HHBB**	203 268	225 872	255 075	283 402	291 021	285 394	284 425	277 705	271 250	282 127	311 933
Up to 5 years	**HHBD**	56 751	67 004	78 777	87 508	83 595	92 512	92 282	87 438	88 852	101 277	85 357
Over 5 and up to 15 years	**HHBE**	91 115	98 260	107 736	122 360	129 032	121 614	114 343	117 092	103 200	97 350	127 650
Over 15 years (including undated)	**HHBF**	55 403	60 608	68 562	73 536	78 395	71 269	77 800	73 175	79 198	83 500	95 960

1 The government guaranteed securities of nationalised industries only. A re-latively small amount of other government guaranteed securities is exclud-ed.

2 Securities with optional redemption dates are classified according to the fi-nal redemption date. The nominal value of index-linked British Government Stock has been raised by the amount of accrued capital uplift.

3 Official holdings were changed following the introduction of the central bank sector in the UK national accounts. These holdings now principally include those of the Debt Management Office and other government departments. The Issue and Banking Departments of the Bank of England are classified within the central bank sector and are therefore part of market holdings.

Source: Bank of England: 020 7601 3598

18.9 Income tax: allowances and reliefs[1]
United Kingdom

		1994 /95	1995 /96	1996 /97	1997 /98	1998 /99	1999 /00	2000 /01	2001 /02	2002 /03	2003 /04	2004 /05
Personal allowances												
Personal allowance	KDZP	3 445	3 525	3 765	4 045	4 195	4 335	4 385	4 535	4 615	4 615	4 745
Married couple's (both partners under 65)[2]	KDZR	1 720	1 720	1 790	1 830	1 900	1 970	..	..	..	..	..
Age allowance:												
Personal (aged 65-74)	KSOH	4 200	4 630	4 910	5 220	5 410	5 720	5 790	5 990	6 100	6 610	6 830
Personal (aged 75 or over)	KSOI	4 370	4 800	5 090	5 400	5 600	5 980	6 050	6 260	6 370	6 720	6 950
Married couple's (either partner between 65-74 but neither partner 75 or over)[2,3]	KEDI	2 665	2 995	3 115	3 185	3 305	5 125	5 185	5 365	5 465	5 565	5 725
Married couple's (either partner 75 or over)[2]	KEIY	2 705	3 035	3 155	3 225	3 345	5 195	5 255	5 435	5 535	5 635	5 795
Minimum married couple's allowance	C58D	1 720	1 720	1 790	1 830	1 900	1 970	2 000	2 070	2 110	2 150	2 210
Income limit[4]	KEOO	14 200	14 600	15 200	15 600	16 200	16 800	17 000	17 600	17 900	18 300	18 900
Additional personal allowance[2]	KEPG	1 720	1 720	1 790	1 830	1 900	1 970	..	..	..	..	..
Widow's bereavement allowance	KEPH	1 720	1 720	1 790	1 830	1 900	1 970	..	..	..	..	..
Blind person's allowance												
Single or married (one spouse blind)	KSOJ	1 200	1 200	1 250	1 280	1 330	1 380	1 400	1 450	1 480	1 510	1 560
Married (both spouses blind)	KSOK	2 400	2 400	2 500	2 560	2 660	2 760	2 800	2 900	2 960	3 020	3 120
Life Assurance Relief												
Percentage of gross premium	KFDR	12.5 or Nil	12.5 or Nil	12.5 or Nil	12.5 or Nil	12.5 or Nil	12.5 or Nil	12.5 or Nil	12.5 or Nil	12.5 or Nil	12.5 or Nil	12.5 or Nil

1 See chapter text.
2 The allowance was restricted to 20 per cent in 1994-95, 15 per cent from 1995-96 and 10 per cent from 1999-00
3 At least one of the partners must be aged 65 before April 2000 to be entitled to the married couple's allowance (MCA). From 2000-01 only people born before 6 April 1935 are entitled to MCA.

4 If the total income, less allowable deductions of a taxpayer aged 65 or over exceeds the limit, the age-related allowances are reduced by £1 for each £2 of income over the aged income level until the basic levels of the personal and married couple's allowances are reached.

Source: Board of Inland Revenue: 020 7147 3082

18.10 Rates of Income tax
United Kingdom

	1995/96		1996/97		1997/98		1998/99		1999/00	
	Bands of taxable income (£)[1]	Rate of tax - Percent-ages	Bands of taxable income (£)[1]	Rate of tax - Percent-ages	Bands of taxable income (£)[1]	Rate of tax - Percent-ages	Bands of taxable income (£)[1]	Rate of tax - Percent-ages	Bands of taxable income (£)[1]	Rate of tax - Percent-ages
Lower rate or starting rate[2]	1 - 3 200	20	1 - 3 900	20	1 - 4 100	20	1 - 4 300	20	1 - 1 500	10[4]
Basic rate	3 201 - 24 300	25[3]	3 901 - 25 500	24[4]	4 101 - 26 100	23[4]	4 301 - 27 100	23[4]	1 501 - 28 000	23[6]
Higher rate	over 24 300	40	over 25 500	40	over 26 100	40	over 27 100	40	over 28 000	40[7]

	2000/01		2001/02		2002/03		2003/04		2004/05	
	Bands of taxable income (£)[1]	Rate of tax - Percent-ages	Bands of taxable income (£)[1]	Rate of tax - Percent-ages	Bands of taxable income (£)[1]	Rate of tax - Percent-ages	Bands of taxable income (£)[1]	Rate of tax - Percent-ages	Bands of taxable income (£)[1]	Rate of tax - Percent-ages
Starting rate	1 - 1 520	10[5]	1 - 1 880	10[5]	1 - 1 920	10[5]	1 - 1 960	10[5]	1 - 2 020	10[5]
Basic rate	1 521 - 28 400	22[6]	1 880 - 29 400	22[6]	1 920 - 29 900	22[6]	1 960 - 30 500	22[6]	2 020 - 31 400	22[6]
Higher rate	over 28 400	40[7]	over 29 400	40[7]	over 29 900	40[7]	over 30 500	40[7]	over 31 400	40[7]

1 Taxable income is defined as gross income for income tax purposes less any allowances and reliefs available at the taxpayer's marginal rate.
2 In 1999/00 the starting rate replaced the lower rate.
3 The basic rate of tax on dividend income is 20%.
4 The basic rate of tax on dividends and savings income is 20%.
5 The starting rate also applies to savings and dividends.
6 The basic rate of tax on dividends is 10% and savings income is 20%
7 The higher rate of tax on dividends is 32.5%.

Source: Board of Inland Revenue: 020 7147 3082

18.11 Rateable values[1]
England and Wales
At 1 April each year

		1994	1995	1996	1997	1998	1999	2000	2001	2002	2003	2004
Number of properties (Thousands)												
Commercial	KMIN	1 227	1 223	1 228	1 225	1 223	1 219	1 223	1 230	1 234	1 236	1 239
Shops and cafes	KMIO	565	562	497	491	488	484	478	476	473	469	466
Offices	KMIP	251	252	255	255	257	258	261	269	273	279	284
Other	KMIQ	411	409	476	479	478	477	484	485	487	488	490
On-licensed premises	KMIR	55	60	59	59	59	60	61	61	60	60	60
Entertainment and recreational:	KMIS	92	87	87	87	81	80	79	79	80	80	80
Cinemas	KMIT	1	1	1	1	1	1	1	1	1	1	1
Theatres and music-halls	KMIU	1	1	1	1	1	1	1	1	1	1	1
Other	KMIV	91	86	85	86	80	79	76	76	77	77	78
Public utility	KMIW	15	9	8	8	9	9	8	8	8	8	8
Educational and cultural	KMIX	41	41	41	41	41	41	41	42	42	42	43
Miscellaneous	KMIY	58	56	55	55	56	61	67	70	70	72	74
Industrial	KMIZ	247	248	249	249	250	250	250	251	250	250	250
Total	KMIH	1 734	1 723	1 726	1 725	1 719	1 720	1 729	1 740	1 745	1 749	1 754
Value of assessments (£ million)												
Commercial	KMHG	20 662	19 626	19 822	19 859	19 733	19 652	26 320	27 255	27 622	27 713	27 878
Shops and cafes	KMHH	7 068	7 780	6 094	5 959	5 860	5 840	6 801	6 972	6 953	6 863	6 845
Offices	KMHI	8 027	5 587	5 630	5 641	5 624	5 575	8 625	9 191	9 388	9 555	9 591
Other	KMHJ	5 568	6 260	8 098	8 259	8 249	8 237	10 894	11 092	11 281	11 295	11 441
On-licensed premises	KMHK	642	968	969	970	980	997	1 311	1 347	1 345	1 334	1 320
Entertainment and recreational	KMHL	988	1 009	1 018	1 033	1 040	1 045	1 310	1 369	1 430	1 416	1 362
Cinemas	KMHM	24	32	32	36	39	45	79	92	104	106	96
Theatres and music-halls	KMHN	19	21	21	21	21	20	24	25	26	26	26
Other	KMHO	946	956	965	975	979	980	1 207	1 252	1 300	1 284	1 240
Public utility	KMHP	3 424	3 455	3 469	3 488	3 380	3 361	3 828	3 411	3 460	3 444	3 410
Educational and cultural	KMHQ	1 813	1 873	1 883	1 894	1 773	1 672	1 829	1 872	1 902	1 895	1 904
Miscellaneous	KMHR	1 319	1 429	1 500	1 494	1 464	1 439	2 142	2 172	2 220	2 218	2 022
Industrial	KMHS	5 280	5 550	5 584	5 561	5 540	5 463	6 249	6 202	6 157	6 034	5 935
Total	KMHA	34 129	33 912	34 245	34 299	33 909	33 649	42 985	43 626	44 136	44 053	43 831

1 See chapter text.

Source: Board of Inland Revenue: 020 7438 6314

18.12 Local authorities: gross loan debt outstanding[1]
At 31 March each year

£ billion

		2000	2001	2002	2003	2004
United Kingdom						
Total debt	KQBR	51.5	52.2	52.2	51.2	50.5
Public Works Loan Board	KQBS	46.1	47.1	46.9	44.6	41.3
Northern Ireland Consolidated Fund	KQBT	0.3	0.3	0.3	0.3	0.3
Other debt	KQBU	5.2	4.8	5.0	6.3	8.8
England						
Total debt	C300	38.0	38.5	38.3	38.2	37.7
of which Public Works Loan Board	C30P	34.1	34.8	34.4	33.4	31.1
Wales						
Total debt	C30Q	3.4	3.5	3.6	3.7	3.6
of which Public Works Loan Board	C30R	3.0	3.2	3.3	3.3	3.1
Scotland						
Total debt	KQBX	9.8	9.9	10.0	8.8	8.8
of which Public Works Loan Board	KQBY	*8.9*	*9.1*	*9.3*	*7.9*	*7.1*
Northern Ireland						
Total debt	KQBZ	0.3	0.3	0.3	0.3	0.3
of which Northern Ireland Consolidated Fund	KQBT	0.3	0.3	0.3	0.3	0.3

1 The sums shown exclude inter-authority loans.

Sources: Office of the Deputy Prime Minister: 020 7944 4176;
Public Works Loan Board: 020 7862 6610;
Department of Finance and Personnel for Northern Ireland: 028 9185 8130

18.13 Revenue expenditure of local authorities

£ million

	2001/02 outturn	2002/03 outturn	2003/04 budget	2004/05 budget
England				
Education[1]	26 121	28 404	30 186	32 510
Transport	3 052	3 438	3 738	5 363
of which:				
Highways	1 969	1 948	2 341	2 203
Public transport	1 082	1 490	1 397	3 159
Social Services[2]	11 505	12 984	14 083	15 585
Housing (excluding HRA)[3]	6 523	7 505	7 717	12 590
Cultural, environmental and planning	6 430	6 924	7 565	8 137
of which:				
Cultural	1 840	1 921	2 680	2 819
Environmental	3 483	3 786	3 457	3 786
Planning and development	1 107	1 217	1 428	1 532
Police	7 912	8 246	9 140	9 739
Fire	1 608	1 698	1 852	2 029
Courts	398	401	391	398
Central services	2 465	2 703	2 973	2 905
Other	414	338	604	582
Net current expenditure	66 427	72 641	78 249	89 838
Capital financing	1 861	1 922	2 317	2 544
Capital Expenditure charged to Revenue Account	672	694	661	524
Interest receipts	-917	-851	-657	-660
Other non-current expenditure[4]	2 349	2 507	2701	2 800
Specific grants outside Aggregate External Finance (AEF)	-8 443	-11 011	-10 799	-15 649
Revenue expenditure	61 952	65 906	72 473	79 397
Specific and special grants inside AEF	-6 552	-8 923	-9 187	-12 240
Net revenue expenditure	55 400	56 996	63 286	67 157
Other adjustments	-49	-30	-23	-2
Use of reserves	-8	177	-247	-594
Budget requirement	55 343	57 144	63 016	66 561
SSA reduction grant	-2		-	-
Police grant	-3 798	-3 808	-4 079	-4 168
Revenue support grant	-21 093	-19 889	-24 215	-26 964
Central Support Protection Grant	-1		-	-
Council Tax Benefit Subsid Limitation Scheme	83		-	-
Non-domestic rates	-15 137	-16 632	-15 611	-15 004
General Greater London Authority Grant	-23	-28	-36	-36
Other items	-126	-138	-130	-90
Council tax requirement	15 246	16 648	18 946	20 299
Scotland				
Net revenue expenditure on general fund	7 727	8 565	..	..

£ million

	2001/02 outturn	2002/03 outturn	2003/04 budget	2004/05 budget
Wales[5]				
Education	1 650.9	1 738.7	1 892.8	2 005.1
Personal social services	746.5	856.6	938.5	1 014.5
Council fund housing, including housing benefit[6]	287.0	329.6	332.9	639.3
Local environmental services[7]	207.7	227.6	284.5	299.9
Roads and transport	188.4	217.3	247.7	249.6
Libraries, culture, heritage, sport and recreation	195.0	207.6	148.5	161.2
Planning, economic development, community development and tourism	63.2	69.8	92.0	98.0
Magistrates', coroners' and other courts	24.6	25.7	28.9	30.1
Council tax benefit and administration[8]	33.6	33.9	35.7	31.3
Local tax collection	17.0	16.2	16.4	..
Debt financing costs: counties	244.1	238.0	260.6	269.5
Central administrative and other revenue expenditure: counties[9,10]	159.4	182.2	245.6	259.2
Total county and county borough council expenditure	3 800.3	4 127.1	4 507.7	5 057.6
Police operational expenditure	419.2	451.6	487.2	519.3
Other police expenditure[9]	15.8	8.1	16.3	29.2
Total police expenditure	435.1	459.8	503.5	548.5
Fire operational expenditure	100.7	106.4	112.7	124.0
Other fire expenditure[9]	3.1	2.6	3.0	2.7
Total fire expenditure	103.8	109.0	115.7	126.7
National park operational expenditure	10.0	10.7	12.0	13.9
Other national park expenditure[9]	1.2	2.1	2.4	2.6
Total national park expenditure	11.2	12.8	14.4	16.6
Gross revenue expenditure	4 350.4	4 708.6	5 141.2	5 749.3
less specific and special government grants (except council tax benefit grant)	-601.1	-778.8	-846.8	-1 287.9
Net revenue expenditure	3 749.2	3 929.8	4 294.4	4 461.4
Putting to (-)/drawing from (+) reserves	7.8	27.8	-33.0	-50.7
Buget requirement	3 757.0	3 957.6	4 261.4	4 410.6
Plus discretionary non-domestic rate relief	1.7	1.9	2.2	2.2
less revenue support grant	-2 146.8	-2 340.5	-2 533.4	-2 591.0
less police grant	-194.6	-196.1	-209.2	-212.0
less re-distributed non-domestic rates income	-697.0	-643.0	-660.0	-672.0
less transitional grant	-4.0	-4.8	..	..
Council tax requirement	716.4	775.7	861.0	924.1
of which:				
Paid by council tax benefit grant from the Department for Work and Pensions	113.0	120.0	128.8	143.3
Paid directly by council tax payers	603.4	655.6	732.2	780.8

1 Includes mandatory student awards and inter-authority education recoupment.
2 Includes supported employment.
3 Includes mandatory rent allowances and rent rebates.
4 Includes:
  (i) Gross expenditure on council tax benefit.
  (ii) Expenditure on council tax reduction scheme.
  (iii) Discretionary (non-domestic) rate relief.
  (iv) Flood defence payments to the Environment Agency
  (v) Bad debt provision.
5 Service expenditure is shown excluding that financed by sales, fees and charges, but including that financed by specific and special government grants. For definitions of the below please e-mail: LGFS.Transfer@Wales.gsi.gov.uk

6 Includes housing benefit, and private sector housing costs such as provision for the homeless. Excludes council owned housing. For 2004-05, includes rent rebates granted to HRA tenants which is 100% grant funded.
7 Includes cemetery and cremation and mortuary service, environmental health, street cleansing, waste collection and disposal.
8 Net of council tax benefit grant.
9 Includes central administrative costs of corporate management, democratic representation and certain costs, such as those relating to back-year or additional pension contributions which should not be allocated to individual services. The figure also includes capital expenditure charged to the revenue account and is net of any interest expected to accrue on balances.
10 The figure includes emergency planning, agricultural services, coastal and licensing.

Sources: Office of the Deputy Prime Minister: 020 7944 4158;
Scottish Executive, Economic Advice & Statistics: 0131 244 7033;
National Assembly for Wales: 029 2082 5355

18.14 Funding of revenue expenditure
England and Wales
Years ending 31 March

£ million

		1994/95	1995/96	1996/97	1997/98	1998/99	1999/00	2000/01	2001/02	2002/03	2003/04 [1]	2004/05 [1]
England												
Revenue expenditure[2]												
2004/05 prices £m[3]	KRTM	56 377	56 328	56 575	56 017	57 828	60 497	63 903	67 342	69 307	74 146	79 397
Cash £m	KRTN	43 602	44 827	46 532	47 256	50 189	53 651	57 329	61 952	65 906	72 473	79 397
Government grants[4]												
Cash £m	KRTO	23 679	23 335	23 003	23 840	25 291	26 421	27 809	31 469	32 643	37 517	43 408
Percentage of revenue expenditure	KRTP	54	52	49	50	50	49	49	51	50	52	55
Non- domestic rates[5]												
Cash £m	KRTQ	10 692	11 361	12 743	12 034	12 531	13 619	15 407	15 144	16 639	15 618	15 004
Percentage of revenue expenditure	KRTR	25	25	27	25	25	25	27	24	25	22	19
Community charges and council taxes[6]												
Cash £m	KRTS	9 239	9 777	10 461	11 241	12 332	13 278	14 200	15 246	16 648	18 946	20 299
Percentage of revenue expenditure	KRTT	21	22	22	24	25	25	25	25	25	26	26
Wales[7]												
Revenue expenditure	ZBXH	2 755	2 932	2 990	3 121	3 246	3 424	3 605	3 860	4 065	4 488	4 975
General government grants[8]	ZBXI	1 881	1 873	2 001	1 957	2 009	2 093	2 234	2 345	2 541	2 743	2 817
Specific government grants[9]	ZBXG	73	70	73	75	84	80	94	111	135	193	514
Share of redistributed non- domestic rates	ZBXJ	464	520	459	584	612	656	638	697	643	660	672
Community charge/council tax income[10]	ZBXK	354	394	449	483	542	596	670	716	776	861	924
Other[11]	ZBXL	−17	75	9	22	..	−1	−31	−10	−30	31	49

1 Budget figures
2 Expenditure financed from revenue support grant, specific grants within Aggregate External Finance, special grants, non domestic rates, community charges/council taxes and balances. Also include spending met by SSA Reduction Grant (1994/95 onwards), Police Grant (1995/96 onwards), Central Support Reduction Grant (1999/00 onwards) and Greater London Local Authority Grant (2000/01 onwards). This series is not the total of the others. The difference is due to funding by balances and other adjustments.
3 Revenue expenditure at 2004/05 prices have been calculated using the GDP deflator.
4 Revenue support grants, specific and special grants within AEF, SSA Reduction grant (1994/95 to 2001/02), Police grant (1995/96 onwards), Central Support Reduction Grant (1999/00 to 2001/02) and General Greater London Authority Grant (2000/01 onwards).
5 Distributables amount from non-domestic rate pool including City Offset (1994/95 to 2003/04).
6 1994/95 onwards: gross of council tax benefit. 1994/95 to 1995/96: gross of council tax transitional reduction scheme.

7 Revenue expenditure is gross revenue expenditure excluding that funded by specific grants outside AEF. This excludes expenditure on services, which are mainly administered by the local authorities on behalf of local government, for example mandatory students awards, so that the measure is a better reflection of total local authority expenditure. Revenue expenditure is often referred to as expenditure on a total standard spending basis (total assumed spending for 2003/04).
8 Includes all unhypothecated grants, namely revenue support grant, police grant, council tax reduction scheme grant and the adjustment to reverse the transfer out of nursery voucher monies in 1997-98.
9 Comprises specific and supplementary grants within aggregate external finance, excluding police grant.
10 This includes community council precepts, and income covered by community charge/council tax benefit grant, but excludes council tax reduction scheme grant.
11 This includes use of, or contributions to, local authority reserves and other minor adjustments.

Sources: Office of the Deputy Prime Minister: 020 7944 4158;
National Assembly for Wales: 029 2082 5355

18.15 Local authority capital expenditure and receipts
England
Final outturn: Years ending 31 March

£ million

		1998/99	1999/00	2000/01	2001/02	2002/03	2003[1]/04
Expenditure[2]							
Education	KRUD	995	1 139	1 533	2 064	2 287	2 749
Personal Social Services	KRUE	140	134	156	158	199	263
Transport	KRUC	1 053	1 086	1 410	1 877	2 461	2 400
Housing	KRUB	2 513	2 406	2 779	3 110	3 828	3 461
Arts and libraries	GEKZ	150	195	194	213	208	178
Agriculture and fisheries	GELA	57	48	45	38	65	19
Sport and recreation	KRUH	235	241	291	314	307	337
Other[3]	GELB	1 140	1 299	1 341	1 513	1 631	2 149
Fire and civil defence	GELC	49	50	46	62	72	65
Police and probation	GELD	263	286	291	359	408	508
Magistrates courts	GELE	33	28	22	33	40	33
Total	KRUR	6 630	6 912	8 109	9 741	11 508	12 162
Receipts[4]							
Education	KRUT	82	102	119	146	233	224
Personal social services	KRUV	52	51	63	71	75	89
Transport	KRUU	64	105	98	138	107	135
Housing	KRUS	1 630	2 249	2 441	2 245	3 474	3 706
Arts and libraries	GELF	6	2	19	19	22	3
Agriculture and fisheries	GELG	51	48	44	42	49	56
Sport and recreation	KRUX	10	8	12	12	21	12
Other[3]	GELH	687	960	600	801	975	1 239
Fire and civil defence	GELI	3	5	8	7	10	18
Police and probation	GELJ	76	118	104	86	70	81
Magistrates court	GELK	–	2	4	12	4	6
Total	KRVB	2 662	3 651	3 512	3 579	5 040	5 571

1 Provisional outturn. The figures shown here have been adjusted based on historical differences between provisional and final outturn
2 Includes aquisition of share or loan capital.
3 Environmental services, consumer protection and employment services.
4 Includes disposal of share or loan capital and disposal of other investments.

Source: Office of the Deputy Prime Minister: 020 7944 4076

18.16 Capital expenditure and income
England

£ million

	Expenditure			Income				
	Expenditure on land works, etc	Capital assigned to repayment of debt	All expenditure	Loans	Government grants	Miscellaneous	All income	Gross debt at end of year
Financial year								
	KRVC	KRVD	KRVE	KRVF	KRVG	KRVH	KRVI	KRVJ
1972/73	2 418	213	2 631	2 030	122	531	2 682	16 105
1973/74	3 286	225	3 511	2 781	143	619	3 544	18 300
1974/75[1]	3 712	127	3 839	3 209	128	498	3 835	18 884
1975/76	3 917	198	4 115	3 285	177	647	4 109	21 930
1976/77	3 783	312	4 095	3 097	249	803	4 149	24 534
1977/78	3 487	352	3 839	2 677	255	981	3 913	26 282
1978/79	3 621	390	4 011	2 627	351	1 139	4 117	27 103
1979/80	4 249	331	4 580	2 992	385	1 367	4 745	30 187
1980/81	4 476	413	4 889	2 900	492	1 864	5 256	32 076
1981/82	4 061	563	4 623	2 527	470	2 177	5 174	34 069
1982/83	5 090	634	5 724	3 358	416	3 100	6 874	36 231
1983/84	5 890	562	6 452	3 538	379	3 294	7 211	38 698
1984/85	6 352	515	6 867	3 381	327	3 283	6 991	40 554
1985/86	5 748	348	6 096	3 008	360	3 239	6 607	40 138
1986/87	5 899	328	6 227	2 814	388	3 878	7 081	43 033
1987/88	6 091	486	6 577	2 953	297	4 286	7 536	44 904
1988/89	7 166	658	7 824	2 985	270	6 122	9 376	47 295
1989/90	9 590	474	10 064	2 919	440	6 110	9 469	48 695

	Gross capital expenditure	Income					Capital receipts set aside[2]	Credit ceiling[3]	Provision for credit liabilities[3]
		Credit approvals used	Government grants	Capital receipts	Other income	Total income			
Financial year									
At 1 April 1990	-	-	-	-	-	-	4 241	42 167	4 241
	KRVK	KRVL	KRVM	KRVN	KRVO	KRVP	KRVQ	KRVR	KRVS
1990/91	6 869	2 786	907	3 165	542	7 400	2 022	41 125	5 677
1991/92	6 572	3 140	1 041	2 251	674	7 106	1 353	41 234	6 502
1992/93	6 567	3 229	1 210	2 110	619	7 168	908	37 051	6 282
1993/94	7 124	2 948	1 279	3 310	651	8 188	356	37 941	6 041
1994/95	6 950	2 722	1 176	2 458	724	7 080	1 409	37 673	6 921
1995/96	6 910	2 264	1 484	1 966	1 278	6 992	1 160	37 103	7 677
1996/97	6 419	2 120	1 388	2 183	1 132	6 823	1 039	37 261	8 172
1997/98	6 298	2 099	1 262	2 349	1 129	6 839	1 186	36 711	7 540
1998/99	6 630	2 334	1 160	2 662	1 413	7 569	1 130	36 782	7 108
1999/00	6 912	2 301	1 161	3 651	1 487	8 600	1 483	36 364	7 201
2000/01	8 109	3 216	1 298	3 512	2 219	10 245	1 642	36 628	7 231
2001/02	9 741	2 551	2 027	3 579	2 994	11 151	1 403	36 732	7 081
2002/03	11 508	3 216	2 474	5 040	2 858	13 588	1 922	36 608	6 940

1 Reorganisation of local government in April 1974 transferred responsibility for various services to regional health and water authorities.
2 Excluding Social Housing Grant and European Regional Development Fund (ERDF) grants.
3 At end of year.

Source: Office of the Deputy Prime Minister: 020 7944 4076

18.17 Expenditure of local authorities
Scotland
Year ending 31 March

£ thousand

		1993/94	1994/95	1995/96	1996/97	1997/98	1998/99	1999/00	2000/01	2001/02	2002/03
Out of revenue:[1] Total	KQTA	8 713 471	9 111 751	9 690 424	9 196 125	9 566 936	10 033 985	10 439 999	10 924 634	11 553 927	12 858 533
General Fund Services:	KQTB	6 589 420	6 904 228	7 324 381	7 151 759	6 679 396	7 021 038	7 429 626	7 884 168	8 428 217	9 290 268
Education	KQTC	2 537 582	2 563 049	2 654 158	2 629 961	2 512 725	2 649 170	2 855 945	3 037 780	3 283 827	3 533 853
Libraries, museums and galleries	KQTD	125 791	132 055	149 427	138 483	121 387	124 648	131 696	134 174	138 318	152 308
Social work	KQTE	914 436	1 045 638	1 222 693	1 289 928	1 315 387	1 394 142	1 519 191	1 632 843	1 793 732	2 173 752
Law, order and protective services	KQTF	804 616	828 480	866 567	816 315	931 795	952 940	1 006 000	1 047 034	1 088 791	1 130 693
Roads and Transport[2]	KQTG	650 555	684 452	676 116	716 570	440 712	546 945	527 018	564 738	506 326	601 454
Environmental services	KQTH	322 534	330 039	351 689	329 674	343 565	349 413	373 050	393 333	414 975	484 177
Planning	KQTI	202 027	211 346	226 073	210 827	163 380	179 078	198 285	194 771	223 414	265 315
Leisure and recreation	KQTJ	396 874	405 083	451 952	426 422	364 853	368 023	375 579	387 115	401 904	426 495
Other services	KQTL	516 842	580 561	591 766	562 462	456 219	430 790	435 155	465 612	572 136	515 661
Other general fund expenditure[3]	KQTM	118 163	123 525	133 940	31 117	29 373	25 889	7 707	26 768	4 794	6 560
Housing	KQTN	1 738 427	1 806 022	1 924 930	2 000 684	1 658 935	1 754 686	1 821 380	1 886 189	1 954 444	2 224 209
Trading services:	KQTO	503 787	525 026	575 053	74 799	75 976	79 644	87 321	80 355	61 899	74 062
Water supply	KQTP	239 291	255 081	274 773	..	..	..	..	..	..	..
Sewerage	KQTQ	200 036	209 323	233 525	..	..	..	..	..	..	..
Passenger transport	KQTR	681	685	794	2 849	1 524	121	336	162	343	427
Ferries	KQTS	7 203	7 574	7 744	6 831	7 512	8 930	9 709	10 005	9 650	11 493
Harbours, docks and piers	KQTT	16 215	16 804	15 301	13 482	12 884	15 697	15 923	13 604	10 912	12 222
Road bridges	KQTV	10 948	7 579	11 755	12 759	16 064	16 408	8 231	8 606	6 914	7 267
Slaughterhouses	KQTW	985	976	1 000	794	850	228	4	..	..	..
Markets	KQTX	8 462	8 615	10 336	14 278	13 479	13 161	14 106	23 844	16 657	17 995
Other trading services	KQTY	19 966	18 389	19 825	23 806	23 663	25 099	39 012	24 134	17 423	24 658
Loan charges:[4] Total	KQTZ	1 346 433	1 383 167	1 451 179	1 121 448	1 126 637	1 152 728	1 109 379	1 100 690	1 114 161	1 269 994
Allocated to :											
General Fund services	KMHV	649 212	677 377	710 801	639 380	651 982	710 371	701 515	708 822	739 351	738 870
Housing	KMHW	505 407	499 904	504 162	475 507	471 274	438 556	402 936	386 512	369 943	525 201
Trading services	KMHX	191 814	205 886	236 216	6 561	3 381	3 801	4 928	5 356	4 867	5 923
On capital works:[5] Total	KQUA	1 428 545	1 518 362	1 528 167	889 572	813 900	815 981	816 473	802 672	929 631	972 049
General Fund Services:	KQUB	699 250	760 564	767 795	540 127	540 096	541 769	557 119	538 843	610 485	662 869
Education	KQUC	85 619	113 121	114 128	101 898	112 753	125 341	136 508	127 781	143 268	157 439
Libraries, museums and galleries	KQUD	11 077	12 822	16 757	11 602	9 974	13 231	10 261	5 834	8 683	19 018
Social work	KQUE	29 040	29 067	30 298	20 658	19 660	22 554	22 097	21 539	31 359	30 116
Law, order and protective services	KQUF	32 951	33 635	35 847	41 326	37 701	37 727	37 132	35 761	39 901	53 268
Roads and Transport	KQUG	189 525	198 178	187 988	116 881	108 227	113 954	108 500	117 485	147 975	147 357
Environmental services	KQUH	18 905	16 595	14 580	10 226	21 193	18 397	14 936	17 944	16 396	17 957
Planning	KQUI	76 477	102 152	103 221	51 182	69 648	50 854	52 045	47 684	33 312	40 241
Leisure and recreation	KQUJ	74 563	65 411	57 243	36 232	29 692	40 926	52 365	44 516	39 240	50 558
Administrative buildings and equipment	KQUK	17 888	23 994	14 693	40 014	45 374	35 107	35 824	34 633	53 189	68 438
Other services	KQUL	163 205	165 589	193 040	110 108	85 814	83 678	87 451	85 666	97 162	78 477
Housing	KQUM	467 811	497 997	517 593	345 713	270 005	268 135	255 019	255 189	300 054	284 418
Trading Services:	KQUN	261 484	259 801	242 779	3 732	3 799	6 077	4 335	8 640	19 092	24 762
Water supply	KQUO	128 081	123 564	107 064	..	..	..	..	..	..	..
Sewerage	KQUP	127 047	130 634	131 684	..	..	..	..	..	..	..
Ferries	KQUR	..	376	355	521	770	268	1 030	23	467	1
Harbours, docks and piers	KQUS	2 300	1 982	1 218	934	1 175	1 626	1 389	6 192	15 898	20 361
Airports	KQUT	184	173	763	1 149	439	..	..	607	663	1 031
Road bridges	KQUU	799	830	805	277	973	2 791	600	964	882	2 386
Slaughterhouses	KQUV	1 068	139	63	112	69	54	12	..	40	116
Other trading services	KMHY	2 005	2 103	827	739	373	1 338	1 304	854	1 142	867

1 Gross expenditure *less* inter-authority and inter-account transfers.
2 Including general fund support for transport (LA and NON-LA).
3 General fund contributions to Housing and Trading services (excluding transport), are also included in the expenditure figures for these services. From 1996/97 water and sewerage are excluded from other general fund expenditure.

4 From 1997/98 loan charges are not included within individual service totals.
5 Expenditure out of loans, government grants and other capital receipts.

Source: Scottish Executive, Local Government Finance Statistics: 0131 244 7033

Income of local authorities: classified according to source
Scotland
Year ending 31 March £ thousand

		1992 /93	1993 /94	1994 /95	1995 /96	1996 /97	1997 /98	1998 /99	1999 /00	2000 /01	2001 /02	2002 /03
Revenue account												
Rates[1]	KQXA	1 336 395	1 258 863	1 198 575	1 310 721	1 313 531	1 326 129	1 437 646	1 440 522	1 662 691	1 553 926	1 718 104
Community charges	KQXB	932 994	..	..	..	..	..	..	..	..	..	..
Council tax	KPUC	..	822 830	918 502	976 465	9 681 531	70 405	1 146 366	1 193 693	1 273 316	1 363 399	1 459 212
Government grants												
Revenue Support Grant	KQXC	3 546 958	3 582 127	3 741 567	3 716 567	3 649 694	3 520 461	3 483 815	3 537 043	3 440 842	3 935 328	4 557 867
Rate rebate grant	KQXG	33 741	41 772	39 860	4 456	496	..	..	..	..	..	..
Community charge grant[2]	KIMJ	15 512	..	..	..	..	..	..	..	..	..	..
Community charge rebate grants	KQXH	153 231	..	..	..	..	..	..	..	..	..	..
Council tax rebate grants	KPUD	..	166 015	186 219	193 937	226 132	260 424	274 940	275 789	279 459	285 131	293 606
Other grants and subsidies	KQXI	1 049 899	1 118 978	1 179 327	1 236 160	1 347 706	1 480 890	1 642 045	1 778 216	1 891 839	2 061 297	2 141 543
Sales	KQXJ	54 399	61 970	59 182	64 284	59 059	46 874	39 595	43 660	49 826	..	..
Fees and charges[3]	KQXK	1 435 951	1 421 565	1 471 320	1 528 270	1 539 611	1 625 952	1 668 223	1 682 385	1 776 455	1 789 428	1 954 337
Other income[4]	KQXL	184 581	194 151	209 819	207 005	238 985	290 427	324 932	398 894	453 458	490 574	712 423
Capital account												
Sale of fixed assets	KQXM	413 083	441 600	529 528	500 838	499 143	327 569	335 037	303 582	149 504	165 016	207 388
Revenue contributions to capital	KQXP	111 710	163 228	134 156	197 606	119 641	149 423	204 982	213 564	210 912	147 760	239 778
Transfer from special funds	KMHZ	1 751	7 902	10 679	9 035	2 652	36 929	26 959	125 365	27 317	37 087	39 650
Other receipts[5]	KMGV	42 631	32 554	38 736	29 571	45 067	32 118	45 028	39 014	45 351	90 360	75 846

1 Excluding government grants towards rate rebates and domestic element of revenue support grant (RSG). Including domestic water rate receipts.
2 Payment to local authorities in respect of the £140 reduction in community charge awarded.
3 From 2001-02 onwards, fees & charges incorporates sales.
4 From 1996-97 Other Income includes income from Health Boards and Trusts, Other Public Bodies and Interest on Revenue Balances.
5 2001-02 figure includes £41,238K public sector contributions.

Source: Scottish Executive, Local Government Finance Statistics: 0131 244 7033

Income of local authorities from government grants[1]
Scotland
Year ending 31 March £ thousand

		1993 /94	1994 /95	1995 /96	1996 /97	1997 /98	1998 /99	1999 /00	2000 /01	2001 /02	2002 /03
General fund services	KQYA	428 927	450 056	468 660	487 734	557 536	690 569	818 537	935 452	1 032 591	952 692
Education	KQYB	21 791	17 452	17 186	18 324	61 960	92 368	225 668	324 340	380 726	251 333
Libraries, museums and galleries	KQYC	108	247	123	137	326	627	507	634	1 137	5 359
Social work	KQYD	36 734	48 091	50 230	57 576	59 892	62 167	71 611	78 611	86 533	114 591
Law, order and protective services	KQYE	288 835	295 600	312 812	330 767	359 811	366 961	382 246	401 485	423 636	445 275
Roads and Transport[2]	KQYF	1 993	4 315	4 788	403	237	97 649	68 429	57 702	49 900	57 664
Environmental services	KQYG	84	82	42	119	159	89	71	301	2 272	5 407
Planning and Economic Development	KQYH	1 310	867	3 030	3 337	4 885	2 695	4 311	4 375	20 351	19 434
Leisure and recreation	KQYI	1 476	1 609	1 830	1 509	1 856	1 509	1 491	2 377	3 322	2 968
Other services	KQYK	76 596	81 793	78 619	75 562	68 410	66 504	64 203	65 627	64 714	50 661
Housing	KQYL	684 519	723 604	762 172	856 435	920 700	948 232	959 276	956 239	1 028 529	1 188 626
Trading services	KQYM	4 954	4 009	4 557	..	..	..	403	148	177	225
Water supply	KQYN	4 823	4 009	4 459	..	..	..	..	..	..	..
Ferries	KQYO	47	..	..	..	..	..	..	..	..	..
Other trading services	KQYP	84	..	98	..	..	..	403	148	177	225
Grants not allocated to specific services[3]	KMGY	3 789 914	3 781 426	3 721 023	3 650 190	3 520 461	3 483 815	3 537 043	3 440 842	3 935 328	4 557 867
Total	KMGZ	4 908 314	4 959 095	4 956 412	4 994 362	4 998 697	5 122 616	5 315 259	5 332 681	5 996 625	6 699 410

1 Including grants for capital works.
2 The significant increase in 1998/99 is due to the different reporting of a grant in aid of expenditure on rail passenger services in the Strathclyde Passenger Transport area.
3 Revenue support grant, community charge grant and community charge rebate grants.

Source: Scottish Executive, Local Government Finance Statistics: 0131 244 7033

18.20 Expenditure of local authorities[1]
Northern Ireland
Years ending 31 March

£ thousand

		1992 /93	1993 /94	1994 /95	1995 /96	1996 /97	1997 /98	1998 /99	1999 /00	2000 /01	2001[2] /02	2002[3] /03
Libraries, museums and art galleries	KQVB	4 644	5 647	7 214	8 481	10 956	13 928	14 571	19 900	23 097	24 181	32 728
Environmental health services:												
Refuse collection and disposal	KQVC	33 582	39 952	42 109	41 284	52 267	56 246	56 360	62 226	65 289	73 395	89 448
Public baths	KQVD	1 505	1 562	1 648	1 703	1 838	2 585	2 634	1 750	1 724	1 423	..
Parks, recreation grounds, etc	KQVE	80 601	91 258	101 319	100 418	111 884	115 302	118 396	158 304	170 999	184 406	194 224
Other sanitary services	KQVF	27 593	32 074	34 582	35 706	39 545	39 682	42 923	44 214	45 552	48 784	52 075
Housing (grants and small dwellings acquisition)[4]	KQVG	792	873	553	472	489	545	358	37	28	27	12
Trading services:												
Cemeteries	KQVI	5 044	5 352	5 984	5 489	5 120	5 626	5 887	5 973	6 151	6 538	7 106
Other trading services (including markets, fairs and harbours)	KQVJ	7 335	7 123	6 587	4 254	8 672	7 016	10 779	9 366	7 209	7 769	18 280
Miscellaneous	KQVK	53 011	46 825	51 741	54 987	63 792	63 375	161 790	86 649	89 881	98 037	86 203
Total expenditure	KQVA	214 107	230 666	251 737	252 794	294 563	304 305	413 698	388 419	409 930	444 560	480 076
Total loan charges	KQVL	21 693	19 194	20 797	21 122	24 363	34 823	26 413	..	..	..	..
Loan charges included in terms of expenditure above:												
Allocated to rate fund services	KQVM	18 785	..	..	..	..	..	..	..	..	..	..
Allocated to trading services	KQVN	2 689	..	..	..	..	..	..	..	..	..	..
Not allocated	KQVO	219	..	..	..	..	..	..	..	..	..	..

1 Out of revenue and special funds.
2 Includes estimates for Antrim and Newtownabbey district councils.
3 Includes estimates for Antrim, Fermanagh and Newtownabbey district councils.
4 Expenditure met out of loans, government grants for capital works, sales of property and other capital receipts.

Source: Department of the Environment for Northern Ireland: 028 9054 0711

External trade and investment

Chapter 19

External trade and investment

External trade

(Table 19.1 and 19.3 to 19.6)

The statistics in this section are on a Balance of Payments (BoP) basis; compiled from information provided to HM Customs and Excise by importers and exporters on an Overseas Trade Statistics (OTS) basis, which values exports 'f.o.b.'(free on board) and imports 'c.i.f.' (including insurance and freight). In addition to deducting these freight costs and insurance premiums from the OTS figures, coverage adjustments are made to convert the OTS data to a BoP basis. Adjustments are also made to the level of all exports and EU imports to take account of estimated under-recording. The adjustments are set out and described in the annual ONS Pink Book (*United Kingdom Balance of Payments*). These adjustments are made to conform to the definitions in the 5th edition of the IMF Balance of Payments Manual.

Aggregate estimates of trade in goods, seasonally adjusted and on a BoP basis are published monthly in the ONS First Release *UK Trade*. More detailed figures are available from the ONS Datashop and are also published in the *Monthly Review of External Trade Statistics* (Business Monitor MM24). Detailed figures for EU and non-EU trade on an OTS basis are published by The Stationery Office in *Overseas Trade Statistics of the United Kingdom*.

A fuller description of how trade statistics are compiled can be found in *Statistics on Trade in Goods* (Government Statistical Service Methodological Series).

Overseas Trade Statistics

HM Customs and Excise provide accurate and up to date information via the website *www.uktradeinfo.com*. They also produce the publications *Overseas Trade Statistics*.

Import penetration and export sales ratios

(Table 19.2)

The ratios were first introduced in the August 1977 edition of *Economic Trends* in an article 'The Home and Export Performance of United Kingdom Industries'. The article described the conceptual and methodological problems involved in measuring such variables as import penetration.

The industries are grouped according to the 1992 Standard Industrial Classification. The four different ratios are defined as follows:

Ratio 1:   percentage ratio of imports to home demand

Ratio 2:   percentage ratio of imports to (home demand plus exports)

Ratio 3:   percentage ratio of exports to total manufacturers' sales

Ratio 4:   percentage ratio of exports to (total manufacturers' sales plus imports).

Home demand is defined as total manufacturers' sales plus imports minus exports. *This is only an approximate estimate as different sources are used for the total manufacturers' sales and the import and export data. Total manufacturers' sales are determined by the ProdCom inquiry and import and export data are provided by Customs & Excise.*

Ratio 1 is commonly used to describe the import penetration of the home market. Allowance is made for the extent of a domestic industry's involvement in export markets by using Ratio 2; this reduces as exports increase.

Similarly Ratio 3 is the measure normally used to relate exports to total sales by UK producers and Ratio 4 makes an allowance for the extent that imports of the same product are coming into the UK.

International trade in services

(Tables 19.7 and 19.8)

These data relate to overseas trade in services and cover both production and non-production industries (excluding the Public Sector). In terms of types of services traded this equates to trade in royalties, various forms of consultancy, computing and telecommunications services, advertising and market research and other business services. A separate inquiry covers the Film and Television industries. The surveys cover receipts from the provision of services to residents of other countries (exports) and payments to residents of other countries for services rendered (imports).

Sources of data

The International Trade in Services (ITIS) surveys (which consist of a quarterly component addressed to the largest businesses and an annual component for the remainder) are based on a sample of companies derived from the Inter-departmental Business register. The companies are asked to show the amounts for their imports and exports against the geographical area to which they were paid or from which they were received – irrespective of where they were first earned.

The purpose of the ITIS survey is to record international transactions which impact on the UK's Balance of Payments, hence companies are asked to exclude from their earnings trade expenses such as the cost of services purchased abroad. Exports and imports of Services are excluded where they are included within an invoice for the import or export of goods; in this case they will already be counted in the estimate for Trade in Goods. However, earnings from third country trade, i.e. from arranging the sale of goods between two countries other than the UK and where the goods never physically enter the UK (known as merchanting), are included. Earnings from commodity trading are also included. Together these two comprise 'Trade Related Services'.

'Royalties' are the largest part of the total trade in services collected in the ITIS survey: these cover transactions for items such as printed matter, sound recordings, performing rights, patents, licences, trademarks, designs, copyrights, manufacturing rights, the use of technical 'know-how' and technical assistance.

Balance of payments

(Tables 19.9 to 19.12)

Tables 19.9 to 19.12 are derived from *United Kingdom Balance of Payments* 2004 edition – the ONS Pink Book. The following general notes to the tables provide brief definitions and explanations of the figures and terms used. Further notes are included in the Pink Book.

Summary of Balance of Payments

The Balance of Payments consists of the current account, the capital account, the financial account and the International Investment Position. The *current account* consists of trade in goods and services, income and current transfers. *Income* consists of investment income and compensation of employees. The *capital account* mainly consists of capital transfers and the *financial account* covers financial transactions. The *International Investment Position* covers balance sheet levels of UK external assets and liabilities. Every credit entry in the balance of payments accounts should, in theory, be matched by a corresponding debit entry so that total current, capital and financial account credits should be equal to, and therefore offset by, total debits. In practice there is a discrepancy termed *net errors and omissions*.

The Current Account

Trade in goods

The goods account covers exports and imports of goods. Imports of motor cars from Japan, for example, are recorded as debits in the trade in goods account whereas exports of vehicles manufactured in the UK are recorded as credits. Trade in goods forms a component of the expenditure measure of Gross Domestic Product (GDP).

Trade in services

The services account covers exports and imports of services (e.g. civil aviation). Passenger tickets for travel on UK aircraft sold abroad, for example, are recorded as credits in the services account whereas the purchases of airline tickets from foreign airlines by UK passengers are recorded as debits. Trade in services, along with trade in goods, forms a component of the expenditure measure of Gross Domestic Product (GDP).

Income

The income account consists of compensation of employees and investment income and is dominated by the latter. Compensation of employees covers employment income from cross-border and seasonal workers which is less significant in the UK than in other countries. Investment income covers earnings (e.g. profits, dividends and interest payments and receipts) arising from cross-border investment in financial assets and liabilities. For example, earnings on foreign bonds and shares held by financial institutions based in the UK are recorded as credits in the investment income account, whereas earnings on UK company securities held abroad are recorded as investment income debits. Investment income forms a component of Gross National Income (GNI) but not Gross Domestic Product (GDP).

Current transfers

Current transfers are composed of central government transfers (e.g. taxes and payments to, and receipts from, the European Union) and other transfers (e.g. gifts in cash or kind received by private individuals from abroad or receipts from the EU, where the UK government acts as an agent for the ultimate beneficiary of the transfer). Current transfers do not form a component either of Gross Domestic Product (GDP) or of Gross National Income (GNI). For example, payments to the UK farming industry under the EU Agricultural Guarantee Fund are recorded as credits in the current transfers account while payments of EU agricultural levies by the UK farming industry are recorded as debits in the current transfers account.

External trade and investment

Capital Account

Capital account transactions involve transfers of ownership of fixed assets, transfers of funds associated with acquisition or disposal of fixed assets and cancellation of liabilities by creditors without any counterparts being received in return. The main components are migrants transfers, EU transfers relating to fixed capital formation (regional development fund and agricultural guidance fund) and debt forgiveness. Funds brought into the UK by new immigrants would, for example, be recorded as credits in the capital account, while funds sent abroad by UK residents emigrating to other countries would be recorded as debits in the capital account. The size of capital account transactions are quite minor compared with the current and financial accounts.

Financial Account

While investment income covers earnings arising from cross-border investments in financial assets and liabilities, the financial account of the balance of payments covers the flows of such investments. Earnings on foreign bonds and shares held by financial institutions based in the UK are, for example, recorded as credits in the investment income account, but the acquisition of such foreign securities by UK based financial institutions are recorded as net debits in the financial account or portfolio investment abroad. Similarly the acquisitions of UK company securities held by foreign residents are recorded in the financial account as net credits or portfolio investment in the UK.

International Investment Position

While the financial account covers the flows of foreign investments and financial assets and liabilities, the International Investment Position records the levels of external assets and liabilities. While the acquisition of foreign securities by UK based financial institutions are recorded in the financial account, as net debits, the total holdings of foreign securities by UK-based financial institutions are recorded as levels of UK external assets. Similarly the holdings of UK company securities held by foreign residents are recorded as levels of UK liabilities.

Foreign direct investment

(Tables 19.13 to 19.18)

Direct investment refers to investment that adds to, deducts from or acquires a lasting interest in an enterprise operating in an economy other than that of the investor, the investor's purpose being to have an effective voice in the management of the enterprise. (For the purposes of the statistical inquiry, an effective voice is taken as equivalent to a holding of 10 per cent or more in the foreign enterprise.) Other investments in

which the investor does not have an effective voice in the management of the enterprise are mainly portfolio investments and these are not covered here. Cross-border investment by public corporations or in property (which is regarded as direct investment in the national accounts) is not covered here, but is shown in the balance of payments. Similarly foreign direct investment earnings data are shown net of tax in Tables 19.15 and 19.18 but are gross of tax in the balance of payments.

Direct investment is a financial concept and is not the same as capital expenditure on fixed assets. It covers only the money invested in a related concern by the parent company and the concern will then decide how to use the money. A related concern may also raise money locally without reference to the parent company.

The investment figures are published on a net basis, that is, they consist of investments net of disinvestments by a company into its foreign subsidiaries, associate companies and branches.

Definitional changes from 1997

The new European System of Accounts (ESA(95)) definitions were introduced from the 1997 estimates. The changes were as follows:

i) Previously for the measurement of direct investment, an effective voice in the management of an enterprise was taken as the equivalent of a 20 per cent shareholding. This is now 10 per cent.

ii) The Channel Islands (Jersey, Guernsey etc.) and the Isle of Man have been excluded from the definition of the economic territory of the UK. Prior to 1987 these islands were considered to be part of the United Kingdom.

iii) Interest received or paid was replaced by interest accrued in the figures on earnings from direct investment. There is deemed to be little or no impact arising from this definitional change on the estimates.

New register sources available from 1998 have led to revisions for the figures from that year onwards. These sources gave an improved estimate of the population satisfying the criteria for foreign direct investment.

The definitional changes have been introduced from 1997 and the register changes from 1998. The data prior to these years have not been reworked in Tables 19.13 to 19.18. For clarity, the Offshore Islands are identified separately on the tables. The breaks in the series for the other definitional changes are not quantified but are relatively small. More detailed information on the effect of these changes appears in the Business Monitor, MA4 – *Foreign Direct Investment* 2002, which was published in February 2003 and is available on the National Statistics website.

Sources of data

The figures in Tables 19.13 to 19.18 are based on annual inquiries into foreign direct investment for 2002. These were sample surveys which involved sending around 1250 forms to UK businesses investing abroad and 2,250 forms to UK businesses in which foreign parents and associates had invested. The tables also contain some revisions to 2001 as a result of new information coming to light in the course of the latest surveys. Further details from the latest annual surveys, including analyses by industry and by components of direct investment, are available in Business Monitor MA4. Initial figures were published on the National Statistics website in a First Release, *Foreign Direct Investment 2002*, in December 2003. Data for 2003 will be published in a First Release in December 2004, followed by the full Business Monitor MA4 in February 2005.

Country allocation

The analysis of inward investment is based on the country of ownership of the immediate parent company. Thus, inward investment in a UK company may be attributed to the country of the intervening overseas subsidiary, rather than the country of the ultimate parent. Similarly, the country analysis of outward investment is based on the country of ownership of the immediate subsidiary. As an example, to the extent that overseas investment in the UK is channelled through holding companies in the Netherlands, the underlying flow of investment from this country is overstated and the inflow from originating countries is understated.

Further information

More detailed statistics on foreign direct investment are available on request from Simon Harrington, Office for National Statistics, Financial & Accounting Surveys Division, Room 2.301, Government Buildings, Cardiff Road, Newport, South Wales, United Kingdom, NP10 8XG. Telephone: 01633 813314, Fax: 01633 812855, e-mail *simon.harrington@ons.gsi.gov.uk*.

19.1 Trade in goods[1]
United Kingdom
Balance of payments basis

£ million and indices (2001=100)

		1993	1994	1995	1996	1997	1998	1999	2000	2001	2002	2003
Value (£ million)												
Exports of goods	**BOKG**	122 229	135 143	153 577	167 196	171 923	164 056	166 166	187 936	190 055	186 517	187 846
Imports of goods	**BOKH**	135 295	146 269	165 600	180 918	184 265	185 869	195 217	220 912	230 703	233 192	235 136
Balance on trade in goods	**BOKI**	−13 066	−11 126	−12 023	−13 722	−12 342	−21 813	−29 051	−32 976	−40 648	−46 675	−47 290
Price index numbers												
Exports of goods	**BQKR**	107.2	109.3	113.2	113.9	108.0	102.7	100.5	101.7	100.0	100.0	101.6
Imports of goods	**BQKS**	101.8	105.3	112.1	111.9	104.4	98.1	97.7	100.9	100.0	97.5	96.8
Terms of trade[2]	**BQKT**	105.3	103.8	101.0	101.8	103.4	104.7	102.9	100.8	100.0	102.6	105.0
Volume index numbers												
Exports of goods	**BQKU**	59.1	65.0	71.4	76.8	83.2	84.2	86.8	97.4	100.0	98.3	97.8
Imports of goods	**BQKV**	56.2	58.7	62.3	68.2	74.9	81.3	86.7	94.8	100.0	104.1	105.6

1 See chapter text. Statistics of trade in goods on a balance of payments basis are obtained by making certain adjustments in respect of valuation and coverage to the statistics recorded in the *Overseas Trade Statistics*. These adjustments are described in detail in *The Pink Book 2004*.
2 Export price index as a percentage of the import price index.

Source: Office for National Statistics: 020 7533 6064

19.2

Import penetration and export sales ratios for products of manufacturing industry[1,2]

United Kingdom: Standard Industrial Classification 1992

Ratios

			2000	2001	2002
Ratio 1 Imports/Home Demand		SIC Division			
Other mining and quarrying	BBAM	14	162	150	162
Food products and beverages	BBAN	15	22	23	23
Tobacco products	BBAO	16	8	15	21
Textiles	BAZJ	17	60	65	70
Wearing apparel: Dressing and dyeing of fur	BAZK	18	86	92	93
Tanning and dressing of leather: Luggage, handbags, saddlery, harness and footwear	BBAP	19	94	92	96
Wood products of wood and cork (except furniture) articles of straw and plaiting materials	BBAQ	20	38	35	38
Pulp, paper and paper products	BBAR	21	39	37	39
Publishing, printing and reproduction of recorded media	BBAS	22	10	10	11
Chemicals and chemical products	BAZL	24	65	72	80
Rubber and plastic products	BBAT	25	30	30	32
Other non metallic mineral products	BBAU	26	21	21	23
Basic metals	BBAV	27	74	73	73
Fabricated metal products (except machinery and equipment)	BBAW	28	46	74	73
Machinery and equipment not elsewhere classified	BBAX	29	60	62	65
Office machinery and computers	BBAY	30	110	133	146
Electrical machinery not elsewhere classified	BBAZ	31	64	66	69
Radio, television and communication equipment and apparatus	BBBA	32	112	131	253
Medical, precision and optical instruments, watches and clocks	BBBB	33	80	85	83
Motor vehicles, trailers and semi-trailers	BBBC	34	136	122	134
Other transport equipment	BBBD	35	74	88	79
Furniture and manufacturing not elsewhere classified	BBBE	36	52	56	60
Total	BAZY		58	61	64
Ratio 2 Imports/Home Demand plus Exports					
Other mining and quarrying	BBBH	14	64	61	53
Food products and beverages	BBBI	15	19	20	21
Tobacco products	BBBJ	16	5	8	11
Textiles	BAZN	17	45	49	52
Wearing apparel: Dressing and dyeing of fur	BAZO	18	68	74	76
Tanning and dressing of leather: Luggage, handbags, saddlery, harness and footwear	BBBK	19	72	74	77
Wood products of wood and cork (except furniture) articles of straw and plaiting materials	BBBL	20	36	33	36
Pulp, paper and paper products	BBBM	21	33	33	34
Publishing, printing and reproduction of recorded media	BBBN	22	8	9	9
Chemicals and chemical products	BAZP	24	38	40	42
Rubber and plastic products	BBBO	25	24	24	26
Other non metallic mineral products	BBBP	26	18	18	20
Basic metals	BBBQ	27	46	46	46
Fabricated metal products (except machinery and equipment)	BBBR	28	31	42	44
Machinery and equipment not elsewhere classified	BBBS	29	37	39	40
Office machinery and computers	BBBT	30	61	64	69
Electrical machinery not elsewhere classified	BBBU	31	41	41	42
Radio, television and communication equipment and apparatus	BBBV	32	56	54	59
Medical, precision and optical instruments, watches and clocks	BBBW	33	45	47	46
Motor vehicles, trailers and semi-trailers	BBBX	34	70	72	73
Other transport equipment	BBBY	35	40	44	45
Furniture and manufacturing not elsewhere classified	BBBZ	36	42	44	48
Total	BBBF		39	41	42

19.2
continued

Import penetration and export sales ratios for products of manufacturing industry[1,2]
United Kingdom: Standard Industrial Classification 1992

Ratios

			2000	2001	2002
Ratio 3 Exports/Sales		SIC Division			
Other mining and quarrying	BBCM	14	168	152	143
Food products and beverages	BBCN	15	14	14	15
Tobacco products	BBCO	16	44	51	52
Textiles	BAZR	17	45	49	53
Wearing apparel: Dressing and dyeing of fur	BAZS	18	66	77	77
Tanning and dressing of leather: Luggage, handbags, saddlery, harness and footwear	BBCP	19	83	76	88
Wood products of wood and cork (except furniture) articles of straw and plaiting materials	BBCQ	20	7	6	7
Pulp, paper and paper products	BBCR	21	20	18	20
Publishing, printing and reproduction of recorded media	BBCS	22	13	13	13
Chemicals and chemical products	BAZT	24	68	74	81
Rubber and plastic products	BBCT	25	25	24	25
Other non metallic mineral products	BBCU	26	18	18	18
Basic metals	BBCV	27	70	68	70
Fabricated metal products (except machinery and equipment)	BBCW	28	47	75	72
Machinery and equipment not elsewhere classified	BBCX	29	60	62	63
Office machinery and computers	BBCY	30	114	145	171
Electrical machinery not elsewhere classified	BBDK	31	62	65	67
Radio, television and communication equipment and apparatus	BBDL	32	113	128	187
Medical, precision and optical instruments, watches and clocks	BBDM	33	79	85	82
Motor vehicles, trailers and semi-trailers	BBDN	34	161	147	170
Other transport equipment	BBDO	35	77	89	78
Furniture and manufacturing not elsewhere classified	BBDP	36	34	38	39
Total	BBCK		53	56	59
Ratio 4 Exports/Sales plus Imports					
Other mining and quarrying	BBDS	14	60	60	67
Food products and beverages	BBDT	15	12	11	12
Tobacco products	BBDU	16	42	47	46
Textiles	BAZV	17	25	25	26
Wearing apparel: Dressing and dyeing of fur	BAZW	18	21	20	19
Tanning and dressing of leather: Luggage, handbags, saddlery, harness and footwear	BBDV	19	23	20	21
Wood products of wood and cork (except furniture) articles of straw and plaiting materials	BBDW	20	5	4	4
Pulp, paper and paper products	BBDX	21	13	12	13
Publishing, printing and reproduction of recorded media	BBDY	22	12	12	12
Chemicals and chemical products	BAZX	24	42	45	47
Rubber and plastic products	BBDZ	25	19	18	18
Other non-metallic mineral products	BBEA	26	15	15	14
Basic metals	BBEB	27	37	37	38
Fabricated metal products (except machinery and equipment)	BBEC	28	32	43	40
Machinery and equipment not elsewhere classified	BBED	29	38	38	38
Office machinery and computers	BBEE	30	45	52	52
Electrical machinery not elsewhere classified	BBEF	31	37	38	39
Radio, television and communication equipment and apparatus	BBEG	32	50	59	77
Medical, precision and optical instruments, watches and clocks	BBEH	33	43	45	44
Motor vehicles, trailers and semi-trailers	BBEI	34	49	41	45
Other transport equipment	BBEJ	35	46	50	43
Furniture and manufacturing not elsewhere classified	BBEK	36	20	21	20
Total	BBDQ		32	33	34

1 See chapter text.

2 Division 13 (Mining of metal ores) has not been published since 1995. Division 23 (Coke, refined petroleum products and nuclear fuel) and SIC 24610 (Manufacture of explosives) are excluded from the analysis. SIC 27100 (Basic iron and steel and ferro-alloys) is not incorporated in PRODCOM and therefore also does not form part of the analysis.

Source: Office for National Statistics: 01633 813065

19.3 United Kingdom exports: by commodity[1,2]
Seasonally adjusted

£ million

		1994	1995	1996	1997	1998	1999	2000	2001	2002	2003
0. Food and live animals	BOGG	6 305	7 079	6 997	6 581	6 286	5 925	5 827	5 499	5 693	6 410
of which:											
01. Meat and meat preparations	BOGS	1 229	1 466	1 081	925	746	657	642	428	517	604
02. Dairy products and eggs	BQMS	692	820	732	745	745	689	660	621	628	728
04 & 08. Cereals and animal feeding stuffs	BQMT	1 523	1 702	2 008	1 800	1 714	1 568	1 604	1 392	1 447	1 679
05. Vegetables and fruit	BQMU	398	456	470	455	408	437	403	405	434	473
1. Beverages and tobacco	BQMZ	3 734	4 113	4 331	4 522	3 930	4 022	4 081	4 151	4 298	4 416
11. Beverages	BQNB	2 865	2 986	3 138	3 305	2 875	3 004	3 065	3 225	3 318	3 491
12. Tobacco	BQOW	869	1 127	1 193	1 217	1 055	1 018	1 016	926	980	925
2. Crude materials	BQOX	2 397	2 725	2 583	2 489	2 267	2 087	2 447	2 429	2 645	3 061
of which:											
24. Wood, lumber and cork	BQOY	45	46	52	52	55	66	72	72	82	107
25. Pulp and waste paper	BQOZ	50	66	57	64	47	54	78	80	106	179
26. Textile fibres	BQPA	571	636	611	568	493	447	496	446	477	492
28. Metal ores	BQPB	663	771	657	642	560	518	759	819	932	1 190
3. Fuels	BOPN	9 492	9 942	11 578	11 016	7 513	9 929	17 057	16 381	15 997	16 502
33. Petroleum and petroleum products	ELBL	9 079	9 384	10 928	10 239	7 018	9 123	15 584	14 811	14 318	14 589
32, 34 & 35. Coal, gas and electricity	BOQI	413	558	650	777	495	806	1 473	1 570	1 679	1 913
4. Animal and vegetable oils and fats	BQPI	171	221	207	264	245	197	156	150	211	261
5. Chemicals	ENDG	18 806	20 999	22 166	21 901	22 102	23 071	24 992	27 607	28 386	31 274
of which:											
51. Organic chemicals	BQPJ	4 731	4 923	5 152	4 974	4 914	5 494	5 718	6 108	5 700	6 026
52. Inorganic chemicals	BQPK	1 120	1 236	1 190	1 183	1 153	1 137	1 491	1 643	1 371	1 459
53. Colouring materials	CSCE	1 479	1 618	1 641	1 578	1 542	1 534	1 555	1 528	1 583	1 629
54. Medicinal products	BQPL	4 010	4 926	5 333	5 416	5 850	6 279	7 217	9 100	10 098	11 876
55. Toilet preparations	CSCF	2 012	2 124	2 409	2 569	2 446	2 462	2 597	2 718	2 820	3 099
57 & 58. Plastics	BQQA	2 800	3 276	3 294	3 166	3 194	3 144	3 366	3 422	3 524	3 695
6. Manufactures classified chiefly by material	BQQB	19 574	22 459	23 142	22 675	21 243	20 302	22 673	22 837	21 837	23 049
of which:											
63. Wood and cork manufactures	BQQC	170	189	228	250	253	278	255	262	271	322
64. Paper and paperboard manufactures	BQQD	2 049	2 350	2 343	2 309	2 197	2 020	2 096	2 088	2 014	2 095
65. Textile manufactures	BQQE	2 950	3 282	3 471	3 421	3 259	3 020	3 051	3 026	2 844	2 948
67. Iron and steel	BQQF	3 660	4 345	4 059	3 637	3 321	2 576	2 848	2 885	2 913	3 305
68. Non-ferrous metals	BQQG	2 233	2 864	2 680	2 774	2 433	2 130	3 171	3 044	2 548	2 566
69. Metal manufactures	BQQH	2 648	3 086	3 346	3 368	3 591	3 553	3 595	3 864	3 666	3 763
7. Machinery and transport equipment[3]	BQQI	55 852	65 353	73 366	79 002	78 011	78 875	87 812	87 804	84 396	79 477
71 - 716, 72, 73 & 74. Mechanical machinery	BQQK	16 272	18 337	20 481	22 329	22 695	21 888	22 140	24 488	22 717	24 164
716, 75, 76 & 77. Electrical machinery	BQQL	24 900	30 652	32 939	34 252	34 464	36 012	42 681	42 230	38 695	30 545
78. Road vehicles	BQQM	9 654	11 644	14 278	14 811	14 550	15 077	15 604	13 929	16 313	17 485
79. Other transport equipment	BQQN	5 026	4 720	5 668	7 610	6 302	5 898	7 387	7 157	6 671	7 283
8. Miscellaneous manufactures[3]	BQQO	17 315	18 859	20 873	21 530	20 563	20 263	21 206	22 158	21 981	22 529
of which:											
84. Clothing	CSCN	2 717	3 056	3 356	3 259	2 976	2 804	2 722	2 592	2 506	2 696
85. Footwear	CSCP	479	519	595	605	535	532	514	494	455	427
87 & 88. Scientific and photographic	BQQQ	5 357	5 900	6 594	6 974	6 705	6 732	7 333	7 856	7 218	7 297
9. Other commodities and transactions	BOQL	1 497	1 827	1 953	1 943	1 896	1 495	1 685	1 039	1 073	867
Total United Kingdom exports	BOKG	135 143	153 577	167 196	171 923	164 056	166 166	187 936	190 055	186 517	187 846

1 See chapter text. The numbers on the left hand side of the table refer to the code numbers of the *Standard International Trade Classification*, Revision 3, which was introduced in January 1988.
2 Balance of payments consistent basis.
3 Sections 7 and 8 are shown by broad economic category in table G2 of the *Monthly Review of External Trade Statistics*.

Source: Office for National Statistics: 020 7533 6064

19.4 United Kingdom imports: by commodity[1,2]
Seasonally adjusted

£ million

		1994	1995	1996	1997	1998	1999	2000	2001	2002	2003
0. Food and live animals	BQQR	11 660	12 923	14 030	13 318	13 223	13 336	13 310	14 286	14 874	16 423
of which:											
01. Meat and meat preparations	BQQS	1 884	2 237	2 540	2 231	2 006	2 144	2 366	2 692	2 795	3 246
02. Dairy products and eggs	BQQT	1 092	1 077	1 194	1 101	1 112	1 167	1 165	1 243	1 289	1 521
04 & 08. Cereals and animal feeding stuffs	BQQU	1 682	1 781	1 915	1 991	1 806	1 719	1 762	1 964	1 988	2 216
05. Vegetables and fruit	BQQV	3 285	3 820	4 173	3 898	4 017	4 040	3 894	4 102	4 371	4 746
1. Beverages and tobacco	BQQW	2 228	2 638	3 392	3 593	4 027	4 451	4 350	4 220	4 518	4 662
11. Beverages	EGAT	1 829	2 065	2 479	2 610	2 881	3 064	2 910	2 858	3 026	3 223
12. Tobacco	EMAI	399	573	913	983	1 146	1 387	1 440	1 362	1 492	1 439
2. Crude materials	ENVB	5 041	5 893	5 859	5 670	5 076	4 861	5 816	5 934	5 421	5 514
of which:											
24. Wood, lumber and cork	ENVC	1 300	1 142	1 202	1 239	1 100	1 088	1 193	1 160	1 213	1 337
25. Pulp and waste paper	EQAH	578	979	656	572	477	510	763	612	490	492
26. Textile fibres	EQAP	576	636	639	590	452	413	412	398	360	336
28. Metal ores	EHAA	1 028	1 358	1 474	1 460	1 314	1 308	1 811	2 008	1 455	1 437
3. Fuels	BQAT	6 342	6 161	7 284	6 824	4 892	5 428	10 016	10 502	9 588	11 452
33. Petroleum and petroleum products	ENXO	5 142	5 061	6 118	5 679	3 976	4 675	9 048	9 232	8 580	10 479
32, 34 & 35. Coal, gas and electricity	BPBI	1 200	1 100	1 166	1 145	916	753	968	1 270	1 008	973
4. Animal and vegetable oils and fats	EHAB	498	561	686	603	555	568	491	520	537	614
5. Chemicals	ENGA	14 156	17 481	18 095	17 405	17 379	18 619	20 633	22 836	23 984	26 052
of which:											
51. Organic chemicals	EHAC	3 421	4 670	4 719	4 462	4 508	4 788	5 374	5 548	5 671	6 094
52. Inorganic chemicals	EHAE	1 063	1 086	1 233	1 107	1 015	1 056	1 046	1 179	1 069	1 094
53. Colouring materials	CSCR	788	930	1 000	975	1 003	956	1 002	982	950	1 000
54. Medicinal products	EHAF	2 254	2 785	3 061	3 100	3 305	4 124	4 714	6 182	7 289	8 159
55. Toilet preparations	CSCS	1 193	1 364	1 477	1 506	1 617	1 774	2 005	2 267	2 498	2 723
57 & 58. Plastics	EHAG	3 672	4 597	4 338	4 168	3 903	3 819	4 144	4 103	4 063	4 394
6. Manufactures classified chiefly by material	EHAH	23 844	27 760	28 700	28 007	27 695	26 930	29 232	30 225	28 736	29 837
of which:											
63. Wood and cork manufactures	EHAI	997	1 037	1 078	1 083	1 089	1 145	1 245	1 347	1 441	1 449
64. Paper and paperboard manufactures	EHAJ	4 180	5 200	4 961	4 550	4 504	4 321	4 407	4 867	4 581	4 732
65. Textile manufactures	EHAK	4 401	4 806	5 075	5 003	4 862	4 380	4 365	4 316	4 152	4 075
67. Iron and steel	EHAL	2 905	3 620	3 604	3 337	3 205	2 473	2 731	3 055	3 047	3 223
68. Non-ferrous metals	EHAM	2 915	3 753	3 720	3 625	3 709	2 942	3 711	3 792	3 226	3 323
69. Metal manufactures	EHAN	2 812	3 239	3 492	3 561	3 721	3 789	4 065	4 337	4 492	4 754
7. Machinery and transport equipment[3]	EHAO	59 993	68 044	76 120	80 518	83 300	90 183	102 420	105 680	107 190	100 866
71 - 716, 72, 73 & 74. Mechanical machinery	EHAQ	13 095	15 148	16 540	17 037	17 156	17 313	17 867	18 767	18 913	18 945
716, 75, 76 & 77. Electrical machinery	EHAR	26 146	31 487	35 299	35 792	36 900	42 423	53 631	51 195	49 919	43 542
78. Road vehicles	EHAS	15 893	17 831	20 238	21 704	22 472	24 000	23 117	26 365	28 447	29 790
79. Other transport equipment	EHAT	4 859	3 578	4 043	5 985	6 772	6 447	7 805	9 353	9 911	8 589
8. Miscellaneous manufactures[3]	EHAU	21 325	22 522	24 987	26 568	27 917	29 042	32 798	35 220	36 894	38 107
of which:											
84. Clothing	CSDR	4 779	5 178	6 059	6 630	7 023	7 483	8 495	9 160	9 806	10 330
85. Footwear	CSDS	1 427	1 514	1 770	1 912	1 859	2 041	2 001	2 244	2 372	2 371
87 & 88. Scientific and photographic	EHAW	4 837	5 382	6 001	6 067	6 102	6 170	7 273	7 691	7 056	7 055
9. Other commodities and transactions	BQAW	1 182	1 617	1 765	1 759	1 805	1 799	1 846	1 280	1 450	1 609
Total United Kingdom imports	BOKH	146 269	165 600	180 918	184 265	185 869	195 217	220 912	230 703	233 192	235 136

1 See chapter text. The numbers on the left hand side of the table refer to the code numbers of the *Standard International Trade Classification*, Revision 3, which was introduced in January 1988.
2 Balance of payments consistent basis.
3 Sections 7 and 8 are shown by broad economic category in table G2 of the *Monthly Review of External Trade Statistics*.

Source: Office for National Statistics: 020 7533 6064

19.5 United Kingdom exports: by area[1,2]
Seasonally adjusted

£ million

		1994	1995	1996	1997	1998	1999	2000	2001	2002	2003
European Union:[3]	LGCK	..	..	..	..	98 995	101 191	111 955	113 893	114 129	109 807
EMU members:	QAKW	71 644	83 271	89 124	89 504	89 241	91 771	101 464	103 493	103 250	99 159
Austria	CHMY	1 052	1 122	1 263	1 159	1 190	1 168	1 146	1 224	1 265	1 255
Belgium & Luxembourg	CHNQ	7 367	8 298	8 522	8 451	8 445	9 241	10 322	9 893	10 555	11 283
Finland	CHMZ	1 316	1 716	1 810	1 570	1 434	1 354	1 471	1 610	1 443	1 478
France	ENYL	13 655	15 265	17 093	16 601	16 449	16 907	18 577	19 242	18 763	18 747
Germany	ENYO	17 339	20 242	20 715	20 685	20 590	20 464	22 789	23 647	22 068	20 656
Greece	CHNT	933	1 038	1 147	1 047	1 045	1 153	1 229	1 113	1 198	1 236
Irish Republic	CHNS	7 163	7 794	8 661	9 357	9 604	10 783	12 372	13 829	15 424	12 153
Italy	CHNO	6 836	7 883	8 027	8 214	8 608	7 831	8 429	8 400	8 511	8 538
Netherlands	CHNP	9 593	12 346	13 484	13 923	12 983	13 632	15 167	14 596	14 014	13 502
Portugal	CHNU	1 259	1 469	1 677	1 752	1 722	1 712	1 660	1 578	1 518	1 443
Spain	CHNV	5 131	6 098	6 725	6 745	7 171	7 526	8 302	8 361	8 491	8 868
Non-EMU members:[3]	BQIA	..	..	..	..	9 754	9 420	10 491	10 400	10 879	10 648
of which:											
Czech Rep	FKML	383	571	719	709	695	742	926	1 083	1 029	1 008
Denmark	CHNR	1 821	2 108	2 214	2 093	2 057	2 054	2 315	2 267	2 730	2 163
Hungary	QALC	263	296	351	435	483	492	611	621	749	857
Poland	ERDR	716	953	1 358	1 354	1 175	1 179	1 286	1 308	1 305	1 453
Sweden	CHNA	3 411	4 157	4 420	4 451	4 392	4 035	4 211	3 950	3 875	3 800
Other Western Europe:	HCJD	5 772	6 417	7 279	7 851	7 392	6 244	7 223	6 957	6 331	6 609
of which:											
Iceland	EPLW	110	138	152	157	158	159	193	154	131	140
Norway	EPLX	2 047	2 002	2 039	2 609	2 658	1 999	2 018	1 862	1 695	1 879
Switzerland	EPLV	2 480	2 729	3 166	2 955	2 892	2 768	3 061	3 581	3 079	2 779
Turkey	EOBA	821	1 149	1 545	1 734	1 562	1 198	1 800	1 179	1 286	1 633
North America:	HBZQ	19 722	20 450	22 341	23 817	24 091	27 582	33 714	33 774	32 256	33 246
of which:											
Canada	EOBC	1 935	1 804	1 963	2 146	2 147	2 532	3 487	3 240	3 106	3 229
Mexico	EPJX	393	277	316	428	516	577	675	689	704	688
USA	EOBB	17 081	17 901	19 753	20 853	21 082	24 040	29 276	29 562	28 192	29 005
Other OECD countries:	HCII	7 843	9 467	11 116	10 900	6 321	6 728	8 028	7 686	7 480	7 823
of which:											
Australia	EPMA	1 957	2 140	2 492	2 454	2 188	2 155	2 699	2 344	2 120	2 289
Japan	EOBD	3 047	3 814	4 296	4 180	3 127	3 300	3 672	3 744	3 588	3 710
New Zealand	EPMB	422	440	474	409	336	324	305	314	310	349
South Korea	ERDM	987	1 162	1 314	1 222	666	949	1 350	1 284	1 462	1 466
Oil exporting countries:	HDII	5 811	6 296	7 906	9 426	7 289	5 524	6 031	6 472	6 226	7 626
of which:											
Brunei	QALF	422	251	548	536	247	124	96	58	61	128
Dubai	QALI	624	701	746	866	830	790	966	1 011	938	1 385
Indonesia	FKMR	371	518	809	674	369	385	404	313	324	452
Kuwait	QATB	319	548	565	481	325	293	338	358	308	374
Nigeria	QATE	467	430	426	410	454	447	524	686	711	740
Saudi Arabia	ERDI	1 534	1 621	2 425	3 656	2 605	1 481	1 557	1 523	1 386	1 820
Rest of the World	HCHW	19 122	21 413	22 796	23 881	19 968	18 897	20 985	21 273	20 095	22 735
of which:											
Brazil	FKMO	539	679	853	1 030	899	739	775	819	880	826
China	ERDN	868	832	741	922	860	1 211	1 468	1 735	1 493	1 923
Egypt	QALL	378	385	434	501	505	539	498	458	462	457
Hong Kong	ERDG	2 356	2 664	2 943	3 215	2 671	2 312	2 673	2 717	2 411	2 483
India	ERDJ	1 340	1 689	1 718	1 576	1 242	1 450	2 058	1 797	1 754	2 283
Israel	ERDL	1 060	1 113	1 277	1 178	1 079	1 295	1 516	1 376	1 428	1 359
Malaysia	ERDK	1 346	1 192	1 169	1 206	677	934	907	1 045	877	1 030
Pakistan	FKMU	362	342	347	271	228	221	207	234	240	292
Philippines	FKMX	364	436	398	601	301	239	273	397	352	376
Russia	ERDQ	728	871	1 018	1 233	929	532	668	903	981	1 418
Singapore	ERDH	1 811	2 072	2 158	2 047	1 598	1 597	1 625	1 613	1 445	1 583
South Africa	EPME	1 452	1 837	1 894	1 646	1 520	1 281	1 413	1 558	1 597	1 770
Taiwan	ERDP	752	965	945	1 036	867	865	1 015	890	848	894
Thailand	ERDO	769	838	981	863	386	463	582	601	528	571

1 See chapter text.
2 Balance of payments consistent basis.
3 Includes the ten countries which joined the EU on 1 May 2004: Cyprus, Czech Republic, Estonia, Hungary, Latvia, Lithuania, Malta, Poland, Slovakia, Slovenia.

Source: Office for National Statistics: 020 7533 6064

315

19.6 United Kingdom imports: by area[1,2]
Seasonally adjusted

£ million

		1994	1995	1996	1997	1998	1999	2000	2001	2002	2003
European Union:[3]	LGDC	..	..	..	..	104 737	109 286	117 217	126 077	135 794	135 362
EMU members	QAKX	76 082	87 323	93 503	93 507	95 466	99 258	105 678	113 842	122 706	121 485
Austria	CHNB	1 027	925	1 155	1 393	1 411	1 453	1 410	1 888	2 393	2 757
Belgium & Luxembourg	CHNY	7 121	8 130	8 895	9 390	9 831	10 156	10 927	12 159	13 188	13 056
Finland	CHNC	2 271	2 500	2 643	2 544	2 328	2 364	2 765	2 962	2 788	2 647
France	ENYP	15 037	16 457	18 090	18 020	17 956	18 415	18 642	20 116	20 427	20 105
Germany	ENYS	21 860	26 234	27 173	25 632	25 095	26 817	28 461	29 884	32 418	33 433
Greece	CHOB	348	429	395	396	363	399	443	476	587	631
Irish Republic	CHOA	5 897	7 045	7 236	7 391	7 802	8 708	10 261	12 136	13 167	9 834
Italy	CHNW	7 496	8 264	8 805	9 548	9 744	9 385	9 516	9 855	10 666	11 399
Netherlands	CHNX	10 064	11 516	12 407	12 328	13 408	13 772	15 379	15 387	16 128	16 561
Portugal	CHOC	1 283	1 467	1 661	1 763	1 790	1 822	1 734	1 624	1 759	1 948
Spain	CHOD	3 678	4 356	5 043	5 102	5 738	5 967	6 140	7 355	9 185	9 114
Non-EMU members:[3]	BQIB	..	..	..	..	9 271	10 028	11 539	12 235	13 088	13 877
of which:											
Czech Rep	FKMM	271	312	353	450	557	575	807	1 107	1 241	1 408
Denmark	CHNZ	2 170	2 199	2 356	2 316	2 156	2 342	2 631	2 921	3 591	3 367
Hungary	QALD	232	358	402	465	537	661	686	710	841	1 117
Poland	ERED	533	616	570	597	651	668	923	1 174	1 253	1 533
Sweden	CHND	4 196	4 537	4 769	4 693	4 361	4 649	4 950	4 666	4 324	4 537
Other Western Europe:	HBTS	9 374	10 341	11 315	10 755	9 701	10 554	13 040	12 404	12 427	13 187
of which:											
Iceland	EPMW	233	244	255	229	251	282	365	286	288	295
Norway	EPMX	3 711	4 175	4 751	4 666	3 440	3 546	5 563	5 596	5 182	6 300
Switzerland	EPMV	4 677	4 981	5 183	4 636	4 755	5 341	5 485	4 604	4 582	3 749
Turkey	EOBU	610	768	892	990	1 103	1 204	1 450	1 692	2 157	2 610
North America:	HCRB	19 379	22 293	25 130	27 277	27 815	28 035	33 460	34 904	29 522	27 432
of which:											
Canada	EOBW	1 827	2 300	2 409	2 480	2 519	3 026	4 009	3 693	3 528	3 654
Mexico	EPJY	233	288	326	371	366	395	613	686	501	490
USA	EOBV	17 233	19 615	22 287	24 329	24 785	24 360	28 416	29 589	24 903	22 820
Other OECD countries:	HDJQ	12 312	13 762	13 699	14 636	13 205	13 805	15 717	14 268	13 187	12 927
of which:											
Australia	EPNA	1 035	1 068	1 230	1 320	1 363	1 338	1 543	1 792	1 709	1 779
Japan	EOBX	8 584	9 276	8 545	9 031	9 124	9 118	10 214	9 151	8 184	8 045
New Zealand	EPNB	527	555	602	555	517	565	544	549	529	550
South Korea	ERDY	1 068	1 505	1 935	2 147	2 201	2 784	3 416	2 776	2 765	2 553
Oil exporting countries:	HCPC	3 049	2 930	3 266	3 351	3 201	3 228	4 258	3 971	3 755	3 942
of which:											
Brunei	QALG	275	111	251	282	161	66	95	34	32	52
Dubai	QALJ	123	169	208	286	337	433	401	398	497	723
Indonesia	FKMS	728	814	852	862	854	931	1 081	1 128	1 000	883
Kuwait	QATC	223	133	158	168	164	121	314	297	269	316
Nigeria	QATF	117	163	254	100	121	112	89	65	90	83
Saudi Arabia	ERDU	757	649	654	841	791	783	977	931	670	718
Rest of the World	HCIF	19 704	22 215	26 880	27 730	27 210	30 309	37 220	39 079	38 507	42 286
of which:											
Brazil	FKMP	891	936	942	911	883	910	1 114	1 287	1 356	1 465
China	ERDZ	1 592	1 843	2 110	2 379	2 816	3 384	4 826	5 775	6 687	8 291
Egypt	QALM	245	235	271	256	277	255	411	408	414	428
Hong Kong	ERDS	2 988	3 364	3 904	4 146	4 391	4 909	5 917	5 793	5 528	5 468
India	ERDV	1 249	1 363	1 542	1 546	1 382	1 426	1 651	1 825	1 793	2 081
Israel	ERDX	555	659	796	839	875	996	1 025	947	872	855
Malaysia	ERDW	1 166	1 414	2 280	1 931	1 892	1 961	2 288	1 951	1 720	1 857
Pakistan	FKMV	348	344	375	362	340	318	363	426	466	518
Philippines	FKMY	237	335	858	726	855	983	1 155	1 163	939	708
Russia	EREC	781	916	1 222	1 418	1 406	1 324	1 496	2 061	1 938	2 441
Singapore	ERDT	1 836	2 101	2 465	2 585	2 343	2 348	2 395	2 079	1 946	2 654
South Africa	EPNE	941	1 058	1 170	1 323	1 351	1 636	2 553	2 861	2 670	2 930
Taiwan	EREB	1 535	1 640	2 001	2 230	2 217	2 626	3 561	2 803	2 371	2 187
Thailand	EREA	884	987	1 140	1 166	1 264	1 291	1 602	1 617	1 544	1 636

1 See chapter text.
2 Balance of payments consistent basis.
3 Includes the ten countries which joined the EU on 1 May 2004: Cyprus, Czech Republic, Estonia, Hungary, Latvia, Lithuania, Malta, Poland, Slovakia, Slovenia.

Source: Office for National Statistics: 020 7533 6064

19.7 Services supplied (exports) and purchased (imports),[1] 2002

£ million

	Exports	Imports	Net
Business services			
Legal	1 746	486	1 260
Accounting	728	252	477
Management consulting	1 064	491	573
Advertising	1 316	709	606
Market research	387	150	236
Research and development	2 873	644	2 229
Insurance: premiums	6	160	-154
claims	20	-	20
Insurance broking	1 075	16	1 059
Financial Services	3 429	738	2 690
Property	14	23	-9
Management charges	1 060	647	413
Procurement	48	80	-32
Publishing services	128	52	76
Recruitment and training	406	268	138
Other business services	2 792	983	1 809
Telecommunications services			
Communications	1 307	1 453	-146
Computer	2 058	1 002	1 057
Information	625	194	432
Technical services			
Architectural	70	24	46
Engineering (consulting, process etc.)	3 049	769	2 280
Surveying	62	30	33
Construction	194	105	90
Agriculture and mining	31	76	-45
Other technical	1 932	363	1 569
Miscellaneous services			
Operational leasing	185	245	-60
Cultural services			
TV and radio services	148	26	123
Music services (excluding royalties)	35	14	21
Other cultural	311	143	168
Royalties	5 077	3 447	1 630
Trade related services			
Own account earning	436	148	289
Commission	1 444	534	910
Commodity trading	192	321	-129
Management services to affiliated companies	1 720	1 140	580
All other services	1 638	1 262	377
World Total	**37 608**	**16 992**	**20 616**

1 See chapter text. Data excludes the following industries: Financial, Film and TV, Travel and Transport, Public Sector (including Education) and Law Society members.

Source: Office for National Statistics: 01633 813109

19.8 International trade in services:[1] by country, 2002

£ million

	Exports	Imports	Net
European Union			
Austria	121	88	33
Belgium/Luxembourg	1 210	650	560
Denmark	420	127	293
Finland	426	70	356
France	1 732	1 380	352
Germany	2 871	1 606	1 265
Greece	116	61	56
Irish Republic	2 196	530	1 665
Italy	841	457	384
Netherlands	2 069	1 263	806
Spain	558	306	252
Sweden	545	324	221
Portugal and EU Institutions	195	67	127
EFTA			
Iceland	16	3	14
Liechtenstein	23	2	21
Norway	706	606	100
Switzerland	2 099	591	1 508
Other European countries			
Czech Republic	62	40	22
Poland	125	36	89
Russia	172	114	59
Channel Islands	459	77	382
Isle of Man	16	9	7
Turkey	71	26	46
Rest of Europe	313	219	95
Europe Unallocated	1 067	261	806
Africa			
South Africa	299	76	223
Rest of Africa	580	237	343
Africa Unallocated	63	21	42
America			
Brazil	75	53	22
Canada	363	236	127
Mexico	57	49	8
USA	9 849	4 307	5 543
Rest of America	1 145	290	855
America Unallocated	255	98	157
Asia			
China	239	72	167
Hong Kong	225	154	72
India	135	148	-13
Indonesia	52	19	33
Israel	117	103	14
Japan	1 716	484	1 232
Malaysia	162	19	143
Pakistan	34	46	-11
Phillippines	33	11	22
Saudi Arabia	212	25	187
Singapore	710	110	600
South Korea	173	34	139
Taiwan	94	38	56
Thailand	39	20	20
Rest of Asia	1 833	966	867
Asia Unallocated	141	44	97
Australia and Oceania			
Australia	341	252	88
New Zealand	39	30	9
Rest of Australia and Oceania	23	6	17
Oceania Unallocated	12	5	6
Rest of World Unallocated and other orgainisations	161	125	37
World Total	**37 608**	**16 992**	**20 616**
Economic Zones			
OCED	28 107	13 550	14 558
NAFTA	9 793	4 591	5 202
Central and Eastern Europe	401	167	235
OPEC	1 891	947	944
ASEAN	1 022	188	834
CIS	381	206	175
NICs1	1 203	335	868
Offshore Financial centres	2 087	520	1 567
ACP	528	318	209

1 See chapter text. Data excludes the following industries: Financial, Film and TV, Travel and Transport, Public Sector (including Education) and Law Society members.

Source: Office for National Statistics: 01633 813109

318

19.9 Summary of balance of payments,[1] 2003
United Kingdom

£ million

	Credits	Debits
1. Current account		
A. Goods and services	277 539	310 212
1. Goods	187 846	235 136
2. Services	89 693	75 076
2.1. Transportation	12 958	17 194
2.2. Travel	13 928	29 740
2.3. Communications	1 957	1 898
2.4. Construction	105	76
2.5. Insurance	6 419	789
2.6. Financial	13 417	3 481
2.7. Computer and information	4 268	1 779
2.8. Royalties and licence fees	6 055	4 516
2.9. Other business	27 400	12 288
2.10. Personal, cultural and recreational	1 294	685
2.11. Government	1 892	2 630
B. Income	126 340	104 243
1. Compensation of employees	1 116	1 057
2. Investment income	125 224	103 186
2.1 Direct investment	55 660	24 246
2.2 Portfolio investment	32 418	31 747
2.3 Other investment (including earnings on reserve assets)	37 146	47 193
C. Current transfers	13 163	23 017
1. Central government	4 199	10 939
2. Other sectors	8 964	12 078
Total current account	**417 042**	**437 472**
2. Capital and financial accounts		
A. Capital account	2 721	1 478
1. Capital transfers	2 575	1 208
2. Acquisition/disposal of non-produced, non-financial assets	146	270
B. Financial account	354 303	336 848
1. Direct investment	9 765	32 052
Abroad		32 052
1.1. Equity capital		13 594
1.2. Reinvested earnings		18 181
1.3. Other capital[2]		277
In United Kingdom	9 765	
1.1. Equity capital	1 223	
1.2. Reinvested earnings	8 465	
1.3. Other capital[3]	77	
2. Portfolio investment	91 257	34 748
Assets		34 748
2.1. Equity securities		20 938
2.2. Debt securities		13 810
Liabilities	91 257	
2.1. Equity securities	5 987	
2.2. Debt securities	85 270	
3. Financial derivatives (net)		5 401
4. Other investment	253 281	266 206
Assets		266 206
4.1 Trade credits		72
4.2 Loans		70 724
4.3 Currency and deposits		195 161
4.4 Other assets		249
Liabilities	253 281	
4.1. Trade credits	–	
4.2. Loans	82 992	
4.3. Currency and deposits	171 160	
4.4. Other liabilities	−871	
5. Reserve assets		−1 559
5.1. Monetary gold		–
5.2. Special drawing rights		−2
5.3. Reserve position in the IMF		−251
5.4. Foreign exchange		−1 116
Total capital and financial accounts	**357 024**	**338 326**
Total current, capital and financial accounts	**774 066**	**775 798**
Net errors and omissions	1 732	

1 See chapter text.
2 Other capital transaction on direct investment abroad represents claims on affiliated enterprises less liabilities to affiliated enterprises
3 Other capital transactions on direct investment in the United Kingdom represents liabilities to direct investors less claims on direct investors

Source: Office for National Statistics

19.10 Summary of balance of payments: balances (credits less debits)[1]
United Kingdom

£ million

	Current account										
	Trade in goods	Trade in services	**Total goods and services**	Compensation of employees	Investment income	**Total income**	**Current transfers**	**Current balance**	Capital account	Financial account	Net errors & omissions
	LQCT	KTMS	KTMY	KTMP	HMBM	HMBP	KTNF	HBOG	FKMJ	HBNT	HHDH
1949	−137	−43	−180	−20	206	186	29	35	−12	−103	80
1950	−54	−4	−58	−21	378	357	39	338	−10	−447	119
1951	−692	32	−660	−21	322	301	29	−330	−15	426	−81
1952	−272	123	−149	−22	231	209	169	229	−15	−229	15
1953	−244	123	−121	−25	207	182	143	204	−13	−177	−14
1954	−210	115	−95	−27	227	200	55	160	−13	−174	27
1955	−315	42	−273	−27	149	122	43	−108	−15	34	89
1956	50	26	76	−30	203	173	2	251	−13	−250	12
1957	−29	121	92	−32	223	191	−5	278	−13	−313	48
1958	34	119	153	−34	261	227	4	384	−10	−411	37
1959	−116	118	2	−37	233	196	–	198	−5	−68	−125
1960	−404	39	−365	−35	201	166	−6	−205	−6	−7	218
1961	−144	51	−93	−35	223	188	−9	86	−12	23	−97
1962	−104	50	−54	−37	301	264	−14	196	−12	−195	11
1963	−123	4	−119	−38	364	326	−37	170	−16	−30	−124
1964	−551	−34	−585	−33	365	332	−74	−327	−17	392	−48
1965	−263	−66	−329	−34	405	371	−75	−33	−18	49	2
1966	−111	44	−67	−39	358	319	−91	161	−19	22	−164
1967	−601	157	−444	−39	354	315	−118	−247	−25	179	93
1968	−708	341	−367	−48	303	255	−119	−231	−26	688	−431
1969	−214	392	178	−47	468	421	−109	490	−23	−794	327
1970	−18	455	437	−56	527	471	−89	819	−22	−818	21
1971	205	590	795	−63	481	418	−90	1 123	−23	−1 330	230
1972	−736	665	−71	−52	407	355	−142	142	−35	477	−584
1973	−2 573	803	−1 770	−68	1 074	1 006	−336	−1 100	−39	1 031	108
1974	−5 241	1 118	−4 123	−92	1 184	1 092	−302	−3 333	−34	3 185	182
1975	−3 245	1 447	−1 798	−102	518	416	−313	−1 695	−36	1 569	162
1976	−3 930	2 532	−1 398	−140	1 100	960	−534	−972	−12	507	477
1977	−2 271	3 306	1 035	−152	−280	−432	−889	−286	11	−3 286	3 561
1978	−1 534	3 777	2 243	−140	138	−2	−1 420	821	−79	−2 655	1 913
1979	−3 326	4 076	750	−130	155	25	−1 777	−1 002	−103	864	241
1980	1 329	3 829	5 158	−82	−1 683	−1 765	−1 653	1 740	−4	−2 157	421
1981	3 238	3 951	7 189	−66	−1 058	−1 124	−1 219	4 846	−79	−5 312	545
1982	1 879	3 198	5 077	−95	−1 273	−1 368	−1 476	2 233	6	−1 233	−1 006
1983	−1 618	4 076	2 458	−89	280	191	−1 391	1 258	75	−3 287	1 954
1984	−5 409	4 491	−918	−94	1 284	1 190	−1 566	−1 294	107	−7 130	8 317
1985	−3 416	6 767	3 351	−120	−877	−997	−2 924	−570	185	−1 657	2 042
1986	−9 617	6 403	−3 214	−156	1 850	1 694	−2 094	−3 614	135	−122	3 601
1987	−11 698	6 813	−4 885	−174	1 091	917	−3 570	−7 538	333	10 764	−3 559
1988	−21 553	4 450	−17 103	−64	817	753	−3 500	−19 850	235	17 201	2 414
1989	−24 724	3 643	−21 081	−138	−654	−792	−4 448	−26 321	270	18 001	8 050
1990	−18 707	4 337	−14 370	−110	−2 869	−2 979	−4 932	−22 281	497	15 083	6 701
1991	−10 223	4 102	−6 121	−63	−3 244	−3 307	−1 231	−10 659	290	5 269	5 100
1992	−13 050	5 482	−7 568	−49	177	128	−5 534	−12 974	421	5 089	7 464
1993	−13 066	6 581	−6 485	35	−226	−191	−5 243	−11 919	309	11 330	280
1994	−11 126	6 379	−4 747	−170	3 518	3 348	−5 369	−6 768	33	2 126	4 609
1995	−12 023	8 481	−3 542	−296	2 397	2 101	−7 574	−9 015	533	5 005	3 477
1996	−13 722	10 272	−3 450	93	1 111	1 204	−4 755	−7 001	1 260	3 961	1 780
1997	−12 342	13 418	1 076	83	3 822	3 905	−5 918	−937	982	−5 056	5 011
1998	−21 813	13 309	−8 504	−10	12 916	12 906	−8 374	−3 972	516	2 219	1 237
1999	−29 051	13 134	−15 917	201	−1 317	−1 116	−7 383	−24 416	773	20 944	2 699
2000	−32 976	13 426	−19 550	150	5 058	5 208	−9 752	−24 094	1 527	24 944	−2 377
2001	−40 648	13 216	−27 432	66	11 586	11 652	−6 611	−22 391	1 206	23 816	−2 631
2002	−46 675	15 577	−31 098	67	21 408	21 475	−8 599	−18 222	868	8 849	8 505
2003	−47 290	14 617	−32 673	59	22 038	22 097	−9 854	−20 430	1 243	17 455	1 732

1 See chapter text.

Source: Office for National Statistics

19.11 Balance of payments:[1] current account
United Kingdom

£ million

		1993	1994	1995	1996	1997	1998	1999	2000	2001	2002	2003
Credits												
Exports of goods and services												
Exports of goods	LQAD	122 229	135 143	153 577	167 196	171 923	164 056	166 166	187 936	190 055	186 517	187 846
Exports of services	KTMQ	41 411	45 365	49 932	56 773	61 104	66 278	72 628	79 071	82 314	87 203	89 693
Total exports of goods and services	KTMW	163 640	180 508	203 509	223 969	233 027	230 334	238 794	267 007	272 369	273 720	277 539
Income												
Compensation of employees	KTMN	595	681	887	911	1 007	840	960	1 032	1 087	1 121	1 116
Investment income	HMBN	72 333	73 702	87 132	91 621	95 337	103 667	99 729	134 436	141 178	124 393	125 224
Total income	HMBQ	72 928	74 383	88 019	92 532	96 344	104 507	100 689	135 468	142 265	125 514	126 340
Current transfers												
Central government	FJUM	2 826	2 138	1 730	2 828	2 173	1 767	3 542	2 465	4 991	3 655	4 199
Other sectors	FJUN	9 565	9 454	10 751	17 121	10 823	10 527	9 768	8 305	9 567	8 558	8 964
Total current transfers	KTND	12 391	11 592	12 481	19 949	12 996	12 294	13 310	10 770	14 558	12 213	13 163
Total	HBOE	248 959	266 483	304 009	336 450	342 367	347 135	352 793	413 245	429 192	411 447	417 042
Debits												
Imports of goods and services												
Imports of goods	LQBL	135 295	146 269	165 600	180 918	184 265	185 869	195 217	220 912	230 703	233 192	235 136
Imports of services	KTMR	34 830	38 986	41 451	46 501	47 686	52 969	59 494	65 645	69 098	71 626	75 076
Total imports of goods and services	KTMX	170 125	185 255	207 051	227 419	231 951	238 838	254 711	286 557	299 801	304 818	310 212
Income												
Compensation of employees	KTMO	560	851	1 183	818	924	850	759	882	1 021	1 054	1 057
Investment income	HMBO	72 559	70 184	84 735	90 510	91 515	90 751	101 046	129 378	129 592	102 985	103 186
Total income	HMBR	73 119	71 035	85 918	91 328	92 439	91 601	101 805	130 260	130 613	104 039	104 243
Current transfers												
Central government	FJUO	4 343	4 977	5 022	5 297	5 260	6 787	7 482	8 015	7 584	9 296	10 939
Other sectors	FJUP	13 291	11 984	15 033	19 407	13 654	13 881	13 211	12 507	13 585	11 516	12 078
Total current transfers	KTNE	17 634	16 961	20 055	24 704	18 914	20 668	20 693	20 522	21 169	20 812	23 017
Total	HBOF	260 878	273 251	313 024	343 451	343 304	351 107	377 209	437 339	451 583	429 669	437 472
Balances												
Trade in goods and services												
Trade in goods	LQCT	−13 066	−11 126	−12 023	−13 722	−12 342	−21 813	−29 051	−32 976	−40 648	−46 675	−47 290
Trade in services	KTMS	6 581	6 379	8 481	10 272	13 418	13 309	13 134	13 426	13 216	15 577	14 617
Total trade in goods and services	KTMY	−6 485	−4 747	−3 542	−3 450	1 076	−8 504	−15 917	−19 550	−27 432	−31 098	−32 673
Income												
Compensation of employees	KTMP	35	−170	−296	93	83	−10	201	150	66	67	59
Investment income	HMBM	−226	3 518	2 397	1 111	3 822	12 916	−1 317	5 058	11 586	21 408	22 038
Total income	HMBP	−191	3 348	2 101	1 204	3 905	12 906	−1 116	5 208	11 652	21 475	22 097
Current transfers												
Central government	FJUQ	−1 517	−2 839	−3 292	−2 469	−3 087	−5 020	−3 940	−5 550	−2 593	−5 641	−6 740
Other sectors	FJUR	−3 726	−2 530	−4 282	−2 286	−2 831	−3 354	−3 443	−4 202	−4 018	−2 958	−3 114
Total current transfers	KTNF	−5 243	−5 369	−7 574	−4 755	−5 918	−8 374	−7 383	−9 752	−6 611	−8 599	−9 854
Total (Current balance)	HBOG	−11 919	−6 768	−9 015	−7 001	−937	−3 972	−24 416	−24 094	−22 391	−18 222	−20 430

1 See chapter text.

Source: Office for National Statistics

321

19.12 Balance of payments:[1] summary of international investment position, financial account and investment income

United Kingdom

£ billion

		1993	1994	1995	1996	1997	1998	1999	2000	2001	2002	2003
Investment abroad												
International investment position												
Direct investment	HBWD	172.6	176.1	203.7	201.6	223.3	299.6	428.1	607.4	603.3	576.1	632.1
Portfolio investment	HHZZ	469.8	429.8	499.3	548.2	651.0	703.8	838.3	906.1	937.4	844.1	969.1
Other investment	HLXV	684.4	708.6	808.1	852.6	1 068.2	1 105.5	1 130.4	1 435.0	1 580.9	1 642.5	1 924.9
Reserve assets	LTEB	29.7	30.7	31.8	27.3	22.8	23.3	22.2	28.8	25.6	25.4	23.7
Total	HBQA	1 356.5	1 345.2	1 542.9	1 629.7	1 965.3	2 132.2	2 418.9	2 977.3	3 147.2	3 088.1	3 549.7
Financial account transactions												
Direct investment	-HJYP	18.2	22.7	28.7	22.3	38.2	73.3	125.0	155.0	41.3	24.4	32.1
Portfolio investment	-HHZC	89.6	−21.8	39.3	59.6	52.0	32.1	21.3	65.5	86.5	1.0	34.7
Other investment	-XBMM	45.3	27.8	47.5	138.7	168.3	19.0	56.8	269.9	173.5	96.8	266.2
Reserve assets	-AIPA	0.7	1.0	−0.2	−0.5	−2.4	−0.2	−0.6	7.3	−2.3	−2.3	−1.9
Total	-HBNR	153.5	27.3	113.6	219.1	255.0	127.3	199.8	492.8	289.9	120.8	336.8
Investment income												
Direct investment	HJYW	17.4	21.9	24.8	28.5	29.4	29.8	33.1	44.9	46.6	52.7	55.7
Portfolio investment	HLYX	16.7	16.4	19.7	20.2	23.8	29.3	25.7	33.0	34.9	32.5	32.4
Other investment	AIOP	36.8	33.8	41.0	41.3	40.7	43.4	39.8	55.5	58.7	38.4	36.4
Reserve assets	HHCB	1.5	1.6	1.7	1.6	1.4	1.1	1.2	1.0	1.0	0.8	0.8
Total	HMBN	72.3	73.7	87.1	91.6	95.3	103.7	99.7	134.4	141.2	124.4	125.2
Investment in the UK												
International investment position												
Direct investment	HBWI	135.9	129.9	146.2	152.6	173.7	213.6	250.3	310.4	363.6	367.6	377.4
Portfolio investment	HLXW	306.9	320.0	406.3	480.0	583.3	692.8	828.9	998.2	958.5	894.0	1 043.8
Other investment	HLYD	882.3	877.4	1 013.0	1 064.9	1 282.1	1 359.0	1 410.4	1 704.8	1 898.6	1 937.8	2 181.0
Total	HBQB	1 325.1	1 327.3	1 565.5	1 697.5	2 039.1	2 265.5	2 489.5	3 013.4	3 220.7	3 199.5	3 602.2
Financial account transactions												
Direct investment	HJYU	10.9	7.1	13.8	17.6	22.8	45.1	55.2	80.6	37.3	19.3	9.8
Portfolio investment	HHZF	28.8	30.7	37.3	43.0	26.8	20.9	114.1	164.5	48.1	51.1	91.3
Other investment	XBMN	125.2	−8.3	67.5	162.5	200.4	63.6	51.5	272.6	228.2	59.2	253.3
Total	HBNS	164.9	29.5	118.6	223.1	250.0	129.6	220.8	517.7	313.7	129.6	354.3
Investment income												
Direct investment	HJYX	11.1	10.6	13.8	16.6	14.9	8.6	17.0	27.4	21.4	18.9	24.2
Portfolio investment	HLZC	14.2	17.2	20.6	23.7	26.6	29.1	31.2	30.7	34.5	31.7	31.7
Other investment	HLZN	47.2	42.5	50.3	50.1	50.0	53.0	52.9	71.3	73.7	52.4	47.2
Total	HMBO	72.6	70.2	84.7	90.5	91.5	90.8	101.0	129.4	129.6	103.0	103.2
Net investment												
International investment position												
Direct investment	HBWQ	36.7	46.2	57.5	49.0	49.5	85.9	177.8	297.1	239.7	208.5	254.6
Portfolio investment	CGNH	162.9	109.8	93.0	68.2	67.7	11.0	9.4	−92.2	−21.1	−49.9	−74.7
Other investment	CGNG	−197.9	−168.8	−204.9	−212.3	−213.9	−253.6	−280.0	−269.8	−317.7	−295.3	−256.1
Reserve assets	LTEB	29.7	30.7	31.8	27.3	22.8	23.3	22.2	28.8	25.6	25.4	23.7
Net investment position	HBQC	31.4	17.9	−22.6	−67.8	−73.8	−133.2	−70.6	−36.1	−73.4	−111.4	−52.4
Financial account transactions												
Direct investment	HJYV	−7.2	−15.6	−14.9	−4.7	−15.4	−28.3	−69.8	−74.4	−4.0	−5.1	−22.3
Portfolio investment	HHZD	−60.8	52.5	−2.0	−16.6	−25.2	−11.2	92.8	99.0	−38.4	50.1	56.5
Other investment	HHYR	79.8	−36.1	20.0	23.8	32.0	44.6	−5.3	2.7	54.7	−37.6	−12.9
Reserve assets	AIPA	−0.7	−1.0	0.2	0.5	2.4	0.2	0.6	−7.3	2.3	2.3	1.9
Net transactions	HBNT	11.3	2.1	5.0	4.0	−5.1	2.2	20.9	24.9	23.8	8.8	17.5
Investment income												
Direct investment	HJYE	6.2	11.4	10.9	11.9	14.5	21.3	16.1	17.6	25.2	33.8	31.4
Portfolio investment	HLZX	2.5	−0.8	−0.9	−3.5	−2.8	0.2	−5.5	2.3	0.4	0.8	0.7
Other investment	CGNA	−10.4	−8.7	−9.4	−8.8	−9.3	−9.6	−13.1	−15.7	−15.0	−14.0	−10.8
Reserve assets	HHCB	1.5	1.6	1.7	1.6	1.4	1.1	1.2	1.0	1.0	0.8	0.8
Net earnings	HMBM	−0.2	3.5	2.4	1.1	3.8	12.9	−1.3	5.1	11.6	21.4	22.0

1 See chapter text.

Source: Office for National Statistics

19.13 Net outward foreign direct investment by United Kingdom companies:[1,2] by area and main country

£ million

		1993	1994	1995	1996	1997	1998	1999	2000	2001	2002	2003
Europe	GQBX	6 171	9 241	9 184	13 321	19 964	23 286	44 140	127 448	13 743	27 300	16 278
EU	CAUU	6 146	8 278	9 457	13 432	17 368	11 777	38 821	124 564	11 140	29 720	11 557
Austria	CBJD	13	102	90	102	16	26	−18	240	1 628	797	125
Belgium	HIIL	160	132	136	433	966	−609	−94	1 643	103	1 046	−45
Denmark	CAUW	237	64	416	−176	47	−105	111	−67	−423	543	−61
Finland	CBJE	10	26	112	28	−5	80	217	−196	61	1 124	102
France	CAUX	471	423	1 515	2 375	2 380	−46	2 171	6 398	2 794	4 112	5 134
Germany	CAUY	1 333	1 261	1 478	1 184	1 078	1 463	1 308	113 762	724	8 473	1 249
Greece	CAUZ	44	84	163	106	302	221	−52	624	156	−65	229
Irish Republic	CAVA	1 082	100	776	755	450	1 165	..	4 679	2 698	1 674	962
Italy	CAVB	282	298	406	421	447	554	190	327	612	572	519
Luxembourg	HIIM	–	–	302	558	571	491	246	−1 495	1 019	−2 046	1 291
Netherlands	CAVC	2 436	4 615	2 953	6 577	9 804	7 772	6 781	−4 335	4 324	13 152	30
Portugal	CAVD	25	169	159	56	112	6	180	105	144	88	392
Spain	CAVE	−31	460	431	735	864	232	617	1 574	−1 564	288	747
Sweden	CBJG	84	546	522	277	335	529	..	1 309	−1 134	−35	886
EFTA	CAVG	−84	645	−594	−12	2 195	8 806	3 251	408	−1 569	994	1 755
of which												
Norway	CBJF	92	662	−255	96	1 997	782	226	−75	508	−329	−256
Switzerland	CBJH	−177	−16	−338	−110	197	8 015	3 024	483	−2 077	1 329	2 016
Other European Countries	GQBY	110	317	322	−97	402	2 703	2 068	2 476	4 173	−3 414	2 966
of which												
Russia[3]	GLAA	11	115	39	132	448	−171	231	246	498	108	1 994
UK offshore islands	GLAC	–	–	–	–	−933	2 476	1 296	1 952	1 346	−1 249	294
America	GQBZ	8 673	8 464	13 460	3 277	13 953	48 972	73 891	29 558	23 987	−5 150	18 581
of which												
Bermuda	CBKZ	586	349	291	142	−43	469	−91	−270	801	−4 371	−272
Brazil	CBLA	38	291	473	692	337	323	855	596	352	17	760
Canada	CAVK	5	−4	244	−159	823	406	849	2 566	4 142	536	2 737
Chile	GQCA	101	76	220	89	168	169	−693	295	292	1 021	290
Colombia	GQCB	−245	204	123	100	241	346	340	58	57	−385	99
Mexico	GLAD	44	42	79	110	760	152	106	195	−139	939	206
Panama	GLAE	−100	94	75	103	..	311	153	19	−19	19	57
USA	CAVJ	7 975	6 549	11 840	1 837	10 509	46 116	70 006	24 249	15 865	−984	18 342
Asia	GQCI	1 596	2 049	1 657	2 823	2 251	1 718	4 572	−3 568	524	5 538	3 475
Near and Middle East Countries	CBKF	−239	253	154	28	350	1 674	−914	43	822	376	83
of which												
Gulf Arabian countries[4]	GQCC	−236	250	116	30	260	1 620	−677	−13	738	369	−105
Other Asian Countries	GQCD	1 834	1 796	1 503	2 794	1 901	45	5 486	−3 611	−297	5 162	3 392
of which												
China	HIIN	21	6	51	204	71	−234	604	410	662	757	214
Hong Kong	CAVN	456	128	734	730	−359	1 554	312	−3 309	590	1 186	879
India	GLAF	139	87	61	110	171	209	148	287	135	276	214
Indonesia	GLAG	69	92	−28	155	170	97	−31	122	−31	70	481
Japan	CAVM	−49	245	169	378	383	14	1 929	1 390	−4 219	388	338
Malaysia	CBKN	363	286	28	184	731	619	227	−250	−321	334	246
Singapore	CBKQ	528	590	−48	535	352	−2 473	1 373	−3 387	1 681	1 619	−46
South Korea	GLAH	44	27	47	32	−26	281	172	−30	–	174	322
Thailand	GLAI	103	177	245	194	103	88	28	257	173	−55	156
Australasia and Oceania	GQCE	658	959	2 596	1 843	827	208	730	−595	1 478	3 677	−1 054
of which												
Australia	CBJO	655	625	2 258	1 472	737	221	715	−482	1 787	3 322	−490
New Zealand	CBJP	71	264	67	244	255	−111	78	−53	−323	337	−548
Africa	GQCF	262	327	707	561	623	−25	1 175	1 401	1 152	2 196	3 425
of which												
Kenya	GLAJ	33	9	67	24	73	39	51	137	42	32	62
Nigeria	CBJY	347	−197	−271	−94	234	−145	160	57	74	220	17
South Africa	CAVO	314	170	466	−25	401	−197	386	629	325	2 265	2 249
Zimbabwe	CBKD	36	28	16	25	1	36	74	38	40	33	37
World Total	CDQD	17 358	21 040	27 604	21 823	37 619	74 159	124 508	154 242	40 884	33 561	40 703
OECD	GQCG	14 864	16 880	23 686	17 545	33 212	68 175	115 813	153 389	28 633	36 096	35 061
Central and Eastern Europe[5]	GQCH	41	168	194	201	214	465	111	263	1 543	654	860

1 See chapter text. Minus sign indicates net disinvestment overseas.
2 Net investment includes unremitted profits.
3 Prior to 1995 Russia covers other former USSR countries, the Baltic States and Albania.
4 Includes Abu Dhabi, Bahrain, Dubai, Iraq, Kuwait, Oman, Other Gulf States, Qatar, Saudi Arabia and Yemen.
5 Includes Albania, Bulgaria, Croatia, Czech Republic, Estonia, Hungary, Latvia, Lithuania, Poland, Romania, Serbia and Montenegro, Slovakia, Bosnia and Herzegovina, Macedonia FYR and Slovenia.

Sources: ONS Foreign Direct Investment Inquiries: 01633 813314; Bank of England

United Kingdom outward foreign direct international investment position: book value of net assets: by area and main country[1]

At year end

£ million

		1993	1994	1995	1996	1997	1998	1999	2000	2001	2002	2003
Europe	GQCJ	57 853	66 705	76 434	87 582	99 263	117 181	170 905	384 204	368 465	390 359	446 354
EU	CDLN	53 914	61 674	72 808	83 902	92 072	96 817	149 804	355 725	326 207	338 116	388 904
Austria	CDLZ	379	454	734	578	461	506	731	1 054	2 428	2 679	3 283
Belgium	HIIO	2 687	3 189	3 055	2 860	4 019	2 862	5 110	7 299	6 175	10 364	10 417
Denmark	CDLP	1 301	1 538	2 803	2 273	2 123	2 295	3 048	2 143	2 607	3 165	2 963
Finland	CDMA	104	117	271	215	217	254	390	597	640	580	588
France	CDLQ	8 619	10 357	12 913	13 128	11 368	10 217	12 774	21 845	24 683	31 928	37 381
Germany	CDLR	5 974	8 442	9 215	8 943	8 328	10 319	10 892	23 354	13 448	13 924	12 113
Greece	CDLS	294	203	500	465	366	508	393	1 001	1 155	498	426
Irish Republic	CDLT	4 169	4 436	4 587	6 282	6 182	7 792	27 000	33 305	23 033	29 944	32 404
Italy	CDLU	2 287	2 475	2 698	3 196	3 064	3 149	3 035	3 643	4 267	5 505	10 123
Luxembourg	HIIP	–	–	117	2 465	1 683	2 698	5 952	52 499	64 042	62 556	82 743
Netherlands	CDLV	23 190	25 228	29 906	37 676	48 240	50 175	69 257	182 944	164 973	158 478	174 365
Portugal	CDLW	1 195	932	1 210	1 190	1 023	1 067	1 074	1 069	918	629	880
Spain	CDLX	2 820	3 157	3 399	3 477	3 748	3 299	3 674	5 907	7 091	7 156	9 734
Sweden	CDMD	894	1 146	1 401	1 154	1 250	1 675	6 475	19 064	10 747	10 712	11 485
EFTA	CDLY	3 303	4 113	2 522	2 161	1 533	10 547	9 298	10 708	18 931	22 069	23 899
of which												
Norway	CDMC	803	1 513	1 244	1 171	1 116	470	3 874	4 236	4 340	4 904	4 594
Switzerland	CDME	2 500	2 594	1 279	988	415	10 072	5 421	6 466	14 584	17 164	18 932
Other European Countries	GQCK	636	918	1 103	1 520	5 658	9 818	11 803	17 771	23 327	30 175	33 550
of which												
Russia[2]	GQAA	7	26	120	238	401	201	247	283	1 062	744	772
UK offshore islands	GQAB	–	–	–	–	2 690	6 937	9 057	14 930	16 579	15 203	23 273
America	GQCU	77 003	75 390	83 275	67 592	80 324	139 031	208 078	173 409	176 685	167 345	178 168
of which												
Bermuda	CDOA	4 869	5 403	5 504	5 295	4 942	4 689	5 075	6 054	6 689	4 929	4 196
Brazil	CDOB	1 963	2 059	2 323	2 421	2 214	1 607	2 374	3 281	2 976	2 050	2 130
Canada	CDML	7 162	4 919	5 395	4 563	5 748	4 952	5 627	10 142	10 328	8 209	8 819
Chile	GQCT	481	439	666	670	970	1 101	1 080	1 506	1 895	2 036	1 803
Colombia	GQCS	839	1 071	1 207	1 274	1 197	559	986	1 691	1 272	1 752	2 444
Mexico	GQAC	419	334	350	553	1 327	801	1 036	1 018	887	1 450	1 187
Panama	GQAD	435	507	467	744	..	..	750	226	204	192	152
USA	CDMM	57 380	55 174	62 159	49 170	59 083	121 408	186 410	141 355	143 359	131 800	146 457
Asia	GQCL	14 118	16 095	18 038	19 916	19 389	20 957	24 148	24 616	30 044	28 914	33 094
Near and Middle East Countries	CDNH	698	754	788	676	917	2 675	1 030	1 760	2 344	1 619	1 389
of which												
Gulf Arabian countries[3]	GQCM	617	660	704	586	658	2 374	626	704	1 482	1 027	1 007
Other Asian Countries	GQCR	13 419	15 341	17 250	19 239	18 472	18 283	23 118	22 856	27 700	27 295	31 705
of which												
China	HIIQ	183	118	174	458	469	233	1 254	1 505	2 106	3 212	2 090
Hong Kong	CDNN	3 569	3 373	4 033	4 636	4 406	5 330	5 533	4 745	6 638	5 872	6 928
India	GQAE	490	601	498	532	703	705	869	1 204	1 488	1 409	1 521
Indonesia	GQAF	272	295	418	391	801	641	421	611	1 612	1 014	1 305
Japan	CDMP	1 936	2 613	2 397	2 437	1 605	1 855	3 628	4 613	1 754	1 896	2 323
Malaysia	CDNQ	1 750	2 119	1 813	2 164	2 411	1 908	2 088	2 423	2 390	1 214	1 153
Singapore	CDNT	3 706	4 445	5 287	5 822	5 186	5 632	6 072	3 286	5 947	6 797	9 971
South Korea	GQAG	155	183	250	238	154	219	603	443	547	927	1 381
Thailand	GQAH	404	511	920	1 053	1 009	630	375	682	831	1 513	1 347
Australasia and Oceania	GQCN	12 287	13 517	13 985	14 636	13 312	12 179	11 652	10 080	15 487	16 652	18 106
of which												
Australia	CDMO	10 299	11 153	11 365	12 213	10 598	9 071	9 475	8 101	13 700	13 936	16 503
New Zealand	CDMQ	1 443	1 689	1 670	1 640	1 663	1 625	1 855	1 701	1 560	2 524	1 419
Africa	GQCQ	4 570	5 409	4 955	4 876	5 873	4 232	9 876	9 383	8 948	13 516	16 775
of which												
Kenya	GQAI	165	673	276	237	361	415	389	373	294	278	287
Nigeria	CDNA	754	681	335	321	1 060	463	508	906	1 044	1 012	1 028
South Africa	CDMR	2 622	2 202	2 827	2 429	2 527	1 698	6 620	3 747	4 148	8 765	11 267
Zimbabwe	CDNF	248	331	262	200	192	114	171	130	166	62	48
World Total	CDOO	165 831	177 116	196 687	194 601	218 162	293 581	424 660	601 692	599 628	616 786	692 496
OECD	GQCO	136 247	142 332	159 476	157 652	175 434	249 340	368 986	536 232	522 287	527 681	598 002
Central & Eastern Europe[4]	GQCP	106	460	427	622	1 782	2 178	1 313	2 032	4 349	6 449	6 682

1 See chapter text.
2 Prior to 1995 Russia covers other former USSR countries, the Baltic States and Albania.
3 Includes Abu Dhabi, Bahrain, Dubai, Iraq, Kuwait, Oman, Other Gulf States, Qatar, Saudi Arabia and Yemen.
4 Includes Albania, Bulgaria, Croatia, Czech Republic, Estonia, Hungary, Latvia, Lithuania, Poland, Romania, Serbia and Montenegro, Slovakia, Bosnia and Herzegovina, Macedonia FYR and Slovenia.

Sources: ONS Foreign Direct Investment Inquiries: 01633 813314;
Bank of England

19.15 Net earnings from foreign direct investment overseas by United Kingdom companies:[1,2] by area and main country

£ million

		1993	1994	1995	1996	1997	1998	1999	2000	2001	2002	2003
Europe	GQCV	5 182	7 033	8 289	9 700	10 440	11 349	14 355	21 760	24 719	26 598	27 852
EU	CAWG	4 450	6 138	7 251	8 557	8 994	9 822	11 244	17 399	21 437	22 376	22 975
Austria	CBLQ	35	52	73	82	65	49	45	77	68	267	312
Belgium	HIIR	412	387	264	169	160	473	242	480	570	545	..
Denmark	CAWI	207	115	286	208	191	215	220	248	227	54	187
Finland	CBLR	22	30	43	–	36	58	95	95	73	95	103
France	CAWJ	50	607	619	999	1 036	994	1 222	1 693	1 610	1 904	2 005
Germany	CAWK	381	834	1 032	951	844	828	1 241	946	679	2 199	1 620
Greece	CAWL	58	–202	–106	172	122	77	162	72	95	120	120
Irish Republic	CAWM	669	516	639	847	1 112	1 245	1 367	1 638	2 123	1 553	2 253
Italy	CAWN	113	219	272	327	268	327	403	539	585	517	640
Luxembourg	HIIS	–	–	44	190	138	160	159	1 672	2 163	1 822	1 552
Netherlands	CAWO	2 459	2 986	3 248	3 748	4 143	4 481	5 246	8 348	11 465	11 395	12 081
Portugal	CAWP	53	162	188	184	96	162	152	174	182	115	168
Spain	CAWQ	39	234	338	493	561	464	389	749	627	672	539
Sweden	CBLT	–48	200	310	188	224	288	300	668	970	1 115	1 058
EFTA	CAWS	639	792	899	963	991	848	1 618	2 393	1 010	1 643	1 742
of which												
Norway	CBLS	119	267	224	311	242	134	248	409	450	293	303
Switzerland	CBLU	520	524	675	652	747	705	1 369	1 983	559	1 349	1 439
Other European Countries	GQCW	95	103	139	180	454	680	1 494	1 968	2 272	2 579	3 134
of which												
Russia[3]	GQAJ	2	3	12	24	–30	–214	–	62	297	334	344
UK offshore islands	GQAK	–	–	–	–	225	685	1 081	1 172	916	1 127	1 455
America	GQCX	6 126	8 007	10 254	10 698	11 867	11 976	12 841	14 886	13 529	14 716	17 605
of which												
Bermuda	CBNK	428	446	509	506	70	440	466	344	–90	203	1 373
Brazil	CBNL	193	348	432	650	380	322	113	256	344	378	296
Canada	CAWW	283	357	374	571	913	844	868	1 140	864	1 015	1 004
Chile	GQCY	139	195	263	265	236	147	143	236	156	199	273
Colombia	GQCZ	16	–22	28	23	53	2	78	293	190	200	234
Mexico	GQAL	43	48	52	74	145	95	186	105	–48	295	232
Panama	GQAM	69	51	45	67	..	180	..	46	45	44	55
USA	CAWV	4 621	5 894	7 803	8 034	9 339	9 672	9 681	11 142	10 646	11 461	12 605
Asia	GQDA	2 792	3 449	2 501	3 776	3 249	4 137	2 768	4 434	4 356	4 755	4 634
Near and Middle East Countries	CBMS	283	297	262	241	475	921	485	908	596	398	455
of which												
Gulf Arabian countries[4]	GQDB	273	293	260	212	424	878	443	721	420	335	346
Other Asian Countries	GQDC	2 509	3 152	2 239	3 536	2 774	3 215	2 283	3 527	3 761	4 357	4 179
of which												
China	HIIT	16	16	3	49	40	6	27	74	340	255	268
Hong Kong	CAYB	972	1 427	1 362	1 463	623	959	881	708	341	610	617
India	GQAN	–190	121	100	81	124	194	188	311	324	496	518
Indonesia	GQAO	60	48	71	87	143	114	54	81	150	132	183
Japan	CAWY	142	199	212	281	313	167	545	505	382	181	339
Malaysia	CBNA	248	221	248	332	360	247	352	400	277	448	479
Singapore	CBND	977	781	–144	883	795	1 291	28	902	1 276	1 053	918
South Korea	GQAP	8	29	40	34	17	34	13	37	111	233	227
Thailand	GQAQ	78	84	75	101	95	16	130	90	166	162	160
Australasia and Oceania	GQDD	1 233	2 131	2 044	2 269	1 950	1 532	1 434	1 591	1 651	2 337	2 081
of which												
Australia	CBMB	991	1 776	1 587	1 747	1 503	1 092	1 139	1 393	1 337	1 818	1 531
New Zealand	CBMC	213	302	322	319	278	147	263	171	304	488	524
Africa	GQDE	1 465	737	807	1 055	965	658	1 097	1 567	1 849	2 973	2 911
of which												
Kenya	GQAR	34	41	46	35	94	78	67	71	70	64	80
Nigeria	CBML	498	–27	–35	61	46	49	65	88	95	282	121
South Africa	CAWZ	488	366	438	503	521	399	656	734	983	1 784	1 693
Zimbabwe	CBMQ	54	58	58	50	58	53	73	60	61	37	43
World Total	GLAB	16 796	21 355	23 894	27 498	28 470	29 652	32 496	44 237	46 103	51 379	55 083
OECD	GQDF	11 454	15 578	18 567	20 621	22 601	22 810	25 812	34 824	36 732	40 229	42 119
Central & Eastern Europe[5]	GQDG	11	–24	16	15	118	75	252	465	791	802	1 004

1 See chapter text. A minus sign indicates net losses.
2 Net earnings equal profits of overseas branches plus UK companies' receipts of interest and their share of profits of overseas subsidiaries and associates. Earnings are after deducting provisions for depreciation and overseas tax on profits, dividends and interest.
3 Prior to 1995 Russia covers other former USSR countries, the Baltic States and Albania.

4 Includes Abu Dhabi, Bahrain, Dubai, Iraq, Kuwait, Oman, Other Gulf States, Qatar, Saudi Arabia and Yemen.
5 Includes Albania, Bulgaria, Croatia, Czech Republic, Estonia, Hungary, Latvia, Lithuania, Poland, Romania, Serbia and Montenegro, Slovakia, Bosnia and Herzegovina, Macedonia FYR and Slovenia.

Sources: ONS Foreign Direct Investment Inquiries: 01633 813314;
Bank of England

19.16 Net inward foreign direct investment in the United Kingdom:[1,2] by area and main country

£ million

		1993	1994	1995	1996	1997	1998	1999	2000	2001	2002	2003
Europe	GQDH	2 202	3 065	4 626	6 931	8 394	22 892	39 398	53 839	17 213	15 431	9 172
EU	CAYO	1 589	3 367	3 555	4 673	6 905	12 654	39 676	52 394	17 500	15 722	7 658
Austria	CBOB	13	60	21	20	18	154	−13	175	−149	..	..
Belgium	HIIU	−427	357	101	200	143	186	588	137	−23	−333	183
Denmark	CAYQ	97	76	68	151	228	227	398	481	195	114	600
Finland	CBOC	−42	32	−36	2	193	129	228	87	26	5	66
France	CAYR	−37	310	1 004	1 321	2 647	778	3 217	31 722	8 779	1 460	569
Germany	CAYS	656	71	2 090	835	1 123	484	26 278	10 564	279	11 340	1 865
Greece	CAYT	..	..	..	..	..	1	3	..	4	7	..
Irish Republic	CAYU	49	224	−35	221	1 127	724	78	384	755	210	262
Italy	CAYV	80	177	328	−184	−32	99	23	469	2 848	−208	−500
Luxembourg	HIIV	−	−	419	−193	31	882	−36	688	196	1	−121
Netherlands	CAYW	1 244	1 915	−633	2 610	1 180	9 019	7 860	4 629	4 256	1 756	3 745
Portugal	CAYX	..	..	..	..	..	5	11	−6	7	−18	..
Spain	CAYY	14	21	17	66	71	99	119	..	224	232	516
Sweden	CBOE	−56	119	184	−379	147	−132	924	657	106	493	417
EFTA of which	CAZB	550	−176	1 036	2 211	1 512	9 859	−660	740	−944	−298	1 413
Norway	CBOD	49	−131	124	1 060	182	−116	−502	−392	−227	−137	−179
Switzerland	CBOF	501	−44	912	1 151	1 320	9 967	−165	1 119	−775	−162	1 416
Other European Countries of which	GQDI	64	−125	36	47	−21	379	382	704	658	8	101
Russia[3]	GQAS	49	−	19	61	19	..	..	..	19	8	..
UK offshore islands	GQAT	−	−	−	−	−74	426	325	646	622	−8	44
America of which	GQDJ	5 993	2 344	8 750	7 210	10 615	18 770	17 159	15 032	16 056	−2 051	3 773
Canada	CAZF	33	−246	−438	444	374	58	519	1 882	−261	562	−340
USA	CAZE	5 142	2 138	9 293	6 742	10 045	18 596	15 953	12 741	15 025	−2 157	2 977
Asia	GQDK	570	186	−189	412	402	1 421	−2 189	7 725	3 132	2 551	−831
Near and Middle East Countries	GQAU	115	78	58	64	103	81	137	88	287	−26	−38
Other Asian Countries of which	GQAV	456	110	−248	348	299	1 340	−2 326	7 637	2 845	2 579	−792
Hong Kong	GQAW	106	45	−124	10	15	60	17	921	70	63	63
Japan	CAZH	277	4	−379	209	288	968	−2 646	5 765	2 572	2 352	−944
Singapore	GQAX	14	2	40	1	41	15	329	800	78	157	−73
South Korea	GQAY	43	2	85	−8	−78	187	−112	−18	1	−26	−5
Australasia and Oceania of which	GQDL	995	387	−647	992	714	986	−133	1 483	92	31	310
Australia	CBOJ	995	260	−708	1 096	721	1 093	..	1 440	112	14	320
New Zealand	CBOK	−	127	60	−104	−6	−107	..	40	−24	18	−9
Africa of which	GQAZ	111	63	117	118	170	808	143	416	63	71	8
South Africa	CAZJ	58	50	125	109	149	585	130	378	51	63	21
World Total	CBDH	9 871	6 046	12 654	15 662	20 296	44 877	54 376	78 495	36 555	16 033	12 432
OECD	GQBA	8 636	5 346	12 511	15 235	19 758	43 306	52 590	74 995	33 980	16 194	11 053
Central & Eastern Europe[4]	GQBB	−	−141	15	−19	14	−16	2	8	10	−	8

1 See chapter text. A minus sign indicates net disinvestment in the UK.
2 Net investment includes unremitted profits.
3 Prior to 1995 Russia covers other former USSR countries, the Baltic States and Albania.
4 Includes Albania, Bulgaria, Croatia, Czech Republic, Estonia, Hungary, Latvia, Lithuania, Poland, Romania, Serbia and Montenegro, Slovakia, Bosnia and Herzegovina, Macedonia FYR and Slovenia.

Sources: ONS Foreign Direct Investment Inquiries: 01633 813314; Bank of England

19.17 United Kingdom inward foreign direct international investment position: book value of net liabilities: by area and main country[1]

At year end
£ million

		1993	1994	1995	1996	1997	1998	1999	2000	2001	2002	2003
Europe	GQDM	47 770	47 281	52 144	55 856	58 037	81 385	118 793	150 203	166 532	157 313	157 465
EU	CDOT	40 266	39 998	43 493	43 774	44 927	69 248	107 249	136 686	150 995	142 397	140 020
Austria	CDPF	93	428	412	280	79	334	253	565	385	1 003	317
Belgium	HIIW	1 801	2 221	1 000	610	959	1 354	1 929	2 200	2 208	1 765	1 965
Denmark	CDOV	1 339	1 072	1 127	850	927	1 560	1 971	2 758	3 955	2 358	2 452
Finland	CDPG	300	356	352	334	444	729	921	1 042	1 084	767	819
France	CDOW	7 880	7 728	8 289	9 147	13 880	16 265	19 797	48 947	35 213	37 195	38 090
Germany	CDOX	5 921	5 589	8 854	9 508	10 078	11 573	36 250	26 140	29 731	37 737	32 197
Greece	CDOY	..	..	..	..	..	..	47	..	92	89	86
Irish Republic	CDOZ	681	956	686	703	1 837	2 807	3 098	3 474	4 209	4 544	4 546
Italy	CDPA	875	839	1 223	988	824	1 406	1 540	2 415	6 522	5 788	4 587
Luxembourg	HIIX	–	–	1 170	623	896	1 455	2 214	1 854	2 330	4 985	5 750
Netherlands	CDPB	18 477	18 511	17 173	18 692	12 131	28 227	33 891	41 565	60 920	39 512	43 546
Portugal	CDPC	..	..	..	78	..	..	179	..	129	97	115
Spain	CDPD	346	178	164	78	247	463	1 015	475	606	2 303	2 838
Sweden	CDPI	2 542	2 105	2 908	1 871	2 521	2 910	4 144	3 929	3 613	4 254	2 713
EFTA	CDPE	7 225	7 111	8 188	11 735	12 379	9 103	9 203	10 103	10 465	10 951	14 466
of which												
Norway	CDPH	701	506	665	1 571	1 866	1 559	560	854	832	1 019	871
Switzerland	CDPJ	6 519	6 605	7 523	10 164	10 422	7 444	8 516	9 091	9 341	9 717	13 108
Other European Countries	GQDN	280	172	463	348	731	3 035	2 341	3 414	5 072	3 966	2 979
of which												
Russia[2]	GQBC	43	24	80	212	..	258	192	..	..	..	..
UK offshore islands	GQBD	–	–	–	–	341	2 465	1 780	2 774	4 366	3 393	2 359
America	GQDU	55 209	55 918	59 420	62 253	77 408	101 645	104 331	113 882	151 338	138 156	149 336
of which												
Canada	CDPM	4 101	4 593	2 652	3 517	4 129	4 090	7 070	9 307	8 693	8 718	10 912
USA	CDPN	49 537	49 829	55 129	55 956	70 270	93 419	93 469	101 245	136 967	124 597	132 632
Asia	GQDO	7 655	7 782	7 934	8 072	9 166	10 308	7 050	17 890	19 388	20 323	19 528
Near and Middle East Countries	GQBE	1 427	2 027	1 324	1 274	1 450	1 380	1 026	1 370	1 788	1 697	1 485
Other Asian Countries	GQBF	6 228	5 755	6 609	6 797	7 715	8 928	6 024	16 520	17 600	18 626	18 043
of which												
Hong Kong	GQBG	262	233	19	31	56	331	445	..	3 613	2 992	..
Japan	CDPQ	5 427	5 105	5 542	5 888	6 562	7 387	4 174	10 545	10 900	11 791	11 716
Singapore	GQBH	415	421	500	503	757	447	834	1 656	1 591	1 684	832
South Korea	GQBI	–3	–203	12	–206	–305	–66	–202	–245	108	448	655
Australasia and Oceania	GQDP	9 560	9 644	8 527	7 707	7 354	7 839	7 147	10 661	11 167	8 462	14 325
of which												
Australia	CDPP	8 598	7 968	7 021	6 169	6 003	5 938	5 450	9 875	10 997	8 309	14 160
New Zealand	CDPR	844	1 676	1 506	1 538	1 351	1 554	1 055	780	149	134	147
Africa	GQBJ	811	712	861	766	991	1 641	953	1 312	917	427	560
of which												
South Africa	CDPS	618	549	665	578	743	1 228	767	969	757	250	387
World Total	CDPZ	121 005	121 336	128 885	134 654	152 956	202 817	238 274	293 949	349 342	324 680	341 214
OECD	GQBK	116 082	116 171	123 761	128 475	145 336	190 717	227 529	278 358	329 296	307 395	324 736
Central & Eastern Europe[3]	GQBL	21	10	258	14	24	63	103	110	84	58	70

1 See chapter text.
2 Prior to 1995 Russia covers other former USSR countries, the Baltic States and Albania.
3 Includes Albania, Bulgaria, Croatia, Czech Republic, Estonia, Hungary, Latvia, Lithuania, Poland, Romania, Serbia and Montenegro, Slovakia, Bosnia and Herzegovina, Macedonia FYR and Slovenia.

Sources: ONS Foreign Direct Investment Inquiries: 01633 813314;
Bank of England

19.18 Net earnings from foreign direct investment in the United Kingdom:[1,2] by area and main country

£ million

		1993	1994	1995	1996	1997	1998	1999	2000	2001	2002	2003
Europe	GQDQ	4 833	3 661	5 432	6 401	5 746	1 485	6 643	15 304	11 250	5 475	10 313
EU	CBDJ	3 556	3 659	4 657	5 631	5 231	2 908	6 232	13 798	10 066	4 430	9 071
Austria	CBOR	−5	94	30	55	13	12	15	79	93	176	139
Belgium	HIIY	224	272	170	174	90	379	216	−27	79	38	156
Denmark	CBDL	92	18	152	137	171	269	208	373	259	253	282
Finland	CBOS	−52	2	88	74	80	70	106	207	197	70	77
France	CBDM	633	227	836	705	1 239	648	1 871	2 186	1 632	1 322	2 737
Germany	CBDN	576	507	700	706	563	−185	−171	2 233	−633	−1 109	1 625
Greece	CBDO	..	..	..	..	..	23	28	21	46	64	5
Irish Republic	CBDP	74	92	155	141	222	397	251	422	426	561	580
Italy	CBDQ	97	246	196	318	430	249	189	155	375	−148	75
Luxembourg	HIIZ	–	–	79	35	49	29	133	164	74	87	198
Netherlands	CBDR	1 820	2 076	2 070	3 053	2 034	640	2 947	7 611	6 972	2 455	2 712
Portugal	CBDS	..	..	..	..	..	−5	2	9	6	13	49
Spain	CBDT	55	17	42	69	106	85	127	88	203	52	296
Sweden	CBOU	46	107	127	146	219	300	309	280	337	599	140
EFTA of which	CBDW	1 188	−33	685	709	408	−1 411	311	1 451	816	735	816
Norway	CBOT	27	12	11	−58	121	−171	−212	120	59	40	–
Switzerland	CBOV	1 161	−45	675	768	277	−1 248	518	1 323	749	692	788
Other European Countries of which	GQDR	88	36	89	60	108	−9	100	55	368	310	425
Russia[3]	GQBM	55	1	15	31	..	..	12	..	..	..	..
UK offshore islands	GQBN	–	–	–	–	33	42	47	−34	313	267	335
America of which	GQDV	4 917	4 992	5 824	7 589	6 775	6 365	7 857	8 482	7 385	7 314	10 749
Canada	CBEA	234	506	228	281	65	198	368	774	147	659	620
USA	CBDZ	4 441	4 372	5 606	6 986	6 512	5 848	7 586	7 789	7 204	6 623	9 728
Asia	GQDS	106	172	459	300	−332	−597	137	1 227	1 099	1 214	−822
Near and Middle East Countries	GQBO	16	−8	112	89	96	46	137	68	154	33	112
Other Asian Countries of which	GQBP	90	181	347	211	−428	−643	–	1 159	945	1 182	−934
Hong Kong	GQBQ	52	4	−2	28	21	−185	26	36	11	−52	−456
Japan	CBEC	45	171	334	151	−502	−391	−61	925	684	1 022	−594
Singapore	GQBS	4	1	5	–	41	−79	88	235	114	100	63
South Korea	GQBT	7	15	−6	−6	−11	−20	−60	−85	3	16	−54
Australasia and Oceania of which	GQDT	418	327	472	594	860	629	508	222	82	432	859
Australia	CBOZ	410	330	479	566	830	602	..	195	17	396	825
New Zealand	CBPA	8	−1	−6	28	..	85	..	21	15	3	5
Africa of which	GQBU	19	25	49	44	55	7	127	180	154	99	60
South Africa	CBED	9	21	38	35	46	−23	114	167	122	97	51
World Total	CBEV	10 293	9 176	12 235	14 928	13 103	7 889	15 272	25 415	19 971	14 534	21 158
OECD	GQBV	9 998	9 118	12 081	14 388	12 583	7 838	14 905	24 907	18 988	13 904	20 416
Central & Eastern Europe[4]	GQBW	1	24	60	13	18	−12	11	5	5	2	1

1 See chapter text. A minus sign indicates net losses.
2 Net earnings equal profits of UK branches plus overseas investors' receipts of interest and their share of the profits of UK subsidiaries and associates. Earnings are after deducting provisions for depreciation and UK tax on profits and interest.
3 Prior to 1995 Russia covers other former USSR countries, the Baltic States and Albania.
4 Includes Albania, Bulgaria, Croatia, Czech Republic, Estonia, Hungary, Latvia, Lithuania, Poland, Romania, Serbia and Montenegro, Slovakia, Bosnia and Herzegovina, Macedonia FYR and Slovenia.

Sources: ONS Foreign Direct Investment Inquiries: 01633 813314; Bank of England

Research and development

Chapter 20

Research and development

Research and experimental development (R&D) is defined for statistical purposes as 'creative work undertaken on a systematic basis in order to increase the stock of knowledge, including knowledge of man, culture and society, and the use of this stock of knowledge to devise new applications'.

R&D is financed and carried out mainly by businesses, the Government, and institutions of higher education. A small amount is performed by non-profit-making bodies. Gross Expenditure on R&D (GERD) is an indicator of the total amount of R&D performed within the UK: it has been approximately two per cent of GDP in recent years. Detailed figures are reported each year in a First Release published in March and the August edition of the ONS's *Economic Trends*. Table 20.1 shows the main components of GERD. ONS conducts an annual survey of expenditure and employment on R&D performed by Government, and of Government funding of R&D. The survey collects data on outturn and planning years. Until 1993 the detailed results were reported in the *Annual Review of Government Funded R&D* produced by the Office of Science and Technology (OST). From 1997 the results have appeared in OST's *Science, Engineering and Technology Statistics* publication. Table 20.2 gives some broad totals for gross expenditure by Government (expenditure before deducting funds received by Government for R&D). Table 20.3 gives a breakdown of net expenditure (receipts are deducted).

ONS conducts an annual survey of R&D in business. Tables 20.4 and 20.5 give a summary of the main trends up to 2002. The latest set of results from the survey will be available in a First Release dated 26 November 2004 and a Business Monitor (MA14) published on 21 January 2005.

Statistics on expenditure and employment on R&D in Higher Education Institutions (HEIs) are based on information collected by Higher Education Funding Councils and HESA (Higher Education Statistics Agency). In 1994 a new methodology was introduced to estimate expenditure on R&D in HEIs. This is based on the allocation of various Funding Council Grants. Full details of the new methodology are contained in SET Statistics available on the Office of Science and Technology website at *www.ost.gov.uk/setstats/*.

The most comprehensive international comparisons of resources devoted to R&D appear in Main Science and Technology Indicators published by the organisation for Economic Co-operation and Development (OECD). The Statistical Office of the European Union and the United Nations also compile R&D statistics based on figures supplied by member states. To make international comparisons more reliable the OECD have published a series of manuals giving guidance on how to measure various components of R&D inputs and outputs. The most important of these is the Frascati Manual, which defines R&D and recommends how resources for R&D should be measured. The UK follows the Frascati Manual as far as possible. For information on available aggregated data on Research and Development please contact Julie Owens on 01633 812789 (e-mail *Julie.Owens@ons.gsi.gov. uk*).

20.1 Cost of research and development: by sector[1]
United Kingdom

	1996 £m	1996 %	1997 £m	1997 %	1998 £m	1998 %	1999 £m	1999 %	2000 £m	2000 %	2001 £m	2001 %	2002 £m	2002 %
Sector carrying out the work **Cash terms (£ million)**														
Government	1 495	10	1 427	10	1 487	10	1 450	9	1 489	8	1 160	6	1 053	5
Research councils	575	4	590	4	591	4	622	4	646	4	670	4	699	4
Business enterprise	9 297	65	9 556	65	10 133	66	11 302	67	11 510	66	12 336	67	13 110	67
Higher education	2 792	19	2 893	20	3 040	20	3 324	20	3 648	21	4 034	21	4 416	23
Private non-profit	177	1	190	1	203	1	231	1	255	1	269	1	290	1
Total	14 336	100	14 657	100	15 454	100	16 929	100	17 547	100	18 469	100	19 568	100
Sector providing the funds **Cash terms (£ million)**														
Government	2 402	17	2 332	16	2 535	16	2 601	15	2 547	15	2 842	15	2 178	11
Research councils	1 092	8	1 135	8	1 117	7	1 185	7	1 250	7	1 358	7	1 464	7
Higher education funding councils	1 027	7	1 033	7	1 085	7	1 157	7	1 276	7	1 474	8	1 626	8
Higher education	120	1	123	1	130	1	142	1	158	1	177	1	196	1
Business enterprise[2]	6 817	48	7 321	50	7 356	48	8 213	49	8 648	49	8 741	46	9 138	47
Private non-profit	545	4	578	4	621	4	701	4	815	5	888	5	963	5
Abroad	2 331	16	2 136	15	2 610	17	2 929	17	2 854	16	3 385	18	4 003	20
Total	14 336	100	14 657	100	15 454	100	16 929	100	17 547	100	18 866	100	19 568	100

1 See chapter text.
2 Including research associations and public corporations.

Source: Office for National Statistics: 01633 812789

20.2 Gross central government expenditure on research and development[1]
United Kingdom

	1997/98 Intra-mural	1997/98 Extra-mural[2]	1998/99 Intra-mural	1998/99 Extra-mural[2]	1999/00 Intra-mural	1999/00 Extra-mural[2]	2000/01 Intra-mural	2000/01 Extra-mural[2]	2001/02 Intra-mural	2001/02 Extra-mural[2]	2002/03 Intra-mural	2002/03 Intra-mural
Defence	750	..	801	..	798	..	932	..	419	1 685	288	2 502
Research councils	608	852	608	865	644	894	667	1 024	695	1 244	725	1 457
Higher education institutes	-	1 033	-	1 085	-	1 157	-	1 276	-	1 474	-	1 626
Other programmes	253	681	266	714	274	810	283	841	282	982	297	1 178
Total (excluding NHS)	1 635	..	1 692	..	1 703	4 577	1 778	4 859	1 396	5 385	1 310	6 763

1 See chapter text.
2 Including work performed overseas and excluding monies spent with other
  government departments.

Source: Office for National Statistics: 01633 812789

20.3 Net central government expenditure on research and development:[1] by European Union objectives for research and development expenditure

United Kingdom
£ million

		1992 /93	1993 /94	1994 /95	1995 /96	1996 /97	1997 /98	1998 /99	1999 /00	2000 /01	2001 /02	2002 /03
Exploration and exploitation of the earth	KDVP	120.5	98.8	106.8	105.2	95.4	81.3	78.5	79.5	85.5	106.0	138.3
Infrastructure and general planning of land-use	KDVQ	85.6	96.7	98.1	94.1	98.8	98.9	103.5	104.4	102.4	100.3	101.0
Control of environmental pollution	KDVR	69.5	108.7	117.2	131.8	128.7	136.2	142.8	147.0	151.1	129.1	126.5
Protection and promotion of human health (ex NHS)	KDVS	341.5	383.1	397.2	416.0	427.4	444.8	450.1	519.5	530.6	571.6	597.8
Production, distribution and rational utilisation of energy	KDVT	120.0	96.8	55.5	52.3	43.2	41.0	28.0	29.0	31.9	36.8	40.3
Agricultural production and technology	KDVU	261.1	284.6	263.4	281.9	257.0	268.9	255.5	260.6	266.6	265.2	267.8
Industrial production and technology	KDVV	394.1	458.7	184.4	165.8	144.6	116.9	61.6	56.5	109.2	237.0	423.4
Social structures and relationships	KDVW	141.9	149.1	141.9	137.1	120.7	113.8	154.7	217.6	270.2	268.8	293.4
Exploration and exploitation of space	KDVX	149.1	187.4	161.5	153.0	164.1	164.4	142.5	142.7	146.3	139.8	155.5
Research financed from general university funds	KDVY	963.3	968.4	1 017.9	1 018.6	1 027.5	1 033.3	1 085.1	1 157.1	1 276.1	1 473.5	1 626.4
Non-oriented research	KDVZ	337.1	267.3	612.5	653.5	680.5	671.0	677.0	700.5	789.3	918.2	1 071.6
Other civil research	KDWA	23.8	34.0	22.2	24.7	20.5	21.6	25.8	20.6	22.3	19.7	36.3
Defence	KDWB	2 080.5	2 278.5	2 033.6	2 071.7	2 237.0	2 317.2	2 144.2	2 275.9	2 245.1	2 063.0	2 739.7
Total (excluding NHS)	KDWC	5 088.0	5 412.1	5 212.2	5 305.7	5 445.4	5 509.3	5 349.3	5 710.9	6 026.6	6 329.0	7 618.0

1 See chapter text.

Source: Office for National Statistics: 01633 812789

20.4 Intramural expenditure on Business Enterprise research and development:[1] by industry

United Kingdom: At Current Prices and Constant 2002 Prices
£ million

		Total				Civil				Defence		
		2000	2001	2002		2000	2001	2002		2000	2001	2002
Current Prices												
Chemicals	KDWF	3 528	3 562	3 887	KDWP	3 527	3 562	3 885	KDWZ	–	–	2
Mechanical engineering	KDWG	776	907	826	KDWQ	463	470	524	KDXA	314	437	302
Electrical machinery	KJRT	1 558	1 599	1 565	KJTC	1 163	1 200	1 204	KJUL	395	399	361
Aerospace	KDWJ	1 094	1 189	1 244	KDWT	1 023	1 106	..	KDXD	71	82	..
Transport equipment	KDWK	1 091	1 260	1 347	KDWU	457	621	645	KDXE	634	639	702
Other manufacturing	KDWL	1 183	1 271	1 272	KDWV	948	1 130	..	KDXF	235	141	..
Manufacturing: Total	KDWE	9 231	9 788	10 140	KDWO	7 582	8 089	8 626	KDWY	1 649	1 699	1 514
Services	KDWM	1 905	2 280	2 645	KDWW	1 883	2 155	2 511	KDXG	22	125	135
Agriculture, hunting and forestry; fishing	HFRV	135	96	122	HFSA	135	96	122	MKFC	..	..	..
Extractive industries	HFRW	46	43	52	HFSB	46	43	52	MKFD	..	..	..
Electricity, gas and water supply	HFRX	160	99	116	HFSC	160	99	116	MKFE	..	..	..
Construction	HFRY	34	30	35	HFSE	34	30	35	MKFF	..	..	..
Other: Total	HFRU	374	268	324	HFRZ	374	268	324	MKFB	..	..	..
Total	KDWD	11 510	12 336	13 110	KDWN	9 838	10 513	11 461	KDWX	1 671	1 824	1 649
2002 Prices												
Chemicals	HFXA	3 721	3 664	3 887	HFXJ	3 720	3 664	3 885	HFYO	–	–	2
Mechanical engineering	HFXB	819	933	826	HFXK	488	483	524	HFYP	331	449	302
Electrical machinery	HFXC	1 643	1 645	1 565	HFYH	1 227	1 234	1 204	HFYQ	417	410	361
Aerospace	HFXD	1 154	1 223	1 244	HFYI	1 079	1 138	..	HFYR	75	84	..
Transport equipment	HFXE	1 151	1 296	1 347	HFYJ	482	639	645	HFYS	669	657	702
Other manufacturing	HFXF	1 248	1 307	1 272	HFYK	1 000	1 162	..	HFYT	248	145	..
Manufacturing: Total	HFWZ	9 737	10 067	10 140	HFXI	7 998	8 320	8 626	HFYN	1 739	1 747	1 514
Services	HFXG	2 009	2 345	2 645	HFYL	1 986	2 216	2 511	HFYU	23	129	135
Agriculture, hunting and forestry: fishing	HFSG	142	99	122	HFSL	142	99	122	MKFH	..	..	..
Extractive industries	HFSH	49	44	52	HFSM	49	44	52	MKFI	..	..	..
Electricity, gas and water supply	HFSI	169	102	116	HFSN	169	102	116	MKFJ	..	..	..
Construction	HFSJ	36	31	35	HFSO	36	31	35	MKFK	..	..	..
Other: Total	HFSF	395	276	324	HFSK	395	276	324	MKFG	..	..	..
Total	HFWY	12 141	12 688	13 110	HFXH	10 377	10 813	11 461	HFYM	1 763	1 876	1 649

1 See chapter text.

Source: Office for National Statistics: 01633 812789

20.5 Sources of funds for research and development within Business Enterprises[1]
United Kingdom

£ million and percentages

		Total				Civil				Defence		
		2000	2001	2002		2000	2001	2002		2000	2001	2002
Cash terms (£ million)												
Government funds	KDYM	1 013	1 101	884	KDYU	228	191	193	KDZC	785	911	691
Overseas funds	KDYN	2 470	3 012	3 567	KDYV	2 003	2 585	3 026	KDZD	467	427	541
Mainly own funds	KDYO	8 026	8 223	8 658	KDYW	7 607	7 738	8 242	KDZE	418	485	417
Total	KDYL	11 510	12 336	13 110	KDYT	9 838	10 513	11 461	KDZB	1 671	1 824	1 649
Percentages												
Government funds	KDYQ	9	9	7	KDYY	2	2	2	KDZG	47	50	42
Overseas funds	KDYR	21	24	27	KDYZ	20	25	26	KDZH	28	23	33
Mainly own funds	KDYS	70	67	66	KDZA	77	74	72	KDZI	25	27	25
Total	KDYP	100	100	100	KDYX	100	100	100	KDZF	100	100	100

1 See chapter text.

Source: Office for National Statistics: 01633 812789

Agriculture, fisheries and food

Chapter 21

Agriculture, fisheries and food

Output and input

(Tables 21.1 and 21.2)

For both tables, output is a net of VAT collected on the sale of non-edible products. Figures for total output include subsidies on products, but not other subsidies.

Unspecified crops include turf, other minor crops and arable area payments for fodder maize. Eggs include the value of duck eggs and exports of eggs for hatching. Landlords' expenses are included within farm maintenance, miscellaneous expenditure and depreciation of buildings and works. Also included within 'other farming costs' are livestock and crop costs, water costs, insurance premia, bank charges, professional fees, rates, and other farming costs.

Other subsidies

Agri-Environment schemes include Environmentally and Nitrate Sensitive Areas, Countryside Stewardship, Countryside Premium, Tir Cymen, Tir Gofal, Moorland, Habitat, Farm Woodland and Organic Farming Schemes. Included in 'other' subsidies are guidance premium for beef and sheep meat production, Pilot Beef and Sheep Extensification Scheme, non-agricultural horse grazing and farm accounts grant as well as historic data for fertiliser and lime grant and payments to small scale cereal producers.

Compensation of employees and interest charges

Total compensation of employees excludes the value of work done by farm labour on own account capital formation in buildings and work. 'Interest' relates to interest charges on loans for current farming purposes and buildings and less interest on money held on short-term deposit.

Rent

Rent paid (after deductions) is the rent paid on all tenanted land including 'conacre' land in Northern Ireland, less landlords' expenses and the benefit value of dwellings on that land. Rent received (after deductions) is the rent received by farming landowners from renting of land to other farmers, less landlords' expenses and the benefit value of dwellings on that land. Total net rent is the net rent flowing out of the

agricultural sector paid to non-farming landowners, including that part of tenanted land in Northern Ireland. (Although there has been some updating of the technical procedures for calculating this figure, it corresponds with the previous net rent variable.)

Agricultural censuses and surveys

(Tables 21.3, 21.5 and 21.13)

The coverage for holdings includes all main and minor holdings for each country. Northern Ireland data are now based on all active farm business.

Estimated quantity of crops and grass harvested

(Table 21.4)

The estimated yields of sugar beet and hops are obtained from production figures supplied by British Sugar plc, and the main hop producers in England and Wales. In Great Britain potato yields are estimated in consultation with the British Potato Council.

Forestry

(Table 21.6)

Statistics for state forestry are from their management information systems.

For private forestry in Great Britain, statistics on new planting and restocking are based on records of the Woodland Grant Scheme, and timber removals are estimated from a survey of the largest timber harvesting companies. Woodland area figures are based on data obtained from censuses of woodlands and adjusted to reflect subsequent changes. Figures are based on results from the 1995–1999 National Inventory of Woodlands and Trees.

Average weekly earnings and hours of agricultural and horticultural workers

(Tables 21.11 and 21.12)

Since 1998, data on the Earnings and Hours of Agricultural and Horticultural workers have been collected via an annual telephone survey. This annual survey collects information for a snapshot in time, relating to the month of September. The survey covers seven main categories of workers and in 2001 data were collected on 1,274 workers. Prior to 1998, data were collected from a monthly postal survey, which mainly covered male full-time workers.

The survey provides data which are used by the Agricultural Wages Board when considering wage claims and by the Department for Environment, Food and Rural Affairs (DEFRA) in considering the cost of labour in agriculture and horticulture.

Data on earnings represents the total earnings of regular full-time male workers, aged 20 and over. Figures include all payments-in-kind, valued where applicable in accordance with the Agricultural Wages Order. The earnings and hours of hire farm managers are excluded. Part-time workers are defined as those working less than 39 basic hours per week. Casual workers are those employed on a temporary basis.

The survey was reviewed in 2002 and it was concluded that the frequency of the survey should be increased to four times per year to enable the production of more representative annual estimates. The annual sample size has been retained and has been split between four quarterly surveys. Results for other quarters can be found on the Defra website.

Fisheries

(Tables 21.14 and 21.15)

Data relating to the weight and value of landings of fish in the United Kingdom (Table 21.14) is generally obtained from sales notes completed at fish market auctions.

Fishing fleet information (Table 21.15) is obtained from vessel registers maintained by the Department for Environment, Food and Rural Affairs in England and Wales and the Scottish Executive Agriculture and Fisheries Department.

Estimated average household food consumption – 'Family Food' Expenditure & Food Survey

(Table 21.16)

The Expenditure & Food Survey replaced both the National Food Survey and the Family Expenditure Survey in April 2001. The new survey is a voluntary sample survey of private households throughout the United Kingdom and the results are produced for the financial year ending 31 March each year. This represents a break in the continuity of the data as results from the National Food Survey were produced for Great Britain and for the calendar year ended 31 December.

The basic unit of the survey is the household which is defined as a group of persons living at the same address and sharing common catering arrangements. Each individual aged 16 or over in the household visited is asked to keep diary records, for a two-week period, of daily expenditure on and weight/volume of food and drink brought into the home and

expenditure on food and drink eaten out. Children aged between 7 and 15 are asked to keep simplified diaries.

For the year 2001/02 the sample size includes nearly 7,500 households and over 18,000 persons.

21.1 Production and income account at current prices[1]
United Kingdom

£ million

		1993	1994	1995	1996	1997	1998	1999	2000	2001	2002	2003[2]
Output[3]												
1. Total cereals:	C5X5	2 704.3	2 658.8	3 285.0	3 593.0	2 906.9	2 502.3	2 324.8	2 335.9	2 022.8	2 177.3	2 333.6
Wheat	KFKA	1 782.5	1 723.4	2 078.7	2 315.1	1 851.0	1 652.3	1 524.9	1 577.9	1 227.0	1 478.9	1 532.4
Rye	VQBG	3.4	4.3	5.1	5.6	5.4	5.0	3.5	3.1	2.8	2.2	2.3
Barley	KFKB	844.5	846.8	1 108.5	1 183.4	976.8	781.3	733.9	685.1	724.1	621.6	720.8
Oats and summer cereal mixtures	KFKC	71.7	81.7	89.0	85.6	70.6	60.5	58.2	65.0	64.9	69.9	72.7
Other cereals	VQBH	2.3	2.5	3.7	3.3	3.1	3.2	4.2	4.8	4.1	4.7	5.4
2. Total industrial crops	VQBI	1 204.6	1 055.8	1 150.8	1 107.1	1 007.7	1 011.7	1 011.8	776.4	810.2	899.4	1 067.2
Oilseeds	VQBJ	594.3	415.9	427.8	473.7	457.5	485.3	502.6	283.2	291.4	303.6	435.5
Oilseed rape	KFKG	410.3	376.9	387.3	434.3	406.0	417.4	370.5	248.9	275.5	297.9	417.1
Other oil seeds	KIBT	183.9	39.0	40.6	39.4	51.5	67.9	132.1	34.3	15.9	5.7	18.4
Sugar beet	KFKH	352.9	342.7	354.9	358.2	329.1	298.5	279.6	252.1	256.4	282.9	320.9
Other industrial crops	VQBK	257.4	297.2	368.0	275.2	221.1	227.9	229.6	241.1	262.4	312.9	310.8
Fibre plants	VQBL	1.6	13.5	14.2	17.0	15.2	12.8	11.4	8.4	3.5	1.9	3.1
Hops	KFKI	20.8	20.2	16.7	19.5	19.6	14.1	13.3	11.5	9.9	8.1	6.8
Others[4]	VQBM	235.0	263.5	337.1	238.6	186.3	201.0	204.9	221.3	249.0	302.9	301.0
3. Total forage plants	VQBO	219.3	182.7	171.5	170.8	159.4	141.1	145.4	138.7	169.6	156.3	171.1
4. Total vegetables and horticultural products	VQBP	1 481.4	1 602.9	1 696.7	1 759.8	1 632.9	1 638.6	1 677.6	1 569.1	1 714.3	1 702.6	1 810.8
5. Total potatoes (including seeds)	KFKO	390.1	710.2	1 095.1	636.3	390.0	629.4	749.2	452.7	655.3	478.9	512.0
6. Total fruit	KFKQ	272.7	246.6	257.6	292.0	198.7	258.8	256.9	228.6	237.5	242.7	290.0
7. Other crop products including seeds	VQBQ	42.5	42.1	41.5	43.3	47.6	43.7	46.2	40.4	39.9	26.9	33.9
8. Total crop output (Sum 1 to 7)	VQBR	6 314.8	6 499.0	7 698.2	7 602.3	6 343.3	6 225.7	6 211.7	5 541.8	5 649.7	5 684.1	6 218.5
9. Total livestock production	VQBS	6 919.9	7 056.4	7 236.3	7 441.9	7 020.6	6 040.0	5 560.8	5 516.4	5 177.0	5 718.6	5 972.5
Primarily for meat	KFLA	6 036.9	6 214.9	6 540.4	6 852.0	6 297.7	5 445.4	5 163.6	5 127.0	4 577.2	5 024.5	5 219.0
Cattle	KFKU	2 371.9	2 467.8	2 579.4	2 545.9	2 276.5	1 975.8	2 047.2	1 993.1	1 786.3	2 126.9	2 181.6
Pigs	KFKW	1 042.5	1 036.8	1 169.7	1 363.2	1 201.5	882.8	784.8	794.0	748.6	681.6	669.8
Sheep	VQBT	1 226.6	1 218.0	1 305.3	1 273.9	1 176.5	1 109.6	984.4	953.9	621.6	888.0	975.4
Poultry	KFXX	1 267.4	1 362.3	1 351.7	1 526.2	1 494.1	1 328.4	1 198.3	1 233.4	1 265.7	1 170.3	1 230.9
Other animals	KFKY	128.5	130.0	134.3	142.8	149.1	148.8	148.9	152.6	154.9	157.7	161.2
Gross fixed capital formation	KFLI	883.0	841.6	695.9	589.9	722.9	594.6	397.2	389.4	599.8	694.2	753.5
Cattle	KUJZ	616.9	565.3	408.4	289.3	377.9	296.9	206.9	188.5	344.7	381.0	465.1
Pigs	LUKB	14.0	13.9	15.4	19.1	15.2	5.6	6.8	5.6	5.3	7.4	6.9
Sheep	LUKA	135.2	152.3	151.1	152.4	198.6	155.3	56.7	63.8	122.4	177.4	153.8
Poultry	LUKC	116.9	110.0	121.0	129.2	131.1	136.8	126.8	131.4	127.4	128.4	127.7
10. Total livestock products	KFLF	3 659.1	3 799.3	3 948.5	4 006.6	3 625.5	3 132.4	3 042.5	2 791.5	3 201.7	2 876.2	3 101.2
Milk	KFLB	3 187.4	3 310.4	3 497.7	3 494.7	3 153.6	2 709.0	2 653.4	2 393.0	2 821.6	2 466.2	2 626.6
Eggs	KFLC	417.8	420.6	380.6	448.3	411.6	378.5	342.0	353.2	341.6	356.3	408.5
Raw wool	KFLD	29.8	46.2	45.9	39.9	35.1	23.9	21.4	22.7	17.3	19.1	20.8
Other animal products	KFLE	24.0	22.1	24.4	23.7	25.3	21.0	25.7	22.6	21.3	34.5	45.3
11. Total livestock output (9+10)	VQBV	10 579.0	10 855.7	11 184.8	11 448.6	10 646.1	9 172.4	8 603.3	8 307.8	8 378.8	8 594.8	9 073.7
12. Total other agricultural activities	LUOS	533.3	629.0	713.0	791.1	722.3	689.2	726.0	638.1	636.9	649.6	652.3
Agricultural services	LUKD	471.1	501.8	552.9	608.0	575.0	570.2	609.5	587.0	608.5	606.5	614.0
Leasing out quota	VQBW	62.2	127.1	160.1	183.1	147.2	119.1	116.5	51.2	28.3	43.1	38.3
13. Total inseparable non-agricultural activities	LUOT	295.1	322.5	326.6	362.1	371.6	421.1	430.4	465.8	604.2	542.0	577.7
14. Gross output at basic prices (8+11+12+13)	KFLT	17 722.2	18 306.2	19 922.6	20 204.1	18 083.4	16 508.3	15 971.4	14 953.5	15 269.5	15 470.6	16 522.2
15. Total subsidies (less taxes) on product	LUOU	1 763.3	1 686.1	2 106.9	2 782.1	2 587.8	2 436.1	2 373.2	2 187.0	1 923.3	2 130.1	2 183.9
16. Output at market prices (14-15)	LUOV	15 958.9	16 620.1	17 815.7	17 422.0	15 495.6	14 072.2	13 598.2	12 766.5	13 346.2	13 340.4	14 338.3
of which transactions within the agricultural industry												
Feed wheat	LUNQ	81.3	74.7	55.4	67.0	77.3	78.8	64.4	39.8	43.1	39.0	79.0
Feed barley	LUNR	232.9	200.9	198.9	205.6	192.8	163.6	147.9	136.9	151.9	142.9	159.3
Feed oats	LUNS	21.3	21.5	16.5	16.1	11.8	11.5	14.5	12.6	13.1	10.5	10.8
Seed potatoes	LUNT	12.7	13.8	41.1	33.7	9.2	12.7	28.8	8.3	17.3	15.5	5.3
Straw	LUNU	207.2	235.8	308.0	211.6	160.3	173.0	174.8	190.4	219.2	271.3	269.2
Contract work	LUNV	471.1	501.8	552.9	608.0	575.0	570.2	609.5	587.0	608.5	606.5	614.0
Leasing of quota	LUNW	62.2	127.1	160.1	183.1	147.2	119.1	116.5	51.2	28.3	43.1	38.3
Total capital formation in livestock	LUNX	883.0	841.6	695.9	589.9	722.9	594.6	397.2	389.4	599.8	694.2	753.5

£ million

		1993	1994	1995	1996	1997	1998	1999	2000	2001	2002	2003[2]
Intermediate consumption												
17.Seeds	KFME	296.9	326.2	384.0	380.5	337.2	332.1	327.4	263.4	291.1	276.1	288.4
Cereals	KFMC	113.5	112.3	121.2	123.7	103.5	84.2	87.1	71.2	74.7	63.8	72.0
Other	KFMD	183.4	213.9	262.8	256.8	233.8	247.9	240.3	192.2	216.4	212.3	216.4
18.Energy	VQDO	594.7	586.5	590.9	647.4	629.9	598.3	621.9	694.7	685.7	647.4	614.5
Electricity	VQDQ	245.7	243.4	237.0	247.6	232.7	231.0	221.7	230.2	242.0	236.5	209.1
Fuels	VQDV	349.1	343.1	353.8	399.8	397.2	367.3	400.2	464.6	443.7	410.9	405.4
19.Fertilisers	KFMM	753.0	768.7	926.0	1 043.3	1 006.9	831.7	756.0	737.8	760.3	757.3	707.0
20.Pesticides	KFMN	547.5	557.3	590.0	646.9	674.6	653.7	621.0	579.4	530.9	533.6	508.1
21.Veterinary expenses	KCPC	253.2	274.3	289.2	297.7	307.8	288.0	270.0	255.8	242.7	250.4	258.0
22.Animal feed	KFMB	2 934.1	2 874.5	3 040.2	3 185.4	2 804.0	2 444.4	2 260.9	2 139.6	2 367.3	2 218.9	2 364.7
Compounds	LUNY	1 764.2	1 689.1	1 806.2	1 959.5	1 772.2	1 523.5	1 402.4	1 283.3	1 398.2	1 376.9	1 348.1
Straights	LUNZ	834.4	888.3	963.3	937.3	749.9	667.0	631.7	667.0	760.9	649.6	767.5
Feed purchased from other farms	LUOA	335.5	297.1	270.8	288.6	281.9	253.9	226.8	189.3	208.1	192.4	249.1
23.Total maintenance[5]	VQDW	949.8	977.3	1 089.4	1 110.4	1 091.2	1 024.6	1 016.5	942.6	982.4	957.8	1 041.8
Materials	KFMO	637.6	631.3	721.4	745.4	720.9	699.2	698.2	650.4	659.3	633.7	698.7
Buildings	KCPB	312.2	346.1	368.1	365.0	370.3	325.4	318.2	292.1	323.1	324.0	343.2
24.Agricultural services	LUOE	471.1	501.8	552.9	608.0	575.0	570.2	609.5	587.0	608.5	606.5	614.0
25.Other goods and services[5,6]	VQDX	1 915.4	2 060.5	2 186.7	2 277.4	2 314.7	2 251.3	2 267.9	2 087.7	2 056.8	2 085.1	2 149.2
26.Total intermediate consumption (Sum 17 to 25)	KCPM	8 715.7	8 927.1	9 649.4	10 197.1	9 741.4	8 994.2	8 750.9	8 288.1	8 525.6	8 333.1	8 545.6
27.Gross value added at basic prices (14-26)	LUOG	9 006.5	9 379.1	10 273.2	10 007.0	8 342.0	7 514.1	7 220.5	6 665.4	6 743.9	7 137.4	7 976.6
28.Total consumption of Fixed Capital	KCPS	2 542.5	2 549.5	2 592.1	2 622.8	2 675.0	2 594.7	2 432.1	2 480.9	2 559.8	2 558.5	2 607.0
Equipment	KCPR	1 137.9	1 175.8	1 226.2	1 291.1	1 318.6	1 323.0	1 309.7	1 255.4	1 249.4	1 247.5	1 198.1
Buildings[5,7]	LUOH	568.2	581.5	640.1	681.4	671.9	683.8	701.5	691.6	686.8	689.7	649.6
Livestock	VQEA	836.5	792.2	725.8	650.2	684.6	587.9	421.0	533.9	623.6	621.3	759.3
Cattle	LUOI	576.9	528.3	415.3	313.7	391.9	314.7	208.3	278.2	321.9	341.5	453.1
Pigs	LUOK	14.0	14.7	16.7	17.4	14.6	8.4	7.6	7.9	6.2	7.8	7.3
Sheep	LUOJ	139.3	143.3	175.8	191.6	157.1	119.0	69.6	120.1	169.1	142.6	173.0
Poultry	LUOL	106.3	105.9	118.0	127.6	120.9	145.8	135.4	127.7	126.5	129.4	125.9
29.Net value added at basic prices (27-28)	KCPT	6 464.0	6 829.6	7 681.0	7 384.3	5 666.9	4 919.5	4 788.4	4 184.5	4 184.1	4 579.0	5 369.6
30.Compensation of employees[8]	LUOR	1 786.6	1 827.5	1 836.3	1 880.9	1 929.8	1 975.3	2 029.0	1 893.3	1 942.6	1 957.7	1 909.6
31.Other taxes on production	VQEB	−63.6	−68.1	−73.2	−81.5	−84.4	−88.9	−92.3	−92.1	−77.8	−80.8	−90.5
32.Other subsidies on production	VQEC	189.5	261.3	266.4	243.1	188.9	209.5	318.3	296.7	536.5	558.8	623.0
Animal disease compensation	LUOM	10.4	6.8	6.9	5.5	15.3	14.3	19.8	29.4	23.2	54.1	60.6
Set-aside	LUON	142.0	206.3	198.4	159.5	90.2	87.7	170.0	127.3	180.1	142.5	176.8
Agri-environment schemes[9]	ZBXC	37.0	48.2	61.1	77.9	83.4	107.5	128.5	140.1	168.3	197.5	223.5
Other including Less Favoured Areas schemes[10]	VQED	–	–	–	0.2	0.1	–	–	–	164.9	164.6	162.2
33.Net value added at factor cost (29+31+32)	LUOQ	6 589.9	7 022.7	7 874.3	7 545.8	5 771.5	5 040.1	5 014.3	4 389.1	4 642.7	5 057.0	5 902.1
34.Rent	KCPV	178.5	181.6	175.5	228.7	255.8	250.1	239.7	223.7	251.4	239.7	295.5
Paid[11]	ZBXE	178.5	181.6	175.5	302.8	335.8	330.6	322.1	302.5	329.6	337.4	387.2
Received[12]	ZBXF	..	..	..	74.1	80.1	80.5	82.4	78.9	78.2	97.7	91.7
35.Interest[13]	KCPU	524.0	536.2	587.3	553.3	621.2	688.6	594.2	623.4	549.9	467.8	466.4
Total income from farming (33-30-34-35)	KCQB	4 100.7	4 477.4	5 275.2	4 882.9	2 964.7	2 126.1	2 151.4	1 648.8	1 898.8	2 391.7	3 230.7

1 See chapter text.

2 Provisional.

3 Output is net of VAT collected on the sale of non-edible products. Figures for total output include subsidies on products, but not other subsidies.

4 Includes straw and minor crops.

5 Landlords' expenses are included within 'Total maintenance', 'Other goods and services' and 'Total consumption of Fixed Capital of buildings'.

6 Includes livestock and crop costs, water costs, insurance premiums, bank charges, professional fees, rates and other farming costs.

7 A more empirically based methodology for calculating landlords' consumption of fixed capital was introduced in 2000. The new series has been linked with the old one using a smoothing procedure for the transition year of 1996.

8 Excludes the value of work done by farm labour on own account capital formation in buildings and works.

9 Includes Environmentally and Nitrate Sensitive Areas, Countryside Stewardship and other management schemes, and Moorland, Habitat, Farm Woodland and Organic Farming Schemes.

10 Land area based schemes which replaced the Hill Livestock Compensatory Allowance Scheme in 2001. These are Tir Mynydd in Wales, Less Favoured Area Compensatory Scheme in Northern Ireland, Less Favoured Areas Support Scheme in Scotland and Hill Farm Allowance in England.

11 Rent paid on all tenanted land (including 'conacre' land in Northern Ireland) less landlords' expenses, landlords' consumption of fixed capital and the benefit value of dwellings on that land.

12 Rent received by farming landowners from renting of land to other farmers less landlords' expenses. This series starts in 1996 following a revision to the methodology of calculating net rent.

13 Interest charges on loans for current farming purposes and buildings and works less interest on money held on short term deposit.

Source: Department for Environment, Food and Rural Affairs: 01904 455080

21.2 Output and input volume indices[1]
United Kingdom

Indices (1995=100)

		1993	1994	1995	1996	1997	1998	1999	2000	2001	2002	2003
Outputs[2]												
1. Total cereals:	VQAN	89.1	91.3	100.0	111.6	106.6	103.2	100.1	108.4	86.6	104.1	97.5
Wheat	LUKH	90.1	93.2	100.0	112.2	104.1	107.5	103.4	116.2	81.2	111.4	99.7
Rye	VQAO	82.1	92.9	100.0	103.6	103.6	82.1	82.1	78.6	82.1	71.4	67.9
Barley	LUKI	88.4	87.4	100.0	112.0	112.7	95.7	94.6	93.6	95.9	88.4	91.7
Oats and summer cereal mixtures	LUKJ	77.9	97.4	100.0	95.6	93.6	95.0	86.9	103.3	100.2	121.9	116.2
Other cereals	VQAP	93.6	89.1	100.0	87.9	85.2	98.5	146.0	176.2	121.5	141.5	135.5
2. Total industrial crops:	VQAQ	101.4	96.1	100.0	110.3	115.5	113.3	120.5	85.6	82.4	92.5	97.6
Oil seeds	VQAR	112.1	103.1	100.0	116.6	131.2	139.9	161.6	81.9	83.7	100.7	126.3
Oilseed rape	VQAS	95.8	101.8	100.0	117.5	131.0	135.0	134.7	93.0	96.3	119.6	145.7
Other oil seeds	LUKN	239.0	116.0	100.0	107.3	131.7	177.6	374.9	52.9	47.7	22.6	73.1
Sugar beet	C5X4	114.6	103.4	100.0	123.6	131.5	118.6	125.5	107.7	98.9	113.4	108.7
Other industrial crops	VQAU	75.8	81.4	100.0	89.7	80.4	74.3	66.7	67.3	63.5	65.0	61.5
Fibre plants	VQAV	12.6	97.2	100.0	130.5	132.4	108.8	106.7	69.8	42.2	23.9	39.5
Hops	LUKP	127.8	108.3	100.0	126.2	119.6	81.9	69.8	62.1	58.6	58.7	44.1
Others[3]	VQAW	75.5	79.3	100.0	86.0	75.9	72.6	65.0	67.5	64.3	66.3	62.8
3. Total forage plants	VQAX	146.9	122.4	100.0	101.7	117.3	109.6	119.6	124.5	144.0	144.8	146.1
4. Total vegetables and horticultural Products:	VQAY	105.2	103.6	100.0	101.4	99.9	97.5	99.4	97.1	94.0	93.2	91.7
Fresh vegetables	LUKX	106.9	105.9	100.0	105.8	100.8	98.7	99.6	93.7	90.4	83.4	84.3
Plants and flowers	LUKZ	102.3	99.9	100.0	94.7	98.0	95.0	98.5	101.0	98.4	107.7	102.3
5. Total potatoes (including seeds)	LUKW	105.1	98.3	100.0	107.7	102.3	90.3	107.2	94.4	100.0	100.7	86.8
6. Total fruit	LUKY	119.8	105.2	100.0	103.5	70.2	89.2	92.3	84.3	90.5	82.0	89.0
7. Other crop products including seeds	VQAZ	111.9	109.3	100.0	90.8	99.6	92.0	102.4	98.6	98.0	68.2	81.0
8. Total crop output (Sum 1 to 7)	VQBA	98.9	97.0	100.0	107.9	104.6	101.8	104.5	100.0	91.5	98.8	96.1
9. Total livestock production	VQBB	96.8	100.9	100.0	89.0	95.1	96.7	94.5	89.9	82.9	87.9	86.9
Mainly for meat processing	LULH	96.4	100.4	100.0	88.2	94.1	96.0	94.3	90.2	81.3	86.8	86.7
Cattle	LULC	93.6	100.4	100.0	74.7	81.0	83.1	84.6	82.0	72.8	84.3	86.0
Pigs	LULE	103.2	106.4	100.0	101.0	110.8	112.3	103.1	86.9	79.7	76.1	67.2
Sheep	LULD	102.4	99.7	100.0	88.4	93.9	99.4	99.1	95.1	68.2	77.5	78.3
Poultry	LULF	90.6	96.3	100.0	103.6	106.1	105.2	100.5	101.4	105.1	102.3	104.2
Other animals	LULG	100.7	100.1	100.0	101.8	102.3	102.3	101.7	101.7	101.4	101.6	101.0
Gross fixed capital formation	LULR	101.0	105.4	100.0	98.2	106.2	104.2	97.4	86.1	99.7	99.7	92.6
Cattle	LULN	100.5	100.6	100.0	99.8	98.4	96.0	96.6	84.4	97.9	93.1	93.9
Pigs	LULP	113.6	115.6	100.0	109.9	115.5	87.1	97.7	66.6	56.2	83.9	67.3
Sheep	LULO	98.1	125.4	100.0	90.8	117.9	122.7	92.4	62.6	97.4	108.4	77.9
Poultry	LULQ	99.8	100.5	100.0	101.7	109.1	102.9	97.0	100.4	96.2	95.6	95.2
10. Total livestock products	LULM	101.0	102.2	100.0	99.5	100.8	99.6	101.3	98.7	99.7	100.7	102.0
Milk	LULI	100.8	102.4	100.0	99.6	100.5	99.0	101.4	98.6	99.8	100.9	102.0
Eggs	LULJ	102.2	101.7	100.0	100.1	103.7	105.4	101.8	101.4	102.1	99.8	99.8
Raw wool	LULK	99.7	96.7	100.0	95.1	97.0	103.3	95.3	91.7	76.2	79.2	77.4
Other animal products	LULL	111.2	92.6	100.0	86.3	90.8	80.8	95.9	80.5	71.3	113.0	141.0
11. Total livestock output (9+10)	VQBC	98.3	101.3	100.0	92.6	97.1	97.7	96.9	92.9	88.5	92.2	92.0
12. Total other agricultural activities	VQBD	83.9	95.0	100.0	108.7	104.1	103.7	109.0	93.8	93.5	95.3	95.5
Agricultural services	VQBE	96.9	98.8	100.0	107.8	109.4	115.2	123.2	116.3	120.6	120.2	121.7
Leasing out quota	VQBF	41.2	82.2	100.0	111.7	87.1	68.1	65.6	28.0	15.2	22.8	19.7
13. Total inseparable non-agricultural Activities	LULX	97.8	103.2	100.0	108.7	108.0	119.0	120.0	125.7	158.7	138.1	142.1

		1993	1994	1995	1996	1997	1998	1999	2000	2001	2002	2003
14.Gross output (at basic prices) (8+11+12+13)	LULY	97.9	99.5	100.0	99.0	100.4	100.0	100.8	96.4	91.5	95.9	94.8
15.Total subsidies (less taxes) on product	VQEE	101.3	98.7	100.0	97.1	103.9	105.0	106.5	98.7	84.5	97.2	97.6
16.Output at market prices (14-15)	VQEG	97.6	99.6	100.0	99.2	99.8	99.2	99.8	96.0	92.6	95.7	94.4
of which transactions within the agricultural industry												
Feed wheat	LULZ	141.2	145.7	100.0	121.5	176.0	209.9	175.0	120.1	115.1	123.9	196.1
Feed barley	LUMA	107.3	105.0	100.0	105.2	125.8	123.5	113.6	112.2	121.4	128.9	121.2
Feed oats	LUMB	94.9	119.4	100.0	89.2	81.6	100.1	118.2	108.8	112.4	105.6	104.7
Seed potatoes	LUMC	121.4	87.8	100.0	119.1	84.1	82.3	82.1	70.4	80.0	83.5	35.4
Straw	LUMD	72.9	77.6	100.0	84.5	73.3	69.5	61.1	63.8	60.4	62.4	58.8
Contract work	LUME	96.9	98.8	100.0	107.8	109.4	115.2	123.2	116.3	120.6	120.2	121.7
Leasing of quota	LUMF	41.2	82.2	100.0	111.7	87.1	68.1	65.6	28.0	15.2	22.8	19.7
Total capital formation in livestock	LUMG	101.0	105.4	100.0	98.2	106.2	104.2	97.4	86.1	99.8	99.7	92.6
Intermediate Consumption												
17.Seeds	LUMO	96.7	98.1	100.0	102.4	99.2	95.2	95.1	90.5	94.5	90.1	92.2
Cereals	LUMM	95.9	95.0	100.0	104.5	95.1	83.1	86.3	73.0	75.1	66.2	75.9
Other	LUMN	97.0	99.6	100.0	101.4	101.1	100.6	99.2	98.6	103.5	101.1	99.9
18.Energy	VQEH	100.4	97.6	100.0	106.3	103.3	108.3	101.6	92.4	94.3	93.4	81.3
Electricity	VQEI	98.9	101.2	100.0	99.5	97.4	106.6	101.3	93.7	102.2	104.1	85.7
Fuels	VQEJ	101.6	95.2	100.0	110.9	107.4	109.5	102.0	92.0	90.8	88.5	79.4
19.Fertilisers	VQEK	100.4	93.4	100.0	105.3	114.7	107.5	100.5	88.0	77.5	80.9	69.9
20.Pesticides	LUMQ	95.8	93.0	100.0	103.1	106.7	111.2	108.1	106.7	101.0	102.6	97.8
21.Veterinary expenses	LUMW	88.1	95.3	100.0	102.1	104.1	96.3	90.2	86.5	83.2	86.6	85.9
22.Animal feed	LUML	95.5	100.2	100.0	97.8	94.5	94.7	95.4	91.8	95.0	92.6	96.3
Compounds	LUMH	98.4	100.4	100.0	101.3	97.3	94.9	97.5	89.6	92.3	91.7	91.6
Straights	LUMI	85.2	96.0	100.0	88.7	79.6	83.6	84.0	90.8	94.4	86.4	96.3
Feed purchased from other farms	LUMJ	113.1	114.1	100.0	107.5	133.2	139.8	126.5	113.8	119.7	126.5	136.4
23.Total maintenance[4]	VQEL	93.5	93.5	100.0	97.5	94.6	88.7	87.0	79.1	80.6	75.8	78.5
Materials	LUMU	94.4	90.8	100.0	97.7	93.8	91.1	89.0	81.2	80.0	73.6	76.4
Buildings	LUMT	91.7	99.0	100.0	97.1	96.3	84.0	83.1	75.2	82.0	80.6	83.2
24.Agricultural services	VQEM	96.9	98.8	100.0	107.8	109.4	115.2	123.2	116.3	120.6	120.2	121.7
25.Other goods and services[4,5]	VQEO	93.2	97.3	100.0	103.8	103.2	96.1	93.0	83.0	79.3	77.5	77.3
26.Total intermediate consumption (Sum 17 to 25)	LUNE	95.4	97.2	100.0	101.5	101.0	98.5	96.7	89.5	88.6	87.2	86.3
27.Gross value added at basic prices (14-26)	LUNF	100.4	101.7	100.0	96.6	100.1	102.2	106.3	105.7	95.3	107.8	106.5
28.Total consumption of Fixed Capital	LUNN	96.3	97.7	100.0	101.7	98.8	96.7	95.1	94.9	93.7	89.2	88.7
Equipment	LUNI	98.9	99.2	100.0	101.3	101.2	96.6	93.8	92.7	92.7	92.6	93.2
Buildings[4,6]	LUNG	100.1	100.3	100.0	101.5	101.4	100.5	98.9	96.4	95.2	93.2	86.9
Livestock	VQES	89.8	93.5	100.0	102.5	91.9	93.4	94.8	100.5	96.5	80.9	83.9
Cattle	LUNJ	88.3	88.8	100.0	106.0	93.7	92.8	94.8	107.6	92.7	80.1	87.3
Pigs	LUNL	102.2	110.4	100.0	92.7	101.0	108.2	97.5	82.7	56.9	82.3	65.2
Sheep	LUNK	88.0	102.6	100.0	96.7	80.6	82.7	92.5	97.2	117.1	76.9	75.4
Poultry	LUNM	92.8	98.7	100.0	103.0	103.5	111.1	105.4	100.5	98.5	99.2	96.7
29.Net value added at basic prices (27-28)	LUNO	101.9	103.2	100.0	94.9	101.0	105.4	112.9	112.1	95.4	119.8	118.0

1 See chapter text.
2 Output is net of VAT collected on the sale of non-edible products. Figures for total output include subsidies on products, but not other subsidies.
3 Includes straw and minor crops.
4 Landlords' expenses are included within 'Total maintenance', 'Other goods and services' and 'Total consumption of Fixed Capital of buildings'.

5 Includes livestock and crop costs, water costs, insurance premiums, bank charges, professional fees, rates, and other farming costs.
6 A more empirically based methodology for calculating landlords' depreciation was introduced in 2000. The new series has been linked with the old one using a smoothing procedure for the transition year of 1996.

Source: Department for Environment, Food and Rural Affairs: 01904 455080

21.3 Agriculture land-use
United Kingdom
Area at the June census[1]

Thousand hectares

		1993	1994	1995	1996	1997	1998	1999	2000	2001	2002	2003
Total agricultural area	BFAH	18 890	18 850	18 746	18 750	18 653	18 604	18 579	18 311	18 555	18 388	18 438
Crops	BFAA	4 520	4 470	4 544	4 722	4 990	4 971	4 709	4 665	4 454	4 573	4 478
Bare fallow	BFAB	50	46	43	37	29	34	33	37	43	33	29
Total tillage	KIJR	4 569	4 516	4 586	4 759	5 020	5 005	4 742	4 702	4 497	4 605	4 507
All grass under 5 years old	KFEM	1 582	1 456	1 407	1 395	1 405	1 301	1 226	1 226	1 205	1 230	1 201
Total arable land	KFEN	6 152	5 972	5 993	6 154	6 425	6 306	5 968	5 928	5 702	5 835	5 708
All grasses 5 years old and over	KFEO	5 274	5 388	5 375	5 354	5 282	5 364	5 449	5 364	5 584	5 422	5 683
Total tillage and grass	KFEP	11 426	11 360	11 368	11 507	11 706	11 671	11 417	11 292	11 286	11 257	11 391
Sole right rough grazing	BFAD	4 879	4 825	4 785	4 760	4 657	4 621	4 575	4 445	4 435	4 484	4 329
Set aside	DMNF	677	728	633	509	306	313	572	567	800	611	689
All other land on agricultural holdings including woodland	BFAE	680	712	734	751	763	773	789	780	801	802	792
Total land on agricultural holdings	BFAF	17 661	17 626	17 520	17 527	17 432	17 377	17 352	17 083	17 323	17 154	17 202
Common rough grazing (estimated)	BFAG	1 229	1 224	1 226	1 223	1 221	1 227	1 227	1 228	1 232	1 234	1 236
Crops	BFAA	4 520	4 470	4 544	4 722	4 990	4 971	4 709	4 665	4 454	4 573	4 478
Cereals	BFAJ	3 033	3 043	3 182	3 359	3 514	3 418	3 141	3 348	3 014	3 245	3 059
Wheat	BFAK	1 759	1 811	1 859	1 976	2 036	2 045	1 847	2 086	1 635	1 996	1 837
Barley	BFAL	1 166	1 108	1 193	1 269	1 359	1 253	1 179	1 128	1 245	1 101	1 078
Oats	BFAM	92	109	112	96	100	98	92	109	112	126	122
Mixed corn	BFAN	3	3	3	3	2	2	2	2	3	4	4
Rye[2]	BFAO	6	7	8	8	9	10	8	7	5	5	4
Triticale	DMNH	7	6	7	7	8	11	13	16	14	14	15
Other arable crops (excluding potatoes)	DMNI	1 128	1 073	993	937	1 125	1 210	1 211	979	1 103	993	1 098
Oilseed rape	BFAP	377	404	354	356	445	507	417	332	404	357	460
Sugar beet not for stock feeding[2]	BFAQ	197	195	196	199	196	189	183	173	177	169	162
Hops[3]	DMNJ	3	3	3	3	3	3	3	2	1	2	2
Peas for harvesting dry and field beans	DMNK	244	228	195	178	197	213	202	208	276	249	235
Linseed	DMNL	150	58	54	49	73	100	209	71	31	12	32
Other crops	DMNM	157	185	195	204	210	200	197	192	214	204	207
Potatoes	BFAR	171	164	172	178	166	164	178	166	165	158	145
Horticultural	BFAV	188	189	187	189	184	180	179	172	173	176	176
Vegetables grown in the open	DMNN	126	127	130	132	126	125	126	119	120	124	125
Orchard fruit[4]	BFBG	32	32	28	28	30	30	28	28	28	26	25
Soft fruit	DMNO	13	13	12	12	11	10	9	10	9	9	9
Ornamentals	DMNP	14	14	15	14	14	14	13	14	14	15	14
Glasshouse crops	DMNQ	2	2	2	2	2	2	2	2	2	2	2

1 Includes estimates for minor holdings for all countries. See chapter text.
2 Figures are for England and Wales only.
3 Figures are for England only.
4 Includes non-commercial orchards.

Source: Agricultural Departments: 01904 455332

21.4 Estimated quantity of crops and grass harvested[1]
United Kingdom

Thousand tonnes

		1993	1994	1995	1996	1997	1998	1999	2000	2001	2002	2003
Agricultural crops												
Wheat	**BADO**	12 890	13 320	14 310	16 100	15 020	16 449	14 867	16 704	11 580	15 973	14 288
Barley (Winter and Spring) .	**BADP**	6 038	5 950	6 840	7 790	7 830	6 623	6 581	6 492	6 660	6 126	6 370
Oats	**BADQ**	479	600	615	590	575	586	541	640	621	753	749
Sugar beet[2]	**BADR**	9 666	8 720	8 431	10 420	11 084	10 002	10 584	9 079	8 335	9 557	9 296
Potatoes	**BADS**	7 072	6 542	6 404	7 228	7 128	6 422	7 131	6 636	6 649	6 966	5 918

		1992 /93	1993 /94	1994 /95	1995 /96	1996 /97	1997 /98	1998 /99	1999 /00	2000 /01	2001 /02	2002 /03
Horticultural crops												
Field vegetables												
Brussels sprouts	**BADT**	97.6	101.8	93.5	74.3	82.6	74.2	70.5	79.5	62.0	54.8	46.0
Cabbage (including savoys and spring greens)	**BADU**	403.3	409.1	381.4	401.8	377.5	304.9	310.9	294.8	268.1	273.4	254.9
Cauliflowers	**BADV**	309.0	311.8	267.6	247.3	217.1	191.0	192.0	168.4	151.3	109.5	116.6
Carrots	**BADW**	531.7	604.8	566.6	524.6	679.5	591.4	625.6	702.1	472.3	614.1	560.7
Turnips and swedes	**BADX**	160.6	140.9	137.1	124.2	135.6	106.9	121.2	126.3	121.8	128.3	106.5
Beetroot	**BADY**	103.6	84.1	88.9	72.1	72.1	72.4	66.3	61.1	71.5	64.5	56.3
Onions, dry bulb	**BADZ**	216.5	322.5	245.0	254.3	313.3	329.3	376.4	405.8	379.2	305.4	350.3
Peas, green for market (in pod weight)	**BAEA**	5.7	5.7	5.6	8.4	6.7	8.2	7.0	7.0	6.7	6.1	7.2
Peas, green for processing (shelled weight)	**BAEB**	210.9	208.5	181.0	198.0	215.5	167.9	152.1	143.1	177.1	162.3	169.6
Lettuce	**BAEC**	173.9	144.8	179.2	191.9	187.5	157.7	152.0	155.5	138.0	122.7	110.7
Protected crops												
Tomatoes	**BAED**	122.5	109.5	108.9	112.8	115.5	114.0	107.6	116.6	113.1	109.1	100.9
Cucumbers	**BAEE**	90.4	104.2	83.2	88.4	85.6	81.7	83.8	83.8	79.8	71.5	73.6
Lettuce	**BAEF**	44.3	37.1	33.1	29.7	26.5	24.1	20.6	19.9	18.7	20.9	16.0
Fruit												
Dessert apples	**BFCD**	178.1	180.2	167.7	118.5	116.3	71.1	113.3	133.6	100.2	106.5	67.0
Cooking apples	**BFCE**	181.6	147.0	144.8	129.6	108.7	82.4	98.5	119.4	99.2	113.7	73.5
Soft fruit	**BFCF**	94.1	93.1	76.6	75.6	82.2	59.4	61.2	65.7	63.5	64.3	62.8
Pears	**BFBQ**	23.4	38.7	25.6	35.3	40.1	24.4	28.1	18.1	33.9	35.6	34.8

1 See chapter text.
2 Figures are adjusted to constant 16% sugar content.

Source: Agricultural Departments: 01904 455332

21.5 Cattle, sheep, pigs and poultry on agricultural holdings[1]
United Kingdom

At June each year

Thousands

		1993	1994	1995	1996	1997	1998	1999	2000	2001	2002	2003
Total cattle and calves	**BFCG**	11 851	11 954	11 857	12 040	11 637	11 519	11 423	11 135	10 602	10 345	10 517
of which:												
dairy cows	**BFCH**	2 668	2 716	2 603	2 587	2 478	2 439	2 440	2 336	2 251	2 227	2 192
beef cows	**BFCI**	1 784	1 809	1 840	1 864	1 862	1 947	1 924	1 842	1 708	1 657	1 700
heifers in calf	**BFCJ**	803	775	775	818	848	787	763	718	701	728	680
Total sheep and lambs	**BFCM**	44 436	43 813	43 304	42 086	42 823	44 471	44 656	42 264	36 716	35 834	35 846
of which:												
ewes and shearlings	**CKUQ**	20 881	20 861	20 830	20 550	20 696	21 260	21 458	20 449	17 921	17 630	17 599
lambs under one year old	**BFCP**	22 394	21 758	21 350	20 443	21 032	22 138	22 092	20 857	17 769	17 310	17 335
Total pigs	**BFCQ**	7 853	7 892	7 627	7 590	8 072	8 146	7 284	6 482	5 845	5 588	5 047
of which:												
sows in pig and other sows for breeding	**CKUU**	698	691	654	649	683	675	603	537	527	483	443
gilts in pig	**CKUR**	117	106	101	107	116	103	85	73	71	74	73
Total fowls	**KPSV**	131 093	126 653	127 035	..	..	..	..	..	..	..	165 324
of which:												
table fowls including broilers	**CKUT**	79 940	75 696	77 177	..	..	98 244	101 625	105 689	112 531	105 137	116 774
laying fowls[2]	**CKUV**	32 965	32 682	31 837	..	34 286	29 483	29 258	28 687	29 895	28 778	29 274
growing pullets	**CKUW**	10 750	10 388	10 210	..	11 510	9 860	9 583	9 461	9 367	9 784	8 286

1 Includes estimates for minor holdings for all countries. See chapter text.
2 Excludes fowls laying eggs for hatching.

Sources: Department for Environment, Food and Rural Affairs;
Farming Statistics: 01904 455332

21.6 Forestry[1]
United Kingdom

		1980	1990	1999	2000	2001	2002	2003	2004
Woodland area[2] - (Thousand hectares)									
United Kingdom	C5OF	2 175	2 400	2 775	2 793	2 790	2 800	2 807	2 817
England[3]	C5OG	948	958	1 097	1 103	1 100	1 104	1 110	1 115
Wales[3]	C5OI	241	248	288	289	289	288	285	286
Scotland[3]	C5OH	920	1 120	1 308	1 318	1 317	1 324	1 327	1 330
Northern Ireland	C5OJ	67	74	82	83	83	84	85	86
Forestry Commission/Forest Service	C5OK	946	956	891	886	861[4]	855	848	842
Other[5]	C5OL	1 230	1 443	1 884	1 907	1 929	1 945	1 960	1 976
Conifer	C5OM	1 372	1 576	1 656	1 663	1 660	1 658	1 652	1 651
Broadleaved[6]	C5ON	804	824	1 120	1 131	1 130	1 143	1 155	1 166

		1993 /94	1994 /95	1995 /96	1996 /97	1997 /98	1998 /99	1999 /00	2000 /01	2001 /02	2002 /03	2003 /04
New Planting[7] - (Thousand hectares)												
United Kingdom	C5OO	18.6	19.9	16.4	17.2	16.7	16.7	17.4	18.3	13.9	13.0	13.0
England	C5OP	6.2	5.1	4.4	4.4	4.1	4.9	5.5	5.5	4.9	5.3	5.3
Wales	C5OR	0.6	0.6	0.4	0.4	0.5	0.6	0.7	0.4	0.3	0.3	0.5
Scotland	C5OQ	10.5	13.4	10.6	11.7	11.4	10.5	10.4	11.7	8.0	6.7	6.8
Northern Ireland	C5OS	1.3	0.9	1.0	0.8	0.6	0.7	0.8	0.7	0.7	0.6	0.5
Forestry Commission/Forest Service	C5OT	1.8	1.2	0.6	0.6	0.2	0.2	0.3	0.3	0.8	0.9	0.3
Other[8]	C5OU	16.8	18.7	15.8	16.6	16.4	16.5	17.2	18.0	13.1	12.1	12.8
Conifer	C5OV	7.4	9.4	7.4	7.7	7.0	6.6	6.5	5.2	3.9	4.0	2.9
Broadleaved	C5OW	11.2	10.5	8.9	9.5	9.7	10.1	10.9	13.2	10.0	8.9	10.1
Restocking[7] - (Thousand hectares)												
United Kingdom	C5OX	16.8	14.6	13.9	15.0	14.1	14.0	15.1	15.2	13.7	14.3	14.7
England	C5OY	6.4	4.9	4.2	4.3	4.3	4.0	3.8	3.8	3.3	3.2	2.9
Wales	C5P2	2.4	2.6	2.3	3.0	2.7	3.0	2.6	2.2	1.9	1.9	1.8
Scotland	C5OZ	7.6	6.6	6.8	7.2	6.3	6.3	8.0	8.0	7.8	8.5	8.9
Northern Ireland	C5P3	0.5	0.6	0.6	0.6	0.7	0.6	0.6	1.1	0.8	0.7	1.0
Forestry Commission/Forest Service	C5P4	8.4	8.4	8.4	8.4	8.5	8.5	8.8	8.9	9.1	9.1	9.9
Other[8]	C5P5	8.5	6.2	6.6	6.6	5.6	5.6	6.3	6.2	4.6	5.2	4.8
Conifer	C5P6	11.5	11.0	10.9	11.4	11.2	11.3	11.9	12.2	11.4	12.0	12.1
Broadleaved	C5P7	5.3	3.6	3.0	3.4	2.9	2.8	3.2	2.9	2.3	2.3	2.6

		1995	1996	1997	1998	1999	2000	2001	2002	2003
Wood Production (volume - Thousand cubic metres overbark standing)										
United Kingdom	C5P8	8 830	8 730	9 150	9 070	9 580	9 730	9 730	9 930	11 150
Great Britain										
Softwood	C5PA	7 610	7 610	7 990	8 000	8 510	8 630	8 630	8 840	10 040
Forestry Commission	C5PB	4 130	4 290	4 570	4 830	5 440	5 530	5 140	5 210	5 370
Private woodland	C5PC	3 480	3 320	3 420	3 170	3 070	3 100	3 480	3 630	4 670
Hardwood[9]	C5PD	970	870	890	790	740	720	710	690	620
Northern Ireland[10]	C5PE	250	250	260	290	320	380	400	410	480

1 See chapter text.
2 Areas as at 31 March.
3 For England, Wales and Scotland, 1980 woodland area figures are the published results from the 1979-1982 Census of Woodlands and Trees and figures for 1990 are adjusted to reflect subsequent changes. From 1998 onwards they are based on results from the 1995-1999 National Inventory of Woodlands and Trees, adjusted to reflect subsequent changes.
4 The apparent fall in woodland cover in 2001 is due to the reclassification of Forestry Commission open land within the forest.
5 Includes private woodland and non-Forestry Commission / Forest Service public woodland.

6 Broadleaved includes coppice. For data based on 1979-82 Census, all scrub and other non-plantation woodland have been assumed to be broadleaved.
7 Figures shown are for the areas of new planting and restocking in the year to 31 March.
8 Includes grant aided planting on non-Forestry Commission/ Forest Service woodland. It excludes areas planted without the aid of grants.
9 Hardwood is timber from broadleaved species. Most hardwood production comes from private woodlands; the figures are estimates based on reported deliveries to wood processing industries.
10 Most Northern Ireland production is from the Forest Service. The figures shown include Forest Service estimates of private sector production.

Sources: Forest Service Agency;
Department of Agriculture and Rural Development (Northern Ireland);
Forestry Commission: 0131 334 0303

345

21.7 Sales for food of agricultural produce and livestock
United Kingdom

			1993	1994	1995	1996	1997	1998	1999	2000	2001	2002	2003
Cereals:		Thousand											
Wheat[1]	KCQK	tonnes	3 930	4 300	4 673	4 842	4 737	4 676	4 826	4 707	4 885	4 768	4 825
Barley	KCQL	"	2 804	3 232	3 818	3 734	3 453	3 525	3 454	3 802	2 669	3 015	3 121
Oats[2]	KCQM	"	208	215	216	235	259	273	270	263	283	311	323
Potatoes[3]	KCQN	"	6 382	6 519	5 961	6 146	6 279	5 997	6 210	6 675	6 606	6 892	6 448
Milk[4]:		Million litres											
Utilised for liquid consumption	KCQO	Million litres	7 026	6 926	6 922	6 838	6 748	6 739	6 853	6 768	6 761	6 756	6 635
Utilised for manufacture	KCQP	"	6 880	7 134	6 918	6 934	7 059	6 821	6 988	6 550	6 741	6 965	7 280
Total available for domestic use[5]	KCQQ	"	14 228	14 420	14 255	14 194	14 258	13 973	14 234	13 737	13 940	14 099	14 323
Hen eggs in shell	KCQR	Million dozens	791	787	774	775	794	792	743	747	806	825	866
Animals slaughtered:													
Cattle and calves:													
Cattle	KCQS	Thousands	2 944	3 089	3 266	2 291	2 264	2 297	2 217	2 275	2 072	2 184	2 175
Calves	KCQT	"	19	22	26	24	20	32	75	152	92	98	87
Total	KCQU	"	2 963	3 111	3 292	2 315	2 284	2 329	2 292	2 427	2 164	2 282	2 262
Sheep and lambs	KCQV	"	18 864	18 962	19 311	18 049	16 660	18 688	19 116	18 442	12 964	14 993	14 924
Pigs:													
Clean pigs	MBGD	"	14 265	14 681	14 021	13 897	15 132	15 872	14 350	12 370	10 446	10 260	9 115
Sows and boars	KCQZ	"	356	389	355	324	363	415	379	321	180	314	240
Total	KCRA	"	14 620	15 069	14 376	14 221	15 496	16 286	14 728	12 692	10 626	10 575	9 355
Poultry[6]	KCRB	Millions	721	761	783	823	850	857	863	843	866	861	880

Note: The figures for cereals and for animals slaughtered relate to periods of 52 weeks

1 Flour millers' receipts of home-grown wheat.
2 Oatmeal millers' receipts of home-grown oats.
3 Total sales for human consumption in the UK.
4 Data to 1994 sourced from the Milk Marketing Boards. Data from 1995 sourced from surveys run by the agricultural departments. 1994 includes two months of data sourced from the surveys run by the agricultural departments.

5 The totals of liquid consumption and milk used for manufacture may not add up to the total available for domestic use because of adjustments for dairy wastage, stock changes and other uses, such as farmhouse consumption, milk fed to stock and on farm waste.
6 Total fowls, ducks, geese and turkeys.

Source: Department for Environment, Food and Rural Affairs: 01904 455332

21.8 Stocks of food and feedingstuffs[1]
United Kingdom
At end December each year

Thousand tonnes

		1993	1994	1995	1996	1997	1998	1999	2000	2001	2002	2003
Wheat and flour (as wheat)	KCRC	1 255	1 237	1 074	1 031	992	1 000	869	826	719	823	842
Barley (GB only)	KCRD	1 432	1 406	1 574	1 534	1 472	1 327	1 404	1 372	1 315	1 295	1 336
Maize	KCRE	23	32	33	25	45	67	43	37	36	66	52
Oilcake and meal[2]	KCRF	92	108	103	89	79	69	72	..	..	..	..
Oilseeds and nuts (crude oil equivalent)	KCRG	17	28	34	28	19	13	20	10	17	10	13
Vegetable oil (as crude oil)	KCRI	90	109	96	101	101	99	98	84	96	89	86
Marine oil (as crude oil)	KCRJ	8	18	17	10	4	–	–	–	–	–	–
Butter[3]	KCRK	34	19	11	14	7	11	22	17	18	19	17
Meat and offal[4]	KCRL	199	103	77	129	162	157	84	54	57	49	47
Raw coffee[5]	KCRM	12	13	11	8	7	8	7	8	13	9	9
Tea[6]	KCRN	44	43	38	39	37	38	38	28	31	29	25
Sugar	KCRO	1 069	1 016	766	807	1 003	928	..	..	..	..	..

1 Recorded stocks, including stocks in bond or held by the main processors.
2 Excluding castor meal, cocoa cake and meal.
3 In addition to stocks in public cold stores surveyed by DEFRA, closing stocks include all intervention stocks in private cold stores.

4 Stocks of imported and home-produced meat and offal held in public cold stores, excluding poultrymeat, bacon and ham.
5 Including manufacturers' stocks and additional public warehouses.
6 Covering stocks held by primary wholesalers and held in public/private warehouses.

Source: Department for Environment, Food and Rural Affairs: 01904 455332

Thousand tonnes

		1993	1994	1995	1996	1997	1998	1999	2000	2001	2002	2003
Flour milling:												
Wheat milling: total	KFTA	5 302	5 355	5 343	5 501	5 535	5 707	5 668	5 617	5 667	5 616	5 572
Home produced	KFTB	3 847	4 171	4 603	4 772	4 667	4 582	4 701	4 609	4 790	4 648	4 726
Imported	KFTC	1 455	1 184	740	729	868	1 125	966	1 008	877	968	846
Flour produced	KFTD	4 170	4 282	4 298	4 454	4 439	4 526	4 497	4 486	4 487	4 413	4 370
Offals produced	KFTE	1 139	1 094	1 081	1 111	1 111	1 221	1 181	1 148	1 169	1 179	1 170
Oat milling:												
Oats milled by oatmeal millers	KFTF	207	209	217	250	259	272	266	261	287	312	322
Products of oat milling	KFTG	105	102	110	123	129	154	157	155	171	186	191
Seed crushing:												
Oilseeds and nuts processed	KFTH	1 903	2 035	2 122	2 466	2 587	2 683	2 398	2 380	2 252	2 332	2 210
Crude oil produced, including production of maize oil	KFTI	658	739	779	862	909	915	832	820	786	805	769
Oilcake and meal produced, excluding castor meal, cocoa cake and meal	KFTJ	1 187	1 242	1 305	1 541	1 614	1 687	1 484	1 475	1 396	1 451	1 361
Production of home-killed meat: total including meat subsequently canned	KFTK	2 260	2 380	2 383	2 084	2 158	2 273	2 139	2 064	1 767	1 881	1 837
Beef	KFTL	858	915	973	701	695	704	675	703	649	690	694
Veal	KFTM	1	1	1	1	1	1	2	4	2	3	2
Mutton and lamb	KFTN	349	352	364	345	321	356	361	361	259	300	300
Pork	KFTO	783	807	752	769	871	934	826	727	606	632	584
Offal[1]	KFTP	268	305	293	268	270	278	275	269	249	256	257
Production of poultry meat[2]	KFTQ	1 289	1 344	1 397	1 461	1 502	..	..	..	..	..	..
Production of bacon and ham, including meat subsequently canned	KFTR	216	233	247	243	242	240	237	214	203	200	203
Production of milk products:												
Butter[3]	KFTS	141	148	133	130	139	137	141	132	126	136	148
Cheese (including farmhouse)	KFTT	338	341	362	377	377	366	368	340	395	380	363
Condensed milk: includes skim concentrate and condensed milk used in manufacture of chocolate crumb	KFTU	191	196	181	206	214	192	177	162	161	174	158
Milk powder: excluding buttermilk and whey powder												
Full cream	KFTV	71	83	90	83	96	97	102	105	87	105	101
Skimmed	KFTW	132	142	117	108	109	107	102	83	71	87	115
Cream, fresh and sterilised; including farm cream[3]	KFTX	255	274	281	281	268	266	275	270	290	290	290
Sugar: production from home-grown sugar-beet (as refined sugar)	KFTY	1 433	1 263	1 469	1 324	1 524	1 439	1 548	1 325	1 222	1 430	1 368
Production of compound fats:												
Margarine and other table spreads	KFTZ	493	487	490	491	461	448	421	388	409	415	442
Solid cooking fats	KFUA	129	109	110	123	109	131	125	135	121	114	131
Production of other processed foods:												
Syrup and treacle[4]	KFUC	52	50	48	..	..	..	..	..	..	..	..
Chocolate confectionery	KSJS	563	573	592	608	569	567	553	544	559	584	600
Sugar confectionery	KSJT	302	322	322	351	345	337	317	307	322	338	333
Cocoa beans excluding re-exports	KFVX	171	163	160	189	174	172	168	..	..	..	..
Breakfast cereals, other than oatmeal and oatmeal flakes	KFUJ	302	325	335	343	359	349	354	334	344	343	323
Glucose	KFUM	580	593	607	642	637	644	630	657	701	727	735
Compound feedingstuffs: total	KFUP	11 135	11 402	11 609	11 801	11 304	11 206	11 404	10 604	10 888	10 762	10 771
Cattle food	KFUQ	4 269	4 347	4 476	4 430	3 926	3 844	4 264	4 038	4 327	4 212	4 490
Calf food	KFUR	261	286	307	277	227	198	187	184	180	177	193
Pig food	KFUS	2 558	2 547	2 453	2 566	2 659	2 740	2 435	2 082	1 930	1 777	1 536
Poultry food	KFUT	3 122	3 179	3 243	3 280	3 324	3 213	3 139	3 064	3 246	3 458	3 340
Other compounds	KFUU	925	1 043	1 130	1 249	1 168	1 210	1 378	1 236	1 204	1 138	1 212

Note: The figures relate to periods of 52 weeks (53 weeks in 1998) with the following exceptions which are on a calendar year basis: butter, cheese, cream, canned meat, soft drinks, condensed milk and milk powder, canned vegetables, canned and bottled fruit, jam and marmalade, and soups.

1 Including poultry offal.
2 Total of fowl, ducks, geese and turkeys (carcase weight).
3 Includes cream from the residual elements of low fat milk production.
4 This survey ceased at the end of 1995.

Source: Department for Environment, Food and Rural Affairs: 01904 455332

21.10 Food and animal feedingstuffs: disposals

		1993	1994	1995	1996	1997	1998	1999	2000	2001	2002	2003
Flour	KFPU	4 125	4 250	4 297	4 457	4 434	4 529	4 487	4 489	4 481	4 408	4 359
Sugar (as refined sugar): total disposals	KFPV	2 154	2 196	2 177	2 200	2 040	2 143	..	..	..	..	..
For food in the United Kingdom[1]	KFPW	2 123	2 165	2 157	2 180	2 007	2 106	..	..	..	..	..
Syrup and treacle[2]	KFPX	52	50	48	..	..	..	..	..	..	..	..
Meat and fish:												
Fresh and frozen meat and offal, including usage for canning:												
Beef and veal	KFPY	1 094	1 228	1 206	804	865	872	942	921	907	996	1 001
Mutton and lamb	KFPZ	470	474	504	501	468	496	497	496	373	423	435
Pork	KFVA	895	922	917	954	1 035	1 113	1 059	997	861	941	998
Offal[3]	KFVB	316	351	354	312	321	316	324	328	305	316	328
Poultry-meat[4,5]	KFVC	1 361	1 459	1 499	1 581	1 561	1 650	1 720	1 707	1 716	1 715	1 705
Bacon and ham, including usage for canning	KFVD	453	457	476	505	481	472	466	483	483	493	503
Dairy products:												
Butter	KFVI	279	284	255	240	256	238	244	255	240	251	268
Cheese	KFVJ	523	559	577	617	614	632	645	595	664	668	684
Condensed milk[6]	KFVK	202	208	195	217	229	205	190	177	172	187	179
Milk powder, excluding buttermilk and whey powder:												
Full cream	KFVM	75	91	97	94	105	107	112	117	92	115	116
Skimmed	KFVN	144	149	138	95	103	91	127	162	86	89	125
Hen eggs in shell[7]	KFVO	821	837	818	833	838	819	795	822	912	959	999
Oils (as crude oil):												
Vegetable oil	KFVP	1 492	1 567	1 905	1 960	2 010	1 780	2 449	2 452	2 052	2 036	2 195
Marine oil for the manufacture of margarine and compound fat	KFVQ	91	105	100	52	31	8	8	2	2	2	2
Potatoes	KFVR	8 288	7 835	7 055	7 661	7 938	7 626	7 584	8 297	7 793	8 382	7 684
Other foods:												
Chocolate confectionery	KFVT	667	696	674	698	668	681	681	669	672	668	679
Sugar confectionery, excluding medicated	KFVU	366	382	380	416	410	409	393	393	400	387	387
Tea excluding re-exports	KFVV	157	149	141	148	152	145	133	144	133	136	..
Raw coffee	KFVW	116	119	105	116	118	122	115	109	105	116	..
Barley:												
For brewing and distilling and for food	KFVY	2 724	3 134	3 616	3 621	3 481	3 544	3 366	3 694	2 623	2 878	3 074
Maize (including maize meal): total disposals	KFVZ	1 437	1 367	1 411	1 389	1 439	1 448	1 256	1 184	1 243	1 231	913
Animal feed	KCRT	175	158	156	174	184	197	216	232	260	271	187
Oilcake and meal	KCRQ	3 891	4 152	4 462	4 429	4 041	3 677	4 035	..	..	..	..
Wheat milling offals	KCRR	1 186	1 137	1 132	1 157	1 158	1 273	1 209	1 176	1 205	1 220	1 216
Fish and poultry meal for animal feed,[8] (figures relate to sales)	KCRS	382	385	378	257	233	216	194	192	180	162	145

Note: The figures relate to periods of 52 weeks with the following exceptions which are on a calendar year basis: fish and potatoes; condensed milk; milk powder; butter and sugar.

1 Including sugar used in the manufacture of other foods subsequently exported. Excluding sugar in imported manufactured foods.
2 This survey ceased at the end of 1995.
3 Including poultry offal.
4 Carcase weight.
5 Total of fowls, ducks, geese and turkeys.
6 Includes skim concentrate and condensed milk used in the manufacture of chocolate crumb.
7 Million dozen eggs
8 Before a ban on 29 March 1996 this included poultry meat as well as mammalian meat and bonemeal.

Source: Department for Environment, Food and Rural Affairs: 01904 455332

21.11 Average weekly and hourly earnings and hours of full-time male agricultural workers[1]

England and Wales: At September each year

		1998	1999	2000	2001	2002	2003
Average weekly earnings (£)	LQML	301.24	301.22	298.24	332.66	366.82	352.88
95% confidence interval		(+/-£12.69)	(+/-£11.88)	(+/-£13.84)	(+/-£15.08)	(+/-£18.88)	(+/-£30.30)
Average weekly hours worked	LQMM	50.7	50.9	49.0	51.9	54.1	51.1
95% confidence interval		(+/-1.5)	(+/-1.4)	(+/-1.4)	(+/-1.7)	(+/-2.1)	(+/-3.0)
Average earnings/hours (£)	LQMN	5.94	5.92	6.09	6.42	6.78	6.91
95% confidence interval		(+/-£0.18)	(+/-£0.15)	(+/-£0.18)	(+/-£0.20)	(+/-£0.19)	(+/-£0.31)
Number of workers in the sample		274	292	234	251	204	72

1 See chapter text.

Source: Department for Environment, Food and Rural Affairs: 01904 455332

21.12 Average weekly and hourly earnings and hours of agricultural workers[1] : by type 2003

England and Wales: At September

	Full-time		Part-time		Casual		
	Male	Female	Male	Female	Male	Female	Managers
Average weekly earnings (£)	352.88	267.51	121.66	117.30	236.02	120.22	471.76
95% confidence interval	(+/-£30.30)	(+/-£23.84)	(+/-£20.43)	(+/-£15.27)	(+/-£37.00)	(+/-£39.78)	(+/-£45.36)
Average weekly hours worked	51.1	41.6	20.3	21.5	37.8	22.6	
95% confidence interval	(+/-3.0)	(+/-1.4)	(+/-3.2)	(+/-2.5)	(+/-5.3)	(+/-7.2)	..
Average earnings/hour (£)	6.91	6.43	5.99	5.47	6.24	5.33	
95% confidence interval	(+/-£0.31)	(+/-£0.51)	(+/-£0.41)	(+/-£0.38)	(+/-£0.32)	(+/-£0.41)	..
Number of workers in the sample	72	43	43	35	52	21	50

1 See chapter text.

Source: Department for Environment, Food and Rural Affairs: 01904 455332

21.13 Workers employed in agriculture [1,2]: by type

United Kingdom

At June each year

Thousands

	Regular					Seasonal or casual			All			Salaried managers[3]
		Full - time		Part - time								
	Total	Male	Female	Male	Female	Total	Male	Female	Total	Male	Female	
	BANC	BAMY	BAMZ	BANA	BANB	BANF	BAND	BANE	BANI	BANG	BANH	KAYG
1993	165.3	96.5	13.7	29.8	25.3	85.4	55.0	30.4	250.7	181.3	69.4	7.6
1994	161.0	93.6	13.2	30.0	24.2	82.2	53.9	28.4	243.2	177.5	65.7	7.8
1995	157.4	90.4	13.0	30.0	24.1	83.7	56.5	27.2	241.2	176.8	64.3	7.7
1996	156.4	89.2	12.6	31.2	23.4	81.5	55.6	25.8	237.9	176.0	61.9	7.8
1997	154.4	87.5	12.6	31.2	23.1	80.9	55.3	25.5	235.2	174.0	61.2	7.8
1998[4,5]	155.6	88.0	13.1	29.7	24.7	79.5	55.6	23.8	235.0	172.8	62.2	12.1
1999	144.7	82.7	11.9	27.5	22.6	73.0	51.8	21.2	217.7	162.0	55.6	13.8
2000	128.9	73.4	10.3	24.6	20.6	64.4	45.9	18.5	193.3	143.9	49.4	11.1
2001[6]	120.8	69.0	10.9	22.0	18.9	63.2	44.6	18.6	184.0	135.6	48.5	13.4
	123.5	70.3	11.2	22.5	19.4	64.1	45.4	18.8	187.6	138.2	49.4	14.1
2002	116.3	64.7	11.5	21.7	18.4	64.2	46.2	18.0	180.6	132.6	47.9	13.4
2003	108.4	60.4	10.0	21.0	17.0	62.6	44.8	17.8	170.9	126.2	44.8	12.7

1 See chapter text. Includes estimates for minor holdings for all countries.
2 Figures exclude school children, farmers, partners, directors and their spouses and most trainees.
3 Great Britain only.
4 Results from 1998 onwards are not comparable with previous years, due to changes in the labour questions on the June Agricultural and Horticultural Census in England, Wales and Scotland.

5 From 1998, all farmers managing holdings for limited companies or other institutions in England and Wales were asked to classify themselves as salaried managers.
6 Due to an English register improvement only the top figure for 2001 is directly comparable with 2000, while the bottom figure for 2001 is only comparable with data from 2002.

Sources: Department for Environment, Food and Rural Affairs;
Farming Statistics: 01904 455332

349

21.14 Landings of fish by United Kingdom vessels: live weight and value[1]
into United Kingdom

		Quantity (thousand tonnes)							Value (£ thousand)					
		1998	1999	2000	2001	2002	2003		1998	1999	2000	2001	2002	2003
Total all species	KSJU	552.5	506.5	464.7	458.3	465.6	444.6	KSLN	484 005	464 131	422 063	423 687	414 689	391 599
Total wet fish	KSJV	428.3	389.8	337.6	322.2	334.9	315.3	KSLO	323 297	297 831	268 816	256 364	250 845	221 091
Brill	KSJX	0.4	0.3	0.4	0.4	0.4	0.4	KSLP	1 674	1 405	1 839	2 032	1 785	1 810
Catfish	KSJY	0.8	0.7	0.8	0.7	0.5	0.6	KSLQ	1 070	1 006	1 081	896	738	740
Cod	KSJZ	72.7	46.8	37.0	28.1	25.7	15.5	KSLR	79 450	62 587	50 635	37 368	35 009	22 729
Dogfish	KSKA	7.4	6.9	7.3	7.0	5.8	6.5	KSLS	5 535	5 295	5 862	6 280	5 433	6 308
Haddock	KSKB	82.8	71.3	50.3	42.3	51.9	40.7	KSLT	57 131	59 286	51 181	36 295	34 631	27 517
Hake	KSKC	2.5	3.9	3.5	2.2	2.1	1.9	KSLU	5 117	7 839	6 941	5 303	5 646	4 138
Lemon Soles	KSKD	4.7	4.5	4.0	3.6	2.3	2.2	KSLV	10 620	10 374	9 934	9 937	7 313	6 719
Ling	KSKE	10.0	8.8	7.6	6.9	7.2	4.5	KSLW	8 291	8 502	7 571	7 384	7 654	4 600
Megrims	KSKF	5.3	5.0	5.0	4.3	4.0	3.6	KSLX	8 573	9 326	8 914	7 035	7 991	8 172
Monks or Anglers	KSKG	18.5	15.5	14.7	15.1	13.1	10.1	KSLY	38 540	35 591	33 609	33 789	27 927	20 807
Plaice	KSKH	11.5	9.5	8.6	7.7	5.9	4.4	KSLZ	13 185	12 549	9 869	9 011	6 645	5 422
Pollack (Lythe)	KSKI	2.6	2.3	2.5	2.6	2.5	2.5	KSMA	2 423	2 734	3 197	3 300	3 026	3 668
Saithe	KSKJ	10.1	10.4	10.2	9.7	9.9	8.5	KSMB	4 971	4 878	4 089	4 258	4 130	3 527
Sand Eels	KSKK	11.6	6.8	9.7	1.3	1.2	0.3	KSMC	742	283	400	..	55	16
Skates and Rays	KSKL	6.8	5.6	5.5	5.5	5.3	5.7	KSMD	6 403	5 380	5 677	5 679	5 299	5 715
Soles	KSKM	2.0	2.0	1.9	2.1	2.1	2.3	KSME	13 960	13 829	11 295	13 223	12 751	14 058
Turbot	KSKN	0.6	0.5	0.5	0.5	0.6	0.5	KSMF	3 614	2 918	2 859	3 277	4 192	2 795
Whiting	KSKO	26.7	25.4	23.3	15.1	11.4	8.2	KSMG	13 380	14 010	14 317	9 913	6 603	5 055
Whiting, Blue	KSKP	27.8	38.4	17.7	20.0	8.6	9.7	KSMH	2 003	1 476	743	936	561	670
Witches	KSKQ	1.9	2.2	2.4	2.7	2.2	2.4	KSMI	1 587	2 202	2 352	2 678	2 478	3 263
Other Demersal[2]	KSKR	12.7	15.7	14.6	17.7	15.1	12.9	KSMJ	15 612	18 559	16 025	19 765	18 513	20 168
Total Demersal[3]	KSKS	319.3	282.6	227.3	195.5	178.1	143.2	KSMK	293 882	280 028	248 392	218 414	198 381	167 898
Herring[4]	KSKT	39.5	45.3	39.5	43.8	42.5	55.2	KSML	4 897	5 057	4 073	10 447	6 873	7 020
Horse Mackerel	KSKU	5.1	2.1	2.7	3.5	1.8	2.0	KSMM	783	304	440	587	367	265
Mackerel[4]	KSKV	54.4	41.3	54.6	63.9	96.6	106.5	KSMN	21 754	9 544	13 848	23 877	42 694	44 624
Pilchards	KSKW	4.7	3.5	2.9	6.8	5.8	2.7	KSMO	765	550	602	1 665	1 005	535
Sprats	KSKX	5.0	14.3	8.3	5.1	5.7	5.5	KSMP	1 112	2 053	1 040	607	677	659
Tuna	KSKY	..	0.1	..	..	–	–	KSMQ	44	111	20	..	–	1
Other Pelagic	KSKZ	0.2	0.6	2.3	3.6	4.4	0.1	KSMR	60	184	401	762	848	89
Total Pelagic	KSLA	108.9	107.2	110.3	126.7	156.8	172.1	KSMS	29 416	17 803	20 424	37 949	52 464	53 193
Cockles	KSLB	12.1	14.2	20.3	19.0	14.3	26.8	KSMT	4 162	2 526	2 953	3 832	4 170	16 918
Crabs	KSLC	27.2	23.0	25.7	25.0	23.3	23.8	KSMU	32 290	26 983	28 036	27 830	26 014	25 494
Lobsters	KSLD	1.6	1.8	1.2	1.1	1.2	1.3	KSMV	14 489	14 928	12 458	11 436	11 680	12 816
Mussels	KSLE	12.7	8.4	7.5	14.9	17.2	3.1	KSMW	3 502	2 107	1 442	4 835	4 515	760
Nephrops	KSLF	28.6	31.1	28.3	28.4	28.4	27.6	KSMX	56 810	74 327	60 778	68 433	68 754	64 023
Periwinkles	KSLG	2.0	1.2	1.1	0.8	0.2	0.3	KSMY	1 892	1 165	1 089	791	221	252
Queens	KSLH	8.1	5.9	5.3	8.7	10.8	7.3	KSMZ	2 887	2 563	2 292	3 667	4 156	2 831
Scallops	KSLI	20.1	19.1	19.7	19.5	18.8	19.2	KSNA	30 156	29 145	30 741	29 853	27 963	29 084
Shrimps/Prawns	KSLJ	2.2	2.0	1.6	2.6	1.5	0.7	KSNB	2 594	2 931	2 062	3 566	2 574	1 093
Squid	KSLK	2.2	2.1	1.4	1.4	2.1	3.0	KSNC	4 362	4 190	2 716	3 903	4 908	6 768
Other shellfish	KSLL	7.6	8.0	14.8	14.9	13.1	16.2	KSND	7 564	5 434	8 680	9 177	8 889	10 469
Total shellfish	KSLM	124.2	116.7	127.0	136.2	130.7	129.3	KSNE	160 708	166 299	153 247	167 323	163 844	170 508

1 See chapter text.
2 Includes roes and livers.
3 Includes fish roes.

4 Includes transshipments, i.e. caught by UK boats but not actually landing at UK ports. These quantities are transshipped to foreign vessels in coastal waters and are later recorded as exports.

Source: Department for Environment, Food and Rural Affairs: 01904 455332

21.15 Fishing fleet[1]
United Kingdom
At 31 December each year

		1993	1994	1995	1996	1997	1998	1999	2000	2001	2002	2003
By size												
10m and under	KSNF	7 666	7 195	6 320	5 606	5 474	5 487	5 409	5 273	5 227	5 287	5 113
10.01 - 12.19m	KSNG	1 361	1 167	1 016	800	732	628	577	547	536	514	486
12.20 - 17.00m	KSNH	751	680	622	540	523	491	468	467	442	409	405
17.01 - 18.29m	KSNI	220	193	187	164	162	154	154	131	143	129	121
18.30 - 24.38m	KSNJ	657	610	574	509	471	443	414	406	405	322	271
24.39 - 30.48m	KSNK	210	211	212	223	227	226	224	219	218	185	156
30.49 - 36.58m	KSNL	124	126	127	114	104	89	80	77	75	65	63
over 36.58m	KSNM	119	116	117	117	119	121	122	122	123	122	120
Total over 10m	KSNN	3 442	3 103	2 855	2 467	2 338	2 152	2 039	1 969	1 942	1 746	1 622
Total UK fleet[2]	KSNO	11 108	10 297	9 174	8 073	7 812	7 639	7 448	7 242	7 169	7 033	6 735
By segment												
Pelagic gears	KSNP	69	68	67	58	49	50	46	44	47	45	42
Beam trawl	KSNQ	240	212	220	215	153	123	114	111	116	113	162
Demersal trawls and seines	KXET	..	..	..	1 040	..	..	..	..	..	..	..
Demersal trawls	KSIX	988	854	856	..	..	..	..	..	..	..	..
Nephrop trawls	KSIY	560	593	528	411	..	..	..	..	..	..	..
Seines	KSIZ	203	197	165	..	..	..	..	..	..	..	..
Demersal, Seines and Nephrops	JZCI	..	..	..	..	1 428	1 318	1 235	1 208	1 158	969	853
Lines and Nets	KSNR	329	300	267	224	214	187	172	165	146	136	118
Shellfish: mobile	KSNS	181	206	194	265	227	241	243	211	229	228	191
Shellfish: fixed	KSNT	312	305	283	339	352	311	301	297	301	304	307
Distant water	KSNU	14	13	12	15	13	14	12	13	11	10	8
Under 10m	KSNV	8 128	7 607	6 757	6 091	6 022	6 027	5 916	5 769	5 713	5 773	5 587
Non-active/non-TAC	KSNW	668	472	371	–	–	–	–	–	–	–	–
Other: Mussel Dredgers	JZCJ	..	..	..	..	3	2	2	2	7	15	15
Total UK fleet[3]	KSNX	11 692	10 827	9 720	8 658	8 461	8 273	8 041	7 820	7 728	7 593	7 283

1 See chapter text.
2 Excluding Channel Islands and Isle of Man.
3 Including Channel Islands and Isle of Man.

Source: Department for Environment, Food and Rural Affairs: 01904 455332

Grammes per person per week

		Great Britain										United Kingdom	
		1992	1993	1994	1995	1996	1997	1998	1999	2000		2001 /02	2002 /03
Liquid wholemilk[2] (ml)	KPQM	995	898	870	812	776	712	693	634	664	VQEW	599	555
Fully skimmed (ml)	KZBH	213	217	207	204	137	158	164	167	164	VQEX	160	166
Semi skimmed (ml)	KZBI	752	814	863	899	935	978	945	958	975	VQEZ	931	919
Other milk and cream (ml)	KZBJ	262	249	252	255	259	248	243	248	278	VQFA	333	350
Cheese	KPQO	114	109	106	108	111	109	104	104	110	VQFB	112	112
Butter	KPQP	41	40	39	36	39	38	39	37	39	VQFC	42	37
Margarine	KPQQ	79	70	43	41	36	26	26	20	21	VQFD	13	13
Low and reduced fat spreads	KZBK	51	52	74	72	79	77	69	71	68	VQFE	72	70
All other oils and fats (ml for oils)	KPQR	74	69	70	69	71	62	62	58	58	VQFF	70	70
Eggs (number)	KPQS	2	2	2	2	2	2	2	2	2	VQFG	2	2
Preserves and honey	KPQT	45	42	43	39	41	41	38	33	33	VQFH	35	34
Sugar	KPQU	156	151	144	136	144	128	119	107	105	VQFI	112	111
Beef and veal	KPQV	141	133	131	121	101	110	109	110	124	VQFJ	118	118
Mutton and lamb	KPQW	71	66	54	54	66	56	59	57	55	VQFK	51	51
Pork	KPQX	72	80	77	71	73	75	76	69	68	VQFL	61	61
Bacon and ham, uncooked	KPQY	77	77	77	76	77	72	76	68	71	VQFM	68	69
Bacon and ham, cooked (including canned)	KPQZ	33	35	38	39	33	41	40	39	41	VQFN	45	45
Poultry uncooked	JZCH	216	222	209	215	233	221	218	201	214	VQFO	206	199
Cooked poultry (not purchased in cans)	KYBP	15	16	20	22	23	33	33	35	39	VQFQ	43	44
Other cooked and canned meats	KPRB	68	60	63	63	62	52	49	48	51	VQFR	54	59
Offals	KPRC	12	11	9	9	7	7	5	5	5	VQFS	6	6
Sausages, uncooked	KPRD	61	60	61	63	63	63	60	58	60	VQFT	66	66
Other meat products	KPRE	183	194	203	211	207	209	216	221	239	VQFU	313	319
Fish, fresh and processed (including shellfish)	KPRF	67	71	71	68	72	70	70	70	67			
Canned fish	KPRG	32	30	30	29	31	31	29	31	32			
Fish and fish products, frozen	KPRH	43	44	44	46	50	46	46	42	44			
Fish, fresh chilled or frozen											VQAI	51	48
Other fish and fish products											VQAJ	105	106
Potatoes (excluding processed)	KPRI	901	875	812	803	805	745	715	673	707	VQFY	647	617
Fresh green vegetables	KPRJ	250	240	245	225	233	251	246	245	240	VQAK	229	231
Other fresh vegetables	KPRK	475	477	464	470	489	497	486	500	492	VQAL	502	505
Frozen potato products	KYBQ	92	98	103	99	113	106	111	113	120			
Other frozen vegetables	KPRL	106	105	107	101	94	94	88	87	80			
Potato products not frozen	JZCF	75	80	82	89	92	90	89	86	82			
Canned beans	KPRM	120	112	111	117	125	122	118	112	114			
Other canned vegetables (excl. potatoes)	KPRN	124	114	103	110	113	104	99	92	97			
Other processed vegetables (excl. potatoes)	LQZH	50	52	55	48	55	52	54	59	54			
All processed vegetables											VQAM	620	613
Apples	KPRO	187	179	180	183	175	179	181	169	180	VQGN	175	172
Bananas	KPRP	144	151	162	176	185	195	198	202	206	VQGO	203	208
Oranges	KPRQ	72	62	65	66	63	62	63	50	54	VQGP	55	62
All other fresh fruit	KPRR	216	224	238	247	263	276	274	290	304	VQGS	318	351
Canned fruit	KPRS	51	48	46	45	43	44	37	38	38	VQGT	40	39
Dried fruit, nuts and fruit and nut products	KPRT	38	39	36	34	36	35	34	30	35	VQGU	39	41
Fruit juices (ml)	KPRU	222	236	240	244	258	277	304	284	303	VQGX	327	333
Flour	KPRV	81	82	62	57	70	54	55	56	67	VQGY	55	61
Bread	KPRW	755	757	758	756	752	746	742	717	720	VQGZ	769	756
Buns, scones and teacakes	KPRX	40	39	38	36	47	43	41	40	43	VQHA	37	41
Cakes and pastries	KPRY	76	79	85	85	87	93	88	87	89	VQHB	139	122
Biscuits	KPRZ	148	142	138	135	150	138	137	132	141	VQHC	166	174
Breakfast cereals	KPSA	132	129	134	135	140	135	136	134	143	VQHE	133	132
Oatmeal and oat products	KPSB	15	14	11	11	13	16	11	13	15	VQHF	12	13
Other cereals and cereal products	JZCG	217	218	218	251	304	293	270	284	291	VQHG	345	366
Tea	KPSC	39	36	38	39	38	36	35	32	34	VQHK	34	34
Instant coffee	KPSD	14	13	13	12	13	11	12	11	11	VQHL	13	12
Canned soups	KPSE	70	66	68	64	72	70	71	67	71	VQHM	79	80
Pickles and sauces	KPSF	72	77	77	80	84	92	96	91	107	VQHN	121	123

1 See chapter text.
2 Including also school and welfare milk.

Sources: Expenditure and Food Survey;
Department for Environment Food and Rural Affairs: 01904 455077

Production

Chapter 22

Production

Annual Business Inquiry

(Table 22.1)

The Annual Business Inquiry (ABI) estimates cover all UK businesses registered for Value Added Tax (VAT) and/ or Pay As You Earn (PAYE), classified to the 1992 Standard Industrial Classification (SIC(92)) headings listed in the tables. The ABI obtains details on these businesses from the ONS Inter-Departmental Business Register (IDBR).

As with all its statistical inquiries, ONS is concerned to minimise the form-filling burden of individual contributors and as such the ABI is a sample inquiry. The sample was designed as a stratified random sample of about 69,600 businesses, the inquiry population is stratified by SIC(92) and employment using the information from the register.

The inquiry results are grossed up to the total population, so that they relate to all active UK businesses on the IDBR for the sectors covered.

The results meet a wide range of needs for government, economic analysts and the business community at large. In official statistics the inquiry is an important source for the national accounts and input-output tables, but also provides weights for the indices of production and producer prices. Inquiry results also enable the United Kingdom to meet statistical requirements of the European Union.

Data from 1995 and 1996 were calculated on a different basis from those for 1997 and later years. In order to provide a link between the two data series, the 1995 and 1996 data were subsequently reworked to provide estimates on a consistent basis.

Revised Annual Business Inquiry results down to SIC(92) 4 digit class level for 1995–2001, giving both analysis and tabular detail, are now available free of charge from the National Statistics website at *www.statistics.gov.uk/ abi/*, with further extracts and bespoke analyses available on request. This service replaces existing publications.

Manufacturers' sales by industry

(Table 22.2)

This table shows the total manufacturers' sales for products classified to the 1992 Standard Industrial Classification and collected under the PRODCOM (Products of the European Community) Inquiry since its introduction in 1993. Some data are not available for confidentiality reasons or where data have not been published for a given period. Detailed product sales data together with exports and imports data are available in the Product Sales and Trade quarterly and annual reports (PRQ and PRA series).

Number of local units in manufacturing industries in 2003

(Table 22.3)

This table shows the number of local units (sites) in manufacturing by employment sizebands. The classification breakdown is at division level (2 digit) as classified to the 2003 Standard Industrial Classification held on the Inter-Departmental Business Register (IDBR). This register became fully operational in 1995 and combines information on VAT traders and PAYE employers in a statistical register comprising two million enterprises (businesses), representing nearly 99 per cent of economic activity. Business Monitor PA1003 *Size Analysis of United Kingdom Businesses* 2003 provides further details and contains detailed information on enterprises in the UK including size, classification and location. Additionally, this information is available for manufacturing local units.

For further information on the IDBR see the National Statistics website at *www.statistics.gov.uk/idbr.*

Production of primary fuels

(Table 22.4)

This table shows indigenous production of primary fuels. It includes the extraction or capture of primary commodities and the generation or manufacture of secondary commodities. Production is always gross; that is, it includes the quantities used during the extraction or manufacturing process. Primary fuels are coal, natural gas (including colliery methane), oil, primary electricity (i.e. electricity generated by hydro, nuclear wind and tide stations and also electricity imported from France through the interconnector) and renewables (includes solid renewables such as wood, straw and waste and gaseous renewables such as landfill gas and sewage gas). The figures are presented on a common basis, expressed in million tonnes of oil equivalent. Estimates of the gross calorific values used for converting the statistics for the various fuels to these are given in the *Digest of UK Energy Statistics* (published by The Stationery Office and available on the Department of Trade and Industry (DTI) website at *www.dti.gov.uk/energy/inform/dukes/*). Chapter 1 of the *Digest of UK Energy Statistics* gives more information on these figures.

Total inland energy consumption

(Table 22.5)

This table shows energy consumption by fuel and final energy consumption by fuel and class of consumer. Primary energy consumption covers consumption of all primary fuels (defined above) for energy purposes. This measure of energy consumption includes energy that is lost by converting primary fuels into secondary fuels, i.e. the energy lost burning coal to generate electricity or the energy used by refineries to separate crude oil into fractions, in addition to losses in distribution. The other common way of measuring energy consumption is to measure the energy content of the fuels supplied to consumers. This is called final energy consumption. It is net of fuel used by the energy industries, conversion, transmission and distribution losses. The figures are presented on a common basis, measured as energy supplied and expressed in million tonnes of oil equivalent. Estimates of the gross calorific values used for converting the statistics for the various fuels to these are given in the *Digest of UK Energy Statistics* (published by The Stationery Office and available on the DTI website at *www.dti.gov.uk/energy/inform/dukes/*). So far as practicable the user categories have been grouped on the basis of the SIC(2003) although the methods used by each of the supply industries to identify end users are slightly different. Chapter 1 of the *Digest of UK Energy Statistics* gives more information on these figures.

Coal

(Table 22.6)

Since 1995, aggregate data on coal production have been obtained from the Coal Authority. In addition, main coal producers provide data in response to an annual DTI inquiry which covers production (deepmined and opencast), trade, stocks and disposals. HM Customs and Excise also provide trade data for solid fuels. The DTI collects information on the use of coal from UK Iron and Steel Statistics Bureau, and consumption of coal for electricity generation is covered by data provided by the electricity generators.

Gas

(Table 22.7)

Production figures, covering the production of gas from the UKCS offshore and onshore gas fields and gas obtained during the production of oil, are obtained from returns made under the DTI's Petroleum Production Reporting System. Additional information is used on imports and exports of gas and details from the operators of gas terminals in the UK to complete the picture.

It is no longer possible to present information on fuels input into the gas industry and gas output and sales in the same format as in previous editions of this table. As such, users are directed to Chapter 4 of the 2002 edition of the *Digest of UK Energy Statistics*, where more detailed information on gas production and consumption in the UK is available.

DTI carry out an annual survey of gas suppliers to obtain details of gas sales to the various categories of consumer. Estimates are included for the suppliers with the smallest market share since the DTI inquiry covers only the largest suppliers (i.e. those more than about 0.5 per cent share of the UK market up to 1997 and those known to supply more than 1,750 GWh per year from 1998 onwards).

Electricity

(Tables 22.8 to 22.10)

The electricity Tables 22.8 to 22.10 cover all generators and suppliers of electricity in the United Kingdom.

The relationship between generation, supply, availability and consumption is as follows:

Electricity generated

less	electricity used on works
equals	electricity supplied (gross)
less	electricity used in pumping at pumped storage stations
equals	electricity supplied (net)
plus	imports (net of exports) of electricity
equals	electricity available
less	losses and statistical differences
equals	electricity consumed.

In Table 22.8 'major power producers' are those generating companies corresponding to the old public sector supply system, i.e. AES Electric Ltd., American Electric Power., Anglian Power Generation., Baglan Generation Ltd., Barking Power Ltd., BNFL Magnox, British Energy plc., Coolkeeragh Power Ltd., Corby Power Ltd., Coryton Energy Company Ltd., Deeside Power, Derwent Cogeneration Ltd., EDF Energy Plc, Edison Mission Energy Ltd., Enfield Energy Centre Ltd., Entergy Power Group Ltd., Fellside Heat and Power Ltd., Fibrogen Ltd., Fibropower Ltd., Fibrothetford Ltd., Fife Power Ltd., Great Yarmouth Power Ltd., Humber Power Ltd., Innogy plc., International Power plc., Killingholme Power Ltd., Lakeland Power Ltd., Medway Power Ltd., National Grid Company (Kielder), NIGEN, Peterborough Power Ltd., PowerGen plc. (including former TXU Europe Power Ltd stations), Premier

Production

Power Ltd., Regional Power Generators Ltd., Rocksavage Power Company Ltd., Saltend Co-generation Company Ltd., Scottish Power plc., Scottish and Southern Energy plc., Seabank Power Ltd., SELCHP Ltd. (South East London Combined Heat & Power Ltd.), Sita Tyre Recycling Ltd., South Coast Power Ltd., South Western Electricity, Sutton Bridge Power Ltd., Teesside Power Ltd.

In Table 22.10 all fuels are converted to the common unit of million tonnes of oil equivalent, i.e. the amounts of oil which would be needed to produce the output of electricity generated from those fuels.

More detailed statistics on energy are given in the *Digest of United Kingdom Energy Statistics* 2003. Readers may wish to note that the production and consumption of fuels are presented using commodity balances. A commodity balance shows the flows of an individual fuel through from production to final consumption, showing its use in transformation and energy industry own use.

Oil and oil products

(Tables 22.11 to 22.13)

The data on the production of crude oil, condensates and natural gases given in Table 22.11 are collected by the DTI direct from the operators of production facilities and terminals situated on UK territory, either onshore or offshore, i.e. on the UK Continental Shelf. Data are also collected from the companies on their trade in oil and oil products. These data are used in preference to the foreign trade as recorded by HM Customs and Excise in the Overseas Trade Statistics.

Data on the internal UK oil industry (i.e. on the supply, refining and distribution of oil and oil products in the UK) are collected by the UK Petroleum Industry Association. These data, reported by individual refining companies and wholesalers, and supplemented where necessary by data from other sources, provide the contents of Tables 22.12 and 22.13. The data are presented in terms of deliveries to the inland UK market. This is regarded as an acceptable proxy for actual consumption of products. The main shortcoming is that, whilst changes in stocks held by companies in central storage areas are taken into account, changes in the levels of stocks further down the retail ladder (such as stocks held on petrol station forecourts) are not. This is not thought to result in a significant degree of difference in the data.

Iron and steel

(Tables 22.14 to 22.16)

Iron and steel industry

The general definition of the UK iron and steel industry is based on groups 271 'ECSC iron and steel', 272 'Tubes', and 273 'Primary Transformation' of the UK Standard Industrial Classification (1992), except those parts of groups 272 and 273 which cover cast iron pipes, drawn wire, cold formed sections and Ferro alloys.

The definition excludes certain products which may be made by works within the industry, such as refined iron, finished steel castings, steel tyres, wheels, axles and rolled rings, open and closed die forgings, colliery arches and springs. Iron foundries and steel stockholders are also considered to be outside of the industry.

Statistics

The statistics for the UK iron and steel industry are compiled by the Iron and Steel Statistics Bureau (ISSB Ltd). from data collected from UK steel producing companies with the exception of trade data which is based on HM Customs data.

Crude steel is the total of usable ingots, usable continuously cast semi-finished products and liquid steel for castings.

Production of finished products is the total production at the mill of that product after deduction of any material which is immediately scrapped.

Deliveries are based on invoiced tonnages and will include deliveries made to steel stockholders and service centres by the UK steel industry.

For more detailed information on definitions etc please contact ISSB Ltd. on 020 7343 3900.

Minerals

(Table 22.19)

Table 22.19 gives, separately for Great Britain and Northern Ireland, the production of minerals extracted from the ground. The figures for chemicals and metals are estimated from the quality of the ore which is extracted. The data come from an annual census of the quarrying industry which, for Great Britain, is conducted by ONS for the Office of the Deputy Prime Minister (ODPM) and the DTI.

Building Materials

(Table 22.20)

Table 22.20 gives the production of a number of building materials which are closely associated with material extracted from the ground. The data come from surveys conducted by ONS on behalf of the DTI.

Construction

(Tables 22.21 to 22.22)

Table 22.21 shows the value of contractors' output in the construction industry in Great Britain. Contractors' output is defined as the amount chargeable to customers for building and civil engineering work done in the relevant period. The data come from surveys run by the DTI. As well as being an important input to the National Accounts, it is used by the government and the construction industry in their efforts to fully understand the industry, and also by Eurostat.

Table 22.22 shows the value of new orders in the construction industry; this is also collected by DTI. This information relates to contracts for new construction work awarded to main contractors by clients in both the public and private sectors; it also includes speculative work, undertaken on the initiative of the firm, where no contract is awarded. New orders are used as a good indicator of future output.

Motor vehicle production

(Table 22.25)

The figures represent the output of United Kingdom based manufacturers classified to Class 34.10 (motor vehicles) of the Standard Industrial Classification 2003. They are derived from the Motor Vehicle Production Inquiry (MVPI).

These figures include vehicles produced in the form of kits for assembly. The value of the kit must be 50 per cent or more of the value of a corresponding complete vehicle.

Drink and tobacco

(Tables 22.26 and 22.27)

Data for these tables are derived by Customs and Excise from the systems for collecting excise duties. Alcoholic drinks and tobacco products become liable to duty when released for consumption in the UK. Figures for releases include both home-produced products and commercial imports. Production figures are also available for potable spirits distilled and beer brewed in the UK.

Alcoholic drink

(Table 22.26)

The figures for Imported and other spirits released for home consumption include gin and other UK produced spirits, for which a breakdown is not available.

Since June 1993 beer duty has been charged when the beer leaves the brewery or other registered premises. Previously duty was chargeable at an earlier stage (the worts stage) in the brewing process, and an allowance was made for wastage. Figures prior to 1994 include adjustments to bring them into line with current data. The change in June 1993 also led to the availability of data on the strength; a series in hectolitres of pure alcohol is shown from 1994.

Made wine with alcoholic strength from 1.2 per cent to 5.5 per cent is termed 'coolers'. Included in coolers are alcoholic lemonade and similar products of appropriate strength. From 28 April 2002, duty on spirit-based 'coolers' (ready to drink products) is charged at the same rate as spirits per litre of alcohol. Made wine coolers include only wine based 'coolers' from this period.

Tobacco Products

(Table 22.27)

Releases of cigarettes and other tobacco products tend to be higher in the period before a Budget. Products may then be stocked, duty paid, before being sold.

22.1

Production and construction:[1] summary table
United Kingdom
Standard Industrial Classfication 1992: Estimates for all firms

£ million

	Total turnover	Gross value added	Stocks and work in progress		Capital expenditure *less* disposals	Total employment costs
			At end of year	Change during year		

Standard Industrial Classification: Revised 1992

Production and construction
Sections C-F

	ZIYQ	KSCD	KSCE	KSCF	KSCG	AWKC
1998	631 265	212 933	70 062	365	34 097	112 326
1999	644 749	220 338	66 400	1 539	30 007	114 584
2000	675 149	228 161	66 571	3 962	27 478	115 943
2001	674 274	229 773	65 831	713	28 823	117 560
2002	673 544	229 672	72 137	457	27 861	119 800

Production industries (Revised definitions)
Sections C-E

	ZIYR	KSCL	KSCM	KSCN	KSCO	AWKH
1998	528 819	178 459	55 354	−601	32 275	93 692
1999	533 384	181 189	54 867	204	28 139	93 774
2000	553 601	185 886	54 945	3 200	25 261	94 209
2001	544 210	182 243	52 732	−824	25 716	93 993
2002	531 081	179 061	51 641	−1 035	23 911	93 590

Mining and quarrying
Section C

	ZIYS	KSCT	KSCU	KSCV	KSCW	AWKI
1998	23 953	13 120	1 138	55	6 303	2 542
1999	26 270	15 245	1 138	−5	4 058	2 469
2000	36 513	22 289	957	−2	2 810	2 669
2001	37 057	22 560	958	64	4 272	2 698
2002	34 346	19 097	900	25	5 022	2 840

Mining and quarrying of energy producing materials
Subsection CA

	ZIYT	KSDB	KSDC	KSDD	KSDE	KSDF
1998	19 866	11 512	732	23	5 985	1 862
1999	21 975	13 615	850	−19	3 738	1 765
2000	31 704	20 489	657	−24	2 572	1 905
2001	32 237	20 765	658	33	4 008	1 945
2002	29 759	17 634	631	3	4 780	2 124

Mining and quarrying except energy producing materials
Subsection CB

	ZIYU	KSDJ	KSDK	KSDL	KSDM	KSDN
1998	4 087	1 609	406	32	318	680
1999	4 295	1 630	289	14	320	704
2000	4 809	1 800	300	21	237	765
2001	4 820	1 795	300	31	264	752
2002	4 587	1 463	269	22	243	716

Manufacturing (Revised definition)
Section D

	ZIYV	KSDR	KSDS	KSDT	KSDU	AWKL
1998	460 677	149 892	52 675	−643	20 386	87 079
1999	461 771	150 449	52 005	309	18 125	87 334
2000	469 146	148 793	52 167	3 150	17 004	87 456
2001	461 898	145 230	50 038	−816	16 278	87 574
2002	450 137	144 227	49 058	−915	13 596	86 817

22.1 Production and construction:[1] summary table
United Kingdom
continued

Standard Industrial Classfication 1992: Estimates for all firms

£ million

	Total turnover	Gross value added	Stocks and work in progress		Capital expenditure *less* disposals	Total employment costs
			At end of year	Change during year		

Standard Industrial Classification: Revised 1992

Manufacture of food; beverages and tobacco
Subsection DA

	ZIYW	KSDZ	KSEA	KSEB	KSEC	AWKM
1998	73 482	19 351	8 023	−221	2 763	9 333
1999	73 655	19 977	7 958	−62	2 725	9 885
2000	73 872	20 184	7 605	−88	2 271	9 929
2001	74 692	20 324	7 633	87	2 638	10 045
2002	76 699	20 799	9 233	27	2 534	10 448

Manufacture of textile and textile products
Subsection DB

	ZIYX	KSEH	KSEI	KSEJ	KSEK	AWKN
1998	17 365	6 699	2 906	−140	552	4 476
1999	16 137	5 930	2 610	−67	460	4 035
2000	14 358	5 506	2 285	−19	275	3 541
2001	13 229	5 051	2 046	41	258	3 096
2002	12 147	4 496	1 853	14	303	2 893

Manufacture of leather and leather products
Subsection DC

	ZIYY	KSEP	KSEQ	KSER	KSES	AWKO
1998	2 005	689	301	−11	42	461
1999	1 819	673	243	−2	38	360
2000	1 728	676	230	−18	9	330
2001	1 758	595	230	−28	23	320
2002	1 541	571	228	−3	18	275

Manufacture of wood and wood products
Subsection DD

	ZIYZ	KSEX	KSEY	KSEZ	KSFA	AWKP
1998	5 797	2 270	593	6	255	1 360
1999	5 838	2 101	508	−14	238	1 246
2000	6 186	2 303	610	30	227	1 292
2001	6 571	2 315	585	−17	219	1 374
2002	7 048	2 471	664	38	188	1 627

Manufacture of pulp, paper and paper products; publishing and printing
Subsection DE

	ZIZA	KSFF	KSFG	KSFH	KSFI	AWKQ
1998	42 734	18 309	2 660	−28	1 957	10 277
1999	43 387	19 280	2 608	71	1 719	10 260
2000	45 291	19 492	2 544	125	1 813	10 857
2001	44 922	19 425	2 606	25	1 657	10 856
2002	45 436	19 308	2 615	115	1 464	10 956

Manufacture of coke, refined petroleum products and nuclear fuel
Subsection DF

	ZIZB	KSFN	KSFO	KSFP	KSFQ	AWKR
1998	23 322	2 289	885	−196	730	923
1999	25 310	3 087	1 333	449	766	912
2000	27 855	2 302	1 199	114	623	920
2001	25 369	2 401	1 000	−190	705	898
2002	24 153	2 649	1 287	190	473	1 099

22.1
continued

Production and construction:[1] **summary table**
United Kingdom
Standard Industrial Classfication 1992: Estimates for all firms

£ million

			Stocks and work in progress			
	Total turnover	Gross value added	At end of year	Change during year	Capital expenditure *less* disposals	Total employment costs

Standard Industrial Classification: Revised 1992

Manufacture of chemicals, chemical products and man-made fibres
  Subsection DG

	ZIZC	KSFV	KSFW	KSFX	KSFY	AWKS
1998	44 825	14 341	5 659	114	3 161	7 374
1999	46 282	14 939	5 911	75	2 830	7 710
2000	47 544	15 069	6 249	481	2 729	7 549
2001	48 915	15 821	6 205	−8	2 473	7 959
2002	48 675	16 401	6 198	−15	2 141	8 305

Manufacture of rubber and plastic products
  Subsection DH

	ZIZD	KSGD	KSGE	KSGF	KSGG	AWKT
1998	20 420	8 062	2 021	54	1 102	4 855
1999	19 520	7 554	1 898	24	1 088	4 940
2000	19 743	7 644	1 824	59	961	4 767
2001	19 869	7 716	1 833	−1	742	4 769
2002	19 631	7 466	1 757	19	682	4 702

Manufacture of other non-metallic mineral products
  Subsection DI

	ZIZE	KSGL	KSGM	KSGN	KSGO	AWKU
1998	11 346	4 904	1 420	29	656	2 771
1999	11 710	4 865	1 364	−106	747	2 759
2000	12 014	5 154	1 460	94	621	2 821
2001	11 656	4 895	1 332	−4	488	2 828
2002	12 185	4 986	1 393	23	605	2 778

Manufacture of basic iron and of ferro-alloys
  Subsection DJ

	ZIZF	KSGT	KSGU	KSGV	KSGW	AWKV
1998	44 399	17 030	4 255	−203	2 024	10 713
1999	40 879	15 941	4 047	99	1 464	10 450
2000	41 028	15 912	4 063	192	1 334	10 340
2001	40 660	15 316	3 920	−43	1 122	10 098
2002	38 506	14 716	3 617	77	1 153	9 672

Manufacture of machinery and equipment not elsewhere specified
  Subsection DK

	ZIZG	KSHB	KSHC	KSHD	KSHE	AWKW
1998	35 580	13 414	5 084	46	982	8 637
1999	33 306	12 254	5 044	−230	954	8 356
2000	33 821	12 286	4 826	−40	872	8 437
2001	32 825	11 770	4 460	−73	792	8 302
2002	31 455	11 373	4 183	−85	683	8 050

Manufacture of electrical and optical equipment
  Subsection DL

	ZIZH	KSHJ	KSHK	KSHL	KSHM	AWKX
1998	61 037	19 202	6 832	−10	2 688	11 568
1999	64 891	19 587	7 014	119	1 861	11 881
2000	69 110	20 504	8 521	1 700	2 331	12 587
2001	63 227	15 813	7 280	−1 130	1 950	12 576
2002	53 148	16 133	6 079	−669	866	11 331

Production and construction:[1] summary table
United Kingdom
Standard Industrial Classfication 1992: Estimates for all firms

£ million

| | Total turnover | Gross value added | Stocks and work in progress | | Capital expenditure *less* disposals | Wages and salaries |
			At end of year	Change during year		

Standard Industrial Classification: Revised 1992

Manufacture of transport equipment
Subsection DM

	ZIZI	KSHR	KSHS	KSHT	KSHU	AWKY
1998	63 009	17 179	10 463	−193	2 948	10 840
1999	63 239	17 955	9 648	−128	2 749	10 866
2000	60 440	15 553	9 048	454	2 444	10 520
2001	61 366	17 322	9 206	444	2 740	10 740
2002	62 280	16 505	8 308	−739	2 064	10 821

Manufacture not elsewhere classified
Subsection DN

	ZIZJ	KSHZ	KSIA	KSIB	KSIC	AWKZ
1998	15 356	6 153	1 574	110	528	3 493
1999	15 798	6 306	1 820	82	485	3 674
2000	16 156	6 208	1 703	67	496	3 565
2001	16 839	6 468	1 701	81	471	3 714
2002	17 231	6 354	1 640	94	422	3 860

Electricity, gas and water supply
Section E

	ZIZK	KSIH	KSII	KSIJ	KSIK	AWLA
1998	44 189	15 446	1 542	−14	5 586	4 071
1999	45 342	15 496	1 723	−100	5 955	3 970
2000	47 942	14 804	1 821	52	5 448	4 084
2001	45 256	14 453	1 736	−72	5 165	3 721
2002	46 598	15 737	1 682	−145	5 292	3 933

Construction
Section F

	ZIZL	KSIP	KSIQ	KSIR	KSIS	AWLB
1998	102 446	34 474	14 708	966	1 822	18 634
1999	111 365	39 150	11 533	1 335	1 869	20 810
2000	121 549	42 275	11 626	762	2 216	21 734
2001	130 064	47 530	13 099	1 537	3 107	23 567
2002	142 463	50 611	20 496	1 492	3 950	26 210

1 See chapter text.

Source: Office for National Statistics: 01633 812435

Industry		SIC (92)	1999	2000	2001	2002
Other mining and quarrying						
Quarrying of stone for construction	KSPF	14110	..	..	44	45
Quarrying of limestone, gypsum and chalk	KSPG	14120	222	209	237	227
Quarrying of slate	KSPH	14130	3	3	4	6
Operation of gravel and sand pits	KSPJ	14210	1 615	1 700	..	..
Mining of clays and kaolin	KSPK	14220	320	306	300	220
Mining of chemical and fertilizer minerals	KSPL	14300	99	125	155	82
Production of salt	KSPM	14400	153	158	159	177
Other mining and quarrying not elsewhere classified	KSPN	14500	71	63	64	57
Manufacture of food products and beverages						
Production and preserving of meat	KSPO	15110	3 184	3 199	3 040	3 435
Production and preserving of poultry meat	KSPP	15120	1 687	1 876	..	..
Bacon and ham production	KSPQ	15131	1 147	1 111	1 133	1 001
Other meat and poultry meat processing	KSPR	15139	3 766	4 038	4 024	3 852
Processing and preserving of fish and fish products	KSPS	15200	1 536	1 558	1 686	1 639
Processing and preserving of potatoes	KSPT	15310	..	..	..	1 226
Fruit and vegetable juice	KSPU	15320	543	545	543	553
Processing and preserving of fruit and vegetables not elsewhere classified	KSPV	15330	1 962	2 163	2 433	2 472
Crude oils and fats	KSPW	15410	508	425	530	505
Refined oils and fats	KSPX	15420	464	485	459	509
Margarine and similar edible fats	KSPY	15430	471	..	..	465
Operation of dairies	KTEH	15510	5 632	5 646	5 678	5 371
Ice cream	KSPZ	15520	553	498	..	485
Grain mill products	KSQA	15610	2 702	2 666	2 485	2 816
Starches and starch products	KSQB	15620	379	377	401	399
Prepared feeds for farm animals	KSPI	15710	1 903	1 982	1 947	2 252
Prepared pet foods	KSQC	15720	1 146	1 167	1 113	1 004
Bread; fresh pastry goods and cakes	KSQD	15810	4 005	4 032	3 919	4 015
Rusks and biscuits; preserved pastry goods and cakes	KSQE	15820	..	..	2 886	3 005
Sugar	KSQF	15830	1 127	1 047	1 140	1 110
Cocoa; chocolate and sugar confectionery	KSQG	15840	..	3 396	3 320	3 470
Macaroni, noodles, couscous and similar farinaceous products	KSQH	15850	..	481	440	
Processing of tea and coffee	KSQI	15860	1 450	1 398	1 380	1 391
Condiments and seasonings	KSQJ	15870	..	..	1 129	1 136
Homogenised food preparations and dietetic foods	KSQK	15880	196	158	134	130
Manufacture of other food products not elsewhere classified	KSQL	15890	1 809	1 846	1 911	1 753
Distilled potable alcoholic beverages	KSQM	15910	2 176	1 987	1 959	2 109
Production of ethyl alcohol from fermented materials	KSQN	15920	101	..	..	101
Wines	KSQO	15930	..	63	60	68
Cider and other fruit wines	KSQP	15940	565	475	438	480
Other non-distilled fermented beverages	KSQQ	15950	–	–	–	–
Beer	KSQR	15960	4 660	3 685	3 624	3 472
Malt	KSQS	15970	264	234	247	266
Mineral waters and soft drinks	KSQT	15980	2 811	2 748	..	..
Manufacture of tobacco products						
Tobacco products	KSQU	16000	2 443	2 282	1 796	1 825
Manufacture of textiles						
Preparation and spinning of textile fibres	KSQV	17100	891	798	672	556
Textile weaving	KSQW	17200	972	902	825	737
Finishing of textiles	KSQX	17300	629	575	518	530
Soft furnishings	KSQY	17401	444	458	544	529
Canvas goods, sacks etc	KSQZ	17402	161	137	137	120
Household textiles	KSRA	17403	942	987	897	783
Carpets and rugs	KSRB	17510	1 029	973	902	841
Cordage, rope, twine and netting	KSRC	17520	80	79	102	..

22.2
continued

Manufacturers' sales: by industry[1]
United Kingdom
Standard Industrial Classification 1992

£ million

Industry	SIC (92)	1999	2000	2001	2002
Manufacture of textiles continued					
Nonwovens and articles made from nonwovens, except apparel	KSRD 17530	158	..	169	167
Lace	KSRE 17541	39	34	28	23
Narrow fabrics	KSRF 17542	223	210	193	187
Other textiles not elsewhere classified	KSRG 17549	498	516	491	438
Knitted and crocheted fabrics	KSRH 17600	..	374	..	244
Knitted and crocheted hosiery	KSRI 17710	363	..	282	..
Knitted and crocheted pullovers, cardigans and similar	KSRJ 17720	664	582	407	351
Manufacture of wearing apparel; dressing and dyeing of fur					
Leather clothes	KSRK 18100	14	16	13	..
Workwear	KSRL 18210	279	261	244	271
Men's outerwear	KSRM 18221	613	421	329	297
Other women's outerwear	KSRN 18222	1 001	915	789	873
Men's underwear	KSRO 18231	437	294	230	224
Women's underwear	KSRP 18232	779	737	612	553
Hats	KSRQ 18241	63	..	..	45
Other wearing apparel and accessories	KSRR 18249	604	568	458	426
Dressing/dyeing of fur; articles of fur	KSRS 18300	6	5	7	6
Tanning and dressing of leather; manufacture of luggage, handbags, saddlery, harness and footwear					
Tanning and dressing of leather	KSRT 19100	310	316	308	..
Luggage, handbags and the like, saddlery and harness	KSRU 19200	207	198	189	183
Footwear	KSRV 19300	761	608	620	550
Manufacture of wood and of products of wood and cork, except furniture; manufacture of articles of straw and plaiting materials					
Sawmilling and planing of wood, impregnation of wood	KSRW 20100	699	638	640	694
Veneer sheets	KSRX 20200	716	711	697	712
Builders' carpentry and joinery	KSRY 20300	1 938	2 221	2 926	2 649
Wooden containers	KSRZ 20400	456	423	409	412
Other products of wood	KSSA 20510	400	330	424	484
Articles of cork, straw and plaiting materials	KSSB 20520	15	15	11	10
Manufacture of pulp, paper and paper products					
Paper and paperboard	KSSC 21120	3 277	3 344	3 127	3 384
Corrugated paper and paperboard, sacks and bags	KSSD 21211	567	567	538	546
Cartons, boxes, cases and other containers	KSSE 21219	3 340	3 266	3 381	3 054
Household and sanitary goods and toilet requisites	KSSF 21220	..	..	..	..
Paper stationery	KSSG 21230	657	684	667	616
Wallpaper	KSSH 21240	268	..	..	..
Other articles of paper and paperboard not elsewhere classified	KSSI 21250	740	816	824	833
Publishing, printing and reproduction of recorded media					
Publishing of books	KSSJ 22110	3 051	3 184	3 224	3 236
Publishing of newspapers	KSSK 22120	3 659	3 929	3 885	4 110
Publishing of journals and periodicals	KSSL 22130	6 701	7 000	7 195	6 979
Publishing of sound recordings	KSSM 22140	238	259	..	252
Other publishing	KSSN 22150	523	453	516	456
Printing of newspapers	KSSO 22210	..	181	..	175
Printing not elsewhere classified	KSSP 22220	9 611	9 831	9 369	9 313
Bookbinding and finishing	KSSQ 22230	434	496	472	443
Composition and plate-making	KSSR 22240	538	593	556	495
Other activities related to printing	KSSS 22250	813	911	815	803
Reproduction of sound recording	KSST 22310	..	555	380	..
Reproduction of video recording	KSSU 22320	..	173	198	204
Reproduction of computer media	KSSV 22330	..	..	93	77
Manufacture of chemicals and chemical products					
Industrial gases	KSSW 24110	530	..	538	508
Dyes and pigments	KSSX 24120	1 049	1 095	1 073	1 022
Other inorganic basic chemicals	KSSY 24130	1 251	1 155	1 148	1 109
Other organic basic chemicals	KSSZ 24140	4 151	5 412	5 716	5 454
Fertilizers and nitrogen compounds	KSTA 24150	737	714	592	699

£ million

Industry		SIC (92)	1999	2000	2001	2002
Manufacture of chemicals and chemical products continued						
Plastics in primary forms	KSTB	24160	3 500	3 775	3 640	3 414
Synthetic rubber in primary forms	KSTC	24170	..	351	324	..
Pesticides and other agro-chemical products	KSTD	24200	725	1 049	1 137	483
Paints, varnishes and similar coatings, printing ink and mastic	KSTE	24300	2 627	2 600	2 530	2 729
Basic pharmaceutical products	KSTF	24410	521	666	679	864
Pharmaceutical preparations	KSTG	24420	7 298	7 264	8 004	8 290
Soap and detergents, cleaning and polishing preparations	KSTH	24510	1 922	1 917	1 963	1 891
Perfumes and toilet preparations	KSTI	24520	2 529	2 656	2 640	2 377
Explosives	KSTJ	24610	107	109	..	..
Glues and gelatines	KSTK	24620	353	318	376	358
Essential oils	KSTL	24630	526	..	582	548
Photographic chemical material	KSTM	24640	..	605	342	307
Prepared unrecorded media	KSTN	24650	141	131	..	124
Other chemical products not elsewhere classified	KSTO	24660	2 315	2 382	2 078	1 939
Man-made fibres	KSTP	24700	673	739	656	602
Manufacture of rubber and plastic products						
Rubber tyres and tubes	KSTQ	25110	963	855	808	805
Retreading and rebuilding of rubber tyres	KSTR	25120	120	98	105	..
Other rubber products	KSTS	25130	1 705	1 634	1 624	1 560
Plastic plates, sheets, tubes and profiles	KSTT	25210	3 095	3 185	3 115	3 392
Plastic packing goods	KSTU	25220	2 699	2 638	2 691	..
Builders' ware of plastic	KSTV	25230	3 208	3 588	4 041	4 308
Other plastic products	KSTW	25240	4 244	4 289	3 712	3 333
Manufacture of other non-metallic mineral products						
Flat glass	KSTX	26110	187	231	..	..
Shaping and processing of flat glass	KSTY	26120	766	776	825	895
Hollow glass	KSTZ	26130	714	680	..	478
Glass fibres	KSUA	26140	271	262	263	284
Manufacturing and processing of other glass including technical glassware	KSUB	26150	271	314	276	..
Ceramic household and ornamental articles	KSUC	26210	563	563	486	471
Ceramic sanitary fixtures	KSUD	26220	213	222	199	..
Ceramic insulators and insulating fittings	KSUE	26230	26	..	..	25
Other technical ceramic products	KSUF	26240	27	28	26	18
Other ceramic products	KSUG	26250	..	16	..	15
Refractory ceramic products	KSUH	26260	454	420	415	376
Ceramic tiles and flags	KSUI	26300	101	87	91	85
Bricks, tiles and construction products in baked clay	KSUJ	26400	627	618	632	..
Cement	KSUK	26510	..	..	..	..
Lime	KSUL	26520	..	70	..	..
Plaster	KSUM	26530	105	..	113	118
Concrete products for construction purposes	KSUN	26610	..	1 799	1 763	..
Plaster products for construction purposes	KSUO	26620	..	321	..	..
Ready mixed concrete	KSUP	26630	1 224	1 216	1 250	941
Mortars	KSUQ	26640	92	104	..	103
Fibre cement	KSUR	26650	88	..	..	75
Other articles of concrete, plaster and cement	KSUS	26660	96	97	..	105
Cutting, shaping and finishing of stone	KSUT	26700	280	328	342	..
Abrasive products	KSUU	26810	218	206	192	172
Other non-metallic mineral products not elsewhere classified	KSUV	26820	732	684	706	708
Manufacture of basic metals						
Cast iron tubes	KSUW	27210	..	207	..	..
Steel tubes	KSUX	27220	1 053	1 026	1 155	1 015
Cold drawing	KSUY	27310	128	137	124	121

22.2
continued

Manufacturers' sales: by industry[1]
United Kingdom
Standard Industrial Classification 1992

£ million

Industry	SIC (92)	1999	2000	2001	2002
Manufacture of basic metals continued					
Cold rolling of narrow strip	KSUZ	27320	103	106	97	89
Cold forming or folding	KSVA	27330	..	..	125	111
Wire drawing	KSVB	27340	311	294	263	240
Other first processing of iron and steel not elsewhere classified	KSVC	27350	77	81	81	78
Precious metals production	KSVD	27410	259	277	433	271
Aluminium production	KSVE	27420	2 017	2 213	2 200	2 007
Lead, zinc and tin production	KSVF	27430	368	351	372	354
Copper production	KSVG	27440	762	787	740	653
Other non-ferrous metal production	KSVH	27450	518	581	589	500
Casting of iron	KSVI	27510	572	579	519	512
Casting of steel	KSVJ	27520	155	161	164	128
Casting of light metals	KSVK	27530	295	300	298	303
Casting of other non-ferrous metals	KSVL	27540	399	403	420	387
Manufacture of fabricated metal products, except machinery and equipment					
Metal structures and parts of structures	KSVM	28110	5 272	4 818	5 240	4 959
Builders' carpentry and joinery of metal	KSVN	28120	858	848	947	966
Tanks, reservoirs and containers of metal	KSVO	28210	..	..	344	365
Central heating radiators and boilers	KSVP	28220	597	599	588	527
Steam generators, except central heating hot water boilers	KSVQ	28300	569	574	456	447
Forging, pressing, stamping and roll forming of metal	KSVR	28400	2 153	2 079	1 911	1 778
Treatment and coating of metals	KSVS	28510	1 135	1 073	1 121	1 020
General mechanical engineering	KSVT	28520	2 586	2 735	2 759	2 892
Cutlery	KSVU	28610	407	..	..	..
Tools	KSVV	28620	952	1 012	993	852
Locks and hinges	KSVW	28630	630	617	588	545
Steel drums and similar containers	KSVX	28710	141	..	138	127
Light metal packaging	KSVY	28720	..	..	..	1 091
Wire products	KSVZ	28730	560	524	480	478
Fasteners, screw machine products, chain and spring	KSWA	28740	687	666	599	588
Other fabricated metal products not elsewhere classified	KSWB	28750	1 660	1 595	1 631	1 587
Manufacture of machinery and equipment not elsewhere classified					
Engines and turbines, except aircraft, vehicles and cycle engines	KSWC	29110	1 759	1 759	1 983	1 731
Pumps	KSWD	29121	1 025	1 031	990	1 021
Compressors	KSWE	29122	1 224	1 352	1 236	1 112
Taps and valves	KSWF	29130	1 171	1 193	1 162	1 149
Bearings, gears, gearing and driving elements	KSWG	29140	1 017	1 031	980	912
Furnaces and furnace burners	KSWH	29210	336	299	292	281
Lifting and handling equipment	KSWI	29220	2 869	2 861	2 937	2 708
Non-domestic cooling and ventilation equipment	KSWJ	29230	2 587	..	..	..
Other general purpose machinery not elsewhere classified	KSWK	29240	2 034	2 072	2 079	1 976
Agricultural tractors	KSWL	29310	919	..	811	872
Other agricultural and forestry machinery	KSWM	29320	530	538	425	441
Machine tools	KSWN	29400	1 935	1 818	1 624	1 312
Machinery for metallurgy	KSWO	29510	75	85	93	90
Machinery for mining	KSWP	29521	385	385	429	461
Earth-moving equipment	KSWQ	29522	..	..	976	931
Equipment for concrete crushing and screening and roadworks	KSWR	29523	..	..	..	..
Machinery for food, beverage and tobacco processing	KSWS	29530	642	595	582	568
Machinery for textile, apparel and leather production	KSWT	29540	246	220	155	137
Machinery for paper and paperboard production	KSWU	29550	242	209	201	207
Other special purpose machinery not elsewhere classified	KSWV	29560	1 996	2 052	2 087	1 791
Weapons and ammunition	KSWW	29600	1 649	1 504	1 384	1 498

22.2
continued

Manufacturers' sales: by industry[1]
United Kingdom
Standard Industrial Classification 1992

£ million

Industry	SIC (92)	1999	2000	2001	2002
Manufacture of machinery and equipment not elsewhere classified continued					
Electric domestic appliances	KSYR 29710	1 826	1 905	1 920	1 871
Non-electric domestic appliances	KSWX 29720	530	499	518	508
Manufacture of office machinery and computers					
Office machinery	KSWY 30010	1 191	1 169	..	753
Computers and other information processing equipment	KSWZ 30020	9 823	11 544	8 441	5 815
Manufacture of electrical machinery and apparatus not elsewhere classified					
Electric motors, generators and transformers	KSXA 31100	2 228	2 377	2 508	2 070
Electricity, distribution and control apparatus	KSXB 31200	2 785	2 770	2 629	2 350
Insulated wire and cable	KSXC 31300	1 295	1 379	1 361	875
Accumulators, primary cells and batteries	KSXD 31400	499	557	406	377
Lighting equipment and electric lamps	KSXE 31500	1 266	1 199	1 132	1 093
Electrical equipment for engines and vehicles not elsewhere classified	KSXF 31610	1 112	..	..	995
Other electrical equipment not elsewhere classified	KSXG 31620	1 653	1 925	1 999	1 838
Manufacture of radio, television and communication equipment and apparatus					
Electronic valves and tubes and other electronic components	KSXH 32100	3 854	4 454	3 747	3 412
Telegraph and telephone apparatus and equipment	KSXI 32201	4 845	5 505	4 616	2 214
Radio and electronic capital goods	KSXJ 32202	2 996	3 595	..	..
Television and radio receivers, sound or video recording etc	KSXK 32300	3 090	3 294	3 210	2 693
Manufacture of medical, precision and optical instruments, watches and clocks					
Medical and surgical equipment and orthopaedic appliances	KSXL 33100	1 663	1 657	1 943	2 145
Instruments and appliances for measuring, checking, testing etc	KSXM 33200	5 025	5 227	5 482	5 194
Industrial process control equipment	KSXN 33300	779	686	701	802
Optical instruments and photographic equipment	KSXO 33400	980	938	962	749
Watches and clocks	KSXP 33500	90	69	53	54
Manufacture of motor vehicles, trailers and semi-trailers					
Motor vehicles	KSXQ 34100	22 336	19 725	17 937	20 491
Bodies (coachwork) for motor vehicles (excluding caravans)	KSXR 34201	797	834	851	811
Trailers and semi-trailers	KSXS 34202	921	874	925	873
Caravans	KSXT 34203	377	412	403	456
Parts and accessories for motor vehicles and their engines	KSXU 34300	8 806	8 480	8 437	8 775
Manufacture of other transport equipment					
Building and repairing of ships	KSXV 35110	2 453	1 561	1 599	1 663
Building and repairing of pleasure and sporting boats	KSXW 35120	459	501	584	601
Railway and tramway locomotives and rolling stock	KSXX 35200	974	1 301	1 416	1 501
Aircraft and spacecraft	KSXY 35300	13 982	12 784	11 745	11 509
Motorcycles	KSXZ 35410	..	..	..	..
Bicycles	KSYA 35420	112	114	102	95
Invalid carriages	KSYB 35430	123	116	119	111
Other transport equipment not elsewhere classified.	KSYC 35500	99	84	86	83
Manufacture of furniture; manufacturing not elsewhere classified					
Chairs and seats	KSYD 36110	2 442	2 519	2 722	2 630
Other office and shop furniture	KSYE 36120	1 251	1 409	1 315	1 208
Other kitchen furniture	KSYF 36130	1 065	975	927	1 002
Other furniture	KSYG 36140	2 197	2 102	2 153	2 201
Mattresses	KSYH 36150	531	547	575	570
Striking of coins and medals	KSYI 36210	..	..	..	..
Jewellery and related articles not elsewhere classified	KSYJ 36220	565	603	491	360
Musical instruments	KSYK 36300	50	51	42	42
Sports goods	KSYL 36400	242	246	270	299
Games and toys	KSYM 36500	521	550	446	455
Imitation jewellery	KSYN 36610	32	29	34	22
Brooms and brushes	KSYO 36620	162	165	155	..
Miscellaneous stationers' goods	KSYP 36631	246	216	..	194
Other manufacturing not elsewhere classified	KSYQ 36639	533	492	466	439

1 See chapter text. PRODCOM data is published on the ONS website in the PRA and PRQ series of reports.

Source: Office for National Statistics: 01633 813065

22.3 Number of local units in manufacturing industries, March 2004[1]
United Kingdom
Standard Industrial Classification 2003 Division by Employment Sizeband

Numbers

					Employment size						
		0 - 4	5 - 9	10 - 19	20 - 49	50 - 99	100 - 249	250 - 499	500 - 999	1,000+	Total
Division											
15/16	Food products; beverages and tobacco	3 245	2 035	1 400	1 135	575	580	270	130	40	9 410
17	Textiles and textile products	2 380	885	610	550	290	190	40	10	0	4 960
18	Wearing apparel; dressing and dyeing of fur	2 305	865	570	400	105	50	15	0	0	4 305
19	Leather and leather products	365	180	90	75	35	25	5	0	0	770
20	Wood and wood products	4 790	1 640	945	600	170	75	20	0	0	8 240
21	Pulp, paper and paper products	925	360	295	385	215	205	40	10	0	2 430
22	Publishing, printing and reproduction of recorded media	18 715	4 525	2 635	1 715	605	370	120	30	15	28 735
23	Coke, refined petroleum products and nuclear fuel	75	35	30	30	20	10	10	5	5	220
24	Chemicals, chemical products and man-made fibres	1 485	635	510	580	350	290	115	60	20	4 045
25	Rubber and plastic products	2 590	1 425	1 210	1 175	570	365	100	20	5	7 455
26	Other non-metallic mineral products	3 395	1 115	730	585	290	200	45	10	0	6 370
27	Basic metals	930	380	265	325	195	125	40	15	5	2 285
28	Fabricated metal products, except machinery and equipment	14 395	5 440	3 745	2 715	825	365	60	15	0	27 565
29	Machinery and equipment not elsewhere classified	5 905	2 385	1 890	1 590	655	395	135	35	15	13 005
30	Office machinery and computers	560	160	85	95	60	50	10	10	5	1 030
31	Electrical machinery and apparatus not elsewhere classified	2 385	825	705	685	305	215	80	25	0	5 230
32	Radio, television and communication equipment and apparatus	1 365	350	260	290	120	105	40	25	5	2 565
33	Medical, precision and optical instruments, watches and clocks	2 030	855	625	605	265	165	55	20	5	4 635
34	Motor vehicles, trailers and semi-trailers	1 060	440	345	400	190	195	110	35	30	2 800
35	Other transport equipment	1 165	410	240	210	135	120	55	35	25	2 390
36/37	Manufacturing not elsewhere classified	12 290	3 325	1 715	1 055	375	225	65	20	0	19 065
Total manufacturing (15/37)		82 350	28 270	18 900	15 205	6 340	4 325	1 435	510	185	157 510

1 See chapter text. The count of units refers to local units, i.e. individual sites, rather than whole businesses. All counts have been rounded to avoid disclosure.

Source: Office for National Statistics: 01633 812293

22.4 Production of primary fuels[1]
United Kingdom

		1993	1994	1995	1996	1997	1998	1999	2000	2001	2002	2003
Coal	HFZQ	41.6	29.7	32.8	31.1	30.3	25.8	23.2	19.6	20.0	18.8	17.6
Petroleum[2]	HGCY	109.6	138.9	142.7	142.1	140.4	145.3	150.2	138.3	127.8	127.0	116.2
Natural Gas[3]	HGDB	60.5	64.6	70.8	84.2	85.9	90.2	99.1	108.4	105.8	103.6	102.9
Primary electricity[4]	HGDN	22.0	21.7	21.7	22.4	23.5	24.0	22.9	20.2	21.2	20.7	20.4
Renewables and waste[5]	HGDO	1.2	1.6	1.7	1.8	1.9	2.1	2.2	2.3	2.5	2.7	3.1
Total Production	HGDP	234.9	256.6	269.7	281.6	282.1	287.2	297.7	288.7	277.4	272.8	260.3

1 See chapter text.
2 Crude oil plus all condensates and petroleum gases extracted at gas separation plants.
3 Includes colliery methane.

4 Includes nuclear, hydro and other non-thermal renewables (wind, tide etc).
5 Includes biofuels and waste, solar heating and photovoltaics, and geothermal aquifers.

Source: Department of Trade and Industry: 020 7215 2710

22.5 Total inland energy consumption
United Kingdom
Heat supplied basis

		1993	1994	1995	1996	1997	1998	1999	2000	2001	2002	2003
Inland energy consumption of primary fuels and equivalents[1]	KLWA	220.7	217.5	218.4	230.1	226.8	230.8	230.4	233.2	236.8	230.6	232.7
Coal[2]	KLWB	54.9	51.3	48.9	45.7	40.8	40.9	36.7	38.1	41.2	37.8	40.4
Petroleum[3]	KLWC	78.1	76.7	75.4	77.8	75.5	76.1	76.0	75.9	75.6	74.1	74.1
Primary electricity	KLWD	23.4	23.1	23.1	23.8	25.0	25.0	24.2	21.4	22.1	21.3	20.6
Natural gas	KLWE	62.9	64.9	69.2	81.0	83.5	86.9	91.4	95.6	95.3	94.7	94.5
Renewables and waste	GYUY	1.2	1.6	1.7	1.8	1.9	2.1	2.2	2.3	2.6	2.8	3.2
less Energy used by fuel producers and losses in conversion and distribution	KLWF	68.0	64.9	68.0	73.0	72.9	75.0	74.2	74.7	75.2	73.2	74.8
Total consumption by final users[1]	KLWG	152.7	152.5	150.4	157.0	153.9	155.8	156.2	158.5	161.5	157.4	158.0
Final energy consumption by type of fuel												
Coal (direct use)	KLWH	7.6	6.9	5.3	4.4	4.3	3.7	3.5	2.0	3.0	2.1	1.2
Coke and breeze	KLWI	3.8	3.9	3.9	1.0	0.8	0.9	1.0	1.0	0.8	0.9	0.7
Other solid fuel[4]	KLWJ	0.8	0.8	0.7	0.8	0.7	0.7	0.5	0.5	0.5	0.3	0.3
Coke oven gas	KLWK	0.6	0.6	0.6	0.4	0.5	0.4	0.2	0.2	0.2	0.1	0.1
Natural gas (direct use)	KLWL	49.3	49.9	50.1	56.5	54.2	55.9	55.1	57.1	57.8	56.1	56.7
Electricity	KLWM	24.6	24.4	25.3	26.5	26.8	27.1	27.8	28.3	28.6	28.6	29.0
Petroleum (direct use)[5]	KLWN	65.4	65.2	63.7	66.1	65.4	66.0	65.7	66.2	67.5	66.3	67.4
Renewables	GYVA	0.7	0.9	1.0	1.0	0.9	0.9	0.7	0.6	0.6	0.7	0.7
Final energy consumption by class of consumer												
Agriculture	KLWP	1.4	1.4	1.3	1.4	1.3	1.4	1.3	1.2	1.3	1.1	0.9
Iron and steel industry	KLWQ	7.0	6.9	6.9	4.2	4.2	4.0	3.8	3.8	3.8	3.2	2.9
Other industries	KLWR	29.5	30.8	29.4	30.3	30.4	30.5	30.9	30.9	32.0	31.2	31.7
Railways[6]	KLWS	1.3	1.3	1.3	1.3	1.2	1.3	1.2	1.2	1.2	1.1	1.0
Road transport	KLWT	39.5	39.7	39.3	40.8	41.3	41.0	41.4	41.1	41.1	41.9	41.8
Water transport	KLWU	1.3	1.2	1.2	1.3	1.3	1.2	1.1	1.0	0.8	0.7	1.2
Air transport	KLWV	7.9	8.1	8.5	8.9	9.3	10.2	11.0	12.0	11.8	11.7	11.9
Domestic	KLWW	45.5	43.9	42.7	48.1	44.8	46.1	46.1	46.9	48.5	47.8	47.9
Public administration	KLWX	8.1	8.3	8.5	8.8	8.4	8.1	8.4	8.1	8.1	7.1	6.8
Commercial and other services	KLWY	11.2	11.0	11.3	11.9	11.7	12.0	11.9	12.2	12.8	11.7	11.8

1 Includes heat sold from 1999.
2 Includes net trade and stock change in other solid fuels.
3 Refinery throughput of crude oil, *plus* net foreign trade and stock change in petroleum products. Petroleum products not used as fuels (chemical feedstock, industrial and white spirits, lubricants, bitumen and wax) are excluded.

4 Includes briquettes, ovoids, Phurnacite, Coalite, etc, and wood, waste etc, used for heat generation.
5 Includes manufactured liquid fuels from 1994.
6 Includes fuel used at transport premises.

Source: Department of Trade and Industry: 020 7215 2710

22.6 Coal: supply and demand[1]
United Kingdom

Million tonnes

			1993	1994	1995	1996	1997	1998	1999	2000	2001	2002	2003
Supply													
Production of deep-mined coal	KLXA		50.5	31.9	35.2	32.2	30.3	25.7	20.9	17.2	17.3	16.4	15.6
Production of opencast coal	KLXB		17.0	16.8	16.4	16.3	16.7	14.3	15.3	13.4	14.2	13.1	12.1
Total	KLXC		67.5	48.7	51.5	48.5	47.0	40.0	36.2	30.6	31.5	29.5	27.8
Recovered slurry, fines, etc	KLXD		0.7	0.1	1.5	1.7	1.5	1.1	0.9	0.6	0.4	0.5	0.5
Imports	KLXE		18.4	15.1	15.9	17.8	19.8	21.2	20.3	23.4	35.5	28.7	31.9
Total	KLXF		86.6	64.9	68.9	68.0	68.3	62.4	57.4	54.6	67.5	58.7	60.2
Change in colliery stocks	KLXG	KSOL	1.8	−4.2	−4.2	−3.0	0.7	−0.2	0.6	−3.5	−0.1	0.9	−0.9
Change in stocks at opencast sites	KLXH		0.5	−0.5									
Total supply	KLXI		84.5	69.6	73.1	70.9	67.6	62.7	56.8	58.2	67.5	57.8	61.0
Home consumption													
Total home consumption	KLXW		86.6	81.7	76.9	71.4	63.1	63.2	55.7	58.9	64.2	58.6	62.4
Overseas shipments and bunkers	KLXX		1.1	1.2	0.9	1.0	1.1	1.0	0.8	0.7	0.5	0.5	0.5
Total consumption and shipments	KLXY		87.7	82.9	77.8	72.4	64.2	64.1	56.5	59.5	64.8	59.2	62.9
Change in distributed stocks[2]	KLXZ		−3.6	−13.9	−4.4	−0.9	3.0	−1.2	0.6	−1.2	2.9	−1.2	−1.7
Balance[3]	KLYA		0.4	0.6	−0.3	−0.5	0.3	−0.3	−0.3	−0.2	−0.2	−0.2	−0.1
Stocks at end of year													
Distributed[2]	KLYB		29.9	16.0	11.6	10.8	13.8	12.6	13.2	12.0	15.0	13.7	12.0
At collieries	KLYC	KSOM	12.7	8.5	7.1	4.2	4.8	4.6	5.2	1.6	1.6	2.5	1.6
At opencast sites	KLYD		3.3	2.8									
Total stocks	KLYE		45.9	27.3	18.7	14.9	18.6	17.2	18.3	13.7	16.5	16.2	13.6

1 See chapter text. Figures relate to periods of 52 weeks. For 1998, figures relate to 52 weeks estimate for period ended 26 December 1998.
2 Excludes distributed stocks held in merchant yards etc, mainly for the domestic market, and stocks held by the industrial sector.
3 This is the balance between supply and consumption, shipments and changes in known distributed stocks.

Source: Department of Trade and Industry: 020 7215 2717

22.7 Fuel input and gas output: gas sales[1]
United Kingdom
Public supply

Giga-watt hours

		1993	1994	1995	1996	1997	1998	1999	2000	2001	2002	2003
Analysis of gas sales												
Fuel producers												
Power stations[2]	KIKK	81 778	114 575	145 790	201 929	251 787	267 703	315 400	324 413	312 103	329 629	324 075
Coal extraction and manufacture of solid fuels	KIKL	415	266	368	344	193	67	14	6	4	–	–
Coke ovens	KIKM	191	1	1	–	–	–	–	–	–	–	–
Petroleum refineries	KIKN	2 449	1 933	2 922	2 907	3 002	3 753	4 155	3 641	4 189	3 350	2 157
Nuclear fuel production	KIKO	565	550	467	874	923	989	1 021	472	1 210	402	219
Production and distribution of other energy	KIKP	178	114	352	437	487	549	629	619	451	709	893
Total final producers	KIKQ	85 576	117 439	149 900	206 491	256 392	273 061	321 219	329 151	317 957	334 090	327 344
Final users:												
Iron and steel industry	KIKR	15 577	20 327	19 988	20 940	20 577	20 105	21 622	22 551	20 901	19 522	19 121
Other industries	KIKS	132 719	143 979	150 697	12 646	13 429	14 415	13 905	15 153	14 808	10 916	11 475
Domestic	KIKT	340 162	329 710	326 010	375 841	345 532	355 895	358 066	369 909	379 426	376 372	385 985
Public administration	KIKU	38 725	41 119	46 308	51 411	52 315	51 976	43 253	44 552	46 232	42 694	43 646
Agriculture	KIKV	1 277	1 227	1 210	1 417	1 440	953	1 155	1 522	2 329	2 346	1 494
Miscellaneous	KIKW	58 917	58 790	61 502	65 080	59 022	64 695	62 079	64 382	64 550	55 371	56 685
Total final users	KIKX	587 377	595 152	605 715	527 335	492 315	508 039	500 080	518 069	528 246	507 221	518 406
Total sales	KIKY	672 952	712 592	755 615	733 826	748 707	781 100	821 299	847 220	846 203	841 311	845 750

1 See chapter text. The breakdown of consumption by industrial users is made according to the 1980 Standard Industrial Classification.
2 Includes auto-production of electricity.

Source: Department of Trade and Industry: 020 7215 2717

22.8 Electricity: generation, supply and consumption[1]
United Kingdom

Gigawatt-hours

		1993	1994	1995	1996	1997	1998	1999	2000	2001	2002	2003
Electricity generated												
Major power producers: total	KLUA	305 434	306 726	313 958	326 235	324 133	333 764	336 608	341 783	353 067	353 994	362 600
Conventional thermal and other[2]	AWLC	..	175 187	170 056	160 791	133 591	134 009	118 762	131 062	132 753	126 694	146 382
Combined cycle gas turbine stations	KJCS	22 811	36 971	48 720	65 880	86 974	93 832	114 620	117 935	123 846	132 016	121 076
Nuclear stations	KLUC	89 353	88 282	88 964	94 671	98 146	99 486	95 133	85 063	90 093	87 848	88 686
Hydro-electric stations:												
Natural flow	KLUE	3 522	4 317	4 096	2 801	3 337	4 237	4 431	4 331	3 215	3 927	2 568
Pumped storage	KLUF	1 437	1 463	1 552	1 556	1 486	1 624	2 902	2 694	2 422	2 652	2 734
Renewables other than hydro	KLUG	165	506	570	536	599	576	761	698	729	856	1 154
Other generators: total	KLUH	17 669	18 252	20 084	24 632	26 534	28 938	31 543	35 285	31 721	33 513	36 019
Conventional thermal and other[2]	AWLD	..	14 263	15 387	18 334	18 629	19 091	19 419	19 094	16 619	16 051	17 766
Combined cycle gas turbine stations	KJCT	607	1 505	2 126	3 535	4 412	5 428	7 141	10 859	8 979	10 577	10 759
Hydro-electric stations (natural flow)	KLUK	780	777	742	592	832	881	905	755	840	860	660
Renewables other than hydro	KILA	1 417	1 707	1 829	2 171	2 661	3 538	4 078	4 577	5 283	6 028	6 842
All generating companies: total	KLUL	323 102	324 978	334 042	350 867	350 667	362 702	368 151	377 068	384 788	387 507	398 619
Conventional thermal and other[2]	AWYH	..	189 451	185 443	179 125	152 220	153 100	138 181	150 156	149 372	142 745	164 148
Combined cycle gas turbine stations	KJCU	23 418	38 475	50 846	69 415	91 386	99 260	121 761	128 794	132 825	142 593	131 835
Nuclear stations	KLUN	89 353	88 282	88 964	94 671	98 146	99 486	95 133	85 063	90 093	87 848	88 686
Hydro-electric stations:												
Natural flow	KLUP	4 302	5 094	4 838	3 393	4 169	5 118	5 336	5 086	4 055	4 787	3 228
Pumped storage	KLUQ	1 437	1 463	1 552	1 556	1 486	1 624	2 902	2 694	2 422	2 652	2 734
Renewables other than hydro	KLUR	1 582	2 213	2 399	2 707	3 260	4 114	4 839	5 275	6 012	6 884	7 996
Electricity used on works: Total	KLUS	19 287	17 491	17 411	16 078	16 560	17 408	16 706	16 304	17 394	17 172	18 238
Major generating companies	KLUT	17 391	16 696	16 510	14 967	15 411	16 140	15 461	14 952	16 066	15 746	16 747
Other generators	KLUU	1 896	795	901	1 111	1 149	1 268	1 245	1 352	1 328	1 426	1 491
Electricity supplied (gross)												
Major power producers: total	KLUV	287 264	290 780	299 000	311 268	308 722	317 624	321 147	326 831	336 991	338 248	345 854
Conventional thermal and other[2]	AWYI	..	167 866	163 818	155 086	127 419	127 788	112 919	124 828	126 435	120 495	139 137
Combined cycle gas turbine stations	KJCV	22 611	36 815	48 525	65 604	86 682	93 005	112 768	116 110	121 344	129 384	118 546
Nuclear stations	KLUX	80 979	79 962	80 598	85 820	89 341	90 590	87 672	78 334	82 985	81 090	81 911
Hydro-electric stations:												
Natural flow	KLUZ	3 513	4 265	4 051	2 763	3 299	4 225	4 409	4 316	3 203	3 914	2 559
Pumped storage	KLVA	1 388	1 417	1 502	1 507	1 439	1 569	2 804	2 603	2 340	2 562	2 641
Renewables other than hydro	KLVB	136	455	506	488	542	447	574	640	683	802	1 059
Other generators: total	KLVC	16 522	18 207	20 909	23 521	25 385	27 670	30 298	33 933	30 393	32 087	34 528
Conventional thermal and other[2]	AWYJ	..	14 333	16 338	17 492	17 815	18 250	18 643	18 499	15 996	15 428	17 155
Combined cycle gas turbine stations	KJCW	584	1 466	2 100	3 358	4 192	5 157	6 785	10 318	8 531	10 049	10 222
Hydro-electric stations (natural flow)	KLVF	772	769	733	584	822	869	894	743	829	849	653
Renewables other than hydro	KIKZ	1 360	1 639	1 738	2 085	2 555	3 393	3 977	4 374	5 037	5 764	6 506
All generating companies: total	KLVG	303 815	308 987	319 909	334 789	334 107	345 294	351 445	360 764	367 384	370 335	380 382
Conventional thermal and other[2]	AWYK	..	182 199	180 156	172 578	145 234	146 038	131 562	143 327	142 431	135 923	156 292
Combined cycle gas turbine stations	KJCX	23 195	38 281	50 625	68 962	90 874	98 162	119 553	126 428	129 875	139 433	128 768
Nuclear stations	KLVI	80 979	79 962	80 598	85 820	89 341	90 590	87 672	78 334	82 985	81 090	81 911
Hydro-electric stations:												
Natural flow	KLVK	4 285	5 034	4 784	3 347	4 121	5 094	5 303	5 059	4 032	4 763	3 212
Pumped storage	KLVL	1 388	1 417	1 502	1 507	1 439	1 569	2 804	2 603	2 340	2 562	2 641
Renewables other than hydro	KLVM	1 496	2 094	2 244	2 573	3 097	3 840	4 551	5 014	5 720	6 566	7 565
Electricity used in pumping												
Major power producers	KLVN	1 948	2 051	2 282	2 430	2 477	2 594	3 774	3 499	3 210	3 463	3 546
Electricity supplied (net): Total	KLVO	301 868	306 936	317 627	332 359	331 630	342 700	347 671	357 266	364 174	366 871	376 836
Major power producers	KLVP	285 316	288 729	296 718	308 838	306 245	315 030	317 373	323 332	333 781	334 785	342 308
Other generators	KLVQ	16 552	18 207	20 909	23 521	25 385	27 670	30 298	33 933	30 393	32 087	34 528
Net imports	KGEZ	16 716	16 887	16 313	16 755	16 574	12 468	14 244	14 174	10 399	8 414	2 160
Electricity available	KGIZ	318 584	323 830	333 940	349 114	348 203	355 168	361 915	371 440	374 573	375 286	378 996
Losses in transmission etc	KGKW	22 838	31 000	30 020	29 335	27 138	29 818	29 862	31 143	32 069	31 029	30 822
Electricity consumption: Total	KGKX	295 746	292 830	303 920	319 779	321 065	325 350	332 053	340 297	342 504	344 257	348 174
Fuel industries	KGKY	9 615	7 518	8 070	9 211	8 624	8 406	8 037	9 703	8 625	10 027	9 629
Final users: total	KGKZ	286 130	285 310	295 849	310 567	312 441	316 944	324 016	330 593	333 879	334 229	338 546
Industrial sector	KGLZ	96 842	96 120	101 780	107 631	108 102	108 443	112 250	115 286	112 495	113 442	115 028
Domestic sector	KGMZ	100 456	101 407	102 210	107 513	104 455	109 410	110 308	111 842	115 337	114 534	115 761
Other sectors	KGNZ	88 833	87 790	91 860	95 423	99 884	99 091	101 457	103 465	106 047	106 253	107 757

1 See chapter text.
2 Includes electricity supplied by gas turbines and oil engines and plants producing electricity from renewable resources other than hydro.

Source: Department of Trade and Industry: 020 7215 5190

22.9 Electricity: plant capacity and demand
United Kingdom
At end of December[1]

Megawatts

		1995	1996		1997	1998	1999	2000	2001	2002	2003
Major power producers:[2]											
Total declared net capability	KGON	64 923	66 100	GUFY	68 288	68 390	70 245	72 193	73 382	70 615	71 746
Conventional steam stations	KGOO	38 453	38 242	GUFZ	37 395	35 081	35 647	34 835	34 835	30 687	30 367
Combined cycle gas turbine stations	KJCZ	8 364	9 034	GUGA	12 252	14 638	16 110	19 349	20 517	21 800	23 585
Nuclear stations[3,4]	KGOP	12 037	12 762	GUGB	12 946	12 956	12 956	12 486	12 486	12 486	12 098
Gas turbines and oil engines	KGOQ	1 895	1 890	GUGC	1 526	1 492	1 301	1 291	1 291	1 432	1 489
Hydro-electric stations:											
Natural flow	KGOR	1 314	1 314	GUGD	1 311	1 327	1 327	1 327	1 348	1 304	1 302
Pumped storage	KGOS	2 788	2 788	GUGE	2 788	2 788	2 788	2 788	2 788	2 788	2 788
Renewables other than hydro	KGOT	72	71	GUGF	70	108	117	117	117	117	117
Other generators:											
Total capacity of own generating plant[5]	KGOU	3 818	4 025	GUGG	4 625	4 990	5 388	6 258	6 296	6 376	6 778
Conventional steam stations[6]	KGOV	3 257	3 234	GUGH	3 240	3 248	3 315	3 544	3 464	3 345	3 405
Combined cycle gas turbine stations	KJDA	153	343	GUGI	757	1 005	1 243	1 709	1 777	1 854	1 950
Hydro-electric stations (natural flow)	KGOX	111	118	GUGJ	145	148	150	158	160	162	166
Renewables other than hydro	KILB	297	330	GUGK	483	589	680	847	895	1 015	1 257
All generating companies: Total capacity[5]	KGOY	68 741	70 126	GUGL	72 913	73 380	75 633	78 451	79 678	76 991	78 524
Conventional steam stations[6]	KGOZ	41 710	41 476	GUGM	40 635	38 329	38 962	38 379	38 299	34 032	33 772
Combined cycle gas turbine stations	KJDC	8 517	9 377	GUGN	13 009	15 643	17 353	21 058	22 294	23 654	25 535
Nuclear stations[3]	KGPM	12 037	12 762	GUGO	12 946	12 956	12 956	12 486	12 486	12 486	12 098
Gas turbines and oil engines	KGPN	1 895	1 890	GUGP	1 526	1 492	1 301	1 291	1 291	1 432	1 489
Hydro-electric stations:											
Natural flow	KGPO	1 425	1 432	GUGQ	1 456	1 475	1 477	1 485	1 508	1 466	1 468
Pumped storage	KGPP	2 788	2 788	GUGR	2 788	2 788	2 788	2 788	2 788	2 788	2 788
Renewables other than hydro	KGPQ	369	401	GUGS	553	697	797	964	1 012	1 132	1 374
Major power producers:[2]											
Simultaneous maximum load met[7]	KGPR	52 362	55 611	GUGT	56 965	56 312	57 849	58 452	58 589	61 717	60 501
System load factor[8] (percentages)	KGQY	*67.3*	*65.4*	GUGU	*66.2*	*67.5*	*66.7*	*67.4*	*68.7*	*64.8*	*67.0*

1 1995 and 1996 are at end of March.
2 See chapter text.
3 The 1995 figure includes 300 MW of the 1,188 MW capacity of Sizewell B which began to produce electricity in March 1995.
4 Nuclear generators are now included under "major power producers" only.
5 Capacity figures for other generators are as at end-December of the previous year.

6 For other generators, conventional steam stations cover all types of stations not separately listed.
7 Maximum load in year to end of March.
8 The average hourly quantity of electricity available during the year ending March expressed as a percentage of the maximum demand.

Source: Department of Trade and Industry: 020 7215 5190

22.10 Electricity: fuel used in generation
United Kingdom

Million tonnes of oil equivalent

		1993	1994	1995	1996	1997	1998	1999	2000	2001	2002	2003
Major power producers:[1] total all fuels	KGPS	72.3	71.7	72.7	74.6	71.5	74.9	73.6	74.4	77.4	75.8	77.9
Coal	FTAJ	38.3	35.9	35.0	32.4	27.1	28.7	24.5	27.8	30.6	28.6	32.0
Oil[2]	FTAK	4.4	3.6	3.1	3.0	1.2	0.8	0.8	0.8	0.8	0.7	0.7
Gas[3]	KGPT	6.3	9.1	11.4	15.2	19.3	20.3	24.2	24.4	23.8	25.0	24.5
Nuclear[4]	FTAL	21.6	21.2	21.3	22.2	22.0	23.4	22.2	19.6	20.8	20.1	20.0
Hydro (natural flow)	FTAM	0.3	0.4	0.4	0.2	0.3	0.4	0.4	0.4	0.3	0.3	0.2
Other fuels used by UK companies[3]	KGPU	0.1	0.1	0.1	0.1	0.2	0.2	0.2	0.2	0.3	0.3	0.4
Net imports	KGPV	1.4	1.5	1.4	1.4	1.4	1.1	1.2	1.2	0.9	0.7	0.2
Other generators: total all fuels	KGPW	4.5	3.5	5.8	6.0	6.7	7.1	7.3	8.0	7.5	8.0	8.7
Transport undertakings												
Gas	KGPX	0.2	0.2	0.2	0.2	0.2	0.2	0.2	0.2	0.2	0.2	–
Undertakings in industrial sector												
Coal	KGPY	1.3	1.2	1.3	1.2	1.2	1.2	1.0	0.9	1.0	1.0	1.0
Oil	KGPZ	1.4	0.5	1.0	1.0	0.8	0.7	0.7	0.8	0.6	0.6	0.6
Gas	KGQM	0.8	0.6	1.6	1.8	2.2	2.5	2.7	3.3	2.9	3.2	3.4
Hydro (natural flow)	KGQO	0.1	0.1	0.1	0.1	0.1	0.1	0.1	0.1	0.1	0.1	0.1
Other fuels	KGQP	1.0	1.0	1.7	1.8	2.2	2.4	2.6	2.8	2.7	3.0	3.6
All generating companies: total fuels	KGQQ	76.8	75.2	78.6	80.6	78.2	82.0	80.9	82.4	84.9	83.8	86.7
Coal	KGQR	39.6	37.1	36.3	33.6	28.3	29.9	25.5	28.7	31.6	29.6	32.9
Oil	KGQS	5.8	4.1	4.1	4.0	2.0	1.5	1.5	1.5	1.4	1.3	1.3
Gas[3]	KGQT	7.0	9.9	13.3	17.2	21.7	23.0	27.1	27.9	26.9	28.4	27.9
Nuclear[4]	KGQU	21.6	21.2	21.3	22.2	22.0	23.4	22.2	19.6	20.8	20.1	20.0
Hydro (natural flow)	KGQV	0.4	0.4	0.4	0.3	0.4	0.4	0.5	0.4	0.3	0.4	0.3
Other fuels used by UK companies[3,5]	KGQW	1.0	1.1	1.8	1.9	2.4	2.6	2.9	3.0	3.0	3.2	4.0
Net imports	KGQX	1.4	1.5	1.4	1.4	1.4	1.1	1.2	1.2	0.9	0.7	0.2

1 See chapter text.
2 Includes oil used in gas turbine and diesel plant for lighting up coal fired boilers and Orimulsion.
3 For 1991 gas used by major power producers was included with other fuels for reasons of confidentiality.

4 Nuclear generators are now included under "major power producers" only.
5 Main fuels included are coke oven gas, blast furnace gas, waste products from chemical processes and sludge gas.

Source: Department of Trade and Industry: 020 7215 5190

22.11 Indigenous petroleum production, refinery receipts, imports and exports of oil[1]

Thousand tonnes

		1993	1994	1995	1996	1997	1998	1999	2000	2001	2002	2003
Total indigenous petroleum production[2]	KMBA	100 188	126 812	129 894	129 742	128 234	132 363	137 099	126 245	116 678	115 944	106 073
Crude petroleum:[3]												
Refinery receipts total	KMBB	97 400	93 771	93 572	96 660	97 023	93 797	88 286	88 014	83 343	84 784	84 585
Foreign trade[4]												
Imports	KMBF	61 701	53 096	48 749	50 099	49 994	47 958	44 869	54 387	53 551	56 968	54 177
Exports	AXRB	64 415	83 205	84 578	81 563	79 400	84 610	91 797	92 918	86 930	87 144	74 898
Net imports	AXRC	−2 714	−30 109	−35 829	−31 464	−29 406	−36 652	−46 928	−38 531	−33 378	−30 176	−20 720
Petroleum products												
Foreign trade												
Imports[4]	BHMI	10 064	10 441	9 878	9 315	8 705	11 327	13 896	14 212	17 466	15 269	17 286
Exports[4]	AXRD	23 060	22 157	21 614	23 681	26 755	24 375	21 730	20 677	19 088	23 444	23 323
Net imports[4]	AXRE	−12 996	−11 716	−11 736	−14 366	−18 049	−12 957	−7 834	−6 464	−1 622	−8 175	−6 037
International marine bunkers	BHMK	2 478	2 313	2 465	2 664	2 961	3 080	2 329	2 079	2 274	1 913	1 764

1 See chapter text. The term 'indigenous' is used in this table to cover oil produced on the UK Continental Shelf. This includes small amounts produced onshore.
2 Crude oil *plus* condensates and petroleum gases derived at onshore treatment plants.

3 Includes process (partly refined) oils.
4 Foreign trade as recorded by the petroleum industry and may differ from figures published in *Overseas Trade Statistics*.

Source: Department of Trade and Industry: 020 7215 5184

22.12 Throughput of crude and process oils and output of refined products from refineries[1]

United Kingdom

Thousand tonnes

		1992	1993	1994	1995	1996	1997	1998	1999	2000	2001	2002
Throughput of crude and process oils	KMAU	92 334	96 274	93 162	92 743	96 661	97 024	93 797	88 285	88 014	83 343	85 389
less: Refinery fuel:	KMAA	6 080	6 383	6 256	6 481	6 623	6 572	6 468	5 969	5 245	5 162	4 873
Losses	KMAB	471	308	261	129	152	86	1 005	1 554	1 672	1 250	845
Total output of refined products	KMAC	85 783	89 583	86 645	86 133	89 885	90 366	86 615	81 195	81 582	77 239	79 750
Gases:												
Butane and propane	KMAE	1 583	1 575	1 605	1 815	1 828	1 950	1 961	1 975	1 981	1 764	2 157
Other petroleum	KMAF	172	162	132	133	144	139	394	361	287	295	582
Naphtha and other feedstock	KMAG	3 040	2 696	2 794	2 711	2 824	2 854	2 316	2 430	3 081	3 405	3 090
Aviation spirit	KMAH	–	–	–	–	–	–	–	16	30	101	28
Motor spirit	KMAJ	27 980	28 394	27 562	27 254	28 046	28 260	27 166	25 230	23 445	21 455	23 178
Industrial and white spirit	KMAK	150	159	143	143	136	128	135	129	122	122	121
Kerosene:												
Aviation turbine fuel	KMAL	7 681	8 341	7 697	7 837	8 305	8 342	7 876	7 249	6 484	5 910	5 603
Burning oil	KMAM	2 450	2 707	2 967	2 924	3 510	3 336	3 442	3 553	3 078	3 088	3 344
Gas/diesel oil	KMAN	25 650	27 361	27 137	27 169	28 903	28 778	27 532	25 750	28 219	26 746	28 383
Fuel oil	KMAO	12 388	13 183	11 378	10 969	11 479	11 747	11 125	10 446	10 390	10 119	8 621
Lubricating oil	KMAP	1 163	1 264	1 296	1 261	1 111	1 231	1 125	907	702	656	516
Bitumen	KMAQ	2 336	2 450	2 569	2 459	2 189	2 258	2 172	1 644	1 438	1 707	1 909
Petroleum wax	KMAR	62	59	64	46	41	65	59	261	437	416	447
Petroleum coke	KMAS	535	621	679	759	714	598	678	648	820	765	890
Other products	KMAT	593	613	623	653	655	680	634	596	1 068	690	881

1 See chapter text. Crude and process oils comprise all feedstocks, other than distillation benzines, for treatment at refinery plants. Refinery production does not cover further treatment of finished products for special grades such as in distillation plant for the preparation of industrial spirits.

Source: Department of Trade and Industry: 020 7215 5184

22.13 Deliveries of petroleum products for inland consumption[1]
United Kingdom

		1993	1994	1995	1996	1997	1998	1999	2000	2001	2002	2003
Total (including refinery fuel)	KMCA	82 173	81 213	80 175	82 013	79 073	78 437	77 985	77 197	76 646	76 304	77 825
Total (excluding refinery fuel)	KMCB	75 970	74 957	73 694	75 390	72 501	71 969	72 009	71 796	71 586	70 722	72 435
Butane and propane	ECAQ	1 992	2 486	2 481	2 439	2 426	2 368	2 249	2 030	2 097	2 438	2 887
Other Petroleum Gases (includes Ethane)	ECAR	1 261	1 459	1 489	1 482	1 561	1 534	1 829	1 886	2 077	2 054	2 070
Naphtha	ECAS	3 117	2 866	2 885	3 010	2 640	2 882	3 100	2 344	1 592	1 480	2 215
Aviation spirit	KMCI	27	29	29	32	37	36	45	52	59	50	46
Motor spirit:												
Retail deliveries:												
Leaded Premium / Lead Replacement Petrol	KMCK	11 046	9 503	7 993	7 043	6 138	4 595	2 629	1 462	838	401	183
Super Premium Unleaded	KMCL	1 439	1 323	925	698	506	409	473	403	420	706	861
Premium Unleaded	KMCM	10 754	11 536	12 603	14 228	15 188	16 432	18 307	19 008	19 100	19 167	18 291
Total Retail Deliveries	ECAT	23 239	22 362	21 521	21 969	21 832	21 436	21 409	20 873	20 358	20 274	19 335
Commercial consumers:												
Leaded Premium / Lead Replacement Petrol	KMCO	217	178	149	135	112	91	61	44	34	19	19
Super Premium Unleaded	KMCP	25	26	17	11	9	4	6	6	9	17	22
Premium Unleaded	KMCQ	286	277	285	294	298	318	311	480	538	499	542
Total Commercial Consumers	ECAU	528	481	451	440	419	413	378	530	581	535	583
Total Motor spirit	BHOD	23 767	22 843	21 972	22 409	22 251	21 849	21 787	21 403	20 939	20 809	19 918
Industrial and white spirits	KMCS	164	170	178	184	195	179	174	170	151	157	147
Kerosene:												
Aviation turbine fuel	BHOE	7 106	7 284	7 660	8 049	8 411	9 241	9 939	10 806	10 614	10 519	10 765
Burning oil	KMCT	2 625	2 655	2 774	3 336	3 343	3 575	3 633	3 839	4 236	3 463	3 457
Gas/diesel oil:												
Derv fuel:												
Retail Deliveries	ECAV	3 765	4 345	4 814	5 537	6 127	6 602	7 137	7 181	7 846	8 153	9 057
Commercial Consumers	ECAW	8 041	8 569	8 643	8 828	8 849	8 541	8 371	8 451	8 213	8 774	8 655
Total Derv fuel	BHOI	11 806	12 914	13 457	14 365	14 976	15 143	15 508	15 632	16 059	16 927	17 712
Other gas/diesel oil (includes Mdf)	ECAX	8 516	8 167	7 879	8 349	8 053	8 005	7 196	7 528	6 960	6 099	6 327
Fuel oil	BHOK	10 770	9 275	7 975	6 854	3 936	2 935	2 415	1 833	2 806	2 088	2 370
Lubricating oils	BHOL	806	795	895	864	872	813	790	801	846	829	868
Bitumen	BHOM	2 523	2 595	2 420	2 146	2 015	1 967	1 928	1 975	1 935	2 385	2 320
Petroleum wax	KMCU	48	47	44	44	44	18	37	32	33	51	57
Petroleum coke	KMCV	778	911	1 008	1 210	1 095	887	660	776	702	774	830
Miscellaneous products	KMCW	661	461	548	617	646	537	719	463	475	596	449

1 See chapter text.

Source: Department of Trade and Industry: 020 7215 5184

22.14 Iron and steel:[1] Summary of steel supplies, deliveries and stocks
United Kingdom

		1993	1994	1995	1996	1997	1998	1999	2000	2001	2002	2003
Supply, disposal and consumption - (Finished product weight - Thousand tonnes)												
UK producers' home deliveries	KLTA	7 567	7 827	8 257	8 383	8 626	8 260	7 652	7 255	6 762	6 506	6 227
Imports excluding steelworks receipts	KLTB	4 132	5 012	5 384	5 147	5 894	6 466	6 014	6 387	6 978	6 793	6 719
Total deliveries to home market (a)	KLTC	11 698	12 839	13 641	13 530	14 520	14 726	13 666	13 642	13 740	13 299	12 946
Total exports (producers, consumers, merchants)	KLTD	7 621	8 120	8 228	8 917	9 060	8 008	7 623	7 446	6 512	6 320	7 033
Exports by UK producers	KLTE	7 536	7 873	7 828	8 305	8 534	7 876	7 416	7 163	6 182	5 594	6 202
Derived consumers' and merchants' exports (b)	KLTF	85	247	400	612	526	132	207	283	330	708	832
Net home disposals (a)-(b)	KLTG	11 614	12 592	13 241	12 918	13 994	14 594	13 460	13 359	13 410	12 591	12 114
Consumers' and merchants' stock change	KLTH	60	390	..	..	..	..	..	..	..	..	..
Estimated home consumption	KLTI	11 554	12 202	13 241	12 918	13 994	14 594	13 460	13 359	13 410	12 591	12 114
Stocks - (Finished product weight - Thousand tonnes)												
Producers												
- ingots & semis	KLTJ	1 005	946	1 068	767	946	717	747	727	705	690	776
- finished steel	KLTK	1 425	1 389	1 274	1 515	1 358	1 495	1 318	1 039	981	932	847
Consumers	KLTL	1 300	1 470	..	..	..	..	..	..	..	..	..
Merchants	KLTM	1 060	1 280	..	..	..	..	..	..	..	..	..
Estimated home consumption - (Crude steel equivalent - Million tonnes)												
Crude steel production[2]	KLTN	16.62	17.28	17.60	17.99	18.50	17.32	16.28	15.15	13.54	11.67	13.27
Producers' stock change	KLTO	−0.09	−0.12	0.01	−0.07	0.03	−0.11	−0.19	−0.33	−0.14	−0.08	..
Re-usable material	KLTP	0.08	0.09	0.08	0.07	0.06	0.02	..	..	..	..	..
Total supply from home sources	KLTQ	16.79	17.49	17.67	18.13	18.53	17.45	16.47	15.48	13.68	11.75	13.27
Total imports[3]	KLTR	5.44	6.58	7.05	7.01	7.49	8.38	7.81	8.43	9.11	9.86	9.32
Total exports[3]	KLTS	8.95	9.55	9.63	10.26	10.43	9.25	8.70	8.61	7.53	7.39	8.65
Net home disposals	KLTT	13.28	14.52	15.09	14.88	15.59	16.58	15.58	15.30	15.26	14.22	13.94
Consumers' and merchants' stock change	KLTU	0.07	0.48	..	..	..	..	..	..	..	..	..
Estimated home consumption	KLTV	13.21	14.04	15.09	14.88	15.59	16.58	15.58	15.30	15.26	14.22	13.94

1 See chapter text. The figures relate to periods of 52 weeks.
2 Includes liquid steel for castings.
3 Based on HM Customs Statistics, reflecting total trade rather than producers' trade.

Source: Iron and Steel Statistics Bureau: 020 8686 9050 ext 126

22.15 Iron and steel:[1] Iron ore, manganese ore, pig iron and iron and steel scrap
United Kingdom

Thousand tonnes

		1993	1994	1995	1996	1997	1998	1999	2000	2001	2002	2003
Iron ore[2]	KLOF	17 507	18 161	18 670	19 720	20 820	19 532	18 754	16 991	15 113	13 185	15 691
Manganese ore[2]	KLOG	152	64	32	48	37	22	14	36	4	4	–
Pig iron (and blast furnace ferro-alloys)												
Average number of furnaces in blast during period	KLOH	8	8	8	9	9	9	9	8	7	5	6
Production												
Steelmaking iron	KLOI	11 534	11 943	12 236	12 830	13 054	12 746	12 139	10 890	9 870	8 561	10 228
Speigeleisen and ferromanganese	KLOK	45	..	..	..	..	..	..	..	..	..	..
In blast furnaces: total	KLOL	11 579	11 943	12 236	12 830	13 054	12 746	12 139	10 890	9 870	8 561	10 228
In steel works	KLOM	11 554	11 889	12 121	12 753	13 044	12 746	12 139	10 890	9 870	8 561	10 228
Consumption of pig iron: total	KLOO	11 554	11 889	12 121	12 753	13 044	12 746	12 139	10 890	9 870	8 561	10 228
Iron and steel scrap												
Steelworks and steel foundries												
Circulating scrap	KLOQ	2 303	2 326	2 390	2 639	2 459	2 380	2 488	2 287	2 019	1 882	1 926
Purchased receipts	KLOR	4 149	4 533	4 688	4 130	5 418	4 045	3 433	3 327	3 001	2 271	2 617
Consumption	KLOS	6 550	6 874	7 012	6 828	7 207	6 408	5 884	5 675	5 006	4 216	4 469
Stocks (end of period)	KLOT	267	253	319	260	236	253	290	229	224	161	234

1 See chapter text. The figures relate to periods of 52 weeks.
2 Consumption.

Source: Iron and Steel Statistics Bureau: 020 8686 9050 ext 126

22.16 Iron and steel:[1] Furnaces and production of steel
United Kingdom

		1993	1994	1995	1996	1997	1998	1999	2000	2001	2002	2003
Steel furnaces (numbers[2])	KLPA	202	202	192	192	192	190	181	181	181	173	..
Oxygen converters	KLPC	11	11	11	11	11	11	11	11	11	8	..
Electric	KLPD	191	191	181	181	181	179	170	170	170	165	..
Production of crude steel	KLPF	16 625	17 286	17 604	17 992	18 499	17 315	16 284	15 155	13 543	11 667	13 268
by process												
Oxygen converters	KLPH	12 330	12 909	13 082	13 758	13 986	13 426	12 634	11 551	10 271	8 956	10 630
Electric	KLPI	4 295	4 377	4 522	4 234	4 513	3 889	3 650	3 604	3 272	2 711	2 639
by cast method												
Cast to ingot	KLPK	2 140	2 033	2 174	1 892	1 660	784	534	539	369	339	354
Continuously cast	KLPL	14 319	15 079	15 250	15 912	16 653	16 346	15 637	14 470	13 024	11 182	12 766
Steel for castings	KLPM	166	174	180	188	186	185	127	146	150	146	148
by quality												
Non alloy steel	KLPN	15 558	16 062	16 243	16 708	17 193	16 145	15 263	14 004	12 482	10 657	12 294
Stainless and other alloy steel	KLPO	1 067	1 224	1 361	1 284	1 306	1 170	1 035	1 151	1 061	1 010	974
Production of finished steel products (All quantities)[3]												
Rods and bars for reinforce-ment (in coil and lengths)	KLPP	1 229	1 269	1 154	1 182	1 118	1 133	893	812	755	487	294
Wire rods and other rods and bars in coil	KLPQ	1 427	1 524	1 642	1 536	1 565	1 492	1 407	1 408	1 389	1 394	1 316
Hot rolled bars in lengths	KLPR	1 140	1 275	1 311	1 499	1 716	1 791	1 542	1 545	1 449	1 267	1 107
Bright steel bars[4]	KLPS	295	363	424	357	385	336	311	337	296	271	273
Light sections other than rails	KLPT	294	306	286	298	302	318	264	183	201	188	116
Heavy sections	KGQZ	2 408	2 412	2 549	2 557	2 397	2 346	2 303	1 915	1 931	1 873	1 774
Hot rolled plates, sheets and strip in coil and lengths	KLPW	7 230	7 715	8 077	8 512	8 956	8 454	7 893	7 278	5 821	5 708	5 178
Cold rolled plates and sheets in coil and lengths[4]	KLPX	3 635	3 835	4 100	4 221	4 437	4 288	3 914	3 612	2 944	2 854	2 958
Cold rolled strip[4]	KLPZ	229	243	267	246	255	259	233	218	201	179	186
Tinplate	KLQW	829	767	791	739	754	772	736	753	602	562	493
Other coated sheet	KLQX	1 865	2 021	2 306	2 366	2 534	2 610	2 475	2 471	1 773	1 786	1 811
Tubes and pipes[4]	KLQY	1 155	1 136	1 183	1 317	1 310	1 276	1 100	1 061	1 096	940	1 066
Forged bars[4]	KLQZ	2	2	3	3	3	3	2	1	1	–	..

1 See chapter text. The figures relate to periods of 52 weeks.
2 Number in existence at end of period. Includes steel furnaces at steel foundries.
3 Includes material for conversion into other products listed in the table.
4 Based on producers' deliveries.

Source: Iron and Steel Statistics Bureau: 020 8686 9050 ext 126

22.17 Non-ferrous metals
United Kingdom

		1993	1994	1995	1996	1997	1998	1999	2000	2001	2002	2003
Copper												
Production of refined copper:												
Primary	KLAA	10.7	11.1	12.0	13.0	9.1	6.4	1.7	–	–	–	–
Secondary	KLAB	35.9	35.6	43.0	43.6	51.3	47.4	48.6	–	–	–	–
Home consumption:												
Refined	KLAC	325.0	377.3	397.9	396.0	408.3	374.1	305.3	322.7	285.9	260.8	242.2
Scrap (metal content)	KLAD	77.9	88.0	81.0	81.0	69.0	64.6	112.5	132.4	127.0	120.0	120.0
Stocks (end of period)[1,2]	KLAE	9.3	8.1	7.5	6.6	12.8	7.5	7.3	10.4	7.3	7.3	7.3
Analysis of home consumption												
(refined and scrap):[3,4] total	KLAF	403.0	468.0	493.2	477.3	477.4	438.7	417.8	455.5	212.7	..	..
Wire[5]	KLAG	253.9	306.2	321.4	309.4	312.5	287.2	276.1	310.2	151.8	..	..
Rods, bars and sections	KLAH	53.2	54.9	59.0	58.3	58.3	53.6	46.9	43.6	21.6	..	..
Sheet, strip and plate	KLAI	30.7	33.0	37.1	34.0	36.5	30.5	27.7	32.3	16.9	..	..
Tubes	KLAJ	65.2	73.9	75.7	75.6	70.1	67.4	67.1	69.4	22.4	..	..
Zinc												
Slab zinc:												
Production	KLAL	102.4	101.3	106.0	96.9	107.7	99.6	132.8	99.6	99.6	99.6	16.6
Home consumption	KLAM	195.9	196.5	198.4	195.7	194.8	187.9	198.9	206.5	197.1	202.4	199.7
Stocks (end of period)	KLAN	11.4	10.5	9.8	10.5	10.1	10.6	10.9	10.9	9.5	9.2	8.9
Other zinc (metal content):												
Consumption	KLAO	45.4	45.0	46.8	41.3	41.5	37.3	41.6	46.3	48.2	51.8	52.5
Analysis of home consumption												
(slab and scrap): total	KLAP	241.3	241.5	245.2	237.1	236.3	226.2	236.7	242.5	231.2	234.6	233.7
Brass	KLAQ	41.6	42.6	45.2	39.1	41.6	36.6	33.6	34.4	32.2	30.0	30.0
Galvanized products	KLAR	105.1	107.4	110.7	110.3	108.4	103.8	116.6	120.9	111.8	117.3	115.5
Zinc sheet and strip	KLAS	4.0	4.6	3.0	3.0	3.3	3.3	3.3	3.3	3.3	3.4	3.3
Zinc alloy die castings	KLAT	46.5	46.5	46.5	46.5	46.5	46.5	46.5	46.5	46.5	46.5	46.5
Zinc oxide	KLAU	20.7	21.6	21.6	20.7	20.6	20.4	21.1	21.8	21.8	22.2	22.9
Other products	KLAV	23.4	18.8	18.2	17.5	16.1	11.0	11.0	11.0	11.0	11.0	11.0
Refined lead												
Production[6,7]	KLAW	363.8	352.5	320.7	351.4	384.1	349.7	347.3	327.9	366.3	374.6	356.2
Home consumption[7,8]												
Refined lead	KLAX	263.6	267.6	285.4	272.8	270.4	275.5	283.3	294.0	298.3	305.7	308.3
Scrap and remelted lead[7]	KLAY	35.2	38.5	41.6	43.4	39.1	38.4	32.2	40.9	40.7	41.5	40.1
Stocks (end of period)[9]												
Lead bullion	KLAZ	20.7	10.2	9.5	32.9	15.5	20.9	17.1	10.0	17.2	21.6	24.0
Refined soft lead at consumers	KLBA	25.0	23.5	24.9	28.8	29.1	27.4	25.7	25.8	26.1	25.6	25.4
In LME Warehouses (UK)	KLBB	9.5	6.1	0.4	3.0	2.4	0.1	0.1	–	–	–	–
Analysis of home consumption												
(refined and scrap): total	KLBC	298.8	306.1	327.0	316.2	309.5	313.9	315.5	333.5	338.9	347.1	349.0
Cables	KLBD	8.9	9.3	9.8	9.8	9.7	9.7	9.7	9.6	9.6	9.8	9.8
Batteries (excluding oxides)	KLBE	48.7	52.5	52.7	52.3	54.7	51.6	47.4	50.5	48.2	49.2	52.0
Oxides and compounds:												
Batteries	KLBF	53.9	55.2	56.2	54.9	56.1	54.4	53.1	55.9	54.7	54.3	55.8
Other uses	KLBG	56.3	53.9	53.8	56.1	54.5	56.4	57.0	56.8	53.8	51.4	49.4
Sheets and pipes	KLBH	82.7	84.6	101.2	94.1	91.1	96.1	94.9	102.3	102.3	107.9	109.7
Solder	KLBJ	7.4	7.4	7.4	7.4	7.4	7.4	7.4	7.4	7.4	7.4	7.2
Alloys	KLBK	14.1	15.3	15.9	12.1	9.4	9.4	11.9	15.2	24.3	27.5	25.7
Other uses	KLBL	26.8	27.9	30.0	29.5	26.6	28.9	34.1	35.8	38.6	39.9	39.4

Thousand tonnes

		1993	1994	1995	1996	1997	1998	1999	2000	2001	2002	2003
Tin												
Tin ore (metal content):												
Production	KLBM	2.2	1.9	2.0	2.1	2.3	0.4	–	..	..	..	..
Tin metal:[10]												
Production[11]	KLBO	–	–	–	–	–	..	..	..	..	..	..
Home consumption[11]	VQIX	10.5	10.6	10.5	10.5	10.4	10.6	9.6	10.0	10.3	9.9	9.9
Exports and re-exports[12]	KLBQ	0.3	1.2	2.7	0.6	0.3	3.4	0.1	0.1	0.4	0.3	0.3
Stocks (end of period):												
Consumers	KLBR	1.0	1.0	1.0	1.0	1.0	1.0	1.0	1.0	1.0	1.0	1.0
Analysis of home consumption												
(excluding scrap): total	KLBT	10.4	10.5	10.6	10.5	10.4	17.5	16.5	17.0	18.8	18.4	18.4
Tinplate	KLBU	3.6	3.6	3.6	3.6	2.8	2.6	3.0	3.0	3.0	3.0	3.0
Alloys	KLBV	3.4	3.3	3.4	3.5	3.4	12.1	11.2	11.6	2.6	2.6	2.6
Solder	KLBW	1.5	1.5	1.1	1.1	1.1	1.1	0.6	0.8	1.5	1.5	1.5
Other uses	KLBX	2.3	2.4	0.4	0.4	0.4	0.4	0.4	0.4	0.4	0.4	0.4
Aluminium												
Ingot production												
Primary	KLBY	239.0	231.2	237.9	240.0	247.7	258.4	269.7	305.1	340.8	344.3	342.7
Secondary[13]	KLCA	236.2	224.3	229.7	260.0	242.7	274.8	285.3	237.7	248.6	207.2	206.5
Wrought remelt production[14]	C6EW	416.8	519.7	546.5	527.8	561.2	583.5	596.2	567.0	585.3	565.1	557.2
Wrought and cast despatches												
Bar, section and tube[15]	C6EX	136.2	142.7	142.1	149.6	160.8	168.0	181.7	184.7	177.1	168.3	158.7
Plate, sheet, strip and circles	C6EY	309.3	346.4	359.2	327.9	350.4	352.5	349.7	419.1	384.8	312.2	274.3
Castings	KLCH	133.0	143.4	147.0	156.0	152.4	148.0	137.3	134.9	129.0	126.9	127.5
Exports												
Primary ingot	C6EZ	29.5	95.2	159.4	53.1	219.6	68.7	233.6	347.7	203.4	214.7	244.3
Secondary ingot	KLCC	98.3	124.8	145.8	152.2	153.3	156.6	143.1	84.2	59.9	35.7	26.9
Extruded products	C6F2	33.2	40.9	65.8	45.8	56.8	59.7	47.5	25.5	20.7	15.3	14.2
Rolled products	C6F3	156.8	177.7	185.6	155.5	157.7	160.1	166.6	222.9	198.3	208.8	193.9
Refined nickel												
Production (including ferro-nickel)	KLCM	28.4	28.4	35.1	38.6	36.1	39.1	39.5	38.0	33.8	33.8	26.8

1 Unwrought copper (electrolytic, fire refined and blister).
2 Reported stocks of refined copper held by consumers and those held in London Metal Exchange (LME) warehouses in the United Kingdom.
3 2001 figures only cover the period January to June.
4 Copper content.
5 Consumption for high-conductivity copper and cadmium copper wire represented by consumption of wire rods, production of which for export is also included.
6 Lead reclaimed from secondary and scrap material and lead refined from bullion and domestic ores.

7 Figures for production and consumption of refined lead include antimonial lead, and for scrap and remelted lead, exclude secondary antimonial lead.
8 Including toll transactions involving fabrication.
9 Excluding goverment stocks.
10 Including production from imported scrap and residues refined on toll.
11 Primary and secondary metal.
12 Including re-exports on toll transactions.
13 Predominantly from old scrap.
14 Predominantly using recycled scrap from fabrication.
15 Excluding forging bars

Sources: World Bureau of Metal Statistics: 01920 461274;
Aluminium Federation: 0121 456 1103

22.18 Fertilisers[1]
Years ending 30 June

Thousand tonnes

		1994	1995	1996	1997	1998	1999	2000	2001	2002	2003	2004
Nutrient Content												
Nitrogen (N):												
Straight	KGRM	553	602	685	615	664	618	637	479	521	594	590
Compounds	KGRN	413	449	444	420	406	430	398	400	419	413	378
Phosphate (P_2O_5)	KGRO	236	272	284	287	296	291	253	228	235	226	206
Potash (K_2O)	KGRP	299	343	353	356	360	357	309	269	289	275	247
Compounds - total product	KGRQ	2 378	2 656	2 688	2 664	2 620	2 727	2 523	2 228	2 329	2 233	2 072

1 Deliveries to UK agriculture by Members of the Agricultural Industries Confederation - Fertiliser Sector.

Source: Agricultural Industries Confederation: 01733 385230

22.19 Minerals: production[1]
United Kingdom

Thousand tonnes

		1993	1994	1995	1996	1997	1998	1999	2000	2001	2002	2003
Great Britain												
Limestone	KLEA	90 069	102 844	90 933	82 442	84 252	85 382	82 714	80 810	83 492	88 013	84 445
Sandstone	KLEB	12 100	13 494	15 017	12 581	12 457	13 545	11 870	12 056	11 897	11 788	11 665
Igneous rock	KLEC	49 209	50 014	49 641	43 731	42 370	39 838	45 294	44 633	45 053	44 544	45 305
Clay/shale	KLED	10 891	12 464	13 930	11 804	11 322	12 230	11 355	10 838	10 426	10 306	10 680
Industrial sand	KLEE	3 587	4 038	4 344	4 861	4 704	4 662	4 092	4 095	3 848	3 833	4 073
Chalk	KLEF	9 076	10 236	9 949	9 239	9 550	9 934	9 667	9 213	8 205	8 587	8 066
Fireclay	KLEG	479	679	708	536	338	577	545	595	459	491	528
Barium sulphate	KLEH	33	34	74	93	57	64	59	54	70	56	..
Calcium fluoride	KLEI	70	50	46	..	58	52	46	21	46	22	..
Copper	KLEJ	–	–	–	–	–	–	–	–	–	–	–
Lead	KLEK	..	2	..	..	..	1	1	..	1	..	..
Tin	KLEL	2.2	1.9	2.0	2.1	2.0	–	–	–	–	–	–
Zinc	KLEM	..	..	..	..	–	–	–	–	–	–	–
Iron ore: crude	KLEN	..	2	2	1	2	2	1	1	1	1	–
Iron ore: iron content	KLEO	1	1	1	1	1	1	1	1	..	..	–
Calcspar	KLEP	3	..	..	..	13	15	..	..	12	..	–
China clay	KLEQ / KILC	2 852	2 977	3 076	2 654	2 798	2 866	2 841	2 779	2 804	2 467	2 378
Ball clay	KIMS	..	913	..	..	..	..	..	..	..	..	..
Chert and flint	KLER	..	..	..	..	..	..	6	..	2	2	..
Fuller's earth	KLES	153	193	150	183	162	111	83	103	..	33	19
Lignite	KLET	3	2	–	–	–	–	–	–	–	–	–
Rock salt	KLEU	..	..	..	..	..	..	..	..	..	..	..
Salt from brine	KLEV	..	..	..	..	..	..	..	..	..	..	..
Salt in brine	KLEW	4 076	4 009	3 548	3 512	3 561	..	..	..	..	..	..
Anhydrite	KLEX	..	..	..	–	–	–	–	–	–	–	–
Dolomite	KLEY	17 985	17 616	17 966	16 555	17 282	15 632	13 698	13 069	14 314	12 946	..
Gypsum	KLEZ	..	..	..	..	..	..	..	..	..	..	..
Slate[2]	KLFA	462	402	275	408	347	425	361	479	551	742	832
Soapstone and talc	KLFB	5	5	4	5	5	5	6	5	5	6	6
Sand and gravel (land-won)	KLFC	79 380	86 341	78 031	70 489	74 362	73 016	74 785	74 877	74 599	69 889	68 090
Sand and gravel (marine dredged)	KLFD	10 090	11 331	11 625	11 508	12 004	12 952	13 424	14 356	13 611	12 832	12 131
Northern Ireland												
Sand and gravel	KLFG	4 318	5 109	5 262	7 684	5 138	5 300	5 517	5 073	6 194	5 512	4 894
Basalt and igneous rock (other than granite)	KLFH	8 557	6 480	7 564	6 974	6 286	6 107	7 861	9 480	6 448	6 681	6 051
Limestone	KLFI	3 236	..	3 703	4 122	3 500	3 892	4 219	3 538	4 746	4 514	4 887
Sandstone[3]	KLFJ	3 959	5 480	4 779	4 941	6 042	6 584	3 615	2 844	8 070	6 574	6 594
Granite	KLFL	..	..	..	–	–	–	–	–	–	–	–
Others[4]	KLFN	647	896	812	1 392	625	473	1 579	3 098	753	242	1 055

1 See chapter text.
2 Includes waste used for constructional fill, and powder and granules used in manufacturing.

3 Prior to 1993 the 'Sandstone' heading was called 'Grit and conglomerate'. The new heading is all encompassing and was confirmed as correct with the Geological Survey in Northern Ireland.
4 Rock salt, Chalk, Diatomite and Fireclay.

Source: Office for National Statistics: 01633 812082

22.20 Building materials and components: production[1]
Great Britain

			1993	1994	1995	1996	1997	1998	1999	2000	2001	2002	2003
Building bricks[2]	KLGA	Millions	2 639	3 114	3 256	3 046	2 997	3 000	2 939	2 864	2 754	2 750	2 772
Common bricks	GRTD	"	436	464	480	401	422	385	367	342	320	332	315
Facing bricks	GRTE	"	1 978	2 421	2 546	2 430	2 386	2 411	2 369	2 287	2 211	2 209	2 244
Engineering bricks	GRTF	"	225	229	230	216	190	204	204	235	223	210	213
Clay bricks (including sand-lime)	GRTG	"	2 447	2 900	3 065	2 880	2 828	2 830	2 759	2 694	2 595	2 600	2 606
Concrete bricks	GRTH	"	192	214	191	166	169	171	180	170	159	150	167
Cement (grey Portland)[3]	KLGB	Thousand tonnes	11 039	12 307	11 805	12 214	12 638	12 409	12 697	12 452	11 090	11 089	11 215
Sand and gravel	GRTI	"	89 470	97 672	89 656	81 997	86 366	85 968	88 209	89 234	88 210	82 721	80 221
Building sand[4]	KLGC	"	17 406	18 534	17 389	14 655	15 337	13 810	13 941	14 219	13 772	13 221	13 617
Concreting sand	KLGD	"	28 021	30 977	29 390	28 659	30 130	30 244	31 730	31 167	31 656	31 224	31 411
Gravel[5]	KLGE	"	44 043	48 162	42 877	38 683	40 899	41 914	42 538	43 847	42 782	38 276	35 193
Crushed rock	GRTJ	"	149 576	161 757	150 838	132 894	133 787	131 716	132 598	130 307	133 759	126 568	122 885
Coated roadstone	KLGF	"	27 238	28 512	28 972	26 270	23 906	23 131	22 260	21 785	23 340	23 281	23 139
Uncoated roadstone	KLGG	"	54 412	51 121	49 307	40 893	40 186	36 816	38 114	36 509	34 638	27 323	28 950
Fill and ballast	KLGH	"	52 141	65 779	56 140	50 982	51 396	51 623	52 144	53 417	47 225	49 622	42 208
Concrete aggregate	KLGI	"	15 786	16 345	16 419	14 748	18 300	20 146	20 080	18 595	28 556	26 342	28 588
Ready mixed concrete[6]	GRXA	Thousand cubic metres	20 771	22 931	21 676	20 892	22 327	22 983	23 550	23 043	23 008	22 597	22 289
Concrete building blocks	GRTK	Thousand square metres	74 287	87 548	78 287	75 866	82 537	84 662	87 767	90 219	87 922	91 474	95 645
Dense aggregate	KLGN	"	30 116	36 997	36 933	34 996	37 250	39 439	38 439	37 629	36 598	35 744	36 745
Lightweight aggregate	KLGO	"	19 235	22 048	18 147	16 316	17 783	19 110	20 830	22 991	22 684	23 478	24 991
Aerated concrete	KLGP	"	24 936	28 503	23 207	24 554	27 505	26 113	28 497	29 599	28 639	32 252	33 909
Concrete roofing tiles	KLGM	"	24 574	28 149	26 118	24 651	24 958	24 981	25 972	26 765	24 825	25 023	21 437
Roofing and architectural slates	GRXB	Tonnes	37 321	44 910	42 030	48 474	44 578	46 159	46 998	41 214	45 604	50 530	50 094
Fibre cement products	KLGK	Thousand tonnes	128.7	154.1	160.5	146.2	163.5	160.9	156.2	..	..	..	..

1 See chapter text.
2 Excluding refractory and glazed bricks.
3 United Kingdom up until 2000. Great Britain for 2001 and 2002.
4 Includes sand and gravel used for coating.
5 Includes hoggin.
6 United Kingdom.

Source: Department of Trade & Industry: 020 7215 1555

22.21 Construction: Value of output in Great Britain[1]
Standard Industrial Classification 1992

£ million

		1993	1994	1995	1996	1997	1998	1999	2000	2001	2002	2003
All work: total	FGAY	46 323	49 439	52 643	55 243	58 352	62 060	65 704	69 676	74 690	83 593	93 284
New work: total	BLAB	23 556	25 086	26 672	27 926	29 928	32 491	35 587	37 660	39 970	45 370	50 353
New housing: total	KLQA	6 628	7 417	7 135	7 013	7 983	8 430	8 418	9 985	10 233	12 089	15 362
For public sector	BLAC	1 415	1 671	1 660	1 421	1 232	1 069	1 012	1 319	1 437	1 716	2 032
For private sector	BLAD	5 213	5 746	5 475	5 592	6 751	7 361	7 406	8 666	8 797	10 373	13 330
Infrastructure: total	KIAM	5 544	5 149	5 660	6 338	6 311	6 182	6 200	6 453	7 147	8 077	7 363
Other new work: total (excluding infrastructure)	KLQB	11 384	12 521	13 877	14 575	15 635	17 879	20 969	21 222	22 594	25 204	27 628
For public sector	BLAE	4 045	4 384	4 661	4 441	3 756	4 151	4 919	4 854	5 330	6 865	8 875
For private sector	KLQC	7 339	8 137	9 217	10 134	11 879	13 728	16 049	16 369	17 263	18 339	18 753
Private Industrial	BLAF	2 208	2 489	3 008	3 119	3 491	3 810	3 973	3 716	3 702	3 374	3 644
Private Commercial	BLAG	5 131	5 648	6 209	7 015	8 388	9 917	12 076	12 653	13 562	14 965	15 109
Repair and maintenance: total	BLAH	22 767	24 353	25 971	27 317	28 423	29 569	30 117	32 016	34 729	38 222	42 931
Housing: total	KLQD	12 809	13 767	14 595	15 035	15 754	16 202	16 370	16 907	17 626	19 170	21 315
For public sector	BLBK	5 439	5 963	6 465	6 637	6 629	6 506	6 485	6 552	6 632	6 412	7 451
For private sector	BLBL	7 370	7 804	8 130	8 398	9 126	9 696	9 885	10 354	10 994	12 758	13 864
Public other work	BLAJ	4 916	5 211	5 398	5 252	5 079	5 220	5 371	5 685	6 111	6 712	7 930
Private other work	BLAK	5 042	5 375	5 978	7 030	7 590	8 147	8 376	9 424	10 992	12 340	13 686

1 See chapter text. Output by contractors, including unrecorded estimates by small firms and self-employed workers, and output by public sector direct labour departments - classified to construction in the *1992 Standard Industrial Classification.*

Source: Department of Trade and Industry: 020 7215 1953

22.22 Construction: Value of new orders obtained by contractors[1]
Great Britain
Standard Industrial Classification 1992

£ million

		1993	1994	1995	1996	1997	1998	1999	2000	2001	2002	2003
New work: total	FHAA	19 965	21 285	22 065	22 834	24 806	27 477	26 079	28 120	29 643	33 411	33 951
Public housing	BLBC	1 668	1 386	1 182	1 073	995	933	969	910	1 084	1 129	1 340
Private housing[2]	BLBD	4 874	5 721	4 905	5 416	6 253	5 997	5 901	6 085	6 525	8 088	9 471
New housing: total	FGAU	6 542	7 106	6 087	6 487	7 248	6 930	6 869	6 995	7 610	9 217	10 812
Infrastructure:												
Water	KIBV	421	412	500	640	733	957	760	1 084	531	936	677
Sewerage	KIBW	447	389	394	481	656	737	789	380	540	524	423
Electricity	KIBX	211	170	218	294	382	359	254	244	279	294	255
Roads	KIBY	1 435	1 356	1 531	1 710	928	821	957	1 445	1 572	1 999	1 424
Gas, communications, air	KIBZ	642	494	904	745	693	745	713	1 085	584	485	699
Railways	KIDP	623	412	351	524	416	573	471	539	1 271	1 052	1 189
Harbours	KIDQ	220	218	273	270	182	287	250	215	377	264	228
Total	BAWT	3 998	3 451	4 170	4 664	3 991	4 479	4 195	4 992	5 154	5 555	4 894
of which												
- Public	KIDS	2 472	2 211	2 327	1 671	1 352	1 505	1 495	1 430	2 085	2 491	1 781
- Private	KIDT	1 525	1 240	1 843	2 993	2 639	2 974	2 700	3 562	3 068	3 064	3 113
Other public non-housing:												
Factories	KIDU	111	111	94	91	72	84	72	64	30	65	121
Warehouses	KIDV	23	38	29	14	27	20	24	12	10	11	27
Oil, steel, coal	KIDW	30	12	13	4	4	2	5	1	8	1	4
Schools and colleges	KIDX	655	658	710	707	749	770	791	986	1 498	1 397	1 988
Universities	KIDY	353	376	373	355	273	405	345	329	378	667	760
Health	KIDZ	697	752	717	681	491	769	635	685	813	1 065	1 114
Offices	KIFP	684	469	393	379	391	292	390	291	395	854	588
Entertainment	KIFQ	281	308	285	259	342	432	435	359	392	400	543
Garages	KIFR	42	49	51	28	34	19	36	44	30	53	34
Shops	KIFS	26	14	21	12	35	35	29	34	38	53	50
Agriculture	KIFT	44	22	12	8	33	17	9	12	46	16	10
Miscellaneous	KIFU	450	844	508	418	441	660	503	999	479	1 328	903
Total	BAWU	3 397	3 654	3 206	2 956	2 894	3 504	3 273	3 815	4 117	5 910	6 142
Private industrial:[2]												
Factories	KIFW	1 221	1 451	2 055	1 603	2 184	1 878	1 698	1 444	1 588	1 341	1 442
Warehouses	KIFX	429	498	594	663	901	1 014	821	1 110	911	866	867
Oil, steel, coal	KIFY	27	51	76	71	64	79	38	34	43	40	74
Total	BAWV	1 677	1 999	2 725	2 337	3 149	2 971	2 558	2 589	2 542	2 247	2 383
Private commercial:[2]												
Schools, universities	KIHP	134	115	105	156	189	351	393	577	702	850	873
Health	KIHQ	179	255	288	277	356	651	411	455	349	575	744
Offices	KIHR	1 471	1 777	2 123	2 169	2 506	3 472	3 566	4 384	4 748	3 947	3 253
Entertainment	KIHS	751	928	940	1 407	1 847	2 244	2 224	1 873	1 674	1 861	1 521
Garages	KIHT	308	300	301	265	344	315	266	169	190	199	194
Shops	KIHU	1 278	1 453	1 871	1 795	1 937	2 154	1 901	1 889	2 212	2 570	2 675
Agriculture	KIBN	108	120	124	123	148	146	100	77	105	107	158
Miscellaneous	KIBO	122	127	126	198	198	259	321	305	242	374	301
Total	BAWW	4 351	5 075	5 877	6 390	7 525	9 593	9 184	9 729	10 221	10 482	9 721

1 See chapter text. Classified to construction in the *1992 Standard Industrial Classification.*
2 Figures for private sector include work to be carried out by contractors on their own initiative for sale.

Source: Department of Trade and Industry: 020 7215 1953

22.23 Total engineering: Total turnover of UK based manufacturers[1]

Standard Industrial Classification 2003

£ million

Activity heading Product group		1998	1999	2000	2001	2002	2003
Class 29: Manufacture of machinery and equipment not elsewhere classified							
2911 Manufacture of engines and turbines except aircraft, vehicle and cycle engines	MXVO	1 494.4	1 359.4	1 445.3	1 911.8	1 823.9	1 717.0
2912 Manufacture of pumps and compressors	MXXO	2 494.9	2 393.0	2 481.5	2 337.4	2 537.3	2 607.9
2913 Manufacture of taps and valves	MXZH	1 504.4	1 218.5	1 346.2	1 358.2	1 330.9	1 281.5
2914 Manufacture of bearings, gears, gearing and driving elements	MYCT	1 477.7	1 344.9	1 282.8	1 227.0	1 004.9	882.4
2922 Manufacture of lifting and handling equipment	MYLS	3 752.8	3 881.5	3 687.8	3 348.7	3 080.7	2 995.3
2923 Manufacture of non-domestic cooling and ventilation equipment	MYPT	3 359.7	3 082.0	3 160.0	3 411.9	3 298.7	3 194.5
2924 Manufacture of other general purpose machinery not elsewhere classified	MYRM	2 494.7	2 715.0	2 693.3	2 947.6	2 573.4	2 650.2
2941/3 Manufacture of other machine tools	MYYP	868.6	839.5	777.3	834.3	745.7	842.1
2942 Manufacture of metalworking machine tools	MYWY	1 002.0	866.9	937.0	912.6	738.6	689.9
2952 Manufacture of machinery for mining, quarrying and construction	MZCE	2 449.4	2 339.0	2 434.8	2 392.4	2 215.9	2 549.3
2953 Manufacture of machinery for food, beverage and tobacco processing	MZFS	648.6	576.0	593.8	629.1	710.8	802.9
2954 Manufacture of machinery for textile, apparel and leather production	MZJP	298.8	203.1	207.6	194.7	158.0	145.9
2956 Manufacture of other special purpose machinery not elsewhere classified	MZQF	2 515.1	2 360.8	2 153.9	2 148.8	2 187.1	2 240.0
2971 Manufacture of electric domestic appliances	MZTZ	2 098.1	2 008.9	2 046.7	2 230.9	2 196.4	2 177.3
Class 30: Manufacture of electrical and optical equipment							
3001 Manufacture of office machinery	MZXQ	1 318.1	1 409.3	1 528.6	1 481.1	1 129.8	919.0
3002 Manufacture of computers and other information processing equipment	VBCE	13 483.6	13 452.6	12 410.7	12 086.4	8 915.6	7 533.4
Class 31 : Manufacture of electrical machinery and apparatus not elsewhere classified							
3110 Manufacture of electric motors, generators and transformers	VBEB	2 892.8	3 150.0	3 302.5	3 287.6	2 732.3	2 620.9
3120 Manufacture of electricity distribution and control apparatus	VBFU	3 560.7	3 813.9	4 213.0	4 090.5	3 661.5	3 464.2
3130 Manufacture of insulated wire and cable	VBHW	1 905.6	1 739.2	1 753.7	1 414.7	1 271.6	1 140.0
3140 Manufacture of accumulators, primary cells and primary batteries	VBJW	632.0	587.5	606.2	493.7	444.6	441.7
3150 Manufacture of lighting equipment and electric lamps	VBLP	1 880.5	1 913.2	1 865.8	1 712.1	1 487.0	1 402.6
3161 Manufacture of other electrical equipment for engines and vehicles not otherwise classified	VBNI	1 265.8	1 068.5	1 030.6	1 034.2	1 042.5	1 037.3
3162 Manufacture of other electrical equipment not elsewhere classified	VBPK	3 422.2	3 438.5	2 756.5	2 728.1	2 480.9	2 384.4
Class 32: Manufacture of radio, television and communication equipment and apparatus							
3210 Manufacture of electronic valves and tubes and other electronic components	VBRI	5 551.7	4 652.9	6 695.8	4 460.0	4 063.0	4 132.7
3220 Manufacture of television and radio transmitters and apparatus for line telephony and line telegraphy	VBTF	7 840.7	11 881.6	15 349.1	10 527.5	7 112.6	5 829.7
3230 Manufacture of television and radio receivers, sound or video recording or reproducing apparatus and associated goods	VBVJ	3 945.1	3 826.5	4 044.2	4 038.0	3 192.4	3 262.4
Class 33: Manufacture of medical, precision and optical instruments, watches and clocks							
3310 Manufacture of medical and surgical equipment and orthopaedic appliances	VBXH	2 331.9	2 597.0	2 691.2	2 967.5	3 167.7	3 538.7
3320 Manufacture of instruments and appliances for measuring, checking, testing, navigating and other purposes, except industrial process control equipment	VBZF	6 533.1	6 261.8	6 541.0	7 104.8	6 378.5	6 698.1
3340 Manufacture of optical instruments and photographic equipment	VCCV	1 061.7	935.1	998.4	999.6	1 027.2	1 031.0

1 The figures shown represent the output of UK based manufacturers classified to Subsections DK and DL of the Standard Industrial Classification 2003. The figures shown are derived from the monthly production inquiry (MPI) and include estimates for non-responders and for establishments which are not sampled. Orders on hand figures are given for the end of the period to which they relate.

Source: Office for National Statistics: 01633 812786

22.24 Volume index numbers of turnover and orders for the engineering industries
United Kingdom

Standard Industrial Classification 1992

Indices (2000=100)

	Total			Home			Export		
	Orders on hand[1]	New orders[2]	Turnover	Orders on hand[1]	New orders[2]	Turnover	Orders on hand[1]	New orders[2]	Turnover

Total Engineering industries
SIC 1992 Division 29, 30, 31, 32 and 33

	JIQI	JIQH	JIQJ	JIQC	JIQB	JIQD	JIQF	JIQE	JIQG
1997	84.5	83.0	85.3	86.5	85.1	87.7	81.3	80.2	82.1
1998	81.9	84.2	87.8	79.1	82.5	88.3	86.7	86.4	87.3
1999	92.0	91.8	91.9	92.8	94.2	93.5	90.8	88.6	89.9
2000	103.4	100.0	100.0	104.9	100.0	100.0	100.8	100.0	100.0
2001	94.4	89.5	95.3	104.6	94.5	98.4	77.2	82.9	91.2
2002	91.7	80.4	84.1	104.2	87.3	91.1	70.5	71.2	74.8
2003	92.9	81.0	83.6	109.1	91.5	93.7	65.4	66.9	70.3

Manufacture of Machinery and Equipment
SIC 1992 Division 29

	JINX	JINW	JINY	JINR	JINQ	JINS	JINU	JINT	JINV
1997	109.4	106.5	106.3	111.4	110.9	108.8	105.0	98.9	101.8
1998	92.6	97.9	106.0	91.0	97.7	106.8	96.1	98.3	104.6
1999	95.1	99.5	100.4	96.9	105.1	103.6	91.2	89.9	94.6
2000	99.9	100.0	100.0	99.1	100.0	100.0	101.7	100.0	100.0
2001	95.0	97.2	100.8	95.1	100.8	103.3	94.9	91.0	96.4
2002	99.1	95.3	95.5	100.3	98.3	97.2	96.5	90.1	92.4
2003	110.6	99.9	97.2	120.3	105.5	97.5	89.2	90.3	96.5

Manufacture of Electrical and Optical Equipment
SIC 1992 Division 30, 31, 32 and 33

	JIPQ	JIPP	JIPR	JIPK	JIPJ	JIPL	JIPN	JIPM	JIPO
1997	68.6	72.6	75.7	67.9	71.8	76.2	69.6	73.5	75.2
1998	75.1	78.0	79.5	70.3	74.7	78.2	82.1	82.2	81.1
1999	90.0	88.4	88.1	89.7	88.6	88.0	90.5	88.1	88.2
2000	105.7	100.0	100.0	109.3	100.0	100.0	100.4	100.0	100.0
2001	94.0	86.1	92.8	111.7	91.2	95.8	68.4	80.0	89.4
2002	86.9	73.8	78.9	107.1	81.5	87.8	57.7	64.5	68.5
2003	81.5	72.5	77.4	100.8	84.3	91.7	53.6	58.5	60.9

1 At end of period, rather than the average value for that period, so the annual value shown for 2000 may not equal 100.
2 Net of cancellations.

Source: Office for National Statistics: 01633 812786

383

22.25 Motor vehicle production[1]
United Kingdom

Numbers

Motor vehicles

		1993	1994	1995	1996	1997	1998	1999	2000	2001	2002	2003
SIC 1992, Class 34-10 Passenger cars: total	JCYM	1 375 524	1 466 823	1 532 084	1 686 134	1 698 001	1 748 258	1 786 623	1 641 452	1 492 365	1 629 744	1 657 558
1 000 c.c. and under	GKAB	98 034	98 178	95 198	108 645	119 894	112 044	113 204	96 043	93 695	79 545	23 985
Over 1 000 c.c. but not over 1 600 c.c.	GKAD	709 615	729 397	814 873	845 084	829 079	814 595	776 111	676 438	632 747	711 553	750 840
Over 1 600 c.c. but not over 2 800 c.c.	GKAF	515 487	573 357	528 444	635 861	653 147	720 556	758 478	723 294	634 573	720 067	740 486
Over 2 800 c.c.	GKAH	52 388	65 891	93 569	96 544	95 881	101 063	138 830	145 677	131 350	118 579	142 247
Commercial vehicles: total	JCYG	193 467	227 815	233 001	238 314	237 706	227 379	185 905	172 442	192 873	191 267	188 871
Of which: Light commercial vehicles	GKDH	171 141	197 285	199 346	205 372	210 942	203 629	162 176	145 655	169 705	168 311	166 359
Trucks: Under 7.5 tonnes	GKDJ	4 755	8 154	9 523	8 913	6 254	5 006	4 107	5 160	5 000	4 600	4 151
Over 7.5 tonnes	GKDL	8 269	10 016	11 727	10 128	7 932	7 002	6 443	6 849	7 359	7 357	7 779
Motive units for articulated vehicles	GKCV	2 283	2 794	3 476	2 631	2 574	2 492	2 739	2 673	2 539	1 795	2 095
Buses, coaches and mini buses	GKDN	7 019	9 566	8 939	11 270	10 004	9 250	10 440	12 105	8 270	9 204	8 487

1 See chapter text. Figures for motor vehicles relate to periods of 52 weeks (53 weeks in 1993).

Source: Office for National Statistics: 01633 812620

22.26 Alcoholic drink[1]
United Kingdom

			1993	1994	1995	1996	1997	1998	1999	2000	2001	2002	2003
Spirits[2] Production	KMEA	Thousand hectolitres of alcohol	3 974	4 106	4 507	4 868	5 297	5 145	4 705	4 210	4 368	4 508	4 553
Released for home consumption Home produced whisky	KMEE	"	374	383	310	321	312	289	323	314	321	321	318
Spirit-based Ready-to-drink[3]	SNET	"	..	..	..	..	..	..	..	..	..	57	124
Imported and other	KMEG	"	504	531	481	495	533	505	596	615	647	737	744
Total	KMEH	"	878	914	791	815	845	794	919	929	968	1 115	1 187
Beer[4] Production	BFNK	Thousand hectolitres "	56 746	58 333	56 800	58 072	59 139	56 652	57 854	55 279	56 802	56 672	58 014
Released for home consumption	BAYL	"	59 177	60 575	59 129	59 894	61 114	58 835	58 917	57 007	58 234	59 384	60 301
Production	JYXJ	Thousand hectolitres of pure alcohol	..	2 345	2 298	2 360	2 406	2 333	2 364	2 299	2 358	2 352	2 414
Released for home consumption	JYXK		..	2 453	2 410	2 448	2 504	2 439	2 428	2 382	2 429	2 473	2 515
Wine of fresh grapes Released for home consumption Fortified	KMEM	Thousand hectolitres	335	329	330	331	323	370	316	289	287	325	296
Still table	KMEN	"	6 471	6 759	6 576	6 995	7 653	7 979	8 391	8 864	9 534	10 319	10 647
Sparkling	KMEO	"	296	297	315	358	382	416	576	543	515	578	640
Total	KMEP	"	7 102	7 385	7 221	7 684	8 358	8 765	9 284	9 696	10 336	11 222	11 584
Made-wine Released for home consumption Other than coolers	KMEQ	"	505	470	516	513	485	406	416	431	364	367	339
Coolers[3]	KJDD	"	485	549	903	1 781	1 153	1 244	1 802	2 800	3 712	1 606	423
Cider and perry Released for home consumption	KMER	"	4 496	4 811	5 575	5 656	5 513	5 548	6 022	6 006	5 911	5 939	5 876

1 See chapter text.
2 Potable spirits distilled.
3 Made wine with alcoholic strength 1.2% to 5.5%. Includes alcoholic lemonade of appropriate strength and similar products. From 28 April 2002, duty on spirit-based "coolers" is charged at the same rate as spirits per litre of alcohol. Coolers for calendar year 2002 includes only wine based "coolers".

4 A new system was introduced for beer duty in June 1993. The figures in this table include adjustments to data prior to this date to bring them into line with current data.

Source: HM Customs and Excise: 020 7865 5323

22.27 Tobacco products: released for home consumption[1]
United Kingdom

			1993[2]	1994	1995	1996	1997	1998	1999	2000	2001	2002	2003
Cigarettes:		Thousand million											
Home produced	KMFA	"	85.8	82.4	70.8	73.8	71.1	67.8	28.2	49.3	47.7	49.6	49.1
Imported	KMFB	"	9.5	10.2	9.5	9.5	9.9	7.5	6.0	7.3	6.8	6.5	4.9
Total	KMFC	"	95.2	92.6	80.3	83.3	81.0	75.3	34.2	56.6	54.5	56.1	54.0
Cigars:		Million kg											
Home produced	KMFD	"	1.7	1.6	1.5	1.4	1.3	1.2	0.9	1.0	0.9	0.9	0.8
Imported	KMFE	"	0.1	0.1	0.1	0.1	0.1	0.1	0.1	0.1	0.1	0.1	0.1
Total	KMFF	"	1.8	1.7	1.6	1.5	1.4	1.3	1.0	1.1	1.0	1.0	0.9
Hand-rolling tobacco:													
Home produced	KMFG	"	3.5	3.0	2.4	2.1	1.8	1.7	2.0	2.1	2.8	2.8	2.9
Imported	KMFH	"	0.1	0.1	0.1	0.1	0.1	0.1	–	–	–	–	–
Total	KMFI	"	3.6	3.2	2.6	2.3	1.9	1.8	2.0	2.2	2.8	2.8	2.9
Other smoking and chewing tobacco:													
Home produced	KMFJ	"	1.8	1.5	1.3	1.2	1.1	1.0	0.6	0.7	0.7	0.6	0.5
Imported	KMFK	"	0.1	0.1	0.1	0.1	0.1	0.1	0.1	0.1	0.1	0.1	0.1
Total	KMFL	"	1.9	1.6	1.4	1.3	1.2	1.1	0.7	0.8	0.8	0.7	0.6

1 See chapter text.
2 1993 contained two Budgets, in March and November.

Source: HM Customs and Excise: 020 7865 5323

Banking, insurance etc

Chapter 23

Banking, insurance etc

Other banks' balance sheet

(Table 23.3)

The implementation of the review of banking statistics at end-September 1997 has resulted in several changes to this table:

(a)   The table now includes the business of all monthly and quarterly reporting banks in the UK; it formerly covered only the business of monthly reporting institutions.

(b)   The Channel Islands and Isle of Man are no longer treated as part of the UK for statistical purposes. Banking institutions in the Channel Islands and Isle of Man no longer have the option of being within the UK banking sector and their business, along with the business of offshore island branches of UK mainland banks, is now excluded from the figures within this table. Additionally, the business of the UK banking sector with offshore island residents and entities has been reclassified from UK residents to non-residents.

(c)   The table now contains more comprehensive detail of business with building societies. This business was previously included indistinguishably within the UK private sector elements of the table.

(d)   The aggregate balance sheet of the banking sector has been inflated because it is now reported on an accrual basis rather than a cash basis (accrued amounts payable/receivable are shown under liabilities and assets respectively). Additionally, acceptances have been brought onto the balance sheet and are shown under both liabilities and assets.

With effect from 1998, the balance sheet of the Banking Department of the Bank of England is excluded from this table, and other banks' business with the Issue Department is reclassified from 'UK public sector' to 'UK banks'.

Data for 1999 reflect the acquisition of Birmingham Midshires Building Society by Halifax during that year.

Data for end-2000 reflect the entry of Bradford and Bingley plc to the banking sector during the year. Data for end-2000 also reflect the new reporting during the year of agency business as a result of collateral management via repos and reverse repos.

Bank lending to, and bank deposits from, UK residents

(Tables 23.4 and 23.5)

These are series of statistics based on the Standard Industrial Classification 1992.

Table 22.4 comprises loans, advances (including under reverse repos), finance leasing, acceptances, facilities and holdings of sterling and euro commercial paper. It includes lending under the Department of Trade and Industry special scheme for domestic shipbuilding. Holdings of investments and bills and adjustments for transit items are not included.

Table 22.5 includes borrowing under sale and repurchase agreements (repro). Adjustments for transit items are not included.

Figures for both tables are supplied by monthly reporting banks and grossed to cover quarterly reporters. They exclude lending to building societies and to residents of the Channel Islands and Isle of Man.

Building societies

(Table 23.13)

Building society figures are sourced from societies' annual returns and for each year relate to accounting years ending on dates between 1 February and 31 January of the following year. Figures are society-only as opposed to group consolidated.

Consumer credit

(Table 23.14)

Figures for net lending refer to changes in amounts outstanding adjusted to remove distortions caused by revaluations of debt outstanding, such as write-offs. Lending by retailers refers to self-financed credit advanced by food retailers, clothing retailers, household goods retailers, mixed business retailers (other than co-operative societies) and general mail order houses. Class 3 loans are advanced under the terms of the Building Societies' Act 1986. Loans on personal accounts exclude loans for house purchase and bridging finance.

Data relating to the narrower coverage cover finance houses and other specialist credit grantors, bank credit cards (operated under the VISA and Mastercard systems), and secured loans by building societies. A high proportion of credit advanced in certain types of agreement, notably on credit cards, is repaid within a month. This reflects use of such agreements as a method of payment rather than a way of obtaining credit.

23.1 Bank of England
At December

£ million

		1993	1994	1995	1996	1997	1998	1999	2000	2001	2002	2003
Issue Department												
Liabilities:												
Notes in circulation	AEFA	18 218	20 055	21 262	22 407	23 715	24 573	27 232	29 412	32 226	33 639	35 524
Notes in Banking Department	AEFB	12	5	7	12	5	7	8	8	4	1	6
Assets:												
Government securities[1]	AEFC	6 816	11 468	14 552	16 524	16 416	15 826	17 264	13 498	13 996	13 841	13 573
Other securities[2]	AEFD	11 414	8 592	6 717	5 896	7 304	8 754	9 976	15 921	18 234	19 799	21 957
Banking Department												
Liabilities:												
Public deposits[3]	AEFF	6 205	938	1 159	1 001	1 192	237	195	391	437	414	542
Bankers' deposits[4]	AEFH	1 700	1 855	2 001	2 021	2 800	1 388	1 357	1 520	2 354	1 722	2 320
Reserves and other accounts[5]	AEFI	3 175	3 385	3 941	3 193	3 214	5 163	50 506	8 471	9 834	12 215	15 190
Total[6]	AEFE	11 095	6 192	7 114	6 229	7 221	6 802	52 072	10 397	12 639	14 366	18 065
Assets:												
Government securities	AEFJ	1 174	1 050	1 090	1 232	1 373	1 352	1 444	1 504	1 795	1 510	1 672
Advances and other accounts	AEFK	9 411	4 696	5 499	2 339	5 388	3 302	46 895	6 533	6 413	6 938	9 173
Premises, equipment and other securities[5]	AEFL	498	441	518	2 646	455	2 141	3 724	2 352	4 428	5 917	7 214
Notes and coin	AEFM	12	5	7	12	5	7	8	8	4	1	6
Total	KCYT	11 095	6 192	7 114	6 229	7 221	6 802	52 071	10 397	12 640	14 366	18 065

1 Including the historic liability of the Treasury of £11 million until 1993 (repaid on 27 July 1994).
2 Including gilt and Treasury bill repurchase agreements from 1994 (previously in "Government securities").
3 Excluding local government and public corporations' deposits which are included under Reserves and other accounts.
4 These consist of operational deposits held mainly by the clearing banks and non-operational cash ratio deposits for which institutions authorised under the Financial Services and Markets Act, deposit - taking UK branches of "European Authorised Institutions" and (from 1998) building societies are liable.
5 Large increases from 1999 arise from the Bank of England's role in TARGET, as a result of which other European central banks may hold substantial credit balances or overdrafts with the Bank.
6 The only liability not shown separately is the Bank's capital (held by the Treasury) which has been constant at £14.6 million.

Source: Bank of England: 020 7601 3236

23.2 Value of inter-bank clearings[1]
United Kingdom

£ billion

		1993	1994	1995	1996	1997	1998	1999	2000	2001	2002	2003
Bulk paper clearings												
Cheque (formerly general)	KCYY	1 065	1 075	1 097	1 161	1 200	1 214	1 226	1 214	1 210	1 178	1 141
Credit (formerly credit clearing)	KCYZ	97	93	92	94	94	92	88	82	80	75	69
High-value clearings												
Town	KCZA	1 069	681	59	–	–	–	–	–	–	–	–
CHAPS Sterling only	KCZB	23 545	25 053	26 719	28 881	36 032	41 501	44 704	49 146	52 913	51 896	51 613
Electronic clearing (BACS)	KCZC	836	941	1 055	1 250	1 432	1 602	1 761	1 922	2 166	2 382	2 574

1 Excludes inter-branch clearings and clearings in Scotland and Northern Ireland.

Source: Association for Payment Clearing Services (APACS): 020 7711 6323

23.3 Other banks' balance sheet[1]

£ million

		1994	1995	1996	1997[2]	1998[3]	1999[4]	2000[5,6]	2001	2002	2003
Sterling liabilities											
Notes outstanding & cash loaded cards	TBFA	2 456	2 576	2 717	2 832	2 929	3 311	3 359	3 866	3 957	4 207
Sight deposits[7]											
UK banks	TBFB	16 222	16 983	20 138	44 573	37 839	33 463	40 054	59 573	101 905	99 208
UK building societies	TBFC	..	..	..	950	1 277	841	1 168	1 466	2 403	1 736
UK public sector[8]	TBFD	3 301	3 824	3 641	3 781	3 003	3 450	3 403	4 283	3 997	5 679
Other UK residents	TBFE	164 451	192 297	211 179	271 233	295 068	325 392	372 725	415 180	457 077	502 359
Non-residents	TBFF	16 425	18 690	17 707	37 730	43 528	44 581	55 489	55 837	57 218	65 157
Time deposits											
UK banks	TBFG	75 629	90 044	95 798	99 782	111 970	112 530	110 955	125 261	141 401	164 433
UK building societies	TBFH	–	–	–	5 682	4 361	4 253	4 688	4 856	4 487	3 643
UK public sector[8]	TBFI	4 908	7 896	6 087	9 059	9 748	8 064	8 241	8 306	8 936	8 934
Other UK residents	TBFJ	166 505	190 707	210 045	284 629	295 924	282 789	301 007	302 715	306 453	313 244
of which TESSAs	TBFK	7 517	10 314	9 389	20 394	21 568	22 868	24 265	9 752	5 235	1 832
of which SAYE	TBFL	–	–	–	2 254	2 604	2 840	2 726	2 439	2 367	2 226
of which cash ISAs	TFDG	..	..	..	..	..	5 210	13 684	31 298	42 269	52 118
Non-residents	TBFM	62 905	68 274	63 995	91 040	97 953	116 967	134 844	150 964	151 304	166 449
Acceptances granted	TBFN	–	–	–	19 952	16 658	12 854	10 012	10 627	9 954	2 856
Liabilities under sale and repurchase agreements											
of which British govt. securities	TBFU	–	–	22 668	47 297	55 561	56 145	83 819	83 330	78 155	114 468
UK banks[8,9]	TBFP	–	–	13 718	29 089	43 314	48 213	56 408	60 551	52 079	95 922
UK building societies	TBFQ	..	..	..	20	32	200	36	–	107	170
UK public sector[8,9]	TBFR	–	–	2 279	6 044	–	–	14 351	5 127	1 402	1 521
Other UK residents	TBFS	–	–	7 703	18 114	20 918	17 165	22 974	25 732	19 759	19 906
Non-residents	TBFT	–	–	683	5 664	5 469	5 542	9 849	8 643	19 072	18 475
CDs and other short-term paper issued	TBFV	63 880	70 277	96 390	119 266	138 248	158 826	151 153	153 768	157 354	148 606
Total sterling deposits	TBFW	574 224	658 993	749 364	1 046 609	1 125 311	1 175 130	1 297 356	1 392 890	1 494 908	1 618 298
Sterling items in suspense and transmission	TBFX	8 412	10 423	12 120	16 054	15 714	17 307	15 261	16 702	13 318	18 371
Net derivatives	TBFY	..	..	..	8 186	8 342	8 324	10 992	4 029	2 491	−10 672
Accrued amounts payable	TBFZ	..	..	..	20 713	24 632	22 122	23 726	22 836	21 541	22 624
Sterling capital and other internal funds	TBGA	78 775	82 160	90 464	103 462	103 868	100 575	133 436	148 294	173 320	204 295
Total sterling liabilities	TBGB	663 868	754 152	854 666	1 197 856	1 280 796	1 326 769	1 484 130	1 588 618	1 709 535	1 857 123
Foreign currency liabilities											
Sight and time deposits											
UK banks[10]	TBGC	105 813	104 769	91 314	90 858	77 128	77 684	99 447	106 368	111 536	139 018
UK building societies	TBGD	..	..	..	1 027	639	681	233	279	373	550
UK public sector[8]	TBGE	..	..	..	226	149	126	1 808	926	833	865
Other UK residents	TBGF	..	..	..	64 188	60 513	65 203	79 627	95 666	81 590	89 034
Non-residents	TBGG	618 769	696 380	605 439	716 573	766 934	736 792	914 888	1 001 321	997 398	1 055 183
Acceptances granted	TBGH	..	..	..	743	729	619	689	638	754	751
Sale and repurchase agreements											
UK banks	TBGJ	–	–	17 114	21 311	30 669	25 170	38 901	54 499	90 407	224 743
UK building societies	TBGK	..	..	..	–	–	–	–	–	–	–
UK public sector	TBGL	..	..	..	22	–	–	468	1	71	844
Other UK residents	TBGM	..	..	..	25 716	26 742	21 997	35 145	52 438	54 463	73 477
Non-residents	TBGN	–	–	61 307	100 936	118 909	115 357	139 656	154 976	211 276	289 674
CDs and other short-term paper issued	TBGO	67 869	89 032	101 005	131 620	124 151	151 009	199 510	224 225	234 731	255 590
Total foreign currency deposits	TBGP	851 856	972 832	975 619	1 153 220	1 206 562	1 194 637	1 510 373	1 691 336	1 783 432	2 129 730
Items in suspense and transmission	TBGQ	14 779	13 881	21 272	35 713	25 026	30 548	46 678	47 363	38 355	60 465
Net derivatives	TBGR	..	..	..	8 654	2 656	3 704	−4 472	−3 854	5 816	14 774
Accrued amounts payable	TBGS	..	..	..	21 996	25 184	18 080	18 568	17 756	16 312	15 708
Capital and other internal funds	TBGT	21 081	26 430	25 535	31 676	46 952	69 798	89 359	85 489	87 047	81 778
Total foreign currency liabilities	TBGU	887 716	1 013 143	1 022 426	1 251 258	1 306 380	1 316 767	1 660 506	1 838 090	1 930 961	2 302 455
Total liabilities	TBGV	1 551 584	1 767 295	1 877 092	2 449 114	2 587 177	2 643 536	3 144 636	3 426 708	3 640 497	4 159 579

23.3 Other banks' balance sheet[1]

continued

£ million

		1994	1995	1996	1997[2]	1998[3]	1999[4]	2000[5,6]	2001	2002	2003
Sterling assets											
Notes and coins	TBGW	4 983	5 357	4 812	5 225	6 699	9 047	8 007	6 566	6 621	7 464
With UK central bank											
Cash ratio deposits	TBGX	1 490	1 682	1 888	2 566	1 068	1 141	1 275	1 386	1 495	1 609
Other	TBGY	103	113	533	216	383	676	117	143	249	54
Market loans											
UK banks[7]	TBGZ	88 582	103 006	109 500	139 996	148 138	144 537	149 174	181 350	237 771	263 004
UK bank CDs	TBHB	23 632	26 767	36 922	62 584	65 510	75 071	65 156	68 868	68 728	55 053
UK bank commercial paper	TBHC	..	..	..	29	130	208	8	52	62	5
UK building societies CDs etc and deposits	TBHD	5 358	4 387	4 891	4 242	4 505	5 093	4 748	3 933	4 293	7 201
Non-residents	TBHE	44 582	47 470	50 585	79 368	84 162	74 403	94 381	102 404	89 848	109 665
Acceptances granted											
UK building societies	TBHF	..	..	..	–	–	–	–	–	–	–
UK public sector[8]	TBHG	..	..	..	–	–	–	–	–	–	–
Other UK residents	TBHH	..	..	..	18 573	15 394	11 933	9 496	9 992	9 111	2 777
Non-residents	TBHI	..	..	..	1 379	1 264	920	516	635	842	79
Bills											
Treasury bills	TBHJ	4 166	10 404	1 652	554	779	2 749	1 612	8 474	18 752	18 211
UK bank bills	TBHA	..	..	..	18 221	14 110	11 426	7 011	8 098	8 491	1 319
UK building societies	TBHK	..	..	..	–	–	–	–	–	–	–
Other UK	TBHL	..	..	..	1 116	1 221	818	1 202	1 601	485	1 013
Non-residents	TBHM	..	..	..	309	207	206	287	744	979	733
Claims under sale and repurchase agreements											
of which British govt. securities	TBHT	–	–	26 030	47 158	56 639	64 943	86 362	84 068	77 460	114 091
UK banks	TBHO	–	–	16 853	27 611	41 969	39 667	46 088	46 585	37 197	77 691
UK building societies	TBHP	..	..	..	345	134	91	116	327	86	114
UK public sector	TBHQ	..	..	..	–	–	–	9 067	4 692	5 159	5 231
Other UK residents	TBHR	..	..	..	21 283	23 803	30 338	35 058	36 222	31 363	35 885
Non-residents	TBHS	..	..	..	6 873	5 907	6 310	7 266	7 010	14 271	12 981
Advances											
UK public sector	TBHU	3 526	3 549	2 912	3 872	3 403	2 567	2 746	2 442	3 783	4 414
Other UK residents[11]	TBHV	380 615	426 936	460 107	636 162	672 812	732 649	823 787	891 790	986 835	1 062 650
Non-residents	TBHW	12 163	13 403	16 759	21 102	21 039	23 364	24 494	29 483	31 380	34 603
Banking dept. lending to central govt. (net)	TBNU	–947	–1 801	948	–2 741	–	–	–	–	–	–
Investments											
British government stocks	TBHX	14 366	17 135	19 910	23 078	14 714	9 243	2 867	499	–3 545	–8 525
Other public sector	TBHY	303	409	303	283	215	124	88	116	158	385
UK banks[12]	TBHZ	..	..	..	11 922	13 415	13 584	22 935	23 965	23 542	34 971
UK building societies	TBIA	4 769	4 639	4 898	2 875	2 223	2 506	2 251	2 099	1 835	1 700
Other UK residents[13]	TBIB	..	..	..	45 134	48 781	57 391	77 647	82 013	76 773	84 813
Non-residents	TBIC	..	..	..	9 343	11 834	13 775	20 572	23 462	22 821	22 505
Items in suspense and collection	TBID	16 477	17 613	19 830	23 526	23 888	23 441	21 982	24 024	19 577	22 434
Accrued amounts receivable	TBIE	..	..	..	15 003	17 352	15 173	15 919	13 528	15 486	17 204
Other assets	TBIF	10 242	10 525	10 267	12 218	12 593	13 036	12 654	12 876	12 685	11 955
Total sterling assets[14]	TBIG	668 960	755 937	852 075	1 192 264	1 257 652	1 321 486	1 468 527	1 595 380	1 727 136	1 889 200

23.3 Other banks' balance sheet[1]

continued

£ million

		1994	1995	1996	1997[2]	1998[3]	1999[4]	2000[5,6]	2001	2002	2003
Foreign currency assets											
Market loans and advances											
UK banks[10]	TBIH	99 885	98 305	83 920	90 367	72 263	74 250	93 269	104 107	114 809	137 417
UK banks' CDs etc	TBII	7 226	9 345	7 793	13 633	11 065	14 364	13 171	13 298	10 128	13 162
UK building societies CDs etc. and deposits	TBIJ				83	259	451	173	354	357	591
UK public sector[8]	TBIK	28	38	36	25	45	20	30	13	83	91
Other UK residents	TBIL	76 538	102 061	72 213	76 356	83 968	88 847	107 707	118 106	117 669	134 894
Non-residents	TBIM	534 589	604 783	505 953	598 541	616 832	599 146	743 781	783 057	783 168	779 983
Claims under sale and repurchase agreement											
UK banks	TBIO	–	–	21 189	24 184	31 900	28 008	41 801	61 188	91 488	225 027
UK building societies	TBIP	..	..	..	–	–	–	–	–	–	–
UK public sector[8]	TBIQ	..	..	..	22	–	–	737	23	486	1 420
Other UK residents	TBIR	..	..	..	55 945	39 764	33 027	57 876	73 237	86 866	100 817
Non-residents	TBIS	–	–	75 376	121 101	147 562	146 756	199 990	219 449	256 663	382 672
Acceptances granted	TBIT	..	..	..	743	729	619	689	638	754	751
Bills	TBIU	10 490	14 429	9 660	12 728	15 239	19 508	21 878	25 399	20 803	31 429
Investments											
British government stocks	TBIV	..	..	..	3 453	4 755	4 473	3 518	890	226	19
Other public sector	TBIW	..	..	..	–	–	–	–	4	18	7
UK banks	TBIX	..	..	..	2 850	4 310	8 607	11 706	10 633	10 298	11 688
UK building societies	TBIY	997	728	701	414	526	631	939	850	1 170	1 570
Other UK residents	TBIZ	..	..	..	4 055	4 584	5 679	12 298	18 129	20 130	21 846
Non-residents	TBJA	128 507	154 398	161 045	186 288	234 563	243 147	297 404	324 073	326 035	334 371
Items in suspense and collection	TBJB	15 572	17 598	21 664	40 175	30 229	29 706	44 885	55 026	44 037	60 804
Accrued amounts receivable	TBJC	..	..	..	23 673	27 821	20 163	21 279	18 969	19 434	18 129
Other assets	TBJD	1 868	1 817	1 809	2 215	3 111	4 648	2 978	3 880	8 735	13 683
Total foreign currency assets[15]	TBJE	882 624	1 011 358	1 025 017	1 256 850	1 329 525	1 322 050	1 676 109	1 831 322	1 913 355	2 270 372
Total assets	TBJF	1 551 584	1 767 295	1 877 092	2 449 114	2 587 177	2 643 536	3 144 636	3 426 702	3 640 491	4 159 572
Holdings of own sterling acceptances	TBJG	18 274	18 721	21 521	1 823	2 137	1 725	1 231	916	1 220	411
Holdings of own FC acceptances	TBJH	640	1 153	1 031	291	170	150	135	118	58	104
Eligible banks' total sterling acceptances	TBJI	18 168	18 476	21 220	21 366	18 722	14 523	10 597	11 320	10 805	3 035
Eligible liabilities	TBJJ	440 032	507 279	564 648	766 683	807 803	849 289	952 062	1 012 194	1 087 877	1 163 917

1 The implementation of the review of banking at end-September 1997 has resulted in several changes to this table. Details are given in the chapter text.

2 Data for 1997 reflect the entry of Northern Rock plc to the banking sector during the year.

3 With effect from 1998 the balance sheet of the Banking Department of the Bank of England is excluded from these data.

4 Data for 1999 reflect the acquisition of Birmingham Midshires Building Society by Halifax during that year.

5 Data for 2000 reflect the entry of Bradford & Bingley plc to the banking sector during the year.

6 Data for 2000 reflect the new reporting during the year of agency business as a result of collateral management via repos and reverse repos.

7 Sterling sight deposits from UK banks and sterling market loans to UK banks in 2003 were depressed by £19 bn following the consolidation of two banks balance sheets.

8 From 2000 the UK public sector series reflects assumption by the Debt Management Office (an executive agency of HM Treasury) of responsibility for government cash management.

9 There is a break in this series in 1998 as a result of the reclassification of the Issue Department of the Bank of England from UK public sector to UK banks.

10 Foreign currency sight and time deposits from UK banks and foreign currency market loans and advances to UK banks in 2001 and 2003 were each depressed by £14.5 bn and £0.5 bn respectively as a result of positions being consolidated out on the merger of two banks.

11 During 2000, 2001, 2002 and 2003 sterling advances to other UK residents were reduced by £10.3 bn, £12.9 bn, £16.2 bn and £29.1bn respectively as a result of securitisations and other loan transfers to non-banks or non- residents.

12 Sterling investments in UK banks in 2000 were boosted by Barclay's £5.8 bn investment in Woolwich.

13 Sterling investments in other UK residents in 2000 were boosted by Lloyds TSB's £5.8 bn investment in Scottish Widows Group.

14 Changes in the reporting populations in 1998, 1999, 2000, 2001 and 2003 account for a net decrease of £7.3 bn, £11.3 bn £0.8 bn, £0.7bn and £0.2bn respectively in sterling assets outstanding.

15 Changes in the reporting populations in 1998, 1999, 2000, 2001 and 2003 account for a net decrease of £4.6 bn, £6.6 bn, £0.2 bn, £0.2bn and £0.2bn of foreign currency assets outstanding.

Source: Bank of England: 020 7601 3236

23.4 Industrial analysis of bank lending to UK residents[1]
Not seasonally adjusted

£ million

	UK residents		Agriculture, hunting and forestry	Fishing	Mining & quarrying	Manufacturing			
	Total	of which sterling				Total	Food, beverages & tobacco	Textiles & leather	Pulp, paper, publishing & printing

Amounts outstanding (sterling & other currencies)

Loans & advances (including under repo & sterling commercial paper)

	TBOA	TBOB	TBOC	TBOD	TBOE	TBOF	TBOG	TBOH	TBOI
2002	1 232 712	1 027 315	7 838	441	3 391	50 599	10 378	1 883	5 832
2003	1 346 730	1 108 980	8 060	446	2 763	42 553	8 930	1 639	5 415

Acceptances

	TBQA	TBQB	TBQC	TBQD	TBQE	TBQF	TBQG	TBQH	TBQI
2002	4 737	4 459	9	–	91	1 109	397	59	18
2003	2 004	1 696	–	–	83	502	92	43	6

Total

	TBSA		TBSC	TBSD	TBSE	TBSF	TBSG	TBSH	TBSI
2002	1 237 449		7 847	441	3 482	51 708	10 775	1 942	5 850
2003	1 348 734		8 060	446	2 846	43 054	9 023	1 681	5 421

of which in sterling

	TBUA		TBUC	TBUD	TBUE	TBUF	TBUG	TBUH	TBUI
2002	1 031 774		7 760	414	1 701	34 231	7 479	1 507	4 324
2003	1 110 676		7 967	438	1 638	29 850	7 135	1 144	4 276

Facilities granted

	TCAA		TCAC	TCAD	TCAE	TCAF	TCAG	TCAH	TCAI
2002	1 507 605		9 996	519	10 798	96 946	23 071	2 846	11 553
2003	1 648 333		10 672	525	9 573	84 989	20 904	2 529	11 284

of which in sterling

	TCCA		TCCC	TCCD	TCCE	TCCF	TCCG	TCCH	TCCI
2002	1 230 620		9 886	485	2 900	57 848	12 105	2 298	7 367
2003	1 346 258		10 525	516	2 464	52 608	12 682	1 902	7 206

	Manufacturing					Electricity, gas and water supply		
	Chemicals, man-made fibres, rubber & plastics	Non-metallic mineral products & metals	Machinery, equipment & transport equipment	Electrical, medical & optical equipment	Other manufacturing	Electricity, gas & heated water	Cold water purification & supply	Construction

Amounts outstanding (sterling & other currencies)

Loans & advances (including under repo & sterling commercial paper)

	TBOJ	TBOK	TBOL	TBOM	TBON	TBOO	TBOP	TBOQ
2002	6 007	6 446	7 811	6 674	5 568	6 384	1 696	14 701
2003	5 113	5 323	6 681	4 388	5 064	4 262	1 835	15 430

Acceptances

	TBQJ	TBQK	TBQL	TBQM	TBQN	TBQO	TBQP	TBQQ
2002	104	98	239	106	87	315	10	128
2003	34	44	86	132	64	25	–	39

Total

	TBSJ	TBSK	TBSL	TBSM	TBSN	TBSO	TBSP	TBSQ
2002	6 112	6 544	8 050	6 780	5 656	6 699	1 706	14 829
2003	5 147	5 367	6 767	4 519	5 129	4 288	1 835	15 469

of which in sterling

	TBUJ	TBUK	TBUL	TBUM	TBUN	TBUO	TBUP	TBUQ
2002	4 057	4 230	4 720	3 682	4 233	5 733	1 582	14 287
2003	3 346	3 535	3 990	2 646	3 778	3 594	1 665	14 893

Facilities granted

	TCAJ	TCAK	TCAL	TCAM	TCAN	TCAO	TCAP	TCAQ
2002	13 090	11 094	15 201	11 065	9 025	14 308	5 325	22 821
2003	11 620	9 876	13 079	7 293	8 403	12 250	5 551	25 148

of which in sterling

	TCCJ	TCCK	TCCL	TCCM	TCCN	TCCO	TCCP	TCCQ
2002	7 508	7 000	9 062	6 261	6 246	10 146	4 630	21 302
2003	6 581	6 340	7 910	4 292	5 696	8 119	4 908	23 624

23.4 Industrial analysis of bank lending to UK residents[1]
Not seasonally adjusted

£ million

	Wholesale and retail trade						Real estate, renting, computer and other business activities		
	Total	Sale & repair of motor vehicles & fuel	Other wholesale trade	Other retail trade & repair	Hotels and restaurants	Transport, storage & communication	Total	Development, buying, selling, renting of real estate	Renting of machinery & equipment

Amounts outstanding (sterling & other currencies)

Loans & advances (including under repo & sterling commercial paper)

	TBOR	TBOS	TBOT	TBOU	TBOV	TBOW	TBOX	TBOY	TBPA
2002	36 306	9 018	11 906	15 382	17 839	30 572	115 622	86 380	7 175
2003	34 084	8 560	11 313	14 211	20 283	26 641	132 767	100 106	7 454

Acceptances

	TBQR	TBQS	TBQT	TBQU	TBQV	TBQW	TBQX	TBQY	TBRA
2002	900	16	646	238	18	42	518	373	35
2003	475	19	385	70	1	1	284	251	15

Total

	TBSR	TBSS	TBST	TBSU	TBSV	TBSW	TBSX	TBSY	TBTA
2002	37 207	9 035	12 552	15 620	17 857	30 614	116 140	86 754	7 209
2003	34 559	8 579	11 698	14 281	20 284	26 642	133 051	100 357	7 468

of which in sterling

	TBUR	TBUS	TBUT	TBUU	TBUV	TBUW	TBUX	TBUY	TBVA
2002	30 541	8 693	8 440	13 408	16 078	25 644	111 296	85 627	6 190
2003	29 565	8 206	8 099	13 260	18 980	22 246	127 761	98 958	6 437

Facilities granted

	TCAR	TCAS	TCAT	TCAU	TCAV	TCAW	TCAX	TCAY	TCBA
2002	59 236	12 424	19 873	26 939	22 804	52 215	151 747	109 960	8 298
2003	56 799	11 144	18 386	27 269	25 601	47 501	170 777	125 194	8 328

of which in sterling

	TCCR	TCCS	TCCT	TCCU	TCCV	TCCW	TCCX	TCCY	TCDA
2002	46 880	11 259	13 963	21 658	20 037	35 961	143 159	107 905	7 024
2003	47 192	10 369	13 493	23 331	23 245	34 370	161 381	122 667	7 143

	Real estate, renting, computer and other business activities					Recreational, personal & community service activities		Financial intermediation (excl. insurance & pension funds)	
	Computer & related activities	Legal, accountancy, consultancy & other business activities	Public administration & defence	Education	Health & social work	Recreational, cultural & sporting activities	Personal & community services activities	Total	Financial leasing corporations

Amounts outstanding (sterling & other currencies)

Loans & advances (including under repo & sterling commercial paper)

	TBPB	TBPC	TBPD	TBPE	TBPF	TBPH	TBPG	TBPI	TBPJ
2002	3 632	18 435	9 179	4 083	8 020	8 420	4 472	290 269	37 887
2003	3 154	22 053	10 900	4 575	8 586	8 428	4 686	349 902	39 114

Acceptances

	TBRB	TBRC	TBRD	TBRE	TBRF	TBRH	TBRG	TBRI	TBRJ
2002	32	78	–	–	–	71	6	1 340	124
2003	3	16	–	–	–	30	5	358	8

Total

	TBTB	TBTC	TBTD	TBTE	TBTF	TBTH	TBTG	TBTI	TBTJ
2002	3 664	18 513	9 179	4 083	8 021	8 490	4 477	291 608	38 011
2003	3 157	22 069	10 900	4 575	8 587	8 459	4 691	350 261	39 122

of which in sterling

	TBVB	TBVC	TBVD	TBVE	TBVF	TBVH	TBVG	TBVI	TBVJ
2002	3 092	16 388	8 634	4 054	7 914	7 668	4 120	149 872	35 508
2003	2 514	19 852	9 399	4 508	8 517	7 914	4 232	168 180	35 336

Facilities granted

	TCBB	TCBC	TCBD	TCBE	TCBF	TCBH	TCBG	TCBI	TCBJ
2002	5 047	28 442	10 941	5 213	9 446	13 159	5 769	323 384	41 936
2003	4 591	32 663	13 091	6 045	10 186	13 851	6 560	385 021	43 111

of which in sterling

	TCDB	TCDC	TCDD	TCDE	TCDF	TCDH	TCDG	TCDI	TCDJ
2002	4 059	24 171	10 190	5 158	9 308	11 226	5 240	171 127	39 131
2003	3 599	27 972	11 394	5 953	9 999	11 981	5 981	193 709	38 982

Industrial analysis of bank lending to UK residents[1]
Not seasonally adjusted

£ million

Financial intermediation (excl. insurance & pension funds)

	Non-bank credit grantors, excl. credit unions	Credit unions	Factoring corporations	Mortgage & housing credit corporations	Investment & unit trusts excl. money market mutual funds	Money market mutual funds	Bank holding companies	Securities dealers (f)	Other financial intermediaries
Amounts outstanding (sterling & other currencies)									
Loans & advances (including under repo & sterling commercial paper)									
	TBPK	TBPL	TBPM	TBPN	TBPO	TBPP	TBPQ	TBPR	TBPS
2002	11 761	1	2 935	24 458	8 941	311	18 453	117 733	67 788
2003	15 262	2	3 209	33 667	8 897	1 317	21 354	167 183	59 897
Acceptances									
	TBRK	TBRL	TBRM	TBRN	TBRO	TBRP	TBRQ	TBRR	TBRS
2002	507	15	149	5	–	–	32	42	464
2003	78	–	79	–	3	–	–	–	190
Total									
	TBTK	TBTL	TBTM	TBTN	TBTO	TBTP	TBTQ	TBTR	TBTS
2002	12 269	17	3 085	24 463	8 941	311	18 485	117 775	68 252
2003	15 340	2	3 288	33 667	8 901	1 317	21 354	167 183	60 087
of which in sterling									
	TBVK	TBVL	TBVM	TBVN	TBVO	TBVP	TBVQ	TBVR	TBVS
2002	10 487	17	2 696	24 408	5 255	173	14 993	22 238	34 097
2003	13 589	1	2 744	33 234	4 587	430	16 340	27 279	34 641
Facilities granted									
	TCBK	TCBL	TCBM	TCBN	TCBO	TCBP	TCBQ	TCBR	TCBS
2002	13 513	30	3 289	26 257	20 423	338	18 738	122 169	76 691
2003	17 275	11	3 644	36 492	20 276	1 410	21 719	170 480	70 604
of which in sterling									
	TCDK	TCDL	TCDM	TCDN	TCDO	TCDP	TCDQ	TCDR	TCDS
2002	11 452	20	2 866	26 199	14 883	190	15 084	22 880	38 423
2003	15 187	10	3 060	36 055	14 762	433	16 550	28 406	40 264

	Activities auxiliary to financial intermediation			Individuals & individual trusts		
	Insurance companies & pension funds	Fund management activities	Other	Total	Lending secured on dwellings inc. bridging finance	Other loans & advances
Amounts outstanding (sterling & other currencies)						
Loans & advances (including under repo & sterling commercial paper)						
	TBPT	TBPU	TBPV	TBPW	TBPX	TBPY
2002	13 714	6 558	26 293	576 315	455 101	121 213
2003	17 746	10 248	21 719	620 815	497 458	123 358
Acceptances						
	TBRT	TBRU	TBRV			
2002	172	–	7			
2003	201	–	–			
Total						
	TBTT	TBTU	TBTV	TBTW	TBTX	TBTY
2002	13 886	6 558	26 300	576 315	455 101	121 213
2003	17 947	10 248	21 719	620 815	497 458	123 358
of which in sterling						
	TBVT	TBVU	TBVV	TBVW	TBVX	TBVY
2002	12 728	4 087	7 610	575 819	455 055	120 764
2003	16 594	4 177	8 302	620 255	497 389	122 866
Facilities granted						
	TCBT	TCBU	TCBV	TCBW	TCBX	TCBY
2002	24 660	8 653	27 787	631 881	489 062	142 819
2003	28 543	12 347	22 950	700 354	541 545	158 810
of which in sterling						
	TCDT	TCDU	TCDV	TCDW	TCDX	TCDY
2002	20 497	4 759	8 705	631 178	488 965	142 214
2003	24 423	5 110	9 186	699 570	541 422	158 148

1 See chapter text.

Source: Bank of England: 020 7601 3236

23.5 Industrial analysis of bank deposits from UK residents[1]

£ million

	Total from UK residents	Agriculture, hunting and forestry	Fishing	Mining & quarrying	Manufacturing Total	Food, beverages & tobacco	Textiles & leather	Pulp, paper, publishing & printing
Amounts outstanding (sterling & other currencies)								
Deposit liabilities (including under repos)								
	TDAA	TDAB	TDAC	TDAD	TDAE	TDAF	TDAG	TDAH
2002	934 618	3 403	134	2 869	32 330	3 075	1 126	3 721
2003	1 015 863	3 750	153	3 686	33 277	3 536	1 160	4 176
of which in sterling								
	TDCA	TDCB	TDCC	TDCD	TDCE	TDCF	TDCG	TDCH
2002	797 661	3 296	111	1 682	23 216	2 580	966	3 087
2003	851 642	3 702	129	2 154	23 351	2 835	964	3 003

	Manufacturing Chemicals, man-made fibres, rubber & plastics	Non-metallic mineral products & metals	Machinery, equipment & transport equipment	Electrical, medical & optical equipment	Other manufacturing	Electricity, gas and water supply Electricity, gas & heated water	Cold water purification & supply	Construction
Amounts outstanding (sterling & other currencies)								
Deposit liabilities (including under repos)								
	TDAI	TDAJ	TDAK	TDAL	TDAM	TDAN	TDAO	TDAP
2002	4 603	3 215	6 228	6 680	3 681	4 406	1 250	11 132
2003	4 169	3 281	6 245	7 122	3 589	3 428	2 175	11 750
of which in sterling								
	TDCI	TDCJ	TDCK	TDCL	TDCM	TDCN	TDCO	TDCP
2002	2 665	2 596	4 700	3 829	2 793	3 904	1 223	10 867
2003	2 772	2 540	4 689	3 656	2 891	3 082	2 152	11 525

	Wholesale and retail trade Total	Sale & repair of motor vehicles & fuel	Other wholesale trade	Other retail trade & repair	Hotels and restaurants	Transport, storage & communication	Real estate, renting, computer and other business activities Total	Development, buying, selling, renting of real estate	Renting of machinery & equipment
Amounts outstanding (sterling & other currencies)									
Deposit liabilities (including under repos)									
	TDAQ	TDAR	TDAS	TDAT	TDAU	TDAV	TDAW	TDAX	TDAY
2002	25 622	2 945	11 367	11 310	4 157	18 807	70 989	20 258	1 252
2003	27 262	2 917	11 577	12 768	4 552	19 539	76 731	22 656	1 195
of which in sterling									
	TDCQ	TDCR	TDCS	TDCT	TDCU	TDCV	TDCW	TDCX	TDCY
2002	22 035	2 849	8 470	10 716	4 071	15 646	66 115	19 914	1 185
2003	23 721	2 794	8 859	12 068	4 333	15 008	71 753	22 355	1 124

23.5 Industrial analysis of bank deposits from UK residents[1]

continued

£ million

	Real estate, renting, computer and other business activities					Recreational, personal & community service activities		Financial intermediation (excl. insurance & pension funds)	
	Computer & related activities	Legal, accountancy, consultancy & other business activities	Public administration & defence	Education	Health & social work	Recreational, cultural & sporting activities	Personal & community services activities	Total	Financial leasing corporations

Amounts outstanding (sterling & other currencies)

Deposit liabilities (including under repos)

	TDAZ	TDBA	TDBB	TDBC	TDBD	TDBF	TDBE	TDBG	TDBH
2002	6 559	42 920	13 829	5 294	7 672	8 272	10 847	159 081	3 570
2003	6 584	46 296	15 632	6 215	8 461	9 508	11 903	177 169	3 395

of which in sterling

	TDCZ	TDDA	TDDB	TDDC	TDDD	TDDF	TDDE	TDDG	TDDH
2002	5 595	39 421	12 980	5 159	7 567	7 648	10 552	83 586	2 687
2003	5 227	43 048	14 029	5 783	8 228	8 791	11 544	83 459	2 276

	Financial intermediation (excl. insurance & pension funds)								
	Non-bank credit grantors, excl. credit unions	Credit unions	Factoring corporations	Mortgage & housing credit corporations	Investment & unit trusts excl. money market mutual funds	Money market mutual funds	Bank holding companies	Securities dealers	Other financial intermediaries

Amounts outstanding (sterling & other currencies)

Deposit liabilities (including under repos)

	TDBI	TDBJ	TDBK	TDBL	TDBM	TDBN	TDBO	TDBP	TDBQ
2002	3 699	195	327	3 711	17 855	190	10 231	68 632	50 671
2003	3 157	263	394	6 157	14 377	192	7 590	83 982	57 660

of which in sterling

	TDDI	TDDJ	TDDK	TDDL	TDDM	TDDN	TDDO	TDDP	TDDQ
2002	3 146	195	228	3 513	13 351	142	9 043	18 177	33 103
2003	2 354	263	196	5 835	9 895	133	5 249	18 382	38 876

	Insurance companies & pension funds	Activities auxiliary to financial intermediation		Individuals & individual trusts
		Placed by fund managers	Other	

Amounts outstanding (sterling & other currencies)

Deposit liabilities (including under repos)

	TDBR	TDBS	TDBT	TDBU
2002	55 897	33 045	30 377	435 204
2003	53 396	34 455	36 286	476 535

of which in sterling

	TDDR	TDDS	TDDT	TDDU
2002	49 744	24 357	10 415	433 489
2003	47 254	22 566	14 350	474 726

1 See chapter text.

Source: Bank of England: 020 7601 3236

23.6 Public sector net cash requirement and other counterparts to changes in money stock during the year

Not seasonally adjusted

£ million

		1993	1994	1995	1996	1997	1998	1999	2000	2001	2002	2003
Public sector net cash requirement (surplus)	ABEN	43 134	39 376	35 438	24 695	11 928	−6 526	−1 516	−37 286	−2 781	18 250	38 905
Sales of public sector debt to M4 private sector	KHGZ	−30 566	−23 333	−21 635	−18 972	−16 074	1 603	−1 538	13 536	7 748	−9 193	−32 510
M4 lending[1]	AVBS	22 680	31 604	57 744	59 130	68 208	63 955	78 087	111 225	82 446	107 654	126 462
External and foreign currency finance of the public sector	KHJP	−10 782	623	−3 640	−10 884	−2 453	−4 717	6 198	3 616	3 875	2 486	−13 442
Other external and foreign currency flows[2]	AVBW	14 278	−8 176	−3 456	18 021	24 565	13 975	−44 743	7 074	−21 638	−24 960	−25 772
Net non-deposit liabilities (increase)	AVBX	−14 865	−14 537	−8 565	−12 653	−5 812	−8 165	−3 102	−30 944	−10 783	−25 295	−20 471
Money stock (M4)	AUZI	23 877	25 557	55 885	59 337	80 362	60 125	33 386	67 220	58 868	68 941	73 172

1 Bank and building society lending, plus holdings of commercial bills by the Issue Department of the Bank of England.
2 Including sterling lending to non-residents sector.

Source: Bank of England: 020 7601 5468

23.7 Money stock and liquidity

£ million

		1993	1994	1995	1996	1997	1998	1999	2000	2001	2002	2003
Amounts outstanding at end-year												
Notes and coin in circulation with the M4 private sector[1]	VQKT	17 716	18 661	19 847	20 642	22 242	23 705	26 269	28 174	30 450	31 895	34 025
UK private sector sterling non-interest bearing sight deposits[2,3]	AUYA	34 521	33 502	35 450	38 447	38 937	37 262	43 011	46 604	50 205	46 144	51 160
Money stock (M2)[3,4]	VQXV	394 438	410 396	436 957	460 108	484 659	515 005	559 214	598 260	649 636	704 476	777 248
Money stock M4[3]	AUYM	544 055	567 157	623 385	682 786	721 977	783 240	816 545	884 839	942 433	1 008 684	1 081 136
Changes during the year[5]												
Notes and coin in circulation with the M4 private sector[1]	VQLU	1 023	956	1 177	797	1 611	1 501	2 582	1 957	2 284	1 498	2 198
UK private sector sterling non-interest bearing sight deposits[2,3]	AUZA	4 203	1 092	1 782	3 530	5 349	−624	5 759	3 364	3 830	−5 761	4 576
Money stock (M2)[3,4]	AUZE	18 851	17 624	26 491	24 323	36 028	30 910	42 397	38 953	51 730	54 704	71 518
Money stock M4[3]	AUZI	23 877	25 557	55 885	59 337	80 362	60 125	33 386	67 220	58 868	68 941	73 172

1 The estimates of levels of coin in circulation include allowance for wastage, hoarding, etc.
2 Non-interest bearing deposits are confined to those with institutions included in the United Kingdom banks sector (See Table 23.3).
3 Revised rules on netting of customers' credit balances against their borrowing increased the UK private sector's outstanding balances of deposits and borrowing by £2.5bn at end-December 1993. Within retail deposit, £1.7bn of the increase was in NIB bank deposits. Re-netting during 1994 amounted to £1.7bn. Changes data have been adjusted to exclude these effects. Building societies' data from 1992 onwards are affected by the revised treatment of building society transit items within M4.

4 M2 comprises the UK non-monetary financial institutions and non-public sector, i.e. M4 private sector's holdings of notes and coin together with its sterling denominated retail deposits with UK monetary financial institutions.
5 As far as possible the changes exclude the effect of changes in the number of contributors to the series, and also of the introduction of new statistical returns. Changes are not seasonally adjusted.

Source: Bank of England: 020 7601 5468

23.8 Selected retail banks' base rate[1]
Operative between dates shown

Date of change	New rate	Date of change	New rate	Date of change	New rate
1986 Jan 9	12.50	Aug 9	11.00		
Mar 19	11.50	Aug 25	11.00-12.00	1997 May 6	6.25
Apr 8	11.00-11.50	Aug 26	12.00	Jun 6	6.25-6.50
Apr 9	11.00	Nov 25	13.00	Jun 9	6.50
Apr 21	10.50			Jul 10	6.75
May 23	10.00-10.50	1989 May 24	14.00	Aug 7	7.00
May 27	10.00	Oct 5	15.00	Nov 6	7.25
Oct 14	10.00-11.00				
Oct 15	11.00	1990 Oct 8	14.00	1998 Jun 4	7.50
				Oct 8	7.25
1987 Mar 10	10.50	1991 Feb 13	13.50	Nov 5	6.75
Mar 18	10.00-10.50	Feb 27	13.00	Dec 10	6.25
Mar 19	10.00	Mar 22	12.50		
Apr 28	9.50-10.00	Apr 12	12.00	1999 Jan 7	6.00
Apr 29	9.50	May 24	11.50	Feb 4	5.50
May 11	9.00	Jul 12	11.00	Apr 8	5.25
Aug 6	9.00-10.00	Sep 4	10.50	Jun 10	5.00
Aug 7	10.00			Sep 8	5.00-5.25
Oct 23	9.50-10.00	1992 May 5	10.00	Sep 10	5.25
Oct 29	9.50	Sep 16[2]	12.00	Nov 4	5.50
Nov 4	9.00-9.50	Sep 17[2]	10.00-12.00		
Nov 5	9.00	Sep 18	10.00	2000 Jan 13	5.75
Dec 4	8.50	Sep 22	9.00	Feb 10	6.00
		Oct 16	8.00-9.00		
1988 Feb 2	9.00	Oct 19	8.00	2001 Feb 8	5.75
Mar 17	8.50-9.00	Nov 13	7.00	Apr 5	5.50
Mar 18	8.50			May 10	5.25
Apr 11	8.00	1993 Jan 26	6.00	Aug 2	5.00
May 17	7.50-8.00	Nov 23	5.50	Sep 18	4.75
May 18	7.50			Oct 4	4.50
Jun 2	7.50-8.00	1994 Feb 8	5.25	Nov 8	4.00
Jun 3	8.00	Sep 12	5.75		
Jun 6	8.00-8.50	Dec 7	6.25	2003 Feb 6	3.75
Jun 7	8.50			Jul 10	3.50
Jun 22	8.50-9.00	1995 Feb 2[2]	6.25-6.75	Nov 6	3.75
Jun 23	9.00	Feb 3	6.75		
Jun 28	9.00-9.50	Dec 13	6.50	2004 Feb 5	4.00
Jun 29	9.50			May 6	4.25
Jul 4	9.50-10.00	1996 Jan 18	6.25	Jun 10	4.50
Jul 5	10.00	Mar 8	6.00	Aug 5	4.75
Jul 18	10.00-10.50	Jun 6	5.75		
Jul 19	10.50	Oct 30	5.75-6.00		
Aug 8	10.50-11.00	Oct 31	6.00		

1 Data obtained from Barclays Bank, Lloyds/TSB Bank, HSBC Bank and National Westminster Bank whose rates are used to compile this series.
2 Where all the rates did not change on the same day a spread is shown.

Source: Bank of England: 020 7601 4342

23.9 Average three month sterling money market rates[1]

Percentage rates

	1994	1995	1996	1997	1998	1999	2000	2001	2002	2003	2004
Treasury bills:[2] KDMM											
January	4.88	5.93	6.08	6.01	6.80	5.28	5.72	5.49	3.83	3.80	3.92
February	4.76	6.16	5.94	5.81	6.88	5.04	5.83	5.46	3.87	3.50	4.01
March	4.85	6.09	5.79	5.92	6.95	4.92	5.86	5.23	3.97	3.47	4.13
April	4.87	6.30	5.80	6.09	7.00	4.90	5.92	5.12	3.97	3.45	4.20
May	4.81	6.20	5.82	6.15	7.01	4.93	5.95	4.98	3.95	3.44	4.40
June	4.89	6.37	5.58	6.37	7.29	4.76	5.85	4.99	3.98	3.47	4.61
July	5.12	6.62	5.49	6.63	7.22	4.76	5.83	5.01	3.84	3.31	4.67
August	5.34	6.58	5.54	6.83	7.19	4.85	5.81	4.72	3.77	3.40	4.71
September	5.39	6.51	5.54	6.88	6.94	5.12	5.78	4.43	3.79	3.52	4.69
October	5.44	6.57	5.61	6.94	6.54	5.23	5.75	4.16	3.75	3.65	4.68
November	5.63	6.40	6.05	7.09	6.31	5.20	5.68	3.78	3.80	3.81	4.65
December	5.87	6.20	6.05	7.07	5.72	5.46	5.62	3.83	3.84	3.83	4.67
Eligible bill: KDMY											
January	5.07	6.41	6.18	6.15	7.28	5.63	5.90	5.64	3.91	3.87	3.94
February	4.95	6.54	6.00	5.99	7.24	5.28	6.01	5.56	3.92	3.65	4.06
March	4.90	6.40	5.87	6.01	7.25	5.11	5.98	5.37	3.99	3.54	4.19
April	4.93	6.44	5.83	6.26	7.24	5.02	6.05	5.21	4.04	3.52	4.28
May	4.92	6.54	5.85	6.31	7.20	5.08	6.09	5.06	4.01	3.52	4.42
June	4.94	6.44	5.66	6.50	7.42	4.94	6.03	5.08	4.04	3.45	4.68
July	5.01	6.66	5.57	6.80	7.49	4.89	5.97	5.07	3.94	3.39	4.75
August	5.44	6.64	5.60	6.95	7.40	4.94	5.97	4.82	3.86	3.42	4.85
September	5.54	6.55	5.63	7.02	7.20	5.16	5.95	4.57	3.86	3.59	4.83
October	5.74	6.58	5.76	7.10	6.91	5.42	5.92	4.26	3.82	3.69	4.79
November	5.89	6.49	6.10	7.27	6.52	5.43	5.88	3.85	3.84	3.88	4.78
December	6.12	6.29	6.18	7.31	6.05	5.59	5.78	3.88	3.71	3.90	4.77
Interbank rate: AMIJ											
January	5.39	6.56	6.36	6.32	7.48	5.80	6.06	5.76	3.98	3.91	3.99
February	5.22	6.75	6.16	6.19	7.46	5.43	6.15	5.69	3.98	3.69	4.10
March	5.16	6.66	6.05	6.20	7.48	5.30	6.15	5.47	4.06	3.58	4.23
April	5.21	6.67	6.00	6.38	7.44	5.23	6.21	5.33	4.11	3.58	4.33
May	5.17	6.72	6.02	6.45	7.41	5.25	6.23	5.17	4.08	3.57	4.46
June	5.13	6.64	5.85	6.66	7.63	5.12	6.14	5.19	4.11	3.57	4.73
July	5.20	6.80	5.73	6.96	7.71	5.07	6.11	5.19	3.99	3.42	4.79
August	5.53	6.79	5.75	7.15	7.66	5.18	6.14	4.93	3.92	3.45	4.89
September	5.67	6.72	5.77	7.21	7.38	5.32	6.12	4.65	3.93	3.63	4.87
October	5.91	6.73	5.94	7.26	7.14	5.94	6.08	4.36	3.90	3.73	4.83
November	6.06	6.64	6.30	7.54	6.89	5.78	6.00	3.93	3.91	3.91	4.82
December	6.37	6.49	6.35	7.62	6.38	5.97	5.89	3.99	3.95	3.95	4.81
Certificate of deposits: KOSA											
January	5.29	6.48	6.31	6.27	7.44	5.74	6.02	5.73	3.96	3.90	3.98
February	5.14	6.67	6.11	6.14	7.42	5.38	6.10	5.66	3.96	3.68	4.09
March	5.09	6.59	6.01	6.15	7.43	5.26	6.09	5.44	4.04	3.57	4.22
April	5.12	6.62	5.96	6.33	7.40	5.19	6.17	5.30	4.08	3.57	4.32
May	5.10	6.66	5.98	6.39	7.37	5.22	6.19	5.15	4.06	3.56	4.45
June	5.06	6.56	5.79	6.62	7.59	5.09	6.10	5.16	4.09	3.56	4.72
July	5.11	6.72	5.69	6.92	7.66	5.03	6.08	5.17	3.97	3.41	4.79
August	5.45	6.73	5.71	7.12	7.61	5.14	6.09	4.90	3.90	3.44	4.89
September	5.58	6.66	5.74	7.17	7.34	5.28	6.08	4.62	3.91	3.62	4.87
October	5.81	6.68	5.89	7.22	7.09	5.86	6.05	4.33	3.88	3.72	4.83
November	5.97	6.58	6.25	7.50	6.82	5.72	5.98	3.91	3.89	3.90	4.81
December	6.25	6.44	6.29	7.57	6.32	5.89	5.85	3.96	3.93	3.94	4.80
Local authority deposits: KDPX											
January	5.30	6.52	6.31	6.27	7.43	5.76	6.03	5.73	3.85	3.87	3.91
February	5.12	6.69	6.13	6.15	7.40	5.38	6.09	5.62	3.88	3.61	4.08
March	5.08	6.59	6.02	6.14	7.40	5.27	6.08	5.39	4.01	3.55	4.12
April	5.14	6.60	5.98	6.33	7.38	5.17	6.12	5.26	4.05	3.54	4.31
May	5.12	6.68	6.00	6.38	7.34	5.19	6.14	5.13	4.06	3.54	4.45
June	5.08	6.58	5.80	6.57	7.56	5.07	6.09	5.10	4.05	3.57	4.75
July	5.18	6.76	5.69	6.90	7.64	5.01	6.04	5.12	3.95	3.39	4.82
August	5.44	6.74	5.71	7.11	7.55	5.11	6.06	4.86	3.87	3.43	4.92
September	5.62	6.65	5.72	7.19	7.35	5.19	6.05	4.58	3.88	3.61	4.90
October	5.84	6.68	5.86	7.21	7.08	5.83	6.03	4.29	3.86	3.71	4.85
November	5.99	6.60	6.24	7.49	6.85	5.64	5.96	3.82	3.87	3.90	4.84
December	6.32	6.43	6.30	7.56	6.35	5.88	5.80	3.87	3.93	3.92	4.82

1 A full definition of these series is given in Section 7 of the ONS Financial Statistics Explanatory Handbook.
2 Average rate of discount at weekly (Friday) tender.

Source: Bank of England: 020 7601 3644

23.10 Average foreign exchange rates[1]

	1994	1995	1996	1997	1998	1999	2000	2001	2002	2003	2004
Sterling exchange rate index (1990 = 100) AGBG											
January	92.0	88.5	83.2	95.9	104.7	99.6	108.5	104.4	106.9	104.0	102.4
February	90.4	87.4	83.8	97.4	104.7	100.8	108.4	104.1	107.4	102.4	104.8
March	89.8	85.6	83.5	97.4	106.8	102.8	108.4	105.0	106.5	100.6	105.0
April	89.2	84.5	83.8	99.5	107.1	103.4	110.1	105.8	107.1	99.8	105.2
May	88.9	84.3	84.6	99.0	103.4	104.2	108.5	106.6	106.6	97.9	104.6
June	89.1	84.1	86.0	100.4	105.4	104.7	104.6	106.8	103.6	99.6	105.8
July	87.9	83.6	85.7	104.5	105.3	103.5	105.6	107.2	105.3	99.4	105.9
August	87.8	84.4	84.7	102.5	104.6	103.3	107.4	105.1	105.4	99.0	105.2
September	88.1	84.8	86.1	100.4	103.3	104.7	106.2	106.1	106.5	99.2	103.3
October	89.1	84.3	88.4	101.1	100.7	105.4	109.2	105.8	106.7	99.8	102.2
November	89.1	83.3	92.0	103.8	100.6	105.7	107.3	106.1	105.9	100.4	101.7
December	89.1	82.9	93.8	104.4	100.4	106.7	106.4	106.5	105.5	100.3	103.2
Sterling/US Dollar AUSS											
January	1.4939	1.5747	1.5306	1.6587	1.6353	1.6509	1.6402	1.4769	1.4323	1.6169	1.8234
February	1.4799	1.5720	1.5364	1.6246	1.6407	1.6276	1.5998	1.4529	1.4231	1.6046	1.8673
March	1.4917	1.6005	1.5271	1.6063	1.6620	1.6220	1.5802	1.4454	1.4225	1.5836	1.8267
April	1.4837	1.6074	1.5145	1.6295	1.6733	1.6105	1.5837	1.4350	1.4434	1.5747	1.8005
May	1.5029	1.5868	1.5152	1.6334	1.6366	1.6154	1.5075	1.4259	1.4593	1.6230	1.7876
June	1.5252	1.5949	1.5418	1.6446	1.6507	1.5950	1.5089	1.4014	1.4863	1.6606	1.8275
July	1.5463	1.5953	1.5539	1.6702	1.6437	1.5747	1.5088	1.4139	1.5546	1.6242	1.8429
August	1.5427	1.5681	1.5502	1.6034	1.6320	1.6073	1.4910	1.4365	1.5377	1.5950	1.8216
September	1.5651	1.5584	1.5597	1.6015	1.6822	1.6243	1.4355	1.4635	1.5561	1.6131	1.7922
October	1.6057	1.5779	1.5862	1.6329	1.6952	1.6572	1.4511	1.4517	1.5574	1.6787	1.8065
November	1.5886	1.5623	1.6626	1.6890	1.6620	1.6214	1.4256	1.4358	1.5723	1.6901	1.8603
December	1.5595	1.5398	1.6647	1.6597	1.6705	1.6132	1.4625	1.4409	1.5863	1.7507	1.9275
Sterling/Euro THAP											
January	1.3295	1.2525	1.1631	1.3559	1.5166	1.4236	1.6201	1.5753	1.6222	1.5222	1.4447
February	1.3082	1.2331	1.1707	1.3906	1.5196	1.4534	1.6266	1.5786	1.6348	1.4893	1.4774
March	1.2915	1.2038	1.1692	1.3944	1.5507	1.4902	1.6377	1.5901	1.6224	1.4649	1.4890
April	1.2840	1.1890	1.1763	1.4243	1.5490	1.5051	1.6730	1.6084	1.6282	1.4505	1.5022
May	1.2719	1.1893	1.1923	1.4217	1.4834	1.5185	1.6655	1.6304	1.5914	1.4030	1.4894
June	1.2709	1.1828	1.2094	1.4499	1.5110	1.5374	1.5882	1.6434	1.5515	1.4234	1.5050
July	1.2455	1.1693	1.2007	1.5247	1.5091	1.5204	1.6052	1.6433	1.5665	1.4277	1.5023
August	1.2420	1.1836	1.1845	1.5043	1.4912	1.5146	1.6478	1.5955	1.5723	1.4286	1.4933
September	1.2469	1.1903	1.2066	1.4591	1.4617	1.5458	1.6471	1.6060	1.5861	1.4338	1.4676
October	1.2563	1.1759	1.2407	1.4623	1.4200	1.5491	1.6994	1.6024	1.5868	1.4334	1.4455
November	1.2613	1.1612	1.2873	1.4914	1.4290	1.5706	1.6664	1.6166	1.5694	1.4426	1.4311
December	1.2672	1.1589	1.3192	1.5053	1.4254	1.5953	1.6302	1.6151	1.5566	1.4246	1.4401

1 Working day average. A full definition of these series is given in Section 7 of the ONS Explanatory Handbook.

Source: Bank of England: 020 7601 3644

23.11 Average zero coupon yields[1]

	1994	1995	1996	1997	1998	1999	2000	2001	2002	2003	2004
Nominal Five Year Yield ZBRG											
January	5.89	8.63	6.85	7.15	6.18	4.30	6.28	5.07	4.90	4.15	4.61
February	6.23	8.53	7.12	6.82	6.10	4.46	6.13	5.04	4.94	3.88	4.63
March	6.96	8.45	7.45	7.07	6.09	4.69	5.89	4.86	5.22	3.94	4.56
April	7.58	8.25	7.52	7.28	5.93	4.66	5.80	4.96	5.21	4.10	4.80
May	7.97	7.95	7.53	6.94	5.95	4.95	5.82	5.14	5.22	3.85	5.01
June	8.45	7.77	7.46	6.96	6.04	5.28	5.61	5.25	5.05	3.72	5.15
July	8.27	7.89	7.30	7.01	6.12	5.49	5.58	5.26	4.88	3.98	5.07
August	8.47	7.70	7.19	6.97	5.80	5.75	5.65	5.03	4.54	4.36	4.96
September	8.71	7.47	7.18	6.72	5.32	6.00	5.65	4.90	4.31	4.46	4.83
October	8.64	7.56	6.97	6.51	4.94	6.25	5.46	4.74	4.36	4.73	4.66
November	8.49	7.21	7.18	6.69	4.92	5.86	5.33	4.55	4.38	4.91	4.58
December	8.49	6.88	7.20	6.46	4.51	5.90	5.14	4.88	4.34	4.71	4.43
Nominal Ten Year Yield ZBRH											
January	6.39	8.57	7.46	7.52	5.96	4.24	5.62	4.75	4.85	4.39	4.76
February	6.78	8.50	7.80	7.15	5.91	4.39	5.44	4.90	4.90	4.25	4.78
March	7.43	8.45	8.08	7.41	5.85	4.60	5.18	4.64	5.18	4.35	4.67
April	7.79	8.31	8.06	7.58	5.69	4.53	5.14	4.90	5.19	4.49	4.92
May	8.24	8.07	8.10	7.08	5.73	4.83	5.23	5.05	5.22	4.24	5.06
June	8.65	8.04	8.09	7.04	5.60	5.07	5.05	5.11	5.05	4.13	5.13
July	8.47	8.20	7.96	6.92	5.65	5.24	5.09	5.10	4.95	4.43	5.04
August	8.54	8.07	7.86	6.97	5.41	5.25	5.18	4.88	4.68	4.59	4.95
September	8.77	7.93	7.86	6.70	5.03	5.51	5.25	4.91	4.47	4.68	4.86
October	8.64	8.09	7.56	6.37	4.93	5.68	5.09	4.77	4.60	4.88	4.72
November	8.51	7.78	7.56	6.46	4.83	5.11	4.98	4.58	4.62	5.03	4.65
December	8.43	7.52	7.52	6.22	4.44	5.19	4.80	4.83	4.55	4.87	4.49
Nominal Twenty Year Yield ZBRI											
January	6.57	8.23	7.89	7.74	5.94	4.36	4.45	4.33	4.69	4.46	4.70
February	6.88	8.16	8.19	7.39	5.88	4.44	4.38	4.42	4.72	4.40	4.73
March	7.45	8.15	8.37	7.59	5.78	4.60	4.25	4.45	4.99	4.56	4.63
April	7.69	8.09	8.30	7.73	5.61	4.53	4.35	4.76	5.02	4.69	4.81
May	7.98	7.92	8.38	7.16	5.67	4.75	4.40	4.87	5.08	4.49	4.91
June	8.18	7.98	8.41	7.08	5.42	4.77	4.37	4.98	4.93	4.44	4.89
July	8.08	8.24	8.34	6.80	5.45	4.67	4.38	4.90	4.82	4.71	4.82
August	8.15	8.14	8.26	6.86	5.30	4.53	4.49	4.69	4.57	4.69	4.70
September	8.29	8.05	8.27	6.64	4.91	4.62	4.63	4.88	4.40	4.74	4.65
October	8.23	8.30	7.98	6.36	4.87	4.56	4.61	4.92	4.54	4.82	4.59
November	8.18	7.98	7.81	6.37	4.73	4.07	4.39	4.53	4.60	4.88	4.50
December	8.08	7.80	7.67	6.17	4.47	4.20	4.30	4.65	4.59	4.77	4.40
Real Ten Year Yield ZBRJ											
January	2.73	3.87	3.42	3.45	3.10	2.00	2.10	2.22	2.52	2.00	1.94
February	2.86	3.86	3.54	3.27	3.06	1.91	2.17	2.27	2.50	1.74	1.96
March	3.09	3.87	3.67	3.43	3.00	1.85	2.05	2.33	2.53	1.79	1.81
April	3.25	3.79	3.63	3.56	2.91	1.70	2.08	2.56	2.43	1.96	1.93
May	3.48	3.57	3.72	3.57	2.92	1.91	2.14	2.58	2.43	1.81	2.05
June	3.76	3.56	3.77	3.66	2.85	1.89	2.12	2.54	2.33	1.67	2.10
July	3.84	3.58	3.70	3.62	2.77	1.90	2.14	2.56	2.42	1.83	2.07
August	3.78	3.48	3.58	3.60	2.65	2.19	2.25	2.42	2.33	1.95	2.04
September	3.81	3.45	3.57	3.52	2.59	2.31	2.28	2.51	2.20	2.04	1.97
October	3.82	3.63	3.41	3.23	2.67	2.26	2.33	2.53	2.36	2.15	1.89
November	3.81	3.52	3.43	3.25	2.40	2.05	2.34	2.39	2.33	2.21	1.88
December	3.83	3.43	3.42	3.11	2.11	1.98	2.23	2.58	2.24	2.03	1.76
Real Twenty Year Yield ZBRK											
January	3.07	3.89	..	3.67	3.06	2.07	2.01	1.88	2.26	2.07	1.96
February	3.23	3.89	3.79	3.49	3.05	1.99	1.95	1.88	2.30	1.96	1.90
March	3.45	3.88	3.81	3.59	2.98	1.93	1.78	1.99	2.32	2.05	1.77
April	3.51	3.80	3.75	3.68	2.85	1.81	1.84	2.25	2.25	2.13	1.85
May	3.68	3.64	3.82	3.66	2.83	1.99	1.91	2.32	2.25	2.04	1.88
June	3.91	3.69	3.86	3.69	2.63	1.97	1.87	2.27	2.17	1.99	1.88
July	3.93	3.71	3.81	3.57	2.58	2.00	1.90	2.24	2.24	2.16	1.87
August	3.84	3.62	3.75	3.57	2.53	2.14	1.96	2.16	2.15	2.14	1.82
September	3.88	3.61	3.76	3.48	2.49	2.26	1.96	2.31	2.06	2.18	1.80
October	3.87	3.73	3.61	3.22	2.59	2.22	1.99	2.32	2.22	2.22	1.77
November	3.85	3.61	3.62	3.18	2.36	1.92	1.94	2.12	2.25	2.21	1.71
December	3.87	3.56	3.62	3.06	2.14	1.87	1.87	2.24	2.21	2.08	1.60

1 Working day average. Calculated using the Variable Roughness Penalty (VRP) model.

Source: Bank of England: 020 7601 3644

23.12 Average rates on representative British Government Stocks[1]

Percentage rates

	1994	1995	1996	1997	1998	1999	2000	2001	2002	2003	2004
5 Year Conventional Rate KORP											
January	5.76	8.61	6.78	7.19	6.33	4.25	6.36	5.17	4.94	4.15	4.59
February	6.05	8.52	7.02	6.86	6.24	4.41	6.23	5.13	4.96	3.88	4.46
March	6.72	8.44	7.56	7.08	6.26	4.65	6.01	4.94	5.23	3.93	4.44
April	7.33	8.26	7.43	7.30	6.11	4.66	5.95	4.97	5.26	4.08	4.66
May	7.74	7.96	7.61	6.98	6.14	4.93	5.97	5.15	5.48	3.83	4.89
June	8.22	7.79	7.52	7.01	6.31	5.27	5.78	5.32	5.10	3.68	5.08
July	8.06	7.90	7.35	7.09	6.14	5.49	5.75	5.34	4.92	3.72	4.98
August	8.31	7.69	7.21	7.02	5.84	5.80	5.81	5.09	4.57	4.30	4.88
September	8.61	7.45	7.20	6.78	5.34	6.04	5.81	4.94	4.25	4.42	4.76
October	8.57	7.54	7.01	6.59	4.88	6.24	5.66	4.78	4.38	4.70	4.57
November	8.44	7.16	7.22	6.79	4.86	5.89	5.50	4.59	4.40	4.88	4.52
December	8.49	6.83	7.26	6.60	4.45	5.91	5.27	4.88	4.34	4.68	..
10 year Conventional Rate KORQ											
January	6.23	8.66	7.42	7.53	6.07	4.16	5.75	4.86	4.84	4.37	4.78
February	6.61	8.59	7.75	7.17	6.02	4.32	5.56	4.88	4.91	4.25	4.75
March	7.29	8.53	8.05	7.41	5.97	4.54	5.29	4.75	5.15	4.51	4.65
April	7.68	8.39	8.05	7.60	5.81	4.48	5.25	4.95	5.23	4.64	4.91
May	8.13	8.12	8.08	7.13	5.85	4.77	5.35	5.13	5.51	4.26	5.07
June	8.54	8.08	8.04	7.10	5.77	5.02	5.15	5.09	5.06	4.38	5.19
July	8.37	8.23	7.91	7.01	5.67	5.20	5.18	5.16	4.94	4.23	5.10
August	8.52	8.10	7.81	7.05	5.56	5.24	5.27	4.92	4.66	4.59	4.99
September	8.80	7.92	7.80	6.77	5.10	5.52	5.32	4.92	4.46	4.69	4.89
October	8.70	8.08	7.51	6.47	4.93	5.70	5.15	4.76	4.57	4.89	4.73
November	8.57	7.75	7.56	6.59	4.87	5.16	5.06	4.58	4.59	5.04	4.66
December	8.53	7.45	7.54	6.34	4.49	5.24	4.88	4.88	4.52	4.94	..
20 Year Conventional Rate KORR											
January	6.53	8.45	7.73	7.71	6.04	4.36	4.91	4.52	4.81	4.46	4.73
February	6.88	8.43	8.04	7.35	5.98	4.47	4.80	4.58	4.83	4.37	4.80
March	7.49	8.40	8.28	7.58	5.90	4.64	4.64	4.56	5.12	4.51	4.69
April	7.81	8.30	8.26	7.74	5.73	4.58	4.71	4.84	5.14	4.64	4.91
May	8.18	8.09	8.31	7.21	5.79	4.83	4.77	4.98	5.45	4.44	5.03
June	8.48	8.08	8.31	7.15	5.59	4.92	4.68	5.10	5.03	4.38	5.07
July	8.35	8.30	8.21	6.93	5.63	4.88	4.70	5.05	4.92	4.59	4.99
August	8.46	8.19	8.12	6.98	5.43	4.82	4.79	4.83	4.65	4.67	4.88
September	8.65	8.06	8.11	6.74	5.02	4.97	4.90	4.94	4.46	4.74	4.83
October	8.56	8.26	7.84	6.45	4.92	4.97	4.84	4.80	4.59	4.85	4.73
November	8.46	7.93	7.77	6.50	4.79	4.46	4.64	4.55	4.65	4.93	4.64
December	8.39	7.70	7.67	6.32	4.49	4.56	4.51	4.75	4.61	4.80	..
10 Year Index-Linked Rate KORS											
January	2.70	3.89	3.42	3.44	3.01	2.00	2.11	2.21	2.61	2.07	1.88
February	2.81	3.87	3.57	3.23	2.94	1.94	2.16	2.30	2.53	1.81	1.90
March	3.07	3.86	3.70	3.41	2.89	1.90	2.06	2.34	2.55	1.88	1.76
April	3.25	3.79	3.66	3.55	2.80	1.74	2.08	2.55	2.45	1.90	1.94
May	3.51	3.58	3.74	3.52	2.83	1.96	2.15	2.61	2.58	1.74	2.10
June	3.78	3.58	3.80	3.62	2.81	1.93	2.13	2.56	2.35	1.59	2.17
July	3.85	3.61	3.82	3.68	2.67	1.93	2.14	2.57	2.46	1.67	2.12
August	3.82	3.52	3.59	3.59	2.55	2.20	2.25	2.45	2.37	1.89	2.04
September	3.85	3.46	3.57	3.47	2.59	2.32	2.29	2.56	2.24	1.99	1.95
October	3.84	3.65	3.41	3.17	2.66	2.26	2.33	2.55	2.42	2.08	1.83
November	3.84	3.54	3.42	3.23	2.39	2.03	2.32	2.42	2.39	2.16	1.85
December	3.85	3.45	3.41	3.01	2.11	1.99	2.20	2.65	2.30	1.97	..
20 Year Index-Linked rate KORT											
January	2.96	3.91	3.58	3.62	3.01	2.06	2.01	1.96	2.35	2.10	1.95
February	3.11	3.89	3.70	3.43	3.01	1.97	1.98	1.99	2.36	1.99	1.94
March	3.35	3.89	3.82	3.55	2.92	1.93	1.83	2.09	2.39	2.07	1.80
April	3.45	3.81	3.77	3.65	2.80	1.81	1.90	2.35	2.32	2.10	1.91
May	3.64	3.64	3.84	3.61	2.79	1.99	1.97	2.41	2.43	2.00	1.99
June	3.88	3.67	3.88	3.65	2.61	1.97	1.94	2.38	2.23	1.93	2.01
July	3.90	3.71	3.72	3.68	2.56	1.97	1.96	2.36	2.30	2.05	1.99
August	3.83	3.62	3.75	3.54	2.51	2.12	2.03	2.25	2.21	2.09	1.93
September	3.87	3.60	3.74	3.43	2.51	2.23	2.04	2.39	2.12	2.13	1.89
October	3.86	3.74	3.60	3.17	2.58	2.18	2.08	2.38	2.29	2.17	1.84
November	3.85	3.62	3.59	3.16	2.35	1.91	2.02	2.19	2.31	2.16	1.80
December	3.86	3.55	3.58	3.02	2.12	1.88	1.94	2.33	2.26	2.04	..

1 Working day average.

Source: Bank of England: 020 7601 3644

23.13 Building societies[1,2]
United Kingdom

		1994	1995[3]	1996[3]	1997[3]	1998[3]	1999[3]	2000[4]	2001	2002	2003
Number and balance sheets											
Societies on register (numbers)	KRNA	96	94	88	82	78	72	68	65	65	63
Share investors (thousands)	KRNB	38 150	38 998	37 768	19 234	21 195	21 774	22 237	20 311	20 724	20 901
Depositors (thousands)	KRNC	5 369	6 143	6 718	882	820	642	660	501	440	452
Borrowers (thousands)	KRND	7 222	6 906	6 586	2 703	2 934	2 868	2 925	2 579	2 520	2 520
Assets and liabilities (£ million)											
Liabilities:											
Shares	KRNE	201 812.2	200 682.0	196 546.4	90 092.8	103 289.8	109 137.7	119 298.5	119 815.2	132 372.9	142 477.1
Deposits and loans	KRNF	69 925.2	67 513.8	73 919.1	31 033.7	33 311.2	34 746.6	44 262.4	37 358.9	37 933.0	49 552.6
Taxation and other	KRNG	2 939.2	3 306.2	3 727.4	1 338.8	1 586.4	1 665.4	1 664.0	1 244.9	1 088.4	1 179.0
General reserves	KRNH	16 312.3	17 218.3	17 940.3	7 331.2	7 926.4	8 301.5	8 987.1	8 511.2	9 043.4	9 489.8
Other Capital	KRNI	4 125.7	3 498.0	4 762.3	1 643.9	1 550.7	1 529.2	1 861.0	1 416.1	1 709.2	2 534.7
Assets:											
Mortgages	KRNK	240 297.2	236 841.0	241 472.9	107 531.5	118 288.4	123 183.4	137 072.3	130 229.6	140 839.7	159 938.2
Investments and cash	KHVZ	50 786.7	50 894.1	51 016.7	21 869.8	27 102.0	29 917.8	36 574.2	35 925.9	38 952.7	43 067.9
Other	KRNN	4 030.7	4 483.2	4 405.9	2 039.1	2 274.1	2 279.2	2 426.6	2 190.7	2 354.4	2 226.9
Total	KRNJ	295 114.6	292 218.3	296 895.5	131 440.4	147 664.5	155 380.4	176 073.0	168 346.2	182 146.8	205 233.1
Current transactions (£ million)											
Mortgage advances	KRNU	34 829.0	34 673.0	38 488.0	28 771.7	21 988.3	23 997.9	28 233.6	29 320.0	33 077.0	43 392.4
Management expenses	KRNX	3 136.7	3 352.6	3 555.3	2 270.5	1 501.7	1 573.8	1 640.7	1 528.0	1 623.6	1 746.4

1 See chapter text.
2 The figures for each year relate to accounting years ending on dates between 1 February of that year and 31 January of the following year.
3 The societies which have converted to the banking sector, namely Cheltenham & Gloucester (August 1995), National & Provincial (August 1996), Alliance & Leicester (April 1997), Halifax (June 1997), Woolwich (July 1997), Bristol & West (July 1997), Northern Rock (October 1997), and Birmingham Midshires (April 1999) have been included in flow figures (using flows up to the date of conversion), but have been excluded from the end of year balances.

4 Bradford & Bingley, which converted to the banking sector in December 2000, is included within flow figures and the end of year balances.

Source: Financial Services Authority: 020 7066 1000

23.14 Consumer credit[1]
United Kingdom

£ million

		1994	1995	1996	1997	1998	1999	2000	2001	2002	2003
Total amount outstanding	VZRD	58 055	68 202	77 478	88 081	102 222	116 155	128 041	141 718	157 844	170 546
Total net lending	VZQC	5 742	8 234	11 213	12 015	14 511	14 858	14 235	17 719	21 154	18 739
Retailers	AAPP	83	−133	75	208	7	103	−285	−27	59	−396
Building societies' class 3 loans	ALPY	89	238	383	120	–	11	111	68	187	179
Banks	AIKN	3 704	5 606	7 682	9 027	11 709	10 999	13 195	16 181	17 352	14 127
of which											
Credit cards	VZQS	1 483	2 103	3 029	3 507	4 858	5 676	6 686	6 229	7 579	8 206
Loans on personal accounts	VTGA	..	..	..	..	..	..	..	..	..	..
Other	VZQT	4 259	6 132	8 184	8 509	9 656	9 182	7 550	11 492	13 577	10 533
Insurance companies	RSBK	−179	39	−83	6	−16	224	−265	−19	4	−129
Non-bank credit companies	−AGSJ	1 856	2 222	2 805	2 287	2 409	2 928	676	980	2 865	4 370
Other specialist lenders	VZQQ	2 045	2 485	3 156	2 654	2 810	3 521	1 478	1 516	3 553	4 958
Total gross lending	VZQG	75 039	89 114	103 215	116 079	133 710	147 015	158 711	175 056	193 938	206 503
Narrower coverage[2]											
Total amount outstanding	RLWE	37 027	..	..	..	..	..	..	..	..	..
Total net lending	RLWF	5 515	..	..	..	..	..	..	..	..	..
Total new credit advanced	RLBY	62 050	..	..	..	..	..	..	..	..	..

1 See chapter text.
2 Data no longer available from 1995.

Source: Office for National Statistics: 01633 812789

23.15 End-year assets and liabilities of investment trust companies, unit trusts[1] and property unit trusts[2]

United Kingdom

£ million

		1993	1994	1995	1996	1997	1998	1999	2000	2001	2002	2003
Investment trust companies												
Short-term assets and liabilities (net):	CBPL	623	273	627	1 076	1 426	2 263	71	423	161	–	73
Cash and UK bank deposits	AHAG	387	443	1 009	1 087	1 577	2 647	1 227	2 202	2 513	1 821	1 346
Other short-term assets	CBPN	1 030	772	738	794	1 714	1 734	1 097	1 082	656	805	1 189
Short-term liabilities	-CBPS	−794	−942	−1 120	−805	−1 865	−2 118	−2 253	−2 861	−3 008	−2 626	−2 462
Medium and long-term liabilities and capital:	-CBPO	−36 140	−40 180	−43 882	−50 911	−54 821	−49 985	−57 616	−60 412	−54 630	−38 054	−48 076
Issued share and loan capital	-CBPQ	−8 286	−10 978	−13 250	−8 330	−9 350	−8 837	−8 565	−8 934	−8 796	−8 711	−9 873
Foreign currency borrowing	-CBPR	−473	−354	−1 061	−638	−658	−607	−880	−994	−933	−780	−682
Other borrowing	-CBQA	−849	−1 354	−622	−823	−1 296	−1 723	−1 716	−2 503	−3 251	−2 246	−2 181
Reserves and provisions, etc	-AHBC	−26 532	−27 494	−28 949	−41 120	−43 517	−38 818	−46 455	−47 981	−41 650	−26 317	−35 340
Investments:	CBPM	35 300	39 586	43 410	50 034	51 618	46 575	56 491	59 948	54 822	37 748	48 035
British government securities	AHBF	1 013	2 490	1 194	1 422	1 255	815	1 217	821	645	471	303
UK company securities:												
Loan capital and preference shares	CBGZ	854	1 000	846	832	1 320	1 351	1 425	1 654	1 516	946	1 079
Ordinary and deferred shares	CBGY	14 892	15 926	19 384	25 046	27 916	24 587	28 010	33 456	30 338	19 475	23 292
Overseas company securities:												
Loan capital and preference shares	CBHA	533	896	740	279	1 165	768	979	963	1 143	677	646
Ordinary and deferred shares	AHCC	16 886	17 873	19 485	21 047	17 747	17 741	23 330	21 355	19 476	14 453	20 294
Other investments	CBPT	1 122	1 401	1 761	1 408	1 631	1 055	1 530	1 699	1 704	1 945	2 464
Unit trusts												
Short-term assets and liabilities:	CBPU	2 673	3 266	3 116	3 822	4 627	6 883	5 894	8 340	7 979	8 041	10 256
Cash and UK bank deposits	AGYE	2 579	3 102	3 326	3 895	4 731	6 020	4 797	6 969	5 748	5 321	5 243
Other short-term assets	CBPW	1 013	1 364	986	1 201	467	1 343	1 545	2 319	2 763	3 072	5 990
Short-term liabilities	-CBPX	−919	−1 200	−1 196	−1 274	−571	−480	−448	−948	−532	−352	−977
Foreign currency borrowing	-AGYK	−39	−21	−1	–	–	–	–	–	–	–	–
Investments:	CBPZ	88 479	83 495	104 069	125 841	143 108	163 048	213 553	222 844	204 899	210 002	245 516
British government securities	CBHT	959	1 414	1 774	2 716	3 087	3 771	3 627	4 693	4 690	7 077	9 125
UK company securities:												
Loan capital and preference shares	CBHU	2 906	2 970	3 298	5 029	6 494	9 290	13 322	14 654	16 318	21 152	23 972
Ordinary and deferred shares	RLIB	49 657	43 335	59 122	67 509	85 742	93 291	119 496	116 808	103 704	82 851	116 407
Overseas company securities:												
Loan capital and preference shares	CBHV	864	1 001	2 145	1 288	1 834	1 801	3 032	3 212	4 113	5 916	9 840
Ordinary and deferred shares	RLIC	32 904	33 473	36 062	47 346	42 898	51 119	70 256	79 601	71 329	63 152	75 074
Other assets	CBQE	1 189	1 302	1 668	1 953	2 593	3 657	3 820	3 876	4 800	9 997	11 098
Property unit trusts												
Short-term assets and liabilities (net)	AGVC	212	253	186	343	351	254	205	285	247	242	459
Property	CBQG	1 492	2 197	1 807	2 582	3 875	2 740	2 722	3 488	2 078	4 026	5 125
Other assets	AGVL	60	11	11	11	167	197	436	380	151	677	373
Long-term borrowing	-AGVM	−42	–	−131	−45	−246	−106	−75	−391	−90	−75	−76

Note: Assets are shown as positive: liabilities as negative.
1 Including open ended investment companies (OEICs).
2 Investments are at market value.

Source: Office for National Statistics: 01633 812789

23.16 Self-administered pension funds: market value of assets

United Kingdom

End year

£ million

		1992	1993	1994	1995	1996	1997	1998	1999	2000	2001	2002
Total pension funds[1]												
Total net assets	AHVA	381 997	480 547	443 467	508 581	543 879	656 874	699 191	812 228	765 199	711 572	610 441
Short-term assets	RYIQ	18 492	20 279	22 617	26 114	31 521	35 368	39 005	32 703	36 638	31 337	30 700
British government securities	AHVK	25 188	34 279	41 854	52 659	57 783	80 533	91 084	98 882	92 458	83 754	84 461
UK local authority long-term debt	AHVO	34	81	250	83	89	156	183	133	177	125	42
Overseas government securities	AHVT	10 529	11 044	11 092	11 721	11 800	13 079	15 493	16 684	19 206	20 383	16 031
UK company securities												
Ordinary shares	AHVP	202 311	251 099	219 189	256 625	276 001	339 687	334 648	357 230	299 318	260 696	186 437
Other	AHVQ	5 905	5 758	3 935	7 064	6 180	5 618	8 168	9 258	16 978	22 301	30 450
Overseas company securities												
Ordinary shares	AHVR	63 276	84 118	74 813	82 164	84 163	104 187	108 884	148 335	135 514	127 893	104 392
Other	AHVS	1 787	2 103	3 045	1 184	4 909	3 851	3 842	5 099	12 736	11 781	11 386
UK loans and mortgages	RLDQ	232	260	44	34	83	160	22	14	7	3	–
UK land, property and ground rent	AHWA	19 914	21 932	24 353	21 317	21 637	24 176	24 355	31 107	32 945	30 617	31 658
Authorised unit trust units	AHVU	8 569	13 188	13 345	15 212	21 767	21 979	30 596	33 731	34 587	38 083	36 530
Property unit trusts	AHVW	1 745	1 905	2 463	2 485	2 666	3 219	3 211	5 498	4 835	5 280	5 869
Other assets	RKPL	28 794	38 761	31 318	36 352	30 628	32 978	47 136	82 273	90 841	90 139	82 490
Total liabilities	GQFX	4 781	4 261	4 852	4 412	5 347	8 118	7 436	8 719	11 041	10 819	10 005

1 These figures cover funded schemes only and therefore exclude the main superannuation arrangements in the central government sector.

Source: Office for National Statistics: 01633 812726

23.17 Insurance companies: balance sheet market values
United Kingdom
End year

£ million

		1992	1993	1994	1995	1996	1997	1998	1999	2000	2001	2002
Long-term insurance companies												
Assets												
Total current assets (gross)	RYEW	18 101	16 925	16 690	24 171	31 699	42 795	46 165	56 360	62 937	63 855	58 122
Agents' and reinsurance balances (net)	AHNY	799	457	−209	−157	−232	155	1 383	508	384	620	6 373
Other debtors[1]	RKPN	4 198	4 368	4 562	7 565	12 982	15 708	18 210	18 613	21 045	27 285	34 391
British government securities	AHNJ	50 970	72 575	64 921	80 268	90 996	107 847	127 903	126 223	116 734	119 513	131 305
UK local authority securities etc	AHNN	667	772	815	1 322	1 088	914	1 722	1 456	1 170	1 407	1 427
UK company securities[2]	RKPO	172 204	237 020	217 034	272 554	304 587	386 734	438 666	539 834	557 293	505 691	443 535
Overseas company securities	RKPP	32 101	49 087	48 195	59 950	62 378	73 428	82 122	120 665	107 439	127 259	110 738
Overseas government securities	AHNS	8 793	8 874	6 871	8 793	7 554	8 471	17 515	18 494	18 004	21 285	19 762
Loans and mortgages	RKPQ	8 345	7 885	6 833	7 305	6 653	8 271	11 027	10 914	9 687	10 048	10 994
UK land, property and ground rent	AHNX	30 074	33 939	35 914	35 596	36 209	42 275	45 903	50 387	49 705	53 726	52 658
Overseas land, property and ground rent	RGCP	124	144	151	118	114	98	252	206	1 975	498	158
Other investments	RKPR	2 663	3 096	4 644	2 162	3 886	3 416	5 654	8 334	8 385	7 420	9 513
Total	RFXN	329 039	435 142	406 421	499 647	557 914	690 112	796 522	951 994	954 760	938 609	878 979
Net value of direct investment in:												
Non-insurance subsidiaries and associate companies in the United Kingdom	RYET	2 569	2 288	2 547	2 773	3 033	3 426	3 035	3 045	6 133	4 486	4 577
UK associate and subsidiary insurance companies and insurance holding companies	RYEU	639	1 186	504	701	575	−239	148	2 245	3 586	4 206	4 569
Overseas subsidiaries and associates	RYEV	773	1 016	1 034	987	986	1 104	1 087	3 638	4 002	5 581	5 463
Total assets	RKBI	333 020	439 632	410 506	504 108	562 508	694 403	800 792	960 922	968 481	952 882	893 588
Liabilities												
Borrowing:												
Borrowing from UK banks	RGDF	1 162	1 234	1 570	1 907	2 234	3 027	3 252	6 064	8 272	8 790	4 958
Other UK borrowing	RGDE	1 007	553	982	796	1 349	786	1 040	3 070	2 823	5 350	7 406
Borrowing from overseas	RGDD	603	381	176	79	90	104	148	159	38	81	800
Long-term business:												
Funds	RKDC	280 276	354 711	357 263	424 866	470 893	581 009	669 301	800 184	838 485	831 051	794 177
Claims admitted but not paid	RKBM	951	1 035	1 085	1 419	1 441	1 436	1 712	2 032	2 249	2 547	3 234
Provision for taxation net of amounts receivable:												
UK authorities	RYPI	−1 119	−141	−470	502	2 568	4 207	5 443	6 344	5 381	3 951	2 803
Overseas authorities	RYPJ	−14	−20	29	−11	9	25	67	314	67	45	−20
Provision for recommended dividends	RYPK	46	83	76	195	276	368	359	201	183	87	32
Other creditors and liabilities	RYPL	3 763	4 020	4 399	5 979	6 303	8 083	12 509	17 042	19 031	18 468	23 261
Excess of assets over above liabilities:												
Excess of value of assets over liabilities in respect of long-term funds	RKBR	43 511	74 160	42 608	63 255	71 817	89 790	96 456	116 951	79 173	63 337	36 517
Minority interests in UK subsidiary companies	RKTI	30	30	–	3	–	2	–	25	–	–	–
Shareholders' capital and reserves in respect of general business	RKBS	1 952	890	1 143	2 050	2 576	3 862	6 299	6 139	10 287	17 044	18 629
Other reserves including profit and loss account balances	RKBT	852	2 696	1 645	3 068	2 952	1 704	4 206	2 396	2 492	2 130	1 791
Total liabilities	RKBI	333 020	439 632	410 506	504 108	562 508	694 403	800 792	960 922	968 481	952 882	893 588

23.17
continued

Insurance companies: balance sheet market values
United Kingdom
End year

£ million

		1992	1993	1994	1995	1996	1997	1998	1999	2000	2001	2002
Other than long-term insurance companies												
Assets												
Total current assets (gross)	RYME	6 523	6 467	7 426	8 318	11 559	12 628	8 524	10 468	8 772	12 264	17 671
Agents' and reinsurance balances (net)	AHMX	6 380	5 887	6 123	7 494	11 569	9 405	10 528	12 177	8 362	7 941	9 492
Other debtors[1]	RKPS	1 765	1 847	2 118	3 403	6 097	5 998	6 277	7 720	7 179	9 056	14 437
British government securities	AHMJ	8 378	11 474	12 320	14 363	16 893	15 666	16 409	15 938	14 561	15 064	18 390
UK local authority securities etc	AHMN	49	59	50	56	42	16	14	10	8	6	10
UK company securities[2]	RKPT	10 480	14 533	14 312	17 425	17 825	18 845	18 440	19 140	18 585	17 101	15 362
Overseas company securities	RKPU	3 747	4 163	3 578	4 422	5 072	6 594	8 676	6 284	8 190	6 402	7 394
Overseas government securities	AHMS	4 660	5 324	5 064	6 511	9 546	8 215	10 459	7 980	6 849	7 134	7 156
Loans and mortgages	RKPV	1 147	1 234	1 321	1 337	1 593	1 385	1 346	1 070	1 429	1 348	1 063
UK land, property and ground rent	AHMW	2 398	2 375	2 121	2 100	2 077	2 842	1 146	1 085	1 069	860	805
Overseas land, property and ground rent	RYNK	185	80	89	128	120	149	107	83	45	4	1
Other investments	RKPW	633	418	536	665	716	2 465	2 366	2 072	2 294	1 608	2 182
Total	RKAL	46 345	53 861	55 058	66 222	83 106	84 208	84 281	84 027	77 343	78 789	93 965
Net value of direct investment in:												
Non-insurance subsidiaries and associate companies in the United Kingdom	RYNR	2 617	2 214	2 474	2 449	3 195	6 950	5 553	7 074	7 038	10 456	11 706
UK associate and subsidiary insurance companies and insurance holding companies	RYNS	1 087	1 835	1 738	1 642	7 170	4 204	6 424	5 617	5 400	8 837	7 190
Overseas subsidiaries and associates	RYNT	9 908	12 275	11 854	15 485	14 859	16 402	14 239	17 775	15 993	14 260	9 014
Total assets	RKBY	59 957	70 185	71 124	85 798	108 330	111 764	110 497	114 493	105 774	112 342	121 875
Liabilities												
Borrowing:												
Borrowing from UK banks	RYMB	434	721	1 382	1 584	1 524	3 029	1 825	1 392	783	481	1 384
Other UK borrowing	RYMC	1 677	1 989	2 354	2 370	2 536	2 996	1 551	3 186	4 239	10 621	10 472
Borrowing from overseas	RYMD	1 296	1 103	1 626	1 876	1 976	1 202	1 600	3 045	1 867	1 964	2 916
General business technical reserves	RKCT	38 005	39 746	42 374	47 493	58 618	59 527	60 775	59 455	60 236	60 995	62 776
Long-term business:												
Funds	RKTF	–	–	–	–	–	–	–	–	–	–	–
Claims admitted but not paid	RKTK	–	–	–	–	–	–	–	–	–	–	–
Provision for taxation net of amounts receivable:												
UK authorities	RYPO	–295	235	397	841	807	1 253	1 197	939	874	594	941
Overseas authorities	RYPP	24	14	22	16	22	7	11	11	11	7	5
Provision for recommended dividends	RYPQ	650	794	874	1 098	1 407	2 048	1 318	1 817	2 682	1 957	958
Other creditors and liabilities	RYPR	1 921	1 987	2 551	2 955	3 886	3 873	3 793	4 981	6 293	6 410	8 025
Excess of assets over above liabilities:												
Excess of value of assets over liabilities in respect of long-term funds	RKCG	–	–	–	–	–	–	–	–	–	–	–
Minority interests in UK subsidiary companies	RKCH	33	80	52	22	24	60	68	29	33	276	4
Shareholders' capital and reserves in respect of general business	RKCI	14 552	21 355	17 628	25 545	35 069	35 172	34 397	35 372	24 699	26 190	31 982
Other reserves including profit and loss account balances	RKCJ	1 660	2 161	1 864	1 998	2 461	2 597	4 215	4 265	4 056	2 847	2 411
Total liabilities	RKBY	59 957	70 185	71 124	85 798	108 330	111 764	110 497	114 493	105 774	112 342	121 875

1 Including outstanding interest, dividends and rents (net).
2 Including authorised unit trust units.

Source: Office for National Statistics: 01633 812726

407

23.18 Individual insolvencies
United Kingdom

Numbers

		1993	1994	1995	1996	1997	1998	1999	2000	2001	2002	2003
England and Wales												
Bankruptcies[1]	AIHW	31 016	25 634	21 933	21 803	19 892	19 647	21 611	21 550	23 447	24 292	28 021
Individual voluntary arrangements[2,3]	AIHI	5 687	5 105	4 386	4 468	4 549	4 902	7 195	7 978	6 298	6 295	7 583
Total	AIHK	36 703	30 739	26 319	26 271	24 441	24 549	28 806	29 528	29 775	30 587	35 604
Scotland												
Sequestrations[4]	KRHA	6 828	2 182	2 188	2 503	2 502	3 016	3 195	2 965	3 048	3 215	3 328
Northern Ireland												
Bankruptcies[5]	KRHB	474	438	399	415	393	394	401	347	292	334	516
Individual voluntary arrangements[3,6]	KJRK	67	84	64	101	84	122	173	260	177	206	314
Total	KRHD	541	522	463	516	477	516	574	607	469	540	830

1 Comprises receiving and administration orders under the Bankruptcy Act 1914 and bankruptcy orders under the Insolvency Act 1986. Orders later consolidated or rescinded are included in these figures.
2 Introduced under the Insolvency Act 1986.
3 For statistical purposes deeds of arrangement are now included with individual voluntary arrangements.
4 Sequestrations awarded but not brought into operation are included in these figures.

5 Comprises bankruptcy adjudication orders, arrangement protection orders and orders for the administration of estates of deceased insolvents. Orders later set aside or dismissed are included in these figures.
6 Introduced under the Insolvency Northern Ireland order 1989.

Source: Department of Trade and Industry: 020 7215 3291/3305

23.19 Company insolvencies
United Kingdom

Numbers

		1993	1994	1995	1996	1997	1998	1999	2000	2001	2002	2003
England and Wales												
Compulsory liquidations	AIHR	8 244	6 597	5 519	5 080	4 735	5 216	5 209	4 925	4 675	6 230	5 234
Creditors' voluntary liquidations	AIHS	12 464	10 131	9 017	8 381	7 875	7 987	9 071	9 392	10 297	10 075	8 950
Total	AIHQ	20 708	16 728	14 536	13 461	12 610	13 203	14 280	14 317	14 972	16 305	14 184
Scotland												
Compulsory liquidations	KRGA	286	242	252	266	254	338	364	344	378	556	436
Creditors' voluntary liquidations	KRGB	265	202	189	175	223	228	208	239	224	232	195
Total	KRGC	551	444	441	441	477	566	572	583	602	788	631
Northern Ireland												
Compulsory liquidations	KRGD	73	69	72	68	60	53	58	83	60	49	95
Creditors' voluntary liquidations	KRGE	85	52	37	54	53	46	45	53	40	53	48
Total	KRGF	158	121	109	122	113	99	103	136	100	102	143

Source: Department of Trade and Industry: 020 7215 3291/3305

23.20 Industry analysis: bankruptcies[1]
England and Wales

Numbers

		1993	1994	1995	1996	1997	1998	1999	2000	2001	2002	2003
Industry												
Self-employed												
Agriculture and horticulture	**KRFY**	277	231	218	168	155	157	183	173	183	132	151
Manufacturing:												
Food, drink and tobacco	**KRFZ**	34	33	30	31	18	21	17	18	10	19	14
Chemicals	**KRLA**	7	23	8	5	5	7	4	2	2	6	2
Metals and engineering	**KRLB**	612	523	396	411	413	378	385	306	339	257	242
Textiles and clothing	**KRLC**	160	95	114	91	76	81	87	81	75	33	46
Timber and furniture	**KRLD**	207	176	158	118	98	96	94	90	88	59	82
Paper, printing and publishing	**KRLE**	161	142	142	117	104	101	112	80	75	70	58
Other	**KRLF**	169	133	146	117	116	110	111	84	79	111	100
Total	**KRLG**	1 350	1 125	994	890	830	794	810	661	668	555	544
Construction and transport:												
Construction	**KRLH**	4 361	3 362	2 783	2 713	2 182	1 919	1 911	1 741	1 783	1 637	1 781
Transport and communication	**KRLI**	1 754	1 402	1 138	1 227	1 162	1 060	1 187	1 120	1 134	1 095	1 116
Total	**KHGP**	6 115	4 764	3 921	3 940	3 344	2 979	3 098	2 861	2 917	2 732	2 897
Wholesaling:												
Food, drink and tobacco	**KRLJ**	114	94	103	77	62	53	45	49	40	48	33
Motor vehicles	**KRLK**	21	28	33	36	28	20	22	29	20	14	15
Other	**KRLL**	191	160	122	101	78	92	83	83	61	44	47
Total	**KHGQ**	326	282	258	214	168	165	150	161	121	106	95
Retailing:												
Food, drink and tobacco	**KRLM**	1 107	981	782	662	546	514	438	424	347	311	251
Motor vehicles and filling stations	**KRLN**	412	343	316	327	276	238	241	237	199	138	128
Other	**KRLO**	2 087	1 615	1 566	1 268	1 048	971	1 032	801	792	680	609
Total	**KHGR**	3 606	2 939	2 664	2 257	1 870	1 723	1 711	1 462	1 338	1 129	988
Services:												
Financial institutions	**KRLP**	292	241	185	125	105	79	54	45	39	31	24
Business services	**KRLQ**	1 843	1 537	1 354	1 176	1 117	1 057	1 162	1 127	1 107	1 057	1 023
Hotels and catering	**KRLR**	2 437	2 102	1 956	1 736	1 603	1 309	1 376	1 263	1 187	1 041	1 038
Total	**KHGS**	4 572	3 880	3 495	3 037	2 825	2 445	2 592	2 435	2 333	2 129	2 085
Other	**KHGT**	2 315	1 893	1 732	2 161	2 077	2 157	2 179	2 199	2 279	2 071	2 379
Total	**KRLT**	18 561	15 114	13 282	12 667	11 269	10 420	10 723	9 952	9 839	8 854	9 139
Other individuals												
Employees	**KRLU**	2 507	2 279	1 981	2 471	2 625	3 141	4 357	4 601	5 525	5 900	7 101
No occupation and unemployed	**KRLV**	4 816	3 696	2 859	3 294	3 051	3 384	4 457	4 856	5 848	6 965	8 978
Directors and promoters of companies	**KRLW**	862	628	484	368	310	272	330	296	328	323	420
Occupation unknown	**KRLX**	4 270	3 917	3 327	3 003	2 637	2 430	1 744	1 845	1 937	2 250	2 383
Total	**KRLY**	12 455	10 520	8 651	9 136	8 623	9 227	10 888	11 598	13 638	15 438	18 882
Total bankruptcies	**KRLZ**	31 016	25 634	21 933	21 803	19 892	19 647	21 611	21 550	23 477	24 292	28 021

1 From January 1991 Industrial Analysis excludes Deeds of Arrangement.

Source: Department of Trade and Industry: 020 7215 3291/3305

23.21 Industry analysis: company insolvencies[1]
England and Wales

Numbers

Industry		1993	1994	1995	1996	1997	1998	1999	2000	2001	2002	2003
Industry												
Agriculture and horticulture	KRMA	157	166	99	89	51	65	75	67	90	76	52
Manufacturing:												
Food, drink and tobacco	KRMB	213	142	130	163	93	89	67	104	71	61	69
Chemicals	KRMC	91	108	69	65	31	57	35	61	37	46	30
Metals and engineering	KRMD	1 381	932	681	658	591	594	698	683	704	739	828
Textiles and clothing	KRME	917	736	567	568	596	526	419	423	320	304	244
Timber and furniture	KRMF	333	252	267	249	181	149	190	187	199	179	92
Paper, printing and publishing	KRMG	777	579	452	438	364	426	387	386	484	545	376
Other	KRMH	878	859	681	599	613	652	780	678	717	768	430
Total	KRMI	4 590	3 608	2 847	2 740	2 469	2 493	2 576	2 522	2 532	2 642	2 069
Construction and transport:												
Construction	KRMJ	3 189	2 401	1 844	1 610	1 419	1 325	1 529	1 474	1 509	1 840	1 728
Transport and communication	KRMK	1 082	774	706	682	540	504	443	526	481	652	694
Total	KHGU	4 271	3 175	2 550	2 292	1 959	1 829	1 972	2 000	1 990	2 492	2 422
Wholesaling:												
Food, drink and tobacco	KRML	231	244	205	183	158	139	187	150	125	142	108
Motor vehicles	KRMM	142	112	83	95	41	60	38	29	24	64	208
Other	KRMN	639	638	678	429	340	364	394	391	363	512	788
Total	KHGV	1 012	994	966	707	539	563	619	570	512	718	1 104
Retailing:												
Food, drink and tobacco	KRMO	388	299	246	236	219	186	193	200	114	132	159
Motor vehicles and filling stations	KRMP	229	226	195	227	132	120	142	141	172	174	59
Other	KRMQ	1 388	1 186	1 127	956	891	847	919	853	833	902	578
Total	KHGW	2 005	1 711	1 568	1 419	1 242	1 153	1 254	1 194	1 119	1 208	796
Services:												
Financial institutions	KRMR	421	259	198	222	111	101	118	57	28	35	48
Business services	KRMS	2 415	1 807	1 525	1 500	1 528	1 617	1 831	1 605	1 618	3 215	3 886
Hotels and catering	KRMT	912	777	692	708	609	626	562	530	538	740	566
Total	KJRS	3 748	2 843	2 415	2 430	2 248	2 344	2 511	2 192	2 184	3 990	4 500
Other	KHGX	4 925	4 231	4 091	3 784	4 102	4 756	5 273	5 772	6 545	5 179	3 241
Total company insolvencies	KHGY	20 708	16 728	14 536	13 461	12 610	13 203	14 280	14 317	14 972	16 305	14 184

1 Including partnerships.

Source: Department of Trade and Industry: 020 7215 3291/3305

Service industry

Chapter 24

Service industry

Annual Business Inquiry

(Tables 24.1, 24.3 and 24.4)

For details of the Annual Business Inquiry, see the text accompanying Table 22.1.

Retail trade: index numbers of value and volume

(Table 24.2)

The main purpose of the Retail Sales Inquiry (RSI) is to provide up to date information on short period movements in the level of retail sales. In principle, the RSI covers the retail activity of every business classified in the retail sector (Division 52 of the 2003 Standard Industrial Classification) in Great Britain. A business will be classified to the retail sector if its main activity is one of the individual 4 digit SIC categories within Division 52. The retail activity of a business is then defined by its retail turnover, i.e. the sale of all retail goods (note that petrol, for example, is not a retail good).

The RSI is compiled from the information returned to the statutory inquiries into the distribution and services sector. The inquiry is addressed to a stratified sample of 5,000 businesses classified to the retail sector, the stratification being by 'type of store' (the individual 4 digit SIC categories within Division 52) and by size. The sample structure is designed to ensure that the inquiry estimates are as accurate as possible. In terms of the selection, this means that:

> each of the individual 4 digit SIC categories are represented, their coverage depending upon the relative size of the category and the variability of the data;

> within each 4 digit SIC category, the larger retailers tend to be fully enumerated with decreasing proportions of medium and smaller retailers.

The structure of the inquiry is updated periodically, by reference to the more comprehensive results of the Annual Business Inquiry (ABI). The monthly inquiry also incorporates a rotation element for the smallest retailers. This helps to spread the burden more fairly, as well as improving the representativeness between successive benchmarks.

During 2003, the retail sales index was rebased using detailed information from the 2000 annual business inquiry. The reference year is now set at 2000=100.

The latest summary statistics are published each month by First Release. More disaggregated value indices (not seasonally adjusted) are published each month in Business Monitor SDM28, via the National Statistics website: *www.statistics.gov.uk/rsi*.

24.1 Retail businesses[1]
United Kingdom

£ million and percentages

		1999	2000	2001	2002
Number of businesses	ZABE	216 826	214 876	210 691	207 513
Total turnover[2]	ZABL	230 822	241 418	251 624	265 211
Value Added Tax in total turnover	ZABM	22 494	23 695	25 249	26 997
Retail turnover[2]	ZABN	209 962	218 013	227 298	238 199
Non-retail turnover[2]	ZABO	20 860	23 406	24 327	27 011
Other income					
Value of commercial insurance claims received	ZABP	85	88	89	107
Subsidies received from UK government sources and the EC	ZAEN	19	7	24	3
Employment costs[3]	ZABQ	25 072	26 475	28 036	29 804
Gross wages and salaries	ZABR	22 430	23 857	25 320	26 945
Redundancy and severance payments	ZABS	329	144	130	129
Employers' National Insurance contributions	ZABT	1 547	1 650	1 733	1 809
Contributions to pension funds	ZABU	767	824	853	921
Stocks					
Increase during year	ZABV	1 271	735	900	1 264
Value at end of year	ZABW	21 095	21 150	21 509	22 325
Total turnover[3] divided by end-year stocks (Quotient)	ZABX	9.9	10.3	10.5	10.7
Purchases of goods, materials and services[3]	ZABY	161 841	168 520	175 593	185 765
Goods bought for resale without processing	ZABZ	135 830	141 330	147 791	155 677
Energy and water products for own consumption	ZACA	1 826	1 921	2 028	1 909
Goods and materials	ZACB	3 484	3 413	3 544	3 964
Hiring, leasing or renting of plant, machinery and vehicles	ZACC	761	828	788	918
Commercial insurance premiums	ZACD	582	616	688	826
Road transport services	ZACE	1 627	1 784	1 945	2 109
Telecommunication services	ZACF	506	558	603	561
Computer and related services	ZACG	636	661	581	662
Advertising and marketing services	ZACH	2 771	2 772	2 881	3 040
Other services	ZACI	13 818	14 638	14 745	16 099
Taxes, duties and levies	ZACJ	3 987	4 132	4 432	4 572
National non-domestic (business) rates	ZACK	3 253	3 353	3 616	3 728
Other amounts paid for taxes, duties and levies	ZACL	734	779	816	845
Capital expenditure					
Cost of acquisitions	ZACM	8 215	8 312	8 469	9 422
Proceeds from disposals	ZACN	2 270	1 683	1 606	1 251
Net capital expenditure	ZACO	5 945	6 629	6 863	8 171
Amount included in acquisitions for assets under finance leasing arrangements	ZACP	498	531	474	586
Work of a capital nature carried out by own staff (included in acquisitions)	ZACQ	78	79	144	125
Gross margin					
Amount	ZACR	72 655	75 929	78 913	83 165
As a percentage of adjusted turnover[4]	ZACS	*34.9*	*34.9*	*34.9*	*34.9*
Approximate gross value added at basic prices	ZACT	47 287	49 415	51 201	53 185

413

		1999	2000	2001	2002
Total turnover	ZABL	230 822	241 418	251 624	265 211
Retail turnover	ZABN	209 962	218 013	227 298	238 199
1 Fruit (including fresh, chilled, dried, frozen, canned and processed)	DSSX	3 960	3 999	4 112	4 000
2 Vegetables (including fresh, chilled, dried, frozen, canned and processed)	DSSY	5 403	5 802	6 662	6 880
3 Meat (including fresh, chilled, smoked, frozen, canned and processed)	DSSZ	11 334	10 729	11 133	11 640
4 Fish, crustaceans and molluscs (including fresh, chilled, frozen, canned and processed)	DSTA	2 092	2 180	2 200	2 365
5 Bakery products and cereals (including rice and pasta products)	DSTC	8 510	9 067	9 424	9 695
6 Sugar, jam, honey, chocolate and confectionery (including ice-cream)	DSTD	6 009	6 040	6 289	6 492
7 Alcoholic drink	DSTE	9 947	10 579	10 625	11 310
8 Non-alcoholic beverages (including tea, coffee, fruit drinks and vegetable drinks)	DSTF	5 546	5 587	5 717	6 477
9 Tobacco (excluding smokers requisites, eg pipes, lighters, etc)	DSTG	8 845	8 293	8 616	9 028
10 Milk, cheese and eggs (including yoghurts and cream)	DSTH	6 866	6 933	7 032	7 233
11 Oils and fats (including butter and margarine)	DSTI	1 113	1 245	1 314	1 227
12 Food products not elsewhere classified (including sauces, herbs, spices and soups)	DSTJ	10 121	9 998	9 986	9 201
13 Pharmaceutical products	DSTK	1 930	2 432	2 744	2 951
14 National Health Receipts	DSTL	5 799	6 412	6 981	7 618
15 Other medical products and therapeutic appliances and equipment	DSTN	2 267	2 690	2 737	2 862
16 Other appliances, articles and products for personal care	DSTO	7 506	8 099	8 543	9 331
17 Other articles of clothing, accessories for making clothing	DSTP	1 356	1 520	1 253	1 383
18 Garments	DSTQ	26 092	25 542	26 777	28 260
19 Footwear (excluding sports shoes)	DSTR	4 213	4 380	4 629	5 260
20 Travel goods and other personal effects not elsewhere classified	DSTT	644	683	848	928
21 Household textiles (including furnishing fabrics, curtains, etc)	DSTV	3 478	3 369	3 568	3 588
22 Household and personal appliances whether electric or not	DSUA	5 088	5 477	6 499	6 578
23 Glassware, tableware and household utensils (including non-electric)	DSUB	2 815	2 651	2 748	2 773
24 Furniture and furnishings	DSUC	10 353	10 630	11 065	12 048
25 Audio and visual equipment (including radios, televisions and video recorders)	DSUE	3 770	4 064	4 500	4 743
26 Recording material for pictures and sound (including audio and video tapes, blank and pre-recorded records, etc)	DSUG	3 080	3 436	3 304	3 632
27 Information processing equipment (including printers, software, calculators and typewriters)	DSUL	2 953	3 205	3 175	2 953
28 Decorating and DIY supplies	DSUM	5 019	5 488	6 279	6 489
29 Tools and equipment for house and garden	DSUN	2 165	2 451	2 669	3 020
30 Books	DSUP	2 226	2 252	2 366	2 738
31 Newspapers and periodicals	DSUQ	3 503	3 541	3 652	3 749
32 Stationery and drawing materials and miscellaneous printed matter	DSUW	3 648	3 768	3 601	3 843
33 Carpets and other floor coverings (excluding bathroom mats, rush and door mats)	DSUX	2 944	3 123	3 182	3 384
34 Photographic and cinematographic equipment and optical instruments	DSUZ	968	1 062	1 059	1 383
35 Telephone and telefax equipment (including mobile phones)	DSVA	1 503	2 264	2 398	2 198
36 Jewellery, silverware and plate; watches and clocks	DSVB	2 806	3 448	3 774	4 377
37 Works of art and antiques (including furniture, floor coverings and jewellery)	DSVF	1 666	1 585	1 820	1 501
38 Equipment and accessories for sport, camping, recreation and musical instruments	DSVH	3 520	3 725	3 861	3 647
39 Spare part and accessories for all types of vehicle and sales of bicycles	DSVI	558	652	752	1 024
40 Games, toys, hobbies (including video game software, video game computers that plug into the tv, video-games cassettes and CD-ROMs)	DSVM	3 744	4 204	4 624	5 355
41 Other goods not elsewhere classified (including sale of new postage stamps and sales of liquid and solid fuels)	DSVN	5 029	5 420	3 745	4 036
42 Non-durable household goods (including household cleaning, maintenance products) and paper products and other non-durable household goods	DSVO	3 609	4 043	4 352	4 427
43 Natural or artificial plants and flowers	DSVQ	2 456	2 653	3 028	3 130
44 Pets and related products (including pet food)	DSVR	2 241	2 348	2 724	2 449
45 Repair of household and personal items	DSVS	1 266	944	927	993

1 See chapter text.
2 Inclusive of VAT.
3 Exclusive of VAT.
4 Turnover is adjusted to take out VAT.

Source: Office for National Statistics: 01633 812435

24.2 Retail trade: Index numbers of value and volume of sales[1]
Great Britain
Not seasonally adjusted

		Sales in 2000 £ million	1994	1995	1996	1997	1998	1999	2000	2001	2002	2003	2004
Value													
All retailing	**EAFY**	207 149	77.3	80.2	84.6	89.9	93.4	96.5	100.0	105.9	111.1	113.8	118.9
Large	**EAFZ**	153 022	71	76	81	87	92	96	100	106	113	118	124
Small	**EAGA**	54 128	96	94	97	97	99	98	100	104	106	101	105
Predominantly food stores	**EAFS**	89 041	75.8	80.3	84.6	88.9	93.4	96.6	100.0	106.1	110.4	114.8	119.6
Predominantly non-food stores	**EAFT**	106 359	77.4	79.8	84.4	90.6	93.2	96.3	100.0	106.0	112.2	114.6	120.1
Non specialised predominantly non-food stores	**EAGE**	18 781	76.4	79.2	85.7	91.5	92.6	95.2	100.0	105.0	107.8	109.1	111.1
Textiles, clothing, footwear and leather	**EAFU**	27 880	80.8	83.5	87.0	93.4	93.8	96.0	100.0	105.8	112.3	118.1	123.5
Household goods stores	**EAFV**	27 699	71.2	73.4	79.2	86.8	91.6	95.7	100.0	108.6	116.0	117.0	121.4
Other specialised non-food stores	**EAFW**	31 999	79.0	81.2	84.5	89.3	93.1	96.8	100.0	104.5	111.6	112.9	121.4
Other retail sale (non-store) and repair	**EAFX**	11 749	88.9	85.3	87.6	91.8	97.1	98.8	100.0	103.2	106.8	98.2	103.5
Volume													
All retailing	**EAHC**	207 149	81.8	82.8	85.4	89.9	92.5	95.7	100.0	106.1	112.7	116.4	123.3
Predominantly food stores	**EAGW**	89 041	86.0	87.7	89.3	92.9	95.5	97.2	100.0	104.1	108.1	111.9	116.4
Predominantly non-food stores	**EAGX**	106 359	77.3	78.6	82.1	87.4	89.9	94.3	100.0	107.7	116.5	121.2	129.5
Non specialised predominantly non-food stores	**EAHI**	18 781	81.2	82.0	86.9	91.5	91.5	94.0	100.0	105.9	110.8	113.6	117.3
Textiles, clothing, footwear and leather	**EAGY**	27 880	77.3	79.3	82.7	88.1	88.8	92.9	100.0	109.4	120.9	128.7	137.9
Household goods stores	**EAGZ**	27 699	66.7	68.5	73.2	80.3	85.8	92.6	100.0	110.9	120.8	126.7	135.4
Other specialised non-food stores	**EAHA**	31 999	85.8	85.8	86.9	90.7	93.6	97.1	100.0	104.6	112.1	114.3	124.3
Other retail sale (non-store) and repair	**EAHB**	11 749	88.6	83.5	84.6	88.2	93.2	96.2	100.0	106.1	113.4	108.1	118.4

1 See chapter text.

Source: Office for National Statistics: 01633 812609

£ million and percentages

		Sale, maintenance and repair of motor vehicles and motorcycles; retail sale of automotive fuel (SIC 92 50.00)					Sale of motor vehicles (SIC 92 50.10)			
		1999	2000	2001	2002		1999	2000	2001	2002
Number of businesses	MKEQ	72 298	71 413	70 942	70 338	MKER	29 761	27 948	26 801	25 856
Total turnover	CMRH	128 956	129 675	136 398	141 582	EWRI	88 644	86 755	92 063	96 958
Motor trades turnover	CMRI	125 752	126 357	131 908	135 840	FDFZ	87 918	86 160	91 015	95 704
Retail sales of:										
New cars	CMRJ	25 992	24 377	28 891	30 400	FDGA	25 073	23 185	27 583	28 776
Other new motor vehicles and motorcycles	CMRK	3 598	3 543	4 011	4 600	FDGB	2 977	2 476	3 514	4 087
Sales to other dealers of:										
New cars	CMRL	16 780	16 241	16 720	21 174	FDGC	16 752	16 228	16 693	21 069
Other new motor vehicles and motorcycles	CMRM	2 936	3 101	3 282	3 621	FDGD	2 622	2 741	2 844	3 058
Gross sales of used motor vehicles and motorcycles	CMRN	28 233	30 126	29 434	27 890	FDGE	26 063	28 254	26 906	26 291
Turnover from sales of petrol, diesel, oil and other petroleum products	CMRO	15 448	17 090	16 750	16 792	FDGF	1 335	1 112	1 087	789
Other motor trades sales and receipts (including parts and accessories, workshop receipts)	CMRP	32 765	31 881	32 819	31 362	FDGG	13 095	12 164	12 387	11 633
Non-motor trades turnover	CMRQ	3 204	3 318	4 490	5 742	FDHJ	726	594	1 049	1 254
Purchases of goods, materials and services										
Total purchases	CMNR	111 324	112 157	116 458	120 420	FDGH	78 607	76 980	80 657	84 156
Energy, water and materials	CMRS	1 280	1 354	1 441	1 408	FDGI	632	629	630	577
Used motor vehicles and motorcycles	COBU	25 223	26 931	26 166	24 421	FDGJ	23 444	25 367	24 100	22 945
Parts used solely in repair and servicing activities	CMRT	6 249	5 181	5 787	6 389	FDGK	2 720	2 050	2 290	2 645
Other goods for resale	CMRU	71 895	71 589	75 855	80 632	FDGL	47 629	44 428	49 125	53 245
Hiring, leasing and renting of plant, machinery and vehicles	CMRV	247	282	270	315	FDGM	74	64	62	132
Commercial insurance premiums	CMRW	360	398	435	461	FDGN	177	163	190	214
Road transport services	CMRX	356	402	452	511	FDGO	196	240	268	313
Telecommunication services	CMRY	282	280	274	275	FDGP	151	137	127	131
Computer and related services	CMRZ	232	229	269	290	FDGQ	142	140	162	175
Advertising and marketing services	CMSA	1 713	1 630	1 644	1 837	FDGR	1 462	1 373	1 412	1 598
Other services	CMSB	3 488	3 881	3 866	3 882	FDGS	1 979	2 388	2 289	2 180
Taxes, duties and levies										
Total taxes and levies	CMSC	904	873	936	992	FDGT	543	482	529	517
National (non-domestic business) rates	CMSD	535	538	586	519	FDGU	246	225	261	231
Other amounts paid for taxes, duties and levies	CMSE	369	335	350	474	FDGV	297	257	268	286
Capital expenditure										
Cost of acquisitions	CMSF	1 964	1 938	2 093	2 210	FDGW	1 211	1 112	1 289	1 380
Cost of disposals	CMSG	685	658	798	845	FDGX	461	463	553	594
Net capital expenditure	CMSH	1 280	1 280	1 295	1 365	FDGY	749	649	736	787
Work of a capital nature carried out by own staff (included in acquisitions)	CMSI	21	9	14	12	FDGZ	13	6	9	6
Stocks										
Increase during year	CMSJ	1 042	616	828	1 229	FDHA	995	561	667	1 038
Value at end of year	CMSK	13 738	13 364	12 155	13 287	FDHB	10 797	10 405	9 005	10 088
Total turnover divided by end-year stocks (Quotient)	CMSL	9.4	9.7	11.2	10.7	FDHC	8.2	8.3	10.2	9.6
Employment costs										
Total employment costs	CMSM	8 179	8 261	9 069	9 422	FDHD	4 285	4 341	4 751	5 021
Gross wages and salaries paid	COBP	7 295	7 376	8 127	8 429	FDHE	3 815	3 859	4 232	4 458
National insurance and pension contributions	COBQ	884	885	942	993	FDHF	469	483	520	563
Gross margin										
Amount	COBR	26 398	26 279	29 335	31 196	FDHG	15 676	15 255	17 169	19 132
As a percentage of adjusted turnover	COBS	*21.5*	*20.3*	*21.5*	*22.0*	FDHH	*18.2*	*17.6*	*18.6*	*19.7*
Approximate gross value added at basic prices	COBT	18 726	18 214	20 710	22 235	FDHI	11 064	10 335	12 039	13 822

24.3 Motor trades[1]
United Kingdom
continued

£ million and percentages

		Maintenance and repair of motor vehicles (SIC 92 50.20)					Sale of motor vehicle parts and accessories (SIC 92 50.30)			
		1999	2000	2001	2002		1999	2000	2001	2002
Number of businesses	MKES	26 089	27 202	27 862	28 438	MKET	7 630	7 757	7 800	7 715
Total turnover	FDHK	11 118	11 218	11 890	11 924	FDIW	11 128	11 094	11 752	11 006
Motor trades turnover	FDHL	10 951	10 992	11 493	11 621	FDIX	11 085	11 014	11 557	10 509
Retail sales of:										
New cars	FDHM	724	977	1 099	1 368	FDIY	46	–	22	53
Other new motor vehicles and motorcycles	FDHN	61	567	..	153	FDIZ	34	83	..	161
Sales to other dealers of:										
New cars	FDHO	22	12	..	4	FDJA	1	–	..	97
Other new motor vehicles and motorcycles	FDHP	8	32	..	–	FDJB	–	–	..	–
Gross sales of used motor vehicles and motorcycles	FDHQ	1 416	1 169	1 574	1 088	FDJC	112	82	173	143
Turnover from sales of petrol, diesel, oil and other petroleum products	FDHR	656	387	371	342	FDJD	73	60	200	87
Other motor trades sales and receipts (including parts and accessories, workshop receipts)	FDHS	8 063	7 847	8 424	8 666	FDJE	10 819	10 789	11 096	9 968
Non-motor trades turnover	FDHT	167	226	397	303	FDJF	44	81	195	497
Purchases of goods, materials and services										
Total purchases	FDHU	7 236	7 375	7 817	7 787	FDJG	8 825	8 903	9 387	8 623
Energy, water and materials	FDHV	298	366	367	513	FDJH	257	260	299	178
Used motor vehicles and motorcycles	FDHW	1 150	965	1 347	929	FDJI	103	71	145	91
Parts used solely in repair and servicing activities	FDHX	3 080	2 606	2 734	3 024	FDJJ	290	293	574	538
Other goods for resale	FDHY	1 590	2 313	2 127	2 163	FDJK	7 359	7 424	7 405	7 015
Hiring, leasing and renting of plant, machinery and vehicles	FDHZ	115	138	146	73	FDJL	49	57	45	50
Commercial insurance premiums	FDIA	116	147	147	139	FDJM	36	52	64	65
Road transport services	FDIB	33	21	30	12	FDJN	76	92	86	63
Telecommunication services	FDIC	66	71	65	69	FDJO	46	49	60	53
Computer and related services	FDID	35	42	44	33	FDJP	39	31	50	61
Advertising and marketing services	FDIE	92	90	98	109	FDJQ	118	89	76	70
Other services	FDIF	661	615	713	722	FDJR	452	484	581	438
Taxes, duties and levies										
Total taxes and levies	FDIG	172	183	196	190	FDJS	97	104	104	89
National (non-domestic business) rates	FDIH	132	141	146	139	FDJT	85	87	80	73
Other amounts paid for taxes, duties and levies	FDII	39	42	49	51	FDJU	13	18	25	16
Capital expenditure										
Cost of acquisitions	FDIJ	389	358	396	371	FDJV	193	212	207	168
Cost of disposals	FDIK	86	75	89	84	FDJW	67	50	91	105
Net capital expenditure	FDIL	303	283	307	287	FDJX	126	162	115	63
Work of a capital nature carried out by own staff (included in acquisitions)	FDIM	7	2	3	2	FDJY	1	1	2	3
Stocks										
Increase during year	FDIN	−3	−43	79	59	FDJZ	31	35	43	17
Value at end of year	FDIO	747	670	809	814	FDKA	1 403	1 440	1 492	1 403
Total turnover divided by end-year stocks (Quotient)	FDIP	14.9	16.7	14.7	14.6	FDKB	7.9	7.7	7.9	7.8
Employment costs										
Total employment costs	FDIQ	1 930	1 919	2 176	2 293	FDKC	1 295	1 353	1 461	1 345
Gross wages and salaries paid	FDIR	1 725	1 715	1 961	2 071	FDKD	1 151	1 210	1 312	1 206
National insurance and pension contributions	FDIS	205	204	215	222	FDKE	144	144	149	138
Gross margin										
Amount	FDIT	5 283	5 236	5 741	5 846	FDKF	3 401	3 328	3 654	3 370
As a percentage of adjusted turnover	FDIU	*65.7*	*46.7*	*48.3*	*49.0*	FDKG	*31.4*	*30.0*	*31.1*	*30.6*
Approximate gross value added at basic prices	FDIV	3 898	3 883	4 134	4 176	FDKH	2 332	2 219	2 392	2 391

		Sale, maintenance and repair of motorcycles and related parts and accessories (SIC 92 50.40)					Retail sale of automotive fuel (SIC 92 50.50)			
		1999	2000	2001	2002		1999	2000	2001	2002
Number of businesses	MKEU	2 077	2 277	2 402	2 513	MKEV	6 741	6 229	6 077	5 816
Total turnover	FDKI	1 665	1 827	1 722	1 795	FDLV	16 401	18 781	18 971	19 898
Motor trades turnover	FDKJ	1 626	1 819	1 707	1 732	FDLW	14 173	16 372	16 136	16 273
Retail sales of:										
New cars	FDKK	17	22	–	–	FDLX	130	192	186	203
Other new motor vehicles and motorcycles	FDKL	526	416	433	189	FDLY	–	1	3	11
Sales to other dealers of:										
New cars	FDKM	–	–	–	–	FDLZ	5	–	–	3
Other new motor vehicles and motorcycles	FDKN	306	328	436	563	FDMA	1	–	1	–
Gross sales of used motor vehicles and motorcycles	FDKO	342	386	329	180	FDMB	300	234	452	187
Turnover from sales of petrol, diesel, oil and other petroleum products	FDKP	3	1	1	–	FDMC	13 382	15 530	15 091	15 574
Other motor trades sales and receipts (including parts and accessories, workshop receipts)	FDKQ	432	667	508	799	FDMD	356	414	404	295
Non-motor trades turnover	FDKR	40	8	15	63	FDME	2 228	2 409	2 835	3 625
Purchases of goods, materials and services										
Total purchases	FDKT	1 423	1 488	1 367	1 472	FDMF	15 232	17 411	17 230	18 383
Energy, water and materials	FDKU	10	26	33	40	FDMG	82	71	112	100
Used motor vehicles and motorcycles	FDKV	314	330	228	136	FDMH	213	197	345	319
Parts used solely in repair and servicing activities	FDKW	55	124	75	112	FDMI	105	109	114	70
Other goods for resale	FDKX	958	889	919	1 021	FDMJ	14 357	16 534	16 278	17 188
Hiring, leasing and renting of plant, machinery and vehicles	FDKY	1	1	4	4	FDMK	8	22	11	55
Commercial insurance premiums	FDKZ	7	9	11	9	FDML	24	27	24	34
Road transport services	FDLA	6	6	4	31	COBV	46	42	64	91
Telecommunication services	FDLB	4	6	6	5	COBW	15	17	16	17
Computer and related services	FDLC	3	3	3	4	COBX	13	12	10	17
Advertising and marketing services	FDLD	22	24	24	38	COBY	18	53	33	21
Other services	FDLE	44	68	60	70	COBZ	351	326	222	471
Taxes, duties and levies										
Total taxes and levies	FDLF	18	22	20	15	COCA	73	81	87	182
National (non-domestic business) rates	FDLG	7	12	15	..	COCB	65	74	84	..
Other amounts paid for taxes, duties and levies	FDLH	11	11	5	..	COCC	9	8	3	..
Capital expenditure										
Cost of acquisitions	FDLI	23	29	25	36	COCD	149	227	176	255
Cost of disposals	FDLJ	3	11	20	5	COCE	67	59	45	57
Net capital expenditure	FDLK	20	18	5	31	COCF	82	168	131	198
Work of a capital nature carried out by own staff (included in acquisitions)	FDLL	1	–	–	1	COCG	–	–	–	–
Stocks										
Increase during year	FDLM	−24	27	−11	33	COCH	43	36	50	82
Value at end of year	FDLN	291	361	378	290	COCI	502	488	471	692
Total turnover divided by end-year stocks (Quotient)	FDLO	5.7	5.1	4.6	6.2	COCJ	32.7	38.5	40.3	28.8
Employment costs										
Total employment costs	FDLP	128	90	132	147	COCK	541	557	548	616
Gross wages and salaries paid	FDLQ	115	81	120	131	COCL	488	512	503	563
National insurance and pension contributions	FDLR	13	9	13	17	COCM	53	46	45	53
Gross margin										
Amount	FDLS	313	501	488	557	COCN	1 725	1 960	2 283	2 291
As a percentage of adjusted turnover	FDLT	*19.5*	*27.4*	*28.3*	*31.0*	CMQN	*10.6*	*10.4*	*12.0*	*11.5*
Approximate gross value added at basic prices	FDLU	218	370	346	356	CMQO	1 215	1 407	1 799	1 491

1 See chapter text. Figures are exclusive of VAT.

Source: Office for National Statistics: 01633 812435

24.4 Catering and allied trades[1]
United Kingdom

£ million and percentages

		Total catering and allied trades (SIC 92 55.00)					Hotels and motels (SIC 92 55.11 and 55.12)			
		1999	2000	2001	2002		1999	2000	2001	2002
Number of businesses	MKEK	114 353	116 568	118 988	122 714	MKEL	11 381	11 188	10 890	10 800
Total turnover[2]	CMKX	51 315	55 058	57 738	60 869	CMLW	10 970	11 595	12 047	11 816
Taxes and levies[3]										
Total taxes and levies	CMLM	1 295	1 343	1 505	1 585	CMML	269	300	371	373
National (non-domestic business) rates	CMLJ	1 156	1 251	1 347	1 473	CMMI	260	292	350	359
Other amounts paid for taxes duties and levies	CMLL	139	92	158	112	CMMK	9	8	21	14
Capital expenditure[3]										
Capital acquisitions	CMLP	4 793	4 945	4 923	4 587	CMMO	1 333	1 402	1 201	1 145
Capital disposals	CMLQ	649	484	520	673	CMMP	203	106	81	229
Net capital expenditure	CMLK	4 144	4 461	4 404	3 914	CMMJ	1 130	1 296	1 120	916
Work of a capital nature carried out by your own staff (included in acquisitions)	CMLR	49	35	28	25	CMMQ	8	10	6	12
Stocks[3]										
Increase during year	CMLN	60	36	63	46	CMMM	−5	−3	−	−9
Value at end of year	CMLO	1 067	1 077	1 247	1 119	CMMN	208	181	207	224
Purchases of goods and services[3]										
Total purchases	CMLI	23 856	25 130	26 160	27 524	CMMH	3 817	3 947	4 135	4 318
Energy, water and materials	CMKZ	8 848	10 136	10 938	10 730	CMLY	1 667	1 793	1 766	1 777
Goods for resale	CMLA	8 028	7 757	7 556	8 115	CMLZ	450	383	469	407
Hiring, leasing of plant, machinery etc.	CMLB	306	344	277	352	CMMA	65	64	50	50
Commercial insurance premiums	CMLC	272	370	374	422	CMMB	67	71	82	99
Road transport services	CMLD	100	101	99	113	CMMC	25	28	19	17
Telecommunication services	CMLE	213	232	235	236	CMMD	60	56	63	58
Computer and related services	CMLF	105	115	130	137	CMME	36	29	31	43
Advertising and marketing services	CMLG	608	628	597	681	CMMF	167	182	177	205
Other services	CMLH	5 377	5 446	5 956	6 738	CMMG	1 280	1 340	1 475	1 661
Employment costs[3]										
Total employment costs	CMKY	11 012	11 668	12 965	13 553	CMLX	2 605	2 775	3 005	3 021
Gross wages and salaries paid	CMKV	10 169	10 777	11 971	12 526	CMLU	2 392	2 539	2 755	2 763
National insurance and pension contributions	CMKW	844	891	994	1 027	CMLV	213	236	250	259
Gross margin[4]										
Amount	CMQP	36 159	39 528	41 918	44 099	CMQS	8 922	9 542	9 825	9 634
As a percentage of turnover	CMQQ	*81.5*	*83.4*	*84.5*	*84.2*	CMQT	*95.0*	*95.9*	*95.2*	*95.5*
Value added at basic prices[4]	CMQR	20 568	22 326	23 466	24 895	CMQU	5 595	6 012	6 191	5 770
Accommodation										
Number of establishments	CMLS	23 667	25 589	23 584	22 915	CMMR	12 583	13 803	12 470	12 920
Letting bedplaces	CMLT	1 731 601	1 788 115	1 903 585	2 044 983	CMMS	757 491	780 158	819 116	1 023 562

£ million and percentages

		Camping sites and other provision of short-stay accommodation (SIC 92 55.21 to 55.23)					Restaurants or cafes, take-away food shops (SIC 92 55.30)			
		1999	2000	2001	2002		1999	2000	2001	2002
Number of businesses	MKEM	3 688	3 851	3 928	4 175	MKEN	49 955	51 395	52 633	54 340
Total turnover[2]	CMMV	1 932	2 152	2 220	2 617	CMNU	14 618	16 934	18 323	18 941
Taxes and levies[3]										
Total taxes and levies	CMNK	61	69	77	74	CMOJ	386	405	466	502
National (non-domestic business) rates	CMNH	53	63	74	73	CMOG	360	383	398	462
Other amounts paid for taxes duties and levies	CMNJ	8	6	3	1	CMOI	26	23	67	40
Capital expenditure[3]										
Capital acquisitions	CMNN	274	228	291	364	CMOM	1 048	1 305	1 351	1 228
Capital disposals	CMNO	38	46	22	38	CMON	137	128	128	110
Net capital expenditure	CMNI	236	182	269	326	CMOH	911	1 176	1 223	1 117
Work of a capital nature carried out by your own staff (included in acquisitions)	CMNP	7	5	7	–	CMOO	7	2	5	4
Stocks[3]										
Increase during year	CMNL	3	−4	48	4	CMOK	26	12	14	26
Value at end of year	CMNM	85	84	141	88	CMOL	291	274	298	294
Purchases of goods and services[3]										
Total purchases	CMNG	852	887	1 102	1 176	CMOF	7 079	7 962	8 544	8 621
Energy, water and materials	CMMX	184	201	233	248	CMNW	3 183	3 791	4 231	4 194
Goods for resale	CMMY	220	243	311	348	CMNX	1 934	2 120	2 154	1 983
Hiring, leasing of plant, machinery etc.	CMMZ	5	9	6	9	CMNY	53	45	42	62
Commercial insurance premiums	CMNA	28	35	32	29	CMNZ	70	92	94	120
Road transport services	CMNB	10	10	4	10	CMOA	29	36	33	37
Telecommunication services	CMNC	12	14	15	12	CMOB	61	64	62	67
Computer and related services	CMND	6	9	20	7	CMOC	19	29	35	28
Advertising and marketing services	CMNE	66	57	78	71	CMOD	200	232	203	245
Other services	CMNF	321	308	402	443	CMOE	1 530	1 555	1 689	1 884
Employment costs[3]										
Total employment costs	CMMW	355	405	428	483	CMNV	2 985	3 318	3 790	4 026
Gross wages and salaries paid	CMMT	325	370	392	446	CMNS	2 762	3 071	3 508	3 746
National insurance and pension contributions	CMMU	30	35	36	37	CMNT	223	247	282	280
Gross margin[4]										
Amount	CMQV	1 460	1 615	1 623	1 908	CMQY	10 665	12 375	13 533	14 224
As a percentage of turnover	CMQW	*85.3*	*85.4*	*83.8*	*83.2*	CMQZ	*84.5*	*85.2*	*86.0*	*87.6*
Value added at basic prices[4]	CMQX	865	1 003	888	1 122	CMRA	5 592	6 564	7 164	7 643
Accommodation										
Number of establishments	CMNQ	4 913	4 827	4 564	4 247	CMOP	1 033	1 053	1 106	1 806
Letting bedplaces	CMRR	844 311	860 261	940 003	895 207	CMOQ	45 449	60 329	55 590	55 382

Catering and allied trades[1]
United Kingdom

£ million and percentages

		Licensed clubs with entertainment, independent, tenanted, managed public houses or wine bars (SIC 92 55.40)[5]					Canteen operator, catering contractor (SIC 92 55.51 and 55.52)			
		1999	2000	2001	2002		1999	2000	2001	2002
Number of businesses	MKEO	44 647	45 139	46 320	47 914	MKEP	4 682	4 995	5 217	5 485
Total turnover[2]	CMOT	18 423	18 578	19 163	20 913	CMPS	5 372	5 799	5 985	6 582
Taxes and levies[3]										
Total taxes and levies	CMPI	551	538	559	612	CMQH	28	31	33	24
National (non-domestic business) rates	CMPF	460	484	497	557	CMQE	23	30	28	22
Other amounts paid for taxes duties and levies	CMPH	92	54	62	55	CMQG	5	1	4	2
Capital expenditure[3]										
Capital acquisitions	CMPL	2 032	1 861	1 895	1 709	CMQK	106	148	185	141
Capital disposals	CMPM	263	196	273	284	CMQL	8	7	15	12
Net capital expenditure	CMPG	1 769	1 665	1 622	1 425	CMQF	99	141	169	130
Work of a capital nature carried out by your own staff (included in acquisitions)	CMPN	25	18	11	8	CMQM	2	–	–	–
Stocks[3]										
Increase during year	CMPJ	24	32	−11	18	CMQI	12	−1	11	7
Value at end of year	CMPK	392	432	486	416	CMQJ	92	104	115	97
Purchases of goods and services[3]										
Total purchases	CMPE	9 386	9 486	9 423	10 316	CMQD	2 721	2 848	2 956	3 094
Energy, water and materials	CMOV	2 028	2 366	2 756	2 491	CMPU	1 785	1 986	1 951	2 020
Goods for resale	CMOW	4 924	4 525	4 166	4 848	CMPV	500	486	455	529
Hiring, leasing of plant, machinery etc.	CMOX	147	193	145	190	CMPW	35	32	34	40
Commercial insurance premiums	CMOY	91	152	141	147	CMPX	17	20	24	26
Road transport services	CMOZ	15	15	16	26	CMPY	21	13	27	23
Telecommunication services	CMPA	67	80	77	79	CMPZ	14	18	17	19
Computer and related services	CMPB	28	34	23	38	CMQA	15	14	20	22
Advertising and marketing services	CMPC	161	137	114	135	CMQB	14	20	25	25
Other services	CMPD	1 925	1 982	1 984	2 359	CMQC	321	261	405	389
Employment costs[3]										
Total employment costs	CMOU	3 206	3 170	3 647	3 800	CMPT	1 861	1 999	2 095	2 224
Gross wages and salaries paid	CMOR	2 975	2 954	3 390	3 539	CMPQ	1 715	1 842	1 926	2 034
National insurance and pension contributions	CMOS	231	216	257	261	CMPR	146	157	169	190
Gross margin[4]										
Amount	CMRB	10 762	11 343	12 126	12 992	CMRE	4 349	4 653	4 811	5 341
As a percentage of turnover	CMRC	*68.1*	*71.3*	*74.2*	*72.7*	CMRF	*89.9*	*90.3*	*91.3*	*90.9*
Value added at basic prices[4]	CMRD	6 383	6 432	6 902	7 569	CMRG	2 133	2 315	2 321	2 790
Accommodation										
Number of establishments	CMPO	5 137	5 906	5 445	3 941					
Letting bedplaces	CMPP	84 351	87 366	88 877	70 832					

1 See chapter text.
2 Inclusive of VAT.
3 Exclusive of VAT.

4 The total turnover figure used to calculate these data excludes VAT.
5 Includes figures for managed public houses owned by breweries.

Source: Office for National Statistics: 01633 812435

Sources

This index of sources gives the titles of official publications or other sources containing statistics allied to those in the tables of this *Annual Abstract*. These publications provide more detailed analyses than are shown in the *Annual Abstract*. This index includes publications to which reference should be made for short-term (monthly or quarterly) series. Further advice on published statistical sources is available from the National Statistics Customer Contact Centre on the numbers provided on page ii.

Table number and subject in Abstract	Government department or other organisation	Official publication or other source
1. Area		
1.1	Ordnance Survey	
	Ordnance Survey of Northern Ireland	
	Office for National Statistics	Regional Trends (annual, Palgrave Macmillan)
2. Parliamentary elections		
Elections		
2.1	University of Plymouth for the Electoral Commission	British Electoral Facts 1832–1999 (Ashgate) Dod's Parliamentary Companion (annual)
By–elections		
2.2	University of Plymouth for the Electoral Commission	Vachers Parliamentary Companion (quarterly) Social Trends (annual, Palgrave Macmillan)
3. International development		
3.1, 3.2	Department for International Development	Statistics on International Development (annual)
4. Defence		
4.1 – 4.11	Ministry of Defence/DASA	UK Defence Statistics 2003 (The Stationery Office (TSO))
5. Population and vital statistics		
Population		**Census**
5.1 – 5.3, 5.5	Office for National Statistics	*England and Wales*: Census reports 1911, 1921, 1931, 1951, 1961, 1971, 1981, 1991 and 2001 Census 1991, Key Population and Vital Statistics; Great Britain Digest of Welsh Statistics (annual, National Assembly for Wales)
	General Register Office (Scotland)	*Scotland:* Census reports 1951, 1961, 1971, 1981 1991 and 2001 Census 1991, Key statistics for urban areas: Scotland

Table number and subject in Abstract	Government department or other organisation	Official publication or other source
	Northern Ireland Statistics and Research Agency	*Northern Ireland:* Census of population 1951, 1961, 1966 and 1971, 1981, 1991 and 2001
		Resident population: mid–year estimates
5.1 – 5.3, 5.5	Office for National Statistics	*England and Wales*: Series FM (Family statistics), DH (Deaths), MB (Morbidity), PP (Population estimates and projections), MN (Migration) and VS (Key population and vital statistics)
		Series PP1, Population estimates: The Registrar General's estimates of the population of regions and local government areas of England and Wales
		Population Trends (quarterly, Palgrave Macmillan)
		Health Statistics Quarterly, (Palgrave Macmillan)
	General Register Office (Scotland)	*Scotland:* Annual report of the Registrar General for Scotland
		Annual estimate of the population of Scotland
	Northern Ireland Statistics and Research Agency	*Northern Ireland:* Annual report of the Registrar General
5.6	Office for National Statistics	
Projections		
5.1 – 5.3	Government Actuary's Department	
	Office for National Statistics	Series PP2, Population projections – national figures
Migration		
5.7, 5.8, 5.9	Office for National Statistics	International Migration – first release of 2002 estimates
		Series MN (International migration)
		Population Trends (quarterly, Palgrave Macmillan)
5.10, 5.11	Home Office	Control of immigration statistics United Kingdom (annual)
Vital statistics		
5.4, 5.12 – 5.22	Office for National Statistics	*England and Wales:* Series FM (Births, marriages and divorce statistics), DH (Deaths), MB (Morbidity), PP (Population estimates and projections), MN (International migration) and VS (Key population and vital statistics)
		Population Trends (quarterly, Palgrave Macmillan)
5.4, 5.12 – 5.21	General Register Office (Scotland)	*Scotland:* Annual report of the Registrar General for Scotland
		Quarterly return of births, deaths and marriages
	Northern Ireland Statistics and Research Agency	*Northern Ireland:* Annual report of the Registrar General
		Quarterly return of births, deaths and marriages

Sources

Table number and subject in Abstract	Government department or other organisation	Official publication or other source
5.14	Northern Ireland Court Service	Northern Ireland Judicial Statistics (annual)
5.18	Scottish Executive	
5.22	Government Actuary's Department	*England and Wales*: Interim Life Table *Scotland:* Interim Life Table *Northern Ireland:* Annual Report of the Registrar General
5.23	Office for National Statistics General Register Office (Scotland) Northern Ireland Statistics and Research Agency	

6. Education

6.1 – 6.11	Department for Education and Skills	Education and Training Statistics for the United Kingdom (annual, TSO)
	National Assembly for Wales	Digest of Welsh Statistics (annual) Statistics of education and training in Wales (annual and ad–hoc, NAfW)
	Scottish Executive (SE)	Scottish educational statistics (annual and ad–hoc, SE) Scottish Social Statistics (annual)
	Northern Ireland Department of Education (DENI)	Annual Abstract of Statistics, Northern Ireland (annual, DENI) Northern Ireland education statistics (annual and ad–hoc, DENI)
	Northern Ireland Department for Employment and Learning (DELNI)	Northern Ireland further and higher education statistics (annual and ad–hoc, DELNI)

7. Labour market

Labour Force Survey 7.1 – 7.3, 7.6, 7.8 – 7.10 7.12, 7.15 – 7.17	Office for National Statistics	Labour Market Trends (monthly, Palgrave Macmillan)
7.4, 7.5	Office for National Statistics	
7.7	Cabinet Office	Civil Service Statistics (annual) Monthly Digest of Statistics (Palgrave Macmillan)
Claimant count 7.11, 7.13 7.14, 7.25	Office for National Statistics	Labour Market Trends (monthly, Palgrave Macmillan)

Table number and subject in Abstract	Government department or other organisation	Official publication or other source
7.18	Office for National Statistics	Labour Market Trends (monthly, Palgrave Macmillan) Monthly Digest of Statistics (Palgrave Macmillan)
Annual Survey of Hours and Earnings 7.19, 7.20, 7.23, 7.24	Office for National Statistics	Annual Survey of Hours and Earnings (annual, ONS)
Average Earnings Index 7.21, 7.22	Office for National Statistics	Labour Market Trends (monthly, Palgrave Macmillan) Monthly Digest of Statistics (Palgrave Macmillan)
7.26	Department of Trade and Industry	

8. Personal income, expenditure and wealth

8.1	Office for National Statistics	Economic Trends, May (monthly, Palgrave Macmillan)
8.2	Board of Inland Revenue	Inland Revenue Statistics (annual, TSO) Economic Trends (monthly, Palgrave Macmillan)
8.3 – 8.5	Office for National Statistics	Expenditure and Food Survey, Family Spending (annual, Palgrave Macmillan)

9. Health

National health service

9.1	Department of Health service	Appropriation Accounts (annual) Health and Personal Social Services Statistics for England (annual)
	National Assembly for Wales	Health Statistics Wales (annual)
9.2	The Scottish Executive, NHS National Services Scotland	
9.3	Department of Health, Social Services and Public Safety (Northern Ireland)	Summary of Health and Personal Social Services (Northern Ireland) Accounts (annual) Hospital Statistics (annual)
9.4, 9.5	Department of Health	Health and Personal Social Services Statistics for England (annual)
	National Assembly for Wales Scottish Health Service, NHS National Services Scotland	Department of Health, Medical and Dental Workforce Census

Sources

Table number and subject in Abstract	Government department or other organisation	Official publication or other source
Public health		
9.6	Office for National Statistics General Register Office (Scotland) Northern Ireland Statistics and Research Agency	
9.7	HPA Communicable Disease Surveillance Centre	Communicable Disease Statistics Series MB2 (annual) Annual Review of Communicable Diseases
	NHS in Scotland NHS National Services Scotland	Scottish Health Statistics (annual)
	Communicable Disease Surveillance Centre (NI)	Annual report of the Registrar General Northern Ireland Quarterly return of births, deaths and marriages
9.8 – 9.10	Health and Safety Executive	Health and Safety Statistics (annual)

10. Social protection

Social security pensions, benefits and allowances		
10.1	Department for Work and Pensions Board of Inland Revenue Department of Health, Social Services and Public Safety (Northern Ireland)	National Insurance Fund Account (annual)
10.2	Board of Inland Revenue	
10.3, 10.5	Department for Work and Pensions (Information and Analysis Directorate) Ministry of Defence (Pay and Pensions) Board of Inland Revenue	
10.4	Board of Inland Revenue	
10.6 – 10.8, 10.12 – 10.18	Department for Work and Pensions (Information and Analysis Directorate)	
10.9, 10.11	Board of Inland Revenue	

Table number and subject in Abstract	Government department or other organisation	Official publication or other source
Working Family Tax Credit 10.10	Board of Inland Revenue Department for Work and Pensions (Information and Analysis Directorate)	Quarterly Enquiry United Kingdom (quarterly)
Social services 10.19 – 10.23	Office for National Statistics Department for Education and Skills	Appropriation (annual) Northern Ireland Annual Abstract of Statistics
10.19	HM Treasury	HM Treasury Expenditure Statistical Analyses
Housing and community amenities 10.24	Office for National Statistics	

11. Crime and justice

11.1	Home Office	Police Service Strength England and Wales 2002/03 Home Office Statistical Bulletin 11/03
	Scottish Executive Justice Department	Scotland: Report of Her Majesty's Chief Inspector of Constabulary for Scotland (annual)
	The Police Service of Northern Ireland	The Chief Constable's Annual Report
11.2	Home Office	Crime in England and Wales 2003/04 Home Office Statistical Bulletin 10/04
11.3 – 11.9	Home Office	Criminal Statistics, England and Wales (annual) (TSO) Offender Management Caseload Statistics 2003 (annual) Digest of Welsh Statistics (annual, Welsh Office)
11.10 – 11.11	Home Office	Offender Management Caseload Statistics 2003
11.12	Home Office	HM Prison Service Annual Report and Accounts April 2003 – March 2004
11.13	Scottish Executive Justice Department	Recorded Crime in Scotland, 2003
11.14 – 11.17	Scottish Executive Justice Department	Criminal Proceedings in Scottish Courts, 2002
11.18, 11.19	Scottish Executive Justice Department	Prison Statistics Scotland, 2002 Scottish Prison Service Annual Report and Accounts 2001–02

Sources

Table number and subject in Abstract	Government department or other organisation	Official publication or other source
11.20	The Police Service of Northern Ireland	
11.21 – 11.24	Northern Ireland Office	A Commentary on Northern Ireland Crime Statistics 2003
12. Lifestyles		
12.1	Department for Culture, Media and Sport	Department for Culture, Media and Sport Annual Report 2002
12.2	Department for Culture, Media and Sport	Table B17 – Labour Market Trends (monthly, Palgrave Macmillan)
12.3	Cinema Advertising Association	
12.4	UK Film Council	
12.5	VisitBritain	Sightseeing in the UK 2002
12.6	VisitBritain Wales Tourist Board VisitScotland Northern Ireland Tourist Board	The UK Tourist: Statistics (annual) www.staruk.org.uk The national tourism statistics website
12.7 – 12.8	Office for National Statistics	Travel Trends (annual, Palgrave Macmillan) Overseas Travel and Tourism First Release Monthly Digest of Statistics (Palgrave Macmillan) International Passenger Survey MQ6 Overseas Travel and Tourism
12.9	Target Group Index, BMRB International	
12.10	Department for Culture, Media and Sport	Camelot – National Lottery Press Releases
	Gaming Board for Great Britain	The Gaming Board for Great Britain Annual Report www.gbgb.org.uk
13. Environment		
13.1, 13.20	Office for National Statistics	Environmental Accounts 2004 Autumn edition (biennial) www.statistics.gov.uk/statbase/ Product.asp?vlnk=3698
13.2 – 13.7, 13.9, 13.13, 13.14, 13.16 –13.18, 13.21	Department for Environment, Food and Rural Affairs	e–Digest of Environmental Statistics (annual) www.defra.gov.uk/environment/statistics/index.htm The Environment in your Pocket (annual)

Table number and subject in Abstract	Government department or other organisation	Official publication or other source
13.8	Centre for Ecology and Hydrology, Wallingford	www.ceh–nerc.ac.uk/data/NWA.htm
	The Met Office	www.met–office.gov.uk
13.10	Scottish Environmental Protection Agency	www.sepa.org.uk/pdf/data/classification/water
13.11	Centre for Ecology and Hydrology, Wallingford	www.ceh–nerc.ac.uk/data/NWA.htm
	Environment Agency	www.environment–agency.gov.uk
	Water plcs	
13.12	Office of Water Services (OFWAT)	Companies 2004 June Return to OFWAT (annual)
13.15	Environment Agency	
13.19	The Chartered Institute of Environmental Health The Royal Environmental Health Institute of Scotland	
14. Housing		
14.1	Office of the Deputy Prime Minister National Assembly for Wales Scottish Executive Department for Social Development, Northern Ireland	
14.2	Office for National Statistics	General Household Survey
	Northern Ireland Statistics Research Agency	Continuous Household Survey
14.3	Office of the Deputy Prime Minister	www.housing.odpm.gov.uk/statistics (Live Tables 241–247)
	National Assembly for Wales	Welsh Housing Statistics (annual, NAfW)
	Scottish Executive	Statistical Bulletins on Housing (SE)
	Department for Social Development, Northern Ireland	Northern Ireland Housing Statistics (annual)

429

Sources

Table number and subject in Abstract	Government department or other organisation	Official publication or other source
14.4	Office of the Deputy Prime Minister	www.odpm.gov.uk/stellent/groups/odpm_housing/documents/ page/odpm_house_604024.xls
14.5	Office of the Deputy Prime Minister National Assembly for Wales	
14.6	Council of Mortgage Lenders Office of the Deputy Prime Minister	
14.7	The Court Service Northern Ireland Court Service	
14.8	Office of the Deputy Prime Minister National Assembly for Wales Scottish Executive	Scottish Executive Sales 1 Form
14.9	Office for the Deputy Prime Minister	Homelessness Statistical Release (quarterly) www.odpm.gov.uk/stellent/groups/odpm_housing/ documents/page/odpm_house_604144.xls P1E homelessness returns (quarterly)

15. Transport and communications

General		
15.1, 15.2, 15.4	Department for Transport	
15.3	Office for National Statistics	
Road transport		
15.5 – 15.12	Department for Transport	Transport Statistics Great Britain (annual, TSO) Vehicle Licensing Statistics (annual, TSO) Monthly Digest of Statistics (Palgrave Macmillan) Road accidents in Great Britain (annual, TSO) Road accidents Wales (annual, National Assembly for Wales)
15.11	Driving Standards Agency	
15.13, 15.14	Department of Regional Development, Northern Ireland	Transport Statistics NI
Rail transport		
15.20, 15.21	Department for Transport	Transport Statistics Great Britain (annual, TSO) Health and Safety Executive: Industry and Services (annual) Bulletin of Rail Statistics (quarterly)

Table number and subject in Abstract	Government department or other organisation	Official publication or other source
15.22, 15.23	Department of Regional Development, Northern Ireland	
Air transport 15.24 – 15.28	Civil Aviation Authority	Monthly Digest of Statistics (Palgrave Macmillan) Civil Aviation Authority; Annual Statements of Movements, Passengers and Cargo Civil Aviation Authority; Monthly Statements of Movements, Passengers and Cargo Accidents to aircraft on the British Register (annual)
Sea transport 15.29, 15.30	Department for Transport	Maritime Statistics (annual, TSO) Monthly Digest of Statistics (Palgrave Macmillan)
Passenger 15.31	Department for Transport Civil Aviation Authority	Monthly Digest of Statistics (Palgrave Macmillan) movement
Communications 15.32	Royal Mail Parcel Force Capita Business Services Ltd. Post Office Counters Ltd.	Monthly Digest of Statistics (Palgrave Macmillan) Post Office report and accounts (annual)

16. National accounts

16.1 – 16.22	Office for National Statistics	United Kingdom National Accounts (annual, Palgrave Macmillan) Monthly Digest of Statistics (Palgrave Macmillan)

17. Prices

Producer prices 17.1, 17.2	Office for National Statistics	Producer Price Index Press Notice (monthly) Business Monitor MM22, Producer Price Indices Monthly Digest of Statistics (Palgrave Macmillan)
Consumer prices 17.3 – 17.6	Office for National Statistics	Monthly Digest of Statistics (Palgrave Macmillan) Labour Market Trends (monthly, Palgrave Macmillan) Focus on Consumer Price Indices (monthly, ONS)
17.7, 17.8	Department for Environment, Food and Rural Affairs	Agriculture in the UK (annual) Agricultural Price Indices, Statistical notice (monthly) Monthly Digest of Statistics (Palgrave Macmillan)

Sources

Table number and subject in Abstract	Government department or other organisation	Official publication or other source
17.9	Department for Environment, Food and Rural Affairs	Economic Trends (monthly, Palgrave Macmillan) Agriculture in the UK (annual) UK Economic Accounts (quarterly, Palgrave Macmillan)

18. Government finance

Central government

18.1 – 18.3	Office for National Statistics	Financial Statistics (monthly, Palgrave Macmillan)
18.4	HM Treasury	Consolidated Fund and National Loans Fund Accounts
	Office for National Statistics	Financial Statistics (monthly, Palgrave Macmillan)
18.5	Office for National Statistics	United Kingdom National Accounts (annual, Palgrave Macmillan)
18.6 – 18.7	HM Treasury	Consolidated Fund and National Loans Fund Accounts
	Office for National Statistics	Financial Statistics (monthly, Palgrave Macmillan)
18.8	Bank of England	

Central government

18.9, 18.10	Board of Inland Revenue	Inland Revenue website

Rateable values

18.11	Board of Inland Revenue	Inland Revenue website

Local authorities

18.12, 18.13	Office of the Deputy Prime Minister	Local government financial statistics (England) (annual)
	National Assembly for Wales	Welsh local government financial statistics (annual)
	Public Works Loan Board	Annual report of the Public Works Loan Board
	Scottish Executive, Economic Advice and Statistics	Local financial returns (Scotland) (annual)
	Department of Finance and Personnel for Northern Ireland	
	Department of the Environment for Northern Ireland	
	Chartered Institute of Public Finance and Accountancy	

Table number and subject in Abstract	Government department or other organisation	Official publication or other source
18.14	Office of the Deputy Prime Minister	Local government financial statistics (England) (annual)
	National Assembly for Wales	Welsh local government financial statistics (annual)
18.15, 18.16	Office of the Deputy Prime Minister	Local government financial statistics (England) (annual)
18.17 – 18.19	Scottish Executive, Economic Advice and Statistics	Local financial returns (Scotland) (annual)
18.20	Department of the Environment for Northern Ireland	District Council – Summary of Statement of Accounts (annual)

19. External trade and investment

19.1 – 19.8	HM Customs and Excise	OTS1 – Overseas Trade Statistics – Extra EC, (formerly MM20) (monthly)
		OTS2 – Overseas Trade Statistics – Intra EC and World, (formerly MM20A) (monthly)
		OTSQ – Overseas Trade Statistics – Intra EC, (formerly MQ20) (quarterly)
		OTSA – Overseas Trade Statistics – Extra and Intra EC, (formerly MA20) (annual)
	Office for National Statistics	Business Monitor MM24, Monthly Review of External Trade Statistics (monthly, ONS)
		Overseas Trade Analysed in Terms of Industries MQ10 (quarterly, ONS)
		Monthly Digest of Statistics (monthly, Palgrave Macmillan)
19.9 – 19.18	Office for National Statistics	United Kingdom Balance of Payments (annual, Palgrave Macmillan)
	Bank of England	Quarterly figures: UK Economic Accounts
		Financial Statistics (monthly, Palgrave Macmillan)
		Foreign Direct Investment MA4 (annual, ONS)

20. Research and development

20.1 – 20.5	Office for National Statistics	Business Monitor MA14, Research and Development in UK Business (annual, ONS)

21. Agriculture, fisheries and food

Agriculture

21.1, 21.2	Department for Environment, Food and Rural Affairs	Agriculture in the United Kingdom (annual)

Sources

Table number and subject in Abstract	Government department or other organisation	Official publication or other source
21.3 – 21.5	Department for Environment, Food and Rural Affairs	Agricultural Statistics; United Kingdom (annual) Scottish Agricultural Economics (annual) Welsh Agricultural Statistics (annual, National Assembly for Wales)
21.6	Forestry Commission	Great Britain: Forestry Statistics (annual)
	Department of Agriculture and Rural Development (Northern Ireland)	Northern Ireland Annual Abstract of Statistics
21.7, 21.8	Department for Environment, Food and Rural Affairs	DEFRA Statistical Notice
Food 21.9 – 21.12	Department for Environment, Food and Rural Affairs	Monthly Digest of Statistics (Palgrave Macmillan)
21.13	Department for Environment, Food and Rural Affairs	Agricultural Statistics, United Kingdom (annual)
Fisheries 21.14, 21.15	Department of Environment, Food and Rural Affairs	England and Wales: Sea fisheries statistical tables (annual)
	Scottish Executive Agricultural Departments	Scotland: Fisheries of Scotland report (annual) Scottish Sea fisheries statistics (annual, TSO)
Family Food 21.16	Department for Environment, Food and Rural Affairs	Expenditure and Food Survey

22. Production

Production and construction 22.1	Office for National Statistics	Annual Business Inquiry www.statistics.gov.uk/abi/
Manufacturers sales 22.2	Office for National Statistics	ProdCom: Product Sales and Trade Annual Reports – PRA series (annual, ONS) Product Sales and Trade Quarterly Reports – PRQ series (quarterly, ONS)
22.3	Office for National Statistics	UK Business: Activity, Size and Location (formerly Business Monitor PA1003) (annual, ONS)

Table number and subject in Abstract	Government department or other organisation	Official publication or other source
Energy 22.4 – 22.13	Department of Trade and Industry (Energy Market Units)	Digest of United Kingdom Energy Statistics (annual) Energy Trends (monthly and quarterly) Annual Business Inquiry www.statistics.gov.uk/abi/
Iron and steel 22.14 – 22.16	Iron and Steel Statistics Bureau	Iron and steel industry: annual statistics: Iron and Steel Statistics Bureau Corporation Regional Trends (annual, Palgrave Macmillan)
Industrial materials 22.17	World Bureau of Metal Statistics Aluminium Federation	World Metal Statistics (monthly) Annual Business Inquiry www.statistics.gov.uk/abi/
22.18	Fertiliser Manufacturers' Association	Monthly Digest of Statistics (Palgrave Macmillan) Annual Business Inquiry www.statistics.gov.uk/abi/
Minerals 22.19	Office of the Deputy Prime Minister	Minerals (Business Monitor PA 1007) (annual, ONS) Natural Environment Research Council: United Kingdom
	Department of Trade and Industry	Minerals Yearbook
	Department of Economic Development (Northern Ireland)	Northern Ireland Annual Abstract of Statistics
Building Materials 22.20	Department of Trade and Industry	Monthly Statistics of Building Materials and Components (DTI) Monthly Digest of Statistics (Palgrave Macmillan)
Construction (output) 22.21	Department of Trade and Industry	Construction Statistics Annual (DTI)
Construction (new orders) 22.22	Department of Trade and Industry	Construction Statistics Annual (DTI)
Engineering 22.23, 22.24	Office for National Statistics	Annual Business Inquiry www.statistics.gov.uk/abi/ Business Monitor PA1003 – Size Analysis of United Kingdom Businesses 2002

Sources

Table number and subject in Abstract	Government department or other organisation	Official publication or other source
Motor vehicle production 22.25	Office for National Statistics	Business Monitor PM 34.10, (monthly, ONS) Annual Business Inquiry www.statistics.gov.uk/abi/
Drink and tobacco 22.26, 22.27	HM Customs and Excise	Annual report of the Commissioners of HM Customs
	Office for National Statistics	Monthly Digest of Statistics (Palgrave Macmillan)

23. Banking, insurance, etc

Banking 23.1	Bank of England	Bank of England Annual Report and Accounts
23.2	Association for Payment Clearing Services	Yearbook of Payment Statistics 2004
23.3 – 22.5	Bank of England	Bank of England, Statistical Interactive Database
23.6	Bank of England	Bank of England, Statistical Interactive Database
23.7	Bank of England	Bank of England, Statistical Interactive Database
23.8	Bank of England	Bank of England Quarterly Bulletin
23.9 – 23.12	Bank of England	Monthly Digest of Statistics (Palgrave Macmillan) Financial Statistics (monthly, Palgrave Macmillan)
Other financial institutions 23.13	Financial Services Authority	Building Societies: Statistical Tables www.fsa.gov.uk/pubs/annual/ar03_04/bs_statistics.html
23.14	Office for National Statistics	Business Monitor SDQ7, Assets and Liabilities of Finance Houses and Other Credit Companies (quarterly, ONS)
23.15	Office for National Statistics	Financial Statistics (monthly, Palgrave Macmillan) Monthly Digest of Statistics (Palgrave Macmillan) Business Monitor MQ5, Insurance Companies; Pension Funds and Trusts Investments (quarterly, ONS) First Release
23.16, 23.17	Office for National Statistics	Financial Statistics (monthly, Palgrave Macmillan) Business Monitor MQ5, Insurance Companies; Pension Funds and Insolvency Trusts Investments (quarterly, ONS)

Table number and subject in Abstract	Government department or other organisation	Official publication or other source
23.18 – 23.21	Department of Trade	Insolvency Annual Report (DTI)and Industry Companies (DTI) Financial Statistics (monthly, Palgrave Macmillan)

24. Service industry

Retail trades

24.1	Office for National Statistics	Annual Business Inquiry www.statistics.gov.uk/abi/
24.2	Office for National Statistics	Business Monitor SDM 28, (Monthly, ONS) www.statistics.gov.uk

Motor trades

24.3	Office for National Statistics	Annual Business Inquiry www.statistics.gov.uk/abi/

Catering

24.4	Office for National Statistics	Annual Business Inquiry www.statistics.gov.uk/abi/

Index — figures indicate table numbers

Index